AF655453

SYĀDVĀDAMAÑJARĪ

OF

MALLIṢEṆA

With the Anyayoga-Vyavaccheda-Dvātriṃśikā

OF

HEMACANDRA

EDITED WITH

INTRODUCTION, NOTES AND APPENDICES

BY

A.B. DHRUVA

FOREWORD

BY

PUSH RAJ JAIN

AKSHAYA PRAKASHAN
DELHI

© Publisher

First published: Poona 1933
First Reprint: Delhi 2005
Second Reprint: Delhi 2023

ISBN 81-88643-12-2

Published by Harish Chandra for
Akshaya Prakashan,
208, M.G. House, 2 Community Centre,
Wazirpur Industrial Area, Delhi - 110052.
Email: harish@akshayaprakashan.com
Phone: 011-41610957, Mob. : 9818452269

Printed at D.K.Fine Arts Press
A-6, Nimri Community Centre
Delhi - 110052

The Department of Public Instruction, Bombay

SYĀDVĀDAMAÑJARĪ

OF

MALLIṢEṆA

with the Anyayoga-Vyavaccheda-Dvātriṃśikā

OF

HEMACANDRA

EDITED WITH

INTRODUCTION, NOTES AND APPENDICES

BY

A. B. DHRUVA, M.A., LL.B., I.E.S. *(Retired)*

Principal, Central Hindu College, and

University Professor of Sanskrit and Pro-Vice-Chancellor,

Benares Hindu University

FIRST EDITION

1933

Bombay Sanskrit and Prakrit Series **No. LXXXIII**

Our little systems have their day;
They have their day and cease to be:
They are but broken lights of Thee,
And thou, O Lord, art more than they.

—*Tennyson*

॥ ॐ नमः श्रीसर्वज्ञाय ॥

स्याद्वादमञ्जरी

श्रीमल्लिषेणसूरिप्रणीता

श्रीहेमचन्द्रसूरिनिर्मितान्ययोगव्यवच्छेद-
द्वात्रिंशिकास्तवनटीकारूपा

भारतशिक्षासेवाधिकारनिवृत्तेन
श्रीकाशीविश्वविद्यालये
उपकुलपतिपदारोपितेन केन्द्रभूतहिन्दुपाठशालामुख्याचार्येण
सर्वशास्त्रान्तर्गतसंस्कृतविद्याध्यापकेन
एम्. ए., एलएल. बी. इत्युपपदधारिणा
आनन्दशङ्कर बापुभाई ध्रुवशर्मणा

संशोधिता
उपोद्घात–विवरण–परिशिष्टादिपरिकरैः प्रसाध्य च
संपादिता

सा च पुण्यपत्तनस्थ-
भाण्डारकरप्राच्यविद्यासंशोधनमन्दिराधिकृतैः
मुम्बय्यां तत्त्वविवेचकयन्त्रालये मुद्रयित्वा प्राकाश्यं नीता
वि० सं० १९८९, शाके १८५४
१९३३ खिस्ताब्दे

श्रीसिद्धसेनदिवाकरपादाः—

उदधाविव सर्वसिन्धवः
समुदीर्णास्त्वयि नाथ दृष्टयः ।
न च तासु भवान् प्रदृश्यते
प्रविभक्तासु सरित्स्विवोदधिः ॥

FOREWORD

It is wrongly presumed by many that Jainism is other-worldly. By this they mean that Jainism is concerned only with *Mokṣa*, the world after death, the methods of attaining it and that it offers no solutions to problems of the lived world. They look on Jainism as a religion of asceticism and regard it as an uncritical and blind faith in many gods and deities. They believe that Jainism is primarily concerned with laying down various rituals and ceremonies dedicated to these gods and deities. According to them, Jainism offers no critique of other religions, or lays down any plan for social transformation with the consequence that it has become irrelevant to the contemporary modern world and its attendant life style.

This criticism of Jainism is either ill-informed or based on extraneous considerations. Contrary to these misconceptions the fact, however, is that Jainism is imbued with the spirit of full dedication to *Puruṣārthas*, the good and well-being of the entire living and non-living creation. In the struggle for liberation from worldly bondage, *Jīva* (soul) cannot depend on any adventitious help from fate or gods. There is of course *Jinavāṇī* that embodies the teachings of the *Tīrthaṁkaras*. But *Jinavāṇī* only shows the way, it does not replace the effort. It is only a guide, a help. Every *Jīva* (soul) has to pursue its own struggle, and make efforts to set itself free from the constrains and compulsions of life to which all flesh, under the sun, is subjected to. Jainism, perhaps, is the only religion that sets store by human endeavour to accomplish life's goals. It describes in vivid and precise detail the complex process of *kārmic* bondage and suggests a way of release from it.

Jainism is a faith with a long and chequered history. A large number of āchāryas (teachers) at different times have expounded the tenets and doctrines of Jainism in all their richness and complexity. *Syādvādamañjarī* fulfils this purpose admirably. It is a learned commentary by Malliṣeṇa on the lyrical and devotional work *Anyayoga-Vyavaccheda-Dvātriṃśikā* composed by Hemacandrāchārya who flourished in the twelfth century A.D.

Syādvādamañjarī discusses threadbare the multitudinous variety of problems man has to deal with vis-a-vis this world and the world beyond. It deals with the problem of permanence *versus* change or the eternal *versus* the transitory, and shows how the arguments and the counter arguments advanced by each of the two sides annihilate each other. It expatiates on the sanctity of all life, the state of emancipated souls, the theory of Knowledge, the nature of reality etc. In short, it discusses ontological, metaphysical, epistemological and ethical issues which form the core of Jainism. It treats highly complicated issues of Philosophy in an erudite, lucid but scholarly manner. It supports its thesis by sophisticated but eloquent and easy to grasp arguments. It closely examines the doctrinal positions of the Cārvākas, Buddhist, Sāṁkhya, Mīmāṁsaka, Nyāya, Vaiśeṣika schools of Indian Philosophy. It lays bare the limitations of the theories propounded by these schools of thought and goes on to explicate the celebrated Jain Doctrine of *Naya* (forms).

The doctrine of *Naya* (forms) or relativity of knowledge is among the unique contributions of Jainism. It implies that reality is perceived by mind in different ways depending upon the point of view of the observer. Jains assert reality as possessed of origination (*Utpāda*) cessation (*Vyaya*) and persistence (*Dhrauvya*). In their view existence (*Sat*) is a combination of appearance, disappearance and persistence. What appears and disappears are modes. What persists is substance. The modes are impermanent, but the substance is permanent. According to them existence (*Sat*) is a combination of impermanence and permanence, modes and substance. This *sat* (truth or existence) has numberless aspects (*Anantdharmātka*). It appears differently to different persons because each one sees it from his particular point of view.

The principle that lays down systematically these *Nayas* (forms) is called *Syādvāda* or *Saptbhangī Naya*. This principle demonstrates how one and the same thing may be viewed synthetically or analytically; as one or as many; as one substance or as many attributes or modes. An idea of the importance of this principle can be had from the fact that Mahatma Gandhi recognized the pragmatic utility of this principle in the affairs of day to day life. He acknowledged his indebtedness to this principle when he said that he, no less than his critics, had a valid position, on a particular issue as each took his stand from his particular point of view. This is what constitutes essence of *Syādvāda*. In fact, *Syādvādamañjarī* which dilates at length on this principle, occupied the pride of place in the reading list of Mahatma Gandhi.

Gandhiji wanted to organize Indian Society in accordance with the Indian thought. He believed that prolonged exposure to foreign rule had benumbed India's capacity to follow its own *Shāstric* tradition. I believe that a philosophical text like *Syādvādamañjarī* would help India revive its own ancient thought, life style and glory.

The present edition of *Syādvādamañjarī* was first published in 1933 with a long introduction and exhaustive notes by Professor A.B.Dhruva. Professor Dhruva was deeply influenced by Mahatma Gandhi and maintained a long correspondence with him. The book has been out of print for a long time now, causing inconvenience to university teachers and students as they have to study it, in part or whole, as a part of their prescribed syllabi at the Post-graduate level.

The reprint is now being brought out by Shri Harishji of Akshaya Prakashan. It will, I believe, fulfil a long-felt need of teachers, students and scholars as well as lay persons who are interested in Indian Philosophy in general and Jainism in particular. They shall, I am sure, welcome this reprint and benefit from it.

Dept. of Sanskrit
PG DAV College (E)
University of Delhi.

Dr Push Raj Jain

Mokṣadā Ekādaśī
December 22, 2004

CONTENTS

PREFACE

I undertook to edit the Syâdvâdamañjarî many years ago, but other interests and preoccupations held up the work for a long time. Eventually I mustered up the 'will to do' and did it, but I regret that the press-copy could not be carried through the press as expeditiously as I had wished. This was due to a number of causes (which it is useless to relate), of which dilatoriness of the press was *not* one. In fact, I am grateful to Dr. S. K. Belvalkar, sometime Superintendent of the Bombay Sanskrit and Prakrit Series and now Secretary of the B. O. R. Institute, and to the Manager of the Tatva-Vivechaka Press for the infinite patience they have shown in putting up with the delay. My thanks are also due to Mr. Narvane for noting the Various Readings of the Text; also to Mr. Bhâskara Datta Miśra, M.A., LL.B., of the Sanskrit Department of the Central Hindu College for arranging the items of the Index (both English and Sanskrit) in alphabetical order.

In the interval a number of editions of the Syâdvâda-mañjarî were published of which the most noteworthy and scholarly was the one brought out by Sheth Motilal Ladhaji as a number of the "Ârhata-Mata-Prabhâkara Series" (often referred to as "AMP" in this book) published at Poona. I acknowledge my particular indebtedness to this publication for the facility it has provided for tracing the sources of the quotations made in this work. Even though many of these are well known and could have been easily traced by me independently, it is no small relief to find that some one has already done the work which it is useless to duplicate.

It may be useful to mention some of the main features of this edition. As is well-known the "Bombay Sanskrit and Prakrit Series" to which this publication belongs is intended for the average University student as well as for the advanced scholar. Accordingly, the Notes have been made sufficiently copious. Their main purpose has been to elucidate every argument as fully and clearly as possible. However, a fair amount of knowledge of Sanskrit on the part of the student has been assumed, and consequently no effort has been made to give the meanings of words and phrases. Secondly, in the body of the Notes as well as in the Appendices to the Notes large extracts have been given from Brâhmaṇa, Buddhist and other Jaina works with various ends in view: to enable the advanced student to weigh for himself the cogency of the arguments on both sides, or to give an idea of the indebtedness of the author to earlier writers, or to show how he has correctly recapitulated the position of the school under review, or to invite the attention of the reader to the influence which Malliṣeṇa has exercised upon later writers. Thirdly, some explanation is due for the length of the Introduction. It is mainly intended to stimulate the study of Indian Philosophy as one whole with numerous branches whose history ranges over a wide expanse both of time and thought. It is desirable that the student should, even at the threshold of his entering upon the study of such a comprehensive point of view as the Syâdvâda, have some idea of the different schools of thought and their history if he is to unite them into a single whole.

One word about the Syâdvâda before I close. While the Vedântin seeks intellectual peace in the Absolute by transcending the antinomies of Intellect, the Jaina finds it in the fact of the Relativity of Knowledge and the consequent revelation of the many-sidedness of Reality—the one leading to religious mysticism, the other to intellectual toleration. It may be that, in actual practice, the followers of both the schools have fallen short of the Ideal, but the Ideal in both cases was great and that was all the Masters could be expected to provide.

Benares
Hindu University,
February 16, 1933

A. B. DHRUVA

Introduction.

I HEMACANDRA AND MALLIṢEṆA

'स्याद्वादमञ्जरी' is a commentary by Malliṣeṇa on 'अन्ययोगव्यवच्छेदिका द्वात्रिंशिका' of Hemacandra, the great Jaina scholar, preacher and author, who lived in the time of Siddharāja Jayasiṃha and his successor, Kumârapâla, two famous kings of Gujarat in the first and the second half of the twelfth century of the Christian era. Not much is known about the personal history of Malliṣeṇa, except what he himself has told us at the end of the Syâdvâdamañjarî, that he was a disciple of Udayaprabhasûri*, and that he composed and completed his work on "Saturday, Âśvina Kṛṣṇa Amâvasyâ in the Śaka year 1214† with the help of Jinaprabhasûri."

But his greater predecessor—Hemacandrâcârya has been the hero of numerous biographical accounts which have been interwoven with those of his royal patron Siddharâja and his royal disciple Kumârapâla. Some of the stories related in these books are obviously coloured§, but all taken together present certain facts which are well—authenticated not only by their recurrence in the several accounts, but by their inherent probability in view of their historical setting and of the great learning which is clearly manifest in the works of their hero. Here are a few indisputable facts:

---

* Author of धर्माभ्युदय, not to be confounded with धर्मशर्माभ्युदय of Haricandra.

† मनु-रवि-मित (मनु=१४, रवि=१२).

§ Dr. Bühler puts the matter very clearly in the following words: "The objects with which the Caritas and Prabandhas were composed, were to edify the Jaina community, to convince them of the glory and power of the Jaina religion, or, in cases where the subject is a purely secular one, to provide them with an agreeable entertainment."

Hemacandra was born in 1134 Vikrama Saṃvat, that is, 1078 A. C. at Dhandhukâ* in a family belonging to Moḍha Vâṇia caste. His birth–name was Caṅgadeva or Câṁgodeva his father's Cacca, Câca or Câciga†, and his mother's Pâhini§. Once upon a time, when Caṁgadeva was only five years old, a Jaina monk named Devacandra happened to visit Dhandhukâ. While he was there at a Jaina temple, Pâhinî went there with her boy to do the usual obeisance to the Jaina tîrthaṁkaras. While she was going round the shrine, the boy went and sat on a seat beside the Âcârya. Struck by the boy's daring, and on marking certain signs of high promise on his person, Devacandra went to the house of Pâhinî and requested her to give him her boy for admission into the Jaina order of asceticism. After a slight hesitation and with such pain as a mother would naturally feel when asked to part with her child, Pâhinî gave away the young Caṁgodeva to the Âcârya. The father was all this time abroad. When he returned home and heard the story he was very angry but was eventually made to agree by Udayana, the Jaina minister of Siddharâja, who pacified the father and himself organised the function of the boy's dîkṣâ. The incident is related somewhat differently by Mr. C. R. Dalal in his Introduction to Yaśaḥpâla's "Mohaparâjaya". He writes: "Once Devacandra Sûri of Pûrṇatalla gaccha came to Dhandhukâ. Among the Jains who came for paying their respects and hearing his lectures, there was one young lad, Caṅgadeva, with his maternal uncle Nemicandra. Chaṅgadeva hearing the lecture requested him to initiate him. The Sûri asked who he was. His maternal uncle said that he was his sister's son. The boy's heart was

---

* 'बन्धूक' says प्रभावकचरित ("बन्धूकामिव बन्धूकं देशे तत्रास्ति सत्पुरम्"). Obviously this is a misreading of धन्धूक which has crept into manuscripts.

† Bom. Gaz. p. 191.

§ गेहिनी पाहिनी तस्य देहिनी मन्दिरेन्दिरा—Prabhâvakacarita. चाहिणी—Kumârapâlapratibodha.

turned to religion. The Âcârya replied that the boy should enter the order as he would, thereby, be able to do good to the people like a Tîrthaṁkara, and asked him to take the permission of his father for initiation. Cacha, however, refused but the boy persisted and followed the Âcârya and took the vow at Cambay"*. That the boy should have gone to the Âcârya with his maternal uncle is not unlikely, but this and other minor differences of detail do not affect the main events of Hemacandra's life. On his thus entering the order of Jaina asceticism, Caṅgodeva (the future Hemacandra) was given the name of " Somacandra ". Asceticism in those days was combined with scholarship, and the first duty of the young neophyte was, as usual, to study Logic, Grammar and Literature§. At the temple of Neminâtha on mount Girnar, Somacandra, says the legend, meditated upon the goddess Sarasvatî (' Brâhmî ') who out of the abundance of her grace bestowed upon him the *Sârasvata mantra*, and told him that he need not go to any other land for perfecting his scholarship. Somacandra thus became a great scholar. A few years later in recognition of his profound scholarship, his old âcârya gave him the mantra and title of *Sûri*, with a change of his name, from Somacandra to *Hemacandra*. The ceremony was performed at Nagor, says one authority. When H E M A-C A N D R A visited Aṇahillapura, the capital of Gujarat, he was introduced to Siddharâja. Siddharâja, who had seen a work on grammar composed by Bhoja, King of Mâlava, was anxious to see a similar work produced in Gujarat. When he consulted his literary advisers, all eyes fell on Hemacandra. Hemacandra undertook to prepare the work. When completed, the new Grammar was carried with great eclat in a procession on the back of an elephant, and copies of it were sent to different provinces of India. The work

* Stambhatîrtha = Skambhatîrtha = Khambhât of the modern geography of Gujarat.

§ तर्कलक्षणसाहित्यविद्याः पर्यच्छिनद् द्रुतम् ।

which was named "Siddha-Hema-S'abdânuśâsana" after the combined names of the patron and the author, consists of Sûtras, with such appendices as belonged to Pâṇini's grammar, viz. Dhâtupâṭha, Uṇādi, Liṁgânuśâsana etc. together with Vṛttis (commentaries), long and short, by Hemacandra himself. During Siddharâja's reign, Hemacandra also composed two other works, "Abhidhânacintâmaṇi" (also called "Haimî Nâmamâlâ") and "Anekârtha-Saṁgraha" on the lines of similar sections in the famous Kośa of Amarasiṃha, the Buddhist lexicographer whose work was read then as now by Brâhmaṇas as well as Buddhists. It has been observed that Siddharâja honoured Hemacandra as a scholar rather than as a spiritual guide,—a position which he acquired during the reign of his successor, Kumârapâla. This is no doubt true to a great extent, but it is also true that the influence on Siddharâja which Hemacandra originally acquired by his scholarship gradually grew, till on many occasions his advice in religious matters was sought and accepted by Siddharâja. As Professor Tawney, the translator of Prabandha-cintâmaṇi, remarks, Hemacandra "gained his favour, at first by his literary eminence, and subsequently made good use of his gifts as a courtier to advocate the claims of his own faith." He did it, however, with great patience and wonderful tact; for example, when he accompanied Siddharâja to Somanâtha, he advised the King to give up for the time being wine and meat as a practice of *brahmacarya*, and not on the Jaina round of its offending against the principle of the humane religion. Moreover, when he was asked by Siddharâja to pay his obeisance to god S'iva at Somanâtha, his utterance was a marvellous stroke of literary and religious genius. He bowed to the god in the following words:

"भवबीजाङ्कुरजनना रागाद्याः क्षयमुपागता यस्य ।
ब्रह्मा वा विष्णुर्वा हरो जिनो वा नमस्तस्मै ॥
यत्र यत्र समये यथा तथा योऽसि सोऽस्यभिधया यया तया ।
वीतदोषकलुषः स चेद्भवानेक एव भगवन्नमोऽस्तु ते ॥"

While Hemacandra's influence on Siddharâja, 'a latitudinarian in religious views,' was considerable, that on Kumârapâla was immense. Under his influence Kumârapâla not only gave up meat-eating, but promulgated the principle of *ahiṁsâ* throughout his kingdom, visited Jaina temples and celebrated Jaina festivals. Hemacandra composed a large number of works, some educational and literary, others frankly sectarian and polemical. The writings of this encyclopaedic author "are said to have amounted to "three crores and half verses"*. Of these the first and perhaps the most celebrated is "सिद्धहेमशब्दानुशासन" (-व्याकरण). The work was written mainly on the lines of Pâṇini's Grammar with appendices as mentioned above; but, unlike the latter, it also contains sections on Prâkṛtas and Apabhraṃśa, which till this day remain a standard work on the grammar of these derived languages. The works on Grammar were followed by those of Kośas (lexicons) vix., "अभिधानचिन्तामणि", "अनेकार्थसंग्रह" (with Vṛtti), "निघण्टु" and "देशीनाममाला". The last named work is particularly interesting as it places on record what in the days of Hemacandra were regarded as *des'ya* as distinguished from Prâkṛta S'abdas¶. To illustrate the rules of his Grammar, Hemacandra composed a Mahâkâvya called "Dvyâśraya", or "Kumârapâla caritram", which is both Sanskrit and Prâkṛta and sings the glories of Caulukya (Solanki) Kings including Kumârapâla, the Prakrit portion dealing with Kumârapâla's reign being a later addition made in the time of Kumârapâla. The next group of Hemacandra's works is that relating to Poetics and Prosody. This comprises "काव्यानुशासन" with a Vṛtti called "अलंकारचूडामणि", and a commentary on the same called विवेक; and "छन्दोनुशासन" with a commentary.

---

* C. R. Dalal's Introduction to Yaśaḥpâla's "Mohaparâjaya," G. O. S.

¶ Some of Hemcandra's 'deśya' words, however, are Prâkrta and are traceable to Sanskrit. This does not diminish the value of Hemacandra's list.

It now remains to note only those works whose subject matter is exclusively Jaina. These are: " *Trişaşti-S'alâkâ -Puruşa-caritram* " or the " Biographies of Sixty-three Supermen" of Jainism, with " Pariśiṣṭas" or supplements which he is said to have composed at Kumârapâla's request. They are written in verse, in simple readable style, and are interwoven with much general information regarding the principles and practices of Jaina morality and religion. Of a similar character is another work, "अध्यात्मयोगशास्त्र". Another work of this class is a series of twenty "वीतरागस्तुतिs" or " Devotional Stanzas addressed to the Passion-free", *i. e.* the great saints of Jainism. These include two well-known "द्वात्रिंशिकाs" or Sets of Thirty-Two Stanzas, the "अयोगव्यवच्छेदिका" and the " अन्ययोगव्यवच्छेदिका " *i. e.* that in which the author disproves the allegation that Jainism is wrong, and that in which he answers the claims of other systems that they are right†. It is the last (" अन्ययोगव्यवच्छेदिका ") work—with its commentary—" स्याद्वादमञ्जरी "—by Mallişeṇa with which we are here concerned.

[Original authorities and books of reference on the life and works of Hemacandra :—

" Praśasti in Trişaṣṭi-Śalâkâ-Puruṣa-caritra" of Hemacandra.

" Prabhâvakacaritram " of Candraprabhasûri.

" Hemakumâracaritra " of Somaprabhâcârya.

" Kumârapâlapratibodha " of ,,

" Kumârapâlaprabandha " of Jinamaṇḍanagaṇi.

" Prabandhacintâmaṇi of Merutuṁgâcârya.

" Prabandhakośa " of Candraśekhara.

Dr. Bühler's " Ûber das Leben das Jaina Mõnches Hemacandra "

---

† 'अयोग'—non-possession (of truth); 'अन्ययोग'—others possession (of truth).

Dr. Peterson's Reports on Bombay Mss.

C. R. Dalal's Introduction to Yaśaḥpâla's "Moharâja-parâjaya" (G. O. S.).

Munirâja Jinavijaya's Introduction to "Kumârapâla-Pratibodha" (G. O. S.).

Introduction to "Pramâṇa-mîmâṃsâ" (Ârhatamata-prabhâkara edition).

"व्याकरणं पञ्चाङ्गं प्रमाणशास्त्रं प्रमाणमीमांसाम् ।
छन्दोलंकृतिचूडामणी च शास्त्रे विभुर्व्यधित ॥
एकार्थानेकार्था देश्या निर्घण्ट इति च चत्वारः ।
विहिताश्च नामकोशाः भुवि कवितानट्युपाध्यायाः ॥
त्र्युत्तरंषष्टिशलाका नरेशव्रतगृहिव्रतविचारे ।
अध्यात्मयोगशास्त्रं विदधे जगदुपकृतिविधासुः ॥
लक्षणसाहित्यगुणं विदधे च द्याश्रयं महाकाव्यम् ।
चक्रे विंशतिमुच्चैः स वीतरागस्तवानां च ॥
इति तद्विहितग्रन्थसंख्यैव हि न विद्यते ।
नामापि न विदन्त्येत्वां मादृशा मन्दबुद्धयः ॥"

—Prabhâvakacarita, Hemasûri-prabandha, vv. 832 to 836.

Aufrecht's "Catalogus Catalogorum"—extracted in the Introduction to "Kâvyânuśâsana" of the Kâvyamâlâ Series: अनेकार्थकोषः, अनेकार्थशेषः, अभिधानचिन्तामणि (नाममाला व्याख्या), अलंकारचूडामणिः (काव्यानुशासनव्याख्या), उणादिसूत्रवृत्तिः, काव्यानुशासनम्, छन्दोनुशासनम्, छन्दोनुशासनवृत्तिः, देशिनाममाला सवृत्ति [द्याश्रयं काव्यं सवृत्ति], धातुपाठः सवृत्तिः, धातुपारायणं सवृत्ति, धातुमाला, नाममाला, नाममालाशेषः, निघण्टुशेषः, [प्रमाणमीमांसा सवृत्तिः], बलाबलसूत्रबृहद्वृत्तिः, बालभाषाव्याकरणसूत्रवृत्तिः, [योगशास्त्रम् विभ्रमसूत्रम्], लिङ्गानुशासनं सवृत्ति, शब्दानुशासनं सवृत्ति, शेषसंग्रहः, शेषसंग्रहसारोद्धारः

The Introduction to the "Pramâṇa-mîmâṃsâ" (A.M.P. Edition) contains an exhaustive list of Hemacandra's works, but his authorship of some of them is doubtful. Aufrecht's list also contains some confusion.]

The "अन्ययोगव्यवच्छेदिका द्वात्रिंशिका"—or "The Set of Thirty-two Stanzas"—which is cast in the form of a devotional panegyric addressed to the last Tîrthaṁkara, Mahâvîra, is virtually a criticism of the Brâhmaṇa and Bauddha systems of philosophy. But before we attempt a general review of its contents as unfolded in the text and its commentary, the Syâdvâdamañjarî, it will be useful to give a short account of the evolution Indian Philosophy.

It is usual to confine such an account to the historical rise and growth of the different 'Darśanas', but I think it will make for better understanding of the gist of each system if an attempt is made to indicate their *logical* relations in the movement of thought before proceeding to consider their *historical or chronological* order.

II EVOLUTION OF THE DARS'ANAS:

(a) *Logical.*†

The History of the Indian Darśanas has been generally regarded not as a history in the sense of an evolving process of thought, but only as a record of brilliant guesses and speculations which have occurred from time to time to men of genius and scholastic ability. This view, however, refutes itself by its very simplicity and unphilosophical character. Another view—that all Darśanas are broken lights of a single Truth, and as such are complementary of one another—has been propounded fully in Madhusûdanasarasvati's "Prasthâna-bheda", and partially in Vijñânabhikṣu's "Sâṃkhya-Pravacanabhâṣya" and Annaṃbhaṭṭa's "Tarkadîpikâ". This is a late tradition founded upon stray thoughts and points of view presented in earlier writings, such as the Nyâya-Kusumâñjali of Udayanâcârya. From a practical point of view of those who are not interested in the history of

† This Section has been reproduced with a few changes from my "Presidential Address" in the Indian Philosophical Section of the 'Indian Philosophical Congress' held at Benares in 1928.

philosophy for its own sake, but only in the *use* to be made of it for man's spiritual benefit, this view is natural and unimpeachable. Moreover, such a synthesis had its analogues in the well-known attempts to harmonize the texts of the Brâhmaṇas, of the Upaniśads, and of the Smṛtis, which lapse of time had consecrated. But the historian cannot overlook the fact that the founders of the Darśanas did not meet at a council, distribute their work, and part, each to execute his own appointed piece. It is undeniably true that there were honest differences of opinion amongst them, which developed in the course of time into bitter controversies. However, it is possible to reconcile in a higher synthesis the point of the historian with that of the practical religious man. For, the differences of opinion, though real and quite sharp, originate from differences of outlook, which *mark successive steps in a single evolutionary process.* Let us follow this thought-movement through its different stages.

The period of the Great Vision—that is my word for "Veda", which means knowledge or thought, but which being philologically connected with Latin *videre*, to see, I prefer to render by the word 'vision'—closed with the teaching that "All this is Brahma" ('सर्वं खल्विदं ब्रह्म'), and "Thou art That" ('तत्त्वमसि'). The earlier Ṛṣis, so at least it was thought, had *seen* the Truth. The generation that followed had heard but not seen it: it had received the tradition, but had not had the sight. The later sages, therefore, asked the question: 'How is it I do not see that 'all is Brahman' and that 'I am Brahman'? and tried to devise means for converting faith into experience, श्रुति into दर्शन. And their first answer to the question was: 'Because I am confounding matter and mind, or to go deeper, Nature and Spirit, which it is necessary for me to distinguish (विवेकख्याति)—this is Wisdom ('सांख्य'=समीचीना ख्यातिः).' But note that this answer just carries us one step forward and no further. For the question still remains: 'How am I to turn this intellectual distinction into a reality of experience?' That points to the next step which was to show the practical method ('योग') of the separation of Nature and Spirit. This was the योग—the practical complement of the theoretical सांख्य. The essential difference between सांख्य and योग is more correctly formulated as the difference between the theoretical and the practical side of a single system of philosophy than as the difference between two Sâṁkhyas, one of which was 'nirîśvara' and the other 'seśvara' (atheistic and theistic), as is sometimes done. But the mysticism of both Sâṁkhya and Yoga did not appeal to the scientifically-minded who thought that it was necessary to investigate the properties ('विशेष') of Nature and Spirit—(अनात्मन् and आत्मन्)—as we do those of any other natural object of experience. In order to carry on this investigation, the वैशेषिक (the investigator of '*viśeṣas*' or distinctive properties) divided Reality into certain categories and studied them in detail. But is not our investigation bound to go wrong unless our method is right ? Hence the necessity of a sound system of Logic ('न्याय'). Thus न्याय became a necessary complement to वैशेषिक. But Natural Philosophy (वैशेषिक) and Logic (न्याय) cannot altogether satisfy man's spiritul needs. Moreover, people were frightened by the growing rationalism of the new schools. They compared the rationalists of their day to 'jackals howling against one another' (M. Bh. S'ântiparva). Consequently, "Back to the Vedas" was the next cry. And the first attempt in this direction was to 'reflect upon' ('मीमांसा') and systematize the teachings of the sacrificial section of the Veda viz. the 'Brâhmaṇas" This was 'मीमांसा'—'पूर्वमीमांसा'—'कर्ममीमांसा', 'अध्वरमीमांसा'. But the mechanical religion of पूर्वमीमांसा was soon found unsatisfactory, and was superseded by the spiritual religion of उत्तरमीमांसा or ब्रह्ममीमांसा which was a systematization of the teachings of the Upaniṣads—the 'वेदान्त', the conclusion, the end, or the siddhânta of the Veda. The last two were *revivalist* schools whose ancient prototypes were the schools of the 'Yâjñikas' (ritualists) and 'Brahmavids' (the teachers of the Upaniṣads) respectively.

Such is the *logical* development of the six Darśanas of the Brâhmaṇas. To prevent misunderstanding, it should be noted that no system wiped out of existence its predecessor, and so all the systems sometimes appear running parallel to one another like mountain-streams. But this does not militate against the *logical* principle of evolution which gave them birth, and which binds them together in a single movement of thought.

Next, let us turn to Buddhism and Jainism. We treat them separately from the Brâhmaṇa darśanas, not because they had no organic relations with those darśanas, but because the *essential idea* of each of the schools falls within the inner history of that school itself, howsoever much some of its details may have been determined by the influence of neighbouring schools.

When the spiritual life and thought of the age of the Upaniṣads had, in certain quarters, degenerated into barren intellectualism on the one hand and superstitious sacerdotalism on the other, there sprang those two movements of Religion which we know as Buddhism and J A I N I S M. Although their real beginnings go back to an earlier date when they were parts of one stupendous whole which we know as the Indian Religion, and even though with Gautama Buddha and Mahâvîrasvâmin they were protests against the religion of their day and not independent religions as they are ordinarily represented, still they took a definite shape and acquired an individuality in the teachings of these two reformers who lived about the fifth or sixth century before the Christian era

To the problem of the post-Upaniṣadic age—How to reach Brahman ?‡—the answer of Gautama Buddha was: By getting rid of *tṛṣṇâ* which is the root of all misery; and by ceasing to believe in the self (*'âttavâda'*) which is the centre of all selfishness which causes transmigrations from life to death

‡ See "Tevijja Sûtta."

and from death to another life, ad infinitum; and lastly, by undergoing a course of discipline which would help in achieving the goal. To justifiy the ending of tṛṣṇâ and prove it to be futile—in fact, in order to shift the standard of values from the external to the internal world, and even to destroy both altogether in the interests of 'tṛṣṇoccheda' or 'vâsanâkṣaya', the Buddhist philosopher slipped into metaphysins inspite of the Master's repeated warning against it. Eventually the numerous schisms, which arose in the Buddhist Church soon after the death of the Master, became crystallised in the four famous schools of Buddhist Philosophy, viz., the schools of the Vaibhâṣikas, the Sautrântikas, the Yogâcâras and the Mâdhyamikas, maintaining respectively the doctrines of Direct Realism, Indirect Realism, Idealistic Phenomenalism, and Nihilistic Mediism—four logical steps in the process of thought from common sense to the highest wisdom, according to Buddhism. The Mâdhyamikas, or Madhyamakas as they were sometimes called, were advocates of the metaphysical 'Middle Path' an expression probably intended to correspond to the ethical 'Middle Path' ('madhyama pratipad') of Gautama Buddha. The two extremes which they repudiate are भाव and अभाव which at the middle or meeting-point destroy each other, leaving nothing but शून्यता as the core of Reality. This शून्यता which is deduced as a logical consequence of the doctrine of the Middle Path is not to be confounded with अभाव, which is relative as distinguished from the former which is absolute.

" अस्तीति नास्तीति उभेऽपि अन्ता
शुद्धी अशुद्धीति इमेऽपि अन्ता ।
तस्मादुभे अन्त विवर्जयित्वा
मध्ये हि स्थानं प्र (v.l. मध्येऽपि स्थानं न) करोति पण्डितः॥"

—Samâdhirâja Sûtra.

"अतो भावाभावान्तद्वयरहितत्वात् सर्वस्वभावानुत्पत्तिलक्षणा शून्यता मध्यमा प्रतिपत् मध्यमो मार्ग इत्युच्यते"—Mâdhyamika Vṛtti.

Of these, Sarvâstivâda or the doctrine that "All is real" associated with the school of the Vaibhâṣikas, is said to be the earliest. But obviously, if there is any point in the 'सर्व' (all) of 'सर्वास्तिवाद' it must have been preceded by a doctrine in which a part of Reality was affirmed and the rest denied. This must be evidently the doctrine of Idealism, in which ideas are declared to be the only reals. The conjecture is justified by our knowledge of the earlier schools of Buddhism, of which one was called the school of Prajñaptivâdins or Idealists, and another of Vibhajyavâdins or part-Realists. Thus originally there must have been only two schools of Buddhist Philosophy, the school of Idealism and that of Realism. From the direct Realism of the Vaibhâṣikas the first step in the direction of Idealism is the Indirect Realism or half-hearted Idealism of the Sautrântikas which in its turn logically leads to the complete Idealism of the Yogâcâra school. The latter, which was a resuscitation of the Vibhajyavâda and Prajñaptivâda§, passed into what is called S'ûnyavâda or Absolute Nihilism, but what, as noticed above, should more accurately be called

---

§ These doctrines were at first expressed in terms of the reality of Time. But Time in Buddhism, it should be noted, stands for the contents of Time. Thus, 'घटक्षण'=घट. In the "Abhidharmakośa," the name 'Vibhajyavâdin' has been traced to the fact that the school answer the old question: 'Does all exist?" with a distinction; the present and the past which has not yet borne its fruit exist; the future and the past which has borne its fruit do not exist (see Keith's "Buddhist Philosophy", p. 153). The reason for the distinction is plain in the half-hearted idealism of the Vibhajyavâda. For, while the future and the past which has already borne its fruit and is no more, exist only in idea, the present and the past which has yet to bear its fruit are real and cannot be denied. It will be noticed that, for what I consider to be valid reasons, I have modified the interpretations of the words 'Sarvâstivâdin' and 'Vibhajyavâdin' which are generally given.

Nihilistic Mediism, of the Mâdhyamikas, or Madhyamakas, in accordance with its logic contained in the Mâdhyamika Vṛtti.

The Jaina Darśana is only one : it formulates the doctrine of the relativity of Truth and thereby shows that each of the different schools represents a certain aspect of Truth (नय) and is so far true. Thus partial truth ('विकलादेश') belongs to the several darśanas while absolute and complete truth is revealed in the Jaina method of Syâdvâda ('सकलादेश'). The doctrine of Naya ('नय') or 'leading point of view' as indicated by its comparative simplicity is perhaps older than the Syâdvâda ('स्याद्वाद') which is highly complicated. Besides, there is nothing in common between them except that both of them are expressions of the same point of view–viz. अनेकान्तवाद, *i.e.* the doctrine of the many-sidedness of Truth. They cannot therefore be regarded as two stages of a single process of thought, but must be traced to separate sources united in a common point of view.

Such are the logical relations of the different systems of Indian Philosophy *inter se.* Each of the systems, moreover, has a history which discloses a similar evolution of doctrines, determined partly by their inner principle of growth and partly by the influence of other systems. Thus, for example, Sâṁkhya which was originally theistic, as is clear from the evidence of the Upaniṣads, the Bhagavadgîtâ, the Mahâbhârata and the Purâṇas, had become atheistic about the time of the later sections of the Mahâbhârata, Sâṁkhya-kârikâs and the Bâdarâyaṇa Sûtras under the pressure of its own doctrine of Prakṛti, which being charged with the energy of evolutionary activity rendered God superfluous and made him drop off from the system like an unused limb, until restored artificially at long last by the author of the Sâṁkhya–Pravacana-Bhâṣya under the influence of Vedânta. Another possible hypothesis, which I put forward somewhat hesitatingly, for explaining the atheistic character of mediaeval Sâṁkhya is that the atheistic Sâṁkhya was not a descendant of the Sâṁkhya of the S'vetâśvatara Upaniṣad, but of one of those systems which have been referred to and rejected in its introductory stanza "कालः स्वभावो नियतिर्यदृच्छा" etc. Similarly, such particular doctrines as those of पुरुष and प्रकृति have undergone evolution in the course of ages. पुरुष was originally the thinking substance, and it was therefore absurd to deny that he was essentially प्रमातृ. This view is held by Vyâsa, the commentator of Pâtañjala Sûtras. But it was felt that this was inconsistent with the transcendental nature of पुरुष, the basic doctrine of the Sâṁkhya philosophy, and it was consequently discarded and पुरुष was made mere साक्षिन् instead of प्रमातृ, a view later rejected or modified by Vijñânabhikṣu in the Sâṁkhya-Pravacana-Bhâṣya. Similarly, Prakṛti was at first either the power of God or the primordial substance from which had emanated the manifold universe like a tree from a seed. Afterwards it came to be regarded as an independent energy, which was another name for the potential unmanifested world. Later, the character of this Prakṛti or Avyakta came to be defined in a way which shows that the problem of philosophy had shifted from cosmogony to psychology and ethics. Prakṛti comes to be conceived as a complex of सत्त्व, रजस्, and तमस्, the three principles which represent respectively सुख, दुःख and मोह in our life. Here is a unique form of idealism which is not cognitive, or conative, or imaginative, but emotional, that is to say, an idealism in which the world is not conceived either as Idea or as Will or as Imagination but as Emotion, which it is the business of Puruṣa to get rid of. The Emotionalism, or Emotional Idealism if one can use such an expression without committing a paradox, was evidently preceded by a stage represented in the Bhagavadgîtâ in which the cognitive conative and emotional elements of idealism were still held together in the functions assigned to सत्त्व, रजस and तमस्. Moreover, Vijñânabhikṣu restores the view in which Prakṛti is regarded as the *dravya* or *dharmin* of which सुख, दुःख and मोह are dharmas or attributes as well as constituent elements.

A tenet of the Sâṃkhyas which is particularly interesting to us from the point of view of Jainism is their unreserved condemnation of 'hiṃsâ' including *sacrificial hiṃsâ*. (See Vijñânabhikṣu's commentary on the Sâṃkhya Sûtras quoted in the Supplementary XI. Notes on St. XI). This attitude seems to be due to the association of the Sâṃkhya with the Bhâgavata Dharma (see the Mahâbhârata, S'ânti Parva). There is a story in the Mahâbhârata which connects Kapila with opposition to sacrificial hiṃsâ. Hopkins notices a passage in the Mahâbhârata xii, 269, 9 where Kapila is presented in the light of an adverse critic from the point of view of orthodox Brahmanism. "On seeing a cow led out for sacrifice, Kapila, filled with compassion, cried out "O ye Vedas!" an exclamation of reproof against the Vedas, as inculcating cruelty to animals. At this he was attacked by the inspired cow with a long discourse, challenging him to show why the Vedas should be regarded as authoritative in any regard, if not in regard to the slaughter of animals. Kapila appears in this tale as a teacher of unorthodox non-injury and maintains to the end (so that his view is presented as really correct) that not the sacrifice of animals but the 'sacrifice (worship) of knowledge' is the best". Prof. Hopkins is mistaken in the view that in this passage there is any intention of representing Kapila as "unorthodox." Kapila's exclamation " " O ye Vedas! " only means " O Ye Vedas!" what sins are committed in thy name!' The whole point of the story is to suggest that there was a higher kind of sacrifice in Vedism itself, which had as much right to be considered orthodox as the sacrifice of animals, because the original meaning of the word 'यज्ञ', as its root (यज्) would indicate, was only worship of God,

The system of Yoga which came into existence as a complement to Sâṁkhya retained its pristine purity probably for a century or two after the death of Gautama Buddha. In the Sûtras of Patañjali the white light of spirituality is somewhat dimmed by a black jet of miraculous 'विभूति's and 'सिद्धि's. Later, the system split into two branches, the Haṭha Yoga and the Rāja Yoga, of which the former sometimes associated itself with certain degraded forms of S'akti-worship and Mahâyâna Buddhism, while the latter namely Râjayoga restored purity to the system under the influence of Vedânta.

The problem of the Vaiśeṣika was to distinguish Âtman from Anâtman by the scientific method of investigating properties ('विशेष') of things. Its consequent silence, more or less, on the problem of God in the Sûtras has been misunderstood as a mild form of atheism. But subsequently it allied itself with Nyâya which is enthusiastic about developing a system of logic, and by means of it, proving the existence of God, Soul and Immortality. In its later stages the Nyâya mistook the means for the end, and spent all its energies in building up a science of Logic, discussing its minutest details with a hair-splitting subtlety which has no parallel in the history of human thought.

The system of Pûrvamîmâṃsâ was at first a logic of Vedic interpretation, but since it was undertaken in the interests of the religion of the sacrifice, the sacrifice occupied a large place in the religious philosophy of that system. Every detail of the sacrifice became a fetish, till at last in the philosophy of the system God was not, and the gods were little more than *some things* which were expressed by words in the dative case in the formulae of offerings. Yet the principle which was responsible for this evolution, or degeneration as some may call it, was far from ignoble. If the Brâhmaṇas came to be regarded as the centre of Vedic literature, and sacrifice has the essence of religion, it was because *doing* and not *being* was regarded as the ideal of life. Secondly, in attributing to the sacrifice a compelling power which governed gods as well as men, the system of Pûrvamîmâṃsâ placed Law above the arbitrary will of gods. Besides this, by defining Pramâṇa as that which makes known what was not knowu already, it virtully separated the spheres of Reason and Faith: so that the Veda ruled only where the senses and reason had no authority, that is, in matters which transcended their sphere. The school also distinguished between the main proposition and obiter dicta, and between a precept and the legend by which the precept was supported. It thus winnowed the wheat from the tares, and made for rationalisation of religion, although apparently no system could be more dogmatic.

The evolution of the doctrines of Vedānta is too well known to need much elaboration*. However, a brief review of the philosophy of the Âcâryas may be attempted just to mark the principal stages of its evolution. The earliest school of the Vedantic theology was *Bhedâbheda-vâda* *i. e.* Difference--cum-Unity, in which *bheda and abheda* were regarded as equally real, and the ideal of life was supposed to consist in recognizing this fact or in progressing from one to the other (These were the doctrines of आश्मरथ्य and औडुलोमि) respectively. Next came the *Upâdhi-vâda* in which *abheda* was regarded as essential and real, and *bheda* as dependent upon *upâdhi*, yet equally real. This more or less self-contradictory formula of the भेदाभेदवाद† and उपाधिवाद was superseded by the 'केवलाद्वैत' of S'aṃkara in which the Unity was declared to be real and the difference as unreal. The next stage was to refuse to relegate Individual Spirits and Nature to the category of the Unreal, and to substitute for S'aṃkara's Absolute-Monism-with-Mâyâ the doctrine of a *triune* (three-in-one) *complex Reality* ('विशिष्टाद्वैत') consisting of the three principles of

* This school has not received the attention of Hemacandra and Malliṣeṇa beyond one Stanza and its commentary; moreover, a portion of the history of its development falls after the age of these Jaina critics.

† This should not be unwelcome to the Jaina.

God, Nature and Man, individual spirits, of which the two latter were forms of the first, but all the three were equally real. To the next Âcârya—Vallabha—all the preceding doctrines including Śaṁkara's Kevalâdvaita which was based on Mâyâvâda appeared to be a departure from rigorous Advaitism, inasmuchas in all of them something over and above Brahman was posited. Hence he claimed for his own doctrine of simple Brahman-without-Mâyâ the title of Brahmavâda or 'शुद्धाद्वैत' *i. e.* pure advaita as distinguished from the 'Kevalâdvaita' of Śaṁkara and the 'Viśiṣṭâdvaita' of Râmânuja. The advaitisms of Râmânuja and Vallabha remained stereotyped, but that of Śaṁkara assumed several forms. To use the simplest metaphor for illustrating the unreality of individual selves as against the reality of the Universal Self is to say that the former are 'प्रतिबिम्ब's or reflections of the latter. This was 'बिम्बप्रतिबिम्बवाद' and it was as old as the Upaniṣads. But the difficulty felt in its acceptance was that this presupposes the existence of a separate medium of reflection, such as water or glass, whereas Mâyâ or Avidyâ cannot be said to be separate from Brahman. To meet this objection another theory, known as 'अवच्छेदवाद' or the theory of delimitation, was started. According to it the individual selves were not the reflections of Brahman in a separate medium, but Brahman delimited or circumscribed by the walls of individuality. But walls, too, are something other than the space which they enclose. To avoid this element of dvaitism, another interesting metaphor was suggested, namely, 'कर्णराधेयवत्' *i.e.* as Karṇa, the famous Mahâbhârata warrior, mistook himself as the son of Rādhā, when in truth he was the son of Pṛthā, in the same way Brahman mistakes itself for jîva. Such was the progressive attempt at illustrating the unity of jîva and Brahman. Similarly, the objective world (विषयचैतन्य-प्रमेयचैतन्य) is at first made parallel with the subject (विषयिचैतन्य-प्रमातृचैतन्य), both being regarded as modes of a single Ideal Reality (चैतन्य). This form of Idealism which might appear to be a concession to Realism is carried further in the same direction, so that we have next a distinction drawn between ईश्वरसृष्टि and जीवसृष्टि *i. e.* the world which is a creation of God, and the world which is a creation of the individual self: thus the external world which I see round about me is God-made, whereas the personal interest which I take in it is what makes it *my* world; so that Mokṣa, in as-much-as it is *my* Mokṣa, is the cessation of the latter, not of the former. This is obviously a greater concession to Realism than that contained in the parallelism of विषयिचैतन्य and विषयचैतन्य. Next, the pendulum swings back full length and Idealism is reinstated with a vengeance; thus, the external reality may be regarded as a creation of the individual mind which, in its turn, may be supposed to be a fictitious manifestation of Brahman: this is known as दृष्टिसृष्टि; *i. e.* to see is to create, as opposed to the earlier सृष्टिदृष्टि, that is, you see what is created already. This doctrine is coupled with एकजीववाद where एकजीव may be हिरण्यगर्भ, in which case the world would be a dream of the cosmic soul: this is objective Idealism. The last and the extreme point to which Idealism could go but which it had never reached so boldly since the days of Gauḍapâda and the Buddhist Nihilists and Śaṁkara, as he appears in the commentary on Gauḍapāda's kârikâs, is that the external Reality does not exist at all, being no better than 'the footprint of a bird in the sky' ('वीनां खे वै पश्यन्ति ते पदम्').¶

Such is the evolution of the Darśanas, of the schools of the Âcâryas, and of the doctrines of some Śâṁkara commentators.

(b) *Historical or Chronological*

Let us now turn from the logical to the chronological evolution of the Darśanas. The task of determining their chronology is not hopeless, but it is certainly very difficult,

---

¶ For the different schools of S'âṁkara philosophy see Das-Gupta's very valuable "History of Indian Philosophy" vol. II which I received after the foregoing paragraphs were ready for print.

because a number of confusions have to be avoided in drawing conclusions. First, it is to be remembered that early thought in the shape of stray ideas and references does not make a 'darśana' in the sense of a system of philosophy, which represents a later stage in its history; for example, in the case of Sâṁkhya and Yoga long centuries of thought and practice had to roll away before these darśanas came to be formulated in Sûtras. Secondly, the age of the sûtras of a darśana should not be confounded with that of its beginning; for, sûtras came only after the darśana had already undergone some systematization. Thirdly, the extant sûtras are not necessarily the first of their kind but the last, that have supplanted their predecessors by the law of the survival of the fittest; the Vedânta Sûtras of Bâdarâyaṇa are an example to the point. Fourthly, while determining the age of particular sûtras by means of external and internal evidence, it should be borne in mind that they were revised, and enlarged from time to time "as new opponents and new points of view presented themselves;" and consequently such evidence cannot be taken to be conclusive as regards the entire work. Fifthly, each of the darśanas, apart from the sûtras, has had its history, and has not remained the same in every large and small detail, and therefore the form in which we find a darśana presented in latter-day summaries and manuals is not the form in which it has really existed throughout the ages. This long list of caveats is sufficient to account for the complexity of the chronological problem and the resulting difficulty of arriving at indubitable conclusions. A large mass of controversial literature relating to the history of the darśanas has thus grown, which it is impossible to present and discuss within the space at our disposal. All that we can do is to mention a few salient points, leaving the reader to gather more information from standard books and articles bearing upon the subject.

(1) The Sâṃkhya and the Yoga are the two oldest 'Darśanas' the former being found in a sufficiently evolved form in the later Upaniṣads, and the practices of the latter being also

old* and known to Gautama Buddha as an established method of discovering Truth. And yet the extant sûtras of the Sâṁkhya system seem to be unknown to Vācaspatimis'ra (9th century A.C.) and even to Mâdhava, the author of the Sarva-darśana-Saṁgraha; (1380 A. C.) and they appear for the first time with the Vṛtti of Aniruddha (1500 A. C.) and a little later with the Bhâṣya of Vijñânabhikṣu (second half of the sixteenth century A.C.). Even if such a late date be not warranted, it is significant that no sûtra of the work has been quoted by any writer earlier than Aniruddha and Vijñânabhikṣu†, that Śaṁkara while dealing with the system extensively does not quote a single one of the sûtras, and that the author of the Kârikâs mentions the Ṣaṣṭitantra as his source and not the sûtras. All this taken with the fact that the sûtras contain references to the philosophical doctrines of later Buddhism raises a high probability that the sûtras of this school belong to a very late date§. Whoever

---

* Recently Marshall has opined that it existed even in the pre-Vedic civilisation of the Indus valley.

† Apart from the fact that Aniruddha had already written the Vṛtti, it may be taken as certain that Vijñânabhikṣu has not committed forgery since the work contains some sûtras such as "ईश्वरासिद्धेः" which Vijñânabhikṣu finds exceedingly inconvenient for his theistic position.

§ It is not unreasonable to contend that on the other hand this is only an argument from silence, and that like Bhâsa's plays which have been recently published, the Sâṁkhya Sûtras may have remained buried for centuries until Aniruddha and Vijñânabhikṣu—like Ganapati Sastri in the other case—unearthed them. This is rendered plausible by the fact that the fifth chapter of the work contains parables which, it is said, were found in the old Ṣaṣṭitantra, but are absent from all the later works except the sûtras. The nucleus of the sûtras may thus go back to the period of the Mahâbhârata, but not the work in its present form which discusses the tenets of all the other darśanas including those of later Buddhism,

be the author of the sûtras there is no doubt that the first teacher of the Sâṃkhya system was Kapila, whom tradition knows as "आदि विद्वान्" or the first philosopher. He is a semi-historical person to whom a reference seems to have been made in the S'vetâśvatara Upaniṣad‡. Kapila taught this 'holy and

‡ It is curious that the author of the Bhagavadgîtā who speaks frequently of "Sâṃkhya" does not refer to Kapila in connection with Sâṃkhya, but refers to him in a different context—in the chapter on the 'vibhûtis' or glorious manifestations of God—as an ideal "siddha" ['सिद्धानां कपिलो मुनिः']. But this difficulty is to some extent reduced by the occurrence of numerous passages in the Mahâbhârata where Kapila is mentioned as the teacher of the Sâṃkhya. The word 'Kapila' in the passage in the Śvetâśvatara Upaniṣad in which it occurs ["ऋषिं प्रसूतं कपिलं यस्तमग्रे ज्ञानैर्बिभर्ति जायमानं च पश्येत्"] has been interpreted by one commentator as the 'tawny' sungod, and this interpretation has been accepted and supported by Max Müller probably under the impression that the commentary was S'aṁkara's, which it is not. It is not possible to rule out this interpretation as absurd, but it is less probable than the other which makes a reference to the sage of that name. That 'Kapila' was known as a historical person long before the time of Gautama Buddha is clear from the name of the birth-place of Gautama which was 'Kapila-vastu', 'the residence of Kapila'. [Keith's remarks to the contrary on p. 50 of his "Sâṃkhya System" in the "Heritage of India" Series are unconvincing.] Moreover, it is noteworthy that S'aṁkara, in the course of his Bhâṣya on the Vedânta Sûtras, in meeting the claim of the Sâṃkhyas that their system was the best exponent of the Vedic teaching inasmuch as the Veda (S'vet. Up.) itself declares Kapila as "perfect in knowledge", says that 'Kapila' in the passage might very well refer to some other Kapila than the teacher of atheistic Sāṃkhya, such as one who was elsewhere called 'Vâsudeva Kapila,' the sage who burnt the sons of Sagara.

foremost system' to Âsuri, and Âsuri taught it to Pañcaśikha, who amplified it*. From the last-named the system passed down, from master to pupil†, to "Bhârgava, Ulûka, Vâlmîki, Hârîta, Devala and others¶, and finally to Îśvarakṛṣṇa, who made an abridgment of it in a series of stanzas in âryâ metre," a work which is known as the "Sâṃkhyakârikâs." This work, says the author, "contains all that is found in the Ṣaṣṭitantra, less the Parables and the controversies with other schools." In the Mahâbhârata xii, 319, 59, along with Kapila, Âsuri and Pañcaśikha, as teachers of the spiritual doctrine with a twentyfifth principle, are mentioned Jaigîṣavya, Asita Devala, Parâśara, Vârṣagaṇya, Bhṛgu, Śuka, Gautama, Ârṣṭiṣeṇa, Garga, Nârada, Pulastya, Sanatkumâra, S'ukra and Kâśyapa. The teaching of many of these, as we know from other sources, was by no means distinctively Sâmkhya and this, therefore, only goes to prove that the Sâmkhya, at one time, was a general term for philosophy and was hardly distinguishable from Vedânta. The Chinese tradition reveals one more name, that of Vodhu, as a teacher of the Sâṃkhya system of the epic age. Among writers who succeeded Îśvarakṛṣṇa in the literary history of the Sâṁkhya were Vârṣagaṇya (= "Rainhost" in Chinese) Vindhyavâsin, Mâṭhara, Vâcaspati and Vijnânabhikṣu. As Vârṣagaṇya figures in the list given in the MBh, which knows nothing of Îśvarakṛṣṇa, he cannot be later than Îśvarakṛṣṇa, and so far the Chinese tradition must be wrong.

Of the next exponent of the Sâṃkhya system—Âsuri—we know nothing except that a verse has been attributed to

---

* "एतत्पवित्रमग्र्यं मुनिरासुरयेऽनुकम्पया प्रददौ ।
आसुरिरपि पञ्चशिखाय तेन च बहुलीकृतं तन्त्रम् ॥"
—Sâṃkhyakârikâ of Îśvarakṛṣṇa No. 70.

† "भार्गवोलूकवाल्मीकिहारीतदेवलप्रभृतीनागतम् ।
—Mâṭharavṛtti on the Sâṃkya-kârikâ No. 71.

¶ "शिष्यपरंपरयागतमीश्वरकृष्णेन चैतदार्याभिः ।
संक्षिप्तमार्यमतिना सम्यक् विज्ञाय सिद्धान्तम् ॥"—S. K. 71.

§ See Syâdvâdamañjarî on St. XV.

him in which he says that pleasure and pain which are really forms of 'Buddhi' are reflected in the 'Puruṣa' like the moon in water. (Syâd. St. xv).

About Pañcaśikha, however, we know a great deal more from the Mahâbhârata where his system has been presented in detail and he is associated with the teaching of the Pañcarâtra doctrines, a distinctly theistic school of the Sâṃkhya known as early as in the time of the Śatapatha Brâhmaṇa. Several quotations are made from his works by later writers such as Vâcaspati and others*. The famous work known as Ṣaṣṭitantra† has been attributed to him by a Chinese tradition, 'though doubtless by an error'§ since his teachings, as given in the Mahâbhârata, differ in several of their details from those found in the Sâṃkhya-kârikâs which profess to be founded upon it. Some attribute this work to " Vârṣagaṇya who, they say, is is a definite

---

* Hopkins has made a short sketch of Pañcaśikha's Sâṃkhya in his " Great Epic of India." See pp. 142-155. See also Keith's " Sâṃkhya System " pp. 39-44.

† Some think that 'षष्टितन्त्रानुशिष्टि'—is only a common name, and like 'योगानुशासनम्' means only the 'teaching of the philosophy of the sixty principles'. This, however, is less probable. As a work it may be referred to about 150 B. C. if it is Varṣagaṇya's as has been suggested.

§ Keith; contra Hiriyanna. See the latter's article on " The Ṣaṣṭitantra and Vârṣagaṇya " in J. O. R. Madras Vol. III, Pt. ii. where he argues in favour of the Chinese tradition that Pañcaśikha was the author of " Ṣaṣṭitantra," a book of 60,000 verses. This meaning of the word 'Ṣaṣṭitantra' is different from the one given by Vâcaspatimiśra in his Sâṃkhya-tattva-Kaumudî on the authority of a 'RâjaVârtika', and contained also in the Ahirbudhnya Saṃhitâ. See Keith's Sâṃkhya System pp. 62-65, and Wood's Yoga Sûtra, Preface.

historical figure, perhaps the first historical figure in the Sāṃkhya and Yoga tradition."

Vârṣagaṇya (= the "Rainhost" in Chinese) is mentioned in the Mahâbhârata as one of the teachers of the Sâṃkhya-Yoga. Vācaspati describes him in the "Bhâmatî" as one of the teachers who expounded Yoga-Śâstra ("योगशास्त्रव्युत्पादयिता"). Consequently it is probable that he belonged to the age when the Sâṃkhya and the Yoga were regarded as two branches of a single Śâstra. Some have gone the length of suggesting that he was a Vedântin—in all probability a 'pariṇâmavâdin'*. The great "Ṣaṣṭitantra" has been ascribed to him, in the "Ahirbudhnya Saṃhitâ"; and if the table of contents given in the latter book can be trusted, Vârṣagaṇya, as the author of the work, was a follower of theistic Sâṃkhya. Only four or five quotations from his work now remain, in one of which he is cited as opposing the atomic theory of the Vaiśeṣikas, in another as dealing with the fourfold character of Ignorance, in a third as declaring that the phenomenal forms of the Guṇas (Prakṛti) were a mere illusion and so on. Mâṭhara, the author of a commentary on the Sâṃkhya-Kârikâs is mentioned in the Anuyogadvâra, a work of the S'vetâmbara Jaina canon, which was given its present form between the third and the fifth century of the Christian era† and therefore cannot be later than the second half of the second or the first half of the third century.

Of Vindhyavâsin we know something from a Chinese source and also from a verse in Kumârila's S'lokavârtika, Anumâna Pari v. 143, where he is said to have held the view that the Inference of fire from smoke relates to particulars

---

* See Hiriyanna's article in J. O. R. Madras Vol. II Pt. ii.

† Weber.

and not to universals*. To this some more light has been added recently by the publication of the "Tattvasaṃgraha" of S'ântarakṣita and its commentary by Kamalaśîla. In Parmârtha's "Life of Vasubandhu" which is found in Chinese it is recorded that Vindhyavāsin was successful in a debate with Buddhamitra, a teacher of Vasubandhu and after this triumph he returned to his home on the Vindhya mountain and died there. Attempts have been made to identify him with Îśvarakṛṣṇa. But Kamalaśîla in his commentary on the Tattvasaṃgraha quotes a verse in which "Rudrila" is given as the proper name of Vindhyavâsin§.

The last but not the least of the important landmarks in the history of the Sâṃkhya system is Vijñânabhikṣu, a devout and learned theist who wrote a Bhāṣya known as the "Sâṃkhya Pravacana Bhâṣya" on the Sûtras attributed to Kapila, wherein he interprets the Sâṃkhya system in the light of the Mahâbhârata and the Purâṇas, and thus restores the theistic character which at one time belonged to the Sâṃkhya system but had been replaced by atheism in the latter half of the Mahâbhârata period, and during the whole of the Kârikâ period from Iśvarakṛṣṇa to Vâcaspatimiśra, the author of the Saṁkhyatattvakaumudî.

The history of the Sâṃkhya thought may be divided into five periods, which can be approximately fixed:—

---

* संदिह्यमानसद्भाववस्तुबोधात् प्रमाणता ।
विशेषदृष्टमेतच्च लिखितं विन्ध्यवासिना ॥

§ यदेव दधि तत्क्षीरं यत्क्षीरं तद्दधीति च ।
वदता रुद्रिलेनैव ख्यापिता विन्ध्यवासिता ॥

G. O. S. Tattvasaṃgraha p. 22 Com.

Here Rudrila the 'Vindhyavāsin' is ridiculed as 'a dweller in the forest who cannot distinguish between milk and curds.' The reference is to the Sāṃkhya's 'Satkāryavāda',

1. The Sâṃkhya of the Upaniṣads and that of the Bhagavadgîtâ, [circa 1000 to 800 B. C.]

2. The Sâṃkhya just before the age of Gautama Buddha. Of this however, we know very little.

3. The Sâṃkhya of the Mahābhārata and the Purâṇas: the earlier and the later stage, the former theistic, the latter atheistic. [circa 600 to 200 B. C.]

4. The Sāṃkhya as known to Bādarāyaṇa, the author of the Vedānta sûtras, and the Sâṃkhya of the Kārikās [circa 300 B. C. to 200 A. D.] both distinctly atheistic.

5. The Sâṃkhya of Vijñânabhikṣu which is distinctly theistic. (16th century A. D.)

(2) The Yoga Dars'ana appears in its fully developed form in the existing "Yoga Sûtras" of Patâñjali who, if he is identical with the famous author of the "Vyâkaraṇa Mahâbhâṣya" belongs to the middle of the second century B.C. The identity, however, has been questioned on fairly reasonable, but by no means conclusive, grounds.† This darśana, owing to its mystic as well as practical character, has been favoured by the Brāhmaṇas, the Bauddhas and the Jainas alike, and has been passed over by Malliṣeṇa without criticism except in one or two places where the doctrines which are criticised are held by the Yogins as a common property with the Sāṃkhyas. As observed before, the system is undoubtedly pre-Buddhistic. Tradition ascribes its origin to "Hiraṇyagarbha" (see S'vetāśvatara Upaniṣad), who, like "Kapila"§, may be either a historical person or the Cosmic Spirit of the "Golden Egg" of the famous "Hiraṇya-garbha Sûkta" of the Ṛgveda, Maṇḍala X. This, again, is not

---

† See Wood's "Yoga Sûtras"; and Dāsgupta's "History of Indian Philosophy" pp. 231–32.

§ The problem of interpretation is exactly similar.

inconsistent with another tradition which makes Yâjñavalkya the first ṛṣi who received his inspiration of Yoga from the Sun-god who is the spirit of the "Golden Egg". As already observed the Yoga darśana reveals two distinct strands, one mystic and truly religious, the other superstitious and gross. The case is similar to, or perhaps the same as that presented by the Atharvaveda and must be similarly explained. It is due to the amalgamation, or rather the crude mixture of the religious ideas and practices of the Âryans and the pre-Âryan inhabitants of India, and also of those of the upper and lower strata of the Âryans themselves. The principal works of this school which are of philosophical interest are:—the Yogasûtras of Patañjali; the Bhâṣya thereon which is attributed to one Vyâsa, who cannot be the same as the author of the Mahābhārata and the Purâṇas in their earlier form; Vâcaspati's commentary called "Tattva-Vaiśâradî"; "Bhojavṛtti" a brief commentary attributed to King Bhoja, and lastly, Vijñâna bhikṣu's "Yoga-Vârtika" on the Bhâṣya. There are numerous other works dealing with 'Haṭha Yoga' and Tântric elements in the system, a mixture of occult philosophy and superstition—which we need not pause to notice, as they possess little that is germane to our study of the Syâdvâdamañjarî.

(3 and 4). The Vais'eṣika and the Nyâya, as observed before, originated as separate systems, but the former which was in its origin a child of the Pûrva-Mîmâṃsâ, soon became a supplement—an adopted child, to use a metaphor—of the latter. Thus, Vâtsyâyana, the Nyâya-bhâṣyakâra, treats the Vaiśeṣika as a 'prati-tantra Siddhânta' of Nyâya. In the post-Christian Buddhist age their alliance seemed to be so complete that the Sûtras of the Nyâya School were sometimes referred to as taken from that of the Vaiśeṣikas. For example, Vasubandhu seems to have used the word 'Vaiśeṣika' in this wider sense,*

* See Tucci's "Pre-Diṅnâga Buddhist Texts (G. O. S.), Introduction pp. xxvi-xxvii,

and the commentator of Âryadeva refers to the quotations which the latter has made in his "S'ataśâstra" from the N. S. as those of the V. S. Yet for a long time the two systems received separate treatment and their authors remained separately attached to their respective systems. Udayana, in the tenth century, was the first important writer who wrote on both, though separately. The alliance thus initiated by unity of authorship ended in complete fusion in later times, so much so that the two systems often came to be designated by a single name, "Nyâya" or "Tarka".

The Vaiśeṣika and the Nyâya are beyond doubt later than the Sâṃkhya and the Yoga, and we owe their origin mainly to the spirit of inquiry which stirred the Indian mind about the time of Gautama Buddha. Of the two again, the Vaiśeṣika is older. This tradition seems to have been preserved as late as the time of Uddyotakara, who calls the author of the Nyâya Sûtras 'ऋषि' and that of the Vaiśeṣika Sûtras 'परमर्षि'. The Vaiśeṣika darśana deals directly with the problem of the 'viśeṣas' or properties of things, its system of logic being subsidiary to the process, and not vice versa as with the Nyâya. The Sûtras of the Vaiśeṣika system are ascribed to a sage named Kaṇâda or Ulûka, whose latter name occurs in the Mahâbhârata as that of a Sâṃkhya-Yoga‡ teacher—a fact which must be taken as indicating that the darśanas had not yet come to be clearly marked off from one another. The author of the Nyâya-sûtras was Gautama, who may or may not be identical with the author of the "Gautama Dharma Sûtras".†

‡ Could not this have been the origin of the designation 'यौगस' as applied to the Vaiśeṣikas?

† Except that 'Gautama' is a very common name among sages, there is nothing to favour the former alternative; at the same time it cannot be peremptorily rejected as a "worthless identification." That it would involve a very early date for the Nyâya-sûtras need not worry us. See my paper in the "Proceedings of the First Oriental Conference.".

Some grounds may be urged in favour of the priority of the Nyâya to the Vaiśeṣika Sûtras,‡ but the evidence on the other side is preponderating, and "it is difficult, therefore, to evade the impressions that Kaṇâda is older of the two" §—Kaṇâda and Gautama, or rather, the Vaiśeṣika Sûtras and the Nyâya Sûtras. As a work, the latter are far better arranged than the former which appear to be an older collection bearing on various topics made without a plan. Besides this, the Nyâya Sûtras reproduce, the physiology and the physics of the Vaiśeṣika Sûtras, "in some cases repeating actual phrases from the latter in a way which proves indebtedness." ¶ Contrariwise, the Vaiśeṣika Sûtras have their own terminology of inference and fallacies which is not borrowed from the Nyâya, although at a later stage when the two schools were amalgamated, it was the Nyâya terminology that was adopted in the syncretic system. We must therefore hold that the Vaiśeṣika and the Nyâya, unlike the Sâṃkhya and the Yoga, were originally two separate systems, which had sprung from two different though related motives—search for properties and search for the instruments of the knowledge of those properties—; and that the Vaiśeṣika had even evolved its own subsidiary system of logic—which though subsidiary was in some details better developed; and yet it was eventually the logic of the Nyâya school that came to be the complement of the Vaiśeṣika system.

It is now generally agreed that the Vaiśeṣika System and even the Vaiśeṣika Sûtras (the two, be it remembered, are not identical) are older than the system and the sûtras of the Nyâya, since, unlike the Nyâya, the Vaiśeṣika does not refer to the doctrines of the Buddhist school, to which numerous references have been made in the Nyâya Sûtras. This conforms with the statement made in Aśva.

‡ See Keith's "Indian Logic and Atomism" p. 21.

§ Keith, ibid p. 22.

¶ Randle.

ghoṣa's "Sûtrâlaṃkâra"* which places the origin of the Vaiśeṣika system before Buddha.† Even if such an early date for the Vais'eṣika darśana be denied, there can be no doubt that it must have originated long before the time of As'vaghoṣa. According to Ui "the origin of the Vais'eṣika was in the time of Mahâvîra and Buddha (the sixth-fifth century B.C.)", although the "systematization [i. e. the composition of the Sûtras] of the Vaiśeṣika is later than 300 B. C., probably in the first century B.C."‡ The latter conclusion is deduced from the following facts: First, "certain notions found in the Nyâya system and the six categories of the Vaiśeṣika are met in the Caraka Saṃhitâ written by the physician of King Kaniṣka (1st century of the Christian era)§; secondly, Kauṭilya's "Artha-śâstra" (supposed to be a work of the third century before Christ) divides 'Ânvîkṣikî' into 'Sâṃkhya', 'Yoga' and 'Lokâyata', but makes no mention of 'Vaiśeṣika', which shows that the systematization of the Vaiśeṣika is later than 300 B.C., at the earliest and it probably took place in the first century B.C., some time after the sixth schism (18 A. D.) of Jainism.¶ As the date of Kauṭilya's "Arthas'âstra" is now generally accepted to be a century or two after the Christian era, and not 300 B.C., as it was uncritically believed at one time, the above argument may appear to be shaky. But it should be noted that the Introductory chapter of the "Artha-śâstra" in

* As'vaghoṣa's authorship of the work has been questioned. But the tradition recorded there still remains and cannot be set aside as worthless.

† Ui's "Vais'eṣika Philosophy".

‡ Ui; Dr. Faddegon following Sulai.

§ Faddegon. According to Keith, "not only is Caraka's date uncertain, but his work has suffered refashioning, and the anthenticity of the text cannot be admitted."

¶ The value of this tradition which is recorded in the Avas'yaka is questioned by Keith who thinks that the passage in which it occurs is probably an interpolation.

which the reference is made to the branches of "Ânvîkṣikî" may well have been older, the chapters which underwent revision being only those which related to the subject-matter of the "Arthaśâstra". Even taking the later date which is assigned to the " Arthas'âstra ", it cannot be asserted that the Vais'eṣika was unknown as late as the second century A. D. For As'va ghoṣa in his "Sûtrâlaṃkâra" refers to "Vaiśeṣika Śâstra".* Thirdly, the doctrine of सामान्य and विशेष as presented in the "Vais'eṣika Sûtras" is less advanced than that which is attributed to one Rohagutta, who it is said imported it into Jainism about the time of the sixth Jaina schism (A. D. 18.).‡

Whatever doubt may be cast on the value of the evidence mentioned above, we are on absolutely solid ground when we come to later Buddhist writers. A series of them—Nâgârjuna, Ârya Deva and Harivarman—ranging roughly from the second to the end of the third century A. D.—show progressively detailed knowledge of the characteristic doctrines of the Vais'eṣika system.§ There can be no doubt, therefore, that the lower limit of the date of the " Vais'eṣika Sûtras " is the end of the first century A. D. While the upper limit may be several centuries before the Christian era, and may go as far back as the time of Gautama Buddha as believed by the author of the "Sûtrālaṃkāra".¶

---

* The passage runs thus : " Once there lived a Brāhmaṇa Kauśika by name, who had thoroughly mastered the Sāṃkhya S'āstra, the Vaiśeṣika Śāstra and the S'āstra of Jñātiputra."—Ui's Vais'eṣika Philosophy p. 40.

‡ सामण्णं तिविहं: १ महासामण्णं, २ सत्तासामण्णं, ३ सामण्ण–विसेस–सामण्णं । तत्र महासामान्यं सत्स्वपि पदार्थेषु पदार्थत्वबुद्धिकारि । सत्तासामान्यं भूपदार्थसद्बुद्धिविधायि । सामान्यविशेषसामान्यम् द्रव्यत्वादि । अन्ये तु व्याचक्षते—महासामान्यं द्रव्यत्वादि सामान्यविशेषः पृथिवीत्वादिः । विसेसो एकविहो । एवं...अण्णे भणंति । सामण्णं दुविहं । परं अपरं च । विसेसो दुविहो अंतविसेसो अनंतविसेसो च ॥

§ See Ui's Vais'. Phil. pp. 42–64.

¶ For a summary of Ui's views, which I have accepted

For the date of the Nyāya Sûtras, the *locus classicus* is Jacobi's article on "The Dates of the Philosophical sûtras of the Brāhmans" published in the Journal of the American Oriental Society Vol. XXXI. Starting with an examination of certain Nyāya sûtras (N. S. IV. ii. 26-35) which criticise Buddhist doctrines, he arrives at the conclusion that they refer to the Śûnyavâda of the Mādhyamika school of Nâgârjuna, and not to the Vijñânavâda of the Yogâcâra school of Vasubandhu and Asaṅga, as is supposed by the commentators. Consequently, the N. Sûtras should be referred to the period following that of Nâgârjuna (3rd century) and preceding that of Vasubandhu and Asaṅga (middle of the 4th century). This deduction of Jacobi has long held the field, and it is only lately that the opinion is gaining ground that it is wrong to suppose that Indian Idealism was inaugurated by Vasu-

---

with certain substantial modifications in the above paragraphs, see "Ui's Vais'eṣika Philosophy" p. 65. It may be quoted here for ready reference. "Jacobi's researches into the dates of the sûtras of the six systems fix the date of V. S. at about 200-500 A. D. and Suali, following Jacobi's proofs places the date in 250-300 A. D. Jacobi bases his proof mainly upon the relation of the Sûtras to the Buddhist schools, the Śûnyavāda and the Vijñanavāda. V. S. does not directly relate to the Buddhist schools. Consequently he deduces the date from the date of N. S. But, as stated above, V. S. is quoted by the author of N. S., and such quotations are found in the work of Nâgârjuna; and Deva makes a complement to Nâgârjuna's quotations. Therefore V. S. would appear to have been composed before Nâgârjuna. But the date of V.S. cannot be earlier than Rohagutta and As'vaghoṣa. The conclusion is that V. S. was composed about 50-150 A. D. If Nâgârjuna is not so early as 113-213, the date of V. S. will be placed at a time later than 50-150 A. D. At any rate the date is earlier than Nâgârjuna, and the contents of V. S. do not contradict this supposition."

bandhu, since the idealistic views had already been expounded in such works as "Laṅkâvatâra sûtra,"* and "Saṁdhi vimocana", and already systematised by Maitreya etc.†

The different views held on this subject have been clearly summed up by Dr. Tucci, who writes "Jacobi maintained that N.S. and V.S. were composed between 200 and 450 A.D.‡ Suali proposed for V. S. the date 250–300 and for N. S. the date 300–350. Stcherbatsky had first maintained that N. S. assumed its definite shape after the 5th century; then, he changed his view and held that no certain conclusion could be derived from the fact that there are in N. S. references to Buddhist Idealism, since the Idealism is not that of Vasubandhu, but an older one. Ui§ proposed the date 150–250. Prof. Dasgupta is rather sceptical as regards the possibility of fixing the exact date when the sûtras were codified. I think he is quite right, because we are still not in a position to determine the various strata that were superimposed in the actual redaction of the sûtras".¶

I am inclined to hold that among the different strata that are traceable in the composition of the Sûtras, the one

---

* Keith discredits the evidence of "Laṅkāvatāra" on the ground that "the sûtra in its present form is not earlier than the sixth century A. D., as it prophesies the Hûṇa rule of that period."

† Tucci's "Pre-Diṅnāga Buddhist Texts on Logic", Introduction xxvi (G. O. S.). See for the early date of Indian Idealism my paper in the "Proceedings of the First Oriental Conference".

‡ J. A. O. S. Vol. XXXI.

§ Ui proposes the date 200–250 A. D. for systematisation of the doctrine and 300–350 for the redaction of N. S.,—a view which is endorsed by Tucci.

¶ "Pre-Diṅnāga Texts of Logic, from Chinese Sources" Introduction p. xxiv.

to which belongs the sûtra relating to "the division of Anumâna ("Trividham Anumānam" I. i. 5) is the oldest. The work as a whole, however, may be referred to the latter half of the second century B. C., to some date about 150 B. C. in the age of the 'Âhnikas' or Daily Lessons, such as the 'Navāhnika' of Patañjali's Vyākaraṇa Mahābhāṣya. This general statement is subject to the qualification that some of the sûtras are demonstrably earlier and some later than the age to which the bulk of the sûtras belong. To this conclusion regarding the date of the sûtras I arrive from the fact that the sûtra relating to the division of Anumāna is obscure even to Vâtsyâyana, the author of the Nyâyabhâṣya, and therefore considerable time must be supposed to have elapsed between the age of the sûtra and that of Vâtsyâyana. Now, it is possible to arrive at the lower limit of the date of Vātsyāyana with the help of the date of the "Anuyoga-dvāra", a work of the younger Jaina Canon, and that of Mâṭhara-Vṛtti, a commentary on Îs'varakṛṣṇa's "Sāṁkhya-kârikâ." Thus:—If we compare Vâtsyâyana's account of the "three kinds of Anumâna" referred to in the N. S. "त्रिविधमनुमानं पूर्ववत् शेषवत् सामान्यतोदृष्टं च" (I. i. 5) with Mâṭhara's exposition of the subject we cannot help concluding that the Mâṭharavṛtti on the Sâṁkhyakârikâ represents a definite step forward in the history of Indian Logic.* And similarly, if we compare the account of the same as given in the "Anuyogadvâra" with that found in Vâtsyâyana's Bhâṣya, we cannot but be impressed by the great mass of details which the former presents as distinguished from the latter. This is as it should be; for, the "Anuyogadvâra" is even later than Mâṭhara, to whose work it refers† as an important branch of learning studied in those days.

* With its 33 kinds of Fallacy, 9 of पक्ष, 14 of हेतु and 10 of निदर्शन. Cf. the list of Fallacies in the Nyāyapravesa Pt. I (G. O. S.)

† The passage is repeated with slight variations in the "Nandîsûtra", another work of the Jaina canon.

If we accept Weber's view that the Jaina Siddhānta was given its present shape between the third and fifth century A. D., the latest date for the passage of the Anuyogadvâra will be the beginning of the fifth century A. D. The same passage occurs with slight alterations in the Nandîsûtra, and supposing the Nandîsûtra is a work of Devardhigaṇin (end of the fifth century A. D.), the passage in question from Anuyoga will have to be placed some time before it. Now, if Vâtsyâyana is later than Nâgârjuna (250 A. D.—Dr. Vidyâbhûṣaṇa), Vâtsyâyana and Mâṭhara have to be accommodated in the interval between 250 A. D. (the date of Nâgârjuna) and 400 A. D. (the date of the passage of the Anuyogadvāra). Allowing a margin of 50 years on either side, the remaining period of 50 years is all too short to account for the great development of Logic, such as we have noted above, between Vâtsyâyana and Māṭhara. If, on the contrary, we accept the Jaina Śvetâmbara tradition as it stands—and we cannot set it aside except for very cogent reasons—and assign the present edition of Anuyoga to Âryarakṣita* who lived in the second half of the first century A.D., the dates of the Sâṃkhyakârikâ (= 'Kaṇagasttari') and the Mâṭhara-Vṛtti will have to be shifted to the first century B. C. and early part of the first century A. D., respectively. Now, one strong reason for assigning the passage in Anuyoga to the latter part of the first century A. D., rather than to some period between the third and the fifth century A. D., is that the passage refers to Buddhistic scriptures in an altogether general way—it calls them merely 'बुद्धसासण'† while the Sâṁkhya works referred to are no less than three, which are mentioned specifically over and above the general 'काविलियं' (the philosophy of Kapila). Had the Anuyogadvāra been written in the 3rd or 5th century

---

* The Jaina tradition ascribes not only the division of Anuyoga, but also the compilation or composition of Anuyogadvāra to Âryarakṣita (see Âvaśyaka I. 774).

† बुद्धवयणं—Nandîsûtra.

A. D., in the age of such eminent Buddhistic teachers as Nâgârjuna, Âryadeva, Asaṅga and Buddhaghoṣa, we would have found them or their works mentioned individually, as has been done in the case of the Sâṁkhya authors. The list clearly reveals an atmosphere of flourishing Brahmanism which, as we know, characterized the three or four centuries from the death of Aśoka to the coronation of Kaniṣka. That the Mahâbhârata and the Râmâyaṇa were popular works read at certain hours of the day among the people in the time of the Anuyogadvâra does not impair the conclusion we have arrived at. For we know that they were read in the remote Indian colony of Cambodia about 600 A.D., and the custom of reading them as sacred literature may have been established in India several centuries before. Land grants dated in the 5th century A. D., and found in various parts of India, quote Mahābhārata as an authority possessed of the character of a Smṛti or Dharmaśāstra—a status and breadth of popularity which it cannot have acquired in a couple of centuries.

Having thus seen that the Mâṭhara-Vṛtti may with a great deal of probability be referred to the first century A. D., we place Vâtsyâyana a century or two earlier, which will account for the vast development of the Science of Logic which took place in the interval between Vâtsyâyana and Mâṭhara.

The date here proposed for Vâtsyâyana may appear to be a violent outrage upon the general opinion of Orientalists in regard to this matter, who place him in the fourth or fifth century A.D. But I submit that the arguments by which their theory is supported are in the first place inconclusive; and, secondly, they have not been co-ordinated with the evidence of the works cited above, a point of view which has been entirely overlooked by these scholars. Even if Dr. Jacobi is right in holding that Vâtsyâyana's revised edition of the Nyâya-Sûtras discusses the Śûnyavâda or Nihilism of the Mâdhyamika school of Nâgârjuna (about 200–250 A. D.) but not the

Vijñânavâda or Idealism of the Yogâcâra school of Asaṅga and Vasubandhu, he cannot take the latter part of the 5th century A. D. (to which Vasubandhu was assigned by Dr. Takakusu) as the lower limit of the date of Vâtsyâyana. For the date of Vasubandhu, has been pushed back to the third century A. D. by the researches of Peri, and, therefore Vātsyâyana will have to be placed at the latest in the early part of that century. Again, even on Weber's hypothesis of the date of the Jaina Siddhânta, if Anuyoga belongs to circa 400 A. D., and Mâṭhara to 350, Vâtsyâyana cannot be later than 250 A. D. Although Dr. Jacobi's and Dr. Vidyâbhûṣaṇa's date of Vâtsyâyana is thus carried back nearly 200 years, it requires to be pushed up still further by nearly three centuries if we are to do full justice to the authority of the Śvetâmbara tradition about the composition of Anuyogadvâra. The only difficulty in the way is the supposed posteriority of Vâtsyâyana to Nâgârjuna and to the author of the " Laṅkâvatârasûtra ". It is said that certain aphorisms in the Nyâyasûtra 'do not constitute an essential part of the Nyâyasûtra, and were evidently interpolated into it before or during the time of Vâtsyâyana, who wrote a commentary on them.' I wonder how such a statement could be made, despite the fact that the impugned passages discuss (1) the question of the reality of the external world and its cause, which arises directly from the topics of 'प्रवृत्ति' and 'दोष' and (2) another about the nature of बुद्धि whether it is नित्य or अनित्य or क्षणिक wherein the Buddhist standpoint comes naturally to be considered as an extreme view in opposition to that of the Sâṁkhya. It is remarkable that there is not a single Nyâyasûtra of a convincing character which reproduces *verbatim* the corresponding text or part of the text of Nâgârjuna's Mâdhyamika Sûtra. The few that seem to do so contain either the siddhânta or the dṛṣṭântas which may have come down from an earlier period and repeated *verbatim* according to the general custom of Indian writers, who love to make an *anuvâda* of an opponent's position in his own words, and, besides, show little disposition to vary the dṛṣṭântas*. Besides, the very fact that in the parallels which Dr. Vidyâbhûṣaṇa has cited there is often a difference of words without a difference of sense points to the conclusion that the author of the Sûtras had used some work of Mâdhymika philosophy other than the Mâdhyamika Vṛtti of Nâgârjuna. Thus, for example, Nâgârjuna's 'गतं न गम्यते' etc. which Dr. Vidyâbhûṣaṇa cites as the original of the Nyâya Sûtra 'वर्तमानाभावः पततः पतितपतितव्यकालोपपत्तेः' appears to me to be really not its original but only a parallel, the original being some other work earlier than both. Prof. Viduśekhara Bhaṭṭâcârya has rightly observed: "Certainly Nâgârjuna established the Mâdhyamika school. But it does not follow from it that all the materials for building the new structure were his own. He chiefly collected them from the works previous to him, such as the Prajñâpâramitâ, Lankâvatâra", etc.

Now the Lankâvatâra itself clearly indicates that it is based upon older traditions of the Mâdhyamika philosophy. The very mythological setting of the treatise, in which Buddha teaches the doctrine of Śûnyatâ to Râvaṇa, shows that the author wants the reader to accept the doctrine as an old heritage. Besides, it is clearly declared to have been taught by 'former Buddhas,'† which need not be taken literally, but which does point to a date long prior to the composition of the Lankâvatâra Sûtra. Besides, one of the passages of the Laṁkâvatâra shows that the doctrine of *Kṣaṇikatâ* had been criticized by earlier writers and the author had therefore to

* Of this we have numerous instances in the commentaries on the "Trividham Anumâna" which are cited by me in my paper on the subject. Moreover, in the "Laṅkāvatāra", we read the illustration मरीचि-उदक-चन्द्र. Is it contended that the Upanisad which contains the illustration of जलचन्द्र is posterior to Laṅkāvatāra ?

† "लङ्कावतारसूत्रं वै पूर्वबुद्धानुवर्णितम् ।"

stand on his defence and explain what it really meant and *what it did not mean.* Thus, we read:

निर्व्यापारं क्षणिकं विविक्तं कायवर्जितम् ।
अनुत्पत्तिं च धर्माणां क्षणिकार्थं वदाम्यहम् ।
उत्पत्त्यनन्तरं भग्नं न वै देशेमि बालिशाः ।

All this is not surprising if we remember that the doctrine of Kṣaṇikatâ, Nairâtmya or Śûnyatâ, is of the very essence of Buddhism, and its logical representation must have been attempted centuries before the age of Nâgârjuna and Laṅkâvatâra Sûtra. The controversy of 'Sâssatavâda' and 'Ucchedavâda' is at least as old as Buddhism, perhaps even the Upaniṣads (see Bṛ. Up.); moreover, the very existence of a school of Buddhist thinkers who call themselves Sarvâstitvavâdins (a sub-division of the Sthaviras and one of the primitive schools of Buddhism) implies that there existed a rival school which denied that "All exists." This may be either the school of Vijñânavâdins who held that "not all, but only vijñânas exist", or those who denied the existence of every thing, including even the *vijñânas.*†

We may therefore claim that the Buddhistic doctrines which are noticed in the Nyâya-Sûtras do not compel us to believe that they belong to a period posterior to the Laṁkâvatâra Sûtra or the Mâdhyamika Vṛtti.

After quoting Dr. Keith who says "We need not, of course, take seriously the conception of Nâgârjuna as the creator of the Śûnyavāda philosophy", Dr. Randle rightly adds: "Therefore references to the S'ûnyavâda in the Nyâya Sûtra

---

† The two doctrines were more or less inseparably bound up together, and even as late as the Nyāya Sûtra it is difficult to decide whether a particular adhikaraṇa contains a refutation of the one or the other. So also in the quotation from 'Vṛttikāra' which occurs in S'ābara Bhāṣya of the P. Mîmâṃsa Sûtras.

are not necessarily references to Nâgârjuna: unless the phrases in N. S. which are parallel to phrases in Mk. (Mâdhyamika Kârikâ) first originated with Nâgârjuna. It is possible to regard these as 'tags' which are repeated by Nâgârjuna from earlier S'ûnyatâvâda writers: in which case Vidyâbhûṣaṇa's argument for the priority of Nâgârjuna to the N. S. passages in question and Jacobi's assumption that the date of Nâgârjuna gives the earliest limit for the composition of the Nyâya Sûtra fall to the ground."

("Indian Logic in the Early Schools" p. 18, footnote)

The principal authors of the Vaiśeṣika and Nyāya schools up to the age of Malliṣeṇa are:

1. Râvaṇa—the author of a work known as "Râvaṇa-Bhâṣya"† which is not extant but seems to have been known to Śaṁkarâcârya.§ He is earlier than the author of the "Laṅkâvatâra Sûtra". Could it not be that the "काश्यप" of the Kârikâs quoted by Praśastapâda in the section on Inference and Fallacies ("......इत्येवं काश्यपोऽब्रवीत्") was Râvaṇa, 'son of Kaśyapa'? A work consisting of kârikâs or mnemonic lines would thus fall between Kaṇâda and Praśastapâda.

2. Pras'astapâda—the author of a Vaiś. work called "Padârtha-Dharma-Saṃgraha," popularly known as "Praśastapâda Bhâṣya," which is not a regular Bhâṣya or exposition of each Vaiśeṣika sûtra but an independent work running along the lines of the Vaiś. Sûtras. In his hands the Vaiś. system has undergone much development. Among his special contributions to the system, Keith notes "his recognition in place of the seventeen qualities of Kaṇâda of twenty-four; the development of the doctrine of generality and particularity and inherence, which assume

† See Keith's I. L. A. p. 27 and M. M. Kuppuswāmi Śāstri's article in the Madras J. O. S. Vol. III Pt. I.

§ See Śāṃkara Bhāṣya on Br. Sûtra II. ii. 11 and "Prakaṭārthavivaraṇa" thereon.

new shapes in his hands; the occurrence of a complete theory of creation in which the Supreme Lord appears as creator; and the elaboration of logical doctrine, which is particularly evident in the case of the doctrine of fallacies." As regards his date, the general view is that he belonged to the fifth century A. D. and was posterior to the Buddhist logician Diṅnâga who should be referred to 400 A. D.‡ After examining all the pros and cons of the problem, however, I come to think that the balance of probability is in favour of Praśastapâda's priority to Diṅnâga—a view which Stcherbatsky has now urged against his own theory of an earlier date.¶

3. Vâtsyâyana—the author of the N. Bhâṣya. It is difficult to surmise which of the two viz., Vâtsyâyana and Râvaṇa, was earlier. For, the work of Râvaṇa is lost and consequently there is no internal evidence to help us. But there is no doubt that Vâtsyâyana was acquainted with the Vaiśeṣika system. For his date, see supra.

4. Uddyotakara—He wrote his epoch-making work—the "Nyāya-vārtika"—to answer the criticisms of the "bad (Buddhist) logicians who had attacked the system of Akṣapāda (Gautama)". His work has been very helpful in reconstructing the history of mediaeval Buddhist Logic (See Randle's "Fragments from Diṅnāga"). Bāṇa, a contemporary and court poet of King Harṣa (A. D. 620-644), mentions Subandhu's "Vāsavadattā", and the latter refers to Uddyotakara; consequently Uddyotakara cannot be later than the first half of the seventh century and was probably a little earlier.

5. Vâcaspatimis'ra—an author of great versatility and depth of thought. He has written works on Sāṃkhya, Yoga,

‡ Keith's I. L. A. p. 27.

¶ See my Introduction to the "Nyāya-praveśa" Part I (G. O. S.) pp. xv to xxi where the problem has been fully discussed.

Vedānta and P. Mîmāṃsā. These are: "Nyâyaśûci-nibandha;" "Nyâyavârtikatâtparyaṭîkâ", a commentary on Uddyotakara's "Nyâya-Vârtika"; Sâṁkhyatattvakaumudî, a commentary on Îśvarakṛṣṇa's "Sâṁkhyakârikâ; "Tattvavaiśâradî", a commentary on "Vyâsa-Bhâṣya" on Patañjali's "Yogasûtras"; "Vidhiviveka" and "Nyâyakaṇikâ", both works of P. Mîmâṃsâ. He flourished in the ninth century (about 850) A. D., as appears from the date given in his Nyâya-śûcînibandha, 898—which has been understood to be the Vikrama Saṁvat year corresponding to 841 of the Christian era.

6. Bhâsarvajña—author of the "Nyâyasâra". This work is noteworthy because of its giving a distinct place to S'aivism within the framework of Logic. This association was hitherto an historical accident due to the writers on Nyâya and Vaiśeṣika being Śaivites in religion. In the Nyâyasâra, S'aivism for the first time finds a distinct place in the system. The work is further important for our purpose, as Malliṣeṇa quotes in one place the "Nyāyabhûṣaṇa" which is a commentary on the "Nyâyasâra", and is referred to by Ratnakîrti, a Buddhist writer of the tenth century.

7. Udayana or Udayanâcârya:—He has written several works both on Nyāya and Vaiśeṣika, though separately. These are: "Lakṣaṇāvali", a book of logical definitions; "Kiraṇāvali" a commentary on Praśastapāda's Vaiś. Bhāṣya; "Nyāyavârtika-tātparaya-pariśuddhi", a commentary on Vācaspati's N. Vārt. Tātparya; "Kusumâñjali", a famous work on the proofs of the existence of God and allied questions such as life before and hereafter, being a counterblast to the "Îśvarabhaṅga-kārikā" of Kalyāṇarakṣita, a Buddhist writer of the 9th century; and "Âtmatattva-viveka", a work on the nature of the soul in which the author criticises the Buddhist doctrines of Apoha, Kṣaṇabhaṅga and S'ruti-aprāmāṇya. His date is definitely fixed at 984 A. D. on the evidence of his own statement in his "Lakṣaṇāvali". He brought fresh vigour to the Nyāya school and is very frequently quoted by later writers as a great

authority on the tenets of that school which was now being amalgamated with the Vaiśeṣika. Besides being a logician and a metaphysician he was a religious teacher of the S'aivite school. It may be noted in passing that just as the Sâṁkhya was associated with Vaiṣṇavism, Yoga partly with S'âktism, so was Nyâya-Vaiśeṣika with S'aivism. The last fact—of the association of Nyāya-Vais. with S'aivism—has been duly noted by the Jaina author of the "Ṣaḍdarśana—Samuccaya". (See Notes).

8. Śrîdhara, the author of the "Nyâyakandali," a very important work written as a commentary on Praśastapâda's Bhâṣya of the Vaiśeṣika system, and freely extracted in the Syâdvâdamañjarî. He composed this work, as he tells us, in A. D. 991.

9. Jayanta—the author of the "Nyâyamañjarî",:—a full and free exposition of the important principles of the Nyâyadarśana, along the lines of the Sûtras. Jayanta could not have lived earlier than the 9th century since he quotes Vâcaspati (841 A. D.); neither could he be later than the 12th century as he is referred to in the "Syâdvâda-ratnâkara" by Devasûri (1086–1169 A. D.); and by Ratnaprabha (1181 A.D.) in the "Ratnâkarâvatârika," who was an elder contemporary of Hemacandra. A few verses from Jayanta's "Nyâyamañjarî" have been extracted by Malliṣeṇa under Stanza VIII. Like Udayana, he too opposes Kalyâṇarakṣita and Dharmottara.

10. Gaṅgeśa :—The author of the "Tattvacintâmaṇi", in which the logic of the Nyâya darśana attains its final shape. He (A.D. 1150–1200) was the founder of the Nuddea (Navadvîpa) school of "Navya–Nyâya," which in the subtleties of its logical definitions went far beyond the founder of the school. But the development of the new school is later, and therefore it is of little interest to us as readers of the "Syâdvâdamañjarî."

(5) Pûrvamîmāṃsā :—As the Vaiśeṣika was engaged in determining the properties of things, and the Nyāya in formulating the principles of Logic, the main function of the Pûrva-Mîmâṃsâ school—which is demonstrably older than both—was to lay down the principles of Interpretation, originally that of Vedic texts relating to the Sacrifice. But its constant contact with rival systems which attacked the authority of the Veda drew it into the arena of epistemology and metaphysics. Thus, from the 'Vṛtti' of the 'Vṛttikâra of the Pûrva-Mîmâṃsâ'. Whom Śabarasvāmin, the Bhâṣyakâra of the P. Mîmâṃsâ Sûtras, quotes, we observe this new element in the darśana, which has been further developed by Prabhâkara and Kumârila and their later exponents Śâlikanâtha and Pârthasârathimiśra. While the epistemological and metaphysical problems were foreign to the original purpose of Mîmâṃsâ, the system found its natural development in the direction of logic, with the result that the Mîmâṃsâ came to be called also "Nyâya," and was the parent of what is now known as the "Nyâya-darṣana".* But the great popularity of the darśana and its importance as a philosophical system date from the time of its revival under Kumârila, who criticised many of the favourite doctrines of Buddhist philosophy with great vigour and dialectic skill.

The principal writers of this school are :—

1. The "Vṛttikâra," to be identified with Upavarṣa or Bodhâyana.†

2. The Bhâṣyakâra, Śabarasvâmin ‡ His quotation from

---

* The ten-membered syllogism which Vātsyāyana notes in his commentary on I. i. 32 seems to be an early effort of the Mîmāṃsā school in this line.

† After Jaimini,—the sûtrakāra of P. Mîmāṃsā. To both of these is attributed a commentary on the two (Pûrva and Uttara or Karma and Brahma-) Mîmāṃsās.

‡ See Keith's "Karmamîmāṃsā" p. 9: Madras J. O. R. Vol. I. Part III—"Vṛttikāragrantha" By Dr. A. Sankaran,

"Vṛttikâra" and the latter's reference to 'S'ûnyavâda' and 'Nirâlambanavâda' of the Buddhists, Nâgârjuna etc. suggest "that 400 A.D. is the earliest date to which he can be assigned." The force of this argument, however, has much diminished since these schools are now dated before Nâgârjuna and Vasubandhu.

3. Prabhâkara and Kumârila. They belong to the 7th or 8th century A. D. Their relative chronology is a much debated problem which is still unsettled.* The latter who wrote "Vârtikas" or supplementary commentaries called the "Ślokavârtika" and "Tantravârtika" on Śabarasvâmin's Bhâṣya is particularly famous for his strong criticism of Buddhist logic and philosophy. He was generally supposed to belong to the latter half of the †8th century A.D., and was believed to be an elder contemporary of Śaṁkarâcârya. This date, however, has now been pushed back a few decades in the light of a recent publication in the G. O. S. For, while his criticism of Dharmakîrti who flouished in the first half of the 7th century A. D. furnishes the upper limit of his date, the lower limit is supplied by references made to his views by Śântarakṣita, the author of the "Tattva-saṃgraha" who is

---

* A review of the arguments of both sides is impossible within the space at our disposal. See Das-Gupta's "Indian Philosophy" p. 69; Keith's "Karmamîmāṃsā" pp. 9–10; Dr. Ganganath Jha's "Prabhākara school"; Prof. Kuppuswami Sâstri's paper in the Proceedings of the Second (Calcutta) Oriental Conference; "Introduction to Pûrvamîmāṃsā" by Pasupatinath Sastri; "Introduction to Prabhākara-Vijaya" by Pt. Ananta Kṛṣṇa Sastri; and "Kumārila and Prabhâkara" by Pt. Chinnaswami Sastri; "Prabhâkaras: Old and new" by Prof. Hiriyanna, Madras J. O. R. Vol. IV Pt. II.

† See Dr. K. B. Pathak's article in the Journal of the Bombay Branch of the R. A. S. Vol. XVIII.

'full of Kumârila' and lived in the first half of the 8th century A. D.‡

Other important writers on Pûrvamîmāṁsā are later than Hemacandra and Malliṣeṇa and consequently we need not note them here.

(6) The Philosophy of "Vedânta," like that of (Pûrva-) Mîmâṃsâ, is at once old and new. As the name signifies the philosophy originates from the Upaniṣads, the end ('anta') or conclusion ('siddhānta') of the Veda. But its great popularity is due to its revival under S'aṁkarâcârya in the 9th century A. D. It is called "Brahma-mîmâṃsâ" as opposed to " Karma-Mîmâṃsâ, " or " Uttara-Mîmâṃsâ " as opposed to " Pûrva-Mîmâṃsâ." This difference of nomenclature is founded upon the difference of view of the relation of the one system to the other. S'aṁkara considers 'Karma' and 'Jñâna' to be essentially inconsistent and therefore rejects the claim of the 'Karma-Mîmâṃsâ' to be regarded as a necessary antecedent to 'Brahma-Mîmâṃsâ.' It is probably that the two were treated at one time as parts of a single study. As Bodhâyana has remarked "संहितमेतच्छास्त्रम्". There can be no point, however, in the remark that the two form one continuous whole, unless the two were really separate but were to be joined, or a doubt had been cast on their continuity before the time of Bodhâyana. That the two must have originated separately admits of little doubt. But later a tendency towards syncretism must have set in, which accounts for the above remark of Bodhâyana; and this is further corroborated by the fact that Upavarṣa commented on both of them and thus practically treated the two as parts of a single whole. It should be noted, however, that this does not make the two really one, since they have originated in fundamentally different types of thought, and are ascribed to different writers.

‡ Dr. B. Bhattacârya's foreword to the "Tattva-saṃgraha" Vol. I p. LXXXIII (G. O. S.).

The "Sûtras" of the Vedânta darśana which are ascribed to Bâdarâyaṇa are presumably old, but the work as it stands at present would seem to be posterior to post-Christian Buddhist schools which it criticises.† Some attempt has been made§ to show that the sûtras relating to the criticism of Buddhism, like similar sûtras of the Nyâyadarśana, if correctly interpreted, would appear to refer to S'ûnyavâda and not to Vijñānavāda, and therefore their date must fall between that of Nāgārjuna and Vasubandhu. But this argument has lost its point, since as already remarked evidence is growing to show that Vijñānavāda existed even before Vasubandhu, and probably Śûnyavâda also before Nâgârjuna. The underlying assumption that a particular 'Vâda' began with its 'âcârya' may well be set aside; for, an 'âcârya' is not an originator but only a promulgator of the doctrines of his school. But the bulk of the Sûtras, since the Sāṃkhya which they criticise is atheistic, cannot be dated earlier than the later Mahâbhârata period when the Sâṃkhya had begun to gravitate towards atheism.

The only doctrine of "Vedânta" which Hemacandra and Malliṣeṇa have noticed is that of Śaṁkara's school, and there again that of "Mâyâ" only, which S'aṁkara and his grand-teacher—Gauḍapâda—are said to have borrowed from Buddhism. There can be no doubt that the language of Gauḍapâda's "Kârikâs" in certain places savours of Buddhist influence, but there is a fundamental difference between the Vedântin's "Brahman" and the Buddhist's "Śûnya", which cannot be ignored. As regards S'aṁkarâcârya also, a similar

† A reference to "Brahma Sûtras" is to be found in the "Bhagavadgîta" ["ब्रह्मसूत्रपदैश्चैव हेतुमद्भिर्विनिश्चितैः"]. That this work could not have been the same as the "Brahmasûtras" which we have at present is beyond question. But it is difficult to decide whether it was the nucleus of the work which we now have or was entirely different.

§ By Jacobi in the article mentioned above.

charge has been made,* but it does not seem to be well founded. The doctrine of "Mâyâ" is only a description by analogy of "Nirupâkhyatâ," and the latter is implied in the antinomy which is said to surround the nature of Brahman in the Upaniṣads and is distinctly declared in the Bh. Gitâ which says "न सत्तन्नासदुच्यते." Moreover, in tracing the doctrine to the Buddhist source, the originality of the latter is taken for granted. It has never been investigated whether the word 'संवृति' of Mahâyâna Buddhism could carry any sense unless there was a Reality which was 'संवृत' *i. e.* covered or obscured, and whether 'शून्य' could mean such a Reality at all. Is not the word 'संवृति' suggested by the "अपावृणु" of "हिरण्मयेन पात्रेण सत्यस्यापिहितं मुखम्। तत्त्वं पूषन्नपावृणु सत्यधर्माय दृष्टये।" and "विवृणुते" of "तस्यैष आत्मा विवृणुते तनूं स्वाम्॥"? Moreover, is not 'नामरूप' of the Buddhist 'chain of causes' a reminiscence of the same word or words occurring in the Upaniṣad? Besides, in the "Kathâvatthu" ("Points of Controversy"—P. T. S.) where the question "whether Matter is subjective" is discussed, the word used is 'sârammana' (= skt sârambhaṇa) and the commentator there notes the two meanings of the word 'ârammaṇa'—a word which comes down from the famous text of the Upaniṣadic Idealism, viz., "वाचारम्भणं विकारो नामधेयं मृत्तिकेत्येव सत्यम्" (Chândogya), which is the sheet-anchor of Śaṁkara's Vedânta.

It should be remembered in this connection that Mahâyâna Buddhism was a development of the original Buddhism under the influence of Brahmanism and local creeds; and that the dialectical method of the Mâdhyamika school was anticipated in the earlier speculations relating to the nature of Brahman, in the Syâdvâda of the Jaina, and in such pre-Buddhistic thought as that of Saṁjaya recorded in the Buddhist canon.

---

* That he has been called 'प्रच्छन्नबौद्ध' is no proof of his being really so. It is after all an argumentum ad bacculum which is not meant to be taken seriously.

The philosophical literature of Vedânta is immense. It can be classified, however, under the following heads:

(1) Philosophy of the Upaniṣads.

(2) The Vedânta of the post-Upaniṣadic period of the Mahâbhârata and the Bhagavadgîtā.

(3) The Vedânta of the Sûtrakâras—first, that of the predecessors of Bâdarâyaṇa, such as Auḍulomi, Âśmarathya, Kâśakṛtsna etc., and afterwards that of Bâdarâyaṇa.

(4) The Vedânta of pre-Śâṁkara commentators of the Upaniṣads and the Sûtras—such as the Vṛttikâra etc.

(5) The Vedânta of S'âṁkara.

(6) Post-S'âṁkara Vedânta of his followers.*

(7) The Vedânta of the other Âcâryas, such as Râmânuja, Vallabha and Madhva, and of minor teachers, such as Vijñânabhikṣu, which differed radically from that of S'aṁkara and flourished side by side with that of his followers.¶

It would be going too far beyond the scope of this section if we were to enter into the chronology and the teachings of these schools, especially because Hemacandra and Malliṣeṇa had mainly concerned themselves with a single problem of Vedânta—viz., the Mâyâvâda—which is the characteristic feature of the Vedânta of S'aṁkara.

Among the post-Bâdarâyaṇa and *pre-S'âṁkara Vedântins* we may note:

1. Bodhâyana—the Vṛttikâra of the Brahmasûtras of Bâdarâyaṇa. Some identifiy him with—

---

* For a summary of the Vedānta of the followers of S'aṁkara and their dates see Dr. Das-Gupta's "History of Indian Philosophy" Vol. II.

¶ For the minor schools of Vedānta, before and after Saṁkara, see Prof. Hiriyanna's articles in the Madras Journal of Oriental Research.

2. Upavarṣa—who is said to have written a commentary on the Pûrva and Uttara-Mîmâṃsâs. Sufficient evidence in favour of the identification of Bodhâyana with Upavarṣa is, however, wanting. Both of these must have flourished before the Christian era, if the nucleus of the Bâdarâyaṇa sûtras is distinguished from their present form.

3. Dramiḍâcârya—an âcârya who belonged to the Dravida country.

4. Ṭaṁka—who is also supposed to be the same as Âtreya or Brahma-nandin—and is known as "Vâkyakâra".

5. Bhartṛprapañca—Like Auḍulomi he stood for the doctrines of "Bhedâbheda" and "Brahma-Pariṇāma". His identity with Bhartṛihari is doubtful.

Among the early exponents of the S'âṁkara school we have—

6. Maṇḍana—Different from 'Maṇḍana-miśra' who, if we are to believe a late tradition, was a pupil of Kumârila and a great Pûrva-Mîmâṃsist whom S'aṃkarâ vanquished in a debate and converted to Vedântism. There was one Maṇḍana who was a Vedântin. He was probably a contemporary (A.D. 800) of Śaṁkara (who died in A. D. 820), and advocated an extreme form of subjective Idealism or Solipsism, which was revived later by a S'aṁkara Vedântin, the author of the Vedânta–Siddhânta–Muktâvali. He composed Brahmasiddhi and several other works of importance.

7. Sureśvara—(circa 820 A. D.) said to be the name of Maṇḍanamiśra after he became a saṁnyâsin and a disciple of Śaṃkarâcârya, according to the tradition of the "Sâṁkara-Digvijaya". At any rate, he is not to be identified with Maṇḍana, the solipsist, from whose view S'ureśvara's is distinguished carefully by Sureśvara's pupil Sarvajñamuni, the author of the "Saṁkṣepa S'ârîraka", and by his commentator. He was the author of Bṛhadâraṇyaka Bhâṣya Vârtika and

Naiṣkarmyasiddhi—works of great importance in the history of Sâṁkara Vedânta.

8. Padmapâda—(circa 820 A. D.) another disciple of Śaṃkarâcârya who wrote a work called "Pañcapâdikâ". On it Prakâśatman wrote "Pañcapâdikâ-vivaraṇa" about 1200 A.D., and the latter received a commentary from Vîdyâraṇya (1350 A. D.) called "Vivaraṇa-Prameya Saṃgraha".

A little later, but still ranking among the early S'aṃkarites are:—

9. Vâcaspatimiśra—(about 840 A.D.) the famous writer on Sâṃkhya, Yoga, Nyâya, Pûrva-Mîmâṃsâ and Vedânta. His great work of the last school is a valuable commentary on S'aṃkara's S'ârîraka Bhâṣya of the Vedânta Sûtras, named Bhâmatî after his wife.

10. Sârvajñâtma Muni (900 A. D.)—a disciple of Sureśvarâcârya and a younger contemporary of Vâcaspati-miśra. His famous work "Saṃkṣepa-S'ârîraka" is more than a mere abridgment of S'aṃkara's S'ârîraka Bhâṣya as it modestly calls itself.

To the later S'âṃkara schools belong:—

11. Prakaṭârtha—a work of the 11th or 12th century A. D. It is a commentary on Śâṁkara S'ârîraka Bhâṣya, and has been commented upon in a work of about 1200 A. D. called "Prakaṭârtha vivaraṇa".

12. S'rî Harṣa—(1150 A. D.) the author of the famous "Khaṇḍanakhaṇḍakhâdya", a work full of the subtle dialectics of Vedânta composed in the interests of "Anirva-canîyatâkhyâti" Vâda.

13. Prakâśatman (1200 A. D.)—the author of Pañca-pâdikâ-vivaraṇa.

14. Citsukhâcârya—(1220 A. D.)—the author of the famous "Citsukhî", a work which is much admired in the school of S'âṃkara Vedânta.

15. Vidyâraṇya (1350 A. D.)—the greatest name in the history of later Sâṃkara Vedânta, and mediaeval Brâhmanism. He wrote a commentary called "Vivaraṇapremeyasaṃgraha" on the "Pañcapâdikâvivaraṇa" of Prakâśâtman, Pañcadaśî, a comprehensive work on S'âṃkara Vedânta written in verse in a popular style, and "Jîvanmuktiviveka", a valuable work on Vedântic life.

Among the latest representatives of S'âṁkara Vedânta we have to note—

16. Madhusûdana Sarasvati—the author of the famous "Advaitasiddhi" and a commentary on the Bhagavadgîtâ and some Bhakti works. He lived in the early part of the sixteenth century.

17. Prakâśânanda—the author of the famous "Vedânta Siddhânta-Muktâvalî" lived in the latter half of the 16th century. He is a powerful advocate of "Dṛṣṭisṛṣṭivâda"—or pan-egoism an extreme form of idealism preached in Yoga-Vâsiṣṭha and by Maṇḍana. (See supra)

18. Appayadîkṣita—a great writer of the seventeenth century on Alaṁkara, Vedânta and of numerous Bhakti works; the author of the "Siddhântaleśa", a digest of Sâṃkara Vedânta which is a monument to his vast knowledge of Śaṃkara schools and his wonderful power of abridgment.

It will be remembered that in tracing the logical evolution of darśanas we dealt with Brahmanical systems only. We omitted Buddhist and Jaina darśanas from the account not because they were in any way less important, but because they did not constitute links in the same logical chain. No historical account of Indian philosophy, however, can be complete without a statement of the essential tenets of the Buddhist and Jaina darśanas and of the stages through which they have passed. A short note on the Lokâyata or Cârvaka should also be added, since it has been noticed both by Hemacandra and Malliṣeṇa in our book.

(7) Buddhism—The teachings of Gautama Buddha, the historical founder of Buddhism, are supposed to have been embodied in the "Tipiṭaka", or the three Baskets of the Pâli canon, consisting of Sutta, Vinaya and Abhidhamma. The last is undoubtedly later than the other two, but even these in their present form belong linguistically to the age succeeding that of Aśoka's Edicts, and are thus divided by several centuries from the original source. Attempts have, therefore, been made to reconstruct Gautama's original teachings* as distinguished from those attributed to him in the Pâli canon. But like all reconstructions, this is based upon certain assumptions†

---

* See "Śākya or Buddhist origins" by Mrs. Rhys Davids.

† Stcherbatsky rejects this method. He writes "It is thus assumed that there has been a primitive Buddhism, very much different, even, as it would seem, quite contrary to what later on finds its expression in the Pāli canon. Pessimism, Nihilism, Soul-denial, psychology without a Soul, annihilation as ultimate end, all those features that mark out Buddhism among other religions, Indian as well as non-Indian, did not exist. It was the Buddhism of the Buddha himself which was so radically different from anything that appeared later in historical times, as Buddhism. The consequence of this hypothesis of a simple creed preceding historical Buddhism is an attempt to interpret the latter in the light of the former". Dr. Stcherbatsky thus rejects the hypothesis of 'a simple creed' of Gautama preceding historical Buddhism and regards the founder as a speculative philosopher whose philosophic position he defines as follows:—

"As far as we can understand his [Gautama Buddha's] philosophical position, it seems that he was deeply impressed by the contradiction of assuming an eternal, pure, spiritual principle which, for incomprehensible reasons, must have been polluted by all the filth of mundane existence in order, later on, to revert to its original purity. He was thus led to a denial of every permanent principle. Matter and Mind

which we fear go too far. This much, however, can be safely asserted—that Gautama Buddha was primarily an ethical teacher, and not a speculative philosopher, whose ethical teaching was based not on a system of theology or metaphysics but on psychology—or to be more definite, on the psychology of Pain with which all sentiency was bound up. In the interests of this particular type of ethics, he asserted certain propositions which, in the course of time, came to be understood too literally by his followers, who supported them by arguments which involved them in controversies with Brâhmaṇas and Jainas. For example, one great error which

---

appeared to him as split in an infinite process of evanescent elements (dharmas), the only ultimate realities, beside Space and Annihilation. The conception of an impersonal world-process was probably prepared by the idea of an impersonal unique substance of the world, as developed in the Upaniṣads. The analysis of the world into its elements of Matter and Mind was probably, to a certain extent, prepared by the work of the Sâṁkhya school. The originality of Buddha's position consisted in denying substantiality altogether, and converting the world-process in a concerted appearance of discrete evanescent elements. Forsaking the Monism of the Upaniṣads and the Dualism of the Sâṁkhyas, he established a system of the most radical Pluralism. That the essence and the starting-point of Buddhism were speculative appears very clearly, if we give credit to the records about the other wandering teachers who were the contemporaries of Buddha and often engaged in controversies with him. The questions at issue between them were of a speculative nature. Ethical questions, the explanation of retribution, were predominant, but they always were narrowly linked together with some system of ontology and some doctrine of a Final Release."—Stcherbatsky's "Conception of Buddhist Nirvâṇa" pp. 2–5.

I do not think Dr. Stcherbatsky is right in his view that Gautama Buddha was essentially a speculative philosopher.

Gautama Buddha found to be the root of all evil was belief in an entity called *Âtman* which engendered selfishness both in this world and the world hereafter. Belief in *permanence* and *reality* of the world with its many supposed joys was another hallucination which gave rise to longings of all sorts, including thirst for life and its pleasures. Gautama declared that all was painful (दुःख), all was transitory (क्षणिक), all was emptiness, that is to say, nothing at all (शून्य), or nothing but ideas (प्रज्ञप्ति or विज्ञान), or a mere creation of mental habits (वासना), or imagination (विकल्प). All these doctrines which in their rudimentary form may well be supposed to be part of the original teaching of Gautama Buddha and which are clearly stated in the Pâli canon, are elaborately treated in the third and last stage of the history of Buddhism—that known as "Mahâyâna" or "Sanskrit Buddhism" which is the only form of Buddhism known to most of the Brâhmaṇa and Jaina writers.

Of the three stages into which the history of Buddhism is divisible viz.—

(1) Original teaching of Gautama Buddha,
(2) Buddhism of the Pâli canon and
(3) Sanskrit Buddhism,

it is the last with which we as students of Syâdvâdamañjarî are concerned.

Its principal schools are those of—

(1) The *Vaibhâṣikas*—the followers of the 'Vibhâṣâ' or commentaries, who declare that *all* is real;

(2) the *Sautrântikas*, or followers of the Sûtras or texts, who hold that the external world is not directly perceived but only indirectly inferred from the images which it creates in the mind;

(3) the *Yogâcâras*—who assert that ideas are the only reals, there being no external reality either directly perceived or mediately inferred. They are so called because their leaders incidentally practised Yoga, and their idealism was naturally suggested by this practice which is mainly concerned with mental life.

(4) the *Mâdhyamikas*—who deny reality of both the ends, being (bhâva) and non-being (abhâva), and affirm it of the centre (मध्य) only, which is neither being nor non-being but simply 'śûnya' or Emptiness.

According to a tradition referred to by Mr. Sogen, "the Vaibhâṣikas arose in the third century after Buddha's death; the Sautrântikas in the fourth; the Mâdhyamika school, as Aryadeva states, came into existence five hundred years after the Nirvâṇa of Buddha; and Asaṅga, the founder of the Yogâcâras or the Vijñânavâdins, is, at least, as late as the third century of the Christian era." This chronological order was till lately generally accepted; the Mâdhyamikas and the Yogâcâras were supposed to be later than the first two, and as between them the Mâdhyamika was considered earlier than the Yogâcâra in accordance with the relative chronology of their respective âcâryas, viz., Nâgârjuna and Asaṅga or Vasubandhu. The fallacy of arguing from the date of the âcârya to the date of the originator of the school is obvious; for âcâryas are only propagators and not the founders of their schools. As I have already shown,* Vijñânavâda existed long before the time of Asaṅga and Vasubandhu, and so there is no reason to make it posterior to the Śûnyavâda of Nâgârjuna. From the position of the Sautrântika who is half an idealist, the next step is naturally to that of the Yogâcâra who is a complete idealist,† rather than to the Mâdhyamika who is a Nihilist.¶

---

* See Supra p. xxv.

† Curiously, this historical sequence of Buddhist darśanas agrees with the mental evolution of Vasubandhu, 'who began his career as a Vaibhâṣika or Sarvâstivâdin,' but 'had strong Sautrântika sympathies' and was 'later converted by his eldest brother Asaṅga to the Yogâcâra school'.

¶ For a contrary opinion see Keith's "Buddhist Philosophy" p. 228.

(8) Cârvâka—Of the systems which have been criticised in the " Dvâtrimśikâ " and the " Syâdvâdamañjarî ", the last but not the least interesting is that of the " Cârvâka ", 'the philosopher of alluring speech' (चारुवाक्) or 'one who swallows' (from चर्व), that is, nullifies the distinctions of virtue and vice. The system is also known as 'Lokâyata' *i. e.* the philosophy of worldly life. By a curious irony the origin of this school is attributed to Bṛhaspati, the preceptor of the gods. He is said to have invented it in order to delude asuras or daityas, the enemies of gods. Probably the system was founded by one Bṛhaspati, who is not to be identified with Bṛhaspati, the 'lord of Prayer' of the Veda or the preceptor of the gods of the later Itihâsa and Purâṇas. Or, it may be that the philosophy of the asuras, that of a comfortable worldly life, with its numerous discoveries of crafts and means of producing wealth, was naturally attributed to one who was considered to be the store of all knowledge, viz., Bṛhaspati, the preceptor of gods. This Lokâyata system which degenerated later into quibbling sophism and a low form of epicureanism was originally 'Nature-lore'—freely recognised as a branch of Brahmanical learning, which included 'wise sayings, riddles, rhymes, and theories handed down by tradition as to cosmogony, the elements, the stars, the weather, scraps of astronomy, of elemetary physics, even of anatomy and knowledge of the nature of precious stones, and of birds and beasts and plants.' It figures as a respectable branch of learning in Kauṭilya's "Arthaśâstra" which refers to an earlier school of the 'followers of Bṛhaspati.' A work on 'Arthaśâstra' called 'Bṛhaspati Sûtras' is available, which after enumerating such wealth-producing avocations as agriculture, cattle-breeding and commerce, says that in the matter of the acquisition of wealth 'Lokâyata' is the supreme śâstra. The philosophic background of this science of worldly life is to be traced to the materialistic outlook which was known even in the age of the Upaniṣads.§ Later,

§ See the Dialogue of Maitreyî and Yâjñavalkya, where

it a became a definite school of thought attributed to one a Ajita Keśakambalin, which is duly noticed in the "Sâmañña Phala Sutta" of the Buddhist canon. This teacher is there reported to have taught his doctrine, which closely resembles that of the Cârvâka school, as follows: "There is no such thing, O King, as alms or sacrifice or offering. There is neither fruit nor result of good or evil deeds. There is no such thing as this world or the next. A human being is built up of the four elements. ("नत्थि दिन्नं यिट्ठं हुतं......सुकटदुक्कटानं कम्मानं फलं विपाको...अयं लोको परो लोको...चातुंमहाभूतिको अयं पुरिसो"......) When he dies the earthy in him returns and relapses to the earth, the fluid to the water, the heat to the fire, the windy to the air, and his faculties pass into space.... It is a doctrine of fools, this talk of gifts. It is an empty lie, mere idle talk when men say there is profit therein. Fools and wise alike, on the dissolution of the body, are cut off, annihilated, and after death they are not." At a later stage in Buddhist and Jaina works this school of the Lokâyatika or Cârvâka is condemned as the school of sophists ('Vaitaṇḍikas'). It seems that just as Science and Atheism–cum–Materialism are not essentially identical, and yet they have often coalesced in the history of Western thought, so the Lokâyata (Nature-lore and economics) and the Cârvâka (epicureanism) in India, though originally different, became one at a later stage. Bṛhaspati Sûtra co-ordinates the Lokayatas or Laukayatikas with the Kâpâlikas, and Guṇaratna, a commentator of "Ṣaḍdarśana Samuccaya" refers to the Kâpâlikas as one of the two schools of 'Nastikas', that is, Lokâyatas or Cârvâkas; one of which, it is said, recognises four elements and the other five.

The history of the system can be divided into the following stages:—

Maitreyî is said to have looked aghast when Yājñavalkya remarked that at the time of death man was absorbed in the elements and nothing remained behind.

(1) The Upaniṣad period (Vide the Dialogue of Yâjña-valkya and Maitreyî).

(2) The early Buddhist period (Vide the account of the philosophy of Ajita Keśakambalin, the Materialist, in the Sâmañña Phalá Sutta).

(a) Lokâyata—i. e. Nature Lore or Physical Science (Vide Dialogues of Buddha S. B. B. Vol. II. p. 166).

(b) Bṛhaspati's and Kauṭilya's Artha-sâstra i. e. Science and art of producing wealth.

(3) Later Buddhist period—when the Lokâyatas were stigmatized as sophists indulging in irresponsible arguments and quibbles.

(4) Association with immoral and superstitious life e. g. that of the Kâpâlikas. (Vide Guṇaratna's commentary on the Ṣaḍdarśana Sammuccaya).

(9) Jainism—Jainism is par excellence *the* doctrine of ahiṃsâ—ahiṃsâ not only of physical life but also of intellectual outlook (darśana). In the latter, moreover, it did not stop short at a mere negative attitude of toleration towards other schools, but took the positive step of investigating *how* each of those schools erred. As a result it came to the conclusion that the errors of those schools were only *partial truths* as seen from particular angles of vision—that none of them was wholly wrong, and if each of them would see things from the point of view of the opponent as well as from their own, there would be perfect harmony all round. The principle of the relativity of knowledge which constitutes this doctrine is an important discovery; yet, in its general form, it is not such as might not occur to common sense. Consequently, we are not surprised that in the "Udâna Sutta" of Pâli Buddhism there occurs a story—the "Parable of the Blind Men and the Elephant"*—

* Pâli जच्चन्धवग्गो=Skt. जात्यन्धवर्गः—the Section of "The Born Blind,"

where certain blind men are said to have come by an elephant and when asked to describe the shape of the animal, each of them gave a description according to the particular limb which he happened to have felt.‡

This general principle of Relativity and Consistency of Contradictories has been tacitly admitted in their systems both by Brâhmaṇa and Buddhist writers, but they know not what they think, says the Jaina. The original contribution, therefore, which Jainism may be said to have made to Philosophy as a result of what I have called their attitude of 'intellectual ahiṃsâ' is its investigation of the different angles of vision or Pathways to Reality (नयs) and its formulation of the doctrine of the Possibility (स्याद्वाद) of apparent contradictories in a real whole. According to Jainism, while its own 'darśana' visualises the *whole* truth ('सकलादेश') other darśanas possess only the gleams of the *broken* light ('विकलादेश'). Both these doctrines, the Nayavâda and the Syâdvâda are varieties of Anekântavâda, i. e. the doctrine of the many-sidedness of Truth. But beyond this there is nothing in common between them, and consequently they do not represent two stages in a single movement of thought, and must therefore be traced to separate origins united in a common viewpoint. Of the two, it is difficult to decide which is earlier. That both of them are anterior to the rupture of Jainism into Śvetâmbara and Digambara about the first century of the Christian era admits of little doubt; for, in spite of the differences of the two sects regarding the Jaina canon, they both uphold the Nayavâda and the Syâdvâda. Of the two the Nayavâda would seem to be earlier by reason of its comparative simplicity, and this view is in harmony with the fact that Umâsvâti, the author of the Tattvâdhigama Sûtra (First century A. D.), while he refers to the different

‡ इमेसु किर सज्जंति एके समण ब्राह्मणा ।
विग्गह नं विवदंति जना एकांगदस्सिनो ॥—Udâna.

—एकांगदस्सिनो those who see a single limb only.

kinds of Nayas,* makes no mention of the Syâdvâda and its seven propositions.† And yet it is highly probable that the Syâdvâda existed long before his days. We find the doctrine in an earlier, or possibly erroneous or misunderstood form, recorded in the Buddhist Suttas, where, however, it is not attributed to the 'Nigganṭhas' or Jainas but to 'some recluses and Brâhmaṇas'. This would show that the doctrine had possibly non–Jaina beginnings. There, referring to a class of thinkers whom the speaker characterizes as 'amarâvikkhepikas', that is 'eel-wrigglers' or equivocators, Gautama Buddha says: "Thus fearing and abhorring the wrong in an expressed opinion ('मुसावादभया'), he will neither declare anything to be good, nor to be bad, but on a question being put to him on this or that, he resorts to eel-wriggling, to equivocation and says: 'I do not take it thus, I don't take it the other way. But I advance no different opinion. And I don't deny your position. And I don't say it is neither the one nor the other.'

Thus does he equivocate, and in like manner about each of such propositions as the following:

(a) 1. There is not another world.
2. There both is, and is not another world.
3. There neither is nor is not another world.

(d) 1. A man who has penetrated to the truth continues to exist after death.
2. He does not.
3. He both does, and does not.
4. He neither does, nor does not.

---

* नैगमसंग्रहव्यवहारर्जुसूत्रशब्दा नयाः । T. S. I. 34.

† The T. Sûtra which is supposed to refer to the subject is अर्पितानर्पितसिद्धेः (T. S. V. 31), which however refers only to the general principle of Relativity or Anekânta. In the Bhâṣya, three of the seven propositions are mentioned, viz. affirmation (सत्), denial (असत्) and indescribability (अवक्तव्य), yet not all the seven.

In the "Sâmañña-Phala Sutta" ("The Fruits of the life of a Recluse"),* another work of the Buddhist Pâli canon, the same kind of prevarication is attributed to one Sañjâya of the Belaṭṭha clan, who said: "If you ask me whether there is another world-well if I thought there were, I would say so. And I don't think it is other-wise. And I don't deny it. And I don't say there neither is nor is not another world."

These passages at once put one in mind of the Jaina "Syâdvâda". It is possible that the Buddhist here does injustice to the school which in answer to certain definite questions refused to commit itself to a definite proposition, because in its opinion the proposition would convey only a partial truth and would consequently be 'मुसावाद'. It does not necessarily prove that the positive side to the doctrine was wanting. If, however, in view of the fact that the doctrine is attributed to the 'recluses and Brâhmaṇas' we hold that it could not have been the "Syâdvâda" of the Jainas, it must be understood as an early reference to the 'anirvacanîyatâvâda' of the Vedântin, which led to the "Syâdvâda" of the Jaina as the next positive step.

The teaching of Mahâvîra Svâmin, like that of Gautama Buddha, was primarily ethical, and consequently logic and metaphysics may well be expected to occupy a subordinate place in the early Jaina canon. Accordingly, there occur in it only a few rare references to the principle of Syâdvâda which are relied upon by later writers as providing the Scriptural authority for their doctrine; moreover, these references occur in connection with concrete problems of spiritual philosophy which were debated in the schools and are not evolved as principles of abstract logic.

Hitherto only one or two passages have been traced in the Jaina canon which contain a reference to the Syâdvâda. They occur in the Bhagavatîsûtra and are quoted by the

* S. B. B. Dialogues of the Buddha, Vol. II.

author of the "Nayacakra" who says: "सर्वनयानां जिनप्रवचनस्यैव निबन्धमत्वात् किमस्य निबन्धनमिति चेत्—उच्यते। निबन्धनं चास्य "आया (Skt. आत्मा) भन्ते नाणे (=Skt. ज्ञानं) अन्नाणे (अज्ञानं)" इति स्वामी गौतमस्वामिना पृष्टो व्याकरोति 'गोदमा णाणे नियमा' अतो ज्ञानं नियमादात्मनि ज्ञानस्यान्यव्यतिरेकेण वृत्त्यदर्शनात् ॥ 'आया पुण सिय (=Skt. स्यात्) णाणे सिय अन्नाणे'.*

The Syâdvâda as found in the Bhagavatîsûtra consists of three propositions¶ only—those of अस्ति (affirmation), नास्ति (negation) and अवक्तव्य (indescribability) Thus: "गोयमा अप्पणो आदिट्ठे आया (=आत्मा), परस्य आदिट्ठे नो आया (= न आत्मा), तदुभयस्य आदिट्ठे अवत्तव्वं (अवक्तव्यं) आता ति यणो आता ति य" इति. Among other early references we have one in Bhadrabâhu's "Sûtrakṛtaṅga-niryukti", and another in "Tattvârtha-Bhâṣya"—which has already been noted. Later, the doctrine is found in its fully developed form of 'Seven Propositions' in the "Pravacana-sâra" and "Pañcâstikâya" of Kundakundâcârya, in the "Âptamîmâṃsâ" of Samantabhadra, in the "Sammati-Tarka" and Nyâyâvatâra of Siddhasena Divâkara, in the "Tattvârtha-Râjavârtika" of Akalaṅka, in the "Tattvârtha Ślokavârtika" of Vidyânandin, in the "Pramâṇanaya-tattvâlokâ-laṁkâra of Devasûri and several other independent works and commentaries both of the Digambara and S'vetâmbara sects. But the most exhaustive treatise devoted entirely to the subject is the famous "Saptabhaṁgî-taraṁgiṇî" of Vimaladâsa, a Digambara writer of a much later date. Except the formal difference in the order of the third and fourth propositions of the "Sapta-Bhaṁgî" inter se,—which, again, does not coincide with the difference of Jaina religious sects—there

* I am indebted for this quotation to an article in the "Jaina Sâhitya Saṃśodhaka" by Mr. Rasiklal C. Parikh, whose attention was first drawn to it by Muni Śrî Jinavijayaji.

¶ These came to be known as "मूलभङ्ग"s when later they came to be developed into seven.

has been no change in the Saptabhaṁgî ever since it became a set of seven propositions instead of three. In regard to Nayas, their number has been variously given. The author of the "Tattvârthâdhigama Sûtra" first mentions *five* nayas—नैगमसंग्रहव्यवहारर्जुसूत्रशब्दा नयाः (I. 34) and next adds "आद्यशब्दौ द्वित्रिभेदौ (I. 35), but does not name these subdivisions. These are added, however, in the Bhâṣya, viz., देशपरिक्षेपी and सर्वपरिक्षेपी, sub-divisions of नैगम, and सांप्रत, समभिरूढ and एवंभूत, sub-divisions of शब्द. These, omitting the subdivisions of नैगम which are regarded as unimportant, make *seven*. Siddhasena Divâkara mentions only *six* nayas, omitting नैगम from the earlier list. Some books, such as the "Anekântajayapatâkâ" of Haribhadra, discuss only the more comprehensive proposition of "Anekânta", with special reference to the problems of द्रव्य and पर्याय, नित्य and अनित्य, सामान्य and विशेष etc.

As important as the Syâdvâda and the Nayavâda but occupying a less spectacular place in Jainism, is its definition of Reality—" उत्पादव्ययध्रौव्ययुक्तं सत् ", which like the other two doctrines is a characteristic example of the Jaina's "अनेकान्तवाद".

The principal writers who have contributed to the philosophical literature of Jainism fall in two distinct lines, that of the Śvetâmbaras and that of the Digambaras. While the Digambaras insist upon nudity as essential in ascetic life, and question the authenticity of the canonical works* recognised by the S'vetâmbaras, and while they are divided in the matter of certain miscellaneous dogmas such as the possibility of spiritual emancipation of women there is no important difference in their philosophical tenets. And yet the two traditions

---

* These according to the Śvetâmbara tradition were first collected at a Council held at Pâṭaliputra about 300 B. C. under the presidency of Sthûlabhadra, and were finally redacted and reduced to writing by Devardhigaṇi at Vallabhi about the beginning of the 6th century A. D.

run in separate lines, the writers of one sect rarely quoting or referring to those of the other. Consequently, all the authors whom Malliṣeṇa quotes belong to the Śvetâmbara tradition, except one or two who command respect throughout the Jaina community.

The history of the philosophical writings of Jainism may be divided into the following periods:

I. The period of the canonical works, many of which were composed before the Christian era, and some were added in the interval between the composition and the final redaction of the texts. To this early period belong speculations about the many-sidedness of Reality, about the spirit and nature of matter and the affection of the former by the latter.

II. Next comes the age of the beginnings of systematic works, of which the earliest writers are Umâsvâti and Kundakundâcârya.

(1) Umâsvâti is claimed as a Digambara by the Digambaras and as a S'vetâmbara by the S'vetâmbaras. He was either too high-souled to belong to either of the two warring sects, or, what is more probable, by his time the sects had not ranged themselves in hostile or separate camps. He belongs to the first century A. D. His great work, "Tattvârthâdhigama Sûtra", probably suggested by the 28th chapter of Uttarâdhyayana, has had the honour of becoming a basis of numerous commentaries and subcommentaries both of the S'vetâmbara and the Digambara sect. The Bhâṣya on the Sûtras is regarded as Umâsvâti's own composition by the S'vetâmbaras, while the Digambaras attribute to him only the Sûtras. Among the numerous commentaries and subcommentaries of the Sûtras the following may be noted as chief: The "Bhâṣya", by Umâsvati himself or some other writer of the S'vetâmbara sect; "Sarvârthasiddhi" (Digambara) of Pûjyapâda Devanandi (5th century A. D.) "Gandhahasti Bhaṣya", attributed to Samantabhadra by Digambaras and to Siddhasena Divâkara

by S'vetâmbaras, but considered to be a work of Siddhasenagaṇi, a writer who lived some time between the 7th and the 9th century of the Vikrama Saṁvat according to Pandit Sukhlal; "Râjavârtika" by Bhatta Akalaṁka (Digambara: 8th century A. D.), and S'lokavârtika by Vidyânandi (Digambara: 9th century A. D.).

(2) Kundakundâcârya—an eminent Digambara writer, also of the 1st century A. D. His most famous works are "Pravacanasâra", and "Pañcâstikâya". The first like the "Tattvârthâdhigama" of Umâśvâti is a comprehensive summary of Jainism.

III. The third period which opens with Siddhasena-Divâkara (S'vetâmbara) and Samantabhadra (Digambara) is the golden age of Jaina philosophy. These two writers recognising the fact that the use of Sanskrit for Jaina works was as much a need of their times as that of Prâkrit was of the age of Mahâvîra, wrote in Sanskrit, and their example was followed widely by later writers on Jaina philosophy.

Siddhasena–Divâkara, a Brâhmaṇa convert to the S'vetâmbara sect of Jainism, is assigned to the end of the 6th century A. D. by Dr. Satischandra, and to the last quarter of the 7th century A.D. by Dr. Jacobi and Dr. P. L. Vaidya. This is done by all on somewhat inconclusive grounds, but the date can be taken as fixed within these broad limits. Besides the famous "Dvâtriṃśikâs" or "Sets of Thirty-two Stanzas" he composed two standard works of Jaina Logic, the Nyâyâvatâra and the "Saṃmati–or Sanmati Tarka". The former was commented upon by Siddharṣi in the beginning of the 10th century A. D., and the latter by Abhayadevasûri about the same time.

2. Samantabhadra, a Digambara contemporary of Siddhasena–Divâkara, wrote "Âpta–Mîmâṃsâ" said to be the introductory part of the "Gandhahasti Bhâṣya", which, according to Digambaras, is a work of Samantabhadra,

3. Haribhadra—There have been two Haribhadras, one of whom belongs to this age. He is a voluminous writer on Jaina religion and philosophy. To the latter branch belongs the famous "Ṣaḍdarśana-Samuccaya", which is a very careful and impartial though brief statement of the different systems of Indian philosophy.

4. Bhatta Akalaṃka or Akalaṃka Deva—a famous Digambara writer of the latter part of the 8th century wrote the monumental "Râja-Vârtika" on the "Tattvârtha" of Umâsvâti and "Aṣṭaśati", a commentary on Samantabhadra's "Âpta-Mîmâṃsâ". He also wrote "Nyâyaviniścaya", "Tattvârtha-Vârtika-Vyâkhyânâlaṁkâra" and numerous other works.

5. Vidyânand or -nandi,—a Digambara writer of the early part of the 9th century A. D. He wrote a commentary called " Aṣṭasahasrî " on the " Aṣṭaśati " of Akalaṃka, and "Tattvârtha-śloka-vârtika"—both polemical works of great value to advanced students of Jaina philosophy.

6. Mânikyanandin—another Digambara author of the 9th century, who wrote "Parikṣâmukhasûtra", a manual of Jaina Logic.

IV. The next, and for our purpose the last, period of Jaina philosophy extends from Devasûri and Hemacandra (12th century A. D.) to Guṇaratna (15th century A. D.)

1. Devasûri (1086–1169 A. D.—Dr. Satischandra) an elder contemporary of Hemacandra wrote "Pramâṇa-naya-tattvâlokâlaṃkara" and its commentary "Syâdvâda-ratnâkara".

2. Hemacandra: (1088–1172 A. D.—Dr. Satischandra) a contemporary of Devasûri. A most voluminous writer who besides writing some " Dvâtriṃsikâs " on the model of Siddhasena-Divâkara's similar works, wrote a work on Jaina Logic called "Pramâṇa-Mîmâṃsâ"; and further, he provided

the Jaina readers with standard works on Vyâkaraṇa and Alaṃkâra to replace those composed by Brâhmaṇas. He is, therefore, called "Kalikâla Sarvajña" for his versatility.

Ratnaprabhasûri: (1181 A. D.)—He wrote "Syâdvâda-ratnâkarâ-vatârikâ", a shorter commentary on the "Syâdvâda-ratnâkara" on Pramâṇanayatattvalokâlaṃkara.

Malliṣeṇasûri—(1292 A. D.) The author of our text—the Syâdvâdamañjarî which is mainly a review of Brâhmaṇı, Bauddha and Câṛvâka systems, in the shape of a commentary on Hemacandra's "Anyayoga-vyavacheda-Dvâtriṃśikâ".

Among later miscellaneous writers, Râjaśekhara (1348 A. D.) wrote a "Pañjikâ" on "Ratnâkarâvatârikâ" of Ratnaprabha, and Jñânacandra (1350) a "tippaṇa" on the same. The age may be said to have closed with Guṇaratna (1409) who has written a very lucid and exhaustive commentary on the "Ṣaḍdarśana-Saṃuccaya" of Haribhadra.

IV. A BIRD'S-EYE VIEW OF THE WORK.

Stanzas I-III.

The first three stanzas are introductory.

St. I.

This contains the characterisation of the last Tîrthaṁkara, Śrî Vardhamâna, otherwise known as Mahâvîra Svâmin, as an ideal teacher possessed of what are technically known in Jainism as the four 'अतिशय's or excellences: (1) ज्ञानातिशय—Excellence of wisdom, that is wisdom which is unfailing and best, expressed in one word as 'केवलज्ञान';* (2) अपायापगमातिशय—Excellence consisting in freedom from all evil, viz. the passions; (3) वचनातिशय—Excellence as a teacher, since he has taught the doctrine of Syâdvâda which has stood invulnerable

* The word has about it a Sâṁkhya tinge which, as we know from the history of Sâṁkhya and Jainism, is not accidental.

against all attacks of rival systems; (4) पूजातिशय—Excellence consisting in the fact that he has deserved and received worship from all beings, gods as well as men. With regard to (2), note that it is a special feature of Jainism that it leaves no room for doubt that 'चारित्र' or moral life is as important as 'ज्ञान' in an ideal man. Cf. सम्यग्दर्शनज्ञानचारित्राणि मोक्षमार्गः Tattvârtha I. 1. As regards (4) it may be remembered that Vaiṣṇavism, with its theory of human incarnations of God, Jainism and Buddhism have lifted the ideal man to a position above that of gods.

St. II.

Of the innumerable qualities of the Master, the one which will engage the attention of the author is his "यथार्थवाद" *i. e.* his philosophy which is true to facts, that is to say, the many-sidedness of Truth or Reality—the fundamental doctrine of Jaina philosophy.

St. III.

The author implores all readers, whether Jaina or not, to ponder upon the truth of Jaina philosophy, which emerges out of the examination of the partial truths of other systems. In other words, the object of the author is not to revile other systems but to serve the cause of Truth—which is not absolutely confined to any single system. Compare the object of the "khaṇḍana-khaṇḍa-khâdya, in the interests of Vedânta.

Stanzas IV-IX: *Criticism of the Vaiśeṣika System.*

St. IV.

First, of its doctrines of सामान्य and विशेष:

Freely rendered the Stanza means: "Things are of themselves—*suo moto*—capable of co-ordination with things of their own class, and differentiation from things of a different class; their nature is not to be explained by assuming realities—(सामान्य and विशेष)—*other* than the things themselves. Those fools err, who declare that the two, viz., सामान्य and विशेष, are distinct realities (distinct inter se and distinct from the things in which they are supposed to inhere), since they are not such."

The Jaina view on the point, like that of several other schools, is that things are *by themselves* co-ordinated with things of their own class and differentiated from things of other classes, and consequently there is no need to assume, as the Vaiśeṣikas do, the two hypothetical realities, सामान्य and विशेष. This, besides being a gratuitous assumption, according to the Jaina view, involves the absurdity of making two such *contradictory* things as सामान्य and विशेष reside in one and the same thing, unless you reconcile them in the Jaina manner by regarding them as two relative aspects—and aspects only—of one and the same thing.

Although the later Vaiśeṣikas regarded सामान्य and विशेष as *two* distinct realities *over and above* द्रव्य, गुण and कर्म in which they were supposed to inhere, they seem to have been originally meant as merely *logical categories* ('बुद्ध्यपेक्ष' i. e. relative to thought as the Vaiś. Sûtrakâra calls them, Vaiś.S.I. ii. 3) or at most, as *hypothetical* realities assumed to account for certain ideas which none can dispute, viz. co-ordination (अनुवृत्ति) and differentiation (व्यावृत्ति). The Jaina position is very clearly formulated by Mallisena in the following words: "स्वभाव एव ह्ययं सर्वभावानां यदनुवृत्तिव्यावृत्तिप्रत्ययौ स्वत एव जनयन्ति। तथाहि घट एव तावत् पृथुबुध्नोदराद्याकारवान् प्रतीतिविषयीभवन् सन् अन्यानपि तदाकृतिभृतः पदार्थान् घटरूपतया घटैकशब्दवाच्यतया च प्रत्याययन् सामान्याख्यां लभते। स एव चेतरेभ्यः सजातीयविजातीयेभ्यो द्रव्यक्षेत्रकाल-भावैरात्मानं व्यावर्तयन् विशेषव्यपदेशमश्नुते। इति न सामान्यविशेषयोः पृथक्-पदार्थान्तरत्वकल्पनं न्याय्यम्॥ Mark that सामान्य and विशेष are regarded by the Jaina as two relative *aspects* of a single reality, not even two related realities, that is to say, they are only *aspects* of Reality, and these, again, are *relative*, not absolutely opposed.

St. V.

All things including दीप and आकाश (*generally believed to be* अनित्य and नित्य respectively) are subject to the law of

स्याद्वाद—that is to say, a दीप which is regarded as an exemplar of अनित्य things is *also* नित्य, and आकाश which is regarded as a type of नित्य things is *also* अनित्य. All reality, according to Jainas, is *both* नित्य and अनित्य; one might almost say, *at once* नित्य and अनित्य, although from different points of view, so that there is no logical contradiction. The Jaina characterises Reality or सत् as "उत्पादव्ययध्रौव्ययुक्तम्". (See Tattvârtha).

Light when extinguished has not passed into nothingness and ceased to be; it has only changed its form which is now darkness. Like light, darkness is also a द्रव्य (substance)§—and not a mere अभाव (Cf. तमः=तेजःसामान्याभावः—Tarkadîpikâ) as the Vaiśeṣikas think,—which is possessed of a black colour and a cool feel. Similarly, आकाश is both नित्य and अनित्य. The Jaina rejects the definition of नित्य which is generally given by other schools, viz., अप्रच्युतानुत्पन्नस्थिरैकरूपं नित्यम्, which means absolute changelessness. He defines it thus: " तद्भावाव्ययं नित्यम् " (ध्रौव्ययुक्तं) *i. e.* नित्य is that which *continues* to exist inspite of उत्पाद and विनाश. To what would उत्पाद and विनाश belong, argues the Jaina, if nothing continues? Therefore a continuous reality, he says, must be posited for the very possibility of उत्पाद and विनाश. In fact, says the Jaina, modes and substance *i. e. change and permanence* exist *together*: neither is possible without the other (द्रव्यं पर्यायवियुतं पर्याया द्रव्यवर्जिताः । क्व कदा केन किंरूपा दृष्टा मानेन केन वा ? ॥ दव्वं पज्जवविउअं दव्वविउत्ता य पज्जवा नत्थि—Sammatitarka). Malliṣeṇa observes that the tenet of the Yoga school agrees with that of the Jaina in this matter.

Note that the Jaina differs equally from (1) those who hold that all is eternal, and (2) those who hold that all is evanescent, and also from (3) those who hold that some things are eternal and some evanescent. According to him all things

§ Mark that द्रव्य or substance is not to be confounded with matter. The former is anything that can stand under attributes, and need not be solid, liquid or gaseous, as matter is.

are *both* eternal and evanescent although from different points of view. (See "Brahmajāla Sutta" of the Buddhists for the earlier exponents of these extreme doctrines.) In a way, says the Jaina, even the Vaiśeṣika absolutist admits—without being aware of it—that पृथ्वी is both नित्य and अनित्य *i. e.* not only are some cases of पृथ्वी नित्य and some अनित्य, but पृथ्वीत्व co-exists simultaneously with both नित्यत्व and अनित्यत्व. In conclusion, Malliṣeṇa reproduces the criticism of absolute eternalism and absolute non-eternalism from Hemacandra's "Pramāṇa-Mîmāṃsā" (I. i. 33) almost verbatim, and winds up with the observation that the Vaiśeṣika admits the 'अनेकान्तवाद' of the Jaina in some of his doctrines without being aware of it; *e. g.* the Vaiśeṣika holds that चित्ररूप is a conglomeration of several mutually exclusive रूपs, which belongs to a single whole substance; similarly, many things in the Vaiśeṣika school are supposed to be कालान्तरावस्थायि, *i. e.* enduring for a certain limited length of time; this means that one and the same thing both endures and perishes, that is, it possesses two contradictory aspects (कालान्तरावस्थायि वस्तु तदपि नित्यानित्यमेव).

St. VI.

The doctrine of the Nyāya-Vaiśeṣika school which is next criticised is that of the existence and nature of God. God according to this school is—

(1) the maker of the world;

(2) one;

(3) all-pervading, by his presence and knowledge—*i. e.* ubiquitous and omniscient;

(4) independent; and

(5) eternal.

The prima facie case for this doctrine is made out as follows:—

(1) That He is the maker of the earth, the mountains etc. (that is to say, of all objects of Nature wherein we do not see the hand of man) can be inferred from the fact that all these

realities are *effects* and therefore require a *cause* (a maker); that they are effects may be easily deduced from another obvious fact that they are limited in their nature. The point of the argument is this: A *definite* nature implies a *conscious maker*, a maker who has made this rather than that. It may be urged that the argument involves a paralogism or the fallacy of *arguing from a part to the whole*. The Naiyâyika† guards against this attack by making his pakṣa *not the whole* of Reality—the totality of being—but confining it to such *particular* things as the earth, the mountains etc.,* (whether such a concept of God is right is a different question,) leaving as dṛṣṭânta all other things which are known to be of *our* making, that is, made by sentient beings. The argument is thus from particulars to adjacent particulars, and not from *some* to *all* which includes the some and thus involves a fallacy. In short, he argues for 'a power that is not we'.

No (1): is criticised by Malliṣeṇa, mainly on two grounds: First, that the *anumâna* is precluded by *pratyakṣa* which definitely bears witness to the fact that these things (earth, mountains etc.) have no maker.‡ Secondly, in the cases in which we have observed making, the making belongs to persons *with a body*. If to escape the difficulty you say that he can put on a body through his infinite power or that he may possess it owing to our own adṛṣṭa, it is a gratuitous assumption which amounts to begging the question.

No (2): He is *one*. For, the world is one consistent whole, and not a congeries of several conflicting forces, since it is a cosmos and not a chaos. To this the Jaina replies: Not neces-

† Here as elsewhere in many places the Naiyāyika and the Vaiśeṣika are to be understood as one.

‡ Throughout here I have used the words 'make' and 'maker', because 'create' and 'creator' or 'author' may prove misleading in the case of the Nyāya–Vais'eṣika idea of God who is not supposed to have created the world out of nothing but has fashioned it out of atoms as a potter makes his pots.

sarily so. For, *many* may co-operate to produce a single result: we often find many co-operating to produce a single result without any conflict of wills and consequent confusion e. g the bees that make their hive.

No (3): Since His making takes place in all parts of the universe, he must be supposed to be *everywhere*, and he must be also *all-knowing*. It he is everywhere, he, says the Jaina, absorbs everything into his own self, leaving nothing to exist outside it. If he knows everything, he knows, we suppose, even hell and knowledge in his case being direct experience, he is to be supposed to experience hell! [Mark that in the preceding argument the Vais'eṣika had confined God's making to things which are not of our making, and he cannot, therefore, now argue that he is *omni*present and *omni*scient. Consistently he can only say God is present where we are not present, or God experiences what we do not experience.]

The Jaina continues: we may agree that certain souls are all-knowing, in which case God would be one of such souls, that is to say, he would be on a par with emancipated souls. "But mark," says Malliṣeṇa revising his position, " that knowledge does not actually travel from the knower to the known; and therefore, omniscience does not necessarily involve omnipresence. Moreover, 'what is the proof of his omniscience ?'—he asks. It cannot be *pratyakṣa*, for we cannot have pratyakṣa (direct perception) of his omniscience, unless we ourselves are omniscient, or become so in the process. It cannot be *anumâna*, for you cannot argue from the finite to the infinite. (See Caird's "Introduction to the Philosophy of Religion"). It cannot be *arthâpatti*, that is, a hypothesis or assumption necessary for explaining the wonderful variety and richness of the world. For, the adṛṣṭa of living beings including the vegetable kingdom will explain one part of it, and the remaining part which belongs to the inanimate kingdom may well be existing eternally so, and eventually become the object of the joys and sorrows of sentient beings. It cannot be *śabda* or the authoritative text of the sacred scriptures. For, the scriptures on which you rely are full of contradictions and are therefore unreliable.

No (4): By the very nature of the case he is said to be independent. Then, why does he create a world so full of misery and inequalities unless he is wantonly cruel and unjust? If misery is a punishment for a foul deed and inequality is due to our varying karmans, this hypothesis of *karman* will suffice to explain everything, and God will be superfluous.

No (5): He is said to be *eternal*. If so, he should be eternally active, or eternally inactive. In the former case, his work would at no point be finished, and so nothing could be ever accomplished. In the latter case, nothing could even begin. Moreover, how could he have eternally conflicting natures viz., making and unmaking at the same time?

It is said that very likely "the (Vaiśeṣika) system was originally atheistic".* and some of the sûtras which the old Sanskrit commentators have interpreted as containing a reference to God, have been understood by modern scholars as possibly referring to dharma or prajâpati." But at no stage of its history has the Vaiśeṣika system been avowedly atheistic or even suspected of atheism. The silence of the Sûtras about the existence of God must be explained as due to the main problem of the system being the nature of âtman and anâtman and the investigation of the properties (विशेषs) of things by first classifying them into categories. The Nyâya-sûtras are also sparing in references to the problem of God. There is only one reference, occurring in three connected sûtras (Ns. Adh. IV, ii. 19-21) which run as follows :—ईश्वरः कारणं पुरुषकर्माफल्यदर्शनात् (19), न पुरुषकर्माभावो फलानिष्पत्तेः (20), and तत्कारितत्वादहेतुः (21). In regard to this Section, as Dr. Ganganath Jha duly notes, "there is a difference among commentators. According to the Bhâṣya, the Vârtika and Vis'vanātha's Vṛtti it is

* See Faddegon's Vaiś. System—p. 354.

meant to propound the Naiyâyika Siddhânta, that the universe has been created by God; and in accordance with his view, Sû. 19 puts forward the final Siddhânta, Sû. 20 puts forward an objection against the Siddhânta, and Sû. 21 answers that objection from the standpoint of the Siddhânta." But in view of the fact that the interpretation of Sû. 19 as a Siddhânta sûtra is inconsistent with the introductory assertion of the Bhaṣya that "अतःपरं प्रावादुकानां दृष्टयः प्रदर्श्यन्ते" *i. e.* "we now proceed to show up the doctrines of philosophers, tall-talkers or sophists", the Tâtparya, followed by the Pariśuddhi and Prakâs'a, has taken it as representing the criticism of the Vedânta doctrine that God is the *constituent* cause of the "Universe". By this interpretation Sû. 19 represents the Vedânta view, Sû. 20 shows the untenability of that view, and Sû. 21 puts forward the references to the question of the existence of God. Thus, there is only one section of three Sûtras and that too occurs not in the constructive but in the destructive part of the work which deals with the doctrines of "talkers". This, again, is explained in two different ways, neither of which seems to be entirely satisfactory. The difficulty of interpretation is inherent in the fact that the section consists of only three Sûtras, an odd number, of which the first is expected to be a pûrvapakṣa and if the second is its answer—the Siddhânta—what about the next? Should not this as the last sûtra of the set be expected to be the Siddhânta? The difficulty, however, can be surmounted to some extent only by taking the third Sûtra as a continuation of the second. But this is not the only trouble. As Dr. Ganganath Jha says:—"There is also a wider issue involved in this Section. The commentators are agreed that the Siddhânta view here put forward is that God is the Creator of the Universe. Now the question arises—How is it that this cardinal doctrine of the system has been inserted by Gautama as a side-issue? He has put it forward only among "certain philosophical doctrines", and not as *the true doctrine*. Nor is it easy to reconcile the doctrine of God being the creator with the view that there is no such thing as 'beginning of creation' as is often found reiterated by the Vârtika (e. g. on p. 445 and p. 466); if there is no beginning, God may be the *Controller*, the *Ruler*, He cannot be the *Creator*. From the Bhâṣya also (p. 301, l. 3) it seems that God is held to be only the *Seer*, *Knower*, *Omniscient*, *All-powerful*.*" †

But, with all respect for Dr. Ganganath Jhâ, I think that in denying "creative power" to the God of the Nyâya Bhâṣya he has overlooked a sentence which has gone before, wherein the author says: "यथा पिताऽपत्यानां तथा पितृभूत ईश्वरो भूतानाम्." This analogy, however, is somewhat different from that which occurs in later Nyâya books which compare him to a potter who makes his pots from clay.

It should be noted that long before the time of Malliṣeṇa, the Nyâya-Vaiśeṣika Theism had acquired the definite form in which it is formulated in all later manuals, and which was given to it in the "Nyâyasâra" of Bhâsarvajña, the "Nyâya-Kusumâñjalî" of Udayana and the Nyâyakandalî of Śrîdhara. It is the last mentioned book on which Malliṣeṇa has largely drawn for the statement of the pûrvapakṣa.

It may be noted in passing that the theism of the Nyâya-Vaiśeṣika differs from the theisms of Vedânta and Yoga which Malliṣeṇa does not note. The theism of the Vedânta differs essentially from that of the Nyâya-Vaiśeṣika in two respects: First, it regards God as both the *nimitta* and the *upâdâna* or *vivarta* kâraṇa of the world; that is to say, God according to it is not only the maker of the world, but also the stuff out of which it is made; in other words, He has created the world out of Himself and is not a mere architect as the Nyâya-Vaiśeṣika holds. Secondly, He is not demonstrable, that is,

---

* Dr. Ganganath Jha's Translation of N. S. etc. Vol. IV, p. 77 footnote on or Bhāṣya on N. S. 4-1-19.

† आगमाच्च द्रष्टा बोद्धा सर्वज्ञाता ईश्वर इति "—N. S. Bhāṣya.

proved by inference, but is revealed* by his own *voice*, that is, as the voice itself declares, 'in the creation, maintenance and destruction of the external world or Nature' ('जन्माद्यस्य यतः'), and 'in the commandments of right and wrong' ('शास्त्रयोनित्वात्'). With Yoga, God is neither a creator nor an architect, but an Ideal, *the* Ideal Man: not *an* ideal man or type generalised from ideal men as in Jainism, but an eternally existing and real Ideal Man.†

St. VII.

The doctrine of the Vaiśeṣikas which is next criticised is that of 'समवाय', also called 'वृत्ति'—which is supposed to connect two absolutely distinct things viz. धर्म and धर्मिन्, it itself being distinct from both, that is, the third. This, says the Jaina, is contrary to all experience. We never perceive three things, one binding the other two, like cement binding the stones. Next समवाय, it is said, is one, eternal and all-pervasive. If so, the moment one thing perished, its समवाय would perish, and with it all things in the world to which it belonged! ['विनश्यदेकवस्तुसमवायाभावे च समस्तवस्तुसमवायाभावः प्रसज्यते']. Just as you say 'here—in the तन्तु—exists this पट,' and therefrom deduce समवाय, in the same way, since you say 'here is समवाय' you will have to admit समवायान्तर and so ad infinitum—" इत्येवं दुस्तरानवस्था महानदी " ! It may be noted, that on all the three points, the new school of the Nyâya-Vaiśeṣikas have admitted the justice of these criticisms, so that according to the 'नवीनs' समवाय is not प्रत्यक्ष but अनुमेय, it is not एक but नाना, it is not नित्य but अनित्य, so that nothing remains of the old doctrine, except that the समवाय is a peculiar type of relation.

St. VIII.

In this stanza Hemacandra and Malliṣeṇa attack three more doctrines of the Vaiśeṣikas. These are:

---

* Unlike the later Naiyāyikas the earlier Naiyāyikas seem to have held the same view: Cf. N. Bh. "बुद्ध्यादिभिश्चात्मलिङ्गैर्निरुपाख्यमीश्वरं प्रत्यक्षानुमानागमविषयातीतं कः शक्त उपपादयितुम् ?"

† See Yoga Sûtra, Vyāsa-Bhāṣya.

1. 'सत्ता' (the highest सामान्य or Universal)—which is supposed to reside not in all that exists, that is in all reals, but *in certain reals only*, viz., द्रव्य, गुण and कर्मन्, the remaining being denied the right.* The latter are सामान्य, विशेष and समवाय, together with अभाव, the last being added by commentators to Kaṇâda's list of categories. But Malliṣeṇa does not care to notice this, because it was a later addition, although it was made long before his time.

2. चैतन्य which one would expect to be regarded as the very essence of आत्मन् is treated by the Vaiśeṣikas as an *adventitious* (औपाधिक) quality (आत्मनश्च व्यतिरिक्तं ज्ञानाख्यं गुणम्) which comes temporarily into आत्मन् as a result of the working of the machinery of cognition (ज्ञान) viz , अर्थ इन्द्रियेण संयुज्यते, इन्द्रियं मनसा, मन आत्मना. ज्ञान is thus something different from आत्मन्. [This applies to प्रत्यक्ष. But in the case of the other varieties of प्रमा, so far as the adventitious character of cognition is concerned, the position is the same viz., one ज्ञान through the working of मनस् causes another ज्ञान to come into आत्मन्.]

3. Liberation of आत्मन् is not a positive state of संवित् (consciousness) and आनन्द (joy), but a *negative* condition in which there is no consciousness and no joy. ("आत्यन्तिक-दुःखध्वंसो मोक्षः "–Tarka).

1 (a). The commentator begins by setting forth the principles of the Vaiśeṣika philosophy, quoting Kaṇâda's Vaiś. sûtras and Udayana's famous verse relating to the restrictions on the field of जाति (सामान्य par excellence). He makes a long extract from Praśastapâda's Bhâṣya on the first point, and quotes from Jayanta's Nyâyamañjarî on the second and the third. According to the Vaiś. school, there is a definite reality called 'सत्ता' or परसामान्य.

---

* Udayanâcârya points out in his Kiraṇâvali ("व्यक्तेरभेदः etc.") certain conditions in which an apparent सामान्य (°त्व) is not a *real* सामान्य ('जाति') See Notes for the conditions and their reasons.

(i) It is not a द्रव्य. For it is lacking in the characteristic nature of a द्रव्य, which is to be either made up of many द्रव्यs as its constituents (e. g. a पट which is made of many तन्तुs) and not to be complete in a single द्रव्य (e. g. पट which is not complete in a single तन्तु unlike सत्ता or सामान्य which is complete in each single द्रव्य, (e. g. तन्तुत्व in each तन्तु), *or* to be made up of no constituent द्रव्य at all (e. g. आकाश which has no constituent as structural parts whatsoever).

(ii) It is not a गुण, because it exists in गुणs, which no गुण does. (गुणे गुणानङ्गीकारात्).

(iii) It is not कर्म, for the same reason, mutatis mutandis.

1 (b). Similarly, there exist विशेषs as a special category. For just as a सामान्य—of which सत्ता is the highest—is the principle of co-ordination (अनुवृत्ति) of individuals, so is विशेष the principle of differentiation or distinction (व्यावृत्ति). By its very nature विशेष belongs to each particular separately, and therefore there should be as many विशेषs as there are particulars in the Universe. Possession of different सामान्यs and possession of different अवयवs are two other principles which serve to distinguish things. For example, घटत्व distinguishes घटs from पटs, and the possession of parts which are not identical with the parts of another घट distinguishes the first घट from the second. Hence it is not necessary to assume any विशेषs in these two cases. But these methods of distinction will not do in the case of परमाणुs of the same substance, which are distinct from one another and yet alike, or in the case of आकाश which being a single whole does not possess either सामान्य or अवयवs. (See "Dinakarî".)

1 (c). समवाय is the *bond* of things which are inseparable, such as पट and its तन्तुs, or पट and its गुणs, or पट and पटत्व, etc. and it is therefore not one of the things themselves.

2 and 3. The ground of the Vaiśeṣikas for regarding ज्ञान and आनन्द as adventitious, and not essential is obvious: We are conscious of our ideas coming and going, and so also of

pleasure and pain which belong to us and are positive in character. Passing states cannot be the essence of things: they belong to us, they are ours, they are not we.

Criticism:—Malliṣeṇa criticises these three doctrines as follows:—

1. 'सत्ता' is *being*, and everything that *is* must possess सत्ता. Moreover, its function is to co-ordinate, and therefore wherever things appear to be alike in one respect or another and are thus capable of co-ordination, there is the field for सामान्य. We can co-ordinate all things that *exist*, and consequently सत्ता can reside in *all*. The difficulties raised by Udayana do not arise, because the Jaina is not prepared to admit 'सामान्य' as a real apart from and over and above the particulars which it co-ordinates, nor does he regard particulars as simply particulars incapable of being referred to a universal. According to the Jaina, सामान्य is only an aspect and not a real per se; and further, सामान्य and विशेष are two aspects of the same real, and are not mutually exclusive. Remember that the ancient Vaiśeṣikas who spoke of a 'सामान्य-विशेष'—the two-in-one—were, according to the Jaina view, wiser than their successors who made the categories so many water-tight compartments. In the doctrine that सत्ता exists only in द्रव्य, गुण and कर्मन् and not in the remaining categories one may see a sound distinction made between *real* categories and *conceptual* categories (see remarks under St. IV).

2. The distinction between ज्ञान and आत्मन्, it may be urged, is the distinction between करण and कर्तृ. But the distinction is false. The करण is not always external to कर्तृ: We speak of a serpent making a coil of himself by himself, where कर्तृ, कर्म and करण are all one. Again, it has been urged that we are conscious of *possessing* ज्ञान and not *being* ज्ञान itself and consequently ज्ञान must be regarded as distinct from आत्मन्. Answer: No, ज्ञान is not external to आत्मन्, it is not a possession of something externally related to it. It is a production or drawing out of something from the आत्मन् itself and is there-

fore only an aspect or mode (परिणाम) of आत्मन् and nothing distinct.

3. As regards सुख, the Jaina would distinguish between 'सांसारिकसुख' which is perishable and मोक्षसुख which is everlasting.

All these weaknesses of the Vaiśeṣika doctrine would seem to arise from two fundamental errors: First, conceptual realities are hypostatised; and secondly, he takes a mechanical view of the Universe where things are taken as essentially so many particulars which come together and separate like actors on a stage—and so carry on mutual intercourse as realities external to each other. The first of these opens up a much deeper question, whether the logical or conceptual is not the real. This we cannot afford to discuss here. The second is to some extent the position of particularists and pluralists of modern European and American philosophy.

St. IX.

The doctrine next examined is that of the विभुत्व of आत्मन् —that आत्मन् is everywhere—, a doctrine which on the face of it, says the Jaina, is contrary to our experience. For, all are agreed that a thing must be where its quality is found, e. g., घट exists where its form exists and not elsewhere. It may be argued: Don't we smell from a distance? Answer: No; the particles which possess the smell fly to our nose. But it may be asked: Does not magic work at a distance? Answer: No; the presiding deity of the magical formula or practice who resides elsewhere is working there. Having thus justified his position in a general way, Malliṣeṇa lays down a syllogism for attacking the Vaiśeṣika doctrine of the विभुत्व of आत्मन्:—आत्मा सर्वगतो न भवति। सर्वत्र तद्गुणानुपलब्धेः। यो यः सर्वत्रानुपलभ्यमानगुणः स स सर्वगतो न भवति यथा घटः। तथा चायम्। तस्मात् तथा। व्यतिरेके व्योमादि ॥ and then proceeds to answer the objections of the opponent, such as, the हेतु is असिद्ध etc. In the course of his answer he urges that the अदृष्ट of our आत्मन् is supposed to act even at a distance—and it cannot be there hanging in the air, so to say, without an underlying substratum; consequently, our

आत्मन् must be supposed to be existing even there. And since अदृष्ट works everywhere, the underlying substance, viz., आत्मन्, must also exist everywhere. But the Jaina denies that अदृष्ट is acting there and everywhere. Things, he says, have their own nature—a fact which is ultimate and does not admit of question or explanation—and that nature is not caused by अदृष्ट. To say that the natures of things are determined by अदृष्ट is to leave no room for your God. Next, since the Vaiśeṣika holds that आत्मन्s are many, if each of them is विभु also, as he believes, what a wonderful clash and interpenetration of आत्मन्s would ensue! Moreover, each of them would enter the आत्मन् of God Himself, and each would thereby become a creator! It may be urged: Unless आत्मन् was विभु, how could the आत्मन् draw to himself the particles for the body in which he has to dwell in the next life? Or, even if he could, would not his body-sized आत्मन्, as a consequence, be सावयव and therefore a कार्य just like the body itself? The Jaina, however, is prepared to accept the logical consequence. [More accurately, he says that आत्मन् has प्रदेशs though not अवयवs]. The Jaina believes that आत्मन् is सावयव, is परिणामिन् and does change from time to time. He is no believer in absolute changelessness of आत्मन्, or for the matter of that, in absolute changelessness of anything whatsoever. It may be asked in support of the विभुत्व theory: If आत्मन् were body-sized, how could आत्मन् enter the body? For, two मूर्त things cannot occupy the same space at the same time. The Jaina answers the objection by denying मूर्तत्व (रूपादिमत्त्व etc.) in one sense (materiality) and affirming it in another (असर्वगतत्व). The Jaina expresses and explains his view that आत्मन् is subject to change and is yet eternal, as follows: "पर्यायतस्तस्यानित्यत्वेपि द्रव्यतो नित्यत्वात्" He further points out that for some time after a body is cut, its parts continue to throb and retain the आत्मन् in them.

It may be noted that the Jaina is the only Indian schoolman who holds that आत्मन् is middle-(body-)sized. The only other philosopher who holds an analogous though not the same doctrine is Râmânujâcârya, according to whom the ज्ञान of आत्मन्, though not the आत्मन् himself, is 'संकोचविकासशालिन्.' In order to appreciate the Jaina position one has to reinterpret it and understand it in the only sense in which it is possible to defend it—viz., that the phenomenon of consciousness is limited to the body, though the consciousness belongs to आत्मन् and is the essence of आत्मन्. Similarly, when Śaṁkara speaks of the विभुत्व or नित्यत्व of आत्मन् what he means is आत्मन् is a reality which is not bounded by time or space. And the same in the case with the Sâṃkhya. Also, it may be added, one must free आत्मन् from all material analogies, and must abandon the conception of आत्मन् as a द्रव्य like घट, पट, शरीर etc. which is the fundamental error of what Kant calls "Rational (i.e. 'uncritical' or 'dogmatic' in the Kantian sense of the word) Psychology." Let us remember, in this connection, that when the Vaiśeṣika speaks of आत्मन् as a 'द्रव्य' or substance, he does not mean material substance, but only a substance which possesses qualities (cf. DesCartes); not, however, as a mere logical subject possessing predicates, for such a view would deprive आत्मन् of all reality making him merely nominal.

Stanza X: *Criticism of Nyâya.*

St. X.

The system under criticism in this stanza and its commentary is that of the Naiyâyikas, who are here called 'यौग's and are distinguished from the Vaiśeṣikas.

In a work of Logic, says the Jaina, what one should expect is an exposition of the laws of correct thinking, and perhaps of the fallacies which one is likely to commit unknowingly. But it is outrageous that "Nyâyasûtras"—a work which professes to deal with subjects which should be carefully studied in order to achieve the summum bonum—the author should treat such subjects as वितण्डा, छल etc. which are various forms of irresponsible, dishonest and sophistical reasoning. The Brâhmaṇa apologist may plead that Gautama has not in any way recommended these, but that out of mercy for the intellectually weak, he has only drawn their attention to such logical traps as the enemy is likely to devise for his ruin. Malliṣeṇa ridicules such an apologia. He next proceeds to deal with the definitions of certain terms which are contained in the fundamental sûtra of Nyâya: "प्रमाण-प्रमेय etc.".

1. प्रमाण. Malliṣeṇa examines and rejects the definition given in the Nyâya Bhâṣya by Vâtsyâyana, and in the Nyâya-sâra" by Bhâsarvajña, viz:—(1) 'अर्थोपलब्धिहेतुः प्रमाणम्' and (2) 'सम्यगनुभवसाधनं प्रमाणम्'. In neither of the two definitions, he says, the essential fact that प्रमाण is ज्ञान is brought out. On the contrary, in the Nyâya system इन्द्रियार्थसंनिकर्ष and not the rudimentary ज्ञान which springs from it is regarded as a करण of प्रत्यक्ष. Moreover, in the case of the first definition, the word हेतु which occurs there is too wide and might include कर्तृ and कर्म as well as करण. The correct definition of प्रमाण, says Malliṣeṇa, is 'स्वपरव्यवसायि ज्ञानं प्रमाणम्" (cf. Pramâṇa-Naya-Tattvâ-lokâ-laṁkâra).

2. प्रमेयम्—Criticism: शरीर etc. are included in आत्मन् and do not require to be separately mentioned. प्रेत्यभाव and अपवर्ग are similarly states of आत्मन्. A more fundamental objection is that आत्मन् is not a प्रमेय but प्रमातृ. दोषs can be included in प्रवृत्ति, and are only activities of मनस् which has been separately mentioned. दुःख and इन्द्रियार्थ are फल as one of the Brâhmaṇa logicians, Jayanta, admits. In conclusion Malliṣeṇa says that the right definition of प्रमेय is "द्रव्यपर्यायात्मकं वस्तु प्रमेयम्."

It may be pointed out that Malliṣeṇa forgets that there are two meanings of the word 'प्रमेय'—प्रमातुं योग्यम् and प्रमातुं शक्यम्—of which the former is intended in the Nyâyasûtra, and the latter in the Vaiśeṣika; in other words, the पदार्थs of the Nyâyasûtras are topics (प्रमातुं योग्याः), not categories, unlike the पदार्थs of the Vaiśeṣika which are categories (प्रमातुं शक्याः).

Malliṣeṇa next explains various kinds of छल, जाति and निग्रहस्थान as is done in the Nyâyasûtras and observes once more at the close that this subject is unworthy of the attention of one who lays claim to 'वैराग्य'. Let us remember, however, that Hemacandra has devoted a section of his Pramâṇa-Mîmâṃsâ to the treatment of these very subjects.

Stanzas XI-XII: *Criticism of Pûrva-Mîmâṃsâ.*

St. XI.

The author next criticises the defence of हिंसा as made by certain Vedists.* After quoting texts from Brâhmaṇa scriptures which prescribe हिंसा, Malliṣeṇa condemns it and pithily asks: "हिंसा चेद् धर्महेतुः कथम्? धर्महेतुश्चेद् हिंसा कथम्?" To say that हिंसा is 'वेदविहिता' and therefore 'धर्महेतु' is to condemn the Veda, and is, moreover, a contradiction in terms. He rejects the weak plea of the Vedists that हिंसा though ordinarily a sin is not a sin when it is prescribed by the Veda. Malliṣeṇa has no difficulty in rejecting this plea as an outrage upon our sense of right and wrong. It may be said that just as the Jainas make an exception in the case of the हिंसा of insects, worms and reptiles which are unavoidably killed in the process of building a Jaina temple, so the Vedist makes an exception of the Vedic यज्ञ which involves हिंसा. Malliṣeṇa meets this plea by pointing out that the हिंसा which takes place while building a temple is unavoidable; moreover, the service which a Jaina temple renders to the spiritual life of the community far outweighs the evil of the हिंसा. The हिंसा involved in a Vedic yajña is not necessary for obtaining स्वर्ग which, as the Brâhmaṇa scriptures admit, can be obtained by the practice of यम etc. The Vedists say: "ओषध्यः etc." "If this be so, hell will be a desert and

---

* The context of the Stanzas and the latter part of the com. on St. XI show that the system criticised is principally that of Pûrva Mîmâṃsā which is primarily responsible for this doctrine. But as the Naiyāyikas have held the same view in regard to sacrificial slaughters of animals I have used the word "Vedists" as including both. Just as this may apply both to Pûrva Mîmāṃsā and Nyâya, so the next Stanza also applies to both.

heaven an overpopulated city!" Mallisena endorses the remark of "पारमर्षाः"—the followers of 'परमर्षि' कपिल,* the Sâṃkhyas —who say:

"यूपं छित्त्वा पशून् हत्वा कृत्वा रुधिरकर्दमम्।
यद्येवं गम्यते स्वर्गे नरके केन गम्यते ॥"

—Quoted in Mâṭhara Vṛtti †

Besides, Malliṣeṇa points out that the Vedic promise of स्वर्ग in such a case does not stand to reason and must be taken to be false like many another rites in connection with marriage etc. Malliṣeṇa then quotes other dicta of Brâhmaṇa philosophers such as those of the Vedantins who like the Sâṃkhyas have condemned हिंसा even for a यज्ञ. Malliṣeṇa condemns also the Śrâddha ceremony which was a great occasion with the Vedist Brâhmaṇas for slaughtering animals and eating animal food.

Lastly, Malliṣeṇa takes up the scholastic problem whether the Veda is to be regarded as 'पौरुषेय' or 'अपौरुषेय'. He says that language and its utterance can never be 'अपौरुषेय' and every sentence has a certain 'तात्पर्य' which implies an author and is thus 'पौरुषेय'. Secondly, the logic of Exception requires that exceptions should relate to the same matter to which the general rule is applied. Here, on the other hand, exceptions are for the purpose of propitiating gods, guests and manes, whereas the general rule (the prohibitory texts "न हिंस्यात् सर्वा भूतानि") is for avoiding sin and its consequences. Where is the necessity of propitiating them by हिंसा when other methods are available? The desire of स्वर्ग in such a case is as foolish as "स्वपुत्रघाताद् नृपतित्वलिप्सा."

---

* Kapila is well known as 'परमर्षि' (see S. K. St. 62). There is considerable affinity between Sâṃkhya and Jainism despite many important differences.

† See Mâṭhara Vṛtti, Sâṃkhya Sûtras etc. on अहिंसा. Many of the quotations here made by Malliṣeṇa seem to have been taken from Mâṭhara Vṛtti.

A short historical note on this subject may be added: There is no doubt that animal slaughter both for food and propitiation of gods and manes was very common among ancient Aryans. At the same time from the evidence of the sermons of Mahâvîra Svâmin and Gautama Buddha it is easy to see that अहिंसा was also an ancient practice which they tried to revive. There is a famous passage in the Aitareya Brâhmaṇa which clearly shows that a strong tendency in favour of अहिंसा must have set in long before its time. Had the passage been post-Buddhistic, अहिंसा even for a Vedic sacrifice would not have been complacently recommended in that Vedic work at a time when the preachings of Jainism and Buddhism were laying their axe at the root of Vedic practices. The Jñana and Bhakti movements had a large share in making the Vedic हिंसा obsolete. Of this we have ample evidence in the Mahâbhârata and the ruling philosophy of the day,—the Sâṃkhya,—which was already in the field when Jainism and Buddhism came to be, preached. It should be borne in mind in this connection that what the two reformers condemned was not the whole of the Vedic religious life even in their day. Apart from the couplet which has been cited by Malliṣeṇa as that of the Sâṃkhyas, there is a whole adhikaraṇa in the Sâṃkhya Sûtras, which though much later may well be supposed to record old Sâṃkhya traditions—devoted to repudiation of हिंसा altogether even from the Vedic sacrifice.

The history of हिंसा and अहिंसा has passed through the following stages:

1. First Stage: When हिंसा was practised by the people generally, both for food and for worship of gods and manes.

2. Second Stage: When it was discarded from food, but was retained in worship. This is easy to understand. For, while a secular practice can be easily changed, superstitions in which gods and ancestors are supposed to be involved die hard.

3. Third Stage: When the moral sense of the people was so far awakened by a deeper sense of religion—of Jñâna and

bhakti—that it revolted against all forms of हिंसा whether religious or secular.

St. XII.

Next, Hemacandra and his commentator examine the Pûrva-Mîmâṃsâ theory (that of the particular school of P. Mîmâṃsâ which was established by Kumârila Bhaṭṭa) regarding the nature of ज्ञान. The problems raised therein are: (1) How do we know that we know?—i. e. how is knowledge itself known, that is, brought to consciousness? (2) How do we know objects?

The Jaina holds that ज्ञान or consciousness has this dual nature: (1) it reveals itself ('स्वावबोधक्षम') and (2) it reveals also the world of objects ('अर्थावबोधक्षम'). He thus rejects the view of Kumârila that ज्ञान itself is known by a process of *implication* (अर्थापत्ति or आक्षेप), being implied in the fact of ज्ञातता of the object, which is its effect. With it he also rejects a similar theory of the "यौगs" (the Nyâya-Vaiśeṣikas) who regard ज्ञान as अनुव्यवसायगम्य i. e. known by a *further act of knowing* (अनुव्यवसाय) directed upon the first fact of knowledge. The commentator could well have added that the Jaina view excludes also the idealistic position that knowledge does not disclose any external reality, ideas being the only ultimate reality of objects (विज्ञानवाद). For, this is the point of अर्थ in the dvandva compound 'स्वार्थ' (स्व+अर्थ) in the first line of the Stanza ('स्वार्थावबोधक्षम एव बोधः'). Hemacandra says that the doctrine of the self-revelation of ज्ञान is a perfectly sound proposition and yet some weak-kneed philosophers have succumbed to the criticism levelled against it by their opponents,—which they need not have done.

As regards the main part of the substance of the Stanza—whether ज्ञान is self-revealed or alter-revealed—the commentator states and examines Kumârila's theory of ज्ञातता, and the implication of ज्ञान in ज्ञातता. The argument against the self-revelation theory is that "ज्ञानं स्वसंविदितं न भवति। स्वात्मनि

क्रियाविरोधात् । न हि सुशिक्षितोऽपि बटुः स्वस्कन्धमधिरोढुं क्षमः । न च सुतीक्ष्णाप्यासिधारा स्वं छेत्तुमाहितव्यापारा ॥" The reply to that is based on the *analogy of* प्रदीप which reveals itself, while revealing other objects also, and does not require to be revealed by another प्रदीप. The argument of the opponent which was based upon such analogies as those of नट and असि is met by an appeal to experience and its irresistible authority ('अनुभवसिद्धेऽर्थे विरोधासिद्धेः'). Moreover, how could Kumârila assume that ज्ञातता was an obvious fact on which he could base his argument of implication? What reason is there for assuming that ज्ञातता is self-revealed any more than that ज्ञान is self-revealed? In fact we are conscious of the self-revelation of ज्ञान rather than that of ज्ञातता. There is one more important objection to meet: If ज्ञान is ज्ञेय i. e. अनुभूति is अनुभाव्य, it is no more अनुभूति ('अनुभूतेरनुभाव्यत्वे घटादिवदननुभूतित्वप्रसङ्गः'). The answer to that is made with the help of the Jaina theory of aspects or relativity of knowledge ('अर्थापेक्षयानुभूतित्वात्; स्वापेक्षया चानुभाव्यत्वात्' । on the analogy: 'स्वपितृपुत्रापेक्षयैकस्य पुत्रपितृत्ववद् विरोधाभावात्').

Malliṣeṇa winds up his examination of Bhaṭṭa's complex theory of the knowledge by analysing it into three steps (त्रिपुटीप्रत्यक्षकल्पना):—

(1) Sensation (इन्द्रियबुद्धि) arising from contact with reality ('सत्संप्रयोगे इन्द्रियबुद्धिजन्यलक्षणं ज्ञानम्').

(2) Knowledge of the Reality ('अर्थप्राकट्यम्').

(3) Knowledge that the Reality was known: deduction of the existence of knowledge (कारण) from that of the fruit of that knowledge (कार्य) viz. the knownness (ज्ञातता) of the object ('तस्मादर्थापत्तिस्तया प्रवर्तकज्ञानस्योपलम्भः').

Malliṣeṇa next turns his attack towards the Nyâya–Vaiśeṣika who puts forward his अनुव्यवसाय theory as follows: "ज्ञानं स्वान्यप्रकाश्यम् । ईश्वरज्ञानान्यत्वे सति प्रमेयत्वात् घटवत् ।" and meets the charge of अनवस्था by saying that as a matter of fact there is no demand for any further act of knowledge (जिज्ञासा):—" न

चैवमनवस्था। अर्थावसायिज्ञानोत्पादमात्रेणैवार्थसिद्धौ प्रमातुः कृतार्थत्वात्।" In doing so he points out:

(1) That the हेतु is 'कालात्ययापदिष्ट' (This is a slip. It should be really सत्प्रतिपक्ष—otherwise known as प्रकरणसम—in the old Brâhmaṇa logic) since the अनुमान above set forth can be met by a counter-अनुमान as follows: "विवादाध्यासितं ज्ञानं स्वसंविदितम्। ज्ञानत्वात्। ईश्वरज्ञानवत्।" With reference to the example, Malliṣeṇa makes an interesting remark regarding the Jaina attitude towards the problem of the existence of God "पुरुषविशेषस्येश्वरतया जैनैरपि स्वीकृतत्वेन तज्ज्ञानस्य तेषां प्रसिद्धिः"—otherwise the example would we fictitious.

(2) That the हेतु is 'व्यर्थविशेष्य,' प्रमेयत्वात् in the हेतु serving no purpose.

(3) That it is 'अप्रयोजक', as the argument 'स्वान्यप्रकाश्यम् ईश्वरज्ञानान्यत्वे सति प्रमेयत्वात्' is applicable to things जड which are 'परमुखोत्प्रेक्षिन्' and not to ज्ञान—"ईश्वरज्ञानान्यत्वे प्रमेयत्वे च सत्यपि यदेव जडं स्तम्भादि तदेव स्वस्मादन्येन प्रकाश्यते।" As regards the denial of the possibility of अनवस्था—on the ground that there is no demand for any further act of knowledge, Malliṣeṇa refuses to admit that it is possible to stop at any point after the regressus has begun.

Stanzas XIII-XIV: *Criticism of Vedânta.*

St. XIII.

From the Pûrva-Mîmâṃsâ, the critic next turns to Uttara-Mîmâṃsâ or Vedânta, and there to that particular school of Vedânta which in the time of the author occupied the fore-ground, and here again to that particular tenet of the school which has made it famous—viz. मायावाद.

Hemacandra's criticism of मायावाद is simple: (1) If माया *is*, there is no more अद्वैत; for ब्रह्मन् is one, and माया would be another, thus making two. (2) If माया is *not*, how will there be this world, which it is sought to account for by assuming माया? Moreover, to say that something is माया—false—and that it serves to account for the world is a contradiction in terms. For, unless something exists how can it do the duty of accounting for another thing ?

Mallisena next proceeds to elaborate the criticism. The Vedântin's argument, he says, runs thus: "अयं तु प्रपञ्चो मिथ्यारूपः। प्रतीयमानत्वात्। यदेवं तदेवं यथा शक्तिः।" etc. the world is *unreal*, because it *appears:* that is to say, all phenomena, by the simple fact of their phenomenality, are mere appearances. Mallisena now challenges the opponent to explain the meaning of मिथ्यारूपत्व.

(1) If it means *absolute non-existence* it is accepting the position of असत्ख्याति*—which the Vedântin would not take up, lest it might expose him to the charge of being considered a शून्यवादिन् (Buddhist). (2) If it means *mis-take* i. e. one thing appearing as another, it is विपरीतख्याति, which too the Advaitins cannot adopt as it involves two reals—the thing which is mis-*taken* and the thing as it is *mis*-taken. (3) If it means that it cannot be definitely characterised as either existent or non-existent (अनिर्वाच्य)—explanation may well be demanded as regards the meaning of this 'अनिर्वाच्यत्व'. If 'अनिर्वाच्यत्व'=निःस्वभावत्व, it will involve सत्ख्याति or असत्ख्याति according as 'स्वभाव' in निःस्वभावत्व is taken to be a भाव or अभाव. Again, if निःस्वभावत्व= प्रतीत्यगोचरत्व, how can such a world (प्रपञ्च) be even talked about ? Moreover, it will be inconsistent with the hetu प्रतीयमानत्वात् as प्रतीत्यगोचरत्व means अप्रतीयमानत्व. If निःस्वभावत्व only means that it does not really possess its own भाव i. e. it is not what it appears to be, this is again विपरीतख्याति (See supra).

Besides, the whole argument is प्रत्यक्षबाधित. The Vedântin now becomes desperate and argues as follows: The very fact of the world being प्रत्यक्ष is the reason for regarding it as a mere *phenomenon*, and therefore *unreal*. According to this school of

---

* The philosophy of 'Khyâtis' is too intricate to be expounded in this short resume. The reader may therefore be referred to Randle's valuable account of the 'Khyâtis' in his "Indian Logic in the Early Schools" pp. 59–76.

thought—a particular School of Śâṁkara Vedântins—प्रत्यक्ष is only a sensation in which what is revealed is the thing-in-itself and not its predicate (निर्विशेष ब्रह्म), and it is afterwards transformed into perception (प्रत्यक्ष) by the addition of an element (which falls outside the province of प्रत्यक्ष) whereby a definite character as against all other characters is predicated of the subject. This is what we call the world (प्रपञ्च). This added element is not based on प्रत्यक्ष. Malliṣeṇa syas that this is all wrong: प्रत्यक्ष is not merely sensation; it bears testimony to the existence of a certain character and exclusion of other characters; besides this, it reveals the fact that the world consists of *many* things, every one of which possesses its own nature to the exclusion of every other nature. Moreover, the argument is अनुमानबाधित. Thus: प्रपञ्चो मिथ्या न भवति असद्विलक्षणत्वात् आत्मवत्। But you will say when one अनुमान is confronted by another अनुमान there must be something to turn the balance. Very well here it is:—If प्रतीयमानत्व is to be taken as a reason for मिथ्यात्व, ब्रह्मन् is मिथ्या too.

Adopting a somewhat different form of argument, Malliṣeṇa makes out a prima facie case for the Vedântin on the grounds of प्रत्यक्ष, अनुमान and आगम, and afterwards attacks each one of them. The Vedântin's argument, he says, would be briefly this: प्रत्यक्ष only affirms, it does not deny ("आहुर्विधातृ प्रत्यक्षं न निषेद्धृ विपश्चितः"); that is to say, it affirms Reality and, therefore, whatever involves exclusion—the world of objects each one of which is supposed to possess a certain nature as against a certain other nature—falls outside the domain of प्रत्यक्ष. अनुमान also supports the same veiw, and so does आगम (the Veda) which, it is well known, affirms ब्रह्मन् as the sole Reality. Malliṣeṇa rejects all these arguments as " the outpourings of a drunken man." For, no man, in his senses, says M., would question that there is no affirmation which is not at the same time a negation (exclusion): the two are the *positive and negative aspects of a singal Reality, which are presented together.* Therefore the Vedântin's argument which makes all *Being* one single reality, with nothing by its side to be excluded, is contrary to all experience. In fact, all our experience bears witness to definite characters of things. All ज्ञान is determinate (सविकल्पक) and things are *many*.

St. XIV.

The problem of the reality of *one* or *many*, which is involved in the Vedântin's position discussed under the preceding Stanza, presents itself in another form in this Stanza: What do words express—सामान्य or विशेष ?—universal or particulars, one or many ? Some P. Mîmâṃsakas, the Advaita Vedântins and the Sâṃkhyas are universalists, and some of them singularists also; the Buddhists are particularists and pluralists; and the Vaiśeṣikas and Naiyâyikas are both. According to the Jaina, they are all *partially right*. The first group of thinkers look to the unity of substance ('द्रव्यास्तिकनयानुपातिनः' or 'संग्रहानयालम्बिनः;'); the second confine their attention to its manifold modes or changes (पर्यायास्तिकनयानुसारिणः:'); the third considers both, but treats them as separate, self-sufficient realities ('नैगमनयानुरोधिनः'). Malliṣeṇa points out wherein each of them errs, what aspect each of them has ignored. The last school—that of the Nyâya-Vaiśeṣika—comes nearest to the Jaina position; yet it fails to appreciate the *relativity* of सामान्य and विशेष—the Universal and the Particular, the One and the Many.

Malliṣeṇa remarks after detailing the three partial truths: "तदेतत् पक्षत्रयमपि न क्षमते क्षोदम्। प्रमाणबाधितत्वात्। सामान्यविशेषोभयात्मकस्यैव वस्तुनो निर्विगानमनुभूयमानत्वात् ...... ।" तदेवमाबालगोपालप्रतीतिप्रसिद्धेऽपि वस्तुनः सामान्यविशेषात्मकत्वे तदुभयैकान्तवादः प्रलापमात्रम्। नहि क्वचित् कदाचित् केनचित् सामान्यं विशेषविनाकृतमनुभूयते, विशेषा वा तद्विनाकृताः। केवलं दुर्नयप्रभावितमतिव्यामोहवशादेकमपलप्यान्यतरद् व्यवस्थापयन्ति बालिशाः। सोऽयमन्धगजन्यायः॥" Not only do सामान्य and विशेष both call for recognition, but they do so for *recognition as relation* i. e. as two aspects of a single reality. ("सामान्यस्य विशेषाणां च कथंचित् परस्पराव्यतिरेकेणैकानेकरूपतया व्यवस्थितत्वात्। विशेषेभ्योऽतिरिक्तत्वाद्धि सामान्यमप्यनेकमिष्यते। सामान्यात् तु विशेषाणामव्यतिरेकेण तेषामप्येकरूपता॥")

Like वाच्य i.e. अर्थ or Reality expressed by words, the वाचक (शब्द) too is सामान्यविशेषात्मक. Incidentally, Mallişeṇa proceeds to prove that शब्द or sound is not a quality but a material substance (पौद्गलिक). The five हेतुs brought forward by the Vaiśeṣikas to deny that it is a material substance are examined, and shown to be हेत्वाभासs. They are: 1 स्पर्शशून्यत्वात्, 2 अतिनिबिडप्रदेशे प्रवेश-निर्गमयोरप्रतिघातात्, 3 पूर्वं पश्चाच्चावयवानुपलब्धेः, 4 सूक्ष्ममूर्तद्रव्यान्तरा-प्रेरकत्वात्, and 5 गगनगुणत्वात्. (For explanation of these hetus and their answers see Notes). Mallişeṇa next submits another explanation of the Stanza: A thing has a nature which is at once one and many. ('एकरूपमपि सत् अनेकरूपम्'). All things possess a double nature of भाव and अभाव ('सर्वभावानां हि भावाभावा-त्मकं स्वरूपम्'). For, if they were only भाव, no nature could be denied, and one thing would be everything ('एकान्तभावात्मकत्वे वस्तुनो वैश्वरूप्यं स्यात्'). If they were only अभाव, all things would have only a negative nature. The Jaina position is summed up in the formula "सर्वमस्ति स्वरूपेण पररूपेण नास्ति च," and in the oft-quoted lines:

> जे एगं जाणइ से सव्वं जाणइ ।
> जे सव्वं जाणइ से एगं जाणइ ।
> एको भावः सर्वथा येन दृष्टः सर्वे भावाः सर्वथा तेन दृष्टः ।
> सर्वे भावाः सर्वथा येन दृष्टाः एको भावः सर्वथा तेन दृष्टः ॥

One statement made by Mallişeṇa should be carefully noted: "न हि वयं येनैव प्रकारेण सत्त्वं तेनैवासत्त्वं येनैव चासत्त्वं तेनैव सत्त्वमभ्युपेमः किं तु स्वरूपद्रव्यक्षेत्रकालभावैः सत्त्वं, पररूपद्रव्यक्षेत्रकालभावै-स्त्वसत्त्वम् । तदा क्व विरोधावकाशः" ॥ Thus, Jainism is not only a philosophy of mere Reconciliation, but of Reconciliation based on Relativity.

The Buddhists in their zeal to make a thing even स्वरूपेण असत् affirm in effect that it is पररूपेण सत्, that is, they must deny the second half of our proposition viz. पररूपेण नास्ति. Thus, one thing could be anything and everything ('घटादेः सर्वात्मकत्वप्रसङ्गः').

Stanza XV: *Criticism of the Sâṁkhya.*

St. XV.

In the Sâṁkhya system—

(1) चित् (चैतन्यशक्ति or पुरुष) has nothing to do with the knowledge of अर्थs, to know things being regarded as a function of बुद्धि. बुद्धि is regarded as जड being an evolute of प्रकृति, and not a धर्म of चित् or पुरुष. Here is a twofold offence against truth, says the critic: The function of पुरुष should be to know, and बुद्धि should be a धर्म of पुरुष and not a product of प्रकृति.

(2) आकाश and other भूतs are said to have sprung from the subtle तन्मात्रs viz. शब्द etc.

This is quite contrary to what we observe, says Malliṣeṇa, regarding their relation: शब्द etc. are the धर्मs or गुणs of the पञ्चमहाभूतs and not the germs of the latter.

(3) बन्ध and मोक्ष, say the Sâṁkhyas, do not really belong to पुरुष, he being ever free.

Then why so much ado about मोक्ष and मोक्षशास्त्र? asks Malliṣeṇa.

Malliṣeṇa first gives a summary of the Sâṁkhya system by quoting from the Sâṁkhyakârikâs, and shows that it has gone wrong in the matter of the points mentioned by Hemacandra.

(1) If चित्शक्ति does not know things, it surrenders its very nature. All talk about चित्शक्ति or पुरुष being reflected in बुद्धि and thereby enabling the बुद्धि to know is absurd. For only a material thing can be reflected. (Is this not taking the metaphor too literally ?)

The Sâṁkhya is afraid that if he attributes knowledge to पुरुष, he would make him as प्रमातृ the principle of activity and therefore subject to परिणाम. But he forgets, says the Jaina, that without some sort of activity and consequent परिणाम he cannot so much as make himself reflected, and without parting with its original nature he cannot have सुखदुःख-भोग;

and if he parts with it he cannot help being सक्रिय so far. The theory that पुरुष is really free from activity and therefore from भोग and yet appears to be subject to it on the analogy of a स्फटिक which receives its apparent colour from the जपाकुसुम which is lying near it is rejected by Mallisena on the ground that here too the स्फटिक is subject to a real change of state, for it is only a स्फटिक—a transparent crystal—which takes the reflection and not an opaque stone (अन्धउपल). Mallisena thus disposes of the position of the Sâṁkhya declared in a text of "Patanjali" (or rather the commentary by Vyâsa from which the quotation is made), in that of वादमहार्णव in regard to the theory of भोग, as formulated by Âsuri in the same connection, and as formulated by Vindhyavâsin also.

Note that as between Âsuri and Vindhyavâsin, Âsuri speaks of the reflection of पुरुष in बुद्धि like that of the moon in a sheet of water, the stirring of the water making the moon stir also, as it were. Vindhyavâsin on the other hand speaks of the colouring of पुरुष by बुद्धि like that of a pure white स्फटिक assuming the colour of the जपाकुसुम which is near it. Thus, the two speak of two different reflections: while one speaks of the reflection of पुरुष in बुद्धि, the other that of बुद्धि in पुरुष. "The Vâda-Mahârṇava" accordingly speaks of reciprocal reflections, and so does also Vijñânabhikṣu, the last great exponent of Sâṁkhya philosophy.

Mallisena next deals with certain minor details of the Sâṁkhya system.

(2) धर्म, ज्ञान, वैराग्य and ऐश्वर्य and their opposites really belong to आत्मन् and not to बुद्धि as the Sâṁkhya holds.

(3) Further, अहङ्कार is not a product of बुद्धि: it is an attribute of आत्मन् which बुद्धि, which is said to be अचेतन, cannot produce.

(4) आकाश etc. are not a product of पञ्चतन्मात्रs, and it is surprising, says Mallisena, that the Sâṁkhya who claims to be the foremost of those who believe in the absolute eternality of

things (as an advocate of सत्कार्यवाद and consequent नित्यैकान्तवाद) should speak of आकाश—apparently a type of eternal things—as a product!

(5) वाक् etc. are regarded by the Sâṁkhyas as इन्द्रियs. But they are not. For, an इन्द्रिय is that which does what nothing else can do—a condition not fulfilled by वाक् etc.

(6) It is vain to think that there is no बन्ध and no मोक्ष. For, there is a *real* confusion of प्रकृति and पुरुष which makes our बन्ध.

Malliṣeṇa then deals with the three kinds of बन्ध mentioned in Sâṁkhya works: (1) प्राकृतिक, (2) वैकारिक and (3) दाक्षिण—that is, (1) that which consists in regarding प्रकृति as the highest ideal of worship like पुरुष, (2) that which consists in regarding the विकारs of प्रकृति such as भूतs, इन्द्रियs, अहङ्कार and बुद्धि as the objects of worship just like पुरुष, and (3) that which consists in practising the religion of ritualism. Malliṣeṇa points out they are all different kinds of causes which create what the Jaina calls 'कर्मबन्ध'. Unless बन्ध is real and not imaginary as the Sâṁkhya wants us to believe, there is no sense in speaking of मोक्ष.

(7) As regards the Sâṁkhya idea of मोक्ष that it consists of the cessation of the activity of प्रकृति, Malliṣeṇa points out that the activity of प्रकृति can never cease, inasmuch as activity is her very nature. If प्रकृति can choose to retire from the stage like an actress she may also choose to return there some day and so cause बन्ध once more! मोक्ष really consists of the real exhaustion of all Karman. The Jaina conception of the nature of आत्मन् and his मोक्ष is essentially the same as that of the Sâṁkhya with this important difference, however, that while the Sâṁkhya regards ज्ञान, क्रिया, बन्ध and मोक्ष as erroneously connected with आत्मन्, the Jaina regards them as its real states.

Stanzas XVI—XVIII: *Criticism of Buddhism.*

The authors next criticise Buddhism, particularly Buddhist Idealism,

St. XVI.

I. The identity of प्रमाण and फल (प्रमिति), according to the Buddhist, does not bring an external object into touch with consciousness, as is generally supposed, or to be more accurate, it does not make (external) reality an object of (internal) knowledge; what it does is, it defines consciousness, that is to say, it produces *conditioned* consciousness; thus, nothing enters into consciousness from without, the act of knowing being nothing but consciousness in every part.

This position is criticised on the following grounds:

The relation between प्रमाण and फल is a *causal* relation—which implies that the two cannot be simultaneous, nor can the two be successive, each enduring for a single kṣaṇa only and leaving no trace behind, for causality is not possible under such conditions. Besides, the causal relation is a relation and as such it implies two correlates, consciousness and something other than consciousness. Malliṣeṇa takes a passage from Dharmakîrti's Nyâyabindu and its ṭikâ by Dharmottara, as a representative text of this school of thought and criticises it on the ground that no such make-shift as the substitution of व्यवस्थाप्यव्यवस्थापकभाव for जन्यजनकभाव as between संवेदन and सारूप्य can succeed in doing away with the necessity of recognising *two* instead of *one* factor in the act of knowledge (व्यवस्थाप्यव्यवस्थापकभावस्यापि च संबन्धत्वेन द्विष्ठत्वादेकस्मिन्नसंभवात्) The Jaina rejects at the same time the extreme dualism of the Nyâya Vaiśeṣika School—for the simple reason that प्रमाण and फल (प्रमिति) both belong to one and the same person, so that their unity in आत्मन् *somehow* cannot be denied altogether. Note that this hardly differs from the Buddhist's "किंचिद्रूपं प्रमाणं किंचित् प्रमाणफलम् " except in that it would substitute कथंचित् for किंचित् and reject absolute dualism even of the aspects which the Buddhist formula cannot wholly exclude.

II. Another favourite doctrine of the Buddhists is their 'क्षणभङ्गवाद'—the doctrine of Momentariness. The main ground on which it rests is that nothing can perish unless it is *in its nature* to perish, which means that perishability is its nature, and since the nature of a thing does not depend upon anything other than the thing itself, perishability amounts to actual perishing. As regards the apparent persistence of a thing (e. g. घट) in time, the Buddhists' explanation is that here *similarity is mistaken for identity*, nothing (घट) being existent for more than a single क्षण, the seemingly persistent thing (घट) being nothing more than a series of perishing things (घटs).

The doctrine of क्षणभङ्ग is rejected by the Jaina on the ground that it is one-sided, the aspect of *permanence* (ध्रौव्य) being as necessary as that of *change*, that is, production (उत्पाद) and destruction (नाश). The former (permanence) belongs to द्रव्य and the latter (change) to its पर्यायs which are aspects of the same द्रव्य. This doctrine of *Permanence-cum—Evanescence* (i. e. persistence and change) has been criticised by the Buddhist as involving a contradiction, being as absurd as the statement that Devadatta is at once living and dying). But the Jaina sees no absurdity in such a proposition. According to him, while we are living we are also dying, for the 'petals of life' are falling away from us all the while we are living.

The argument advanced by the Buddhist philosopher Mokṣâkaragupta against the doctrine of Permanence in order to establish that of Momentariness falls flat on the Jaina, for it is welcome to him in so far as it proves one half of the whole truth in which he believes.

III. Next is criticised Buddhist *Realism*, according to which the विषय of ज्ञान is also a tenet of the Nyâya-Vaiśeṣika school, but the special trouble of the Buddhist is due to his क्षणभङ्गवाद which makes the realistic position as difficult to maintain as the idealistic position which was discussed above. Moreover, says the Jaina, it is not true that the अर्थ has to be real in order to be a कारण of ज्ञान, for there can be जलज्ञान even when there is no real जल but only मृगतृष्णिका. The Buddhist Realist may perhaps argue that the प्रकाशक (the revealer, ज्ञान)

implies the प्रकाश्य (the revealed, अर्थ)—प्रकाश्य (अर्थ) which is also the *cause* of its प्रकाशक (ज्ञान). This argument is answered by citing the example of प्रदीप and घट between which no causal relation exists although one is प्रकाशक and the other प्रकाश्य. Further, it is pointed out that the cause need not be real, it may be only ideal. For example, स्मृति is not caused by अर्थ but by ज्ञान (अनुभव) and yet it is the very breath of अनुमानप्रमाण.

Buddhist Realism is divided into two schools, that of 'Presentationists' and 'Representationists' (वैभाषिक and सौत्रान्तिक respectively), the latter being midway between Realism and Idealism.* The former holds that ज्ञान is produced by अर्थ ('तदुत्पत्ति'), the latter that it bears the form ('तदाकारता') of अर्थ. The point of the realistic argument consists in this that unless the reality of अर्थ were recognised as a cause of ज्ञान, anything would be the object of that ज्ञान, and that all distinction between right and wrong knowledge would vanish. The critic dispenses with the *causality* in the अर्थ and substitutes *capacity* in the ज्ञान, by way of a rejoinder to the Realist. Moreover, he sees no likeness (तदाकारता) between ज्ञान and अर्थ (e. g. the feeling of heat is not *like* heat in the fire). Likeness, again, cannot account for epistemological relation: thus the reflection of the moon in the water does not apprehend the moon in the sky.

Taking up the Second Half of the Stanza, Malliṣeṇa attacks the school of Buddhist Idealism (विज्ञानवाद of the योगाचार) which asserts that ideas (ज्ञानs) are the only reals, there being no causal (यत्कारणकं ज्ञानं) or corresponding (यदाकारकं ज्ञानं) world of external reality. It attacks the reality of the external world, discarding the problem of epistemology, i. e. of the theory of knowledge, as an imaginary bugbear, by subjecting it to a number of dilemmas, such as, are the wholes identical with parts, that is, are the bodies nothing more than the constituting atoms, or are they something over and above them; are they permanent or transitory;

is the object in consciousness or outside it etc. None of the positions survives critical scrutiny, with the result that the belief in external world cannot be regarded as due to its external reality, but must be accounted for by the hypothesis of वासना due to अविद्या (nescience).

This is criticised as follows :

This idealistic position which makes our belief in external reality a huge mis-take involves the reality of something that is mis-taken, that is taken amiss, which strikes at the root of this extreme Idealism.

All knowledge is of something which is other than the knowledge itself and is the विषय of that knowledge; it is a क्रिया which is directed towards something which is other than the क्रिया itself.

(3) Atoms are real. That body is not separable from them is no reason why their reality should be questioned.

Moreover, it possesses objective reality which is the same for all subjects.

(4) The object is not the subject. The fact of self-consciousness implies that there is a reality other than the self from the consciousness of which the consciousness of the self is distinguished.

Moreover, an object possesses objective reality, which is the same for all subjects.

(5) The अनुमान by which the non-existence of external reality is sought to be proved can have no value against the evidence of प्रत्यक्ष which decides the question in favour of its existence.

(6) That ज्ञान and its विषय are found *together* is an unwarranted assumption.

(7) The two have distinct natures, e.g. one is experienced as in us, the other outside us; one is already there, which the other notes afterwards.

The last stanza and its commentary having dealt with the क्षणभङ्गवाद which was held by the Vaibhâṣika in common with all the other schools of Buddhism, and also the half-hearted and the extreme forms of Idealism (विज्ञानवाद) which were propounded by the Sautrântika and the Yogâcâra schools, the critics next proceed to attack the शून्यवाद of the Mâdhyamikas, generally understood to mean the doctrine of absolute and universal emptiness or void. It may be noted here that the doctrine attributed to the Mâdhyamika in the stanza quoted by Malliṣeṇa towards the close of his commentary on St. XVII makes शून्यता a synonym of the Para-Brahman of the S'âmkara Vedântins, and many a Mahâyana hymn may be cited in which शून्यता is glorified in language which the Vedântin employs with respect to his Para-Brahman. But this is really a confusion between शून्यता and पूर्णता.*

Malliṣeṇa, like all other critics of the 'शून्यवाद', has under-stood it as the doctrine of the Universal Void or Emptiness.

An obvious objection which is taken to this doctrine is that it leaves no ground even for itself to stand upon, its only logical position being dead *silence* (" ततश्चास्य मूकतैव युक्ता, न पुनः शून्यवादोपन्यासाय तुण्डताण्डवाडम्बरम् "). Yet it may be interesting to examine the argument which is advanced in its favour. The argument is a sophistical demonstration of the logical impossibility of the supposed reals, viz., प्रमातृ, प्रमेय, प्रमाण and प्रमिति. This, says Malliṣeṇa, the Buddhist tries to prove in extenso in " तत्त्वोपप्लवसिंह, " a work which is not now available, but which was, according to its author, as the title implies, 'a lion that confounds the animals of Reality'.

This postion is met by showing that प्रमातृ etc. are by no means impossible; on the contrary they can be shown to be undeniably real. In fact, शून्यवाद, if it is to be worthy of

* ॐ पूर्णमिदं पूर्णमदः पूर्णात् पूर्णमुदच्यते ।
पूर्णस्य पूर्णमादाय पूर्णमेवावशिष्यते ॥—Upaniṣad.

credence, must be supported by प्रमाण, which, however, will mean negation of शून्यवाद.

St. XVIII.

Next, we have a criticism of the Buddhist's क्षणभङ्गवाद in its application to the problem of आत्मन्. In the absence of an abiding आत्मन्, says the critic,—

(1) There can be no moral retribution in our life (भव). The Buddhist no doubt substitutes for the single आत्मन् a *series* of विज्ञानs of which each preceding one is supposed to be connected with each succeeding one, and vice versa. But who connects them? What is the synthesizing principle?

(2) Similarly, there is no room for Liberation (मोक्ष). For, if there is no आत्मन्, who is to be liberated from the bondage of life (संसार)? The heap of वासनाs which has to be destroyed must belong to some one, to that very person who has been in bondage (बद्ध).

(3) Even such an ordinary psychological fact as स्मृति—memory—becomes impossible.

St. XIX.

The doctrine next criticised is that of वासना—a kind of makeshift which is intended to do duty for the principle of permanence which the Buddhist denies.

All Indian philosophers are firm believers in transmigration of the soul, and the Buddhist who denies the existence of the soul and yet believes in transmigration has somehow to make it possible. This he does by adopting the theory of वासना. It is intended to account for the apparent continuity of our psychic experience not only in our present life but also of the past and the future. But the problem which he has to face is that of reconciliation of वासना with क्षणभङ्ग. Hemacandra and with him Malliṣeṇa point out how the task is hopeless. They put forward this trilemma: Are वासना and क्षणसंतति (lit, a series of moments, that is, things conditioned by moments) one (अभेद) or separate (भेद) or neither one nor the other (अनुभय) ?—and they show how the Buddhist doctrine breaks on the spearheads of this triśûla. In the first case, nothing is gained by the addition of वासना. In the second case, it must either conform to the principle of क्षणभङ्ग or not—if it does, no gain; if it does not, the universality of the principle of क्षणभङ्ग is so far violated. In the third case, the position becomes impossible; for it must be either the one (अभेद) or the other (भेद). There is only one escape from all these troubles and that is by taking shelter underneath the shady tree of the Jaina doctrine of अनेकान्त i. e. भेद–cum–अभेद. As Hemacandra graphically puts it, the birds that have flown away far across the wide sea without any hope of finding a resting place must return to their home (स्याद्वाद) on the mast of the ship.

In connection with this hypothesis—भेदाभेद—Malliṣeṇa generously points out how in this case the difference is merely verbal. He says : " स्याद्वादवादिनामपि हि प्रतिक्षणं नवनवपर्याय-परंपरोत्पत्तिरभिमतैव । तथा च क्षणिकत्वम् । अतीतानागतवर्तमानपर्याय-परंपरानुसंधायकं चान्वयिद्रव्यम् तच्च वासनेति संज्ञान्तरभावेप्यभिमतमेव । न खलु नामभेदाद् वादः कोऽपि कोविदानाम् ". Malliṣeṇa further shows how वासना is not possible without a permanent something on which it should rest (" स्थिरस्य संबद्धस्य च वस्त्रादेर्मृगमदादिना वास्यत्वं दृष्टम् ").

Stanza XX: *Criticism of the Cârvâka.*

St. XX.

The two principles of the Cârvâka which are criticised are:

(1) That प्रत्यक्ष is the only प्रमाण ; not even अनुमान.

(2) That there is no soul, beyond the physical body, and consequently, there is no moral responsibility and no life after death (भूतचिद्वाद).

1. The first is impugned on the following grounds: As a result of your doctrine, we cannot be aware of the mind

of other persons, as we have evidently no प्रत्यक्ष or direct experience of it. We cannot classify our cognitions as प्रमाण and अप्रमाण (न च संनिहितार्थबलेनोत्पद्यमानं पूर्वापरपरामर्शशून्यं प्रत्यक्षं पूर्वापरकालभाविनीनां ज्ञानव्यक्तीनां प्रामाण्याप्रामाण्यव्यवस्थापकं निमित्तमुपलक्षयितुं क्षमते ।) Moreover, we should not forget that we call even प्रत्यक्ष a प्रमाण on the strength of our experience and generalisation from observed cases—that is to say, our belief in the credibility of our senses rests on Inference.

2. The materialistic view of the soul is condemned by M. with the help of a long passage quoted from "Dravyâlamkâra", where it is shown that consciousness is not the product of भूतs (न भूतकार्यमुपयोगः), and even an ugly and a diseased body may hold a beautiful and healthy soul.

Stanzas XXI-XXX: *The Jaina Doctrine.*

St. XXI: *Nature of Reality: Permanence and Change.*

The authors assert here the Jaina doctrine of Reality as possessed of उत्पाद, व्यय and ध्रौव्य as against those who obsessed by the phenomena of the first two overlook the third, viz. the Buddhists, and also those who contrariwise, notice only the third and forget the first two, for example, the S'âmkara Vedântins. Recall here the pre-Buddhistic schools noted in the Brahmajâlasutta, the Eternalists (सस्सतिका=शाश्वतिकाः) and the non-eternalists (असस्सतिका=अशाश्वतिकाः).

St. XXII: *Reality, manysided.*

The Jaina insistence upon the entirety or wholeness of truth has found expression in various forms. In the preceding stanza it was expressed as "उत्पादव्ययध्रौव्ययुक्तं सत्." Now, another proposition in which it is set forth is "अनन्तधर्मात्मकमेव तत्त्वम्"—Truth has numberless aspects.

St. XXIII: *"Saptabhamgî".*

Next the author points out how one and the same thing may be viewed synthetically or analytically as *one* or as *many* —as one substance or as many attributes or modes. This fact has been expressed in the famous 'set of Seven Forms'—the "सप्तभङ्गी". For a full statement of the seven forms see the text of the Syâdvâdamañjarî under St. XXII and the Notes thereon.

St. XXIV : *No contradiction of the so called opposites.*

The authors now explain how the synthesis of opposites recommended in the previous Stanza does not involve any contradiction, inasmuch as the opposites are conditioned by 'upâdhis' and are relative to them.

St. XXV : *No contradiction—continued: application of the principle to certain problems of philosophy.*

The सप्तभङ्गी, be it remembered, gives only the *forms* of the propositions. The principle has to be applied to actual problems of philosophy on which various schoolmen stand divided owing to their viewpoints being partial. The problems are: (1) Permanence versus Change; (2) Universal versus Particular; (3) Expressible versus Inexpressible i.e. Positivism versus Transcendentalism; (4) Being versus Non-being, or Real versus Unreal.

St. XXVI : *Criticism of the absolutely eternal and the absolutely transitory.*

Of these the author takes up the first, viz., Permanence versus Change or the Eternal versus the Transitory, and shows how the arguments of the two sides destroy each other, with the result that the doctrine of Syâdvâda emerges from their mutual conflict. Compare here Kant's philosophy of antinomies.

St. XXVII : *Criticism of Absolutism continued.*

Absolutists cannot solve the problems of सुख-दुख (भोग), पुण्य-पाप, and बन्ध-मोक्ष.

St. XXVIII : *Durnaya, Naya, and Pramâṇa.*

The author next refers to the Jaina philosophy of दुर्नय, नय and प्रमाण. (1) दुर्नय is the mis-take of *partial* truth for the whole truth, to the exclusion of the latter; (2) नयs are the statements of partial truths, without the recognition that they are only partial; and (3) प्रमाण is the *whole* truth. The commentator here sets forth the famous doctrine of the नयs.

The doctrine of नय or Relativity of Knowledge is the most remarkable contribution of Jainism to Philosophy. It means that Reality is conveyed (from √नी) to the mind differently from different points of view, or to take it from the other end, the mind approaches Reality differently from different points of view. A very useful and fundamental division of नयs which is made is that into (1) द्रव्यास्ति(र्थि)क नय and (2) पर्यायास्ति(र्थि)क नय, i. e. (1) that which regards द्रव्य or substance and (2) that which regards पर्याय or modes. The नयs are also divided into five, six or seven kinds. Of these seven the first four are अर्थनयs and the last three शब्दनयs, or to adopt the fundamental divisions of द्रव्य and पर्याय, the first three are द्रव्यार्थिक and the last four पर्यायार्थिक. These are:

(1) नैगम—(variously derived) which notes both the universal and the particular;

(2) संग्रह—which notes the universal only;

(3) व्यवहार—the point of view of daily life, which does not penetrate below the surface of things;

(4) ऋजुसूत्र—It confines itself to the present, and takes note of actual phenomena—the attributes or changes occurring in a substance and not the substance itself.

(5) शब्द—which pays attention to the character of the world. This, while it distinguishes between the different connotations of words, does not do so in regard to their denotation.

(6) समभिरूढ—This नय goes further in the direction of attaching much importance to the form of the word. It makes distinctions of things corresponding to the etymologies of the words. Thus no two synonyms denote the same thing.

(7) एवंभूत—This नय takes the word as signifying an object while it possesses the क्रिया connoted by the etymology.

The Jaina observes that the Naiyâyika and the Vaiśeṣika systems are cases of नैगमनय, so far as they recognise both the universal (सामान्य) and the particular (विशेष). The Vedânta and the Sâṁkhya are cases of संग्रहनय, the former because it merges all particulars in the universal सत्, and the latter in so far as it represents an attempt at marshalling particulars under certain general concepts, and regarding the former as forms of the latter, the effect being contained in the cause. The Cârvâka's way of looking at things is that of व्यवहारनय. The Buddhists follow ऋजुसूत्रनय, inasmuch as they accept phenomena and deny the noumenon; and the grammarians are by the very nature of their profession inclined towards शब्द etc.

It is obvious that the whole set of seven Nayas could not have come into existence all at once. As a matter of fact, they represent a gradual growth as is a apparent from the number of नयs recognised at different times (see Notes) and also from their varying importance.

See the text of the Syâdvâdamañjarî on this Stanza and Notes for fuller account.

St. XXIX : *The number of Souls.*

The souls are divisible into six kinds but their number is endless.

St. XXX : *The doctrine of the Syâdvâda, all comprehensive and impartial.*

The teaching of the Master is important and all-comprehensive. He has hardly to attack any of the other systems, as those systems quarrel inter se and destroy each other. In other words, the Jaina philosophy emerges as the whole truth from the mutual conflicts of the several schools. For details see the Text, Notes and Supplementary Notes with Appendices.

This note presupposes the existence of the schools. If so, it only points to a late date of the Jaina point of view as compared with that of the other schools between which it mediates.

Stanzas XXXI–XXXII: *Conclusion.*

St. XXXI–XXXII: *Praise of the Lord Mahâvîra.*

The Dvâtriṁśikâ closes as it began with the panegyric of the Tîrthaṁkara.

V. AN ESTIMATE OF THE WORK.

From this short summary of the contents the reader will see what a wide range of philosophical topics has been covered in this work. None of the rival sytems has been examined in its entirety, but only those tenets have been selected for criticism from each of the schools in which the Jaina is really interested, and these are some of the greatest problems of religion and philosophy, such as the problems of the universal and the particular, the permanent and the changing, God, the one, omnipresent, omnipotent and omniscient maker of the world, the sanctity of all life, the state of the liberated souls, the theory of knowledge, the nature of Reality etc. The examination, moreover, is not in the nature of irresponsible criticism (vitaṇḍâ), but care has been taken to present the Jaina view on each of the points that has been considered; and, in conclusion, a clear statement has been made of the Jaina doctrine of Naya and Syâdvâda—in one phrase, of the Relativity of Knowledge which is determined by the point of view from which Reality is approached. For this great achievement it is difficult to apportion credit between Hemacandra, the author of the Anyayogavyavaccheda-Dvâtriṃśikâ, and Malliṣeṇa, the writer of the Syâdvâdamañjarî. The former is a genuine devotional lyric, pulsating with reverence for the Master, and is at the same time a review of some of the tenets of the rival schools on which the Jaina sees reason to differ. Devotion and thought are here haphily blended together in one whole, and are expressed in such noble and dignified language that it deserves to rank as a piece of literature no less than that of philosophy. To Malliṣeṇa belongs the credit of constructing a systematic work out of the brief critical remarks which Hemacandra throws out at random. His knowledge of the different systems, however, is not equally deep. In some of the systems such as the Nyâya-Vaiśeṣika he is evidently well read, while of others such as the Vedânta he has touched only the fringe. But on the whole, he has conducted the examination of the different systems with knowledge and mastery of detail, and that too, in a wonderfully lucid style, which lifts his work from the position of a mere parasitical commentary to that of an original work of independent value.

॥ ॐ नमः श्रीसर्वज्ञाय ॥

श्रीमल्लिषेणसूरिप्रणीता

स्याद्वादमञ्जरी

श्रीहेमचन्द्रसूरिनिर्मितान्ययोगव्यवच्छेद-
द्वात्रिंशिकास्तवनटीकारूपा

यस्य ज्ञानमनन्तवस्तुविषयं यः पूज्यते दैवतै-
र्नित्यं यस्य वचो न दुर्नयकृतैः कोलाहलैर्लुप्यते ।
रागद्वेषमुखा द्विषां च परिषत् क्षिप्ता क्षणाद्येन सा
स श्रीवीरविभुर्विधूतकलुषां बुद्धिं विधत्तां मम ॥ १ ॥

निःसीमप्रतिभैकजीवितधरौ निःशेषभूमिस्पृशां
पुण्यौघेन सरस्वतीसुरगुरू स्वाङ्गैकरूपौ दधत् ।
यः स्याद्वादमसाधयन्निजवपुर्दृष्टान्ततः सोस्तु मे
सद्बुद्ध्यम्बुनिधिप्रबोधविधये श्रीहेमचन्द्रः प्रभुः ॥ २ ॥

ये हेमचन्द्रं मुनिमेतदुक्त-
ग्रन्थार्थसेवामिषतः श्रयन्ते ।
संप्राप्य ते गौरवमुज्ज्वलानां
पदं कलानामुचितं भवन्ति ॥ ३ ॥

मातर्भारति संनिधेहि हृदि मे येनेयमाप्तस्तुते-
र्निर्मातुं विवृतिं प्रसिद्ध्यति जवादारम्भसंभावना ।
यद्वा विस्मृतमोष्ठयोः स्फुरति यत्सारस्वतः शाश्वतो
मन्त्रः श्रीउदयप्रभेतिरचनारम्यो ममाहर्निशम् ॥ ४ ॥

इह हि विषमदुःषमाररजनितिमिरतिरस्कारभास्करानुकारिणा वसुधातलावतीर्णसुधासारिणीदेश्यदेशनावितानपरमार्हतीकृतश्रीकुमारपालक्ष्मापालप्रवर्तिताभयदानाभिधानजीवातुसंजीवितनानाजीवप्रदत्ताशीर्वादमाहात्म्यकल्पावधिस्थायिविशदयशःशरीरेण निरवद्यचातुर्विद्यनिर्माणैकब्रह्मणा श्रीहेमचन्द्रसूरिणा जगत्प्रसिद्धश्रीसिद्धसेनदिवाकरविरचितद्वात्रिंशद्द्वात्रिंशिकानुसारिश्रीवर्धमानजिनस्तुतिरूपमयोगव्यवच्छेदान्ययोगव्यवच्छेदाभिधानं द्वात्रिंशिकाद्वितयं विद्वज्जनमनस्तत्त्वावबोधनिबन्धनं विदधे। तत्र च प्रथमद्वात्रिंशिकायाः सुखोन्नेयत्वाद्व्याख्यानमुपेक्ष्य द्वितीयस्यास्तस्या निःशेषदुर्वादिपरिषदधिक्षेपदक्षायाः कतिपयपदार्थविवरणकरणेन स्वस्मृतिबीजप्रबोधविधिर्विधीयते। तस्याश्चेदमादिकाव्यम्—

अनन्तविज्ञानमतीतदोष–
मबाध्यसिद्धान्तममर्त्यपूज्यम् ।
श्रीवर्धमानं जिनमाप्तमुख्यं
स्वयंभुवं स्तोतुमहं यतिष्ये ॥ १ ॥

श्रीवर्धमानं जिनमहं स्तोतुं यतिष्य इति क्रियासंबन्धः। किंविशिष्टम्। अनन्तमप्रतिपाति विशिष्टं सर्वद्रव्यपर्यायविषयत्वेनोत्कृष्टं ज्ञानं केवलाख्यं विज्ञानं ततोनन्तं विज्ञानं यस्य सोनन्तविज्ञानस्तम्। तथातीता निःसत्ताकीभूतत्वेनातिक्रान्ता दोषा रागादयो यस्मात्स तथा तम्। तथाबाध्यः परैर्बाधितुमशक्यः सिद्धान्तः स्याद्वादश्रुतलक्षणो यस्य स तथा तम्। तथामर्त्या देवास्तेषामपि पूज्यमाराध्यम् ॥

अत्र च श्रीवर्धमानस्वामिनो विशेषणद्वारेण चत्वारो मूलातिशयाः प्रतिपादिताः । तत्रानन्तविज्ञानमित्यनेन भगवतः केवलज्ञानलक्षणविशिष्टज्ञानानन्त्यप्रतिपादनाज्ज्ञानातिशयः । अतीतदोषमित्यनेनाष्टादशदोषसंक्षयाभिधानादपायापगमातिशयः । अबाध्यसिद्धान्तमित्यनेन कुतीर्थिकोपन्यस्तकुहेतुसमूहाशक्यबाधस्याद्वादरूपसिद्धान्तप्रणयनभणनाद्वचनातिशयः । अमर्त्यपूज्यमित्यनेनाकृत्रिमभक्तिभरनिर्भरसुरासुरनिकायनायकनिर्मितमहाप्रातिहार्यसपर्यापरिज्ञापनात्पूजातिशयः ॥

अत्राह परः । अनन्तविज्ञानमित्येतावदेवास्तु नातीतदोषमिति । गतार्थत्वात् । दोषात्ययं विनाऽत्यन्तविज्ञानत्वस्यानुपपत्तेः ॥ अत्रोच्यते । कुनयमतानुसारिपरिकल्पिताप्तव्यवच्छेदार्थमिदम् । तथा चाहुराजीविकनयानुसारिणः—

ज्ञानिनो धर्मतीर्थस्य कर्तारः परमं पदम् ।
गत्वागच्छन्ति भूयोपि भवं तीर्थनिकारतः ॥

इति । तन्नूनं न तेतीतदोषाः । कथमन्यथा तेषां तीर्थनिकारदर्शनेपि भवावतारः ॥

आह । यद्येवमतीतदोषमित्येवास्त्वनन्तविज्ञानमित्यतिरिच्यते । दोषात्ययेवश्यंभावित्वादनन्तविज्ञानत्वस्य ॥ न । कैश्चिद्दोषाभावेपि तदनभ्युपगमात् । तथा च तद्वचनम्—

सर्वं पश्यतु वा मा वा तत्त्वमिष्टं तु पश्यतु ।
कीटसंख्यापरिज्ञानं तस्य नः क्वोपयुज्यते ॥

तथा—तस्मादनुष्ठानगतं ज्ञानमस्य विचार्यताम् ।
प्रमाणं दूरदर्शी चेदेते गृध्रानुपास्महे ॥

तन्मतव्यपोहार्थमनन्तविज्ञानमित्यदुष्टमेव । विज्ञानानन्त्यं विना एकस्याप्यर्थस्य यथावत्परिज्ञानाभावात् । तथा चार्षम्—

जे एगं जाणइ से सव्वं जाणइ ।
जे सव्वं जाणइ से एगं जाणइ ॥

तथा— एको भावः सर्वथा येन दृष्टः
सर्वे भावाः सर्वथा तेन दृष्टाः ।
सर्वे भावाः सर्वथा येन दृष्टा
एको भावः सर्वथा तेन दृष्टः ॥

इति ॥

ननु तर्ह्यबाध्यसिद्धान्तमित्यपार्थकम् । यथोक्तगुणयुक्तस्याव्यभिचारिवचनत्वेन तदुक्तसिद्धान्तस्य बाधायोगात् ॥ न । अभिप्रायापरिज्ञानात् । निर्दोषपुरुषप्रणीत एवाबाध्यसिद्धान्तो नापरेऽपौरुषेयाद्या असंभवादिदोषाघ्रातत्वात् इति ज्ञापनार्थम् । आत्ममात्रतारकमूकान्तकृत्केवल्यादिरूपमुण्डकेवलिनो यथोक्तसिद्धान्तप्रणयनासमर्थस्य व्यवच्छेदार्थं वा विशेषणमेतत् ॥

अन्यस्त्वाह । अमर्त्यपूज्यमिति न वाच्यम् । यावता यथोद्दिष्टगुणगरिष्ठस्य त्रिभुवनविभोरमर्त्यपूज्यत्वं न कथंचन व्यभिचरतीति ॥ सत्यम् । लौकिकानां ह्यमर्त्या एव पूज्यतया प्रसिद्धास्तेषामपि भगवानेव पूज्य इति विशेषणेनानेन ज्ञापयन्नाचार्यः परमेश्वरस्य देवाधिदेवत्वमावेदयति ॥

एवं पूर्वार्धे चत्वारोतिशया उक्ताः ॥

अनन्तविज्ञानत्वं च सामान्यकेवलिनामप्यवश्यं भावीत्यतस्तद्व्यवच्छेदाय श्रीवर्धमानमिति विशेष्यपदमपि विशेषणरूपतया

व्याख्यायते ॥ श्रिया चतुस्त्रिंशदतिशयसमृद्ध्यनुभवात्मकभावार्हन्त्यरूपया वर्धमानं वर्धिष्णुम् ॥ नन्वतिशयानां परिमिततयैव सिद्धान्ते प्रसिद्धत्वात्कथं वर्धमानतोपपत्तिः ॥ इति चेन्न । यथा निशीथचूर्णौ भगवतां श्रीमदर्हतामष्टोत्तरसहस्रसंख्यबाह्यलक्षणसंख्याया उपलक्षणत्वेनान्तरङ्गलक्षणानां सत्त्वादीनामानन्त्यमुक्तम् । एवमतिशयानामधिकृतपरिगणनायोगेऽप्यपरिमितत्वमविरुद्धम् । ततो नातिशयश्रिया वर्धमानत्वं दोषाश्रय इति ॥

अतीतदोषता चोपशान्तमोहगुणस्थानवर्तिनामपि संभवतीत्यतः क्षीणमोहाख्याप्रतिपातिगुणस्थानप्राप्तिप्रतिपत्त्यर्थं जिनमिति विशेषणम् । रागादिजेतृत्वाज्जिनः । समूलकाषंकषितरागादिदोष इति । अबाध्यसिद्धान्तता च श्रुतकेवल्यादिष्वपि दृश्यतेतस्तदपोहायाप्तमुख्यमिति विशेषणम् । आप्तिर्हि रागद्वेषमोहानामैकान्तिक आत्यन्तिकश्च क्षयः । सा येषामस्ति ते खल्वाप्ताः । अर्शादित्वान्मत्वर्थीयोऽच्प्रत्ययः । तेषु मध्ये मुखमिव सर्वाङ्गानां प्रधानत्वेन मुख्यम् । शाखादेर्यः इति तुल्ये यः । अमर्त्यपूज्यता च तथाविधगुरूपदेशपरिचर्यापर्याप्तविद्याचरणसंपन्नानां सामान्यमुनीनामपि न दुर्घटा । अतस्तन्निराकरणाय स्वयंभुवमिति विशेषणम् । स्वयमात्मनैव परोपदेशनिरपेक्षतयावगततत्त्वो भवतीति स्वयंभूः स्वयं संबुद्धः । तमेवंविधं चरमजिनेन्द्रं स्तोतुं स्तुतिविषयीकर्तुमहं यतिष्ये यत्नं करिष्यामि ॥ अत्र चाचार्यो भविष्यत्कालप्रयोगेण योगिनामप्यशक्यानुष्ठानं भगवद्गुणस्तवनं मन्यमानः श्रद्धामेव स्तुतिकरणेऽसाधारणं कारणं ज्ञापयन्यत्नकरणमेव मदधीनं न पुनर्यथावस्थितभगवद्गुणस्तवनसिद्धिरिति सूचितवान् । अहमिति च गतार्थत्वेपि परोपदेशान्यानुवृत्त्यादिनिरपेक्षतया निजश्रद्धयैव स्तुतिप्रारम्भ इति ज्ञापनार्थम् ॥

अथवा । श्रीवर्धमानादिविशेषणचतुष्टयमनन्तविज्ञानादिपदचतुष्टयेन सह हेतुहेतुमद्भावेन व्याख्यायते । यत एव श्रीवर्धमानमत एवानन्तविज्ञानम् । श्रिया कृत्स्नकर्मक्षयाविर्भूतानन्तचतुष्कसंपद्रूपया वर्धमानम् । यद्यपि श्रीवर्धमानस्य परमेश्वरस्यानन्तचतुष्कसंपत्तेरुत्पत्त्यनन्तरं सर्वकालं तुल्यत्वाच्चयापचयौ न स्तस्तथापि निरपचयत्वेन शाश्वतिकावस्थानयोगाद्वर्धमानत्वमुपचर्यते । यद्यपि च श्रीवर्धमानविशेषणेनानन्तचतुष्कान्तर्भावित्वेनानन्तविज्ञानत्वमपि सिद्धं तथाप्यनन्तविज्ञानस्यैव परोपकारसाधकतमत्वाद्भगवत्प्रवृत्तेश्च परोपकारैकनिबन्धनत्वादनन्तविज्ञानत्वं शेषानन्तत्रयात्पृथङ्निर्धार्याचार्येणोक्तम् ॥

ननु यथा जगन्नाथस्यानन्तविज्ञानं परार्थं तथानन्तदर्शनस्य केवलज्ञानपरपर्यायस्य पारार्थ्यमव्याहतमेव । केवलज्ञानकेवलदर्शनाभ्यामेव हि स्वामी क्रमप्रवृत्तिभ्यामुपलब्धं सामान्यविशेषात्मकं पदार्थसार्थं परेभ्यः प्ररूपयति । तत्किमर्थं तन्नोपात्तम् ॥ इति चेदुच्यते । विज्ञानशब्देन तस्यापि संग्रहाददोषः । ज्ञानमात्राया उभयत्रापि समानत्वात् । य एव ह्यभ्यन्तरीकृतसमताख्यधर्मा विषमताधर्मविशिष्टा ज्ञानेन गम्यन्तेर्थास्त एव ह्यभ्यन्तरीकृतविषमताधर्माः समताधर्मविशिष्टा दर्शनेन गम्यन्ते । जीवस्वाभाव्यात् । सामान्यप्रधानमुपसर्जनीकृतविशेषमर्थग्रहणं दर्शनमुच्यते । तथा प्रधानविशेषमुपसर्जनीकृतसामान्यं च ज्ञानमिति ॥

तथा यत एव जिनमत एवातीतदोषम् । रागादिजेतृत्वाद्धि जिनः । न चाजिनस्यातीतदोषता ॥ तथा यत एवाप्तमुख्यमत एवाबाध्यसिद्धान्तम् । आप्तो हि प्रत्ययित उच्यते । तत आप्तेषु मुख्यं श्रेष्ठमाप्तमुख्यम् । आप्तमुख्यत्वं च प्रभोरविसंवादिवचनतया

विश्वविश्वासभूमित्वात् । अत एवाबाध्यसिद्धान्तम् । नहि यथावज्ज्ञानावलोकितवस्तुवादी सिद्धान्तः कुनयैर्बाधितुं शक्यते ॥ यत एव स्वयंभुवमत एवामर्त्यपूज्यम् । पूज्यते हि देवदेवो जगत्त्रयविलक्षणलक्षणेन स्वयंसंबुद्धत्वगुणेन सौधर्मेन्द्रादिभिरमर्त्यैरिति ॥

अत्र च श्रीवर्धमानमिति विशेषणतया यद्व्याख्यातं तदयोगव्यवच्छेदाभिधानप्रथमद्वात्रिंशिकाप्रथमकाव्यतृतीयपादवर्तमानं श्रीवर्धमानाभिधमात्मरूपम् इति विशेष्यमनुवर्तमानं बुद्धौ संप्रधार्य विज्ञेयम् । तत्र ह्यात्मरूपमिति विशेष्यपदम् । आवृत्त्या वा विशेषणमपि विशेष्यतया व्याख्येयम् ॥

इति प्रथमवृत्तार्थः ॥ १ ॥

अस्यां च स्तुतावन्ययोगव्यवच्छेदाधिकृतः तस्य च तीर्थान्तरीयपरिकल्पिततत्त्वाभासनिरासेन तेषामाप्तत्वव्यवच्छेदः स्वरूपम् । तच्च भगवतो यथावस्थितवस्तुतत्त्ववादित्वख्यापनेनैव प्रामाण्यमश्नुते । अतः स्तुतिकारस्त्रिजगद्गुरोर्निःशेषगुणस्तुतिश्रद्धालुरपि सद्भूतवस्तुवादित्वाख्यं गुणविशेषमेव वर्णयितुमात्मनोभिप्रायमाविष्कुर्वन्नाह—

अयं जनो नाथ तव स्तवाय
गुणान्तरेभ्यः स्पृहयालुरेव ।
विगाहतां किंतु यथार्थवाद-
मेकं परीक्षाविधिदुर्विदग्धः ॥ २ ॥

हे नाथ अयं मल्लक्षणो जनः तव गुणान्तरेभ्यो यथार्थवाद-

व्यतिरिक्तेभ्योनन्यसाधारणशारीरलक्षणादिभ्यः स्पृहयालुरेव श्रद्धालुरेव। किमर्थम्। स्तवाय स्तुतिकरणाय। इयं तादर्थ्ये चतुर्थी। पूर्वत्र तु—स्पृहेर्व्याप्यं वा इतिलक्षणा। तव गुणान्तराण्यपि स्तोतुं स्पृहावानेवायं जन इति भावः॥ ननु यदि गुणान्तरस्तुतावपि स्पृहयालुता तत्किमर्थं तत्रोपेक्षा। इत्याशङ्क्योत्तरार्धमाह। किंत्वित्यभ्युपगमविशेषद्योतने निपातः। एकमेकमेव। यथार्थवादं यथावस्थितवस्तुतत्त्वप्रख्यापनाख्यं त्वदीयं गुणम्। अयं जनो विगाहतां स्तुतिक्रियया समन्ताद्व्याप्नोतु। तस्मिन्नेकस्मिन्नपि हि गुणे वर्णिते तन्त्रान्तरीयदैवतेभ्यो वैशिष्ट्यख्यापनद्वारेण वस्तुतः सर्वगुणस्तवनसिद्धेः॥

अथ प्रस्तुतगुणस्तुतिः सम्यक्परीक्षाक्षमाणां दिव्यदृशामेवौचितीमञ्चति नार्वाग्दृशां भवादृशामित्याशङ्कां विशेषणद्वारेण निराकरोति। यतोयं जनः परीक्षाविधिदुर्विदग्धोधिकृतगुणविशेषपरीक्षणविधौ दुर्विदग्धः पण्डितंमन्य इति यावत्। अयमाशयः। यद्यपि जगद्गुरोर्यथार्थवादित्वगुणपरीक्षणं मादृशां मतेरगोचरस्तथापि भक्तिश्रद्धातिशयात् तस्यामहमात्मानं विदग्धमिव मन्य इति विशुद्धश्रद्धाभक्तिव्यक्तिमात्ररूपत्वात्स्तुतेः॥

इति वृत्तार्थः॥ २॥

अथ ये कुतीर्थ्याः कुशास्त्रवासनावासितस्वान्ततया त्रिभुवनस्वामिनं स्वामित्वेन न प्रतिपन्नाः तानपि तत्त्वविचारणां प्रति शिक्षयन्नाह—

गुणेष्वसूयां दधतः परेमी
मा शिश्रियन्नाम भवन्तमीशम्।

तथापि संमील्य विलोचनानि
विचारयन्तां नयवर्त्म सत्यम् ॥ ३ ॥

अमी इति अदसस्तु विप्रकृष्टे इति वचनात्तत्त्वातत्त्वविमर्शबाह्यतया दूरीकरणार्हत्वाद्विप्रकृष्टाः परे कुतीर्थिकाः भवन्तं त्वाम् अनन्यसामान्यसकलगुणनिलयमपि मा ईशं शिश्रियन्मा स्वामित्वेन प्रतिपद्यन्ताम् । यतो गुणेष्वसूयां दधतः गुणेषु बद्धमत्सराः । गुणेषु दोषाविष्करणं ह्यसूया । यो हि यत्र गुणे मत्सरीभवति स तदाश्रयं नानुरुध्यते । यथा माधुर्यमत्सरी करभः पुण्ड्रेक्षुकाण्डम् । गुणाश्रयश्च भवान् ॥ एवं परतीर्थिकानां भगवदाज्ञाप्रतिपत्तिं प्रतिषिध्य स्तुतिकारो माध्यस्थ्यमिवास्थाय तान्प्रति हितशिक्षामुत्तरार्धेनोपदिशति । तथापि त्वदाज्ञाप्रतिपत्तेरभावेपि । लोचनानि नेत्राणि । संमील्य मिलितपुटीकृत्य । सत्यं युक्तियुक्तम् । नयवर्त्म न्यायमार्गम् । विचारयन्तां विमर्शविषयीकुर्वन्तु ॥

अत्र च विचारयन्तामित्यात्मनेपदेन फलवत्कर्तृविषयेणैवं ज्ञापयत्याचार्यो यदवितथनयपथविचारणया तेषामेव फलं वयं केवलमुपदेष्टारः । किं तत्फलम् इति चेत्प्रेक्षावत्तेति ब्रूमः । संमील्य विलोचनानीति च वदतः प्रायस्तत्त्वविचारणमेकाग्रताहेतुनयननिमीलनपूर्वकं लोके प्रसिद्धमित्यभिप्रायः ॥ अथवा अयमुपदेशस्तेभ्योऽरोचमान एवाचार्येण वितीर्यते । ततोऽस्वदमानोप्ययं कटुकौषधपानन्यायेनायतिसुखत्वाद्भवद्भिर्नेत्रे निमील्य पेय एवेत्याकूतम् ॥

ननु च यदि पारमेश्वरे वचसि तेषामविवेकातिरेकादरोचकता तत्किमर्थं तान् प्रत्युपदेशक्लेश इति ॥ नैवम् । परोपकारसार-

प्रवृत्तीनां महात्मनां प्रतिपाद्यगतां रुचिमरुचिं वानपेक्ष्य हितोपदेशप्रवृत्तिदर्शनात् । तेषां हि परार्थस्यैव स्वार्थत्वेनाभिमतत्वात् । न च हितोपदेशादपरः पारमार्थिकः परार्थः । तथा चार्षम् ।

रूसउ वा परो मा वा विसं वा परियत्तउ ।
भासियव्वा हिया भासा सपक्खगुणकारिया ॥

इति । उवाच च वाचकमुख्यः—

न भवति धर्मः श्रोतुः सर्वस्यैकान्ततो हितश्रवणात् ।
ब्रुवतोनुग्रहबुद्ध्या वक्तुस्त्वेकान्ततो भवति ॥ १ ॥

इति वृत्तार्थः ॥ ३ ॥

अथ यथावन्नयवर्त्मविचारमेव प्रपञ्चयितुं पराभिमेततत्त्वानां प्रामाण्यं निराकुर्वन्नादितस्तावत्काव्यषट्केनौलूक्यमताभिमततत्त्वानि दूषयितुकामस्तदन्तःपातिनौ प्रथमतरं सामान्यविशेषौ दूषयन्नाह—

स्वतोनुवृत्तिव्यतिवृत्तिभाजो
भावा न भावान्तरनेयरूपाः ।
परात्मतत्त्वादतथात्मतत्त्वाद्-
द्वयं वदन्तोऽकुशलाः स्खलन्ति ॥ ४ ॥

अभवन् भवन्ति भविष्यन्ति चेति भावाः पदार्था आत्मपुद्गलादयस्ते । स्वत इति सर्वं हि वाक्यं सावधारणमामनन्ति

इति । स्वत एव आत्मीयस्वरूपादेव । अनुवृत्तिव्यतिवृत्तिभाजः । एकाकारा प्रतीतिरेकशब्दवाच्यता चानुवृत्तिः । व्यत्तिवृत्तिः व्यावृत्तिः । सजातीयविजातीयेभ्यः सर्वथा व्यवच्छेदः । ते उभे अपि संवलिते भजन्त आश्रयन्तीति अनुवृत्तिव्यतिवृत्तिभाजः । सामान्यविशेषोभयात्मका इत्यर्थः ॥

अस्यैवार्थस्य व्यतिरेकमाह । न भावान्तरनेयरूपा इति । नेति निषेधे । भावान्तराभ्यां पराभिमताभ्यां द्रव्यगुणकर्मसमवायेभ्यः पदार्थान्तराभ्यां भावव्यतिरिक्तसामान्यविशेषाभ्यां नेयं प्रतीतिविषयं प्रापणीयं रूपं यथासंख्यमनुवृत्तिव्यतिवृत्तिलक्षणं स्वरूपं येषां ते तथोक्ताः । स्वभाव एव ह्ययं सर्वभावानां यदनुवृत्तिव्यावृत्तिप्रत्ययौ स्वत एव जनयन्ति । तथाहि । घट एव तावत्पृथुबुध्नोदराद्याकारवान्प्रतीतिविषयीभवन्सन्नन्यानपि तदाकृतिभृतः पदार्थान्घटरूपतया घटैकशब्दवाच्यतया च प्रत्याययन्सामान्याख्यां लभते । स एव चेतरेभ्यः सजातीयविजातीयेभ्यो द्रव्यक्षेत्रकालभावैरात्मानं व्यावर्तयन्विशेषव्यपदेशमश्नुते । इति न सामान्यविशेषयोः पृथक्पदार्थान्तरत्वकल्पनं न्याय्यम् । पदार्थधर्मत्वेनैव तयोः प्रतीयमानत्वात् । न च धर्मा धर्मिणः सकाशादत्यन्तं व्यतिरिक्ताः । एकान्तभेदे विशेषणविशेष्यभावानुपपत्तेः । करभरासभयोरिव धर्मधर्मिव्यपदेशाभावप्रसङ्गाच्च । धर्माणामपि च पृथक्पदार्थान्तरत्वकल्पन एकस्मिन्नेव वस्तुनि पदार्थानन्त्यप्रसङ्गः । अनन्तधर्मकत्वाद्वस्तुनः ॥

तदेवं सामान्यविशेषयोः स्वतत्त्वं यथावदनवबुध्यमाना अकुशलाः अतत्त्वाभिनिविष्टदृष्टयः तीर्थान्तरीयाः स्खलन्ति

न्यायमार्गाद्भ्रश्यन्ति निरुत्तरीभवन्तीत्यर्थः । स्खलनेन चात्र प्रामाणिकजनोपहसनीयता ध्वन्यते । किं कुर्वाणाः द्वयमनुवृत्तिव्यावृत्तिलक्षणं प्रत्ययद्वयं वदन्तः । कस्मादेतत्प्रत्ययद्वयं वदन्तः इत्याह । परात्मतत्त्वात् । परौ पदार्थेभ्यो व्यतिरिक्तत्वादन्यौ परस्परनिरपेक्षौ च यौ सामान्यविशेषौ तयोर्यदात्मतत्त्वं स्वरूपमनुवृत्तिव्यावृत्तिलक्षणं तस्मात् तदाश्रित्येत्यर्थः गम्ययपः कर्माधारे इत्यनेन पञ्चमी । कथंभूतात् परात्मतत्त्वात् । इत्याह । अतथात्मतत्त्वात् । मा भूत्पराभिमतस्य परात्मतत्त्वस्य सत्यरूपतेति विशेषणमिदम् । यथा येनैकान्तभेदलक्षणेन प्रकारेण परैः प्रकल्पितं न तथा तेन प्रकारेणात्मतत्त्वं स्वरूपं यस्य तत्तथा । तस्मात् । यतः पदार्थेष्वविष्वग्भावेन सामान्यविशेषौ वर्त्तेते तैश्च तौ तेभ्यः परत्वेन कल्पितौ । परत्वं चान्यत्वम् । तच्चैकान्तभेदाविनाभावि ॥

किंच पदार्थेभ्यः सामान्यविशेषयोरेकान्तभिन्नत्वे स्वीक्रियमाण एकवस्तुविषयमनुवृत्तिव्यावृत्तिरूपं प्रत्ययद्वयं नोपपद्येत । एकान्ताभेदे चान्यतरस्यासत्त्वप्रसङ्गः सामान्यविशेषव्यवहाराभावश्च स्यात् । सामान्यविशेषोभयात्मकत्वेनैव वस्तुनः प्रमाणेन प्रतीतेः । परस्परनिरपेक्षपक्षस्तु पुरस्तान्निर्लोठयिष्यते । अत एव तेषां वादिनां स्खलनक्रिययोपहसनीयत्वमभिव्यज्यते । यो ह्यन्यथास्थितं वस्तुस्वरूपमन्यथैव प्रतिपद्यमानः परेभ्यश्च तथैव प्रज्ञापयन्स्वयं नष्टः परान्नाशयति न खलु तस्मादन्य उपहासपात्रम् ॥

इति वृत्तार्थः ॥ ४ ॥

अथ तदभिमतावेकान्तनित्यानित्यपक्षौ दूषयन्नाह—

आदीपमाव्योम समस्वभावं
स्याद्वादमुद्रानतिभेदि वस्तु ।
तन्नित्यमेवैकमनित्यमन्य-
दिति त्वदाज्ञाद्विषतां प्रलापाः ॥ ५ ॥

आदीपं दीपादारभ्य । आव्योम व्योम मर्यादीकृत्य । सर्वम् । वस्तु पदार्थस्वरूपम् । समस्वभावं समः तुल्यः स्वभावः स्वरूपं यस्य तत्तथा । किंच वस्तुनः स्वरूपं द्रव्यपर्यायात्मकत्वमिति ब्रूमः । तथा च वाचकमुख्यः—उत्पादव्ययध्रौव्ययुक्तं सत् इति । समस्वभावत्वं कुतः । इति विशेषणद्वारेण हेतुमाह-स्याद्वादमुद्रानतिभेदि । स्यादित्यव्ययमनेकान्तद्योतकम् । ततः स्याद्वादोऽनेकान्तवादः । नित्यानित्याद्यनेकधर्मशबलैकवस्त्वभ्युपगम इति यावत् । तस्य मुद्रा मर्यादा तां नातिभिनत्ति नातिक्रामतीति स्याद्वादमुद्रानतिभेदि । यथा हि न्यायैकनिष्ठे राजनि राज्यश्रियं शासति सति सर्वाः प्रजास्तन्मुद्रां नातिवर्तितुमीशते तदतिक्रमे तासां सर्वार्थहानिभावात् एवं विजयिनि निष्कण्टके स्याद्वादमहानरेन्द्रतदीयमुद्रां सर्वेपि पदार्था नातिक्रामन्ति तदुल्लङ्घने तेषां स्वरूपव्यवस्थाहानिप्रसक्तेः ॥

सर्ववस्तूनां समस्वभावत्वकथनं च पराभीष्टस्यैकं वस्तु व्योमादि नित्यमेवान्यच्च प्रदीपाद्यनित्यमेवेति वादस्य प्रतिक्षेपबीजम् । सर्वे हि भावा द्रव्यार्थिकनयापेक्षया नित्याः पर्यायार्थिकनयादेशात्पुनरनित्याः । तत्रैकान्तानित्यतया परैरङ्गीकृतस्य प्रदीपस्य तावन्नित्यानित्यत्वव्यवस्थापने दिङ्मात्रमुच्यते ॥ तथाहि । प्रदीप-

पर्यायापन्नास्तैजसाः परमाणवः स्वरसतस्तैलक्षयाद्वाताभिघाताद्वा ज्योतिःपर्यायं परित्यज्य तमोरूपं पर्यायान्तरमासादयन्तोपि नैकान्तेनानित्याः । पुद्गलद्रव्यरूपतयावस्थितत्वात्तेषाम् । न ह्येतावतैवानित्यत्वं यावता पूर्वपर्यायस्य विनाश उत्तरपर्यायस्य चोत्पादः । न खलु मृद्द्रव्यं स्थासककोशकुशूलशिवकघटाद्यवस्थान्तराण्यापद्यमानमप्येकान्ततो विनष्टम् । तेषु मृद्द्रव्यानुगमस्याबालगोपालं प्रतीतत्वात् । न च तमसः पौद्गलिकत्वमसिद्धम् । चाक्षुषत्वान्यथानुपपत्तेः । प्रदीपालोकवत् । अथ यच्चाक्षुषं तत्सर्वं स्वप्रतिभासे आलोकमपेक्षते । न चैवं तमः । तत्कथं चाक्षुषम् ॥ नैवम् । उलूकादीनामालोकमन्तरेणापि तत्प्रतिभासात् । यैस्त्वस्मदादिभिरन्यच्चाक्षुषं घटादिकमालोकं विना नोपलभ्यते तैरपि तिमिरमालोकयिष्यते । विचित्रत्वाद्भावानाम् । कथमन्यथा पीतश्वेतादयोपि स्वर्णमुक्ताफलाद्या आलोकापेक्षदर्शनाः । प्रदीपचन्द्रादयस्तु प्रकाशान्तरनिरपेक्षाः । इति सिद्धं तमश्चाक्षुषम् ॥ रूपवत्त्वाच्च स्पर्शवत्त्वमपि प्रतीयते । शीतस्पर्शप्रत्ययजनकत्वात् । यानि त्वनिबिडावयवत्वमप्रतिघातित्वमनुद्भूतस्पर्शविशेषत्वमप्रतीयमानखण्डावयविद्रव्यप्रविभागत्वमित्यादीनि तमस पौद्गलिकत्वनिषेधाय परैः साधनान्युपन्यस्तानि तानि प्रदीपप्रभादृष्टान्तेनैव प्रतिषेध्यानि । तुल्ययोगक्षेमत्वात् । न च वाच्यं तैजसाः परमाणवः कथं तमस्त्वेन परिणमन्त इति । पुद्गलानां तत्तत्सामग्रीसहकृतानां विसदृशकार्योत्पादकत्वस्यापि दर्शनात् । दृष्टो ह्यार्द्रेन्धनसंयोगवशाद्भास्वररूपस्यापि वह्नेरभास्वररूपधूमरूपकार्योत्पादः । इति सिद्धो नित्यानित्यः प्रदीपः । यदापि निर्वाणादर्वाग्देदीप्यमानो दीपस्तदापि नवनवपर्यायोत्पादविनाशभाक्त्वात्प्रदीपत्वान्वयाच्च नित्यानित्य एव ॥

एवं व्योमाप्युत्पादव्ययध्रौव्यात्मकत्वान्नित्यानित्यमेव । तथा-ह्यवगाहकानां जीवपुद्गलानामवगाहदानोपग्रह एव तल्लक्षणम् । अवकाशदमाकाशम् इति वचनात् । यदा चावगाहका जीवपुद्गलाः प्रयोगतो विस्रसातो वैकस्मान्नभःप्रदेशात्प्रदेशान्तरमुपसर्पन्ति तदा तस्य व्योम्नस्तैरवगाहकैः सममेकस्मिन्प्रदेशे विभाग उत्तरस्मिंश्च प्रदेशे संयोगः । संयोगविभागौ च परस्परं विरुद्धौ धर्मौ । तद्भेदे चावश्यं धर्मिणो भेदः । तथा चाहुः—अयमेव हि भेदो भेदहेतुर्वा यद्विरुद्धधर्माध्यासः कारणभेदश्चेति । ततश्च तदाकाशं पूर्वसंयोगविनाशलक्षणपरिणामापत्त्या विनष्टमुत्तरसंयोगोत्पादाख्यपरिणामानुभवाच्चोत्पन्नम् । उभयत्राकाशद्रव्यस्यानुगतत्वाच्चोत्पादव्यययोरेकाधिकरणम् । तथा च यत्—अप्रच्युतानुत्पन्नस्थिरैकरूपं नित्यम् इति नित्यलक्षणमाचक्षते तदपास्तम् । एवंविधस्य कस्यचिद्वस्तुनोऽभावात् । तद्भावाव्ययं नित्यम् इति तु सत्यं निसलक्षणम् । उत्पादविनाशयोः सद्भावेपि तद्भावात् अन्वयिरूपाद्यन्न व्येति तन्नित्यमिति तदर्थस्य घटमानत्वात् । यदि ह्यप्रच्युतादिलक्षणं नित्यमिष्यते तदोत्पादव्यययोर्निराधारत्वप्रसङ्गः । न च तयोर्योगे नित्यत्वहानिः ॥

द्रव्यं पर्यायवियुतं पर्याया द्रव्यवर्जिताः ।
क्व कदा केन किंरूपा दृष्टा मानेन केन वा ॥

इति वचनात् । न चाकाशं न द्रव्यम् । लौकिकानामपि घटाकाशं पटाकाशमिति व्यवहारप्रसिद्धेराकाशस्य निसानित्यत्वम् । घटाकाशमपि हि यदा घटापगमे पटेनाक्रान्तं तदा पटाकाशमिति व्यवहारः । न चायमौपचारिकत्वादप्रमाणमेव । उपचारस्यापि किंचित्साधर्म्यद्वारेण मुख्यार्थस्पर्शित्वात् । नभसो हि

यत्किल सर्वव्यापकत्वं मुख्यं परिमाणं तदाधेयघटपटादिसंबन्धिनियतपरिमाणवशात्कल्पितभेदं सत्प्रतिनियतदेशव्यापितया व्यवह्रियमाणं घटाकाशपटाकाशादि तत्तद्व्यपदेशनिबन्धनं भवति। तत्तद्घटादिसंबन्धे च व्यापकत्वेनावस्थितस्य व्योम्नोवस्थान्तरापत्तिः। ततश्चावस्थाभेदेवस्थावतोपि भेदः। तासां ततोऽविष्वग्भावात्। इति सिद्धं नित्यानित्यत्वं व्योम्नः ॥

स्वायंभुवा अपि हि नित्यानित्यमेव वस्तु प्रपन्नाः। तथा चाहुस्ते—त्रिविधः खल्वयं धर्मिणः परिणामो धर्मलक्षणावस्थारूपः। सुवर्णं धर्मि। तस्य धर्मपरिणामो वर्धमानरुचकादिः। धर्मस्य तु लक्षणपरिणामोऽनागतत्वादिः। यदा खल्वयं हेमकारो वर्धमानकं भङ्क्त्वा रुचकमारचयति तदा वर्धमानको वर्तमानतालक्षणं हित्वातीततालक्षणमापद्यते। रुचकस्तु अनागततालक्षणं हित्वा वर्तमानतालक्षणमापद्यते। वर्तमानतापन्न एव तु रुचको नवपुराणभावमापद्यमानोवस्थापरिणामवान्भवति। सोयं त्रिविधः परिणामो धर्मिणः। धर्मलक्षणावस्थाश्च धर्मिणो भिन्नाश्चाभिन्नाश्च। तथा च ते धर्म्यभेदात्तन्नित्यत्वेन नित्याः। भेदाच्चोत्पत्तिविनाशविषयत्वम्। इत्युभयमुपपन्नमिति ॥

अथोत्तरार्धं वित्रियते ॥ एवं चौत्पादव्ययध्रौव्यात्मकत्वे सर्वभावानां सिद्धेपि तद्वस्त्वेवमाकाशात्मादिकं नित्यमेव अन्यच्च प्रदीपघटादिकमनित्यमेव इत्येवकारोत्रापि संबध्यते। इत्थं हि दुर्नयवादापत्तिः। अनन्तधर्मात्मके वस्तुनि स्वाभिप्रेतनित्यत्वादिधर्मसमर्थनप्रवणाः शेषधर्मतिरस्कारेण प्रवर्त्तमाना दुर्नया इति तल्लक्षणात्। इत्यनेनोल्लेखेन त्वदाज्ञाद्विषतां भवत्प्रणीतशासनविरोधिनां प्रलापाः प्रलपन्त्यसंबद्धवाक्यनीति यावत् ॥

अत्र च प्रथममादीपमिति परप्रसिद्ध्या अनित्यपक्षोल्लेखेपि यदुत्तरत्र यथासंख्यपरिहारेण पूर्वतरं नित्यमेवैकमित्युक्तं तदेवं ज्ञापयति–यदनित्यं तदपि नित्यमेव कथंचित् यच्च नित्यं तदप्यनित्यमेव कथंचित् । प्रक्रान्तवादिभिरप्येकस्यामेव पृथिव्यां नित्यानित्यत्वाभ्युपगमात् । तथा च प्रशस्तकरः—सा तु द्विविधा नित्यानित्या च । परमाणुलक्षणा नित्या कार्यलक्षणा त्वनित्या इति । न चात्र परमाणुकार्यद्रव्यलक्षणविषयद्वयभेदान्नैकाधिकरणं नित्यानित्यत्वमिति वाच्यम् । पृथ्वीत्वस्योभयत्राप्यव्यभिचारात् । एवमबादिष्वपीति । आकाशेपि संयोगविभागाङ्गीकारात्तैरनित्यत्वं युक्त्या प्रतिपन्नमेव । तथा च स एवाह—शब्दकारणत्ववचनात्संयोगविभागौ इति नित्यानित्यपक्षयोः संवलितत्वम् । एतच्च लेशतो भावितमेवेति ॥

प्रलापप्रायत्वं च परवचनानामित्थं समर्थनीयम् ॥ वस्तुनस्तावदर्थक्रियाकारित्वं लक्षणम् । तच्चैकान्तनित्यानित्यपक्षयोर्न घटते ॥ अप्रच्युतानुत्पन्नस्थिरैकरूपो हि नित्यः । स च क्रमेणार्थक्रियां कुर्वीत अक्रमेण वा । अन्योन्यव्यवच्छेदरूपाणां प्रकारान्तरासंभवात् ॥ तत्र न तावत्क्रमेण । स हि कालान्तरभाविनीः क्रियाः प्रथमक्रियाकाल एव प्रसह्य कुर्यात् । समर्थस्य कालक्षेपायोगात् । कालक्षेपिणो वा असामर्थ्यप्राप्तेः । समर्थोपि तत्तत्सहकारिसमवधाने तं तमर्थं करोतीति चेत् न तर्हि तस्य सामर्थ्यम् । अपरसहकारिसापेक्षवृत्तित्वात् । सापेक्षमसमर्थमिति न्यायात् । न तेन सहकारिणोऽपेक्ष्यन्ते अपि तु कार्यमेव सहकारिष्वसत्स्वभवत्तानपेक्षत इति चेत् तत्किं स भावोऽसमर्थः समर्थो वा । समर्थश्चेत् किं सहकारिमुखप्रेक्षणदीनानि तान्यपेक्षते न पुनर्झटिति घटयति । ननु समर्थमपि बीजमिला-

जलानिलादिसहकारिसहितमेवाङ्कुरं करोति नान्यथा । तत्किं तस्य सहकारिभिः किंचिदुपक्रियेत न वा । यदि नोपक्रियेत तदा सहकारिसंनिधानात्प्रागिव किं न तदाप्यर्थक्रियायामुदास्ते । उपक्रियेत चेत्स तर्हि तैरुपकारोऽभिन्नो भिन्नो वा क्रियत इति वाच्यम् । अभेदे स एव क्रियते । इति लाभमिच्छतो मूलक्षतिरायाता । कृतकत्वेन तस्यानित्यत्वापत्तेः । भेदे तु स कथं तस्योपकारः । किं न सह्यविन्ध्यादेरपि । तत्संबन्धात्तस्यायमिति चेत् उपकार्योपकारयोः कः संबन्धः । न तावत्संयोगः । द्रव्ययोरेव तस्य भावात् । अत्र तूपकार्यं द्रव्यमुपकारश्च क्रियेति न संयोगः । नापि समवायः । तस्यैकत्वाद्व्यापकत्वाच्च प्रत्यासत्तिविप्रकर्षाभावेन सर्वत्र तुल्यत्वान्न नियतैः संबन्धिभिः संबन्धो युक्तः । नियतसंबन्धिसंबन्धे चाङ्गीक्रियमाणे तत्कृत उपकारोऽस्य समवायस्याभ्युपगन्तव्यः । तथा च सत्युपकारस्य भेदाभेदकल्पना तदवस्थैव । उपकारस्य समवायादभेदे समवाय एव कृतः स्यात् । भेदे पुनरपि समवायस्य न नियतसंबन्धिसंबन्धत्वम् । तन्नैकान्तनित्यो भावः क्रमेणार्थक्रियां कुरुते ॥ नाप्यक्रमेण । न ह्येको भावः सकलकालकलाकलापभाविनीर्युगपत्सर्वाः क्रियाः करोतीति प्रातीतिकम् । कुरुतां वा । तथापि द्वितीयक्षणे किं कुर्यात् । करणे वा क्रमपक्षभावी दोषः । अकरणे त्वर्थक्रियाकारित्वाभावादवस्तुत्वप्रसङ्गः । इत्येकान्तनित्यात् क्रमाक्रमाभ्यां व्याप्तार्थक्रिया व्यापकानुपलब्धिबलाद्व्यापकनिवृत्तौ निवर्तमाना स्वव्याप्यमर्थक्रियाकारित्वं निवर्तयति । अर्थक्रियाकारित्वं च निवर्तमानं स्वव्याप्यं सत्त्वं निवर्तयति । इति नैकान्तनित्यपक्षो युक्तिक्षमः ॥

एकान्तानित्यपक्षोपि न कक्षीकरणार्हः ॥ अनित्यो हि प्रतिक्षणविनाशी । स च न क्रमेणार्थक्रियासमर्थः । देशकृतस्य कालकृतस्य च क्रमस्यैवाभावात् । क्रमो हि पौर्वापर्यम् । तच्च क्षणिकस्यासंभवि । अवस्थितस्यैव हि नानादेशकालव्याप्तिर्देशक्रमः कालक्रमश्चाभिधीयते । न चैकान्तविनाशिनि सास्ति । यदाहुः—

यो यत्रैव स तत्रैव यो यदैव तदैव सः ।
न देशकालयोर्व्याप्तिर्भावानामिह विद्यते ॥

न च संतानापेक्षया पूर्वोत्तरक्षणानां क्रमः संभवति । संतानस्यावस्तुत्वात् । वस्तुत्वेपि तस्य यदि क्षणिकत्वं न तर्हि क्षणेभ्यः कश्चिद्विशेषः । अथाक्षणिकत्वं तर्हि समाप्तः क्षणभङ्गवादः ॥

नाप्यक्रमेणार्थक्रिया क्षणिके संभवति । स ह्येको बीजपूरादिरूपादिक्षणो युगपदनेकान् रसादिक्षणाञ्जनयन्नेकेन स्वभावेन जनयेन्नानास्वभावैर्वा । यद्येकेन तदा तेषां रसादिक्षणानामेकत्वं स्यादेकस्वभावजन्यत्वात् । अथ नानास्वभावैर्जनयति किंचिद्रूपादिकमुपादानभावेन किंचिद्रसादिकं सहकारित्वेनेति चेत् स्वभावास्तस्यात्मभूता अनात्मभूता वा । अनात्मभूताश्चेत् स्वभावत्वहानिः । यद्यात्मभूतास्तर्हि तस्यानेकत्वमनेकस्वभावत्वात् । स्वभावानां वैकत्वं प्रसज्येत । तदव्यतिरिक्तत्वात्तेषां तस्य चैकत्वात् । अथ य एव एकत्रोपादानभावः स एवान्यत्र सहकारिभाव इति न स्वभावभेद इष्यते । तर्हि नित्यस्यैकरूपस्यापि क्रमेण नानाकार्यकारिणः स्वभावभेदः कार्यसांकर्यं च कथमिष्यते क्षणिकवादिना । अथ नित्यमेकरूपत्वादक्रमम् । अक्रमाच्च क्रमिणां नानाकार्याणां कथमुत्पत्तिरिति चेत् अहो स्वपक्षपाती देवानांप्रियो यः खलु स्वयमेकस्मान्निरंशाद्रूपादिक्षणात्कारणाद्युगपदनेककारण-

साध्यान्यनेककार्याण्यङ्गीकुर्वाणोपि परपक्षे नित्येपि वस्तुनि क्रमेण नानाकार्यकरणेपि विरोधमुद्भावयति । तस्मात्क्षणिकस्यापि भावस्याक्रमेणार्थक्रिया दुर्घटा ॥ इत्यनित्यैकान्तादपि क्रमाक्रमयोर्व्यापकयोर्निवृत्त्यैव व्याप्यार्थक्रियापि व्यावर्तते । तद्व्यावृत्तौ च सत्त्वमपि व्यापकानुपलब्धिबलेनैव निवर्तते । इत्येकान्तानित्यवादोपि न रमणीयः ॥

स्याद्वादे तु पूर्वोत्तराकारपरिहारस्वीकारस्थितिलक्षणपरिणामेन भावानामर्थक्रियोपपत्तिरविरुद्धा । न चैकत्र वस्तुनि परस्परविरुद्धधर्माध्यासायोगादसन्स्याद्वाद इति वाच्यम् । नित्यानित्यपक्षविलक्षणस्य पक्षान्तरस्याङ्गीक्रियमाणत्वात् । तथैव च सर्वैरनुभवात् । तथा च पठन्ति—

भागे सिंहो नरो भागे योऽर्थो भागद्वयात्मकः ।
तमभागं विभागेन नरसिंहं प्रचक्षते ॥ इति ॥

वैशेषिकैरपि चित्ररूपस्यैकस्यावयविनोभ्युपगमादेकस्यैव पटादेश्चलाचलरक्तारक्तावृतानावृतत्वादिविरुद्धधर्माणामुपलब्धेः । सौगतैरप्येकत्र चित्रपटीज्ञाने नीलानीलयोर्विरोधानङ्गीकारात् ॥

अत्र च यद्यप्यधिकृतवादिनः प्रदीपादिकं कालान्तरावस्थायित्वात्क्षणिकं न मन्यन्ते तन्मते पूर्वापरान्तावच्छिन्नायाः सत्ताया एवानित्यतालक्षणात् तथापि बुद्धिसुखादिकं तेपि क्षणिकतयैव प्रतिपन्नाः इति तदधिकारेपि क्षणिकवादचर्चा नानुपपन्ना । यदापि च कालान्तरावस्थायि वस्तु तदापि नित्यानित्यमेव । क्षणोपि न खलु सोस्ति यत्र वस्तूत्पादव्ययध्रौव्यात्मकं नास्ति ॥ इति काव्यार्थः ॥ ५ ॥

अथ तदभिमतमीश्वरस्य जगत्कर्तृत्वाभ्युपगमं मिथ्याभिनिवेशरूपं निरूपयन्नाह ।

कर्तास्ति कश्चिज्जगतः स चैकः
स सर्वगः स स्ववशः स नित्यः ।
इमाः कुहेवाकविडम्बनाः स्यु-
स्तेषां न येषामनुशासकस्त्वम् ॥ ६ ॥

जगतः प्रत्यक्षादिप्रमाणोपलक्ष्यमाणचराचररूपस्य विश्वत्रयस्य कश्चिद् अनिर्वचनीयस्वरूपः पुरुषविशेषः कर्ता स्रष्टा अस्ति विद्यते ॥ ते हीत्थं प्रमाणयन्ति । उर्वीपर्वततर्वादिकं सर्वं बुद्धिमत्कर्तृकम् । कार्यत्वात् । यद्यत्कार्यं तत्तत्सर्वं बुद्धिमत्कर्तृकम् यथा घटः । तथा चेदम् । तस्मात्तथा । व्यतिरेके व्योमादि । यश्च बुद्धिमांस्तत्कर्ता स भगवानीश्वर एवेति ॥

न चायमसिद्धो हेतुः । यतो भूभूधरादेः स्वस्वकारणकलापजन्यतयावयवितया वा कार्यत्वं सर्ववादिनां प्रतीतमेव । नाप्यनैकान्तिको विरुद्धो वा । विपक्षादत्यन्तव्यावृत्तत्वात् । नापि कालात्ययापदिष्टः । प्रत्यक्षानुमानागमाबाधितधर्मधर्म्यनन्तरप्रतिपादितत्वात् ॥ नापि प्रकरणसमः । तत्प्रतिपन्थिधर्मोपपादनसमर्थप्रत्यनुमानाभावात् । न च वाच्यमीश्वरः पृथ्वीपृथ्वीधरादेर्विधाता न भवति अशरीरत्वात् निर्वृतात्मवदिति प्रत्यनुमानं तद्बाधकमिति । यतोत्रेश्वररूपो धर्मी प्रतीतोऽप्रतीतो वा प्ररूपितः । न तावदप्रतीतः । हेतोराश्रयासिद्धिप्रसङ्गात् । प्रतीतश्चेत् येन प्रमाणेन स प्रतीतस्तेनैव किं स्वयमुत्पादितस्वतनुर्न प्रतीयते । इत्यतः कथमशरीरत्वम् । तस्मान्निरवद्य एवायं हेतुरिति ॥

स चैक इति । च पुनरर्थे । स पुनः पुरुषविशेष एकः अद्वितीयः । बहूनां हि विश्वविधातृत्वस्वीकारे परस्परविमतिसंभावनाया अनिवार्यत्वादेकैकस्य वस्तुनोऽन्यान्यरूपतया निर्माणे सर्वमसमञ्जसमापद्येतेति ॥

तथा स सर्वग इति । सर्वत्र गच्छतीति सर्वगः । सर्वव्यापी । तस्य हि प्रतिनियतदेशवर्तित्वे नियतदेशवृत्तीनां विश्वत्रयान्तर्वर्तिपदार्थसार्थानां यथावन्निर्माणानुपपत्तिः । कुम्भकारादिषु तथा दर्शनात् ॥ अथवा सर्वं गच्छति जानातीति सर्वगः सर्वज्ञः । सर्वे गत्यर्थाः ज्ञानार्थाः इति वचनात् । सर्वज्ञत्वाभावे हि यथोचितोपादानकारणाद्यनभिज्ञत्वादनुरूपकार्योत्पत्तिर्न स्यात् ॥

तथा स स्ववशः स्वतन्त्रः । सकलप्राणिनां स्वेच्छया सुखदुःखयोरनुभावनसमर्थत्वात् । तथा चोक्तम्—

ईश्वरप्रेरितो गच्छेत् स्वर्गं वा श्वभ्रमेव वा ।
अन्यो जन्तुरनीशोऽयमात्मनः सुखदुःखयोः ॥

पारतन्त्र्ये तु तस्य परमुखप्रेक्षितया मुख्यकर्तृत्वव्याघातादनीश्वरत्वापत्तिः ॥

तथा स नित्य इति । अप्रच्युतानुत्पन्नस्थिरैकरूपः । तस्य ह्यनित्यत्वे परोत्पाद्यतया कृतकत्वप्राप्तिः । अपेक्षितपरव्यापारो हि भावः स्वभावनिष्पत्तौ कृतक इत्युच्यते । यश्चापरस्तत्कर्ता कल्प्यते स नित्योऽनित्यो वा स्यात् । नित्यश्चेदधिकृतेश्वरेण किमपराद्धम् । अनित्यश्चेत्तस्याप्युत्पादकान्तरेण भाव्यम् । तस्यापि नित्यानित्यत्वकल्पनायामनवस्थादौस्थ्यमिति ॥

तदेवमेकत्वादिविशेषणविशिष्टो भगवानीशस्त्रिजगत्कर्तेति पराभ्युपगममुपदर्श्योत्तरार्धेन तस्य दुष्टत्वमाचष्टे ॥ इमा एता

अनन्तरोक्ताः। कुहेवाकविडम्बनाः कुत्सिता हेवाका आग्रहविशेषाः कुहेवाकाः कदाग्रहा इत्यर्थः त एव विडम्बनाः विचारचातुरीबाह्यत्वेन तिरस्काररूपत्वाद्विगोपकप्रकाराः। स्युः भवेयुः। तेषां प्रामाणिकापसदानाम्। येषां हे स्वामिन् त्वं नानुशासकः न शिक्षादाता॥ तदभिनिवेशानां विडम्बनारूपत्वज्ञापनार्थमेव पराभिप्रेतपुरुषविशेषणेषु प्रत्येकं तच्छब्दप्रयोगमसूयागर्भमाविर्भावयांचकार स्तुतिकारः। तथा चैवमेव निन्दनीयं प्रति वक्तारो वदन्ति। स मूर्खः स पापीयान् स दरिद्र इत्यादि। त्वमित्येकवचनसंयुक्तयुष्मच्छब्दप्रयोगेण परमेशितुः परमकारुणिकतयानपेक्षितस्वपरपक्षविभागमद्वितीयं हितोपदेशकत्वं ध्वन्यते। अतोत्रायमाशयः। यद्यपि भगवानविशेषेण सकलजगज्जन्तुजातहितावहां सर्वेभ्य एव देशनावाचमाचष्टे तथापि सैव केषांचिन्निचितनिकाचितपापकर्मकलुषितात्मनां रुचिरूपतया न परिणमते। अपुनर्बन्धकादिव्यतिरिक्तत्वेनायोग्यत्वात्। तथा च कादम्बर्यां बाणोपि बभाण—अपगतमले हि मनसि स्फटिकमणाविव रजनिकरगभस्तयो विशन्ति सुखमुपदेशगुणाः। गुरुवचनममलमपि सलिलमिव महदुपजनयति श्रवणस्थितं शूलमभव्यस्य इति। अतो वस्तुवृत्त्या न तेषां भगवाननुशासक इति॥ न चैतावता जगद्गुरोरसामर्थ्यसंभावना। न हि कालदष्टमनुज्जीवयन् समुज्जीवितेतरदष्टको विषभिषगुपालम्भनीयः। अतिप्रसङ्गात्। स हि तेषामेव दोषः। न खलु निखिलभुवनाभोगमवभासयन्तोपि भानवीया भानवः कौशिकलोकस्यालोकहेतुतामभजमाना उपालम्भसंभावनास्पदम्। तथा च श्रीसिद्धसेनः—

सद्धर्मबीजवपनानघकौशलस्य
यल्लोकबान्धव तवापि खिलान्यभूवन्।

तन्नाद्भुतं खगकुलेष्विह तामसेषु
सूर्यांशवो मधुकरीचरणावदाताः ॥

अथ कथमिव तत्कुहेवाकानां विडम्बनारूपत्वमिति । ब्रूमः । यत्तावदुक्तं परैः क्षित्यादयो बुद्धिमत्कर्तृकाः कार्यत्वाद्घटवदिति । तदयुक्तम् । व्याप्तेरग्रहणात् । साधनं हि सर्वत्र व्याप्तौ प्रमाणेन सिद्धायां साध्यं गमयेदिति सर्ववादिसंवादः ॥ स चायं जगन्ति सृजन् सशरीरोऽशरीरो वा स्यात् ॥ सशरीरोपि किमस्मदादिवदृश्यशरीरविशिष्ट उत पिशाचादिवददृश्यशरीरविशिष्टः । प्रथमपक्षे प्रत्यक्षबाधः । तमन्तरेणापि च जायमाने तृणतरुपुरंदरधनुरभ्रादौ कार्यत्वस्य दर्शनात् प्रमेयत्वादिवत्साधारणानैकान्तिको हेतुः । द्वितीयविकल्पे पुनरदृश्यशरीरत्वे तस्य माहात्म्यविशेषः कारणम् आहोस्विदस्मदाद्यदृष्टवैगुण्यम् । प्रथमप्रकारः कोशपानप्रत्यायनीयः । तत्सिद्धौ प्रमाणाभावात् । इतरेतराश्रयदोषापत्तेश्च । सिद्धे हि माहात्म्यविशेषे तस्यादृश्यशरीरत्वं प्रत्येतव्यम् । तत्सिद्धौ च माहात्म्यविशेषसिद्धिरिति । द्वैतीयिकस्तु प्रकारो न संचरत्येव विचारगोचरे । संशयानिवृत्तेः । किं तस्यासत्त्वाददृश्यशरीरत्वं वान्ध्येयादिवत् किं वास्मदाद्यदृष्टवैगुण्यात्पिशाचादिवदिति निश्चयाभावात् ॥ अशरीरश्चेत्तदा दृष्टान्तदार्ष्टान्तिकयोर्वैषम्यम् । घटादयो हि कार्यरूपाः सशरीरकर्तृका दृष्टाः । अशरीरस्य च सतस्तस्य कार्यप्रवृत्तौ कुतः सामर्थ्यम् आकाशादिवत् । तस्मात्सशरीराशरीरलक्षणे पक्षद्वयेपि कार्यत्वहेतोर्व्याप्त्यसिद्धिः ॥ किं च त्वन्मतेन कालात्ययापदिष्टोप्ययं हेतुः । धर्म्येकदेशस्य तरुविद्युदभ्रादेरिदानीमप्युत्पद्यमानस्य विधातुरनुपलभ्यमानत्वेन प्रत्यक्षबाधितधर्म्यनन्तरं हेतुभणनात् । तदेवं न कश्चिज्जगतः कर्ता ॥

एकत्वादीनि तु जगत्कर्तृत्वव्यवस्थापनायानीयमानानि तद्वि-

शेषणानि षण्ढं प्रति कामिन्या रूपसंपन्निरूपणप्रायाण्येव । तथापि तेषां विचारासहत्वख्यापनार्थं किंचिदुच्यते ॥ तत्रैकत्वचर्चस्तावत् । बहूनामेककार्यकरणे वैमत्यसंभावनेति नायमेकान्तः । अनेककीटिकाशतनिष्पाद्यत्वेपि शक्रमूर्ध्नोनेकशिल्पिकल्पितत्वेपि प्रासादादीनां नैकसरघानिर्वर्तितत्वेपि मधुच्छत्रादीनां चैकरूपताया अविगानेनोपलम्भात् । अथैतेष्वप्येक एवेश्वरः कर्तेति ब्रूषे । एवं चेद्भवतो भवानीपतिं प्रति निष्प्रतिमा वासना तर्हि कुविन्दकुम्भकारादितिरस्कारेण पटघटादीनामपि कर्ता स एव किं न कल्प्यते । अथ तेषां प्रत्यक्षसिद्धं कर्तृत्वं कथमपह्नोतुं शक्यम् । तर्हि कीटिकादिभिः किं तेषां विराद्धं यत्तेषामसदृशतादृशप्रयाससाध्यं कर्तृत्वमेकहेलयैवापलप्यते । तस्माद्वैमत्यभयान्महेशितुरेकत्वकल्पना भोजनादिव्ययभयात्कृपणस्यात्यन्तवल्लभपुत्रकलत्रादिपरित्यजनेन शून्यारण्यानीसेवनमिव ॥

तथा सर्वगतत्वमपि तस्य नोपपन्नम् । तद्धि शरीरात्मना ज्ञानात्मना वा स्यात् । प्रथमपक्षे तदीयेनैव देहेन जगत्त्रयस्य व्याप्तत्वादितरनिर्मेयपदार्थानामाश्रयानवकाशः । द्वितीयपक्षे तु सिद्धसाध्यता । अस्माभिरपि निरतिशयज्ञानात्मना परमपुरुषस्य जगत्त्रयक्रोडीकरणाभ्युपगमात् । यदि परमेवं भवत्प्रमाणीकृतेन वेदेन विरोधः । तत्र हि शरीरात्मना सर्वगतत्वमुक्तम् । विश्वतश्चक्षुरुत विश्वतोमुखो विश्वतःपाणिरुत विश्वतःपात् इत्यादिश्रुतेः ॥ यच्चोक्तं तस्य प्रतिनियतदेशवर्तित्वे त्रिभुवनगतपदार्थानामनियतदेशवृत्तीनां यथावन्निर्माणानुपपत्तिरिति । तत्रेदं पृच्छ्यते । स जगत्त्रयं निर्मिमाणस्तक्षादिवत्साक्षाद्देहव्यापारेण निर्मिमीते यदि वा संकल्पमात्रेण । आद्ये पक्ष एकस्यैव भूभूधरादेर्विधानेऽक्षोदी-

यसः कालक्षेपस्य संभवाद्बंहीयसाप्यनेहसा न परिसमाप्तिः । द्वितीयपक्षे तु संकल्पमात्रेणैव कार्यकल्पनायां नियतदेशस्थायित्वेपि न किंचिद्दूषणमुत्पश्यामः । नियतदेशस्थायिनां सामान्यदेवानामपि संकल्पमात्रेणैव तत्तत्कार्यसंपादनप्रतिपत्तेः ॥ किं च तस्य सर्वगतत्वेनाङ्गीक्रियमाणे शुचिषु निरन्तरसन्तमसेषु नरकादिस्थलेष्वपि तस्य वृत्तिः प्रसज्यते । तथा चानिष्टापत्तिः । अथ युष्मत्पक्षेपि यदा ज्ञानात्मना सर्वजगत्त्रयं व्याप्नोतीत्युच्यते तदा शुचिरसस्वादादीनामप्युपलम्भसंभावनान्नरकादिदुःखस्वरूपसंवेदनात्मकतया दुःखानुभवप्रसङ्गाच्चानिष्टापत्तिस्तुल्यैवेति चेत् तदेतदुपपत्तिभिः प्रतिकर्तुमशक्तस्य धूलिभिरिवावकरणम् । यतोज्ञानमप्राप्यकारि स्वस्थलस्थमेव विषयं परिच्छिनत्ति न पुनस्तत्र गत्वा । तत्कुतो भवदुपालम्भः समीचीनः । तर्हि भवतोप्यशुचिज्ञानमात्रेण तद्रसास्वादानुभूतिः । तद्भावे हि स्रक्चन्दनाङ्गनारसवत्यादिचिन्तनमात्रेणैव तृप्तिसिद्धौ तत्प्राप्तिप्रयत्नवैफल्यप्रसक्तिरिति ॥ यत्तु ज्ञानात्मना सर्वगतत्वे सिद्धसाधनं प्रागुक्तं तच्छक्तिमात्रमपेक्ष्य मन्तव्यम् । तथा च वक्तारो भवन्ति । अस्य मतिः सर्वशास्त्रेषु प्रसरतीति । न च ज्ञानं प्राप्यकारि । तस्यात्मधर्मत्वेन बहिर्निर्गमाभावात् । बहिर्निर्गमे चात्मनोऽचैतन्यापत्त्याऽजीवत्वप्रसङ्गः । न हि धर्मो धर्मिणमतिरिच्य क्वचन केवलो विलोकितः । यच्च परे दृष्टान्तयन्ति यथा सूर्यस्य किरणा गुणरूपा अपि सूर्यान्निष्क्रम्य भुवनं भासयन्त्येवं ज्ञानमप्यात्मनः सकाशाद्बहिर्निर्गत्य प्रमेयं परिच्छिनत्तीति तत्रेदमुत्तरम् । किरणानां गुणत्वमसिद्धम् । तेषां तैजसपुद्गलमयत्वेन द्रव्यत्वात् । यश्च तेषां प्रकाशात्मा गुणः स तेभ्यो न जातु पृथग्भवतीति । तथा च धर्मसंग्रहिण्यां श्रीहरिभद्राचार्यपादाः—

किरणा गुणा न दव्वं तेसिं पयासो गुणो न वा दव्वं ।।
जं नाणं आयगुणो कहमदव्वो स अन्नत्थ ।। १ ।।
गन्तूण न परिछिंदइ नाणं णेयं तयम्मि देसम्मि ।
आयत्थं चिय नवरं अचिन्तसत्ती उ विण्णेयं ।। २ ।।
लोहोवलस्स सत्ती आयत्था चेव भिन्नदेसंपि ।
लोहं आगरिसंती दीसइ इह कज्ज पच्चक्खा ।। ३ ।।
एवमिह नाणसत्ती आयत्था चेव हंदि लोगंतं ।
जइ परिछिंदइ सम्मं को णु विरोहो भवे तत्थ ।। ४ ।।

इत्यादि ।।

अथ सर्वगः सर्वज्ञ इति व्याख्यानं तत्रापि प्रतिविधीयते । ननु तस्य सार्वज्ञ्यं केन प्रमाणेन गृहीतम् । प्रत्यक्षेण परोक्षेण वा । न तावत्प्रत्यक्षेण । तस्येन्द्रियार्थसंनिकर्षोत्पन्नतयातीन्द्रियग्रहणासामर्थ्यात् । नापि परोक्षेण । तद्ध्यनुमानं शाब्दं वा स्यात् । न तावदनुमानम् । तस्य लिङ्गग्रहणेन लिङ्गिलिङ्गसंबन्धस्मरणपूर्वकत्वात् । न च तस्य सर्वज्ञत्वेनुमेये किंचिदव्यभिचारि लिङ्गं पश्यामः।तस्यात्यन्तविप्रकृष्टत्वेन तत्प्रतिबद्धलिङ्गसंबन्धग्रहणाभावात्। अथ तस्य सर्वज्ञत्वं।विना जगद्वैचित्र्यमनुपपद्यमानं सर्वज्ञत्वमर्थादापादयतीति चेन्न । अविनाभावाभावात्। न हि जगद्वैचित्री तत्सार्वज्ञ्यं विनान्यथा नोपपन्ना । द्विविधं हि जगत्। स्थावरजङ्गमभेदात् । तत्र जङ्गमानां वैचित्र्यं स्वोपात्तशुभाशुभकर्मपरिपाकवशेनैव । स्थावराणां तु सचेतनानामियमेव गतिरचेतनानां तु तदुपभोगयोग्यतासाधनत्वेनानादिकालसिद्धमेव वैचित्र्यमिति ।। नाप्यागमस्तत्साधकः । स हि तत्कृतोन्यकृतो वा स्यात् । तत्कृत एव चेत्तस्य सर्वज्ञतां साधयति तदा तस्य महत्त्वक्षतिः ।

स्वयमेव स्वगुणोत्कीर्तनस्य महतामनधिकृतत्वात् । अन्यच्च तस्य शास्त्रकर्तृत्वमेव न युज्यते । शास्त्रं हि वर्णात्मकम् । ते च ताल्वादिव्यापारजन्याः । स च शरीर एव संभवी । शरीराभ्युपगमे च तस्य पूर्वोक्ता एव दोषाः । अन्यकृतश्चेत्सोऽन्यः सर्वज्ञोऽसर्वज्ञो वा । सर्वज्ञत्वे तस्य द्वैतापत्त्या प्रागुक्ततदेकत्वाभ्युपगमबाधस्तत्साधकप्रमाणचर्चायामनवस्थापातश्च । असर्वज्ञश्चेत्कस्तस्य वचसि विश्वासः । अपरं च भवदभीष्ट आगमः प्रत्युत तत्प्रणेतुरसर्वज्ञत्वमेव साधयति । पूर्वापरविरुद्धार्थवचनोपेतत्वात् । तथाहि न हिंस्यात्सर्वभूतानीति प्रथममुक्त्वा पश्चात्तत्रैव पठितम् ।

षट्शतानि नियुज्यन्ते पशूनां मध्यमेऽहनि ।
अश्वमेधस्य वचनान्न्यूनानि पशुभिस्त्रिभिः ॥

तथा अग्नीषोमीयं पशुमालभेत सप्तदश प्राजापत्यान्पशूनालभेत इत्यादिवचनानि कथमिव न पूर्वापरविरोधमनुरुध्यन्ते ॥

तथा नानृतं ब्रूयात् इत्यादिना अनृतभाषणं प्रथमं निषिध्य पश्चाद् ब्राह्मणार्थमनृतं ब्रूयात् इत्यादि । तथा—

न नर्मयुक्तं वचनं हिनस्ति
न स्त्रीषु राजन्न विवाहकाले ।
प्राणात्यये सर्वधनापहारे
पञ्चानृतान्याहुरपातकानि ॥

तथा अदत्तादानमेकधा निरस्य पश्चादुक्तम्—यद्यपि ब्राह्मणो हठेन परकीयमादत्ते छलेन वा तथापि तस्य नादत्तादानम् । यतः सर्वमिदं ब्राह्मणेभ्यो दत्तं ब्राह्मणानां तु दौर्बल्याद्वृषलाः परिभुञ्जते । तस्मादपहरन् ब्राह्मणः स्वमादत्ते स्वमेव ब्राह्मणो भुङ्क्ते स्वं वस्ते स्वं ददाति इति ॥ तथा । अपुत्रस्य गतिर्नास्ति इति लपित्वा

अनेकानि सहस्राणि कुमारब्रह्मचारिणाम् ।
दिवं गतानि विप्राणामकृत्वा कुलसन्ततिम् ॥

इत्यादि ॥ कियन्तो वा दधिमाषभोजनात्कृपणा विवेच्यन्ते । तदेवमागमोपि न तस्य सर्वज्ञतां वक्ति । किं च सर्वज्ञः सन्नसौ चराचरं चेद्विरचयति तदा जगदुपप्लवकरणस्वैरिणः पश्चादपि कर्तव्यनिग्रहान्सुरवैरिण एतदधिक्षेपकारिणश्चास्मदादीन्किमर्थं सृजतीति । तन्नायं सर्वज्ञः ॥

तथा स्ववशत्वं स्वातन्त्र्यम् । तदपि तस्य न क्षोदक्षमम् ॥ स हि यदि नाम स्वाधीनः सन् विश्वं विधत्ते परमकारुणिकश्च त्वया वर्ण्यते तत्कथं सुखिताद्यवस्थाभेदवृन्दस्थपुटितं घटयति भुवनमेकान्तशर्मसंपत्कान्तमेव तु किं न निर्मिमीते । अथ जन्मान्तरोपार्जिततत्तत्तदीयशुभाशुभकर्मप्रेरितः संस्तथा करोतीति । दत्तस्तर्हि स्ववशत्वाय जलाञ्जलिः । कर्मजन्ये च त्रिभुवनवैचित्र्ये शिपिविष्टहेतुकविष्टपसृष्टिकल्पनायाः कष्टैकफलत्वादस्मन्मतमेवाङ्गीकृतं प्रेक्षावता । तथाचायातोऽयं घटकुट्यां प्रभातमितिन्यायः । किं च प्राणिनां धर्माधर्मावपेक्षमाणश्चेदयं सृजति प्राप्तं तर्हि यदयमपेक्षते तन्न करोतीति । न हि कुलालो दण्डादि करोति । एवं कर्मापेक्षश्चेदीश्वरो जगत्कारणं स्यात्तर्हि कर्मणीश्वरत्वमीश्वरोनीश्वरः स्यादिति ॥

तथा नित्यत्वमपि तस्य स्वगृह एव प्रणिगद्यमानं हृद्यम् ॥ स खलु नित्यत्वेनैकरूपः सन् त्रिभुवनसर्गस्वभावोऽतत्स्वभावो वा । प्रथमविधायां जगन्निर्माणात्कदाचिदपि नोपरमेत । तदुपरमे तत्स्वभावत्वहानिः । एवं च सर्गक्रियाया अपर्यवसानादेकस्यापि

कार्यस्य न सृष्टिः । घटो हि स्वारम्भक्षणादारभ्य परिसमाप्तिरूपान्त्यक्षणं यावन्निश्चयनयाभिप्रायेण न घटव्यपदेशमासादयति । जलाहरणाद्यर्थक्रियायामसाधकतमत्वात् । अतत्स्वभावपक्षे तु न जातु जगन्ति सृजेत्स्वभावायोगाद्गगनवत् । अपि च तस्यैकान्तनित्यस्वरूपत्वे सृष्टिवत्संहारोपि न घटते । नानारूपकार्यकरणेऽनित्यत्वापत्तेः । स हि येनैव स्वभावेन जगन्ति सृजेत्तेनैव तानि संहरेत् स्वभावान्तरेण वा । तेनैव चेत् सृष्टिसंहारयोर्यौगपद्यप्रसङ्गः । स्वभावाभेदात् । एकस्वभावात्कारणादनेकस्वभावकार्योत्पत्तिविरोधात् । स्वभावान्तरेण चेत् नित्यत्वहानिः । स्वभावभेद एव हि लक्षणमनित्यतायाः । यथा पार्थिवशरीरस्याहारपरमाणुसहकृतस्य प्रत्यहमपूर्वापूर्वोत्पादेन स्वभावभेदादनित्यत्वम् । इष्टश्च भवतां सृष्टिसंहारयोः शम्भौ स्वभावभेदः । रजोगुणात्मकतया सृष्टौ तमोगुणात्मकतया संहरणे सात्त्विकतया च स्थितौ तस्य व्यापारस्वीकारात् । एवं चावस्थाभेदस्तद्भेदे चावस्थावतोपि भेदान्नित्यत्वक्षतिः ॥ अथास्तु नित्यस्तथापि कथं सततमेव सृष्टौ न चेष्टते । इच्छावशाच्चेन्ननु ता अपीच्छाः स्वसत्तामात्रनिबन्धनात्मलाभाः सदैव किं न प्रवर्तयन्तीति स एवोपालम्भः । तथा शम्भोरष्टगुणाधिकरणत्वे कार्यभेदानुमेयानां तदिच्छानामपि विषमरूपत्वहानिः केन वार्यते । किं च प्रेक्षावतां प्रवृत्तिः स्वार्थकरुणाभ्यां व्याप्ता । ततश्चायं जगत्सर्गे व्याप्रियते स्वार्थात्कारुण्याद्वा । न तावत् स्वार्थात् तस्य कृतकृत्यत्वात् । न च कारुण्यात् । परदुःखप्रहाणेच्छा हि कारुण्यम् । ततः प्राक्सर्गाज्जीवानामिन्द्रियशरीरविषयानुत्पत्तौ दुःखाभावेन कस्य प्रहाणेच्छा कारुण्यम् । सर्गोत्तरकाले तु दुःखिनोवलोक्य कारुण्याभ्युपगमे दुरुत्तरमितरेतराश्रयं कारुण्येन सृष्टिः सृष्ट्या च कारुण्यम् । इति नास्य जगत्कर्तृत्वं कथमपि सिद्ध्यति । तदेवमेवं-

विधदोषकलुषिते पुरुषविशेषे यस्तेषां सेवाहेवाकः स खलु केवलं बलवन्मोहविडम्बनापरिपाक इति । अत्र च यद्यपि मध्यवर्तिनो नकारस्य घण्टालालान्यायेन योजनादर्थान्तरमपि स्फुरति यथा इमाः कुहेवाकविडम्बनास्तेषां न स्युर्येषां त्वमनुशासक इति तथापि सोऽर्थः सहृदयैर्न हृदयधारणीयोऽन्ययोगव्यवच्छेदस्याधिकृतत्वादिति काव्यार्थः ॥

अथ चैतन्यादयो रूपादयश्च धर्मा आत्मादेर्घटादेश्च धर्मिणोऽत्यन्तं व्यतिरिक्ता अपि समवायसंबन्धेन संबद्धाः सन्तो धर्मधर्मिव्यपदेशमश्नुवते तन्मतं दूषयन्नाह ।

न धर्मधर्मित्वमतीवभेदे
वृत्त्यास्ति चेन्न त्रितयं चकास्ति ।
इहेदमित्यस्ति मतिश्च वृत्तौ
न गौणभेदोऽपि च लोकबाधः ॥ ७ ॥

धर्मधर्मिणोरतीवभेदे [अतीवेत्यत्रेवशब्दो वाक्यालङ्कारे तं च प्रायोऽतिशब्दात्किवृत्तेश्च प्रयुञ्जते शाब्दिकाः यथा—आवर्जिता किञ्चिदिव स्तनाभ्याम् उद्वृत्तः क इव सुखावहः परेषामित्यादि] ततश्च एकान्तभिन्नत्वेऽङ्गीक्रियमाणे धर्मधर्मित्वं न स्याद् अस्य धर्मिण इमे धर्मा एषां च धर्माणामयमाश्रयभूतो धर्मीत्येवं सर्वप्रसिद्धो धर्मधर्मिव्यपदेशो न प्राप्नोति । तयोरत्यन्तभिन्नत्वेपि तत्कल्पनायां पदार्थान्तरधर्माणामपि विवक्षितधर्मधर्मित्वापत्तेः ॥ एवमुक्ते सति परः प्रत्यवतिष्ठते । वृत्त्यास्तीति । अयुतसिद्धानामाधार्याधारभूतानामिहप्रत्ययहेतुः संबन्धः समवायः । स च समवयनात्समवाय इति द्रव्यगुणकर्मसामान्य-

विशेषेषु पञ्चसु पदार्थेषु वर्तनाद्वृत्तिरिति चाख्यायते । तया वृत्त्या समवायसंबन्धेन तयोर्धर्मधर्मिणोरितरेतरविनिर्लुण्ठितत्वेपि धर्मधर्मिव्यपदेश इष्यते । इति नानन्तरोक्तो दोष इति ॥ अत्राचार्यः समाधत्ते । चेदिति । यद्येवं तव मतिः सा प्रत्यक्षप्रतिक्षिप्ता । यतो न त्रितयं चकास्ति । अयं धर्मी इमे चास्य धर्मा अयं चैतत्संबन्धनिबन्धनं समवाय इत्येतत्त्रितयं वस्तुत्रयं न चकास्ति ज्ञानविषयतया न प्रतिभासते । यथा किल शिलाशकलयुगलस्य मिथोऽनुसन्धायकं रालादिद्रव्यं तस्मात्पृथक् तृतीयतया प्रतिभासते नैवमत्र समवायस्यापि प्रतिभानं किं तु द्वयोरेव धर्मधर्मिणोरिति शपथप्रत्यायनीयोयं समवाय इति भावार्थः ॥ किं चायं तेन वादिना एको नित्यः सर्वव्यापको ऽमूर्तश्च परिकल्प्यते । ततो यथा घटाश्रिताः पाकजरूपादयो धर्माः समवायसंबन्धेन समवेतास्तथा किं न पटेपि । तस्यैकत्वनित्यत्वव्यापकत्वैः सर्वत्र तुल्यत्वात् । यथाकाश एको नित्यो व्यापकोऽमूर्तश्च सन् सर्वैः संबन्धिभिर्युगपदविशेषेण संबध्यते तथा किं नायमपीति । विनश्यदेकवस्तुसमवायाभावे च समस्तवस्तुसमवायाभावः प्रसज्यते । तत्तदवच्छेदकभेदान्नायंदोष इति चेदेवमनित्यत्वापत्तिः । प्रतिवस्तुस्वभावभेदादिति । अथ कथं समवायस्य न ज्ञाने प्रतिभासनं यतस्तस्येहेतिप्रत्ययः सावधानं साधनम् । इहप्रत्ययश्चानुभवसिद्ध एव । इह तन्तुषु पटः इहात्मनि ज्ञानम् । इह घटे रूपादय इति प्रतीतेरुपलम्भात् । अस्य च प्रत्ययस्य केवलधर्मधर्म्यनालम्बनत्वादस्ति समवायाख्यं पदार्थान्तरं तद्धेतुरिति पराशङ्कामभिसन्धाय पुनराह । इहेदमित्यस्ति मतिश्च वृत्ताविति । इहेदमिति इहेदमिति आश्रयाश्रयिभावहेतुक इहप्रत्ययो वृत्तावप्यस्ति समवायसंबन्धेपि विद्यते । चशब्दोऽपिशब्दार्थः । तस्य

च व्यवहितसंबन्धस्तथैव च व्याख्यातम् । इदमत्र हृदयम् । यथा त्वन्मते पृथिवीत्वाभिसंबन्धात्पृथिवी तत्र पृथिवीत्वं पृथिव्या एव स्वरूपमस्तित्वाख्यं नापरं वस्त्वन्तरं तेन स्वरूपेणैव समं योसावभिसंबन्धः पृथिव्याः स एव समवाय इत्युच्यते । प्राप्तानामेव प्राप्तिः समवायः इति वचनात् । एवं समवायत्वाभिसंबन्धात्समवाय इत्यपि किं न कल्प्यते । यतस्तस्यापि यत्समवायत्वं स्वस्वरूपं तेन सार्धं संबन्धोस्त्येव । अन्यथा निःस्वभावत्वाच्छशविषाणवदवस्तुत्वमेव भवेत् । ततश्च इह समवाये समवायत्वमित्युल्लेखेन इहप्रत्ययः समवायेपि युक्त्या घटत एव । ततो यथा पृथिव्यां पृथिवीत्वं समवायेन समवेतं समवायेपि समवायत्वमेवं समवायान्तरेण संबन्धनीयं तदप्यपरेणेत्येवं दुस्तरानवस्था महानदी ॥ एवं समवायस्यापि समवायत्वाभिसंबन्धे युक्त्या उपपादिते साहसिक्यमालम्ब्य पुनः पूर्वपक्षवादी वदति । ननु पृथिव्यादीनां पृथिवीत्वाभिसंबन्धनिबन्धनं समवायो मुख्यः । तत्र त्वतलादिप्रत्ययाभिव्यङ्ग्यस्य संगृहीतसकलावान्तरजातिलक्षणव्यक्तिभेदस्य सामान्यस्योद्भवात् । इह तु समवायस्यैकत्वेन व्यक्तिभेदाभावे जातेरनुद्भूतत्वाद्गौणोयं युष्मत्परिकल्पित इहेतिप्रत्ययसाध्यः समवायत्वाभिसंबन्धस्तत्साध्यश्च समवाय इति । तदेतन्न चेतश्चमत्कारकारणम् । यतोत्रापि जातिरुद्भवन्ती केन निरुध्येत । व्यक्तेरभेदेनेति चेन्न । तत्तदवच्छेदकवशात्तद्भेदोपपत्तौ व्यक्तिभेदकल्पनाया दुर्निवारत्वात् । अन्यो हि घटसमवायोन्यश्च पटसमवाय इति व्यक्त एव समवायस्यापि व्यक्तिभेद इति तत्सिद्धौ सिद्ध एव जात्युद्भवः । तस्मादन्यत्रापि मुख्य एव समवायः । इहप्रत्ययस्योभयत्राप्यव्यभिचारात् ॥

तदेतत्सकलं सपूर्वपक्षं समाधानं मनसि निधाय

सिद्धान्तवादी प्राह । न गौणभेद इति । गौण इति योयं भेदः स नास्ति । गौणलक्षणाभावात् । तल्लक्षणं चेत्थमाचक्षते—

अव्यभिचारी मुख्योऽविकलोऽसाधारणोऽन्तरङ्गश्च ।
विपरीतो गौणोर्थः सति मुख्ये धीः कथं गौणे ॥

तस्माद्धर्मधर्मिणोः संबन्धने मुख्यः समवायः समवाये च समवायत्वाभिसंबन्धे गौण इत्ययं भेदो नानात्वं नास्तीति भावार्थः। किं च योयमिह तन्तुषु पट इत्यादिप्रत्ययात्समवायसाधनमनोरथः स खल्वनुहरते नपुंसकादपत्यप्रसवमनोरथम्। इह तन्तुषु पट इत्यादेर्व्यवहारस्यालौकिकत्वात् । पांशुलपादानामपीह पटे तन्तुरित्येवं प्रतीतिदर्शनात् । इह भूतले घटाभाव इत्यत्रापि समवायप्रसङ्गात्। अत एवाह अपि च लोकबाध इति। अपिचेति दूषणाभ्युच्चये। लोकः प्रामाणिकलोकः सामान्यलोकश्च। तेन बाधो विरोधो लोकबाधः। तदप्रतीतव्यवहारसाधनात्। बाधशब्दस्य ईहाद्याः प्रत्ययभेदे इति पुंस्त्रीलिङ्गता । तस्माद्धर्मधर्मिणोरविष्वग्भावलक्षण एव संबन्धः प्रतिपत्तव्यो नान्यः समवायादिरिति काव्यार्थः ॥ ७ ॥

अथ सत्ताभिधानं पदार्थान्तरमात्मनश्च व्यतिरिक्तं ज्ञानाख्यं गुणमात्मविशेषगुणोच्छेदस्वरूपां च मुक्तिमज्ञानादङ्गीकृतवतः परानुपहसन्नाह ।

सतामपि स्यात्क्वचिदेव सत्ता
चैतन्यमौपाधिकमात्मनोन्यत् ।
न संविदानन्दमयी च मुक्तिः
सुसूत्रमासूत्रितमत्वदीयैः ॥ ८ ॥

वैशेषिकाणां द्रव्यगुणकर्मसामान्यविशेषसमवायाख्याः षट्पदार्थास्तत्त्वतयाभिप्रेताः ॥ तत्र पृथिव्यापस्तेजोवायुराकाशः कालो दिग् आत्मा मन इति नव द्रव्याणि ॥ गुणाश्चतुर्विंशतिः। तद्यथा—रूपरसगन्धस्पर्शसंख्यापरिमाणानि पृथक्त्वं संयोगविभागौ परत्वापरत्वे बुद्धिः सुखदुःखे इच्छाद्वेषौ प्रयत्नश्चेति सूत्रोक्ताः सप्तदश । चशब्दसमुच्चिताश्च सप्त—द्रवत्वं गुरुत्वं संस्कारः स्नेहो धर्माधर्मौ शब्दश्च। इत्येवं चतुर्विंशतिर्गुणाः । संस्कारस्य वेगभावनास्थितिस्थापकभेदात्त्रैविध्येऽपि संस्कारत्वजात्यपेक्षया एकत्वाच्छौर्यौदार्यादीनां चात्रैवान्तर्भावान्नाधिक्यम् ॥ कर्माणि पञ्च । तद्यथा-उत्क्षेपणमवक्षेपणमाकुञ्चनं प्रसारणं गमनमिति। गमनग्रहणाद् भ्रमणरेचनस्यन्दनाद्यविरोधः ॥ अत्यन्तव्यावृत्तानां पिण्डानां यतः कारणादन्योन्यस्वरूपानुगमः प्रतीयते तदनुवृत्तिप्रत्ययहेतुः सामान्यम् । तच्च द्विविधं परमपरं च । तत्र परं सत्ता भावो महासामान्यमिति चोच्यते। द्रव्यत्वाद्यवान्तरसामान्यापेक्षया महाविषयत्वात्। अपरसामान्यं च द्रव्यत्वादि । एतच्च सामान्यविशेष इत्यपि व्यपदिश्यते । तथाहि द्रव्यत्वं नवसु द्रव्येषु वर्तमानत्वात्सामान्यं गुणकर्मभ्यो व्यावृत्तत्वाद्विशेषः । ततः कर्मधारये सामान्यविशेष इति । एवं द्रव्यत्वापेक्षया पृथिवीत्वादिकमपरं तदपेक्षया घटत्वादिकम् । एवं चतुर्विंशतौ गुणेषु वृत्तेर्गुणत्वं सामान्यं द्रव्यकर्मभ्यो व्यावृत्तेश्च विशेषः। एवं गुणत्वापेक्षया रूपत्वादिकं तदपेक्षया नीलत्वादिकम् । एवं पञ्चसु कर्मसु वर्तनात्कर्मत्वं सामान्यं द्रव्यगुणेभ्यो व्यावृत्तत्वाद्विशेषः । एवं कर्मत्वापेक्षया उत्क्षेपणत्वादिकं ज्ञेयम् ॥ तत्र सत्ता द्रव्यगुणकर्मभ्योऽर्थान्तरं कया युक्त्येति चेत् । उच्यते । न द्रव्यं सत्ता द्रव्यादन्येत्यर्थः । एकद्रव्यवत्त्वात्। एकैकस्मिन् द्रव्ये वर्तमानत्वादित्यर्थः। द्रव्यत्ववत्।

यथा द्रव्यत्वं नवसु द्रव्येषु प्रत्येकं वर्तमानं द्रव्यं न भवति किं तु सामान्यविशेषलक्षणं द्रव्यत्वमेव एवं सत्तापि । वैशेषिकाणां हि अद्रव्यं वा द्रव्यम् अनेकद्रव्यं वा द्रव्यम् । तत्राद्रव्यमाकाशः कालो दिग् आत्मा मनः परमाणवः । अनेकद्रव्यं तु द्व्यणुकादिस्कन्धः । एकद्रव्यं तु द्रव्यमेव न भवति । एकद्रव्यवती च सत्ता । इति द्रव्यलक्षणविलक्षणत्वान्न द्रव्यम् । एवं न गुणः सत्ता । गुणेषु भावाद् । गुणत्ववत् । यदि हि सत्ता गुणः स्यान्न तर्हि गुणेषु वर्तेत । निर्गुणत्वाद् गुणानाम् । वर्तते च गुणेषु सत्ता । सन् गुण इति प्रतीतेः । तथा न सत्ता कर्म । कर्मसु भावात् । कर्मत्ववत् । यदि च सत्ता कर्म स्यान्न तर्हि कर्मसु वर्तेत । निष्कर्मत्वात् कर्मणाम् । वर्त्तते च कर्मसु सत्ता । सत् कर्मेति प्रतीतेः । तस्मात् पदार्थान्तरं सत्ता ॥

तथा विशेषा नित्यद्रव्यवृत्तयोन्त्या अत्यन्तव्यावृत्तिहेतवस्ते द्रव्यादिवैलक्षण्यात् पदार्थान्तरम् । तथा च प्रशस्तकरः—अन्तेषु भवा अन्त्याः । स्वाश्रयविशेषकत्वाद्विशेषाः । विनाशारम्भरहितेषु नित्यद्रव्येष्वण्वाकाशकालदिगात्ममनःसु प्रतिद्रव्यमेकैकशो वर्तमाना अत्यन्तव्यावृत्तिबुद्धिहेतवः । यथास्मदादीनां गवादिष्वश्वादिभ्यस्तुल्याकृतिगुणक्रियावयवोपचयावयवविशेषसंयोगनिमित्त प्रत्ययव्यावृत्तिर्दृष्टा गौः शुक्लः शीघ्रगतिः पीनः ककुद्मान् महाघण्ट इति तथास्मद्विशिष्टानां योगिनां नित्येषु तुल्याकृतिगुणक्रियेषु परमाणुषु मुक्तात्ममनःसु चान्यनिमित्तासंभवाद्येभ्यो निमित्तेभ्यः प्रत्याधारं विलक्षणोयं विलक्षणोयमितिप्रत्ययव्यावृत्तिर्देशकालविप्रकृष्टे च परमाणौ स एवायमिति प्रत्यभिज्ञानं च भवति तेन्त्या विशेषा इति । अमी च विशेषरूपा एव न तु द्रव्यत्वादिवत्सामान्यविशेषोभयरूपा । व्यावृत्तेरेव हेतुत्वात् ॥

तथा अयुतसिद्धानामाधार्याधारभूतानामिहप्रत्ययहेतुः संबन्धः

समवाय इति । अयुतसिद्धयोः परस्परपरिहारेण पृथगाश्रयानाश्रितयोराश्रयाश्रयिभावः इह तन्तुषु पट इत्यादेः प्रत्ययस्यासाधारणं कारणं समवायः । यद्वशात् स्वकारणसामर्थ्यादुपजायमानं पटाद्याधार्यं तन्त्वाद्याधारे संबध्यते यथा छिदिक्रिया छेद्येनेति सोपि द्रव्यादिलक्षणवैधर्म्यात् पदार्थान्तरम् ।। इति षट् पदार्थाः ।।

सांप्रतमक्षरार्थो व्याक्रियते । सतामपीत्यादि । सतामपि सद्बुद्धिवेद्यतया साधारणानामपि षण्णां पदार्थानां मध्ये क्वचिदेव केषुचिदेव पदार्थेषु सत्ता सामान्ययोगः स्यात् भवेत् न सर्वेषु । तेषामेषा वाचोयुक्तिः सदिति । यतो द्रव्यगुणकर्मसु सा सत्ता इति वचनात् यत्रैव सत्प्रत्ययस्तत्रैव सत्ता । सत्प्रत्ययश्च द्रव्यगुणकर्मस्वेव अतस्तेष्वेव सत्तायोगः। सामान्यादिपदार्थत्रये तु न । तदभावात् । इदमुक्तं भवति । यद्यपि वस्तुस्वरूपमस्तित्वं सामान्यादित्रयेपि विद्यते तथापि तदनुवृत्तिप्रत्ययहेतुर्न भवति । य एव चानुवृत्तिप्रत्ययः स एव सदितिप्रत्यय इति तदभावान्न सत्तायोगः तत्र । द्रव्यादीनां पुनस्त्रयाणां षट्पदार्थसाधारणं वस्तुस्वरूपमस्तित्वमपि विद्यते । अनुवृत्तिप्रत्ययहेतुः सत्तासंबन्धोप्यस्ति । निःस्वरूपे शशविषाणादौ सत्तायाः समवायाभावात् । सामान्यादित्रिके कथं नानुवृत्तिप्रत्यय इति चेत् बाधकसद्भावादिति ब्रूमः । तथा हि सत्तायामपि सत्तायोगाङ्गीकारेनवस्था । विशेषेषु पुनस्तदभ्युपगमे व्यावृत्तिहेतुत्वलक्षणतत्स्वरूपहानिः । समवाये तत्कल्पनायां संबन्धाभावः । केन हि संबन्धेन तत्र सत्ता संबध्यते । समवायान्तराभावात् । तथा च प्रामाणिकप्रकाण्डमुदयनः—

व्यक्तेरभेदस्तुल्यत्वं संकरोथानवस्थितिः ।
रूपहानिरसंबन्धो जातिबाधकसंग्रहः ।।

इति । ततः स्थितमेतत्सतामपि स्यात्क्वचिदेव सत्तेति ।।

तथा चैतन्यमित्यादि । चैतन्यं ज्ञानम् । आत्मनः क्षेत्रज्ञात् । अन्यत् अत्यन्तव्यतिरिक्तम् । असमासकरणादत्यन्तमिति लभ्यते । अत्यन्तभेदे सति कथमात्मनः संबन्धि ज्ञानमिति व्यपदेश इति पराशङ्कापरिहारार्थम् औपाधिकमितिविशेषणद्वारेण हेत्वभिधानम् । उपाधेरागतम् औपाधिकम् । समवायसंबन्धलक्षणेनोपाधिना आत्मनि समवेतम् । आत्मनः स्वयं जडरूपत्वात् । समवायसंबन्धोपढौकितमिति यावद् । यद्यात्मनो ज्ञानादव्यतिरिक्तत्वमिष्यते तदा दुःखजन्मप्रवृत्तिदोषमिथ्याज्ञानानामुत्तरोत्तरापाये तदनन्तराभावाद् बुद्ध्यादीनां नवानामात्मविशेषगुणानामुच्छेदावसर आत्मनोप्युच्छेदः स्यात् । तदव्यतिरिक्तत्वात् । अतो भिन्नमेवात्मनो ज्ञानं यौक्तिकमिति ॥ तथा न संविदित्यादि । मुक्तिर्मोक्षः । न संविदानन्दमयी न ज्ञानसुखरूपा । संविद् ज्ञानम् । आनन्दः सौख्यम् । ततो द्वन्द्वः । संविदानन्दौ प्रकृतौ यस्यां सा संविदानन्दमयी । तादृशी न भवति । बुद्धिसुखदुःखेच्छाद्वेषप्रयत्नधर्माधर्मसंस्काररूपाणां नवानामात्मनो वैशेषिकगुणानामत्यन्तोच्छेदो मोक्ष इति वचनात् । चशब्दः पूर्वोक्ताभ्युपगमद्वयसमुच्चये । ज्ञानं हि क्षणिकत्वादनित्यं सुखं च सप्रक्षयतया सातिशयतया च न विशिष्यते संसारावस्थातः । इति तदुच्छेदे आत्मस्वरूपेणावस्थानं मोक्ष इति । प्रयोगश्चात्र—नवानामात्मविशेषगुणानां संतानोत्यन्तमुच्छिद्यते । संतानत्वात् । यो यः संतानः स सोत्यन्तमुच्छिद्यते यथा प्रदीपसंतानः । तथा चायं । तस्मादत्यन्तमुच्छिद्यते इति । तदुच्छेद एव महोदयो न कृत्स्नकर्मक्षयलक्षण इति । न हि वै सशरीरस्य प्रियाप्रिययोरपहतिरस्ति । अशरीरं वा वसन्तं प्रियाप्रिये न स्पृशतः इत्यादयोपि वेदान्तास्तादृशीमेव मुक्तिमादिशन्ति । अत्र हि प्रिया-

प्रिये सुखदुःखे ते चाशरीरं मुक्तं न स्पृशतः। अपि च

यावदात्मगुणाः सर्वे नोच्छिन्ना वासनादयः।
तावदात्यन्तिकी दुःखव्यावृत्तिर्न विकल्प्यते ॥ १ ॥
धर्माधर्मनिमित्तो हि संभवः सुखदुःखयोः।
मूलभूतौ च तावेव स्तम्भौ संसारसद्मनः ॥ २ ॥
तदुच्छेदे च तत्कार्यशरीराद्यनुपप्लवात्।
नात्मनः सुखदुःखे स्त इत्यसौ मुक्त उच्यते ॥ ३ ॥
इच्छाद्वेषप्रयत्नादि भोगायतनबन्धनम्।
उच्छिन्नभोगायतनो नात्मा तैरपि युज्यते ॥४॥
तदेवं धिषणादीनां नवानामपि मूलतः।
गुणानामात्मनो ध्वंसः सोपवर्गः प्रतिष्ठितः ॥५॥
ननु तस्यामवस्थायां कीदृगात्मावशिष्यते।
स्वरूपैकप्रतिष्ठानः परित्यक्तोखिलैर्गुणैः ॥६॥
ऊर्मिषट्कातिगं रूपं तदस्याहुर्मनीषिणः।
संसारबन्धनाधीनदुःखक्लेशाद्यदूषितम् ॥ ७ ॥

कामक्रोधलोभगर्वदम्भहर्षाः ऊर्मिषट्कमिति। तदेतदभ्युपगमत्रयमित्थं समर्थयद्भिः अत्वदीयैस्त्वदाज्ञाबहिर्भूतैः कणादमतानुगामिभिः सुसूत्रमासूत्रितम् सम्यगागमः प्रपञ्चितः। अथ वा सुसूत्रमिति क्रियाविशेषणम्। शोभनं सूत्रं वस्तुव्यवस्थाघटनाविज्ञानं यत्रैवमासूत्रितं कृत्स्नशास्त्रार्थोपनिबन्धः कृत इति हृदयम्। सूत्रं तु सूचनाकारि ग्रन्थे तन्तुव्यवस्थयोः इत्यनेकार्थवचनात्। अत्र सुसूत्रमिति विपरीतलक्षणयोपहासगर्भं प्रशंसावचनम्। यथा—उपकृतं बहु तत्र किमुच्यते सुजनता प्रथिता भवता चिरम् इत्यादि। उपहसनीयता च युक्तिरिक्तत्वात् तदङ्गीकरणम्। तथा हि अविशेषेण सद्बुद्धिवेद्येष्वपि सर्वपदार्थेषु द्रव्यादिष्वेव त्रिषु सत्तासंबन्धः स्वीक्रियते न सामान्या-

दित्रये इति महतीयं पश्यतोहरता । यतः परिभाव्यतां सत्ताशब्दस्य शब्दार्थः। अस्तीति सन्। सतो भावः सत्ता अस्तित्वम्। तद्वस्तुस्वरूपं निर्विशेषमशेषेष्वपि पदार्थेषु त्वयाप्युक्तम् । तत्किमिदमर्धजरतीयं यद्द्रव्यादित्रय एव सत्तायोगो नेतरत्र त्रये इति । अनुवृत्तिप्रत्ययाभावान्न सामान्यादित्रये सत्तायोग इति चेत् न । तत्राप्यनुवृत्तिप्रत्ययस्यानिवार्यत्वात् । पृथिवीत्वगोत्वघटत्वादिसामान्येषु सामान्यं सामान्यमिति विशेषेष्वपि बहुत्वादयमपि विशेषोयमपि विशेष इति समवाये च प्रागुक्तयुक्त्या तत्तदवच्छेदकभेदात् एकाकारप्रतीतेरनुभवात् । स्वरूपत्वसाधर्म्येण सत्ताध्यारोपात् । सामान्यादिष्वपि सत्सदित्यनुगम इति चेत् तर्हि मिथ्याप्रत्ययोयमापद्यते । अथ भिन्नस्वभावेष्वेकानुगमो मिथ्यैवेति चेत् द्रव्यादिष्वपि सत्ताध्यारोपकृत एवास्तु प्रत्ययानुगमः। असति मुख्येध्यारोपस्यासंभवात् । द्रव्यादिषु मुख्योयमनुगतः प्रत्ययः सामान्यादिषु तु गौण इति चेत् न। विपर्ययस्यापि शक्यकल्पनत्वात्। सामान्यादिषु बाधकसंभवान्न मुख्योनुगतः प्रत्ययः द्रव्यादिषु तु तदभावान्मुख्य इति चेत् ननु किमिदं बाधकम्। अथ सामान्येपि सत्ताभ्युपगमेनवस्था विशेषेषु पुनः सामान्यसद्भावे स्वरूपहानिः समवायेपि सत्ताकल्पने तद्वृत्त्यर्थं संबन्धान्तराभाव इति बाधकानीति चेत् न। सामान्येपि सत्ताकल्पने यद्यनवस्था तर्हि कथं न सा द्रव्यादिषु। तेषामपि स्वरूपसत्तायाः प्रागेव विद्यमानत्वात्। विशेषेषु पुनः सत्ताभ्युपगमेपि न रूपहानिः । स्वरूपस्य प्रत्युतोत्तेजनात् । निःसामान्यस्य विशेषस्य क्वचिदप्यनुपलम्भात् । समवायेपि समवायत्वलक्षणायाः स्वरूपसत्तायाः स्वीकारे उपपद्यत एवाविष्वग्भावात्मकः संबन्धः । अन्यथा तस्य स्वरूपाभावप्रसङ्गः । इति बाधकाभावात् तेष्वपि द्रव्यवन्मुख्य एव सत्तासंबन्ध इति व्यर्थं

द्रव्यगुणकर्मस्वेव सत्ताकल्पनम् ॥ किं च तैर्वादिभिर्यो द्रव्यादित्रये मुख्यः सत्तासंबन्धः कक्षीकृतः सोऽपि विचार्यमाणो विशीर्येत । तथा हि—यदि द्रव्यादिभ्योऽत्यन्तविलक्षणा सत्ता तदा द्रव्यादीन्यसद्रूपाण्येव स्युः । सत्तायोगात्सत्त्वमस्त्येवेति चेत् असतां सत्तायोगेपि कुतः सत्त्वम् । सतां तु निष्फलः सत्तायोगः । स्वरूपसत्त्वं भावानामस्त्येवेति चेत् तर्हि किं शिखण्डिता सत्तायोगेन । सत्तायोगात्प्राग् भावो न सन् नाप्यसन् सत्तायोगाच्च सन्निति चेत् वाङ्मात्रमेतत् । सदसद्विलक्षणस्य प्रकारान्तरस्यासंभवात् । तस्मात् सतामपि स्यात्क्वचिदेव सत्तेति तेषां वचनं विदुषां परिषदि कथमिव नोपहासाय जायते ॥ ज्ञानमपि यद्येकान्तेनात्मनः सकाशाद्भिन्नमिष्यते तदा तेन चैत्रज्ञानेन मैत्रस्येव नैव विषयपरिच्छेदः स्यादात्मनः । अथ यत्रैवात्मनि समवायसंबन्धेन समवेतं ज्ञानं तत्रैव भावावभासं करोतीति चेन्न । समवायस्यैकत्वान्नित्यत्वाद्व्यापकत्वाच्च । सर्वत्र वृत्तेरविशेषात्समवायवदात्मनामपि व्यापकत्वादेकज्ञानेन सर्वेषां विषयावबोधप्रसङ्गः । यथा च घटे रूपादयः समवायसंबन्धेन समवेतास्तद्विनाशे च तदाश्रयस्य घटस्यापि विनाश एवं ज्ञानमप्यात्मनि समवेतम् तच्च क्षणिकम् ततस्तद्विनाशे आत्मनोपि विनाशापत्तेरनित्यत्वापत्तिः । अथास्तु समवायेन ज्ञानात्मनोः संबन्धः । किं तु स एव समवायः केन तयोः संबध्यते । समवायान्तरेण चेत् अनवस्था । स्वेनैव चेत् किं न ज्ञानात्मनोरपि तथा । अथ यथा प्रदीपस्वाभाव्यादात्मानं परं च प्रकाशयति तथा समवायस्येदृगेव स्वभावो यदात्मानं ज्ञानात्मानौ च संबन्धयतीति चेत् ज्ञानात्मनोरपि किं न तथास्वभावता येन स्वयमेवैतौ संबध्येते । किं च प्रदीपदृष्टान्तोपि भवत्पक्षे न जाघटीति । यतः प्रदीपस्तावद्द्रव्यं

प्रकाशश्च तस्य धर्मो धर्मधर्मिणोश्च त्वयात्यन्तं भेदोऽभ्युपगम्यते तत्कथं प्रदीपस्य प्रकाशात्मकता। तदभावे च स्वपरप्रकाशकस्वभावताभणितिर्निर्मूलैव । यदि च प्रदीपात्प्रकाशस्यात्यन्तभेदेऽपि प्रदीपस्य स्वपरप्रकाशकत्वमिष्यते तदा घटादीनामपि तदनुषज्यते। भेदाविशेषात् । अपि च तौ स्वपरसंबन्धस्वभावौ समवायाद्भिन्नौ स्यातामभिन्नौ वा । यदि भिन्नौ ततस्तस्यैतौ स्वभावाविति कथं संबन्धः । संबन्धनिबन्धनस्य समवायान्तरस्यानवस्थाभयादनभ्युपगमात् । अथाभिन्नौ ततः समवायमात्रमेव । न तौ । तदव्यतिरिक्तत्वात्तत्स्वरूपवदिति । किं च यथा इह समवायिषु समवाय इति मितिः समवायं विनाप्युपपन्ना तथा इहात्मनि ज्ञानमित्ययमपि प्रत्ययस्तं विनैव चेदुच्यते तदा को दोषः। अथात्मा कर्ता ज्ञानं करणं कर्तृकरणयोश्च वर्द्धकिवासीवद्भेद एव प्रतीतस्तत्कथं ज्ञानात्मनोरभेद इति । तन्न । दृष्टान्तस्य वैषम्यात् । वासी हि बाह्यं करणं ज्ञानं चाभ्यन्तरं तत्कथमनयोः साधर्म्यम् । न चैवं करणस्य द्वैविध्यमप्रसिद्धम् । यदाहुर्लाक्षणिकाः ।

करणं द्विविधं ज्ञेयं बाह्यमाभ्यन्तरं बुधैः ।
यथा लुनाति दात्रेण मेरुं गच्छति चेतसा ॥

यदि हि किंचित्करणमान्तरमेकान्तेन भिन्नमुपदर्श्यते ततः स्यात् दृष्टान्तदार्ष्टान्तिकयोः साधर्म्यम् । न च तथाविधमस्ति । न च बाह्यकरणगतो धर्मः सर्वोऽप्यान्तरे योजयितुं शक्यते। अन्यथा दीपेन चक्षुषा देवदत्तः पश्यतीत्यत्रापि दीपादिवच्चक्षुषोऽप्येकान्तेन देवदत्तस्य भेदः स्यात्। तथा च सति लोकप्रतीतिविरोध इति। अपि च साध्यविकलोऽपि वासीवर्द्धकिदृष्टान्तः। तथा हि नायं वर्द्धकिः काष्ठमिदमनया वास्या घटयिष्य इत्येवं वासीग्रहणपरिणामेनापरिणतः सन् तामगृहीत्वा घटयति किं तु तथा परिणतस्तां गृहीत्वा।

तथा परिणामेन वासिरपि तस्य काष्ठस्य घटने व्याप्रियते पुरुषोपि। इत्येवं लक्षणैकार्थसाधकत्वाद्वासीवर्द्धक्योरभेदोप्युपपद्यते । तत्कथमनयोर्भेद एवेत्युच्यते । एवमात्मापि विवक्षितमर्थमनेन ज्ञानेन ज्ञास्यामीति ज्ञानग्रहणपरिणामवान् ज्ञानं गृहीत्वार्थं व्यवस्यति।ततश्च ज्ञानात्मनोरुभयोरपि संवित्तिलक्षणैककार्यसाधकत्वादभेद एव। एवं कर्तृकरणयोरभेदे सिद्धे संवित्तिलक्षणं कार्यं किमात्मनि व्यवस्थितं आहोस्विद्विषय इति वाच्यम्। आत्मनि चेत् सिद्धं नः समीहितम्। विषये चेत् कथमात्मनोनुभवः प्रतीयते । अथ विषयस्थितसंवित्तेः सकाशादात्मनोनुभवःतर्हि किं न पुरुषान्तरस्यापि । तद्भेदाविशेषात्। अथ ज्ञानात्मनोरभेदपक्षे कथं कर्तृकरणभाव इति चेत् ननु यथा सर्प आत्मानमात्मना वेष्टयतीत्यत्र अभेदे यथा कर्तृकरणभावस्तथात्रापि । अथ परिकल्पितोऽयं कर्तृकरणभाव इति चेत् वेष्टनावस्थायां प्रागवस्थाविलक्षणगतिनिरोधलक्षणार्थक्रियादर्शनात् कथं परिकल्पितत्वम् । न हि परिकल्पनाशतैरपि शैलस्तम्भ आत्मानमात्मना वेष्टयतीति वक्तुं शक्यम् । तस्मादभेदेपि कर्तृकरणभावः सिद्ध एव॥ किं च चैतन्यमितिशब्दस्य चिन्त्यतामन्वर्थः । चेतनस्य भावश्चैतन्यम् । चेतनश्चात्मा त्वयापि कीर्त्यते । तस्य भावः स्वरूपं चैतन्यम् । यच्च यस्य स्वरूपं न तत्ततो भिन्नं भवितुमर्हति । यथा वृक्षाद्वृक्षस्वरूपम् । अथास्ति चेतन आत्मा। परं चेतनासमवायसंबन्धात् न स्वतः तथाप्रतीतेरिति चेत् तदयुक्तम्। यतः प्रतीतिश्चेत्प्रमाणीक्रियते तर्हि निर्बाधमुपयोगात्मक एवात्मा प्रसिद्ध्यति। न हि जातुचित्स्वयमचेतनोहं चेतनायोगाच्चेतनः अचेतने वा मयि चेतनायाः समवाय इति प्रतीतिरस्ति । ज्ञाताहमिति समानाधिकरणतया प्रतीतेः। भेदे तथाप्रतीतिरिति चेत् न । कथंचित्तादात्म्याभावे सामानाधिकरण्य-

प्रतीतेरदर्शनात् । यष्टिः पुरुष इत्यादिप्रतीतिस्तु भेदे सत्युपचारात् दृष्टा न पुनस्तात्त्विकी । उपचारस्य तु बीजं पुरुषस्य यष्टिगतस्तब्धत्वादिगुणैरभेदः । उपचारस्य मुख्यार्थस्पर्शित्वात् । तथा चात्मनि ज्ञाताहमिति प्रतीतिः कथंचिच्चेतनात्मतां गमयति । तामन्तरेण ज्ञाताहमितिप्रतीतेरनुपपद्यमानत्वात् । घटादिवत् । न हि घटादिरचेतनात्मको ज्ञाताहमिति प्रत्येति । चैतन्ययोगाभावादसौ न तथा प्रत्येतीति चेत् न । अचेतनस्यापि चैतन्ययोगाच्चेतनोहमिति प्रतिपत्तेरनन्तरमेव निरस्तत्वात् । इत्यचेतनत्वं सिद्धमात्मनो जडस्यार्थपरिच्छेदं पराकरोति । तं पुनरिच्छता चैतन्यस्वरूपतास्य स्वीकरणीया ॥ ननु ज्ञानवानहमितिप्रत्ययादात्मज्ञानयोर्भेदः अन्यथा धनवानितिप्रत्ययादपि धनधनवतोर्भेदाभावानुषङ्गात् । तदसत् । यतो ज्ञानवानहमिति नात्मा भवन्मते प्रत्येति जडत्वैकान्तरूपत्वात् । घटवत् । सर्वथा जडश्च स्यादात्मा ज्ञानवानहमितिप्रत्ययश्च स्यादस्य विरोधाभावात् इति मा निर्णैषीः । तस्य तथोत्पत्त्यसंभवात् । ज्ञानवानहमिति हि प्रत्ययो नागृहीतज्ञानाख्ये विशेषणे विशेष्ये चात्मनि जातूत्पद्यते । स्वमतविरोधात् । नागृहीतविशेषणा विशेष्ये बुद्धिः इति वचनात् । गृहीतयोस्तयोरुत्पद्यत इति चेत्कुतस्तद्गृहीतिः । न तावत्स्वतः । स्वयंवेदनानभ्युपगमात् । स्वयंविदिते ह्यात्मनि ज्ञाने च स्वतः सा युज्यते नान्यथा । संतानान्तरवत् । परतश्चेत् तदपि ज्ञानान्तरं विशेष्यं नागृहीते ज्ञानत्वविशेषणे ग्रहीतुं शक्यम् । गृहीते हि घटत्वे घटग्रहणमिति ज्ञानान्तरात्तद्ग्रहणेन भाव्यमित्यनवस्थानात् कुतः प्रकृतप्रत्ययः । तदेवं नात्मनो जडस्वरूपता संगच्छते । तदसंगतौ च चैतन्यमापाधिकमात्मनोऽन्यत् इति वाङ्मात्रम् ॥

तथा यदपि न संविदानन्दमयी च मुक्तिरिति व्यवस्थापनायानुमानमवादि संतानत्वादिति तत्राभिधीयते। ननु किमिदं संतानत्वं स्वतन्त्रमपरापरपदार्थोत्पत्तिमात्रं वा एकाश्रयापरापरोत्पत्तिर्वा। तत्राद्यः पक्षः सव्यभिचारः। अपरापरेषामुत्पादुकानां घटपटकटादीनां संतानत्वेऽप्यत्यन्तमनुच्छिद्यमानत्वात्। अथ द्वितीयपक्षः तर्हि तादृशं संतानत्वं प्रदीपे नास्तीति साधनविकलो दृष्टान्तः। परमाणुपाकजरूपादिभिश्च व्यभिचारी हेतुः। तथाविधसंतानत्वस्य तत्र सद्भावेऽप्यत्यन्तोच्छेदाभावात्। अपि च संतानत्वमपि भविष्यति अत्यन्तानुच्छेदश्च भविष्यति। विपर्ययबाधकप्रमाणाभावात्। इति संदिग्धविपक्षव्यावृत्तिकत्वादप्यनैकान्तिकोयम्। किं च स्याद्वादवादिनां नास्ति क्वचिदत्यन्तमुच्छेदो द्रव्यरूपतया स्थास्नूनामेव सतां भावानामुत्पादव्यययुक्तत्वात् इति विरुद्धश्च। इति नाधिकृतानुमानाद्बुध्यादिगुणोच्छेदरूपा सिद्धिः सिध्यति॥ नापि न हि वै सशरीरस्य इत्यादेरागमात्। स हि शुभाशुभादृष्टपरिपाकजन्ये सांसारिकप्रियाप्रिये परस्परानुषक्ते अपेक्ष्य व्यवस्थितः। मुक्तिदशायां तु सकलादृष्टक्षयहेतुकमैकान्तिकमात्यन्तिकं च केवलं प्रियमेव तत्कथं प्रतिषिध्यते। आगमस्य चायमर्थः सशरीरस्य गतिचतुष्टयान्यतमस्थानवर्तिनः आत्मनः प्रियाप्रिययोः परस्परानुषक्तयोः सुखदुःखयोरपहतिरभावो नास्तीति। अवश्यं हि तत्र सुखदुःखाभ्यां भाव्यम्। परस्परानुषक्तत्वं च समासकरणादभ्यूह्यते। अशरीरं मुक्तात्मानम्। वाशब्दस्यैवकारार्थत्वादशरीरमेव सन्तं सिद्धिक्षेत्रमध्यासीनं प्रियाप्रिये परस्परानुषक्ते सुखदुःखे न स्पृशतः। इदमत्र हृदयम्। यथा किल संसारिणः सुखदुःखे परस्परानुषक्ते स्यातां न तथा मुक्तात्मनः किं तु केवलं सुखमेव। दुःखमूलस्य शरीरस्यैवाभावात्। सुखं त्वात्मस्वरूपत्वादवस्थितमेव।

स्वस्वरूपावस्थानं हि मोक्षः । अत एवाशरीरमित्युक्तम् । आगमार्थश्चायमित्थमेव समर्थनीयः । यत एतदर्थानुपातिन्येव स्मृतिरपि दृश्यते ।

सुखमात्यन्तिकं यत्र बुद्धिग्राह्यमतीन्द्रियम् ।
तं वै मोक्षं विजानीयाद्दुष्प्रापमकृतात्मभिः ॥

न चायं सुखशब्दो दुःखाभावमात्रे वर्तते । मुख्यसुखवाच्यतायां बाधकाभावात् । अयं रोगाद्विप्रमुक्तः सुखी जात इत्यादिवाक्येषु च सुखीतिप्रयोगस्य पौनरुक्त्यप्रसङ्गाच्च । दुःखाभावमात्रस्य रोगाद्विप्रयुक्त इतीयतैव गतत्वात् । न च भवदुदीरितो मोक्षः पुंसामुपादेयतया संमतः । को हि नाम शिलाकल्पमपगतसकलसुखसंवेदनमात्मानमुपपादयितुं यतेत । दुःखसंवेदनरूपत्वादस्य सुखदुःखयोरेकस्याभावेऽपरस्यावश्यंभावात् । अत एव त्वदुपहासः श्रूयते ।

वरं वृन्दावने रम्ये क्रोष्टृत्वमभिवाञ्छितम् ।
न तु वैशेषिकीं मुक्तिं गौतमो गन्तुमिच्छति ॥

सोपाधिकसावधिकपरिमितानन्दनिष्यन्दात् स्वर्गादप्यधिकं तद्विपरीतानन्दमम्लानज्ञानं च मोक्षमाचक्षते विचक्षणाः । यदि तु जडः पाषाणनिर्विशेष एव तस्यामवस्थायामात्मा भवेत् तदलमपवर्गेण । संसार एव वरमस्तु । यत्र तावदन्तरान्तरापि दुःखकलुषितमपि कियदपि सुखमनुभुज्यते चिन्त्यतां तावत्किमल्पसुखानुभवो भव्य उत सर्वसुखोच्छेद एव । अथास्ति तथाभूते मोक्षे लाभातिरेकः प्रेक्षादक्षाणाम् । ते ह्येवं विवेचयन्ति । संसारे तावत् दुःखास्पृष्टं सुखं न संभवति दुःखं चावश्यं हेयं विवेकहानं चानयोरेकभाजनपतितविषमधुनोरिव दुःशक्यमत एव द्वे अपि त्यज्येते । अतश्च संसारान्मोक्षः श्रेयान् । यतोत्र दुःखं

सर्वथा न स्यात् । वरमियती कादाचित्कसुखमात्रापि त्यक्ता न तु तस्याः कृते दुःखभार इयान् व्यूढ इति । तदेतत्सत्यम् । सांसारिकसुखस्य मधुदिग्धधाराकरालमण्डलाग्रग्रासवद्दुःखरूपत्वादेव युक्तैव मुमुक्षूणां तज्जिहासा । किंत्वात्यन्तिकसुखविशेषलिप्सूनामेव । इहापि विषयनिवृत्तिजं सुखमनुभवसिद्धं तद्यदि मोक्षे विशिष्टं नास्ति ततो मोक्षो दुःखरूप एवापद्यत इत्यर्थः । ये अपि विषमधुनी एकत्र संपृक्ते त्यज्येते ते अपि सुखविशेषलिप्सयैव । किञ्च यथा प्राणिनां संसारावस्थायां सुखमिष्टं दुःखं चानिष्टं तथा मोक्षावस्थायां दुःखनिवृत्तिरिष्टा सुखनिवृत्तिस्त्वनिष्टैव । ततो यदि त्वदभिमतो मोक्षः स्यात्तदा न प्रेक्षावतां प्रवृत्तिः स्यात् । भवति चेयम् । ततः सिद्धो मोक्षः सुखसंवेदनस्वभावः । प्रेक्षावत्प्रवृत्तेरन्यथानुपपत्तेः । अथ यदि सुखसंवेदनैकस्वभावो मोक्षः स्यात्तदा तद्रागेण प्रवर्तमानो मुमुक्षुर्न मोक्षमधिगच्छेत् । नहि रागिणां मोक्षोस्ति।रागस्य बन्धनात्मकत्वात् । नैवम्। सांसारिकसुखमेव रागो बन्धनात्मको विषयादिप्रवृत्तिहेतुत्वात् ।मोक्षसुखे तु रागो न बन्धनात्मकः । परां कोटिमारूढस्य च स्पृहामात्ररूपोप्यसौ निवर्तते । मोक्षे भवे च सर्वत्र निःस्पृहो मुनिसत्तमः इति वचनात् । अन्यथा भवत्पक्षेपि दुःखनिवृत्त्यात्मकमोक्षाङ्गीकृतौ दुःखविषयकषायकालुष्यं केन निषिध्येत । इति सिद्धं कृत्स्नकर्मक्षयात्परमसुखसंवेदनात्मको मोक्षो न बुद्ध्यादिविशेषगुणोच्छेदरूप इति ॥ अपि च भोः तपस्विन् कथं चिदुच्छेदोस्माकमप्यभिमत एवैषामिति मा विरूपं मनः कृथाः। तथा हि बुद्धिशब्देन ज्ञानमुच्यते । तच्च मतिश्रुतावधिमनःपर्यायकेवलभेदात्पञ्चधा । तत्राद्यं ज्ञानचतुष्टयं क्षायोपशमिकत्वात् केवलज्ञानाविर्भावकाल एव प्रलीनम् । "नट्ठंमि उ छाउमत्थिए नाणे" इत्यागमात् । केवलं तु सर्वद्रव्यपर्यायगतं क्षायिक-

त्वेन निष्कलङ्कात्मस्वरूपत्वादस्त्येव मोक्षावस्थायां सुखं तु वैषयिकं तत्र नास्ति। तद्धेतोर्वेदनीयकर्मणोऽभावात्। यत्तु निरतिशयमक्षयमनपेक्षमनन्तं च सुखं तद्बाढं विद्यते। दुःखस्य चाधर्ममूलत्वात्तदुच्छेदादुच्छेदः। नन्वेवं सुखस्यापि धर्ममूलत्वाद्धर्मस्य चोच्छेदात्तदपि न युज्यते। पुण्यपापक्षयो मोक्षः इत्यागमवचनात्। नैवम्। वैषयिकसुखस्यैव धर्ममूलत्वाद्भवतु तदुच्छेदो न पुनरनपेक्षस्यापि सुखस्योच्छेदः। इच्छाद्वेषयोः पुनर्मोहभेदत्वात् तस्य च समूलकाषंकषितत्वादभावः। प्रयत्नश्च क्रियाव्यापारगोचरो नास्त्येव। कृतकृत्यत्वात्। वीर्यान्तराय क्षयोपनतस्त्वस्त्येव प्रयत्नो दानादिलब्धिवत्। न च क्वचिदुपयुज्यते कृतार्थत्वात्। धर्माधर्मयोस्तु पुण्यपापापरपर्याययोरुच्छेदोऽस्त्येव। तदभावे मोक्षस्यैवायोगात्। संस्कारश्च मतिज्ञानविशेष एव। तस्य च मोहक्षयानन्तरमेव क्षीणत्वादभाव इति। तदेवं न संविदानन्दमयी च मुक्तिरिति युक्तिरिक्तेयमुक्तिरिति काव्यार्थः॥ ८॥

अथ ते वादिनः कायप्रमाणत्वमात्मनः स्वयंसंवेद्यमानमप्यपलप्य तादृशकुशास्त्रशस्त्रसंपर्कविनष्टदृष्टयस्तस्य विभुत्वं मन्यन्ते। अतस्तत्रोपालम्भमाह।

यत्रैव यो दृष्टगुणः स तत्र
कुम्भादिवन्निष्प्रतिपक्षमेतत्।
तथापि देहाद्बहिरात्मतत्त्व-
मतत्त्ववादोपहताः पठन्ति॥ ९॥

यत्रैव देशे यः पदार्थो दृष्टगुणो दृष्टाः प्रत्यक्षादिप्रमाणतोनुभूता गुणा धर्मा यस्य स तथा स पदार्थस्तत्रैव विवक्षितदेश एवोपपद्यते। क्रियाध्याहारो गम्यः। पूर्वस्यैवकारस्यावधारणार्थस्यात्रा-

प्यभिसंबन्धात् तत्रैव नान्यत्रेत्यन्ययोगव्यवच्छेदः । अमुमेवार्थं दृष्टान्तेन द्रढयति । कुम्भादिवदिति । घटादिवत् । यथा कुम्भादेर्यत्रैव देशे रूपादयो गुणा उपलभ्यन्ते तत्रैव तेषामस्तित्वं प्रतीयते नान्यत्र एवमात्मनोपि गुणाश्चैतन्यादयो देह एव दृश्यन्ते न बहिः तस्मात् तत्प्रमाण एवायमिति । यद्यपि पुष्पादीनामवस्थानदेशादन्यत्रापि गन्धादिगुण उपलभ्यते तथापि तेन न व्यभिचारः । तदाश्रया हि गन्धादिपुद्गलास्तेषां च वैस्रासिक्या प्रायोगिक्या वा गत्या गतिमत्त्वेन तदुपलम्भकघ्राणादिदेशं यावदागमनोपपत्तेरिति । अत एवाह । निष्प्रतिपक्षमेतदिति । एतन्निष्प्रतिपक्षं बाधकरहितम् । न हि दृष्टेऽनुपपन्नं नामेति न्यायात् । ननु मन्त्रादीनां भिन्नदेशस्थानामप्याकर्षणोच्चाटनादिको गुणो योजनशतादेः परतोपि दृश्यते इत्यस्ति बाधकमिति चेत् मैवं वोचः । स हि न खलु मन्त्रादीनां गुणः किं तु तदधिष्ठातृदेवतानाम् । तासां चाकर्षणीयोच्चाटनीयादिदेशगमने कौतस्कुतोऽयमुपालम्भः । न जातु गुणा गुणिनमतिरिच्य वर्तन्त इति ॥

अथोत्तरार्धं व्याख्यायते । तथापीत्यादि । तथाप्येवं निःसपत्नं व्यवस्थितेपि तत्त्वे । अतत्त्ववादोपहताः । अनाचार इत्यत्रेव नञः कुत्सार्थत्वात् । कुत्सिततत्त्ववादेन तदभिमताप्ताभासपुरुषविशेषप्रणीतेन तत्त्वाभासप्ररूपणेनोपहता व्यामोहिताः । देहाद्बहिः शरीरव्यतिरिक्तेपि देशे । आत्मतत्त्वमात्मरूपम् । पठन्ति शास्त्ररूपतया प्रणयन्ते॥ इत्यक्षरार्थः ॥

भावार्थस्त्वयम् । आत्मा सर्वगतो न भवति । सर्वत्र तद्गुणानुपलब्धेः । यो यः सर्वत्रानुपलभ्यमानगुणः स सर्वगतो न भवति यथा घटः। तथा चायम् । तस्मात् तथा । व्यतिरेके व्योमादिः॥ न चायमसिद्धो हेतुः । कायव्यतिरिक्तदेशे तद्गुणानां बुद्ध्या-

दीनां वादिना प्रतिवादिना वानभ्युपगमात् । तथा च भट्टः श्रीधरः । सर्वगतत्वेप्यात्मनो देहप्रदेशे ज्ञातृत्वं नान्यत्र शरीरस्योपभोगायतनत्वात् अन्यथा तस्य वैयर्थ्यात् इति । अथास्त्यदृष्टमात्मनो विशेषगुणः । तच्च सर्वोत्पत्तिमतां निमित्तं सर्वव्यापकं च । कथमितरथा द्वीपान्तरादिष्वपि प्रतिनियतदेशवर्त्तिपुरुषोपभोग्यानि कनकरत्नचन्दनाङ्गनादीनि तेनोत्पाद्यन्ते । गुणश्च गुणिनं विहाय न वर्तते । अतोनुमीयते सर्वगत आत्मेति । नैवम् । अदृष्टस्य सर्वगतत्वसाधने प्रमाणाभावात् । अथास्त्येव प्रमाणं वह्नेरूर्द्ध्वज्वलनं वायोस्तिर्यग्गमनं चादृष्टकारितमिति चेन्न । तयोस्तत्स्वभावत्वादेव तत्सिद्धेर्दहनस्य दहनशक्तिवत् । साप्यदृष्टकारिता चेत् तर्हि जगत्त्रयवैचित्रीसूत्रणेपि तदेव सूत्रधारायतां किमीश्वरकल्पनया । तन्नायमसिद्धो हेतुः ॥ नचानैकान्तिकः । साध्यसाधनयोर्व्याप्तिग्रहणेन व्यभिचाराभावात् ॥ नापि विरुद्धः । अत्यन्तं विपक्षव्यावृत्तत्वात् । आत्मगुणाश्च बुद्ध्यादयः शरीर एवोपलभ्यन्ते ततो गुणिनापि तत्रैव भाव्यम् ॥ इति सिद्धः कायप्रमाण आत्मा ॥ अन्यच्च । त्वया आत्मनां बहुत्वमिष्यते । नानात्मानो व्यवस्थात इति वचनात् । ते च व्यापकाः । ततस्तेषां प्रदीपप्रभामण्डलानामिव परस्परानुवेधे तदाश्रितशुभाशुभकर्मणामपि परस्परं संकरः स्यात् । तथाचैकस्य शुभकर्मणा अन्यः सुखी भवेदितरस्याशुभकर्मणा अन्यो दुःखीत्यसमञ्जसमापद्येत । अन्यच्च एकस्यैवात्मनः स्वोपात्तशुभकर्मविपाकेन सुखित्वं परोपार्जिताशुभकर्मविपाकसंबन्धेन च दुःखित्वमिति युगपत्सुखदुःखसंवेदनप्रसङ्गः । अथ स्वावष्टब्धभोगायतनमाश्रित्यैव शुभाशुभयोर्भोगः तर्हि स्वोपार्जितमप्यदृष्टं कथं भोगायतनाद्बहिर्निष्क्राम्य वह्नेरूर्द्ध्वज्वल-

नादिकं करोतीति चिन्त्यमेतत् ॥ आत्मनां च सर्वगतत्वे एकैकस्य सृष्टिकर्तृत्वप्रसङ्गः । सर्वगतत्वेनेश्वरान्तरानुप्रवेशस्य संभावनीयत्वात् । ईश्वरस्य वा तदन्तरनुप्रवेशे तस्याप्यकर्तृत्वापत्तिः । न हि क्षीरनीरयोरन्योन्यसंबन्धे एकतरस्य पानादिक्रिया अन्यतरस्य न भवतीति युक्तं वक्तुम् ॥ किंच आत्मनः सर्वगतत्वे नरनारकादिपर्यायाणां युगपदनुभवानुषङ्गः । अथ भोगायतनाभ्युपगमान्नायं दोष इति चेत् ननु स भोगायतनं सर्वात्मनावष्टभ्नीयादेकदेशेन वा । सर्वात्मना चेदस्मदभिमताङ्गीकारः । एकदेशेन चेत् सावयवत्वप्रसङ्गः । परिपूर्णभोगाभावश्च ॥ अथात्मनो व्यापकत्वाभावे दिग्देशान्तरवर्तिपरमाणुभिर्युगपत्संयोगाभावादाद्यकर्माभावः तदभावादन्त्यसंयोगस्य तन्निर्मितशरीरस्य तेन तत्संबन्धस्य चाभावादनुपायसिद्धः सर्वदा सर्वेषां मोक्षः स्यात् । नैवम् । यद्येन संयुक्तं तदेव तं प्रत्युपसर्पतीति नियमासंभवात् । अयस्कान्तं प्रत्ययसस्तेनासंयुक्तस्याप्याकर्षणोपलब्धेः । अथासंयुक्तस्याप्याकर्षणे तच्छरीरारम्भं प्रत्येकमुखीभूतानां त्रिभुवनोदरविवरवर्तिपरमाणूनामुपसर्पणप्रसङ्गान्न जाने तच्छरीरं कियत्प्रमाणं स्यादिति चेत् संयुक्तस्याप्याकर्षणे कथं स एव दोषो न भवेत् । आत्मनो व्यापकत्वेन सकलपरमाणूनां तेन संयोगात् । अथ तद्भावाविशेषेऽप्यदृष्टवशाद्विवक्षितशरीरोत्पादनानुगुणा नियता एव परमाणव उपसर्पन्ति । तदितरत्रापि तुल्यम् ॥ अथास्तु यथाकथंचिच्छरीरोत्पत्तिः तथापि सावयवं शरीरं प्रत्यवयवमनुप्रविशन्नात्मा सावयवः स्यात् । तथा चास्य पटादिवत् कार्यत्वप्रसङ्गः । कार्यत्वे चासौ विजातीयैः सजातीयैर्वा कारणैरारभ्येत । न तावद्विजातीयैः । तेषामनारम्भकत्वात् । न हि तन्तवो घटमारभन्ते । न च सजातीयैः । यत आत्मत्वाभिसंब-

न्धादेवैतेषां कारणानां सजातीयत्वम्। पार्थिवादिपरमाणूनां विजातीयत्वात्। तथा चात्मभिरात्मा आरभ्यत इत्यायातम्। तच्चायुक्तम्। एकत्र शरीरेऽनेकात्मनामात्मारम्भकाणामसंभवात्। संभवे वा प्रतिसन्धानानुपपत्तिः। नह्यन्येन दृष्टमन्यः प्रतिसन्धातुमर्हति। अतिप्रसङ्गात्। तदारभ्यत्वे चास्य घटवदवयवक्रियातो विभागात्संयोगविनाशाद्विनाशः स्यात्। तस्माद्व्यापक एवात्मा युज्यते। कायप्रमाणतायामुक्तदोषसद्भावात्। इति चेन्न। सावयवत्वकार्यत्वयोः कथंचिदात्मन्यभ्युपगमात्। तत्र सावयवत्वं तावदसंख्येयप्रदेशात्मकत्वम्। तथा च द्रव्यालङ्कारकारौ। आकाशोपि सदेशः सकृत्सर्वमूर्ताभिसंबन्धार्हत्वात् इति। यद्यप्यवयवप्रदेशयोर्गन्धहस्त्यादिषु भेदोस्ति तथापि नात्र सूक्ष्मेक्षिका चिन्त्या। प्रदेशेष्वप्यवयवव्यवहारात्। कार्यत्वं तु वक्ष्यामः॥ नन्वात्मनां कार्यत्वे घटादिवत् प्राक्प्रसिद्धसमानजातीयावयवारभ्यत्वप्रसक्तिः। अवयवा ह्यवयविनमारभन्ते यथा तन्तवः पटमिति चेन्न वाच्यम्। न खलु घटादावपि कार्ये प्राक्प्रसिद्धसमानजातीयकपालसंयोगात्मत्वं दृष्टम्। कुम्भकारादिव्यापारान्वितान्मृत्पिण्डात्प्रथममेव पृथुबुध्नोदराद्याकारस्यास्योत्पत्तिप्रतीतेः। द्रव्यस्य हि पूर्वाकारपरित्यागेन उत्तराकारपरिणामः कार्यत्वम्। तच्च बहिरिवान्तरप्यनुभूयत एव। ततश्चात्मापि स्यात्कार्यः। न च पटादौ स्वावयवसंयोगपूर्वककार्यत्वोपलम्भात् सर्वत्र तथाभावो युक्तः। काष्ठे लोहलेख्यत्वोपलम्भाद्वज्रेपि तथाभावप्रसङ्गात्। प्रमाणबाधनमुभयत्र तुल्यम्। न चोक्तलक्षणकार्यत्वाभ्युपगमेप्यात्मनोऽनित्यत्वानुषङ्गात्प्रतिसन्धानाभावोऽनुषज्यते। कथंचिदनित्यत्वे सत्येवास्योपपद्यमानत्वात्। प्रतिसन्धानं हि यमहमद्राक्षं तमहं स्मरामीत्यादिरूपम्। तच्चैकान्तनित्यत्वे कथमुपपद्यते। अवस्थाभेदात्। अन्या ह्यनुभवावस्था अन्या च

स्मरणावस्था । अवस्थाभेदे चावस्थावतोपि भेदादेकरूपत्वक्षतेः कथंचिदनित्यत्वं युक्त्यायातं केन वार्यताम् ॥ अथात्मनः शरीरपरिमाणत्वे मूर्तत्वानुषङ्गात् शरीरेनुप्रवेशो न स्यात् । मूर्ते मूर्तस्यानुप्रवेशविरोधात् । ततो निरात्मकमेवाखिलं शरीरं प्राप्नोतीति चेत् किमिदं मूर्तत्वं नाम । असर्वगतद्रव्यपरिमाणत्वं रूपादिमत्त्वं वा । तत्र नाद्यः पक्षो दोषाय । संमतत्वात् । द्वितीयस्त्वयुक्तः । व्याप्त्यभावात् । नहि यदसर्वगतं तन्नियमेन रूपादिमदित्यविनाभावोस्ति । मनसोऽसर्वगतत्वेपि भवन्मते तदसंभवात् । आकाशकालदिगात्मनां सर्वगतत्वं सर्वसंयोगिसमानदेशत्वं वेत्युक्तत्वान्मनसो वैधर्म्यात्सर्वगतत्वप्रतिषेधनात् । अतो नात्मनः शरीरेऽनुप्रवेशानुपपत्तिर्येन निरात्मकं तत् स्यात् । असर्वगतद्रव्यपरिमाणलक्षणमूर्तत्वस्य मनोवत्प्रवेशाप्रतिबन्धकत्वात् । रूपादिमत्त्वलक्षणमूर्तत्वोपेतस्यापि जलादेर्वालुकादावनुप्रवेशो न निषिध्यते आत्मनस्तु तद्रहितस्यापि तत्रासौ प्रतिषिध्यत इति महच्चित्रम् ॥ अथात्मनः कायप्रमाणत्वे बालशरीरपरिमाणस्य सतो युवशरीरपरिमाणस्वीकारः कथं स्यात् । किं तत्परिमाणपरित्यागात् तदपरित्यागाद्वा । परित्यागाच्चेत् तदा शरीरवत्तस्यानित्यत्वप्रसङ्गात्परलोकाद्यभावानुषङ्गः । अथापरित्यागात् तन्न । पूर्वपरिमाणापरित्यागे शरीरवत्तस्योत्तरपरिमाणोत्पत्त्यनुपपत्तेः । तदयुक्तम् । युवशरीरपरिमाणावस्थायामात्मनो बालशरीरपरिमाणपरित्यागे सर्वथा विनाशासंभवात् । विफणावस्थोत्पादे सर्पवत् । इति कथं परलोकाभावोनुषज्यते । पर्यायतस्तस्यानित्यत्वेपि द्रव्यतो नित्यत्वात् ॥ अथात्मनः कायप्रमाणत्वे तत्खण्डने खण्डनप्रसङ्ग इति चेत् कः किमाह शरीरस्य खण्डने कथंचित्तत्खण्डनस्येष्टत्वात् । शरीरसंबद्धात्मप्रदेशेभ्यो हि कतिपयात्मप्रदेशानां खण्डितशरीरप्रदेशेवस्थानादात्मनः

खण्डनम् । तच्चात्र विद्यत एव । अन्यथा शरीरात्पृथग्भूतावयवस्य कम्पोपलब्धिर्न स्यात् । न च खण्डितावयवानुप्रविष्टस्यात्मप्रदेशस्य पृथगात्मत्वप्रसङ्गः । तत्रैवानुप्रवेशात् । न चैकत्र संतानेऽनेक आत्मानः । अनेकार्थप्रतिभासिज्ञानानामेकप्रमात्राधारतया प्रतिभासाभावप्रसङ्गात् । शरीरान्तरव्यवस्थितानेकज्ञानावसेयार्थसंवित्तिवत् । कथं खण्डितावयवयोः संघट्टनं पश्चादिति चेत् एकान्तेन छेदानभ्युपगमात् । पद्मनालतन्तुवच्छेदस्यापि स्वीकारात् । तथाभूतादृष्टवशात्तत्संघट्टनमविरुद्धमेवेति तनुपरिमाण एवात्माङ्गीकर्तव्यो न व्यापकः । तथा चात्मा व्यापको न भवति । चेतनत्वात् । यत्तु व्यापकं न तच्चेतनं यथा व्योम । चेतनश्चात्मा । तस्मान्न व्यापकः । अव्यापकत्वे चास्य तत्रैवोपलभ्यमानगुणत्वेन सिद्धा कायप्रमाणता । यत्पुनरष्टसमयसाध्यकेवलिसमुज्ज्ञातदशायामार्हतानामपि चतुर्दशरज्ज्वात्मकलोकव्यापित्वेनात्मनः सर्वव्यापकत्वं तत्कादाचित्कमिति न तेन व्यभिचारः । स्याद्वादमन्त्रकवचावगुण्ठितानां च नेदृशबिभीषिकाभ्यो भयमिति काव्यार्थः ॥ ९ ॥

वैशेषिकनैयायिकयोः प्रायः समानतन्त्रत्वादौलूक्यमते क्षिप्ते यौगमतमपि क्षिप्तमेवावसेयम् । पदार्थेषु च तयोरपि न तुल्या प्रतिपत्तिरिति सांप्रतमक्षपादप्रतिपादितपदार्थानां सर्वेषां चतुर्थपुरुषार्थं प्रत्यसाधकतमत्वे वाच्येपि तदन्तःपातिनां छलजातिनिग्रहस्थानानां परोपन्यासनिरासमात्रफलतया अत्यन्तमनुपादेयत्वात् तदुपदेशदातुर्वैराग्यमुपहसन्नाह ।

स्वयंविवादग्रहिले वितण्डा-
पाण्डित्यकण्डूलमुखे जनेऽस्मिन् ।

मायोपदेशात्परमर्म भिन्द-
न्नहो विरक्तो मुनिरन्यदीयः ॥ १० ॥

अन्ये अविज्ञाततत्त्वदाज्ञासारतयाऽनुपादेयनामानः परे। तेषामयं शास्तृत्वेन संबन्धी अन्यदीयः। मुनिः अक्षपादऋषिः। अहो विरक्तः अहो वैराग्यवान्। अहो इत्युपहासगर्भमाश्चर्यं सूचयति। अन्यदीय इत्यत्र ईयकारके इति दोन्तः। किं कुर्वन्नित्याह परमर्म भिन्दन्। जातावेकवचनप्रयोगात् परमर्माणि व्यथयन्। बहुभिरात्मप्रदेशैरधिष्ठिता देहावयवा मर्माणीति पारिभाषिकी संज्ञा। तत उपचारात्साध्यस्वतत्त्वसाधनाव्यभिचारितया प्राणभूतः साधनोपन्यासोपि मर्मेव मर्म। कस्मात्तद्भिन्दन्। मायोपदेशाद्धेतोः। मायापरवञ्चनम्। तस्या उपदेशश्छलजातिनिग्रहस्थानलक्षणपदार्थचयप्ररूपणद्वारेण शिष्येभ्यः प्रतिपादनं तस्मात्। गुणादस्त्रियां न वा इत्यनेन हेतौ तृतीयाप्रसङ्गे पञ्चमी। कस्मिन्विषये मायामयमुपदिष्टवान् इत्याह। अस्मिन् प्रत्यक्षोपलक्ष्यमाणे जने तत्त्वविमर्शबहिर्मुखतया प्राकृतप्राये लोके। कथंभूते। स्वयमात्मना परोपदेशनिरपेक्षमेव। विवादग्रहिले। विरुद्धः परस्परकक्षीकृतपक्षाधिक्षेपदक्षो वादो वचनोपन्यासो विवादः। तथा च भगवान् हरिभद्रसूरिः।

लब्धिख्यात्यर्थिना तु स्याद् दुःस्थितेनामहात्मना।
छलजातिप्रधानो यः स विवाद इति स्मृतः॥

तेन ग्रहिल इ ग्रहगृहीत इव विवादग्रहिलः। तत्र यथा ग्रहाद्यपस्मारपरवशः पुरुषो यत्किंचनप्रलापी स्यादेवमयमपि जन इति भावः। तथा वितण्डा प्रतिपक्षस्थापनाहीनं वाक्यम्। वितण्ड्यते आहन्यतेऽनया प्रतिपक्षसाधनमिति व्युत्पत्तेः। अभ्युपेत्य

पक्षं यो न स्थापयति स वैतण्डिक इत्युच्यते इति न्यायवार्त्तिकम्। वस्तुतस्तु अपरामृष्टतत्त्वातत्त्वविचारं मौखर्यं वितण्डा। तत्र यत्पाण्डित्यमविकलं कौशलं तेन कण्डूलमिव कण्डूलं मुखं लपनं यस्य स तथा तस्मिन्। कण्डूः खर्जूः। कण्डूरस्यास्तीति कण्डूलः। सिध्मादित्वान्मत्वर्थीयो लप्रत्ययः। यथा किलान्तरुत्पन्नकृमिकुलजनितां कण्डूतिं निरोद्धुमपारयन्पुरुषो व्याकुलतां कलयाति एवं तन्मुखमपि वितण्डापाण्डित्येनासंबद्धप्रलापचापलमाकलयत्कण्डूलमित्युपचर्यते। एवं च स्वरसत एव स्वस्वाभिमतव्यवस्थापनाविसंष्ठुलो वैतण्डिकलोकः। तत्र च तत्परमाप्तभूतपुरुषविशेषपरिकल्पितपरवञ्चनप्रचुरवचनोपदेशश्चेत्सहायः समजनि तदा स्वत एव ज्वालाकलापजटिले प्रज्वलति हुताशन इव कृतो घृताहुतिप्रक्षेप इति। तैश्च भवाभिनन्दिभिर्वादिभिरेतादृशोपदेशदानमपि तस्य मुनेः कारुणिकत्वकोटावारोपितम्। तथा चाहुः।

दुःशिक्षितकुतर्कांशलेशवाचालिताननाः।
शक्याः किमन्यथा जेतुं वितण्डाटोपमण्डिताः॥
गतानुगतिको लोकः कुमार्गं तत्प्रतारितः।
मा गादिति छलादीनि प्राह कारुणिको मुनिः॥

कारुणिकत्वं च वैराग्यान्न भिद्यते। ततो युक्तमुक्तम् अहो विरक्त इति स्तुतिकारेणोपहासवचनम्॥ अथ मायोपदेशादितिसूचनासूत्रं वितन्यते। अक्षपादमते किल षोडश पदार्थाः। प्रमाणप्रमेयसंशयप्रयोजनदृष्टान्तसिद्धान्तावयवतर्कनिर्णयवादजल्पवितण्डाहेत्वाभासछलजातिनिग्रहस्थानानां तत्त्वज्ञानान्निःश्रेयसाधिगम इति वचनात्। न चैतेषां व्यस्तानां समस्तानां वा

अधिगमो निःश्रेयसावाप्तिहेतुः। न ह्येकेनैव क्रियाविरहितेन ज्ञानमात्रेण मुक्तिर्युक्तिमती। असमग्रसामग्रीकत्वात्। विघटितैकचक्ररथेन मनीषितनगरप्राप्तिवत्। न च वाच्यं न खलु वयं क्रियां प्रतिक्षिपामः किंतु तत्त्वज्ञानपूर्विकाया एव तस्या मुक्तिहेतुत्वमिति ज्ञापनार्थं तत्त्वज्ञानान्निःश्रेयसाधिगम इति ब्रूम इति। न ह्यमीषां संहते अपि ज्ञानक्रिये मुक्तिप्राप्तिहेतुभूते। वितथत्वात्तज्ज्ञानक्रिययोः। न च वितथत्वमसिद्धम्। विचार्यमाणानां षोडशानामपि तत्त्वाभासत्वात्। तथा हि। तैः प्रमाणस्य तावल्लक्षणमित्थं सूत्रितम् अर्थोपलब्धिहेतुः प्रमाणमिति। एतच्च न विचारसहम्। यतोऽर्थोपलब्धौ हेतुत्वं यदि निमित्तत्वमात्रं तत्सर्वकारकसाधारणमिति कर्तृकर्मादेरपि प्रमाणत्वप्रसङ्गः। अथ कर्तृकर्मादिविलक्षणं हेतुशब्देन करणमेव विवक्षितं तर्हि तज्ज्ञानमेव युक्तं न चेन्द्रियसन्निकर्षादि। यस्मिन् हि सत्यर्थ उपलब्धो भवति स तत्करणम्। न चेन्द्रियसन्निकर्षसामग्र्यादौ सत्यपि ज्ञानाभावेऽर्थोपलम्भः। साधकतमं हि करणम्। अव्यवहितफलं तदिष्यते। व्यवहितफलस्यापि करणत्वे दुग्धभोजनादेरपि तथाप्रसङ्गः। तन्न ज्ञानादन्यत्र प्रमाणत्वम्। अन्यत्रोपचारात्। यदपि न्यायभूषणसूत्रकारेणोक्तं सम्यगनुभवसाधनं प्रमाणमिति तत्रापि साधनग्रहणात्कर्तृकर्मनिरासेन करणस्यैव प्रमाणत्वं सिध्यति। तथाप्यव्यवहितफलत्वेन साधकतमत्वं ज्ञानस्यैवेति न तत्सम्यग्लक्षणम्। स्वपरव्यवसायि ज्ञानं प्रमाणम् इति तु तात्त्विकं लक्षणम्॥

प्रमेयमपि तैरात्मशरीरेन्द्रियार्थबुद्धिमनःप्रवृत्तिदोषप्रेत्यभावफलदुःखापवर्गभेदाद् द्वादशविधमुक्तम्। तच्च न सम्यक्॥ यतः शरीरेन्द्रियबुद्धिमनःप्रवृत्तिदोषफलदुःखानामात्मन्येवान्तर्भावो युक्तः। संसारिण आत्मनः कथंचित्तदविष्वग्भूतत्वात्। आत्मा च

प्रमेय एव न भवति। तस्य प्रमातृत्वात्॥ इन्द्रियबुद्धिमनसां तु करणत्वात्प्रमेयत्वाभावः॥ दोषास्तु रागद्वेषमोहास्ते च प्रवृत्तेर्न पृथग्भवितुमर्हन्ति । वाङ्मनःकायव्यापारस्य शुभाशुभफलस्य विंशतिविधस्य तन्मते प्रवृत्तिशब्दवाच्यत्वात् । रागादिदोषाणां च मनोव्यापारात्मकत्वात्॥ दुःखस्य शब्दादीनामिन्द्रियार्थानां च फल एवान्तर्भावः। प्रवृत्तिदोषजनितं सुखदुःखात्मकं मुख्यं फलं तत्साधनं तु गौणम् इति जयन्तवचनात्॥ प्रेत्यभावापवर्गयोः पुनरात्मन एव परिणामान्तरापत्तिरूपत्वान्न पार्थक्यमात्मनः सकाशादुचितम्॥ तदेवं द्वादशविधं प्रमेयमिति वाग्विस्तरमात्रम् । द्रव्यपर्यायात्मकं वस्तु प्रमेयम् इति तु समीचीनं लक्षणम्। सर्वसंग्राहकत्वात्॥

एवं संशयादीनामपि तत्त्वाभासत्वं प्रेक्षावद्भिरनुप्रेक्षणीयम्। अत्र तु प्रतीतत्वाद् ग्रन्थगौरवभयाच्च न प्रपञ्चितम् । न्यक्षेण ह्यत्र न्यायशास्त्रमवतारणीयं तच्चावतार्यमाणं ग्रन्थान्तरतामवगाहत इत्यास्ताम्॥

तदेवं प्रमाणादिषोडशपदार्थानामविशिष्टेपि तत्त्वाभासत्वे प्रकटकपटनाटकसूत्रधाराणां त्रयाणामेव छलजातिनिग्रहस्थानानां मायोपदेशादितिपदेनोपक्षेपः कृतः॥ तत्र परस्य वदतोऽर्थविकल्पोपपादनेन वचनविघातश्छलम् । तत्त्रिधा । वाक्छलं सामान्यच्छलमुपचारच्छलं चेति। तत्र साधारणे शब्दे प्रयुक्ते वक्तुरभिप्रेतादर्थादर्थान्तरकल्पनया तन्निषेधो वाक्छलम् । यथा नवकम्बलोऽयं माणवक इति नूतनविवक्षया कथिते परः संख्यामारोप्य निषेधति कुतोस्य नव कम्बला इति । संभावनयातिप्रसङ्गिनोपि सामान्यस्योपन्यासे हेतुत्वारोपणेन तन्निषेधः सामान्यच्छलम्। यथा अहो नु खल्वसौ ब्राह्मणो विद्याचरणसंपन्न इति ब्राह्मणस्तुतिप्रसङ्गे कश्चिद्वदति संभवति ब्राह्मणे विद्याचरणसंपदिति

तच्छलवादी ब्राह्मणत्वस्य हेतुतामारोप्य निराकुर्वन्नभियुङ्क्ते यदि ब्राह्मणे विद्याचरणसंपद् भवति व्रात्येपि सा भवेद्व्रात्योपि ब्राह्मण एवेति। औपचारिके प्रयोगे मुख्यप्रतिषेधेन प्रत्यवस्थानमुपचारच्छलम् । यथा मञ्चाः क्रोशन्तीत्युक्ते परः प्रत्यवतिष्ठते कथमचेतनाः मञ्चाः क्रोशन्ति मञ्चस्थाः पुरुषाः क्रोशन्तीति ॥ तथा सम्यग्हेतौ हेत्वाभासे वा वादिना प्रयुक्ते झटिति तद्दोषतत्त्वाप्रतिभासे हेतुप्रतिबिम्बनप्रायं किमपि प्रत्यवस्थानं जातिर्दूषणाभास इत्यर्थः। सा च चतुर्विंशतिभेदा। साधर्म्यादिप्रत्यवस्थानभेदेन । यथा साधर्म्यवैधर्म्योत्कर्षापकर्षवर्ण्यावर्ण्यविकल्पसाध्यप्राप्त्यप्राप्तिप्रसङ्गप्रतिदृष्टान्तानुत्पत्तिसंशयप्रकरणाहेत्वर्थापत्त्यविशेषोपपत्त्युपलब्ध्यनुपलब्धिनित्यानित्यकार्यसमाः । तत्र साधर्म्येण प्रत्यवस्थानं साधर्म्यसमा जातिर्भवति । अनित्यः शब्दः कृतकत्वाद् घटवदिति प्रयोगे कृते साधर्म्यप्रयोगेणैव प्रत्यवस्थानं नित्यः शब्दो निरवयवत्वादाकाशवत्। न चास्ति विशेषहेतुर्घटसाधर्म्यात्कृतकत्वादनित्यः शब्दो न पुनराकाशसाधर्म्यान्निरवयवत्वान्नित्य इति । वैधर्म्येण प्रत्यवस्थानं वैधर्म्यसमा जातिर्भवति । अनित्यः शब्दः कृतकत्वाद् घटवदित्यत्रैव प्रयोगे स एव प्रतिहेतुर्वैधर्म्येण प्रयुज्यते नित्यः शब्दो निरवयवत्वात् अनित्यं हि सावयवं दृष्टं घटादीति । न चास्ति विशेषहेतुर्घटसाधर्म्यात् कृतकत्वादनित्यः शब्दो न पुनस्तद्वैधर्म्यान्निरवयवत्वान्नित्य इति । उत्कर्षापकर्षाभ्यां प्रत्यवस्थानमुत्कर्षापकर्षसमे जाती भवतः । तत्रैव प्रयोगे दृष्टान्तधर्मं कंचित्साध्यधर्मिण्यापादयन्नुत्कर्षसमां जातिं प्रयुङ्क्ते । यदि घटवत् कृतकत्वादनित्यः शब्दो घटवदेव मूर्तो भवतु न चेन्मूर्तो घटवदनित्योपि माभूदिति शब्दे धर्मान्तरोत्कर्षमापादयति ।

अपकर्षस्तु घटः कृतकः सन्नश्रावणो दृष्टः एवं शब्दोप्यस्तु नो चेद् घटवदनित्योपि माभूदिति शब्दे श्रावणत्वधर्ममपकर्षतीति । इत्येताश्चतस्रो दिङ्मात्रदर्शनार्थं जातय उक्ताः । एवं शेषा अपि विंशतिरक्षपादशास्त्रादवज्ञेयाः । अत्र तु अनुपयोगित्वान्न लिखिताः॥ तथा विप्रतिपत्तिरप्रतिपत्तिश्च निग्रहस्थानम् । तत्र विप्रतिपत्तिः साधनाभासे साधनबुद्धिर्दूषणाभासे च दूषणबुद्धिरिति । अप्रतिपत्तिः साधनस्यादूषणं दूषणस्य चानुद्धरणम् । तच्च निग्रहस्थानं द्वाविंशतिविधम् । तद्यथा । प्रतिज्ञाहानिः प्रतिज्ञान्तरं प्रतिज्ञाविरोधः प्रतिज्ञासंन्यासः हेत्वन्तरम् अर्थान्तरम् निरर्थकम् अविज्ञातार्थम् अपार्थकम् अप्राप्तकालम् न्यूनम् अधिकम् पुनरुक्तम् अननुभाषणम् अज्ञानम् अप्रतिभा विक्षेपः मतानुज्ञा पर्यनुयोज्योपेक्षणं निरनुयोज्यानुयोगः अपसिद्धान्तः हेत्वाभासाश्च । तत्र हेतावनैकान्तिकीकृते प्रतिदृष्टान्तधर्मं स्वदृष्टान्तेभ्युपगच्छतः प्रतिज्ञाहानिर्नाम निग्रहस्थानम् । यथा अनित्यः शब्द ऐन्द्रियकत्वाद् घटवदिति प्रतिज्ञासाधनाय वादी वदन् परेण सामान्यमैन्द्रियकमपि नित्यं दृष्टमिति हेतावनैकान्तिकीकृते यद्येवं ब्रूयात् सामान्यवद्धटोपि नित्यो भवत्विति स एवं ब्रुवाणः शब्दानित्यत्वप्रतिज्ञां जह्यात् । प्रतिज्ञातार्थप्रतिषेधे परेण कृते तत्रैव धर्मिणि धर्मान्तरं साधनीयमभिदधतः प्रतिज्ञान्तरं नाम निग्रहस्थानं भवति । अनित्यः शब्द ऐन्द्रियकत्वादित्युक्ते तथैव सामान्येन व्यभिचारे चोदिते यदि ब्रूयात् युक्तं सामान्यमैन्द्रियकं नित्यं तद्धि सर्वगतम् असर्वगतस्तु शब्दः इति तदिदं शब्देऽनित्यत्वलक्षणपूर्वप्रतिज्ञातः प्रतिज्ञान्तरमसर्वगतः शब्द इति निग्रहस्थानम् । अनया दिशा शेषाण्यपि विंशतिर्ज्ञेयानि । इह तु न लिखितानि । पूर्वहेतोरेव ॥ इत्येवं मायाशब्देनात्र छलादित्रयं सूचितम् । तदेवं परवञ्चनात्मकान्यपि

छलजातिनिग्रहस्थानानि तत्त्वरूपतयोपदिशतोऽक्षपादर्षेर्वैराग्यव्यावर्णनं तमसः प्रकाशात्मकत्वप्रख्यापनमिव कथमिव नोपहसनीयमिति काव्यार्थः ॥ १० ॥

अधुना मीमांसकभेदाभिमतं वेदविहितहिंसाया धर्महेतुत्वमुपपत्तिपुरसरं निरस्यन्नाह ।

न धर्महेतुर्विहितापि हिंसा
नोत्सृष्टमन्यार्थमपोद्यते च ।
स्वपुत्रघातान्नृपतित्वलिप्सा-
सब्रह्मचारि स्फुरितं परेषाम् ॥ ११ ॥

इह खल्वर्चिर्मार्गप्रतिपक्षधूममार्गाश्रिता जैमिनीया इत्थमाचक्षते । या हिंसा गार्ध्याद् व्यसनितया वा क्रियते सैवाधर्मानुबन्धहेतुः प्रमादसंपादितत्वात् शौनिकलुब्धकादीनामिव । वेदविहिता तु हिंसा प्रत्युत धर्महेतुः देवतातिथिपितॄणां प्रीतिसंपादकत्वात् तथाविधपूजोपचारवत् । न च तत्प्रीतिसंपादकत्वमासिद्धम् । कारीरीप्रभृतियज्ञानां स्वसाध्ये वृष्ट्यादिफले यः खल्वव्यभिचारः स तत्प्रीणितदेवताविशेषानुग्रहहेतुकः । एवं त्रिपुरार्णववर्णितच्छगलजाङ्गलहोमात्परराष्ट्रवशीकृतिरपि तदनुकूलितदैवतप्रसादसंपाद्या । अतिथिप्रीतिस्तु मधुपर्कसंस्कारादिसमास्वादजा प्रत्यक्षोपलक्ष्यैव । पितॄणामपि तत्तदुपयाचितश्राद्धादिविधानेन प्रीणितानां स्वसंतानवृद्धिविधानं साक्षादेव वीक्ष्यते । आगमश्चात्र प्रमाणम् । स च देवप्रीत्यर्थमश्वमेधगोमेधनरमेधादिविधानाभिधायकः प्रतीत एव । अतिथिविषयस्तु महोक्षं वा महाजं वा श्रोत्रियाय प्रकल्पयेत् इत्यादिः । पितृप्रीत्यर्थस्तु–

द्वौ मासौ मत्स्यमांसेन त्रीन्मासान् हारिणेन तु ।
औरभ्रेणाथ चतुरः शाकुनेनेह पञ्च तु ॥

इत्यादिः । एवं पराभिप्रायं हृदि संप्रधार्याचार्यः प्रतिविधत्ते न धर्मेत्यादि ॥ विहितापि वेदप्रतिपादितापि । आस्तां तावदविहिता हिंसा प्राणिप्राणव्यपरोपणरूपा । न धर्महेतुः न धर्मानुबन्धनिबन्धनम् । यतोऽत्र प्रकट एव स्ववचनविरोधः । तथाहि । हिंसा चेद्धर्महेतुः कथम् धर्महेतुश्चेद्धिंसा कथम् । श्रूयतां धर्मसर्वस्वं श्रुत्वा चैवावधार्यतामित्यादिः । न हि भवति माता च वन्ध्या चेति । हिंसा कारणं धर्मस्तु तत्कार्यमिति पराभिप्रायः । नचायं निरपायः । यतो यद्यस्यान्वयव्यतिरेकावनुविधत्ते तत्तस्य कार्यम् । यथा मृत्पिण्डादेर्घटादिः । न च धर्मो हिंसात एव भवतीति प्रातीतिकम् । तपोविधानदानध्यानादीनां तदकारणत्वप्रसङ्गात् । अथ न वयं सामान्येन हिंसां धर्महेतुं ब्रूमः किं तु विशिष्टामेव विशिष्टा च सैव या वेदविहितेति चेत् ननु तस्या धर्महेतुत्वं किं वध्यजीवानां मरणाभावेन मरणेऽपि तेषामार्त्तध्यानाभावात्सुगतिलाभेन वा । नाद्यः पक्षः । प्राणत्यागस्य तेषां साक्षादवेक्ष्यमाणत्वात् । न द्वितीयः । परचेतोवृत्तीनां दुर्लक्षतयार्त्तध्यानाभावस्य वाङ्मात्रत्वात् । प्रत्युत हा कष्टम् अस्ति न कोपि कारुणिकः शरणमिति स्वभाषया विरसमारसत्सु तेषु वदनदैन्यनयनतरलतादीनां लिङ्गानां दर्शनात् । दुर्ध्यानस्य स्पष्टमेव निष्टङ्क्यमानत्वात् ॥ अथेत्थमाचक्षीथाः यथा अयःपिण्डो गुरुतया मज्जनात्मकोपि तनुतरपत्रादिकरणेन संस्कृतः सन् जलोपरि प्लवते यथा च मारणात्मकमपि विषं मन्त्रादिसंस्कारविशिष्टं सद् गुणाय जायते यथा वा दहनस्वभावोप्यग्निः सत्यादिप्रभावप्रतिहतशक्तिः सन्न हि प्रदहति एवं मन्त्रादिविधिसंस्काराम्न खलु

वेदविहिता हिंसा दोषपोषाय । न च तस्याः कुत्सितत्वं शङ्कनीयं तत्कारिणां याज्ञिकानां लोके पूज्यत्वदर्शनादिति । तदेतन्न दक्षाणां क्षमते क्षोदम् । वैषम्येण दृष्टान्तानामसाधकतमत्वात् । अयःपिण्डादयो हि पत्रादिभावान्तरापन्नाः सन्तः सलिलतरणादिक्रियासमर्थाः । नच वैदिकमन्त्रसंस्कारविधिनापि विशस्यमानानां पशूनां काचिद्वेदनानुत्पादादिरूपा भावान्तरापत्तिः प्रतीयते । अथ तेषां वधानन्तरं देवतापत्तिर्भावान्तरमस्त्येवेति चेत्किमत्र प्रमाणम् । न तावत्प्रत्यक्षम् । तस्य संबद्धवर्तमानार्थग्राहकत्वात् । संबद्धं वर्तमानं च गृह्यते चक्षुरादिना इति वचनात् । नाप्यनुमानम् । तत्प्रतिबद्धलिङ्गानुपलब्धेः । नाप्यागमः । तस्याद्यापि विवादास्पदत्वात् । अर्थापत्त्युपमानयोस्त्वनुमानान्तर्गततया तद्दूषणेनैव गतार्थत्वम् । अथ भवतामपि जिनायतनादिविधाने परिणामविशेषात्पृथिव्यादिजन्तुजातघातनमपि यथा पुण्याय कल्पत इति कल्पना तथास्माकमपि किं नेष्यते । वेदोक्तविधिविधानरूपस्य परिणामविशेषस्य निर्विकल्पं तत्रापि भावात् । नैवम् । परिणामविशेषोपि स एव शुभफलो यत्रानन्योपायत्वेन यतनयापकृष्टप्रतनुचैतन्यानां पृथिव्यादिजीवानां वधेपि स्वल्पपुण्यव्ययेनापरिमितसुकृतसंप्राप्तिः न पुनरितरः । भवत्पक्षे तु सत्स्वपि तत्तच्छ्रुतिस्मृतिपुराणेतिहासप्रतिपादितेषु यमनियमादिषु स्वर्गावाप्त्युपायेषु तांस्तान्देवानुद्दिश्य प्रतिप्रतीकं कर्तनकदर्थनया कान्दिशीकान्कृपणपञ्चेन्द्रियान् शौनिकाधिकं मारयतां कृत्स्नसुकृतव्ययेन दुर्गतिमेवानुकूलयतां दुर्लभः शुभपरिणामविशेषः । एवं च यं कंचन पदार्थं किंचित्साधर्म्यद्वारेणैव दृष्टान्तीकुर्वतां भवतामतिप्रसङ्गः संगच्छते । न च जिनायतनविधापनादौ पृथिव्यादिजीववधेपि न गुणः । तथाहि तद्दर्शनाद्गुणानुरागितया भव्यानां बोधिलाभः पूजा-

तिशयविलोकनादिना च मनःप्रसादः ततः समाधिःततश्च क्रमेण निश्रेयसप्राप्तिरिति । तथा च भगवान्पञ्चलिङ्गीकारः ।

पुढवाइयाण जइवि हु होइ विणासो जिणालयाहिंतो ।
तव्विसया वि सुदिट्ठिस्स णियमओ अत्थि अणुकंपा ॥ १ ॥
एयाहिंतो बुद्धा विरया रक्खंति जेण पुढवाई ।
इत्तो निव्वाणगया अबाहिया आभवमिमाणं ॥२॥
रोगिसिरावेहो इव सुविज्जकिरिया व सुप्पउत्ताओ ।
परिणामसुंदरच्चिय चिट्ठा से बाहजोगे वि ॥ ३ ॥

इति । वैदिकवधविधाने तु न कंचित्पुण्यार्जनानुगुणं गुणं पश्यामः । अथ विप्रेभ्यः पुरोडाशादिप्रदानेन पुण्यानुबन्धी गुणोस्त्येवेति चेत् न । पवित्रसुवर्णादिप्रदानमात्रेणैव पुण्योपार्जनसंभवात् । कृपणपशुगणव्यपरोपणसमुत्थमांसदानं केवलं निर्घृणत्वमेव व्यनक्ति । अथ न प्रदानमात्रं पशुवधक्रियायाः फलं किं तु भूत्यादिकम् । यदाह श्रुतिः श्वेतं वायव्यमजमालभेत भूतिकामः इत्यादि । एतदपि व्यभिचारपिशाचग्रस्तत्वादप्रमाणमेव । भूतेश्चौपयिकान्तरैरपि साध्यत्वात् । अथ तत्र सत्वे हन्यमानानां छागादीनां प्रेत्यसङ्गतिप्राप्तिरूपोस्त्येवोपकार इति चेत् वाङ्मात्रमेतत् । प्रमाणाभावात् । न हि ते निहताः पशवः संगतिलाभमुदितमनसः कस्मैचिदागत्य तथाभूतमात्मानं कथयन्ति । अथास्त्यागमाख्यं प्रमाणम् । यथा

औषध्यः पशवो वृक्षास्तिर्यञ्चः पक्षिणस्तथा ।
यज्ञार्थं निधनं प्राप्ताः प्राप्नुवन्त्युच्छ्रितं पुनः ॥

इत्यादि । नैवम् । तस्य पौरुषेयापौरुषेयविकल्पाभ्यां निराकरिष्यमाणत्वात् । न च श्रौतेन विधिना पशुविशसनविधायिना स्वर्गावाप्तिरुपकार इति वाच्यम् । यदि हि हिंसयापि स्वर्गप्राप्तिः

स्यात्तर्हि बाढं पिहिता नरकपुरप्रतोल्यः । शौनिकादीनामपि स्वर्गप्राप्तिप्रसङ्गात् । तथा च पठन्ति पारमर्षाः ।

यूपं छित्वा पशून् हत्वा कृत्वा रुधिरकर्दमम् ।
9 यद्येवं गम्यते स्वर्गे नरके केन गम्यते ॥

किंच अपरिचितास्पष्टचैतन्यानुपकारिपशुहिंसनेनापि त्रिदिवपदवीप्राप्तिस्तदा परिचितस्पष्टचैतन्यपरमोपकारिमातापित्रादिव्यापादनेन यागकारिणामधिकतरपदप्राप्तिः प्रसज्यते । अथ अचिन्त्यो हि मणिमन्त्रौषधीनां प्रभावः इति वचनाद्वैदिकमन्त्राणामचिन्त्यप्रभावत्वात् तत्संस्कृतपशुवधे संभवत्येव स्वर्गप्राप्तिरिति चेत् न । इह लोके विवाहगर्भाधानजातकर्मादिषु तन्मन्त्राणां व्यभिचारोपलम्भाददृष्टे स्वर्गादावपि तद्व्यभिचारोनुमीयते । दृश्यन्ते हि वेदोक्तमन्त्रसंस्कारविशिष्टेभ्योपि विवाहादिभ्योनन्तरं वैधव्याल्पायुष्कतादारिद्र्याद्युपद्रवविधुराः परःशताः । अपरे च मन्त्रसंस्कारं विना कृतेभ्योपि तेभ्योनन्तरं तद्विपरीताः । अथ तत्र क्रियावैगुण्यं विसंवादहेतुरिति चेत् न । संशयानिवृत्तेः । किं तत्र क्रियावैगुण्यात् फले विसंवादः किं वा मन्त्राणामसामर्थ्यादिति न निश्चयः । तेषां फलेनाविनाभावासिद्धेः । अथ यथा युष्मन्मते आरोग्गबोहिलाभं समाहिवरमुत्तमं दिंतु इत्यादीनां वाक्यानां लोकान्तर एव फलमिष्यते एवमस्मदभिमतवेदवाक्यानामपि नेह जन्मनि फलमिति किं न प्रतिपद्यते । ततश्च विवाहादौ नोपलम्भावकाश इति चेत् अहो वचनवैचित्री । यथा वर्तमानजन्मनि विवाहादिषु प्रयुक्तैर्मन्त्रसंस्कारैरागामिनि जन्मनि तत्फलमेवं द्वितीयादिजन्मान्तरेष्वपि विवाहादीनामेव प्रवृत्तिधर्माणां पुण्यहेतुत्वाङ्गीकारेनन्तभवानुसन्धानं प्रसज्यते । एवं च न कदाचन संसारस्य परिसमाप्तिः । तथा च न कस्यचिदपवर्गप्राप्तिः । इति प्राप्तं भवदभिमतवेदस्यापर्यव-

सितसंसारवल्लरीमूलकन्दत्वम्। आरोग्यादिप्रार्थना तु असत्यामृषाभाषापरिणामविशुद्धिकारणत्वान्न दोषाय। तत्र हि भावारोग्यादिकमेव विवक्षितम्। तच्च चातुर्गतिकसंसारलक्षणभावरोगपरिक्षयस्वरूपत्वादुत्तमफलम्। तद्विषया च प्रार्थना कथमिव विवेकिनामनादरणीया। न च तज्जन्यपरिणामविशुद्धेस्तत्फलं न प्राप्यते। सर्ववादिनां भावशुद्धेरपवर्गफलसंपादनेऽविप्रतिपत्तेरिति। न च वेदनिवेदिता हिंसा न कुत्सिता। सम्यग्दर्शनज्ञानसंपन्नैरर्चिर्मार्गप्रपन्नैर्वेदान्तवादिभिश्च गर्हितत्वात्। तथा च तत्त्वदर्शिनः पठन्ति।

देवोपहारव्याजेन यज्ञव्याजेन येऽथवा।
घ्नन्ति जन्तून् गतघृणा घोरां ते यान्ति दुर्गतिम्॥

वेदान्तिका अप्याहुः।

अन्धे तमसि मज्जामः पशुभिर्ये यजामहे।
हिंसा नाम भवेद्धर्मो न भूतो न भविष्यति॥

तथा अग्निर्मामेतस्माद्धिंसाकृतादेनसो मुञ्चतु। छान्दसत्वान्मोचयतु इत्यर्थः। इति। व्यासेनाप्युक्तम्।

ज्ञानपालिपरिक्षिप्ते ब्रह्मचर्यदयाम्भसि।
स्नात्वातिविमले तीर्थे पापपङ्कापहारिणि॥ १॥
ध्यानाग्नौ जीवकुण्डस्थे दममारुतदीपिते।
असत्कर्मसमित्क्षेपैरग्निहोत्रं कुरूत्तमम्॥२॥
कषायपशुभिर्दुष्टैर्धर्मकामार्थनाशकैः।
शममन्त्रहुतैर्यज्ञं विधेहि विहितं बुधैः॥३॥
प्राणिघातात्तु यो धर्ममीहते मूढमानसः।
स वाञ्छति सुधावृष्टिं कृष्णाहिमुखकोटरात्॥४॥

इत्यादि ॥ यच्च याज्ञिकानां लोकपूज्यत्वोपलम्भादित्युक्तं तदप्यसारम् । अबुधा एव हि पूजयन्ति तान् न तु विविक्तबुद्धयः । अबुधपूज्यता तु न प्रमाणम् । तस्याः सारमेयादिष्वप्युपलम्भात् ॥ यदप्यभिहितं देवतातिथिपितृप्रीतिसंपादकत्वाद्वेदविहिता हिंसा न दोषायेति तदपि वितथम् । यतो देवानां संकल्पमात्रोपनताभिमताहारपुद्गलरसास्वादसुहितानां वैक्रियशरीरत्वाद् युष्मदावार्जितजुगुप्सितपशुमांसाद्याहुतिगृहीताविच्छैव दुःसंभवा । औदारिकशरीरिणामेव तदुपादानयोग्यत्वात् । प्रक्षेपाहारस्वीकारे च देवानां मन्त्रमयदेहत्वाभ्युपगमबाधः । न च तेषां मन्त्रमयदेहत्वं भवत्पक्षे न सिद्धम् । चतुर्थ्यन्तपदमेव देवता इति जैमिनिवचनप्रामाण्यात् । तथा च मृगेन्द्रः ।

शब्देतरत्वे युगपद्भिन्नदेशेषु यष्टृषु ।
न सा प्रयाति सांनिध्यं मूर्तत्वादस्मदादिवत् ॥

इति । सेति देवता । हूयमानस्य च वस्तुनो भस्मीभावमात्रोपलम्भात्तदुपयोगजनिता देवानां प्रीतिः प्रलापमात्रम् । अपि च योयं त्रेताग्निः स त्रयस्त्रिंशत्कोटिदेवतानां मुखम् । अग्निमुखा वै देवा इति श्रुतेः । ततश्चोत्तममध्यमाधमदेवानामेकेनैव मुखेन भुञ्जानानामन्योच्छिष्टभुक्तिप्रसङ्गः । तथा चैते तुरुष्केभ्योप्यतिरिच्यन्ते । तेपि तावदेकत्रैवामत्रे भुञ्जते न पुनरेकेनैव वदनेन । किं च । एकस्मिन् वपुषि वदनबाहुल्यं क्वचन श्रूयते यत्पुनरनेकशरीरेष्वेकं मुखमिति महदाश्चर्यम् । सर्वेषां च देवानामेकस्मिन्नेव मुखेङ्गीकृते यदा केनचिदेको देवः पूजादिनाराद्धोन्यश्च निन्दादिना विराद्धस्ततश्चैकेनैव मुखेन युगपदनुग्रहनिग्रहवाक्योच्चारणसंकरः प्रसज्येत । अन्यच्च । मुखं देहस्य नवमो भागस्तदपि येषां दाहात्मकं तेषामेकैकशः सकलदेहदाहा-

त्मकत्वं त्रिभुवनभस्मीकरणपर्यवसितमेव संभाव्यत इत्यलमतिचर्चया ॥ यश्च कारीरीयज्ञादौ वृष्ट्यादिफलेऽव्यभिचारस्तत्प्रीणितदेवतानुग्रहहेतुक उक्तः सोप्यनैकान्तिकः । क्वचिद् व्यभिचारस्यापि दर्शनात् । यत्रापि न व्यभिचारस्तत्रापि न त्वदाहिताहुतिभोजनजन्मा तदनुग्रहः । किं तु स देवताविशेषोतिशयज्ञानी स्वोद्देशनिर्वर्तितं पूजोपचारं यदा स्वस्थानावस्थितः सन् जानीते तदा तत्कर्तारं प्रति प्रसन्नचेतोवृत्तिस्तत्कार्याणीच्छावशात्साधयति । अनुपयोगादिना पुनरजानानो जानानोपि वा पूजाकर्तुरभाग्यसहकृतः सन्न साधयति । द्रव्यक्षेत्रकालभावादिसहकारिसाचिव्यापेक्षस्यैव कार्योत्पादस्योपलम्भात् । स च पूजोपचारः पशुविशसनव्यतिरिक्तैः प्रकारान्तरैरपि सुकरस्तत्किमनया पापैकफलया शौनिकवृत्त्या । यच्च छगलजाङ्गलहोमात्परराष्ट्रवशीकृतिसिद्ध्या देव्याः परितोषानुमानं तत्र कः किमाह । कासांचित्क्षुद्रदेवतानां तथैव प्रत्यङ्गीकारात् । केवलं तत्रापि तद्वस्तुदर्शनज्ञानादिनैव परितोषो न पुनस्तद्भुक्त्या । निम्बपत्रकटुकतैलधूमांशादीनां हूयमानद्रव्यादीनामपि तद्भोज्यत्वप्रसङ्गात् । परमार्थतस्तु तत्तत्सहकारिसमवधानसचिवाराधकानां भक्तिरेव तत्तत्फलं जनयति अचेतने चिन्तामण्यादौ तथादर्शनात् । अतिथीनां तु प्रीतिः संस्कारसंपन्नपक्वान्नादिनापि साध्या । तदर्थं महोक्षमहाजादिप्रकल्पनं निर्विवेकतामेव ख्यापयति । पितॄणां पुनः प्रीतिरनैकान्तिकी श्राद्धादिविधानेनापि भूयसां संतानवृद्धेरनुपलब्धेः । तदविधानेपि च केषांचिद्गर्दभशूकराजादीनामिव सुतरां तद्दर्शनात् । ततश्च श्राद्धादिविधानं मुग्धजनविप्रतारणमात्रफलमेव । ये हि लोकान्तरं प्राप्तास्ते तावत्स्वकृतकर्मानुसारेण सुरनारकादिगतिषु सुखमसुखं वा भुञ्जाना एवासते ते कथमिव

तनयादिभिरावर्जितं पिण्डमुपभोक्तुं स्पृहयालवोऽपि स्युः । तथा च युष्मद्यूथिनः पठन्ति ।

मृतानामपि जन्तूनां श्राद्धं चेत्तृप्तिकारणम् ।
तन्निर्वाणप्रदीपस्य स्नेहः संवर्द्धयेच्छिखाम् ॥

इति कथं श्राद्धविधानाद्यार्जितं पुण्यं तेषां समीपमुपैतु । तदन्यकृतत्वात् तस्य जडत्वात् निश्चरणत्वाच्च । अथ तेषामुद्देशेन श्राद्धादिविधानेऽपि पुण्यं दातुरेव तनयादेः स्यादिति चेन्न । तेन तज्जन्यपुण्यस्य स्वाध्यवसायादुत्तारितत्वात् । एवं च तत्पुण्यं नैवेतरस्यापि इति विचाल एव विलीनं त्रिशङ्कुज्ञातेन । किं तु पापानुबन्धिपुण्यत्वात् तत्त्वतः पापमेव । अथ विप्रोपभुक्तं तेभ्य उपतिष्ठत इति चेत् क इवैतत्प्रत्येतु । विप्राणामेव मेदुरोदरतादर्शनात् । तद्वपुषि च तेषां संक्रमः श्रद्धातुमपि न शक्यते । भोजनावसरे तत्संक्रम लिङ्गस्य कस्याप्यनवलोकनात् । विप्राणामेव च तृप्तेः साक्षात्करणात् । यदि परं त एव स्थूलकवलैराकुलतरमतिगार्द्ध्याद्भक्षयन्तः प्रेतप्राया इति मुधैव श्राद्धादिविधानम् । यदपि गयाश्राद्धादियाचनमुपलभ्यते तदपि तादृशविप्रलम्भकविभङ्गज्ञानिव्यन्तरादिकृतमेव निश्चेयम् ॥ यदप्युदितम् आगमश्चात्र प्रमाणमिति तदप्यप्रमाणम् । स हि पौरुषेयो वा स्यादपौरुषेयो वा । पौरुषेयश्चेत् सर्वज्ञकृतः तदितरकृतो वा । आद्यपक्षे युष्मन्मतव्याहतिः । तथा च भवत्सिद्धान्तः ।

अतीन्द्रियाणामर्थानां साक्षाद्द्रष्टा न विद्यते ।
नित्येभ्यो वेदवाक्येभ्यो यथार्थत्वविनिश्चयः ॥

द्वितीयपक्षे तु तत्र दोषवत्कर्तृकत्वेनानाश्वासप्रसङ्गः । अपौरुषेयश्चेन्न । संभवत्येव स्वरूपनिराकरणात् तुरङ्गशृङ्गवत् । तथाह्युक्तिर्वचनमुच्यत इति चेति पुरुषक्रियानुगतं रूपमस्य एतत्क्रियाभावे कथं भवितुमर्हति । नचैतत्केवलं क्वचिद्ध्वनदुपलभ्यते ।

उपलब्धावप्यदृश्यवक्त्राशङ्कासंभवात् । तस्माद्यद्वचनं तत्पौरुषेयमेव वर्णात्मकत्वात् कुमारसंभवादिवचनवत् । वचनात्मकश्च वेदः । तथा चाहुः ।

ताल्वादिजन्मा ननु वर्णवर्गो
वर्णात्मको वेद इति स्फुटं च ।
पुंसश्च ताल्वादि ततः कथं स्या-
दपौरुषेयोऽयमिति प्रतीतिः ॥

इति श्रुतेरपौरुषेयत्वमुररीकृत्यापि तावद्भवद्भिरपि तदर्थव्याख्यानं पौरुषेयमेवाङ्गीक्रियते । अन्यथाग्निहोत्रं जुहुयात्स्वर्गकाम इत्यत्र श्वमांसं भक्षयेदिति किं नार्थः । नियामकाभावात् । ततो वरं सूत्रमपि पौरुषेयमभ्युपगतम् । अस्तु वा अपौरुषेयः तथापि तस्य न प्रामाण्यम् । आप्तपुरुषाधीना हि वाचां प्रमाणतेति । एवं च तस्याप्रामाण्ये तदुक्तस्तदनुपातिस्मृतिप्रतिपादितश्च हिंसात्मको यागश्राद्धादिविधिः प्रामाण्यविधुर एवेति ॥ अथ योऽयं न हिंस्यात् सर्वभूतानि इत्यादिना हिंसानिषेधः स औत्सर्गिको मार्गः । सामान्यतो विधिरित्यर्थः । ततश्चापवादेनोत्सर्गस्य बाधितत्वान्न श्रौतो हिंसाविधिर्दोषाय । उत्सर्गापवादयोरपवादो विधिर्बलीयानिति न्यायात् । भवतामपि हि न खल्वेकान्तेन हिंसानिषेधः । तत्तत्कारणजाते पृथिव्यादिप्रतिसेवनानामनुज्ञानात् । ग्लानाद्यसंस्तरे आधाकर्मादिग्रहणभणनाच्च । अपवादपदं च याज्ञिकी हिंसा देवतादिप्रीतेः पुष्टालम्बनत्वादिति परमाशङ्क्य स्तुतिकार आह । नोत्सृष्टमित्यादि । अन्यार्थमिति मध्यवर्ति पदं डमरुकमणिन्यायेनोभयत्रापि संबन्धनीयम् । अन्यार्थमुत्सृष्टम् अन्यस्मै कार्याय प्रयुक्तम् । उत्सर्गवाक्यमन्यार्थप्रयुक्तेन वाक्येन नापोद्यते नापवादगोचरीक्रियते । यमेवार्थमाश्रित्य शास्त्रे उत्सर्गः प्रवर्तते

तमेवाश्रित्यापवादोपि प्रवर्तते । तयोर्निम्नोन्नतादिव्यवहारवत्परस्परसापेक्षत्वेनैकार्थसाधनविषयत्वात् । यथा जैनानां संयमपरिपालनार्थं नवकोटिविशुद्धाहारग्रहणमुत्सर्गः तथाविधद्रव्यक्षेत्रकालभावापत्सु च निपतितस्य गत्यन्तराभावे पञ्चकादियतनयाऽनेषणीयादिग्रहणमपवादः सोपि च संयमपरिपालनार्थमेव । न च मरणैकशरणस्य गत्यन्तराभावोऽसिद्ध इति वाच्यम् ।

सव्वत्थसजंमं संजमाओ अप्पाणमेव रक्खिज्जा ।
मुच्चइ अइवायाओ पुणो विसोही नयाऽविरई ॥

इत्यागमात् । तथा आयुर्वेदेपि यमेवैकं रोगमधिकृत्य कस्यांचिदवस्थायां किंचिद्वस्त्वपथ्यं तदेवावस्थान्तरे तत्रैव रोगे पथ्यम् ।

उत्पद्यते हि सावस्था देशकालामयान्प्रति ।
यस्यामकार्यं कार्यं स्यात्कर्म कार्यं तु वर्जयेत् ॥

इति वचनात् । यथा बलवदादेर्ज्वरिणो लङ्घनं क्षीणधातोस्तु तद्विपर्ययः। एवं देशाद्यपेक्षया ज्वरिणोपि दधिपानादि योज्यम् । तथा च वैद्याः ।

कालाविरोधि निर्दिष्टं ज्वरादौ लङ्घनं हितम् ।
ऋतेऽनिलश्रमक्रोधशोककामकृतज्वरान् ॥

एवं च यः पूर्वमपथ्यपरिहारो यत्र तत्रैवावस्थान्तरे तस्यैव परिभोगः। स खलूभयोरपि तस्यैव रोगस्य शमनार्थः। इति सिद्धमेकविषयत्वमुत्सर्गापवादयोरिति ॥ भवतां चोत्सर्गोन्यार्थोऽपवादश्चान्यार्थः। न हिंस्यात्सर्वभूतानि इत्युत्सर्गो हि दुर्गतिनिषेधार्थः अपवादस्तु वैदिकहिंसाविधिर्देवतातिथिपितृप्रीतिसंपादनार्थः। अतश्च परस्परनिरपेक्षत्वे कथमुत्सर्गोपवादेन बाध्यते । तुल्यबलयोर्विरोध इति न्यायात् । भिन्नार्थत्वेपि तेन तद्बाधनेतिप्रसङ्गात् । न च वाच्यं

वैदिकहिंसाविधिरपि स्वर्गहेतुतया दुर्गतिनिषेधार्थ एवेति तस्योक्तयुक्त्या स्वर्गहेतुत्वनिर्लोठनात् । तमन्तरेणापि च प्रकारान्तरैरपि तत्सिद्धिभावाद्गत्यन्तराभावे ह्यपवादपक्षकक्षीकारः ॥ न च वयमेव यागविधेः सुगतिहेतुत्वं नाङ्गीकुर्महे किं तु भवादाप्ता अपि । यदाह व्यासमहर्षिः ।

पूजया विपुलं राज्यमग्निकार्येण संपदः ।
तपः पापविशुद्ध्यर्थं ज्ञानं ध्यानं च मुक्तिदम् ॥

अत्राग्निकार्यशब्दवाच्यस्य यागादिविधेरुपायान्तरैरपि लभ्यानां संपदामेव हेतुत्वं वदन्नाचार्यस्तस्य सुगतिहेतुत्वमर्थात्कदर्थितवानेव । तथा च स एव भावाग्निहोत्रं ज्ञानपालीत्यादिश्लोकैः स्थापितवान् । तदेवं स्थिते तेषां वादिनां चेष्टामुपमया दूषयति स्वपुत्रेत्यादि । परेषां भवत्प्रणीतवचनपराङ्मुखानाम् । स्फुरितं चेष्टितम्।स्वपुत्रघातान्नृपतित्वलिप्सासब्रह्मचारि निजसुतनिपातनेन राज्यप्राप्तिमनोरथसदृशम्। यथा किल कश्चिदविपश्चित्पुरुषः परुषाशयतया निजमङ्गजं व्यापाद्य राज्यश्रियं प्राप्तुमीहते न च तस्य तत्प्राप्तावपि पुत्रघातपातककलङ्कपङ्कः क्वचिदपयाति एवं वेदविहितहिंसया देवतादिप्रीतिसिद्धावपि हिंसासमुत्थं दुष्कृतं न खलु पराहन्यते। अत्र च लिप्साशब्दं प्रयुञ्जानः स्तुतिकारो ज्ञापयति यथा तस्य दुराशयस्यासदृशतादृक्कर्मणा निर्मूलितसत्कर्मणो राज्यप्राप्तौ केवलं समीहामात्रमेव न पुनस्तत्सिद्धिः एवं तेषां दुर्वादिनां वेदविहितहिंसामनुतिष्ठतामपि देवतादिपरितोषणे मनोराज्यमेव । न पुनस्तेषामुत्तमजनपूज्यत्वमिन्द्रादिदिवौकसां च तृप्तिः । प्रागुक्तयुक्त्या निराकृतत्वात् ॥ इति काव्यार्थः ॥ ११ ॥

सांप्रतं नित्यपरोक्षज्ञानवादिनां मीमांसकभेदभट्टानामेकात्मसमवायिज्ञानान्तरवेद्यज्ञानवादिनां च यौगानां मतं विकुट्टयन्नाह ।

स्वार्थावबोधक्षम एव बोधः
प्रकाशते नार्थकथान्यथा तु ॥
परे परेभ्यो भयतस्तथापि
प्रपेदिरे ज्ञानमनात्मनिष्ठम् ॥ १२ ॥

बोधो ज्ञानम् । स च स्वार्थावबोधक्षम एव प्रकाशते । स्वस्यात्मस्वरूपस्यार्थस्य च पदार्थस्य योवबोधः परिच्छेदः तत्र क्षम एव समर्थ एव प्रतिभासत इत्ययोगव्यवच्छेदः । प्रकाशत इति क्रिययावबोधस्य प्रकाशरूपत्वसिद्धेः सर्वप्रकाशानां स्वार्थप्रकाशकत्वेन बोधस्यापि तत्सिद्धिः । विपर्यये दूषणमाह । नार्थकथान्यथा तु इति । अन्यथेति अर्थप्रकाशनेऽविवादात् ज्ञानस्य स्वसंविदितत्वानभ्युपगमेर्थकथैव न स्यात् । अर्थकथा पदार्थसंबन्धिनी वार्ता । सदसद्रूपात्मकं स्वरूपमिति यावत् । तुशब्दोवधारणे । भिन्नक्रमश्च । स चार्थकथया सह योजित एव । यदि हि ज्ञानं स्वसंविदितं नेष्यते तदा तेनात्मज्ञानाय ज्ञानान्तरमपेक्षणीयं तेनाप्यपरमित्याद्यनवस्था । ततो ज्ञानं तावत्स्वावबोधव्यग्रतामग्नम् । अर्थस्तु जडतया स्वरूपज्ञापनासमर्थ इति को नामार्थस्य कथामपि कथयेत् । तथापि एवं ज्ञानस्य स्वसंविदितत्वे युक्त्या घटमानेपि । परे तीर्थान्तरीयाः । ज्ञानं कर्मतापन्नम् । अनात्मनिष्ठम् न विद्यते आत्मनः स्वस्य निष्ठा निश्चयो यस्य तदनात्मनिष्ठम् । अस्वसंविदितमित्यर्थः । प्रपेदिरे प्रपन्नाः । कुत इत्याह । परेभ्यो भयतः । परे पूर्वपक्षवादिनस्तेभ्यः सकाशात् ज्ञानस्य स्वसंविदितत्वं नोपपद्यते स्वात्मनि क्रियाविरोधादित्युपालम्भसंभावनासंभवं यद्भयं तस्मात् तदाश्रित्येत्यर्थः ॥

इत्थमक्षरगमनिकां विधाय भावार्थः प्रपञ्च्यते ॥ भट्टास्तावदिदं वदन्ति । यत् ज्ञानं स्वसंविदितं न भवति । स्वात्मनि क्रियाविरोधात् । न हि सुशिक्षितोपि नटबटुः स्वस्कन्धमधिरोढुं पटुः । न च सुतीक्ष्णाप्यसिधारा स्वं छेत्तुमाहितव्यापारा । ततश्च परोक्षमेव ज्ञानमिति ॥ तदेतन्न सम्यक् । यतः किमुत्पत्तिः स्वात्मनि विरुध्यते ज्ञप्तिर्वा । यद्युत्पत्तिः सा विरुध्यताम् । न हि वयमपि ज्ञानमात्मानमुत्पादयतीति मन्यामहे । अथ ज्ञप्तिः । नेयमात्मनि विरुद्धा । तदात्मनैव ज्ञानस्य स्वहेतुभ्य उत्पादात् प्रकाशात्मनेव प्रदीपालोकस्य । अथ प्रकाशात्मैव प्रदीपालोक उत्पन्न इति परप्रकाशकोस्तु आत्मानमप्येतावन्मात्रेणैव प्रकाशयतीति कोऽयं न्याय इति चेत् तत्किं तेन वराकेणाप्रकाशितेनैव स्थातव्यम् आलोकान्तराद्वास्य प्रकाशेन भवितव्यम् । प्रथमे प्रत्यक्षबाधः । द्वितीयेपि सैवानवस्थापत्तिश्च ॥ अथ नासौ स्वमपेक्ष्य कर्मतया चकास्तीत्यस्वप्रकाशकः स्वीक्रियते । आत्मानं न प्रकाशयतीत्यर्थः । प्रकाशरूपतयोत्पन्नत्वात्स्वयं प्रकाशत एव इति चेत् चिरं जीव । न हि वयमपि ज्ञानं कर्मतयैव प्रतिभासमानं स्वसंवेद्यं ब्रूमः । ज्ञानं स्वयं प्रतिभासत इत्यादावकर्मकस्य तस्य चकासनात् । यथा तु ज्ञानं स्वं जानामीति कर्मतयापि तद्भाति तथा प्रदीपः स्वं प्रकाशयतीत्ययमपि कर्मतया प्रथित एव । यस्तु स्वात्मनि क्रियाविरोधो दोष उद्भावितः सोऽयुक्तः । अनुभवसिद्धेर्थे विरोधासिद्धेः । घटमहं जानामीत्यादौ कर्तृकर्मवज्ज्ञप्तेरप्यवभासमानत्वात् । न चाप्रत्यक्षोपलम्भस्यार्थदृष्टिः प्रसिध्यति । न च ज्ञानान्तरादुपलम्भसंभावना । तस्याप्यनुपलब्धस्य प्रस्तुतोपलम्भप्रत्यक्षीकाराभावात् । उपलम्भान्तरसंभावने चानवस्था । अर्थोपलम्भात्तस्योपलम्भेऽन्योन्याश्रयदोषः ॥ अथार्थप्राकट्यमन्यथा नोपपद्यते यदि ज्ञानं

न स्यादित्यर्थापत्त्या तदुपलम्भ इति चेन्न । तस्या अपि ज्ञापकत्वेनाज्ञाताया ज्ञापकत्वायोगात् । अर्थापत्त्यन्तरात्तज्ज्ञानेऽनवस्थेतरेतराश्रयदोषापत्तेस्तदवस्थः परिभवः । तस्मादर्थोन्मुखतयेव स्वोन्मुखतयापि ज्ञानस्य प्रतिभासात्स्वसंविदितत्वम् ॥ नन्वनुभूतेरनुभाव्यत्वे घटादिवदननुभूतित्वप्रसङ्गः । प्रयोगस्तु ज्ञानमनुभवरूपमप्यनुभूतिर्न भवति अनुभाव्यत्वाद् घटवत् अनुभाव्यं च भवद्भिरिष्यते ज्ञानम् । स्वसंवेद्यत्वात् । नैवम् । ज्ञातुर्ज्ञातृत्वेनेवानुभूतेरनुभूतित्वेनैवानुभवात् । न चानुभूतेरनुभाव्यत्वं दोषः । अर्थापेक्षयानुभूतित्वात् स्वापेक्षया चानुभाव्यत्वात् । स्वपितृपुत्रापेक्षयैकस्य पुत्रत्वपितृत्ववद्विरोधाभावात् ॥ अनुमानाच्च स्वसंवेदनसिद्धिः । तथाहि । ज्ञानं स्वयं प्रकाशमानमेवार्थं प्रकाशयति प्रकाशकत्वात् प्रदीपवत् । संवेदनस्य प्रकाश्यत्वात्प्रकाशकत्वमसिद्धमिति चेन्न । अज्ञाननिरासादिद्वारेण प्रकाशकत्वोपपत्तेः । ननु नेत्रादयः प्रकाशका अपि स्वं न प्रकाशयन्तीति प्रकाशकत्वहेतोरनैकान्तिकतेति चेत् नात्र नेत्रादिभिरनैकान्तिकता । तेषां लब्ध्युपयोगलक्षणभावेन्द्रियरूपाणामेव प्रकाशकत्वात् ॥ भावेन्द्रियाणां च स्वसंवेदनरूपतैवेति न व्यभिचारः । तथा संवित् स्वप्रकाशा । अर्थप्रतीतित्वात् । यः स्वप्रकाशो न भवति नासावर्थप्रतीतिर्यथा घटः ॥ तदेवं सिद्धेपि प्रत्यक्षानुमानाभ्यां ज्ञानस्य स्वसंविदितत्वे सत्संप्रयोगे इन्द्रियबुद्धिजन्मलक्षणं ज्ञानं ततोर्थप्राकट्यं तस्मादर्थापत्तिः तया प्रवर्तकज्ञानस्योपलम्भ इत्येवंरूपा त्रिपुटीप्रत्यक्षकल्पना भट्टानां प्रयासफलैव ॥

यौगास्त्वाहुः । ज्ञानं स्वान्यप्रकाश्यम् । ईश्वरज्ञानान्यत्वे सति प्रमेयत्वात् । घटवत् । समुत्पन्नं हि ज्ञानमेकात्मसमवेतानन्तरोद्भविष्णुमानसप्रत्यक्षेणैव लक्ष्यते न पुनः स्वेन । न चैवमनवस्था । अर्थावसायिविज्ञानोत्पादमात्रेणैवार्थसिद्धौ प्रमातुः कृतार्थत्वात् । अर्थज्ञान-

जिज्ञासायां तु तत्रापि ज्ञानमुत्पद्यत एवेति ॥ तदयुक्तम् । पक्षस्य प्रत्यनुमानबाधितत्वेन हेतोः कालात्ययापदिष्टत्वात् । तथा हि । विवादास्पदं ज्ञानं स्वसंविदितं ज्ञानत्वात् ईश्वरज्ञानवत् । न चायं वाद्यप्रतीतो दृष्टान्तः । पुरुषस्येश्वरतया जैनैरपि स्वीकृतत्वेन तज्ज्ञानस्य तेषां प्रसिद्धेः । व्यर्थविशेष्यश्चात्र तव हेतुः । समर्थविशेषणोपादानेनैव साध्यसिद्धेः। अग्निसिद्धौ धूमवत्त्वे सति द्रव्यत्वादितिवत् ईश्वरज्ञानान्यत्वादित्येतावतैव गतत्वात् । न हीश्वरज्ञानादन्यत्स्वसंविदितमप्रमेयं वा ज्ञानमस्ति यद्व्यवच्छेदाय प्रमेयत्वादिति क्रियेत । भवन्मते तदन्यज्ञानस्य सर्वस्य प्रमेयत्वात् । अप्रयोजकश्चायं हेतुः । सोपाधित्वात् । साधनाव्यापकः साध्येन समव्याप्तिश्च खलूपाधिरभिधीयते । तत्पुत्रत्वादिना श्यामत्वे साध्ये शाकाद्याहारपरिणामवत् । उपाधिश्चात्र जडत्वम् । तथा हि ईश्वरज्ञानान्यत्वे प्रमेयत्वे च सत्यपि यदेव जडं स्तम्भादि तदेव स्वस्मादन्येन प्रकाश्यते । स्वप्रकाशे परमुखप्रेक्षित्वं हि जडस्य लक्षणम् । न च ज्ञानं जडस्वरूपम् । अतः साधनाव्यापकत्वं जडत्वस्य । साध्येन समव्याप्तिकत्वं चास्य स्पष्टमेव । जाड्यं विहाय स्वप्रकाशाभावस्य तं च त्यक्त्वा जाड्यस्य क्वचिदप्यदर्शनादिति ॥ यच्चोक्तं समुत्पन्नं हि ज्ञानमेकात्मसमवेतेत्यादि तदप्यसत्यम् । इत्थमर्थज्ञानतज्ज्ञानयोरुत्पद्यमानयोः क्रमानुपलक्षणात् । आशूत्पादात्क्रमानुपलक्षणमुत्पलपत्रशतव्यतिभेदवदिति चेत् तन्न।जिज्ञासाव्यवहितस्यार्थज्ञानस्योत्पादप्रतिपादनात् । न च ज्ञानानां जिज्ञासासमुत्पाद्यत्वं घटते । अजिज्ञासितेष्वपि योग्यदेशेषु विषयेषु तदुत्पादप्रतीतेः । न चार्थज्ञानमयोग्यदेशम् । आत्मसमवेतस्यास्य समुत्पादात्।इति जिज्ञासामन्तरेणैवार्थज्ञाने ज्ञानोत्पादप्रसङ्गः । अथोत्पद्यतां नामेदं को दोष इति चेत् तन्न । नन्वेवमेव तज्ज्ञानज्ञानेप्यपरज्ञानोत्पादप्रसङ्गः

तत्रापि चैवमेवायमित्यपरापरज्ञानोत्पादपरंपरायामेवात्मनो व्यापारान्न विषयान्तरसंचारः स्यादिति ॥ तस्माद्यज्ज्ञानं तदात्मबोधं प्रत्यनपेक्षितज्ञानान्तरव्यापारम् । यथा गोचरान्तरग्राहिज्ञानात्प्राग्भाविगोचरान्तरग्राहिधारावाहिज्ञानप्रबन्धस्यान्त्यज्ञानम् । ज्ञानं च विवादाध्यासितं रूपादिज्ञानमिति न ज्ञानस्य ज्ञानान्तरज्ञेयता युक्तिं सहत इति काव्यार्थः ॥ १२ ॥

अथ ये ब्रह्माद्वैतवादिनोऽविद्याऽपरपर्यायमायावशात्प्रतिभासमानत्वेन विश्वत्रयवर्तिवस्तुप्रपञ्चमपारमार्थिकं समर्थयन्ते तन्मतमुपहसन्नाह ।

माया सती चेद्द्वयतत्त्वसिद्धि-
रथासती हन्त कुतः प्रपञ्चः ।
मायैव चेदर्थसहा च तत्किं
माता च वन्ध्या च भवत्परेषाम् ॥ १३ ॥

तैर्वादिभिस्तात्त्विकात्मब्रह्मव्यतिरिक्ता या माया अविद्या प्रपञ्चहेतुः परिकल्पिता सा सद्रूपाऽसद्रूपा वा द्वयी गतिः । सती सद्रूपा चेत्तदा द्वयतत्त्वसिद्धिः । द्वाववयवौ यस्य तद्द्वयं तथाविधं यत्तत्त्वं परमार्थस्तस्य सिद्धिः । अयमर्थः । एकं तावत्त्वदभिमतं तात्त्विकमात्मब्रह्म द्वितीया च माया तत्त्वरूपा सद्रूपतयाङ्गीक्रियमाणत्वात् । तथा चाद्वैतवादस्य मूले निहितः कुठारः । अथेति पक्षान्तरद्योतने । यदि असती गगनाम्भोजवदवस्तुरूपा सा माया ततः । हन्तेत्युपदर्शने आश्चर्ये वा । कुतः प्रपञ्चः । अयं त्रिभुवनोदरविवरविवर्तिपदार्थसार्थरूपप्रपञ्चः कुतः । न कुतोपि संभवीत्यर्थः । मायाया अवस्तुत्वेनाभ्युपगमात् अवस्तुनश्च तुरङ्गशृङ्गस्येव सर्वोपा-

ख्याविरहितस्य साक्षात्क्रियमाणेदृशविवर्तजननेऽसमर्थत्वात् । किलेन्द्रजालादौ मृगतृष्णादौ वा मायोपदर्शितार्थानामर्थक्रियायामसामर्थ्यं दृष्टम् । अत्र तु तदुपलम्भात्कथं मायाव्यपदेशः श्रद्धीयताम् । अथ मायापि भविष्यति अर्थक्रियासमर्थपदार्थोपदर्शनक्षमा च भविष्यति इति चेत्तर्हि स्ववचनविरोधः । न हि भवति माता च वन्ध्या चेति । एनमेवार्थं हृदि निधायोत्तरार्धमाह । मायैव चेदित्यादि। अत्रैवकारोऽप्यर्थः।अपिश्च समुच्चयार्थः।अग्रेतनचकारश्च तथा। उभयोश्च समुच्चयार्थयोर्यौगपद्यद्योतकत्वं प्रतीतमेव। यथा रघुवंशे ते च प्रापुरुदन्वन्तं बुबुधे चादिपूरुषः इति । तदयं वाक्यार्थो माया च भविष्यति अर्थसहा च भविष्यति । अर्थसहा अर्थक्रियासमर्थपदार्थोपदर्शनक्षमा। चेच्छब्दोऽत्र योज्यते इति चेत् । एवं परमाशङ्क्य तस्य स्ववचनविरोधमुद्भावयति। तत्किं भवत्परेषां माता च वन्ध्या च । किमिति संभावने । संभाव्यते एतत् भवतो ये परे प्रतिपक्षास्तेषां भवत्परेषां भवद्व्यतिरिक्तानां भवदाज्ञापृथग्भूतत्वेन तेषां वादिनां यन्माता च भविष्यति वन्ध्या च भविष्यतीत्युपहासः। माता हि प्रसवधर्मिणी वनितोच्यते। वन्ध्या च तद्विपरीता। ततश्च वन्ध्या चेत्कथं माता माता चेत्कथं वन्ध्या। तदेवं मायाया अवास्तव्या अप्यर्थसहत्वेऽङ्गीक्रियमाणे प्रस्तुतवाक्यवत्स्पष्ट एव स्ववचनविरोधः। इति समासार्थः॥

व्यासार्थस्त्वयम्। ते वादिन इदं प्रणिगदन्ति। तात्त्विकमात्मब्रह्मैवास्ति।

सर्वं स्वल्विदं ब्रह्म नेह नानास्ति किंचन ।
आरामं तस्य पश्यन्ति न तत्पश्यति कश्चन ॥

इति समयात् । अयं तु प्रपञ्चो मिथ्यारूपः प्रतीयमानत्वात् यदेवं तदेवं यथा शुक्तिशकले कलधौतं तथा चायं तस्मात्तथा। तदेतद्वार्तम्। तथाहि । मिथ्यारूपत्वं तैः कीदृग्विवक्षितं किमत्यन्ता-

सत्त्वम् उतान्यस्यान्याकारतया प्रतीतत्वम् आहोस्विदनिर्वाच्यत्वम्। प्रथमपक्षेऽसत्ख्यातिप्रसङ्गः । द्वितीये विपरीतख्यातिस्वीकृतिः । तृतीये तु किमिदमनिर्वाच्यत्वम् । निःस्वभावत्वं चेन्निसः प्रतिषेधार्थत्वे स्वभावशब्दस्यापि भावाभावयोरन्यतरार्थत्वेऽसत्ख्यातिसत्ख्यात्यभ्युपगमप्रसङ्गः । भावप्रतिषेधेऽसत्ख्यातिरभावप्रतिषेधे सत्ख्यातिरिति। प्रतीत्यगोचरत्वं निःस्वभावत्वमिति चेदत्र विरोधः । स प्रपञ्चो हि न प्रतीयते चेत्कथं धर्मितयोपात्तः कथं च प्रतीयमानत्वं हेतुतयोपात्तं तथोपादाने वा कथं न प्रतीयते । यथा प्रतीयते न तथेति चेत् तर्हि विपरीतख्यातिरियमभ्युपगता स्यात् । किं चेयमनिर्वाच्यता प्रपञ्चस्य प्रत्यक्षबाधिता घटोयमित्याद्याकारं हि प्रत्यक्षं प्रपञ्चस्य सत्यतामेव व्यवस्यति । घटादिप्रतिनियतपदार्थपरिच्छेदात्मनस्तस्योत्पादात् । इतरेतरविविक्तवस्तूनामेव च प्रपञ्चशब्दवाच्यत्वात्। अथ प्रत्यक्षस्य विधायकत्वात्कथं प्रतिषेधे सामर्थ्यम्। प्रत्यक्षं हि इदमिति वस्तुस्वरूपं गृह्णाति नान्यत्स्वरूपं प्रतिषेधति ।

आहुर्विधातृ प्रत्यक्षं न निषेद्धृ विपश्चितः ।
नैकत्व आगमस्तेन प्रत्यक्षेण प्रबाध्यते ॥

इति वचनात् इति चेन्न । अन्यरूपनिषेधमन्तरेण तत्स्वरूपपरिच्छेदस्याप्यसंपत्तेः । पीतादिव्यवच्छिन्नं हि नीलं नीलमिति गृहीतं भवति नान्यथा । केवलवस्तुस्वरूपप्रतिपत्तेरेवान्यप्रतिषेधप्रतिपत्तिरूपत्वात् । मुण्डभूतलग्रहणे घटाभावग्रहणवत् । तस्माद्यथा प्रत्यक्षं विधायकं प्रतिपन्नं तथा निषेधकमपि प्रतिपत्तव्यम् । अपि च विधायकमेव प्रत्यक्षमित्यङ्गीकृते यथा प्रत्यक्षेण विद्या विधीयते तथा किं नाविद्यापीति । तथा च द्वैतापत्तिः । ततश्च सुव्यवस्थितः प्रपञ्चः । तदमी वादिनोऽविद्याविवेकेन सन्मात्रं प्रत्यक्षात्प्रतियन्तोपि न निषेधकं तदिति ब्रुवाणाः कथं नोन्मत्ता इति सिद्धं प्रत्यक्ष-

बाधितः पक्ष इति ॥ अनुमानबाधितश्च । प्रपञ्चो मिथ्या न भवति असद्विलक्षणत्वात् आत्मवत् । प्रतीयमानत्वं च हेतुर्ब्रह्मात्मना व्यभिचारी । स हि प्रतीयते न च मिथ्या । अप्रतीयमानत्वे त्वस्य तद्विषयवचसामप्रवृत्तेर्मूकतैव तेषां श्रेयसी । साध्यविकलश्च दृष्टान्तः। शुक्तिशकलकलधौतेपि प्रपञ्चान्तर्गतत्वेन अनिर्वचनीयतायाः साध्यमानत्वात् । किं चेदमनुमानं प्रपञ्चाद्भिन्नमभिन्नं वा । यदि भिन्नं तर्हि सत्यमसत्यं वा । यदि सत्यं तद्वदेव प्रपञ्चस्यापि सत्यत्वं स्यात् । अद्वैतवादप्राकारे खण्डिपातात् । अथासत्यं तर्हि न किंचित्तेन साधयितुं शक्यम् । अवस्तुत्वात् । अभिन्नं चेत् पञ्चस्वभावतया तस्यापि मिथ्यारूपत्वापत्तिः । मिथ्यारूपं च तत्कथं स्वसाध्यसाधनायालम् ॥ एवं च प्रपञ्चस्यापि मिथ्यारूपत्वासिद्धेः कथं परमब्रह्मणस्तात्त्विकत्वं स्याद्यतो बाह्यार्थाभावो भवेदिति ॥

अथवा प्रकारान्तरेण सन्मात्रलक्षणस्य परमब्रह्मणः साधनं दूषणं चोपन्यस्यते । ननु परमब्रह्मण एवैकस्य परमार्थसतो विधिरूपस्य विद्यमानत्वात्प्रमाणविषयत्वम् । अपरस्य द्वितीयस्य कस्यचिदप्यभावात् । तथा हि । प्रत्यक्षं तदावेदकमस्ति । प्रत्यक्षं द्विधा भिद्यते । निर्विकल्पकसविकल्पकभेदात् । ततश्च निर्विकल्पकप्रत्यक्षात्सन्मात्रविषयात्तस्यैकस्यैव सिद्धिः । तथाचोक्तम् ।

अस्ति ह्यालोचनाज्ञानं प्रथमं निर्विकल्पकम् ।
बालमूकादिविज्ञानसदृशं शुद्धवस्तुजम् ।

न च विधिवत्परस्परव्यावृत्तिरप्यध्यक्षत एव प्रतीयत इति द्वैतसिद्धिः । तस्य निषेधाविषयत्वात् । आहुर्विधातृ प्रत्यक्षं न निषेद्धृ इत्यादिवचनात् । यच्च सविकल्पकप्रत्यक्षं घटपटादिभेदसाधकं तदपि सत्तारूपेणान्वितानामेतेषां प्रकाशकत्वात् सत्ताऽद्वैतस्यैव साधकम् । सत्तायाश्च परमब्रह्मरूपत्वात् । तदुक्तं यदद्वैतं तद्ब्रह्मणो रूपमिति ॥

अनुमानादपि तत्सद्भावो विभाव्यत एव । तथा हि विधिरेव तत्त्वम् । प्रमेयत्वात् । यतः प्रमाणविषयभूतोऽर्थः प्रमेयः । प्रमाणानां च प्रत्यक्षानुमानागमोपमानार्थापत्तिसंज्ञकानां भावविषयत्वेनैव प्रवृत्तेः । तथा चोक्तम् ।

प्रत्यक्षाद्यवतारः स्याद्भावांशो गृह्यते यदा ।
व्यापारस्तदनुत्पत्तेरभावांशे जिघृक्षिते ॥

यच्चाभावाख्यं प्रमाणं तस्य प्रामाण्याभावान्न तत्प्रमाणम् । तद्विषयस्य कस्यचिदप्यभावात् । यस्तु प्रमाणपञ्चकविषयः स तु विधिरेव । तेनैव च प्रमेयत्वस्य व्याप्तत्वात् । सिद्धं प्रमेयत्वेन विधिरेव तत्त्वम् । यत्तु न विधिरूपं तन्न प्रमेयम् यथा खरविषाणम् । प्रमेयं चेदं निखिलं वस्तुतत्त्वम् । तस्माद्विधिरूपमेव । अतो वा तत्सिद्धिः । ग्रामारामादयः पदार्थाः प्रतिभासान्तःप्रविष्टाः । प्रतिभासमानत्वात् । यत्प्रतिभासते तत्प्रतिभासान्तःप्रविष्टं यथा प्रतिभासस्वरूपम् । प्रतिभासन्ते च ग्रामारामादयः पदार्थाः । तस्मात्प्रतिभासान्तःप्रविष्टाः ॥ आगमोऽपि परमब्रह्मण एव प्रतिपादकः समुपलभ्यते । पुरुष एवेदं सर्वं यद्भूतं यच्च भाव्यं उतामृतत्वस्येशानो यदन्नेनातिरोहति । यदेजति यन्नैजति । यद्दूरे यदन्तिके । यदन्तरस्य सर्वस्य यदुत सर्वस्यास्य बाह्यतः । इत्यादिः । श्रोतव्यो मन्तव्यो निदिध्यासितव्यः अनुमन्तव्य इत्यादिवेदवाक्यैरपि तत्सिद्धेः । कृत्रिमेणाप्यागमेन तस्यैव प्रतिपादनात् । उक्तं च ।

सर्वं वै खल्विदं ब्रह्म नेह नानास्ति किंचन ।
आरामं तस्य पश्यन्ति न तत्पश्यति कश्चन ॥

इति प्रमाणतस्तस्यैव सिद्धेः ॥ परमपुरुष एक एव तत्त्वम् । सकलभेदानां तद्विवर्तत्वात् । तथा हि सर्वे भावा ब्रह्मविवर्ताः । सत्त्वैकरूपेणान्वितत्वात् । यद्यद्रूपेणान्वितं तत्तदात्मकमेव यथा घटघटीशरावो-

दञ्चनादयो मृद्रूपेणैकेनान्विता मृद्विवर्ताः । सत्त्वैकरूपेणान्वितं च सकलं वस्तु । इति सिद्धं ब्रह्मविवर्तत्वं निखिलभेदानामिति ॥

तदेतत्सर्वं मदिरारसास्वादगद्गदोद्गदितमिवाभासते । विचारासहत्वात् । सर्वं हि वस्तु प्रमाणसिद्धं न तु वाङ्मात्रेण । अद्वैतमते च प्रमाणमेव नास्ति । तत्सद्भावे द्वैतप्रसङ्गात् । अद्वैतसाधकस्य प्रमाणस्य द्वितीयस्य सद्भावात् । अथ मतं लोकप्रत्यायनाय तदपेक्षया प्रमाणमप्यभ्युपगम्यते । तदसत् । त्वन्मते लोकस्यैवासंभवात् । एकस्यैव नित्यनिरंशस्य परब्रह्मण एव सत्त्वात् ॥ अथास्तु यथाकथंचित्प्रमाणमपि । तत्किं प्रत्यक्षमनुमानमागमो वा तत्साधकं प्रमाणमुररीक्रियते । न तावत्प्रत्यक्षम् । तस्य समस्तवस्तुजातगतभेदस्यैव प्रकाशकत्वात् । आबालगोपालं तस्यैव प्रतिभासनात् । यच्च निर्विकल्पकं प्रत्यक्षं तदावेदकमित्युक्तं तदपि न सम्यक् । तस्य प्रामाण्यानभ्युपगमात् । सर्वस्यापि प्रमाणतत्त्वस्य व्यवसायात्मकस्यैव विसंवादकत्वेन प्रामाण्योपपत्तेः । सविकल्पकेन तु प्रत्यक्षेण प्रमाणभूतेनैकस्यैव विधिरूपस्य परब्रह्मणः स्वप्नेऽप्यप्रतिभासनात् । यदप्युक्तम् आहुर्विधातृ प्रत्यक्षमित्यादि तदपि न पेशलम् । प्रत्यक्षेण ह्यनुवृत्तव्यावृत्ताकारात्मकवस्तुन एव प्रकाशनात् । एतच्च प्रागेव क्षुण्णम् । न ह्यनुस्यूतमेकमखण्डं सत्तामात्रं विशेषनिरपेक्षं सामान्यं प्रतिभासते येन यदद्वैतं तद्ब्रह्मणो रूपमित्याद्युक्तं शोभेत । विशेषनिरपेक्षस्य खरविषाणवदप्रतिभासनात् । तदुक्तम् ।

निर्विशेषं हि सामान्यं भवेत्खरविषाणवत् ।
सामान्यरहितत्वेन विशेषास्तद्वदेव हि ॥

ततः सिद्धे सामान्यविशेषात्मन्यर्थे प्रमाणविषये कुत एवैकस्य परब्रह्मणः प्रमाणविषयत्वम् ॥ यच्च प्रमेयत्वादित्वादित्यनुमानमुक्तं तदप्येतेनैवापास्तं बोद्धव्यम् । पक्षस्य प्रत्यक्षबाधितत्वेन हेतोः काला-

त्ययापदिष्टत्वात् । यच्च तत्सिद्धौ प्रतिभासमानत्वं साधनमुक्तं तदपि साधनाभासत्वेन न प्रकृतसाध्यसाधनायालम् । प्रतिभासमानत्वं हि निखिलभावानां स्वतः परतो वा । न तावत्स्वतः । घटपटमुकुटशकटादीनां स्वतः प्रतिभासमानत्वेनासिद्धेः । परतः प्रतिभासमानत्वं च परं विना नोपपद्यत इति । यच्च परमब्रह्मविवर्तवर्तित्वमखिलभेदानामित्युक्तं तदप्यन्वेत्रन्वीयमानद्वयाविनाभावित्वेन पुरुषाद्वैतं प्रतिबध्नात्येव । न च घटादीनां चैतन्यान्वयोप्यस्ति । मृदाद्यन्वयस्यैव तत्र दर्शनात् । ततो न किंचिदेतदपि । अतोनुमानादपि न तत्सिद्धिः । किं च पक्षहेतुदृष्टान्ता अनुमानोपायभूताः परस्परं भिन्ना अभिन्ना वा । भेदे द्वैतसिद्धिः । अभेदे त्वेकरूपतापत्तिः । तत्कथमेतेभ्योनुमानमात्मानमासादयति । यदि च हेतुमन्तरेणापि साध्यसिद्धिः स्यात्तर्हि द्वैतस्यापि वाङ्मात्रतः कथं न सिद्धिः । तदुक्तम् ।

हेतोरद्वैतसिद्धिश्चेद् द्वैतं स्याद्धेतुसाध्ययोः ।
हेतुना चेद्विना सिद्धिर्द्वैतं वाङ्मात्रतो न किम् ॥

पुरुष एवेदं सर्वमित्यादेः सर्वं वै खल्विदं ब्रह्मेत्यादेश्चागमादपि न तत्सिद्धिः । तस्यापि द्वैताविनाभावित्वेन अद्वैतं प्रति प्रामाण्यासंभवात् । वाच्यवाचकभावलक्षणस्य द्वैतस्यैव तत्रापि दर्शनात् । तदुक्तम् ।

कर्मद्वैतं फलद्वैतं लोकद्वैतं विरुध्यते ।
विद्याऽविद्याद्वयं न स्याद्बन्धमोक्षद्वयं तथा ॥

ततः कथमागमादपि तत्सिद्धिः ॥ ततो न पुरुषाद्वैतलक्षणमेकमेव प्रमाणस्य विषयः । इति सुव्यवस्थितः प्रपञ्चः । इति काव्यार्थः ॥ १३ ॥

अथ स्वाभिमतसामान्यविशेषोभयात्मकवाच्यवाचकभावसमर्थनपुरःसरं तीर्थान्तरीयप्रकल्पिततदेकान्तगोचरवाच्यवाचकभावनिरासद्वारेण तेषां प्रतिभावैभवाभावमाह ।

अनेकमेकात्मकमेव वाच्यं
द्वयात्मकं वाचकमप्यवश्यम् ।
अतोन्यथा वाचकवाच्यक्लृप्ता–
वतावकानां प्रतिभाप्रमादः ॥ १४ ॥

वाच्यमभिधेयं चेतनमचेतनं वस्तु । एवकारस्याप्यर्थत्वात् । सामान्यरूपतया एकात्मकमपि व्यक्तिभेदेनानेकम् अनेकरूपम् । अथ वाऽनेकरूपमप्येकात्मकमन्योन्यसंवलितत्वात् इत्थमपि व्याख्याने न दोषः । तथा वाचकमभिधायकं शब्दरूपं तदप्यवश्यं निश्चितं द्वयात्मकम् । सामान्यविशेषोभयात्मकत्वात् । एकानेकात्मकमित्यर्थः । उभयत्र वाच्यलिङ्गत्वेप्यव्यक्तत्वान्नपुंसकत्वम् । अवश्यमितिपदं वाच्यवाचकयोरुभयोरप्येकानेकात्मकत्वं निश्चिन्वत्तदेकान्तं व्यवच्छिनत्ति । अत उपदर्शितप्रकारादन्यथा सामान्यविशेषैकान्तरूपेण प्रकारेण । वाचकवाच्यक्लृप्तौ वाच्यवाचकभावकल्पनायाम् । अतावकानाम् अत्वदीयानाम् अन्ययूथ्यानाम् । प्रतिभाप्रमादः प्रज्ञास्खलितम् । इत्यक्षरार्थः ॥ अत्र चाल्पस्वरत्वेन वाच्यपदस्य प्राग्निपाते प्राप्तेपि यदादौ वाचकग्रहणं तत्प्रायोऽर्थप्रतिपादनस्य शब्दाधीनत्वेन वाचकस्यार्च्यत्वज्ञापनार्थम् । तथा च शाब्दिकाः ।

न सोस्ति प्रत्ययो लोके यः शब्दानुगमादृते ।
अनुविद्धमिव ज्ञानं सर्वं शब्देन भासते ॥

इति ॥

भावार्थस्त्वेवम् । एके तीर्थिकाः सामान्यरूपमेव वाच्यतया अभ्युपग-

च्छान्ति। ते च द्रव्यास्तिकनयानुपातिनो मीमांसकभेदा अद्वैतवादिनः सांख्याश्च। केचिच्च विशेषरूपमेव वाच्यं निर्वचन्ति। ते च पर्यायास्तिकनयानुसारिणः सौगताः। अपरे च परस्परानिरपेक्षपदार्थपृथग्भूतसामान्यविशेषयुक्तं वस्तु वाच्यत्वेन निश्चिन्वते। ते च नैगमनयानुगामिनः काणादा आक्षपादाश्च। एतच्च पक्षत्रयमपि किंचिच्चर्च्यते॥ तथा हि संग्रहनयावलम्बिनो वादिनः प्रतिपादयन्ति। सामान्यमेव तत्त्वम्। ततः पृथग्भूतानां विशेषाणामदर्शनात्। तथा सर्वमेकम्। अविशेषेण सदितिज्ञानाभिधानानुवृत्तिलिङ्गानुमितसत्ताकत्वात्। तथा द्रव्यत्वमेव तत्त्वम्। ततोऽर्थान्तरभूतानां धर्माधर्माकाशकालपुद्गलजीवद्रव्याणामनुपलब्धेः। किं च यैः सामान्यात्पृथग्भूता अन्योन्यव्यावृत्त्यात्मका विशेषाः कल्प्यन्ते तेषु विशेषत्वं विद्यते न वा। नो चेन्निःस्वभावताप्रसङ्गः। स्वरूपस्यैवाभावात्। अस्ति चेत्तर्हि तदेव सामान्यम्। यतः समानानां भावः सामान्यम्। विशेषरूपतया च सर्वेषां तेषामविशेषेण प्रतीतिः सिद्धैव। अपि च विशेषाणां व्यावृत्तिप्रत्ययहेतुत्वं लक्षणम्। व्यावृत्तिप्रत्यय एव विचार्यमाणो न घटते। व्यावृत्तिर्हि विवक्षितपदार्थे इतरपदार्थप्रतिषेधः। विवक्षितपदार्थश्च स्वस्वरूपव्यवस्थापनमात्रपर्यवसायी कथं पदार्थान्तरप्रतिषेधे प्रगल्भते। न च स्वरूपसत्त्वादन्यत्तत्र किमपि येन तन्निषेधः प्रवर्त्तते। तत्र च व्यावृत्तौ क्रियमाणायां स्वात्मव्यतिरिक्तविश्वत्रयवर्तिनोऽतीतवर्तमानानागताः पदार्थास्तस्माद्व्यावर्तनीयाः। ते च नाज्ञातस्वरूपा व्यावर्तयितुं शक्याः। ततश्चैकस्यापि विशेषस्य परिज्ञाने प्रमातुः सर्वज्ञत्वं स्यात्। न चैतत्प्रातीतिकं यौक्तिकं वा। व्यावृत्तिश्च निषेधः। स चाभावरूपत्वात्तुच्छः कथं प्रतीतिगोचरमञ्चति। खपुष्पवत्। तथा येभ्यो व्यावृत्तिस्ते असद्रूपा सद्रूपा वा। असद्रूपाश्चेत्तर्हि खरविषाणात्किं न व्यावृत्तिः। सद्रूपाश्चेत्सामान्यमेव। या चेयं व्यावृत्तिर्विशेषैः

क्रियते सा सर्वासु विशेषव्यक्तिष्वेका अनेका वा। अनेका चेत्तस्या अपि विशेषत्वापात्तिः। अनेकरूपत्वैकजीविततत्वाद्विशेषाणाम्। ततश्च तस्या अपि विशेषत्वान्यथानुपपत्तेर्व्यावृत्त्या भाव्यम्। व्यावृत्तेरपि च व्यावृत्तौ विशेषाणामभाव एव स्यात्। तत्स्वरूपभूताया व्यावृत्तेः प्रतिषिद्धत्वात्। अनवस्थापाताच्च। एका चेत्सामान्यमेव संज्ञान्तरेण प्रतिपन्नं स्यात्। अनुवृत्तिप्रत्ययलक्षणाव्यभिचारात्। किं चामी विशेषाः सामान्याद्भिन्ना अभिन्ना वा। भिन्नाश्चेन्मण्डूकजटाभारानुकाराः। अभिन्नार्थाश्चेत्तदेव तत्स्वरूपवत्। इति सामान्यैकान्तवादः॥ पर्यायनयान्वयिनस्तु भाषन्ते। विविक्ताः क्षणक्षयिणो विशेषा एव परमार्थः। ततो विष्वग्भूतस्य सामान्यस्याप्रतीयमानत्वात्। न हि गवादिव्यक्त्यनुभवकाले वर्णसंस्थानात्मकव्यक्तिरूपमपहायान्यत्किंचिदेकमनुयायि प्रतिभासते। तादृशस्यानुभवाभावात्। तथा च पठन्ति।

एतासु पञ्चस्ववभासिनीषु प्रत्यक्षबोधे स्फुटमङ्गुलीषु।
साधारणं रूपमवेक्षते यः शृङ्गं शिरस्यात्मन ईक्षते सः॥

एकाकारपरामर्शप्रत्ययस्तु स्वहेतुदत्तशक्तिभ्य एवोत्पद्यत इति न तेन सामान्यसाधनं न्याय्यम्। किं च यदिदं सामान्यं परिकल्प्यते तदेकमनेकं वा। एकमपि सर्वगतमसर्वगतं वा। सर्वगतं चेत्किं न व्यक्त्यन्तरालेषूपलभ्यते। सर्वगतैकत्वाभ्युपगमे च तस्य यथा गोत्वं सामान्यं गोव्यक्तीः क्रोडीकरोति एवं किं न घटपटादिव्यक्तीरपि। अविशेषात्। असर्वगतं चेद्विशेषरूपापत्तिरभ्युपगमबाधश्च। अथानेकम् गोत्वाश्वत्वघटत्वपटत्वादिभेदभिन्नत्वात् तर्हि विशेषा एव स्वीकृताः। अन्योन्यव्यावृत्तिहेतुत्वात्। न हि यद्गोत्वं तदश्वत्वात्मकमिति। अर्थक्रियाकारित्वं च वस्तुनो लक्षणम्। तच्च विशेषेष्वेव

स्फुटं प्रतीयते । न हि सामान्येन काचिदर्थक्रिया क्रियते । तस्य निष्क्रियत्वात्।वाहदोहादिकास्वर्थक्रियासु विशेषाणामेवोपयोगात्। तथेदं सामान्यं विशेषेभ्यो भिन्नमभिन्नं वा। भिन्नं चेदवस्तु। विशेषविश्लेषेणार्थक्रियाकारित्वाभावात् । अभिन्नं चेद्विशेषा एव तत्स्वरूपवत् । इति विशेषैकान्तवादः।। नैगमनयानुगामिनस्त्वाहुः। स्वतन्त्रौ सामान्यविशेषौ। तथैव प्रमाणेन प्रतीतत्वात् । तथा हि सामान्यविशेषावत्यन्तं भिन्नौ । विरुद्धधर्माध्यासितत्वात् । यावेवं तावेवं यथा पाथःपावकौ । तथा चैतौ । तस्मात्तथा । सामान्यं हि गोत्वादि सर्वगतं तद्विपरीताश्च शबलशाबलेयादयो विशेषाः । ततः कथमेषामैक्यं युक्तम् । न सामान्यात्पृथग्विशेषस्योपलम्भ इति चेत् कथं तर्हि तस्योपलम्भ इति वाच्यम्। सामान्यव्याप्तस्येति चेत् न तर्हि स विशेषोपलम्भः। सामान्यस्यापि तेन ग्रहणात्। ततश्च तेन बोधेन विविक्तविशेषग्रहणाभावात् तद्वाचकं ध्वनिं तत्साध्यं च व्यवहारं न प्रवर्तयेत्प्रमाता। न चैतदस्ति। विशेषाभिधानव्यवहारयोः प्रवृत्तिदर्शनात्। तस्माद्विशेषमभिलषता तत्र च व्यवहारं प्रवर्त्तयता तद्ग्राहको बोधो विविक्तोऽभ्युपगन्तव्यः । एवं सामान्यस्थाने विशेषशब्दं विशेषस्थाने च सामान्यशब्दं प्रयुञ्जानेन सामान्येपि तद्ग्राहके बोधो विविक्तोङ्गीकर्तव्यः । तस्मात्स्वस्वग्राहिणि ज्ञाने पृथक्प्रतिभासमानत्वाद्भावपीतरेतरविशकलितौ । ततो न सामान्यविशेषात्मकत्वं वस्तुतो घटते । इति स्वतन्त्रसामान्यविशेषवादः ।।

तदेतत्पक्षत्रयमपि न क्षमते क्षोदम्।प्रमाणबाधितत्वात् ।सामान्यविशेषोभयात्मकस्यैव वस्तुनो निर्विगानमनुभूयमानत्वात्। वस्तुनो हि लक्षणमर्थक्रियाकारित्वम्। त च्चानेकान्तवाद एवाविकलं कलयन्ति परीक्षकाः। तथा हि यथा गौरित्युक्त खुरककुत्सास्नालाङ्गूलविशाणाद्यवयवसंपन्नं वस्तुस्वरूपं सर्वव्यक्त्यनुयायि प्रतीयते तथा महि-

ष्यादिव्यावृत्तिरपि प्रतीयते। यत्रापि च शबला गौरित्युच्यते तत्रापि यथा विशेषप्रतिभासस्तथा गोत्वप्रतिभासोपि स्फुट एव। शबलेतिकेवलविशेषणोच्चारणेपि अर्थात्प्रकरणाद्वा गोत्वमनुवर्त्तते । अपि च शबलत्वमपि नानारूपम्। तथा दर्शनात्। ततो वक्त्रा शबलेत्युक्ते क्रोडीकृतसकलशबलसामान्यं विवक्षितगोव्यक्तिगतमेव शबलत्वं व्यवस्थाप्यते । तदेवमाबालगोपालं प्रतीतिप्रसिद्धेपि वस्तुनः सामान्यविशेषात्मकत्वे तदुभयैकान्तवादः प्रलापमात्रम् । न हि क्वचित्कदाचित्केनचित्सामान्यं विशेषविनाकृतमनुभूयते विशेषा वा तद्विनाकृताः। केवलं दुर्नयप्रभावितमतिव्यामोहवशादेकमपलप्याऽन्यतरद्व्यवस्थापयन्ति बालिशाः। सोयमन्धगजन्यायः ॥ येपि च तदेकान्तपक्षोपनिपातिनः प्रागुक्ता दोषास्तेपि अनेकान्तवादप्रचण्डमुद्गरजर्जरितत्वान्नोच्छ्वसितुमपि क्षमाः ॥ स्वतन्त्रसामान्यविशेषवादिनस्त्वेवं प्रतिक्षेप्याः। सामान्यं प्रतिव्यक्ति कथंचिद्भिन्नम् । कथंचिदभिन्नम् । कथंचित्तदात्मकत्वाद्। विसदृशपरिणामवत्। यथैव हि काचिद्व्यक्तिरुपलभ्यमानाद्व्यक्त्यन्तराद्विशिष्टा विसदृशपरिणामदर्शनादवतिष्ठते तथा सदृशपरिणामात्मकसामान्यदर्शनात्समानेति। तेन समानो गौरयम्। सोऽनेन समान इति प्रतीतेः। न चास्य व्यक्तिस्वरूपादभिन्नत्वात्सामान्यरूपताव्याघातः। यतो रूपादीनामपि व्यक्तिस्वरूपादभिन्नत्वमस्ति न चैतेषां गुणरूपताव्याघातः। कथंचिद्व्यतिरेकस्तु रूपादीनामिव सदृशपरिणामस्याप्यस्त्येव। पृथग्व्यपदेशादिभाक्त्वात्। विशेषा अपि नैकान्तेन सामान्यात्पृथग्भवितुमर्हन्ति । यतो यदि सामान्यं सर्वगतं सिद्धं भवेत् तदा तेषामसर्वगतत्वेन ततो विरुद्धधर्माध्यासः स्यात्। न च तस्य तात्सिद्धम्। प्रागुक्तयुक्त्या निराकृतत्वात्। सामान्यस्य विशेषाणां च कथंचित्परस्पराव्यतिरेकेणैकानेकरूपतया व्यवस्थितत्वात्। विशेषेभ्योऽव्यतिरिक्तत्वाद्धि सामान्यमप्य-

नेकमिष्यते सामान्यात्तु विशेषाणामव्यतिरेकात्तेप्येकरूपा इति ॥ एकत्वं च सामान्यस्य संग्रहनयार्पणात्सर्वत्र विज्ञेयम् । प्रमाणार्पणात्तस्य कथंचिद्विरुद्धधर्माध्यासितत्वम् । सदृशपरिणामरूपस्य विसदृशपरिणामवत् कथंचित्प्रतिव्यक्ति भेदात् । एवं चासिद्धं सामान्यविशेषयोः सर्वथाविरुद्धधर्माध्यासितत्वम् । कथंचिद्विरुद्धधर्माध्यासितत्वं चेद्विवक्षितं तदास्मत्कक्षाप्रवेशः। कथंचिद्विरुद्धधर्माध्यासस्य कथंचिद्भेदाविनाभूतत्वात्। पाथःपावकदृष्टान्तोपि साध्यसाधनविकलः। तयोरपि कथंचिदेव विरुद्धधर्माध्यासितत्वेन भिन्नत्वेन च स्वीकरणात्। पयस्त्वपावकत्वादिना हि तयोर्विरुद्धधर्माध्यासो भेदश्च। द्रव्यत्वादिना पुनस्तद्वैपरीत्यमिति। तथा च कथं न सामान्यविशेषात्मकत्वं वस्तुनो घटत इति ॥ ततः सुष्ठूक्तं वाच्यमेकमनेकरूपमिति ॥

एवं वाचकमपि शब्दाख्यं द्वयात्मकम् सामान्यविशेषात्मकम्। सर्वशब्दव्यक्तिष्वनुयायि शब्दत्वमेकं शाङ्खशार्ङ्गतीव्रमन्दोदात्तानुदात्तस्वरितादिविशेषभेदादनेकम् । शब्दस्य हि सामान्यविशेषात्मकत्वं पौद्गलिकत्वाद्व्यक्तमेव। तथाहि पौद्गलिकः शब्दः। इन्द्रियार्थत्वात्। रूपादिवत्। यच्चास्य पौद्गलिकत्वनिषेधाय स्पर्शशून्याश्रयत्वात् अतिनिबिडप्रदेशे प्रवेशनिर्गमयोरप्रतिघातात् पूर्वं पश्चाच्चावयवानुपलब्धेः सूक्ष्ममूर्तद्रव्यान्तराप्रेरकत्वात् गगनगुणत्वाच्चेति पञ्चहेतवो यौगैरुपन्यस्तास्ते हेत्वाभासाः। तथा हि शब्दपर्यायस्याश्रयो भाषावर्गणा न पुनराकाशम्। तत्र च स्पर्शो निर्णीयत एव । यथा शब्दाश्रयः स्पर्शवान् । अनुवातप्रतिवातयोर्विप्रकृष्टनिकटशरीरिणोपलभ्यमानानुपलभ्यमानेन्द्रियार्थत्वात् । तथाविधगन्धाधारद्रव्यपरमाणुवत्। इत्यसिद्धः प्रथमः । द्वितीयस्तु गन्धद्रव्येण व्यभिचारादनैकान्तिकः। वर्त्यमानजात्यकस्तूरिकादिगन्धद्रव्यं हि पिहितद्वारापवरकस्यान्तर्विशति बहिश्च निर्याति न चापौद्गलिकम्।अथ तत्र सूक्ष्मरन्ध्र-

संभवान्नातिनिबिडत्वमतस्तत्र तत्प्रवेशनिष्क्रमौ । कथमन्यथोद्घाटितद्वारावस्थायामिव न तदेकार्णवत्वम् । सर्वथा नीरन्ध्रे तु प्रदेशे न तयोः संभव इति चेत् तर्हि शब्देऽप्येतत्समानमित्यसिद्धो हेतुः । तृतीयस्तु तडिल्लतोल्कादिभिरनैकान्तिकः । चतुर्थोऽपि तथैव । गन्धद्रव्यविशेषसूक्ष्मरजोधूमादिभिर्व्यभिचारात् । न हि गन्धद्रव्यादिकमपि नासायां निविशमानं तद्विवरद्वारदेशोद्भिन्नश्मश्रुप्रेरकं दृश्यते । पञ्चमः पुनरसिद्धः । तथाहि न गगनगुणः शब्दः । अस्मदादिप्रत्यक्षत्वात् । रूपादिवत् । इति सिद्धः पौद्गलिकत्वात्सामान्यविशेषात्मकः शब्द इति ॥ न च वाच्यम् आत्मन्यपौद्गलिकेऽपि कथं सामान्यविशेषात्मकत्वं निर्विवादमनुभूयत इति । यतः संसार्यात्मनः प्रतिप्रदेशमनन्तानन्तकर्मपरमाणुभिः सह वह्नितापितघनकुट्टितनिर्विभागपिण्डीभूतसूचीकलापवत् लोलीभावमापन्नस्य कथंचित्पौद्गलिकत्वाभ्यनुज्ञानादिति । यद्यपि स्याद्वादवादिनां पौद्गलिकमपौद्गलिकं च सर्वं वस्तु सामान्यविशेषात्मकं तथाप्यपौद्गलिकेषु धर्माधर्माकाशकालेषु तदात्मकत्वमर्वाग्दृशां न तथाप्रतीतिविषयमायातीति पौद्गलिकेषु पुनस्तत्साध्यमानं तेषां सुश्रद्धानमित्यप्रस्तुतमपि शब्दस्य पौद्गलिकत्वमत्र सामान्यविशेषात्मकत्वसाधनायोपन्यस्तमिति । अत्रापि नित्यशब्दवादिसंमतः शब्दैकत्वैकान्तोऽनित्यशब्दवाद्यभिमतः शब्दानेकत्वैकान्तश्च प्राग्दर्शितदिशा प्रतिक्षेप्यः । अथवा वाच्यस्य घटादेरर्थस्य सामान्यविशेषात्मकत्वे तद्वाचकस्य ध्वनेरपि तत्त्वम् । शब्दार्थयोः कथंचित्तादात्म्याभ्युपगमात् । यदाहुर्भद्रबाहुस्वामिपादाः ।

अभिहाणं अभिहेयाउ होइ भिण्णं अभिण्णं च ।
खुरअग्गिमोयगुच्चारणम्मि जम्हा उ वयणसवणाणं ॥
नवि छेओ नवि दाहो न पूरणं तेण भिन्नं तु ।

जम्हा य मोयगुच्चारणम्मि तत्थेव पच्चओ होइ ॥
न य होइ स अन्नत्थे तेण अभिन्नं तदत्थाओ ।

एतेन

विकल्पयोनयः शब्दा विकल्पाः शब्दयोनयः ।
कार्यकारणता तेषां नार्थं शब्दाः स्पृशन्त्यपि ॥

इति प्रत्युक्तम् । अर्थाभिधानप्रत्ययास्तुल्यनामधेया इति वचनात् । शब्दस्य ह्येतदेव तत्त्वं यदभिधेयं याथात्म्येनासौ प्रतिपादयति । स च तत्तथाप्रतिपादयन् वाच्यस्वरूपपरिणामपरिणत एव वक्तुं शक्तो नान्यथा । अतिप्रसङ्गात् । घटाभिधानकाले पटाद्यभिधानस्य प्राप्तेरिति ॥

अथवा भङ्ग्यन्तरेण सकलं काव्यमिदं व्याख्यायते । वाच्यं वस्तु घटादिकम् । एकात्मकमेव एकरूपमेव सत् अनेकम् अनेकस्वरूपम् । अयमर्थः । प्रमाता तावत्प्रमेयं लक्षणेन निश्चिनोति । तच्च सजातीयविजातीयव्यवच्छेदादात्मलाभं लभते । यथा घटस्य सजातीया मृन्मयपदार्था विजातीयाश्च पटादयः । तेषां व्यवच्छेदस्तल्लक्षणम् । पृथुबुध्नोदराद्याकारः कम्बुग्रीवो जलधारणादिक्रियासमर्थः पदार्थविशेषो घट इत्युच्यते । तेषां च सजातीयानां स्वरूपं तत्र बुद्ध्यारोप्य व्यवच्छिद्यते । अन्यथा प्रतिनियततत्स्वरूपपरिच्छेदानुपपत्तेः । सर्वभावानां हि भावाभावात्मकं स्वरूपम् । एकान्तभावात्मकत्वे वस्तुनो वैस्वरूप्यं स्यात् । एकान्ताभावात्मकत्वे च निःस्वभावता स्यात् । तस्मात्स्वरूपेण सत्त्वात्पररूपेण चासत्त्वाद्भावाभावात्मकं वस्तु । यदाह ।

सर्वमस्ति स्वरूपेण पररूपेण नास्ति च ।
अन्यथा सर्वसत्त्वं स्यात्स्वरूपस्याप्यसंभवः ॥

ततश्चैकस्मिन् घटे सर्वेषां घटव्यतिरिक्तपदार्थानामभावरूपेण वृत्तेर-

नेकात्मकत्वं घटस्य सूपपादम् । एवं चैकस्मिन्नर्थे ज्ञाते सर्वेषामर्थानां ज्ञानम् । सर्वपदार्थपरिच्छेदमन्तरेण तन्निषेधात्मन एकस्य वस्तुनो विविक्ततया परिच्छेदासंभवात्।आगमोऽप्येवमेव व्यवस्थितः।

जे एगं जाणइ से सव्वं जाणइ । जे सव्वं जाणइ से एगं जाणइ ।

तथा

एको भावः सर्वथा येन दृष्टः सर्वे भावाः सर्वथा तेन दृष्टाः ।
सर्वे भावाः सर्वथा येन दृष्टा एको भावः सर्वथा तेन दृष्टः ॥

ये तु सौगताः परासत्त्वं नाङ्गीकुर्वते तेषां घटादेः सर्वात्मकत्वप्रसङ्गः।तथा हि यथा घटस्य स्वरूपादिनापि सत्त्वं तथा यदि पररूपादिनापि स्यात् तथा च सति स्वरूपादिसत्त्ववत्पररूपादिसत्त्वप्रसक्तेः कथं न सर्वात्मकत्वं भवेत् । परासत्त्वेन तु प्रतिनियतोऽसौ सिध्यति। अथ न नाम नास्ति परासत्त्वं किं तु स्वसत्त्वमेव तादिति चेत् अहो वैदग्धी।न खलु यदेव सत्त्वं तदेवासत्त्वं भवितुमर्हति। विधिप्रतिषेधरूपतया विरुद्धधर्माध्यासेनानयोरैक्यायोगात् । अथ युष्मत्पक्षेऽप्येवं विरोधस्तदवस्थ एवेति चेत् अहो वाचाटता देवानां प्रियस्य । न हि वयं येनैव प्रकारेण सत्त्वं तेनैवासत्त्वं येनैवासत्त्वं तेनैव सत्त्वमभ्युपेमः किं तु स्वरूपद्रव्यक्षेत्रकालभावैः सत्त्वं पररूपद्रव्यक्षेत्रकालभावैस्त्वसत्त्वम् तदा क्व विरोधावकाशः॥यौगास्तु प्रगल्भन्ते सर्वथापृथग्भूतपरस्पराभावाभ्युपगममात्रेणैव पदार्थप्रतिनियमसिद्धेः किं तेषामसत्त्वात्मकत्वकल्पनयेति । तदसत् । यदा हि पटाद्यभावरूपो घटो न भवति तदा घटो घटादिरेव स्यात् यथा च घटाभावाद्भिन्नत्वाद् घटस्य घटरूपता तथा पटादेरपि स्याद् । घटाभावाद्भिन्नत्वादेव । इत्यलं विस्तरेण ॥ एवं वाचकमपि शब्दरूपं द्वयात्मकम् । एकात्मकमपि सदनेकमित्यर्थः । यथोक्तन्यायेन शब्दस्यापि भावाभावात्मकत्वात् । अथ वा एकविषयस्यापि वाचक-

स्यानेकविषयत्वोपपत्तेः । यथा किल घटशब्दः संकेतवशात्पृथुबुध्नोदराद्याकारवति पदार्थे प्रवर्तते वाचकतया तथा देशकालाद्यपेक्षया तद्वशादेव पदार्थान्तरेष्वपि च तथा प्रवर्तमानः केन वार्यते । भवन्ति हि वक्तारो योगिनः शरीरं प्रति घट इति । संकेतानां पुरुषेच्छाधीनतयाऽनियतत्वात् । तथा चौरशब्दोन्यत्र तस्करे रूढोपि दाक्षिणात्यानामोदने प्रसिद्धः । यथा च कुमारशब्दः पूर्वदेशे आश्विनमासे रूढः । एवं कर्कटिशब्दादयोपि तत्तद्देशापेक्षया योन्यादिवाचका ज्ञेयाः । कालापेक्षया पुनर्यथा जैनानां प्रायश्चित्तविधौ धृतिश्रद्धासंहननादिमति प्राचीनकाले षड्गुरुशब्देन शतमशीत्यधिकमुपवासानामुच्यते स्म सांप्रतकाले तु तद्विपरीते तेनैव षड्गुरुशब्देनोपवासत्रयमेव संकेत्यते जीतकल्पव्यवहारानुसारात् । शास्त्रापेक्षया तु यथा पुराणेषु द्वादशीशब्देनैकादशी त्रिपुरार्णवे चालिशब्देन मदिराभिषक्तं मैथुनशब्देन मधुसर्पिषोर्ग्रहणमित्यादि । न चैवं सङ्केतस्यैवार्थप्रत्यायने प्राधान्यम् । स्वाभाविकसामर्थ्यसाचिव्यादेव तस्य तत्र प्रवृत्तेः । सर्वशब्दानां सर्वार्थप्रत्यायनशक्तियुक्तत्वाद्यत्र च देशकालादौ पदार्थप्रतिपादनशक्तिसहकारी सङ्केतस्तत्र तमर्थं प्रतिपादयति । तथा च निर्जितदुर्जयपरप्रवादाः श्रीदेवसूरिपादाः । स्वाभाविकसामर्थ्यसमयाभ्यामर्थबोधनिबन्धनं शब्दः । अत्र शक्तिपदार्थसमर्थनं ग्रन्थान्तरादवसेयम्॥अतोऽन्यथेत्यादि उत्तरार्द्धं पूर्ववत् । प्रतिभाप्रमादस्तु तेषां सदसदेकान्ते वाच्यस्य प्रतिनियतार्थविषयत्वे च वाचकस्योक्तयुक्त्या दोषसद्भावाद् व्यवहारानुपपत्तेः ॥ तदयं समुदायार्थः । सामान्यविशेषात्मकस्य भावाभावात्मकस्य च वस्तुनः सामान्यविशेषात्मको भावाभावात्मकश्च ध्वनिर्वाचक इति । अन्यथा प्रकारान्तरैः पुनर्वाच्यवाचकभावव्यवस्थामातिष्ठमानानां प्रतिभैव प्रमाद्याति न

तु तद्भणितयो युक्तिस्पर्शमात्रमपि सहन्ते । कानि तानि वाच्यवाचकभावप्रकारान्तराणि परवादिनामिति चेदेते ब्रूमः । अपोह एव शब्दार्थ इत्येके ।

अपोहः शब्दलिङ्गाभ्यां न वस्तुविधिनोच्यते ॥

इति वचनात् । अपरे च सामान्यमात्रमेव शब्दानां गोचरः । तस्य क्वचित्प्रतिपन्नस्यैकरूपतया सर्वत्र संकेतविषयतोपपत्तेः । न पुनर्विशेषाः। तेषामानन्त्यतः कार्त्स्न्येनोपलब्धुमशक्यतया तद्विषयतानुपपत्तेः । विधिवादिनस्तु विधिरेव वाक्यार्थोऽप्रवृत्तप्रवर्तनस्वभावत्वात्तस्येत्याचक्षते । विधिरपि तत्तद्वादिविप्रतिपत्त्याऽनेकप्रकारः । तथाहि वाक्यरूपः शब्द एव प्रवर्तकत्वाद्विधिरित्येके । तद्व्यापारो भावनापरपर्यायो विधिरित्यन्ये । नियोग इत्यपरे । प्रैषादय इत्येके । तिरस्कृततदुपाधिप्रवर्तनामात्रमित्यन्ये । एवं फलतदभिलाषकर्मादयोपि वाच्याः । एतेषां निराकरणं सपूर्वोत्तरपक्षं न्यायकुमुदचन्द्रादवसेयमिति काव्यार्थः ॥ १४ ॥

इदानीं सांख्याभिमतप्रकृतिपुरुषादितत्त्वानां विरोधावरुद्धत्वं ख्यापयन् तद्बालिशताविलसितानामपरिमितत्वं दर्शयति ।

चिदर्थशून्या च जडा च बुद्धिः
शब्दादितन्मात्रजमम्बरादि ।
न बन्धमोक्षौ पुरुषस्य चेति
कियज्जडैर्न ग्रथितं विरोधि ॥ १५ ॥

चित् चैतन्यशक्तिरात्मस्वरूपभूता अर्थशून्या विषयपरिच्छेदविरहिता अर्थाध्यवसायस्य बुद्धिव्यापारत्वादित्येका कल्पना । बुद्धिश्च महत्तत्त्वाख्या जडानवबोधरूपा इति द्वितीया । अम्बरादि व्योमप्रभृति भूतपञ्चकं शब्दादितन्मात्रजम् शब्दादीनि पञ्चतन्मा-

त्राणि सूक्ष्मसंज्ञानि तेभ्यो जातमुत्पन्नं शब्दादितन्मात्रजम् इति तृतीया। अत्र चशब्दो गम्यः। पुरुषस्य च प्रकृतिविकृत्यनात्मकस्यात्मनो न बन्धमोक्षौ किं तु प्रकृतेरेव। तथा च कापिलाः।

तस्मान्न बध्यते नापि मुच्यते नापि संसरति कश्चित्।
संसरति बध्यते मुच्यते च नानाश्रया प्रकृतिः॥

तत्र बन्धः प्राकृतिकादिः। मोक्षः पञ्चविंशतितत्त्वज्ञानपूर्वकोऽपवर्ग इति चतुर्थी। इतिशब्दस्य प्रकारार्थत्वादेवंप्रकारमन्यदपि। विरोधीति विरुद्धं पूर्वापरविरोधादिदोषाघ्रातम्। जडैर्मूर्खैस्तत्त्वावबोधविधुरधीभिः कापिलैः कियन्न ग्रथितं कियन्न स्वशास्त्रेषूपनिबद्धम्। कियदित्यसूयागर्भम्। तत्प्ररूपितविरुद्धार्थानामानन्त्येनेयत्ताऽनवधारणात्। इति संक्षेपार्थः॥

व्यासार्थस्त्वयम्। सांख्यमते किल दुःखत्रयाभिहतस्य पुरुषस्य तदपघातहेतुतत्त्वजिज्ञासा उत्पद्यते। आध्यात्मिकमाधिदैविकमाधिभौतिकं चेति दुःखत्रयम्। तत्राध्यात्मिकं द्विविधं शारीरं मानसं च। शारीरं वातपित्तश्लेष्मणां वैषम्यनिमित्तम्। मानसं कामक्रोधलोभमोहेर्ष्याविषयादर्शननिबन्धनम्। सर्वं चैतदान्तरोपायसाध्यत्वादाध्यात्मिकं दुःखम्। बाह्योपायसाध्यं दुःखं द्वेधा आधिभौतिकमाधिदैविकंचेति। तत्राधिभौतिकं मानुषपशुपक्षिमृगसरीसृपस्थावरनिमित्तम्। आधिदैविकं यक्षराक्षसग्रहाद्यावेशहेतुकम्। अनेन दुःखत्रयेण रजःपरिणामभेदेन बुद्धिवर्तिना चेतनाशक्तेः प्रतिकूलतयाऽभिसंबन्धः अभिघातः। तत्त्वानि च पञ्चविंशतिः। तद्यथा अव्यक्तमेकं महदहंकारपञ्चतन्मात्रैकादशेन्द्रियपञ्चमहाभूतभेदात् त्रयोविंशतिविधं व्यक्तं पुरुषश्चिद्रूप इति। तथा चेश्वरकृष्णः।

मूलप्रकृतिरविकृतिर्महदाद्याः प्रकृतिविकृतयः सप्त।
षोडशकस्तु विकारो न प्रकृतिर्न विकृतिः पुरुषः॥

प्रीत्यप्रीतिविषादात्मकानां लाघवोपष्टम्भगौरवधर्माणां परस्परोपकारिणां त्रयाणां गुणानां सत्त्वरजस्तमसा साम्यावस्था प्रकृतिः । प्रधानमव्यक्तमित्यनर्थान्तरम् । तच्चानादिमध्यान्तमनवयवं साधारणमशब्दमस्पर्शमरूपमरसमगन्धमव्ययम् । प्रधानाद्बुद्धिर्महदित्यपरपर्यायोत्पद्यते । योऽयमध्यवसायो गवादिषु प्रतिपत्तिः एवमेतत् नान्यथा गौरेवायं नाश्वः स्थाणुरेष नायं पुरुष इत्येषा बुद्धिः । तस्यास्त्वष्टौ रूपाणि धर्मज्ञानवैराग्यैश्वर्यरूपाणि चत्वारि सात्त्विकानि अधर्मादीनि तु तत्प्रतिपक्षभूतानि चत्वारि तामसानि । बुद्धेरहंकारः । स चाभिमानात्मकः । अहं शब्देऽहं स्पर्शेऽहं रूपेऽहं गन्धेऽहं रसेऽहं स्वामी अहमीश्वरः असौ मया हतः ससत्त्वोहममुं हनिष्यामि इत्यादिप्रत्ययरूपः । तस्मात्पञ्चतन्मात्राणि शब्दतन्मात्रादीन्यविशेषरूपाणि सूक्ष्मपर्यायवाच्यानि । शब्दतन्मात्राद्धि शब्द एवोपलभ्यते न पुनरुदात्तानुदात्तस्वरितकम्पितषड्जादिभेदाः । षड्जादयः शब्दविशेषादुपलभ्यन्ते । एवं स्पर्शरूपरसगन्धतन्मात्रेष्वपि योजनीयमिति । तत एव चाहङ्कारादेकादशेन्द्रियाणि च । तत्र चक्षुः श्रोत्रं घ्राणं रसनं त्वगिति पञ्चबुद्धीन्द्रियाणि वाक्पाणिपादपायूपस्थाः पञ्च कर्मेन्द्रियाणि एकादशं मन इति । पञ्चतन्मात्रेभ्यश्च पञ्चमहाभूतानि उत्पद्यन्ते । तद्यथा शब्दतन्मात्रादाकाशं शब्दगुणं शब्दतन्मात्रसहितात्स्पर्शतन्मात्राद्वायुः शब्दस्पर्शगुणः शब्दस्पर्शतन्मात्रसहिताद्रूपतन्मात्रात्तेजः शब्दस्पर्शरूपगुणं शब्दस्पर्शरूपतन्मात्रसहिताद्रसतन्मात्रादापः शब्दस्पर्शरूपरसगुणाः शब्दस्पर्शरूपरसतन्मात्रसहिताद्गन्धतन्मात्रात् शब्दस्पर्शरूपरसगन्धगुणा पृथ्वी जायत इति । पुरुषस्तु—

अमूर्तश्चेतनो भोगी नित्यः सर्वगतोऽक्रियः ।
अकर्ता निर्गुणः सूक्ष्म आत्मा कापिलदर्शने ॥

इति । अन्धपङ्गुवत् प्रकृतिपुरुषयोः संयोगः । चिच्छक्तिश्च विषयपरिच्छेदशून्या । यत इन्द्रियद्वारेण सुखदुःखादयो विषया बुद्धौ प्रतिसंक्रामन्ति बुद्धिश्चोभयमुखदर्पणाकारा ततस्तस्यां चैतन्यशक्तिः प्रतिबिम्बते । ततः सुख्यहं दुःख्यहम् इत्युपचारः । आत्मा हि स्वं बुद्धेरव्यतिरिक्तमभिमन्यते । आह च पतञ्जलिः । शुद्धोपि पुरुषः प्रत्ययं बौद्धमनुपश्यति तमनुपश्यन्नतदात्मापि तदात्मक इव प्रतिभासते इति । मुख्यतस्तु बुद्धेरेव विषयपरिच्छेदः । तथा च वाचस्पतिः । सर्वो व्यवहर्ता आलोच्य नन्वहमत्राधिकृत इत्यभिमत्य कर्तव्यमेतन्मयेति अध्यवस्यति ततश्च प्रवर्त्तत इति लोकतः सिद्धम् । तत्र कर्तव्यमिति योयं निश्चयश्चितिसन्निधानापन्नचैतन्याया बुद्धेः सोध्यवसायो बुद्धेरसाधारणो व्यापार इति । चिच्छक्तिसन्निधानाच्चाचेतनापि बुद्धिश्चेतनावतीवाभासते । वादमहार्णवोप्याह । बुद्धिदर्पणसंक्रान्तमर्थप्रतिबिम्बकं द्वितीयदर्पणकल्पे पुंस्यध्यारोहति तदेव भोक्तृत्वमस्य नत्वात्मनो विकारापत्तिः इति । तथा चासुरिः ।

विविक्ते दृक्परिणतौ बुद्धौ भोगोस्य कथ्यते ।
प्रतिबिम्बोदयः स्वच्छे यथा चन्द्रमसोम्भसि ॥

विन्ध्यवासी त्वेवं भोगमाचष्टे ।

पुरुषोऽविकृतात्मैव स्वनिर्भासमचेतनम् ।
मनः करोति सांनिध्यादुपाधिः स्फटिकं यथा ॥

न च वक्तव्यं पुरुषश्चेदगुणोऽपरिणामी कथमस्य मोक्षः । मुचेर्बन्धनविश्लेषार्थत्वात्सवासनक्लेशकर्माशयानां च बन्धनसमाम्नातानां पुरुषेऽपरिणामिन्यसंभवात् । अत एव नास्य प्रेत्यभावापरनामा संसारोस्ति निष्क्रियत्वादिति । यतः प्रकृतिरेव नानापुरुषाश्रया सती बध्यते संसरति मुच्यते च न पुरुष इति बन्ध-

मोक्षसंसाराः पुरुषे उपचर्यन्ते । यथा जयपराजयौ भृत्यगतावपि स्वामिन्युपचर्येते तत्फलस्य कोशलाभादेः स्वामिनि संबन्धात् तथा भोगापवर्गयोः प्रकृतिगतयोरपि विवेकाग्रहात्पुरुषे संबन्ध इति ॥

तदेतदखिलमालजालम् । चिच्छक्तिश्च विषयपरिच्छेदशून्या चेति परस्परविरुद्धं वचः । चिती संज्ञाने । चेतनं चित्यते वानयेति चित् । सा चेत्स्वपरपरिच्छेदात्मिका नेष्यते तदा चिच्छक्तिरेव सा न स्याद् । घटवत् । न चामूर्तायाश्चिच्छक्तेर्बुद्धौ प्रतिबिम्बोदयो युक्तः । तस्य मूर्तधर्मत्वात् । न च तथा परिणाममन्तरेण प्रतिसंक्रमोपि युक्तः । कथंचित्सक्रियाकताव्यतिरेकेण प्रकृत्युपधानेप्यन्यथात्वानुपपत्तेः । अप्रच्युतप्राचीनरूपस्य च सुखदुःखादिभोगव्यपदेशानर्हत्वात् । तत्प्रच्यवे च प्राक्तनरूपत्यागेनोत्तररूपाध्यासिततया सक्रियत्वापत्तिः । स्फटिकादावपि तथा परिणामेनैव प्रतिबिम्बोदयसमर्थनात् । अन्यथा कथमन्धोपलादौ न प्रतिबिम्बः । तथा परिणामाभ्युपगमे च बलादायातं चिच्छक्तेः कर्तृत्वं साक्षाद्भोक्तृत्वं च । अथ अपरिणामिनी भोक्तृशक्तिरप्रतिसंक्रमा च परिणामिन्यर्थे प्रतिसंक्रातेव तद्वृत्तिमनुभवतीति पतञ्जलिवचनादौपचारिक एवायं प्रतिसंक्रम इति चेत् तर्हि उपचारस्तत्त्वचिन्तायामनुपयोगीति प्रेक्षावतामनुपादेय एवायम् । तथा च प्रतिप्राणिप्रतीतं सुखदुःखादिसंवेदनं निराश्रयमेव स्यात् । न चेदं बुद्धेरुपपन्नम् । तस्या जडत्वेनाभ्युपगमात् । अत एव जडा च बुद्धिरित्यपि विरुद्धम् । न हि जडस्वरूपायां बुद्धौ विषयाध्यवसायः साध्यमानः साधीयस्तां दधाति । ननूक्तमचेतनापि बुद्धिश्चिच्छक्तिसांनिध्याच्चेतनावतीवावभासत इति । सत्यमुक्तमयुक्तं तूक्तम् । न हि चैतन्यवति पुरुषादौ प्रतिसंक्रान्ते दर्पणस्य चैतन्यापत्तिश्चैतन्याचैतन्ययोरपरावर्तिस्वभाव-

त्वेन शक्रेणाप्यन्यथाकर्तुमशक्यत्वात् । किं चाचेतनापि चेतनावतीव प्रतिभासत इति इवशब्देनारोपो ध्वन्यते । न चारोपोऽर्थक्रियासमर्थः । न खल्वतिकोपनत्वादिना समारोपिताग्नित्वो माणवकः कदाचिदपि मुख्याग्निसाध्यां दाहपाकाद्यर्थक्रियां कर्तुमीश्वरः। इति चिच्छक्तेरेव विषयाध्यवसायो घटते न जडरूपाया बुद्धेरिति ॥ अत एव धर्माद्यष्टरूपताद्यपि तस्या वाङ्मात्रमेव। धर्मादीनामात्मधर्मत्वात् । अत एव चाहंकारोपि न बुद्धिजन्यो युज्यते । तस्याभिमानात्मकत्वेनात्मधर्मस्याचेतनादुत्पादायोगात् ॥ अम्बरादीनां च शब्दादितन्मात्रजत्वं प्रतीतिपराहतत्वेनैव विहितोत्तरम् । अपि च सर्ववादिभिस्तावदविगानेन गगनस्य नित्यत्वमङ्गीक्रियते। अयं च शब्दतन्मात्रात्तस्याविर्भावमुद्भावयन्नित्यैकान्तवादिनां च धुरि आसनं न्यासयन्नसंगतप्रलापीव प्रतिभाति ।न च परिणामिकारणं स्वकार्यस्य गुणो भवितुमर्हतीति शब्दगुणमाकाशमित्यादि वाङ्मात्रम् ॥ वागादीनां चेन्द्रियत्वमेव न युज्यते । इतरासाध्यकार्यकारित्वाभावात् । परप्रतिपादनग्रहणविहरणमलोत्सर्गादिकार्याणामितरावयवैरपि साध्यत्वोपलब्धेः। तथापि तत्त्वकल्पन इन्द्रियसंख्या न व्यवतिष्ठते । अन्याङ्गोपाङ्गादीनामपीन्द्रियत्वप्रसङ्गात् ॥ यच्चोक्तं नानाश्रयायाः प्रकृतेरेव बन्धमोक्षौ संसारश्च न पुरुषस्येति तदप्यसारम् । अनादिभवपरंपरानुबद्धया प्रकृत्या सह यः पुरुषस्य विवेकाग्रहणलक्षणोऽविष्वग्भावः स एव चेन्न बन्धस्तदा को नामान्यो बन्धः स्यात् । प्रकृतिः सर्वोत्पत्तिमतां निमित्तमिति च प्रतिपद्यमानेनायुष्मता संज्ञान्तरेण कर्मैव प्रतिपन्नम् ।तस्यैवैवंस्वरूपत्वात् अचेतनत्वाच्च ॥ यस्तु प्राकृतिकवैकारिकदाक्षिणभेदात्त्रिविधो बन्धः । तद्यथा प्रकृतावात्मज्ञानाद्ये प्रकृतिमुपासते तेषां प्राकृतिको बन्धः।ये विकारानेव भूतेन्द्रियाहंकारबुद्धीः पुरुषबुद्ध्योपासते तेषां वैकारिकः। इष्टा-

पूर्त्तेर्दाक्षिणः । पुरुषतत्त्वानभिज्ञो हीष्टापूर्तिकारी कामोपहतमना बध्यत इति ।

इष्टापूर्तं मन्यमाना वरिष्ठं नान्यच्छ्रेयो येभिनन्दन्ति मूढाः ।
नाकस्य पृष्ठे ते सुकृतेन भूत्वा इमं लोकं हीनतरं वा विशन्ति॥

इति वचनात् । स त्रिविधोपि कल्पनामात्रम् । कथंचिन्मिथ्यादर्शनाविरतिप्रमादकषाययोगेभ्योऽभिन्नस्वरूपत्वेन कर्मबन्धहेतुष्वेवान्तर्भावात् । बन्धसिद्धौ च सिद्धस्तस्यैव निर्बाधः संसारः । बन्धमोक्षयोश्चैकाधिकरणत्वाद्य एव बद्धः स एव मुच्यत इति पुरुषस्यैव मोक्षः । आबालगोपालं तथाप्रतीतेः । प्रकृतिपुरुषविवेकदर्शनात्प्रवृत्तेरुपरतायां प्रकृतौ पुरुषस्य स्वरूपेणावस्थानं मोक्ष इति चेत् न । प्रवृत्तिस्वभावायाः प्रकृतेरौदासीन्यायोगात् । अथ पुरुषार्थनिबन्धना तस्याः प्रवृत्तिः । विवेकख्यातिश्च पुरुषार्थः । तस्यां जातायां निवर्तते । कृतकार्यत्वात् ।

रङ्गस्य दर्शयित्वा निवर्तते नर्तकी यथा नृत्यात् ।
पुरुषस्य तथात्मानं प्रकाश्य विनिवर्तते प्रकृतिः ॥

इति वचना । इति चेत् नैवम् । तस्या अचेतनाया विमृश्यकारित्वाभावात् । यथेयं कृतेपि शब्दाद्युपलम्भे पुनस्तदर्थं प्रवर्त्तते तथा विवेकख्यातौ कृतायामपि पुनस्तदर्थं प्रवर्तिष्यते । प्रवृत्तिलक्षणस्य स्वभावस्यानपेतत्वात् । नर्तकीदृष्टान्तस्तु स्वेष्टविघातकारी । यथा हि नर्तकी नृत्यं पारिषदेभ्यो दर्शयित्वा निवृत्तापि पुनस्तत्कुतूहलात्प्रवर्तते तथा प्रकृतिरपि पुरुषायात्मानं दर्शयित्वा निवृत्तापि पुनः कथं न प्रवर्ततामिति । तस्मात्कृत्स्नकर्मक्षये पुरुषस्यैव मोक्ष इति प्रतिपत्तव्यम् ॥ एवमन्यासामपि तत्कल्पनानां तमोमोहमहामोहतामिस्रान्धतामिस्रभेदात्पञ्चधाविद्यास्मितारागद्वेषाभिनिवेशरूपो विपर्ययः । ब्राह्मप्राजापत्यसौम्यैन्द्रगान्धर्वयक्षराक्ष-

सपैशाचभेदादष्टविधो दैवः सर्गः। पशुमृगपक्षिसरीसृपस्थावरभेदात्पञ्चविधस्तैर्यग्योनः। ब्राह्मणत्वाद्यवान्तरभेदाविवक्षया चैकविधो मानुष इति चतुर्दशधा भूतसर्गः। बाधिर्यकुष्ठितान्धत्वजडताऽजिघ्रतामूकताकौण्यपङ्गुत्वक्लैब्योदावर्तमत्ततारूपैकादशेन्द्रियवधतुष्टिनवकविपर्ययसिद्ध्यष्टकविपर्ययलक्षणसप्तदशबुद्धिवधभेदादष्टाविंशतिधा शक्तिः। प्रकृत्युपादानकालभोगाख्याः अम्भःसलिलौघवृष्ट्यपरपर्यायवाच्याश्चतस्र आध्यात्मिक्यः। शब्दादिविषयोपरतयश्चार्जनरक्षणक्षयभोगहिंसादोषदर्शनहेतुजन्मानः पञ्च बाह्यास्तुष्टयः। ताश्च पारसुपारपारापारानुत्तमाम्भउत्तमाम्भःशब्दव्यपदेश्याः। इति नवधा तुष्टिः। त्रयो दुःखविघाता इति मुख्यास्तिस्रः सिद्धयः प्रमोदमुदितमोदमानाख्याः। तथाध्ययनं शब्द ऊहः सुहृत्प्राप्तिर्दानमिति दुःखविघातोपायतया गौण्यः पञ्च तारसुतारतारतारररम्यकसदामुदिताख्याः। इत्येवमष्टधा सिद्धिः। धृतिश्रद्धासुखविविदिषाविज्ञप्तिभेदात्पञ्च कर्मयोनयः। इत्यादीनां संवरप्रतिसंवरादीनां च तत्त्वकौमुदीगौडपादभाष्यादिप्रसिद्धानां विरुद्धत्वमुद्भावनीयमिति काव्यार्थः॥ १५॥

इदानीं ये प्रमाणादेकान्तेनाभिन्नं प्रमाणफलमाहुः ये च बाह्यार्थप्रतिक्षेपेण ज्ञानाद्वैतमेवास्तीति ब्रुवते तन्मतस्य विचार्यमाणत्वे विशरारुतामाह।

न तुल्यकालः फलहेतुभावो
हेतौ विलीने न फलस्य भावः।
न संविदद्वैतपथेऽर्थसंवि-
द्विलूनशीर्णं सुगतेन्द्रजालम्॥ १६॥

बौद्धाः किल प्रमाणात्तत्फलमेकान्तेनाभिन्नं मन्यन्ते । तथा च तत्सिद्धान्तः । उभयत्र तदेव ज्ञानं प्रमाणं फलम्। अधिगमरूपत्वात्। उभयत्रेति प्रत्यक्षेऽनुमाने च तदेव ज्ञानं प्रत्यक्षानुमानलक्षणं फलं कार्यम् । कुतः । अधिगमरूपत्वात् इति परिच्छेदरूपत्वात् । तथा हि परिच्छेदरूपमेव ज्ञानमुत्पद्यते । न च परिच्छेदादृतेऽन्यज्ज्ञानफलम् । अभिन्नाधिकरणत्वात् । इति सर्वथा न प्रत्यक्षानुमानाभ्यां भिन्नं फलमस्तीति।। एतच्च न समीचीनं यतो यद्यस्मादेकान्तेनाभिन्नं तत्तेन सहैवोत्पद्यते यथा घटेन घटत्वम्। तैश्च प्रमाणफलयोः कार्यकारणभावोऽभ्युपगम्यते । प्रमाणं कारणं फलं कार्यमिति । स चैकान्ताभेदे न घटते । न हि युगपदुत्पद्यमानयोस्तयोः सव्येतरगोविषाणयोरिव कार्यकारणभावो युक्तः । नियतप्राक्कालभावित्वात्कारणस्य । नियतोत्तरकालभावित्वात्कार्यस्य । एतदेवाह न तुल्यकालः फलहेतुभाव इति । फलं कार्यं हेतुः कारणं तयोर्भावः स्वरूपं कार्यकारणभावः । स तुल्यकालः समानकालो न युज्यत इत्यर्थः । अथ क्षणान्तरितत्वात्तयोः क्रमभावित्वं भविष्यतीत्याशङ्क्याह । हेतौ विलीने न फलस्य भाव इति । हेतौ कारणे प्रमाणलक्षणे विलीने क्षणिकत्वादुत्पत्त्यनन्तरमेव निरन्वयं विनष्टे फलस्य प्रमाणकार्यस्य न भावः सत्ता । निर्मूलत्वात्। विद्यमाने हि फलहेतावस्येदं फलमिति प्रतीयते नान्यथा। अतिप्रसङ्गात्। किं च हेतुफलभावः संबन्धः स च द्विष्ठ एव स्यात् । न चानयोः क्षणक्षयैकदीक्षितो भवान्संबन्धं क्षमते। ततः कथमयं हेतुः इदं फलमिति प्रतिनियता प्रतीतिः । एकस्य ग्रहणेप्यन्यस्याग्रहणे तदसंभवात् ।

द्विष्ठसंबन्धसंवित्तिर्नैकरूपप्रवेदनात् ।
द्वयोः स्वरूपग्रहणे सति संबन्धवेदनम् ।।

इति वचनात् । यदपि धर्मोत्तरेणाऽर्थसारूप्यमस्य प्रमाणं तद्वशा-

दर्थप्रतीतिसिद्धेरिति न्यायबिन्दुसूत्रं विवृण्वता भणितं नीलनिर्भासं हि विज्ञानं यतस्तस्मान्नीलस्य प्रतीतिरवसीयते येभ्यो हि चक्षुरादिभ्यो ज्ञानमुत्पद्यते न तद्वशात्तज्ज्ञानं नीलस्य संवेदनं शक्यतेऽवस्थापयितुम् नीलसदृशं त्वनुभूयमानं नीलस्य संवेदनमवस्थाप्यते न चात्र जन्यजनकभावनिबन्धनः साध्यसाधनभावो येनैकस्मिन्वस्तुनि विरोधः स्यात् अपि तु व्यवस्थाप्यव्यवस्थापकभावेन तत एकस्य वस्तुनः किंचिद्रूपं प्रमाणं किंचित्प्रमाणफलं न विरुध्यते व्यवस्थापनहेतुर्हि सारूप्यं तस्य ज्ञानस्य व्यवस्थाप्यं च नीलसंवेदनरूपमित्यादि तदप्यसारम्। एकस्य निरंशस्य ज्ञानलक्षणस्य व्यवस्थाप्यव्यवस्थापकत्वलक्षणस्वभावद्वयायोगात्। व्यवस्थाप्यव्यवस्थापकभावस्यापि च संबन्धत्वेन द्विष्ठत्वात् एकस्मिन्नसंभवात्। किं चार्थसारूप्यमर्थाकारता तच्च निश्चयरूपमनिश्चयरूपं वा। निश्चयरूपं चेत्तदेव व्यवस्थापकमस्तु। किमुभयकल्पनया। अनिश्चितं चेत् स्वयमव्यवस्थितं कथं नीलादिसंवेदनव्यवस्थापने समर्थम्। अपि च केयमर्थाकारता। किमर्थग्रहणपरिणामः आहोस्विदर्थाकारधारित्वम्। नाद्यः। सिद्धसाधनात्। द्वितीयस्तु ज्ञानस्य प्रमेयाकारानुकरणाज्जडत्वापत्त्यादिदोषाघ्रातः। तन्न प्रमाणादेकान्तेन फलस्याभेदः साधीयान्। सर्वथातादात्म्ये हि प्रमाणफलयोर्न व्यवस्था। तद्भावविरोधात्। न हि सारूप्यमस्य प्रमाणमधिगतिः फलमिति सर्वथातादात्म्ये सिद्ध्यति। अतिप्रसङ्गात्। ननु प्रमाणस्यासारूप्यव्यावृत्तिः सारूप्यम् अनधिगतिव्यावृत्तिरधिगतिरिति व्यावृत्तिभेदादेकस्यापि प्रमाणफलव्यवस्थेति चेत् नैवम्। स्वभावभेदमन्तरेणान्यव्यावृत्तिभेदस्याप्यनुपपत्तेः। कथं च प्रमाणस्य फलस्य चाप्रमाणाफलव्यावृत्त्या प्रमाणफलव्यवस्थावत्प्रमाणान्तरफलान्तरव्या-

वृत्त्याप्यप्रमाणत्वस्याफलत्वस्य च व्यवस्था न स्यात् । विजातीयादिव सजातीयादपि व्यावृत्तत्वाद्वस्तुनः । तस्मात्प्रमाणात्फलं कथंचिद्भिन्नमेवैष्टव्यम् । साध्यसाधनभावेन प्रतीयमानत्वात् । ये हि साध्यसाधनभावेन प्रतीयेते ते परस्परं भिद्येते । यथा कुठारच्छिदिक्रिये इति ॥ एवं यौगाभिप्रेतः प्रमाणात्फलस्यैकान्तभेदोपि निराकर्तव्यः । तस्यैकप्रमातृतादात्म्येन प्रमाणात्कथंचिदभेदव्यवस्थितेः । प्रमाणतया परिणतस्यैवात्मनः फलतया परिणतिप्रतीतेः । यः प्रमिमीते स एवोपादत्ते परित्यजत्युपेक्षते चेति सर्वव्यवहारिभिरस्खलितमनुभवात् । इतरथा स्वपरयोः प्रमाणफलव्यवस्थाविप्लवः प्रसज्यत इत्यलम् ॥

अथवा पूर्वार्द्धमिदमन्यथा व्याख्येयम् । सौगताः किलेत्थं प्रमाणयन्ति । सर्वं सत् क्षणिकम् । यतः सर्वं तावत् घटादिकं वस्तु मुद्गरादिसंनिधौ नाशं गच्छद्दृश्यते तत्र येन स्वरूपेणान्त्यावस्थायां घटादिकं विनश्यति तच्चैतत्स्वरूपमुत्पन्नमात्रस्य विद्यते तदानीमुत्पादानन्तरमेव तेन नष्टव्यमिति व्यक्तमस्य क्षणिकत्वम् । अथेदृश एव स्वभावस्तस्य हेतुतो जातो यत्कियन्तमपि कालं स्थित्वा विनश्यति । एवं तर्हि मुद्गरादिसंनिधानेपि एष एव तस्य स्वभाव इति पुनरप्यनेन तावन्तमेव कालं स्थातव्यम् इति नैवं विनश्येदिति । सोयमदित्सोर्वणिजः प्रतिदिनं पत्रलिखितश्वस्तनदिनभणनन्यायः । तस्मात्क्षणद्वयस्थायित्वेनाप्युत्पत्तौ प्रथमक्षणवत् द्वितीयेपि क्षणे क्षणद्वयस्थायित्वात्पुनरपरक्षणद्वयमवतिष्ठेत । एवं तृतीयेपि क्षणे तत्स्वभावत्वान्नैव विनश्येदिति । स्यादेतत् । स्थावरमेव तत्स्वहेतोर्जातं परं बलेन विरोधकेन मुद्गरादिना विनाश्यत इति । तदसत् । कथं पुनरेतद्घटिष्यते । न च तद्विनश्यति स्थावरत्वात् विनाशश्च तस्य विरोधिना बलेन क्रियत इति ।

न ह्येतत्संभवति । जीवति च देवदत्तो मरणं चास्य भवतीति । अथ विनश्यति तर्हि कथमविनश्वरं तद्वस्तु स्वहेतोर्जातमिति । न हि म्रियते चामरणधर्मा चेति युज्यते वक्तुम् । तस्मादविनश्वरत्वे कदाचिदपि नाशायोगात् दृष्टत्वाच्च नाशस्य नश्वरमेव तद्वस्तु स्वहेतोरुपजातमेवाङ्गीकर्तव्यम् । तस्मादुत्पन्नमात्रमेव विनश्यति । तथा च क्षणक्षयित्वं सिद्धं भवति । प्रयोगस्त्वेवम् । यद्विनश्वररूपं तदुत्पत्तेरनन्तरानवस्थायि यथान्त्यक्षणवर्तिघटस्य स्वरूपम् विनश्वरस्वरूपं च रूपादिकमुदयकाले इति स्वभावहेतुः । यदि क्षणक्षयिणो भावाः कथं तर्हि स एवायमिति प्रत्यभिज्ञा स्यात् । उच्यते । निरन्तरसदृशापरापरोत्पादादविद्यानुबन्धाच्च पूर्वक्षणविनाशकाल एव तत्सदृशं क्षणान्तरमुदयते तेनाकारविलक्षणत्वाभावादव्यवधानाच्चात्यन्तोच्छेदेपि स एवायमित्यभेदाध्यवसायी प्रत्ययः प्रसूयते । अत्यन्तभिन्नेष्वपि लूनपुनरुत्पन्नकुशकाशकेशादिषु दृष्ट एवायं स एवायमिति प्रत्ययस्तथेहापि किं न संभाव्यते । तस्मात्सर्वं सत् क्षणिकमिति सिद्धम् ॥अत्र च पूर्वक्षणउपादानकारणं उत्तरक्षण उपादेयमिति पराभिप्रायमङ्गीकृत्याह न तुल्यकाल इत्यादि । ते विशकलितमुक्तावलीकल्पा निरन्वयविनाशिनः पूर्वक्षणा उत्तरक्षणान् जनयन्तः किं स्वोत्पत्तिकाल एव जनयन्ति उत क्षणान्तरे । न तावदाद्यः । समकालभाविनोर्युवतिकुचयोरिवोपादानोपादेयभावाभावात् । अतः साधूक्तम् न तुल्यकालः फलहेतुभाव इति । न च द्वितीयः ।तदानीं निरन्वयविनाशेन पूर्वक्षणस्य नष्टत्वादुत्तरक्षणजनने कुतः संभावनापि । न चानुपादानस्योत्पत्तिर्दृष्टा । अतिप्रसङ्गात् । इति सुष्ठु व्याहृतं हेतौ विलीने न फलस्य भाव इति ॥ पदार्थस्त्वनयोः पादयोः प्रागेवोक्तः । केवलमत्र फलमुपादेयं हेतुरुपादानं तद्भाव उपादानोपादेयभाव इत्यर्थः ॥ यच्च क्षणिकत्वस्था-

पनाय मोक्षाकरगुप्तेनानन्तरमेव प्रलपितं तत् स्याद्वादवादे निरवकाशमेव। निरन्वयनाशवर्जं कथंचित्सिद्धसाधनात्। प्रतिक्षणं पर्यायनाशस्यानेकान्तवादिभिरभ्युपगमात् । यदप्यभिहितं न ह्येतत्संभवति जीवति च देवदत्तो मरणं चास्य भवतीति तदपि संभवादेव न स्याद्वादवादिनां क्षतिमावहति। यतो जीवनं प्राणधारणं मरणं चायुर्दलिकक्षयस्ततो जीवतोपि देवदत्तस्य प्रतिसमयमायुर्दलिकानामुदीर्णानां क्षयादुपपन्नमेव मरणम्। न च वाच्यमन्त्यावस्थायामेव कृत्स्नायुर्दलिकक्षयात् तत्रैव मरणव्यपदेशो युक्त इति। तस्यामप्यवस्थायां न्यक्षेण तत्क्षयाभावात्। तत्रापि ह्यवशिष्टानामेव तेषां क्षयो न पुनस्तत्क्षण एव युगपत्सर्वेषाम्। इति सिद्धं गर्भादारभ्य प्रतिक्षणं मरणम्। इत्यलं प्रसङ्गेन ॥

अथवाऽपरथा व्याख्या। सौगतानां किलार्थेन ज्ञानं जन्यते तच्च ज्ञानं तमेव स्वोत्पादकमर्थं गृह्णातीति। नाकारणं विषय इति वचनात्। ततश्चार्थः कारणं ज्ञानं च कार्यमिति। एतच्च न चारु। यतो यस्मिन् क्षणेऽर्थस्य स्वरूपसत्ता तस्मिन्नद्यापि ज्ञानं नोत्पद्यते। तस्य तदा स्वोत्पत्तिमात्रव्यग्रत्वात् । यत्र च क्षणे ज्ञानं समुत्पन्नं तत्रार्थोऽतीतः। पूर्वापरकालभावनियतश्च कार्यकारणभावः। क्षणातिरिक्तं चावस्थानं नास्ति। ततः कथं ज्ञानस्योत्पत्तिः । कारणस्य विलीनत्वात्। तद्विलये च ज्ञानस्य निर्विषयतानुषज्यते । कारणस्यैव युष्मन्मते तद्विषयत्वात्। निर्विषयं च ज्ञानमप्रमाणमेवाकाशकेशज्ञानवत् । ज्ञानसहभाविनश्चार्थक्षणस्य न ग्राह्यत्वम्। तस्याकारणत्वात्। अत आह न तुल्यकाल इत्यादि। ज्ञानार्थयोः फलहेतुभावः कार्यकारणभावः तुल्यकालो न घटते। ज्ञानसहभाविनोऽर्थक्षणस्य ज्ञानानुत्पादकत्वात्। युगपद्भाविनोः कार्यकारणभावायोगात्। अथ प्राचोऽर्थक्षणस्य ज्ञानोत्पादकत्वं भविष्यति। तन्न।

यत आह हेतौ इत्यादि। हेतौ अर्थरूपे ज्ञानकारणे विलीने क्षणिकत्वान्निरन्वयं विनष्टे न फलस्य ज्ञानलक्षणकार्यस्य भाव आत्मलाभः स्यात्। जनकस्यार्थक्षणस्यातीतत्वान्निर्मूलमेव ज्ञानोत्थानं स्यात्। जनकस्यैव च ग्राह्यत्वे इन्द्रियाणामपि ग्राह्यत्वापत्तिः। तेषामपि ज्ञानजनकत्वात्। न चान्वयव्यतिरेकाभ्यामर्थस्य ज्ञानहेतुत्वं दृष्टम्। मृगतृष्णादौ जलाभावेपि जलज्ञानोत्पादात्। अन्यथा तत्प्रवृत्तेरसंभवात्। भ्रान्तं तज्ज्ञानमिति चेत् ननु भ्रान्ताभ्रान्तविचारः स्थिरीभूय क्रियतां त्वया। सांप्रतं प्रतिपद्यस्व तावदनर्थजमपि ज्ञानम्। अन्वयेनार्थस्य ज्ञानहेतुत्वं दृष्टमेवेति चेत् न। न हि तद्भावे भावलक्षणोऽन्वय एव हेतुफलभावनिश्चयनिमित्तम्। अपि तु तदभावेऽभावलक्षणो व्यतिरेकोपि। स चोक्तयुक्त्या नास्त्येव। योगिनां चातीतानागतार्थग्रहणे किमर्थस्य निमित्तत्वम्। तयोरसत्त्वात्।

ण णिहाणगया भग्गा पुंजो णत्थि अणागए।
णिव्वुया णेव चिट्ठन्ति आरग्गे सरिसोवमा॥

इति वचनात्। निमित्तत्वे चार्थक्रियाकारित्वेन सत्त्वादतीतानागतत्वक्षतिः। न च प्रकाश्यादात्मलाभ एव प्रकाशकस्य प्रकाशकत्वम्। प्रदीपादेर्घटादिभ्योऽनुत्पन्नस्यापि तत्प्रकाशकत्वात्। जनकस्यैव च ग्राह्यत्वाभ्युपगमे स्मृत्यादेः प्रमाणस्याप्रामाण्यप्रसङ्गः। तस्यार्थाजन्यत्वात्। न च स्मृतिर्न प्रमाणम्। अनुमानप्राणभूतत्वात् साध्यसाधनसंबन्धस्मरणपूर्वकत्वात्तस्य। जनकमेव चेद्ग्राह्यं तदा स्वसंवेदनस्य कथं ग्राहकत्वम्। तस्य हि ग्राह्यं स्वरूपमेव। न च तेन तज्जन्यते। स्वात्मनि क्रियाविरोधात्। तस्मात्स्वसामग्रीप्रभवयोर्घटप्रदीपयोरिवार्थज्ञानयोः प्रकाश्यप्रकाशकभावसंभवान्न ज्ञाननिमित्तत्वमर्थस्य। नन्वर्थाजन्यत्वे ज्ञानस्य कथं प्रतिनियतकर्मव्यवस्था। तदुत्पत्तितदाकारताभ्यां हि सोपपद्यते। तस्मादनुत्पन्नस्यातदाका-

रस्य च ज्ञानस्य सर्वार्थान्प्रत्यविशेषात्सर्वग्रहणं प्रसज्येत । नैवम् । तदुत्पत्तिमन्तरेणाप्यावरणक्षयोपशमलक्षणया योग्यतयैव प्रतिनियतार्थप्रकाशकत्वोपपत्तेः । तदुत्पत्तावपि च योग्यतावश्यमेष्टव्या । अन्यथाऽशेषार्थसांनिध्ये तत्तदर्थासांनिध्येपि कुतश्चिदेवार्थात् कस्यचिदेव ज्ञानस्य जन्मेति कौतस्कुतोऽयं विभागः । तदाकारता त्वर्थाकारसंक्रान्त्या तावदनुपपन्ना । अर्थस्य निराकारत्वप्रसङ्गात् । ज्ञानस्य साकारत्वप्रसङ्गाच्च । अर्थेन च मूर्तेनामूर्तस्य ज्ञानस्य कीदृशं सादृश्यमित्यर्थविशेषग्रहणपरिणाम एव साभ्युपेया । ततः

अर्थेन घटयत्येनां न हि मुक्त्वार्थरूपताम् ।
तस्मात्प्रमेयाधिगतेः प्रमाणं मेयरूपता ॥

इति यत्किञ्चिदेतत् । अपि च व्यस्ते समस्ते वैते ग्रहणकारणं स्याताम् । यदि व्यस्ते तदा कपालाद्यक्षणो घटान्त्यक्षणस्य जलचन्द्रो वा नभश्चन्द्रस्य ग्राहकः प्राप्नोति । यथासंख्यं तदुत्पत्तेस्तदाकारत्वाच्च । अथ समस्ते तर्हि घटोत्तरक्षणः पूर्वघटक्षणस्य ग्राहकः प्रसजति । तयोरुभयोरपि सद्भावात् । ज्ञानरूपत्वे सत्येते ग्रहणकारणमिति चेत् तर्हि समानजातीयज्ञानस्य समनन्तरज्ञानग्राहकत्वं प्रसज्येत । तयोर्जन्यजनकभावसद्भावात् । तन्न योग्यतामन्तरेणान्यद्ग्रहणकारणं पश्याम इति ॥

अथोत्तरार्द्धं व्याख्यातुमुपक्रम्यते । तत्र च बाह्यार्थनिरपेक्षं ज्ञानाद्वैतमेव ये बौद्धविशेषा मन्वते तेषां प्रतिक्षेपः।तन्मतं चेदम् । ग्राह्यग्राहकादिकलङ्कानाङ्कितं निष्प्रपञ्चं ज्ञानमात्रं परमार्थसत् । बाह्यार्थस्तु विचारमेव न क्षमते । तथाहि । कोऽयं बाह्यार्थः । किं परमाणुरूपः स्थूलावयविरूपो वा । न तावत्परमाणुरूपः । प्रमाणाभावात् । प्रमाणं हि प्रत्यक्षमनुमानं वा । न तावत्प्रत्यक्षं तत्साधनबद्धकक्षम् । तद्धि योगिनां स्यात् अस्मदादीनां वा ।

नाद्यम् । अत्यन्तविप्रकृष्टतया श्रद्धामात्रगम्यत्वात् । न द्वितीयम् । अनुभवबाधितत्वात् । न हि वयमयं परमाणुरयं परमाणुरिति स्वप्नेपि प्रतीमः । स्तम्भोऽयं कुम्भोऽयमित्येवमेव नः सदैव संवेदनोदयात् । नाप्यनुमानेन तत्सिद्धिः । अणूनामतीन्द्रियत्वेन तैः सह अविनाभावस्य क्वापि लिङ्गे ग्रहीतुमशक्यत्वात् । किं चामी नित्या अनित्या वा स्युः । नित्याश्चेत् क्रमेणार्थक्रियाकारिणो युगपद्वा । न क्रमेण । स्वभावभेदेनानित्यत्वापत्तेः । न युगपद् । एकक्षण एव कृत्स्नार्थक्रियाकरणात् क्षणान्तरे तदभावादसत्त्वापत्तिः । अनित्याश्चेत् क्षणिकाः कालान्तरस्थायिनो वा । क्षणिकाश्चेत् सहेतुका निर्हेतुका वा । निर्हेतुकाश्चेत् नित्यं सत्त्वमसत्त्वं वा स्यात् । निरपेक्षत्वात् । अपेक्षातो हि कादाचित्कत्वम् । सहेतुकाश्चेत् किं तेषां स्थूलं किंचित्कारणं परमाणवो वा । न स्थूलम् । परमाणुरूपस्यैव बाह्यार्थस्याङ्गीकृतत्वात् । न च परमाणवः । ते हि सन्तोऽसन्तः सदसन्तो वा स्वकार्याणि कुर्युः । सन्तश्चेत् किमुत्पत्तिक्षण एव क्षणान्तरे वा । नोत्पत्तिक्षणे । तदानीमुत्पत्तिमात्रव्यग्रत्वात्तेषाम् । अथ

भूतिर्येषां क्रिया सैव कारणं सैव चोच्यते ।

इति वचनात् भवनमेव तेषामपरोत्पत्तौ कारणमिति चेत् एवं तर्हि रूपाणवो रसाणूनां ते च तेषामुपादानं स्युः । उभयत्र भवनाविशेषात् । न च क्षणान्तरे । नष्टत्वात् । अथासन्तस्ते तदुत्पादकाः । तर्हि एकं स्वसत्ताक्षणमपहाय सदा तदुत्पत्तिप्रसङ्गः । तदसत्त्वस्य सर्वदाऽविशेषात् । सदसत्पक्षस्तु

प्रत्येकं यो भवेद्दोषो द्वयोर्भावे कथं न सः ।

इति वचनाद्विरोधाघ्रात एव । तन्नाणवः क्षणिकाः । नापि कालान्तरस्थायिनः । क्षणिकपक्षसदृक्षयोगक्षेमत्वात् । किं चामी कियत्कालस्थायिनोपि किमर्थक्रियापराङ्मुखास्तत्कारिणो वा ।

आद्ये खपुष्पवदसत्त्वापत्तिः । उदग्विकल्पे किमसद्रूपं सद्रूपमुभयरूपं वा ते कार्यं कुर्युः । असद्रूपं चेच्छशविषाणादेरपि किं न करणम् । सद्रूपं चेत् सतोपि करणेऽनवस्था । तृतीयभेदस्तु प्राग्वद्विरोधदुर्गन्धः । तन्नाणुरूपोऽर्थः सर्वथा घटते ॥

नापि स्थूलावयविरूपः । एकपरमाण्वसिद्धौ कथमनेकतत्सिद्धिः । तदभावे च तत्प्रचयरूपः स्थूलावयवी वाङ्मात्रम् । किं चायमनेकावयवाधार इष्यते । ते चावयवा यदि विरोधिनः तर्हि नैकः स्थूलावयवी । विरुद्धधर्माध्यासात् । अविरोधिनश्चेत्प्रतीतिबाधः । एकस्मिन्नेव स्थूलावयविनि चलाचलरक्तारक्तावृतानावृतादिविरुद्धावयवानामुपलब्धेः । अपि चासौ तेषु वर्तमानः कात्स्न्र्येनैकदेशेन वा वर्तते । कात्स्न्र्येन वृत्तावेकस्मिन्नेवावयवे परिसमाप्तत्वादनेकावयववृत्तित्वं न स्यात् । प्रत्यवयवं कात्स्न्र्येन वृत्तौ चावयविबहुत्वापत्तेः । एकदेशेन वृत्तौ च तस्य निरंशत्वाभ्युपगमबाधः । सांशत्वे वा तेंऽशास्ततो भिन्ना अभिन्ना वा । भिन्नत्वे पुनरप्यनेकांशवृत्तेरेकस्य कात्स्न्र्यैकदेशविकल्पानतिक्रमादनवस्था । अभिन्नत्वे न केचिदंशाः स्युः । इति नास्ति बाह्योऽर्थः कश्चित् । किन्तु ज्ञानमेवेदं सर्वं नीलाद्याकारेण प्रतिभाति । बाह्यार्थस्य जडत्वेन प्रतिभासायोगात् । यथोक्तम् ।

स्वाकारबुद्धिजनका दृश्या नेन्द्रियगोचराः ।

अलङ्कारकारेणाप्युक्तम् ।

यदि संवेद्यते नीलं कथं बाह्यं तदुच्यते ।
न चेत्संवेद्यते नीलं कथं बाह्यं तदुच्यते ॥

यदि बाह्योऽर्थो नास्ति ॥ किंविषयस्तर्ह्ययं घटपटादिप्रतिभास इति चेत् ननु निरालम्बन एवायमनादिवितथवासनाप्रवर्तितः । निर्विषयत्वात् । आकाशकेशज्ञानवत् स्वप्नज्ञानवद्वेति । अत एवोक्तम्

नान्योऽनुभाव्यो बुद्ध्यास्ति तस्या नानुभवोऽपरः ।
ग्राह्यग्राहकवैधुर्यात्स्वयं सैव प्रकाशते ॥
बाह्यो न विद्यते ह्यर्थो यथा बालैर्विकल्प्यते ।
वासनालुठितं चित्तमर्थाभासं प्रवर्तते ॥

इति ॥

तदेतत्सर्वमवद्यम् । ज्ञानमिति हि क्रियाशब्दः। ततो ज्ञायतेऽनेनेति ज्ञानं ज्ञप्तिर्वा ज्ञानमिति। अस्य च कर्मणा भाव्यम् । निर्विषयाया ज्ञप्तेरघटनात् । न चाकाशकेशादौ निर्विषयमपि दृष्टं ज्ञानमिति वाच्यम् । तस्याप्येकान्तेन निर्विषयत्वाभावात् । न हि सर्वथाऽगृहीतसत्यकेशज्ञानस्य तत्प्रतीतिः । स्वप्नज्ञानमप्यनुभूतदृष्टाद्यर्थविषयत्वान्न निरालम्बनम् । तथा च महाभाष्यकारः ।

अणुहूयदिट्ठचिंतिय सुयपयइवियारदेवयाणूवा ।
सुमिणस्स निमित्ताइं पुण्णं पावं च णाभावो ॥

यश्च ज्ञानविषयः स बाह्योर्थः । भ्रान्तिरियमिति चेत् चिरं जीव । भ्रान्तिर्हि मुख्येऽर्थे क्वचिद्दृष्टे सति करणापाटवादिना अन्यत्र विपर्यस्तग्रहणे प्रसिद्धा । यथा शुक्तौ रजतभ्रान्तिः । अर्थक्रियासमर्थेऽपि वस्तुनि यदि भ्रान्तिरुच्यते तर्हि प्रलीना भ्रान्ताभ्रान्तव्यवस्था । तथा च सत्यमेतद्वचः ।

आशामोदकतृप्ता ये ये चास्वादितमोदकाः ।
रसवीर्यविपाकादि तुल्यं तेषां प्रसज्यते ॥

न चामून्यर्थदूषणानि स्याद्वादिनां बाधां विदधते । परमाणुरूपस्य स्थूलावयविरूपस्य चार्थस्याङ्गीकृतत्वात् । यच्च परमाणुपक्षखण्डनेऽभिहितं प्रमाणाभावादिति तदसत् । तत्कार्याणां घटादीनां प्रत्यक्षत्वे तेषामपि कथंचित्प्रत्यक्षत्वं योगिप्रत्यक्षेण च साक्षात्प्रत्यक्षत्वमवसेयम् । अनुपलब्धिस्तु सौक्ष्म्यात् । अनुमानादपि तत्सि-

द्भिः। यथा सन्ति परमाणवः स्थूलावयविनिष्पत्त्यन्यथानुपपत्तेरित्यन्तर्व्याप्तिः । न चाणुभ्यः स्थूलोत्पाद इत्येकान्तः। स्थूलादपि सूत्रपटलादेः स्थूलस्य पटादेः प्रादुर्भावविभावनात्। आत्माकाशादेरपुद्गलत्वकक्षीकाराच्च । यत्र पुनरणुभ्यस्तदुत्पत्तिस्तत्र तत्तत्कालादिसामग्रीसव्यपेक्षक्रियावशात्प्रादुर्भूतं संयोगातिशयमपेक्ष्येयमवितथैव। यदपि किं चायमनेकावयवाधार इत्यादि न्यगादि तत्रापि कथंचिद्विरोध्यनेकावयवाविष्वग्भूतवृत्तिरवयव्यभिधीयते। तत्र च यद्विरोध्यनेकावयवाधारतायां विरुद्धधर्माध्यासनमभिहितं तत्कथंचिदुपेयत एव तावत्।अवयवात्मकस्य तस्यापि कथंचिदनेकरूपत्वात्। यच्चोपन्यस्तम् अपि चासौ तेषु वर्तमानः कार्त्स्न्येनैकदेशेन वा वर्तेतेत्यादि तत्रापि विकल्पद्वयानभ्युपगम एवोत्तरम्। अविष्वग्भावेनावयविनोऽवयवेषु वृत्तेः स्वीकारात्। किं च यदि बाह्योऽर्थो नास्ति किमिदानीं नियताकारं प्रतीयते। नीलमेतदिति विज्ञानाकारोऽयमिति चेत् न। ज्ञानाद्बहिर्भूतस्य संवेदनात्। ज्ञानाकारत्वे त्वहं नीलमिति प्रतीतिः स्यात् न त्विदं नीलमिति। ज्ञानानां प्रत्येकमाकारभेदात् कस्यचिदहमिति प्रतिभासः कस्यचिन्नीलमेतदिति चेत् न। नीलाद्याकारवदहमित्याकारस्य व्यवस्थिततत्त्वाभावात्। तथा च यदेकेनाहमिति प्रतीयते तदेवापरेण त्वमिति प्रतीयते। नीलाद्याकारस्तु व्यवस्थितः सर्वैरप्येकरूपतया ग्रहणात्। भक्षितहृत्पूरादिभिस्तु यद्यपि नीलादिकं पीतादितया गृह्यते तथापि तेन न व्यभिचारः। तस्य भ्रान्तत्वात्। स्वयं स्वस्य संवेदनेऽहमिति प्रतिभासत इति चेत् ननु किं परस्यापि संवेदनमस्ति। कथमन्यथा स्वशब्दस्य प्रयोगः। प्रतियोगिशब्दो ह्ययं परमपेक्षमाण एव प्रवर्तते। स्वरूपस्यापि भ्रान्त्या भेदप्रतीतिरिति चेत् हन्त प्रत्यक्षेण प्रतीतो भेदः कथं न वास्तवः। भ्रान्तं प्रत्यक्षमिति चेत् ननु कुत

एतत् । अनुमानेन ज्ञानार्थयोरभेदसिद्धेरिति चेत् किं तदनुमानमिति पृच्छामः । यद्येन सह नियमेनोपलभ्यते तत्ततो न भिद्यते यथा सच्चन्द्रादसच्चन्द्रः । नियमेनोपलभ्यते च ज्ञानेन सहार्थः इति व्यापकानुपलब्धिः । प्रतिषेध्यस्य ज्ञानार्थयोर्भेदस्य व्यापकः सहोपलम्भानियमःतस्यानुपलब्धिः। भिन्नयोर्नीलपीतयोर्युगपदुपलम्भनियमाभावात् । इत्यनुमानेन तयोरभेदासिद्धिरिति चेत् न । संदिग्धानैकान्तिकत्वेनास्यानुमानाभासत्वात् । ज्ञानं हि स्वपरसंवेदनम्। तत् परसंवेदनतामात्रेणैव नीलं गृह्णाति स्वसंवेदनतामात्रेणैव च नीलबुद्धिम् । तदेवमनयोर्युगपद्ग्रहणात्सहोपलम्भनियमोऽस्ति अभेदश्च नास्ति इति सहोपलम्भनियमरूपस्य हेतोर्विपक्षाद्व्यावृत्तेः संदिग्धत्वात् संदिग्धानैकान्तिकत्वम् । असिद्धश्च सहोपलम्भनियमः । नीलमेतदिति बहिर्मुखतयाऽर्थेनुभूयमाने तदानीमेवान्तरस्य नीलानुभवस्याननुभवात् इति कथं प्रत्यक्षस्यानुमानेन ज्ञानार्थयोरभेदसिद्धया भ्रान्तत्वम् । अपि च प्रत्यक्षस्य भ्रान्तत्वेनाबाधितविषयत्वादनुमानस्यात्मलाभः लब्धात्मके चानुमाने प्रत्यक्षस्य भ्रान्तत्वमित्यन्योन्याश्रयदोषोऽपि दुर्निवारः। अर्थाभावे च नियतदेशाधिकरणा प्रतीतिः कुतः। न हि तत्र विवक्षितदेशेऽयमारोपयितव्यो नान्यत्रेत्यस्ति नियमे हेतुः । वासनानियमात्तदारोपनियम इति चेत् न। तस्या अपि तद्देशनियमकारणाभावात्।सति ह्यर्थसद्भावे यद्देशोऽर्थस्तद्देशोऽनुभवस्तद्देशा च तत्पूर्विका वासना । बाह्यार्थाभावे तु तस्याः किंकृतो देशनियमः । अथास्ति तावदारोपनियमः। न च कारणविशेषमन्तरेण कार्यविशेषो घटते बाह्यश्चार्थो नास्ति तेन वासनानामेव वैचित्र्यं तत्र हेतुः । इति चेत् तद्वासनावैचित्र्यं बोधाकारादन्यदनन्यद्वा । अनन्यच्चेत् बोधाकारस्यैकत्वात्कस्तासां परस्परतो विशेषः । अन्यच्चेत् अर्थे कः प्रद्वेषः येन सर्वलोकप्रतीतिरपह्नू-

यते । तदेवं सिद्धो ज्ञानार्थयोर्भेदः । तथा च प्रयोगः । विवादाध्यासितं नीलादि ज्ञानाद्व्यतिरिक्तम्। विरुद्धधर्माध्यस्तत्वात्। विरुद्धधर्माध्यासश्च ज्ञानस्य शरीरान्तः अर्थस्य च बहिः । ज्ञानस्यापरकाले अर्थस्य च पूर्वकाले वृत्तिमत्त्वात् । ज्ञानस्य आत्मनः सकाशादर्थस्य स्वकारणेभ्य उत्पत्तेः । ज्ञानस्य प्रकाशरूपत्वादर्थस्य च जडरूपत्वादिति ।। अतो न ज्ञानाद्वैतेऽभ्युपगम्यमाने बहिरनुभूयमानार्थप्रतीतिः कथमपि संगतिमङ्गति । न च दृष्टमपह्नोतुं शक्यम् इति । अत एवाह स्तुतिकारः न संविदद्वैतपथेऽर्थसंविद् इति । सम्यग् अवैपरीत्येन विद्यतेअवगम्यते वस्तुस्वरूपमनयेति संवित्। स्वसंवेदनपक्षे तु संवेदनं संवित् ज्ञानं तस्या अद्वैतम् । द्वयोर्भावो द्विता द्वितैव द्वैतं प्रज्ञादित्वात् स्वार्थिकेऽणि । न द्वैतमद्वैतम् । बाह्यार्थप्रतिक्षेपादेकत्वम्। संविदद्वैतं ज्ञानमेवैकं तात्त्विकं न बाह्योऽर्थ इत्यभ्युपगम इत्यर्थः।तस्य पन्थाः मार्गः संविदद्वैतपथः तस्मिन् ज्ञानाद्वैतवादपक्ष इति यावत् । किमित्याह । नार्थसंवित् । येयं बहिर्मुखतयाऽर्थप्रतीतिः साक्षादनुभूयते सा न घटते इत्युपस्कारः । एतच्चानन्तरमेव भावितम् । एवंस्थिते सति किमित्याह । विलूनशीर्णं सुगतेन्द्रजालमिति । सुगतो मायापुत्रः तस्य संबन्धि तेन परिकल्पितं क्षणक्षयादिवस्तुजातम् । इन्द्रजालमिवेन्द्रजालम् । मतिव्यामोहविधातृत्वात् । सुगतेन्द्रजालं सर्वमिदं विलूनशीर्णम् । पूर्वं विलूनं पश्चात् शीर्णं विलूनशीर्णम् । यथा किंचित्तृणस्तम्बादि विलूनमेव शीर्यते विनश्यति एवं तत्कल्पितमिन्द्रजालं तृणप्रायं धारालयुक्तिशस्त्रिकया छिन्नं सद्विशीर्यत इति ॥ अथ वा यथा निपुणेन्द्रजालिककल्पितमिन्द्रजालमवास्तवतत्तद्वस्त्वद्भुततोपदर्शनेन तथाविधबुद्धिदुर्विदग्धं जनं विप्रतार्य पश्चादिन्द्रधनुरिव निरवयवं विलूनशीर्णतां कलयति तथा सुगतपरिकल्पितं तत्तत्प्रमाणतत्तत्फलाभेदक्षणक्षयज्ञानार्थहेतुकतत्त्वज्ञानाद्वैता-

भ्युपगमादि सर्वं प्रमाणानभिज्ञं लोकं व्यामोहयमानमपि युक्त्या विचायमाणं विशरारुतामेव सेवत इति। अत्र च सुगतशब्द उपहासार्थः। सौगता हि शोभनं गतं ज्ञानमस्येति सुगत इत्युशन्ति । ततश्चाहो तस्य शोभनज्ञानता येनेत्थमयुक्तियुक्तमुक्तमिति काव्यार्थः॥१६॥

अथ तत्त्वव्यवस्थापकप्रमाणादिचतुष्टयव्यवहारापलापिनः शून्यवादिनः सौगतजातीयांस्तत्कक्षीकृतपक्षसाधकस्य प्रमाणस्याङ्गीकारानङ्गीकारलक्षणपक्षद्वयेपि तदभिमतार्थासिद्धिप्रदर्शनपूर्वकमुपहसन्नाह ।

विना प्रमाणं परवन्न शून्यः
स्वपक्षसिद्धेः पदमश्नुवीत ।
कुप्येत्कृतान्तः स्पृशते प्रमाण-
महो सुदृष्टं त्वदसूयिदृष्टम् ॥ १७ ॥

शून्यः शून्यवादी प्रमाणं प्रत्यक्षादिकं विना अन्तरेण स्वपक्षसिद्धेः स्वाभ्युपगतशून्यवादनिष्पत्तेः पदं प्रतिष्ठां नाश्नुवीत न प्राप्नुयात्। किंवत् परवत् इतरप्रामाणिकवत्। वैधर्म्येणायं दृष्टान्तः। यथा इतरे प्रामाणिकाः प्रमाणेन साधकतमेन स्वपक्षसिद्धिमश्नुवते एवं नायम् । अस्य मते प्रमाणप्रमेयादिव्यवहारस्यापारमार्थिकत्वात्। सर्व एवायमनुमानानुमेयव्यवहारो बुद्ध्यारूढेन धर्मधर्मिभावेन न बहिःसदसत्त्वमपेक्षते इत्यादिवचनात् । अप्रमाणकश्च शून्यवादाभ्युपगमः कथमिव प्रेक्षावतामुपादेयो भविष्यति । प्रेक्षावत्त्वव्याहतिप्रसङ्गात् । अथ चेत्स्वपक्षसंसिद्धये किमपि प्रमाणमयमङ्गीकुरुते तत्रायमुपालम्भः कुप्येदित्यादि । प्रमाणं प्रत्यक्षाद्यन्यतमत्स्पृशते आश्रयमाणाय प्रकरणादस्मै शून्यवादिने कृतान्तः तत्सिद्धान्तः कुप्येत् कोपं कुर्यात् सिद्धान्तबाधः स्यादित्यर्थः। यथा

किल सेवकस्य विरुद्धवृत्त्या कुपितो नृपतिः सर्वस्वमपहरति एवं तत्सिद्धान्तोपि शून्यवादविरुद्धं प्रमाणभावमङ्गीकुर्वाणस्य तस्य सर्वस्वभूतं सम्यग्वादित्वमपहरति । किं च स्वागमोपदेशेनैव तेन वादिना शून्यवादः प्ररूप्यते इति स्वीकृतमागमस्य प्रामाण्यमिति कुतस्तस्य स्वपक्षसिद्धिः । प्रमाणाङ्गीकरणात् । किं च प्रमाणं प्रमेयं विना न भवतीति प्रमाणानङ्गीकरणे प्रमेयमपि विशीर्णम् । ततश्चास्य मूकतैव युक्ता न पुनः शून्यवादोपन्यासाय तुण्डताण्डवडम्बरम् । शून्यवादस्यापि प्रमेयत्वात् । अत्र च स्पृशिधातुं कृतान्तशब्दं च प्रयुञ्जानस्य सूरेरयमभिप्रायः । यद्यसौ शून्यवादी दूरे प्रमाणस्य सर्वथाङ्गीकारः यावत्प्रमाणस्पर्शमात्रपि विधत्ते तदा तस्मै कृतान्तो यमराजः कुप्येत् । तत्कोपो हि मरणफलः । ततश्च स्वसिद्धान्तविरुद्धमसौ प्रमाणयन्निग्रहस्थानापन्नत्वान्मृत एवेति । एवं सति अहो इत्युपहासप्रशंसायाम् तुभ्यमसूयन्ति गुणेषु दोषानाविष्कुर्वन्तीत्येवंशीलास्त्वदसूयिनः तन्त्रान्तरीयाः तैर्दृष्टं मत्यज्ञानचक्षुषा निरीक्षितम् अहो सुदृष्टं साधुदृष्टम् । विपरीतलक्षणयोपहासान्न सम्यग्दृष्टमित्यर्थः । अत्रासूयधातोस्ताच्छीलिकणकप्राप्तावपि बाहुलकाण्णिन् । असूयाऽस्त्येषामित्यसूयिनः त्वय्यसूयिनः त्वदसूयिनः इति मत्वर्थीयान्तं वा । त्वदसूयुदृष्टमिति पाठेपि न किंचिदचारु । असूयुशब्दस्योदन्तस्योदयनाद्यैर्न्यायतात्पर्यपरिशुद्ध्यादौ मत्सरिणि प्रयोगादिति ॥

इह शून्यवादिनामयमभिसंधिः । प्रमाता प्रमेयं प्रमाणं प्रमितिरिति तत्त्वचतुष्टयं परपरिकल्पितमवस्त्वेव । विचारासहत्वात् । तुरङ्गशृङ्गवत् । तत्र प्रमाता तावदात्मा तस्य च प्रमाणग्राह्यत्वाभावादभावः । तथा हि न प्रत्यक्षेण तत्सिद्धिः । इन्द्रियगोचरातिक्रान्तत्वात् । यत्तु अहंकारप्रत्ययेण तस्य मानसप्रत्यक्षत्वसाधनं

तदप्यनैकान्तिकम् । तस्याहं गौरः श्यामो वेत्यादौ शरीराश्रयतयाप्युपपत्तेः । किं च यद्ययमहंकारप्रत्यय आत्मगोचरः स्यात्तदा न कादाचित्कः स्यात् । आत्मनः सदा सन्निहितत्वात् । कादाचित्कं हि ज्ञानं कदाचित्कारणपूर्वकं दृष्टं यथा सौदामनीज्ञानमिति । नाप्यनुमानेन । अव्यभिचारिलिङ्गाग्रहणात् । आगमानां च परस्परविरुद्धार्थवादिनां नास्त्येव प्रामाण्यम् । तथा हि एकेन कथमपि कश्चिदर्थो व्यवस्थापितोऽभियुक्ततरेणापरेण स एवान्यथा व्यवस्थाप्यते । स्वयमव्यवस्थितप्रामाण्यानां च तेषां कथमन्यव्यवस्थापने सामर्थ्यम् । इति नास्ति प्रमाता ॥ प्रमेयं च बाह्योऽर्थः स चानन्तरमेव बाह्यार्थप्रतिक्षेपक्षणे निर्लोठितः ॥ प्रमाणं च स्वपरावभासिज्ञानम् । तच्च प्रमेयाभावे कस्य ग्राहकमस्तु । निर्विषयत्वात् । किं चैतदर्थसमकालं तद्भिन्नकालं वा तद्ग्राहकं कल्प्येत । आद्यपक्षे त्रिभुवनवर्तिनोपि पदार्थास्तत्रावभासेरन् । समकालत्वाविशेषात् । द्वितीये तु निराकारं साकारं वा तत्स्यात् । प्रथमे प्रतिनियतपदार्थपरिच्छेदानुपपत्तिः । द्वितीये तु किमयमाकारो व्यतिरिक्तोऽव्यतिरिक्तो वा ज्ञानात् । अव्यतिरेके ज्ञानमेवायं तथा च निराकारपक्षदोषः । व्यतिरेके यद्ययं चिद्रूपः तदानीमाकारोपि वेदकः स्यात् । तथा चायमपि निराकारः साकारो वा तद्वेदको भवेत् । इत्यावर्तनेनानवस्था । अथाचिद्रूपः किमज्ञातो ज्ञाता वा तज्ज्ञापकः स्यात् । प्राचीने विकल्पे चैत्रस्येव मैत्रस्यापि तज्ज्ञापकोऽसौ स्यात् । तदुत्तरे तु निराकारेण साकारेण वा ज्ञानेन तस्यापि ज्ञानं स्यात् । इत्याद्यावृत्तावनवस्थैवेति ॥ इत्थं प्रमाणाभावे तत्फलरूपा प्रमितिः कुतस्तनी । इति सर्वशून्यतैव परं तत्त्वमिति । तथा च पठन्ति ।

यथा यथा विचार्यन्ते विशीर्यन्ते तथा तथा ।
यदेतत्स्वयमर्थेभ्यो रोचते तत्र के वयम् ॥

इति पूर्वपक्षः। विस्तरतस्तु प्रमाणखण्डनं तत्त्वोपप्लवसिंहादवलोकनीयम् ॥

अत्र प्रतिविधीयते । ननु यदिदं शून्यवादव्यवस्थापनाय देवानांप्रियेण वचनमुपन्यस्तं तच्छून्यमशून्यं वा । शून्यं चेत् सर्वोपाख्याविरहितत्वात्खपुष्पेणेव नामेन किंचित्साध्यते निषिध्यते वा । ततश्च निष्प्रतिपक्षा प्रमाणादितत्त्वचतुष्टयीव्यवस्था । अशून्यं चेत् प्रलीनस्तपस्वी शून्यवादः । भवद्वचनेनैव सर्वशून्यताया व्यभिचारात् । तत्रापि निष्कण्टकैव सा भगवती । तथापि प्रामाणिकसमयपरिपालनार्थं किञ्चित्तत्साधनं दूष्यते । तत्र यत्तावदुक्तं प्रमातुः प्रत्यक्षेण न सिद्धिरिन्द्रियगोचरातिक्रान्तत्वात् इति तत्सिद्धसाधनम् । यत्पुनरहंप्रत्ययेन तस्य मानसप्रत्यक्षत्वमनैकान्तिकमित्युक्तं तदसिद्धम् । अहं सुखी अहं दुःखीत्यन्तर्मुखस्य प्रत्ययस्य आत्मालम्बनतयैवोपपत्तेः । तथा चाहुः ।

सुखादि चेत्यमानं हि स्वतन्त्रं नानुभूयते ।
मतुबर्थानुवेधात्तु सिद्धं ग्रहणमात्मनः ॥
इदं सुखमिति ज्ञानं दृश्यते न घटादिवत् ।
अहं सुखीति तु ज्ञप्तिरात्मनोऽपि प्रकाशिका ॥

यत्पुनरहं गौरः अहं श्याम इत्यादिबहिर्मुखः प्रत्ययः स खल्वात्मोपकारकत्वेन लक्षणया शरीरे प्रयुज्यते । यथा प्रियभृत्येऽहमिति व्यपदेशः । यच्चाहंप्रत्ययस्य कादाचित्कत्वं तत्रेयं वासना । आत्मा तावदुपयोगलक्षणः । स च साकारानाकारोपयोगयोरन्यतरस्मिन्नियमेनोपयुक्त एव भवति । अहंप्रत्ययोपि चोपयोगविशेष एव । तस्य च कर्मक्षयोपशमवैचित्र्यादिन्द्रियानिन्द्रियालोकविषयादिनिमित्तसव्यपेक्षतया प्रवर्तमानस्य कादाचित्कत्वमुपपन्नमेव । यथा बीजं सत्यामप्यङ्कुरोपजननशक्तौ पृथिव्युदकादिसहकारिकारणकलाप-

समवहितमेवाङ्कुरं जनयति नान्यथा । न चैतावता तस्याङ्कुरोत्पादने कादाचित्केऽपि तदुत्पादनशक्तिरपि कादाचित्की । तस्याः कथंचिन्नित्यत्वात् । एवमात्मनः सदा सन्निहितत्वेऽप्यहंप्रत्ययस्य कादाचित्कत्वम् । यदप्युक्तं तस्याव्यभिचारि लिङ्गं किमपि नोपलभ्यते इति तदप्यसारम् । साध्याविनाभाविनोऽनेकस्य लिङ्गस्य तत्रोपलब्धेः । तथा हि । रूपाद्युपलब्धिः सकर्तृका । क्रियात्वात् । छिदिक्रियावत् । यश्चास्याः कर्ता स आत्मा । न चात्र चक्षुरादीनां कर्तृत्वम् । तेषां कुठारादिवत् करणत्वेनास्वतन्त्रत्वात् । करणत्वं चैषां पौद्गलिकत्वेनाचेतनत्वात् । परप्रेर्यत्वात् । प्रयोक्तृव्यापारनिरपेक्षप्रवृत्त्यभावात् । यदीन्द्रियाणामेव कर्तृत्वं स्यात्तदा तेषु विनष्टेषु पूर्वानुभूतार्थस्मृतेर्मया दृष्टं स्पृष्टम् आघ्रातम् आस्वादितं श्रुतमिति प्रत्ययानामेककर्तृकत्वप्रतिपत्तेश्च कुतः संभवः । किंच इन्द्रियाणां स्वस्वविषयनियतत्वेन रूपरसयोः साहचर्यप्रतीतौ न सामर्थ्यम् । अस्ति च तथाविधफलादे रूपग्रहणानन्तरं तत्सहचरितरसानुस्मरणम् । दन्तोदकसंप्लवान्यथानुपपत्तेः । तस्मादुभयोर्गवाक्षयोरन्तर्गतः प्रेक्षक इव द्वाभ्यामिन्द्रियाभ्यां रूपरसयोर्दर्शी कश्चिदेकोऽनुमीयते । तस्मात्करणान्येतानि । यश्चैषां व्यापारयिता स आत्मा । तथा साधनोपादानपरिवर्जनद्वारेण हिताहितप्राप्तिपरिहारसमर्था चेष्टा प्रयत्नपूर्विका । विशिष्टक्रियात्वात् । रथक्रियावत् । शरीरं च प्रयत्नवदधिष्ठितम् । विशिष्टक्रियाश्रयत्वात् रथवत् यश्चास्याधिष्ठाता स आत्मा । सारथिवत् । तथात्रैव पक्षे इच्छापूर्वकविकृतवाय्वाश्रयत्वात् । भस्त्रावत् । वायुश्च प्राणापानादिश्चास्याधिष्ठाता स आत्मा । भस्त्राध्मापयितृवत् । तथा अत्रैव पक्षे इच्छाधीननिमेषोन्मेषवदवयवयोगित्वात् । दारुयन्त्रवत् । तथा शरीरस्य वृद्धिक्षतभग्नसंरोहणं च प्रयत्नवत्कृतम् । वृद्धिक्षतभग्नसंरोहणत्वात् । गृहवृद्धिक्षतभग्नसंरो-

ह्णवत् । वृक्षादिगतेन वृद्ध्यादिना व्यभिचार इति चेत् न । तेषामपि एकेन्द्रियजन्तुत्वेन सात्मकत्वात् । यश्चैषां कर्ता स आत्मा । गृहपतिवत् । वृक्षादीनां च सात्मकत्वमाचाराङ्गादेरवसेयम् । किंचिद्वक्ष्यते च । तथा प्रेर्यं मनः । अभिमतविषयसंबन्धनिमित्तक्रियाश्रयत्वात् । दारकहस्तगतगोलकवत् । यश्चास्य प्रेरकः स आत्मा इति । तथा आत्मचेतनक्षेत्रज्ञजीवपुरुषादयः पर्याया न निर्विषयाः । पर्यायत्वात् । घटकुटकलशादिपर्यायवत् । व्यतिरेके षष्ठभूतादि । यश्चैषां विषयः स आत्मा । तथा अस्त्यात्मा । असमस्तपर्यायवाच्यत्वात् । यो यः साङ्केतिकशुद्धपर्यायवाच्यः स सोऽस्तित्वं न व्यभिचरति । यथा घटादि । व्यतिरेके खरविषाणनभोम्भोरुहादयः । तथा सुखादीनि द्रव्याश्रितानि गुणत्वात् रूपवत् । योऽसौ गुणी स आत्मा । इत्यादिलिङ्गानि । तस्मादनुमानतोऽप्यात्मा सिद्धः ॥ आगमानां च येषां पूर्वापरविरुद्धार्थत्वं तेषामप्रामाण्यमेव । यस्त्वाप्तप्रणीत आगमः स प्रमाणमेव । कषच्छेदतापलक्षणोपाधित्रयविशुद्धत्वात् । कषादीनां च स्वरूपं पुरस्ताद्वक्ष्यामः । न च वाच्यमाप्तः क्षीणसर्वदोषः तथाविधं चाप्तत्वं कस्यापि नास्तीति । यतो रागादयः कस्यचिदत्यन्तमुच्छिद्यन्ते । अस्मदादिषु तदुच्छेदप्रकर्षापकर्षोपलम्भात् । सूर्याद्यावरकजलदपटलवत् । तथा चाहुः ।

देशतो नाशिनो भावा दृष्टा निखिलनश्वराः ।
मेघपङ्क्त्यादयो यद्वदेवं रागादयो मताः ॥

इति । यस्य च निरवयवतयैते विलीनाः स एवाप्तो भगवान् सर्वज्ञः । अथानादित्वाद्रागादीनां कथं प्रक्षय इति चेन्न । उपायतस्तद्भावात् । अनादेरपि सुवर्णमलस्य क्षारमृत्पुटपाकादिना विलयोपलम्भात् । तद्वदेवानादीनामपि रागादिदोषाणां प्रतिपक्षभूतरत्नत्रया-

भ्यासेन विलयोपपत्तेः। क्षीणदोषस्य च केवलज्ञानाव्यभिचारात्सर्वज्ञत्वम्। तत्सिद्धिस्तु ज्ञानतारतम्यं क्वचिद्विश्रान्तं तारम्यत्वात् आकाशपरिमाणतारतम्यवत्। तथा सूक्ष्मान्तरितदूरार्थाः कस्यचित्प्रत्यक्षा अनुमेयत्वात् क्षितिधरकन्धराधिकरणधूमध्वजवत्। एवं चन्द्रसूर्योपरागादिसूचकज्योतिर्ज्ञानाविसंवादान्यथानुपपत्तिप्रभृतयोऽपि हेतवो वाच्याः। तदेवमाप्तेन सर्वविदा प्रणीत आगमः प्रमाणमेव। तदप्रामाण्यं हि प्रणायकदोषनिबन्धनम्।

रागाद्वा द्वेषाद्वा मोहाद्वा वाक्यमुच्यते ह्यनृतम्।
यस्य तु नैते दोषास्तस्यानृतकारणं किं स्यात्॥

इति वचनात्। प्रणेतुश्च निर्दोषत्वमुपपादितमेवेति सिद्ध आगमादप्यात्मा। एगे आया इत्यादिवचनात्॥ तदेवं प्रत्यक्षानुमानागमैः सिद्धः प्रमाता॥

प्रमेयं चानन्तरमेव बाह्यार्थसाधने साधितम्। तत्सिद्धौ च प्रमाणं ज्ञानं प्रमेयाभावे कस्य ग्राहकमस्तु निर्विषयत्वादिति प्रलापमात्रम्। करणमन्तरेण क्रियासिद्धेरयोगात्। लवनादिषु तथादर्शनात्। यच्चात्र समकालमित्याद्युक्तं तत्र विकल्पद्वयमपि स्वीक्रियत एव। अस्मदादिप्रत्यक्षं हि समकालार्थाकलनकुशलम्। स्मरणमतीतार्थस्य ग्राहकम्। शब्दानुमाने च त्रैकालिकस्याप्यर्थस्य परिच्छेदके। निराकारं चैतद्द्वयमपि। न चातिप्रसङ्गः। स्वज्ञानावरणवीर्यान्तरायक्षयोपशमविशेषवशादेवास्य नैयत्येन प्रवृत्तेः। शेषविकल्पानामस्वीकार एव तिरस्कारः॥

प्रमितिस्तु प्रमाणस्य फलं स्वसंवेदनसिद्धैव। न ह्यनुभवेऽप्युपदेशापेक्षा। फलं च द्विधा। आनन्तर्यपारंपर्यभेदात्। तत्रानन्तर्येण सर्वप्रमाणानामज्ञाननिवृत्तिः फलम्। पारंपर्येण केवलज्ञानस्य तावत् फलमौदासीन्यम्। शेषप्रमाणानां तु हानोपादानोपेक्षा-

बुद्धयः ॥ इति सुव्यवस्थितं प्रमात्रादिचतुष्टयम् ॥

ततश्च

नासन्न सन्न सदसन्न चाप्यनुभयात्मकम् ।
चतुष्कोटिविनिर्मुक्तं तत्त्वमाध्यात्मिका विदुः ॥

इत्युन्मत्तभाषितम् ॥ किं चेदं प्रमात्रादीनामवास्तवत्वं शून्यवादिना वस्तुवृत्त्या तावदेष्टव्यम् । तच्चासौ प्रमाणादभिमन्यते अप्रमाणाद्वा । न तावदप्रमाणात् । तस्याकिंचित्करत्वात् । अथ प्रमाणात् । तन्न । अवास्तवत्वग्राहकं प्रमाणं सांवृतमसांवृतं वा स्यात् । यदि सांवृतं कथं तस्मादवास्तवाद्वास्तवस्य शून्यवादस्य सिद्धिः । तथा तदसिद्धौ च वास्तव एव समस्तोपि प्रमात्रादिव्यवहारः प्राप्तः । अथ तद्ग्राहकं प्रमाणं स्वयमसांवृतम् । तर्हि क्षीणा प्रमात्रादिव्यवहारावास्तवत्वप्रतिज्ञा । तेनैव व्यभिचारात् । तदेवं पक्षद्वयेपि इतो व्याघ्र इतस्तटीति न्यायेन व्यक्त एव परमार्थतः स्वाभिमतसिद्धिविरोधः ॥ इति काव्यार्थः ॥ १७ ॥

अधुना क्षणिकवादिन ऐहिकामुष्मिकव्यवहारानुपपन्नार्थसमर्थनमविमृश्यकारितं दर्शयन्नाह ।

कृतप्रणाशाकृतकर्मभोग-
भवप्रमोक्षस्मृतिभङ्गदोषान् ।
उपेक्ष्य साक्षात् क्षणभङ्गमिच्छ-
न्नहो महासाहसिकः परस्ते ॥ १८ ॥

कृतप्रणाशदोषमकृतकर्मभोगदोषं भवभङ्गदोषं प्रमोक्षभङ्गदोषं स्मृतिभङ्गदोषमित्येतान् । साक्षादित्यनुभवासिद्धान् । उपेक्ष्य अनादृत्य । साक्षात्कुर्वन्नपि गजनिमीलिकामवलम्बमानः । क्षणभङ्गम् उदया-

नन्तरविनाशरूपक्षणक्षयिताम् । इच्छन् प्रतिपद्यमानः। ते तव। परः प्रतिपक्षः वैनाशिकः सौगत इत्यर्थः। अहो महासाहसिकः। सहसा अविमर्शात्मकेन बलेन वर्तते साहसिकः । भाविनमनर्थमविभाव्य यः प्रवर्तते स एवमुच्यते । महांश्चासौ साहसिकश्च महासाहसिकः अत्यन्तमविमृश्य प्रवृत्तिकारी । इति मुकुलितार्थः ॥

विवृतार्थस्त्वयम्। बौद्धा बुद्धिक्षणपरंपरामात्रमेवात्मानमामनन्ति न पुनर्मौक्तिककणनिकरानुस्यूतैकसूत्रवत्तदन्वयिनमेकम्।तन्मते येन ज्ञानक्षणेन सदनुष्ठानमसदनुष्ठानं वा कृतं तस्य निरन्वयविनाशान्न तत्फलोपभोगः यस्य च फलोपभोगस्तेन तत्कर्म न कृतमिति प्राच्यज्ञानक्षणस्य कृतप्रणाशः स्वकृतकर्मफलानुपभोगात् उत्तरज्ञानक्षणस्य चाकृतकर्मभोगः स्वयमकृतस्य कर्मणः फलोपभोगादिति। अत्र कर्मशब्दः उभयत्रापि योज्यः। तेन कृतप्रणाश इत्यस्य कृतकर्मप्रणाश इत्यर्थो दृश्यः।बन्धानुलोम्याच्चेत्थमुपन्यासः।।तथा भवभङ्गदोषः।भव आजवीभावलक्षणः संसारः तस्य भङ्गो विलोपः स एव दोषः क्षणिकवादे प्रसज्यते । परलोकाभावप्रसङ्ग इत्यर्थः । परलोकिनः कस्यचिदभावात् । परलोको हि पूर्वजन्मकृतकर्मानुसारेण भवति। तच्च प्राचीनज्ञानक्षणानां निरन्वयं नाशात् केन नामोपभुज्यतां जन्मान्तरे। यच्च मोक्षाकरगुप्तेन यच्चित्तं तच्चित्तान्तरं प्रतिसंधत्ते यथेदानीन्तनं चित्तं चित्तं च मरणकालभावि इति भवपरंपरासिद्धये प्रमाणमुक्तं तद्व्यर्थम् । चित्तक्षणानां निरवशेषनाशिनां चित्तान्तरप्रतिसंधानायोगात् । द्वयोरवस्थितयोर्हि प्रतिसंधानमुभयानुगामिना केनचित्क्रियते । यश्चानयोः प्रतिसंधाता स तेन नाभ्युपगम्यते। स ह्यात्माऽन्वयी। न च प्रतिसंधत्ते इत्यस्य जनयतीत्यर्थः । कार्यहेतुप्रसङ्गात् । तेन वादिनाऽस्य हेतोः स्वभावहेतुत्वेनोक्तत्वात् । स्वभावहेतुश्च तादात्म्ये सति भवति । भिन्नकालभाविनोश्च

चित्तचित्तान्तरयोः कुतस्तादात्म्यम् । युगपद्भाविनोश्च प्रतिसंधेयप्रतिसंधायकत्वाभावापत्तिः । युगपद्भावित्वेऽविशिष्टेपि किमत्र नियामकं यदेकः प्रतिसंधायकोऽपरश्च प्रतिसंधेय इति । अस्तु वा प्रतिसंधानस्य जननमर्थः । सोप्यनुपपन्नः । तुल्यकालत्वे हेतुफलभावस्याभावात् । भिन्नकालत्वे च पूर्वचित्तक्षणस्य विनष्टत्वात् उत्तरचित्तक्षणः कथमुपादानमन्तरेणोत्पद्यताम्। इति यत्किंचिदेतत्॥ तथा प्रमोक्षभङ्गदोषः। प्रकर्षेणापुनर्भावेन कर्मबन्धनान्मुक्तिः प्रमोक्षः तस्यापि भङ्गः प्राप्नोति । तन्मते तावदात्मैव नास्ति कः प्रेत्य सुखीभवनार्थं यतिष्यते । ज्ञानक्षणोपि संसारी कथमपरज्ञानक्षणसुखीभवनाय घटिष्यते । न हि दुःखी देवदत्तो यज्ञदत्तसुखाय चेष्टमानो दृष्टः। क्षणस्य तु दुःखं स्वरसनाशित्वात्तेनैव सार्धं दध्वंसे। संतानस्तु न वास्तवः कश्चित् । वास्तवत्वे तु आत्माभ्युपगमप्रसङ्गः। अपि च बौद्धा निखिलवासनोच्छेदे विगतविषयाकारोपप्लवविशुद्धज्ञानोत्पादो मोक्ष इत्याहुस्तच्च न घटते। कारणाभावादेव तदनुपपत्तेः। भावनाप्रचयो हि तस्य कारणमिष्यते। स च स्थिरैकाश्रयाभावाद्विशेषानाधायकः प्रतिक्षणमपूर्ववदुपजायमानो निरन्वयविनाशी गगनलङ्घनाभ्यासवदनासादितप्रकर्षो न स्फुटाभिज्ञानजननाय प्रभवतीत्यनुपपत्तिरेव तस्य। समलचित्तक्षणानां स्वाभाविक्याः सदृशारम्भणशक्तेरसदृशारम्भं प्रत्यशक्तेश्चाकस्मादनुच्छेदात् । किं च समलचित्तक्षणाः पूर्वं स्वरसपरिनिर्वाणाः अयमपूर्वो जातः संतानश्चैको न विद्यते बन्धमोक्षौ चैकाधिकरणौ न विषयभेदेन वर्तेते तत्कस्येयं मुक्तिर्य एतदर्थं प्रयतते। अयं हि मोक्षशब्दो बन्धनविच्छेदपर्यायः। मोक्षश्च तस्यैव घटते यो बद्धः। क्षणक्षयवादे त्वन्यः क्षणो बद्धः क्षणान्तरस्य मुक्तिरिति मोक्षाभावः प्राप्नोति ॥ तथा स्मृतिभङ्गदोषः । तथा

हि पूर्वबुद्ध्यानुभूतेऽर्थे नोत्तरबुद्धीनां स्मृतिः संभवति । ततोऽन्यत्वात् । संतानान्तरबुद्धिवत् । न ह्यन्यदृष्टोऽर्थोऽन्येन स्मर्यते । अन्यथा एकेन दृष्टोऽर्थः सर्वैः स्मर्येत । स्मरणाभावे च कौतस्कुती प्रत्यभिज्ञाप्रसूतिः । तस्याः स्मरणानुभवोभयसंभवत्वात् । पदार्थप्रेक्षणप्रबुद्धप्राक्तनसंस्कारस्य हि प्रमातुः स एवायमित्याकारेणेयमुत्पद्यते । अथ स्यादयं दोषो यद्यविशेषेणान्यदृष्टमन्यः स्मरतीत्युच्यते । किंत्वन्यत्वेपि कार्यकारणभावादेव च स्मृतिः । भिन्नसंतानबुद्धीनां तु कार्यकारणभावो नास्ति तेन संतानान्तराणां स्मृतिर्न भवति । न चैकसांतानिकीनामपि बुद्धीनां कार्यकारणभावो नास्ति येन पूर्वबुद्ध्यनुभूतेर्थे तदुत्तरबुद्धीनां स्मृतिर्न स्यात् । तदप्यनवदातम् । एवमपि अन्यत्वस्य तदवस्थत्वात् । न हि कार्यकारणभावाभिधानेपि तदपगतम् । क्षणिकत्वेन सर्वासां भिन्नत्वात् । न हि कार्यकारणभावात्स्मृतिरित्यत्रोभयप्रसिद्धोस्ति दृष्टान्तः । अथ

यस्मिन्नेव हि संताने आहिता कर्मवासना ।
फलं तत्रैव संधत्ते कर्पासे रक्तता यथा ॥

इति कर्पासरक्ततादृष्टान्तोस्तीति चेत् तदसाधीयः । साधनदूषणयोरसंभवात् । तथा हि अन्वयाद्यसंभवान्न साधनम् । न हि कार्यकारणभावो यत्र तत्र स्मृतिः कर्पासे रक्ततावदित्यन्वयः संभवति । नापि यत्र न स्मृतिस्तत्र न कार्यकारणभाव इति व्यतिरेकोस्ति । असिद्धत्वाद्यनुद्भावनाच्च न दूषणम् । न हि ततोन्यत्वादित्यस्य हेतोः कर्पासे रक्ततावदित्यनेन कश्चिद्दोषः प्रतिपाद्यते । किंच यद्यन्यत्वेपि कार्यकारणभावेन स्मृतेरुत्पत्तिरिष्यते तदा शिष्याचार्यादिबुद्धीनामपि कार्यकारणभावसद्भावेन स्मृत्यादिः स्यात् । अथ नायं प्रसङ्गः एकसंतानत्वे सतीतिविशेषणादिति चेत्

तदप्ययुक्तम्। भेदाभेदपक्षाभ्यां तस्योपक्षीणत्वात्। क्षणपरंपरातस्तस्याभेदे हि क्षणपरंपरैव सा। तथा च संतान इति न किंचिदतिरिक्तमुक्तं स्यात्। भेदे त्वपारमार्थिकः पारमार्थिको वाऽसौ स्यात्। अपारमार्थिकत्वेऽस्य तदेव दूषणम्।अकिंचित्करत्वात्।पारमार्थिकत्वे स्थिरो वा स्यात् क्षणिको वा। क्षणिकत्वे संताननिर्विशेष एवायमिति किमनेन स्तेनभीतस्य स्तेनान्तरशरणस्वीकरणानुकरणिना। स्थिरश्चेत् आत्मैव संज्ञाभेदतिरोहितः प्रतिपन्नः। इति न स्मृतिर्घटते क्षणक्षयवादिनाम्। तदभावे चानुमानस्यानुत्थानमित्युक्तं प्रागेव। अपि च स्मृतेरभावे निहितप्रत्युन्मार्गणप्रत्यर्पणादिव्यवहारा विशीर्येरन्।

इत्येकनवते कल्पे शक्त्या मे पुरुषो हतः।
तेन कर्मविपाकेन पादे विद्धोऽस्मि भिक्षवः॥

इति वचनस्य च का गतिः। एवमुत्पत्तिरुत्पादयति स्थितिः स्थापयति जरा जर्जरयाति विनाशो नाशयति इति चतुःक्षणिकं वस्तु प्रतिजानाना अपि प्रतिक्षेप्याः। क्षणचतुष्कानन्तरमपि निहितप्रत्युन्मार्गणादिव्यवहाराणां दर्शनात्॥तदेवमनेकदोषापातेऽपि यः क्षणभङ्गमभिप्रैति तस्य महत् साहसमिति काव्यार्थः॥१८॥

अथ ताथागताः क्षणक्षयपक्षे सर्वव्यवहारानुपपत्तिं परैः सद्भावितामाकर्ण्येत्थं प्रतिपादयिष्यन्ति। यत्सर्वपदार्थानां क्षणिकत्वेऽपि वासनाबललब्धजन्मना ऐक्याध्यवसायेन ऐहिकामुष्मिकव्यवहारप्रवृत्तेः कृतप्रणाशादिदोषा निरवकाशा एवेति। तदाकूतं परिहर्तुकामस्तत्कल्पितवासनायाः क्षणपरंपरातो भेदाभेदानुभयलक्षणे पक्षत्रयेऽप्यघटमानत्वं दर्शयन् स्वाभिप्रेतभेदाभेदस्याद्वादमकामयमानानपि तानङ्गीकारयितुमाह।

सा वासना सा क्षणसंततिश्च
नाभेदभेदानुभयैर्घटेते ।
ततस्तटादर्शिशकुन्तपोत-
न्यायात्त्वदुक्तानि परे श्रयन्तु ॥ १९ ॥

सा शाक्यपरिकल्पिता त्रुटितमुक्तावलीकल्पानां परस्परविशकलितानां क्षणानामन्योन्यानुस्यूतप्रत्ययजनिका एकसूत्रस्थानीया संतानापरपर्याया वासना । वासनेति पूर्वज्ञानजनितामुत्तरज्ञाने शक्तिमाहुः । सा च क्षणसंततिस्तद्दर्शनप्रसिद्धा प्रदीपकलिकावन्नवनवोत्पद्यमानाऽपरापरसदृशक्षणपरंपरा । एते द्वे अपि अभेदभेदानुभयैर्न घटेते ॥ न तावदभेदेन तादात्म्येन ते घटेते । तयोर्हि अभेदे वासना वा स्यात् क्षणपरंपरा वा । न द्वयम् । यद्धि यस्मादभिन्नं न ततः पृथगुपलभ्यते यथा घटात् घटस्वरूपम् । केवलायां वासनायामन्वयिस्वीकारः। वास्याभावे च किं तया वासनीयमस्तु । इति तस्या अपि न स्वरूपमवतिष्ठते । क्षणपरंपरामात्राङ्गीकरणे च प्राञ्च एव दोषाः ॥ न च भेदेन ते युज्येते। सा हि भिन्ना वासना क्षणिका स्यादक्षणिका वा । क्षणिका चेत् तर्हि क्षणेभ्यस्तस्याः पृथक्कल्पनं व्यर्थम् । अक्षणिका चेदन्वयिपदार्थाभ्युपगमेनागमबाधः । तथा च पदार्थान्तराणां क्षणिकत्वकल्पनाप्रयासो व्यसनमात्रम् ॥ अनुभयपक्षेणापि न घटेते । स हि कदाचिदेवं ब्रूयात् नाहं वासनायाः क्षणश्रेणितोऽभेदं प्रतिपद्ये न च भेदं किं त्वनुभयमिति। तदप्यनुचितम्। भेदाभेदयोर्विधिनिषेधरूपयोरेकतरप्रतिषेधेऽन्यतरस्यावश्यं विधिभावादन्यतरपक्षाभ्युपगमः । तत्र च प्रागुक्त एव दोषः । अथवाऽनुभयरूपत्वेऽवस्तुत्वप्रसङ्गः । भेदाभेदलक्षणपक्षद्वयव्यतिरिक्तस्य मार्गान्तरस्यानस्तित्वात्।अनार्हतानां हि

वस्तुना भिन्नेन वा भाव्यमभिन्नेन वा। तदुभयातीतस्य वन्ध्यास्तनन्धयप्रायत्वात् । एवं विकल्पत्रयेपि क्षणपरंपरावासनयोरनुपपत्तौ पारिशेष्याद्भेदाभेदपक्ष एव कक्षीकरणीयः । न च प्रत्येकं यो भवेद्दोषो द्वयोर्भावे कथं न सः इति वचनादत्रापि दोषतादवस्थ्यमिति वाच्यम्।कुक्कुटसर्पनरसिंहादिवज्जात्यन्तरत्वादनेकान्तपक्षस्य । नन्वार्हतानां वासनाक्षणपरंपरयोरङ्गीकार एव नास्ति तत्कथं तदाश्रयभेदाभेदचिन्ता चरितार्था इति चेन्नैवम् । स्याद्वादवादिनामपि हि प्रतिक्षणं नवनवपर्यायपरंपरोत्पत्तिरभिमतैव ।तथा च क्षणिकत्वम् । अतीतानागतवर्तमानपर्यायपरंपरानुसंधायकं चान्वयि द्रव्यम्।तच्च वासनेतिसंज्ञान्तरभागपि अभिमतमेव। न खलु नामभेदाद्वादः कोपि कोविदानाम् । सा च प्रतिक्षणोत्पादिष्णुपर्यायपरंपरा अन्वयिद्रव्यात् कथंचिद्भिन्ना कथंचिदभिन्ना। तथा तदपि तस्याः स्याद्भिन्नं स्यादभिन्नम् । इति पृथक्प्रत्ययव्यपदेशविषयत्वाद्भेदः। द्रव्यस्यैव च तथा तथा परिणमनादभेदः। एतच्च सकलादेशविकलादेशव्याख्याने पुरस्तात्प्रपञ्चयिष्यामः ॥

अपि च बौद्धमते वासनापि तावन्न घटते इति निर्विषया तत्र भेदादिविकल्पचिन्ता। तल्लक्षणं हि पूर्वक्षणेनोत्तरक्षणस्य वास्यता। न चास्थिराणां भिन्नकालतयाऽन्योन्यासंबद्धानां च तेषां वास्यवासकभावो युज्यते । स्थिरस्य संबद्धस्य च वस्त्रादेर्मृगमदादिना वास्यत्वं दृष्टमिति । अथ पूर्वचित्तसहजाच्चेतनाविशेषात्पूर्वशक्तिविशिष्टं चित्तमुत्पद्यते सोऽस्यशक्तिविशिष्टचित्तोत्पादो वासना । तथा हि पूर्वचित्तं रूपादिविषयं प्रवृत्तिविज्ञानं यत् तत् षड्विधम् । पञ्च रूपादिविज्ञानान्यविकल्पकानि षष्ठं च विकल्पविज्ञानम् । तेन सह जातः समानकालश्चेतनाविशेषोऽहंकारास्पदमालयविज्ञानम् । तस्मात्पूर्वशक्तिविशिष्टचित्तोत्पादो वासनेति । तदपि न । अस्थि-

रत्वाद्वासकेनासंबन्धाच्च । यश्चासौ चेतनाविशेषः पूर्वचित्तसहभावी स न वर्तमाने चेतस्युपकारं करोति । वर्तमानस्याशक्यापनेयोपनेयत्वेनाविकार्यत्वात् । तद्धि यथाभूतं जायते तथाभूतं विनश्यतीति । नाप्यनागत उपकारं करोति । तेन सहासंबद्धत्वात् । असंबद्धं च न भावयतीत्युक्तम् । तस्मात् सौगतमते वासनापि न घटते । अत्र च स्तुतिकारेणाभ्युपेत्यापि तामन्वयिद्रव्यस्थापनाय भेदाभेदादिचर्चा विरचितेति भावनीयम् ॥

अथोत्तरार्धव्याख्या । तत इति ॥ पक्षत्रयेपि दोषसद्भावात् त्वदुक्तानि भवद्वचनानि भेदाभेदस्याद्वादसंवादपूतानि परे कुतीर्थ्याः प्रकरणान्मायासूनवीयाः श्रयन्तु आद्रियन्ताम् । अत्रोपमानमाह तटादर्शीत्यादि । तटं न पश्यतीति तटादर्शी यः शकुन्तपोतः पक्षिशावकः तस्य न्यायः उदाहरणं तस्मात् । यथा किल कथमप्यपारपारावारान्तःपतितः काकादिशकुनिशावको बहिर्निर्जिगमिषया प्रवहणकूपस्तम्भादेस्तटप्राप्तये मुग्धतयोड्डीनः समन्ताज्जलैकार्णवमेवावलोकयंस्तटमदृष्ट्वैव निर्वेदाद्व्यावृत्त्य तदेव कूपस्तम्भादिस्थानमाश्रयते गत्यन्तराभावादेवं तेपि कुतीर्थ्याः प्रागुक्तपक्षत्रयेपि वस्तुसिद्धिमनासादयन्तस्त्वदुक्तमेव चतुर्थं भेदाभेदपक्षमनिच्छयापि कक्षीकुर्वाणास्त्वच्छासनमेव प्रतिपद्यन्ताम् । न हि स्वस्य बलविकलतामाकलय्य बलीयसः प्रभोः शरणाश्रयणं दोषपोषाय नीतिशालिनाम् । त्वदुक्तानीति बहुवचनं सर्वेषामपि तन्त्रान्तरीयाणां पदे पदेऽनेकान्तवादप्रतिपत्तिरेव यथावस्थितपदार्थप्रतिपादनौपयिकं नान्यदिति ज्ञापनार्थम् । अनन्तधर्मात्मकस्य सर्वस्य वस्तुनः सर्वनयात्मकेन स्याद्वादेन विना यथावद्ग्रहीतुमशक्यत्वात् । इतरथान्धगजन्यायेन पल्लवग्राहिताप्रसङ्गात् ॥ श्रयन्तीति वर्तमानान्तं केचित्पठन्ति तथा-

प्यदोषः ॥ अत्र च समुद्रस्थानीयः संसारः । पोतसमानं त्वच्छासनम् । कूपस्तम्भसंनिभः स्याद्वादः । पक्षिपोतोपमा वादिनः । ते च स्वाभिमतपक्षप्ररूपणोड्डयनेन मुक्तिलक्षणतटप्राप्तये कृतप्रयत्ना अपि तस्मादिष्टार्थसिद्धिमपश्यन्तो व्यावृत्य स्याद्वादरूपकूपस्तम्भालङ्कृततावकीनशासनप्रवहणोपसर्पणमेव यदि शरणीकुर्वते तदा तेषां भवार्णवाद्बहिर्निष्क्रमणमनोरथः सफलतां कलयति नापरथेति काव्यार्थः ॥ १९ ॥

एवं क्रियावादिनां प्रावादुकानां कतिपयकुग्रहनिग्रहं विधाय सांप्रतमक्रियावादिनां लौकायतिकानां मतं सर्वाधमत्वादन्ते उपन्यस्यन् तन्मतमूलस्य प्रत्यक्षप्रमाणस्यानुमानादिप्रमाणान्तरानङ्गीकारेऽकिञ्चित्करत्वप्रदर्शनेन तेषां प्रज्ञायाः प्रमादमादर्शयति ।

विनानुमानेन पराभिसंधि-
मसंविदानस्य तु नास्तिकस्य ।
न सांप्रतं वक्तुमपि क्व चेष्टा
क्व दृष्टमात्रं च हहा प्रमादः ॥ २० ॥

प्रत्यक्षमेवैकं प्रमाणमिति मन्यते चार्वाकः । तत्र संनह्यते ॥ अनु पश्चाद् लिङ्गसंबन्धग्रहणस्मरणानन्तरं मीयते परिच्छिद्यते देशकालस्वभावविप्रकृष्टोर्थोनेन ज्ञानविशेषेणेत्यनुमानम् । प्रस्तावात् स्वार्थानुमानम् । तेनानुमानेन लैङ्गिकप्रमाणेन विना पराभिसंधिं पराभिप्रायम् असंविदानस्य सम्यगजानानस्य। तुशब्दः पूर्ववादिभ्यो भेदद्योतनार्थः। पूर्वेषां वादिनामास्तिकतया विप्रतिपत्तिस्थानेषु क्षोदः कृतः नास्तिकस्य तु वक्तुमपि नौचिती कुत एव तेन सह क्षोद इति तुशब्दार्थः । नास्ति परलोकः पुण्यं पापमिति वा मतिरस्य ।

नास्तिकास्तिकदैष्टिकम् इति निपातनान्नास्तिकः। तस्य नास्तिकस्य लौकायतिकस्य । वक्तुमपि न सांप्रतम् वचनमप्युच्चारयितुं नोचितम् । ततस्तूष्णींभाव एवास्य श्रेयान् । दूरे प्रामाणिकपरिषदि प्रविश्य प्रमाणोपन्यासगोष्ठी । वचनं हि परप्रत्यायनाय प्रतिपाद्यते । परेण चाप्रतिपित्सितमर्थं प्रतिपादयन्नासौ सतामवधेयवचनो भवत्युन्मत्तवत् । ननु कथमिव तूष्णींकतैवास्य श्रेयसी यावता चेष्टाविशेषादिना प्रतिपाद्यस्याभिप्रायमनुमाय सुकरमेवानेन वचनोच्चारणमित्याशङ्क्याह क्व चेष्टा क्व दृष्टमात्रं च इति । क्वेति बृहदन्तरे । चेष्टा इङ्गितम् । पराभिप्रायरूपस्यानुमेयस्य लिङ्गम् । क्व च दृष्टमात्रम् । दर्शनं दृष्टम् । भावे क्तः। दृष्टमेव दृष्टमात्रम् प्रत्यक्षमात्रम् । तस्य लिङ्गनिरपेक्षप्रवृत्तित्वात् । अत एव दूरमन्तरमेतयोः । न हि प्रत्यक्षेणातीन्द्रियाः परचेतोवृत्तयः परिज्ञातुं शक्याः । तस्यैन्द्रियकत्वात् । मुखप्रसादादिचेष्टया तु लिङ्गभूतया पराभिप्रायस्य निश्चये अनुमानप्रमाणमनिच्छतोपि तस्य बलादापतितम् । तथा हि । मद्वचनश्रवणाभिप्रायवानयं पुरुषः। तादृग्मुखप्रसादादिचेष्टाऽन्यथानुपपत्तेरिति । अतश्च हहा प्रमादः । हहा इति खेदे । अहो तस्य प्रमादः प्रमत्तता यदनुभूयमानमप्यनुमानं प्रत्यक्षमात्राङ्गीकारेणापह्नुते । अत्र संपूर्वस्य वेत्तेरकर्मकत्व एवात्मनेपदम् अत्र तु कर्मास्ति तत्कथमत्रानश् । अत्रोच्यते । अत्र संवेदितुं शक्तः संविदान इति कार्यम् । वयःशक्तिशीले इति शक्तौ शानविधानात् । ततश्चायमर्थः । अनुमानेन विना पराभिसंहितं सम्यग्वेदितुमशक्तस्येति । एवं परबुद्धिज्ञानान्यथानुपपत्त्याऽयमनुमानं हठादङ्गीकारितः । तथा प्रकारान्तरेणाप्ययमङ्गीकारयितव्यः। तथा हि । चार्वाकः काश्चिज्ज्ञानव्यक्तीः संवादित्वेनाव्यभिचारिणीरुपलभ्यान्याश्च विसंवादित्वेन व्यभिचारिणीः पुनः

कालान्तरे तादृशीतराणां ज्ञानव्यक्तीनामवश्यं प्रमाणतेतरते व्यवस्थापयेत् । न च संनिहितार्थबलेनोत्पद्यमानं पूर्वापरपरामर्शशून्यं प्रत्यक्ष पूर्वापरकालभाविनीनां ज्ञानव्यक्तीनां प्रामाण्याप्रामाण्यव्यवस्थापकं निमित्तमुपलक्षयितुं क्षमते । न चायं स्वप्रतीतिगोचराणामपि ज्ञानव्यक्तीनां परं प्रति प्रामाण्यमप्रामाण्यं वा व्यवस्थापयितुं प्रभवति । तस्माद्यथादृष्टज्ञानव्यक्तिसाधर्म्यद्वारेणेदानीन्तनज्ञानव्यक्तीनां प्रामाण्याप्रामाण्यव्यवस्थापकं परप्रतिपादकं च प्रमाणान्तरमनुमानरूपमुपासीत । परलोकादिनिषेधश्च न प्रत्यक्षमात्रेण शक्यः कर्तुम् । संनिहितमात्रविषयत्वात्तस्य । परलोकादिकं चाप्रतिषिध्य नायं सुखमास्ते प्रमाणान्तरं च नेच्छतीति डिम्भहेवाकः ॥ किंच प्रत्यक्षस्याप्यर्थाव्यभिचारादेव प्रामाण्यम् । कथमितरथा स्नानपानावगाहनाद्यर्थक्रियाऽसमर्थे मरुमरीचिकानिचयचुम्बिनि जलज्ञाने न प्रामाण्यम् । तच्च अर्थप्रतिबद्धलिङ्गशब्दद्वारा समुन्मज्जतोरनुमानागमयोरप्यर्थाव्यभिचारादेव किं नेष्यते । व्यभिचारिणोरप्यनयोर्दर्शनादप्रामाण्यमिति चेत् । प्रत्यक्षस्यापि तिमिरादिदोषान्निशीथिनीनाथयुगलावलम्बिनोऽप्रमाणस्य दर्शनात्सर्वत्राप्रामाण्यप्रसङ्गः । प्रत्यक्षाभासं तदिति चेत् इतरत्रापि तुल्यमेतदन्यत्र पक्षपातात् । एवं च प्रत्यक्षमात्रेण वस्तुव्यवस्थानुपपत्तेः । तन्मूला जीवपुण्यापुण्यपरलोकनिषेधादिवादा अप्रमाणमेव ॥ एवं नास्तिकाभिमतो भूतचिद्वादोपि निराकार्यः । तथा च द्रव्यालङ्कारकार उपयोगवर्णने । न चायं भूतधर्मः । सत्त्वकठिनत्वादिवत् मद्याङ्गेषु भ्रम्यादिमदशक्तिवद्वा प्रत्येकमनुपलम्भात् । अनभिव्यक्तावात्मसिद्धिः । कायाकारपरिणतेभ्यस्तेभ्यः स उत्पद्यत इति चेत् कायपरिणामोपि तन्मात्रभावी न कादाचित्कः । अन्यस्त्वात्मैव स्यात् । अहेतुत्वे न देशादि-

नियमः । मृतादपि च स्यात् । शोणिताद्युपाधिः सुप्तादावप्यस्ति । न च सतस्तस्योत्पत्तिः । भूयोभूयः प्रसङ्गात् । अलब्धात्मनश्च प्रसिद्धमर्थक्रियाकारित्वं विरुध्येत । असतः सकलशक्तिविकलस्य कथमुत्पत्तौ कर्तृत्वम् । अन्यस्यापि प्रसङ्गात् । तन्न भूतकार्यमुपयोगः । कुतस्तर्हि सुप्तोत्थितस्य तदुदयः । असंवेदनेन चैतन्यस्याभावात् । न । जाग्रदवस्थानुभूतस्य स्मरणात् । असंवेदनं तु निद्रोपघातात् । कथं तर्हि कायविकृतौ चैतन्यविकृतिः । नैकान्तः । श्वित्रादिना कश्मलवपुषोपि बुद्धिशुद्धेः । अविकारे च भावनाविशेषतः प्रीत्यादिभेददर्शनात् । शोकादिना बुद्धिविकृतौ कायविकारादर्शनाच्च । परिणामिना विना च न कार्योत्पत्तिः । न च भूतान्येव तथा परिणमन्ति । विजातीयत्वात् । काठिन्यादेरनुपलम्भात् । अणव एवेन्द्रियग्राह्यत्वरूपां स्थूलतां प्रतिपद्यन्ते तज्जात्यादि चोपलभ्यते । तन्न भूतानां धर्मः फलं वा उपयोगः । तथा भवांश्च यदाक्षिपति तदस्य लक्षणम् । स चात्मा स्वसंविदितः । भूतानां तथाभावे बहिर्मुखं स्यात् । गौरोऽहमित्यादि तु नान्तर्मुखम् । बाह्यकरणजन्यत्वात् ॥ अनभ्युपगतानुमानप्रामाण्यस्य चात्मनिषेधोपि दुर्लभः ।

धर्मः फलं च भूतानामुपयोगो भवेद्यदि ।
प्रत्येकमुपलम्भः स्यादुत्पादो वा विलक्षणात् ॥

इति काव्यार्थः ।

एवमुक्तयुक्तिभिरेकान्तवादप्रतिक्षेपमाख्याय सांप्रतमनाद्यविद्यावासनाप्रवासितसन्मतयः प्रत्यक्षोपलक्ष्यमाणमप्यनेकान्तवादं येवमन्यन्ते तेषामुन्मत्ततामाविर्भावयन्नाह ।

प्रतिक्षणोत्पादविनाशयोगि-
स्थिरैकमध्यक्षमपीक्षमाणः ।

जिन त्वदाज्ञामवमन्यते यः
स वातकी नाथ पिशाचकी वा ॥२१॥

प्रतिक्षणं प्रतिसमयम्। उत्पादेन उत्तराकारस्वीकाररूपेण विनाशेन च पूर्वाकारपरिहारलक्षणेन युज्यत इत्येवंशीलं प्रतिक्षणोत्पादविनाशयोगि। किं तत्। स्थिरैकं कर्मतापन्नम्। स्थिरमुत्पादविनाशयोरनुयायित्वात्त्रिकालवर्ति यदेकं द्रव्यं स्थिरैकम्। एकशब्दोत्र साधारणवाची। उत्पादे विनाशे च तत्साधारणम्। अन्वयिद्रव्यत्वात्। यथा चैत्रमैत्रयोरेका जननी साधारणेत्यर्थः। इत्थमेव हि तयोरेकाधिकरणता। पर्यायाणां कथंचिदनेकत्वेपि तस्य कथंचिदेकत्वात्। एवं त्रयात्मकं वस्त्वध्यक्षमपीक्षमाणः प्रत्यक्षमवलोकयन्नपि। हे जिन रागादिजैत्र। त्वदाज्ञाम् आ सामस्त्येनानन्तधर्मविशिष्टतया ज्ञायन्ते अवबुध्यन्ते जीवाजीवादयः पदार्था यया साज्ञा आगमः शासनम् तवाज्ञा त्वदाज्ञा तां त्वदाज्ञां भवत्प्रणीतस्याद्वादमुद्राम्। यः कश्चिदविवेक्यवमन्यते अवजानाति। जात्यपेक्षमेकवचनम् अवज्ञया वा। स पुरुषपशुः वातकी पिशाचकी वा। वातो रोगविशेषोऽस्यास्तीति वातकी वातकीव वातकी वातूल इत्यर्थः। एवं पिशाचकीव पिशाचकी भूताविष्ट इत्यर्थः। अत्र वाशब्दः समुच्चयार्थ उपमानार्थो वा। स पुरुषापसदो वातकिपिशाचकिभ्यामधिरोहति तुलामित्यर्थः। वातातीसारपिशाचात्कश्चान्तः इत्यनेन मत्वर्थीयः कश्चान्तः। एवं पिशाचकीत्यपि। यथा किल वातेन पिशाचेन वाक्रान्तवपुर्वस्तुतत्त्वं साक्षात्कुर्वन्नपि तदावेशवशादन्यथा प्रतिपद्यते एवमयमप्येकान्तवादापस्मारपरवश इति॥

अत्र च जिनेति साभिप्रायम्। रागादिजेतृत्वाद्धि जिनः। ततश्च यः किल विगलितदोषकालुष्यतयावधेयवचनस्यापि तत्रभवतः

शासनमवमन्यते तस्य कथं नोन्मत्ततेति भावः। नाथ हे स्वामिन्। अलब्धस्य सम्यग्दर्शनादेर्लम्भकतया लब्धस्य च तस्यैव निरतिचारपरिपालनोपदेशदायितया च योगक्षेमकरत्वोपपत्तेर्नाथः। तस्यामन्त्रणम्।

वस्तुतत्त्वं चोत्पादव्ययध्रौव्यात्मकम्। तथा हि। सर्वं वस्तु द्रव्यात्मना नोत्पद्यते विपद्यते वा। परिस्फुटमन्वयदर्शनात्। लूनपुनर्जातनखादिष्वन्वयदर्शनेन व्यभिचार इति न वाच्यम्। प्रमाणेन बाध्यमानस्यान्वयस्यापरिस्फुटत्वात्। न च प्रस्तुतोन्वयः प्रमाणविरुद्धः। सत्यप्रत्यभिज्ञानासिद्धत्वात्।

सर्वव्यक्तिषु नियतं क्षणे क्षणेऽन्यत्वमथ च न विशेषः।
सत्योश्चित्यपचित्योराकृतिजातिव्यवस्थानात्॥

इति वचनात्। ततो द्रव्यात्मना स्थितिरेव सर्वस्य वस्तुनः। पर्यायात्मना तु सर्वं वस्तूत्पद्यते विपद्यते च। अस्खलितपर्यायानुभवसद्भावात्। न चैवं शुक्ले शङ्खे पीतादिपर्यायानुभवेन व्यभिचारः। तस्य स्खलद्रूपत्वात्। न खलु सोस्खलद्रूपो येन पूर्वाकारविनाशाजहद्वृत्तोत्तराकारोत्पादाविनाभावी भवेत्। न च जीवादौ वस्तुनि हर्षामर्षौदासीन्यादिपर्यायपरंपरानुभवः स्खलद्रूपः। कस्यचिद् बाधकस्याभावात्। ननूत्पादादयः परस्परं भिद्यन्ते न वा। यदि भिद्यन्ते कथमेकं वस्तु त्र्यात्मकम्। न भिद्यन्ते चेत् तथापि कथमेकं त्रयात्मकम्। तथा च।

यद्युत्पादादयो भिन्नाः कथमेकं त्रयात्मकम्।
अथोत्पादादयोऽभिन्नाः कथमेकं त्रयात्मकम्॥

इति चेत्। तदयुक्तम्। कथंचिद्भिन्नलक्षणत्वेन तेषां कथंचिद्भेदाभ्युपगमात्। तथा हि। उत्पादविनाशध्रौव्याणि स्याद्भिन्नानि भिन्नलक्षणत्वात् रूपादिवदिति। न च भिन्नलक्षणत्वम-

सिद्धम् । असत आत्मलाभः सतः सत्तावियोगो द्रव्यरूपतयानुवर्तनं च खलूत्पादादीनां परस्परमसङ्कीर्णानि लक्षणानि सकललोकसाक्षिकाण्येव ॥ न चामी भिन्नलक्षणा अपि परस्परानपेक्षाः खपुष्पवदसत्त्वापत्तेः । तथाहि । उत्पादः केवलो नास्ति । स्थितिविगमरहितत्वात् कूर्मरोमवत् । तथा विनाशः केवलो नास्ति । स्थित्युत्पत्तिरहितत्वात् तद्वत् । एवं स्थितिः केवला नास्ति । विनाशोत्पादशून्यत्वात् तद्वदेव । इत्यन्योन्यापेक्षाणामुत्पादादीनां वस्तुनि सत्त्वं प्रतिपत्तव्यम् । तथा चोक्तम् ।

घटमौलिसुवर्णार्थी नाशोत्पादस्थितिष्वयम् ।
शोकप्रमोदमाध्यस्थ्यं जनो याति सहेतुकम् ॥
पयोव्रतो न दध्यत्ति न पयोऽत्ति दधिव्रतः ।
अगोरसव्रतो नोभे तस्माद्वस्तु त्रयात्मकम् ॥

इति काव्यार्थः ॥

अथान्ययोगव्यवच्छेदस्य प्रस्तुतत्वादास्तां तावत्साक्षाद्भवान् भवदीयप्रवचनावयवा अपि परतीर्थिकतिरस्कारबद्धकक्षा इत्याशयवान् स्तुतिकारः स्याद्वादव्यवस्थापनाय प्रयोगमुपन्यस्यन् स्तुतिमाह ।

अनन्तधर्मात्मकमेव तत्त्व-
मतोन्यथा सत्त्वमसूपपादम् ।
इति प्रमाणान्यपि ते कुवादि-
कुरङ्गसंत्रासनसिंहनादाः ॥ २२ ॥

तत्त्वं परमार्थभूतं वस्तु जीवाजीवलक्षणमनन्तधर्मात्मकमेव । अनन्तास्त्रिकालविषयत्वादपरिमिता ये धर्माः सहभाविनः क्रमभाविनश्च पर्यायास्त एवात्मा स्वरूपं यस्य तदनन्त-

धर्मात्मकम् । एवकारः प्रकारान्तरव्यवच्छेदार्थः । अत एवाह अतोन्यथा इत्यादि । अतोन्यथा उक्तप्रकारवैपरीत्येन । सत्त्वं वस्तुतत्त्वम् । असूपपादम् सुखेनोपपाद्यते घटनाकोटिसंटङ्कमारोप्यत इति सूपपादम् न तथा असूपपादं दुर्घटमित्यर्थः । अनेन साधनं दर्शितम् । तथाहि । तत्त्वमिति धर्मि । अनन्तधर्मात्मकत्वं साध्यो धर्मः । सत्त्वान्यथानुपपत्तेरिति हेतुः । अन्यथानुपपत्त्येकलक्षणत्वाद्धेतोः । अन्तर्व्याप्त्यैव साध्यस्य सिद्धत्वाद्दृष्टान्तादिभिर्न प्रयोजनम् । यदनन्तधर्मात्मकं न भवति तत्सदपि न भवति यथा वियदिन्दीवरमिति केवलव्यतिरेकी हेतुः । साधर्म्यदृष्टान्तानां पक्षकुक्षिनिक्षिप्तत्वेनान्वयायोगात् । अनन्तधर्मात्मकत्वं चात्मनि तावत्साकारानाकारोपयोगिता कर्तृत्वं भोक्तृत्वं प्रदेशाष्टकनिश्चलता अमूर्तत्वमसंख्यातप्रदेशात्मकता जीवत्वमित्यादयः सहभाविनो धर्माः । हर्षविषादशोकसुखदुःखदेवनरनारकतिर्यक्त्वादयस्तु क्रमभाविनः । धर्मास्तिकायादिष्वप्यसंख्येयप्रदेशात्मकत्वं गत्याद्युपग्रहकारित्वं मत्यादिज्ञानविषयत्वं तत्तदवच्छेदकावच्छेद्यत्वमवस्थितत्वमरूपित्वमेकद्रव्यत्वं निष्क्रियत्वमित्यादयः । घटे पुनरामत्वं पाकजरूपादिमत्त्वं पृथुबुध्नोदरत्वं कम्बुग्रीवत्वं जलादिधारणाहरणसामर्थ्यं मत्यादिज्ञानज्ञेयत्वं नवत्वं पुराणत्वमित्यादयः । एवं सर्वपदार्थेष्वपि नानानयमताभिज्ञेन शाब्दानार्थांश्च पर्यायान्प्रतीत्य वाच्यम् ॥

अत्र चात्मशब्देनानन्तेष्वपि धर्मेष्वनुवृत्तिरूपमन्वयिद्रव्यं ध्वनितम् । ततश्च उत्पादव्ययध्रौव्ययुक्तं सत् इति व्यवस्थितम् । एवं तावदर्थेषु । शब्देष्वपि उदात्तानुदात्तस्वरितविवृतसंवृतघोषवदघोषताल्पप्राणमहाप्राणतादयस्तत्तदर्थप्रत्यायनशक्त्यादयश्चावसेयाः । अस्य हेतोरसिद्धविरुद्धानैकान्तिकत्वादिकण्टकोद्धारः

स्वयमभ्यूह्यः । इत्येवमुल्लेखशेखराणि ते तव प्रमाणान्यपि न्यायोपपन्नसाधनवाक्यान्यपि । आस्तां तावत्साक्षात्कृतद्रव्यपर्यायनिकायो भवान् । तावदेतान्यपि कुवादिकुरङ्गसंत्रासनसिंहनादाः कुवादिनः कुत्सितवादिनः । एकांशग्राहकनयानुयायिनोन्यतीर्थिकाः त एव संसारवनगहनवसनव्यसनितया कुरङ्गा मृगास्तेषां सम्यक्त्रासने सिंहनादा इव सिंहनादाः । यथा सिंहस्य नादमात्रमप्याकर्ण्य कुरङ्गास्त्रासमासूत्रयन्ति तथा भवत्प्रणीतैवंप्रकारप्रमाणवचनान्यपि श्रुत्वा कुवादिनस्त्रस्नुतामश्नुवते । प्रतिवचनप्रदानकातरतां बिभ्रतीति यावत् । एकैकं त्वदुपज्ञं प्रमाणमन्ययोगव्यवच्छेदकमित्यर्थः ॥

अत्र प्रमाणानीति बहुवचनमेवंजातीयानां प्रमाणानां भगवच्छासने आनन्त्यज्ञापनार्थम् । एकैकस्य सूत्रस्य सर्वोदधिसलिलसर्वसरिद्वालुकानन्तगुणार्थत्वात् । तेषां च सर्वेषामपि सर्वविन्मूलतया प्रमाणत्वात् । अथवा इत्यादिबहुवचनान्ता गणस्य संसूचका भवन्तीति न्यायात् इतिशब्देन प्रमाणबाहुल्यसूचनात् पूर्वार्धे एकस्मिन्नपि प्रमाणे उपन्यस्ते उचितमेव बहुवचनम् ॥ इति काव्यार्थः ॥

अनन्तरमनन्तधर्मात्मकत्वं वस्तुनि साध्यं मुकुलितमुक्तम् । तदेव सप्तभङ्गीप्ररूपणद्वारेण प्रपञ्चयन् भगवतो निरतिशयं वचनातिशयं च स्तुवन्नाह ।

अपर्ययं वस्तु समस्यमान-
मद्रव्यमेतच्च विविच्यमानम् ।
आदेशभेदोदितसप्तभङ्ग-
मदीदृशस्त्वं बुधरूपवेद्यम् ॥२३॥

समस्यमानं संक्षेपेणोच्यमानं वस्तु अपर्ययम् अविवक्षितपर्यायम्। वसन्ति गुणपर्याया अस्मिन्निति वस्तु धर्माधर्माकाशपुद्गलकालजीवलक्षणं द्रव्यषट्कम् । अयमभिप्रायः । यदैकमेव वस्त्वात्मघटादिकं चेतनाचेतनं सतामपि पर्यायाणामविवक्षया द्रव्यरूपमेव वक्तुमिष्यते तदा संक्षेपेणाभ्यन्तरीकृतसकलपर्यायनिकायत्वलक्षणेनाभिधीयमानत्वादपर्ययमित्युपदिश्यते । केवलद्रव्यरूपमेवेत्यर्थः। यथात्मायं घटोयमित्यादि । पर्यायाणां द्रव्यानतिरेकात् । अत एव द्रव्यास्तिकनयाः शुद्धसंग्रहादयो द्रव्यमात्रमेवेच्छन्ति । पर्यायाणां तदविष्वग्भूतत्वात् । पर्ययः पर्यवः पर्यायः इत्यनर्थान्तरम् । अद्रव्यमित्यादि । चः पुनरर्थे । स च पूर्वस्माद्विशेषद्योतने भिन्नक्रमश्च। विविच्यमानं चेति विवेकेन पृथग्रूपतयोच्यमानम् । पुनरेतद्वस्तु अद्रव्यमेव । अविवक्षितान्वयिद्रव्यं केवलपर्यायरूपमित्यर्थः ॥

यदा ह्यात्मा ज्ञानदर्शनादीन्पर्यायानधिकृत्य प्रतिपर्यायं विचार्यते तदा पर्याया एव प्रतिभासन्ते न पुनरात्माख्यं किमपि द्रव्यम् । एवं घटोपि कुण्डलौष्ठपृथुबुध्नोदरपूर्वापरादिभागाद्यवयवापेक्षया विविच्यमानः पर्याया एव न पुनर्घटाख्यं तदतिरिक्तं वस्तु । अत एव पर्यायास्तिकनयानुपातिनः पठन्ति ।

भागा एव हि भासन्ते संनिविष्टास्तथा तथा ।
तद्वान्नैव पुनः कश्चिन्निर्भागः संप्रतीयते ॥

इति । ततश्च द्रव्यपर्यायोभयात्मकत्वेपि वस्तुनो द्रव्यनयार्पणया पर्यायनयानर्पणया च द्रव्यरूपता पर्यायनयार्पणया द्रव्यनयानर्पणया च पर्यायरूपता उभयनयार्पणया च तदुभयरूपता । अत एवाह वाचकमुख्यः अर्पितानर्पितसिद्धेः इति । एवंविधं द्रव्यपर्यायात्मकं वस्तु त्वमेव अदीदृशः त्वमेव दर्शितवान् । नान्य इति काक्वावधारणावगतिः ॥

नन्वन्याभिधानप्रत्यययोग्यं द्रव्यमन्याभिधानप्रत्ययविषयाश्च पर्यायाः तत्कथमेकमेव वस्तूभयात्मकमित्याशङ्क्य विशेषणद्वारेण परिहरति आदेशभेदेत्यादि । आदेशभेदेन सकलादेशविकलादेशलक्षणेनादेशद्वयेनोदिताः प्रतिपादिताः सप्तसंख्या भङ्गा वचनप्रकारा यस्मिन् वस्तुनि तत्तथा । ननु यदि भगवता त्रिभुवनबन्धुना निर्विशेषतया सर्वेभ्य एवंविधं वस्तुतत्त्वमुपदर्शितं तर्हि किमर्थं तीर्थान्तरीयाः तत्र विप्रतिपद्यन्त इत्याह बुधरूपवेद्यमिति । बुध्यन्ते यथावस्थितं वस्तुतत्त्वं सारेतरविषयविभागविचारणया इति बुधाः । प्रकृष्टा बुधा बुधरूपाः नैसर्गिकाधिगमिकान्यतरसम्यग्दर्शनविशदीकृतज्ञानशालिनः प्राणिनः । तैरेव वेदितुं शक्यं वेद्यं परिच्छेद्यम् । न पुनः स्वस्वशास्त्रतत्त्वाभ्यासपरिपाकशाणानिशातबुद्धिभिरप्यन्यैः । तेषामनादिमिथ्यादर्शनवासनादूषितमतितया यथास्थितवस्तुतत्त्वानवबोधेन बुधरूपत्वाभावात् । तथा चागमः ।

सदसदविसेसणाउ भवहेउजहिच्छिओवलंभाउ ।
णाणफलाभावाउ मिच्छादिट्ठिस्स अण्णाणं ॥ १ ॥

अत एव तत्परिगृहीतं द्वादशाङ्गमपि मिथ्याश्रुतमामनन्ति । तेषामुपपत्तिनिरपेक्षं यदृच्छया वस्तुतत्त्वोपलम्भसंरम्भात् । सम्यग्दृष्टिपरिगृहीतं तु मिथ्याश्रुतमपि सम्यक्श्रुततया परिणमति सम्यग्दृशाम् । सर्वविदुपदेशानुसारिप्रवृत्तितया मिथ्याश्रुतोक्तस्याप्यर्थस्य यथावस्थितविधिनिषेधविषयतयोन्नयनात् । तथा हि किल वेदे अजैर्यष्टव्यम् इत्यादिवाक्येषु मिथ्यादृशोऽजशब्दं पशुवाचकतया व्याचक्षते सम्यग्दृशस्तु जन्मप्राप्तयोग्यं त्रिवार्षिकं यवव्रीह्यादि पञ्चवार्षिकं तिलमसूरादि सप्तवार्षिकं कङ्गुसर्षपादि धान्यपर्यायतया पर्यवसाययन्ति । अत एव च भगवता श्रीवर्ध-

मानस्वामिना विज्ञानघन एवैतेभ्यो भूतेभ्यः समुत्थाय तान्येवानु विनश्यति न प्रेत्य संज्ञास्ति इत्यादिऋचः श्रीमदिन्द्रभूत्यादीनां द्रव्यगणधरदेवानां जीवादिनिषेधकतया प्रतिभासमाना अपि तद्व्यवस्थापकतया व्याख्याताः । तथा स्मार्ता अपि

न मांसभक्षणे दोषो न मद्ये न च मैथुने ।
प्रवृत्तिरेषा भूतानां निवृत्तिस्तु महाफला ॥

इति श्लोकं पठन्ति । अस्य च यथाश्रुतार्थव्याख्यानेऽसंबद्धप्रलाप एव । यस्मिन् ह्यनुष्ठीयमाने दोषो नास्त्येव तस्मान्निवृत्तिः कथमिव महाफला भविष्यति । इज्याध्ययनदानादेरपि निवृत्तिप्रसङ्गात् । तस्मादन्यदैदंपर्यमस्य श्लोकस्य । तथाहि न मांसभक्षणे कृते अदोषः अपि तु दोष एव । एवं मद्यमैथुनयोरपि । कथं नादोष इत्याह यतः प्रवृत्तिरेषा भूतानाम् । प्रवर्तन्त उत्पद्यन्तेऽस्यामिति प्रवृत्तिः उत्पत्तिस्थानम् । भूतानां जीवानां तत्तज्जीवसंसक्तिहेतुरित्यर्थः । प्रसिद्धं च मांसमद्यमैथुनानां जीवसंसक्तिमूलकारणत्वमागमे ।

आमासु य पक्कासु य विपच्चमाणासु मंसपेसीसु ।
आयंतिअमुववाओ भणिओ उ णिगोअजीवाणं ॥ १ ॥
मज्जे महुम्मि मंसम्मि णवणीयम्मि चउत्थए ।
उप्पज्जंति अणंता तव्वण्णा तत्थ जंतुणो ॥ २ ॥
मेहुणसण्णारूढो णवलक्ख हणेइ सुहुमजीवाणं ।
केवलिणा पण्णत्ता सद्दहिअव्वा सया कालं ॥ ३ ॥

तथाहि

इत्थीजोणीए संभवंति बेइंदिया उ जे जीवा ।
इक्को व दो तिण्णि व लक्खपुहुत्तं च उक्कोसं ॥ ४ ॥

पुरिसेण सह गयाए तेसिं जीवाण होइ उद्दवणं ।
वेणुगदिट्ठंतणं तत्तायसलागणाएणं ॥ ५ ॥

संसक्तायां योनौ द्वीन्द्रिया एते । शुक्रशोणितसंभवास्तु गर्भजपञ्चेन्द्रिया इमे ।

पंचिंदिया मणुस्सा एगणरभुत्तणारिगब्भम्मि ।
उक्कोसं णवलक्खा जायंति एगवेलाए ॥ ६ ॥
णवलक्खाणं मज्झे जायइ इक्कस्स दुण्ह व समत्ती ।
सेसा पुण एमेव य विलयं वच्चंति तत्थेव ॥ ७ ॥

तदेवं जीवोपमर्दहेतुत्वान्न मांसभक्षणादिकमदुष्टमिति प्रयोगः । अथवा भूतानां पिशाचप्रायाणामेषा प्रवृत्तिः । त एवात्र मांसभक्षणादौ प्रवर्तन्ते न पुनर्विवेकिन इति भावः । तदेवं मांसभक्षणादेर्दुष्टतां स्पष्टीकृत्य यदुपदेष्टव्यं तदाह । निवृत्तिस्तु महाफला । तुरेवकारार्थः । तुः स्याद्भेदेवधारणे इति वचनात् । ततश्चैतेभ्यो मांसभक्षणादिभ्यो निवृत्तिरेव महाफला स्वर्गापवर्गफलप्रदा न पुनः प्रवृत्तिरपीत्यर्थः । अत एव स्थानान्तरे पठितम्

वर्षे वर्षेऽश्वमेधेन यो यजेत शतं समाः ।
मांसानि च न खादेद्यस्तयोस्तुल्यं भवेत्फलम् ॥
एकरात्रोषितस्यापि या गतिर्ब्रह्मचारिणः ।
न सा क्रतुसहस्रेण प्राप्तुं शक्या युधिष्ठिर ॥

मद्यपाने तु कृतं सूत्रानुवादैः । तस्य सर्वविगर्हितत्वात् । तानेवंप्रकारानर्थात्कथमिव बुधाभासास्तीर्थिका वेदितुमर्हन्तीति कृतमतिप्रसङ्गेन ॥

अथ केऽमी सप्तभङ्गाः कश्चायमादेशभेद इत्युच्यते । एकत्र जीवादौ वस्तुन्येकैकसत्त्वादिधर्मविषयप्रश्नवशादविरोधेन प्रत्यक्षा-

दिबाधापरिहारेण पृथग्भूतयोः समुदितयोश्च विधिनिषेधयोः पर्यालोचनया कृत्वा स्याच्छब्दलाञ्छितो वक्ष्यमाणैः सप्तभिः प्रकारैर्वचनविन्यासः सप्तभङ्गीति गीयते। तद्यथा। स्यादस्त्येव सर्वमिति विधिकल्पनया प्रथमो भङ्गः १। स्यान्नास्त्येव सर्वमिति निषेधकल्पनया द्वितीयः २। स्यादस्त्येव स्यान्नास्त्येवेति क्रमतो विधिनिषेधकल्पनया तृतीयः ३। स्यादवक्तव्यवेति युगपद्विधिनिषेधकल्पनया चतुर्थः ४। स्यादस्त्येव स्यादवक्तव्यमेवेति विधिकल्पनया युगपद्विधिनिषेधकल्पनया च पञ्चमः ५। स्यान्नास्त्येव स्यादवक्तव्यमेवेति निषेधकल्पनया युगपद्विधिनिषेधकल्पनया च षष्ठः ६। स्यादस्त्येव स्यान्नास्त्येव स्यादवक्तव्यमेवेति क्रमतो विधिनिषेधकल्पनया युगपद्विधिनिषेधकल्पनया च सप्तमः ७॥

तत्र स्यात्कथंचित् स्वद्रव्यक्षेत्रकालभावरूपेणास्त्येव सर्वं कुम्भादि न पुनः परद्रव्यक्षेत्रकालभावरूपेण। तथाहि कुम्भो द्रव्यतः पार्थिवत्वेनास्ति नाप्यादिरूपत्वेन। क्षेत्रतः पाटलिपुत्रकत्वेन न कान्यकुब्जादित्वेन। कालतः शैशिरत्वेन न वासन्तिकादित्वेन। भावतः श्यामत्वेन न रक्तादित्वेन। अन्यथेतररूपापत्त्या स्वरूपहानिप्रसङ्ग इति। अवधारणं चात्र भङ्गेऽनभिमतार्थव्यावृत्त्यर्थमुपात्तम्। इतरथानभिहिततुल्यतैवास्य वाक्यस्य प्रसज्येत। प्रतिनियतस्वार्थानभिधानात्। यदुक्तम्

वाक्येऽवधारणं तावदनिष्टार्थनिवृत्तये।
कर्तव्यमन्यथानुक्तसमत्वात्तस्य कुत्रचित्॥

तथाप्यस्त्येव कुम्भ इत्येतावन्मात्रोपादाने कुम्भस्य स्तम्भाद्यस्तित्वेनापि सर्वप्रकारेणास्तित्वप्राप्तेः प्रतिनियतस्वरूपानुपपत्तिः स्यात्। तत्प्रतिपत्तये स्यादिति शब्दः प्रयुज्यते। स्यात्कथंचित्स्वद्रव्यादिभिरेवायमस्ति न परद्रव्यादिभिरपीत्यर्थः। यत्रापि चासौ

न प्रयुज्यते तत्रापि व्यवच्छेदफलैवकारवद् बुद्धिमद्भिः प्रतीयत एव। यदुक्तम्

सोऽप्रयुक्तोपि वा तज्ज्ञैः सर्वत्रार्थात्प्रतीयते ।
यथैवकारोऽयोगादिव्यवच्छेदप्रयोजनः ॥ १ ॥

इति प्रथमो भङ्गः ॥

स्यात्कथञ्चिन्नास्त्येव कुम्भादिः स्वद्रव्यादिभिरेव परद्रव्यादिभिरपि वस्तुनोऽसत्त्वानिष्टौ हि प्रतिनियतस्वरूपाभावाद्वस्तुप्रतिनियतिर्न स्यात् । न चास्तित्वैकान्तवादिभिरत्र नास्तित्वमसिद्धमिति वक्तव्यम् । कथंचित्तस्य वस्तुनि युक्तिसिद्धत्वात् साधनवत् । नहि क्वचिदनित्यत्वादौ साध्ये सत्त्वादिसाधनस्यास्तित्वं विपक्षे नास्तित्वमन्तरेणोपपन्नम् । तस्य साधनत्वाभावप्रसङ्गात् । तस्माद् वस्तुनोस्तित्वं नास्तित्वेनाविनाभूतं नास्तित्वं च तेनेति । विवक्षावशाच्चानयोः प्रधानोपसर्जनभावः । एवमुत्तरभङ्गेष्वपि ज्ञेयम् । अर्पितानर्पितसिद्धेः इति वाचकवचनात् । इतिं द्वितीयः ॥

तृतीयः स्पष्ट एव ॥

द्वाभ्यामस्तित्वनास्तित्वधर्माभ्यां युगपत्प्रधानतयाऽर्पिताभ्यामेकस्य वस्तुनोऽभिधित्सायां तादृशस्य शब्दस्यासंभवादवक्तव्यं जीवादिवस्तु । तथाहि सदसत्त्वगुणद्वयं युगपदेकत्र सदित्यनेन वक्तुमशक्यम्।तस्यासत्त्वप्रतिपादनासमर्थत्वात्।तथाऽसदित्यनेनापि। तस्य सत्त्वप्रत्यायनसामर्थ्याभावात् । न च पुष्पदन्तादिवत्साङ्केतिकमेकं पदं तद्वक्तुं समर्थम् तस्यापि क्रमेणार्थद्वयप्रत्यायने सामर्थ्योपपत्तेः । शतृशानयोः संकेतितसच्छब्दवत् । अत एव द्वन्द्वकर्मधारयवृत्त्योर्वाक्यस्य च न तद्वाचकत्वम् । इति सकलवाचकरहितत्वादवक्तव्यं वस्तु युगपत्सत्त्वासत्त्वाभ्यां प्रधान-

भावार्पिताभ्यामाक्रान्तं व्यवतिष्ठते। न च सर्वथाऽवक्तव्यम्। अवक्तव्यशब्देनाप्यनभिधेयत्वप्रसङ्गात्। इति चतुर्थः॥

शेषास्त्रयः सुगमाभिप्रायाः॥

न च वाच्यमेकत्र वस्तुनि विधीयमाननिषिध्यमानानन्तधर्माभ्युपगमेनानन्तभङ्गीप्रसङ्गादसंगतैव सप्तभङ्गीति। विधिनिषेधप्रकारापेक्षया प्रतिपर्यायं वस्तुन्यनन्तानामपि सप्तभङ्गीनामेव संभवात्। यथा हि सदसत्त्वाभ्यामेवं सामान्यविशेषाभ्यामपि सप्तभङ्ग्येव स्यात्। तथाहि। स्यात्सामान्यं स्याद्विशेषः स्यादुभयं स्यादवक्तव्यं स्यात्सामान्यावक्तव्यं स्याद्विशेषावक्तव्यं स्यात्सामान्यविशेषावक्तव्यमिति। न चात्र विधिनिषेधप्रकारौ न स्त इति वाच्यम्। सामान्यस्य विधिरूपत्वाद्विशेषस्य च व्यावृत्तिरूपतया निषेधात्मकत्वात्। अथवा प्रतिपक्षशब्दत्वाद्यदा सामान्यस्य प्राधान्यं तदा तस्य विधिरूपता विशेषस्य च निषेधरूपता यदा विशेषस्य पुरस्कारस्तदा तस्य विधिरूपता इतरस्य च निषेधरूपता। एवं सर्वत्र योज्यम्। अतः सुष्ठूक्तम् अनन्ता अपि सप्तभङ्ग्य एव भवेयुः इति। प्रतिपर्यायं प्रतिपाद्यपर्यनुयोगानां सप्तानामेव संभवात्। तेषामपि सप्तत्वं सप्तविधतज्जिज्ञासानियमात्। तस्या अपि सप्तविधत्वं सप्तधैव तत्संदेहसमुत्पादात्। तस्यापि सप्तविधत्वनियमः स्वगोचरवस्तुधर्माणां सप्तविधत्वस्यैवोपपत्तेरिति। इयं च सप्तभङ्गी प्रतिभङ्गं सकलादेशस्वभावा विकलादेशस्वभावा च। तत्र सकलादेशः प्रमाणवाक्यम्। तल्लक्षणं चेदम्। प्रमाणप्रतिपन्नानन्तधर्मात्मकवस्तुनः कालादिभिरभेदवृत्तिप्राधान्यादभेदोपचाराद्वा यौगपद्येन प्रतिपादकं वचः सकलादेशः। अस्यार्थः। कालादिभिरष्टभिः कृत्वा यदभेदवृत्तेर्धर्मधर्मिणोरपृथग्भावस्य प्राधान्यं तस्मात्कालादिभिर्भिन्नात्मनामपि धर्मधर्मिणामभेदा-

ध्यारोपाद्वा समकालमभिधायकं वाक्यं सकलादेशः । तद्विपरीतस्तु विकलादेशो नयवाक्यमित्यर्थः । अयमाशयः । यौगपद्येनाशेषधर्मात्मकं वस्तु कालादिभिरभेदप्राधान्यवृत्त्याऽभेदोपचारेण वा प्रतिपादयति सकलादेशः। तस्य प्रमाणाधीनत्वात् । विकलादेशस्तु क्रमेण भेदोपचाराद्भेदप्राधान्याद्वा तदभिधत्ते । तस्य नयात्मकत्वात् ॥

कः पुनः क्रमः किं च यौगपद्यम् । यदाऽस्तित्वादिधर्माणां कालादिभिर्भेदविवक्षा तदैकशब्दस्यानेकार्थप्रत्यायने शक्त्यभावात् क्रमः । यदा तु तेषामेव धर्माणां कालादिभिरभेदेन वृत्तमात्मरूपमुच्यते तदैकेनापि शब्देनैकधर्मप्रत्यायनमुखेन तदात्मकतामापन्नस्यानेकशेषधर्मरूपस्य वस्तुनः प्रतिपादनसंभवाद्यौगपद्यम् ॥

के पुनः कालादयः । कालः आत्मरूपम् अर्थः संबन्धः उपकारः गुणिदेशः संसर्गः शब्दः । तत्र स्याज्जीवादिवस्त्वस्त्येवेत्यत्र यत्कालमस्तित्वं तत्कालाः शेषानन्तधर्मा वस्तुन्येकत्रेति तेषां कालेनाभेदवृत्तिः (१) । यदेव चास्तित्वस्य तद्गुणत्वमात्मरूपं तदेवान्यानन्तगुणानामपीत्यात्मरूपेणाभेदवृत्तिः (२) । य एव चाधारोऽर्थो द्रव्याख्योस्तित्वस्य स एवान्यपर्यायाणामित्यर्थेनाभेदवृत्तिः (३) । य एव चाविष्वग्भावः कथंचित्तादात्म्यलक्षणः संबन्धोस्तित्वस्य स एव शेषविशेषाणामिति संबन्धेनाभेदवृत्तिः (४) । य एव चोपकारोऽस्तित्वेन स्वानुरक्तत्वकरणं स एव शेषैरपि गुणैरित्युपकारेणाभेदवृत्तिः (५) । य एव गुणिनः संबन्धी देशः क्षेत्रलक्षणोस्तित्वस्य स एवान्यगुणानामिति गुणिदेशेनाभेदवृत्तिः (६) । य एव चैकवस्त्वात्मनास्तित्वस्य संसर्गः स एव शेषधर्माणामिति संसर्गेणाभेदवृत्तिः (७) । अवि-

ष्वग्भावेऽभेदः प्रधानं भेदो गौणः संसर्गे तु भेदः प्रधानमभेदो गौण इति विशेषः। य एव चास्तीति शब्दोऽस्तित्वधर्मात्मकस्य वस्तुनो वाचकः स एव शेषानन्तधर्मात्मकस्यापीति शब्देनाभेदवृत्तिः (८) पर्यायार्थिकनयगुणभावे द्रव्यार्थिकनयप्राधान्यादुपपद्यते द्रव्यार्थिकगुणभावे पर्यायार्थिकप्राधान्ये तु न गुणानामभेदवृत्तिः संभवति। समकालमेकत्र नानागुणानामसंभवात्। संभवे वा तदाश्रयस्य तावद्धा भेदप्रसङ्गात्। नानागुणानां संबन्धिन आत्मरूपस्य च भिन्नत्वात्। आत्मरूपाऽभेदे तेषां भेदस्य विरोधात्। स्वाश्रयस्यार्थस्यापि नानात्वात् अन्यथा नानागुणाश्रयत्वस्य विरोधात्। संबन्धस्य च संबन्धिभेदेन भेददर्शनात् नानासंबन्धिभिरेकत्रैकसंबन्धाघटनात्। तैः क्रियमाणस्योपकारस्य च प्रतिनियतरूपस्यानेकत्वात् अनेकैरुपकारिभिः क्रियमाणस्योपकारस्य विरोधात्। गुणिदेशस्य च प्रतिगुणं भेदात् तदभेदे भिन्नार्थगुणानामपि गुणिदेशाभेदप्रसङ्गात्। संसर्गस्य च प्रतिसंसर्गिभेदात् तदभेदे संसर्गिभेदविरोधात्। शब्दस्य प्रतिविषयं नानात्वात् सर्वगुणानामेकशब्दवाच्यतायां सर्वार्थानामेकशब्दवाच्यतापत्तेः शब्दान्तरवैकल्यापत्तिः। तत्त्वतोऽस्तित्वादीनामेकत्र वस्तुन्येवमभेदवृत्तेरसंभवे कालादिभिर्भिन्नात्मनामभेदोपचारः क्रियते। तदेताभ्यामभेदवृत्त्यभेदोपचाराभ्यां कृत्वा प्रमाणप्रतिपन्नानन्तधर्मात्मकस्य वस्तुनः समसमयं यदभिधायकं वाक्यं स सकलादेशः प्रमाणवाक्यापरपर्यायः। नयविषयीकृतस्य वस्तुधर्मस्य भेदवृत्तिप्राधान्याद्भेदोपचाराद्वा क्रमेण यदभिधायकं वाक्यं स विकलादेशो नयवाक्यापरपर्यायः। इति स्थितम्। ततः साधूक्तम्, आदेशभेदोदितसप्तभङ्गम् ॥ इति काव्यार्थः ॥

अनन्तरं भगवद्दर्शितस्यानेकान्तात्मनो वस्तुनो बुधरूपवेद्यत्वमुक्तम् । अनेकान्तात्मकत्वं च सप्तभङ्गीप्ररूपणेन सुखोन्नेयं स्यादिति सापि निरूपिता । तस्यां च विरुद्धधर्माध्यासितं वस्तु पश्यन्त एकान्तवादिनोऽबुधरूपा विरोधमुद्भावयन्ति तेषां प्रमाणमार्गाच्च्यवनमाह ।

उपाधिभेदोपहितं विरुद्धं
नार्थेष्वसत्त्वं सदवाच्यते च ।
इत्यप्रबुध्यैव विरोधभीता
जडास्तदेकान्तहताः पतन्ति ॥ २४ ॥

अर्थेषु पदार्थेषु चेतनाचेतनेष्वसत्त्वं नास्तित्वं न विरुद्धं न विरोधावरुद्धम् । अस्तित्वेन सह विरोधं नानुभवतीत्यर्थः । न केवलमसत्त्वं न विरुद्धं किंतु सदवाच्यते च । सच्चावाच्यं च सदवाच्ये तयोर्भावौ सदवाच्यते । अस्तित्वावक्तव्यत्वे इत्यर्थः । ते अपि न विरुद्धे ॥ तथा हि । अस्तित्वं नास्तित्वेन सह न विरुध्यते । अवक्तव्यत्वमपि विधिनिषेधात्मकमन्योन्यं न विरुध्यते । अथवा अवक्तव्यत्वं वक्तव्यत्वेन साकं न विरोधमुद्वहति । अनेन च नास्तित्वाऽस्तित्वाऽवक्तव्यत्वलक्षणभङ्गकत्रयेण सकलसप्तभङ्ग्या निर्विरोधतोपलक्षिता । अमीषामेव त्रयाणां मुख्यत्वाच्छेषभङ्गानां च संयोगजत्वेनामीष्वेवान्तर्भावादिति ॥ नन्वेते धर्माः परस्परं विरुद्धास्तत्कथमेकत्र वस्तुन्येषां समावेशः संभवतीति विशेषणद्वारेण हेतुमाह उपाधिभेदोपहितम् इति । उपाधयोऽवच्छेदका अंशप्रकाराः तेषां भेदो नानात्वम् तेनोपहितम् अर्पितम् । सत्त्वस्य विशेषणमेतत् । उपाधिभेदोपहितं सदर्थेष्वसत्त्वं न

विरुद्धम् । सदवाच्यतयोश्च वचनभेदं कृत्वा योजनीयम् । उपाधिभेदोपहिते सती सदवाच्यते अपि न विरुद्धे । अयमभिप्रायः । परस्परपरिहारेण ये वर्तेते तयोः शीतोष्णवत्सहानवस्थानलक्षणो विरोधः । न चात्रैवम् । सत्त्वासत्त्वयोरितरेतरमविष्वग्भावेन वर्तनात् । नहि घटादौ सत्त्वमसत्त्वं परिहृत्य वर्तते। पररूपेणापि सत्त्वप्रसङ्गात् । तथा च तद्व्यतिरिक्तार्थान्तराणां नैरर्थक्यम्। तेनैव त्रिभुवनार्थसाध्यार्थक्रियाणां सिद्धेः। न चासत्त्वं सत्त्वं परिहृत्य वर्तते। स्वरूपेणाप्यसत्त्वप्राप्तेः। तथा च निरुपाख्यत्वात्सर्वशून्यतेति। तदा हि विरोधः स्याद् यद्येकोपाधिकं सत्त्वमसत्त्वं च स्यात्। न चैवम्। यतो न हि येनैवांशेन सत्त्वं तेनैवासत्त्वमपि । किंत्वन्योपाधिकं सत्त्वमन्योपाधिकं पुनरसत्त्वम्। स्वरूपेण हि सत्त्वं पररूपेण चासत्त्वम् । दृष्टं ह्येकस्मिन्नेव चित्रपटावयविन्यन्योपाधिकं तु नीलत्वमन्योपाधिकाश्चेतरे वर्णाः । नीलत्वं हि नीलीरागाद्युपाधिकं वर्णान्तराणि च तत्तद्रञ्जनद्रव्योपाधिकानि। एवं मेचकरत्नेपि तत्तद्वर्णपुद्गलोपाधिकं वैचित्र्यमवसेयम् । न चैभिर्दृष्टान्तैः सत्त्वासत्त्वयोर्भिन्नदेशत्वप्राप्तिः। चित्रपटाद्यवयविन एकत्वात् । तत्रापि भिन्नदेशत्वासिद्धेः। कथंचित्पक्षस्तु दृष्टान्ते दार्ष्टान्तिके च स्याद्वादिनां न दुर्लभः ॥

एवमप्यपरितोषश्चेदायुष्मतस्तर्ह्येकस्यैव पुंसस्तत्तदुपाधिभेदात्पितृत्वपुत्रत्वमातुलत्वभागिनेयत्वपितृव्यत्वभ्रातृव्यत्वादिधर्माणां परस्परविरुद्धानामपि प्रसिद्धिदर्शनात्किं वाच्यम्। एवमवक्तव्यत्वादयोपि वाच्या इति। उक्तप्रकारेणोपाधिभेदेन वास्तवं विरोधाभावमप्रबुध्यैवअज्ञात्वैव। एवकारोऽवधारणे। स च तेषां सम्यग्ज्ञानस्याभाव एव न पुनर्लेशतोऽपि भाव इति व्यनक्ति। ततस्ते विरोध-

भीताः सत्त्वासत्त्वादिधर्माणां बहिर्मुखशेमुष्या संभावितो वा विरोधः सहानवस्थानादिस्तस्माद्भीताः त्रस्तमानसाः । अत एव जडाः तात्त्विकभयहेतोरभावेपि तथाविधपशुवद्भीरुत्वान्मूर्खाः परवादिनः । तदेकान्तहताः तेषां सत्त्वादिधर्माणां य एकान्त इतरधर्मनिषेधेन स्वाभिप्रेतधर्मव्यवस्थापननिश्चयस्तेन हता इव हताः पतन्ति स्खलन्ति पतिताश्च सन्तस्ते न्यायमार्गाक्रमणे न समर्था न्यायमार्गाध्वनीनानां च सर्वेषामप्याक्रमणीयतां यान्तीति भावः । यद्वा पतन्तीति प्रमाणमार्गतश्च्यवन्ते । लोके हि सन्मार्गच्युतः पतित इति परिभाष्यते । अथवा यथा वज्रादिपरिहारेण हतः पतितो मूर्च्छामतुच्छामासाद्य निरुद्धवाक्प्रसरो भवत्येवं तेपि वादिनः स्वाभिमतैकान्तवादेन युक्तिसरणिमननुसरता वज्राशनिप्रायेण निहताः सन्तः स्याद्वादिनां पुरतोऽकिंचित्करा वाङ्मात्रमपि नोच्चारयितुमीशत इति ॥

अत्र च विरोधस्योपलक्षणत्वाद् वैयधिकरण्यम् अनवस्था संकरः व्यतिकरः संशयः अप्रतिपत्तिः विषयव्यवस्थाहानिः इत्येतेपि परोद्भाविता दोषा अभ्यूह्याः ॥ तथाहि । सामान्यविशेषात्मकं वस्त्वित्युपन्यस्ते परे उपालब्धारो भवन्ति । यथा सामान्यविशेषयोर्विधिप्रतिषेधरूपयोर्विरुद्धधर्मयोरेकत्राभिन्ने वस्तुन्यसंभवाच्छीतोष्णवदिति विरोधः । न हि यदेव विधेरधिकरणं तदेव प्रतिषेधस्याधिकरणं भवितुमर्हत्येकरूपतापत्तेः ततो वैयधिकरण्यमपि भवति ॥ अपरं येनात्मना सामान्यस्याधिकरणं येन च विशेषस्य तावप्यात्मानौ एकेनैव स्वभावेनाधिकरोति द्वाभ्यां वा स्वभावाभ्याम् । एकेनैव चेत् तत्र पूर्ववद्विरोधः । द्वाभ्यां वा स्वभावाभ्यां सामान्यविशेषाख्यं स्वभावद्वयमधिकरोति तदानवस्था तावपि स्वभावान्तराभ्यां तावपि स्वभावान्त-

राभ्यामिति ॥ येनात्मना सामान्यस्याधिकरणं तेन सामान्यस्य विशेषस्य च येन च विशेषस्याधिकरणं तेन विशेषस्य सामान्यस्य चेति संकरदोषः ॥ येन स्वभावेन सामान्यं तेन विशेषो येन विशेषस्तेन सामान्यमिति व्यतिकरः ॥ ततश्च वस्तुनोऽसाधारणाकारेण निश्चेतुमशक्तेः संशयः ॥ ततश्चाप्रतिपत्तिः ॥ ततश्च प्रमाणविषयव्यवस्थाहानिः इति ॥ एते च दोषाः स्याद्वादस्य जात्यन्तरत्वान्निरवकाशा एव । अतः स्याद्वादमर्मवेदिभिरुद्धरणीयास्तत्तदुपपत्तिभिरिति । स्वतन्त्रतया निरपेक्षयोरेव सामान्यविशेषयोर्विधिप्रतिषेधरूपयोस्तेषामवकाशात् ॥

अथवा विरोधशब्दोत्र दोषवाची । यथा विरुद्धमाचरतीति । दुष्टमित्यर्थः । ततश्च विरोधेभ्यो विरोधवैयधिकरण्यादिदोषेभ्यो भीता इति व्याख्येयम् । एवं च सामान्यशब्देन सर्वा अपि दोषव्यक्तयः संगृहीता भवन्ति ॥ इति काव्यार्थः ॥

अथानेकान्तवादस्य सर्वद्रव्यसर्वपर्यायव्यापित्वेपि मूलभेदापेक्षया चातुर्विध्याभिधानद्वारेण भगवतस्तत्त्वामृतरसास्वादसौहित्यमुपवर्णयन्नाह ।

स्यान्नाशि नित्यं सदृशं विरूपं
वाच्यं न वाच्यं सदसत्तदेव ।
विपश्चितां नाथ निपीततत्त्व-
सुधोद्गतोद्गारपरंपरेयम् ॥ २५ ॥

स्यादित्यव्ययमनेकान्तद्योतकमष्टास्वपि पदेषु योज्यम् । तदेवाधिकृतमेवैकं वस्तु स्यात्कथंचिन्नाशि विनशनशीलमनित्यमित्यर्थः । स्यान्नित्यमविनाशधर्मीत्यर्थः । एतावता नित्यानित्यलक्षणमेकं विधानम् ॥ तथा स्यात्सदृशम् अनुवृत्तिहेतुसामान्यरूपम् ॥

स्याद्विरूपम् विविधरूपं विसदृशपरिणामात्मकं व्यावृत्तिहेतुविशेषरूपमित्यर्थः । अनेन सामान्यविशेषरूपो द्वितीयः प्रकारः ॥ तथा स्याद्वाच्यं वक्तव्यम् ॥ स्यान्न वाच्यम् अवक्तव्यमित्यर्थः । अत्र च समासे अवाच्यमिति युक्तं तथाप्यवाच्यपदं योन्यादौ रूढमित्यसभ्यतापरिहारार्थं न वाच्यमित्यसमस्तं चकार स्तुतिकारः । एतेनाभिलाप्यानभिलाप्यस्वरूपस्तृतीयो भेदः ॥ तथा स्यात्सत् विद्यमानमस्तिरूपमित्यर्थः । स्यादसत् तद्विलक्षणमिति । अनेन सदसदाख्या चतुर्थी विधा ॥

हे विपश्चितां नाथ संख्यावतां मुख्य इयम् अनन्तरोक्ता निपीततत्त्वसुधोद्गतोद्गारपरंपरा । तवेति प्रकरणात्सामर्थ्याद्वा गम्यते । तत्त्वं यथावस्थितवस्तुस्वरूपपरिच्छेदः तदेव जरामरणापहारित्वाद्विबुधोपभोग्यत्वान्मिथ्यात्वविषोर्मिनिराकरिष्णुत्वादान्तराह्लादकारित्वाच्च सुधा पीयूषं तत्त्वसुधा । नितरामनन्यसामान्यतया पीता आस्वादिता या तत्त्वसुधा तस्या उद्गता प्रादुर्भूता तत्कारणिका उद्गारपरंपरा उद्गारश्रेणिरिवेत्यर्थः । यथा हि कश्चिदाकण्ठं पीयूषरसमापीय तदनुविधायिनीमुद्गारपरंपरां मुञ्चति तथा भगवानपि जरामरणापहारि तत्त्वामृतं स्वैरमास्वाद्य तद्रसानुविधायिनीं प्रस्तुतानेकान्तवादभेदचतुष्टयीलक्षणामुद्गारपरंम्परां देशनामुखेनोद्गीर्णवानित्याशयः ॥

अथवा यैरेकान्तवादिभिर्मिथ्यात्वगरलभोजनमातृप्ति भक्षितं तेषां तत्तद्वचनरूपा उद्गारप्रकाराः प्राक् प्रदर्शिताः । यैस्तु पचेलिमप्राचीनपुण्यप्राग्भारानुगृहीतैर्जगद्गुरुवदनेन्दुनिःस्यन्दि तत्त्वामृतं मनोहत्य पीतं तेषां विपश्चितां यथार्थवादविदुषां हे नाथ इयं पूर्वदलदर्शितोल्लेखशेखरोद्गारपरंपरेति व्याख्येयम् । एते च चत्वारोपि वादास्तेषु तेषु स्थानेषु प्रागेव चर्चिताः । तथा हि । आदी-

पमाव्योम समस्वभावाम् इति वृत्ते नित्यानित्यवादः प्रदर्शितः । अनेकमेकात्मकमेव वाच्यम् इति काव्ये सामान्यविशेषवादः संसूचितः। सप्तभङ्ग्यामभिलाप्यानभिलाप्यवादः सदसद्वादश्च चर्चितः। इति न भूयः प्रयासः ॥ इति काव्यार्थः ॥

इदानीं नित्यानित्यपक्षयोः परस्परदूषणप्रकाशनबद्धलक्षतया वैरायमाणयोरितरेतरोदीरितविविधहेतुहेतिसंनिपातसंजातविनिपातयोरयत्नसिद्धप्रतिपक्षप्रतिक्षेपस्य भगवच्छासनसाम्राज्यस्य सर्वोत्कर्षमाह ।

य एव दोषाः किल नित्यवादे
विनाशवादेपि समास्त एव ।
परस्परध्वंसिषु कण्टकेषु
जयत्यधृष्यं जिनशासनं ते ॥ २६ ॥

किलेति निश्चये । य एव नित्यवादे नित्यैकान्तवादे दोषा अनित्यैकान्तवादिभिः प्रसञ्जिताः क्रमयौगपद्याभ्यामर्थक्रियानुपपत्त्यादयस्त एव विनाशवादेपि क्षणिकैकान्तवादेपि समाः तुल्याः नित्यैकान्तवादिभिः प्रसज्यमाना अन्यूनाधिकाः । तथाहि नित्यवादी प्रमाणयति । सर्वं नित्यं सत्त्वात् । क्षणिके सदसत्कालयोरर्थक्रियाविरोधात् तल्लक्षणं सत्त्वं नावस्थां बध्नातीति ततो निवर्तमानमनन्यशरणतया नित्यत्वेवतिष्ठते । तथाहि क्षणिकोर्थः सन् वा कार्यं कुर्यात् असन्वा। गत्यन्तराभावात् । न तावदाद्यः पक्षः। समसमयवर्तिनि व्यापारायोगात् । सकलभावानां परस्परं कार्यकारणभावप्राप्त्यातिप्रसङ्गाच्च । नापि द्वितीयः पक्षः क्षोदं क्षमते । असतः कार्यकरणशक्तिविकलत्वात् । अन्यथा शशविषाणादयोपि कार्यकरणायोत्सहेरन् । विशेषाभावात् । इति ॥ अनित्यवादी

नित्यवादिनं प्रति पुनरेवं प्रमाणयति । सर्वं क्षणिकं सत्त्वात् । अक्षणिके क्रमयौगपद्याभ्यामर्थक्रियाविरोधात् अर्थक्रियाकारित्वस्य च भावलक्षणत्वात् ततोर्थक्रिया व्यावर्तमाना स्वक्रोडीकृतां सत्तां व्यावर्तयेदिति क्षणिकसिद्धिः । नहि नित्योर्थोर्थक्रियां क्रमेण प्रवर्तयितुमुत्सहते । पूर्वार्थक्रियाकरणस्वभावोपमर्दद्वारेणोत्तरक्रियायां क्रमेण प्रवृत्तेः । अन्यथा पूर्वक्रियाकरणाविरामप्रसङ्गात् । तत्स्वभावप्रच्यवे च नित्यता प्रयाति । अतादवस्थ्यस्यानित्यतालक्षणत्वात् । अथ नित्योपि क्रमवर्तिनं सहकारिकारणमर्थमुदीक्षमाणस्तावदासीत् पश्चात्तमासाद्य क्रमेण कार्यं कुर्यादिति चेत् न । सहकारिकारणस्य नित्येर्थेऽकिंचित्करत्वादकिंचित्करस्यापि प्रतीक्षणेऽनवस्थाप्रसङ्गात् । नापि यौगपद्येन नित्योर्थोर्थक्रियां कुरुते । अध्यक्षविरोधात् । नह्येककालं सकलाः क्रियाः प्रारभमाणः कश्चिदुपलभ्यते । करोतु वा । तथाप्याद्यक्षण एव सकलक्रियापरिसमाप्तेर्द्वितीयादिक्षणेष्वकुर्वाणस्यानित्यता बलादाढौकते । करणाकरणयोरेकस्मिन्विरोधात् । इति ॥ तदेवमेकान्तद्वयेपि ये हेतवस्ते युक्तिसाम्याद्विरुद्धं न व्यभिचरन्तीत्यविचारितरमणीयतया मुग्धजनस्य ध्यान्ध्यं चोत्पादयन्तीति विरुद्धा व्यभिचारिणोऽनैकान्तिकाः । इति ॥ अत्र च नित्यानित्यैकान्तपक्षप्रतिक्षेप एवोक्तः । उपलक्षणत्वाच्च सामान्यविशेषाद्येकान्तवादा अपि मिथस्तुल्यदोषतया विरुद्धा व्यभिचारिण एव हेतूनुपस्पृशन्तीति परिभावनीयम् ॥

अथोत्तरार्धं व्याख्यायते । परस्परेत्यादि । एवं च कण्टकेषु क्षुद्रशत्रुष्वेकान्तवादिषु परस्परध्वंसिषु सत्सु परस्परस्माद् ध्वंसन्ते विनाशमुपयान्तीत्येवंशीलाः सुन्दोपसुन्दवदिति परस्परध्वंसिनः । तेषु हे जिन ते तव शासनं स्याद्वादप्ररूपणनिपुणं द्वादशाङ्गीरूपं प्रवचनं पराभिभावुकानां कण्टकानां स्वयमुच्छिन्नत्वेनैवाभावाद-

धृष्यम् अपराभवनीयम् । शक्तार्हे कृत्याश्च इति कृत्यविधानाद् धर्षितुमशक्यं धर्षितुमनर्हं वा । जयति सर्वोत्कर्षेण वर्तते । यथा कश्चिन्महाराजः पीवरपुण्यपरीपाकः परस्परं विगृह्य स्वयमेव क्षयमुपेयिवत्सु द्विषत्स्वयत्नसिद्धनिष्कण्टकत्वं समृद्धं राज्यमुपभुञ्जानः सर्वोत्कृष्टो भवत्येवं त्वच्छासनमपि । इति काव्यार्थः ॥

अनन्तरकाव्ये नित्यानित्याद्येकान्तवादे दोषसामान्यमभिहितम् । इदानीं कतिपयतद्विशेषान्नामग्राहं दर्शयंस्तत्प्ररूपकाणामसद्भूतोद्भावकतयोद्वृत्ततथाविधरिपुजनजनितोपद्रवमिव परित्रातुर्धरित्रीपतेस्त्रिजगत्पतेः पुरतो भुवनत्रयं प्रत्युपकारकारितामाविष्करोति—

नैकान्तवादे सुखदुःखभोगौ
न पुण्यपापे न च बन्धमोक्षौ ।
दुर्नीतिवादव्यसनासिनैवं
परैर्विलुप्तं जगदप्यशेषम् ॥ २७ ॥

एकान्तवादे नित्यानित्यैकान्तपक्षाभ्युपगमे न सुखदुःखभोगौ घटेते । न च पुण्यपापे घटेते । न च बन्धमोक्षौ घटेते । पुनःपुनर्नञः प्रयोगोऽत्यन्ताघटमानतादर्शनार्थः ॥ तथाहि एकान्तनित्ये आत्मनि तावत् सुखदुःखभोगौ नोपपद्येते । नित्यस्य हि लक्षणम् अप्रच्युतानुत्पन्नस्थिरैकरूपत्वम् । ततो यदा आत्मा सुखमनुभूय स्वकारणकलापसामग्रीवशाद् दुःखमुपभुङ्क्ते तदा स्वभावभेदादनित्यत्वापत्त्या स्थिरैकरूपताहानिप्रसङ्गः । एवं दुःखमनुभूय सुखमुपभुञ्जानस्यापि वक्तव्यम् । अथ अवस्थाभेदादयं व्यवहारः । न चावस्थासु भिद्यमानास्वपि तद्वतो भेदः सर्पस्येव कुण्डलार्जवाद्यवस्थासु इति चेत् न ।

तास्ततो व्यतिरिक्ताः अव्यतिरिक्ता वा । व्यतिरेके तास्तस्येति संबन्धाभावः । अतिप्रसङ्गात् । अव्यातिरेके तु तद्वानेवेति तदवस्थितैव स्थिरैकरूपताहानिः । कथं च तदेकान्तैकरूपत्वेऽवस्थाभेदोपि भवेत् । इति ॥ किंच सुखदुःखभोगौ पुण्यपापनिवर्त्यौ तन्निर्वर्तनं चार्थक्रिया सा च कूटस्थनित्यस्य क्रमेण अक्रमेण वा नोपपद्यत इत्युक्तप्रायम् । अत एवोक्तं न पुण्यपापे इति । पुण्यं दानादिक्रियोपार्जनीयं शुभं कर्म पापं हिंसादिक्रियासाध्यमशुभं कर्म । ते अपि न घटेते । प्रागुक्तनीतेः ॥ तथा न बन्धमोक्षौ । बन्धः कर्मपुद्गलैः सह प्रतिप्रदेशमात्मनो वन्ह्ययःपिण्डवद् अन्योन्यसंश्लेषः । मोक्षः कृत्स्नकर्मक्षयः । तावप्येकान्तनित्ये न स्याताम् । बन्धो हि संयोगविशेषः स च अप्राप्तानां प्राप्तिः इतिलक्षणः । प्राक्कालभाविनी अप्राप्तिरन्यावस्था उत्तरकालभाविनी प्राप्तिश्चान्या । तदनयोरप्यवस्थाभेददोषो दुस्तरः । कथं चैकरूपत्वे सति तस्याकस्मिको बन्धनसंयोगः । बन्धनसंयोगाच्च प्राक् किं नायं मुक्तोऽभवत् । किंच तेन बन्धनेनासौ विकृतिमनुभवति न वा । अनुभवति चेत् चर्मादिवद् अनित्यः । नानुभवति चेत् निर्विकारत्वे सता असता वा तेन गगनस्येव न कोऽप्यस्य विशेषः इति बन्धवैकल्यान्नित्यमुक्त एव स्यात् । ततश्च विशीर्णा जगति बन्धमोक्षव्यवस्था । तथा च पठन्ति ।

वर्षातपाभ्यां किं व्योम्नश्चर्मण्यस्ति तयोः फलम् ।
चर्मोपमश्चेत्सोऽनित्यः खतुल्यश्चेदसत्फलः ॥

बन्धानुपपत्तौ मोक्षस्याप्यनुपपत्तिः । बन्धनविच्छदेपर्यायत्वान्मुक्तिशब्दस्य । इति ॥

एवमनित्यैकान्तवादेपि सुखदुःखाद्यनुपपत्तिः। अनित्यं हि अत्यन्तोच्छेदधर्मकम्। तथाभूते चात्मनि पुण्योपादानक्रियाकारिणो निरन्वयं विनष्टत्वात् कस्य नाम तत्फलभूतसुखानुभवः। एवं पापोपादानक्रियाकारिणोपि निरवयवनाशे कस्य दुःखसंवेदनमस्तु। एवं चान्यः क्रियाकारी अन्यश्च तत्फलभोक्ता इत्यसमञ्जसमापद्यते। अथ

यस्मिन्नेव हि संताने आहिता कर्मवासना।
फलं तत्रैव संधत्ते कर्पासे रक्तता यथा॥

इतिवचनान्नासमञ्जसमित्यपि वाङ्मात्रम्। संतानवासनयोरवास्तवत्वेन प्रागेव निर्लोठितत्वात्। तथा पुण्यपापेपि न घटेते। तयोर्हि अर्थक्रिया सुखदुःखोपभोगः तदनुपपत्तिश्चानन्तरमेवोक्ता। ततोऽर्थक्रियाकारित्वाभावात् तयोरप्यघटमानत्वम्। किंचानित्यः क्षणमात्रस्थायी तस्मिंश्च क्षणे उत्पत्तिमात्रव्यग्रत्वात् तस्य कुतः पुण्यपापोपादानक्रियार्जनम्। द्वितीयादिक्षणेषु चावस्थातुमेव न लभते। पुण्यपापोपादानक्रियाभावे च पुण्यपापे कुतः। निर्मूलत्वात्। तदसत्त्वे च कुतस्तनः सुखदुःखभोगः। आस्तां वा कथंचिदेतत्। तथापि पूर्वक्षणसदृशेनोत्तरक्षणेन भवितव्यम्। उपादानानुरूपत्वाद् उपादेयस्य। ततः पूर्वक्षणाद् दुःखितादुत्तरक्षणः कथं सुखित उत्पद्यते। कथं च सुखितात्ततः स दुःखितः स्यात्। विसदृशभागतापत्तेः। एवं पुण्यपापादावपि। तस्माद्यत्किंचिदेतत्॥ एवं बन्धमोक्षयोरप्यसंभवः। लोकेपि हि य एव बद्धः स एव मुच्यते। निरन्वयनाशाभ्युपगमे चैकाधिकरणत्वाभावात् संतानस्य चावास्तवत्वात् कुतस्तयोः संभावनामात्रमपि। इति परिणामिनि चात्मनि स्वीक्रियमाणं सर्वं निर्बाधमुपपद्यते।

परिणामोऽवस्थान्तरगमनं न च सर्वथा ह्यवस्थानम् ।
न च सर्वथा विनाशः परिणामस्तद्विदामिष्टः ॥

इतिवचनात् । पातञ्जलटीकाकारोऽप्याह । अवस्थितस्य द्रव्यस्य पूर्वधर्मनिवृत्तौ धर्मान्तरोत्पत्तिः परिणामः इति ॥ एवं सामान्यविशेषसदसदभिलाप्यानभिलाप्यैकान्तवादेष्वपि सुखदुःखाद्यभावः स्वयमभियुक्तैरभ्यूह्यः ॥

अथोत्तरार्धव्याख्या । एवमनुपपद्यमानेपि सुखदुःखभोगादिव्यवहारे परैः परतीर्थिकैः अथ च परमार्थतः शत्रुभिः । परशब्दो हि शत्रुपर्यायोप्यस्ति । दुर्नीतिवादव्यसनासिना । नीयते एकदेशविशिष्टोर्थः प्रतीतिविषयमाभिरिति नीतयो नयाः । दुष्टा नीतयो दुर्नीतयो दुर्नयाः । तेषां वदनं परेभ्यः प्रतिपादनं दुर्नीतिवादः । तत्र यद् व्यसनम् अत्यासक्तिः औचित्यनिरपेक्षा प्रवृत्तिरिति यावत् दुर्नीतिवादव्यसनम् । तदेव सद्बोधशरीरोच्छेदनशक्तियुक्तत्वाद् असिरिव असिः कृपाणः दुर्नीतिवादव्यसनासिः । तेन दुर्नीतिवादव्यसनासिना करणभूतेन दुर्नयप्ररूपणहेवाकखड्गेन । एवम् इत्यनुभवसिद्धं प्रकारमाह । अपिशब्दस्य भिन्नक्रमत्वाद् अशेषमपि जगत् निखिलमपि त्रैलोक्यम् । तात्स्थ्यात् तद्व्यपदेश इति त्रैलोक्यगतजन्तुजातम् । विलुप्तम् सम्यग्ज्ञानादिभावप्राणव्यपरोपणेन व्यापादितम् । तत् त्रायस्व इत्याशयः । सम्यग्ज्ञानादयोहि । भावप्राणाः प्रावचनिकैर्गीयन्ते । अत एव सिद्धेष्वपि जीवव्यपदेशः । अन्यथा हि जीवधातुः प्राणधारणार्थेभिधीयते तेषां च दशविधप्राणधारणाभावादजीवत्वप्राप्तिः । सा च विरुद्धा । तस्मात्संसारिणो दशविधद्रव्यप्राणधारणाज्जीवाः । सिद्धाश्च ज्ञानादिभावप्राणधारणात् । इति सिद्धम् ॥ दुर्नयस्वरूपं चोत्तरकाव्ये व्याख्यास्यामः । इति काव्यार्थः ॥

सांप्रतं दुर्नयनयप्रमाणप्ररूपणद्वारेण प्रमाणनयैरधिगमः इति वचनाज्जीवाजीवादितत्त्वाधिगमनिबन्धनानां तेषां प्रमाणनयानां प्रतिपादयितुः स्वामिनः स्याद्वादविरोधिदुर्नयमार्गनिराकरिष्णुमनन्यसामान्यं वचनातिशयं स्तुवन्नाह ।

सदेव सत्स्यात्सदिति त्रिधार्थो
मीयेत दुर्नीतिनयप्रमाणैः ।
यथार्थदर्शी तु नयप्रमाण-
पथेन दुर्नीतिपथं त्वमास्थः ॥ २८ ॥

अर्थ्यते परिच्छिद्यत इत्यर्थः पदार्थः । त्रिधा त्रिभिः प्रकारैः । मीयेत परिच्छिद्येत । विधौ सप्तमी । कैस्त्रिभिः प्रकारैरित्याह । दुर्नीतिनयप्रमाणैः । नीयते परिच्छिद्यते एकदेशविशिष्टोर्थ आभिरिति नीतयः नयाः । दुष्टा नीतयो दुर्नीतयो दुर्नया इत्यर्थः । नया नैगमाद्याः । प्रमीयते परिच्छिद्यतेऽर्थोऽनेकान्तविशिष्टोऽनेनेति प्रमाणं स्याद्वादात्मकं प्रत्यक्षपरोक्षलक्षणम् । दुर्नीतयश्च नयाश्च प्रमाणे च दुर्नीतिनयप्रमाणानि तैः । केनोल्लेखेन मीयेतेत्याह सदेव सत्स्यात्सदिति । सदिति अव्यक्तत्वान्नपुंसकत्वं यथा किं तस्या गर्भे जातमिति । सदेवेति दुर्नयः । सदिति नयः । स्यात्सदिति प्रमाणम् । तथा हि । दुर्नयस्तावत्सदेवेति ब्रवीति । अस्त्येव घट इति । अयं वस्तुन्येकान्तास्तित्वमेवाभ्युपगच्छन्नितरधर्माणां तिरस्कारेण स्वाभिप्रेतमेव धर्मं व्यवस्थापयति । दुर्नयत्वं चास्य मिथ्यारूपत्वात् । मिथ्यारूपत्वं च तत्र धर्मान्तराणां सतामपि निह्नवात् । तथा सदित्युल्लेखवान्नयः । स ह्यस्ति घटः इति घटे स्वाभिमतमस्तित्वधर्मं प्रसाधयन् शेषधर्मेषु गजनिमीलिकामालम्बते । न चास्य दुर्नयत्वम् । धर्मान्तरा-

तिरस्कारात् । न च प्रमाणत्वम् । स्याच्छब्देनालाञ्छितत्वात् । स्यात्सादिति स्यात्कथंचित्सद्वस्तु इति प्रमाणम् । प्रमाणत्वं चास्य दृष्टेष्टाबाधितत्वाद्विपक्षे बाधकसद्भावाच्च । सर्वं हि वस्तु स्वरूपेण सत् पररूपेण चासदित्यसकृदुक्तम् । सदिति दिङ्मात्रदेशनार्थम् ॥ अनया दिशा असत्त्वनित्यत्वानित्यत्ववक्तव्यत्वावक्तव्यत्वसामान्यविशेषाद्यपि बोद्धव्यम् ॥

इत्थं वस्तुस्वरूपमाख्याय स्तुतिमाह यथार्थदर्शी इत्यादि । दुर्नीतिपथं दुर्नयमार्गम् । तुशब्दस्यावधारणार्थस्य भिन्नक्रमत्वात् त्वमेव । आस्थः त्वमेव निराकृतवान् । न तीर्थान्तरदैवतानि । केन कृत्वा । नयप्रमाणपथेन । नयप्रमाणे उक्तस्वरूपे । तयोर्मार्गेण प्रचारेण । यतस्त्वं यथार्थदर्शी । यथार्थोस्ति तथैव पश्यतीत्येवंशीलो यथार्थदर्शी । विमलकेवलज्योतिषा यथावस्थितवस्तुदर्शी । तीर्थान्तरशास्तारस्तु रागादिदोषकालुष्यकलङ्कितत्वेन तथाविधज्ञानाभावान्न यथार्थदर्शिनः । ततः कथं नाम दुर्नयपथमथने प्रगल्भन्ते ते तपस्विनः । नहि स्वयमनयप्रवृत्तः परेषामनयं निषेद्धुमुद्धुरतां धत्ते । इदमुक्तं भवति । यथा कश्चित्सन्मार्गवेदी परोपकारदुर्ललितः पुरुषश्चौरश्वापदकण्टकाद्याकीर्णं मार्गं परित्याज्य पथिकानां गुणदोषोभयविकलं दोषास्पृष्टं गुणयुक्तं च मार्गमुपदर्शयति एवं जगन्नाथोपि दुर्नयतिरस्करणेन भव्येभ्यो नयप्रमाणमार्गं प्ररूपयतीति । आस्थः इत्यस्यतेरद्यतन्यां शास्त्यसूवक्तिख्यातेरङ् इत्यङि श्वयत्यसूवचपतः श्वास्थवोचपप्तम् इति अस्थादेशे स्वरादेस्तासु इति वृद्धौ रूपम् ॥ मुख्यवृत्त्या च प्रमाणस्यैव प्रामाण्यम् । यच्चात्र नयानां प्रमाणतुल्यकक्षताख्यापनं तत्तेषामनुयोगद्वारभूततया प्रज्ञापनाङ्गत्वज्ञापनार्थम् । चत्वारि हि प्रवचनानुयोगमहानगरस्य द्वाराण्युपक्रमो निक्षेपोनुगमो नयश्चेति ।

एतेषां च स्वरूपमावश्यकभाष्यादेर्निरूपणीयम् । इह तु नोच्यते । ग्रन्थगौरवभयात् । अत्र चैकत्र कृतसमासान्तः पथिन्शब्दः । अन्यत्र चाव्युत्पन्नः पथशब्दोऽदन्त इति पथशब्दस्य द्विःप्रयोगो न दुष्यति ॥

अथ दुर्नयनयप्रमाणस्वरूपं किंचिन्निरूप्यते । तत्रापि प्रथमं नयस्वरूपम् । तदनधिगमे दुर्नयस्वरूपस्य दुष्परिज्ञानत्वात् । अत्र चाचार्येण प्रथमं दुर्नयनिर्देशो यथोत्तरं प्राधान्यावबोधनार्थः कृतः । तत्र प्रमाणप्रतिपन्नार्थैकदेशपरामर्शो नयः । अनन्तधर्माध्यासितं वस्तु स्वाभिप्रेतैकधर्मविशिष्टं नयति प्रापयति संवेदनकोटिमारोहयतीति नयः । प्रमाणप्रवृत्तेरुत्तरकालभावी परामर्श इत्यर्थः । नयाश्चानन्ताः । अनन्तधर्मत्वाद्वस्तुनस्तदेकधर्मपर्यवसितानां वक्तुरभिप्रायाणां च नयत्वात् । तथा चवृद्धाः ।

जावइआ वयणपहा तावइआ चेव हुंति नयवाया ।

इति । तथापि चिरंतनाचार्यैः सर्वसंग्राहिसप्ताभिप्रायपरिकल्पनाद्वारेण सप्त नयाः प्रतिपादिताः । तद्यथा । नैगमसंग्रहव्यवहारऋजुसूत्रशब्दसमभिरूढैवंभूता इति । कथमेषां सर्वग्राहकत्वमिति चेदुच्यते । अभिप्रायस्तावदर्थद्वारेण शब्दद्वारेण वा प्रवर्तते । गत्यन्तराभावात् । तत्र ये केचनार्थनिरूपणप्रवणाः प्रमात्रभिप्रायास्ते सर्वेऽप्याद्ये नयचतुष्टयेन्तर्भवन्ति । ये च शब्दविचारचतुरास्ते शब्दादिनयत्रय इति ॥

तत्र नैगमः सत्तालक्षणं महासामान्यम् अवान्तरसामान्यानि च द्रव्यत्वगुणत्वकर्मत्वादीनि तथान्त्यान् विशेषान् सकलासाधारणरूपलक्षणानवान्तर विशेषांश्चापेक्षया पररूपव्यावर्तनक्षमान् सामान्यादत्यन्तविनिर्लुठितस्वरूपानभिप्रैति । इदं च स्वतन्त्रसामान्यविशेषवादे क्षुण्णमिति न पृथक्प्रयत्नः । प्रवचन-

प्रसिद्धनिलयनप्रस्थदृष्टान्तद्वयगम्यश्चायम् ॥

संग्रहस्तु अशेषविशेषतिरोधानद्वारेण सामान्यरूपतया विश्वमुपादत्ते । एतच्च सामान्यैकान्तवादे प्राक् प्रपञ्चितम् ॥

व्यवहारस्त्वेवमाह । यथालोकग्राहमेव वस्त्वस्तु किमनया अदृष्टाव्यवह्रियमाणवस्तुपरिकल्पनकष्टपिष्टिकया । यदेव च लोकव्यवहारपथमवतरति तस्यैवानुग्राहकं प्रमाणमुपलभ्यते नेतरस्य । न हि सामान्यमनादिनिधनमेकं संग्रहाभिमतं प्रमाणभूमिः । तथानुभवाभावात् । सर्वस्य सर्वदर्शित्वप्रसङ्गाच्च । नापि विशेषाः परमाणुलक्षणाः क्षणक्षयिणः प्रमाणगोचराः । तथाप्रवृत्तेरभावात् । तस्मादिदमेव निखिललोकाबाधितं प्रमाणप्रसिद्धं कियत्कालभाविस्थूलतामाबिभ्राणमुदकाद्याहरणाद्यर्थक्रियानिर्वर्तनक्षमं घटादिकं वस्तुरूपं पारमार्थिकम् । पूर्वोत्तरकालभावितत्पर्यायपर्यालोचना पुनरज्यायसी । तत्र प्रमाणप्रसराभावात् । प्रमाणमन्तरेण च विचारस्य कर्तुमशक्यत्वात् । अवस्तुत्वाच्च तेषां किं तद्गोचरपर्यालोचनेन । तथाहि पूर्वोत्तरकालभाविनो द्रव्यविवर्ताः क्षणक्षयिपरमाणुलक्षणा वा विशेषा न कथंचन लोकव्यवहारमुपरचयन्ति । तन्न ते वस्तुरूपाः । लोकव्यवहारोपयोगिनामेव वस्तुत्वात् । अत एव पन्था गच्छति कुण्डिका स्रवति गिरिर्दह्यते मञ्चाः क्रोशन्तीत्यादिव्यवहाराणां प्रामाण्यम् । तथा च वाचकमुख्यः । लौकिकसम उपचारप्रायो विस्तृतार्थो व्यवहारः इति ॥

ऋजुसूत्रः पुनरिदं मन्यते । वर्तमानक्षणविवर्त्यैव वस्तुरूपम् । नातीतमनागतं च । अतीतस्य विनष्टत्वादनागतस्यालब्धात्मलाभत्वात्खरविषाणादिभ्योऽविशिष्यमाणतया सकलशक्तिविरहरूपत्वान्नार्थक्रियानिर्वर्तनक्षमत्वं तदभावाच्च न वस्तुत्वम् । यदे-

वार्थक्रियाकारि तदेव परमार्थसत् इति वचनात् । वर्तमानक्षणालिङ्गितं पुनर्वस्तुरूपं समस्तार्थक्रियासु व्याप्रियत इति तदेव पारमार्थिकम् । तदपि च निरंशमभ्युपगन्तव्यम् । अंशव्याप्तेर्युक्तिरिक्तत्वात् । एकस्यानेकस्वभावतामन्तरेणानेकस्वावयवव्यापनायोगात् । अनेकस्वभावता एवास्तु इति चेत् न । विरोधव्याघ्राघ्रातत्वात् । तथाहि यद्येकः स्वभावः कथमनेकोऽनेकश्चेत्कथमेकः । एकानेकयोः परस्परपरिहारेणावस्थानात् । तस्मात्स्वरूपनिमग्नाः परमाणव एव परस्परोपसर्पणद्वारेण कथंचिन्निचयरूपतामापन्ना निखिलकार्येषु व्यापारभाज इति त एव स्वलक्षणं न स्थूलतां धारयत्पारमार्थिकामिति । एवमस्याभिप्रायेण यदेव स्वकीयं तदेव वस्तु न परकीयम् । अनुपयोगित्वात् । इति ॥

शब्दस्तु रूढितो यावन्तो ध्वनयः कस्मिंश्चिदर्थे प्रवर्तन्ते यथेन्द्रशक्रपुरंदरादयः सुरपतौ तेषां सर्वेषामप्येकमर्थमभिप्रैति किल । प्रतीतिवशात् । यथा शब्दाव्यतिरेकोर्थस्य प्रतिपाद्यते तथैव तस्यैकमनेकत्वं वा प्रतिपादनीयम् । न चेन्द्रशक्रपुरन्दरादयः पर्यायशब्दाविभिन्नार्थवाचितया कदाचन प्रतीयन्ते । तेभ्यः सर्वदा एकाकारपरामर्शोत्पत्तेरस्खलितवृत्तितया तथैव व्यवहारदर्शनात् । तस्मादेक एव पर्यायशब्दानामर्थ इति । शब्द्यते आहूयतेऽनेनाभिप्रायेणार्थ इति निरुक्तात् एकार्थप्रतिपादनाभिप्रायेणैव पर्यायध्वनीनां प्रयोगात् । यथा चायं पर्यायशब्दानामेकमर्थमभिप्रैति तथा तटस्तटी तटमिति विरुद्धलिङ्गलक्षणधर्माभिसंबन्धाद्वस्तुनो भेदं चाभिधत्ते । न हि विरुद्धधर्मकृतं भेदमनुभवतो वस्तुनो विरुद्धधर्मायोगो युक्तः । एवं संख्याकालकारकपुरुषादिभेदादपि भेदोभ्युपगन्तव्यः । तत्र संख्या एकत्वादिः कालोतीतादिः कारकं कर्त्रादि पुरुषः प्रथमपुरुषादिः ॥ समभिरूढस्तु

पर्यायशब्दानां प्रविभक्तमेवार्थमभिमन्यते। तद्यथा इन्दनादिन्द्रः। परमैश्वर्यमिन्द्रशब्दवाच्यं परमार्थतस्तद्वत्यर्थे। अतद्वत्यर्थे पुनरुपचारतो वर्तते। न वा कश्चित्तद्वान्। सर्वशब्दानां परस्पर विभक्तार्थप्रतिपादितया आश्रयाश्रयिभावेन प्रवृत्त्यसिद्धेः। एवं शकनाच्छक्रः पूर्दारणात्पुरन्दर इत्यादिभिन्नार्थत्वं सर्वशब्दानां दर्शयति। प्रमाणयति च। पर्यायशब्दा अपि भिन्नार्थाः। प्रविभक्तव्युत्पत्तिनिमित्तकत्वात्। इह ये ये प्रविभक्तव्युत्पत्तिनिमित्तकास्ते ते भिन्नार्थका यथेन्द्रपशुपुरुषशब्दाः। विभिन्नव्युत्पत्तिनिमित्तकाश्च पर्यायशब्दा अपि। अतो भिन्नार्था इति ॥

एवंभूतः पुनरेवं भाषते। यस्मिन्नर्थे शब्दो व्युत्पाद्यते स व्युत्पत्तिनिमित्तमर्थो यदैव प्रवर्तते तदैव तं शब्दं प्रवर्तमानमभिप्रैति न सामान्येन। यथोदकाद्याहरणवेलायां योषिदादिमस्तकारूढो विशिष्टचेष्टावानेव घटोभिधीयते न शेषः। घटशब्दव्युत्पत्तिनिमित्तशून्यत्वात् पटादिवदिति। अतीतां भाविनीं वा चेष्टामङ्गीकृत्य सामान्येनैवोच्यत इति चेत् न। तयोर्विनष्टानुत्पन्नतया शशविषाणकल्पत्वात्। तथापि तद्द्वारेण शब्दप्रवर्तने सर्वत्र प्रवर्तयितव्यः। विशेषाभावात्। किंच यद्यतीतवर्त्स्यच्चेष्टापेक्षया घटशब्दोऽचेष्टावत्यपि प्रयुज्येत तदा कपालमृत्पिण्डादावपि तत्प्रवर्तनं दुर्निवारं स्यात्। विशेषाभावात्। तस्माद्यत्र क्षणे व्युत्पत्तिनिमित्तमविकलमस्ति तस्मिन्नेव सोऽर्थस्तच्छब्दवाच्य इति ॥

अत्र संग्रहश्लोकाः।

अन्यदेव हि सामान्यमभिन्नज्ञानकारणम्।
विशेषोप्यन्य एवेति मन्यते नैगमो नयः ॥ १ ॥
सद्रूपतानतिक्रान्तं स्वस्वभावमिदं जगत्।
सत्तारूपतया सर्वं संगृह्णन् संग्रहो मतः ॥ २ ॥

व्यवहारस्तु तामेव प्रतिवस्तु व्यवस्थिताम् ।
तथैव दृश्यमानत्वाद्व्यापारयति देहिनः ॥ ३ ॥
तत्रर्जुसूत्रनीतिः स्याच्छुद्धपर्यायसंश्रिता ।
नश्वरस्यैव भावस्य भावात्स्थितिवियोगतः ॥ ४ ॥
विरोधिलिङ्गसंख्यादिभेदाद्भिन्नस्वभावताम् ।
तस्यैवं मन्यमानोयं शब्दः प्रत्यवतिष्ठते ॥ ५ ॥
तथाविधस्य तस्यापि वस्तुनः क्षणवर्तिनः ।
ब्रूते समभिरूढस्तु संज्ञाभेदेन भिन्नताम् ॥ ६ ॥
एकस्यापि ध्वनेर्वाच्यं सदा तन्नोपपद्यते ।
क्रियाभेदेन भिन्नत्वादेवंभूतोऽभिमन्यते ॥ ७ ॥

एत एव च परामर्शा अभिप्रेतधर्मावधारणात्मकतया शेषधर्मतिरस्कारेण प्रवर्तमाना दुर्नयसंज्ञामश्नुवते । तद्बलप्रभावितसत्ताका हि खल्वेते परप्रवादाः । तथा हि । नैगमनयदर्शनानुसारिणौ नैयायिकवैशेषिकौ । संग्रहाभिप्रायप्रवृत्ताः सर्वेऽप्यद्वैतवादाः सांख्यदर्शनं च । व्यवहारनयानुपातिप्रायश्चार्वाकदर्शनम् । ऋजुसूत्राकूतप्रवृत्तबुद्धयस्ताथागताः । शब्दादिनयावलम्बिनो वैयाकरणादयः । उक्तं च सोदाहरणं नयदुर्नयस्वरूपं श्रीदेवसूरिपादैः। तथा च तद्ग्रन्थः । नीयते येन श्रुताख्यप्रमाणविषयीकृतस्यार्थस्यांशस्तदितरांशौदासीन्यतः स प्रतिपत्तुरभिप्रायविशेषो नयः इति । स्वाभिप्रेतादंशादितरांशापलापी पुनर्नयाभासः । स व्याससमासाभ्यां द्विप्रकारः । व्यासतोऽनेकविकल्पः । समासतस्तु द्विभेदो द्रव्यार्थिकः पर्यायार्थिकश्च । आद्यो नैगमसंग्रहव्यवहारभेदात्त्रेधा । धर्मयोर्धर्मिणोर्धर्मधर्मिणोश्च । प्रधानोपसर्जनभावेन यद्विवक्षणं स नैकगमो नैगमः। सच्चैतन्यमात्मनीति धर्मयोः। वस्तुपर्यायवद्द्रव्यमिति धर्मिणोः । क्षणमेकं सुखी विषयासक्तजीव इति

धर्मधर्मिणोः । धर्मद्वयादीनामैकान्तिकपार्थक्याभिसंधिर्नैगमाभासः ॥ यथा आत्मनि सत्त्वचैतन्ये परस्परमत्यन्तं पृथग्भूते इत्यादि ॥ सामान्यमात्रग्राही परामर्शः संग्रहः । अयमुभयविकल्पः परोऽपरश्च । अशेषविशेषेष्वौदासीन्यं भजमानः शुद्धद्रव्यं सन्मात्रमभिमन्यमानः परः संग्रहः । विश्वमेकं सत् अविशेषादिति यथा । सत्ताद्वैतं स्वीकुर्वाणः सकलविशेषान्निराचक्षाणस्तदाभासः । यथा सत्तैव तत्त्वं ततः पृथग्भूतानां विशेषाणामदर्शनात् । द्रव्यत्वादीन्यवान्तरसामान्यानि मन्वानस्तद्भेदेषु गजनिमीलिकामवलम्बमानः पुनरपरसंग्रहः ॥ धर्माधर्माकाशकालपुद्गलजीवद्रव्याणामैक्यं द्रव्यत्वाभेदादित्यादिर्यथा । द्रव्यत्वादिकं प्रतिजानानस्तद्विशेषान्निह्नुवानस्तदाभासः । यथा द्रव्यत्वमेव तत्त्वं ततोर्थान्तरभूतानां द्रव्याणामनुपलब्धेरित्यादि ॥ संग्रहेण गोचरीकृतानामर्थानां विधिपूर्वकमवहरणं येनाभिसंधिना क्रियते स व्यवहारः । यथा यत्सत्तद्द्रव्यं पर्यायो वेत्यादिः । यः पुनरपारमार्थिकद्रव्यपर्यायविभागमभिप्रैति स व्यवहाराभासः । यथा चार्वाकदर्शनम् ॥ पर्यायार्थिकश्चतुर्धा ऋजुसूत्रः शब्दः समभिरूढ एवंभूतश्च ॥ ऋजु वर्तमानक्षणस्थायिपर्यायमात्रं प्राधान्यतः सूत्रयन्नभिप्राय ऋजुसूत्रः । यथा सुखविवर्तः संप्रत्यस्तीत्यादिः । सर्वथा द्रव्यापलापी तदाभासः । यथा तथागतमतम् ॥ कालादिभेदेन ध्वनेरर्थभेदं प्रतिपद्यमानः शब्दः । यथा बभूव भवति भविष्यति सुमेरुरित्यादिः । तद्भेदेन तस्य तमेव समर्थयमानस्तदाभासः । यथा बभूव भवति भविष्यति सुमेरुरित्यादयो भिन्नकालाः शब्दा भिन्नमेवार्थमभिदधति भिन्नकालशब्दत्वात् तादृक्सिद्धान्यशब्दवदित्यादिः ॥ पर्यायशब्देषु निरुक्तिभेदेन भिन्नमर्थं समभिरोहन् समभिरूढः । इन्दनादिन्द्रः शकनाच्छक्रः पूर्दारणात्पुरन्दर इत्यादिषु यथा पर्यायध्वनीनामभिधेयनानात्वमेव

कक्षीकुर्वाणस्तदाभासः यथेन्द्रः शक्रः पुरन्दर इत्यादय शब्दा भिन्नाभिधेया एव भिन्नशब्दत्वात्करिकुरङ्गतुरङ्गशब्दवदित्यादिः ॥ शब्दानां स्वप्रवृत्तिनिमित्तभूतक्रियाविष्टमर्थं वाच्यत्वेनाभ्युपगच्छन्नेवंभूतः । यथेन्दनमनुभवन्निन्द्रः शकनक्रियापरिणतः शक्रः पूर्दारणप्रवृत्तः पुरन्दर इत्युच्यते । क्रियानाविष्टं वस्तु शब्दवाच्यतया प्रतिक्षिपंस्तु तदाभासः । यथा विशिष्टचेष्टाशून्यं घटाख्यं वस्तु न घटशब्दवाच्यं घटशब्दप्रवृत्तिनिमित्तभूतक्रियाशून्यत्वात् पटवदित्यादिः ॥ एतेषु चत्वारः प्रथमेऽर्थनिरूपणप्रवणत्वादर्थनयाः । शेषास्तु त्रयः शब्दवाच्यार्थगोचरतया शब्दनयाः ॥ पूर्वः पूर्वो नयः प्रचुरगोचरः परः परस्तु परिमितविषयः । सन्मात्रगोचरात्संग्रहान्नैगमो भावाभावभूमिकत्वाद्भूमविषयः। सद्विशेषप्रकाशकाद्व्यवहारतः संग्रहः समस्तसत्समूहोपदर्शकत्वाद्बहुविषयः । वर्तमानविषयादृजुसूत्राद्व्यवहारस्त्रिकालविषयावलम्बित्वादनल्पार्थः । कालादिभेदेन भिन्नार्थोपदर्शिनः शब्दादृजुसूत्रस्तद्विपरीतवेदकत्वान्महार्थः प्रतिपर्यायशब्दमर्थभेदमभीप्सतः समभिरूढाच्छब्दस्तद्विपर्ययानुयायित्वात्प्रभूतविषयः । प्रतिक्रियं विभिन्नमर्थं प्रतिजानानादेवंभूतात्समभिरूढस्तदन्यथार्थस्थापकत्वान्महागोचरः ।नयवाक्यमपि स्वविषये प्रवर्तमानं विधिप्रतिषेधाभ्यां सप्तभङ्गीमनुव्रजति । इति ॥ विशेषार्थिना नयानां नामान्वर्थविशेषलक्षणाक्षेपपरिहारादिचर्चस्तु भाष्यमहोदधिगन्धहस्तिटीकान्यायावतारादिग्रन्थेभ्यो निरीक्षणीयः ॥

प्रमाणं तु सम्यगर्थनिर्णयलक्षणं सर्वनयात्मकम् ॥ स्याच्छब्दलाञ्छितानां नयानामेव प्रमाणव्यपदेशभाक्त्वात् । तथा च श्रीविमलनाथस्तवे श्रीसमन्तभद्रः ।

नयास्तव स्यात्पदलाञ्छना इमे रसोपविद्धा इव लोहधातवः ।
भवन्त्यभिप्रेतकला यतस्ततो भवन्तमार्याः प्रणता हितैषिणः ॥

इति । तच्च द्विविधं प्रत्यक्षं परोक्षं च । तत्र प्रत्यक्षं द्विधा सांव्यवहारिकं पारमार्थिकं च । सांव्यवहारिकं द्विविधम् इन्द्रियानिन्द्रियनिमित्तभेदात् । तद् द्वितयमवग्रहेहाऽवायधारणाभेदादेकैकशश्चतुर्विकल्पम् । अवग्रहादीनां स्वरूपं सुप्रतीतत्वान्न प्रतन्यते । पारमार्थिकं पुनरुत्पत्तावात्ममात्रापेक्षम् । तद्द्विविधं क्षायोपशमिकं क्षायिकं च । आद्यमवधिमनःपर्यायभेदाद्द्विधा । क्षायिकं तु केवलज्ञानमिति । परोक्षं च स्मृतिप्रत्यभिज्ञानोहानुमानागमभेदात्पञ्चप्रकारम् । तत्र संस्कारप्रबोधसंभूतमनुभूतार्थविषयं तदित्याकारं वेदनं स्मृतिः । तत्तीर्थकरबिम्बमिति यथा । अनुभवस्मृतिहेतुकं तिर्यगूर्ध्वतासामान्यादिगोचरं संकलनात्मकं ज्ञानं प्रत्यभिज्ञानम् । यथा तज्जातीय एवायं गोपिण्डो गोसदृशो गवयः स एवायं जिनदत्त इत्यादि । उपालम्भानुपलम्भसंभवं त्रिकालीकलितसाध्यसाधनसंबन्धाद्यालम्बनमिदमस्मिन्सत्येव भवतीत्याद्याकारं संवेदनमूहाऽपरनामा तर्कः । यथा यावान् कश्चिद्धूमः स सर्वो वन्हौ सत्येव भवतीति तस्मिन्नसत्यसौ न भवत्येवेति वा । अनुमानं द्विधा स्वार्थं परार्थं च । तत्रान्यथाऽनुपपत्त्येकलक्षणहेतुग्रहणसंबन्धस्मरणकारणकं साध्यविज्ञानं स्वार्थम् । पक्षहेतुवचनात्मकं परार्थम् अनुमानमुपचारात् । आप्तवचनादाविर्भूतमर्थसंवेदनमागमः । उपचारादाप्तवचनं च । इति स्मृत्यादीनां च विशेषस्वरूपं स्याद्वादरत्नाकरात्साक्षेपपरिहारं ज्ञेयमिति । प्रमाणान्तराणां पुनरर्थापत्त्युपमानसंभवप्रातिभैतिह्यादीनामत्रैवान्तर्भावः ॥ संनिकर्षादीनां तु जडत्वादेव न प्रामाण्यम् । इति ॥ तदेवंविधेन नयप्रमाणोपन्यासेन दुर्नयमार्गस्त्वया खिलीकृतः । इति काव्यार्थः ॥

इदानीं सप्तद्वीपसमुद्रमात्रो लोक इति वावदूकानां तन्मात्रलोके परिमितानामेव सत्त्वानां संभवात् परिमितात्मवादिनां दोषदर्शनमुखेन भगवत्प्रणीतं जीवानन्त्यवादं निर्दोषतयाभिष्टुवन्नाह ।

मुक्तोपि वाभ्येतु भवं भवो वा
भवस्थशून्योस्तु मितात्मवादे ।
षड्जीवकायं त्वमनन्तसंख्य-
माख्यस्तथा नाथ यथा न दोषः ॥ २९ ॥

मितात्मवादे संख्यातानामात्मनामभ्युपगमे दूषणद्वयमुपतिष्ठते । तत्क्रमेण दर्शयति । मुक्तोपि वाभ्येतु भवमिति । मुक्तः निर्वृतिमाप्तः । सोपि वा । अपि विस्मये । वाशब्द उत्तरदोषापेक्षया समुच्चयार्थः यथा देवो वा दानवो वेति । भवमभ्येतु संसारमभ्यागच्छतु । इत्येको दोषप्रसङ्गः ॥ भवो वा भवस्थशून्योस्तु । भवः संसारः स वा भवस्थशून्यः संसारिजीवैर्विरहितः अस्तु भवतु । इति द्वितीयो दोषप्रसङ्गः ॥

इदमत्राकूतम् । यदि परिमिता एवात्मानो मन्यन्ते तदा तत्त्वज्ञानाभ्यासप्रकर्षादिक्रमेणापवर्गं गच्छत्सु तेषु संभाव्यते खलु स कश्चित्कालो यत्र तेषां सर्वेषां निर्वृतिः । कालस्यानादिनिधनत्वादात्मनां च परिमितत्वात्संसारस्य रिक्तता भवन्ती केन वार्यताम् । समुन्नीयते हि प्रतिनियतसलिलपटलपरिपूरिते सरसि पवनतपनातपनजनोदञ्चनादिना कालान्तरे रिक्तता । न चायमर्थः प्रामाणिकस्य कस्यचित्प्रसिद्धः । संसारस्य स्वरूपहानिप्रसङ्गात् । तत्स्वरूपं ह्येतद्यत्र कर्मवशवर्तिनः प्राणिनः संसरन्ति समासार्षुः संसरिष्यन्ति चेति । सर्वेषां च निर्वृतत्वे संसारस्य वा रिक्तत्वं हठादभ्युपगन्तव्यम् । मुक्तैर्वा पुनर्भव आगन्तव्यम् । न च क्षीणकर्मणां भवाधिकारः ।

दग्धे बीजे यथात्यन्तं प्रादुर्भवति नाङ्कुरः ।
कर्मबीजे तथा दग्धे न रोहति भवाङ्कुरः ॥

इति वचनात् । आह च पतञ्जलिः । सति मूले तद्विपाको जात्यायुर्भोगा इति। एतट्टीका च। सत्सु क्लेशेषु कर्माशयो विपाकारम्भी भवति नोच्छिन्नक्लेशमूलः । यथा तुषावनद्धाः शालितण्डुला अदग्धबीजभावाः प्ररोहणसमर्था भवन्ति नापनीततुषा दग्धबीजभावा वा तथा क्लेशावनद्धः कर्माशयो विपाकप्ररोही भवति । नापनीतक्लेशो न प्रसंख्यानदग्धक्लेशबीजभावो वेति । स च विपाकस्त्रिविधो जातिरायुर्भोग इति । अक्षपादोऽप्याह । न प्रवृत्तिः प्रतिसन्धानाय हीनक्लेशस्य इति ॥

एवं विभङ्गज्ञानिशिवराजर्षिमतानुसारिणो दूषयित्वा उत्तरार्धेन भगवदुपज्ञमपरिमितात्मवादं निर्दोषतया स्तौति । षड्जीवेत्यादि । त्वं तु हे नाथ तथा तेन प्रकारेण अनन्तसंख्यम् अनन्ताख्यसंख्याविशेषयुक्तम् षड्जीवकायम् । अजीवन् जीवन्ति जीविष्यन्ति चेति जीवाः इन्द्रियादिज्ञानादिद्रव्यभावप्राणधारणयुक्ताः तेषां संधेवानूर्ध्वे इति चिनोतेर्घञि आदेश्च कत्वे कायः समूहो जीवकायः पृथिव्यादिः । षण्णां जीवकायानां समाहारः षड्जीवकायम् । पात्रादिदर्शनान्नपुंसकत्वम् । अथ वा षण्णां जीवानां कायः प्रत्येकं संघातः षड्जीवकायः तं षड्जीवकायम् । पृथिव्यप्तेजोवायुवनस्पतित्रसलक्षणषड्जीवनिकायम् । तथा तेन प्रकारेण । आख्यः मर्यादया प्ररूपितवान् । यथा येन प्रकारेण । न दोषः दूषणमिति । जात्यपेक्षमेकवचनम् । प्रागुक्तदोषद्वयजातीया अन्येऽपि दोषा यथा न प्रादुःष्यन्ति तथा त्वं जीवानन्त्यमुपदिष्टवानित्यर्थः । आख्य इति आङ्पूर्वस्य ख्यातेरङि सिद्धिः । त्वमित्येकवचनं चेदं ज्ञापयति यज्जगद्गुरोरेवैकस्येदृक् प्ररूपणसामर्थ्यं न तीर्थान्तरशास्तॄणामिति ॥

पृथिव्यादीनां पुनर्जीवमित्थं साधनीयम् । यथा सात्मिका विद्रुमशिलादिरूपा पृथिवी छेदे समानधातूत्थानात् अर्शोऽङ्कुरवत् । भौममम्भोपि सात्मकं क्षतभूसजातीयस्य स्वभावस्य संभवात् शालूरवत् । आन्तरिक्षमपि सात्मकम् अभ्रादिविकारे स्वतः संभूय पातात् मत्स्यादिवत् । तेजोपि सात्मकम् आहारोपादानेन वृद्ध्यादिविकारोपलम्भात् पुरुषाङ्गवत् । वायुरपि सात्मकः अपरप्रेरितत्वे तिर्यग्गतिमत्त्वात् गोवत् । वनस्पतिरपि सात्मकः छेदादिभिर्म्लान्यादिदर्शनात् पुरुषाङ्गवत् । केषांचित्स्वापाङ्गनोपश्लेषादिविकाराच्च । अपकर्षतश्चैतन्याद्वा सर्वेषां सात्मकत्वसिद्धिः । आप्तवचनाच्च । त्रसेषु च कृमिपिपीलिकाभ्रमरमनुष्यादिषु न केषांचित्सात्मकत्वे विगानमिति ॥

यथा च भगवदुपज्ञे जीवानन्त्ये न दोषस्तथा दिङ्मात्रं भाव्यते। भगवन्मते हि षण्णां जीवनिकायानामेतदल्पबहुत्वम् । सर्वस्तोकास्त्रसकायिकाः । तेभ्योऽसंख्यातगुणास्तेजस्कायिकाः । तेभ्यो विशेषाधिकाः पृथिवीकायिकाः । तेभ्यो विशेषाधिका अप्कायिकाः । तेभ्योपि विशेषाधिका वायुकायिकाः । तेभ्योनन्तगुणा वनस्पतिकायिकाः । ते च व्यावहारिका अव्यावहारिकाश्च ।

गोला य असंखिज्जा असंखणिगोअ गोलओ भणिओ ।
इक्किक्कम्मि णिगोए अणन्तजीवा मुणेअव्वा ॥
सिज्झंति जत्तिया खलु इह संववहारजीवरासिओ ।
एंति अणाइवणस्सइ रासिओ तत्तिया तम्मि ॥

इति वचनात् । यावन्तश्च यतो मुक्तिं गच्छन्ति जीवास्तावन्तोऽनादिनिगोदवनस्पतिराशेस्तत्रागच्छन्ति । न च तावता तस्य काचित्परिहाणिः।निगोदजीवानन्त्यस्याक्षयत्वात्। निगोदस्वरूपं च समयसागरादवगन्तव्यम् । अनाद्यनन्तेपि काले ये केचिन्निर्वृता

निर्वान्ति निर्वास्यन्ति च ते निगोदानामनन्तभागेपि न वर्तन्ते नावर्तिषत न वर्त्स्यन्ति । ततश्च कथं मुक्तानां भवागमनप्रसङ्गः कथं च संसारस्य रिक्ततापसक्तिरिति । अभिप्रेतं चैतदन्ययूथ्यानामपि । यथा चोक्तं वार्तिककारेण ।

अत एव विशुध्यत्सु मुच्यमानेषु संततम् ।
ब्रह्माण्डलोकजीवानामनन्तत्वादशून्यता ॥
अन्त्यन्यूनातिरिक्तत्वैर्युज्यते परिमाणवत् ।
वस्तुन्यपरिमेये तु नूनं तेषामसंभवः ॥

इति काव्यार्थः ॥

अधुना परदर्शनानां परस्परविरुद्धार्थसमर्थकतया मत्सरित्वं प्रकाशयन् सर्वज्ञोपज्ञसिद्धान्तस्यान्योन्यानुगतसर्वनयमयतया मात्सर्याभावमाविर्भावयाति ।

अन्योन्यपक्षप्रतिपक्षभावा-
द्यथा परे मत्सरिणः प्रवादाः ।
नयानशेषानविशेषमिच्छन्
न पक्षपाती समयस्तथा ते ॥ ३० ॥

प्रकर्षेणोद्यते प्रतिपाद्यते स्वाभ्युपगतोर्थो यैरिति प्रवादाः । यथा येन प्रकारेण । परे भवच्छासनादन्ये । प्रवादा दर्शनानि । मत्सरिणः अतिशायने मत्वर्थीयविधानात् सातिशयासहनताशालिनः क्रोधकषायकलुषितान्तकरणाः सन्तः पक्षपातिन इतरपक्षतिरस्कारेण स्वकक्षीकृतपक्षव्यवस्थापनप्रवणा वर्तन्ते । कस्माद् हेतोर्मत्सरिण इत्याह । अन्योन्यपक्षप्रतिपक्षभावात् । पच्यते व्यक्तीक्रियते साध्यधर्मवैशिष्ट्येन हेत्वादिभिरिति पक्षः । कक्षीकृतधर्मप्रतिष्ठापनाय साधनोपन्यासः । तस्य प्रतिकूलः पक्षः प्रति-

पक्षः। पक्षस्य प्रतिपक्षो विरोधी पक्षः प्रतिपक्षः। तस्य भावः पक्षप्रतिपक्षभावः। अन्योन्यं परस्परं यः पक्षप्रतिपक्षभावः पक्षप्रतिपक्षत्वमन्योन्यपक्षप्रतिपक्षभावः तस्मात्। तथाहि। य एव मीमांसकानां नित्यः शब्द इति पक्षः स एव सौगतानां प्रतिपक्षः। तन्मते शब्दस्यानित्यत्वात्। य एव सौगतानामनित्यः शब्द इति पक्षः स एव मीमांसकानां प्रतिपक्षः। एवं सर्वप्रयोगेषु योज्यम्। तथा तेन प्रकारेण। ते तव। सम्यगेति गच्छति शब्दोर्थमनेनेति पुन्नाम्नि घः समयः संकेतः। यद्वा सम्यग् अवैपरीत्येन ईयन्ते ज्ञायन्ते जीवा जीवादयोर्था अनेन इति समयः सिद्धान्तः। अथवा सम्यगयन्ते गच्छन्ति जीवादयः पदार्थाः स्वस्मिन् रूपे प्रतिष्ठां प्राप्नुवन्त्यस्मिन्निति समय आगमः। न पक्षपाती नैकपक्षानुरागी। पक्षपातित्वस्य हि कारणं मत्सरित्वं परप्रवादेषूक्तम्। त्वत्समयस्य च मत्सरित्वाभावान्न पक्षपातित्वम्। पक्षपातित्वं हि मत्सरित्वेन व्याप्तं व्यापकं च निवर्तमानं व्याप्यमपि निवर्तयतीति मत्सरित्वे निवर्तमाने पक्षपातित्वमपि निवर्तत इति भावः। तव समय इति वाच्यवाचकभावलक्षणे संबन्धे षष्ठी। सूत्रापेक्षया गणधरकर्तृकत्वेपि समयस्यार्थापेक्षया भगवत्कर्तृकत्वाद्वाच्यवाचकभावो न विरुध्यते। अत्थं भासइ अरहा सुत्तं गंथंति गणहरा णिउणं इति वचनात्। अथवा उत्पादव्ययध्रौव्यप्रपञ्चः समयः। तेषां च भगवता साक्षान्मातृकापदरूपतयाभिधानात्। तथा चार्षम्। उप्पन्नेइवा विगमेइवा धुवेइवा इत्यदाषः॥ मत्सरित्वाभावमेव विशेषणद्वारेण समर्थयति। नयानशेषानविशेषमिच्छन् इति। अशेषान् समस्तान्नयान्नैगमादीनविशेषं निर्विशेषं यथा भवत्येवम् इच्छन् आकाङ्क्षन्। सर्वनयात्मकत्वादनेकान्तवादस्य। यथा विशकलितानां मुक्तामणीनामेकसूत्रानुस्यूतानां

हारव्यपदेश एवं पृथगभिसन्धीनां नयानां स्याद्वादलक्षणैकसूत्रप्रोतानां श्रुताख्यप्रमाणव्यपदेश इति । ननु प्रत्येकं नयानां विरुद्धत्वे कथं समुदितानां निर्विरोधिता । उच्यते । यथा हि समीचीनं मध्यस्थं न्यायनिर्णेतारमासाद्य परस्परं विवदमाना अपि वादिनो विवादाद्विरमन्ति एवं नया अन्योन्यं वैरायमाणा अपि सर्वज्ञशासनमुपेत्य स्याच्छब्दप्रयोगोपशमितविप्रतिपत्तयः सन्तः परस्परमत्यन्तं सुहृद्भूयावतिष्ठन्ते । एवं च सर्वनयात्मकत्वे भगवत्समयस्य सर्वदर्शनमयत्वमविरुद्धमेव । नयरूपत्वाद्दर्शनानाम् । न च वाच्यं तर्हि भगवत्समयस्तेषु कथं नोपलभ्यत इति । समुद्रस्य सर्वसरिन्मयत्वेऽपि विभक्तासु तास्वनुपलम्भात् । तथा च वक्तृवचनयोरैक्यमध्यवस्य श्रीसिद्धसेनदिवाकरपादाः ।

उदधाविव सर्वसिन्धवः
समुदीर्णास्त्वयि नाथ दृष्टयः ।
न च तासु भवान्प्रदृश्यते
प्रविभक्तासु सरित्स्विवोदधिः ॥

अन्ये त्वेवं व्याचक्षते । यथान्योन्यपक्षप्रतिपक्षभावात्परे प्रवादा मत्सरिणस्तथा तव समयः सर्वनयान्मध्यस्थतयाङ्गीकुर्वाणो न मत्सरी । यतः कथंभूतः । पक्षपाती पक्षमेकपक्षाभिनिवेशं पातयति तिरस्करोतीति पक्षपाती । रागस्य जीवनाशं नष्टत्वात् । अत्र च व्याख्याने मत्सरीति विधेयपदं पूर्वस्मिंश्च पक्षपातीति विशेषः । अत्र च क्लिष्टाक्लिष्टव्याख्यानविवेको विवेकिभिः स्वयं कार्यः । इति काव्यार्थः ॥

इत्थंकारं कतिपयपदार्थविवेचनद्वारेण स्वामिनो यथार्थवादाख्यगुणमभिष्टुत्य समग्रवचनातिशयव्यावर्णने स्वस्यासामर्थ्यं दृष्टा-

न्तपूर्वकमुपदर्शयन् औद्धत्यपरिहाराय भङ्ग्यन्तरतिरोहितं स्वाभिधानं च प्रकाशयन् निगमनमाह—

वाग्वैभवं ते निखिलं विवेक्तु-
माशास्महे चेन्महनीयमुख्य ।
लङ्घेम जङ्घालतया समुद्रं
वहेम चन्द्रद्युतिपानतृष्णाम् ॥ ३१ ॥

विभव एव वैभवम् । प्रज्ञादित्वात्स्वार्थेऽण् । विभोर्भावः कर्म चेति वा वैभवम् । वाचां वैभवं वाग्वैभवं वचनसंपत्प्रकर्षम् । विभोर्भाव इति पक्षे तु सर्वनयव्यापकत्वम् । विभुशब्दस्य व्यापकपर्यायतया रूढत्वात् । ते तव संबन्धिनं निखिलं कृत्स्नं विवेक्तुं विचारयितुं चेत् यदि वयमाशास्महे इच्छामः । हे महनीयमुख्य महनीयाः पूज्याः पञ्च परमेष्ठिनस्तेषु मुख्यः प्रधानभूतः आद्यत्वात् तस्य संबोधनम् । ननु सिद्धेभ्यो हीनगुणत्वादर्हतां कथं वागतिशयशालिनामपि तेषां मुख्यत्वम् । न च हीनगुणत्वमसिद्धम् । प्रव्रज्यावसरे सिद्धेभ्यस्तेषां नमस्कारकरणश्रवणात् । काऊण नमुक्कारं सिद्धाणमभिग्गहंतु सो गिण्हे इति श्रुतकेवलिवचनात् । मैवम् । अर्हदुपदेशेनैव सिद्धानामपि परिज्ञानात् । तथा चार्षम् । अरहन्तुवएसेण सिद्धा णज्झंति तेण अरिहाई इति । ततः सिद्धं भगवत एव मुख्यत्वम् । यदि तव वाग्वैभवं निखिलं विवेक्तुमाशास्महे ततः किमित्याह । लङ्घेम इत्यादि । तदा इत्यध्याहार्यम् । तदा जङ्घालतया जाङ्घिकतया वेगवत्तया समुद्रं लङ्घेम किल समुद्रमिव अतिक्रमामः । तथा वहेम धारयेम । चन्द्रद्युतीनां चन्द्रमरीचीनां पानं चन्द्रद्युतिपानम् । तत्र तृष्णा तर्षोऽभिलाष इति यावत् चन्द्रद्युतिपानतृष्णा ताम् ।

उभयत्रापि संभावने सप्तमी । यथा कश्चिच्चरणचङ्क्रमणवेगवत्तया यानपात्राद्यन्तरेणापि समुद्रं लङ्घितुमीहते यथा च कश्चिच्चन्द्रमरीचीरमृतमयीः श्रुत्वा चुलुकादिना पातुमिच्छति न चैतद्द्वयमपि शक्यसाधनम् तथा न्यक्षेण भवदीयवाग्वैभववर्णनाकाङ्क्षापि अशक्यारम्भप्रवृत्तितुल्या । आस्तां तावत्तावकीनवचनविभवानां सामस्त्येन विवेचनविधानं तद्विषयाकाङ्क्षापि महत्साहसमिति भावार्थः । अथवा लाघि शोषणे इति धातोर्लङ्घेम शोषयेम समुद्रं जङ्घालतया अतिरहंसा । अतिक्रमणार्थलङ्घेस्तु प्रयोगे दुर्लभं परस्मैपदमनित्यं चात्मनेपदमिति । अत्र च औद्धत्यपरिहारेधिकृतेपि यदाशास्महे इत्यात्मनि बहुवचनमाचार्यः प्रयुक्तवांस्तदिति सूचयति यद्विद्यन्ते जगति मादृशा मन्दमेधसो भूयांसः स्तोतारः इति बहुवचनमात्रेण न खल्वहङ्कारः स्तोतरि प्रभौ शङ्कनीयः प्रत्युत निरभिमानताप्रासादोपरि पताकारोप एवावधारणीयः । इति काव्यार्थः ॥

एषु एकत्रिंशतिवृत्तेषु उपजातिच्छन्दः ॥

एवं विप्रतारकैः परतीर्थिकैर्व्यामोहमये तमसि निमज्जितस्य जगतोभ्युद्धरणेऽव्यभिचारिवचनतासाध्येनान्ययोगव्यवच्छेदेन भगवत एव सामर्थ्यं दर्शयन् तदुपास्तिविन्यस्तमानसानां पुरुषाणामौचितीचतुरतां प्रतिपादयति ।

इदं तत्त्वातत्त्वव्यतिकरकरालेन्धतमसे
जगन्मायाकारैरिव हतपरैर्हा विनिहतम् ।
तदुद्धर्तुं शक्तो नियतमविसंवादिवचन-
स्त्वमेवातस्त्रातस्त्वयि कृतसपर्याः कृतधियः ॥ ३२ ॥

इदं प्रत्यक्षोपलभ्यमानं जगत् विश्वम् उपचाराज्जगद्वर्ती जनः । हतपरैः हता अधमा ये परे तीर्थान्तरीया हतपरे तैः । मायाकारैः इन्द्रजालिकैरिव शाम्बरीयप्रयोगनिपुणैरिवेति यावत् । अन्धतमसे निबिडान्धकारे । हा इति खेदे । विनिहतं विशेषेण निहितं स्थापितं पातितमित्यर्थः । अन्धं करोतीत्यन्धयति अन्धयतीत्यन्धं तच्च तत्तमश्चेत्यन्धतमसम् समवान्धात्तमसः इत्यत्प्रत्ययः तस्मिन्नन्धतमसे । कथंभूतेन्धतमसे इति द्रव्यान्धकारव्यवच्छेदार्थमाह । तत्त्वातत्त्वव्यतिकरकराले । तत्त्वं चातत्त्वं च तत्त्वातत्त्वे तयोर्व्यतिकरो व्यतिकीर्णता व्यामिश्रता स्वभावविनिमयस्तत्त्वातत्त्वव्यतिकरः तेन कराले भयङ्करे । यत्रान्धतमसे तत्त्वे अतत्त्वाभिनिवेशोऽतत्त्वे च तत्त्वाभिनिवेश इत्येवंरूपो व्यतिकरः संजायत इत्यर्थः । अनेन च विशेषणेन परमार्थतो मिथ्यात्वमोहनीयमेवान्धतमसम् । तस्यैवेदृशलक्षणत्वात् । तथा च ग्रन्थान्तरे प्रस्तुतस्तुतिकारपादाः ।

अदेवे देवबुद्धिर्या गुरुधीरगुरौ च या ।
अधर्मे धर्मबुद्धिश्च मिथ्यात्वं तद्विपर्ययात् ॥

ततोयमर्थः । यथा किल ऐन्द्रजालिकास्तथाविधसुशिक्षितपरव्यामोहनकलाप्रपञ्चास्तथाविधमौषधीमन्त्रहस्तलाघवादिप्रायं किंचित्प्रयुज्य परिषज्जनं मायामये तमसि मज्जयन्ति तथा परतीर्थिकैरपि तादृक्प्रकारदुरधीतकुतर्कयुक्तीरुपदर्श्य जगदिदं व्यामोहमहान्धकारे निक्षिप्तमिति । तज्जगदुद्धर्तुं मोहमहान्धकारोपप्लवात् ऋष्टुं नियतं निश्चितं त्वमेव नान्यः शक्तः समर्थः । किमर्थमित्थमेकस्यैवं भगवतः सामर्थ्यमुपवर्ण्यत इति विशेषणद्वारेण कारणमाह । अविसंवादिवचनः । कषच्छेदतापलक्षणपरीक्षात्रयविशुद्धत्वेन फलप्राप्तौ न विसंवदतीत्येवंशीलमविसंवादि । तथाभूतं वचनमुपदेशो यस्यासाववविसंवादिवचनः । अव्यभिचारि-

वागित्यर्थः। यथा च पारमेश्वरी वाग् न विसंवादमासादयति तथा तत्र तत्र स्याद्वादसाधने दर्शितम् । कषादिस्वरूपं चेत्थमाचक्षते प्रावचनिकाः ॥

पाणवहाईआणं पावट्ठाणाण जो उ पडिसेहो।
झाणज्झयणाईणं जो य विही एस धम्मकसो ॥
बज्झाणुट्ठाणेणं जेण ण बाहिज्जए तयं णियमा ।
संभवइ य परिसुद्धं सो पुण धम्मम्मि छेउत्ति ॥
जीवाइभाववाओ बंधाइपसाहगो इहं तावो ।
एएहिं परिसुद्धो धम्मो धम्मत्तणमुवेइ ॥

तीर्थान्तरीयाप्ता हि न प्रकृतपरीक्षात्रयविशुद्धवादिन इति ते महामोहान्धतमस एव जगत्पातयितुं समर्था न पुनस्तदुद्धर्तुम् । अतः कारणात् । कुतः कारणात् । कुमतध्वान्तार्णवान्तःपतितभुवनाभ्युद्धारणासाधारणसामर्थ्यलक्षणात् । हे त्रातः त्रिभुवनपरित्राणप्रवीण । त्वयि काक्वावधारणस्य गम्यमानत्वात् त्वय्येव विषये न देवान्तरे। कृतधियः । करोतिरत्र परिकर्मणि वर्तते यथा हस्तौ कुरु पादौ कुरु इति । कृता परिकर्मिता तत्त्वोपदेशपेशलतत्तच्छास्त्राभ्यासप्रकर्षेण संस्कृता धीर्बुद्धिर्येषां ते कृतधियः चिद्रूपाः पुरुषाः। कृतसपर्याः । प्रादिकं विनाप्यादिकर्मणो गम्यमानत्वात् । कृता कर्तुमारब्धा सपर्या सेवाविधिर्यैस्ते कृतसपर्याः । आराध्यान्तरपरित्यागेन त्वय्येव सेवाहेवाकितां परिशीलयन्ति । इति शिखरिणीच्छन्दोलङ्कृतकाव्यार्थः ॥

समाप्ता चेयमन्ययोगव्यवच्छेदद्वात्रिंशिकास्तवनटीका ॥

येषामुज्ज्वलहेतुहेतिरुचिरः प्रामाणिकाध्वस्पृशां
हेमाचार्यसमुद्भवस्तवनभूरर्थः समर्थः सखा ।
तेषां दुर्नयदस्युसंभवभयास्पृष्टात्मनां संभव-
त्यायासेन विना जिनागमपुरप्राप्तिः शिवश्रीप्रदा ॥ १ ॥
चातुर्वैद्यमहोदधेर्भगवतः श्रीहेमसूरेर्गिरां
गम्भीरार्थविलोकनं यदभवद्दृष्टिः प्रकृष्टा मम ।
द्राघीयः समयादराग्रहपराभूतप्रभूतावमं
तन्नूनं गुरुपादरेणुकणिकासिद्धाञ्जनस्योर्जितम् ॥ २ ॥
अन्यान्यशास्त्रतरुसंगतचित्तहारि-
पुष्पोपमेयकतिचिन्निचितप्रमेयैः ।
दृब्धां मयान्तिमजिनस्तुतिवृत्तिमेनां
मालामिवामलहृदो हृदये वहन्तु ॥ ३ ॥
प्रमाणसिद्धान्तविरुद्धमत्र
यत्किंचिदुक्तं मतिमान्द्यदोषात् ।
मात्सर्यमुत्सार्य तदार्यचित्ताः
प्रसादमाधाय विशोधयन्तु ॥ ४ ॥
उर्व्यामेष सुधाभुजां गुरुरिति त्रैलोक्यविस्तारिणो
यत्रेयं प्रतिभाभरादनुमितिर्निर्दम्भमुज्जृम्भते ।
किं चामी विबुधाः सुधेति वचनोद्गारं यदीयं मुदा
शंसन्तः प्रथयन्ति तामतितमां संवादमेदस्विनीम् ॥ ५ ॥
नागेन्द्रगच्छगोविन्दवक्षोलङ्कारकौस्तुभाः ।
ते विश्ववन्द्या नन्द्यासुरुदयप्रभसूरयः ॥ ६ ॥ युग्मम् ॥
श्रीमल्लिषेणसूरिभिरकारि तत्पदगगनदिनमणिभिः ।
वृत्तिरियं मनुरविमितशाकाब्दे दीपमहसि शनौ ॥ ७ ॥

श्रीजिनप्रभसूरीणां साहाय्योद्भिन्नसौरभा ।
श्रुतावुत्तंसतु सतां वृत्तिः स्याद्वादमञ्जरी ॥ ८ ॥
बिभ्राणे कलिनिर्जयाज्जिनतुलां श्रीहेमचन्द्रप्रभौ
तद्दृब्धस्तुतिवृत्तिनिर्मितिमिषाद्भक्तिर्मया विस्तृता ।
निर्णेतुं गुणदूषणे निजगिरां तन्नार्थये सज्जनां-
स्तस्यास्तत्त्वमकृत्रिमं बहुमतिः सास्त्यत्र सम्यग् यतः ॥ ९ ॥

इति श्रीटीकाकारस्य प्रशस्तिः समाप्ता ॥

NOTES.

The Mangalacarana (Page 1)

The Syâdvâdamañjarî opens with a *mangalâcaraṇa* in four verses. The Jainas, like the Brâhmaṇas, believe in the efficacy of prayer to Higher Powers for successful execution of literary undertakings. cf. "'श्रेयांसि बहुविघ्नानि भवन्ति महतामपि। अश्रेयसि प्रवृत्तानां क्वापि यान्ति विनायकाः ॥' तस्मादशेषप्रत्यूहोपशमनाय मङ्गलमभिधेयम्।......। सर्वमेव वा शास्त्रं मङ्गलं ज्ञानरूपत्वात्।......। मङ्गलशब्दनिरुक्तं च मां गालयत्यपनयति भवादिति मङ्गलम्। मा भूद्गलो विघ्नो गालो वा नाशः शास्त्रस्येति मङ्गलम् ॥"—S'îlânkâcârya's Commentary on the Acârâṅga Sûtras.

Much intellectual energy has been spent in Brahmanical books of Logic (Mimâṁsâ and Nyâya) on demonstrating the necessity of maṅgalācaraṇa and on determining the manner in which it acts towards fulfilling its purpose. The duty of performing a maṅgalâcaraṇa is based upon s'iṣṭâcâra (practice of the good and respectable) which itself presupposes, say the Brâhmaṇas, a vedic commandment. As regards its *modus operandi*, while some hold that it brings an undertaking to a successful completion, removing obstacles if any (समाप्ति or निर्विघ्नसमाप्ति), others think that its function is simply to counteract the bad luck which causes obstacles (विघ्नध्वंस), the completion itself depending upon other natural or supernatural causes. Then, again, while some connect the maṅgala with the completion (समाप्ति) through the removal of obstacles (विघ्नध्वंसस्तु मङ्गलस्य द्वारम्), others believe that a kind of religious merit (अपूर्व) is created by the maṅgala, which removes the obstacles and produces the completion (अपूर्वद्वारैव मङ्गलस्य समाप्तिहेतुता). The scholiasts were not unaware of such incomplete works in Indian literature as Bâṇa's Kâdambarî despite a maṅgalâcaraṇa, and complete works even without a maṅgalâcaraṇa. Consequently, they have endeavoured to explain the breach in the causal law by the hypothesis of maṅgalâcaraṇa done in a previous life (जन्मान्तरीय मङ्गल), and also of comparative quantities and qualities of the maṅgalâcaraṇa and the evil karma. ("समाप्त्यभावश्च क्वचित् प्राचीनविघ्नभूयस्त्वात् क्वचिन्मङ्गलानन्तरोत्पन्नविघ्नात् क्वचिल्लोकावगतकारणाभावात्" "अन्ये तु मङ्गलं प्रधानम् अदृष्टद्वारा आरब्धकर्मसमाप्तिः फलम्...क्वचित्तु फलाभावः कर्मादिवैकल्यात् कारीरीवत्" Tattva-Ci.) Yet, the trend of their belief in the efficacy of maṅgalâcaraṇa would seem to be in the direction of rationalism. For the whole subject, see maṅgalavâda in Tatt.-Ci. N. Kaustubha, N. Mañjarî, Muktâvalî, and its commentaries. ["ननु न मङ्गलं विघ्नध्वंसं प्रति न वा समाप्तिं प्रति कारणं विनापि मङ्गलं नास्तिकादीनां ग्रन्थे निर्विघ्नसमाप्तिदर्शनात् इति चेन्न अविगीतशिष्टाचारविषयत्वेन मङ्गलस्य सफलत्वे सिद्धे तत्र फलजिज्ञासायां संभवति दृष्टफलकत्वे अदृष्टफलकल्पनाया अन्याय्यत्वात् उपस्थितत्वाच्च समाप्तिरेव फलं कल्प्यते । इत्थं च यत्र मङ्गलं न दृश्यते तत्र जन्मान्तरीयं तत्कल्प्यते यत्र च सत्यपि मङ्गले समाप्तिर्न दृश्यते तत्र बलवत्तरो विघ्नो विघ्नप्राचुर्यं वा बोध्यम्... विघ्नध्वंसस्तु मङ्गलस्य द्वारमित्याहुः प्राञ्चः । नव्यास्तु मङ्गलस्य विघ्नध्वंस एव फलं समाप्तिस्तु बुद्धिप्रतिभादिकारणकलापात् ।...नास्तिकादीनां ग्रन्थेषु जन्मान्तरीयमङ्गलजन्यदुरितध्वंसः स्वतःसिद्धविघ्नात्यन्ताभावो वाऽस्तीति न व्यभिचार इत्याहुः ॥ मुक्ता०]

The religious belief in the necessity of propitiating gods before commencing any serious piece of work—even the day's routine—is natural, and so we find that in the vedic ritual, the main sacrifice was often preceded by a small introductory offering made to the gods (cf. "आग्रावैष्णवमेकादशकपालं चरुं निर्वपेद्दर्शपूर्णमासावारिप्समानः"). Similarly, as recorded in the Bharata–Nâṭyaśâstra, a tediously long religious ceremony was performed on the stage, before commencing a dramatic representation. The ceremony which was originally mixed doing (कायिक) and speaking (वाचिक) came, in course of time, to be cut down to the latter; thus, the recitation of Nāndi remained the sole survivor of the old elaborate ceremonies of the Pûrva-raṅga. Thus, the maṅgalâcaraṇa in all literary works is mostly verbal:

"स्तुतिनमस्कारादिषु मङ्गलव्यवहारः शिष्टानाम्...अत एव दुरितनाशकमपि गङ्गास्नानादि न मङ्गलम्" Tatt.-Ci. Such a maṅgalâcaraṇa generally takes one of the three following forms: (i) आशीः Benediction or Prayer, (ii) नमस्क्रिया Salutation, and (iii) वस्तुनिर्देश Description, the last being supposed to be accomplished even by a bare reference to the name of a god, or the use of a word which means 'a god' as, for example, the word देवता in 'अस्त्युत्तरस्यां दिशि देवतात्मा हिमालयो नाम नगाधिराजः,' the first line of Kâlidâsa's Kumârasambhava.

The old practice was probably the performance of maṅgalâcaraṇa *outside the work*, in the shape of the recitation of vedic mantras, of the syllable Om, or of the names of âcâryas and gurus (*vide infra*), and hence its apparent absence from early works. But the duty of performing a maṅgalâcaraṇa is so liberally construed by the later scholiasts, that it is supposed to have been sufficiently discharged by the use of a word like अथ—which is said to be auspicious, but which really means nothing more than 'now'—at the commencement of a work *e. g.* 'अथातो धर्मं व्याख्यास्यामः,' 'अथातो ब्रह्मजिज्ञासा' ["अथशब्दो विघ्ननिवर्तकत्वान्मङ्गलमेव । ओङ्कारश्चाथशब्दश्च द्वावेतौ ब्रह्मणः पुरा । कण्ठं भित्त्वा विनिर्यातौ तेन माङ्गलिकावुभौ–इति स्मृतेः"—Tatt.-Ci.]

Some manuscripts of the Syâdvâdamañjarî open with 'नमः सर्वज्ञाय'—the usual mangalâcaraṇa of namaskâra to be found in Jaina and Bauddha works, the 'सर्वज्ञ' being, of course the Perfect Man, *i. e.*, the Jina or the Buddha. This may be part of the author's maṅgala, or it may be the copyist's.

St. 1. (Page 1 ll. 1-4)

ज्ञानमनन्तवस्तुविषयम्—knowledge of innumerable things, substances and modes, rather than of one endless Reality of the Vedântins ; for, the Jaina is a pluralist. This ज्ञान is technically known as 'केवलज्ञान' (see below). यः पूज्यते दैवतैर्नित्यम्—man, in his spiritual perfection, is higher than gods–a doctrine contributed to the history of world's religious thought by Jainism, Buddhism, and Vaiṣṇavism. दुर्नय—false doctrines or systems. कोलाहल–the jargon arising from their mutual contradictions. रागद्वेषमुखद्विषां परिषद्–the crowd of enemies consisting of or full of passions such as राग and द्वेष. Here रागद्वेषमुखाः द्विषः may mean: (i) enemies beginning with राग and द्वेष *i. e.* all the passions; or (ii) enemies whose mouths are full of राग and द्वेषः *i. e.* the heretical schools. (cf. *infra*). वीरविभुः–The Lord Mahâvîra. For the name see Kalpasûtra, 108 : "परीसहोव सग्गाणं खंतिखमे पडिमाणं पालए धीयं अरइ रइसहे दविए वीरिअसंपन्ने देवेहि से नामं कयं समणे भगवं महावीरे"–"because he stands fast in the midst of dangers and fears, patiently bears hardships and calamities, adheres to the chosen rules of penance, is wise, indifferent to pleasure and pain, rich in control, and gifted with fortitude, the name Venerable Ascetic Mahâvîra has been given him by the gods." [Tr. S. B. E.]; also vide Hemacandra's note on Haribhadra's आवश्यकवृत्तिः " वीरं विदारयत्यष्टप्रकारं कर्म विराजते वा सबाह्याभ्यन्तरेण तपसा सूर वीर विक्रान्तौ इत्यस्य वा वीरयति कर्मशत्रून्प्रति विक्रमते इति वीरः। तदुक्तम्– विदारयति यत्कर्म तपसा च विराजते। तपोवीर्येण युक्तश्च तस्माद्वीर इति स्मृतः ॥"

St. 2. (Page 1 ll. 5-8)

निःसीमप्रतिभैकजीवितधरौ or °धरो—whose very life or being consists of an unbounded play of genius. प्रतिभा—intuition or quick perception. It goes with हेमचन्द्रः or सरस्वतीसुरगुरू (Sarasvatî and Bṛhaspati) according as we read धरो (रः) or °धरौ. निःशेषभूमिस्पृशां पुण्यौघेन—Owing to the mass of puṇya of all those who are born on this earth, the mortals; that is to say, it is our good fortune that a Hemacandra was born in this world. The variant °स्पृशा पुण्यौघेन would give the sense—By the mass of puṇya which in its magnitude covers the whole earth. सरस्वतीसुरगुरू स्वाङ्गैकरूपौ दधत्—Hemacandra representing in his person both Sarasvatî and Bṛhaspati—the former the goddess of learning, and the latter the teacher of gods. स्वाङ्गैकरूपे (v.l.)—loc. sing. or acc. dual in apposition to सरस्वतीसुरगुरू. The former appears to be preferable. यः स्याद्वादमसाधयत्निजवपुर्दृष्टान्ततः who, in virtue of his being both सरस्वती and सुरगुरु, may be said to have demonstrated the Syâdvâda doctrine of Many-in-One or

One-in-Many by his own personal example. सद्बुध्यम्बुनिधि° ...चन्द्रः-The sea is roused into activity by the moon (चन्द्र); so is good thought by हेमचन्द्र. आप्तस्तुतेः-of the Dvâtrimśikâ which is a panegyric of Mahâvîra—the आप्त. आप्त-originally a kinsman (cf. 'य आपिर्नित्यो वरुणः प्रियःसन्' Ṛg. S.) or a friend; and, hence, he who declares the Truth—'आप्तस्तु यथार्थवक्ता.' or is competent to declare the Truth. 'तत्त्वदर्शनकारुण्यकरणपाटवाभिसंबन्ध आप्तिस्तया सह वर्तत इत्याप्तः'-Vâcaspatimis'ra's योग भा. टी.

St 4. (Page 1 ll. 13-16)

विवृति—the present work of Malliṣeṇa—that is the Syâdvâdamañjarî. प्रसिध्यति-proves successful. आरम्भसंभावनां-undertaking of the work, or the work which is respectfully undertaken (= संभावितः आरम्भः) यद्वा विस्मृतम्—an instance of आक्षेपालङ्कार—cf. 'निषेधो वक्तुमिष्टस्य यो विशेषाभिधित्सया । वक्ष्यमाणोक्तविषयः स आक्षेपो द्विधा मतः॥' K. Pr.

From the original stock of the Indian Religion, Jainism and Buddhism branched off as separate religions many years after the time of the great reformers Mahâvîra and Gautama Buddha; and even when eventually Brahmanism, Jainism and Buddhism stood out as rival religions in the country, they influenced each other much more profoundly than their followers cared to admit. Owing to their common origin, they possess mainly the same religious traditions including the Pantheon. The prayer to भारती here is an instance to the point. The prayer, however, is withdrawn ('यद्वा विस्मृतम्') in favour of the author's Jaina master—Udayaprabha-as quickly as the reverence which the Jainas at one time paid to the ancient Indian religion. सारस्वतः शाश्वतो मन्त्रः—The eternal mystic formula of Sarasvatî; here, the name of the author's guru—उदयप्रभ-which is to take the place of the formula. उदयप्रभ wrote आरम्भसिद्धि, धर्माभ्युदय महाकाव्य and उपदेशमालाकर्णिका-वृत्ति, etc.

Page 2.

l. 17 दुःषमार°-The wheel of Time with its spokes (Sk. अरङ, Guj. આરા) is divided by the Jainas into two parts-अवसर्पिणी

and उत्सर्पिणी–*i. e.* the half with the *downward* move, and that with the *upward* move. The former is subdivided into six अरऽ *i. e.* spokes, sectors, or arcs in the descending order of happiness: 1. सुषम-सुषमा (the period of extreme happiness,) 2 सुषमा (the period of happiness), 3 सुषम-दुःषमा (the period of mixed happiness and misery, the former preponderating), 4 दुःषमसुषमा (the period of mixed misery and happiness, the former preponderating), 5 दुःषमा (the period of misery) and 6 दुःषमदुःषमा (the period of extreme misery). The first Tîrthaṅkara–Ṛṣabhadeva–was born during the 3rd and the remaining twenty-three during the 4th period. Ours is the 5th. The same divisions in the reverse order belong to the other half, *viz.*, उत्सर्पिणी. For a detailed account of their characteristics see Mrs. Stevenson's "The Heart of Jainism" pp. 272–278. "The main features of the chronological system of the Gainas equally differ from those of the Buddhists as from those of the Brâhmaṇas. For it is impossible to derive the Utsarpiṇî and Avasarpiṇî eras, with their six Aras, from the Buddhistical four great and eighty smaller Kalpas, which are as it were the acts and scenes in the drama of the successive creations and dissolutions of the universe, nor from the Yugas and Kalpas of the Brâhmaṇas. I am of opinion that the Buddhists have improved on the Brahmanic system of the Yugas, while the Gainas inverted their Utsarpiṇî and Avasarpiṇî eras after the model of the day and night of Brahmā."—Jacobi, S. B. E. Gaina Sûtras, Pt. I p. xxii.

" स च कालो द्विविधः। उत्सर्पिणी अवसर्पिणी चेति। तद्भेदाः प्रत्येकं षट्। अन्वर्थसंज्ञे चैते। अनुभवादिभिरुत्सर्पणशीला उत्सार्पिणी। तैरेवावसर्पणशीला अवसर्पिणी। तत्रावसार्पिणी षड्विधा। सुषमसुषमा, सुषमा, सुषमदुष्षमा, दुष्षमसुषमा, दुष्षमा अतिदुष्षमा। उत्सर्पिण्यपि अतिदुःषमाद्या सुषमसुषमान्ता षड्विधैव भवति।"–Āv. Tîkâ.

"द्वादशारं कालचक्रं हेतुः कालव्यवस्थितेः। कालो द्विविधोऽवसर्पिण्युत्सर्पिणी विभेदतः। अराः षडवसर्पिण्यामेकान्तसुखमादयः। तत्रैकान्तः सुखमारः चतस्रः कोटिकोटयः। सागराणां सुषमा तु तिस्रस्तत्कोटिकोटयः। सुषमदुःषमा ते द्वे दुःखमसु-

षमा पुनः। सैका सहस्रैर्वर्षाणां द्विचत्वारिंशतो मिता। एकविंशतिरब्दानां सहस्राणि तु दुःखमा। एकान्तदुःखमापि स्यात्तावद्वर्षप्रमाणिका। अरका अवसर्पिण्यां य एते समुदीरिताः। उत्सर्पिण्यां त एव स्युः प्रतिलोमक्रमेण तु। तदेवमवसर्पिण्या-मुत्सर्पिण्यां च मीलिताः। सागरोपमकोटीनां कोटयः खलु विंशतिः।" Hem.-आदीश्वरचरित Sarga II, Verses 111, etc.

l. 18 वसुधातलावतीर्ण etc.-सुधासारणी-a canal or stream of nectar. A canal near Mângrol in Kâthiavad is known by the proper name of Sâraṇ. सुधासारिणि (a. v. l.), streaming with nectar, causing nectar to flow. देश्यदेशनावितान-Spreading of the gospel of Jainism among his pupils or those who are prepared or fit to hear it.

परमार्हतीकृत०-For Kumârapâla's conversion to Jainism, and the stories of his enthusiasm for the new faith, see Dvyâsraya Kumârapâlacarita of Hemacandra Prabandha-cintâmaṇi, Pt. iv, pp. 132-133 Tawney's Edition, A. S. B. Râsamâlâ vol. I pp. 182-192, & 194-197, the Bombay Gazetteer, Gujarat pp. 190-193. "The King and the monk [Hemâcârya] returned to Unhilpoor. There Hemâcârya instructed Kumâra Pâl in the purity which proceeded from the mouth of Jin Dev, and caused him to become great among the followers of Urhant. Under the Âcâryâ's directions, the King forbad the destruction of life for a period of fourteen years in the eighteen countries of Goozerat, in which his order was obeyed." (Râsmâlâ vol. I pp. 187-188.) The order is known by the name of 'अमारिघोषणा' or proclamation prohibiting slaughter.

l. 21 चातुर्विद्य—Explained in a marginal note in some of the manuscripts as 'लक्षणागमसाहित्यतर्काश्चातुर्विद्यम्' *i. e.* Grammar, Sacred Canon (Jaina), Literature and Logic. This nearly accords with the four subjects in which Mukulabhaṭṭa (ix century A. D.), the teacher of प्रतीहारेन्दुराज (9th century) is said to have been versed, *viz.*, मीमांसा, व्याकरण, तर्क and साहित्य. In several Gujarat inscriptions, however, the word चातुर्विद्य occurs in the sense of the four Vedas. (see Fleet's Inscriptions.)

l. 22. जगत्प्रसिद्धश्रीसिद्धसेनदिवाकर etc.–Siddhasena Divâkara (for his date and other account see H.J. pp. 76–77) composed 32 sets of 32 stanzas each. Similarly Hemacandra composed two such sets called अयोगव्यवच्छेद॰ and अन्ययोगव्यवच्छेद—द्वात्रिंशिकाs, the former being a *defence* of the Jaina system, and the latter an *attack* on other systems. (cf. similarly, Pâdas i and ii of the Adhyâya II of the Brahmasûtras. The words are of common occurrence in these senses and the method the common method of scholastic treatment. cf. "यथोक्तस्योभयस्य मार्गत्वं द्रढयितुमयोगव्यावृत्तिमन्ययोगव्यावृत्तिं च विधत्ते...तमेवानतिक्रमं स्वपक्षसाधनपरपक्षदूषणाभ्यां द्रढयति "—Sâyaṇa's com. on Aitareya Brâhmaṇa).

l. 23 (1) अयोगव्यवच्छेद lit. exclusion of non-possession, *i. e.* demonstration that truth does not fail to belong to the Jaina system, *that it certainly belongs to it*:. the *constructive* or *positive* part of Hemacandra's work (स्वपक्षसाधन). (2) अन्ययोगव्यवच्छेद—lit. exclusion of the position that truth might belong to other rival systems, *i. e.*, demonstration that truth does *not* belong to other systems: the *destructive* or *negative* part of the undertaking (परपक्षदूषण). *Thirty-two* seems to have been a favourite number with Hemacandra. He got thirty-two Vihâras or Jaina monasteries built by Kumârapâla in expiation of the sin the latter had committed by eating a certain dish which reminded him of flesh. The reason given for the number was that man had thirty-two teeth. see Prabandha–cintâmaṇi ch. iv: "पृथ्वीपतिः......पूर्वभक्षितस्याभक्ष्यस्य प्रायश्चित्तं याचितवान् । द्वात्रिंशद्दशनसंख्यया द्वात्रिंशद्विहारान् कारयेति । "

l. 26. निःशेषदुर्वादिपर्षद॰ (*i. e.* परिषद्)—An assembly or assemblage of all the heretical *i. e.* non-Jaina philosophers. पर्षद्—evidently a contraction of परिषद्–is as old as the Sûtrâs and the Smṛitis and even older. (cf. supra रागद्वेषमुखद्विषां च परिषत् क्षिप्ता क्षणाद् येन).

Stanza I.

ll. 29-30 अनन्तम्=अप्रतिपाति, unlimited, unfailing; विज्ञानम्=विशिष्टं सर्वद्रव्यपर्यायविषयत्वेनोत्कृष्टं ज्ञानं केवलाख्यम्, that extraordinary kind of knowledge called केवलज्ञान (see infra), which is superior to all other kinds of knowledge, since it visualises all dravyas (substances) and all paryâyas (attributes or modes). The following varieties of ज्ञान are enumerated in Jaina works :—

(1) मतिज्ञान *i. e.* such knowledge as we ordinary human beings acquire by means of the इन्द्रियs and मनः. It is divided into अवग्रह, ईहा, अवा(*i. e.* पा)य and धारणा-which are thus explained in the T. Rv. विषयविषयिसंनिपातसमनन्तरमाद्यग्रहणमवग्रहः । अवगृहीतेऽर्थे तद्विशेषाकाङ्क्षणमीहा । (यथा पुरुष इत्यवगृहीते तस्य भाषावयोरूपादिविशेषैराकाङ्क्षणमीहा) । विशेषनिर्ज्ञानाद्याथात्म्यावगमनमवायः । (भाषादिविशेषनिर्ज्ञानात्तस्य याथात्म्येनावगमनमवायः दाक्षिणात्योऽयं युवा गौर इति वा) । निर्ज्ञातार्थाविस्मृतिर्धारणा । (भाषावयोरूपादिविशेषैर्याथात्म्येन निर्णीतस्य पुरुषस्योत्तरकालं स एवायमित्यवस्मरणं यतो भवति सा धारणा) *i. e.* first a bare concept (अवग्रह), next a desire for detailed knowledge (ईहा), then the detailed knowledge (अवाय), and lastly holding the knowledge as a permanent possession in the mind (धारणा).

(2) श्रुतज्ञान—or scriptural knowledge *i. e.* such knowledge as is acquired from scriptures proper, *viz.*, the works of the first gaṇadharas, known as the Twelve Angas, (अङ्गप्रविष्टम्) and the later supplements composed by their successors such as the Uttarâdhyayana, the Dasavaikâlika etc., together with the books of daily prayers and religious practice (अङ्गबाह्यम्):cf. तत्राङ्गप्रविष्टमङ्गबाह्यं चेति द्विविधम्। अङ्गप्रविष्टमाचारादिद्वादशभेदं बुद्ध्यतिशयर्द्धियुक्तगणधरानुस्मृतग्रन्थरचनम् (भगवदर्हत्सर्वज्ञहिमवन्निर्गतवाग्गङ्गार्थविमलसलिलप्रक्षालितान्तःकरणे बुद्ध्यतिशयर्द्धियुक्तैर्गणधरैरनुस्मृतरचनम् , आचाराद्द्विादशविधमङ्गप्रविष्टमित्युच्यते ।) आरातीयाचार्यकृताङ्गार्थप्रत्यासन्नरूपमङ्गबाह्यम् । (यद् गणधरशिष्यैः प्रशिष्यैरारातीयैरधिगतश्रुतार्थतत्त्वैः कालदोषादल्पमेधायुर्बलानां प्राणिनामनुग्रहार्थमुपनिबद्धं संक्षिप्ताङ्गार्थवचनविन्यासं तदङ्गबाह्यम्) T. Rv.

Of course, in the case of Mahâvîra, the श्रुतज्ञान must be understood to refer to his knowledge of the older Jaina scriptures. A difference between मतिज्ञान and श्रुतज्ञान is said to be this, that while the former is limited to things present, the latter extends to things past and future as well (मतिज्ञान

श्रुतज्ञानयोः कः प्रतिविशेष इति। अत्रोच्यते। उत्पन्नाविनष्टार्थग्राहकं साम्प्रतकालविषयं मतिज्ञानम्। श्रुतज्ञानं तु त्रिकालविषयमुत्पन्नविनष्टानुत्पन्नार्थग्राहकम्—T. Bh.) In illustrating the difference thus drawn Mr. Jaini says—"An eclipse to-day may be known by Matijñâna, but one in the time of Alexander, or one to happen next year, can now only be known by S'rutajñâna." All true history is thus श्रुतज्ञान, in the same way as ऐतिह्य is included in शब्दप्रमाण in Brahmanical Logic. This is, however, extending the scope of श्रुतज्ञान beyond its intended limits, it being originally opposed to मतिज्ञान in the sense of Authority or Revelation as distinguished from Experience and Reason.

(3) अवधिज्ञान—Knowledge of the distant in time or space (अवधि-limit or boundary.) It is innate ('भव') in the case of the celestial (देव) and the infernal (नारक) souls; or, acquired by the precipitation or annihilation of karmic matter (क्षयोपशमनिमित्त), in the case of other souls such as men and lower animals (मनुष्य and तिर्यग्योनि). This variety of ज्ञान is concerned with only रूपिद्रव्यs (material objects possessing रूप, रस, etc.)

(4) मनःपर्य(v. l. र्या)यज्ञान—knowledge of what passes in other minds. मनः प्रतीत्य प्रतिसन्धाय वा ज्ञानं मनःपर्ययः (T. Rv.) reaching and reading the mind. It has two varieties—ऋजुमति and विपुलमति *i. e.* simple and complex. The latter is finer (विशुद्धतर) than the former, and, unlike it, is not exposed to the risk of destruction (अप्रतिपाति).

(5) केवलज्ञान—pure or perfect knowledge–which is a characteristic of the soul entirely liberated from the bondage of matter. The word is thus explained :(1)बाह्याभ्यन्तरक्रियाविशेषात् यदर्थं केवन्ते तत्केवलम् (तपःक्रियाविशेषात् वाङ्मनसकार्याश्रयान् बाह्यानाभ्यन्तरांश्च यदर्थानर्थिनः केवन्ते सेवन्ते तत् केवलम्); (2) अव्युत्पन्नो वाऽसहायार्थः केवलशब्दः (केवलमन्नं भुङ्क्ते देवदत्त इति। असहायं व्यञ्जनरहितं भुङ्क्ते इति गम्यते। तथा क्षायोपशमिकज्ञानासम्पृक्तं असहायं केवलमित्यव्युत्पन्नोऽयं शब्दो द्रष्टव्यः) *i. e.* (1) that which is sought and practised, from the root केव्=सेव्; or (2) pure, unmixed, free from other shades of ज्ञान such as क्षायोपशमिक. The second is evidently a better explanation than the first. But, in reality, the word as well

as the idea seems to be a legacy from the Sâṁkhyas and the Vedântins; or, what is more probable, it is a common heritage of the Jainas, the Sâṁkhyas and the Vedântins from the Upaniṣad thinkers according to whom the highest knowledge consisted in realising the purity or absoluteness of Âtmâ, that is, its freedom from the bondage of anâtmâ or Prakṛti. For a brief account of these different kinds of ज्ञान see Appendix III pp. 143–144 of Barnett's Antagadadasāo.

Mahâvîra, say the Jainas, was born with the first three kinds of ज्ञान, *viz.*, मति, श्रुत and अवधि. मनःपर्य(र्या)यज्ञान he gained immediately on entering the state of houselessness, according to S'vetâmbaras; after several months of wandering, penance and meditation, according to Digambaras. केवलज्ञान came to him, according to all authorities, at the end of his twelve years of ascetic life. (see H. J. p. 33).

Page 3.

l. 35 अत्र च श्रीवर्धमानस्वामिनो विशेषणद्वारेण etc.--The four adjectives in the Stanza, *viz.*, (1) अनन्तविज्ञानम्, (2) अतीतदोषम्, (3) अबाध्यसिद्धान्तम् and (4) अमर्त्यपूज्यम् connote respectively the four 'मूलातिशयs' or 'fundamental excellences' of a Tîrthaṃkara. These are (1) ज्ञानातिशय, (2) अपायापगमातिशय, (3) वचनातिशय and (4) पूजातिशय. Their number is extended to thirty-four by some: thus we read in Kundakundâcârya's Niyamasâra gâthâ: घणघाइकम्मरहिया केवलणाणा य परमगुणसहिया। चौत्तिस-अतिसयजुत्ता अरिहंता एरिसा होंति ॥

l. 36 अनन्तविज्ञानम्......him who possesses unbounded knowledge, pure and perfect—(केवलज्ञान). See above.

ll. 37–38 अतीतदोषम्–him who has transcended the *eighteen* kinds of evil. These are enumerated as follows:— "अन्तरायदानलाभवीर्यभोगोपभोगगाः । हासो रत्यरती भीतिर्जुगुप्सा शोक एव च ॥ कामो मिथ्यात्वमज्ञानं निद्रा चाविरतिस्तथा । रागो द्वेषश्च नो दोषास्तेषामष्टादशाप्यमी"। "प्राणातिपात–मृषावाद–अदत्तादान–मैथुन–परिग्रह–क्रोध–मान–माया–लोभ–प्रेम–द्वेष–कलह–अभ्याख्यान—पैशून्य—परपरिवाद–रति–अरति–माया–मृषा–मिथ्यादर्शन–शल्याख्यम् (अकरणीयं कर्म)"–S'îlâṅka's Com. on आचाराङ्ग p. 79.

l. 39 अबाध्यसिद्धान्तम् etc.—him who has taught the doctrine of स्याद्वाद which successfully resists the attacks of heretical teachers.

l. 40 अमर्त्यपूज्यम्–him who has received the highest homage ('महाप्रातिहार्यसपर्या') from the chiefs of gods and demons. An account of how Indra and others waited upon Vardhamâna may be read in Kalpasûtra and Acârânga.

l. 43 अत्राह परः etc.—The author now proceeds to consider certain possible (I do not think anyone actually raised them) objections, with a view to showing the need of each of the adjectives in the Stanza. These are :—

First, it may be objected :—अनन्तविज्ञान necessarily implies दोषात्यय, and so the word 'अतीतदोषम्' in the stanza is superfluous. This is answered by referring to the view of the Âjîvikas according to whom even the emancipated sages—the founders of the Law–are reborn as Saviours, when they find the Law in danger. Compare, in this connection, the distinction between Arhat and Bodhisat in Rhys David's American Lectures on Buddhism and Kern's Indian Buddhism.

The Jaina regards this as a weakness, and so deems it necessary to state explicitly that the Tîrthamkara is not only all-wise, but is also free from all evil, *i. e.*, is liable to re-birth on no account whatsoever.

Âjîvikas were sometimes confounded with Buddhists. Compare "अपरे हि सौगतादयो मोक्षमवाप्यापि तीर्थनिकारादिसंभवे भूयो भूयो भवमवतरन्ति । यदाहुः–ज्ञानिनो धर्मतीर्थस्य कर्तारः परमं पदम् । गत्वा गच्छन्ति भूयोऽपि भवं तीर्थनिकारतः इति । न ते परमार्थतो मोक्षगतिभाजः कर्मक्षयाभावात् । न हि तत्त्वतः कर्मक्षये पुनर्भवावतारः । यदुक्तम्–दग्धे बीजे यथात्यन्तं प्रादुर्भवति नाङ्कुरः कर्मबीजे तथा दग्धे न रोहति भवाङ्कुरः इति" Manibhadra's Laghuvritti on Haribhadra's Ṣaḍ-Sam.

For Âjîvikas see Hoernle's article on the subject in the Enc. of Religion and Ethics Vol. I, Rockhill's Life of Buddha, Appendix II, and Bhandarkar's and Pathak's articles in the Indian Antiquary Vol. XL (1912).

The founder of this community according to Jaina scriptures was one Gos'âla Mankhaliputra (see Uvâsagadasāo and Bhagavatîsûtra. The latter gives an account of his life.) The teachings of Gos'âla were condemned by the Buddhists and the Jainas as unmoral and immoral. King As'oka, however, in the 13th year of his reign (B. C. 251) bestowed a cave on the Âjîvikas, whom in a later Pillar Edict he co-ordinates with the Brâhmaṇas and Nigganthas. In the 6th century Varâhamihira in his astrological works, the Bṛhajjâtaka and the Laghujâtaka, names them as one of the seven classes of religious mendicants. They were also known as 'Ekadaṇḍins' according to his commentator Bhaṭṭotpala and were sometimes identified with Digambaras, (of course, wrongly) as for example by S'îlāṅka (9th century) in his commentary on Sûtrakṛtâṅga, and in the inscriptions of the Chola King Râjarâja. The origin of the word is obscure. Hoernle, surmises that Âjîvikas='Professionals' on account of their leader's peculiar views on the âjîva or profession of a religious mendicant. There is nothing, however, very peculiar about the views to justify the conjecture.

ll. 51–65 on P. 4. (2) Second objection:—' अतीतदोषं ' necessarily implies अनन्तविज्ञान and therefore 'अनन्तविज्ञानं' is superfluous. To it the author replies that according to some heretical thinkers दोषाभाव is quite compatible with limitation in knowledge. Thus, they say, it is immaterial whether one knows everything or not; what matters is whether he knows the essential thing, that is what he ought to know, or not; it does not matter at all if one does not know the number of bacteria in a thing; the ज्ञान that matters is the 'अनुष्ठानगत ज्ञान' *i. e.* the ज्ञान that has a bearing on life or practice; if ज्ञान, 'long sight,' *i. e.* the mere range of knowledge were valuable in itself, without its bearing on life, why not worship vultures who are tall birds with a long range of sight ? Thus, then, absolute purity of life and not unlimited knowledge is the essential characteristic of a Teacher. The Jaina rejects this view of the comparative unimportance of the extent of ज्ञान in a Teacher.

You cannot know a single thing in its entirety, says the Jaina, unless you know all: thus one and all are organically related, and so is the knowledge of one and the knowledge of all. (Here one is reminded of Tennyson's "*Flower in the Cranied Wall*"). Hence, 'अनन्तविज्ञानं' is as much required as 'अनन्तदोषं'. cf. "अथ सर्वमजानन्नेकमपि न जानातीति निश्चिनोति यो न विजानाति युगपदर्थान् त्रैकालिकान् त्रिभुवनस्थान्। ज्ञातुं तस्य न शक्यं सपर्ययं द्रव्यमेकं वा ॥" Pravacanasâra st. 48;

एको भावः सर्वभावस्वभावः ।
सर्वे भावा एकभावस्वभावाः ।
एको भावस्तत्त्वतो येन बुद्धः
सर्वे भावास्तत्त्वतस्तेन बुद्धाः ॥

P. Sâra Tâtparyavṛtti on st. 49.

cf. also "एवं चैकस्मिन्नर्थे ज्ञाते सर्वेषामर्थानां ज्ञानं सर्वपदार्थपरिच्छेदमन्तरेण तन्निषेधात्मन एकस्य वस्तुनो विविक्ततया परिच्छेदासंभवात्। आगमोऽप्येवमेव व्यवस्थितः। "जे एगं जाणइ सो सव्वं जाणइ जो सव्वं जाणइ सो एगं जाणइ।" तथा—

एको भावः सर्वथा येन दृष्टः
सर्वे भावाः सर्वथा तेन दृष्टाः ।
सर्वे भावाः सर्वथा येन दृष्टाः
एको भावः सर्वथा तेन दृष्टः ॥

(Maṇibhadra's Laghuvṛtti on the Ṣaḍ. Sam. of Haribhadra p. 48 Ben. Edition.)

"तथा अनेनैव बुद्धस्यापि महादेवत्वं किंचिज्ज्ञत्वान्निवारितम्। यदाहुस्तच्छिष्यकाः। सर्वं पश्यतु वा मा वा इष्टमर्थं तु पश्यतु। कीटसंख्यापरिज्ञानं तस्य नः (or न) क्वोपयुज्यते। किं च किंचिज्ज्ञत्वमपि तस्य न घटते। एकस्याप्यर्थस्य सकलस्वपरपर्यायविशेषितस्यासर्वज्ञत्वे ज्ञातुमशक्यत्वात्। यत आह। एको भावः सर्वथा येन दृष्टः सर्वे भावाः सर्वथा तेन दृष्टाः। सर्वे भावाः सर्वथा येन दृष्टा एको भावः सर्वथा तेन दृष्टः ॥"—अभयनन्दसूरि's Com. on अष्टप्रकरण of हरिभद्रसूरि. These quotations occur in numerous Jaina works.

Page 4.

l. 67 (3) Third objection:—Does not 'अबाध्यसिद्धान्तम्' necessarily follow from the first two adjectives? One answer is—It does. But, then, you miss one point. According to Jainism, the Siddhânta is propounded by a *person or persons* (who possess the two former qualifications) as distinguished from the Vedas which are supposed by some (the Mîmâṁsakas, for example) to be अपौरुषेय *i. e.* not emanating from a personal author—which is impossible. Hence the word अबाध्यसिद्धान्त in the text for directing our attention to the personality of the founder of the सिद्धान्त, who deserves to be revered not only by mortals, but even by immortals. Another answer : आत्ममात्र तारक° [P. 4. l. 71] : certain kevalins who simply save themselves, and are not authors of any true सिद्धान्त, cf. " आत्मार्थसंप्रवृत्तः स्वप्रयोजनमात्रप्रतिबद्धचित्तोऽसौ सदा निरन्तरं स्याद्भवेत् मुण्डकेवली द्रव्यभावमुण्डनप्रधानस्तथाविधः बाह्यातिशयशून्यः—Haribhadra's सम्यग्दृष्टिद्वात्रिं. १९ Com.

l. 73 (4) Fourth objection:—अमर्त्यपूज्यं is superfluous, since it follows as a matter of course from the qualities above mentioned. Answer : True. But people worship only gods, and do not know that the Jaina arhat is greater than gods, and therefore worthy of greater worship.

l. 79 अनन्तविज्ञानत्वं च etc.–Next, it is suggested that the word 'श्रीवर्धमानं' in the stanza may be taken as a विशेषण also—in which case, it will mean श्रिया (चतुस्त्रिंशदतिशयसमृद्धयनुभवात्मकभावार्हन्त्यरूपया) वर्धमानं = infinitely possessed of the glory of भावार्हन्त्य consisting of the personal experience of the wealth of thirty-four excellences. ' भावार्हन्त्य—not the appearance but the reality, not the external possession but the inward being of Arhathood. The thirty-four excellences have been referred to above (see Notes p. 11) These consist of 19 दैव्य, 4 सहज and 11 कर्मक्षयज. आर्हन्त्य–cf. अर्हतो नुम् च । अर्हतो भावः कर्म वा आर्हत्यम् । आर्हन्ती–Sid. Kaumudî. But अर्हतस्तोऽन्त् च (7·1·46 Hem. S'abd) चतुस्त्रिंशतमतिशयान् सुरेन्द्रादिकृतां पूजां वार्हतीति अर्हन् तस्य भावः कर्म वा आर्हन्त्यम् आर्हन्ती–Hema.

Page 5.

l. 82 वर्धमान—ever increasing, infinite. How is this consistent with the limit of अतिशयs mentioned in the Jaina Siddhânta, such as the number thirty-four etc. ? Ans.–In the Nis'ītha Cûrṇî (Nis'ītha–one of the Aṅga-bâhyas) are enumerated 1008 'external marks' of an Arhat and the number is taken at the same time to be suggestive of an infinite number of internal marks; in the same way, the special mention of 34, does not exclude the possibility of the number being really infinite.

l. 88 अतीतदोषता च etc.—Next. the word जिन in the stanza is justified. The term implies more than 'अतीतदोष' of the first line. On the fourteen Steps to Liberation from Karma known as Guṇasthâna see H. J. pp. 185-192. उपशान्तमोहगुणस्थान is the eleventh and क्षीणमोहगुणस्थान the twelfth step of the ladder. On their difference, see ibid p. 190: "When a man has attained to the eleventh stage, *Upas'ântamoha guṇasthânaka* he has reached a really critical point, where everything depends on how he deals with the sin of greed. If he destroys it, and it becomes quite extinct, he is safe; but if it only remains quiescent, he is in a perilous state, for, like a flood, it may at any moment burst its dam and the force of its current may carry the soul far down the slope he has been climbing, depositing him on either the sixth or the seventh step (*Pramatta* or *Apramatta guṇasthânaka*), or even on the lowest (*Mithyâtva*). On the other hand, if he deal successfully with greed, he becomes an anuttaravâsî Deva and knows that he will become a Siddha after he has undergone one more rebirth as a man.

If a man be on the twelfth step, *Kṣîṇamoha guṇasthânaka*, he has won freedom for ever not only from greed but from all the ghatin karma and though the aghatin karma may still persist, they have little power to bind the soul: in fact, so limited is their power, that at death a soul passes at once through the two remaining stages and enters mokṣa without delay. The Digambara believe that at this stage the first two parts of pure contemplation (S'ukla-dhyâna) are developed."

l. 91 अबाध्यसिद्धान्तता च etc.–Next is justified the word 'आप्तमुख्यम्' in the stanza. Mahâvîra was of course a perfect Kevalin; so were the next three propagators of the siddhânta, *viz.*, Gautama, Sudharman and Jambusvâmin (—B. C. 465).

"The six (? five: Visnu-nandin, Nandi-mitra, Aparâjita, Govardhana, and Bhadrabâhu.) spiritual leaders who followed Jambusvâmin are called *S'rutakevalin,* because, though the complete omniscience which Jambusvâmin and his predecessors attained was denied to them, they possessed complete knowledge of the scriptures (श्रुत)". (H. J. pp 72, 80).

l. 93 अर्शादित्वात् etc.—See Panini 5-2-127 अर्शआदिभ्यः Hemacandra's S'abdânusâsana 7-2-46, where अर्शस् is included in अश्रादिगण.

l. 95 शाखादेर्य—See Hem.'s S'abd. 7-1-114.

l. 95 अमर्त्यपूज्यता च etc.—अमर्त्यपूज्यता may conceivably exist even in such sages as have equipped themselves with wisdom and character by sitting at the feet of great masters and serving them. But their wisdom and character are, after all, acquired, not innate. स्वयंभुवम् etc.-(l. 99) स्वयंसंबुद्धः तं–self-enlightened. यतिष्ये (l. 100). Mark the word, which only means : I will endeavour or strive, thus suggesting the difficulty of doing full justice to the subject. The future tense of the root has also a point in it, *viz.*, that of suggesting faith in the task. अहम्—Though already implied in the first person form यतिष्ये, अहम् is explicitly mentioned in order to suggest that the author proceeds on his own initiative, and is not led to his task by either the advice or the example of others.

Page 6.

l. 106 etc. अथवा श्रीवर्धमानादि.........It is ingeniously pointed out that the four adjectives (1) श्रीवर्धमानं, (2) जिनं, (3) आप्तमुख्यं and (4) स्वयंभुवं, in the last two lines may be connected with the four words (1) अनन्तविज्ञानं, (2) अतीतदोषं, (3) अबाध्यसिद्धान्तं and (4) अमर्त्यपूज्यम् respectively, in the first two lines, as cause and effect. Thus, श्रीवर्धमानं *i. e.* 'infinitely possessed of glory' necessarily implies infinite knowledge 'अनन्तविज्ञानं,' the glory consisting in the possession of the four infinites as a consequence of the destruction of all karmas. यद्यपि–The word वर्धमान primarily signifies growth, but there is no occasion for growth in this case where excellences are possessed in infinite measure from the very birth, therefore the word should be understood in the secondary sense of infinite and eternal possession. अनन्तचतुष्क (l. 110). The 'four infinites' are infinite ज्ञान (knowledge), दर्शन (faith), चारित्र (character or conduct) and वीर्य (spiritual energy). Some substitute सुख for चारित्र in the list of the four anantas or infinites, the first three of which are the well-known रत्नत्रय or "the Three Jewels" of Jainism. (see O. J. p. xli). Some, again, put दर्शन first and ज्ञान second in the list of the three Jewels. For a discussion of the relative positions of दर्शन and ज्ञान and the particular position of ज्ञान between दर्शन and चारित्र, see T. Rv. 30-35 on T. S. 1. See also O. J. pp 52-53. Dr. Bhandarkar's Report Bom. Mss etc. Some authorities mention ज्ञान before दर्शन.

l. 112 etc. यद्यपि च etc.-Since 'श्रीवर्धमानं' connotes the possession of the 'four infinites' including 'infinite knowledge', the word अनन्त विज्ञानं in the first line would seem superfluous. So it is in a way; yet it has been specifically mentioned in order to suggest that infinite knowledge (अनन्तविज्ञान) is the great instrument for beneficence possessed by the Master.

l. 116–125 ननु यथा जगन्नाथस्य etc.—A query: Just as अनन्तज्ञान is the great instrument of beneficence, so is अनन्तदर्शन; why, then, is the latter not mentioned specifically like the former? Answer: The word अनन्तविज्ञान in the stanza not only stands for ज्ञान, but includes दर्शन also—the difference between ज्ञान and दर्शन being only the difference between the particular and the general. Every object has a particular and a general aspect, of which the general is subordinated to the particular in ज्ञान, and the particular to the general in दर्शन. (सामान्यप्रधानमुपसर्जनीकृतविशेषमर्थग्रहणं दर्शनमुच्यते, तथा प्रधानविशेषमुपसर्जनीकृतसामान्यं च ज्ञानम् ll.124-25). Mark, however, that this is a different kind of distinction from that drawn in T. S. and T. Rv., where दर्शन and ज्ञान stand for faith ('श्रद्धान') and knowledge ('पदार्थतत्त्वोपलब्धि') respectively.

l. 126 तथा यत एव–अमर्त्यैरिति—Next, (2) 'जिनम्', (3) 'आप्तमुख्यम्', & (4) 'स्वयंभुवम्' are shown to be connected with (2) अतीतदोषम्, (3) अबाध्यसिद्धान्तम् and (4) अमर्त्यपूज्यम् as cause and effect.

Page 7.

l. 135 अत्र च श्रीवर्धमानमिति...To take 'श्रीवर्धमानम्' as an adjective may appear unusual, but it has a precedent in the अयोगव्यवच्छेदद्वात्रिंशिका stanza 1, line 3 which runs as 'श्रीवर्धमानाभिधमात्मरूपम्' where आत्मरूपम् (आत्म + रूपम् a termination in the sense of प्रशंसा cf. Paninî प्रशंसायां रूपम् 5·3·66) = परमात्मानम् is the विशेष्य and 'श्रीवर्धमानाभिधम्' one of its विशेषणs. With due deference to the author one may question how श्रीवर्धमानाभिधम् could be equated with श्रीवर्धमानम् : on the contrary, one would seem justified in holding that श्रीवर्धमान is a singular term and therefore a substantive in श्रीवर्धमानाभिधम्. Against this it will perhaps be contended that श्रीवर्धमान in °भिधम् is a singular term and a substantive, but it is at the same time a विशेषण–inasmuch as it characterizes the आत्मरूप or परमात्मा. Yet, this does not put श्रीवर्धमानाभिधम् on all fours with श्रीवर्धमानम्.

l. 138 आवृत्त्या वा etc.—The author perceives the weakness of the position he has taken up, and so proposes to treat the word श्रीवर्धमानं as at once a विशेषण and a विशेष्य, the quality (विशेषण) justifying the name (विशेष्य).

Stanza II.

l. 1 अस्यां च स्तुतौ etc.—Introduction to the next stanza. This explains why from amongst all the excellent qualities that belong to Mahâvîra, this particular one, *viz.*, 'यथार्थवाद' has been selected for specific mention in the next stanza.

Page 8.

l. 9 इयं तादर्थ्ये etc.–स्पृह् governs the dative of the noun.

l. 10 पूर्वत्र etc. Hem. 2-2-26-"स्पृहेर्व्याप्यं वा। स्पृहयतेर्धातोर्व्याप्यं वा संप्रदानसंज्ञं भवति । पुष्पेभ्यः पुष्पाणि वा स्पृहयति। व्याप्यमिति किम् ?। पुष्पेभ्यः स्पृहयति वने ।"

l. 13 एकमेकमेव......To praise this one quality is to praise all, since it is the distinguishing trait of Mahâvîra and places him above all other teachers, be they even celestial beings.

l. 20 यतोऽयं etc.—This writer presumes to scan Mahâvîra's intellectual greatness, not because he is really competent to do so, but because he possesses Faith and Love (श्रद्धा and भक्ति), of which an eulogium like the present is but one expression.

Stanza III.

Page 9.

ll. 4-5 अमी...विप्रकृष्टाः-अमी-Those, from अदस्-a pronoun suggesting distance or remoteness. The commentator sees in this word a sly hint that those heretical writers deserve to be avoided.

ll. 9-10 करभः पुण्ड्रेक्षुकाण्डम्—as a camel dislikes a white sugar-cane.

l. 13 संमील्य—The author wishes they closed their eyes in meditation and pondered over these philosophical problems dispassionately.

l. 15 अत्र च विचारयन्तामित्या०.—For the point which the commentator sees in the Âtmanepada, see Pân. 1.3.72 "स्वरितञितः कर्त्रभिप्राये क्रियाफले."

l. 19 etc. अथवा अयमुपदेशस्तेभ्यो etc.—Or, closing the eyes while the great physician, Mahâvîra, administers and thrusts down their throats the bitter yet wholesome medicine of Jaina Siddhântas. Let us recall that Gautama Buddha is similarly characterised as a 'भिषक्' in Buddhistic works.

Page 10.

l. 25 प्रतिपाद्य-One to whom Truth is imparted ; a pupil,—whether willing or otherwise to sit at the Master's feet.

l. 28 इसड वा...Note the philanthropic missionary zeal expressed in this old stanza.

l. 30 वाचकमुख्य : —Umâsvâti or Umâsvâmin, 'the great exponent' of Jaina scriptures, respected alike by the S'vetâmbaras and the Digambaras, probably because the split between the two sects had not yet established itself in his life-time. For an account of the man, and his parentage, see his Tat.Sûtra Ch. x p. 233. Bib. Ind. Ed.

cf. "न्यग्रोधिकाप्रसूतेन विहरता पुरवरे कुसुमनाम्नि। कौ भीषणिना स्वातितनयेन वात्सीसुतेनार्घ्यम्। अर्हद्वचनं सम्यग्गुरुक्रमेणागतं समुपधार्य दुःखार्तं च दुरागमविहतमतिं लोकमवलोक्य। इदमुच्चैर्नागरवाचकेन सत्त्वानुकम्पया दृब्धम्। तत्त्वार्थाधिगमाख्यं स्पष्टमुमास्वातिना शास्त्रम्", from which it appears that his father's name was Svâti and his mother's Vâtsi (Umâ of the Vatsa gotra.) A Similar account is found in the commentary on the Tatt. Sûtra by Siddhasenagaṇi. Dr. Satishchandra is evidently wrong in understanding the word 'नागरवाचक' 'as probably containing a reference to his S'âkhâ (spiritual geneology)' ; the word 'नगर' means Kusumapura or Pâṭaliputra (as they call London 'the Town'), and 'नागरवाचक' is the celebrated teacher who belonged to Paṭaliputra–the scene of Ûmâsvâti's literary and missionary activities. He lived, according to the tradition, for 84 years, 8 months and 6 days and attained Nirvâṇa in Samvat 142 *i. e.* 85 A. D. For further particulars, see Peterson's 4th Report on Sanskrit MSS. p. xvi, Dr. Hoernle's article in the Ind. Ant. Vol. XX p. 351, and Dr. Satishcandrâ's H. I. L. p. 168.

Stanza IV.

The system first examined is the Vaiśeṣika system of Kaṇâda. काव्यषट्केन–from st. IV to IX, both inclusive.

l. 2 औलूक्यमताभिमततत्त्वानि—The categories laid down in the system of Kaṇâda, the Vaiśeṣika system, one of the six great systems of Brahmanical philosophy.

As to the origin of the words कणाद and काणाद, उलूक and औलूक्य, *vide* the following:—"वैशेषिकशास्त्रप्रणेता काणादः स च मांसभक्षी। त्रिकाण्डशेषमेदिनीकोशप्रामाण्यात् काणः काकस्तमत्तीति काणादः काकमांसभक्षीति यावत्। उलूका एव काकमांसं भक्षन्तीति अन्वर्थं तस्य वैशेषिकशास्त्रकर्तुः काणादस्य उलूक इति नाम *।......। कणादस्य महर्षेर्नाम

---

* "Aulûkya given by Mâdhava as a name for the tenets of Kaṇâda rests on a play upon the word Kaṇâda, crow-eater=Ulûka" Weber's H. I. L. p. 246, footnote 264. This wretched derivation has been rightly dismissed by Prof. Keith as 'an idle fiction.'

प्रसह्य काणाद इति पठित्वा काणशब्दं कस्मिंश्चित्कोशे काकवाचकं दृष्ट्वा काकमांसभक्षीति निर्धारितवान् [जैनः ?] । इत्ययुक्तम् । वस्तुतस्तु " कणादः काश्यपः समाविति" त्रिकाण्डशेषकोशात् "काश्यपोऽब्रवीदिति" प्रशस्तपादभाष्याच्च कश्यपस्य महर्षेः पुत्रः कणाद इति । कणाद इति तस्य कापोतीं वृत्तिमनुतिष्ठतो रथ्यानिपतितांस्तण्डुलकणानादाय प्रत्यहं कृताहारनिमित्ता संज्ञा । "स्वयमीश्वरः उलूकरूपधारी प्रत्यक्षीभूय द्रव्यगुणकर्मसामान्यविशेषसमवायलक्षणं पदार्थषट्कमुपदिदेश " इत्यादि पौराणिकीं कथामजानन्तः—

> योगाचारविभूत्या यस्तोषयित्वा महेश्वरम् ।
> चक्रे वैशेषिकं शास्त्रं तस्मै कणभुजे नमः ॥

इति प्रशस्तपादभाष्यमप्यवज्ञाय अपरिचितनिन्दास्तुतिविषया अज्ञातसिद्धान्तपूर्वपक्षास्ते व्यामोहयन्ति श्रोत्रियाद्विजबालकान् " । (Vindhyes'wari prasâda's न्यायवार्तिकभूमिका Ben. Ed. pp. 53–55.) While some Jaina writer may have been responsible for the derivation criticised in the above passage, it by no means represents the Jaina tradition, which is perfectly respectful and is in harmony with the Brahmanical account. Thus, Râjaśekhara, a Jaina writer, says in his Ṣaḍdarśanasamuccaya : "शिवेनोलूकरूपेण कणादस्य मुनेः पुरः । मतमेतत् प्रकथितं तत औलूक्यमुच्यते "॥ Similarly, in his commentary on the Nyâyakandalî, he says "इह किल पूर्वमजिह्मब्रह्माभ्यासदूरीकृतप्रमादाय मुनये कणादाय स्वयमीश्वर उलूकरूपधारी प्रत्यक्षीभूय द्रव्यगुणकर्मसामान्यविशेषसमवायलक्षणं पदार्थषट्कमुपदिदेश । तदनु च स महर्षिर्लोकानुकम्पया षट्पदार्थरहस्यप्रपञ्चनपराणि सूत्राणि रचयाञ्चकार ॥ " Guṇaratna, another distinguished Jaina writer, writes in his commentary on the Ṣaḍdarśanasamuccaya of Haribhadra : 'मुनिविशेषस्य कापोतीं वृत्तिमनुष्ठितवतो रथ्यानिपतितांस्तण्डुलकणानादाय कृताहारस्याहारनिमित्तात् कणाद इति संज्ञाऽजनि । तस्य कणादस्य मुनेः पुरः शिवेनोलूकरूपेण मतमेतत् प्रकाशितम् । तत औलूक्यं प्रोच्यते । कणादस्य शिष्यत्वेन वैशेषिकाः काणादा भण्यन्ते ।', thus endorsing the Brahmanical explanation of the name कणाद as stated in S'rîdhara's Nyāyakandalî: "कणाद इति तस्य कापोतीं वृत्तिमनुतिष्ठतो रथ्यानिपतितांस्तण्डुलकणानादाय प्रत्यहं कृताहारनिमित्ता संज्ञा अत एव निरवकाशकणान् वा भक्षयत्वित्युपालम्भः ॥ " (The last remark of S'rîdhara: refers to the sarcasm on the Atomism of Kaṇâda.)

It will be interesting to turn next to the Buddhist tradition relating to this subject, for which see Prof. Ui's

Introduction to the Daśapadārthī: "Ci-tsân (549-623 A. D.), a Chinese Buddhist, relates the following traditions with regard to the Vaiśeṣika and its founder :—"(The founder's name) Ulūka means an 'owl'......The time when he lived was 800 years before the Buddha. By day he composed a work and by night he wandered about for alms......The sûtra composed by him is called the Vaiśeṣika (-sûtra) and consists of 100,000 s'lokas. The main tenets are the doctrines of the six categories, of the asatkâryavâda, and that self (âtman) is some thing different from cognition (buddhi)." In another passage he states :—"According to the life of Harivarman, there lived a follower of Ulûka (at the time of Harivarman, c. 260 A. D.). He said that the sûtra composed by our teacher Ulûka, is named the Vaiśeṣika (– sûtra), and is subtle or scholastic. Its general tenet is the doctrine of the six categories, and the speciality is that cognition is something different from self.... Vaiśeṣika, the name of the Sûtra, means superior, or excellent, and distinguished (or different). The origin of the name is in the fact that the system is distinguished from, and superior to, the Sāṁkhya." Kwhei-ci states :—"About the end of the time of the creation (sṛṣṭi) when the age of creatures was immeasurable, a teacher (Tîrthaka) came to the world. He was named Ulûka. Ulûka means an 'owl'. In the day time he meditated in a dense forest, secluding himself from worldly affairs, and at night, when people went to rest, he wandered about for food. This mode of living was very similar to that of an owl, so that he got the name Ulûka. He was also called Kaṇabhuj or Kaṇabhakṣa. *Kaṇa* means 'a grain (or a piece) of (rice–) corn', and *bhuj* or *bhakṣa* means 'to eat'. The origin of the name was that he was usually wandering about at night, but as young women were frightened by the sight of him he afterwards went in secret into mills, picked up pieces of corn from rice–bran, and ate them. He was consequently, nicknamed the 'corn-piece eater.' He was further called (the teacher of) the Vaiśeṣika. Vaiśeṣika means 'superior' or 'excellent' (literally, 'conquering.') He composed a work explaining the six categories. The work was named the Vaiśeṣika (- śāstra), since it excelled other works in all respects, or because it was composed by a man of superior intelligence." Kwhēi-ci also calls the founder Kaṇāda; but to the Chinese tradition it is not known that Kaṇāda or Kaṇabhuj means, "atom-eater," and the meaning of the term Vaiśeṣika is 'superior' or 'excellent'. " Atom-eater, " as the nickname of the founder, might not be probable, because an atomic theory is not special to the system, and the Vaiśeṣika is not the first pioneer of the theory. 'Superior' or 'excellent' is a secondary meaning of the term, and the term is not used in this sense in V. S. The explanation of the name Vaiśeṣika that it was derived from the fifth category particularity (Viśeṣa), or the characteristic of the system that an object is precisely analysed and classified, is more probable......Râjaśekhara, in the Nyāyakandalîtîka explains that Kaṇāda was favoured by Íśvara on account of the merit of his ardent ascetic practice. Íśvara appeared to him as *Ulûka-rûpa-dhârî* (bearing the form of an owl.)......But Íśvara is not mentioned in V. S., although later commentators strain the meaning of some passages. Praśastapâda acknowledged Îśvara for the first time in the history of the Vaiśeṣika. Consequently the tradition must have originated in a time later than Praśastapāda who lived in the fifth or sixth century A. D. The Chinese traditional explanation of Ulûka seems to have been derived from an etymological meaning of the term, but it represents an older tradition. Even Aśvaghoṣa alludes to the meaning.*

---

* In his Sûtrālamkāra. But somewhat differently: " Before Buddha came to the world, all creatures were so uncultivated and blind to truth that they looked upon the Vaiśeṣikaśāstra as the best. But after our Buddha, the sun, appeared and shone, wisdom (of creatures) became clear, so that the Vaiśeṣika-śāstra was known not to contain any reasonable explanation and to be good for nothing, like an owl that is flying and energetic at night and conceals itself and is not energetic in the daytime." (Mahâvyutpatti.)

Summary :

I औलूक्य from उलूक ; so called,

(1) because S'iva appeared to the ṛṣi in the form of an owl (उलूकरूपधारी) and taught the Vaiśeṣika Sûtras ;

or (2) because the ṛṣi went about like an owl in the night and collected grains of corn for his food ;

or (3) because his system was all-powerful like an owl in the night, *i. e.* before the appearance of the Buddha, but worthless in the day *i. e.* after his appearance.

II वैशेषिक so called,

(1) because superior to the Sāṃkhya which was the older philosophy ;

or (2) because of its peculiar category called विशेष ;

or (3) because of its favourite method of investigating truth by determining the Viśeṣas or distinguishing properties of things.

III कणाद—

(1) = काणाद—a crow-eater or owl (? see Weber's H. I. L.)

(2) so called, because of his ascetic practice of maintaining himself by eating grains of corn collected in the night ;

(3) so called sarcastically because of his Atomic Theory.

1.3 प्रथमतरं सामान्यविशेषौ–The characteristic method of investigating Truth adopted in the Vaiśeṣika system is to find out the Viśeṣas *i. e.* the differentia or distinguishing properties of things. This gives the name to the system, and is therefore rightly selected first for attack. The Chinese account of the origin of the word Vaiśeṣika meaning superior *i. e.* superior to the Sāṃkhya may be set aside as less likely.

St. स्वतोऽनुवृत्तिव्यतिवृत्तिभाजो...

The Jaina view on the question of सामान्य and विशेष is (1) that they are not required to be recognized as special पदार्थs to account for अनुवृत्ति and व्यावृत्ति (= 'व्यतिवृत्ति' of the Stanza); for, अनुवृत्ति and व्यावृत्ति can very well be explained as arising from the nature of the objects themselves, without the hypothesis of separate categories called सामान्य and विशेष: (2) that they are neither absolutely the same as the objects in which they are supposed to inhere (एकान्त अभेद), nor absolutely distinct from those objects (एकान्त भेद): in fact, they are *both*.

l. 5 अभवन् भवन्ति भविष्यन्ति चेति भावाः—भावs are things past, present or future *i. e.* a भाव does not necessarily connote *present* existence: thus a ध्वंस or a प्रागभाव which the Vaiśeṣika regards as the अ-भाव of a thing is as much a भाव as the thing itself; moreover, the so-called अभाव is not तुच्छ or मिथ्या, *i. e.*, unsubstantial nothing, as some Vedāntins would have it, but is an aspect of भाव and, therefore, the भाव itself.

l. 5-6 आत्मपुद्गलादयः—Sprit, matter, etc.

सर्वं हि वाक्यं etc.—Every proposition is determining and, therefore, exclusive of something *i. e.* it implies 'only' even when the word is not expressly employed. Hence स्वतः in the stanza=स्वत एव, न परतः; स्वत एव = आत्मीयस्वरूपादेव—Things coordinate themselves and distinguish themselves *sui forte*; they do not require such mediators as सामान्य and विशेष to enable them to accomplish the task.

Page 11.

ll. 8-9 एकाकारा प्रतीतिरेकशब्दवाच्यता चानुवृत्तिः-सामान्य and विशेष are assumed by the Vaiśeṣikas to account for अनुवृत्ति and व्यावृत्ति (or 'व्यतिवृत्ति' as it is called in the stanza). Of these अनुवृत्ति is defined as 'एकाकारा प्रतीतिः एकशब्दवाच्यता च' *i. e.* it consists of the fact that a thing (a) appears to possess the same form as certain other things, and (b) is expressible by the same word as those things; in other words, अनुवृत्ति means a common concept (एकाकारा प्रतीतिः) and a common name (एकशब्दवाच्यता च). व्यतिवृत्तिर्व्यावृत्तिः etc. The points of वि and अति are brought out in the explanation attached to the word : thus, व्यतिवृत्तिर्व्यावृत्तिः (the latter is more intelligible, being more commonly employed)=विजातीयेभ्यः (वि) सर्वथा (= अति) व्यवच्छेदः

ll. 9-10 उभे अपि संवलिते etc.—object to 'भजन्ते,' the subject being भावाः

अस्यैवार्थस्य व्यतिरेकमाह—The negative side of the same fact: भावs or things are not presented to the mind through anything other than the भावs themselves('भावा न भावान्तरनेयरूपाः' st. l. 2), *i. e.*, through सामान्य and विशेष, categories which the Vaiśeṣika recognises in addition to द्रव्य, गुण, and कर्म and समवाय. According to this explanation भावान्तर in the compound 'भावान्तरनेयरूपाः' (in l. 2 of the st.) means द्रव्य-गुण-कर्म-समवायेभ्यः पदार्थान्तरनेयं प्रतीतिविषयं प्रापणीयम्–whose character (रूप) of अनुवृत्ति and व्यतिवृत्ति is brought to the mind (नेय) by the additional categories (भावान्तर) of सामान्य and विशेष respectively.

ll. 16, etc. स्वभाव एव etc.—It is the very nature of things to produce ideas of अनुवृत्ति and व्यतिवृत्ति. Thus घटसामान्य (घटत्व) is nothing but the घट itself: a घट possessing a certain form and presenting itself before the mind thereby causes other objects possessing the same form to come before the mind as घटs and be denotable by the term 'घट' (घट एव तावत् पृथुबुध्नोदराद्याकारवान् प्रतीतिविषयीभवन् सन् अन्यानपि तदाकृतिभृतः पदार्थान् घटरूपतया घटैकशब्दवाच्यतया च प्रत्याययन् सामान्याख्यां लभते (ll. 17-20) in other words, things by their very nature, and not through any imaginary category like the सामान्य, bring about their co-ordination with other individuals of their class, and give rise to common terms. The same घट, moreover, becomes विशेष in so far as it distinguishes itself from other individuals of the same (सजातीय) or different (विजातीय) class by virtue of its peculiar द्रव्य (substance), क्षेत्र (place), काल (time), and भाव (nature or quality). Therefore, सामान्य and विशेष need not be recognised as separate categories ('न सामान्यविशेषयोः पृथक्पदार्थत्वकल्पनं न्याय्यम्' l. 22), they being nothing more than certain aspects (अनुवृत्ति aspect and व्यावृत्ति aspect, respectively) of the things of which they are predicated (पदार्थधर्मत्वेनैव तयोः प्रतीयमानत्वात् l. 23). For द्रव्य, क्षेत्र, काल and भाव see Syâdvâda-manjarî on St. XXIII. "तत्र स्यात् कथंचित् स्वद्रव्यक्षेत्रकालभावरूपेणास्त्येव सर्वं कुम्भादि । न पुनः परद्रव्यक्षेत्रकालभावरूपेण । तथा हि । कुम्भो द्रव्यतः पार्थिवत्वेनास्ति नाबादिरूपत्वेन । क्षेत्रतः पाटलिपुत्रकत्वेन न कान्यकुब्जादित्वेन । कालतः शिशिरत्वेन न वासन्तिकादित्वेन । भावतः श्यामत्वेन न रक्तादित्वेन । अन्यथेतररूपापत्त्या स्वरूपहानिप्रसङ्ग इति ॥"

Mark that upto this point Malliṣeṇa has taken the word 'भावान्तर' of the second line of the stanza as referring to सामान्य and विशेष recognised as categories other than the well-known भावs or पदार्थs *viz.* द्रव्य गुण कर्म and समवाय (भावान्तराभ्यां पराभिमताभ्यां द्रव्यगुणकर्मसमवायेभ्यः पदार्थान्तराभ्यां भावव्यतिरिक्तसामान्यविशेषाभ्यां etc.). The explanation involves the use of the word 'भाव' in two different senses in one and the same verse, nay, in one and the same line: 'भाव' in भावाः means things in general, while 'भाव' in 'भावान्तर°' means the पदार्थ or categories, *viz.*, द्रव्य गुण कर्म and समवाय. This is obviously unsatisfactory, and one would, therefore, prefer to take भावान्तर in the sense of 'other than the *things themselves*', and, this is the sense in which the author understands the word in the passage that follows, *viz.*, "पदार्थधर्मत्वेनैव तयोः प्रतीयमानत्वात् । न च धर्मा धर्मिणः सकाशादत्यन्तं व्यतिरिक्ताः" (ll. 22-24). The transition, however, from one explanation to the other is almost unconscious, the argument being continuous, and the words पृथक्पदार्थान्तर (in सामान्यविशेषयोः पृथक्पदार्थान्तरत्वकल्पनं न्याय्यम्) and भावव्यतिरिक्त (in भावव्यतिरिक्तसामान्यविशेषाभ्याम्) lending themselves to a double interpretation, *viz.*, (1) other than the categories द्रव्यगुण–कर्म–समवाय, or (2) other than the things themselves.

l. 23 न च धर्मा धर्मिणः सकाशात् etc.—सामान्य and विशेष are but the धर्मs (*i. e.* not real independent entities, but mere aspects) of the पदार्थs of which they are predicated. Thus :—Are not धर्मs other than the धर्मिन् of which they are predicated? Is not a predicate different from its subject? To this the author replies: No. If धर्मs were absolutely *other* than the धर्मिन्, there could be no such relation between them as विशेष्य and विशेषण

or subject and predicate, any more than between a camel and a donkey, two absolutely distinct entities which could never be related as subject and predicate, ('एकान्तभेदे विशेषणविशेष्यभावानुपपत्तेः । करभरासभयोरिव धर्मधर्मिव्यपदेशाभावप्रसङ्गाच्च' (ll. 24-25) Moreover, if धर्मs were held to be distinct from the धर्मिन् *i. e.* the substratum in which they are supposed to inhere, there would be as many distinct entities in a धर्मिन् as there are धर्मs, that is to say, an infinite number of पदार्थs would have to be admitted on the proposed hypothesis (धर्माणामपि पृथक्पदार्थत्वकल्पने एकस्मिन्नेव वस्तुनि पदार्थानन्त्यप्रसङ्गः । अनन्तधर्मकत्वाद्वस्तुनः-ll. 26-27)

Page 12.

l. 33 परात्मतत्त्वात् etc. St. iv ll. 3-4 – Construe thus :-परौ (पदार्थेभ्यो व्यतिरिक्तत्वात् अन्यौ परस्परनिरपेक्षौ च) यौ सामान्यविशेषौ तयोर्यद् आत्मतत्वं (स्वरूपम्-अनुवृत्तिव्यावृत्तिलक्षणं) तस्मात् (तदाश्रित्य) (ll. 33-34). परौ = 1. Other than (अन्यौ.) 2. strangers to each other (परस्परनिरपेक्षौ). सामान्य and विशेष which are supposed to be other than the पदार्थs of which they are predicated, or other than the categories द्रव्य, गुण, कर्म and समवाय. (For the two explanations see above), and which, moreover, are regarded as two distinct पदार्थs *inter se* (पदार्थेभ्यो व्यतिरिक्तत्वादन्यौ परस्परनिरपेक्षौ च). Their आत्मतत्त्व=their स्वरूप consisting of अनुवृत्ति and व्यावृत्ति respectively. तस्मात्=तदाश्रित्य *i. e.* in reference to that. For the meaning of the पञ्चमी the author cites गम्ययपः कर्माधारे (H. S. 2-2-74) अतथात्मतत्त्वात्-a bahuvrîhi adjective qualifying the tatpuruṣa noun परात्मतत्त्वात्. It means :-Since the alleged otherness is not a fact, is not what it is said to be; literally, = since it does not possess the 'आत्मतत्त्व' *i. e.* the स्वरूप or character which has been ascribed to it by the Vaiśeṣikas, *viz.* that (1) सामान्य and विशेष are absolutely *other* than the पदार्थs of which they are predicated, and (2) are distinct *inter se.* अविष्वग्भावेन-not as separate entities (from वि not, and स्वञ्ज्-ष्वञ्ज् to adhere, hence विष्वग् separate). परत्वं चान्यत्वं etc.—To say that something is पर *i. e.* अन्य is to assert एकान्तभेद (absolute distinction) as its necessary implicate.

ll. 43 etc. किं च पदार्थेभ्यः सामान्यविशेषयोरेकान्तभिन्नत्वे स्वीक्रियमाणे etc.—Now if there were एकान्तभेद between सामान्य and विशेष on the one hand and the पदार्थs on the other, it would be impossible to connect the two cognitions of अनुवृत्ति and व्यावृत्ति with the पदार्थs. For, if the two sides fall absolutely asunder, सामान्य and विशेष could have nothing to do with the पदार्थs. If, on the other hand, we adopt the alternative of एकान्त अभेद—absolute identity—one member of the pair of सामान्य and विशेष would vanish leaving only the other in the field. (एकान्ताभेदे चान्यतरस्यासत्त्वप्रसङ्गः l. 45). For, both being mutually contradictory, they could not be identified with the same पदार्थs. Moreover, if सामान्य and विशेष were merged in the पदार्थ, there would be no explanation of two such evident facts as सामान्य and विशेष (= अनुवृत्ति and व्यावृत्ति) which appear in every experience.

l. 47 परस्परनिरपेक्षपक्षास्तु etc.—The word पर in the stanza was interpreted in the sense of (1) other than the पदार्थs, and (2) distinct *inter se*. The परत्व of सामान्य and विशेष in the latter sense will be discussed later on. See स्या. म. on St. VIII.

I was tempted to interpret the passage in a somewhat different way, that is, as referring to the परत्व or अन्यत्व of सामान्य and विशेष *inter se*. Thus the argument in सामान्यविशेषयोरेकान्त-भिन्नत्वे स्वीक्रियमाणे, etc., would be that if सामान्य and विशेष were regarded as absolutely distinct from *each other*, they could not give rise to the ideas of अनुवृत्ति and व्यावृत्ति in reference to one and the same object—as in fact they did—being contradictory ; if, on the other hand, सामान्य and विशेष were regarded as absolutely *one*, one would be merged in the other leaving only the other in the field, which would be contrary to our everyday experience of *both* सामान्य and विशेष appearing together in one and the same object (सामान्यविशेषोभयात्मकत्वेनैव वस्तुनः प्रमाणेन प्रतीतेः l. 47). But this interpretation, while it possesses the advantage of giving point to एक and द्वय in एकवस्तुविषयं and प्रत्ययद्वयं and also to उभयात्मकत्वेनैव in the last quoted line, is precluded by the fact that the author twice speaks of the परत्व or अन्यत्व as 'पदार्थेभ्यः' and not *inter se*, in this passage ; *vide* पदार्थेभ्यो व्यतिरिक्तत्वादन्यौ and 'पदार्थेभ्यः एकान्तभिन्नत्वे स्वीक्रियमाणे.'

Stanza V.

Divide the Commentary thus :—

I आदीपं... सर्वे हि भावा द्रव्यार्थिकनयापेक्षया नित्याः पर्यायार्थिकनया-देशात् पुनरनित्याः। Introductory.

II तथैकान्तानित्यतया...नित्यानित्य एव। तमः is but a form of तेजः, and so the latter is both नित्य and अनित्य.

III एवं व्योमापि... इति सिद्धं नित्यानित्यत्वं व्योम्नः। आकाश is similarly both नित्य and अनित्य.

IV स्वायंभुवा अपि...उपपन्नमिति। The doctrine of the Yogins on the nature of नित्य and अनित्य.

V (a) अथोत्तरार्धे... कथंचित्. The second half of the Stanza explained.

(b) The doctrine of the Vaiśeṣikas unwittingly in favour of नित्यानित्य.

Page 13.

ll. 2–5. आदीपं etc. :—All things, दीप (a flame of light) and व्योम (âkâśa) alike, possess the common nature of permanance and change. For all Reality is *substance-cum-mode* (वस्तुनः स्वरूपं द्रव्यपर्यायात्मकम्). This is stated by Umâsvâti in the T. Sûtra "उत्पादव्ययध्रौव्ययुक्तं सत्"—of which the terms उत्पाद, व्यय and ध्रौव्य are thus explained in the T. R. Vârtika: 'स्वजात्यपरित्यागेन भावान्तरावाप्तिरुत्पादः,' 'तथापूर्वभावविगमो व्ययः,' 'ध्रुवे स्थैर्यकर्मणोध्रुवतीति ध्रुवः'. Note that द्रव्य is not merely द्रव्य but also पर्याय, and hence, उत्पाद and व्यय in addition to ध्रौव्य; moreover, द्रव्य is not simply पर्याय but is also द्रव्य, and therefore ध्रौव्य in addition to उत्पाद and विनाशः. Thus, everything that exists (सत्) is द्रव्यपर्यायात्मक and उत्पादव्ययध्रौव्ययुक्त. As to the point of 'युक्त' and its implication in regard to the relation of द्रव्य and पर्याय, see the Com. on the T. R.-Vārtika on the T. Sûtra V, 29— which thus sums up the whole position: पर्यायिणः पर्यायाणां च स्यादन्यत्वं स्यादनन्यत्वम्। यथा एकस्य मनुष्यस्य जातिकुलरूपादिभिः अविशिष्टस्य अनेकसंबन्धान्तराविर्भूतपितृपुत्रभ्रातृभागिनेयादयो धर्माः परस्परतो विशिष्टा उपलभ्यन्ते। न तेषां भेदात्तस्य भेदः, नापि तस्याभेदात्तेषामभेदः। ततः पितृत्वादिशक्त्यपेक्षया नाना

मनुष्यत्वापेक्षया न पृथक्। तथा द्रव्यस्यापि बाह्याभ्यन्तरहेतुविशेषापादिताः पर्यायाः कथंचिद्भिन्नाः द्रव्यार्पणात् कथंचिदाभिन्नाः इति नासत्त्वं न लक्ष्यलक्षण-भावाभावः। तस्मादुत्पादादित्रयैक्यवृत्तिः सत्ता तद्युक्तं द्रव्यमित्यवसेयम्।" Note, again, how ध्रौव्य is reconciled with उत्पाद and व्यय. Thus: "व्ययोत्पादाव्यतिरेकाद्द्रव्यस्य ध्रौव्यानुपपत्तिरिति चेन्नाभिहितानवबोधात्।...... द्रव्यार्थावस्थानात् ध्रौव्यमभिहितं व्ययोत्पादाभ्यां व्यतिरेकात्। यदि च व्ययोत्पा-दाभ्यामव्यतिरेकात् ध्रौव्यमभिहितं स्यात् तदव्यतिरेकात् अध्रौव्यं भवेत्। यदि वा व्ययोत्पादाभ्यां व्यतिरेकात् द्रव्यं ध्रुवं, द्रव्यादपि व्यतिरेकात् व्ययोत्पादयो-र्ध्रौव्यं प्रसज्येत।" etc.

l. 6. स्याद्वादमुद्रानतिभेदि—Nothing can break through the seal of स्याद्वाद, i. e., the conditions imposed by the Universal Law of स्याद्वाद–the doctrine of the "May-be" – which denies all absolute propositions, such as, something is absolutely नित्य or अनित्य, every proposition, according to the Jain doctrine, being only *relatively* true, i. e., true from a certain point of view, and untrue from a different point of view. It is thus a doctrine of Relativity of Truth, of fluid as opposed to rigid Truth, and should not be confounded with any form of Scepticism or Agnosticism, ancient or modern.

l. 7. स्यादित्यव्ययम् etc. स्याद् (originally Pot. 3rd pers. sing. of अस् to be) is generally treated by commentators as an indeclinable noun or adjective connoting indefinite possibility.

l. 8. स्याद्वादोऽनेकान्तवादः etc. The doctrine of the "*May-be*" means the doctrine of *Indefinite* aspects of Truth, involving co-existence of such apparently inconsistent dharmas as नित्यत्व and अनित्यत्व.

l. 10. यथा हि न्यायैकनिष्ठे राजनि etc The word मुद्रा suggests the idea of the royal seal, and through it, the analogy of a sovereign whose law all must obey. Nothing can transgress the law of स्याद्वाद, says the author, without committing suicide or throwing itself out of the world-order. (तदुल्लङ्घने तेषां स्वरूपव्यवस्थाहानिप्रसक्तेः It is possible to take स्वरूपव्यवस्था as a षष्ठीतत्पुरुष, but I prefer to take it as a द्वन्द्व, thus drawing from it two ideas instead of one.)

l. 15. सर्ववस्तूनां समस्वभावत्व०. The स्याद्वाद — that all things partake of the common nature of अनैकान्तिकत्व or स्याद्वाद is introduced here with a view to showing that the Vaiśeṣika distinction of नित्य and अनित्य things—e. g. that between व्योम and दीप—is false. Every भाव is at once नित्य and अनित्य—it is नित्य from the standpoint of 'द्रव्यार्थिकनय' and अनित्य from the standpoint of 'पर्यायार्थिकनय,' that is to say, considered as the underlying substance it is नित्य, and as the changing manifestation it is अनित्य. The doctrine of नयs or standpoints follows as a necessary corollary from that of स्याद्वाद. "*Naya* is the method by which things are comprehended from particular standpoints," says Dr. Satischandra. Having defined it, he proceeds to explain the nature of the five nayas mentioned in the T. Sûtra 'नैगम-संग्रह-व्यवहार-ऋजुसूत्र-शब्दानयाः'. The last, viz., शब्द he subdivides, on the authority of Umâsvâti's Bhāṣya into साम्प्रत, समभिरूढ, and एवम्भूत. But the same Sùtra is quoted in the T. R.-Vârtika thus: "नैगम-संग्रह-व्यवहार-ऋजुसूत्र-शब्द-समभिरूढ-एवंभूता नयाः", and these are the 'सप्तनयs'—the *seven* modes of stating truth from different standpoints—according to its commentator. For the explanation of the different नयs in English, see Dr. Satischandra's "Indian Logic: Mediæval School," pp. 11-12 and "History of Indian Logic," pp. 170-71. But more important than this classification, for the purpose of the text, is the fundamental one of नयs into द्रव्यार्थिकनय and पर्यायार्थिकनय, also called द्रव्यास्तिक० and पर्यायास्तिक०.

The following extract from the T. R.-Vārtika and its commentary will be found useful:— "प्रमाणप्रकाशितोऽर्थविशेषप्ररूपको नयः (T. R.-V.)—प्रकर्षेण मानं प्रमाणं सकलादेश इत्यर्थः, तेन प्रकाशितानां न प्रमाणाभासपरिगृहीतानामित्यर्थः, तेषामर्थानामस्तित्व-नास्तित्व-नित्यत्वा-नित्यत्वाद्यन्तात्मनां जीवादीनां ये विशेषाः पर्यायास्तेषां प्रकर्षेण रूपकः प्ररूपकः निरुद्धदोषानुषङ्गद्वारेणेत्यर्थः । एवंलक्षणो नयस्तस्य द्वौ मूलभेदौ द्रव्यास्तिकः पर्यायास्तिक इति। द्रव्यमस्तीति मतिरस्य द्रव्यभवनमेव नातोऽन्ये भावविकाराः नाप्यभावस्तद्व्यतिरेकेणानुपलब्धेरिति द्रव्यास्तिकः। पर्याय एवास्ति इति मतिरस्य जन्यादिभावविकारमात्रमेव भवनं न ततोऽन्यद्द्रव्यमस्ति तद्व्यतिरेकेणानुपलब्धेरिति पर्यायास्तिकः। अथवा द्रव्यमेवार्थोऽस्य न गुणकर्मणी तदवस्थारूपादिति द्रव्यार्थिकः। पर्याय एवार्थोऽस्य रूपाद्युत्क्षेपणादिलक्षणो न ततोऽ-

न्यद्द्रव्यमिति पर्यायार्थिकः। अथवाऽर्य्यते गम्यते निष्पाद्यत इत्यर्थः। कार्यं द्रवति गच्छतीति द्रव्यं कारणम्। द्रव्यमेवार्थोऽस्य कारणमेव कार्यं नार्थान्तरं न च कार्यकारणयोः कश्चिद्रूपभेदः तदुभयमेकाकारमेव पर्वाङ्गुलिवदिति द्रव्यार्थिकः। परि समन्ताद् आयः पर्यायः। पर्याय एवार्थः कार्यमस्य न द्रव्यम् अतीतानागतयोर्विनष्टानुत्पन्नत्वेन व्यवहाराभावात् स एवैकः कार्यकारणव्यपदेशभागिति पर्यायार्थिकः। अथवाऽर्थनमर्थः प्रयोजनं द्रव्यमेवार्थोऽस्य प्रत्ययाभिधानानुप्रवृत्तिलिङ्गदर्शनस्य निह्नोतुमशक्यत्वादिति द्रव्यार्थिकः। पर्यायोऽर्थः प्रयोजनमस्य वाग्विज्ञानव्यावृत्तिनिबन्धव्यवहारप्रसिद्धेरिति पर्यायार्थिकः। तद्भेदा नैगमादयः॥"

(I) द्रव्यास्तिक and (2) पर्यायास्तिक are slight variations of द्रव्यार्थिक and पर्यायार्थिक and they mean respectively (1) the view that द्रव्य is the fundamental reality, the भावविकारs being nothing apart from it, and (2) the view that पर्याय, i. e., भावविकारs are the only reality, the द्रव्य being nothing apart from them. In explaining द्रव्यार्थिक and पर्यायार्थिक, the writer refers to three different meanings of the word अर्थ, viz., (1) Truth or Reality, (2) Effect, and (3) Object or Purpose—so that the two terms would respectively mean (1) अर्थ = वस्तु—Reality: the view that द्रव्य is the only reality, गुण and कर्म (comprised under the common head of पर्याय) being mere states of द्रव्य, and the view tha पर्याय (i. e., गुण such as रूप etc. and कर्म such as उत्क्षेपण) is the only reality, द्रव्य being nothing apart from पर्याय. (2) अर्थ = कार्य, i. e., Effect: the view that द्रव्य, i. e., कारण is the अर्थ, i. e., कार्य; and the view that पर्याय is the अर्थ, i. e., कार्य. (3) अर्थ = प्रयोजन object: the view that द्रव्य is the object of our thought, language, etc. and the view that the same are directed to पर्याय.

ll. 18—26 तत्रैकान्तनित्यतया etc. :—Next follows the proof that प्रदीप is at once नित्य and अनित्य. The obvious difficulty in the way of regarding प्रदीप or तेजः as नित्य is our experience of तमः as the negation of प्रदीप or तेजः. The difficulty is met by the Jaina by treating तमः as a positive substance, a kind of matter—पुद्गल—into which तेजः is at times transformed. The particles of तेजः, according to the Jaina theory, assume the particular form (पर्याय) of प्रदीप, but when the oil is exhausted or there is a blast of wind the particles abandon the form (पर्याय) of light and assume that (पर्यायान्तर) of darkness. Thus, the particles persist as the original matter (पुद्गलद्रव्य), that which changes being only their form (पर्याय). A mere change of form does not mean अनित्यत्व—मृत्तिका, for example, may take numberless forms, such as those of a jar, a storehouse, etc.; yet the मृत्तिका is recognised as the identical substance persisting through all the changes. This, says the author, is patent to the dullest man (आबालगोपालं प्रतीतत्वात्). The case of प्रदीप and तमः is not so patent; yet it is the same. That transformation is not cessation (अनित्यत्व) is shown here in the same way as in the theory of the सत्कार्यवादिन् (Sâṁkhya and Vedânta) which goes as far back as the Upaniṣads, for which see inter alia Sâṁkhya Kârikâ IX and Com., Sâṁkhya Sûtras I. 113–123 and Com., Brahma-Sûtras-II-i-14-18 and S'ankara's commentaries thereon:—

"असदकरणादुपादानग्रहणात् सर्वसंभवाभावात् । शक्तस्य शक्यकरणात् कारणभावाच्च सत्कार्यम् ॥" S. Kâr. IX.

"यथा हि कूर्मस्याङ्गानि कूर्मशरीरे निविशमानानि तिरोभवन्ति निःसरन्ति चाविर्भवन्ति न तु कूर्मस्तदङ्गान्युत्पद्यन्ते प्रध्वंसन्ते वा एवमेकस्या मृदः सुवर्णस्य वा घटमुकुटादयो विशेषा निःसरन्त आविर्भवन्त उत्पद्यन्त इत्युच्यन्ते निविशमानाश्च तिरोभवन्तो विनश्यन्तीत्युच्यन्ते न पुनरसतामुत्पादः सतां वा निरोधः"—S. T. Kaumudi (Com. on S. K.) IX.

"तस्मान्नित्यस्यैव कार्यस्यातीतानागतवर्तमानावस्थाभेदा एव वक्तव्याः। घटोऽतीतो घटो वर्तमानो घटो भविष्यन्निति प्रत्ययानां तुल्यरूपतौचित्यात् । न त्वेकस्य भावविषयत्वमन्ययोश्चाभावविषयत्वमिति । ते एवातीतानागतत्वे अवस्थे ध्वंसप्रागभावव्यवहारं जनयतः ॥" S. Pr. Bh. on S. Sûtra 113.

"अयमेव हि सत्कार्यवादिनामसत्कार्यवादिभ्यो विशेषो यत् तैरुच्यमानौ प्रागभावध्वंसौ सत्कार्यवादिभिः कार्यस्यानागतावस्थे भावरूपे प्रोच्येते । वर्तमानताख्या चाभिव्यक्त्यवस्था घटाद्यतिरिक्तेष्यते । घटादेरवस्थात्रयवत्त्वानुभवादिति·" S. Pr. Bh. on S. Sûtra 83.

Let us note here the views of the different Indian Schools regarding the relation of Cause ('material' cause in the Aristotelian sense) and Effect :

(1) According to the Sāṁkhya and the School of Vedānta which agrees with the Sāṁkhya, the Cause and the Effect are but one entity in two different states : the Effect is not created, but is only pro-duced, that is, drawn out of the Cause. This doctrine is known as **सत्कार्यवाद**. cf. the following:-

"अतस्तस्यैव मृद्धिरण्यादेर्द्रव्यस्यं संस्थानान्तरभाक्त्वमात्रेण बुद्धिशब्दान्तरादय उपपद्यन्ते यथैकस्यैव देवदत्तस्यावस्थाभेदैः बालो युवा स्थविरः इति बुद्धिशब्दान्तरादयः कार्यविशेषाश्च दृश्यन्ते। यदुक्तं सत्यामेव मृदि घटो नष्ट इति व्यवहारात्कारणादन्यत्कार्यमिति तदुत्पत्तिविनाशादीनां कारणभूतस्यैव द्रव्यावस्थाविशेषत्वाभ्युपगमादेव परिहृतम्। तत्तदवस्थस्यैकस्यैव द्रव्यस्य ते ते शब्दास्तानि तानि च कार्याणीति युक्तम्। द्रव्यस्य तत्तदवस्थत्वं कारकव्यापारायत्तमिति तस्यार्थवत्त्वम्। अभिव्यक्त्यनुबन्धीनि चोद्यानि तस्या अनभ्युपगमादेव परिहृतानि। उत्पत्त्यभ्युपगमेऽपि सत्कार्यवादो न निरुध्यते। सत एवोत्पत्तेः। विप्रतिषिद्धमिदमभिधीयते पूर्वमेव सत् तदुत्पद्यत इति। अज्ञातोत्पत्तिविनाशयाथात्म्यस्येदं चोद्यम्। द्रव्यस्योत्तरोत्तरसंस्थानयोगः पूर्वपूर्वसंस्थानसंस्थितस्य विनाशः स्वावस्थस्य तूत्पत्तिः। अतः सर्वावस्थस्य द्रव्यस्य सत्त्वात्सत्कार्यवादो न निरुध्यते। संस्थानस्यासत उत्पत्तावसत्कार्यवादप्रसङ्ग इति चेत् असत्कार्यवादिनोऽप्युत्पत्तेरनुत्पत्तिमत्त्वे सत्कार्यवादप्रसङ्गः। उत्पत्तिमत्त्वे चानवस्था। अस्माकं त्ववस्थानां पृथक् प्रतिपत्तिकार्ययोगानर्हत्वादवस्थावत एवोत्पत्त्यादिकं सर्वमिति निरवद्यम्॥" Râm. Srî Bhâṣya II. 1–15.

(2) According to the Nyāya-Vaiśeṣika, the Cause and the Effect are *two* distinct entities held together by a relation called '**समवाय**'; so that, **घट** was non-existent before its manufacture, and will be non-existent after its destruction, enjoying existence only during the interval. This doctrine is known as **असत्कार्यवाद** (For the Sâṁkhya case set forth in the Kârikâ above quoted and the Nyāya-Vaiśeṣika and criticism thereof, see Nyāyakandalî, Viz. Ed. pp. 143-144.)

(3) According to the School of Vedânta led by S'aṁkara, the Effect is neither the same as, nor distinct from, the Cause; moreover, it cannot be both the same as and distinct from the Cause, the two judgments being contradictory ; hence, it is concluded, the Effect is such as cannot be described adequately either as that which is the same as or distinct from the Cause—

it is 'अनिर्वचनीय,' it is neither सत् nor असत्, either before or after its birth, it is मिथ्या. This doctrine which may be called अनिर्वचनीय-कार्यतावाद is sometimes confused with or placed under सत्कार्यतावाद. But in truth it is सत्कारणवाद rather than सत्कार्यवाद.*

"ये हि दृष्टनष्टस्वरूपा न ते वस्तुसन्तो यथा मृगतृष्णिकोदकादयः। तथा च सर्वं विकारजातं तस्मादवस्तु सत्। तथा हि यदस्ति तदस्त्येव, यथा चिदात्मा। न ह्यसौ कदाचित् क्वचित् कथंचिद्वास्ति किंतु सर्वदा सर्वत्र सर्वथास्त्येव, न नास्ति। न चैवं विकारजातम्। तस्य कदाचित् कथंचित् कुत्राचिदवस्थानात्। तथाहि सत्स्वभावं चेद्विकारजातं कथं कदाचिदसत्। असत्स्वभावं चेत्कथं कदाचित् सत्। सद-सतोरेकत्वविरोधात्। न हि रूपं कदाचित् क्वचित् कथंचिद्वा गन्धो भवति। अथ तस्य सदसत्त्वे धर्मौ ते च स्वकारणाधीनजन्मतया कदाचिदेव भवतः, तत्तर्हि विकार-जातं दण्डायमानं सदातनमिति न विकारः कस्यचित्। अथासत्त्वसमये तन्नास्ति, कस्य तर्हि धर्मोऽसत्त्वम्। न हि धर्मिण्यप्रत्युत्पन्ने तद्धर्मोऽसत्त्वं प्रत्युत्पन्नमुपपद्यते। अथास्य न धर्मः किंत्वर्थान्तरमसत्त्वम्। किमायातं भावस्य। न हि घटे जाते पटस्य किंचिद्भवति। असत्त्वं भावविरोधीति चेत्। न। अकिंचित्करस्य तत्त्वानुपपत्तेः। किंचित्करत्वे वा तत्राप्यसत्त्वेन तदनुयोगसंभवात्। अथास्यासत्त्वं नाम किंचिन्न जायते किं तु स एव न भवति। यथाहुः 'न तस्य किंचिद्भवति न भवत्येव केवलम्' इति। अथैष प्रसज्यप्रतिषेधो निरुच्यताम्। किं तत्स्वभावो भाव उत भावः स्वभावः स इति। तत्र पूर्वस्मिन् कल्पे भावानां तत्स्वभावतया तुच्छतया जग-च्छून्यं प्रसज्येत। तथा च भावानुभवाभावः। उत्तरस्मिंस्तु सर्वभावनित्यतया नाभावव्यवहारः स्यात्। कल्पनामात्रनिमित्तत्वेऽपि निषेधस्य भावनित्यतापत्तिस्तद-वस्थैव। तस्माद्भिन्नमस्ति कारणाद्विकारजातं न वस्तु सत्। अतो विकारजात-मनिर्वचनीयमनृतम्"॥ Bhāmati on Br. S. II. i. 14.

(4) According to the Jaina, as with the S'ânkara Vedântin, there is partial truth in both the conflicting theories mentioned

---

* Das-Gupta rightly observes: "Both the Vedānta and Sāṁkhya theories of causation are sometimes called *Satkârya-vâda.* But correctly speaking, as some discerning commentators have pointed out, the Vedānta theory of causation should be called *Sat-kâraṇavâda,* for according to it the *Kâraṇa* (cause) alone exists (sat) and all *Kâryas* (effects) are illusory appearances of the Kâraṇa; but according to Sâṁkhya, the Kârya exists in a potential state in the Kâraṇa and is hence always existing and real.—Das-Gupta H. I. Phil. vol. I. p. 258.

in (1) and (2); but, while the S'ânkara Vedântin deduces his favourite doctrine of अनिर्वचनीयता or मिथ्यात्व from the contradiction of being (सत्) and non-being (असत्), the Jaina records the views as partial statements of a single truth, both of which he regards as equally true from different points of view. He sees no irrationality (अनिर्वचनीयता and मिथ्यात्व) in the so-called contradiction, and would, moreover, urge that logic should be ruled by facts and not facts by logic. (So also a school of Vedânta criticised by S'ankara. cf. similarly, "नन्वनेकात्मकं ब्रह्म। यथा वृक्षोऽनेकशाख एवमनेकशक्तिप्रवृत्तियुक्तं ब्रह्म। अत एकत्वं नानात्वं चोभयमपि सत्यमेव। यथा वृक्ष इत्येकत्वं शाखा इति नानात्वम्॥") To borrow the words of a literary critic in a different context, "the ingredients of a pudding are no more true or essential than the pudding itself when it is cooked."

On the problem of सत्कार्यवाद or असत्कार्यवाद consider the following passage from Prof Ward's "The Realm of Ends":—

"But widely as the term 'evolution' is used, it is rarely defined; hence it is often without misgiving applied to processes that are diametrically opposed, to the differentiation of a unity and to the integration of a plurality. The history of this term is worth a moment's consideration. We begin with the literal sense, the unrolling of a scroll or volume, whereby what lies written inside it is no longer latent but laid bare—becomes patent and evident. This as a figure is then transferred to the processes of thought; and we talk of evolving or explicating whatever may be implied or involved in a concept, an argument or a theory. We find it later applied with a similar meaning to the supposed unfolding of an organism regarded as completely pre-existing in miniature within the germ. Such was the theory of biological evolution or preformation advocated by Leibnitz. And throughout the 18th century this was the prevalent view among biologists and philosophers alike; but now it is all but superseded by the very different theory of epigenesis or new formation; for which, nevertheless, the term evolution is still retained. So different are the two theories in fact that the earlier, strictly evolutional view would—unless essentially modified—render the Darwinian doctrine of the origin of species impossible. For, according to that earlier theory, 'the germ was more than a marvellous bud-like miniature of the adult, it necessarily included in its turn the next generation, and this the next—in short all future generations. Germ within germ, in ever smaller miniature, after the fashion of an infinite juggler's box, was the corollary logically appended to this theory of preformation.' The successive unfolding of such a system of emboitement or involution, though the plus ultra of evolution, literally understood, is than the direct negative of an evolution, as we understand it to-day. According to this latter theory each new organism is not an 'educt' but a 'product' to use Kantian phrases; its parts are in no sense present in the embryo but are gradually organized, one after another in due order, as the term epigenesis implies and as Harvey, who first used the term, prophetically maintained. It is now known too that in this progressive differentiation the individual retraces the main stages through which the species has advanced as Haeckel in technical language concisely puts it : Ontogeny recapitulates phylogeny."

ll. 26-34. III. न च तमसः पौद्गलिकत्वमसिद्धम् :—The author next shows how तमः may well be regarded as a material substance (पुद्गल). His reasoning is that तमः being quite as visible (चाक्षुषत्वान्यथानुपपत्तेः) as light (आलोक), it is as much a material substance as the latter, the only difference between the two being that one is dark, and the other bright. But it may be objected that तमः is not really visible (चाक्षुष): for, whatever is really visible (चाक्षुष) requires light to make it so; whereas, तमः does not require it; therefore its visibility (चाक्षुषत्व) must be deemed to be only *apparent*. The answer made to this objection is: तमः is seen by owls without the help of light, which shows that the व्याप्ति relied upon by the Vaiśeṣika (viz., whatever is visible requires light to make it so) breaks down. No doubt we do require light to enable us to see

घट पट etc., but this is no reason why we should require it in order to see तमः. So different are the natures of things in this world that you must take the differences as they are, and have no right to obliterate them by adopting a fictitious uniformity. For example, gold, pearls, etc., although all तैजस, are not visible without external light; whereas a lamp, the moon, etc., are visible even without the aid of other light.

l. 34. रूपवत्त्वाच्च etc.—Moreover, तमः possesses not only a colour (dark) which makes it visible, but also tangibility (स्पर्श), viz., cool touch.

ll. 35-38. यानि त्वनिबिड॰ etc.—The following are the grounds relied upon by the Vaiśeṣika, says the author, for holding that तमः cannot be a material substance:—(a) want of density (अनिबिडावयवत्वम्); (b) want of resistance (अप्रतिघातित्वम्); (c) absence of developed—distinct—tangibility(अनुद्भूतस्पर्शविशेषत्वम्); (d) absence of its being a fragment cut off like a chip from a block (अप्रतीयमानखण्डावयविद्रव्यप्रतिभागत्वम्). To all these, he says, he could make a simple reply: None of these conditions, viz., density, resistance, tangibility, and divisibility is fulfilled by light—प्रदीपप्रभा—and yet light is undeniably a material substance.

ll.38-42. न च वाच्यं तैजसाः etc.—The dissimilarity between the तैजस particles and their product—the तमः—may be paralleled by that of वह्नि and धूम, the one refulgent (भास्वररूप) and the other dark.

On the question of the nature of तमः, according to the Nyâya-Vaiśeṣika School, see Vaiś. Sûtras II, 19-20 with S'ankaramiśra's Upaskâra, the section on "Dravya" in Tarkadîpikâ with Nîlakanṭhi and other commentaries; similarly, Nyâya-Siddhânta-muktâvali and its commentaries, Nyâyakandali, Viz. Ed. pp. 9-10, and Sarvadarśana Saṁgraha O. S. Ed. pp. 228-230 where the Vaiśeṣika view is discussed and established.

"यदवाच्यन्धकारादौ भावत्वं निषिध्यते इति तदसंगतम्। तत्र चतुर्धा विवादसंभवात्। तथाहि द्रव्यं तम इति भाट्टा वेदान्तिनश्च भणन्ति। आरोपितं नीलरूपमिति श्रीधराचार्याः। आलोकज्ञानाभाव इति प्राभाकरैकदेशिनः। आलोकाभाव इति

नैयायिकादयः। इति चेत् तत्र द्रव्यत्वपक्षो न घटते। विकल्पानुपपत्तेः। द्रव्यं भवदन्धकाराख्यं पृथिव्याद्यन्यतममन्यद्वा। नाद्यः। यत्रान्तर्भावोऽस्य तस्य यावन्तो गुणास्तावद्गुणकत्वप्रसङ्गात्। न द्वितीयः। निर्गुणस्य तस्य द्रव्यत्वासंभवेन द्रव्यान्तरत्वस्य सुतरामसंभवात्। ननु तमालश्यामलत्वे नोपलभ्यमानं तमः कथं निर्गुणं स्यादिति चेत् तदसारम्। गन्धादिव्याप्तस्य नीलरूपस्य तन्निवृत्तौ निवृत्तेः। अथ नीलं तम इति गतेः का गतिरिति चेत् नीलं नभ इतिवद्भ्रान्तिरेवेत्यलं वृद्धविवधया। अत एव नारोपितरूपं तमः। अधिष्ठानप्रत्ययमन्तरेणारोपायोगात्। बाह्यालोकसहकारिरहितस्य चक्षुषो रूपारोपे सामर्थ्यानुपलम्भाच्च। न चायमचाक्षुषः प्रत्ययः। तदनुविधानस्यानन्यथासिद्धत्वात्। अत एव नालोकज्ञानाभावः। अभावस्य प्रतियोगिग्राहकेन्द्रियग्राह्यत्वनियमेन मानसत्वप्रसङ्गात्। तस्मादालोकाभाव एव तमः। न च विधिप्रत्ययवेद्यत्वेनाभावत्वायोग इति सांप्रतम्। प्रलयविनाशावसानादिषु व्यभिचारात्। न चाभावे भावधर्माध्यारोपो दुरुपपादः। दुःखाभावे सुखत्वारोपस्य संयोगाभावे विभागत्वाभिमानस्य च दृष्टत्वात्। न चालोकाभावस्य घटाद्यभाववद्रूपवदभावत्वेनालोकसापेक्षचक्षुर्जन्यज्ञानविषयत्वं स्यादित्येषितव्यम्। यद्ग्रहे यदपेक्षं चक्षुस्तदभावग्रहेऽपि तदपेक्षत इति न्यायेनालोकग्रह आलोकापेक्षाया अभावेन तदभावग्रहेऽपि तदपेक्षाया अभावात्। न चाधिकरणावश्यंभावः। अभावप्रतीतावधिकरणावश्यंभावानङ्गीकारात्। अपरथा निवृत्तः कोलाहल इति शब्दप्रध्वंसः प्रत्यक्षो न स्यादिति अप्रामाणिकं परवचनम्। तत्सर्वमभिसंधाय भगवान् कणादः प्रणिनाय सूत्रं—द्रव्यगुणकर्मनिष्पत्तिवैधर्म्यादभावस्तमः (क॰ सू॰ ५-२-१९) इति।"

Contra, S'rî-Bhâṣya Chatus-Sûtrî Mad. Ed. p. 77: "आलोकाभावमात्रं वा रूपदर्शनाभावमात्रं वा तमो न द्रव्यान्तरम्। तत्कथं भावरूपाज्ञानसाधने निदर्शनतयोच्यत इति चेत् उच्यते। बहुलत्वविरलत्वाद्यवस्थायोगेन रूपवत्तया चोपलब्धेर्द्रव्यान्तरमेव तम इति निरवद्यम्" । cf. "तमः खलु चलं नीलं परापरविभागवत्। प्रसिद्धद्रव्यवैधर्म्यान्नवभ्यो भेत्तुमर्हति" and for a brief statement of the whole controversy, the following interesting stanza:

"तमो द्रव्यं नैल्याद्धटवदिति माने समुदिते यदीदं रूपि स्यात् किमिह न भवेत् स्पार्शनगुणः। इतीमं सत्तर्कं शिथिलयितुमन्तर्व्यवसिता तमोवृन्दं धत्ते कचभरमिषादिन्दुवदना॥"

1.42. यदापि निर्वाणात् प्राक् etc.—This is another sense in which a दीप is both नित्य and अनित्य, and it does not militate against our common belief as does the former: a दीप (i. e., the flame) is undergoing numberless changes and yet it retains its identity, thus proving itself both नित्य and अनित्य.

IV. ll. 45–55. एवं व्योमापि । उत्पादव्ययध्रौव्यात्मकत्वात् नित्याऽनित्यमेव—Having shown that दीप is both नित्य and अनित्य, the author next proceeds to show the same in the case of व्योम—with this difference that in the former case the difficulty to be met was about नित्यत्व, in the latter it is about अनित्यत्व. उत्पाद and व्यय account for अनित्यत्व, ध्रौव्य for नित्यत्व.

अवगाहकानां etc.—Compare आकाशस्यावगाहः [उपकारः], T. Sûtra Adh. V, Sû. 18. उपग्रहो निमित्तमपेक्षाकारणं हेतुरित्यनर्थान्तरम्. cf. the com. of भावविजयगणि on Uttarâ-Sûtra XXVIII, 9.

"अवगाहिनां धर्मादीनामवकाशदायित्वेनोपकारेणाकाशमनुमीयते । अवकाशदायित्वं चोपकारोऽवगाहः । स चात्मभूतोऽस्य लक्षणमुच्यते । मकरादिगत्युपकारकारिजलादिदृष्टान्ता अत्राप्यनुवर्तनीयाः । नन्वयमवगाहो पुद्गलादिसंबन्धी व्योमसंबन्धी च ततः स उभयोर्धर्मः कथमाकाशस्यैव लक्षणम् ? । उभयजन्यत्वात् द्व्यङ्गुलसंयोगवत् । न खलु द्रव्यद्वयजनितः संयोगो द्रव्येणैकेन व्यपदेष्टुं पार्यते लक्षणं चैकस्य भवितुमर्हतीति । सत्यमेतत् । ततोऽत्रगाहनमनुप्रवेशो यत्र तदाकाशमवगाह्यमवगाहलक्षणं विवक्षितं इतरत्तु पुद्गलादिकमवगाहकम् । यस्माद्व्योमैवासाधारणकारणतयावगाह्यत्वेनोपकरोति." Gunaratna's Com. on Haribhadra's Saddars'ana p. 172.

When souls and material objects (जीवपुद्गलाः) which occupy space travel from one point of space to another, they become separated from one portion of आकाश and get united with another portion of आकाश. These separation and union being contradictory dharmas must belong to two different dharmins, according to the rule "अयमेव हि भेदो etc.—" What constitutes or causes a भेद (difference) is the possession of two contradictory predicates or difference of causes, volitionally or spontaneously (for संयोगतो विश्र(स्र)सातो वा—I would prefer to read प्रयोगतो विस्रसातो वा, संयोगतो being wrongly substituted for प्रयोग owing to the former word occuring several times in the same passage. प्रयोग and विस्रसा are technical terms of Jaina psychology, for which see Rāj. Vâr. on T. Sûtra, v. 225.

"द्रव्यस्य स्वजात्यपरित्यागेन प्रयोगविस्रसालक्षणो विकारः परिणामः—... तत्र प्रयोगः पुद्गलविकारस्तदनपेक्षा विक्रिया विस्रसा...अचेतनस्य च मृदादेः घटसंस्थानादिपरिणामः कुलालादिपुरुषप्रयोगनिमित्तत्वात् प्रयोगजः । इन्द्रधनुरादिनानापरिणामो वैस्रसिकः ।"

i. e., those things must be regarded as distinct which possess contradictory predicates (विरुद्धधर्माध्यासः) or spring from different causes (कारणभेदः). आकाश comes under the first part of the rule, and is thus shown to be two—one that is destroyed and the other that is produced, the former being the one from which the previous संयोग is destroyed, and the latter being the one with which a new संयोग is produced; and yet, in another way, both the आकाशs are one. Thus आकाश may be shown to be both नित्य and अनित्य.

ll. 55–60. तथा च यदप्रच्युता० etc.—It will be observed that the नित्यत्व above set forth is नित्यत्व *in the midst of change*, a conception of नित्यत्व which requires to be justified against that false conception of नित्यत्व which makes it consist in *changelessness*. The Jaina accordingly defines नित्यत्व as 'तद्भावाव्ययं नित्यम्' (T. Sûtra V, 30) which is thus explained in the Râj.V. and its commentary: " प्रत्यभिज्ञानहेतुना तद्भावः । तदेवेदमिति स्मरणं प्रत्यभिज्ञानं तदकस्मान्न भवति इति योऽस्य हेतुः स तद्भावः । तस्य भावस्तद्भावः । येनात्मना प्राग्दृष्टं वस्तु तेनैवात्मना पुनरपि भावात् तदेवेदमिति प्रत्यभिज्ञायते । यद्यत्यन्त-विरोधाभिनवप्रादुर्भावमात्रमेव, स्मरणानुपपत्तेः तदधीनलोकसंव्यवहारो विरुध्यते। ततः तद्भावेनाव्ययं नित्यमिति निश्चीयते।" In the same manner our author says here: "...उभयत्राकाशद्रव्यस्यानुगतत्वाच्चोत्पादव्यययोरेकाकाशाधि-करणत्वम्।...उत्पादविनाशयोः सद्भावेऽपि तद्भावादन्वयिरूपान्न व्येति तन्नित्यमिति तदर्थस्य घटमानत्वात्", and his reason for the rejection of नित्यत्व= changelessness is that it will leave उत्पाद and व्यय without a basis (that to which they should cling, in which they should rest, as predicates), and thus make them impossible. (यदि हि अप्रच्युतादिलक्षणं नित्यमिष्यते तदोत्पादव्यययोर्निराधारत्वप्रसङ्गः). On the general line of argument which deduces नित्यत्व from प्रत्यभिज्ञा or अन्वयित्व, compare S'ankara's Com. on Br. Sûtra II. ii-26. Thus there would seem to be three different views on the subject: 1st, that of the *Vaiśeṣikas*, according to whom nothing is नित्य which is not absolutely changeless, and such are according to them आकाश, परमाणु etc. 2nd, that of the *Vedântins*, who distinguish between two kinds of नित्यत्व—one *relative*, which they call अन्वयित्व or अन्वितत्व or स्थिरत्व, such as belongs to कारण in all its changes (e. g. मृत्तिका in घट, घटविनाश etc.) and which they base on the ground of प्रत्यभिज्ञा just like the Jainas, and the other *absolute* such as belongs to ब्रह्म or आत्मा and to it alone; and 3rd, that of the *Jainas*, according to whom the only नित्यत्व possible is the relative नित्यत्व, absolute नित्यत्व being a pure fiction. In so far as the Vedântin traces स्थिरत्व or अन्वितत्व in the midst of change he would seem to be at one with the Jaina; but, in so far as relative नित्यत्व (what he calls स्थिरत्व or अन्वितत्व) is of small importance in his system, and absolute नित्यत्व alone counts, he may be classed with the Vaiśeṣika in holding the view 'अप्रच्युताऽनुत्पन्नस्थिरैकरूपं नित्यम्'.

ll. 61–64. न च तयोर्योगे नित्यत्वहानिः etc.—The Jaina has to reconcile उत्पाद् and व्यय with नित्यत्व. This he does by pointing to the nature of Reality which, he says, is neither द्रव्य nor पर्याय, but द्रव्य-*cum*-पर्याय. It was this very consideration which made him posit ध्रौव्य along with उत्पाद and व्यय in his definition or rather characterization of सत्; for उत्पाद and व्यय in his system are not only consistent with ध्रौव्य, but would lack the peg to hang on and thus become impossible in the absence of ध्रौव्य. The alleged inconsistency of उत्पाद and व्यय on the one hand and ध्रौव्य on the other is thus dealt with in the Râj.V. and its Com. which takes up the specific question of the नित्यत्व or otherwise of वियत् and answers it in the spirit of स्याद्वादः—

" विरोध इति चेद्धर्मान्तराश्रयणात् (Râj.V.)। स्यान्मतं वियदेव न व्येति उत्पद्यमान एव नोपपद्यते इति विरोधः ततो न युक्तमिति तन्न। किं कारणम्?। धर्मान्तराश्रयणात्। यदि येन रूपेण व्ययोदयकल्पना तेनैव रूपेण नित्यता प्रत्यभिज्ञायेत स्याद्विरोधः। जनकत्वापेक्षयैव पितापुत्रव्यपदेशवत्। न तु धर्मान्तरसंश्रयणात्।"

द्रव्यं पर्यायवियुतं etc. cf. "दव्वं पज्जवविजुअं दव्वविउत्ता य पज्जवा नत्थि"—संमति० I, 12.

ll. 64–74. लौकिकानामपि घटाकाशपटाकाश० etc.—Another way in which आकाश may be shown to be नित्यानित्य is this: When घट is gone and पट takes its place, घटाकाश is replaced by पटाकाश; thus, one आकाश is destroyed and another is produced. It may be objected that this is mere 'उपचार', that is to say, आकाश is not really produced or destroyed, but by a transference of predicates it is said to be produced or destroyed according to the production or destruction of घट, पट, etc., which condition it. To this objection it is replied: The transference of predicates takes place in an उपचार owing to something being common to the primary and the secondary subject. Thus उपचार does not take place without some connection of the predicate with the primary subject (उपचारस्यापि किंचित्साधर्म्यद्वारेण मुख्यार्थस्पर्शित्वात्.) For example, आकाश has primarily सर्वव्यापकत्व-परिमाण, but in accordance with the घट, पट etc., which reside in it, it has different supposed parts (कल्पितभेदं), with reference to which it may be said to possess प्रतिनियतदेशव्यापित्व परिमाण, i. e., a परिमाण which covers a particular space or spot, and the आकाश is thereby known as घटाकाश, पटाकाश, etc., This change of states means change of that to which the states belong (अवस्थाभेदे अवस्थावतोऽपि भेदः) Thus, the production and destruction of घट, पट, etc., and through them of घटाकाश, पटाकाश, etc., amount to the production and destruction of आकाश itself, for घटाकाश, पटाकाश, etc. are but forms or particulars of आकाश. आकाश is thus proved to be अनित्य.

l. 75. स्वायंभुवा अपि etc.—The author proceeds to show how even amongst the Brahmanical schools the Yogins hold the doctrine of नित्यानित्य.

स्वायंभुवाः—The followers of स्वयंभू or हिरण्यगर्भ, one of the ancient teachers of Yoga philosophy, mentioned in the Mahâbhârata, and, according to a certain interpretation of the passage, in the S'vetâśvatara Upaniṣad also. The other names of the same group are कपिल, आसुरि, and पञ्चशिख. Whether हिरण्यगर्भ was a historical or a mythical teacher must remain doubtful. हिरण्यगर्भ of the Ṛgveda Saṃhitâ is beyond doubt the God of monotheism from which has sprung this luminous universe; and probably the कपिल and हिरण्यगर्भ of the S'vetâśvatara Upaniṣad are used in the same sense, although the word 'ऋषि' used in connection with them gives plausibility to their historical character. But long before the time of Gautama Buddha कपिल had become historical, that is, some teacher had come to be invested with the ancient name. And similar must have been the case with हिरण्यगर्भ.

ll. 76-85. त्रिविधः खल्वयं धर्मिणः परिणामो॰ etc.—According to the Yogins (See Pât. Yoga Sûtras and Vyâsa Bhâṣya -III. 13), says the author, a धर्मिन् (a substance possessed of धर्मs, as every substance is) undergoes परिणाम or modification of three kinds: (1) धर्म, (2) लक्षण, and (3) अवस्था—which he thus illustrates: (1) When the substance—gold—is made into ornaments, the ornaments are the 'धर्मपरिणाम' of gold. (2) The धर्म, again, of gold, viz., the ornaments may be changed from one shape to another, when a present shape becomes past and a future shape becomes present. This is called 'लक्षण परिणाम'. (लक्ष्यतेऽनेनेति लक्षणं कालभेदः। तेन हि लक्षितं वस्तु वस्त्वन्तरेभ्यः कालान्तरयुक्तेभ्यो व्यवच्छिद्यते—Vâcaspati Miśra.) (3) Or, a certain shape may become old by sheer lapse of time. This is called 'अवस्थापरिणाम'. All the three kinds of परिणाम belong to one and the same धर्मिन् (सोऽयं त्रिविधः परिणामो धर्मिणः). [But how would you reconcile this remark with another just a few lines above, viz., 'धर्मस्य तु लक्षणपरिणामोऽनागतत्वादिः'? I suppose by referring the लक्षणपरिणाम through the धर्म to the धर्मिन्]. And they are supposed to be at once distinct from and identical with the धर्मिन्. (धर्मलक्षणावस्थाश्च धर्मिणो भिन्नाश्चाभिन्नाश्च). Now, if they are identical with the धर्मिन्, the धर्मिन् being नित्य (persistent or abiding reality), the परिणामs too are नित्य; and if they are distinct from the धर्मिन्, they are subject to उत्पाद and विनाश and are therefore अनित्य. Thus they are both नित्य and अनित्य.

cf. तत्रेदमुदाहरणम्। मृद्धर्मी पिण्डाकाराद्धर्माद्धर्मान्तरमुपसंपद्यमानो धर्मतः परिणमते घटाकार इति। घटाकारोऽनागतं लक्षणं हित्वा वर्तमानलक्षणं प्रतिपद्यत इति लक्षणतः परिणमते। घटो नवपुराणतां प्रतिक्षणमनुभवन्नवस्थापरिणामं प्रतिपद्यत इति। धर्मिणोऽपि धर्मान्तरमवस्था धर्मस्यापि लक्षणान्तरमवस्थेत्येक एव द्रव्यपरिणामो भेदेनोपदर्शित इति।...। त एते धर्मलक्षणावस्थापरिणामा धर्मिस्वरूपमनतिक्रान्ता इत्येक एव परिणामः सर्वानमून् विशेषानभिप्लवते॥ cf. also न धर्मी त्र्यध्वा। धर्मास्तु त्र्यध्वानः। ते लक्षिता अलक्षिताः। तत्र लक्षितास्तां तामवस्थां प्राप्नुवन्तोऽन्यत्वेन प्रतिनिर्दिश्यन्तेऽवस्थान्तरतो न द्रव्यान्तरतः। यथैका रेखा शतस्थाने शतं दशस्थाने दशैका चैकस्थाने यथा चैकत्वेऽपि स्त्री माता चोच्यते दुहिता च स्वसा चेति (Vyâsa Bhâṣya on Pât. Sûtra-III. 13.)

ll. 86-92. अथोत्तरार्धे विव्रियते etc.—All भावs are equally characterized by उत्पाद, व्यय and ध्रौव्य; and, therefore, it is wrong to draw a line of distinction between things and things and say that certain things are absolutely नित्य and नित्य only, e. g., आकाश, आत्मा etc., while certain others are absolutely अनित्य and अनित्य only, e.g. प्रदीप, घट, etc.

l. 89. अनन्तधर्मात्मके वस्तुनि etc.—Compare—येनोत्पादव्ययध्रौव्ययुक्तं यत्सत्तदिष्यते । अनन्तधर्मकं वस्तु तेनोक्तं मानगोचरः ॥ येन कारणेन यदुत्पादव्ययध्रौव्ययुक्तं तत्सत्स्वरूपमिष्यते तेन कारणेनानन्तधर्मकं वस्तुमानगोचरः प्रत्यक्षपरोक्षप्रमाणविषयः । उक्तं कथितमिति संबन्धः । Laghu-Vṛtti on the Ṣaḍ.

Page 17.

ll. 93-96. अत्र च प्रथममादीप० etc.—This is too ingenious. Mallis'eṇa says that in the first line we had दीप and व्योम—the first supposed to be अनित्य and the latter नित्य; but in the second half the order is reversed, नित्य being mentioned first and अनित्य afterwards. This यथासंख्यपरिहार—abandonment of the order—is suggestive of the view that after all there is no such thing as fixed or absolute नित्य and अनित्य, and so they may very well change places!

ll. 96- प्रक्रान्तवादिभिः etc.—The author has shown above that the Yoga doctrine of परिणामs and their relation to the धर्मिन् is a virtual admission of the नित्यानित्य doctrine, that is, of the अनेकान्तवाद of the Jainas. Next he proceeds to show how the 'प्रक्रान्तवादिन् s'—the Vais'eṣikas whose system is being discussed—hold a doctrine which is a virtual admission of the नित्यानित्यवाद. Thus 'प्रशस्तकर'—Pras'astapâda, the Bhâṣyakâra of the Vais'eṣika Sûtras, says, पृथ्वी is of two kinds, नित्य and अनित्य; that consisting of atoms is नित्य, that consisting of effects is अनित्य. Obviously, it may be argued, this is not an admission that पृथ्वी—the identical पृथ्वी—is at once नित्य and अनित्य, but all that is said is that *some* varieties of पृथ्वी (पार्थिव atoms) are नित्य, while *others* (कार्य) are अनित्य. The statements of नित्यत्व and अनित्यत्व thus refer to two separate अधिकरणs (नैकाधिकरणं नित्यानित्यत्वम्). That is to say, नित्यत्व and अनित्यत्व are here predicated of two separate subjects. But this defence is futile. For, पृथ्वीत्व belongs to *all* the varieties, to नित्य as well as to अनित्य पृथ्वी and is 'एकाधिकरण' both with नित्यत्व and अनित्यत्व; in other words, नित्यत्व and अनित्यत्व are both predicated of पृथ्वी. So also are they predicated of जल. Then again, there is a tacit admission of अनित्यत्व about आकाश inasmuch as संयोग and विभाग are predicated of it.

ll. 102–105. तथा च स एवाह । etc.—शब्दकारणत्ववचनात् संयोगविभागाविति—Pra. Bhâṣya in the section on आकाश, p. 58. Viz. Edn. The passage is thus explained in the Nyâyakandalî "संयोगाद्विभागात् शब्दाच्च शब्दस्य निष्पत्तिरिति सूत्रेणाकाशगुणं शब्दं प्रति संयोगविभागौ कारणम् इत्युक्तं तेनाकाशे संयोगविभागौ सिद्धौ व्यधिकरणस्यासमवायिकारणत्वाभावात् (*ibid* p. 62). Of the three ways in which शब्द is produced two are by means of संयोग and विभाग. संयोग and विभाग being thus the असमवायिकारणs of शब्द, they have the same अधिकरण as शब्द, and that is आकाश. आकाश being thus shown to possess संयोग and विभाग, it becomes subject to उत्पाद and व्यय; in other words, it is अनित्य (see above). Now, from its परममहत्परिमाण, it is already known to be नित्य. Therefore, it is नित्यानित्य. The नित्यानित्यत्व of आकाश had already been shown above. But the same is shown once more here as a doctrine which is denied and yet virtually admitted by the Vais'eṣikas in some of their tenets—thus betraying incoherent talk. (l. 105).

Page 17-18.

ll. 105–142. प्रलापप्रायत्वं च etc.—The author now takes up the question of नित्यानित्यत्व–in its general form—i. e., without any such particular application as that to दीप or व्योम as was done above, and points out * the innumerable contradictions and impossible positions to which the doctrine of absolute नित्यत्व or अनित्यत्व leads us.

For example, a real thing is defined as that which *does* something. Now let us see how the doctrine of absolute नित्यत्व or अनित्यत्व will fit in with this. A नित्य thing is one which has

* The whole paragraph of the text is taken almost verbatim from Hemacandra's commentary on his own प्रमाणमीमांसासूत्र—I–i. 33.

neither beginning nor end, but only persistent existence (अप्रच्युतानुत्पन्नस्थिरैकरूप). Now, if it is a reality it must *do* something, as required by the definition of reality; and that either *at once* or *gradually*, for no third alternative is possible according to the law of 'the excluded middle' (अन्योन्यव्यवच्छेदरूपाणां प्रकारान्तरासंभवात्). Of the two, the latter, that is, *gradual* activity is impossible in the present case, for there is nothing to delay the action of the नित्य thing and prevent its doing its work *at once* (समर्थस्य कालक्षेपायोगात्), unless the thing is lacking in the required energy or competency. It may be argued that the thing possesses the *capacity* to do a certain work, but it needs an auxiliary agent to turn that capacity into actuality. But that is virtually admitting that the thing is so far lacking in the required competency (सापेक्षमसमर्थम्-इति न्यायात्); for, what depends upon others is pro tanto lacking in its own strength. It may be answered that it is not the नित्य thing that needs an auxiliary in order to produce an effect, but it is the effect itself which needs it in order to come into being (न तेन सहकारिणोऽपेक्ष्यन्ते, अपि तु कार्यमेव सहकारिष्वसत्सु अभवत् तानपेक्षते). But this is only trying to evade the difficulty: we want a straight answer to this question—Is the thing competent or incompetent? If it is competent, why should it weakly and imploringly look at the face of the auxiliary, and not produce the effect *at once*? You will perhaps say that a seed though perfectly competent to put forth a sprout does so actually only when accompanied by earth, water, etc., and not otherwise. This statement, however, will not stand the test of the following dilemma: Do those companions render any assistance to the principal cause or not? If they do not, the cause (the नित्य thing of our hypothesis) has no more reason to be active after than it had before the advent of those companions. If they do, we ask the question: Is the assistance (उपकार) thus rendered by the companions to the नित्य thing identical with the नित्य thing or is it different? If it (उपकार) is identical with the नित्य thing, it vitiates the very नित्यत्व of the thing and turns it into something अनित्य, it being itself something produced by those auxiliaries. (अभेदे स

एव क्रियते इति लाभमिच्छतो मूलक्षतिरायाता । कृतकत्वेन तस्यानित्यत्वापत्तेः) If, on the other hand, it (उपकार) is different from the नित्य thing itself, how can it affect the नित्य thing at all, any more than the Sahya mountain can affect the Vindhya mountain? (This is only an example to illustrate two disconnected things which have no influence upon each other). It may be argued that the assistance (उपकार) is neither identical with the thing to which it is rendered, nor is it separate from it, but it *belongs* to it (तत्संबन्धात् तस्यायम्). To this argument we reply by a question: What is the relation between the thing assisted (उपकार्य—the नित्य thing of our hypothesis) and the assistance itself (उपकार)? It cannot be संयोग; for, संयोग exists only between two द्रव्यs, whereas in the present case the thing assisted (उपकार्य) is a द्रव्य and the assistance itself (उपकार) is a क्रिया. Nor can the relation be समवाय; for, समवाय is one and all-pervading, and therefore it cannot be connected with any particular correlates (i.e., these, rather than those), all the correlates being equally far from or equally near to the समवाय (प्रत्यासत्ति-विप्रकर्षाभावेन सर्वत्र तुल्यत्वान्न नियतैः संबन्धिभिः संबन्धो युक्तः). If you hold that the समवाय is connected with particular correlates, it means that those correlates influence (उपकार) the समवाय in a certain manner—in which case the old difficulties (see above) about the influence (उपकार), whether regarded as identical with or different from the समवाय recur: thus, if the उपकार is one with the समवाय, it is nothing more than the समवाय; if it is distinct from the समवाय, the समवाय fails to be the relation of any particular correlate. Therefore nothing that is absolutely नित्य can *gradually do* something and thus fulfil the definition of Reality. Now to take the other alternative, viz., the alternative of the नित्य thing doing its work all *at once*. The objection to it is that nothing is ever known to be doing all its work at a single stroke. Supposing it does, what will remain for it to do in the next moment? Supposing, again, that there does remain some work to do, then the position is the same as the one above considered, viz., that of gradual action, of which it is only an alias. Supposing, however, that it has no work to do in the succeeding moment, it fails to fulfil the definition of Reality and is therefore nothing. Thus, both the alternative hypotheses of gradual or successive action and simultaneous action failing in the case of an absolutely नित्य thing, the activity with which they are concomitant also fails, and with the failure of activity comes non-existence or nothingness. Thus collapses the alternative of absolute नित्यत्व.

Page 19-20,

ll. 143–173. Turn we now to the other alternative, viz., that of absolute अनित्यत्व. An अनित्य thing is one which perishes every moment. Such a thing cannot do any kind of work *successively* (क्रमेण); for, in its case no succession either of time or of space is possible. Thus:—Succession means the relation of before and after, which is impossible in the case of that which has absolutely momentary existence. Only a thing that abides can cover several points of space and time. But the thing which perishes every moment cannot do so. How things fare under the absolute-अनित्यत्व-hypothesis is thus described in a verse "यो यत्रैवं स तत्रैव यो यदैव तदैव सः । न देशकालयोर्व्याप्तिर्भावानामिह विद्यते ॥"—i. e., Things occupy only a certain point of space or time, they do not cover any length of space or time. It may be urged that things no doubt perish in a moment and so do not admit of succession (क्रम), but they form a संतान, i. e., a continuous series, which does not so perish and which consequently makes succession possible. But this assumption will not mend matters. For, there is no such reality as a continuous series. Supposing there is such a real series, if the series is momentary, the position is the same as before, that is, the objection in the case of the single members mentioned above applies to the series as well. If, on the other hand, the series be supposed to be capable of persistence in time, the doctrine of momentariness (क्षणभङ्गवाद) vanishes. Nor can an absolutely अनित्य thing (as supposed by the hypothesis) i. e., that which is only momentary(क्षणिक), do all its work *at once* (अक्रमेण). The dilemma with which the advocate of absolute अनित्यत्व—the

Buddhist—is confronted is this: When a single रूपक्षण [the Buddhist is so obsessed by the idea of क्षणिकत्व, that he calls things 'क्षण's'], when a fruit, for example, simultaneously gives rise to numerous effects such as रसक्षण etc., does it do so by virtue of a single nature or of many natures (एकेन स्वभावेन जनयेन्नानास्वभावैर्वा)? In the former case, there could be no diversity of effects among रस etc., since they all arise from a single—uniform—nature. In the latter case i. e., if it produced रूप etc., as उपादान (the stuff of which the effect is made), and रस etc., as सहकारि (auxiliaries), we would ask whether the many natures (which, by hypothesis, belong to the thing) were the thing itself or otherwise? In the latter case, they could not be *natures* (अनात्मभूताश्चेत् स्वभावत्वहानिः). In the former case, the thing itself would have to be regarded as many (यद्यात्मभूतास्तर्हि तस्यानेकत्वम्); or the natures would have to be regarded as one (स्वभावानां वा एकत्वं प्रसज्येत—तदव्यतिरिक्तत्वात् तेषां तस्य चैकत्वात्). It may be argued that there is no plurality of natures in a thing, the thing acting as उपादान in one place and सहकारि in another. But this will mean that the thing which is नित्य and एकरूप (persistent and possessed of a single nature, uniform), successively produces many effects—an admission of plurality of natures and variety of effects. (स्वभावभेदः कार्यसांकर्यं च). If you object: How can that which is नित्य, and एकरूप (uniform) and therefore अक्रम (acting at once and not by successive steps) give rise to effects which are नाना (various) and क्रमिक (arising in succession)? We retort: If from one single partless रूपादिक्षण acting as a cause there can spring—as you hold—at a single flash, without succession, numerous effects requiring numerous causes, why can not a नित्य thing produce successively a variety of effects? That is to say, the anomaly if any, under one supposition is the same as under the other. Therefore, a thing which is absolutely अनित्य i. e., क्षणिक, fails to show itself to be a reality by doing something *at once*, without succession of steps (तस्मात् क्षणिकस्यापि भावस्याक्रमेणार्थक्रिया दुर्घटा). Thus, both the alternatives of क्रम and अक्रम failing, the अर्थक्रिया

which they cover also fails, and with the failure of अर्थक्रिया goes the failure of existence. Thus, collapses the doctrine of absolute अनित्यत्व, of which the Buddhist is a special advocate.

cf. "अर्थक्रिया न युज्येत नित्यक्षणिकपक्षयोः । क्रमाक्रमाभ्यां भावानां सा लक्षणतया मता ॥" Quoted in Hem.'s Com. प्र. मीमांसा १.१.१९.

It is interesting to read, however, the following remark made by a Jaina writer: " अनेन च सल्लक्षणेन नैयायिकादिपरिकल्पितः सत्तायोगः सत्त्वं बौद्धाभिमतं चार्थक्रियालक्षणं सत्त्वं द्वे अपि प्रतिक्षिप्ते वेदितव्ये॥" (Guṇa. Com. on Ṣad. St. 57) where the अर्थक्रिया is mentioned as the Buddhistic definition of Reality.

Page 20.

ll. 174-180. स्याद्वादे तु पूर्वोत्तराकार० etc.—Now the author shows how things, under the Syâdvâda hypothesis, can *act*, while they possess the three-fold characteristics of the abandonment of previous form, acceptance of a new form, and retention of its own identity. The only possible objection to it is that it involves the attribution of contradictory characteristics to one and the same thing. But the objection can be easily met by an appeal to experience—which favours the view that things are multiform in character, and so the only doctrine which tallies with experience and therefore with truth, is that things are neither exclusively नित्य nor अनित्य, but are in reality both—like the Nara-Siṁha (Man-Lion) of mythology: " न नरः सिंहरूपत्वात् न सिंहो नररूपतः" ("भागे सिंहो नरो भागे योऽर्थो भागद्वयात्मकः। तमभागं विभागेन नरसिंहं प्रचक्षते।").

ll. 181-183. वैशेषिकैरपि etc.—The Vais'eṣikas, too, hold doctrines which can be easily shown to savour of Syâdvâda—though they would not like to admit it. Thus, for example, they recognise चित्ररूप (which really amounts to contradictory रूपs) in a single body or substance; one and the same substance is described as moving or stationary; one and the same object—a घट, for example, is supposed to be both red and not-red (the former when it is hot, the latter when it is not so), covered and open etc.

cf. " एकमेव चित्रपटादेरवयविनो रूपं विचित्राकारमभ्युपयन्ति। न च विरोधमाचक्षते। तदुक्तं कन्दल्याम्। विरोधादिकमनेकस्वभावमयुक्तमिति चेन्न। तथा च प्रावादुकप्रवादः। एकं चेत्तत् कथं चित्रं चेत्येतच्चित्रतरं मतम्। इति को विरोध इत्यादि।" Guṇa. Com. on Ṣaḍ. 57.

सौगतैरपि etc.—The Buddhists, similarly, find no contradiction in seeing नील and अ-नील in one and the same चित्रपट. Note that they do not attribute qualities to substances, for they recognise no external reality, but only see certain elements in a particular idea—नील and अनील, for example, in the idea or concept of पट.

ll. 184–188. अत्र च यद्यप्यधिकृतवादिनः etc.—The author finds it necessary to observe that so far as प्रदीप is concerned the Vaiśeṣika unlike the Buddhist does not regard it as क्षणिक (momentary) but only अनित्य (that which has a beginning and an end, not necessarily the short duration of a single moment of time), but even he regards बुद्धि, सुख etc., as क्षणिक just like the Buddhist, and so the question of क्षणिकवाद is not irrelevantly introduced while dealing with the tenets of the Vais'eṣikas. Remember that S'ankara has called the Vais'eṣikas, on this account, 'अर्धवैनाशिकः' i. e., semi-Buddhists. For the क्षणिकत्व of बुद्धि, सुख, etc., in the Vais'eṣika system, see Nyāya-Muktâvali and Com. thereon, Bh. P. Stanza 27.

l. 188. यदापि च कालान्तरावस्थायि etc.—The Vais'eṣika confines क्षणिकत्व to बुद्धि, सुख, etc.—but many a thing he regards as having a certain *duration* in time which is *limited*. Now if you put the ideas of duration, i. e., persistence in time, and limitedness in time together, it will mean the same thing as नित्यानित्यत्व.

l. 189. क्षणोऽपि न खलु सोऽस्ति etc.—There is not a moment of time when a thing does not partake of the three-fold character of उत्पाद, व्यय and ध्रौव्य (see above).

Stanza VI.

Page 21.

The doctrine next criticized is :—

Stanza VI:—(1) There is some maker of the world; (2) He is one; (3) He is everywhere; [(3 *a*) He knows everything.] (4) He is self-dependent; (5) He is eternal.

Criticism :—

I. ll. 3-8 जगतः प्रत्यक्षादि etc.—कश्चित् = अनिर्वचनीयस्वरूप : उर्वीपर्वततर्वादिकं etc.—A syllogism to prove the existence of God. The major premiss on which it rests is 'यद्यत् कार्यं तत्सर्वं बुद्धिमत्कर्तृकं यथा घटः'—

Everything that is *made* requires an intelligent maker—*e.g.* a jar, etc.; the Earth etc. are things made; therefore, (कार्यत्वात्) they have an intelligent maker, whom we call Is'vara or God.

ll. 9. न चायमसिद्धो हेतुः etc.—Here the minor premiss is not "unproven." For, it can be easily shown to be true by *means* of the following argument:—The Earth etc. are things made; because, they spring from definite causes (स्वस्वकारणकलापजन्यतया); also because, they are bodies possessed of parts (अवयवितया).

ll. 10-11. नाप्यनैकान्तिको विरुद्धो वा—Nor is the *hetu* (कार्यत्वात्) in the theistic syllogism either "inconclusive" or "hostile." For, it fully satisfies the condition विपक्षाद्व्यावृत्ति, the violation of which involves the fallacies of "inconclusive" and "hostile" *hetus.* If there be a single case in which the हेतु exists without the साध्य, the हेतु is 'inconclusive' ('अनैकान्तिक'); if the हेतु exists always without the साध्य, it is distinctly 'hostile' ('विरुद्ध'). But in the present case, the हेतु is one which is *never* found where the साध्य is not found (विपक्षाद्व्यावृत्तिः) and is, therefore, a good हेतु (यत्र बुद्धिमत्कार्यकर्तृकत्वं नास्ति तत्र कार्यत्वमपि नास्ति यथा आकाशे).

ll. 11-12. नापि कालात्ययापदिष्टः etc.—Nor is the हेतु "precluded" (बाधित) by प्रत्यक्ष, अनुमान or शब्द having closed the question to the contrary. धर्मधर्म्यनन्तर—*i. e.* stated as a हेतु after the statement of the पक्ष (धर्मिन्) and the साध्य (धर्म).

ll. 13. नापि प्रकरणसमः etc. There is no rival हेतु or अनुमान to prove the opposition. The following may be plausibly advanced as such an अनुमान, but it will fail:

God could not be the maker of the World—the Earth, etc., because he would be wanting in a physical body to accomplish the task, he being like emancipated souls (निर्वृतात्मवत्) whom no one supposes to be world-makers.

This syllogism may be subjected to the following criticism.

Is God–the subject of the proposition to be proved–*known* or *unknown?* If *unknown* the argument involves the fallacy of 'आश्रयासिद्ध' (हेतु affirmed of a subject–पक्ष–which is fictitious). If *known,* there is no reason to think that he is lacking in a body and is, therefore, incapable of making the world. If a body is required for the task, he may be supposed to have got it, by what is called धर्मिग्राहकप्रमाण, that is to say, the प्रमाण which proves a धर्मिन् may be supposed to prove also the धर्मs that are required in the धर्मिन्. [Example: If you assume the existence of a substance called either to explain the phenomenon of light, that substance may be supposed, by the same hypothesis, to possess all those properties that are required to make the phenomenon possible.]

Page 22.

ll. 20. (2) स चैक इति etc.—*God is one.* If there were many gods, *i. e.*, many masters of the world, the world would be thrown into confusion by the conflict of discordant wills; and the very purpose for which we had resorted to the hypothesis of a divine maker, viz., to explain the harmony and order of the Universe, would thereby be defeated.

ll. 24-29. (3a) तथा स सर्वग इति etc.— सर्वगः = *Omnipresent*; because, his activity is wanted everywhere. Or, (3b) सर्वगः = *omniscient*; because intelligent making requires thought or wisdom.

ll. 30-35. (4) तथा स्ववशः—God is *self*-dependent. ईश्वरप्रेरितो etc.—Originally found in the Mahābhārata, Vana-parva. It has has been subsequently reproduced in many works both of Jaina and Brāhmana literature. It means: Impelled by

God, a soul moves to heaven or to hell. No other person is master of his सुख and दुःख. *Self*-dependence is implied in the very notion of one who is the Lord of all.

ll. 36. (5) तथा स नित्यः etc.—He is eternal. A created God is a contradiction in terms. This may be shown by a simple question: Is the Creater of God eternal or not? If he is, why not so God himself? If not, he will have to be supposed to be a creature created by another, and he by another, and so on *ad infinitum.*

Page 23.

l. 45. इमा एताः etc.—कुदेवाकविडम्बना :—ridiculous and false doctrines.

ll. 54. अतोऽत्रा० etc.—The master preaches his doctrine to all, yet all do not benefit by it, because there are some whose minds are so bedimmed by passions that they cannot receive the light of his teaching. It is their fault, not his. कादम्बर्यां बाणोऽपि—See Kād. Nir. ed. p. 196. कौशिक-owl.

ll. 67.-तथा श्रीसिद्धसेनः etc.—Oh friend of the World! Despite your possessing faultless skill in sowing seeds of the right Dharma, even you have had your barren lands. It is not surprising. To birds of darkness (owls) the rays of the sun are as white (ironical : black) as the feet of bees!

Page 24.

ll. 72-75.-II. अथ कथमिव etc.—Here begins a detailed criticism of the theistic syllogism—क्षित्यादयो बुद्धिमत्कर्तृकाः कार्यत्वात् घटवत्.

l. The first objection is that here the व्याप्ति (major premiss) is not known to be sound (व्याप्तेरग्रहणात्). All are agreed that a साधन (हेतु) leads to the inference of साध्य, when the व्याप्ति (*i. e.* its invariable concomittance with the साध्य) is established by प्रमाण. But we are going to show that such व्याप्ति is impossible in the present case.

ll. 75.-स चायं जगन्ति सृजन् etc.—Here is a dilemma: Is God (1) possessed of a *body* or (2) not—when making these worlds? If he is possessed of a body, we should like to know

8

whether the body is (1,a) *visible* like ours, or (1,b) *invisible* like that of a ghost? The former alternative (No. 1,a) is ruled out by प्रत्यक्ष. We do not see any such body working in the production of grass, trees, rain-bows, clouds, etc. Hence the alleged व्याप्ति—यत्र यत्र कार्यत्वं तत्र तत्र सशरीरकर्तृकत्वम्-falls to the ground. The हेतु here is साधारण अनैकान्तिक *i. e.* inconclusive, on account of its being common to things possessed of साध्य and those possessed of साध्याभाव, like the hetu प्रमेयत्व which is inconclusive as to नित्यत्व or अनित्यत्व, being found in things which are नित्य (*e. g.* गगन) and also in things which are अनित्य (*e. g.* घट). The latter alternative (No. 1,b) requires to be made clearer as to whether the invisibility of his body is due to his unique greatness or to any fault of our adṛṣṭa *i. e.* misfortune, caused by the law of Karma—*i.e.* dharma and adharma.—The first of these alternatives is not supported by any proof; moreover, it involves argument in a circle (इतरेतराश्रयदोष) in that his invisible body will be proved when his unique greatness is proved, and his unique greatness will be proved when his invisible body is proved. The second alternative (No. 2) is not free from certain doubts. Thus, a doubt will arise in our mind whether our failure to see his body is due to the fact of his not existing at all (*e. g.* we do not see the body of a son of a barren woman) or to any defect in our adṛṣṭa which incapacitates us for the sight (*e.g.* owing to the same reason we do not see the body of a ghost). Moreover, if God works without a body it is contrary to all our experience of other dṛṣṭântas or examples. For, all the examples of कार्य which we have observed (such as घट etc.) show a maker possessed of a body (such as a potter). Without a body a maker can do nothing: he would be as inactive as आकाश. So the व्याप्ति of the hetu (कार्यत्व) with the sâdhya (सकर्तृकत्व) breaks down when placed on the horns of the dilemma of सशरीरत्व and अशरीरत्व. For the Nyâya-Vais arguments, see न्या. क. Viz. Ed. pp. 55-57, दिनकरी on न्या. मु. on भा. प. St. I.

ll. 90-93-2. Moreover, the *hetu* is 'कालात्ययापदिष्ट' or 'बाधित' as it is otherwise called. For, we see by प्रत्यक्षप्रमाण that certain

कार्यs do spring into existence even without an intelligent maker, *e. g.* a tree, a lightning, a cloud etc., in fact all natural phenomena which we do not see created by man or any other living being.

So we conclude: "न कश्चिज्जगतः कर्ता."

Page 25.

Mallisena next proceeds to examine the so called attributes of God viz. एकत्व, सर्वगत्व etc.

ll. 96. तत्रैकत्वचर्चस्तावत् etc.—God is supposed to be *one*, because, it is said, multiplicity of gods would mean multiplicity of wills, with its necessary corollary,—a conflict of wills and the consequent confusion in the making and management of the world. But the Jaina denies the necessity of the corollary and in support of his position he cites the examples of (1) an anthill made by many ants, (2) that of a palace made by many artizans and (3) that of a beehive made by many bees—all working harmoniously together to a common end.

अथ तेष्वप्येक etc.—Some might see one Supreme Maker behind each of these makers viz. the ants, the bees etc. But they may well be asked: Why not say then that God is the maker of घट, पट etc. instead of the potter, the weaver etc.? * If you say their agency is too visible to be denied we should like to know how the agency of the ants and the bees is any the less visible. cf. Sîl.'s Com. on the Sûtrâkṛ. p. 79 "अपि च—घटादिसंस्थानानां कुम्भकार एव विशिष्टः कर्तोपलक्ष्यते नेश्वरः । यदि पुनरीश्वरः स्यात् किं कुम्भकारेणेति ? । नैतदस्ति । तत्रापीश्वर एव सर्वव्यापितया निमित्तकारणत्वेन व्याप्रियते । नन्वेवं दृष्टहानिरदृष्टकल्पना स्यात् । तथा चोक्तम्—शस्त्रौषधादिसंबन्धाच्चैत्रस्य व्रणरोहणे । असंबद्धस्य किं स्थाणोः कारणत्वं न कल्प्यते ? । तदेवं दृष्टकारणपरित्यागेनादृष्टपरिकल्पना न न्याय्येति । अपि च—देवकुलावटादीनां यः कर्ता स सावयवोऽव्याप्यनित्यो दृष्टः तद्दृष्टान्तसाधितश्चेश्वर एवंभूत एव प्राप्नोति । अन्यथाभूतस्य च दृष्टान्ताभावात् व्याप्त्यसिद्धेर्नानुमानमिति ।" S'il. Com. on सूत्रकृताङ्ग, समयाध्ययन, उद्देशः ३

* [They do say, however, that God is according to them the primary cause, and the potter etc., the secondary causes. See Bh. G., Br. Sûtras etc., cf. Martineau's Study of Rel. Vol. I.]

ll. 105-107.–तस्माद्वैमत्य etc.—To hold that God is one in order to avoid conflict of wills is like getting rid of a family to avoid quarrelling about food !

l. 108.–तथा सर्वगतत्वमपि etc.—If, as you say, he is omnipresent, it must be either through the body (शरीरात्मना) or through the mind (ज्ञानात्मना). In the former case, his body would fill all space, leaving no room for other objects. The latter alternative is all right, for, we too hold that the Supreme Person (परमपुरुष) pervades the whole Universe with his boundless ज्ञान. But it is not a position which you can take up since your Veda asserts the omnipresence of God in the physical sense. For, your texts such as विश्वतश्चक्षुः etc. declare his physical ubiquity.

l. 115.– यच्चोक्तं etc.—A possible reason for regarding God as physically all-pervasive is this : If God occupied only a particular spot he could not well deal with objects at a distance. But this is bad reasoning. Is the Divine Architect, who is the supposed maker of the three worlds, working like a carpenter through the instrumentality of his body, or through that of his mind? The first would be a long and tedious process if his body is to be supposed to be limited in size to avoid the difficulties of the hypothesis of an infinite body. The second process viz. that of working by the mind will not necessitate physical omnipresence of the deity. Minor gods, all are agreed, dwell in limited worlds of their own and yet work by their mind at great distances. Moreover, the physical omnipresence of God would mean his contamination through contact with all sorts of impurities including residence in hell. It may be urged from the other side that this objection will apply equally to the doctrine which we have accepted viz. that of mental omnipresence of the Supreme Person (the Perfect Man). But this is wrong. It is mistaking the very nature of a *mental* process, in which ज्ञान has not to leave the âtman and travel to the object from a distance. Besides, the argument of contamination is absurd : thought of a dirty thing does not fill the mouth with dirt, or the thought of luxuries provide you with the luxuries themselves.

Page 26.

l. 133.-यत्तु ज्ञानात्मना etc.—This is withdrawing a point which was conceded in a foregoing passage (see supra).

l. 138.-यच्च परे दृष्टान्तयन्ति etc.—The case of ज्ञान is sometimes illustrated by the analogy of the light (किरण-rays) of the sun, which, though a guṇa (attribute) of the sun, travels from the sun to the world which it illumines. But the analogy will not bear scrutiny. The rays are not a guṇa of the sun, but a *dravya* made of luminous matter (pudgala), and the luminosity (light-प्रकाश) which belongs to them as a guṇa never travels out of them.

l. 143.-तथा च धर्मसंग्रहिण्यां etc.—See vv. 370-73. The passage occurs in a discussion about the nature of Jîva. The position of the opponent and the Jaina criticism of the same are very clearly brought out in the text and the Com. of the verses quoted here. These have been explained in the Commentary as follows :—

" ' किरणा गुणा ण......'

ननु किरणा गुणा न भवन्ति किंतु द्रव्यम् । यस्तु तेषां किरणानां प्रकाशः स गुणः । न चासौ प्रकाशरूपो गुणोऽद्रव्यो द्रव्यदेशादन्यत्र वर्तते । ज्ञानं पुनरिदं यत् यस्मादात्मगुणस्ततः स कथमद्रव्यो द्रव्यरहितः सन् अन्यत्र आत्मदेशपरित्यागेन भवेत्? । नैव भवेदिति भावः । तस्माल्लोकान्ते ज्ञानदर्शनादयमात्मा सर्वव्यापी प्रतीयत एव ॥ तदेवं चिरादवबुध्यमानेन परेणाभिहिते सत्याचार्यः सम्यगुत्तरमाह-

' गं तुं ण परिछिंदाइ......'

न ज्ञानं यस्मिन् देशे ज्ञेयमस्ति तस्मिन् देशे गत्वा परिच्छिनत्ति न वरं किंतु आत्मस्थमेव सत् तत् दूरदेशस्थस्यापि ज्ञेयस्य परिच्छेदकमचिन्त्यशक्तेर्विज्ञेयम् अमुमेवार्थं दृष्टान्तेन भावयति—

' लोहोवलस्स सत्ती......'

लोहस्याकर्षक उपलः लोहोपलः । अत्राकृष्याकर्षकभावलक्षणसंबन्धे षष्ठी । यथा राज्ञः पुरुष इत्यत्र पोष्यपोषकभावे तस्य शक्तिरात्मस्थैव सती भिन्नदेशमपि भिन्नस्थ-(लस्थ)मपि लोहमाकर्षन्ती दृश्यते । न च दृष्टे अनुपपन्नं नाम । अतीन्द्रियत्वाच्छक्तीनां कथं तस्या दर्शनमिति चेत् । अत आह—' कार्यप्रत्यक्षा ' कार्यं लोहाकर्षणलक्षणं प्रत्यक्षं यस्याः सा कार्यप्रत्यक्षा । एतदुक्तं भवति—तत्कार्यस्य प्रत्यक्षत्वात् सापि दृश्यत इति व्यवह्रियत इत्यदोषः ॥" ध. सं. vv. 370-73 etc., Com.

Page 27.

ll. 144.–किरणा॰—This formulates the objection: The rays of the sun are not guṇas but dravya; and so little wonder that they travel out of the Sun; luminosity is their guṇa, which cannot go out of the dravya. Similarly, ज्ञान is a guṇa of âtman and it cannot travel out of âtman.

गं तुं णं etc.—Wonderful is the nature of ज्ञान it has not to go out to the spot of its object—it remains in âtman and works at a distance. If an analogy is wanted it is afforded in a magnet—which is wellknown for its *actio in distans.*

ll. 153-194.–अथ सर्वगः सर्वज्ञः etc.—Taking सर्वग=omniscient. The doctrine of the omniscience of God can be easily disproved by means of the following dilemma: Is the *omniscience* of God proved by प्रत्यक्ष or परोक्ष (i. e. अनुमान or शब्द)? Not the former. For, प्रत्यक्ष springs from the contact of इन्द्रिय and अर्थ, which is not possible in the case of omniscience which transcends the employment of इन्द्रिय s. Not the latter—in the shape of अनुमान. For, अनुमान is based upon the recollection of an invariable concomittance between लिङ्ग (हेतु) and लिङ्गिन् (साध्य) and we do not know of any लिङ्ग which can prove omniscience—the latter being too far away from the field of our observation.

It may be argued that the अनुमान in the present case is of the nature of अर्थापत्ति, that is to say, omniscience is inferred as necessarily implied in the wonderful variety of the cosmos. But the argument is wrong. There is no necessary implication of omniscience contained in the variety of the Cosmos, which can be easily explained by the law of karma in the case of living beings and by an uncaused natural state of things in the case of inanimate matter. Nor is there any testimony of शब्द or आगम to prove the omniscience. Is the आगम (1) made by God or (2) made by any other person? (1) If it is made by God, it is a wonderful self-laudatory document—hardly worthy of true greatness. Moreover, it is impossible that he could have given out the âgamas without a physical body, the very utterance of the sounds of their letters requiring a throat, a palate etc., (cf. Br. Sû. II. ii. 38-40.) And if he has a body, it is a position which has been already disposed of (see above). (2) If it is made by any other person, is that person (2a) omniscient or (2b) not? (2a) If he is omniscient, God is one such person and here is another—a position which militates against the unity and singularity of God. Besides, the omniscience of the other person will require to be demonstrated by the word of a third person, who must be also omniscient, and so on *ad infinitum*. (2b) If he is not omniscient, what faith can we put in his word ?

Page 28.

ll. 174.-अपरं च भवदभीष्ट etc.—The author next proceeds to show that if God is the source of the Brahmanical scriptures, he is anything but omniscient. For, the Brahmanical scriptures, says the writer, are full of contradictions.

ll. 175-178.-तथाहि etc.—The passage that follows is taken verbatim from Gunaratna's T. R. D. p. 261-62. The conflicting texts quoted therein are selected with reference to the vratas or moral precepts of the Jainas viz. अहिंसा, सत्य, अदत्तादान (अस्तेय), ब्रह्मचर्य together with अपरिग्रह.

ll. 199.-तथा स्ववशत्वं etc.—If God is self-dependent and at the same time all-merciful, why should he create a world full of misery ? There is nothing to prevent him from creating a perfect world. Not even his independent will ? No. For, the will is linked to an all-merciful nature. cf. S'ankara on Br. Sû. II. ii. 37.

l. 201-02.-स्थपुटितं—Full of ; शर्म-happiness.

ll. 202.-अथ जन्मान्तरो० etc.—If you propose to reconcile the misery in the world with God's mercy by the hypothesis of *karma*, it will amount to a surrender of the principle of his independence (cf. S'ankara on Br. Sû. II. ii. 37).

ll. 204.-जलाञ्जलि—Funeral libation of water; equivalent to sounding the death-knell.

शिपिविष्ट–Vishṇu, God. विष्टप–a world. घट्टकुट्यां प्रभातम्— Arriving in the morning at a toll-bar. You drove your cart all night in the hope that you would thereby pass the toll-bar unnoticed in the darkness of the night. But unfortunately you reached the toll-bar just when there was daybreak and the officer at the station had got up to do his duty! Hence 'घट्टकुट्यां प्रभातम्' is an idiomatic expression to state that you have arrived at the very position you wanted to avoid all along.

ll. 207.–किं च प्राणिनां etc.—He is not only *dependent* upon the law of *karma* of his creatures for the allotment of happiness and misery in this world, but a further question arises as to who is the maker of the law of karma (धर्माधर्म)? If he has not made it, he is not Iśvara or Lord in regard to it.

ll. 211.–तथा नित्यत्वमपि etc.—If he is eternal, his nature should be eternal, his creativeness should be eternal—he should be ever creating and creating—a process which would never end, and not a single act of creation would ever be complete. And, since an incomplete act is no act (a घट is not a घट before the last moment of completion is reached and it is fit to perform the work for which it was intended for, सत्त्व=अर्थक्रियाकारित्व.), God would be the maker of nothing. If, on the other hand, creativeness were not part of his nature, he could not create the world any more than âkâśa which never creates any world.

Page 30.

ll. 218.–अपि च तस्य etc.–If he has an absolutely eternal nature, and creativeness is part of that nature, he would be ever creating and creating without any possibility of संहार or destruction. If creation and destruction sprang from a single nature—the two would be simultaneous; moreover, it would mean difference of effects (creation *and* destruction) without difference in the cause (a single nature). If you adopt the hypothesis of two natures, one of which (सृष्टि) is put forth at one time and the other (संहार) at the other time, that is tantamount to a confession that his nature is not eternal, but only occasional.

ll. 225-229.–इष्टश्च भवतां etc.—A plurality of natures is attributed to God in the Brahmanical scriptures. Thus, the nature of रजोगुण is active at the time of creation, of तमोगुण at the time of destruction, and of सत्त्वगुण at the time of its existence: ब्रह्मन्, रुद्र and विष्णु.

एवं चावस्थाभेदे etc.—A change of states in God would mean a changing God.

ll. 229.–अथास्तु नित्यः etc.—Granting that God is eternal, how is it that he is not ever-creating? A possible answer is that it depends upon his free and independent *will* when to be engaged in the act of creation and when not, and hence the creation is occasional. But the answer is futile. On what should his will depend? On him and him only? If so, it should be eternally there, and the creative activity should be eternal and not occasional and spasmodic.

ll. 232.–तथा शम्भोरष्टगुणा० etc.—God is said to have the following attributes: बुद्धि etc. (For this and small differences on the point see Tarkasamgraha and Com., Kârikâvali with Com. Muktâvalî and Dinakari, and Nyâyakandali p. 57). If these have to be inferred from their effects, they will be of a very unsatisfactary kind, unworthy of God. For, the world we see is by no means perfect. From our imperfect or finite world we can only argue to a finite or imperfect God: See E. Caird's Com. on Kant: Rational Theology; John Caird's "Introduction to the Phil. of Religion," and Flint's "Theism."

ll. 233.– किं च प्रेक्षावतां प्रवृत्तिः etc.—The famous dilemma raised by Mill and S'ankara. Creative activity on the part of God may be supposed to spring either from self-interest or pity for his creatures. The former is impossible in the case of God. The latter is not possible without the presupposition of misery of his creatures which he strives to remove. The misery, however, is impossible without a body and organs to suffer it, and these are not existing prior to creation. Thus, the theist finds himself lost in a vicious circle—pity and misery necessary to account for God's creative activity, and the creative activity necessary for the possibility of misery!

Page 31.

ll. 242.– घण्टालाला०—Going both ways like the pendulum of a bell. For the Jaina argument see Ṣaḍ-Darśana-Samuccaya, Tarka-rahasya-dîpikâ pp. 52-53, 115-24, S'il. Com. on the Sûtrakritânga pp. 42-47).

For the Theistic argument examined in the Stanza and the Com. see न्या. कु. p. 54–56.

For the difficulties of the Theistic position consult Sânkara's Com. on the Br. Su. II. i.i, 37-41 Râmânuja's Com. on the same and on I. i. 3. For an attempt at a solution of some of the difficulties see Br. Su. II. i. 30-36 The point of शरीरित्व will be found suggested by a corresponding passage in न्या. कु. pp. 55–56: cf. " Meanwhile the practical needs and experiences of religion seem to me sufficiently met by the belief that beyond each man and in a fashion continuous with him there exists a larger power which is friendly to him and to his ideals. All that the facts require is that the power should be both other and larger than our conscious selves. Anything larger will do, if only it be large enough to trust for the next step. It need not be infinite, it need not be solitary. It might conceivably even be only a larger and more godlike self, of which the present self would then be but the mutilated expression, and the universe might conceivably be a collection of such selves, of different degrees of inclusiveness, with no absolute unity realized in it at all. Thus would a sort of polytheism return upon us......"

"Upholders of the monistic view will say to such a polytheism (which, by the way, has always been the real religion of common people, and is so still to-day) that unless there be one all-inclusive God, our guarantee of security is left imperfect. In the Absolute, and in the Absolute only *all* is saved. If there be different Gods, each caring for his part, some portion of some of us might not be covered with divine protection, and our religious consolation would thus fail to be complete.............Common sense is less sweeping in its demand than philosophy.........I think, in fact, that a final philosophy of religion will have to consider the pluralistic hypothesis more seriously than it has hitherto been willing to consider it"—James's Varieties of Religious Experience p. 526.

" This [a belief in more gods than one] of itself is what reason cannot rest in—what reason is constantly finding out more clearly to be false. The more the universe is examined and understood, the more apparent does it become that it is a single, self-consistent whole—a vast unity in which nothing is isolated or independent. The very notion, therefore, of separate and independent deities, and still more, of course, of discordant or hostile deities ruling over different departments of nature, is opposed to the strivings and findings of reason " Flint's " Theism " pp. 40–41.

For the Design Argument in its old form see Paley's "Natural Theology", and for its defence against later criticism, see Flint's " Theism;" and for a history of the Teleological Argument, Flint's Theism pp. 387–90.

For the whole subject of Theistic proofs, see ibid, Lectures IX to end. Among modern writings on the subject in addition to Flint's " Theism " and Anti-Theistic Theories the reader may consult Kant's criticism of Cartesian proofs and Rational Theology, and the statement of difficulties in the design argument in the old orthodox form and a reinterpretation of the argument in John Caird's "Philosophy of Religion," and Edward Caird's Com. on Kant. Consult also Martineau's " Study of Religion " Vol I, Fraser's "Theism" (Kantian presentation of the subject), Lindsay's "Recent Advances in Theism," Pringle-Pattison's " Idea of God," Ward's " Realm of Ends " and Alexander's " Space, Time and Deity."

Appendices.

1.

किं पुनरीश्वरसद्भावे प्रमाणम्?। आगमस्तावदनुमानं च। महाभूतचतुष्टयमुपलब्धिमत्पूर्वकं, कार्यत्वात्, यत्कार्यं तदुपलब्धिमत्पूर्वकम्। प्रमाणेन पूर्वकोट्यनुपलब्धेरसिद्धं पृथिव्यादिषु कार्यत्वमिति चेत्। तदयुक्तम्। सावयवत्वात्। यत्सावयवं तत्कार्यं, यथा घटः, सावयवं च पृथिव्यादि, तस्मादेतदपि कार्यमेव। ननु व्याप्तिग्रहणादनुमानप्रवृत्तिः। कार्यत्वबुद्धिमत्पूर्वकत्वयोश्च व्याप्तिग्रहणमशक्यं, घटादिषु कर्तृप्रतीतिकाल एवाङ्कुरादिषूत्पद्यमानेषु तदभावप्रतीतेः। न चाङ्कुरादीनामपि पक्षत्वमिति न्याय्यम्। गृहीतायां व्याप्तावनुमानप्रवृत्तिकाले प्रतिवाद्यपेक्षया पक्षादि प्रविभागः। इह तु सर्वदैव प्रतिपक्षप्रतीत्याक्रान्तत्वाद्व्याप्तिग्रहणमेव न सिध्यतीत्युक्तम्। अत्र प्रतिविधीयते। यदि चैवं द्वैतानुपलम्भाद्व्याप्तिग्रहणाभावः, तदानीं मीमांसाभाष्यकृदभिमतं सामान्यतोदृष्टमादित्यगत्यनुमानमपि न सिध्यति। तत्रापि देवदत्तगतिपूर्वकदेशान्तरप्राप्तिग्रहणकाल एवं नक्षत्रादिषु देशान्तरप्राप्तिमात्रोपलम्भात्। अथ तेषु देशविप्रकर्षेणापि गतेरनुपलब्धौ संभवन्त्यां न तया व्याप्तिग्रहणहेतोर्निरुपाधिप्रवृत्तस्य भूयोदर्शनस्य प्रतिरोधस्तुल्यकक्षत्वाभावात्। एवं चेत् अत्राशरीरत्वेनाभ्युपेतस्य कर्तुः स्वरूपविप्रकर्षेणाप्यङ्कुरादिष्वनुपलम्भसंभवान्न तेन निरुपाधिप्रवृत्तस्य भूयोदर्शनस्य सामर्थ्यमुपहन्यते इति समानम्। अपि च। भोः किमनुमानेन कर्तृमात्रं साध्यते पृथिव्यादिनिर्माणसमर्थो वा?। कर्तृमात्रसाधने तावदभिप्रेतासिद्धिः। न ह्यस्मदादिसदृशः कर्ताऽभिप्रेतो भवताम्। न च तेनेदं पृथिव्यादिकार्यमर्वाग्दृशा शक्यनिर्माणम्। पृथिव्यादिनिर्माणसमर्थस्तु कर्ता न सिध्यति। अनन्वयात्। अन्वयबलेन हि दृष्टान्तदृष्टकर्तृसदृशः सिध्यतीति। नायं प्रसङ्गः। कर्तृविशेषस्याप्रसाधनात्। व्याप्तिसामर्थ्याद्बुद्धिमत्पूर्वकत्वे सामान्ये साध्यमाने, पृथिव्यादिनिर्माणसामर्थ्यलक्षणोऽपि विशेषः सिध्यत्येव। निर्विशेषस्य सामान्यस्य सिद्ध्यभावात्। ननु मा सिध्यतु सामान्यमिति चेन्न। कार्यत्वेन सह तद्व्याप्तेरप्रतिक्षेपत्वात्। यदि हि व्याप्तमपि न सिध्यति धूमादप्यग्निसामान्यं न सिध्येत्। अग्निविशेषस्यानन्वितस्यासिद्धेः। निर्विशेषस्यानवस्थानात्। अथेदमुच्यते द्वयमनुमानस्य स्वरूपं व्याप्तिः पक्षधर्मता च। तत्र व्याप्तिसामर्थ्यात् सामान्यं सिध्यति, पक्षधर्मताबलेन चाभिप्रेतो विशेषः पर्वताद्यवच्छिन्नवह्निलक्षणात्मा सिध्यति। अन्यथा पक्षधर्मतायाः क्वोपयोगः?। क्व चानुमानस्य गृहीतग्राहिणः प्रामाण्यम्?। एवं चेत् ईश्वरानुमानेऽपि तुल्यम् अन्यत्राभिनिवेशात्। अथ मतं सिध्यत्यनुमाने विशेषोऽपि। यत्र प्रमाणविरोधो नास्ति तथा हि धूमात् पर्वतनितम्बवृत्तिवह्निविशेषसिद्धौ का नामानुपपत्तिः?। दृष्टो हि देशकालादिभेदः स्वलक्षणानाम्। ईश्वरानुमाने तु विशेषो न सिध्यति। प्रमाणविरोधात्। तथा हि नात्र शरीरपूर्वकत्वं साधनीयम्। शरीरे सत्यवश्यमिन्द्रियप्राप्तावतीन्द्रियोपादानोपकरणादिकारकशक्तिपरिज्ञानासंभवे सति कर्तृत्वासंभवात्। अशरीरपूर्वकत्वं चाशक्यसाधनं सर्वोऽपि कर्ता कारकस्वरूपमवधारयति तत इच्छतीदमहमनेन

निर्वर्तयामीति । ततः प्रयतते । तदनु कायं व्यापारयति । ततः करोति । अनवधारयन्ननिच्छन्नप्रयतमानः कायमव्यापारयन्न करोतीत्यन्वयव्यतिरेकाभ्यां बुद्धिवच्छरीरमपि कार्योत्पत्तावुपायभूतं निखिलोपाधिग्रहणे व्याप्तिग्राहकप्रमाणादेवावधारितं न शक्यते प्रहातुम् । वह्नेरिवेन्धनविकारसामर्थ्यं धूमानुमाने । तत्परित्यागे च बुद्धिरपि परित्यज्यताम् । प्रभावातिशयादशरीरवदबुद्धिमानेवायमीश्वरः करिष्यति । उपादानोपकरणादिस्वरूपानभिज्ञो न शक्नोतीति चेत् कुत एतत् ? । तथानुपलम्भादिति चेत् फलितं ममापि मनोरथद्रुमेण । न तथा यावदिच्छा प्रयत्नव्यवहिता कार्योत्पत्तावुपयुज्यते यथेदमव्यवहितव्यापारं शरीरम् । एवं तर्हि का गतिरत्र बुद्धिमत्कर्तृपूर्वकत्वसामान्यस्य ? । अगतिरेव । उभयोरपि शरीरत्वाशरीरत्वविशेषयोरनुपपत्तेः । निर्विशेषस्य सामान्यस्य सिद्ध्यभावात् । किमनुमानस्य दूषणम् ? । न किंचित् । पुरुष एवायं विशेषाभावाच्छशविषाणायमाने साधनानर्हे सामान्ये साधनं प्रयुञ्जानो निगृह्यते यथा कश्चिन्निशितं कृपाणमच्छेद्यमाकाशं प्रति व्यापारयन् । अथानुमानदूषणं विना न तुष्यति भवान् तदिदमशरीरिपूर्वकतानुमानं व्याप्तिग्राहकप्रमाणबाधितत्वात् कालात्ययापदिष्टं व्याप्तिबलेन चाभिप्रेतमशरीरित्वविशेषं विरुन्धद्विशेषविरुद्धं ततश्च विरुद्धावान्तरप्रभेद एवेति पूर्वपक्षसंक्षेपः ॥ अत्र प्रतिसमाधिः । किं शरीरत्वमेव कर्तृत्वमुत परिदृष्टसामर्थ्यकारकप्रयोजकत्वम् ? । न तावच्छरीरित्वमेव कर्तृत्वम् । सुषुप्तस्योदासीनस्य च कर्तृत्वप्रसङ्गात् । किंतु परिदृष्टसामर्थ्यकारकप्रयोजकत्वम् । तस्मिन् सति कार्योत्पत्तेः । तच्चाशरीरस्यापि निर्वहति यथा स्वशरीरप्रेरणायामात्मनः । अस्ति तत्राप्यस्य स्वकर्मोपार्जितं तदेव शरीरमिति चेत् सत्यमस्ति । परं प्रेरणोपायो न भवति । स्वात्मनि क्रियाविरोधात् । प्रेर्यतयास्तीति चेत् ईश्वरस्यापि प्रेर्यः परमाणुरस्ति । ननु स्वशरीरे प्रेरणाया इच्छाप्रयत्नाभ्यामुत्पत्तेरिच्छाप्रयत्नयोश्च सति शरीरे भावादसत्यभावात् अस्ति तस्य स्वप्रेरणायामिच्छाप्रयत्नजननद्वारेणोपायत्वमिति चेन्न । तस्येच्छाप्रयत्नयोरुपजननं प्रत्येव कारकत्वात् लब्धात्मकयोरिच्छाप्रयत्नयोः प्रेरणाकरणकाले तु तदनुपायभूतमेव शरीरं कर्मत्वादिति व्यभिचारः । अनपेक्षितशरीरव्यापारस्येच्छाप्रयत्नमात्रसचिवस्यैव चेतनस्य कदाचिदचेतनव्यापारं प्रति सामर्थ्यदर्शनात् बुद्धिमदव्यभिचारि तु कार्यत्वमितीश्वरसिद्धिः । इच्छाप्रयत्नोत्पत्तावपि शरीरमपेक्षणीयमिति चेत् अपेक्षतां यत्र तयोरागन्तुकत्वम् । यत्र पुनरिमौ स्वाभाविकावासाते तत्रास्यापेक्षणं व्यर्थम् । न च बुद्धीच्छाप्रयत्नानां नित्यत्वे कश्चिद्विरोधः । दृष्टा हि रूपादीनां गुणानामाश्रयभेदेन द्वयी गतिः नित्यताऽनित्यता च तथा बुद्ध्यादीनामपि भविष्यतीति । सेयमीश्वरवादे वादिप्रतिवादिनोः पराकाष्ठा । अतः परं प्रपञ्चः ॥ आत्माधिष्ठिताः परमाणवः प्रवर्तिष्यन्ते इति चेन्न । तेषां स्वकर्मोपार्जितेन्द्रियागणाधीन संविदां शरीरोत्पत्तेः । सर्वविषयावबोधविरहात् । अस्त्यात्मनामपि सर्वविषयव्यापि सहजचैतन्यमिति चेन्न । सहजं शरीरसंबन्धभाजां तत्केनाविलुप्तं येनेदं सर्वत्रापूर्ववदवभासयति । शरीरावरणतिरोधानात् । तदात्मन्येव समाधीयते न बहिर्मुखं भवतीति चेत्, व्यापकत्वेन तस्य विषयसंबन्धानुच्छेदेन नित्यत्वेन च

विषयप्रकाशस्वभावस्यानिवृत्तौ का तिरोधानवाचोयुक्तिः ? । वृत्तिप्रतिबन्धश्चैतन्यतिरोधानमिति चेत् कथं तर्हि शरीरिणां विषयग्रहणम् ? । क्वचिदस्य वृत्तयो न निरुध्यन्ते इति चेत् कुतोऽयं विशेषः?। इन्द्रियप्रत्यासत्तिविशेषात्। यद्येवमिन्द्रियाधीनश्चैतन्यस्य विषयेषु वृत्तिलाभो न संनिधिमात्रनिबन्धनः ! सत्यपि व्यापकत्वे सर्वार्थेषु वृत्त्यभावादिन्द्रियवैयर्थ्यप्रसङ्गाच्च साधूक्तमशरीरिणामात्मनां न विषयावबोध इति । तथा चैके वदन्ति । पराञ्चि खानि व्यतृणत् स्वयंभूस्तस्मात्पराङ्पश्यति नान्तरात्मेति । अनवबोधे च तेषां नाधिष्ठातार इति तेभ्यः परः सर्वार्थदर्शिसहजज्ञानमयः कर्तृस्वभावः कोऽप्यधिष्ठाता कल्पनीयः। चेतनमधिष्ठातारमन्तरेणाचेतनानां प्रवृत्त्यभावात् । स किमेकोऽनेको वा ? । एक इति वदामः । बहूनामसर्वज्ञत्वेऽस्मदादिवदसामर्थ्यादपरेषामनुपयोगात् । न च समप्रधानानां भूयसां सर्वदैकमत्ये हेतुरस्तीति कदाचिदनुत्पत्तिरपि कार्यस्य स्यात् एकाभिप्रायानुरोधेन सर्वेषां प्रवृत्तावेकस्येश्वरत्वं नापरेषाम्। मठपरिषदामिव कार्योत्पत्त्यनुरोधेन सर्वेषामविरोधे प्रत्येकमनीश्वरत्वम् । तदेवं कार्यविशेषेण सिद्धस्य कर्तृविशेषस्य सर्वज्ञत्वान्न कुत्रचिद्वस्तुनि विशेषानुपलम्भः अतो न तन्निबन्धनं मिथ्याज्ञानं मिथ्याज्ञानाभावे च न तन्मूलौ रागद्वेषौ तयोरभावान्न तत्पूर्विका प्रवृत्तिः प्रवृत्त्यभावे च न तत्साध्यौ धर्माधर्मौ तयोरभावात् तज्जयोरपि सुखदुःखयोरभावः सर्वदैव चानुभवसद्भावात् स्मृतिसंस्कारावपि नासाते इत्यष्टगुणाधिकरणो भगवानीश्वर इति केचित्। अन्ये तु बुद्धिरेव तस्याव्याहता क्रियाशक्तिरित्येवं वदन्त इच्छाप्रयत्नावप्यनङ्गीकुर्वाणाः षड्गुणाधिकरणोऽयमित्याहुः । स किं बद्धो मुक्तो वा ?। न तावद्बद्धो बन्धनसमाज्ञातस्य बन्धहेतोः क्लेशादेरसंभवात्। मुक्तोऽपि न भवति बन्धविच्छेदपर्यायत्वान्मुक्तेः । नित्यमुक्तस्तु स्यात् । यदाह भगवान् पतञ्जलिः क्लेशकर्मविपाकाशयैरपरामृष्टः पुरुषविशेष ईश्वर इति ॥ Nyâyakandali pp. 54–57.

2.

"अक्षपादमते देवः सृष्टिसंहारकृच्छिवः ।
विभुर्नित्यैकसर्वज्ञो नित्यबुद्धिसमाश्रयः ॥

अत्र प्रयोगमेवं शैवा व्याहरन्ते। भूभूधरसुधाकरदिनकरमकराकरादिकं बुद्धिमत्पूर्वकं, कार्यत्वात्।यद्यत्कार्यं तत्तद्बुद्धिमत्पूर्वकं यथा घटः।कार्यं चेदम्।तस्माद्बुद्धिमत्पूर्वकम्। यश्चास्य बुद्धिमान् स्रष्टा स ईश्वर एवेत्यन्वयः। व्यतिरेके गगनम्। न चायमसिद्धो हेतुः । भूभूधरादीनां स्वस्वकारणकलापजन्यत्वेनावयवितया वा कार्यत्वस्य जगति सुप्रसिद्धत्वात्। नापि विरुद्धोऽनैकान्तिको वा। विपक्षादत्यन्तं व्यावृत्तत्वात् । नापि कालात्ययापदिष्टः। प्रत्यक्षागमबाध्यमानसाध्यधर्मधर्मिविषये हेतोः प्रवर्तनात्। नापि प्रकरणसमः ।तत्प्रतिपन्थिपदार्थस्वरूपसमर्थनप्रथितप्रत्यनुमानोदयाभावात्। अथ निर्वृत्तात्मवदशरीरत्वादेव न संभवति सृष्टिसंहारकर्तेश्वर इति प्रत्यनुमानोदयात् कथं न प्रकरणसम इति चेत् । उच्यते । अत्र त्वदीयानुमाने साध्यमान ईश्वरो धर्मी त्वया प्रतीतोऽप्रतीतो वाऽभिप्रेयते । अप्रतीतश्चेत् तदा त्वत्परिकल्पितहेतोराश्रया-

सिद्धिदोषः प्रसज्येत। प्रतीतश्चेत् तर्हि येन प्रमाणेन प्रतीतस्तेनैव स्वयमुद्भावितनिजतनुरपि किमिति नाभ्युपेयत इति कथमशरीरत्वम्। ततो न प्रकरणसमदोषता हेतोः। अतः साधूक्तं सृष्टिसंहारकृच्छिव इति। तथा विभुराकाशवत्सर्वजगद्व्यापकः। नियतैकस्थानवर्तित्वे ह्यनियतप्रदेशवर्तिनां पदार्थानां प्रतिनियतयथावन्निर्माणानुपपत्तेः। न ह्येकस्थानस्थितः कुम्भकारोऽपि दूरतरघटादिघटनायां व्याप्रियते। तस्माद्विभुः। तथा नित्यैकसर्वज्ञः। नित्यश्चासावेकश्च नित्यैकः स चासौ सर्वज्ञश्चेति विशेषणत्रयसमासः। तत्र नित्योऽप्रच्युतानुत्पन्नस्थिरैकरूपः कूटस्थः। ईश्वरस्य ह्यनित्यत्वे पराधीनोत्पत्तिसव्यपेक्षया कृतकत्वप्राप्तिः। स्वोत्पत्तावपेक्षितपरव्यापारो हि भावः कृतक इष्यते। कृतकश्चेज्जगत्कर्ता स्यात् तदा तस्याप्यपरेण कर्त्रा भाव्यमनित्यत्वादेव। अपरस्यापि च कर्तुरन्येन कर्त्रा भवनीयमित्यनवस्थानदी दुस्तरा स्यात्। तस्मान्नित्य एवाभ्युपगमनीयः। नित्योऽपि स एकोऽद्वितीयो मन्तव्यो बहूनां हि जगत्कर्तृत्वस्वीकारे परस्परं पृथक्पृथगन्यान्यविसदृशमतिव्यापृतत्वेनैकैकपदार्थस्य विसदृशनिर्माणे सर्वमसमञ्जसमापद्येतेति युक्तमेक इति विशेषणम्। एकोऽपि सर्वज्ञः सर्वपदार्थानां सामस्त्येन ज्ञाता सर्वज्ञत्वाभावे हि विधित्सितपदार्थोपयोगि जगत्प्रसृमरविप्रकीर्णपरमाणुकणप्रचयसम्यक्सामग्रीमीलनाक्षमतया याथातथ्येन पदार्थानां निर्माणं दुर्घटं भवेत्। सर्वज्ञत्वे पुनः सकलप्राणिनां संमीलितसमुचितकारणकलापानुरूप्येण कार्यं वस्तु निर्मिमाणः स्वार्जितपुण्यपापानुमानेन च स्वर्गनरकयोः सुखदुःखोपभोगं ददानः सर्वथौचितीं नातिवर्तेत। तथा चोक्तं तद्भक्तैः—

ज्ञानमप्रतिघं यस्य वैराग्यं च जगत्पतेः।
ऐश्वर्यं चैव धर्मश्च सहसिद्धं चतुष्टयम्॥
अतो जन्तुरनीशोयमात्मनः सुखदुःखयोः
ईश्वरप्रेरितो गच्छेत्स्वर्गं वा श्वभ्रमेव वा॥ Guṇa Com. on षड्. pp. 51–53.

3.

ननु मा भूत्सुगतादिको देवः, जगत्स्रष्टा त्वीश्वरः किमिति नाङ्गीक्रियते?। तत्साधकप्रमाणाभावादिति ब्रूमः। अथास्त्येव तत्साधकप्रमाणम्। क्षित्यादिकं बुद्धिमत्कर्तृकं, कार्यत्वात् घटादिवत्। न चायमसिद्धो हेतुः। क्षित्यादेः सावयवत्वेन कार्यत्वप्रसिद्धेः। तथाहि उर्वीपर्वततर्वादिकं सर्वं कार्यं, सावयवत्वात्, घटवत्। नापि विरुद्धः। निश्चितकर्तृके घटादौ कार्यत्वदर्शनात्। नाप्यनैकान्तिकः। निश्चिताकर्तृकेभ्यो व्योमादिभ्यो व्यावर्तमानत्वात्। नापि कालात्ययापदिष्टः। प्रत्यक्षागमाबाधितविषयत्वात्। न च वाच्यं घटकर्त्रादिदृष्टान्तदृष्टासर्वज्ञत्वासर्वगतत्वकर्तृत्वादिधर्मानुरोधेन सर्वज्ञादिविशेषणविशिष्टसाध्यविपर्ययसाधनाद्विरुद्धो हेतुः। दृष्टान्तश्च साध्यविकलो घटादौ तथाभूतबुद्धिमतोऽभावात् इति। यतः साध्यसाधनयोर्विशेषेण व्याप्तौ गृह्यमाणायां सकलानुमानोच्छेदप्रसक्तिः। किंतु सामान्येनान्वयव्यतिरेकाभ्यां हि व्याप्तिरवधार्यते। तौ चानन्यथाव्यभिचाराच्च विशेषेषु गृहीतु न

शक्यौ। तेन बुद्धिमत्पूर्वकत्वमात्रेण कार्यत्वस्य व्याप्तिः प्रत्येतव्या, न शरीरित्वादिना। न खलु कर्तृत्वसामर्थ्यां शरीरमुपयुज्यते। तद्व्यतिरेकेणापि ज्ञानेच्छाप्रयत्नाश्रयत्वेन च शरीरकरणे कर्तृत्वोपलम्भात्। अकिंचित्करस्यापि सहचरत्वमात्रेण कारणत्वे वह्निपैङ्गल्यस्यापि धूमं प्रति कारणत्वप्रसङ्गः स्यात्। विद्यमानेऽपि हि शरीरे ज्ञानादीनां समस्तानां व्यस्तानां वाभावे कुलालादावपि कर्तृत्वं नोपलभ्यते। प्रथमं हि कार्योत्पादककारणकलापज्ञानं, ततः करणेच्छा, ततः प्रयत्नः, ततः फलनिष्पत्तिरित्यमीषां त्रयाणां समुदितानामेव कार्यकर्तृत्वे सर्वत्राव्यभिचारः। सर्वज्ञता चास्याखिलकार्यकर्तृत्वात्सिद्धा। प्रयोगोऽत्र। ईश्वरः सर्वज्ञोऽखिलक्षित्यादिकार्यकर्तृत्वात्। यो हि यस्य कर्ता स तदुपादानाद्यभिज्ञः, यथा घटोत्पादकः कुलालो मृत्पिण्डाद्यभिज्ञः। जगतः कर्ता चायम्। तस्मात्सर्वज्ञ इति। उपादानं हि जगतः पार्थिवाप्यतैजसवायवीयलक्षणाश्चतुर्विधाः परमाणवः। निमित्तकारणमदृष्टादि, भोक्तात्मा, भोग्यं तन्वादि। न चैतदनभिज्ञस्य क्षित्यादौ कर्तृत्वं संभवत्यस्मदादिवत्। ते च तदीयज्ञानादयो नित्याः, कुलालादिभ्यो विलक्षणत्वात्। एकत्वं च क्षित्यादिकर्तुरनेककर्तृणामेकाधिष्ठातृनियमितानां प्रवृत्त्युपपत्तेः सिद्धम्। प्रसिद्धा हि स्थपत्यादीनामेकसूत्रधारपरतन्त्राणां महाप्रासादिकार्यकरणे प्रवृत्तिः। नच ईश्वरस्यैकरूपत्वे नित्यत्वे च कार्याणां कादाचित्कत्वं वैचित्र्यं च विरुध्यते इति वाच्यम्। कादाचित्कविचित्रसहकारिलाभेन कार्याणां कादाचित्कत्ववैचित्र्यसिद्धौ विरोधासंभवात्। ननु क्षित्यादेर्बुद्धिमद्धेतुकत्वेऽक्रियादर्शिनोऽपि जीर्णकूपादिष्विव कृतबुद्धिरुत्पद्यते। न चात्र सा उत्पद्यमाना दृष्टा। अतो दृष्टान्तदृष्टस्य हेतोर्धर्मिण्यभावादसिद्धत्वम्। तदप्ययुक्तम्। यतः प्रामाणिकमितरं वापेक्ष्येदमुच्यते। यदीतरं, तर्हि धूमादावप्यसिद्धत्वानुषङ्गः। प्रामाणिकस्य तु नासिद्धत्वं, कार्यत्वस्य बुद्धिमत्कर्तृपूर्वकत्वेन प्रतिपन्नाविनाभावस्य क्षित्यादौ प्रसिद्धेः। पर्वतादौ धूमादिवत्। न च यावन्तः पदार्थाः कृतकाः तावन्तः कृतबुद्धिमात्मन्याविर्भावयन्तीति नियमोऽस्ति। खातप्रतिपूरितायां भुव्यक्रियादर्शिनः कृतबुद्ध्युत्पादाभावात्। किंच बुद्धिमत्कारणाभावोऽत्रानुपलब्धितो भवता प्रसाध्यते। एतच्चायुक्तम्। दृश्यानुपलब्धेरेवाभावसाधकत्वोपपत्तेः। न चेयमत्र संभवति। जगत्कर्तुरदृश्यत्वात्। अनुपलब्धस्य चाभावसाध्यत्वे पिशाचादेरपि तत्प्रसक्तिः स्यादिति ॥

अत्र प्रतिविधीयते। तत्र यत्तावत् क्षित्यादेर्बुद्धिमद्धेतुकत्वसिद्धये कार्यत्वसाधनमुक्तं, तत् किं सावयवत्वं १ प्रागसतः स्वकारणसत्तासमवायः २ कृतमितिप्रत्ययविषयत्वं ३ विकारित्वं, ४ वा स्यात्॥ यदि सावयवत्वं, तदेदमपि किमवयवेषु वर्तमानत्वं १ अवयवैरारभ्यमाणत्वं २ प्रदेशवत्त्वं ३ सावयवमितिबुद्धिविषयत्वं ४ वा। तत्राद्यपक्षेऽवयवसामान्येनानैकान्तिकोऽयं हेतुः तद्ध्यवयवेषु वर्तमानमपि निरवयवमकार्यं च प्रोच्यते। द्वितीयपक्षे तु साध्यसमो हेतुः। यथैव हि क्षित्यादेः कार्यत्वं साध्यं, एवं परमाण्वाद्यवयवारभ्यत्वम पि। तृतीयोऽप्याकाशेनानैकान्तिकः। तस्य प्रदेशवत्त्वेऽप्यकार्यत्वात्। प्रसाधयिष्यते चाग्रतोऽस्य प्रदेशवत्त्वम्। चतुर्थकक्षायामपि

तेनैवानेकान्तः। न चास्य निरवयवत्वं व्यापित्वविरोधात्परमाणुवत् ॥ १ ॥ नापि प्रागसतः स्वकारणसत्तासमवायः कार्यत्वं तस्य नित्यत्वेन तल्लक्षणायोगात्। तल्लक्षणत्वे वा कार्यस्यापि क्षित्यादेस्तद्वन्नित्यत्वानुषङ्गात् कस्य बुद्धिमद्धेतुकत्वं साध्यते। किंच योगिनामशेषकर्मक्षये पक्षान्तःपातिन्यप्रवृत्तत्वेन भागासिद्धोऽयं हेतुः तत्प्रक्षयस्य प्रध्वंसाभावरूपत्वेन सत्तास्वकारणसमवाययोरभावात् ॥ २ ॥ कृतमिति प्रत्ययविषयत्वमपि न कार्यत्वं खननोत्सेचनादिना कृतमाकाशमित्यकार्येऽप्याकाशे वर्तमानत्वेनानैकान्तिकत्वात् ॥३॥ विकारित्वस्यापि कार्यत्वे महेश्वरस्यापि कार्यत्वानुषङ्गः। सतो वस्तुनोऽन्यथाभावो हि विकारित्वम्। तच्चेश्वरकार्यस्याप्यस्तीत्यस्यापरबुद्धिमद्धेतुकत्वप्रसङ्गादनवस्था स्यात् अविकारित्वे चास्य कार्यकारित्वमतिदुर्घटमिति ॥४॥ कार्यस्वरूपस्य विचार्यमाणस्यानुपपद्यमानत्वादसिद्धः कार्यत्वादित्ययं हेतुः। किं च। कादाचित्कं वस्तु लोके कार्यत्वेन प्रसिद्धम्। जगतस्तु महेश्वरवत्सदा सत्त्वात्कथं कार्यत्वम्। तदन्तर्गततरुतृणादीनां कार्यत्वात्तस्यापि कार्यत्वे महेश्वरान्तर्गतानां बुद्ध्यादीनां परमाण्वाद्यन्तर्गतानां पाकजरूपादीनां च कार्यत्वात् महेश्वरादेरपि कार्यत्वानुषङ्गः। तथाचास्याप्यपरबुद्धिमद्धेतुककल्पनायामनवस्थापसिद्धान्तश्चानुषज्येते। अस्तु वा यथाकथंचिज्जगतः कार्यत्वं तथापि कार्यमात्रमिह हेतुत्वेन विवक्षितं तद्विशेषो वा। यद्याद्यः तर्हि न ततो बुद्धिमत्कर्तृविशेषसिद्धिः। तेन समं व्याप्त्यसिद्धेः। किंतु कर्तृसामान्यस्य। तथा च हेतोरकिंचित्करत्वं साध्यविरुद्धसाधनाद्विरुद्धत्वं वा। ततः कार्यत्वं कृतबुद्ध्युत्पादकम्। बुद्धिमत्कर्तृगमकं न सर्वम्। सारूप्यमात्रेण च गमकत्वे बाष्पादेरप्यग्निं प्रति गमकत्वप्रसङ्गः। महेश्वरं प्रत्यात्मत्वादेः सादृश्यात्संसारित्वकिंचिज्ज्ञत्वाखिलजगदकर्तृत्वानुमापकानुषङ्गः। तुल्याक्षेपसमाधानत्वात्। ततो बाष्पधूमयोः केनचिदंशेन साम्येऽपि यथा कुतश्चिद्विशेषाद्धूमोऽग्निं गमयति न बाष्पादिः तथा क्षित्यादीतरकार्यत्वयोरपि कश्चिद्विशेषोऽभ्युपगम्यः ॥

अथ द्वितीयः तर्हि हेतोरसिद्धत्वं कार्यविशेषस्याभावाद्भावे वा जीर्णकूपप्रासादादिवदक्रियादर्शिनोऽपि कृतबुद्ध्युत्पादकत्वप्रसङ्गः। समारोपान्नेति चेत् सोऽप्युभयत्राविशेषतः किं न स्यात्। उभयत्र कर्तुरतीन्द्रियत्वाविशेषात्। अथ प्रामाणिकस्यास्त्येवात्र कृतबुद्धिः ननु कथं तस्य तत्र कृतत्वावगमोऽनेनानुमानेनानुमानान्तरेण वा। आद्येऽन्योन्याश्रयः। तथाहि। सिद्धविशेषणाद्धेतोरस्योत्थानं तदुत्थाने च हेतोर्विशेषणसिद्धिरिति। द्वितीयपक्षेऽनुमानान्तरस्यापि सविशेषणहेतोरेवोत्थानम्। तत्राप्यनुमानान्तरात्तत्सिद्धावनवस्था। तन्न कृतबुद्ध्युत्पादकत्वरूपविशेषणसिद्धिः। तथा च विशेषणासिद्धत्वं हेतोः। खातप्रतिपूरितभूनिदर्शनेन कृतकानामात्मनि कृतबुद्ध्युत्पादकत्वनियमाभावः इति तदप्यसत् तत्राकृत्रिमभूभागादिसारूप्यस्य तदनुत्पादकस्य सद्भावात्तदनुत्पादकस्योपपत्तेः। नच क्षित्यादावप्यकृत्रिमसंस्थानसारूप्यमस्ति, येनाकृत्रिमत्वबुद्धिरुत्पद्यते। तस्यैवानभ्युपगमात्। अभ्युपगमे चापसिद्धान्तप्रसक्तिः स्यादिति। कृतबुद्ध्युत्पादकत्वविशेषणासिद्धेर्विशेषणासिद्धत्वं हेतोः। सिध्यतु वा तथाप्यसौ विरुद्धः। घटादाविव शरीरादिविशिष्टस्यैव बुद्धिमत्कर्तुरत्र प्रसाधनात्। नन्वेवं

दृष्टान्तदार्ष्टान्तिकसाम्यान्वेषणे सर्वत्र हेतूनामनुपपत्तिरिति चेत् न। धूमाद्यनुमाने महानसेतरसाधारणस्याग्नेः प्रतिपत्तेः। अत्राप्येवं बुद्धिमत्सामान्यप्रसिद्धेर्न विरुद्धत्वमित्यप्ययुक्तं दृश्यविशेषाधारस्यैव तत्सामान्यस्य कार्यत्वहेतोः प्रसिद्धेर्नादृश्यविशेषाधारस्य। तस्य स्वप्नेऽप्यप्रतीतेः। खरविषाणाधारतत्सामान्यवत्। ततो यादृशात्कारणाद्यादृशं कार्यमुपलब्धं तादृशादेव तादृश्यमनुमातव्यं यथा यावद्धर्मात्मकाद्वह्नेर्यावद्धर्मात्मकस्य धूमस्योत्पत्तिः सुदृढप्रमाणात्प्रतिपन्ना तादृशादेव धूमात्तादृशस्यैवाग्नेरनुमानमिति। एतेन साध्यसाधनयोर्विशेषेण व्याप्तौ गृह्यमाणायां सर्वानुमानोच्छेदप्रसक्तिरित्याद्यपास्तं द्रष्टव्यमिति। तथाकृष्टप्रभवैस्तरुतृणादिभिर्व्यभिचार्ययं हेतुः। द्विविधानि कार्याण्युपलभ्यन्ते, कानिचिद्बुद्धिमत्पूर्वकाणि यथा घटादीनि कानिचित्तु तद्विपरीतानि यथाकृष्टप्रभवतृणादीनि। तेषां पक्षीकरणादव्यभिचारे स श्यामस्तत्पुत्रत्वादितरतत्पुत्रवदित्यादेरपि गमकत्वप्रसङ्गान्न कश्चिद्धेतुः व्यभिचारी स्यात् व्यभिचारविषयस्य सर्वत्रापि पक्षीकर्तुं शक्यत्वात्। ईश्वरबुद्ध्यादिभिश्च व्यभिचारः तेषां कार्यत्वे सत्यपि समवायिकारणादीश्वराद्भिन्नबुद्धिमत्पूर्वकत्वाभावात्। तदभ्युपगमे चानवस्था। तथा कालात्ययापदिष्टश्चायं अकृष्टप्रभवाङ्कुरादौ कर्तृभावस्याध्यक्षेणाध्यवसायात् अग्नेरनुष्णत्वे साध्ये द्रव्यत्ववत्। ननु तत्राप्यदृश्य ईश्वर एव कर्तेति चेत् तन्न। यतस्तत्र तत्सद्भावोऽस्मादेवान्यतो वा प्रमाणात्सिध्येत्। प्रथमपक्षे चक्रकम्। अतो हि तत्सद्भावे सिद्धेऽस्यादृश्यत्वेनानुपलम्भसिद्धिः तत्सिद्धौ च कालात्ययापदिष्टत्वाभावः ततश्चास्मात्तत्सद्भावसिद्धिरिति। द्वितीयपक्षोऽप्ययुक्तः, तत्सद्भाववेदकस्य प्रमाणान्तरस्यैवाभावात्। अस्तु वा तत्र तत्सद्भावः तथाप्यस्यादृष्टत्वे शरीराभावः कारणं विद्यादिप्रभावः जातिविशेषो वा। प्रथमपक्षे कर्तृत्वानुपपत्तिः अशरीरत्वात् मुक्तात्मवत्। ननु शरीराभावेऽपि ज्ञानेच्छाप्रयत्नाश्रयत्वेन शरीरकरणे कर्तृत्वमुपपद्यत इत्यप्यसमीक्षिताभिधानं शरीरसंबन्धेनैव तत्प्रेरणोपपत्तेः शरीराभावे मुक्तात्मवत्तदसंभवात्। शरीराभावे च ज्ञानाद्याश्रयत्वमप्यसंभाव्यं तदुत्पत्तावस्य निमित्तकारणत्वात्। अन्यथा मुक्तात्मनोऽपि तदुत्पत्तिप्रसक्तेः। विद्यादिप्रभावस्य चादृश्यत्वहेतुत्वे कदाचिदसौ दृश्यते न खलु विद्याभृतां शाश्वतिकमदृश्यत्वं दृश्यते पिशाचादिवत्। जातिविशेषोपि नादृश्यत्वे हेतुरेकस्य जातिविशेषाभावादनेकव्यक्तिनिष्ठत्वात्तस्य। अस्तु वा दृश्योऽदृश्यो वासौ तथापि किं सत्तामात्रेण १ ज्ञानवत्त्वेन २ ज्ञानेच्छाप्रयत्नवत्त्वेन ३ तत्पूर्वकव्यापारेण ४ ऐश्वर्येण ५ वा क्षित्यादेः कारणं स्यात्। तत्राद्यपक्षे कुलालादीनामपि जगत्कर्तृत्वमनुषज्यते सत्त्वाविशेषात्। द्वितीये तु योगिनामपि कर्तृत्वापत्तिः। तृतीयोऽप्यसाम्प्रतः। अशरीरस्य पूर्वमेव ज्ञानाद्याश्रयत्वप्रतिषेधात्। चतुर्थोऽप्यसंभाव्यः। अशरीरस्य कायवाक्कृतव्यापारवत्त्वासंभवात्। ऐश्वर्यमपि ज्ञातृत्वं कर्तृत्वमन्यद्वा। ज्ञातृत्वं चेत् तत्किं ज्ञातृत्वमात्रं सर्वज्ञातृत्वं वा। आद्यपक्षे ज्ञातैवासौ स्यान्नेश्वरः अस्मादाद्यन्यज्ञातृत्ववत्। द्वितीयेऽप्यस्य सर्वज्ञत्वमेव स्यान्नैश्वर्यं सुगतादिवत्। अथ कर्तृत्वं, तर्हि कुम्भकारादीनामप्यनेककार्यकारिणामैश्वर्यप्रसक्तिः। नाप्यन्यत्

इच्छाप्रयत्नव्यतिरेकेणान्यस्यैश्वर्यनिबन्धनस्येश्वरेऽभावात् ॥ किं चेश्वरस्य जगन्निर्माणे यथारुचि प्रवृत्तिः १ कर्मपारतन्त्र्येण २ करुणया ३ क्रीडया ४ निग्रहानुग्रहविधानार्थं ५ स्वभावतो ६ वा । अत्राद्यविकल्पे कदाचिदन्यादृश्येव सृष्टिः स्यात् । द्वितीये स्वातन्त्र्यहानिः । तृतीये सर्वमपि जगत्सुखितमेव करोति । अथेश्वरः किं करोति ! पूर्वार्जितैरेव कर्मभिर्वशीकृता दुःखमनुभवन्ति । तदा तस्य कः पुरुषकारः । अदृष्टापेक्षस्य च कर्तृत्वे किं तत्कल्पनया । जगतस्तदधीनतैवास्तु । चतुर्थपञ्चमयोस्तु रागद्वेषवत्ताभावः प्रसज्यते । तथा हि रागवानीश्वरः क्रीडाकारित्वाद्बालवत् तथा अनुग्रहप्रदत्वाद्राजवत् तथा द्वेषवानसौ निग्रहप्रदत्वात्तद्वदेव इति । अथ स्वभावतः तर्ह्यचेतनस्यापि जगत एव स्वभावतः प्रवृत्तिरस्तु किं तत्कर्तृकल्पनयेति । न कार्यत्वहेतुर्बुद्धिमन्तं कर्तारमीश्वरं साधयति । एवं संनिवेशविशिष्टत्वादचेतनोपादानत्वादभूतभावित्वादित्यादयोऽपि स्वयमुत्थाप्याः तुल्याक्षेपसमाधानत्वात् । किं च क्षित्यादेर्बुद्धिमत्पूर्वकत्वे साध्ये प्रदीयमानाः सर्वेऽपि हेतवो विरुद्धाः । दृष्टान्तानुग्रहेण सशरीरासर्वज्ञासर्वकर्तृपूर्वकत्वसाधनात् । न च धूमात्पावकानुमानेऽप्ययं दोषः तत्र तार्णपार्णादिविशेषाधारवह्निमात्रव्याप्तस्य धूमस्य दर्शनात् । नैवमत्र सर्वज्ञकर्तृविशेषाधिकरणतत्सामान्येन कार्यत्वस्यास्ति व्याप्तिः सर्वज्ञस्य कर्तुरतोऽनुमानात्प्रागसिद्धेः । व्यभिचारिणश्चामी बुद्धिमन्तमन्तरेणापि विद्युदादीनां प्रादुर्भावविभावनात् स्वप्नाद्यवस्थायामबुद्धिमत्पूर्वस्यापि कार्यस्य दर्शनाच्चेति । कालात्ययापदिष्टाश्चैते । प्रत्यक्षागमबाधितपक्षानन्तरं प्रयुक्तत्वात् । तद्बाधा च पूर्वमेव दर्शिता । प्रकरणसमाश्चामी। प्रकरणचिन्ताप्रवर्तकानां हेत्वन्तराणां सद्भावात् । तथा हि। ईश्वरो जगत्कर्ता न भवति निरुपकरणत्वात् दण्डचक्रचीवराद्युपकरणरहितकुलालवत् तथा व्यापित्वादाकाशवत् एकत्वात्तद्वदित्यादय इति । नित्यत्वादीनि तु विशेषणानि तद्व्यवस्थापनायानीयमानानि षण्ढं प्रति कामिन्या रूपसम्पन्निरूपणप्रायाण्यपकर्षणीयान्येव ॥ विचारासहत्वाख्यापनार्थं तु किंचिदुच्यते । तत्रादौ नित्यत्वं विचार्यते । तच्चेश्वरे न घटते । तथा हि । नेश्वरो नित्यः स्वभावभेदेनैव क्षित्यादिकार्यकर्तृत्वात् । अप्रच्युतानुत्पन्नस्थिरैकस्वभावं कूटस्थं नित्यमिति हि नित्यत्वलक्षणाभ्युपगमात् । स्वभावभेदानभ्युपगमे च सृष्टिसंहारादिविरुद्धकार्यकारित्वमतिदुर्घटम् । नापि तज्ज्ञानादीनां नित्यत्वं वाच्यम् । प्रतीतिविरोधात् । ईश्वरज्ञानादयो न नित्या ज्ञानादित्वादस्मदादिज्ञानादिवदित्यनुमानविरोधाच्च । एतेन तदीयज्ञानादयो नित्या इत्यादि यदवादि तदपोहितमवगन्तव्यम् । सर्वज्ञत्वमप्यस्य केन प्रमाणेन ग्राह्यम् । न तावत्प्रत्यक्षेण तस्येन्द्रियार्थसन्निकर्षोत्पन्नत्वेनातीन्द्रियार्थग्रहणासमर्थत्वात् । नाप्यनुमानेन अव्यभिचारिलिङ्गाभावात् । ननु जगद्वैचित्र्यान्यथानुपपत्तिरूपं तदस्त्येवेति चेत् न । तेन सहाविनाभावाभावात् । जगद्वैचित्र्यस्य सार्वज्ञ्यं विनापि शुभाशुभकर्मपरिपाकादिवशेनोपपद्यमानत्वात् । किं चायं यदि सर्वज्ञः तदा जगदुपप्लवकरणस्वैरिणः पश्चादपि कर्तव्यनिग्रहानसुरादींस्तदधिक्षेपकृतोऽस्मदादींश्च किमर्थं सृजतीति नायं सर्वज्ञः । तथा बहूनामेककार्यकरणे वैमत्य-

संभावनाभयेन महेशितुरेकत्वकल्पना भोजनादिव्ययभयात् कृपणस्यात्यन्तवल्लभपुत्रकलत्रमित्रादिपरित्यजनेन शून्यारण्यानीसेवनतुलामाकलयति । अनेककीटिकासरघाशतसंपाद्यत्वेऽपि शक्रमूर्धमधुच्छत्रादिकार्याणामेकरूपतया विगानेनोपलम्भात् । किं चेश्वरस्याखिलजगत्कर्तृत्वेऽभ्युपगम्यमाने शास्त्राणां प्रमाणेतरताव्यवस्थाविलोपः स्यात् । तथा हि । सर्वं शास्त्रं प्रमाणमीश्वरप्रणीतत्वादितरप्रणीतशास्त्रवत् प्रतिवाद्यादिव्यवस्थाविलोपश्च सर्वेषामीश्वरादेशविधायित्वेन तत्प्रतिलोमाचरणानुपपत्तेः प्रतिवाद्यभावप्रसङ्गात् । इति न सृष्टिकरस्य महेश्वरस्य कथंचिदपि सिद्धिः । ततः सद्भूतार्थप्रकाशकत्वाद्वीतराग एव सर्वज्ञो देवो देवत्वेनाभ्युपगमनार्हो नापरः कश्चिदिति स्थितम् ॥ Guṇaratna's Com. on षड्०, pp. 115-124.

4.

यत्प्रमाणं सर्वं धरणिधरणीधरतरुपुरप्राकारादिकं बुद्धिमत्पूर्वकं कार्यत्वात् यद्यत् कार्यं तत्तद्बुद्धिमत्पूर्वकं यथा घटः कार्यं चेदं तस्माद्बुद्धिमत्पूर्वकमिति प्रयोगः । स भगवानीश्वर एवेत्यर्थः । व्यतिरेके गगनम् । न चायमसिद्धो हेतुः । भूभूधरादीनां स्वकारणकलापजन्यत्वेनावयवितया वा कार्यत्वस्य जगत्प्रसिद्धत्वात् । नापि विरुद्धानैकान्तिकदोषौ । विपक्षादत्यन्तव्यावृत्तत्वात् । नापि कालात्ययापदिष्टः । प्रत्यक्षानुमानोपमानागमाबाध्यमानधर्मधर्मित्वात् । नापि प्रकरणसमः । तत्परिपन्थिपदार्थस्वरूपसमर्थनप्रथितप्रत्यनुमानोदयाभावात् । अथ निर्वृतात्मशरीरत्वादेव न संभवति सृष्टिसंहारकर्तेश्वर इति प्रत्यनुमानोदयात् कथं प्रकरणसमदूषणाभाव इति चेत् । उच्यते । अत्र साध्यमान ईश्वररूपो धर्मी प्रतीतोऽप्रतीतो वानुमन्यते सुहृदा । अप्रतीतश्चेद्भवत्परिकल्पितहेतोरेवाश्रयासिद्धिदोषप्रसङ्गः । प्रतीतश्चेत्तर्हि येनैव प्रमाणेन प्रतीतस्तेनैव स्वयमुद्भावितस्वतनुरपि किमर्थं नाभ्युपगम्यते इति कथमशरीरत्वम् । अतो न दुष्टो हेतुरिति साधूक्तं सृष्टिसंहारकृच्छिवः । तथा विभुः सर्वव्यापकः । एकनियतयथावन्निर्माणानुपपत्तेः । न ह्येकस्थानस्थित कुम्भकारोऽपि दूरदूरतरघटघटनायां व्याप्रियते । तस्माद्विभुर्भगवान् । तथा नित्यैकः । नित्यश्चासावेकश्चेति यतो नित्योऽत एव एकः । अप्रच्युतानुत्पन्नस्थिरैकरूपं नित्यम् । भगवतो ह्यनित्यत्वे पराधीनोत्पत्तिसव्यपेक्षतया कृतकत्वप्राप्तिः । स्वोत्पत्तावपेक्षितपरव्यापारो हि भावः कृतक इष्यते इति । अथ चेत्कश्चिज्जगत्कर्तारमपरमभिदधाति स एवानुयुज्यते । सोऽपि नित्योऽनित्यो वा । नित्यश्चेदधिकृतेश्वरेण किमपराद्धम् । अनित्यश्चेत्तस्याप्यन्येनोत्पादकान्तरेण भाव्यमनित्यत्वादेव तस्याप्यन्येनेति नित्यानित्यवादविकल्पशिल्पशतस्वीकारे कल्पान्तेऽपि न जल्पसमाप्तिः । तस्मान्नित्य एव भगवान् । अन्यच्चैकोऽद्वितीयः बहूनां हि जगत्कर्तृत्वस्वीकारे परस्परं पृथक् पृथगन्योन्यसदृशमतिव्यापारतयैकैकपदार्थस्य विसदृशनिर्माणे सर्वमसमञ्जसमापद्येतेति भगवानेक एवेति युक्तियुक्तं नित्यैकेतिविशेषणम् । तथा सर्वज्ञ इति सर्वपदार्थानां सर्वविशेषज्ञाता । सर्वज्ञत्वाभावे हि विधित्सितपदार्थोपयोगयोग्यजगत्प्रसृमरविप्रकीर्णपरमाणुकणप्रचयसम्यक्सामग्रीमीलनाक्षमतया याथातथ्येन पदार्थनिर्माण-

रचना दुर्घटा। सर्वज्ञश्च सन् सकलप्राणिनां संमीलितसमुचितकारणकलापानुरूपपरिमाण्डल्यानुसारेण कार्यवस्तु निर्मिमाणः स्वार्जितपुण्यपापानुमानेन च स्वर्गनरकयोः सुखदुःखोपभोगं ददानः केषां नाभिमतः। तथा चोक्तम्—

ईश्वरप्रेरितो गच्छेत्स्वर्गं वा श्वभ्रमेव वा।
अन्यो जन्तुरनीशोऽयमात्मनः सुखदुःखयोः॥ इति Maṇibhadra's Com. on षड्., pp. 12-13.

5.

यदुक्तम्—तनुभुवनकरणादिकं विमत्यधिकरणभावापन्नं विशिष्टबुद्धिमत्कारणपूर्वकं कार्यत्वाद् घटवदिति तदयुक्तम्। तथाविधविशिष्टकारणपूर्वकत्वेन व्याप्त्यसिद्धेः। कारणपूर्वकत्वमात्रेण तु कार्यं व्याप्तं कार्यविशेषोपलब्धौ कारणविशेषप्रतिपत्तिर्गृहीतप्रतिबन्धस्यैव भवति। न चात्यन्तादृष्टे तथा प्रतीतिर्भवति। घटे तत्पूर्वकत्वं प्रतिपन्नमिति चेत् युक्तं तत्र घटस्य कार्यविशेषत्वप्रतिपत्तेः। न त्वेवं सरित्समुद्रपर्वतादौ बुद्धिमत्कारणपूर्वकत्वेन संबन्धो गृहीत इति। नन्वत एव घटसंस्थानविशेषदर्शनवत्पर्वतादावपि विशिष्टसंस्थानदर्शनाद् बुद्धिमत्कारणपूर्वकत्वस्य साधनं क्रियते। नैतदेवं युक्तम्। यतो न हि संस्थानशब्दप्रवृत्तिमात्रेण सर्वस्य बुद्धिमत्कारणपूर्वकत्वावगतिर्भवति। यदि तु स्यात् मृद्विकारत्वाद्वल्मीकस्यापि घटवत् कुम्भकारकृतिः स्यात्। तथा चोक्तम्—"अन्यथा कुम्भकारेण मृद्विकारस्य कस्यचित्। घटादेः करणात् सिध्येद्वल्मीकस्यापि तत्कृतिः"॥ इति। तदेवं यस्यैव संस्थानविशेषस्य बुद्धिमत्कारणपूर्वकत्वेन संबन्धो गृहीतस्तद्दर्शनमेव तथाविधकारणानुमापकं भवति न संस्थानमात्रमिति। Sûtrakṛtâṅga Com., I. iii., pp.43-44.

6.

अत्राहुः—सावयवत्वादेव जगतः कार्यत्वं न प्रत्याख्यातुं शक्यते। भवन्ति च प्रयोगाः। विवादाध्यासितं भूभूधरादि कार्यं सावयवत्वात् घटादिवत्। तथा विवादाध्यासितमवनिजलधिमहीधरादि कार्यं महत्त्वे सति क्रियावत्त्वात् घटवत्। तनुभुवनादि कार्यं महत्त्वे सति मूर्तत्वात् घटवत् इति। सावयवेषु द्रव्येषु इदमेव क्रियते नान्यत् इति कार्यत्वस्य नियामकं सावयवत्वातिरेकरूपान्तरं नोपलभामहे। कार्यत्वप्रतिनियतं शक्यक्रियत्वं शक्योपादानादिविज्ञानत्वं चोपलभ्यत इति चेत् न कार्यत्वेनानुमितेऽपि विषये ज्ञानशक्ती कार्यानुमेये इत्यन्यत्रापि सावयवत्वादिना कार्यत्वं ज्ञातमिति ते च प्रतिपन्ने एवेति न कश्चिद्विशेषः। तथा हि घटमणिकादिषु कृतेषु कार्यदर्शनानुमितकर्तृगततन्निर्माणशक्तिज्ञानः पुरुषोऽदृष्टपूर्वं विचित्रसंनिवेशं नरेन्द्रभवनमालोक्यावयवसंनिवेशविशेषेण तस्य कार्यत्वं निश्चित्य तदानीमेव कर्तुस्तज्ज्ञानशक्तिवैचित्र्यमनुमिनोति। अतस्तनुभुवनादेः कार्यत्वे सिद्धे सर्वसाक्षात्कारतन्निर्माणादिनिपुणः कश्चित् पुरुषविशेषः सिध्यत्येव............

कुलालादीनां दण्डचक्राद्यधिष्ठानं शरीरद्वारेणैव दृष्टमिति जगदुपादानोपकरणाधिष्ठानमीश्वरस्याशरीरस्यानुपपन्नमिति चेत्। न। संकल्पमात्रेणैव परशरीरगतभूतवे-

हालगरलाद्यपगमविनाशदर्शनात् । कथमशरीरस्य परप्रवर्तनरूपः संकल्प इति चेत् । न शरीरापेक्षः संकल्पः शरीरस्य संकल्पहेतुत्वाभावात् । मन एव हि संकल्पहेतुः । तदभ्युपगतमीश्वरेऽपि कार्यत्वेनैव ज्ञानशक्तिवन्मनसोऽपि प्राप्तत्वात् । मानसः संकल्पः सशरीरस्यैव समनस्कत्वादिति चेत् न । मनसो नित्यत्वेन देहापगमेऽपि मनसः सद्भावेनानैकान्त्यात् । अतो विचित्रावयवसंनिवेशविशेषतनुभुवनादिकार्यनिर्माणे पुण्यपापपरवशः परिमितशक्तिज्ञानः क्षेत्रज्ञोऽपि प्रभवतीति निखिलभुवननिर्माणचतुरोऽचिन्त्यापरिमितज्ञानशक्त्यैश्वर्योऽशरीरः संकल्पमात्रसाधनं परिनिष्पन्नानन्तविस्तारविचित्ररचनप्रपञ्चः पुरुषविशेष ईश्वरोऽनुमानेनैव सिध्यति ।

यदुक्तं सावयवत्वादिना कार्यं सर्वं जगत् कार्यं च तदुचितकर्तृविशेषपूर्वकं दृष्टमिति निखिलजगन्निर्माणतदुपादानोपकरणवेदनचतुरः कश्चिदनुमेय इति । तदयुक्तम् । महीमहार्णवादीनां कार्यत्वेऽप्येकदैवैकेन निर्मिता इत्यत्र प्रमाणाभावात् । न चैकस्य घटस्येव सर्वेषामेकं कार्यत्वम् । येनैकदैवैकः कर्ता स्यात् । पृथग्भूतेषु कार्येषु कालभेदकर्तृभेददर्शनेन कर्तृकालैक्यनियमादर्शनात् ।......

भवन्ति च प्रयोगाः—तनुभुवनादि क्षेत्रज्ञकर्तृकम् कार्यत्वात् घटवत् । ईश्वरः कर्ता न भवति प्रयोजनशून्यत्वात् मुक्तात्मवत् । ईश्वरः कर्ता न भवति अशरीरत्वात्तद्वदेव । न च क्षेत्रज्ञानां स्वशरीराधिष्ठाने व्यभिचारः । तत्राप्यनादेः सूक्ष्मशरीरस्य सद्भावात् । विमतिविषयः कालो न लोकशून्यः कालत्वाद्वर्तमानकालवत् इति ।

अपि च किमीश्वरः सशरीरोऽशरीरो वा कार्यं करोति । न तावदशरीरः अशरीरस्य कर्तृत्वानुपलब्धेः । मानसान्यपि कार्याणि सशरीरस्यैव भवन्ति । मनसो नित्यत्वेऽप्यशरीरेषु मुक्तेषु तत्कार्यादर्शनात् । नापि सशरीरः विकल्पासहत्वात् । नापि सशरीरः विकल्पासहत्वात् । तच्छरीरं किं नित्यम् उतानित्यम् । न तावन्नित्यम् । सावयवस्य तस्य नित्यत्वे जगतोऽपि नित्यत्वाविरोधादीश्वरासिद्धेः । नाप्यनित्यम् । तद्व्यतिरिक्तस्य तच्छरीरहेतोस्तदानीमभावात् । स्वयमेव हेतुरिति चेत् । न अशरीरस्य तदयोगात् । अन्येन शरीरेण सशरीर इति चेत् । न । अनवस्थानात् । स किं सव्यापारो निर्व्यापारो वा । अशरीरत्वादेव न सव्यापारः । नापि निर्व्यापारः कार्यं करोति मुक्तात्मवत् । कार्यं जगदिच्छामात्रव्यापारकर्तृकमित्युच्यमाने पक्षस्याप्रसिद्धविशेषणत्वात् । दृष्टान्तस्य च साध्यहीनता । अतो दर्शनानुगुण्येन ईश्वरानुमानं दर्शनानुगुण्यपराहतम् इति शास्त्रैकप्रमाणकः परब्रह्मभूतः सर्वेश्वरः पुरुषोत्तमः ॥ Râm. S'rî-Bhâṣya, I.i. 3, pp.133-37 (Vâṇî. Ed.)

Stanza VII.

Another doctrine of the Vaiseṣika school which is next criticized is the *Doctrine of Samavâya.*

Stanza VII: If there be an *absolute* distinction between धर्म and धर्मिन्, there can be no such relation as that of धर्म and धर्मिन्. If you say that the relation is due to समवाय (='वृत्ति' = inherence or residence), we would point out that three realities—1 धर्म, 2 धर्मिन् *and* 3 समवाय—are not perceived, but only two, viz., the first and the second. If it be contended that the experience 'this पट is *in* the तन्तुs' bears testimony to the residence—'Vṛtti' (Samavâya)—of the former in the latter, please note that the line of argument will carry you too far, requiring you to recognize a समवाय in a समवाय, and so on *ad infinitum.* If, to meet this difficulty, you draw a distinction between the two समवायs, saying that while one is primary the other is secondary, all that we need say is—the distinction is imaginary. Moreover, it is contrary to common experience to say that the पट is *in* the तन्तुs.

Page 31.

l. 4. धर्मधर्मिणोः etc.—'इव' in 'अतीव' is a rhetorical appendage of अति, having no particular meaning of its own. It is sometimes used after 'किम्' as in the two passages cited in the text. The first is from Kumâra. iii, 54, and the second from S'is'upâla.viii, 18.

l. 7. ततश्चैकान्त etc.—एकान्त–absolute; a synonym of the word 'अतीव' of the Stanza. The Jaina does not deny the distinction *in a certain sense* between धर्म and धर्मिन्; what he denies is *absolute* distinction between them. Compare the view of the S'âṁkara Vedântin who affirms the identity (तादात्म्य) of the two, and while recognizing some distinction denies that it has any *real* existence, the धर्म and the संबन्ध being looked upon as unreal (मिथ्या, अनिर्वचनीय) appearances or aspects of the one Absolute Reality. (See S'âṁkara-Bhâṣya on Br. Sûtra II. ii. 13, and Advaitabrahmasiddhi, on समवाय).

l. 8. अस्य धर्मिणः etc.—The fact that we *relate* them is a disproof of their *absolute* distinction—an argument well-known in Neo-Hegelianism. Were they absolutely distinct, we could not so much as say that a particular धर्म belonged to धर्मिन् A; for, so far as distinction was concerned, it would be in the same position with respect to the धर्मिन् as that occupied by the धर्म of any other object with respect to the said धर्मिन्. In other words, the धर्म would be a total stranger to the particular धर्मिन्, and would be in no way *its*. Thus, A (dravya) and A′ (its guṇa) would be *absolutely* distinct, just as A (the dravya) and B′ (guṇa of another dravya) are absolutely distinct—there being no difference between the position of A′ (the first guṇa) and B′ (the second guṇa) with respect to A (the first dravya), on the hypothesis of absolute distinction.

l. 11. एवमुक्ते सति etc.—'वृत्त्यास्ति'—A possible defence of the Vais'eṣika position.

l. 12. अयुतसिद्धानामाधारा॰ etc.—'समवाय,' or 'वृत्ति' as it is called in the stanza, owing to the residence (वृत्ति) of one thing in the other—is defined as "अयुतसिद्धानामाधार्याधारभूतानामिहप्रत्ययहेतुः संबन्धः" (The definition is taken from Praśasta. Bh. section on समवाय p. 324. Viz. ed.) Of things indissolubly connected as आधार and आधेय we say 'Here is A (आधेय) *residing in* B (आधार)'. This perception of the residential connection (वृत्ति) of A with B is evidence of समवाय. 'अयुतसिद्ध'—roughly, indissolubles—are thus described: "ययोर्द्वयोर्मध्य एकमविनश्यदपराश्रितमेवावतिष्ठते तौ द्वौ अयुतसिद्धौ"—अयुतसिद्धयोः संबन्धः= 'अवयवावयविनोः, गुणगुणिनोः, क्रियाक्रियावतोः, जातिव्यक्तयोः, नित्यद्रव्यविशेषयोः' संबन्धः (Tarkabhâṣâ).

l. 13. 'समवाय,' so-called because it weaves or strings *together* ('समवयनात्') dravya and guṇa. It is also called 'वृत्ति', because it causes गुण etc. to reside (वर्तनात्) in द्रव्य.

Page 32.

l. 15. विनिर्लुण्ठित = separate.

ll. 16-23.-अत्राचार्यः समाधत्ते etc.—Hemacandra's reply to the Vaiśeṣika's vindication of समवाय is that it is unwarranted by

प्रत्यक्ष. There is no प्रत्यक्ष of धर्म, धर्मिन् *and* समवाय. No doubt we see two separate stones rivetted together by lac (राला), but we do not see धर्म and धर्मिन् so rivetted together by a *third* thing corresponding to the lac in the analogy.

ll. 23-29.–किंचायं etc.—Besides, the समवाय is said to be 'एको नित्यः सर्वव्यापको नित्यश्च'—which would make the धर्मs of घट reside in पट quite as well as in घट ! For, the two समवायs (घटधर्मसमवाय and पटधर्मसमवाय) are, as you hold, but "*one*, *eternal*, *omnipresent* and *incorporeal*" and therefore in touch with everything simultaneously, like आकाश. Moreover, when घट perishes its समवाय will be no more (it *must* be no more; for, how can it exist without the घट to which it belongs ?), and as there is but *one* समवाय in the universe, and the one has perished, a घटसमवाय becomes impossible thereafter !

ll. 29-30–तत्तदवच्छेदक etc.—The Vaiśeṣika endeavours to explain the position by the hypothesis of different अवच्छेदकs (limiting circumstances, the media in which the अवच्छेद्य reveals itself) belonging to one समवाय. Thus, समवाय is but one; but घटसमवाय, पटसमवाय, etc. are different in consequence of the different अवच्छेदकs of the समवाय viz. घट, पट, etc., which are the limiting conditions or media in which the समवाय manifests itself. To this Malliṣeṇa replies: एवमनित्यतापत्तिः—This is virtually admitting the plurality of समवायs and their perishableness along with घट, पट etc. It may be noted that later Vaiśeṣikas and Naiyâyikas have abandoned the creed of a single, eternal समवाय—which is admitted by them to be many (नाना) and perishable (अनित्य). The reason for the earlier logicians holding the doctrine of one समवाय probably was this—that they found it absurd to associate the quality of *number* with समवाय—number itself being a guṇa which was connected with dravyas by समवाय, and so when they spoke of *one* समवाय all that they meant was that they could not predicate number of it. Similarly I think when they say दिक् is everywhere (विभ्वी), what they should mean is that there is no limitation of space to it. So about कालो नित्यः.

ll. 30-35.—अथ कथं etc.—The existence of समवाय is not a matter of faith, but is evidenced by the sensuous experience 'इह तन्तुषु पटः' according to the old school of Nyâya, and, I believe, of Vaiśeṣika also. According to the recognised school of the Vaiśeṣikas represented by Pras'astapâda, and also according to the later Naiyâyikas, however, समवाय is अनुमेय—See Muktâvalî on St. XI. and Dinakarî on the same. It was only fair that the Naiyâyikas should admit this and change the old dogma, in deference to the voice of a large number of opponents all ready to swear that they never *perceived* any such thing as समवाय.

ll. 35-38.—इहेदमिति etc.—Construe thus: इहेदमिति वृत्तौ च (=अपि) मतिः—'च'=अपि though placed after मतिः in the stanza is to be construed with वृत्तौ. Just as the आश्रयाश्रयिभाव in इहेदम् *i. e.* इह तन्तुषु पटः implies, according to you, समवाय (=वृत्ति) relation, so, to be consistent, you should hold the same with regard to the समवाय itself. The point is made clear in the passage beginning with "इदमत्र हृदयम्" (P. 33).

ll. 30-35.—अथ कथं समवायस्य न ज्ञाने प्रतिभासनं etc.—How do you say that there is no such awareness of समवाय? For, we are distinctly aware of it when we say that पट is *in* the तन्तुs, or that ज्ञान is *in* the आत्मन् or that रूप is *in* the घट. Here we are conscious not of the धर्म and धर्मिन् only, but also of the residence of the one in the other. Such is the argument of the Vaiśeṣika in favour of समवाय. It is answered in the following lines.

Page 33.

ll. 38-49—इदमत्र हृदयम् etc.—Just as you say पृथ्वीत्वाभिसंबन्धात् पृथ्वी and add that here पृथ्वीत्व is but the स्वरूप or अस्तित्व of पृथ्वी and is not a separate entity, and that the connection of पृथ्वी with पृथ्वीत्व is समवाय, why can we not say समवायत्वाभिसंबन्धात् समवायः, and add that समवायत्व is the स्वरूप of समवाय, and then the connection of समवाय with its स्वरूप, viz., समवायत्व would be another समवाय and so on *ad infinitum*? cf. "समवायस्य समवायान्तरेण वृत्त्यभ्युपगमे तु तत्राप्यपरसमवायकल्पनेऽनवस्थानदी दुस्तरा"—Guṇaratna, p. 252. If समवाय had not the स्वरूपसमवायत्व it would be *nothing*, no better than a शशविषाण which is

निःस्वरूप· 'प्राप्तानामेव प्राप्तिः समवायः'—Contra, 'अप्राप्तानां प्राप्तिः संयोगः'. Difference between संयोग and समवाय—the former joins things that were not joined before; the latter joins things that are already joined *i. e.* it is the name of a relation to explain a relatedness which has been already there.

ll. 50-55–ननु पृथिव्यादीनां etc.—A distinction is drawn by the Vaiśeṣika between the case of पृथ्वीत्व and that of the alleged समवायत्व. The former is a real °त्व and a सामान्य which embraces all the व्यक्तिs *i.e.* individual पृथ्वीs within it, and so the समवाय which connects it with the व्यक्तिs is a 'मुख्य समवाय' *i. e.* समवाय in the primary and real sense of the term, whereas समवाय being but one व्यक्ति, समवायत्व is not a real सामान्य, and therefore its existence in समवाय, and the second समवाय by which it would be expected to exist in it, will be both अमुख्य or गौण *i.e.* secondary and unreal. The distinction between मुख्य and गौण is pointed out *infra* p. 34. ll. 63-64.–तल्लक्षणं चेत्थं etc.

तदेतच्च चेतश्चमत्कार° etc.—The fine distinction which the Vaiśeṣika has drawn between the two cases is unfounded. You say that when there is but one व्यक्ति, as in the case of समवाय, there can be no real जाति or सामान्य. (See Udayanâcârya's famous Kârikâ: "व्यक्तेरभेदस्तुल्यत्वं संकरोऽथानवस्थितिः । रूपहानिरसंबन्धो जातिबाधकसंग्रहः" This will be explained below in Note on St. VIII. ll. 74–75.) But we answer: Where is 'व्यक्तेरभेदः' (only a single individual) in the case of समवाय which would preclude the possibility of जाति or universal? There is a घटसमवाय, there is a पटसमवाय, and so are innumerable समवायs which would require a °त्व quite as much as पृथ्वी. (Recall the admission of the new school of Nyâya noted above in Note on ll. 29-30).

Page 34.

ll. 64-66.–तल्लक्षणं चेत्थं etc.—Distinction between मुख्य and गौण: "मुख्य is that which is invariable; also, complete, characteristic and inner; गौण is the opposite of this."

ll. 67-68.–तस्माद्धर्म etc.—So it is a false distinction to draw that the समवाय which joins धर्म and धर्मिन् is मुख्य, while that which joins समवायत्व with the original समवाय is गौण. "न गौणभेदः" of the Stanza.

l. 73.–अपि च लोकबाधः etc.—Even the man in the street says 'इह पटे तन्तवः'—'there are so many threads in this piece of cloth;' nobody says 'the cloth is in the threads.' So the Vais'eṣika argument of 'इह तन्तुषु पटः' breaks down.

पांसुलपाद—he who walks barefooted on the road and has dusty feet; hence, 'the man in the street;' cf. "पांसुलपादानामपीह पटे तन्तव इत्येवं प्रतीतिदर्शनात्"–Guṇaratna, p. 252. See below Appendix 3.

References: For the Vaiśeṣika case see Vaiś. Sûtras, Praśastapâda's Bhâṣya, Nyâyakandalî, Vaiśeṣika Sûtra-Upaskâra, Muktâvalî, Dinakarî, etc.

For a vigorous criticism of the same see Bâd. Sûtras with the Com. of S'aṁkara, Râmânuja, etc.

Appendices.

1.

"इहेदमिति यतः कार्यकारणयोः स समवायः" Vais'. Sûtras VII-ii-26.

"कार्यकारणयोरित्युपलक्षणम् । अकार्यकारणयोरपि द्रष्टव्यम् । तदुक्तं पदार्थप्रदेशाख्ये प्रकरणे "अयुतसिद्धानामाधार्याधारभूतानां यः संबन्धः इहेतिप्रत्ययहेतुः स समवायः इति असंबद्धयोरविद्यमानत्वमयुतासिद्धिः । इह कुण्डे दधि इह कुण्डे बदराणीतिवत् इह तन्तुषु पटः इह वीरणेषु कटः इह द्रव्ये द्रव्यगुणकर्माणि इह गवि गोत्वम् इहात्मनि ज्ञानम् इहाकाशे शब्द इतीहबुद्धिरुत्पद्यमाना न विना संबन्धमुत्पत्तुमर्हति तेनानुमीयतेऽस्ति कश्चित् संबन्धः । न चासौ संयोग एव । अन्यतरकर्मादीनां तदुत्पादकानामभावात् विभागपर्यवसानाभावाच्च संबन्धिनामयुतसिद्धत्वाच्च नियताधिकरणतयैवोन्नेयत्वात् अप्रत्यक्षत्वात् एकत्वात् नित्यत्वाच्च ॥ नन्वेकश्चेत् समवायस्तदा द्रव्यत्वादीनां संकरप्रसङ्गः कर्मत्वादिसमवायस्य द्रव्ये संभवात् । मैवम् । आधाराधेयनियमादेवासंकरात् । यद्यपि य एव द्रव्यत्वसमवायः स एव गुणत्वकर्मत्वादीनामपि तथापि तेषां न द्रव्यमाधारः तत्र तेषामप्रतीतेः । द्रव्येष्वेव द्रव्यत्वं प्रतीयते गुणेष्वेव गुणत्वं कर्मस्वेव कर्मत्वं न त्वत्यन्तेत्यन्वयव्यतिरेकदर्शनादेव नियमः ।.........। स चायं नित्यः । अकारणकत्वात् । भावानां हि समवायिकारणादुत्पत्तिनियमः । ....। तन्तुषु पटसमवायः पटे रूपसमवायः इति:प्रतीतिः कथमिति चेत् । स्वरूपसंबन्धेन। समवायान्तराङ्गीकारेऽनवस्थापातात् । तर्हीह पटे रूपमित्यपीहप्रत्ययः स्वरूपसंबन्धेनैव स्यात् किं समवायेनेति चेन्न । तत्रातिरिक्तसंबन्धे बाधकाभावात् ॥ ...... समवायो नानानित्यश्चेति प्राभाकराः । तच्चानुपपन्नम् । रूपं नष्टमिति प्रत्ययो न तु रूपसमवायो नष्ट इति कस्यापि प्रत्ययः । प्रत्यक्षः समवाय इति नैयायिकाः । तदप्यनुपपन्नम् । समवायोऽतीन्द्रियः आत्मान्यत्वे सत्यसमवेतभावत्वात् मनोवत् कालादिवद्वा"—Vaiś. Sûtras VII. ii, 26-27-28 Upaskâra,

Stanza VIII.

The commentary on the last stanza was only a preliminary skirmish directed against one single tenet of the Vais'eṣika preparatory to the main offensive which is now going to be vigorously conducted against the whole of the Vais'eṣika philosophy, especially against its doctrine of सामान्य and its conception of the nature of आत्मन् and मोक्ष.

I. Vais'eṣika Categories and their subdivisions.

1. The *Six Padârthas* or the highest Nameables: (1) द्रव्य, (2) गुण, (3) कर्म, (4) सामान्य, (5) विशेष, and (6) समवाय. Later Vaiśeṣikas add (7) अभाव.

The Vaiśeṣika Sûtra says: "धर्मविशेषप्रसूताद्द्रव्यगुणकर्मसामान्यविशेषसमवायानां पदार्थानां साधर्म्यवैधर्म्याभ्यां तत्त्वज्ञानान्निःश्रेयसम्," on which the Pras'astapâda-Bhâṣya runs as follows:—"द्रव्यगुणकर्मसामान्यविशेषसमवायानां षण्णां पदार्थानां साधर्म्यवैधर्म्यतत्त्वज्ञानं निःश्रेयसहेतुः," thus fixing the number of पदार्थs definitely at *six*. Its commentator—S'rîdhara, of the tenth century A. D.—would add 'अभाव' as the seventh to complete the list of the categories; for, अभाव is as real as the rest, and yet it is not mentioned by the Sûtrakâra or the Bhâṣyakâra, not because it is not a real category but because it is dependent upon भाव. The argument, or rather the excuse, for the omission would go too far and would apply to certain other categories such as गुण etc., which are dependent upon द्रव्य. The same weakness belongs to the following remark of Udayana and his commentator: "अभावस्तु स्वरूपवानपि पृथङ् नोद्दिष्टः। प्रतियोगिनिरूपणाधीननिरूपणत्वात्। न तु तुच्छत्वात् [Thus the doctrine differs from that of the S'. Vedânta and Prabhâkara's school]"; "अभावो भाष्यकृता नोपवर्णितः तुच्छत्वादिति केचित्। तन्मतनिरासायाह। अभावस्त्विति। स्वरूपवान् प्रामाणिकः। पृथग्द्रव्यादिवत्तत्त्वज्ञानविषयतया। न तु अत्र भाष्ये नोक्त एव। फलस्य निःश्रेयसस्याभावरूपत्वादित्याशयः। तथानभिधाने हेतुमाह। प्रतियोगीति। प्रतियोगिनिरूपणं शास्त्रान्तरं तच्च प्रकृते न्यायदर्शनम्" [This is a new and very curious explanation of 'प्रतियोगिन्' which could never have been meant by Udayana]। तदधीननिरूपणत्वादित्यर्थः। नन्वेतावताभ्युपगमसिद्धान्तसिद्धत्वमभावे उक्तं तच्च तदा स्याद्यदि स्वतन्त्रे [वैशेषिके] अभावोऽ-

धिकृतः स्यात्। इति स्वतन्त्रेऽधिकृतत्वमाह। उत्पत्तीति। प्रागभाववत एवोत्पत्तिरिति तच्चिन्तायां प्रागभावोऽधिकृतः। विनाशचिन्तायां तु ध्वंसः प्राधान्येनैवाधिकृतः। वैधर्म्यकथनेऽन्योन्याभावात्यन्ताभावावाधिकृतौ। वैधर्म्यस्य व्यतिरेकहेतुतया तत्साध्यतयाऽन्योन्याभावस्य व्यतिरेकव्याप्तौ साध्यहेत्वोरत्यन्ताभावस्य स्वीकृतत्वादिति भावः। अभ्युपगमसिद्धान्तसिद्धस्य च प्राधान्येनानभिधानं न्यायदर्शने मनस इन्द्रियत्वस्य दृष्टमिति हृदयम् ॥"—Kiraṇâvalî-Bhâskara.

This is justifying the recognition of अभाव as a category on the authority of a sister school—the Nyâyadars'ana—and its implied acceptance by the Vaiś. Sûtrakâra himself in the Sûtras which refer to प्रागभाव and प्रध्वंसाभाव, and to अन्योन्याभाव and अत्यन्ताभाव, under the names वैधर्म्य and व्यतिरेक. Here is one example of the conservative liberalism of Indian writers. This explanation, however, does not cure the enumeration in the V.-Sûtra of the defect of being inexhaustive. It only justifies addition. Udayana is on much firmer ground when he says in the Lakṣaṇâvali:" अभिधेयः पदार्थः— । स द्विविधः । भावाभावभेदात् । तत्र नञर्थविषयत्वरहितप्रत्ययविषयो भावः । स च षोढा द्रव्यादिभेदेन" that is to say, that the Sûtrakâra had before his mind only the भावs when he penned this Sûtra.

2. The Nine *Dravyas*: (1) पृथ्वी, (2) अप्, (3) तेजः etc., "क्रियागुणवत् समवायिकारणम्" V.-Sûtra—तमः or अन्धकार which is regarded by Mîmâṁsakas and some others as a positive dravya is according to the Nyâya–Vaiś. nothing but तेजःसामान्याभाव.

3. The twenty-four Guṇas: 17—रूप etc., *plus* 7 द्रवत्व etc. The original Sûtra mentioned only *seventeen* to which Praśastapâda, added *seven*, वेग (Velocity), भावना (Impression—physical and mental), and स्थितिस्थापक (Elasticity)—are but different varieties of संस्कार and so are included in संस्कार by virtue of the jâti संस्कारत्व which belongs to them all. शौर्य, औदार्य etc.—come under the recognised heads of Guṇas. On the number of गुणs cf. "गुणाश्च रूपरसगन्धस्पर्शसंख्यापरिमाणपृथक्त्वसंयोगविभागपरत्वापरत्वबुद्धिसुखदुःखेच्छाद्वेषप्रयत्नाश्चेति कण्ठोक्ताः सप्तदश । च-शब्दसमुच्चिताश्च गुरुत्व-द्रवत्व-स्नेह-संस्कारा-दृष्ट-शब्दाः सप्तैवेत्येवं चतुर्विंशतिर्गुणाः ॥"—P. Bhâṣya; and "ये तु शौर्यौदार्यकारुण्यदाक्षिण्यौद्धत्यादयः तेऽत्रैवान्तर्भवन्ति। शौर्यं बलवतोऽपि परस्य पराजयाय प्रत्युत्साहः स च प्रयत्नविशेष एव। सततं सन्मार्गवर्तिनी

बुद्धिरौदार्यम्। अपरदुःखप्रहाणेच्छा कारुण्यम्। तत्त्वाभिनिवेशिनी बुद्धिर्दाक्षिण्यम्। औद्धत्यमात्मन्युत्कर्षप्रत्ययः। इत्येवमादिः। अदृष्टशब्देन धर्माधर्मयोरुपसंग्रहः। संस्कार इति च वेगस्य भावनायाः स्थितस्थापकस्य चाभिधानम्॥"—"नन्वेवं तर्ह्याधिक्यम्। न। संस्कारजात्यपेक्षया वेगभावनास्थितस्थापकानामेकत्वात्। एवं तर्हि न चतुर्विंशतित्वम्। अदृष्टत्वजात्यपेक्षया धर्माधर्मयोरेकत्वात्। न। अदृष्टत्वजात्यभावात्। निर्गुणेष्वपि गुणेष्वसाधारणधर्मयोगित्वेनोपचाराच्चतुर्विंशतिरिति व्यवहारः॥" N. Kandalî.

4. The five कर्मन्s : उत्क्षेपण, etc.—"गमनग्रहणात्" etc. a remark found in almost every book of the school. For स्यन्दन some read स्पन्दन (vide Pr. Bhâṣya and N. Kandalî). Upaskâra reads स्यन्दन, as in our printed text. कर्म is thus defined:—"एकद्रव्यमगुणं संयोगविभागेष्वनपेक्षकारणमिति कर्मलक्षणम्."

5. सामान्य—Generality—the principle of the co-ordination of individuals in one group. The whole passage bearing on सामान्य and the next two categories—from here to the end of the first section इति षट् पदार्थाः—occurs also in the Laghu Vṛtti on the Ṣad. D-Sam: see pp. 61-62-63 तच्च द्विविधं etc. One would suppose that the highest point to which a generalization could be carried was पदार्थत्व embracing *all* the पदार्थs in one group. But this is not what the Vais'. thinks. Certain categories he sets aside as incapable of possessing सामान्य in the real sense of the term*—which, according to him, belongs to only three categories, viz., द्रव्य, गुण and कर्म. This highest सामान्य he calls सत्ता, also भाव (cf. Vaiś. Sûtra I. ii. 4, भावोऽनुवृत्तेरेव हेतुत्वात् सामान्यमेव) which, be it noted, does not mean Existence simply, but *Existence carried to the highest possible point of generalization*, which stops at the collective group of द्रव्य, गुण and कर्म, and cannot go beyond it. This सत्ता is otherwise called 'महासामान्य,' because it is the highest सामान्य to which *real* generalization can be carried. द्रव्यत्व, गुणत्व etc., are lower than this, but are higher than पृथ्वीत्व, रूपत्व etc., and are called अपरसामान्यs. An अपरसामान्य is not only a सामान्य, but also a विशेष—inas-

* The Vaiś.-Naiyâyikas, therefore, distinguish जाति from उपाधि. For this and सखण्ड and अखण्ड उपाधिs see Muktâvalî and Nîlakaṇṭhî.

much as it co-ordinates its individuals in a group and differentiates them from those of other groups, and is, therefore called, सामान्यविशेष. This fluid conception of सामान्य-विशेष which was held by the old Vaiśeṣikas is endorsed among later writers by Keśavamiśra in his Tarkabhâṣâ.

cf. "सामान्यं विशेष इति बुद्ध्यपेक्षम्"—Vaiś. Sûtra I. ii. 3. "सामान्यं द्विविधं परमपरं च। तत्र परं सत्ता। अपरं सत्ताव्याप्यं द्रव्यत्वादि। तत्र सामान्यस्य तद्विशेषस्य च लक्षणं बुद्धिरेव। अनुवृत्तबुद्धिः सामान्यस्य व्यावृत्तबुद्धिर्विशेषस्य...परमपि सामान्यमपरमपि तथा। परं तु सामान्यं विशेषसंज्ञामपि लभते यथा द्रव्यमिदं द्रव्यमिदमित्यनुवृत्तप्रत्यये सत्येव नायं गुणो नेदं कर्मेति विशेषप्रत्ययः। तथा च द्रव्यत्वादीनां सामान्यानामेव विशेषत्वम्।"—Upaskâra on V. S. I.ii. 3. "भावानुवृत्तेरेव हेतुत्वात् सामान्यमेव।" V.S. I.ii.4. "द्रव्यत्वं गुणत्वं कर्मत्वं च सामान्यानि विशेषाश्च"—V.S.I. ii. 5. "अन्यत्रान्त्येभ्यो विशेषेभ्यः" V. S. I. ii. 6. "अन्त्या विशेषा नित्यद्रव्यवृत्तयोऽभिहितास्तान् वर्जयित्वा सामान्यविशेषाभिधानमित्यर्थः।" Upaskâra, ibid. "सदिति यतो द्रव्यगुणकर्मसु सा सत्ता।" V.S.I. ii. 7. "द्रव्यगुणकर्मभ्योऽर्थान्तरं सत्ता" V. S. I. ii. 8. "न तु द्रव्यगुणकर्मभ्यः पृथग्भावेन सत्ता नानुभूयतेऽतो द्रव्याद्यन्यतममेव सत्ता। यतो हि यद्भिन्नं भवति तत्ततो भेदेनानुभूयते यथा घटः पटात्। न च सत्ता तेभ्यो भेदेनानुभूयते इति तदात्मिकैवेत्यत आह द्रव्येति। द्रव्यादयोऽननुगताः। सत्ता चानुगता। तथा च अनुगतत्वानुगतत्वलक्षणविरुद्धधर्माध्यासेन तेभ्यो भेदस्य सिद्धत्वात्। यत्तु तेभ्योऽन्यत्र नोपलभ्यते तदयुतसिद्धबलात्। घटपटयोस्तु युतसिद्धिः। न च व्यक्तिस्वरूपमेव सत्ता। व्यक्तीनामननुगमात्। स्वरूपत्वं यद्यनुगतं तदा सैव सत्ता। अननुगतैरपि स्वरूपैरनुगतव्यवहारश्चेत्तदा गोत्वादिभिरपि गतम्॥" Upaskâra, ibid. "गुणकर्मसु च भावान्न कर्म न गुणः" V.S.I.ii.9. "न हि कर्म कर्मसु वर्तते न वा गुणो गुणेषु न वा द्रव्यं गुणे कर्मणि वा। सत्ता तु गुणे कर्मणि च वर्तते तेन द्रव्यगुणकर्मवैधर्म्यात्तेभ्यो भिन्नैव सत्ता॥" Upaskâra, ibid. "सामान्यविशेषाभावेन च॥" V. S. I. ii. 10. "यदि सत्ता द्रव्यं गुणः कर्म वा स्यात् तदा सामान्यविशेषवती स्यात्। न च सत्तायां सामान्यविशेषा द्रव्यत्वादय उपलभ्यन्ते। न हि भवति सत्ता द्रव्यं गुणः कर्म वेति केषांचिदनुभवः।" Upaskâra, ibid.

"सामान्यं द्विविधं परमपरं च अनुवृत्तिप्रत्ययकारणम्। तत्र परं सत्ता महाविषयत्वात्। सा चानुवृत्तेरेव हेतुत्वात् सामान्यमेव। द्रव्यत्वाद्यपरमल्पविषयत्वात् तच्च व्यावृत्तेरपि हेतुत्वात् सामान्यं सद् विशेषाख्यामपि लभते।" P.Bhâṣya.

"सामान्यं द्विविधं परमपरं च। स्वविषयसर्वगतमभिन्नात्मकमनेकवृत्ति एकद्विबहुष्वात्मस्वरूपानुगमप्रत्ययकारि स्वरूपाभेदेनाधारेषु प्रबन्धेन वर्तमान-

मनुवृत्तिप्रत्ययकारणम् ।......। तत्र सत्तासामान्यं परमनुवृत्तिप्रत्ययकारणमेव। यथा परस्परविशिष्टेषु चर्मवस्त्रकम्बलादिष्वेकस्मान्नीलद्रव्याभिसंबन्धात् नीलं नीलमिति प्रत्ययानुवृत्तिः तथा परस्परविशिष्टेषु द्रव्यगुणकर्मस्वविशिष्टा सत् सदिति प्रत्ययानुवृत्तिः सा चार्थान्तराद्भवितुमर्हतीति यत्तदर्थान्तरं सा सत्तेति सिद्धा। सत्तानुसंबन्धात् सत्सदिति प्रत्ययानुवृत्तिः। तस्मात् सा सामान्यमेव। अपरं द्रव्यत्वगुणत्वकर्मत्वादि अनुवृत्तिव्यावृत्तिहेतुत्वात् सामान्यं विशेषश्च भवति ।......। एतानि तु द्रव्यत्वादीनि प्रभूतविषयत्वात् प्राधान्येन सामान्यानि स्वाश्रयविशेषकत्वाद्भक्त्या विशेषाख्यानीति ॥" P. Bhâṣya.

"तत्र तयोर्मध्ये परं सत्ता भावो महासामान्यमिति चोच्यते। द्रव्यत्वाद्यवान्तरसामान्यापेक्षया महाविषयत्वात्। अपरसामान्यं द्रव्यत्वादि एतच्च सामान्यविशेष इत्यपि व्यपदिश्यते। तथाहि । द्रव्यत्वं नवसु द्रव्येषु वर्तमानत्वात् सामान्यम् गुणकर्मव्यावृत्तत्वाद्विशेषः ततः कर्मधारये सामान्यविशेष इति। एवं द्रव्यत्वाद्यपेक्षया पृथिवीत्वादिकमपरं तदपेक्षया घटत्वादिकम्। एवं चतुर्विंशतौ गुणेषु वृत्तेर्गुणत्वं सामान्यं द्रव्यकर्मभ्यो व्यावृत्तेश्च विशेषः। एवं गुणत्वापेक्षया रूपत्वादिकं तदपेक्षया नीलत्वादिकम्। एवं पञ्चसु कर्मसु वर्तमानत्वात्कर्मत्वं सामान्यं द्रव्यगुणेभ्यो व्यावृत्तत्वाद्विशेषः। एवं कर्मत्वापेक्षयोत्क्षेपणत्वादिकं ज्ञेयम् ॥ तत्र सत्ता द्रव्यगुणकर्मभ्योऽर्थान्तरं कया युक्त्येति चेत् उच्यते। न द्रव्यं सत्ता द्रव्यादन्येत्यर्थः एकद्रव्यत्वात् एकैकस्मिन् द्रव्ये वर्तमानत्वादित्यर्थः द्रव्यत्ववत्। यथा द्रव्यत्वं नवसु द्रव्येषु प्रत्येकं वर्तमानं द्रव्यं न भवति किंतु सामान्यं विशेषलक्षणं द्रव्यत्वमेव एवं सत्तापि। वैशेषिकाणां हि अद्रव्यं वा द्रव्यं अनेकद्रव्यं वा द्रव्यम्। तत्राद्रव्यं द्रव्यमाकाशं कालो दिग् आत्मानः परमाणवः। अनेकद्रव्यं तु द्व्यणुकादिस्कन्धाः। एकद्रव्यं तु द्रव्यमेव न भवति। एकद्रव्यवती सत्तेति द्रव्यलक्षणविलक्षणत्वान्न द्रव्यम्। एवं न गुणः सत्ता गुणेष्वभावात् गुणत्ववत्। यदि हि सत्ता गुणः स्यात् न तर्हि गुणेषु वर्तेत। निर्गुणत्वाद्गुणानाम्। वर्तते च गुणेषु सत्ता। सन् गुण इति प्रतीतेः। तथा न सत्ता कर्म कर्मसु भावात् कर्मत्ववत्। यदि च सत्ता कर्म स्यात् न तर्हि कर्मसु वर्तेत। निष्कर्मत्वात् कर्मणाम्। वर्तते च कर्मसु भावः । सत्कर्मेति प्रतीतेः। तस्मात् पदार्थान्तरं सत्ता ॥" Maṇibhadra's Com. on Ṣad. Dars'. Sam. pp. 61–62.

"तच्च द्रव्यत्वादिकं स्वाश्रयेषु द्रव्यादिष्वनुवृत्तिप्रत्ययहेतुत्वात् सामान्यमप्युच्यते। स्वाश्रयस्य च विजातीयेभ्यो गुणादिभ्यो व्यावृत्तिप्रत्ययहेतुतया विशेषोऽप्युच्यते। ततोऽपरं सामान्यमुभयरूपत्वात् सामान्यविशेषसंज्ञां लभते। अपेक्षाभेदादेकस्यापि सामान्यविशेषभावो न विरुध्यते ॥"—Guṇaratna's Com. on Ṣad-Dars'. Sam. p. 276.

"परे पुनः प्राहुः । सामान्यं त्रिविधं महासामान्यं सत्तासामान्यं सामान्यविशेषसामान्यं च। तत्र महासामान्यं षट्स्वपि पदार्थेषु पदार्थत्वबुद्धिकारि। सत्ता-

सामान्यं त्रिपदार्थसिद्धबुद्धिविधायि । सामान्यविशेषसामान्यं तु द्रव्यत्वादि ॥ अन्ये त्वाचक्षते । त्रिपदार्थसत्कारि सत्ता । सामान्यं द्रव्यत्वादि । सामान्यविशेषः पृथिवीत्वादिति । लक्षणभेदादेतेषां सत्तादीनां द्रव्यगुणकर्मभ्यः पदार्थान्तरत्वं सिद्धम् ।" ibid. p. 277.

तत्र सत्ता द्रव्यगुणकर्मभ्यो etc.—Next it is shown how सत्ता (the महासामान्य) is a पदार्थ outside the groups of द्रव्य, गुण and कर्म. cf. "द्रव्यगुणकर्मभ्योऽर्थान्तरं सत्ता" Vais'. Sûtra. I. ii. 8.

(1) "न द्रव्यं सत्ता ।": सत्ता is not a द्रव्य, because it is lacking the characteristic mark of a द्रव्य which is that it should be made of many constituent द्रव्यs (अनेकद्रव्यत्व), or of no द्रव्य (अद्रव्यत्व), but never of a single constituent द्रव्य (एकद्रव्य). Like द्रव्यत्व, सत्ता resides in each द्रव्य. And nothing which resides in a single द्रव्य can be a द्रव्य itself. But सत्ता does reside in each single द्रव्य (एकैकस्मिन् द्रव्ये वर्तमानत्वात् ... एकद्रव्यवती च सत्ता इति द्रव्यलक्षणविलक्षणत्वान्न द्रव्यम्). According to the Vaiśeṣika अद्रव्यं वा etc.—"a द्रव्य is without a constituent द्रव्य, or has many constituent द्रव्यs, but never a single (unitary) constituent द्रव्य; for example, आकाश, काल, दिश्, आत्मन् and परमाणुs are द्रव्यs devoid of constituent द्रव्यs, while bodies such as द्व्यणुक (duads), त्र्यणुक (triads), etc., are possessed of *many* constituent द्रव्यs—viz. the parts of which they are composed (See Muktâ–Dinakarî). But the सत्ता fulfils neither of the two conditions: it is एकद्रव्यवती, that is, it exists in a single द्रव्य—*e. g.* गोत्व in a single cow—no less than in many cows; and it is, therefore, not a द्रव्य.

(2) "एवं न गुणः सत्ता ।": सत्ता is not a गुण. For, it resides in a गुण. And a गुण can never reside in a गुण, गुणs being themselves निर्गुण.

(3) "तथा न सत्ता कर्म ।": सत्ता is not a कर्म. For, it resides in a कर्म. And a कर्म cannot reside in a कर्म, कर्मन्s being themselves निष्कर्म.

6. विशेष :—cf. Praśastapâda Bh. and Nyâyakandalî: pp.321-22. विशेषs—rather a certain class of विशेषs, according to the original notion of विशेष which was more comprehensive than the later, are resident in नित्यद्रव्यs and are ultimate, they are absolutely exclusive and thus they serve to distinguish the dravyas

to which they belong from other dravyas (स्वाश्रयविशेषकत्वात्). They reside in each of the नित्यद्रव्यs—one in each individual unit—viz., अणुs, आकाश, काल, दिश्, आत्मन् and मनः. Just as we distinguish cows from horses owing to certain physical features, so do yogins perceive the distinction of atom A from atom B both of which belong to the substance of the same genus, despite all their homogeneity in point of shape, quality, etc. This must be in virtue of something in A which is not in B—and that something is called विशेष. There is one विशेष for each नित्यद्रव्य, and no विशेष belongs to more than one द्रव्य ; therefore, it does not serve as a basis of co-ordination, and so, unlike अपरसामान्यs such as द्रव्यत्व etc which are 'सामान्यविशेष,' these are pure विशेषs.

According to the older conception of विशेष, विशेषs are of two kinds : first, those that are *relative* and consequently not incompatible with सामान्य : these are सामान्यविशेषs (see supra); secondly, those that are *ultimate* and *absolute*. The latter are 'अन्त्य' and 'नित्यद्रव्यवृत्ति' Later Nyâya takes note of the latter only, and in it, it is not अन्त्यविशेष (as distinguished from सामान्यविशेष) which is described as नित्यद्रव्यवृत्ति, but अन्त्य and नित्यद्रव्यवृत्ति are both predicates of the subject विशेष; cf. "अन्त्यो नित्यद्रव्यवृत्तिविशेषः परिकीर्तितः—" Bh. Paricchedа and "अन्तेऽवसाने वर्तते इति अन्त्यः यदपेक्षया विशेषो नास्तीत्यर्थः । घटादीनां द्व्यणुकपर्यन्तानां तत्तदवयवभेदात् परस्परं भेदः। परमाणूनां परस्परं भेदको विशेष एव। स तु स्वत एव व्यावृत्तस्तेन विशेषान्तरापेक्षा नास्तीत्यर्थः ॥"—Muktâvalî on the same. "नन्वेतत्परमाणुत्वादयो व्यावर्तका भविष्यन्ति, किं विशेषेणेति चेन्न। अव्यावृत्तधर्मस्य व्यावर्तकत्वासंभवात्। तत्र व्यावर्तकान्तरापेक्षायामनवस्थानात्। ननु विशेषेष्वेव प्रसङ्ग इति चेन्न। तस्य धर्मिग्राहकमानेन स्वतोव्यावृत्ततयैव सिद्धेः। एवं च नित्यद्रव्येषु विशेषाः सिद्धाः । तद्गुणास्तु न विशेषवन्तः आश्रयरूपेण विशेषेणैव तेषां व्यावृत्तत्वात् आश्रयस्य च विशेषवत्तया व्यावृत्तत्वेन विशेषत्वासंभवात् इति भावः । ईश्वराकाशयोर्नित्यज्ञानशब्दाभ्यां व्यावृत्तेः संभवान्न तत्र विशेष इत्यप्याहुः। नवीनास्तु विशेषेऽतिरिक्ते मानाभावः ॥"

Cf. "अन्यत्रान्त्येभ्यो विशेषेभ्यः" V. Sûtra I. ii. 6.

"ननु य एव विशेषपदार्थ उद्दिष्टः स एव किं सामान्यविशेषत्वेनाभिधीयते इति शिष्याकाङ्क्षामपनयन्नाह। अन्यत्रेति। अन्त्या विशेषा नित्यद्रव्यवृत्तयो येऽभि-

हितास्तान् वर्जयित्वा सामान्यविशेषाभिधानमित्यर्थः। अन्तेऽवसाने भवन्तीत्यन्त्याः। यतो न व्यावर्तकान्तरमस्तीत्याचार्याः। उत्पादविनाशयोरन्तेऽवसाने भवन्तीत्यन्त्या नित्यद्रव्याणि तेषु भवन्तीत्यन्त्या विशेषा इति वृत्तिकृतः। ते हि विशेषा एव व्यावृत्तिबुद्धिहेतवो न तु सामान्यरूपा अपीति॥"—Upaskâra on the same.

तथा च प्रशस्तकरः—तेऽन्त्या विशेषा इति—The passage thus quoted from P. Bhâṣya is found verbatim in the printed editions, with just one slight variation—विप्रकर्षे for विप्रकृष्टे—which too is a reading of one of the MSS. The original passage, which is longer, concludes as follows: "अथान्त्यविशेषेष्विव परमाणुषु कस्मान्न स्वतः प्रत्ययव्यावृत्तिः कल्प्यते इति चेन्न। तादात्म्यात्। इहातदात्मकेष्वन्यनिमित्तः प्रत्ययो भवति। यथा घटादिषु प्रदीपात् न तु प्रदीपे प्रदीपान्तरात्। यथा गवाश्वमांसादीनां स्वत एवाशुचित्वं तद्योगादन्येषां तथेहापि। तादात्म्यादन्त्यविशेषेषु स्वत एव प्रत्ययव्यावृत्तिः तद्योगात् परमाण्वादिष्विति॥ P. Bh. on विशेष.

7. तथा अयुतसिद्धानां etc.—

अयुतसिद्धयोः—The term is explained as परस्परपरिहारेण पृथगाश्रयानाश्रितयोः *i. e.* which do not reside in separate आश्रयs to the exclusion of each other, *e. g.* तन्तुs and पट which do not reside in separate आश्रयs to the exclusion of each other. For the literal meaning of the word अयुतसिद्ध see Ṣaḍ-Darśana-Sam., Guṇaratna's Com. p. 278. "य इहायुतसिद्धानामाधाराधेयभूतभावानां संबन्ध इह प्रत्ययहेतुः स हि भवति समवायः॥ केचिद्धातुपारायणकृतो यु अमिश्रणे इति पठन्ति। तत एवायुतसिद्धानामिति वैशेषिकीये सूत्रे। अयुतसिद्धानामपृथक्सिद्धानामिति व्याख्यातम्।" For the oft-quoted definition see Tarka-Bhâṣâ: "ययोर्द्वयोर्मध्ये एकमविनश्यदपराश्रितमेवावतिष्ठते तावेवायुतसिद्धौ। तदुक्तम् तावेवायुतसिद्धौ द्वौ विज्ञातव्यौ ययोर्द्वयोः। अनश्यदेकमपराश्रितमेवावतिष्ठते॥" See Pras'asta Bhâṣya and Nyâyakandalî.

इह तन्तुषु etc.—समवाय defined as the असाधारणकारण–the special cause–which accounts for such judgments as 'इह तन्तुषु पटः', a judgment of distinction between तन्तुs and पट, and yet of their indissoluble union.

II. Explanation of the text of the Stanza.

1. According to the Vaiśeṣika, of the things existent, viz., the six padârthas, only some possess सत्ता.

अस्तित्व—the very स्वरूप of a thing belongs to सामान्य etc., but it does not form the basis of any अनुवृत्ति or co-ordination in their case, and is, therefore, distinguished from that fuller and more real अस्तित्व which belongs to द्रव्य, गुण and कर्म. The latter is technically known as 'सत्ता', and is the basis of 'सत्प्रत्यय' and 'अनुवृत्तिप्रत्यय' *i.e.* judgments of existence and co-ordination. The reason why no judgment of co-ordination and therefore सामान्य is possible in the case of सामान्य, विशेष and समवाय is that in the case of सामान्य it would lead to 'अनवस्था' (a सामान्य in a सामान्य and so on *ad infinitum*); in the case of विशेष it would contradict its very nature ('रूपहानि') to possess सामान्य; and in the case of समवाय, there will be the lack of that very संबन्ध viz. समवाय, which is required for holding the सामान्य; for, समवाय cannot exist in a समवाय ('असंबन्धात्'). This famous Kârikâ of Udayanâcârya–"व्यक्तेरभेद: etc."—is found in his Kiraṇâvalî, a commentary on P. Bhâṣya.

This stanza of Udayanâcârya has been explained in numerous books on Nyâya. Let us quote two explanations, one given briefly by Guṇaratna in S. D. S. Com.: "अस्य व्याख्या। व्यक्तेरभेद एकमनेकवर्ति सामान्यम्। आकाशे व्यक्तेरभेदान्न जातित्वम् १। पृथिवीत्वे जातौ यदि भूमित्वमुच्यते तदा तुल्यत्वम् २। परमाणुषु जातित्वेऽङ्गीकृते पार्थिवाप्यतैजसवायवीयत्वयोगात् संकरः ३। सामान्ये यदि सामान्यमङ्गीक्रियते तदा मूलक्षतिकारिणी अनवस्थितिः ४। विशेषेषु यदि सामान्यं स्वीक्रियते तदा विशेषस्य रूपहानिः ५। यदि समवाये जातित्वमङ्गीक्रियते तदा संबन्धाभावः ६। केन हि संबन्धेन तत्र सत्ता संबध्यते। समवायान्तराभावात्।" p. 276; the other in Jayanârâyaṇa's Vivṛti of Upaskâra: "तत्रैकव्यक्तिकत्वादाकाशं न जातिः। अन्यूनानतिरिक्तव्यक्तिकत्वाद्घटत्वं कलशत्वं च न जातिद्वयम्। परस्पराऽत्यन्ताभावसमानाधिकरणयोरेकव्यक्तिसमावेशेन संकरेण भूतत्वं मूर्त्तत्वं च न जातिः। अनवस्थाभयात् सामान्यत्वं न जातिः। विशेषस्य व्यावृत्तस्वभावस्य रूपहानिर्विशेषत्वजातिबाधिका। यदि विशेषत्वं जातिः स्यात् तदा जातिमतः स्वतोऽव्यावृत्तत्वासंभवेन स्वतोव्यावृत्तत्वरूपस्य असाधारणधर्मस्य व्याघातः स्यादतो विशेषत्वं न जातिः। अथवा रूपहानिः स्वरूपहानिः। तथा च विशेषा यदि मूर्तवृत्तित्वे सति जातिमन्तः स्युस्तदा गुणाः कर्माणि वा स्युः विभुवृत्तित्वे सति जातिमन्तः स्युस्तदा गुणाः स्युरिति विशेषस्य स्वरूपहानिर्विशेषत्वजातिबाधिका। समवायसंबन्धाभावात् समवायत्वं न जातिः। समवाये समवायान्तरस्वीकारेऽनवस्थाप्रसङ्गात्। उत्पादविनाशशालिनो बहवः समवाया इति मते नैतत्।

अन्यथैकव्यक्तिकत्वादपि समवायत्वं न जातिः स्यात् । एवमभावत्वस्य जातित्वे समवायसंबन्धाभाव एव बाधकः इत्यादिकमूहनीयम् ॥ प्राभाकरास्तु संस्थान-व्यङ्ग्यैव जातिः सा च गुणकर्मणो नास्तीत्याहुः ।"

2. तथा चैतन्यं etc.—Second line of the Stanza. Another curious doctrine of the Vais. is that ज्ञान is *absolutely* distinct from आत्मन् (a particular variety of the general relation of धर्म and धर्मिन् discussed in the last stanza.)

अन्यत्—absolutely distinct; the word is not subordinated to any compound, and it thus yields the idea of *absolute* distinction, not some distinction. The latter the Jaina too is prepared to hold.

अत्यन्तभेदे etc.—Absurd as the doctrine is, it requires to be given some appearance of reasonableness. Hence, औपाधिक in the stanza, which means 'arising from an उपाधि' *i.e.* conditioning circumstance, which in the present case is समवाय. Thus, the line means: चैतन्य or ज्ञान is absolutely distinct from आत्मन् but is connected with आत्मन् by समवायसंबन्ध; in other words, ज्ञान is an adventitious, not an essential, attribute of आत्मन्.

यदात्मनो etc.—If आत्मन् were not distinct from ज्ञान, the cessation of ज्ञान which must take place in the state of मोक्ष would mean the cessation—the death—of आत्मन्. Hence, the Vais. doctrine of आत्मन् as separate from ज्ञान. "दुःख-जन्म-प्रवृत्ति etc.'—is Nyâyasûtra I. i. 9. It means: Pain, Birth, Activity, Passion, Error—of these every preceding one being destroyed, every succeeding one is destroyed also; thus, in the state of मोक्ष, all the special गुणs of आत्मन्, viz. बुद्धि etc., cease to exist.

3. तथा न संविद्—A third curious doctrine of the Vais. is that in the state of मोक्ष, there is no संविद् (ज्ञान) or आनन्दः, बुद्धि, सुख etc. are all extirpated from आत्मन् in that state.

प्रयोगश्चात्र etc.—Syllogism to prove that the nine विशेषगुणs of आत्मन्, viz. बुद्धि etc., must cease to exist in the state of मोक्ष. It is based upon the hetu 'संतानत्वात्', *i. e.* because they are 'streams', i. e. none of them is a permanent nature of आत्मन्, but a stream of qualities continuously flowing on the ground of आत्मन्.

न हि वै सशरीरस्य etc.—This is a text of the Chândogya Upaniṣad, declaring that when आत्मन् is rid of the body–as he must be in the state of मोक्ष—सुख and दुःख touch him no more.

अपि च etc.—The verses quoted here, with the exception of couplet No. 5, occur in न्या. मञ्जरि p. 508. The latter has one more couplet which gives the list of the six ऊर्मिs : "प्राणस्य क्षुत्पिपासे द्वे लोभमोहौ च चेतसः। शीतातपौ शरीरस्य षडूर्मिरहितः शिवः।" A recent edition of the स्याद्वादमञ्जरी quotes in the footnote a somewhat different list: "प्राणस्य क्षुत्पिपासे द्वे मनसः शोकमूढते। जरामृत्यू शरीरस्य षडूर्मिरहितः शिवः।—इति पुराणे." The list of the text differs from both (Text p. 39 l. 118).

सुसूत्रं etc.—सुसूत्रम् (noun)=A good (ironical, and therefore= bad) doctrine, indeed, has been formulated by them! सुसूत्रम् (adverb) = with excellent (ironical) reason. For the irony contained in the word, the commentator compares उपकृतं etc.—which is quoted in the Kâvyaprakâs'a.

III. Criticism of the Vais'eṣika doctrines detailed above :—

1. अविशेषेण etc.—It is a piece of great audacity to restrict सत्ता to the three padârthas द्रव्य, गुण and कर्म, when the idea of existence is undeniably predicable of all the padârthas.

यतः परिभाव्यताम् etc.—Just see how the word सत्ता is formed: it is an abstract noun from सत्–existing, pres. part. of अस् to exist. It is, therefore, wholly equivalent to अस्तित्व—and since अस्तित्व is the very स्वरूप of things, which you are prepared to predicate of all the पदार्थs (see supra)–the plea that अनुवृत्तिप्रत्यय or co-ordination is possible in the case of the first three and is absent from the rest is baseless. For, अनुवृत्तिप्रत्यय is possible in the case of all the categories. For, just as we say पृथ्वीत्व is a सामान्य, गोत्व is a सामान्य, घटत्व is a सामान्य and so on, thus referring to a common idea (अनुवृत्तिप्रत्यय) of सामान्य running through all its specimens, in the same way, we have this विशेष, that विशेष, a third विशेष and so on, which shows that we have a general idea of विशेष which we recognize in all the विशेषs. Similarly in the case of समवाय, there are several समवायs taken with their several अवच्छेदकs —which reveal one general idea of समवाय.

स्वरूपत्वसाधर्म्येण—It may be contended that in consequence of all the categories having a certain स्वरूप of their own, and therefore likeness in this particular, सत्ता which really belongs to the first three is erroneously extended to the rest. Thus, in consequence of false ascription (अध्यारोप) of सत्ता to सामान्य etc., we imagine that the सत्प्रत्यय runs through them also, whereas, as a matter of fact, what belongs to them is mere अस्तित्व (not an अनुवृत्तसत्प्रत्यय) as their वस्तुस्वरूप *i. e.* as the very being of those categories. The Jaina's answer to this argument is that if the ascription of सत्ता to सामान्य etc. be false for the reason that we are thereby ascribing a common nature to things that are really diverse, the same thing could be said about सत्ता as applied to द्रव्य, गुण, and कर्म, and one would be as much an 'अध्यारोप' (false ascription) as the other. The Vais'eṣika might reply that सत्ता as traced in द्रव्य, गुण and कर्म is *real*, while in the rest it is unreal, for there cannot be a false ascription unless there is reality somewhere, and that is in सत्ता as perceived in द्रव्य, गुण and कर्म. But this division of सत्ता into मुख्य and गौण,—मुख्य in the first three cases and गौण in the last three—could be reversed with equal justice, if only the distinction between real and unreal is to be secured somehow.

सामान्यादिषु बाधकसंभवात् etc. But it may be urged that the सत्प्रत्यय in the case of the सामान्य etc. is गौण owing to the difficulties mentioned above (see above). But, in truth, the difficulties are quite imaginary. If the admission of सत्ता in सामान्य leads to अनवस्था, why not in द्रव्यs? In द्रव्यs there is the स्वरूपसत्ता (their very being) already, and admission of another सत्ता (सामान्य) would lead to similar अनवस्था. Then, as to विशेषs, there should be no harm in ascribing to them सत्ता, for that will not interfere with their nature, as is supposed, but will on the contrary, confirm it. Besides, a विशेष which is totally devoid of सामान्य is found nowhere. Lastly, the समवाय would lose its very being, unless it possessed a स्वरूपसत्ता *i. e.* existence of something that makes it what it is viz., समवायत्व which gives it its peculiar character of 'अविष्वग्भावात्मकसंबन्ध' (indissoluble relation).

किं च तैर्वादिभिः—Moreover, the सत्ता cannot be a distinct reality added unto the द्रव्य etc. from without. If सत्ता be *absolutely* distinct from द्रव्य etc. the latter would be असत्. It may be urged that they acquire सत्त्व in consequence of their possessing सत्ता. But the answer to it is—If they are असत् in themselves, सत्ता cannot make them सत्; if they are सत् in themselves, सत्ता can add nothing and is therefore superfluous. If all the भावs have got their स्वरूपसत्त्व–their own individual being–what can सत्ता add to them or it? If it be urged that a भाव is neither सत् nor असत् before it becomes invested with सत्ता and that it becomes सत् after it is so invested, all we need say is that it is useless hair-splitting, for nothing can be neither सत् nor असत्, it must be one or the other or, as we Jainas prefer to maintain, both.

cf. "अथ सामान्यम्। तद्द्विधा–परमपरं च। तत्र परं महासत्ताख्यं द्रव्यादिपदार्थव्यापि। तथा चोक्तम्—"सदिति यतो द्रव्यगुणकर्मसु सा सत्ता"। अपरं च द्रव्यगुणत्वं गुणत्वकर्मत्वात्मकम्। तत्र न तावन्महासत्तायाः पृथक्पदार्थता युज्यते। यतस्तस्यां यः सदिति प्रत्ययः स किमपरसत्तानिबन्धन उत स्वत एव? । तत् यद्यपरसत्तानिबन्धनस्तत्राप्ययमेव विकल्पोऽतोऽनवस्था। अथ स्वत एव ततस्तद्वद् द्रव्यादिष्वपि स्वत एव सत्प्रत्ययो भविष्यतीति किमपरसत्तयाऽजागलस्तनकल्पया विकल्पितया?। किं च—द्रव्यादीनां किं सतां सत्तया सत्प्रत्यय उतासताम्?। तत् यदि सतां स्वत एव सत्प्रत्ययो भविष्यति। किं तया?। असत्पक्षे तु शशविषाणादिष्वपि सत्तायोगात् सत्प्रत्ययः स्यादिति। तथा चोक्तम्—"स्वतोऽर्थाः सन्तु सत्तावत् सत्तया किं सदात्मनाम्?। असदात्मसु नैषा स्यात् सर्वथातिप्रसङ्गतः॥" इत्यादि। एतदेव दूषणमपरसामान्येऽप्यायोज्यम्। तुल्ययोगक्षेमत्वात्। किं च—अस्माभिरपि सामान्यविशेषरूपत्वाद्वस्तुनः कथंचित्तदिष्यत एवेति। तस्य च कथंचित्तद्व्यतिरेकाद् द्रव्यग्रहणेनैव ग्रहणमिति॥ अथ विशेषाः ते चात्यन्तव्यावृत्तिबुद्धिहेतुत्वेन परैराश्रीयन्ते। तत्रेदं चिन्त्यते—या तेषु विशेषबुद्धिः सा नापरविशेषहेतुकाऽऽश्रयितव्या। अनवस्थाभयात्। स्वतः समाश्रयणे च तद्वद् द्रव्यादिष्वपि विशेषबुद्धिः स्यात् किं द्रव्यादिव्यतिरिक्तैर्विशेषैरिति। द्रव्यादिव्यतिरिक्तास्तु विशेषा अस्माभिरप्याश्रीयन्ते सर्वस्य सामान्यविशेषात्मकत्वादिति। एतत्तु प्रक्रियामात्रम्।

तद्यथा—नित्यद्रव्यवृत्तयोऽन्त्या विशेषाः, नित्यद्रव्याणि च चतुर्विधाः परमाणवो मुक्तात्मानो मुक्तमनांसि च—इति निर्युक्तिकत्वादपकर्णयितव्यमिति ।"

2. ज्ञानमपि यद्येव etc.—If ज्ञान is to be supposed to be *absolutely distinct* from आत्मन्, the ज्ञान of Mr. Caitra is in the same position with respect to his आत्मन् as the ज्ञान of Mr. Maitra, that is to say, both the ज्ञानs would be equal strangers to the आत्मन् of Mr. Caitra, and there is no reason why his ज्ञान should serve him better than the ज्ञान of any other person in determining the nature of things; in fact, there is no such thing as *his* ज्ञान, all ज्ञानs being equally foreign to him. An explanation may be offered by the other side: ज्ञान is absolutely distinct from आत्मन्, but it is connected with आत्मन् by समवायसंबन्ध, and hence the ज्ञान of Mr. Caitra is not in the same position with respect to him as the ज्ञान of Mr. Maitra; for, the former is connected with him by समवाय relation which the latter is not. But this explanation can be easily scotched. According to your notion of समवाय, it is एक, नित्य and व्यापक, and therefore it is impossible that ज्ञान should reside in Caitra and not in Maitra; and since आत्मन्s are also व्यापक according to your theory, the ज्ञान, which takes place in one आत्मन् takes place in all the आत्मन्s, and any knowledge which Caitra has acquired will belong to Maitra also!

यथा च घटे etc.—Moreover, according to the Vais'. theory when the रूप of an object is destroyed and another is substituted, the object gets destroyed, also a new object taking its place with the new रूप. Similarly, when ज्ञान perishes आत्मन् would be expected to perish also.

अथास्तु समवायेन etc.—Let us concede that it is possible for ज्ञान to be connected with आत्मन् by समवाय relation. But a question still remains to be answered: By what relation is the समवाय connected with ज्ञान and आत्मन्? By another समवाय? That would mean an unending series of समवायs–अनवस्था. Of itself? Then, why should not ज्ञान and आत्मन् be connected of themselves, without requiring a समवाय relation to effect the connection?

अथ यथा प्रदीपः etc.—A possible argument on the side of the Vais'. As it is the nature of a प्रदीप to illumine, so it is the nature of समवाय to connect. It, therefore, does not require to be brought into connection with ज्ञान and आत्मन् by any other connection. Answer: Why should it not similarly be the nature of ज्ञान and आत्मन् to be self-connected? Moreover, the analogy of प्रदीप will not fit in. प्रदीप is a द्रव्य *i. e.* धर्मिन्, and प्रकाश its धर्म; and, according to you धर्म and धर्मिन् are absolutely distinct. So how could a प्रदीप have प्रकाश for its very self or being? And if प्रकाश be not the very self of प्रदीप, it would be absurd to cite प्रदीप as an example of a द्रव्य which illumines both itself and others. If प्रकाश be absolutely distinct from प्रदीप and yet प्रदीप is capable of illumining itself as well as other objects, there is no reason why घट, पट should not do the same.

अपि च तौ etc.—Next, are the two स्वभावs of समवाय viz., that of connecting itself and of connecting others (आत्मन् and ज्ञान in this case) distinct from the समवाय or one with the समवाय? In the former case, how can they be its स्वभावs, unless they are connected with it by another connection, which would similarly require to be connected by a third, and so on *ad infinitum*? In the latter case, there remains only समवाय in the field, and the old difficulties continue as before. Therefore, just as you say 'इह समवायिषु समवायः' and no second समवाय is required to connect the first समवाय with the समवायिन्s, in the same way why can we not say 'इहात्मनि ज्ञानम्' without requiring a संबन्ध like समवाय to connect ज्ञान with आत्मन्?

अथात्मा कर्ता etc.—It may be urged that a distinction between आत्मन् and ज्ञान is required owing to their being related as कर्तृ and करण, आत्मन् being the कर्तृ and ज्ञान the करण. Answer: The position of ज्ञान is different from that of an ordinary करण such as a scythe (दात्र): ज्ञान is an internal करण, while the scythe is an external करण cf. करणं etc. Now, if an internal करण could be shown which was absolutely distinct from कर्तृ, the argument of absolute distinction between ज्ञान and आत्मन् would hold water, but not otherwise. We say 'दीपेन चक्षुषा देवदत्तः

पश्यति ' : here दीप and चक्षुः are both करणs, but on that account the two are not in the same position of अत्यन्तभेद with respect to देवदत्त.

अपि च साध्यविफलो etc.—Moreover, it should be noted that the example of the carpenter (कर्तृ) and his tool (करण) does not point to an absolute distinction between the two. The carpenter has to resolve—which is a process of आत्मन्—to use the tool and thus undergo a परिणाम of आत्मन् and assimilate the tool with himself in order to work on the wood. So in this sense even the carpenter and his tool may be said to be not absolutely distinct. In the same way, आत्मन् resolves to know a particular object by means of his ज्ञान, undergoes परिणाम and assimilates the ज्ञान with himself, and thus the two becoming one, produce the effect, viz., knowledge of the thing (संवित्ति).

एवं कर्तृकरणयोरभेदे etc.—Now, the unity of कर्तृ and करण being proved, we have one question to put to the opponent: Is the ज्ञान or संवित्ति, which is the effect of the united action of कर्तृ and करण, resident in (a) आत्मन् or (b) विषय? If (a) in आत्मन्, that is all we care to prove. If (b) in विषय, how does that mean consciousness (अनुभव) in आत्मन्? If the consciousness (अनुभव) in the person springs from संवित्ति in the object, why does it not arise in another person? For, there is no difference between the position of one person and another, in as much as the विषय with its संवित्ति is absolutely extraneous to the person.

अथ ज्ञानात्मनोरभेद etc.—If ज्ञान and आत्मन् are one, how is their relation of कर्तृ and करण to be accounted for? Answer: By the analogy of a serpent who makes a coil of his body by his body. It may be said that the कर्तृकरणभाव in the case of the serpent is simply imaginary. Criticism: How can it be said to be imaginary, when we actually see the effect, viz., the coil, which is a new state of rest different from the former state of motion? No amount of imagination could make us believe that a pillar was going to wind itself into a coil.

किं च चैतन्यम् etc.—Next, consider the word चैतन्य. It is the abstract noun from चेतन which means आत्मन्. Thus चैतन्य means the भाव or स्वरूप of आत्मन्. Now, how can a भाव or स्वरूप of a thing be absolutely distinct from a thing?

अथास्ति चेतन etc.—The Vais'. argues that आत्मन् is no doubt चेतन, but that is not without a cause (स्वतः), but is owing to चेतना coming to reside by समवाय relation in आत्मन् as is shown by actual प्रतीति (experience). Answer : If you are prepared to accept the evidence of प्रतीति, you must admit that आत्मन् is by nature 'उपयोगात्मक' *i. e.* of the nature of consciousness. For, nobody is aware of being first अचेतन–that is, lacking in consciousness, and afterwards becoming चेतन in consequence of connection with चेतना, or of चेतना coming to reside by समवाय relation in him who was at first अचेतन. [उपयोग is thus defined in the Tat. Râj. Vârt. "बाह्याभ्यन्तरहेतुद्वयसंनिधाने यथासम्भवमुपलब्धुश्चैतन्यानुविधायी परिणामः उपयोगः" *i. e.* 'उपयोग' is the modification that takes place in the knowing mind (उपलब्धृ) in accordance with its चैतन्य, when the external and internal हेतुs are present.] On the contrary, he is always aware of himself as 'ज्ञाताहम्' which implies सामानाधिकरण्य *i. e.* apposition, unity of आत्मन् and ज्ञान.

भेदे तथा प्रतीतिः etc.—This सामानाधिकरण्य could take place even when there was भेद. Answer : But never, unless there were अभेद in some way or another. In 'यष्टिः पुरुषः' (when we speak of a " man," who is straight and stiff like a stick, as a " stick ") there is no doubt सामानाधिकरण्य (apposition, unity) inspite of भेद. But be it noted that there the सामानाधिकरण्यं is figurative, and not real. The figure, however, arises from the अभेद of certain qualities of the stick and the man, a figure being always based upon a foundation of reality. [see Kâvya-Prakâs'a Ullâsa II]. In the same way, our consciousness of 'ज्ञाताहम्' in आत्मन् shows that the अहम् is essentially ज्ञातृ or चेतन; without this, one could never say 'ज्ञाता अहम्' any more than घट could say so.

चैतन्ययोगाभावात् etc.—But it may be contended that घट can never say ज्ञाताहम् because घट does not possess चैतन्य. But the answer to it is that similarly if आत्मन् does not essentially possess चेतना it can never be aware of being चेतन as shown above. And so, if आत्मन् is अचेतन, it should be जड and incapable of knowing things, which is absurd.

ननु ज्ञानवानहम् etc.—It may be further contended that the consciousness 'ज्ञानवानहम्' would prove a distinction between ज्ञान and अहम्, for the former is that which is possessed (e. g. धन) and the latter is he who possesses (*e. g.* धनवान्). But the contention is untenable. For, who possesses the consciousness ज्ञानवानहम् in your theory? Not the आत्मन्; for, आत्मन् is supposed to be जड *i. e.* devoid of ज्ञान in himself like घट. You cannot assert that आत्मन् is जड (*i. e.* essentially devoid of ज्ञान), and yet be able to say 'ज्ञानवानहम्' without contradiction.

ज्ञानवानहमिति हि प्रत्ययो etc.—For, when I say 'ज्ञानवानहम्' I am supposed to have known both the विशेषण and the विशेष्य-नागृहीत etc.—See K. Pr. Now, let us inquire how the विशेषण and the विशेष्य in the present case are known–whether स्वतः or परतः? It cannot be स्वतः. For, according to the Vais'. ज्ञान (the विशेषण) and आत्मन् (अहम् the विशेष्य) are not self-revealed. It cannot be परतः. For, in that case, one ज्ञान would require to be revealed by another ज्ञान and so on ad infinitum (अनवस्था). Therefore, आत्मन् is not in himself जड (devoid of ज्ञान) by nature, who afterwards comes to possess ज्ञान by समवाय relation as the result of the working of इन्द्रियs etc.

3. तथा यदपि etc.—Next, it is held by the Vais'. that in मुक्ति there is neither ज्ञान nor आनन्द, since ज्ञान and आनन्द are "streams" (संतानs of attributes, a stream of cognitions and a stream of joys, *i. e.* pleasurable feelings) and all "streams" must cease at some point. Criticism: What is meant by their being 'streams'–'संतानत्व?' Does it mean a series of states which go on producing themselves independently of one another, and one after another? Or does it mean the states

which go on springing into existence one by one, but residing in a common abode? The former alternative involves the fallacy of सव्यभिचारहेतु *i. e.* संतानत्व in this sense does not necessarily imply cessation. For, घट, पट etc., are running on in an unceasing stream. The second alternative presents a conception of संतान which does not fit in with the example of प्रदीप. Moreover, in the case of परमाणुपाकजरूप (a new रूप produced in atoms by means of heat), there is a continued stream–संतान–of products, but no absolute cessation. Besides, there may be a continuous stream and no absolute cessation; for, there is nothing to render such a position impossible: a suspicion like this would arise in the mind and make the hetu "inconclusive".

किं च स्याद्वाद etc.—Besides, according to the Syâdvâda of the Jainas there is no अत्यन्त उच्छेद–absolute annihilation of anything, all things being regarded as persisting in the midst of change: cf. उत्पादध्रौव्ययुक्तं सत्.

न हि सशरीरस्य etc.—This text of the Upaniṣad admits of a better interpretation than that placed upon it by the Vaiś. Thus: It need not mean that in the state of मोक्ष when the आत्मन् is free from the body there is an end to both सुख and दुःख; it should only mean that आत्मन् in that condition is free from the pair of सुख and दुःख, that is to say, from such सुख as is bound up with दुःख *i. e.* the सुख of संसार. It does not preclude the existence of pure, unmixed सुख–such as is proper to मुक्ति. Malliṣeṇa seems to read 'वसन्तम्' for 'वाव सन्तम्' in the Upaniṣad. वसन्तम् = सिद्धिक्षेत्रमध्यासीनम्—occupying the state of मुक्ति or Perfection.

स्मृतिरपि etc.—The first half of the verse is the first line of Verse 20, Adhyâya VI of the Bh. Gîtâ. Here सुख need not mean merely दुःखाभाव–a negative condition of the absence of sorrow. For, सुख is not a mere negative state of आत्मन्.

न च भवदुदीरितो मोक्षः etc.—Who would care for the negative state of दुःखाभाव which the Vaiś. holds forth as the state of मुक्ति? Such a state would be no better than that of a stone which too possesses दुःखाभाव (को हि नाम etc.—cf. न्या. म. p. 508). The Vaiś. मुक्ति is well-ridiculed in the famous passage "वरं etc."

अथास्ति etc. Some out of sheer despair of pessimism may prefer even दुःखाभाव to the present condition of mixed सुख and दुःख. But it should be noted that even they throw off the 'poison and honey' only with the desire of being thereby happy. Thus, happiness is always the desired end.

किं च यथा प्राणिनां etc.—Moreover, just as we regard दुःख as undesirable and सुख as desirable in the संसारावस्था, so we should be expected to regard दुःखनिवृत्ति as desirable and सुखनिवृत्ति as undesirable in मोक्षावस्था. If मोक्ष were such a negative state of दुःखाभाव as you suppose it to be, no wise man would care for it. But many wise men do care for it. This implies that मोक्ष is regarded by them as a state of positive joy (सुख).

अथ यदि etc.—Does not even Homer nod? If wise men too long for happiness, they are not wise men to that extent, longing of every kind being inconsistent with wisdom and the source of bondage. Answer: It is the longing for the pleasures of संसार that makes for bondage, not the noble desire which opens up the path to wisdom.

अपि च मोक्तपस्विन् etc.—The Jaina out of the fulness of his merciful heart sympathises with the opponent and tells him how, after all, he does agree with him to some extent, inasmuch as he too admits some sort of उच्छेद्-annihilation.

बुद्धि etc.—बुद्धि in the Vaiś. system means ज्ञान. ज्ञान, says the Jaina, is of five kinds: (1) मति, (2) श्रुत, (3) अवधि, (4) मनःपर्यो(र्य)य, and (5) केवल (See Tattv. Sûtra; also supra). Of these the first four, which are क्षायोपशमिक—*i. e.* arising from उपशम (quelling, precipitation; not, destruction) as well as क्षय (destruction) of Karma—cease as soon as केवलज्ञान arises. But the केवलज्ञान which embraces within its range all द्रव्यs with their पर्यायs (modes) persists in the condition of मोक्ष. In fact, it is the characteristic feature of मोक्ष. Thus, there is a partial agreement with the Vaiś. to the extent of the first four varieties of ज्ञान. नहंभि etc.—See आवश्यक०.

सुखं तु etc.—The सुख arising from worldly objects ceases in the state of मोक्ष, because the वेदनीय कर्म which was the source of the sensations of pleasure and pain in worldly experience has been exhausted. So, in the condition of मोक्ष, there is endless, infinite सुख of spirit, but no दुःख, because अधर्म, the source of दुःख is no more.

नन्वेवं सुखस्यापि etc.—Following the same line of reasoning it may be argued that सुख would also cease, because its source—viz., धर्म–is no more. Answer: धर्म is the source of वैषयिक सुख *i. e.* objective pleasures, and so, धर्म ceasing, वैषयिक सुख would also cease. Not, however, the आत्मसुख *i. e.* the spiritual joy of आत्मन् which is inherent in him. On धर्म and its relation to सुख, and the अपवर्ग transcending धर्म and its सुख as much as अधर्म and its दुःख, compare the Vedânta doctrine.

इच्छा द्वेष etc.—इच्छा and द्वेष of course cease, because they are varieties of मोह.

प्रयत्नश्च etc.—Ordinary प्रयत्न *i. e.* effort in the direction of क्रिया ceases, because in मोक्ष nothing remains to be done. But there still persists the one special kind of प्रयत्न which has brought about the destruction of वीर्यान्तराय, the impediment to मोक्ष consisting of spiritual inertia or slothfulness.

The प्रयत्न, however, is admitted to be " ineffective ". How will it then satisfy the definition of सत्त्व = अर्थक्रियाकारित्व ?

धर्माधर्मयो : etc.—धर्माधर्म alias पुण्यपाप must, of course, cease in the state of मोक्ष.

संस्कार etc.—This is a kind of मतिज्ञान and it ceases as soon as मोह is destroyed.

It will be noticed that Mallisena has thus passed in review all the special attributes of आत्मन् as held in the Vais'. system and shown how far according to himself they persist in the state of मोक्ष.

For a knowledge of the Vaiś. categories the best books to read are the Vaiś. Sûtras, with Upaskâra, Praśastapâda's Bhâṣya and S'rîdhara's Nyâya-Kandalî. For सामान्य and the doctrine of सत्ता consult the same; also, the Muktâvalî and the Dinakarî and the Nîlakaṇṭhî.

For the nature of आत्मन् and its relation to ज्ञान see Madhusûdana's Siddhânta-tattva-bindu Com., and Vedânta Sûtras II.iii. with differences between S'aṁkara and Râmânuja.

Stanza IX.

Different views as regards the size (परिमाण) of आत्मन् :

(i) आत्मन् is विभु (all-pervasive, infinitely vast in size) according to the Vais'eṣikas, Naiyâyikas, Sâṁkhyas, Yogins and Vedântins of the S'âṁkara School. [*N. B.* With the first two its विभुत्व consists in the possession of a positive परिमाण which does not seem to differ in character from that which belongs to आकाश; with the third and the fourth, in its essential freedom from the bondage of प्रकृति; with the last, in the negation of all limiting उपाधिs including spatial limitations.]

(ii) आत्मन् is अणु (infinitesimal) according to the Vedântins of the Râmânuja-and Vallabha-Âcâryas' schools.

(iii) आत्मन् is मध्यमपरिमाण, adjusting itself to the size of the body in which it dwells. This is the Jaina view. This, says the Jaina, is borne out by our consciousness; for we are not conscious of ourselves as either infinitely vast, or infinitely small (infinitesimal), but as co-extensive with our own physical body—[" कायप्रमाणत्वमात्मनः स्वयं संवेद्यमानं..."].

Of these (i) comes up for criticism as a tenet of the Vais'eṣika school which is now under examination.

यत्रैव देशे......एवायमिति—The guṇas of Âtman, such as चैतन्य etc., are found within the limits of the body. From this the natural inference is that Âtman is co-extensive with the body (तत्परिमाणः). This is clear from the example of घट etc., which, as all agree, exist only where their guṇas (रूप etc.,) are found and not elsewhere and yet these fools who ignore facts place the Âtman outside the body! [यत्रैव यो दृष्टगुणः स तत्र कुम्भादिवत्; निष्प्रतिपक्षमेतत् etc.]

यद्यपि पुष्पादीनां etc.—The case of a flower emitting its fragrance beyond itself is no exception.

वैस्रसिकया प्रायोगिकया वा etc.—Involuntary and voluntary; natural and voluntarily (that is volitionally) caused. cf Râjavârt. pp. 200 and 232.

विस्रसा विधिविपर्यये निपातः—पौरुषेयपरिणामापेक्षा विधिः तद्विपर्यये विस्रसाशब्दो निपातो द्रष्टव्यः। प्रयोगः पुरुषकायवाङ्मनःसंयोगलक्षणः। पुद्गलानामपि द्विविधा क्रिया विस्रसा प्रयोगनिमित्ता च। See Tatvârtha.

'न च दृष्टेऽनुपपन्नं नाम'—A very frequently used argument and phrase. cf. S'îl. com. on Sûtrak.

ननु मन्त्रादीनां etc.—The case of मन्त्रs (magic spells or incantations) is cited by the opponent as showing *actio in distans.* But this is explained away by the Siddhântin as really a case of their *devatâs* going out to the spot where the effect takes place.

अनाचार इव—The negative (नञ्-अन्) sometimes connotes not mere negation or absence, but badness (कुत्सा); *e. g.* अनाचार is not mere absence of आचार, but bad आचार. Similarly अतत्त्व० means not only those who ignore truth, but those who espouse the opposite of truth *i. e.* wretched falsehood.

II भावार्थस्त्वयम्: Substance of the Stanza:—

आत्मा सर्वगतो न भवति etc.—A परार्थानुमान with an अन्वयव्यतिरेकि-हेतु and a negative साध्य.

न चायमसिद्धो हेतुः—The author next shows that the हेतु in the above अनुमान is free from all fallacies: The only fallacies that could possibly be suspected in the present case are those of (a) an असिद्ध (स्वरूपासिद्ध) हेतु, (b) an अनैकान्तिक हेतु and (c) a विरुद्ध हेतु. That none of them exists in the present case may be shown as follows:—

(a) सर्वत्र तद्गुणानुपलब्धेः etc.—The above अनुमान is not vitiated by an असिद्ध (that is, स्वरूपासिद्ध) हेतु. For, the हेतु *is* predicable of the पक्ष. The guṇas of आत्मन्—बुद्धि etc., are not found everywhere. Vide the following from S'rîdhara's Nyâyakandalī: "सर्वगतत्वेऽप्यात्मनो देहप्रदेशे ज्ञातृत्वं नान्यत्र। शरीरस्योपभोगार्थत्वात्। अन्यथा तस्य वैयर्थ्यात्" Nyâyakandalī p. 62. आत्मन् is everywhere, but its ज्ञातृत्व takes place within the limits—confines—of the body.

अथास्त्यदृष्ट...आत्मेति etc.—A possible objection: Take an other गुण of आत्मन्—viz. अदृष्ट. It is a निमित्तकारण of everything that rises into being, and is *everywhere.* So, it operates at remotest places and produces effects which I am destined to enjoy or suffer. Now, unless आत्मन् were everywhere—even at the remotest places—its गुण viz. अदृष्ट could not be *there*, and so could not produce the things.

अथास्त्येव etc.—Mark the weak spot in the above argument: The *Pûrva-pakṣin* has not proved that the अदृष्ट cannot operate *from here.* The author, however, makes a bolder attack, directing his criticism against the very doctrine of अदृष्ट, and revealing a situation which makes the existence of God (a favourite doctrine of the Vaiśeṣikas) superfluous. As a proof of अदृष्ट, the Vaiś. cites phenomena which cannot be explained by any known causes—*e. g.* the natural properties of fire, air etc. (वह्नेरूर्ध्वज्वलनं etc.) : All ultimate properties of things are thus determined by अदृष्ट. The author asks : Could not these properties be regarded as *the very nature* of fire, air etc., rather than be accounted for by an obscure cause of which we know nothing and which you dub 'अदृष्ट'? It is silly to attempt to explain the obscure by the obscure. The Vaiśeṣika would reply by a question: What endows them with that nature? What makes their nature what it is?—if not 'अदृष्ट'? The author: Indeed? The 'अदृष्ट' will then account for every variety in Creation, thereby making the doctrine of the existence of God superfluous! [Mark that to account for the variety of Creation is not the same thing as to account for Creation itself—unless Creation and its variety may be regarded as a single fact—one integral or concrete reality—not an impossible position in itself. Moreover, it may be noted that the early Vaiśeṣika philosopher did not explain Creation by the hypothesis of a Divine Creator, but that of the mysterious something—which he called 'अदृष्ट'—the Unseen.]

(b) न चानैकान्तिकः etc.—The हेतु is not 'अनैकान्तिक' *i. e.* inconclusive for want of invariable concomitance between the हेतु and the साध्य—the हेतु 'सर्वत्र तद्गुणानुपलब्धेः' being in every case accompanied by the साध्य—'सर्वगतो न भवति.'

(c) नापि विरुद्धः etc.—Much less is the हेतु—'विरुद्ध' *i. e.* proving the very opposite of what is intended to be proved. There is not a single instance to break the universal concomitance between the हेतु and the साध्य.

अन्यच्च त्वया आत्मनां बहुत्वमिष्यते—See Vaiśeṣika Sû. p. 87; Nyâyakandalī p. 88.

The Vaiś. holds that आत्मन्s are *many* and that each of them is all-pervasive (विभु). This, says the author, would create inter-penetration of आत्मन्s, and the consequent confusion of their कर्मन्s, and also of their सुखदुःख etc.

This difficulty the opponent may perhaps endeavour to meet by holding that the experience of सुख and दुःख takes place, with every individual आत्मन्, *within the limits of the body*. But, in that case, अदृष्ट—whose case is similar to that of सुखदुःख inasmuch as all of them are guṇas of आत्मन्—would be confined to the limits of the body; so that it could not go forth to the spot of the fire and cause it to burn in the particular manner in which it does. And this would be cutting off the ground on which the case of the all-pervasiveness of आत्मन् is attempted to be based. [Vide supra आत्मनां च सर्वगतत्वे...]

Not only would our आत्मन्s—together with their कर्मन्s and their सुखदुःख—get hopelessly mixed up *inter se*, but also with God!

किं च आत्मनः etc.—Moreover, the आत्मन् would be then living in every possible world—earth, heaven and hell—at one and the same time.

अथ भोगायतनाभ्युपगमात् etc.-How does आत्मन् localise himself in the body? *In toto* or *in part?* In the former case, the position reached would be exactly the one which is maintained by the Jaina. In the latter case, आत्मन् would be a substance possessing parts—which is absurd. Moreover, the experience of pleasure and pain would not belong to the whole but only to a part of आत्मन्!

अथात्मनो व्यापकत्वाभावे etc.—The Vaiś. argues: If आत्मन् were not all-pervasive and were consequently far away from the particles of matter which have to be set in motion in order to build a body out of it for its abode, then it could not exercise any influence on the particles and could not eventually produce the body and be its owner, and it would thus be eternally 'मुक्त'—liberated!

The author: This argument could be easily met by denying the necessity of adjacence between the cause and the material on which it has to act: Compare the case of the magnet operating on a piece of iron.

Vaiś.: If distance (असंयोग) were no bar to action, would not the whole world of particles be drawn to आत्मन् and produce a prodigious body?

The author: Are not all the particles equally in contact (संयुक्त) with आत्मन् on your hypothesis of विभुद्रव्य and therefore equally entitled to get corporealized?

The Vaiś.: No; they would be selected for the purpose by अदृष्ट.

The author (Siddhântin): The same principle of selection could work amongst the distant (असंयुक्त) particles, and prevent the imaginary rush for corporealization.

अथास्तु यथा कथञ्चित् etc.—The Vaiśeṣika grants for the sake of argument that the corporealization of आत्मन् is somehow possible. Yet, he says, a difficulty remains: It means then that a *part* of आत्मन् enters every particle of the body in which it becomes incarnate. This will be a fatal position—involving the consequence that आत्मन् is a कार्य *i. e.* a product out of certain ingredients!

Now, according to the law of homogeneity of Cause and and Effect these ingredients should be themselves आत्मन्s. Thus, the position reached is this: Several आत्मन्s dwell in one body and combine to produce a single आत्मन् dwelling in the same body! This is impossible. Supposing it is possible, it means loss of personal identity, and liability to disintegration of components, and therefore death.

To this the Jaina replies : He is prepared to accept the consequences : as a matter of fact, he does hold that somehow—in a certain sense—आत्मन् is possessed of parts (सावयव) and is a product (कार्य). The former *i. e.* सावयवत्व arises from its possessing innumerable प्रदेशs. "आकाश too," say रामचन्द्र and गुणचन्द्र authors of "द्रव्यालङ्कार," "has got देशs (extension), since it can possess contact with all मूर्तद्रव्यs at one and the same time." In certain works (*e.g.* गन्धहस्ति०) a distinction is drawn between अवयव and प्रदेश, but it is too fine and may be left out of consideration for the purposes of the present argument. प्रदेश is sometimes called अवयव, and since the Jaina holds that आत्मन् has got प्रदेशs, he may well make an admission that आत्मन् is सावयव—and in that sense आत्मन् is a कार्य too, in his system.

नन्वात्मनां कार्यत्वे etc.—The Jaina denies the force of the argument contained in the foregoing parallel. He says : Our explanation of the nature of the effect which we call घट is not that it is a new creation arising from the संयोग of the कपालs which are homogeneous with घट, but that the घट arises as a change of state from the original state when it is worked upon by the potter. A द्रव्य is said to be a कार्य, when abandoning one form it assumes another. This is true of the internal quite as much as of the external world. And in this sense आत्मन् must be admitted to be a कार्य. It may be that in making a पट you have to bring together (संयोग) the तन्तुs, but it is not the only manner of producing things (cf. "कार्यारम्भोऽपि नावयवसंयोगेनैव केवलेन भवति, क्षीरजलादीनामप्यन्तरेणाप्यवयवसंयोगान्तरं दधिहिमादिकार्यारम्भदर्शनात्" S'aṁkara on Br. Sû. II. ii. 17). We must recognise the endless variety of ways in which things are produced in nature.

न चोक्तलक्षण etc.—The Jaina turns the tables against the Vaiś. In the matter of the argument that मध्यम परिमाण would involve

कार्यत्व and therefore अनित्यत्व which is inconsistent with the nature of आत्मन्. Far from अनित्यत्व (change) interfering with personal identity it is the *sine qua non* of its consciousness. "I remember what I saw" would be impossible but for difference between him who saw and him who remembers, and the change from one to the other, between the state of seeing and the state of remembering. And this fact is inconsistent with absolute नित्यत्व of आत्मन् *i. e.* unchanging personal identity or consciousness.

अथात्मनः शरीरपरिमाणत्वे etc.—The Vais'. might urge: If आत्मन् were only as large as the body it would be मूर्त (possessed of extension) and in that case, how could it enter the body? For, two things possessed of मूर्तत्व cannot interpenetrate each other, and so the body must remain without a soul (आत्मन्)!

To this the Jaina replies: What is a 'मूर्त द्रव्य'? Does it mean a द्रव्य which has a limited size? In that sense आत्मन् is मूर्त, and we see nothing wrong in holding that proposition. In fact, it is just the proposition we have been urging. Secondly, मूर्तत्व may be interpreted to mean रूपादिमत्त्व *i. e.* possession of रूप etc. But in that sense, मूर्तत्व is not a necessary concomitant of शरीरपरिमाणत्व *i. e.* असर्वगतत्व. Thus, for example, मनस् is असर्वगत but not रूपादिमत्. [मनस् according to the Vais'eṣika school is not सर्वगत. See Vais'. Sú. and Nyâya-Sûtra.]

In the former sense (असर्वगत), a मूर्त can penetrate a मूर्त *e. g.* मनस्. Even in the latter sense, (रूपवत्), मूर्त things are sometimes found to do it *e. g.* water penetrates sands.

अथात्मनः कायपरिमाणत्वे etc.—Another objection to the Jaina doctrine of body-sized आत्मन्: Does the आत्मन् grow in size? If it does, it must part with its former size as it goes on assuming larger sizes—*i. e.* it is अनित्य, and may well be expected to perish with the body. If it does not, its size does not keep pace with the growing size of the body, and this is abandoning the dogma of body-sized आत्मन्.

The author replies : आत्मन् may well relinquish its former size without ceasing to be. Take, for example, the case of a serpent which can change its size at different times by expanding or contracting its hood.

पर्यायतस्तस्य etc.—This contains the gist of the Jaina position which is a recognition of unity-in-difference, change-in-permanence. आत्मन् is substantially नित्य; modally अनित्य.

अथात्मनः कायपरिमाणत्वे तत्खण्डने etc.—Another objection to the doctrine of body-sized आत्मन् is—that the mutilation of the body would involve mutilation of आत्मन्.

Answer : It is so, as a matter of fact. When the body is mutilated, a few out of the total number of the प्रदेशs of आत्मन् continue to remain in the mutilated body, and the rest have gone off with the part of the body cut off. Hence it is that the part cut off is often found throbbing with life— which is a clear evidence of the existence of some प्रदेशs of आत्मन् dwelling in it. Would not the आत्मप्रदेशs dwelling in the part cut off thereby become a separate and independent आत्मन्? No; the आत्मप्रदेशs are dwelling not in the whole but a fraction of the body, and cannot therefore be regarded as a single, independent whole. Besides, there cannot be *many* आत्मन्s dwelling in parts which together make *one* continuous whole. For in that case, there would be no unity of consciousness : the cognitions would fall asunder like those obtained through different bodies.

कथं खण्डितावयवो etc.—If it be asked—How do the parts unite once more ?—the answer is : They were never absolutely separated in the manner in which a lotus-fibre is separated from the parent stock. That is only temporary and the reunion may be brought about by अदृष्ट.

तथा चात्मा etc.—केवलव्यतिरेकि अनुमान with a negative साध्य : It is contended that an आत्मन् being चेतन must be limited in size; for, only an अचेतन—like आकाश—could be unlimited in size. Next, if it is limited in size the limits must be imposed by the body; for, its guṇas—ज्ञान etc.—are manifested in the body.

यत्पुनरष्ट etc.—This refers to the Jaina doctrine that the soul of an अर्हत् may at times fill the whole universe. This, however, is occasional, and therefore does not interfere with our main thesis—that आत्मन् is not विभु but शरीरपरिमाण.

समय—Smallest division of time, moment, instant (Jacobi).

Read समुद्घात for समुज्ज्ञात which is an obvious misprint. Vide Abhayadeva's com. on Bhagavati Sûtra XIII, 10 cited in the note on p. 66 of स्या. मञ्जरी published in the "Ârhata-mata-prabhâkara Series", which explains how according to the Jaina doctrine the कर्मप्रदेशs are drawn together and mixed with आत्मप्रदेशs and thereby the कर्मन्s are suffered and exhausted by the Kevalin (the pure, emancipated) sage. For this, his आत्मप्रदेशs have to spread through the universe.

चतुर्दशरज्ज्वात्मक—For this Jaina Cosmography, see Tattvârthâdhigama Sûtra iii-6, and Lokaprakâśa Sarga 22.

Appendices.

1. For the Jaina view of the nature of Âtman—cf.

जीवोत्ति हवदि चेदा उपओग विसेसिदो मह्नकत्ता ।
भोत्ता य देहमत्तो ण हि मुत्तो कम्मसंजुत्तो ॥
कम्ममलविप्पमुक्को उड्ढं लोगस्स अंतमधिगंता ।

—Pañcâstikâya 27.

जीवो उवओगमओ अमुत्ति कत्ता सदेहपरिमाणो ।
भोत्ता संसारत्थो सिद्धो सो विस्ससोड्ढगई ॥
जीवः उपयोगमयः अमूर्तिः कर्ता स्वदेहपरिमाणः ।
भोक्ता संसारस्थः सिद्धः स विस्रसा ऊर्ध्वगतिः ॥

—Dravyasaṁgraha—2.

जीवसिद्धिः चार्वाकं प्रति; ज्ञानदर्शनोपयोगलक्षणं नैयायिकं प्रति; अमूर्तजीवस्थापनं भट्टचार्वाकद्वयं प्रति; कर्मकर्तृत्वस्थापनं सांख्यं प्रति; स्वदेहप्रमितिस्थापनं नैयायिक-मीमांसक-सांख्य-त्रयं प्रति; कर्मभोक्तृत्वव्याख्यानं बौद्धं प्रति; संसारस्य व्याख्यानं सदाशिवं प्रति; सिद्धत्वव्याख्यानं भट्टचार्वाकद्वयं प्रति; ऊर्ध्वगतिस्वभावकथनं माण्डलिकग्रन्थकारं प्रति—इति मतार्थो ज्ञातव्यः—Com.

This summarises very beautifully the differences of the Jaina school with other schools in regard to the several points concerning the nature of आत्मन्.

2. For the पूर्वपक्ष and its arguments which have been answered in the text, vide the following:—

व्यवस्थातो नाना—Vais. Sutra III. ii-20.

नानाऽत्मानः कुतः व्यवस्थातः—Upaskâra.

यस्य तु नानात्मानः तस्य सर्वेषात्मनां सर्वगतत्वेन सर्वशरीरसंबन्धेऽपि न साधारणो भोगः यस्य कर्मणा यच्छरीरमारब्धं तस्यैव तद् उपभोगायतनं न सर्वस्य । कर्मापि यस्य शरीरेण कृतं तस्यैव तद्भवति नापरस्य । एवं शरीरान्तरनियमः कर्मान्तरनियमात् इत्यनादिः ।

—N. Kandali p. 87.

विभुत्वं चात्मनो वह्नेरूर्ध्वज्वलनाद् वायोस्तिर्यक्पवनादवगतम् । ते ह्यदृष्टकारिते । न च तदाश्रयेणासंबद्धमदृष्टं तयोः कारणं भवितुमर्हति । अतिप्रसङ्गात् । न चात्मसमवेतस्यादृष्टस्य साक्षाद् द्रव्यान्तरसंबन्धो घटते इति स्वाश्रयसंबन्धद्वारेण तस्य संबन्ध इत्यायातम् । ततः समस्तमूर्तद्रव्यसंबन्धलक्षणमात्मनो विभुत्वं सिध्यति । स्वभावत एव वह्नेरूर्ध्वज्वलनं नादृष्टादिति चेत् कोयं स्वभावो नाम ? । अथेन्धनविशेषप्रभवत्वं स्वभाव इति अनिन्धनप्रभवस्य विद्युदादिप्रभवस्य चोर्ध्वज्वलनं न स्यात् । अथातीन्द्रियः कोपि स्वभावः कासुचिद्व्यक्तिष्वस्ति यासामूर्ध्वज्वलनं दृश्यते इति पुरुषगुणे कः प्रद्वेषः ? ।

—N. Kandali p. 88.

"एवं चात्माकात्स्न्र्यम्"—Br. S. II. ii. 34.

यथैकस्मिन् धर्मिणि विरुद्धधर्मासंभवो दोषः स्याद्वादे प्रसक्त एवमात्मनोऽपि जीवस्याकात्स्न्र्यमपरो दोषः प्रसज्येत । कथम् । शरीरपरिमाणो हि जीव इत्यार्हता मन्यन्ते । शरीरपरिमाणतायां च सत्यामकृत्स्नोऽसर्वगतः परिच्छिन्न आत्मेत्यतो घटादिवदनित्यत्वमात्मनः प्रसज्येत । शरीराणां चानवस्थितपरिमाणत्वान्मनुष्यजीवो मनुष्यशरीरपरिमाणो भूत्वा पुनः केनचित् कर्मविपाकेन हस्तिजन्म प्राप्नुवन्न कृत्स्नं हस्तिशरीरं व्याप्नुयात् । पुत्तिकाजन्म च प्राप्नुवन्न कृत्स्नः पुत्तिकाशरीरे संमीयेत । समान एष एकस्मिन्नपि जन्मनि कौमारयौवनस्थाविरेषु दोषः । स्यादेतत् । अनन्तावयवो जीवस्तस्य त एवावयवा अल्पे शरीरे संकुचेयुर्महति च विकसेयुरिति । तेषां पुनरनन्तानां जीवावयवानां समानदेशत्वं प्रतिहन्यते वा न वेति वक्तव्यम् । प्रतिघाते तावन्नानन्तावयवाः परिच्छिन्ने देशे संमीयेरन् । अप्रतिघातेऽप्येकावयवदेशत्वोपपत्तेः सर्वेषामवयवानां प्रथिमानुपपत्तेर्जीवस्याणुमात्रत्वप्रसङ्गः स्यात् । अपि च शरीरमात्रपरिच्छिन्नानां जीवावयवानामानन्त्यं नोत्प्रेक्षितुमपि शक्यम् । अथ पर्यायेण बृहच्छरीरप्रतिपत्तौ केचिज्जीवावयवा उपगच्छन्ति तनुशरीरप्रतिपत्तौ च केचिदपगच्छन्तीत्युच्येत तत्राप्युच्यते—

—S'aṁkara's Com. ibid.

"न च पर्यायादप्यविरोधो विकारादिभ्यः" Br. S. II. ii. 35.

न च पर्यायेणाप्यवयवोपगमापगमाभ्यामेतद्देहपरिमाणत्वं जीवस्याविरोधेनोपपादयितुं शक्यते। कुतः। विकारादिदोषप्रसङ्गात्। अवयवोपगमापगमाभ्यां ह्यनिशमापूर्यमाणस्यापक्षीयमाणस्य च जीवस्य विक्रियावत्त्वं तावदपरिहार्यम्। विक्रियावत्त्वे च चर्मादिवदनित्यत्वं प्रसज्येत। ततश्च बन्धमोक्षाभ्युपगमो बाध्येत कर्माष्टकपरिवेष्टितस्य जीवस्यालाबुवत् संसारसागरे निमग्नस्य बन्धनोच्छेदादूर्ध्वगामित्वं भवतीति। किं चान्यत्। आगच्छतामपगच्छतां चावयवानामागमापायधर्मवत्त्वादेवानात्मत्वं शरीरादिवत्। ततश्चावस्थितः कश्चिदवयव आत्मेति स्यात्। न च स निरूपयितुं शक्यतेऽयमसाविति। किं चान्यत्। आगच्छन्तश्चैते जीवावयवाः कुतः प्रादुर्भवन्त्यपगच्छन्तश्च क्व वा लीयन्त इति वक्तव्यम्। न हि भूतेभ्यः प्रादुर्भवेयुर्भूतेषु च निलीयेरन् अभौतिकत्वाज्जीवस्य। नापि कश्चिदन्यः साधारणोऽसाधारणो वा जीवानामवयवाधारो निरूप्यते। प्रमाणाभावात्। किं चान्यत्। अनवधृतस्वरूपश्चैवं सत्यात्मा स्यात्। आगच्छतामपगच्छतां चावयवानामनियतपरिमाणत्वात्। अत एवमादिदोषप्रसङ्गान्न पर्यायेणाप्यवयवोपगमापगमावात्मन आश्रयितुं शक्येते।

—S'aṁkara's Com. ibid.

"अन्त्यावस्थितेश्चोभयनित्यत्वादविशेषः"

—Br. S. II. ii. 36.

अपि चान्त्यस्य मोक्षावस्थाभाविनो जीवपरिमाणस्य नित्यत्वमिष्यते जैनैः। तद्वत्पूर्वयोरप्याद्यमध्यमयोर्जीवपरिमाणयोर्नित्यत्वप्रसङ्गादविशेषप्रसङ्गः स्यात्। एकशरीरपरिमाणतैव स्यान्नोपचितापचितशरीरान्तरप्राप्तिः। अथवान्त्यस्य जीवपरिमाणस्यावस्थितत्वात् पूर्वयोरप्यवस्थयोरवस्थितपरिमाण एव जीवः स्यात्। ततश्चाविशेषेण सर्वदैवाणुर्महान् वा जीवोऽभ्युपगन्तव्यो न शरीरपरिमाणः॥

S'aṁkara's Com.

Râmânujâcârya holds that आत्मन् is अणुपरिमाण, not subject to संकोच and विकास (expansion and contraction) as in the Jaina system, but its ज्ञान is capable of संकोच and विकास, the perfect विकास being accomplished in the condition of मोक्ष. This विकास is its natural state, which is unnaturally cribbed during बन्ध owing to कर्म. cf. "स्वयमपरिच्छिन्नमेव ज्ञानं संकोचविकासार्हमित्युपपादयिष्यामः अतः क्षेत्रज्ञावस्थायां कर्मणा संकुचितस्वरूपं तत्तत्कर्मानुगुणतरतमभावेन वर्तते"—S'rî. Bh. I. i. 1.

वैशेषिकनैयायिकयोः प्रायः समानतन्त्रत्वात्—On the relation of the Nyâya and Vais'eṣika systems, see Bodas' Introduction to the Tarkasaṁgraha and Keith's "Indian Logic and Atomism" Chap. I and II.

औलूक्यमत—The Vais'eṣika system.

यौगमत—The doctrine of the 'Yaugas' *i. e.* the Naiyâyika system founded by **अक्षपाद**.

"अथादौ नैयायिकानां यौगापराभिधानानां लिङ्गादिव्यक्तिरुच्यते। ते च दण्डधराः प्रौढकौपीनपरिधानाः कम्बलिकाप्रावृताः जटाधारिणो भस्मोद्धूलनपरा यज्ञोपवीतिनो जलाधारपात्रकराः नीरसाहाराः प्रायो वनवासिनो द्रोर्मूले तुम्बकं बिभ्राणाः कन्दमूलफलाशिनः। आतिथ्यकर्मनिरताः सस्त्रीकाः। निस्त्रीकास्तेषूत्तमाः। ते च पञ्चाग्निसाधनपराः करे जटादौ च बाणलिङ्गधराश्चापि भवन्ति।उत्तमां संयमावस्थां प्राप्तास्तु नग्ना भ्रमन्ति। एते प्रातर्दन्तपादादि शौचं विधाय शिवं ध्यायन्तो भस्मनाङ्गं त्रिस्त्रिः स्पृशन्ति। यजमानो वन्दमानः कृताञ्जलिर्वक्ति ओं नमः शिवाय इति। गुरुस्तथैव शिवाय नमः इति प्रतिवक्ति।......। तेषु ये निर्विकारास्ते स्वमीमांसागतमिदं पद्यं दर्शयन्ति॥ न स्वर्धुनी न फणिनो न कपालदाम नेन्दोः कला न गिरिजा न जटा न भस्म। यत्रान्यदेव च न किंचिदुपास्महे तद् रूपं पुराणमुनिशीलितमीश्वरस्य॥ स एव योगिनां सेव्यो ह्यर्वाचीनस्तु भोगभाक्। स ध्यायमानो राज्यादिसुखलुब्धैर्निषेव्यते—॥ उक्तं च तैः स्वयोगशास्त्रे—॥ वीतरागं स्मरन् योगी वीतरागत्वमश्नुते सरागं ध्यायतस्तस्य सरागत्वं तु निश्चितम्॥ येन येन हि भावेन युज्यते यन्त्रवाहकः। तेन तन्मयतां याति विश्वरूपो मणिर्यथा॥ एतत्सर्वं लिङ्गवेषदेवादिस्वरूपं वैशेषिकमतेऽप्यवसातव्यं यतो नैयायिकवैशेषिकाणां हि मिथः प्रमाणतत्त्वानां संख्याभेदे सत्यप्यन्योन्यं तत्त्वानामन्तर्भावनेऽल्पीयानेव भेदो जायते। ते नैतेषां प्रायो मततुल्यतया उभयेऽप्येते तपस्विनोऽभिधीयन्ते। ते च शैवादिभेदेन चतुर्धा भवन्ति। तदुक्तम्—॥ आधारभस्मकौपीनजटायज्ञोपवीतिनः स्वस्वाचारादिभेदेन चतुर्धा स्युस्तपस्विनः। शैवाः पाशुपताश्चैव महाव्रतधरास्तथा। तुर्याः कालमुखा मुख्या भेदा एते तपस्विनाम्॥ तेषामन्तर्भेदा भरटभक्तरलैङ्गिकतापसादयो भवन्ति। भरटादीनां व्रतग्रहणे ब्राह्मणादिवर्णनियमो नास्ति। यस्य तु शिवे भक्तिः स व्रती भरटादिर्भवेत्। परं शास्त्रेषु नैयायिकाः सदा शिवभक्तत्वात् शैवा इत्युच्यन्ते वैशेषिकास्तु पाशुपता इति॥"

—Guṇaratna's com. on the Ṣaḍ-dars'ana-samuccaya.

I have quoted this passage in extenso as it gives interesting details relating to the religious side of the Naiyâyîka and Vais'eṣîka schools. It is difficult to decide whether this was originally a complement of their logical systems or a later supplement in which elements of Vedânta, Yoga and Bhakti schools can be traced.

Stanza X.

Stanza: That in this world, where men are naturally inclined towards disputes and are anxious to babble out their so-called wisdom, the sage of the heretics should injure the hearts of others by preaching to them false doctrines is indeed a singular mark of his dispassionateness!

अन्यदीयो मुनिः —The sage "of others", that is to say, of the heretics, viz., *Akṣapâda,* the Sûtrakâra of the Nyâya system. He is also known as *Gautama* or *Gotama* after his gotra [Gotama is a Prakrit form of Gautama]. For further information see Nyâya-Vârtika Bhûmikâ by Vindhyeshwari Prasad. Dr. Satischandra Vidyabhushana distinguishes between Gautama or Gotama and Akṣapâda, one of whom he believes to have lived in Mithilâ long before the Christian era and the other at Prabhâsa in Kathiawad about 150 A. D. "Akṣapâda", he says, " was the real author of the Nyâya-Sûtra which derived a considerable part of the materials from the Ânvîkṣikî vidyâ of Gautama. Just as Caraka was the redactor of the Agnives'a-tantra or the Âyurveda of Âtreya, Akṣapâda was the redactor of the Ânvîkṣikî of Gautama" [Vide Dr. Vidyabhushana's H. I. L. pp. 47-50.]

Dr. Vidyabhushana's view, however, has not been generally accepted.

Dr. Keith writes: " Of the personalities of Gautama and Kaṇâda we know absolutely nothing. The personal name of the former Akṣapâda has the appearance of being a nickname such as early India seems to have loved, 'one whose eyes are directed at his feet,' but it is variously interpreted and embellished with idle legends. " We may well dismiss the fantastic stories invented to account for his name, such as that of his falling into a well while absorbed in thought and being provided by a merciful God with a pair of eyes in his feet to protect him from further mishaps, and also the other story of Vyâsa falling at his feet and his condescending to see him with his eyes in his feet. But when so much obscurity hangs about the origin of the name, one may venture to submit a conjecture which is at any rate more plausible than the others : Possibly, the philosophy of 'आन्वीक्षिकी' was the philosophy which aimed at 'seeing' that is bringing to human consciousness by means of reasoning—Pramâṇas (=अक्ष and अन्वीक्षा)-the truths relating to the Prameyas--such as 'âtman, s'arîra, etc.' (see N. S.). Its founder was अक्ष and पाद् was an honorific word like the same in Pras'astapâda, the author of the Vais'eṣika Bhâṣya.

मर्म 1.—Vital parts ; those limbs of the body which are thickly studded with आत्मप्रदेशs are its vital parts. [Note that the Jainas believe Âtman to be possessed of प्रदेशs. " जीवा पोग्गलकाया धम्माधम्मा पुणो य आगासं । देसेहिं असंखादा "—*i. e.* the five अस्तिकायs viz. जीव, पुद्गलकाय, धर्म, अधर्म and आकाश are 'असंख्यातप्रदेश'—Pravacanasâra. अणुगुरुदेहपमाणो उवसंहारप्पसप्पदो चेदा । असमुहदो ववहारा णिच्चयणयदो असंखदेसो वा ॥—According to Vyavahâra Naya, the conscious Jîva, being without samudghâta, becomes equal in extent to a small or a large body, by contraction and expansion ; but according to Nis'caya Naya it is existent in innumerable prades'âs. (Dravyasaṁgraha Ed. U. C. Ghosal)] By प्रदेश, however, one need not understand material space or extension. 2. Secondarily, vital parts of their systems, *i. e.*, the essential propositions which are put forward to prove their tenets.

मायोपदेशात् etc.—Teaching deceit, in the shape of छल, जाति and निग्रहस्थान. [These will be explained below.]

गुणाद्स्त्रियां न वा—Hema-S'abdânus'âsana II. ii. 7.

अस्मिन्—To 'this' *i. e.* the vulgar crowd which cannot discriminate between Truth and Error.

विरुद्धः etc.—विवाद defined.

लब्धिख्यात्यर्थिना etc.—A quotation from Haribhadra Sûri-Aṣṭaka XII. 4. विवाद is that set of propositions-consisting of छल (fraudulent arguments) and जाति (objections in the shape of futile analogues)—which a wretched man, not possessed of true greatness of soul, puts forward out of greed of money or fame.

ग्रहिल—Caught, as it were, by an evil spirit.

तथा वितण्डा—वितण्डा cavilling, from तण्ड् to strike; a proposition not founded on a constructive basis of thought; one in which the speaker does not care to enunciate or establish his own position (स्वपक्ष) in regard to a certain truth, and indulges in mere destructive criticism. A quotation from N. Vârtika on N. Sûtra I. i. 1, in support of this meaning. The author adds that the word rather means prattle which is lacking in judgment or discernment and therefore irresponsible.

कण्डूल from कण्डू. For the termination ल see Hema. VII. ii. 21.

एवं च स्वरसतः etc.—When men are naturally so anxious to defend their own positions by hook or by crook, and to cavil at others, if they get expert aid of great thinkers they are sure to abuse it. Such a preaching is 'like adding ghee to burning fire'.

भवाभिनन्दिभिः—Rejoicing in the world and the ways of the world. cf. "असारोऽप्येष संसारः सारवानिव लक्ष्यते। दधिदुग्धाम्बुताम्बूलपुण्यपण्याङ्गनादिभिः"—quoted in the footnote in the A. M. P. edition of the स्या० म०.

तथा चाहुः etc.—The verses occur in न्या. मञ्जरी of जयन्त P. 11. The teaching of this branch of Logic or Nyâya-S'âstra is further justified in the न्या. म. (p. 595) as follows:—

कस्यांचिदवस्थायां स्वप्रतिपत्तिसाधनोपहिततत्त्वज्ञानरक्षायै तान्यपि व्याप्रियन्ते। यदा जानन्नपि परपक्षकृशिमानं स्वपक्षे द्रढिमानं च क्वचिदवसरे परप्रयुक्ते साधने दूषणं सपदि न पश्यति स्वपक्षसाधनं च झगिति न स्मरति तदा छलादिभिरप्युपक्रम्य परमभिभवत्यात्मानं च रक्षतीति। ननु यदि परश्छलादीनि जानीयात्तेषु चानुरूपमुत्तरमभिदधीत कथं जीयेत प्रत्युत जयत्येव। सत्यम्। तथाप्येकान्तपराजयद्वारं संदेह इति युक्तमेव तत्प्रयोगेण स्फुटाटोपकरणम्। नन्वीदृंशि प्रयोजनानि जिगीषतो जनस्य जनपदसदसि भवन्ति तस्यापि निपुणमतिसदसि मुमुक्षोस्तु दूरापेतैव कथेयमिति कथमिह मोक्षशास्त्रे अस्याउपदेशः। नैतदेवम्। मुमुक्षो-

रपि क्वचित्प्रसङ्गे तदुपयोगात्। यथोक्तं तत्त्वाध्यवसायसंरक्षणासीनमनेकशिष्यगणोपास्यमानं रहस्यतत्त्वमुपदिशन्तं शान्तमानसमाचार्यमनार्यः कश्चिद्द्विपश्चिदाभासः कुतश्चिदागत्य दुरधिगतकतिपयाक्षरपरिचयजनितगुरुतरगर्वगद्गदया गिरा भोस्तपस्विन् किमाख्यायते हुङ्कारमान्वीक्षिकी सरलमतिप्रियेयं विद्या क्व वेदाः क्व वेदप्रामाण्यं क्वात्मज्ञानं क्वापवर्गः इत्यादि मन्दं विहस्य सहस्य सहसा दृष्टमेघ इव प्रकटितकाण्डदण्डकाशनितम्बविघ्नासिताश्रममृगवर्गमुद्ग्राहयन्नाकुलयति तदा जलजालमिन्द्रजालपण्डितविलसितमिति जानन्नप्याशाभ्यो यदि तदुपेक्षते न तिरस्करोति सद्यः सम्यक् साधनाप्रतिभासेऽपि यदि छलादिभिरेनं न शमयति तदा तस्मिन् गते तत उत्थाय शिष्यगणा ब्रूयुः कष्टमस्थाने क्लिष्टाः स्मः। योऽस्मात्रस्माकमाचार्यः पण्डितो न्यायविन्तमः। अद्य त्वागत्य सोऽन्येन पण्डितेन पराजितः॥ तच्छ्रुत्वा जन इतरोऽपि सत्पथस्याशैथिल्यात्सपदि तमेव माऽनुयासीत्। तन्नूनं परिभवभूमिकामसह्यां नेतव्यः सदसि स वावदूकपाशः। तद्विघातघटने निरर्गलं जल्पमन्त्रमुपदिष्टवान् मुनिः। आनुषङ्गिकमपि प्रयोजनं तस्य रागिजनतासु वर्णितम्। "—N. Mañjarî.

मायोपदेशादिति etc.—Malliṣeṇa is now going to make this one word the basis of his commentary dealing with the exposition and criticism of some of the points of the Nyâya system.

I. न चैतेषां etc.—A mere knowledge of each of these sixteen पदार्थs taken singly or collectively will not suffice to bring about the summum bonum. ज्ञान and क्रिया are the two wheels of the chariot of साधन, which will not move if either of them is wanting. It may be urged that क्रिया is not discarded altogether, but it has to be preceded by तत्त्वज्ञान if it is to bring about मोक्ष. Even if ज्ञान and क्रिया be joined together they will be of little use in achieving the end. For, the ज्ञान that is provided there is false ज्ञान. This can be shown as follows:

II. 1. तैः प्रमाणस्य लक्षणं etc.—प्रमाण is defined as 'अर्थोपलब्धिहेतुः प्रमाणम्' 'अर्थवत् प्रमाणम्'—N. Bhâṣya I. i. 1. 'उपलब्धिहेतुः प्रमाणम्'—N. Bh. Vârtika I. i. 1; 'उपलब्धिहेतुश्च प्रमाणं प्रमेयं तूपलब्धिविषयः'—N. Bh. II. i. 11. Here if हेतु means only a cause, any cause, not necessarily an instrumental cause or करण, the definition will apply to all the कारकs (things participating in or associated with the क्रिया such as agent (कर्तृ), object (कर्मन्) etc.). If, however, हेतु is taken to mean only करण, ज्ञान and not इन्द्रियार्थसंनिकर्ष is the करण of अर्थोपलब्धि; for, इन्द्रियार्थसंनिकर्ष may take place and yet for want of ज्ञान there may not be अर्थोपलब्धि.

Hence, ज्ञान is the true करण and not इन्द्रियार्थसंनिकर्ष. Besides, a करण must immediately precede the effect, which ज्ञान does but इन्द्रिया० does not, the latter being one step remote.

यदपि न्यायभूषण० etc.—Another definition of प्रमाण is "सम्यगनुभवसाधनं प्रमाणम्" (Nyâyasâra of भासर्वज्ञ I. i.). Here 'साधन' is all right: it means करण, and this excludes कर्तृ and कर्मन् of the अनुभव. It would be a definition applicable to ज्ञान and not to इन्द्रियार्थसंनिकर्ष. The right definition is "स्वपरव्यवसायि ज्ञानं प्रमाणम्"—See Pramâṇa-Naya-Tattvâlokâlaṁkâra. I-2. न्यायभूषण is a commentary on न्यायसार of भासर्वज्ञ, an old Saivite writer on Nyâya.

2. प्रमेयमपि etc.—प्रमेय *i. e.* the object of right knowledge is of twelve kinds : (1) आत्मन्, (2) शरीर, (3) इन्द्रिय, (4) अर्थ, (5) बुद्धि, (6) मनः, (7) प्रवृत्ति, (8) दोष, (9) प्रेत्यभाव, (10) फल, (11) दुःख and (12) अपवर्ग.

तच्च न सम्यग् etc.—The classification is objected to on the ground that शरीर, इन्द्रिय, etc. deserve to be included in आत्मन्. For जीव *i. e.* the आत्मन् who is associated with and subject to संसार and to whom the knowledge of the प्रमेयs is prescribed, cannot be dissociated from his शरीर, इन्द्रिय, etc. [Note, however, that प्रमेय in the Nyâya-Sûtra does not mean a logical category (प्रमातुं शक्यं प्रमेयम्), but topics which deserve to be studied by one desirous of मोक्ष (प्रमातुं योग्यं प्रमेयम्): thus, आत्मन्, शरीर etc., deserve to be studied separately and in detail by a मुमुक्षु, and are in this sense प्रमेय. The criticism therefore misses the point.]

आत्मा च etc.—Another defect in the classification : आत्मन् is not a प्रमेय but a प्रमातृ.

इन्द्रियबुद्धिमनसां etc.—These three are करणs, and not कर्मन्s of प्रमा ; and therefore not प्रमेय.

दोषास्तु etc.—दोषs are thus defined in the N. Sûtra: प्रवर्तनालक्षणा दोषाः (N. S. I. i. 18). They are included in प्रवृत्ति *i. e.* activity of the वाक्, शरीर and मनस्, all of which again are included in three of the प्रमेयs viz. शरीर, इन्द्रिय and मनस्. शुभाशुभफलस्य विंशतिविधस्य *i. e.* Twenty-one kinds of दुःख have been enumerated in the Nyâya-Sâra :—' एकविंशतिभेदास्तु—शरीरं, षडिन्द्रियाणि, षड्विषयाः, षड्बुद्धयः, सुखं, दुःखं चेति। Com. तत्र शरीरं प्रतीतम्। षडिन्द्रियाणि घ्राणरसनचक्षुस्त्वक्श्रोत्रमनांसि। षड् विषयाः गन्धरूपरसस्पर्शशब्दस्मृतिसंकल्पाः। षड्बुद्धयः षडिन्द्रियाणाम्। षड् विषयाः ज्ञप्तयः। आह्लादरूपं सुखं तद्विपरीतं दुःखम्।" The details of दोषs given in Jayanta's Nyâya-Mañjarî are interesting :

तेषां दोषाणां त्रयो राशयो भवन्ति रागो द्वेषो मोह इति। तत्रानुकूलेष्वर्थेष्वलाभलक्षणो रागः। प्रतिकूलेष्वसहनलक्षणो द्वेषः। वस्तुपरमार्थापरिच्छेदलक्षणो मिथ्याव्यवसायो मोहः। ननु चेर्ष्यासूयालोभमानमदमत्सरादिदोषान्तरसंभवात् कथं त्रय एव दोषाः। न। ईर्ष्यादीनां यथानिर्दिष्टेष्वेवान्तर्भावात्। कामो मत्सरः स्पृहा तृष्णा लोभ इति पञ्चप्रकारो रागपक्षः। स्त्रीसंयोगेच्छा कामः। यदन्यस्मै निवेद्यमानमपि वस्तु धनवन्न क्षीयते तदपरित्यागेच्छा मत्सरः। अनात्मीयवस्त्वादित्सा स्पृहा। पुनर्भवप्रतिसंधानहेतुभूतेच्छा तृष्णा। निषिद्धद्रव्यग्रहणेच्छा लोभ इत्यभिलाषप्रकारभेदाद्रागपक्ष एवायम्। द्वेषपक्षोऽपि पञ्चविधः। क्रोध ईर्ष्यासूया द्रोहोऽमर्ष इति। अक्षिभ्रूत्रादिविकारहेतुः प्रज्वलनात्मकः क्रोधः। साधारणेऽपि वस्तुनि परस्य दर्शनाद्यसहनमीर्ष्या। परगुणेष्वक्षमाऽसूया। परापकारो द्रोहः। अदर्शितमुखादिविकारः परं प्रति मन्युरमर्षः इत्यसहनप्रकारभेदादेव द्वेषपक्षः। मोहपक्षस्तु चतुर्विधो मिथ्याज्ञानं विचिकित्सा मानः प्रमाद इति। अतस्मिंस्तदिति ज्ञानं मिथ्याज्ञानम्। किंस्विदिति विमर्शो विचिकित्सा। असद्गुणाध्यारोपेण स्वोत्कर्षबुद्धिर्मानः। कियदेतदित्यवज्ञया कर्तव्याकरणं प्रमादः। स एव मद इति व्याख्यायते। सोऽयं तत्त्वापरिज्ञानप्रकारभेदान्मोहपक्षः। एवं त्रय एवैते दोषाः। शोकहर्षौ तु सुखदुःखे उच्येते न दोषान्तरम्। तेषां तु मोहः पापतमः इतरयोस्तु तदधीनात्मलाभत्वात्। मूढस्य हि रागद्वेषौ भवतो मिथ्यासंकल्पादुत्पद्यमानयोरनुभवात् कुसंकल्पश्च मिथ्याज्ञानप्रवृत्तिरेव। मिथ्याज्ञानस्यैव भगवतः सर्वमिदं विलसितं योऽयमनेकप्रकारः संसारदुःखभारः—N. Mañjarî pp. 500-1.

दुःखस्य शब्दादीनां etc.—दुःख and इन्द्रियार्थs such as शब्द etc. are included in फल—the former as the principal or direct (मुख्य) फल, and the latter as subordinate or indirect (गौण) फल—in-asmuch as the latter is the साधन of the former. "सुखदुःखे मुख्यं फलं तत्साधनं तु शरीरेन्द्रियविषयादि गौणम्"—Jayanta's N. Mañjarî p. 505.

प्रेत्यभावापवर्गयोः etc.—प्रेत्यभाव (Being after death *i. e.* transmigration) and अपवर्ग (= मोक्ष, emancipation) are certain states of आत्मन्, and they may well be taken as included in आत्मन्—says the author. प्रेत्यभाव and अपवर्ग are thus defined in the N.

Sûtra—पुनरुत्पत्तिः प्रेत्यभावः; तद् (दुःखा)त्यन्तविमोक्षोऽपवर्गः (N. S. I. i. 19, 22).

The right definition of प्रमेय, says the author, is the famous Jaina definition "द्रव्यपर्यायात्मकं वस्तु प्रमेयम्."

3. एवं संशयादीनां etc.—संशय etc. are the other terms on the list of the पदार्थs. That they are not 'तत्त्वs' or realities can be easily shown.

तदेवं प्रमाणादि etc.—Only three out of the sixteen padârthas have been selected here for detailed criticism, because they are unbecoming of any one who professes to be a sage. These are छल, जाति and निग्रहस्थान.

III. 1. तत्र परस्य etc.—Definition of छल. छल is a deceitful attack upon the opponent by quibbling upon his words. अविशेषाभिहितेऽर्थे वक्तुरभिप्रायादर्थान्तरकल्पना वाक्छलम् (N. S. I. ii. 52).

Example: When you know that in saying 'नवकम्बलोऽयं ब्राह्मणः' your opponent has used the word 'नव' in the sense of 'new', and still if you purposely take the word in the sense of the number 'nine' and try to put him out by showing how absurd it was to say that the man was 'नवकम्बल' in the sense of "he who possesses nine blankets'—you are indulging in वाक्छल *i. e.* deceitful or dishonest use of language.

2. सामान्यच्छल—Deceit concerning the use of a class-term (सामान्य). संभवतोऽर्थस्यातिसामान्ययोगादसंभूतार्थकल्पना सामान्यच्छलम् (N. S. I. ii. 54). Example: Suppose one says "The Brâhmaṇa is learned and well-behaved" and somebody remarks "Learning and good behaviour are quite natural in a Brâhmaṇa". Then, if you purposely strain the argument beyond the limits intended by the latter speaker and attribute to him what he never intended to lay down, viz. a causal connection between ब्राह्मणत्व and विद्याचरणसंपन्नत्व thus: "If Brâhmaṇas possess learning and good behaviour, a Vrâtya (a low, degraded and illiterate Brâhmaṇa) should possess them too, for he too is a Brâhmaṇa"—then, this would be a case of सामान्यच्छल. I take विद्याचरण=विद्या-आचरण, not विद्या-चरण.

औपचारिके प्रयोगे etc.—When knowing that a term has been used in a figurative sense by the opponent, you purposely take it in the literal sense and attack it, it would be a case of उपचारच्छल—deceit concerning a figurative word. Example: One says " मञ्चाः क्रोशन्ति "—" The benches are crying out "—meaning thereby that the men seated on the benches are crying out. Here, if you purposely take the word मञ्च in the literal sense and object: " Benches are wooden; they cannot be crying out", your objection would be an उपचारच्छल. अभिधानस्य धर्मो यथार्थप्रयोगः । धर्मविकल्पोऽन्यत्र दृष्टस्यान्यत्र प्रयोगः । तस्य निर्देशे धर्मविकल्पनिर्देशे । यथा मञ्चाः क्रोशन्तीति अर्थसद्भावेन प्रतिषेधः मञ्चस्थाः पुरुषाः क्रोशन्ति न तु मञ्चाः क्रोशन्ति । का पुनरत्रार्थविकल्पोपपत्तिः ? । अन्यथा प्रयुक्तस्यान्यार्थकल्पनम् । भक्त्या प्रयोगे प्राधान्येन कल्पनम् । उपचारविषयं छलमुपचारच्छलम् । उपचारो नीतार्थः सहचरणादिनिमित्तेन । तद्भावे तद्वदभिधानमुपचार इति (N. S. Bh. *ibid*) धर्मविकल्पनिर्देशेऽर्थसद्भावप्रतिषेध उपचारच्छलम् (N. S. I. ii. 55).

तथा सम्यग् हेतौ etc.—When an opponent uses a हेतु whether good or bad, the right way of dealing with it is to examine it. If, instead of doing that, you set forth an argument to prove the opposite, it is a case of जाति or bad form of criticism (दूषणाभास). जाति means class; in the present case, an argument based on class (जाति) i. e. based on vicious analogy or likeness. It is of twenty-four kinds (सा च चतुर्विंशति etc.) of which only the first four have been illustrated in the Text.

तत्र साधर्म्येण etc.—The साधर्म्यसमा जाति is that bad method of criticism in which you meet the opponent's argument based on a certain हेतु and like instances with another argument based upon a different हेतु and its own like instances without going to the root of the matter and examining which of the हेतुs has a better right to be accepted. Thus, against the argument शब्दः अनित्यः कृतकत्वात् घटवत् is set up another argument to prove the opposite, such as शब्दो नित्यः निरवयवत्वात् आकाशवत्, without going into the question which of the two हेतुs together with their like instances is more entitled to our acceptance.

वैधर्म्येण etc.—वैधर्म्यसमा जाति–As in the case of साधर्म्यसमा *mutatis mutandis.*

तत्रैव प्रयोगे दृष्टान्तधर्मं etc.—To press the analogy of the दृष्टान्त too far, and thereupon argue the addition (उत्कर्ष) of such a धर्म as would be obviously absurd is उत्कर्षसमा जाति. For an illustration, see the Text. अपकर्षस्तु etc.—Similarly to press the analogy of the दृष्टान्त too far and thereupon to argue the absence (अपकर्ष) of such a धर्म as would be obviously absurd is अपकर्षसमा जाति. For an illustration see the Text.

तथा विप्रतिपत्तिः etc.—विप्रतिपत्तिरप्रतिपत्तिश्च निग्रहस्थानम् (N. S. I. ii.60). निग्रहस्थान or position of defeat is of two kinds: विप्रतिपत्ति and अप्रतिपत्ति. The former consists in abandoning the original position or in taking up a new position or in contradicting the first position. The latter consists in failure to meet the opponent by getting dumb-founded and so on. There are twenty-two kinds of निग्रहस्थानs, which are all enumerated in the Text. The whole Text from छलं त्रिधा to इति निग्रहस्थानम् is taken verbatim from Guṇaratna's Tarkarahasya-Dîpikâ on Ṣaḍdars'ana-Samuccaya. It recurs also in Maṇibhadra's Laghu-vṛtti on the same. The subject should be studied in the Nyâya-Sûtras with Bhâṣya and Vṛtti. Jayanta's Nyâya-Mañjarî also will be found to be very illuminating.

Stanza XI.

Stanza: *Hiṃsâ* (Killing), even though it may be enjoined by the Vedas, cannot produce *Dharma* (religious merit). A general rule such as 'No living being should be killed (injured)' can have no exception in any other sphere. The idea of the heretics is like the desire to get sovereignty for one's self, by performing the ceremony of killing one's own son.

The system next criticised is the *Pûrva-Mîmâṃsâ* of Jaimini.

इह खल्वर्चिमार्गे etc.—अर्चिमार्ग and धूममार्ग–the 'Path of Light' and the 'Path of Smoke' mean the religion of wisdom (ज्ञान)

and the religion of rituals or works (कर्म). They are also known as 'देवयान' and 'पितृयाण'–the Path of Gods and the Path of Manes. The earliest locus classicus of the "Two Paths" is the Bṛhadâraṇyaka Up. (p. 78) followed and slightly varied by the Ch. Up. (p. 145) and the doctrine is found later in the Bhag. Gîtâ as follows :

वेदविहिता तु हिंसा etc.—Animal slaughter practised in the course of a sacrifice is justified on the ground that it is prescribed by the Vedas, and is pleasing to gods, guests, and manes. This will be discussed in order in the sequel.

कारीरी– See Âs'v. S'rauta Sûtras II. iii. 1, 2 ; Kâtyayana Sr. Sût. I. ii. 22.

त्रिपुरार्णव—A tantra work of that name.

अतिथि etc.—That guests are pleased by the offer of meat is a matter of प्रत्यक्ष.—a poor argument, indeed, and perhaps sufficient to condemn the Brâhmaṇa case.

पितृणां etc.—Quotations from Manu and Mahâbhârata etc.

Manu : (i) recognises the custom of meat-eating ; (ii) at the same time he sounds a strong note of disapprobation ; (iii) but he approves of, nay, prescribes animal slaughter and use of meat at sacrifices to gods, in offerings and feasts connected with ancestor-worship and in the reception of guests. The Mahâbhârata which ranges over a much wider field of religious opinions contains many dialogues on the question of the religious ethics of Ahiṃsâ and Hiṃsâ including यज्ञहिंसा. Taken collectively they bear witness to (i) the prevalence of animal slaughter and meat-eating at a certain period of our religious history ; (ii) condemnation from the stand-point of higher ethics at the same time; (iii) the animal slaughter and meat-eating permitted or prescribed in certain cases such as a sacrifice etc. and (iv) even the latter sometimes discountenanced as an institution of the क्षत्रियs (क्षात्रयज्ञ). There was, even at a very early period of our history, a section of religious opinion which condemned animal slaughter even for a sacrifice, and substituted vegetables for animal offerings and regarded the latter as characteristic of 'क्षात्रयज्ञ' only.—See Ait. Br. 4, Mahâbhârata, S'ântiparvan-Nârâyaṇîya section—the story of King Vasu-Uparicara and the Citras'ikhaṇḍins ; and the Bhâgavata Purâṇa.

पितॄणामपि etc.—The performance of special S'râddhas with meat for the manes is laid down for the growth of progeny.

आगमश्चात्र etc.—(i) Scriptures justify the use of flesh at sacrifices where horses, bulls and even human animals (See Ait. Br. iv.) were slaughtered for propitiating *gods*. S'rauta Sûtra. (ii) They lay down its use for the reception of learned *guests*. See Manu., Âpastamba Gṛ. etc. महोक्षं वा etc. quoted from the Yâjñavalkya-Smṛti Âcâ 109. (iii) They also prescribe its use for the propitiation of manes. See Manu S., Gṛihya Sûtras etc. द्वौ मासौ etc. the quotation is from Manu III—268-271.

एवं पराभिप्रायं etc.—In criticising the Hiṃsâvâda of the Brâhmaṇas the author first cites texts from their own scriptures which condemn Hiṃsâ.

न हि भवति माता etc.—To say that हिंसा is धर्महेतु is to say that a woman is both a 'माता' and a 'वन्ध्या'—in other words it is a contradiction in terms.

हिंसाकारण etc.—A cause is that 'whose अन्वय and व्यतिरेक are followed by the कार्य' *i. e.* whose presence and absence determine the presence and absence of the कार्य ; in other words, a cause is an invariable antecedent of the कार्य. Now, can you say that हिंसा is an invariable antecedent of धर्म ? Surely, not. For, धर्म you admit arises from तपः and similar practices. हिंसा, therefore, is not धर्महेतु.

अथ न वयं etc.—The Brâhmaṇa replies : It is not every kind of हिंसा that we regard as meritorious (धर्महेतु) but only a special kind of हिंसा, *viz.* that laid down in the Scriptures.

ननु तस्या धर्म॰ etc.—The Siddhântin (Jaina) asks : How is हिंसा धर्महेतु? Is it that the animals do not *die* although they are *killed?* This is evidently absurd, as we see with our eyes, that when you kill them they die. Or, is it that the animals retain a quiet mind even when they are being slaughtered and afterwards go to heaven ? This, too, is contrary to what we actually observe. How piteous are the cries of the animals when they are being slaughtered ! They make out in their own language (of bleating etc.) what corresponds to such a human cry as "हा कष्टमस्ति etc. "—This is evident from the expression on their face, eyes and so forth.

अथेत्थमाचक्षीथाः etc.—The natural effect of a thing can be counteracted by certain contrivances and processes. Thus, pieces of iron ordinarily heavy and liable to sink can be made to float on water when used as parts of a ship; similarly, a poison can be turned into a medicine. Analogously, हिंसा though bad in itself can become a good act.

न च तस्याः कुत्सितत्वं etc.—It is besides not a disgraceful act, since the Brâhmaṇa priests who practise it, are treated with respect.

Criticism : तदेतत्र दक्षाणां etc.—The analogies are inapplicable. The pieces of iron are used as parts of a ship and are thus capable of floating. The Vedic mantras do not change the poor animals to a state wherein they would be beyond the touch of suffering. You will say: They get turned into gods. But do they ? What evidence ? There can be no sensuous evidence (प्रत्यक्ष). For the state of gods can only be supra-sensible. Nor, is there evidence consisting of inference (अनुमान) pointing in that direction. For, our inference will require a certain mark (a हेतु) on which to base it. There is none such in the present case. Nor is there an authoritative word (शब्द) to establish it. The texts cited have no value inasmuch as their authority is at issue. The two remaining प्रमाणs, viz. अर्थापत्ति and उपमान are included in inference (अनुमान) and need not be considered separately.

अथ भवतामपि जिनायतना॰ etc.—The Brâhmaṇa: In erecting a Jaina temple many a life has to be destroyed. Yet this is justified by the Jainas on the ground of temple-building being a very meritorious and pious act, an act whose merit far outweighs the sin incurred in destroying small lives in the process of building: The case of our animal slaughter at sacrifices is similar.

जैनं etc.—The Jaina : In temple-building, killing of small पृथिवीजीवs is found *inevitable*. Besides, a small loss of पुण्य incurred by destroying small life is far outweighed by the transcendent merit of temple-building. But you cannot plead inevitability in the case of हिंसा. For your own Scriptures lay down यम, नियम and similar other practices as available for securing स्वर्ग. See Gautama Dharma-sûtras, Patañjali's Yoga-sûtras, Manusmṛti etc. It is not so in the case of sacrificial slaughter. For, the same great merit can be secured by the practices above mentioned.

प्रतिप्रतीकं etc.—Cut and tortured in every limb. कान्दिशीकान्-not knowing which way to go ; bewildered. सौ(सौ)निकात्०-far more cruel than a butcher. एवं च यं कंचन-the citing of an analogy on the strength of some little likeness is wrong. It would go too far and affect injuriously many of your own positions.

न च जिनायतन etc.—The outweighing merit of building Jaina temples.

तद्दर्शनात् etc.—The *rationale* of its meritoriousness : how the sight of the idols installed therein influences the mind of the worshipper and so on. तथा च etc.-पञ्चलिङ्गी a work of Jines'vara Sûri, teacher of Abhayadeva.

अथ विप्रेभ्यः etc.– There is the visible merit contained in giving meat-cakes to the Brâhmaṇas who are very much pleased thereby.

पवित्रसुवर्ण etc.—Why not give them the holy दक्षिणाs of gold instead of meat ? A very friendly proposal.

अथ न प्रदानमात्रं etc.—The animal slaughter at sacrifices brings भूति *i. e.* prosperity, says the Brâhmaṇa. But the same can be secured by several other means. Hence, हिंसा is not necessary (व्यभिचार०).

श्वेतं वायव्यं etc.—One desirous of prosperity should sacrifice a white animal to the god Vâyu—an oft-quoted text of the Brâhmaṇas.

अथ तत्र सत्त्वे etc.—The animals get heaven, says the Brâhmaṇa. Who brought the news from heaven ?—asks the Jaina. Here are the Scriptures, answers the Br. The Jaina rejoins that the authority of the Scriptures will be shortly discussed and shown to be hollow. In the meanwhile, he ridicules the idea of स्वर्ग associated with animal-killing.

यदि हि हिंसया etc.—If हिंसा can bring heaven, the streets of hell may be taken as closed. For, who will then have to go to the latter place ? That is to say, if the worst sin could bring heaven, let us declare an end to hell!

पारमर्षाः:—A marginal note says 'मीमांसकाः'. Certainly not they, but the Sâṁkhyas.

किंच अपरिचित॰ etc.—If the offering of a lower life at a sacrifice can bring heaven, why not make an offering of a higher life, for the matter of that, of your father and mother to secure a still better heaven ?

अथ अचिन्त्यो हि etc.—The Br: So marvellous is the efficacy of Vedic mantras pronounced on the victim, that the result is heaven.

इह लोके etc.—The Jaina: The Vedic mantras have been found clearly inefficacious in the matter of marriage, and other ceremonies, many brides becoming widows inspite of the mantras promising a happy and prosperous married life, and many leading a happy married life even without the Vedic mantras pronounced upon them.

अथ तत्र क्रियावैगुण्यं etc.—The last stronghold of a defeated logician. The Br: The ceremony in connection with mantras may have been badly performed.

The Jaina: Who can remove the doubt whether the failure of the result has been due to bad performance of the ceremonies or the mantras were inefficacious ?

अथ यथा युष्माकं etc.—Br: You also pray for "Health etc." (See the verse quoted from आवश्यक 4-6. p. 509), and the fruit of the prayer is admitted by you to be accruing in another world. Similarly, the mantras of marriage ceremony may bear fruit in another life. Jaina; In that case, the Saṁskâras would be producing their fruits in the succeeding lives, and liberation from Saṃsâra would become impossible.

आरोग्यादि॰—The Jaina further explains that the prayer for आरोग्य in आवश्यक, 4-6. p.509, is for mental आरोग्य (भावारोग्य) which makes for truthfulness and other virtues.

न च वेदविहिता etc.—The Jaina quoted passages from Vedântic writers who condemn hiṁsâ, even at sacrifices.

यच्च याज्ञिकानां etc.—As regards the so-called respectability of sacrificial priests, the Jaina says that only fools respect them. He adds : " Even dogs are worshipped by fools."

यदप्यभिहितं etc.—Gods could produce before themselves any delectable food by their mere will; why should they care for your wretched meat ? The gods have a 'वैक्रिय' or वैक्रियिक as distinguished from an 'औदारिक' body which belongs to us. (See Tv. Sû. II. 36 and Râja-V, and Sûtra-kṛt p. 577.) वैक्रियिक=अष्टगुणैश्वर्ययोगादनेकानेकाणुमहच्छरीरविविधकरणं विक्रिया सा प्रयोजनमस्येति वैक्रियिकम् *i. e.* adjustable to various needs. औदारिक= उदारं स्थूलमिति यावत् ततोभवे प्रयोजने वा ठञ्जि औदारिकमिति भवति—gross and rigid.

प्रक्षेपाहार॰ etc.—If the gods be supposed to eat what is thrown into the sacrificial fire, it will conflict with the statement that the gods possess " mantra-bodies ".

चतुर्थ्यन्तपदमेव etc.—The Ritualists (Pûrva-Mimâṁsakas) not only denied the existence of God, but even of gods apart from ' the Vedic word in the dative case '—to which offerings were to be made. See Nirukta, and Pûrva M.Bh. Vârt.

हूयमानस्य॰—The offering simply burns away in the fire and turns to ashes; it is but vain talk to say that it pleases gods.

अपि च योऽयं etc.—A piece of banter. The tretâ fire (See Ait. and S'at. Brs.) is said to be 'the mouth of 33 crores of Gods'; so there is but one mouth for all varieties of gods—' high, medium and low ' : one god would be eating the उच्छिष्ट, (food from the mouth) of another god, thus surpassing even the Turks (Mahomedans) who eat from a common dish, but not from a common mouth ! Moreover, we have heard of many mouths to one body, but not of one mouth to many bodies! Again, suppose a man praises one god and reviles another. One god would thereupon pronounce a blessing, and the other a curse. How are the two operations to be carried out from *one* mouth? Besides, a mouth is but a 1/9 part of the body; if even that 1/9 part is a fire, how dangerous to the three worlds would be the 33 crores of gods!

इत्यलमति०—The writer is rightly disgusted with his own bantering tone.

यश्च कारीरि०—The कारीरी यज्ञ which is prescribed for rain, does not always secure it. Even when rain follows a कारीरि यज्ञ, it is not due to gods eating your offering but owing to their being pleased with the worshipper for his heart's worship. There are many ways of propitiating gods other than the sacrificial butchery which is nothing but sin.

यच्च छगल etc.—(See ante.) The deities may be supposed to have been gratified by the idea, they need not be supposed to have eaten the animal offerings. If what is thrown into fire as an offering reaches gods, why not such deleterious and objectionable substances as leaves of the nimb tree, bad oil etc.?

परमार्थतस्तु etc.—The true theory in this matter is this: the devotion of the worshipper taken along with certain accessories brings about the desired consequences such as rain, victory etc. This is borne out by the fact that a चिन्तामणि (the philosopher's stone) fulfils our objects inspite of its being inanimate.

अतिथीनां तु etc.—Better give your guests nicely prepared vegetable food.

पितॄणां etc.—The offering made to the manes for increase of progeny often fails to secure the end. Besides, without any such offering a donkey or a pig or an ewe has plenty of progeny. Moreover, the manes in their transterrestrial spheres must be engaged in enjoying or suffering the fruits of their earthly works. How could they have any desire for the rice-balls offered by their sons?

अथ विप्रोपभुक्तं etc.—As to the offerings made to the manes through the mouths of the Brâhmaṇas, the theory is simply ridiculous. The Brâhmaṇas get a fat belly by eating; there is nothing to show that the manes enter the body or the stomach of the Brâhmaṇas. In fact the Brâhmaṇas look like प्रेतs (ghosts) when they are engaged in gluttonously devouring the dishes spread before them, and so far no S'râddha ceremony need be performed.

आगमश्चात्र॰ etc.—A dilemma : Is the Brâhmaṇical Âgama —the Veda—पौरुषेय or अपौरुषेय *i. e.* composed by a personal (N.B.—It does not mean a human being—a mistake often committed) being or not? If it is composed by a personal being is that personal being omniscient or not? The *former* alternative is contrary to your statement contained in the following verse अतीं (See तत्त्वार्थसंग्रह of शान्तरक्षित, with पञ्जिका-in which a verse is quoted with the first line the same as in this)—"There is no direct percipient of suprasensible objects; the truth about things is determined by the eternal sentences of the Veda." The *latter*, that the Veda is composed by a personal being who is not omniscient would deprive it of all authority whatsoever. If now you say that the Veda is not composed by a personal being all we need say is, it can never exist any more than 'the horn of a horse'. You speak of the 'वाक्य of the Veda' etc. But वाक्य=utterance, which is clearly an act done by a personal being. We do not hear any sound in the sky; even if we did, we should have to presume a person behind it from whose mouth it emanated. All वचन is पौरुषेय *e.g.* कुमारसंभव of Kâlidâsa.

वचनात्मकश्च वेद: etc.—The Veda is a heap of articulate sounds which requires a body with organs such as the palate etc.

श्रुतेरपौरुषेयत्व etc.—Even after holding that श्रुति is अपौरुषेय, you admit that its interpretation is पौरुषेय *i. e.* the interpretation comes from a personal being or beings-the exponents of the Vedas. Why not then allow श्रुति to be पौरुषेय?

अन्यथाऽग्निहोत्रं etc.—Why is the text relating to अग्निहोत्र interpreted as referring to अग्निहोत्र, and not as referring to anything else under the sun? In other words, why have the Vedic texts certain definite meanings in the same manner as propositions of our ordinary parlance? *E.g.* why is 'अग्निहोत्रं जुहुयात् स्वर्गकामः' (a Vedic text)=अग्निहोत्रं जुहुयात् स्वर्गकामः (as we personal beings use and understand the terms), and not = श्वमांसं भक्षयेत् (any other irrelevant nonsense).

अस्तु वाऽपौरुषेय: etc.—Granting that it is अपौरुषेय, what bearing could that fact have on the question of its प्रामाण्य? प्रामाण्य depends on the words being आप्तपुरुषोक्त, not अपौरुषेय.

अथ योऽयं न हिंस्यात् etc.—विधि is of two kinds : उत्सर्ग (General rule) and अपवाद (Exception); where the two conflict the अपवाद overrides the उत्सर्ग.

अन्यार्थमुत्सृष्टं etc.—But the necessary condition is that the two–उत्सर्ग and अपवाद–must relate to the same matter. Illustrations as given in the text.

भक्तां चोत्सर्गे etc.—In the case of the question at issue, we find that the उत्सर्ग—न हिंस्यात् etc.—is for the purpose of averting hell (दुर्गतिनिषेधार्थः), while the अपवाद is for securing propitiation of gods, guests and manes—an entirely different matter. So one cannot be an अपवाद of the other, but is a contradiction of the other (तुल्यबलयोर्विरोध :—See Artha–Saṁgraha.)

न च वाच्यं etc.—It may be argued that the अपवाद about the Vedic *Hiṃsā*, inasmuch as it relates to securing heaven, relates virtually to averting hell (दुर्गतिनिषेध). Thus the उत्सर्ग and the अपवाद have the same subject-matter.

Criticism : It has been already shown that the Vedic *Hiṃsā* cannot be a means for securing heaven. Moreover, the विधि may be accepted as an अपवाद if there is no other recourse. But in the present case, heaven can be secured in many other ways such as यम, नियम etc.—and therefore the texts about the Vedic *Hiṃsā* had better be thrown overboard as conflicting (विरुद्ध) with the general principle first laid down (न हिंस्यात्), and not treated as an अपवाद.

न च वयमेव etc.—See supra. See also Dr. Bhandarkar's "Vaiṣṇavism" etc.

अत्र च लिप्साशब्द: etc.—A mere ambition which is never destined to be fulfilled.

Stanza XII.

A Brief Exposition :—

स्वार्थविबोधक्षम एव बोधः—Thesis: Knowledge, thought, or consciousness is capable of revealing *itself* and its *object*. Take 'स्वार्थ' as a द्वन्द्व compound of स्व and अर्थ [*i. e.* itself and its object: स्वस्य आत्मस्वरूपस्य अर्थस्य पदार्थस्य च], and not as their षष्ठीतत्पुरुष. 'एव' excludes the opposite of which there are two cases: (1) Revealing itself only, the world of objects being either nil (शून्यवाद), or a matter of mere inference (पदार्थानुमेयतावाद) or identical with ज्ञान itself (विज्ञानवाद); (2) Revealing other objects only, itself being revealed by another ज्ञान which some consider to be अनुव्यवसाय (a kind of second or after-consciousness), and some अनुमान or आक्षेप from its effect, viz., ज्ञातता.

प्रकाशते etc.—प्रकाशते being made predicate of बोध, the latter is suggested to the mind as a kind of light. And what is essentially of the nature of प्रकाश (light) illumines or reveals everything including itself.

विपर्यये etc.—Otherwise, *i. e.* if ज्ञान is not regarded as capable of revealing itself *i. e.* self-luminous (ज्ञानस्य स्वसंविदितत्वानभ्युपगमे). It does not mean 'if ज्ञान is not regarded as capable of revealing objects'. For, all are agreed as to its capacity to do the latter, whatever their difference as regards the nature of the objective world. This eliminates (2) of the foregoing paragraph from our consideration.

अर्थकथा—Talk about objects *i. e.* whether they *are* or *are not* etc.

तुशब्दः—तु=एव; नार्थकथा etc.=अन्यथा अर्थकथैव न.

यदि हि ज्ञानं etc.—Now begins the argument.

If ज्ञान is not regarded as self-luminous, it would require to be revealed by another ज्ञान, that by a third ज्ञान, and so on *ad infinitum.* Thus, while the ज्ञान is at its wit's end in the matter of revealing itself, the अर्थ (objective reality), which is जड, is unable to reveal itself and so 'even the talk of अर्थ becomes impossible.'

तथाप्येवं etc.—Therefore, there is good reason to hold that ज्ञान is self-revealed (स्वसंविदित). And yet other schoolmen maintain that ज्ञान is 'अनात्मनिष्ठ' (St. 1 l. 4) *i. e.* not स्वसंविदित or self-revealed, it being as much an object (कर्मतापन्न) of ज्ञान as any other object in the universe.

निष्ठा = निश्चय *i. e.* संवेदन.

परेभ्यो भयत :—Afraid of their critics, whom they are too dull to meet with arguments, in spite of their case of self-luminousness of ज्ञान being strong.

Fuller Exposition.

I. भाट्टास्तावदिदं etc.—भाट्टा:—The Mîmâṁsakas represented by the school of Kumârila Bhaṭṭa.

ज्ञानं etc.—They hold that ज्ञान is not self-revealed, because revelation is a क्रिया, and no क्रिया can have itself as its object, any more than "a gymnast however much trained can ride upon his own shoulders, or a sword howsoever sharp can cut itself."

तदेतन्न सम्यक् etc.—*Criticism*: What is the exact nature of your difficulty of 'स्वात्मनि क्रियाविरोध'? Is it that the क्रिया of उत्पत्ति cannot be directed towards itself, in other words, nothing can produce itself? Or, does it mean that the क्रिया of ज्ञप्ति cannot be directed towards itself? As to the former alternative, all we need say is that we do not hold it: we quite agree that ज्ञान cannot produce itself. But the second alternative we do maintain: ज्ञप्ति can be directed towards itself. When ज्ञान arises, it arises invested with that particular character, just as प्रदीपालोक—the light of a lamp—springs into existence as प्रकाश or illumination. You will say: If the light of a lamp springs into existence as प्रकाश *i. e.* if प्रकाश be the very nature of light, let it illuminate other objects; why should it be supposed to illuminate itself? Answer: Then, is that poor thing—the light—to remain unilluminated while it illuminates others? Or is it to receive illumination from another light and so on? The first supposition is contrary to experience, the latter involves अनवस्था–*regressus ad infinitum*— You will say : The light does not make itself an object of its illumination, that is to say, it does not illuminate itself, but springs into existence as illumination, and in that sense it is self-illuminating (स्वयंप्रकाश).

Answer : That is all the admission we need. When we say ज्ञान is self-illuminating or स्वयंप्रकाश we do not mean that ज्ञान appears before itself as an object (like घट, पट etc.). But just as we say 'ज्ञानं जानामि' (I know knowledge: I am aware of the fact of my knowledge), in the same way we say प्रदीपः स्वयं प्रकाशयति.

यस्तु etc.—As to the objection that a क्रिया cannot direct itself towards itself, for that would involve contradiction of कर्तृ and कर्म, we reply that the supposed incongruity is justified by experience (अनुभवसिद्धेऽर्थे विरोधासिद्धेः). Just as we experience a कर्ता working towards a कर्म in 'घटमहं जानामि,' so do we experience it in 'ज्ञानमहं जानामि'. If ज्ञान were not here known by itself it could not have been an object of knowledge. The ज्ञान is not known by another ज्ञान, and that by a third ज्ञान etc., as it would involve अनवस्था. It may be said (this is the ज्ञातता theory of the Bhaṭṭa Mîmâṁsakas) that ज्ञान is revealed by the revelation of its objects. Thus : Objects are revealed as a matter of fact; this revealedness (ज्ञातता) of objects becomes impossible except on the hypothesis of a ज्ञान having been already there as its cause. But this theory involves अन्योन्याश्रय-दोष. For, according to it, objects are objects of knowledge owing to ज्ञान, and ज्ञान is possible owing to objects being known. You will reiterate your explanation thus : अर्थ-प्राकट्य (ज्ञातता) is impossible except on the *hypothesis* of ज्ञान. Thus, ज्ञान is known by अर्थापत्तिप्रमाण, *i. e.* the argument of Implication. Criticism : Is that अर्थप्राकट्य or ज्ञातता, which presupposes ज्ञान, as you say, itself ज्ञात or अज्ञात ? If it is अज्ञात, it cannot form the basis of the revelation of ज्ञान. If it is ज्ञात, it involves ज्ञातता in ज्ञातता *ad inf.* (अनवस्था), or one अर्थापत्ति to support another अर्थापत्ति, and so on *ad inf.* Besides,

ज्ञान and ज्ञातता will involve each other, and there will be अन्योन्याश्रय. Therefore ज्ञान is double-faced: it looks towards objects and it looks towards itself, and in this way it is 'स्वसंविदित'.

Objection: If अनुभूति (ज्ञान) be अनुभाव्य (ज्ञानविषय) *i.e.* object of ज्ञान, it would not be अनुभूति any more than घट, पट etc.—(which are अनुभाव्य) are अनुभूति. [Râmânuja's S'rî-Bhâṣya Catuḥ-sûtrî.]

प्रयोगस्तु etc.—Syllogism: ज्ञान, though अनुभव, is not अनुभूति; because it is अनुभाव्य; as, for example, घट; and that ज्ञान is अनुभाव्य you do not deny, because you admit that it is स्वसंवेद्य (संवेद्य=अनुभाव्य).

नैवं etc.—The objection may be thus answered: Just as a ज्ञातृ is experienced as a ज्ञातृ, so अनुभूति is experienced as अनुभूति. That अनुभूति is also अनुभाव्य involves no absurdity (cf. S'rî-Bhâṣya). For, अनुभूति is अनुभूति in relation to the objects; it is अनुभाव्य in relation to itself. Thus things might differ according to their several relations *e.g.* one may be father of his children, but son of his own father and so on.

अनुमानाच्च etc.—that ज्ञान is स्वसंवेद्य can be shown by an अनुमान also. Thus:—ज्ञानं स्वयं प्रकाशमानमेवार्थं प्रकाशयति प्रकाशकत्वात् प्रदीपवत् *i.e.* ज्ञान illuminates objects while it illuminates itself, *because it is an illuminator e.g.* a प्रदीप.

संवेदनस्य प्रकाश्यत्वात् etc.—Objection: संवेदन (ज्ञान) if it is प्रकाश्य cannot be प्रकाशक. Answer: It can be प्रकाशक by removing the screen of अज्ञान.

ननु नेत्रादयः etc.—Objection: The eyes etc. are illuminators but they do not illuminate themselves; so your हेतु in the above syllogism is inconclusive. नात्र नेत्रादिभिः etc.—Answer: They are illuminators as भावेन्द्रियs *i.e.* not as physical organs—the eyeballs—but as sensuous consciousness (भावेन्द्रिय), and sensuous consciousness is self-revealed (स्वसंवेदनरूप). So the above हेतु—'to be an illuminator'—is not inconclusive.

तथा संवित् etc.—Another अनुमान to support स्वसंवेदन of ज्ञान=संवित् स्वप्रकाशा अर्थप्रतीतित्वात् यः स्वप्रकाशः etc.—*i. e.* संवित् (ज्ञान) is स्वप्रकाश, because it is a revelation of अर्थ; that which is not स्वप्रकाश is not a revelation of अर्थ *e. g.* a घट.

एवं सिद्धेऽपि etc.—Thus, when प्रत्यक्ष and अनुमान both prove स्वसंवेदन *i. e.* स्वयंप्रकाशत्व of ज्ञान, it is needless to set up a series of प्रत्यक्षs to account for the revelation of ज्ञान.

सत्संप्रयोगे—See Mîm. Darś. I. 1. and Bhâṣya. ज्ञान arises from the contact of इन्द्रिय and बुद्धि with the world of Reality (सत्). The three steps are as follows: First there arises ज्ञान from the contact of इन्द्रिय and बुद्धि with the world of Reality. [This is the first act of प्रत्यक्ष.] By it the latter is revealed (अर्थप्राकट्य). [This is the second act of प्रत्यक्ष.] From this revealedness I gather, by a kind of inference or implication, that there has been revelation. [This is the third act of प्रत्यक्ष.]

II. यौगास्त्वाहुः—For यौगाः=वैशेषिकs and the नैयायिकs, see Guṇaratna's Com. on Ṣaḍ.

Our ज्ञान, they say, is अन्यप्रकाश्य *i. e.* illuminable by something other than itself, because it is a प्रमेय—a reality—which is not divine omniscience. The point of the argument is this: All प्रमेयs, with the exception of God's own knowledge which surely does not require any other light, are अन्यप्रकाश्य; our ज्ञान is one of them; therefore our ज्ञान is अन्यप्रकाश्य.

समुत्पन्नं हि ज्ञानं etc.—ज्ञान, immediately after it is born, becomes an object of mental perception (मानसप्रत्यक्ष) by a further act of the mind taking place in the same आत्मन्. It is not self-revealed. (The नै० call this अनुव्यवसाय. This view is attributed to Murâri-Miśra in Nyâya books—See their chapter on प्रामाण्यवाद).

न चैवमनवस्था—The charge of अनवस्था levelled against the position of अन्यप्रकाश्यता of ज्ञान (see ante) may be thus met: Ordinarily a प्रमातृ (knower) is satisfied with the knowledge of an object; when, however, there arises in his mind a *desire to know* (*i. e.* to be aware or conscious of) *his own knowledge,* a knowledge of the knowledge takes place. [In Western psychology they call it self-consciousness. But I do not adopt the term because in this passage it is the very point at issue whether the consciousness is self-revealed or other-revealed.]

तदयुक्तं etc.—Answer : (1) The पक्ष (rather, the साध्य of the पक्ष ; or पक्ष with the साध्य) is बाधित by a contrary अनुमान, and the हेतु is therefore कालात्ययापदिष्ट. (When one अनुमान is opposed by another अनुमान, the fallacy is called सत्प्रतिपक्ष or प्रकरणसम हेत्वाभास in Brahmanical Nyâya books. कालात्ययापदिष्ट or बाधित is the name of the हेत्वाभास when the साध्य of the अनुमान is contradicted by another प्रमाण such as प्रत्यक्ष.)

तथा हि विवादास्पदं etc.—Syllogism to prove that ज्ञान is स्वसंविदित (स्वप्रकाश्य), as against the preceding syllogism: ज्ञानं स्वसंविदितं ज्ञानत्वात् ईश्वरज्ञानवत् *i. e.* our ज्ञान is स्वसंविदित, because it is a ज्ञान ; as for example, God's own ज्ञान. The argument is that all ज्ञान by the very nature of it is स्वसंविदित, ours as well as God's.

न चायं वाद्यप्रतीतो etc.—It may be objected by the other side that the दृष्टान्त on which the generalisation is based viz. ईश्वरज्ञान is a pure fiction according to the Jainas—there being no ईश्वर, according to them. But the objection is not correct. The Jainas do admit the existence of ईश्वर as a 'पुरुषविशेष', just as the Yogins do (क्लेशकर्मविपाकाशयैरपरामृष्टः पुरुषविशेष ईश्वरः See Pat.'s Yoga Sû.). [If by पुरुषविशेष we are to understand a single 'पुरुषविशेष', I am afraid the author is making an admission not justified by the general tenor of Jainism. But I suppose we can very well understand this as "जातावेकवचनम्", numerous पुरुषविशेषs being ईश्वरs in Jaina Theology.]

व्यर्थविशेष्याश्चात्र etc.—(2) Besides, the हेतु in the syllogism : ज्ञानं स्वान्यप्रकाश्यम् ईश्वरज्ञानान्यत्वे सति प्रमेयत्वात् घटवत्—is व्यर्थ-विशेष्य or असमर्थविशेष्य as the Naiyâyikas call it (See न्या. सू. वृ. or त. भा.). The विशेष्य viz. प्रमेयत्वात् is redundant, since it adds nothing to the विशेषण 'ईश्वरज्ञानान्यत्वे सति' which is quite sufficient for the purpose of the argument. The stock illustration of 'असमर्थविशेष्य' is पर्वतो वह्निमान् धूमत्वे सति द्रव्यत्वात् where द्रव्यत्वात् is redundant, धूमत्वात् being quite sufficient for the purpose of the argument.

न हीश्वरस्य ज्ञानादन्यत् etc.—That प्रमेयत्वात् is redundant is obvious; for it excludes nothing. There is nothing 'other than ईश्वरज्ञान' which is not प्रमेय and which would accordingly require to be excluded by inserting the word प्रमेयत्वात्. Nor does the omission of प्रमेयत्वात् endanger the साध्य viz. स्वान्यप्रकाश्य making the remainder of the हेतु viz., ईश्वरज्ञानादन्यत्व, sometimes go with साध्याभाव *i. e.* स्वसंविदितत्व.

अप्रयोजकश्चायं etc.—(3) the हेतु is अप्रयोजक or सोपाधिक *i. e.* ineffective, except under conditions which do not exist in the present case. Technically an उपाधि is साध्यव्यापकत्वे (or साध्यसमव्याप्तिकत्वे) सति साधनाव्यापक *i.e.* that which covers or is co-extensive with साध्य, but does not cover the साधन.

तत्पुत्रत्वादिना etc.—The stock-illustration of सोपाधिक हेत्वाभास is अयं (भावी मित्रातनयः) श्यामः मित्रातनयत्वात् अन्यमित्रातनयवत् *i. e.* the next son of Mitrâ must be dark-complexioned because it is a child of Mitrâ, like all the other sons of that lady. This argument is considered to be unsound, inasmuch as it is based upon a हेतु viz. मित्रातनयत्व which is अप्रयोजक *i. e.* ineffective or सोपाधिक *i. e.* depending upon a condition viz. शाकपाकजत्व (to be fed on a particular kind of vegetable food). The point is this: A son of Mitrâ is *not bound* to be dark-complexioned simply because he is a son of that lady, for the dark complexion really arises from one's being fed in the womb on a certain kind of food and not from the simple fact of one's being a son of Mitrâ. In other words, the validity of the अनुमान depends not merely on the uniformity of nature, but on the *necessity* of the uniformity arising from the *law of causation*. The technical definition of an उपाधि in साध्यव्यापकत्वे सति साधनाव्यापकत्वम् (See Nîl. and Muktâvali with com.) will apply to the illustration as follows:—यत्र यत्र श्यामत्वं तत्र तत्र शाकपाकजत्वम्; but not यत्र यत्र मित्रातनयत्वं तत्र तत्र शाकपाकजत्वम्, the coming मित्रातनय being not शाकपाकज.

उपाधिश्चात्र etc.—In the syllogism under discussion जडत्वं is the उपाधि. Thus : the साधन here is ईश्वरज्ञानान्यत्वे सति प्रमेयत्वम्, but it holds good only under the conditions of जडत्व *i. e.* that which is not only ईश्वरज्ञानान्यत् and प्रमेय, but *also* जड; that alone is स्वान्यप्रकाश्य. In fact, जडत्व is the प्रयोजक of स्वान्यप्रकाश्यत्व and is therefore the उपाधि in the present case.

स्वप्रकाशे परमुख°—जड is defined as that which depends upon another for its revelation.

यच्चोक्तं etc.—Moreover, the ज्ञान and the ज्ञान of the ज्ञान (See ante) are not known to be arising one after the other.

आशूत्पादात्—It may be argued that they *do* arise one after the other, but the succession is so quick that we fail to notice it. For example, when we run a needle into a file of lotus-leaves we imagine that we have pierced all of them *simultaneously*, but as a matter of fact it is obvious that they have been pierced one after another.

जिज्ञासाव्यवहित etc.—Answer : Between the first and the second ज्ञान comes the जिज्ञासा of the ज्ञान; so you cannot say that one *immediately* follows the other and so their succession is not noticed.

न च ज्ञानानां etc.—Moreover, ज्ञानs do not necessarily arise from जिज्ञासा; even without the latter, in certain cases, ज्ञान does arise, provided the objects are there in the right place.

न चार्थज्ञानमयोग्य° etc.—Now the first ज्ञान (the ज्ञान of objects) is not in an unsuitable place so that it could not become an object of ज्ञान without a special desire to know it. For, that first ज्ञान is in the आत्मन्—quite a suitable place—and would therefore become known without a जिज्ञासा on our part–the result of which would be that one ज्ञान would spring on another ज्ञान and so on *ad infinitum.* आत्मन् would thus be engaged in knowing its own series of ज्ञानs and could, therefore, never turn to other विषयs. The point is that without a जिज्ञासा, a ज्ञान cannot arise; if it did, there would be nothing to prevent ज्ञानs springing in endless succession—like particles of radium—a show to which there would be no end, so that आत्मन् would never have the opportunity of turning again to the world of objects. Thus जिज्ञासा must be interposed between the ज्ञानs. But when this is done, the proposition 'समुत्पन्नं हि ज्ञानं etc.' (See supra) breaks down.

तस्माज्ज्ञानं etc.—Conclusion : Therefore a ज्ञान does not need another ज्ञान to reveal it; it reveals itself ; as does the last ज्ञान in a धारावाहिक ज्ञान (ज्ञान of the nature of attention where the mind continues to rest on a particular object for a length of time).

Books of reference.

1. Books on प्रामाण्यवाद—and न्या. सि. मञ्जरी pp. 160-65. Pandit Vol. III; तर्कभाषा, तर्ककौमुदी, नीलकण्ठी etc.
2. S'rî–Bhâṣya on अनुभूति.
3. S'loka Vârt. on Sûtra 2-4.

Stanza XIII.

Stanza: If Mâyâ *is*, there arises the dualism of Brahman and Mâyâ. If Mâyâ *is not*, how could the manifold world be explained? To say that there is Mâyâ (something that is not real) and that it can do something is equivalent to saying that a woman is barren and that she is a mother!

तैर्वादिभिः—The Vedântins of the S'âṁkara school. माया = अविद्या (Nescience). It is a much-discussed problem of later S'âṁkara Vedânta whether 'माया' and 'अविद्या' are synonymous or different. Some distinguish between the two, referring one to ब्रह्मन् or ईश्वर and the other to जीव. (For more information, see Siddhântaleśa.)

I Brief Explanation : (समासार्थः).

सा सद्वया etc.—द्वय = twofold, द्वौ अवयवौ यस्य, viz., (1) आत्मन् (ब्रह्मन्) and (2) माया.

यदि असती etc.—ब्रह्मन् being transcendental, माया is supposed to produce the world. But if it (माया) is unreal, how can it produce it ? Does 'the horn of a horse' (an absolute nothing) ever produce anything ? A feat of jugglery or a mirage cannot produce any real effect. Besides, the world is too real to be regarded as a mere show.

अत्रैवकारो etc.—In मायैव, एव = अपि = च. Thus the passage = माया च अर्थसहा च—that something should be माया and *at the same time* अर्थसहा. Cf. a similar use of two चs in the Raghu.-Canto X, 6. ते च प्रापुः etc. अर्थसहा—capable of doing something. अर्थक्रियाकारित्व is given as a definition of सत्ता (Existence or Reality), in Jaina and Bauddha metaphysics. And माया can have no सत्ता—without ceasing to be माया. Thus, to say that माया (unreal) is अर्थसहा (real) is like saying 'माता च वन्ध्या च'.

II. Detailed Explanation (व्यासार्थः).

ते वादिनः etc.—The Vedântins who cite सर्वं खल्विदं ब्रह्म and other texts of the Upaniṣads in support of Monism.

अयं तु प्रपञ्चो etc.—Their syllogism to prove that the world is मिथ्या.

Criticism:—तदेतद्वार्तं etc.—Here begins the criticism. It is all idle talk.

The Vedântin is called upon to state what he means by मिथ्यारूपत्व—Three alternative explanations are possible.

(1) मिथ्यात्व *i. e.* unreality in the sense of *absolute non-existence* (असत्त्व), such as belongs to वन्ध्यापुत्र. This, however, is impossible, as it involves the position of 'असत्ख्याति' (appearance of what is nothing) which the Buddhist takes up but the Vedântin rejects. [See, however, Gauḍapâda's Kârikâs and S'aṁkara's Commentary thereon.]

"असतो मायया जन्म तत्त्वतो नैव युज्यते ।
वन्ध्यापुत्रो न तत्त्वेन मायया वाऽपि जायते ॥"

—Gauḍapâda Kârikâs, Advaita 28.

असद्वादिनामसतो भावस्य मायया तत्त्वतो वा न कथंचन जन्म युज्यते, अदृष्टत्वात्। न हि वन्ध्यापुत्रो मायया तत्त्वतो वा जायते । तस्मादत्रासद्वादो दूरत एवानुपपन्न इत्यर्थः ।—S'aṁkara's Com.

(2) मिथ्यात्व *i.e.* unreality in the sense of mis-take—that is, wrongly taking A for B. This, again, would be विपरीत(अन्यथा-) ख्याति involving the reality of one or both, which too the Vedântin does not accept. [The words of S'aṁkara in the Introductory portion of his S'ârîraka Bhâṣya where he speaks of अविद्या as परत्र पूर्वदृष्टस्यावभासः would seem to be an acceptance of अन्यथाख्याति. See, however, the commentaries on the passage.]

(3) मिथ्यात्व *i. e.* unreality in the sense of what cannot be described as either existent or non-existent (अनिर्वाच्यत्व). [There are numerous passages which can be cited to support this sense of मिथ्यात्व in S'aṁkara's Bhâṣya on the Brahma-Sûtras. In this sense of मिथ्यात्व, the author of the Bhâmatî observes : "न हि ब्रह्मवादिनो नीलाद्याकारां वित्तिमभ्युपगच्छन्ति किं-त्वनिर्वचनीयं नीलादीति ।"—Bh. on S'aṁkara's Com. on II. ii. 28.]

Now the Vedântin may be called upon to explain what he means by अनिर्वाच्यत्व. Does he mean निःस्वभावत्व ? Now what is that भाव or स्वभाव which is denied by the prefix 'निः' in the word निःस्वभाव ?

(a) If it is Being or सत्त्व (भाव) that is denied, it is once more the position of असत्ख्याति which has been already repudiated by them as non-Vedântic.

(b) If it is non-Being or असत्त्व (अभाव) that is denied, it is the position of सत्ख्याति which is also unacceptable and unwelcome to the Mâyâvâdin.

(c) Suppose निःस्वभाव=प्रतीत्यगोचर (that which is unthinkable). But if the world (प्रपञ्च) is unthinkable, how could it be made the subject (पक्ष) of the syllogism अर्थप्रपञ्चो मिथ्यारूपः etc. ? Also the hetu प्रतीयमानत्वात् could not be predicated of the world, if the world is, as you say, प्रतीत्यगोचर. If you explain प्रतीत्यगोचर, not as precluding प्रतीयमानत्व altogether but as implying that it is not known as it ought to be known, that is to say, as ब्रह्मन्, this would be विपरीत (अन्यथा–) ख्याति, which has been already shown to be unacceptable to the Mâyâvâdin.

[For the Khyâtis, see Commentaries on S'aṁkara's Adhyâsa Bhâṣya in the Introduction of the Brahma-Sûtra S'âriraka Bhâṣya, Râmânuja's S'rî-Bhâṣya, Appaya-Dîkṣita's Siddhântales'a, and Mâdhava's Ṣaḍdars'ana-saṁgraha and Jhalkikara's Nyâyakos'a.]

किं चेयमनिर्वाच्यता etc.—The unreality of जगत् is contradicted by प्रत्यक्ष.

अथ प्रत्यक्षस्य etc.—It is urged by the other side that प्रत्यक्ष can *affirm*, it cannot *deny*. Thus, it is said : आहुर्विधातृ॰ : प्रत्यक्ष affirms, it does not deny; therefore, the Unity, which the Veda has declared, प्रत्यक्ष has no power to deny.

अन्यरूपनिषेधमन्तरेण etc.— Affirmation implies negation. You cannot affirm a thing to be yellow without denying that it is black. You cannot know an empty table by itself without denying its contents. Hence we cannot regard प्रत्यक्ष to be purely affirmatory.

अपि च विधायकमेव etc.—Granting that प्रत्यक्ष is only affirmatory, one would like to ask : why should it affirm विद्या and not अविद्या, ब्रह्मन् and not जगत्? If it affirms the latter, there is the dualism of ब्रह्मन् and जगत्.

तदमी वादिनः—There are two schools of S'âṁkara Vedânta. One of them takes its stand upon mere श्रुति and rejects प्रत्यक्ष which comes in the way of the sole reality of Brahman as incompetent to pronounce any opinion on this question, since ब्रह्मन् is beyond its range. The other school holds that प्रत्यक्ष too affirms the said Brahman as pure सत्, as the subject in every proposition. " प्रत्यक्षादिविरोधे शास्त्रस्य बलीयस्त्वमुक्तम् । सति च विरोधे बलीयस्त्वं वक्तव्यम् । विरोध एव न दृश्यते । निर्विशेषसन्मात्रावग्राहित्वात् प्रत्यक्षस्य । "—a S'âṁkara school criticised by Râmânuja. (See Râmânuja's S'rî–Bhâṣya, Appaya-Dîkṣita's Siddhântales'a, etc.). It is the latter school that is referred to in this passage.

To say that प्रत्यक्ष is सन्मात्रग्राहिन् is not only to make it विधायक but also निषेधक, because मात्र implies negation.

अनुमानबाधितश्च etc.—A syllogism to prove that the world *is not* मिथ्या.

प्रपञ्चो मिथ्या न भवति etc.—Moreover, in the Vedântin's syllogism the hetu 'प्रतीयमानत्वात्' is inconclusive, ब्रह्मन् being प्रतीयमान as well as जगत्, and yet not मिथ्या. If, however, you deny प्रतीयमानत्व of ब्रह्मन्, silence would be golden for you. Nor can you cite any दृष्टान्त in support of your reasoning; for, every दृष्टान्त will be found included in the पक्ष, viz., अर्थप्रपञ्च or जगत्, about which मिथ्यात्व (अनिर्वचनीयत्व) is going to be proved. This is what is called अनुपसंहारिन् hetvâbhâsa.

किं चेदमनुमानं etc.—Is the syllogism which is supposed to prove that जगत् is मिथ्या (a) a part of the जगत्, or (b) is it separate from it? (b) If it is separate from it, is it सत्य or असत्य? If it is सत्य, why not the whole जगत्? If it is असत्य, it can prove nothing. (a) If it is part of जगत्, it is मिथ्या like the rest of it, and cannot accomplish its task of proving मिथ्यात्व of जगत्. Thus, it may be shown that Brahman cannot be the sole reality.

Cf. P. N. Tattvâlokâlaṁkâra Ratnâkarâvatârikâ on i. 15. pp. 34–36 Syâdvâda-Ratnâkara.

III. अथवा प्रकारान्तरेण etc.—

Another statement of the Vedântin's case and its refutation: Brahman, the pure सत्, may be proved by every प्रमाण.

1. प्रत्यक्ष—Pratyakṣa is of two kinds—निर्विकल्पक and सविकल्पक, both of which prove the existence of Brahman. The former of these has been thus defined: अस्ति ह्या० etc. It is such a ज्ञान as takes note of the abstract reality devoid of the धर्म. (Quoted from Mîmâṁsâ-S'loka-Vârtika of Kumârila). The latter is well-known. [For two differing views about the nature of सवि० and निर्वि० see Tarka-Bhâṣâ and Râm.'s S'rî-Bh. I. i. 1. "निर्विकल्पकं नामजात्यादियोजनाहीनं वस्तुमात्रावगाहि

किंचिदिदमिति ज्ञानम्–"(T.Bh.) otherwise called निष्प्रकारक or निर्विशेष ज्ञान. Contra. Râmânuja who says: "निर्विकल्पकमपि सविशेषविषयमेव ...निर्विकल्पकं नाम केनचिद्विशेषेण वियुक्तस्य ग्रहणं न सर्वविशेषरहितस्य."]

न च विधिवत् etc.—It may be objected that the निर्विकल्पक प्रत्यक्ष will take note of what ब्रह्मन् is not, quite as much as of what ब्रह्मन् is—in which case it will be bearing witness to the dualism of Brahman and non-Brahman. But the answer to that objection is that the प्रत्यक्ष is only विधायक and not निषेधक (cf. आहुर्विधातृ etc.), and is, therefore, bearing witness to the positive Reality, namely, Brahman. Next, if you take the other variety of प्रत्यक्ष—the सविकल्पक प्रत्यक्ष, it too will be found to be revealing घट, पट etc. as imbued with the principle of *existence* for which our word is "ब्रह्मन्".

2. अनुमानादपि etc.—Here is an अनुमान to prove the same:–(a) विधिरेव तत्त्वं प्रमेयत्वात्, विधि i. e. the Positive Reality, revealed as सत् in our experience, is the only Reality, because it is प्रमेय. For, that to which we can direct our thought must be something positive and not negative. All प्रमाणs—प्रत्यक्ष, अनुमान, शब्द, उपमान and अर्थापत्ति—accordingly refer to something positive "तथाचोक्तं—प्रत्यक्षाद्यवतारः स्यात्" etc. (Mîm. S'l. Vârt. Abhâva-Paricchheda, 17.) etc." The प्रमाणs operate to reveal something positive; when something negative is known, what takes place is not that the प्रमाणs are directed to a negation, but that there is no operation of the प्रमाणs at all. This, of course, means that there is no such प्रमाण as अनुपलब्धि which is supposed to be directed to a negative object (अभाव).

अतो वा तत्सिद्धिः etc.—Another अनुमान to prove ब्रह्मन्. (b) ग्रामारामादयः etc.—The world we see before us is penetrated through and through with thought (प्रतिभासान्तःप्रविष्ट) because it is an object of thought (प्रतिभासमानत्वात्). Whatever is an object of thought is penetrated with thought, e. g. the form of thought (प्रतिभासस्वरूप). So is this whole objective world. And, therefore, it is penetrated with thought. Thought or consciousness is what we call ब्रह्मन्. Thus, the अनुमानप्रमाण also bears witness to the existence of ब्रह्मन्.

3. आगमोऽपि etc.—The quotations, which are well-known, are taken from the Upaniṣads.

कृत्रिम आगम—The Smṛtis which are man-made, as distinguished from S'ruti which is God-made.

सर्वे भावाः etc.—All objects are but appearances of ब्रह्मन्, because they are imbued with सत्त्व (Existence). That with which a thing is imbued is the real essence of that thing. For example, मृत्तिका is the real essence of घट, शराव etc., which are all earthy, that is, imbued with मृत्तिका.

तदेतत्सर्वं etc.—The Vedântin is compared to a man who is drunk.

सर्वं हि वस्तु etc.—Nothing can be accepted as true unless it is proved by प्रमाण. In the *A-dvaita* doctrine, however, there is no room for प्रमाण—for, प्रमाण means *dvaita*, that is, dualism.

अथ मतं etc.—It may be argued that the प्रमाणs have only a व्यावहारिक use, and are intended to satisfy the needs of ' लोक ' *i. e.*, either the vulgar mind (cf. Spinoza) or the demands of objective experience. But such an argument will not do. For, where is the room for ' लोक ' in *A-dvaitism* ?

अथास्तु etc.—Granting that there is scope for प्रमाण even in *A-dvaita*, one would like to know what प्रमाण it is. Is it प्रत्यक्ष ? No. For प्रमाण only reveals the world of plurality. You mentioned निर्विकल्पक प्रत्यक्ष as proving ब्रह्मन्. But we do not recognize its validity as a प्रमाण. For, प्रत्यक्ष is प्रमाण only when its character accords with the character of its object. This can never be unless the प्रत्यक्ष is सविकल्पक *i. e.*, has a certain character as घटज्ञान, पटज्ञान etc. Now सविकल्पक प्रत्यक्ष, which alone deserves to be recognized as प्रमाण amongst the two varieties of प्रत्यक्ष, is never known to reveal the Positive Reality which you speak of, viz., pure ब्रह्मन् abstracted from its various forms constituting the world of plurality. [See also Râmânuja's S'rî-Bhâṣya, I. i. 1.]

यदप्युक्तम् " आहुः " etc.—Then, as regards the remark that प्रत्यक्ष reveals only Positive Reality and is incompetent to reveal

Negation, we say it is not justified by experience. For, प्रत्यक्ष has a double function to perform: it differentiates as well as co-ordinates.

न ह्यनुस्यूतं etc.—We nowhere perceive सामान्य—the one pure and simple existence—divorced from विशेषs. Cf. Râmânuja's S'rî-Bhâṣya, Catus-Sûtrî. I. i. 1. निर्विशेषं हि सामान्यं—Mîm. S'l. Vârt. आकृतिवाद—10.

यच्च प्रमेयत्वादित्यनुमानं etc.—The syllogism referred to is विधिरेव तत्त्वम् प्रमेयत्वात् (See above). Here, 'विधिरेव तत्त्वम्' *i. e.* the proposition that Reality is always positive, is opposed to the evidence of प्रत्यक्ष; for, the latter bears testimony to negation also. The hetu is, therefore, कालात्ययापदिष्ट, otherwise called बाधित.

यच्च तत्सिद्धौ etc.—Another हेतु given to prove the same was 'प्रतिभासमानत्वात्'. (See supra.) As to it, we ask the question whether the 'प्रतिभासमानत्व'—revelation to consciousness—arises 'स्वतः' or 'परतः'? Evidently it does not arise स्वतः (of itself); for, nobody thinks घट, पट etc., to be self-revealed. If, however, the revelation to consciousness is supposed to arise परतः *i. e.* from some *other* source, it involves the admission of something that is other, which means dualism.

यच्च परमब्रह्म etc.—Then, again, as regards the argument that Brahman is that principle of Existence which runs through all things and unites them in one Reality, we may observe that it involves the admission of (1) a principle that runs through the things and (2) the things through which it runs *i. e.* the dualism of अन्वेतृ and अन्वीयमान. Moreover, it is absurd to think that चैतन्य (consciousness, which is but another name for Brahman) runs through घट, पट etc. What runs through घटs is मृत्तिका, through पटs तन्तुs, and so on.

किं च पक्षहेतुदृष्टान्ताः etc.—An अनुमान involves पक्ष and हेतु. Now, tell us whether they are *identical* inter se or *distinct*. If *identical*, it will be impossible to construct a syllogism, which requires different members. If *distinct*, there is the inevitable dualism.

यदि च हेतुमन्तरेण etc.—The verse quoted means: If it is attempted to establish the principle of *Advaita* by means of a हेतु, there will be the dualism of at least the हेतु and the साध्य; if, without the हेतु, anything could be got proved by a mere mandate! The point of the argument is that in proving a साध्य by means of a हेतु we proceed from the 'known' to the 'unknown' which is a clear admission of the dualism of the 'known' and the 'unknown'. हेतोरद्वैतसिद्धिश्चेत् etc.—Âptamîmâṁsâ II. 26.

पुरुष एवेदं etc.—The texts must be interpreted in harmony with dualism, if they are to be interpreted at all. For, without वाच्यवाचकभाव—which means dualism—they can declare nothing. कर्मद्वैतं फलद्वैतं etc.—Âptamîmâṁsâ II. 25. The verse means: कर्म–फल, लोक (इह and पर), विद्या–अविद्या, बन्ध–मोक्ष all involve dualism.

Reference Books: S'aṁkara's Adhyâsa-Bhâṣya and Com. especially Bhâmatî; Siddhânta-tattva-bindu; Siddhânta-leśa; Râmânuja's S'rî-Bhâṣya.

Appendix.

ज्ञानादन्योऽर्थः परः (P.N. T. 15).

मिथ्यात्वमत्र कीदृक्षमाकाङ्क्षितं सूक्ष्मदृशा। किमत्यन्तासत्त्वम्। उतान्यस्यान्याकारतया प्रतीतत्वम्। आहोस्विदनिर्वाच्यत्वम्।

......निःस्वभावत्वपक्षेऽपि निसः प्रतिषेधार्थत्वे स्वभावशब्दस्यापि भावाभावयोरन्यतरार्थत्वे पूर्ववत् प्रसङ्गः। प्रतीत्यगोचरत्वं निःस्वभावत्वमिति चेत् अत्र विरोधः।—प्रपञ्चो न प्रतीयते चेत् कथं धर्मितया प्रतीयमानं च हेतुतयोपाददे। तथोपादाने वा कथं न प्रतीयते। यथा प्रतीयते न तथेति चेत् तथा विपरीतख्यातेरभ्युपगमः स्यात्।

...अथ कथमेतत् प्रत्यक्षं पक्षप्रतिक्षेपकम्। तद्धि विधायकमेव इति तथा तथा ब्रह्मैव विदधाति न पुनः प्रपञ्चसत्यतां प्ररूपयति। सा हि तदा प्ररूपिता स्याद् यदीतरस्मिन्नितरेषां प्रतिषेधः कृतः स्यात्। न चैवम्। निषेधे कुण्ठत्वात् प्रत्यक्षस्येति चेत् तदयुक्तम्—यतो विधायकमिति कोऽर्थः। इदमिति वस्तुस्वरूपं गृह्णाति नान्यस्वरूपं प्रतिषेधति प्रत्यक्षमिति चेत् मैवम्। अन्यरूपनिषेधमन्तरेण तत्स्वरूपपरिच्छेदस्याप्यसंपत्तेः। पीतादिव्यवच्छिन्नं हि नीलमिति गृहीतं भवति नेतरथा।

यदेदमिति वस्तुस्वरूपमेव गृह्णाति प्रत्यक्षमित्युच्यते तदावश्यमपरस्य प्रतिषेधमपि तत् प्रतिपद्यत इत्यभिहितमेव भवति । केवलवस्तुस्वरूपप्रतिपत्तेरेवान्यप्रतिषेधप्रतिपत्तिरूपत्वात् । अपि च विधायकमेव प्रत्यक्षमिति नियमस्याङ्गीकारे विद्यावदविद्याया अपि विधानं तवानुषज्यते । सोऽयमविद्याविवेकेन सन्मात्रं प्रत्यक्षात् प्रतियन्नेव न निषेधकं तदिति ब्रुवाणः कथं स्वस्थः । इति सिद्धं प्रत्यक्षबाधितः पक्ष इति ॥ अनुमानबाधितश्च । प्रपञ्चो मिथ्या न भवति । असद्विलक्षणत्वात् । य एवं स एवं यथा आत्मा । तथा चायम् । तस्मात्तथेति । प्रतीयमानत्वं च हेतुर्ब्रह्मात्मना व्यभिचारी । स हि प्रतीयते न च मिथ्या । अप्रतीयमानत्वे तु अस्य तद्गोचरवचनानामप्रवृत्तेर्मूकतैव तत्र वः श्रेयसी स्यात् । दृष्टान्तश्च साध्यविकलः । शुक्तिशकलकलधौतेऽपि प्रपञ्चान्तर्गतत्वेनानिर्वचनीयतायाः साध्यमानत्वात् । किं च—इदमनुमानं प्रपञ्चाद्भिन्नम् अभिन्नं वा । यदि भिन्नं तर्हि सत्यमसत्यं वा । यदि सत्यं तर्हि तद्वदेव प्रपञ्चस्यापि सत्यत्वं स्यात् । अथासत्यम् । तत्रापि शून्यम् अन्यथाख्यातम् अनिर्वचनीयं वा । आद्यपक्षद्वयेऽपि न साध्यसाधकत्वम् नृशृङ्गवत् शुक्तिकलधौतवच्च । तृतीयपक्षोऽप्यक्षमः । अनिर्वचनीयस्यासंभवित्वेनाभिहितत्वात् ॥......अथासत्यस्वरूपः शब्दः कथं ततस्तस्य सत्यत्वं नाम । न हि स्वयमसत्यमन्यस्य सत्यत्वव्यवस्थापनहेतुः । अतिप्रसङ्गात् । अथ कूटकार्षापणे सत्यकार्षापणोचितक्रयविक्रयव्यवहारजनकत्वेन सत्यकार्षापणव्यवहारवदसत्येऽप्यनुमाने सत्यव्यवहार इति चेत् तर्ह्यसत्यमेव तदनुमानम् । तत्र चोक्तो दोषः ।...प्रपञ्चस्वभावतया तस्यापि मिथ्यात्वप्रसक्तेः । मिथ्यारूपं च तत्कथं नाम स्वसाध्यं साधयेत् ॥

—Com. Ratnâkarâvatârikâ.

Stanza XIV.

Stanza : Things (वाच्य), though many, are also one; though one, they are also many. So are the words denoting them (वाचक) both one and many. Those who are not 'yours', *i.e.* the heretics, in considering things and words to be of a different nature from what is mentioned above, are mistaken.

वाच्यम्=अभिधेयम् viz. चेतनमचेतनं वस्तु.

एव=अपि, also.

सामान्यरूपतया एकात्मकमपि etc.—One as the universal (सामान्य); many as the particulars (व्यक्तिभेदेन).

अथवाऽनेकरूपमपि etc.—The enlargement of the subject and the predicate reversed.

तथा वाचक०—So also words have a double nature of one and many, arising from the double aspect, that of **सामान्य** and of **विशेष**.

अत्र चाल्पस्वरत्वेन etc.—Ordinarily in a dvandva compound the word with the smaller number of syllables is placed first. Yet, here, **वाचक** (three-syllabled word) is placed before **वाच्य** (two-syllabled). This is in accordance with the special provision about the priority of the more important (See Pâṇ. and Kâtyayana). **अल्पाच्तरम्** । But **अभ्यर्हितं च (पूर्वम्)**. The **वाचक** is more important than the **वाच्य** because the latter depends upon the former. As 'the word-philosophers' (the grammarians) say: "There is no idea (**वाच्य=प्रत्यय**), which is not accompanied by its word (**वाचक=शब्द**); all thought (**ज्ञान**) appears penetrated through and through with language. (See Patañjali's M.Bhâṣya and Bhartṛi's. Vâkyapadîya : **न सोऽस्ति प्रत्ययो लोके** etc. I. 124.)

भावार्थस्त्वयम् etc.—**Substance of the Stanza** :

(1) Some schoolmen recognise only the *Universal* (**सामान्य**) as the Reality. They are, in the language of Jaina philosophy, followers of **द्रव्यास्तिकनय** *i. e.* the point of view of the reality of substance (**द्रव्य**). The typical representatives of this school of thought among Brâhmaṇas are preeminently the Advaitins of the Uttara-Mîmâṁsâ (Vedânta) and next the Sâṁkhyas.

(2) Then again there are other schoolmen who regard *particulars* (**विशेष**) to be the only reality. They belong to the **पर्यायास्तिकनय** *i. e.* the point of view of the reality of the changing modes (**पर्याय**). This point of view is represented by the Buddhists.

(3) There is a third school of thought which gives equal treatment to **सामान्य** and **विशेष** as principles of Reality, but recognises them as absolutely distinct entities. This is **नैगम** (= **नैकगम**) point of view—which is advocated by the Vaiśeṣikas and the Naiyâyikas.

I. Discussion of the different schools.

I. संग्रहनयावलम्बिनो etc.—A statement of the सामान्यैकान्तवाद्—which according to the Jainas contains only partial truth from the point of view of the संग्रहनय.

सामान्यमेव etc.—सामान्य is the only reality. For, we do not see any विशेषs apart from the सामान्य. The argument may be stated as follows :

सर्वमेकम् अविशेषेण सदितिज्ञानाभिधानानुवृत्तिलिङ्गानुमितसत्ताकत्वात् *i. e.* From the fact that all things are equally (अविशेषेण) known (ज्ञान) and styled (अभिधान) ' सत् ', we conclude that *All is One.* Its existence is inferred from the one general notion (अनुवृत्ति) and language of सत् which we employ in respect of all things without distinction.

Note that the argument is intended to prove two things : that (1) something *is*; and that (2) something is the *Universal Being*.

तथा द्रव्यत्वमेव etc.—Another argument : द्रव्यत्व is the only reality. For, the so-called particulars of द्रव्य viz. धर्म, अधर्म etc. are nowhere found separated from द्रव्यत्व, *i. e.* they are known not in themselves but only as द्रव्यs; and, therefore, द्रव्यत्व is their only reality.

किं च ये सामान्यात् etc.—A third argument which establishes the sole reality of सामान्य by destroying the case for विशेषs. Supposing विशेषs (defined as अन्योन्यव्यावृत्त्यात्मक *i. e.* consisting of reciprocal distinctions—see Dinakarî on Nyâya-Muktâvali) exist, you have to meet the following dilemma : Do they contain विशेषत्व or not ? In other words, do they conform to the general idea of विशेष or not ? If they do not, they have no nature of their own, and therefore no existence. If they do, that विशेषत्व is a सामान्य—which contradicts your dogma of the sole reality of विशेषs.

अपि च विशेषाणां etc.—विशेषs are defined as the ground or cause of व्यावृत्तिप्रत्यय—the idea of distinction. But we shall show that on reflection that व्यावृत्तिप्रत्यय is found to be an impossibility. What is व्यावृत्ति? 'विवक्षितपदार्थे इतरपदार्थप्रतिषेधः' (Denial of any other पदार्थ in regard to the पदार्थ in hand). Thus the denial of पटत्व in regard to घट is घटस्य पटाद्व्यावृत्ति. Now the question we ask is this: How can the thing—the पदार्थ under consideration—*e. g.* घट, which has enough work, to do in securing its own being, venture to undertake a denial of other things? If it undertakes to do that work, it will find it too stupendous to do. For, innumerable are those 'other things', past, present and future, which it shall have to exclude from itself. They cannot be excluded unless they are *known*. And if they are *known*, the knower is nothing short of an omniscient being!—a being who knows *all* things in the Universe from which a particular thing—a घट—is to be distinguished!

न चैतत् प्रातीतिकं—It is not justified either by experience or by reason.

व्यावृत्तिश्च निषेधः etc.—Besides, व्यावृत्ति is a negation, a nothing—which can be made an object of knowledge no more than 'a flower of the sky'.

तथा येभ्यो व्यावृत्ति etc.—Another dilemma: Are those things, from which the पदार्थ under consideration is distinguished, सत् (existent) or असत् (non-existent)? If they are non-existent the पदार्थ could as well be distinguished from 'the horn of a donkey'. If they are 'सत्', in calling them *all* 'सत्' you have admitted सामान्य!

या चेयं व्यावृत्तिः etc.—व्यावृत्ति (exclusion, distinction) you say, takes place owing to विशेष. Now tell us whether there is *one* व्यावृत्ति for all the विशेषs or one for each, and therefore *many*. In the latter case, the व्यावृत्तिs will be so many विशेषs; for, to be many and *distinct inter se* constitutes the very soul of विशेष. The व्यावृत्तिs will then require other व्यावृत्तिs to account for their विशेषs. (For 'व्यावृत्तिहेतवो विशेषाः'). Now, if a व्यावृत्ति possesses व्यावृत्ति from a व्यावृत्ति, the व्यावृत्ति will be not-व्यावृत्ति, and therefore there will be no विशेषs; moreover, there will be an endless series of व्यावृत्तिs (अनवस्था).

एका चेद् सामान्यमेव etc.—In the former case *i.e.* if व्यावृत्ति is supposed to be *one*, it is an admission of सामान्य under another name, inasmuch as all the विशेषs have then something in common (अनुवृत्ति).

किं चामी विशेषाः etc.—Lastly, one more dilemma: Are the विशेषs distinct from सामान्य or are they identical with it? Distinct they are not found, any more than 'a crest of matted hair' is found 'on the head of a frog.' In other words, they do not exist at all. If they are identical with सामान्य, there is सामान्य and nothing else. Thus is argued out the case for the *sole reality* of सामान्य.

2. पर्यायनयान्वयिनस्तु etc.—A statement of the विशेषैकान्तवाद—which according to the Jainas contains a partial truth from the point of view of पर्यायास्तिकनय.

विविक्ता क्षणक्षयिणो etc.—*Particulars* are the only Reality. They are distinct, self-contained and momentary. No universal is ever found apart from them.

न हि गवादिव्यक्त्यनुभव॰ etc.—When we see cows, we see this cow or that cow and so on, that is *particular* cows—each with her own physical shape, colour etc.—and no such thing as a universal essence—सामान्य—of cows.

तथा च पठन्ति etc.—"Here are five fingers which I distinctly see to be different from one another. He who sees a common form in them might as well see a horn on his own head!" The verse is quoted, says the note in the AMP. edition of स्याद्वादमञ्जरि, from "अशोकविरचितसामान्यदूषणादिक्प्रसारितामन्थ."

एकाकारपरामर्शस्तु etc.—It, then, remains for the विशेषैकान्तवादी to account for the idea of unity which is at the root of class-notions and class-names ('common terms'). It arises, he says, from the particulars themselves, and the particulars are born with the power of causing एकाकारप्रत्यय, which they, therefore, do not need to borrow from elsewhere, *i. e.* from an imaginary सामान्य outside them.

किं च यदिदं सामान्यं etc.—A series of dilemmas for the **सामान्यवादी** to answer: Is this **सामान्य** *one* or *many*? If one, is it everywhere or only at particular places? If it is everywhere, why is it not found in the space between this cow and that cow? Besides, if it is *one* existing *everywhere*, why does not **गोत्व** embrace within its fold **घट**s and **पट**s as it does **गो**s? If it (the **सामान्य**) is not everywhere but only at particular places, it is another name for **विशेष**; and this, again, is contrary to the tenet of the school.

अथानेकं etc.—If, however, you hold that **सामान्य** is *many*, there being such distinct **सामान्य**s as **गोत्व, अश्वत्व, घटत्व, पटत्व** etc., it is an admission of **विशेष**s, since the **सामान्य**s distinguish themselves from each other, **गोत्व** being not the same as **अश्वत्व** and so on.

अर्थक्रियाकारित्व etc.—A positive argument to prove that **विशेष**s are the only reality. Reality is defined as '**अर्थक्रियाकारिन्**' *i.e.* that which *does* something, serving a purpose; in other words, to *be* is to *do* (cf. Modern Pragmatism and Carlyle's characterization of the universe as ' an infinite conjugation ' of the verb *to do*). Now this is what you can affirm only of **विशेष**s and not of **सामान्य**. You cannot ride **अश्वत्व** or milk **गोत्व**; for that you require **अश्व**s and **गो**s, *i. e.* the real particulars, not imaginary universals.

तथेदं सामान्यं etc.—Lastly, is the **सामान्य** different from **विशेष**s or is it identical with it? If it is different, we do not see it so, and it is therefore only a figment of your imagination. If it is identical with the **विशेष**s, we have **विशेष**s only, and no **सामान्य**. Compare a similar argument of the other side at the end of the foregoing section (**सामान्यैकान्तवाद**).

3. **नैगमानुयायिनस्तु**—A third view about **सामान्य** and **विशेष** is that both of them are realities, *distinct inter se*. For, so we actually find them.

सामान्यविशेषौ etc.—That they are *distinct inter se* is thus shown by means of a syllogism :—**सामान्यविशेषावत्यन्तभिन्नौ।**

विरुद्धधर्माध्यासितत्वात् etc. They are *distinct* from each other, because they possess contradictory properties as do water and fire. The contradictory properties are, for example, सर्वगतत्व and असर्वगतत्व : thus while सामान्य is ubiquitous, विशेषs are limited to particular places.

न सामान्यात् पृथग् etc.—You may perhaps object that विशेषs are not found *apart* from सामान्य. We would then ask you: How, then, are they found? You would reply : As invariably *accompanied by* सामान्य. Criticism: Then it is not finding a विशेष but सामान्य *also*. Now if this were true, we should not be using a word to express a विशेष or enter into a व्यवहार founded upon the विशेष. But, as a matter of fact, we do. Therefore we must recognise a विशेष apart from सामान्य.

4. न चैतत् पक्षत्रयमपि etc.—A statement of the *Siddhânta*. All the three views set forth above are partial representations of the truth. There can be no doubt that we see Reality possessed of a *double nature*, that of सामान्य and that of विशेष. Hence the Nyâya-Vâis'eṣika view of घटत्व, पटत्व etc. as सामान्यविशेषs. (See V. Sûtras and Pras'astapâda Bhâṣya).

वस्तुनो हि लक्षणं etc.—अर्थक्रियाकारित्व which is said to be the very essence of Reality (see supra) is consistent only with the thesis above laid down. When we see a cow, we apprehend a certain unity of animal form, such as belongs to all individuals we call 'cows' (वस्तुस्वरूपं सर्वव्यक्त्यनुयायि). But, at the same time we apprehend its distinction from other animals such as buffaloes etc. When, moreover, we speak of 'a brindled cow' thus referring to the विशेष (particular character) of the animal, we must not fail to remember that in doing so we also recognise the fact that the animal is *a cow*. We thus notice सामान्य and विशेष— *the two—in one*. [Note carefully the difference of this view from that of the नैगमनय. The नैगमनयवादिन् recognises सामान्य and विशेष as *distinct inter se* (स्वतन्त्रसामान्यविशेषवादिनः), the सिद्धान्तिन् recognises them as *two-in-one* ('वाच्यमनेकम्'—Stanza)].

अपि च शबलत्वमपि etc.—Similarly, शबलत्व too has a variety of forms. So when we speak of 'a brindled cow' we do not refer to any brindled colour of the animal, but the particular brindled colour which we see in the cow before us. So here, again, the perception of सामान्य is at the same time a perception of विशेष.

न हि क्वचिद् etc.—The two are never experienced separately from each other anywhere.

अन्धगजन्याय—The parable of the Elephant and the Blind Men: The Elephant is not seen wholly by any of the blind men, nor is he the sum total of the partial aspects, but is the one reality which appears different from different points of view or rather touch in the case of the blind men of the parable.

स्वतन्त्रसामान्यविशेष etc.—Syllogism: सामान्य is in a certain way different for each individual and in a certain way it is one with it because made of it, like a dissimilar परिणाम (product), that is, a modification of a substance which though like that substance is also unlike it. Similarly, we may recognise likeness (सामान्य) in different individuals, and say this cow is like that and that cow is like this. Thus, we may demonstrate the unity-in-difference of सामान्य and विशेष. In being one with the व्यक्ति the सामान्य does not lose its nature. For example, रूप and similar qualities are identical with the substance, viz. घट, and yet they do not on that account cease to be गुणs. If you say that it is due to some difference existing between रूप and its substance, we may point out that some difference exists also between like products such as घटs, inasmuch as even different objects of the same class do bear different names.

Next the Siddhântin criticises विशेषैकान्तवाद:—

विशेषा अपि नैकान्तेन etc.—The reader will remember that one of the arguments against keeping the two (सामान्य and विशेष) together was that the two possessed contradictory natures. But the सामान्य, according to our Siddhânta is not सर्वगत, as विशेष also is not, and therefore there is no conflict of the धर्मs of the two.

सामान्यस्य विशेषाणां च etc.—They are somehow blended together. सामान्य is *many* inasmuch as it is inseparable from विशेषs; विशेषs are *one* inasmuch as they are inseparable from सामान्य.

एकत्वं च etc.—सामान्य is *one* from the point of view of संग्रहनय. From the point of view of the *whole* truth (प्रमाण as distinguished from नय—see S. Mañjari on Stanza XXIII), however, it is somehow the subject of contradictory predicates, viz. both one and many, inasmuch as सामान्य is the universal element in like things, and yet it is particularized in consequence of each of the things having its own individuality.

एवं चासिद्धं etc.—So you cannot lay down an *absolute* opposition between सामान्य and विशेष. If you insist upon *opposition somehow,* it is what we are actually contending for against all other schools.

पाथः पावक० etc.—The example of water and fire cited to show the incompatibility of contradictory natures really points to the very conclusion we have been urging. Thus: as water and fire they are opposed ; but as द्रव्य they are one.

II. Next we show how वाचक *i. e.* शब्द also has got a double nature viz. सामान्य and विशेष or one and many. शब्दत्व is *one* in all शब्दs, and it is also *many* in the particular forms of शब्द, such as the शब्द of a शङ्ख, the शब्द of a शार्ङ्ग (bow), the शब्द which is sharp or the शब्द which is soft and so forth.

शब्दस्य हि सामान्यविशेषात्मकत्वं etc.—शब्द is पौद्गलिक (material, that which belongs to matter) and its double nature of सामान्य and विशेष can be easily perceived.

पौद्गलिकः शब्दः etc.—That शब्द is पौद्गलिक may be shown by an अनुमान. Thus: शब्दः पौद्गलिकः इन्द्रियार्थत्वात् रूपादिवत् = शब्द (sound) belongs to matter (and thus material) because it is an object of sensuous perception, just like रूप (colour) etc. (For a contrary view see शब्दनित्यत्वाधिकरण in Kumârila's श्लोकवार्तिक).

यच्चास्य etc.—That शब्द does not belong to matter is maintained by the Vaiśeṣikas ('यौगs' as they are also called) on the following grounds :—

(1) It rests in something that is *intangible* (viz. आकाश).

(2) It experiences *no obstruction* in the way of going in or going out even in a crowded place.

(3) It does not admit of being analysed into *successive parts*.

(4) It does not give a *push* even to any fine corporeal द्रव्य.

(5) It is a quality of आकाश, which is not matter.

These five arguments are met by the Siddhântin as follows :

(1) शब्दपर्यायाश्रयो etc.—The attribute which we call शब्द does not rest in आकाश but in the different kinds (वर्गणा) of भाषा. So the intangibility of आकाश does not affect the argument.

शब्दाश्रयः etc.—The substance which is the abode of शब्द must be tangible because it is an object of our इन्द्रिय, found or not according as the percipient is near or far and the wind is blowing in a favourable or unfavourable direction. Parallel case : the particles of matter which are the abode of गन्ध. The alleged हेतु of the Vaiś. is therefore असिद्ध.

(2) द्वितीयस्तु गन्धद्रव्येण etc.—गन्ध rests in a द्रव्य which experiences no such obstruction, and yet it is admittedly पौद्गलिक. So the alleged हेतु is अनैकान्तिक *i. e.* inconclusive, not invariably pointing to the conclusion desired. It may be urged that the गन्धद्रव्य does experience obstruction ; for, from a tightly-closed box, musk will not emit any smell. The answer to it is: the same is true of शब्द. Therefore the हेतु is असिद्ध, *i. e.* not found in the पक्ष.

(3) तृतीयस्तु etc.—The flash of a lightning does not admit of analysis into successive parts, and yet it is पौद्गलिक. The alleged हेतु is, therefore, अनैकान्तिक.

(4) चतुर्थोऽपि etc.—The particles of a fragrant substance or dust or smoke give no push to other matter, and yet they are beyond question पौद्गलिक. The alleged हेतु is, therefore, अनैकान्तिक.

(5) पञ्चमः पुनरसिद्धः etc.—शब्द may be shown to be not a गुण of आकाश; because it is perceptible by a sense of ours, like रूप which is similarly perceptible. The हेतु is therefore असिद्ध.

सिद्धः पौद्गलिकत्वात् etc.—शब्द being thus shown to be पौद्गलिक, it follows that it is सामान्यविशेषात्मक. It may be asked: Are not even अपौद्गलिक things—*e. g.* आत्मन्—सामान्यविशेषात्मक? Answer: The Jainas hold that the 'संसारी आत्मा' somehow gets attached to पुद्गल and is in a certain sense पौद्गलिक or material.

यद्यपि स्याद्वादिनां etc.—Are not all things—whether पौद्गलिक or अपौद्गलिक—सामान्यविशेषात्मक according to the Jainas? Answer: They are. But the truth cannot be well realised by ordinary thinking in the case of अपौद्गलिक substances such as धर्म, अधर्म, आकाश and काल. But it can be realised easily in the case of a पौद्गलिक द्रव्य. Therefore this long digression to show that शब्द is पौद्गलिक.

अत्रापि नित्यशब्द०—The नित्यशब्दवादी (the Mîmâṁsaka) holds that शब्द is *absolutely one*; the अनित्यशब्दवादी (the Buddhist) holds that it is *absolutely many*. Both may be shown to be part-truths, as is done in the above paragraphs in regard to सामान्य-विशेष.

अथवा वाच्यस्य etc.—The वाच्य having been shown to be सामान्यविशेषात्मक, it follows as a matter of course that वाचक is also सामान्यविशेषात्मक, since in a certain way शब्द and अर्थ (वाचक and वाच्य) are held to be one.

अभिहाणं अभिहेयाउ etc.—अभिधानमभिधेयाद् भवति भिन्नमभिन्नं च।
क्षुराग्निमोदकोच्चारणे यस्मात्तु वदनश्रवणयोर्नापि च्छेदो नापि दाहो न पूरणं।

तेन भिन्नं तु । यस्माच्च मोदकोच्चारणे तत्रैव प्रत्ययो भवति न च भवति अन्यार्थे । तेनाभिन्नं तदर्थात् ॥—Bhadrabâhu. [I have divided the sentences of these stanzas according to the sense, and they should be so construed.]

अभिधान......अभिन्नं च—अभिधान (वाचकशब्द) is distinct from and yet not distinct from अभिधेय (वाच्य). This is the proposition to be proved. Next comes the reason why it is *distinct* from अभिधेय.

क्षुराग्नि...भिन्नं तु—When you utter the word क्षुर (razor), अग्नि (fire) or मोदक (sweet ball), neither the mouth that speaks nor the ear that hears, is cut, or burnt, or filled by it (*i. e.* क्षुर, अग्नि and मोदक respectively). Therefore, अभिधान is *distinct* from अभिधेय. Next comes the reason why अभिधान is *not distinct* from अभिधेय.

यस्माच्च मोदकोच्चारणे...तदर्थात्—When one utters the word मोदक, the thing denoted by the word, viz., मोदक, is presented to the mind and not anything else, it follows that the word ('अभिधान'-शब्द) is *not* distinct from its sense (अभिधेय-अर्थ).

विकल्पयोनयः शब्दाः etc.—Words originate from concepts of things and vice versa; hence, the two are related as cause and effect (respectively and vice versa); at the same time, words do not affect things; (hence, they are distinct from each other).

शब्दस्य ह्येतदेव तत्त्वं etc.—When a वाचक (शब्द) conveys its वाच्य (अर्थ) it becomes transformed into the latter; it is only then that it conveys the sense. Hence it is that a particular word has a particular sense only.

II. Another Interpretation of the Stanza :

वाच्यम्=वस्तु घटादिकम्.

एकात्मकमेव=एकरूपमेव सत्.

अनेकम्=अनेकस्वरूपम्. *i. e.* Reality is at once one and many.

अयमर्थः etc.—When one knows an object (घट), he distinguishes it from like as well as unlike objects (other clayvessels and also पट). Thus, in knowledge, there is a negative element in addition to the positive element. It is only with the help of the former, that we fix the nature of an object, which would otherwise remain nebulous, floating, vague, undefined. Therefore सर्वभावानां भावाभावात्मकं स्वरूपम्.

एकान्तभावात्मके etc.—If a thing had only a *positive* nature, the nature would not be *its own*; it is because of its negative nature, its differentiation from other things, that a thing possesses its specific nature. If, on the other hand, it had only a *negative* nature, it would have no positive contents, and so it would be nothing.

तस्मात्स्वरूपेण etc.—A thing is both भावात्मक and अभावात्मक—t is सत् or भावात्मक in its own form, it is असत् or अभावात्मक as another thing.

सर्वमस्ति स्वरूपेण etc.—This sums up the अनेकान्त (भावाभाव) वाद of the Jainas who believe in *being-cum-nonbeing* of all things from different points of view, viz., स्व and पर.

एवं चैकस्मिन्नर्थे ज्ञाते etc.—Hence, *to know one is to know all.* For, you cannot know a thing unless you distinguish it from all things.

ये तु सौगताः etc.—" स्वरूपादिना सत्त्वं पररूपादिना असत्त्वम् " is the thesis maintained. If you deny the latter, as the Buddhists do, घट would be *everything* ; for, it is then not असत् in any way. If you deny the former, घट would be *nothing* ; for, it has no सत्त्व in any way.

यौगास्तु—The Vaiśeṣikas would say: In order that घट may possess its own proper nature all that you require is mutual अभावs (अन्योन्याभावs) of things which are in themselves separate. Why should the things themselves be regarded as अभावात्मक? Answer: If घट were not पटाभाव, घट would be पट. Just as घट is a घट because घट is other than घटाभाव, so घट would be पट because पट is also other than घटाभाव (as represented by मठ).

एवं वाचकमपि etc.—शब्द is similarly द्वयात्मक *i.e.* भावाभावात्मक; or, एकविषय; and अनेकविषय *e. g.* घट may denote an earthen pot only ; it may denote an earthen pot and also the body of a yogin (a technical sense of the word घट). The संकेत or convention may give rise to a number of अर्थs connected with a single वाचक. चौर a thief ; also rice (the latter being a meaning of the word in the language of the Dākṣiṇâtyas). Similarly कुमार= a boy or prince ; also, the month of Âśvina in the language of the Easterners.

'सद्गुरु'—A technical term of the Jainas. More than 180 fasts, formerly; now only 3, according to the convention of the जीतकल्प, a gatha work of त्रितभद्रगणिक्षमाश्रमण, जीतमाचरितं तस्य कल्पो वर्णना प्ररूपणा जीतकल्पः (A.M.P. Edition, P. 117-Note). Thus the same word may connote different meanings at different times. S'âstras may add certain meanings: Thus, द्वादशी may mean एकादशी under the rules relating to fasts in the Vaishṇava books. अलि=मदिरा in Trip-Tantra.

न चैवं सङ्केतस्य etc.—Convention is not the only ruling principle in fixing the meanings of words. Convention is guided by certain definite considerations also.

कानि तानि etc.—Next are recorded some differences of opinion as regards the Connotation or Denotation of terms, the Import of Propositions.

(1) अपोह—exclusion, negation is conveyed by word, *e.g.* घट means घटेतरव्यावृत्ति (अपोह). This is the Buddhists' view. (See Diṅnâga and Apohasiddhi, a work of Ratnakîrti).

(2) सामान्य—जाति is conveyed by words (व्यक्ति by आक्षेप). for that alone gives fixity to the sense. व्यक्तिs are innumerable and cannot be presented to the mind by a word except through the medium of the जाति (See K. Prakâśa).

विधिवादिनस्तु etc.—All propositions are mandatory according to a school of the Mîmâṁsakas (See Râmânuja's S'rî-Bhâṣya etc.)

विधिरपि—विधि variously defined. See R.'s S'rî-Bhâṣya and Mîmâṁsâ Bhâṣya, Vârtika and Âpodevi (न्यायप्रकाश) and Prakaraṇa-p.

Stanza XV.

Stanza : Here are a few out of the innumerable absurd propositions maintained by the Sâṁkhyas.

(1) That चित् (पुरुष) does not function in the cognition of the objective world.

(2) That बुद्धि is जड *i. e.* an unconscious principle.

(3) That आकाश etc. spring from the तन्मात्रs *i. e.* the essences of शब्द etc.

(4) That बन्ध and मोक्ष do not belong to पुरुष.

Explanation: The Sâṁkhya makes Spirit, the principle of Intelligence (पुरुष), too transcendental, and places everything which an ordinary spiritual philosopher would refer to the Spirit under the category of जड *i. e.* Unintelligent Reality. This draws down upon him from Hemacandra the compliment of "Jaḍa"—unintelligent or idiotic.

The commentator as usual divides his commentary into two parts : (1) A Summary Exposition and (2) A Detailed Exposition.

I. A Summary Exposition :—

This consists of a bare enumeration of the Sâṁkhya tenets mentioned in the Stanza :

(1) चित् चैतन्यशक्तिः etc.—The चित्—the power of चैतन्य—what we call the Self or Âtman—' has no objects ' [' चिद् अर्थशून्या '] *i. e.* it is not its function to cognize the world of objects. That function is assigned to बुद्धि, the first evolute from अव्यक्त or प्रकृति.

(2) बुद्धि—otherwise known as 'महत् तत्त्व' or the Great Principle—is जड *i.e.* devoid of consciousness.

(3) The पञ्चमहाभूतs, viz. आकाश, वायु, तेजः, जल, and पृथ्वी, spring from the पञ्चतन्मात्रs *i. e.* the essences or the subtle (सूक्ष्म) principles of शब्द, स्पर्श, रूप, रस and गन्ध respectively.

(4) पुरुष who is neither प्रकृति nor विकृति—neither Nature nor any of its modifications—has neither बन्ध nor मोक्ष. These belong to प्रकृति. (*Vide* "तस्मान्न प्रकृतिः" Sâṁkhya Kârikâ 62).

(5) बन्ध consists in being of the प्रकृति; मोक्ष is absolution from प्रकृति, which arises from the right understanding of the Twenty-five Principles :—1. पुरुष, 1. प्रकृति, and 23 evolutes (विकृतिs) of प्रकृति.

इति etc.—" What propositions contrary to all sense have not been laid down by these fools ? "—that is, they are capable of perpetrating all kinds of absurdities.

II. Detailed Exposition:—

सांख्यमते etc.—

The Sâṁkhya Doctrine :—Man is so pain-stricken that there arises in him a desire to know the nature of the causes that produce the Pain. On reflection he finds that Pain is are of three kinds : आध्यात्मिक, आधिभौतिक and आधिदैविक.

(1) आध्यात्मिक *i. e.* personal pain, may be either physical or mental. The former is well-known. The latter is caused by Lust, Anger, Greed, Stupor, Envy, Uneasiness and Doubt. The Sanskrit originals of these have been thus explained by a commentary of the S. K :—

"कामः=इष्टविषयाभिलाषः ; क्रोधः=अनिष्टविषयद्वेषः ; लोभः=सत्यपि धने तदादानेच्छा ; मोहः=हानोपादानविवेचनासामर्थ्यम् ; भयम्=अनिष्टदर्शनजन्यत्रासः ; ईर्ष्या=परसंपदुत्कर्षासहिष्णुता ; विषादः=स्नेहास्पदपदार्थविच्छेदनिमित्तो व्याकुलीभावः ; विषयविशेषादर्शनम्=अनवधारणात्मकमनेककोटिकं ज्ञानं संशय इत्यर्थः "—Explanations of these terms vary, sometimes changing the fundamental sense, in different works.

All these दुःखs are called आध्यात्मिक or personal, because their *remedy* lies *in*(अधि) *us*(आत्मन्) आन्तरोपायसाध्यत्वात्—Malliṣeṇa's explanation. Not because they originate in us ?

The next two varieties are caused from without and their remedy is found outside us. These are :

(2) आधिभौतिक—That caused by the भूतs *i. e.* beasts, reptiles, trees etc.

(3) आधिदैविक—That caused by godlings, demigods and other lower spirits.

अनेन दुःखत्रयेण......अभिघात :—All the three kinds of दुःख are effects of the रजस् principle (see below) which, residing in बुद्धि, 'attacks' adversely the चेतनाशक्ति. This contains an explanation of the origin and nature of *Pain.* Pain is that which is experienced by the चेतनाशक्ति as प्रतिकूल or adverse (Cf. The Naiyâyika definition of Pain ; also, those of Spencer etc. As a matter of fact it is very difficult to define pleasure and pain, for they are unanalysable and therefore cannot be split up into differentia and genus or species for the purpose of definition.) Strictly speaking, however, it does not belong to the चेतना but to the बुद्धि, and is a product of the रजस् principle, according to Sâṁkhyas.

The whole passage from सांख्यमते to पञ्चविंशतिः is extracted verbatim from Guṇaratna's Com. p. 97 on the Ṣaḍ. D. Samuccaya, 34 (See Appendix). The Com. is based upon the statements of the Sâṁkhya tenets as found in Vâcaspati-mis'ra's सां. त. कौ. on the सां. का. दुःखत्रयाभिघातात् जिज्ञासा तदपघातके हेतौ (S. K. 1.)—v. l. तदभिघातके of our text.

तत्त्वानि च पञ्चविंशतिः etc.—*The Twenty-five Principles* consist of :—

(1) अव्यक्त—The Unmanifest or the Potential Reality.

(2) महत्तत्त्व—The Great Principle—viz. the Buddhi or Intelligence. It is generally understood as the Cosmic Intelligence *i. e.* Intelligence manifested in the macrocosm, and hence 'महत्'.

(3) अहङ्कार—the Ego. Not to be confounded with पुरुष or आत्मन्. पुरुष or आत्मन् caught in the trammels of प्रकृति appears as अहम्—ego.

(4) पञ्चतन्मात्रs—or the Five Essences of शब्द, स्पर्श etc. which are the seeds of the पञ्च.

22

(5) The *Eleven* इन्द्रियs consisting of the five बुद्धीन्द्रियs or cognitive organs, five कर्मेन्द्रियs or organs of activity, and मनस्, the organ of mentality.

(6) The पञ्चमहाभूतs—Or the Great Material Elements : आकाश etc.

(7) पुरुष—The Cit or Âtman. The last is neither प्रकृति nor विकृति.

तथा चेश्वरकृष्ण: etc.—Guṇaratna also quotes Iśvarakṛishṇa's Kârikâ 3 and explains it. (See Appendix).

Of the 25 principles, *one* is the original प्रकृति which is in no way विकृति ; *seven* beginning with महत्तत्त्व *i.e.* महत्तत्त्व, अहङ्कार and the पञ्चतन्मात्रs are प्रकृति-विकृतिs *i. e.* विकृतिs of their antecedents and प्रकृतिs of their consequents on the list ; *sixteen* are pure विकृतिs : these are the eleven इन्द्रियs and the five महाभूतs ; while *one* viz. पुरुष is neither प्रकृति nor विकृति—he is transcendental.

प्रीत्यप्रीतिविषाद etc.—प्रीति (joy), अप्रीति (grief) and विषाद (stupor or dulness—not dejection merely), लाघव (lightness—not in the English sense of levity, but in the good sense of agility or easy movement), उपष्टम्भ (making a stand, aggressiveness), गौरव (heaviness, lack of agility or ease) are constantly tending to override one another, depend upon another, produce one another and combine with one another. But when they are in a state of equipoise they are called ' प्रकृति '—which is their original and natural condition. Other names for the same are प्रधान, अव्यक्त, etc. Cf. "प्रीत्यप्रीतिविषादात्मकाः प्रकाशप्रवृत्तिनियमार्थाः । अन्योन्याभिभवाश्रयजननमिथुनवृत्तयश्च गुणाः ॥ सत्त्वं लघुप्रकाशकमिष्टमुपष्टम्भकं चलं च रजः । गुरुवरणकमेव तमः प्रदीपवच्चार्थतो वृत्तिः ॥—S. K. 12, 13.

An additional series is found in the Sâṁkhya Kârikâ and its commentary, viz. प्रकाश, प्रवृत्ति and नियम *i. e.* light, activity and arrest or stationariness, mentioned as the functions of सत्त्व, रजस् and तमस् respectively. (See Bhâṣya, S. K. on 'लाघव' etc.).

प्रधानमव्यक्तं etc.—प्रकृति is also known as ' प्रधान ' (' प्रकृष्टं धीयते अस्मिन्निति '), the Great Abode or Reservoir, and ' अव्यक्त '

the Unmanifest or the Potential. [" प्रकृतिः प्रधानं ब्रह्म अव्यक्तं बहुधानकं मायेति पर्यायाः "—S. K. Bhâṣya. "अव्यक्तस्यामी पर्यायशब्दा भवन्ति अव्यक्तं प्रधानं ब्रह्म परं ध्रुवं प्रधानकमक्षरं क्षेत्रं तमः प्रसूतमिति" S. T. Samâsa.]

अव्यक्तस्यामी etc.—[S. T. Samâsa p. 4.] Its characteristics are :—It is without beginning, middle or end; it has no parts; it is common to all, that is to say it is an all-embracing principle; it has no qualities such as शब्द etc. (the qualities are its later evolutes); and it is changeless.

प्रधानात् etc.—From प्रधान springs बुद्धि or महत्तत्व. (cf. ततः प्रकृतेर्बुद्धिः संजायते.—Sad. D. S. p. 100; cf. प्रतिविषयमध्यवसायो—S K. 5; "प्रतिविषयेषु श्रोत्रादीनां शब्दादिविषयेष्वध्यवसायो दृष्टं प्रत्यक्षमित्यर्थः"—S.K.Bh. "का बुद्धिः । अत्रोच्यते अध्यवसायो बुद्धिः सोऽयमध्यवसायो गवादिषु द्रव्येषु यस्मात् प्रतिपत्तिः एवमेतन्नान्यथा । गौरेवायं नाश्वः स्थाणुरेवायं न पुरुषः" —S. T. Samâsa.

अध्यवसायः—Perception; determination of the character of an object positively and negatively; thought, in the fullest sense of the term, including comparison and contrast.

तस्यास्त्वष्टौ etc.—The same as in Guṇaratna's Com. Cf. तस्या अष्टौ रूपाणि । धर्मज्ञानवैराग्यैश्वर्यरूपाणि चत्वारि सात्विकानि अधर्मादीनि तु तत्प्रतिपक्षभूतानि चत्वारि तामसानि । —Guṇaratna p. 100. (Cf. also S. T. S. अस्यास्तु बुद्धेरष्टौ रूपाणि भवन्ति तामसानि p. 5.)

Mark that although we translate बुद्धि by the English word "Intellect", the former in truth stands for much more than what is signified by the latter in English books on Psychology—where it is distinguished sharply from 'Emotion' and 'Will'. The reason for adopting the word 'Intellect' as the best English equivalent for बुद्धि is that the explanation अध्यवसायो बुद्धिः etc. accords best with the meaning of the term "Intellect" implying existential and predicative judgment. The advantage possessed by the Sanskrit term बुद्धि is that it recognises the implication of emotion and will even in intellectual determination. The word बुद्धि means lighting up, or the faculty of lighting up or bringing definitely into consciousness.

धर्म, वैराग्य etc.—Are certain attitudes of the mind which play a part even in the intellectual determination of the character of the world of objects.

बुद्धेरहङ्कारः etc.—(Cf. ततोऽपि बुद्धेरप्यहङ्कारः स्यादुत्पद्यते स चाहं सुभगः अहं दर्शनीयः इत्याद्यभिमानरूपः—Guṇaratna p. 100. Cf. S. T. S. p. 6: अभिमानोऽहङ्कारः also) Parts of this are clear reminiscences of the Bhagavad-Gîtâ which is unquestionably earlier than the Sâṁkhya-Tattva-Samâsa.

तस्मात् पञ्चतन्मात्राणि etc.—Cf. Guṇaratna's तथाहङ्कारादन्यानि अपराणि रूपाणि तन्मात्राणि सूक्ष्मसंज्ञानि पञ्च उत्पद्यन्ते ; also S. T. S. p. 6–7 : अहङ्कारान्वितानि...गन्धतन्मात्रे विशेषः—See Max Müller's "Six Systems of Indian Philosophy" where the Tattva-samâsa is rendered into English.

पञ्चतन्मात्रेभ्यश्च etc.—Cf. S. T. S. : From शब्दतन्मात्रादाकाशं to पृथिवी जायते—taken from the S. T. K.

The points to note here are :—

1. That the महाभूतs, according to the Sâṁkhyas, spring from the तन्मात्रs (essences) of their respective गुणs, and of the गुण or गुणs of the preceding महाभूत or महाभूतs if any: thus, आकाश springs from शब्दतन्मात्र and its गुण is शब्द; वायु springs from शब्दतन्मात्र plus स्पर्शतन्मात्र and its गुणs are शब्द and स्पर्श ; and, so on. Not, as in the Vais'eṣika system where वायु springs from the atoms of वायु, तेजः from the atoms of तेजः etc.—with the exception of आकाश which is supposed to be one eternal reality without constituent parts.

2. The evolution of the महाभूतs does not take place as an evolution of one महाभूत into another, say, of आकाश into वायु, of वायु into तेजः etc., as it does according to Vedânta (cf. वायोरग्निः etc. आकाशाद्वायुः etc. तै. उप०) but of तन्मात्रs into महाभूतs ; neither does one तन्मात्र beget another, it only joins itself with another and begets the next महाभूत in the series. Haribhadra, and Guṇaratna in his summary of the Sâṁkhya, derive each of the महाभूतs from the तन्मात्र of its special guṇa. cf. " रूपात्तेजो रसादापो गन्धाद्भूमिः स्वरान्नभः । स्पर्शाद्वायुस्तथैवं च पञ्चभ्यो भूतपञ्चकम् " Haribhadra's Ṣad. 40.

"रूपतन्मात्रात् सूक्ष्मसंज्ञात्तेजोऽग्निरुत्पद्यते रसतन्मात्रात् पृथिवी समुत्पद्यते स्वराच्छब्दतन्मात्रादाकाशमुद्भवति तथा स्पर्शतन्मात्राद्वायुः प्रादुर्भवति । एवं च पञ्चभ्यस्तन्मात्रेभ्यो भूतपञ्चकं भवति ॥" Guṇaratna's Com.—p. 101.

पुरुषस्तु अमूर्तः etc.—For a statement of the characteristics of पुरुष and reasons for the same quoted also in the Ṣaḍ., see S. T. S. iii.

अन्धपङ्गुवत् etc.—प्रकृति and पुरुष co-operate like the Blind Man and the Lame Man who supply each other's deficiency and bring about rational movement. The reference is to the famous Sâṁkhya Parable of the Blind and the Lame. It is thus set forth in detail in Guṇaratna's Com.—कश्चिदन्धः सार्थेन समं पाटलिपुत्रनगरं प्रस्थितः । स सार्थश्चौरैरभिहतः । अन्धस्तत्रैव रहित इतश्चेतश्च धावन् वनान्तरस्थेन पङ्गुना दृष्टोऽभिहितश्च 'भो भो अन्ध मा भैषीः । अहं पङ्गुर्गमनादिक्रियाविकलत्वेनाक्रियश्चक्षुर्भ्यां सर्वं पश्यन्नस्मि त्वं तु गमनादिक्रियावान्न पश्यसि' । अन्धेनोचे । 'रुचिरमिदम् । अहं भवन्तं स्कन्धे करिष्यामि । एवमावयोर्वर्तनमस्तु' इति । ततोऽन्धेन पङ्गुर्दृष्टत्वगुणेन स्वस्कन्धमारोपितो नगरं प्राप्य नाटकादिकं पश्यन् गीतादिकं चेन्द्रियविषयमन्यमप्युपलभमानो यथा मोदते तथा पङ्गुकल्पः शुद्धचैतन्यस्वरूपः पुरुषोऽप्यन्धकल्पां जडां प्रकृतिं सक्रियामाश्रितो बुद्ध्यध्यवसितं शब्दादिकं स्वात्मनि प्रतिबिम्बितं चेतयमानो मोदते मोदमानश्च प्रकृतिं सुखस्वभावां मोहान्मन्यमानः संसारमधिवसति । (Pp. 105-106.)

चिच्छक्तिश्च etc.—According to the Sâṁkhya epistemology, it is not the Puruṣa or Cits'akti that determines an objective reality, but Buddhi, working in the presence of Puruṣa. This is how the determination of reality takes place :—सुख, दुःख etc. enter बुद्धि through इन्द्रियs. बुद्धि is like a double-faced mirror in which the Cits'akti is reflected on one side and the objective world on the other. The consequence of the Cit being reflected in the Buddhi is that Âtman (Cit) identifies himself with the Buddhi and the determinations of the Buddhi get transferred to the Âtman (Cit), and the Âtman thereupon refers सुख, दुःख etc. to himself, that is to say, regards himself as happy or miserable and so on.

आह च पतञ्जलिः—The pure transcendental पुरुष notices the determinations of बुद्धि and identifies himself with it, although in reality he is distinct from it. Likewise बुद्धि, which is unintelligent in itself, seems possessed of intelligence, as it were, in consequence of its proximity to पुरुष or चित्. The parallel passage in Gunaratna runs as follows: केवलमात्मा स्वं बुद्धेरव्यतिरिक्तमभिमन्यते। सुखदुःखादयश्च विषया इन्द्रियद्वारेण बुद्धौ संक्रामन्ति, बुद्धिश्चोभयमुखदर्पणाकारा ततस्तस्यां चैतन्यशक्तिः प्रतिबिम्बते ततः सुख्यहं दुःख्यहं ज्ञाताहमित्युपचर्यते। आह च पतञ्जलिः 'शुद्धोऽपि पुरुषः बौद्धमनुपश्यति तमनुपश्यन्नतदात्माऽपि तदात्मक इव प्रतिभासते' इति बुद्धिश्चाचेतनापि चिच्छक्तिसंनिधानात् चेतनावतीवावभासेत (p. 105.)

The passage attributed to Patañjali is not found in Patañjali's Yoga-Sûtras, but in Vyâsa's Bhâṣya on the same. (Vyâsa on Pat. Sû. 20.: अस्तु तर्हि विरूपः। नात्यन्तं विरूपः। कस्मात्। शुद्धोऽप्यसौ प्रत्ययानुपश्यः। यतः प्रत्ययं बौद्धमनुपश्यति। तमनुपश्यन्नतदात्मापि तदात्मक इव प्रत्यवभासते। तथा चोक्तम्—अपरिणामिनी हि भोक्तृशक्तिरप्रतिसंक्रमा च परिणामिन्यर्थे प्रतिसंक्रान्तेव तद्वृत्तिमनुपतति॥ p. 91.)

The slip was originally Gunaratna's and was afterwards repeated by Malliṣena who does not seem to have either seen Patañjali's Sûtras or verified the source of the quotation. Possibly Gunaratna too had not, otherwise, he could not have confounded the language of aphorisms with that of a Bhâṣya. Could it be that in the time of Gunaratna the author of the Bhâṣya was supposed to be Patañjali himself, Vyâsa being too ancient to be a commentator of Patañjali? Perhaps not. The very frequent practice of writing among the Jainas—a 'स्वोपज्ञवृत्ति', *i. e.*, the author's own gloss, could have also led to the confusion between the Sûtra-kâra and the Bhâṣya-kâra.

तथा च वाचस्पति: etc.—See commentary on S. T. K. 23. This shows बुद्धि to be not merely a faculty of Intellectual Apprehension but also of Moral Resolve—in other words, it is the attitude of the whole man towards objective reality, which implies a certain intellectual acceptance regarding the nature of that reality and is therefore rendered by the word 'Intellect'. As to the correctness of the commentator's explanation of बुद्धि, Prof. Müller is sceptical. ("Cf. The Six Systems".)

वादमहार्णवोऽप्याह etc.—The whole passage upto "स्फटिकं यथा", including the quotations, is reproduced from Guṇaratna's Commentary on Haribhadra's Ṣaḍ. D. Samuccaya. The analogies of the mirror and the face, the water and the moon, the crystal and the adjacent red flower are easy to follow.

न च वक्तव्यं etc.—Taken from Vâcaspati-miśra's Commentary (S. T. K.) on S. K. 61—स्यादेतत् पुरुषश्चेदगुणोऽपरिणामी कथमस्य मोक्षः। मुचेर्बन्धनविश्लेषार्थत्वात्। सवासनक्लेशकर्माशयानां च बन्धनसंज्ञितानां पुरुषेऽपरिणामिन्यसंभवात्। अत एवास्य न संसारः प्रेत्यभावापरनामास्ति निष्क्रियत्वात्। तस्मात् पुरुषविमोक्षार्थमिति रिक्तं वचः। If पुरुष is अगुण and अपरिणामी he is above modifications of any sort; he is not liable to undergo बन्धन; for the same reason, he is devoid of क्रिया and cannot transmigrate from one life to another. Hence, there is no occasion for मोक्ष in his case.

यतः प्रकृतिः etc.—Cf. तस्मान्न बध्यतेऽसौ न मुच्यते नापि संसरति कश्चित्। संसरति बध्यते मुच्यते च नानाश्रया प्रकृतिः ॥ S. K. 62.

अथा न कश्चित् पुरुषो बध्यते...पुरुषे उपचर्यन्ते। यथा जयपराजयौ भृत्यगतावपि स्वामिन्युपचर्येते। तदाश्रयेण भृत्यानां तद्भागभागित्वात् तत्फलस्य च शोकलाभादेः स्वामिसंबन्धात्। भोगापवर्गयोश्च प्रकृतिगतयोरपि विवेकाग्रहात् पुरुषसम्बन्ध उपपादितः—Vâcaspati.

Guṇaratna also quotes तस्मान्न etc. and comments as follows: न वरममी बन्धमोक्षसंसाराः पुरुष उपचर्यन्ते। यथा जयपराजयौ भृत्यगतावपि स्वामिन्युपचर्येते तत्फलस्य कोशलाभादेः (*v. l.*) स्वामिनि संबन्धात्। तथा भोगापवर्गयोः प्रकृतिगतयोरपि विवेकाग्रहात् पुरुषे संबन्धः etc.—p. 107. Cf. also Vyâsa-Bhâṣya, the original of Vâcaspati, p. 86. The passage means: Just as a king arrogates to himself the victory and the defeat of his army and thereby appropriates and enjoys the treasure of the enemy, in the same way, भोग and मोक्ष, which strictly speaking belong to प्रकृति, are associated with पुरुष by a kind of confusion between the two.

Criticism : The four absurdities of the Sâṁkhya system pointed out in the Stanza:

1. (a) To be चित् and to be devoid of Intelligence or Consciousness is a contradiction in terms. चित्—to know or be conscious; or चिन्त्—to think, from which the word चित् has come, connotes thought or knowledge. [As a matter of fact 'चित्' is Vedic 'कित्'–to know.] If it be not its function to know itself and that which is other than itself viz. the Objective Reality (cf. ' स्वपरव्यवसायि ज्ञानम् प्रमाणम् '—PNT.-kâra I. 2. for this doctrine of the Jainas), the चित् is no longer चित्. For, in that case, it would be no better than such dead matter as घट which does not know itself or anything other than itself. Similarly, Râmânujâcârya holds that Cit knows itself as well as its object (See S'rîbhâṣya I. i. 1).

(b) Moreover, चित् has no form or corporeal shape (is 'अमूर्त') and therefore it is impossible for it to be *reflected* in बुद्धि, reflection being possible only in the case of things which are possessed of corporeal form (तस्य मूर्तधर्मत्वात्). Then, as regards the प्रतिसंक्रम *i. e.*, the response of पुरुष to the influence of प्रकृति, it is impossible without the response producing परिणाम *i. e.* affection or modification of पुरुष. The presence of प्रकृति could bring about no change in पुरुष, unless पुरुष was possessed of कर्तृत्व. Without पुरुष parting with its original character it could not be said to be *subject* to सुख and दुःख. And the moment it is admitted that the original character is lost and a new one acquired, the operation of losing one and acquiring the other is a क्रिया which makes पुरुष a कर्तृ—which is contrary to the Sâṁkhya tenets. The analogy of the crystal points in the same direction. If it be not due to a certain *action* in the crystal that it catches a reflection, how is it that an opaque stone does not catch it? Therefore, it is plain that चित् (पुरुष) is a कर्तृ and a भोक्तृ—that is, a कर्तृ and a भोक्तृ directly and not through बुद्धि. According to Râmânujâcârya, चित् is possessed of कर्तृत्व of itself, but of भोक्तृत्व through प्रकृति—though both really and not fictitiously as S'aṁkara holds. अथापरिणामिनी...पतञ्जलिवचनम्—This, like the foregoing passage, is not found in Patañjali's Sûtras, but in Vyâsa's Bhâṣya; and there, again, it is introduced with the words " तथा चोक्तम् " on which Vâcaspati adds—"पञ्चशिखेन" *i. e.* by Pañcaśikhâcârya, an ancient teacher of the Sâṁkhya System. The passage is thus explained by Vâcaspati-Mis'ra : "तथा चोक्तं पञ्चशिखेन अपरिणामिनी हि भोक्तृशक्तिरात्मा । अत एव बुद्धावप्रतिसंक्रमा च परिणामिनि बुद्धिरूपेऽर्थे संक्रान्तेव तद्वृत्तिं बुद्धिवृत्तिमनुपतति ।"—Pat. Yoga 20 Com.

It is argued that भोक्तृत्वशक्ति is in reality above परिणाम and प्रतिसंक्रम, *i. e.*, modification or activity, but being reflected in बुद्धि which is subject to them, it itself comes to be regarded as subject to them. But how can that which is admittedly a mere उपचार, *i. e.*, a false ascription, be of any use in the investigation of truth ? Moreover, if सुख-दुःख of which we are all undeniably conscious as belonging to ourselves, that is, to our आत्मन्, do not belong to the आत्मन्, they will have to hang in the air so to say, since बुद्धि is incompetent to possess them, it being held to be जड (dead, insensate thing).

2. अत एव च जडा etc.—We cannot very well predicate विषयाध्यवसाय (knowledge of objects) of बुद्धि if the latter is जडा *i. e.* unconscious or insensate.

ननूक्तं...सत्यमयुक्तं तूक्तम् etc.—The explanation is reiterated that the neighbouring चिच्छक्ति is reflected in बुद्धि, and thus बुद्धि becomes possessed of it as it were (चेतनावतीवावभासते). But to it a reply may be easily made that a man is reflected in a mirror, but that does not make the mirror living. चैतन्य and अचैतन्य are inherent in things and cannot be altered even by an omnipotent being. Moreover, the "इव"="as it were" in your statement (चेतनावतीवावभासते) is a clear admission of unreality. Cf. S'aṃkara: "सत्त्वानुरोधित्वाच्चेतनोऽपि तद्यत इवेति चेत् परमार्थतस्तर्हि नैव तद्यत इत्यापतति । इवशब्दप्रयोगात् ।" Br. Sûtrâs II. ii. 10.

अत एव धर्माद्यष्टरूपता etc.—Similarly, the eight spiritual qualities and Egoism (अहङ्कार) belong to आत्मन्, not to बुद्धि.

3. अम्बरादीनां च etc.—That आकाश and the other महाभूतs have sprung from the essences of their qualities is a doctrine contrary to all experience. Apart from the absurdity of matter springing out of the essences of qualities, there is the initial

paradox of calling आकाश अनित्य, which all other schools of thinkers are agreed in regarding as नित्य. (The author is here overlooking the Vedântin—See Ved. Sûtrâs II. iii. and the Bhâṣyas thereon).

नित्यैकान्तवादिनां च धुरि etc.—For the Sâṁkhya claims to be a सत्कार्यवादिन् as against the Naiyâyika and Vaiśeṣika who are असत्कार्यवादिन्s, and are, therefore, stigmatized as "अर्धवैनाशिकs". Besides, how can the परिणामिकारण (*i. e.* the stuff of which an effect is made) be a गुण (quality) of its कार्य ? Or, rather, how can the गुण of a कार्य be its परिणामिकारण *i. e.* be the very stuff of which the कार्य is made ?

वागादीनां च etc.—वाक् etc. cannot be called 'इन्द्रियs' *i. e.* *organs* or *senses* as distinguished from *limbs*. The former are parts of the organism which perform functions which nothing else can perform. The functions परप्रतिपादन, ग्रहण, विहरण, मलोत्सर्ग etc. which are ascribed to वाक्, पाणि, पाद etc.—called कर्मेन्द्रियs —respectively can be performed by other limbs as well, for example, we can communicate our ideas by finger-signs etc. Thus वाक् etc. are limbs and not organs. If they are to be regarded as organs despite this, there will be no fixed number of इन्द्रियs, many other limbs being entitled to the same rank.

4. यथोक्तं नानाश्रयायाः etc.—You admit that पुरुष confounds himself with प्रकृति. This is exactly what one understands by बन्ध. If that is not बन्ध, what else is बन्ध? Therefore, it is absurd to deny—while making this admission—that बन्ध belongs to पुरुष.

यत्तु प्राकृतिक etc.—The Sâṁkhya speaks of three kinds of बन्ध—

(1) प्राकृतिक—that consisting in the worship of प्रकृति, by confounding it with आत्मन्. Cf. तत्र प्रकृतावात्मज्ञानाद् ये प्रकृतिमुपासते तेषां प्राकृतिको बन्धः यः पुराणे प्रकृतिलयान् प्रत्युच्यते पूर्णं शतसहस्रं तु तिष्ठन्त्यव्यक्तचिन्तकाः—S. T. K. on verse 44, p. 290.

(2) वैकारिक—that consisting in the worship of the विकारs, *viz.* भूतs, इन्द्रियs, अहङ्कार and बुद्धि, mistaking them for आत्मन्:

Cf. वैकारिको बन्धस्तेषां ये विकारानेव भूतेन्द्रियाहङ्कारबुद्धीः पुरुषबुद्धयोपासते तान् प्रतीदमुच्यते दशमन्वन्तराणीह तिष्ठन्तीन्द्रियचिन्तकाः। भौतिकास्तु शतं पूर्णं सहस्रं त्वाभिमानिकाः। बौद्धा दश सहस्राणि तिष्ठन्ति विगतज्वराः S. T. K. ibid.

(3) दाक्षिण—that consisting in attachment to 'दक्षिणा' *i. e.* the sacrificial rites with their attendant fees, and the heaven sought to be obtained thereby. Cf. इष्टापूर्तेन दाक्षिणकः। पुरुषतत्त्वानभिज्ञो हीष्टापूर्तकारी कामोपहतमना बध्यते।—S. T. K. ibid.

The passage in the text is reproduced from Guṇaratna's Com. Cf., also, S. T. S.

In truth, all the three—प्राकृतिक, वैकारिक and दाक्षिण—are causes of कर्म and बन्ध. The resulting बन्ध gives rise to संसार; and, मोक्ष too eventually belongs to the same पुरुष to whom belongs the बन्ध. Hence, it is absurd to hold "तस्मान्न बध्यते नैव मुच्यते नापि संसरति etc. See S. K. 62.

प्रकृतिपुरुषविवेकदर्शनात् etc.--The Sâṁkhya explains: मोक्ष consists simply in the पुरुष being restored to his original state, when प्रकृति has ceased to act owing to the distinction between प्रकृति and पुरुष having come to be realized. But this explanation is evidently unsatisfactory. For, is it not the very nature of प्रकृति to be active, with the necessary consequence that the activity should never cease to exist and thus preclude मोक्ष?

The Sâṁkhya would rejoin: The activity of प्रकृति originates from पुरुषार्थ; and, therefore, when the पुरुषार्थ is accomplished, the activity ceases, विवेकख्याति (discrimination between प्रकृति and पुरुष) being a पुरुषार्थ.

रङ्गस्य etc.—Sâṁkhya Kârikâ 59. On the analogy of an actress who retires from the stage after her work is done.

Criticism: First, the unintelligent प्रकृति is not capable of such thought as is pre-supposed in the analogy. Secondly, the प्रकृति will repeat its activity even after विवेकख्याति has taken place, just as it goes in search of a विषय even after it has once enjoyed it—a persistence which can be explained only on the hypothesis of the activity being of the very nature of प्रकृति. Thirdly, the analogy of the actress is fatal to the point sought to be established; for, the actress will always have her part " once more ". So the right view about मोक्ष is that it belongs to पुरुष and that it takes place when all the karmans have been exhausted. The Nyâya-Vaiśeṣika agrees with the Jaina.

Miscellaneous absurdities in the Sâṁkhya system : This supplementary portion in the text is based upon S. T. K. Cf. also S. T. S.

एवमन्यासामपि etc.—S. T. K. pp. 292-302; S. T. S. pp. 27-30. and M. M.'s Six Systems p. 268, where the Tattva-Samâsa is fully translated.

Books of Reference :

1. Sâṁkhya-Kârikâ.
2. Sâṁkhya-Tattva-Kaumudî.
3. Gauḍapâda's Sâṁkhya-Bhâṣya.
4. Sâṁkhya-Tattva-Samâsa.
5. Kapila-Sûtras and the Sâṁkhya-Pravacana-Bhâṣya.
6. Patañjali's Sûtrâs and the Vyâsa-Bhâṣya and Vâcaspati-Miśra's Commentary.
7. Summary in the Ṣaḍdarśana Samuccaya and Guṇaratna's Commentary thereon.
8. Max-Müller and Garbe.

Appendices.

वादमहार्णवोऽप्याह । " बुद्धिदर्पणसंक्रान्तमर्थप्रतिबिम्बकं द्वितीयदर्पणकल्पे पुंस्यध्यारोहति । तदेव भोक्तृत्वमस्य न त्वात्मनो विकारापत्तिरिति । " तथा चासुरिः—" विविक्ते दृक्परिणतौ बुद्धौ भोगोऽस्य कथ्यते । प्रतिबिम्बोदयः स्वच्छे यथा चन्द्रमसोऽम्भसि ॥ विन्ध्यवासी त्वेवं भोगमाचष्टे—" पुरुषोऽविकृतात्मैव स्वनिर्भासमचेतनम् । मनः करोति सांनिध्यादुपाधिः स्फटिकं यथा ॥ " इति—Guṇaratna's Com. p. 104.

तत्र कार्योद्गमने हेतुर्धर्मो लाघवं गौरवप्रतिद्वन्द्वि यतोऽग्नेरूर्ध्वज्वलनं भवति । तदेव लाघवं कस्यचित् तिर्यग्गमने हेतुर्भवति । यथा वायोः । एवं करणानां वृत्तिपटुत्वे हेतुर्लाघवं गुरुत्वे हि मन्दानि स्युः इति । सत्त्वस्य प्रकाशकमुक्तम् । सत्त्व-

तमसी स्वयमक्रियतया स्वस्वकार्यप्रवृत्ति प्रत्यवसीदन्ती रजसोपष्टभ्येते अवसादात् प्रच्याव्य स्वकार्ये उत्साहप्रयत्नं कार्येते। तदिदमुक्तम् "उपष्टम्भकं रज" इति। कस्माद् इत्यत उक्तं "चलम्" इति। तदनेन रजसः प्रवृत्त्यर्थत्वं दर्शितम्। रजस्तु चलतया परितस्त्रैगुण्यं चालयद् गुरुणावृण्वता च तमसा तत्र तत्र प्रवृत्तिप्रतिबन्धकेन क्वचिदेव प्रवर्त्यत इति ततस्ततो व्यावर्त्य तमोनियामकत्वमुक्तं गुरु वरणकमेव तम इति। The co-operation of the three Principles in spite of their mutual incompatibility is explained by means of the following analogies :—

"दृष्टमेतत्—यथा वर्तितैलेऽनलविरोधिनी अथ च मिलिते सहानलेन रूपप्रकाशलक्षणं कार्यं कुरुतः यथा वा वातपित्तश्लेष्माणः परस्परविरोधिनः शरीरधारणलक्षणकार्यकारिण एवं सत्त्वरजस्तमांसि मिथो विरुद्धान्यप्यनुवर्त्स्यन्ति च स्वकार्यं करिष्यन्ति च"—Others deny mutual conflict of the principles since the principles are combined in varying degrees of strength (तुल्यबलानामेव विरोधो नातुल्यबलानाम्).

अहं शब्दे अहं स्पर्शे अहं रूपे अहं रसे। अहं गन्धे अहं स्वामी धनवानहमीश्वरः। अहं भोगी अहं धर्मोऽभिषिक्तोऽसौ मया हतः। अहं हनिष्ये बलिभिः परैरित्येवमादिभिः—प्रत्ययो यः सोऽहङ्कारः S. T. S. p. 6.—where it will be noticed that अभिमान=अहङ्कार is used in a double sense—of egoism *i. e.* self-reference in the cognition of शब्द, स्पर्श etc., and egotism or pride as in अहं भोगी etc.

सांख्यमते किल दुःखत्रयाभिहतस्य पुरुषस्य तदुपघातहेतुस्तत्त्वजिज्ञासेत्पद्यते। आध्यात्मिकमाधिदैविकमधिभौतिकं चेति दुःखत्रयम्। आध्यात्मिकं द्विविधं शारीरं मानसं च। तत्र वातपित्तश्लेष्मणां वैषम्यनिमित्तं यद्दुःखमात्मानं देहमधिकृत्य ज्वरातीसारादि समुत्पद्यते तच्छारीरम्। मानसं च कामक्रोधलोभमोहेर्ष्याविषयादर्शननिबन्धनम्। सर्वं चैतदान्तरोपायसाध्यत्वादाध्यात्मिकं दुःखम्। बाह्योपायसाध्यं दुःखं द्वेधा आधिभौतिकमाधिदैविकं चेति। तत्राधिभौतिकं मानुषपशुपक्षिमृगसरीसृपस्थावरनिमित्तं आधिदैविकं यक्षराक्षसग्रहाद्यावेशहेतुकम्। अनेन दुःखत्रयेण रजःपरिणामभेदेन बुद्धिवर्तिनाभिहतस्य प्राणिनस्तत्त्वानां जिज्ञासा भवति दुःखविघाताय। तत्त्वानि च पञ्चविंशतिर्भवन्ति—Guṇaratna's Com. on Ṣ. D. Sam. p. 97.

मूलप्रकृतिरविकृतिः पुरुषः—तथा महदादयः प्रकृतेर्विकारास्ते च व्यक्ताः सन्तः पुनरव्यक्ता अपि भवन्तीति स्वरूपाद्भ्रश्यन्त्यनित्यत्वात्। प्रकृतिस्त्वविकृता नित्याभ्युपगम्यते। ततो न कदाचिदपि सा स्वरूपाद्भ्रश्यति"—Guṇaratna's Com. p. 102-3.

Stanza XVI.

Stanza : The relation of Cause and Effect cannot be one of simultaneity; nor can an Effect come into existence after the Cause is dead. Monism cannot account for knowledge being the knowledge *of* things. Thus, the jugglery of Sugata (Buddha) has been torn to pieces.

Here begins the *Criticism* of the Bauddha doctrines :

I. The First Half of the Stanza.

I. The Bauddhas hold that the प्रमाण and the फल of ज्ञान are absolutely identical. Thus, says a Buddhist writer, "उभयत्र etc."—In both cases, the ज्ञान itself is both the प्रमाण and the फल, consisting as it does of 'अधिगम'. In both cases *i. e.* in प्रत्यक्ष and अनुमान; the ज्ञान *i. e.* प्रत्यक्ष or अनुमान; फल—the effect. अधिगमरूपत्वात्=परिच्छेदरूपत्वात्—*i. e.* since the ज्ञान is अधिगम or परिच्छेद *i. e.* determination of the nature of an object. There is no फल of ज्ञान except the परिच्छेद itself *i. e.* knowing an object to be such and such; and since the परिच्छेद is प्रत्यक्ष or अनुमान, प्रत्यक्ष or अनुमान is the फल of ज्ञान. But प्रत्यक्ष and अनुमान are प्रमाणs. Therefore a प्रमाण is also the फल. Cf. तदेव च प्रत्यक्षं ज्ञानं प्रमाणफलम् N. Bindu I. 18.

Criticism :

एतच्च न समीचीनं etc.—Things which are absolutely non-distinct come into existence together, *e.g.* घट and its घटत्व. So if प्रमाण and फल were absolutely non-distinct they would come into existence *simultaneously*. But this is contrary to the relation which is supposed to subsist between them, viz., the relation of कार्य (Effect) and कारण (Cause). Witness the case of the left and the right horn of a cow, which come into existence *simultaneously*: are they related as Cause and Effect? No. Cause and Effect demand priority and posteriority of the two respectively. [न तुल्यकालः फलहेतुभावः].

Now take the other alternative, which is to regard the two —प्रमाण and फल—as *successive*. This is also impossible. For, in that case, the कारण viz. प्रमाण would precede the कार्य viz. फल;

and as the Buddhist is a क्षणभङ्गवादी (holding that everything in the universe exists only for a single moment of time), it means that one has already passed off the stage of existence—absolutely, without leaving a trace behind—before the other arrives on the scene.

किं च हेतुफलभावः etc.—Moreover, the relation of Cause and Effect is a *relation*, and as such it must subsist *in two* things. Now, unless both of them *are at one and the same time*, it could not subsist in them. Hence the alternative of *succession* is impossible. How can you say, here is the cause and here is the effect, unless both of them are simultaneously present before you? As the verse (quoted in one place in the Ratnâkarâvatârikâ) says: द्विष्ठसंबन्ध० etc. *i. e.* the knowledge of the relation which subsists in two things cannot take place while only one of the things is known; the relation can be known only when both the correlates are known.

यदपि धर्मोत्तरेण etc.—See न्या· वि· with टीका p. 103, and p. 18-19 respectively. (Peterson's Edition, A. S. Bengal.) The Bauddha logician holds, as against the Naiyâyika, that when I see a नील object (e. g. घट), it is the नील form or likeness (सादृश्य, निर्भास) in the ज्ञान which occupies the place of प्रमाण (instrument of right knowledge) and not the इन्द्रिय such as the eye etc. [नीलनिर्भासं हि यद् विज्ञानं तस्मान्नीलस्य प्रतीतिरवसीयते। येभ्यो हि चक्षुरादिभ्यो ज्ञानमुत्पद्यते न तद्वशात्तज्ज्ञानं नीलस्य संवेदनं शक्यतेऽवस्थापयितुम्। नीलसदृशं त्वनुभूयमानं नीलस्य संवेदनमवस्थाप्यते। N. B. T. p. 19.]

An obvious objection to this view is that it makes प्रमाण and फल—the Cause and Effect—*one*, which is absurd. But the answer to the objection is: that, here प्रमाण and फल are not Cause and Effect in the sense of जनक and जन्य, but व्यवस्थापक and व्यवस्थाप्य : that is to say, one explains the other, not engenders it : it is *ratio* as distinguished from *causa*. Now, this relation of व्यवस्थाप्य and व्यवस्थापक can very well subsist between two aspects of one and the same thing. In the present case, सारूप्य or सादृश्य is the व्यवस्थापक (determinant or regulator), and नीलज्ञान is व्यवस्थाप्य (determined) [See Appendix].

Criticism: The one ज्ञान which is क्षणिक‡ is too simple to have parts and so it is impossible that it should possess a two-fold nature of व्यवस्थाप्य and व्यवस्थापक. The relation of व्यवस्थाप्य and व्यवस्थापक is after all a relation, and as such must require two correlates to subsist in. The explanation that this is a case of व्यवस्थाप्यव्यवस्थापकभाव and not जन्यजनकभाव makes no difference to this requirement. Moreover, one should like to know whether the अर्थसारूप्य which is said to be अर्थाकार (नीलसादृश्य is नीलाकार) is निश्चयरूप or अनिश्चयरूप—that is to say, whether it carries with it the conviction that the सारूप्य=अर्थ *is* there or not. If it does not, how can that which is itself अनिश्चित produce any निश्चय *i. e.* be व्यवस्थापक of the knowledge of reality (अर्थसंवेदन)?

Then, again, what is meant by the 'अर्थाकारता' of ज्ञान? Does it mean the character that is impressed upon the ज्ञान as the result of apprehending the अर्थ (the object)? Or, does it mean that the ज्ञान assumes the form of the अर्थ? In the former case, it is all we wanted to prove viz. that there *was* the अर्थ which imparted its character to the ज्ञान. In the latter case, the ज्ञान would become जड; for, the object into which it is supposed to turn itself is जड. Therefore, it is not proper to hold the doctrine that the प्रमाण and the फल are absolutely one. Were they absolutely one, it would be absurd to draw any such distinction as प्रमाण and फल; for, then you cannot say that सारूप्य is प्रमाण and अधिगति (ज्ञानसंवेदन) is फल.

‡ The Bauddha metaphysician is so ardently committed to the doctrine of क्षणिकता that when he has to speak of a घट, he often speaks of it as घटक्षण—which is to be understood not in the sense of a moment of घट but घट enduring for a moment only. Thus, ज्ञानक्षण=क्षणिकज्ञान.

Suppose you were to explain : There is but *one* reality of which सारूप्य and अधिगति are but two forms—सारूप्य being the name which we give to its असारूप्यव्यावृत्ति (=to be other than non-Sârûpya) and अधिगति the name we give to its अनधिगतिव्यावृत्ति (=to be other than non-Adhigati.) Thus, सारूप्य and अधिगति are not two positive realities, but mere negatives characterizing a single Reality.

Criticism : This is but a futile makeshift. The two व्यावृत्तिs—viz. the असारूप्यव्यावृत्ति and अनधिगतिव्यावृत्ति—cannot be *two*, without implying two स्वभावs. But two स्वभावs are an evident absurdity. Moreover, as प्रमाण and फल are explained as अप्रमाणव्यावृत्ति and अफलव्यावृत्ति, why can we not say that अप्रमाण is प्रमाणान्तरव्यावृत्ति, and अफल=फलान्तरव्यावृत्ति—that is to say, the व्यावृत्तिs may be व्यावृत्तिs not merely from things outside the class, but also from other things of the same class ? We must, therefore, admit some distinction between प्रमाण and फल, of which one is साधन and the other साध्य, like कुठार and छिदिक्रिया,

एवं यौगाभिप्रेतः etc.—The other extreme is held by the Naiyâyikas. They are equally wrong. प्रमाण and फल cannot be altogether separate from each other, since they are *one* with the same प्रमाता or subject, the प्रमाता taking the form of प्रमाण in one case and of फल in the other. प्रमाता is the principle of unity, the synthesizing principle of all its forms and activities. Thus, the same person that knows an object takes that object or abandons it or is indifferent about it. Unless this unity were recognised between the प्रमाण and the फल, the प्रमाण of one person would produce फल in another person, and so everything would get into confusion. If the प्रमाण is to produce its फल, it must be in the same person, which means that we must recognize a principle of unity behind them and not treat them as absolutely separate entities.

II. Another Exposition of the First Half of the Stanza :

सर्वं सत् क्षणिकं etc.—Everything is momentary (क्षणिक), because everything perishes in the presence of the destroying agent. And the same nature which it possesses at the last moment it must possess at the beginning on coming into existence. Thus, a hammer (मुद्गर) cannot produce a new nature in घट when it destroys it; the nature which the घट possesses at the end it must possess at the start—and, thus, it should perish immediately after the start. In other words, it is क्षणिक. The argument is essentially this : A thing perishes. Nothing can make it perish, unless it were in its nature to perish. This nature is as much in it at the start as at the finish, and, therefore, all along the line. And nothing can prevent this nature from realising itself, i. e., the perishable thing from perishing at every moment. But an explanation may be offered by the स्थावरवादिन् : (the advocate of continuity or permanence). The thing acquires from its progenitor a nature which keeps it *stable for some time*, and then allows it to perish. But this explanation proves too much : Even in the presence of the destroying agent it possesses the same nature, and will therefore remain stable in spite of those agents, and so will go on acquiring leases of life ad infinitum and will never perish. (This is illustrated by the analogy of a debtor who puts off his creditors from day to day and never pays the debt.) But it may be rejoined from the other side that a thing is born to persist, but it eventually perishes when it is overwhelmed by the agent of destruction. This explanation, however, will not mend matters. If a thing does not perish because it is by nature stable, it is not open to say that an overwhelming force interferes with that nature and makes it perish, for, nothing can destroy the nature of a thing. (It is like saying Devadatta is living and is dying.) If, however, as we see the thing does perish, it shows that it has not come into existence from its progenitor with stability stamped upon it. (If Devadatta dies, he cannot have been immortal, but was a mortal from his very birth). If a thing is not perishable, it can never perish. But we see it perish. Therefore, we must suppose that when it was born from its parent, it was born perishable and not stable. Thus, perishability being found to be the nature of things, a thing must perish immediately after coming into existence. This is how the Buddhist doctrine of क्षणक्षयिकत्व is established. Cf. Gunaratna's Com. on Ṣaḍ. pp. 29-30: [See Appendix].

प्रयोगस्त्वेवम् etc.—Syllogism to establish the position :—

That which is perishable will not endure after its birth; as, for example, घट which is in its last moment does not endure thereafter. रूप etc. are perishable at the time of their birth. Therefore they will not endure after the moment of their birth. This is known in the Buddhistic Nyâya (logic) as the syllogism based on a 'स्वभावहेतु' (Essential हेतु) as distinguished from a 'कार्यहेतु' (Causal हेतु). The following passage will throw good light on the distinction: "स्वभावहेतुर्यथा वृक्षोऽयं शिंशपात्वात्। कार्यहेतुर्यथा अग्निरत्र धूमात्"—Ṣaḍ. Guṇaratna's Com. section on बौद्धमत. Here in the first syllogism शिंशपात्व and वृक्षत्व are not related as Cause and Effect, but as Essences, whereas अग्नि and धूम of the second syllogism are Cause and Effect. The former is the basis of deductive, and the latter of indirective logic. In the case of the कार्यहेतु we argue from Effect to Cause; in the case of स्वभावहेतु we argue from one essence to another.

क्षणक्षयिणो etc.—यदि etc.—It now remains for the क्षणिकविज्ञानवादिन् to explain how we happen to recognise persistent identity of घट from the first to the last moment of its existence, if, as he says, a घट cannot abide for more than a single moment of time. निरन्तरसदृश etc.—the explanation which the Buddhist gives is that *similarity* is mistaken for *identity*: there is a constant flux of similar घटs, of which every preceding घट produces every succeeding घट; and all of them are so alike and so close in their succession that in spite of absolute break at every point we imagine that there is a single घट from first to last. This is owing to our अविद्या or ignorance. Cf. the doctrine of Heraclites in Greek philosophy, and see Guṇaratna's Com. on Ṣaḍ. p. 30.

Criticism: न तुल्यकालः etc.—According to the क्षणभङ्गवाद, a number of क्षणs *i. e.* क्षणिकघटs (See supra, note) may be, compared to a loose series of pearls—not a string as the Vedântin holds but a loose series of absolutely loose units, in which every preceding क्षण produces every succeeding क्षण. Now, what we would fain know about this theory is—whether the preceding क्षणs produce the succeeding क्षणs simultaneously with their birth, or in the moments which succeed their birth: In other words, are the two क्षणs which are supposed to cause each other, simultaneous or successive? If they are simultaneous, one of them cannot produce the other any more than one hand can produce the other hand: "न तुल्यकालः फलहेतुभावः"—as the line in the Stanza runs. If they are successive, there can be no causal relation between them, in-as-much as one has already passed away into nothingness when the other springs into existence. At the same time, we cannot discard the causal bond; for, without it anything might spring out of anything. Therefore, says the Stanza, "हेतौ विलीने न फलस्य भावः".

As to whether the causal relation is merely a relation of Antecedent and Consequent, see Hume and his critics,—Kant etc.

यच्च क्षणिकत्वस्थापनाय.—The Bauddha criticism of the doctrine of Permanence has no point against the Syâdvâdin as the latter heartily endorses the criticism with the exception of one bit viz. 'निरन्वयनाश' *i. e.* such absolute destruction as leaves no trace behind of the thing destroyed. Hence the Jaina definition of सत्—"उत्पादव्ययध्रौव्यं सत्," the word ध्रौव्यं providing for the exception. The Syâdvâdin's agreement with the Buddhist in the rest of the case may be seen in his doctrine of 'प्रतिक्षणपर्यायनाश' *i. e.* the destruction of the पर्यायs or modes every moment. His difference lies in his recognition of the permanence of the underlying द्रव्य which the Buddhist denies. This double doctrine of Permanence-cum-Evanescence the Buddhist has compared to such propositions as "Devadatta is living; he is dying." But the Jaina Anekântavâdin sees no absurdity in such a proposition. According to him while we live we also die; for, 'petals of life' are falling away from us all the while that we are living. It may be argued that Death is the proper word not for the process of the gradual falling away of the 'petals of life,' but only for the last state of extinction, so that we cannot be said to be dying while living. But this is wrong. Even at the time of the final extinction, what happens is that the last 'petal of life' falls away. Thus, Death is a word which must apply to the whole process of the falling away of the 'petals of life' and thus it is going on in the midst of life. Thus stands the Anekântavâda of Life and Death.

III A Third Way of expounding the First Half of the Stanza:

According to a certain school of the Buddhists, ज्ञान is produced by अर्थ; and the same ज्ञान which is the effect cognises the अर्थ which is its cause. As a Buddhist Sûtra goes, नाकारणं विषयः that is, nothing can be a विषय of ज्ञान which is not also a कारण of the same ज्ञान.

Criticism: The whole theory is inconsistent with the Buddhist's favourite doctrine of क्षणिकता. In the moment in which an अर्थ just exists it cannot produce the ज्ञान; for, one क्षण must be fully taken up in the act of existing, and there is no time left for the second act—the act of producing the ज्ञान. And in the next moment—the moment in which ज्ञान comes into existence—the अर्थ has already passed off according to the hypothesis of क्षणिकता. Remember that the causal relation is a relation of antecedent and consequent. But your antecedent is incapable of entering into a causal relation; since it lasts only for a single moment of time, in which it can do nothing beyond coming into existence.

Moreover, the ज्ञान will be found to be निर्विषय (without a विषय) according to the third theory of क्षणिकता. For, the विषय

has passed away before the ज्ञान comes into being, and when the ज्ञान turns towards the object, it is more than one moment since it has been dead. And a निर्विषयज्ञान is a wrong ज्ञान, being like the ज्ञान of the hairs of Âkâsa !

Suppose ज्ञान and अर्थ are *simultaneous*. Then, the latter will not be a कारण ; for, a कारण is prior to, not simultaneous with, the effect, and therefore according to the principle you have yourself laid down it will not be an object too. Hence the line in the Stanza : "न तुल्यकालः फलहेतुभाव :"

ज्ञानार्थयोः फलहेतुभावः etc.—Construction and interpretation of the first two lines in the light of the foregoing remarks:—

Moreover, the अर्थक्षण which is supposed to be the cause of the ज्ञान having already passed off, the ज्ञान will be found to be निर्मूल *i. e.* निर्विषय (See supra). Then, again, if that which causes ज्ञान were to be regarded on that account to be also the विषय of ज्ञान, इन्द्रियs would be विषयs of ज्ञान also ; for, they were indisputably causes of ज्ञान. But they are not held to be विषयs of ज्ञान. Therefore the hypothesis of the identity of the कारण and the विषय of ज्ञान breaks down. It may be contended that the अर्थ can be easily shown to be a कारण of ज्ञान owing to its holding अन्वय and व्यतिरेक with ज्ञान, just as अग्नि is shown to be a कारण of धूम by अन्वय (यत्र यत्र धूमस्तत्र तत्राग्निः) and व्यतिरेक (यत्र यत्राग्न्यभावस्तत्र तत्र धूमाभावः). But the contention is wrong. ज्ञान does not depend upon अर्थ as धूम depends upon अग्नि, ज्ञान being found even without its corresponding अर्थ *e. g.* जलज्ञान without real जल. Mark that the ज्ञान is जलज्ञान, not मृगतृष्णिकाज्ञान ; for, it is जलज्ञान which accounts for the प्रवृत्ति of the man in the direction of the supposed water. You will perhaps say that in that case ज्ञान exists without the अर्थ, because the ज्ञान is a भ्रम. An answer to it is, भ्रम or no भ्रम, it is ज्ञान; and the ज्ञान has come into being without the अर्थ. This is all we want to prove, and it makes no difference whether the ज्ञान is भ्रम or प्रमा. The case of अर्थ, being entitled to be regarded as a cause of ज्ञान, must depend not only upon the test of अन्वय but also of व्यतिरेक. And that test अर्थ does not satisfy in relation to ज्ञान : we cannot say यत्र अर्थाभावस्तत्र ज्ञानाभावः; for, in the case of मृगतृष्णिका there is जलाभाव, and yet there is जलज्ञान. Moreover, Yogins are able to know अर्थs before they are produced and also after they have passed away, that is to say, here ज्ञान takes place without the actual existence of the अर्थs. If, in this case, the अर्थs are somehow supposed to produce ज्ञान, that activity would be evidence of their existence, that is, they would be present, and not past or future.

ण णिह्राणगया etc.=न निधानगता भग्नाः पुञ्जो नास्त्यनागते। निर्वृत्ता नैव तिष्ठन्ति आराग्रे सर्षपोपमाः ॥

It may be said by way of further argument that a प्रकाशक (*e. g.* ज्ञान) acquires existence from its प्रकाश्य (*e. g.* अर्थ) and then becomes the प्रकाशक of that प्रकाश्य. (The effect reveals the cause.) The argument, however, is fallacious. Witness the case of प्रदीप, which is प्रकाशक of घट and yet the घट is not produced by it. That is to say, the relation of प्रकाश्य and प्रकाशक (*e. g.* अर्थ and ज्ञान) does not necessarily imply the relation of कार्य and कारण. Then, again, if ज्ञान is required to be produced by an अर्थ in order that the अर्थ could be its object, स्मृति which is not produced by an अर्थ could have no corresponding object and it would therefore be अप्रमाण. But स्मृति is प्रमाण. It is the very breath of अनुमान (a प्रमाण) which is founded upon the act of recalling to mind the relation (व्याप्ति) of साध्य and साधन. Next, if according to your theory the जनक (cause, कारण) alone is to be the ग्राह्य (object, विषय) how would you explain the case of स्वसंवेदन (self-revelation of ज्ञान) which is ग्राहक of a thing (ग्राह्य) which is its very स्वरूप and not its जनक ? For, in the single स्वसंवेदन itself there is no room for a causal activity which always implies the dualism of कार्य and कारण ('स्वात्मनि क्रियाविरोधः'). Thus अर्थ and ज्ञान which spring from their respective sets of causes are related as प्रकाश्य and प्रकाशक, not as कार्य and कारण.

The Buddhist : If ज्ञान is not produced by a particular अर्थ ('तदुत्पत्ति'), or does not bear the form or stamp of that अर्थ ('तदाकारता') it would be equally related to all the अर्थs in the universe, and so anything and everything would be the object of that ज्ञान—which is absurd.

Reply : ज्ञान is not produced by the अर्थ, and yet it reveals that particular अर्थ, because it possesses the *capacity* to destroy or keep down the 'obscuring veil of ignorance' in the particular case. Even if you hold the view that ज्ञान is produced by अर्थ, you will have to admit the doctrine of *capacity*, for you will have to explain why a particular अर्थ produces a particular ज्ञान, which you can do only on the hypothesis of a special capacity. Then, again, the particular character of ज्ञान you cannot explain by the hypothesis of अर्थ imparting an आकार (form) to the ज्ञान. For, that would make ज्ञान साकार, and अर्थ निराकार, the latter being no longer required to possess आकार, the आकार of the former being sufficient to account for the व्यवहार of distinctions. What सादृश्य or likeness could there be between अर्थ and ज्ञान, one of which is मूर्त and the other अमूर्त? Therefore the particular अर्थाकारता of ज्ञान must be supposed to be the परिणाम (कार्य) of the apprehension of a particular अर्थ. Next, as regards your contention that ज्ञान apprehends (ग्राहक) objects because it springs from objects (तदुत्पत्ति) and possesses the form of the objects, we would inquire whether these two causes operate together (समस्ते) or separately (व्यस्ते)? In the latter case, the first moment of कपाल would apprehend the last moment of घट, in-as-much as the one has produced the other (तदुत्पत्ति); जलचन्द्र (reflection of the moon in the water) would apprehend नभश्चन्द्र (the moon in the sky) in-as-much as one bears the form of the other (तदाकारता). In the former case (समस्ते), the second क्षण of घट would apprehend the first क्षण of घट, since it fulfils both the conditions, that of 'तदुत्पत्ति' and that of 'तदाकारता'. If, in accounting for the apprehension (ग्राहकता) of objects which belongs to ज्ञान, you add to 'तदुत्पत्ति' and 'तदाकारता' a further condition 'ज्ञानरूपत्वे सति' which none of the above examples satisfies, even then, one ज्ञान would be the ग्राहक of the next similar ज्ञान, since it satisfies all the three conditions above laid down. Hence, the only satisfactory explanation of why ज्ञान apprehends objects is that it possesses fitness to do so while nothing else does.

II. The Second Half of the Stanza:

It criticises a doctrine of a certain other school of the Bauddhas, according to which ज्ञान is the sole reality, the external world being a pure fiction.

The Argument of the Buddhists: ग्राह्यग्राहकादि etc.—Cf. Ṣaḍ. Guṇa. Com. p. 40. [See Appendix] Simple ज्ञान, unspoiled by any such fictitious divisions as ग्राह्य and ग्राहक, and hence free from the complexities of the external world, is the only Reality. For, *the external world is impossible.* This may be proved by a series of dilemmas: Is the external world—the बाह्यार्थ—a heap of atoms or a single body? Not the former, for there is nothing to prove these atoms—neither प्रत्यक्ष nor अनुमान. The प्रत्यक्ष of Yogins makes too great a demand on our faith; while our प्रत्यक्ष is out of the question, we ordinary mortals having never seen atoms even in a dream. Nor is there a possibility of an अनुमान; for, अनुमान requires the observation of invariable concomitance of the हेतु and the साध्य which in the present case is impossible for want of प्रत्यक्ष of the atoms (the alleged साध्य). Another dilemma: Are the atoms नित्य or अनित्य? If नित्य, are they doing their work gradually or all at once? Not *gradually*, for that would mean that they are slowly undergoing change in their nature, that is to say, are अनित्य, which is contrary to our hypothesis. Nor, *all at once*, for in that case, the whole universe would have been accomplished by a coup de force—in the twinkle of an eye—and there could have been no such gradual change as we actually observe; the atoms moreover would have ceased to exist, the effect, viz., universe having taken their place. If अनित्य, are they only momentary or are they lasting only for a limited space of time? In the former case, again, are they caused or uncaused? If they are *uncaused*, they would exist either always or never at all, temporary existence requiring dependence upon a cause. If they are *caused*, are they caused by *gross matter* or by *atoms*? Not the former, because according to you there is no gross matter, the external world being only atoms. If the latter, will you explain whether the atoms are to produce their effects while, existing or not-existing, or both existing and not-existing? If *existing*, whether they are to produce those effects in the first moment of their existence, or in a subsequent moment? Not in the first moment, for it will be taken up in its own act of coming into existence. As has been remarked, Being, Acting and Causality would be all one in this case! If mere Being could be a cause of the production, the atoms of रूप would beget atoms of रस and would become the उपादानकारण of रसाणुs; for, so far as Being is concerned, there is no difference between the atoms of रूप and the atoms of रस, and there will be nothing to regulate the production of रूपाणुs from रूपाणुs only, and not from रसाणुs. If *not-existing* they are to produce their effects, they would be perpetually producing their effects in moments other than those of their existence. The third alternative of combined *existence and non-existence* is no good; for, it can fare no better than the two alternatives of which it is made up, and which have been already disposed of. We, therefore, conclude that the atoms are not क्षणिक.

Next, let us see whether they could be कालान्तरावस्थायिन् *i. e.* existing longer than one moment, but still for a limited space of time. This alternative is liable to the same criticism as the one to which the other alternative–that of क्षणिकता–was subjected.

Besides, we ask whether the atoms in this case, are अर्थक्रियाकारिन्—*i. e.* doing something and producing some effect —or not? If *not*, they are *nothing*, no better than the fictitious 'sky-flower'. If they *are*, there are three possible positions to take up: first, that the effect which the atoms are producing is (a) existing or (b) not-existing or (c) both existing and not existing. (a) If it is not-existing, the atoms may as well have produced 'the horn of a hare', that is, nothing. (b) If it is existing, the atoms have been producing something that is already there which means अनवस्था. (c) If it is both existing and not-existing, it is a foolish position to take up, a position which shares the difficulties of both.

Therefore, there is no such reality as *Atoms.*

Nor does the external would consist of *Bodies.* When you could not prove a परमाणु how can you hope to prove a body (अवयविन्) which consists of many परमाणुs? Without परमाणुs a body, which is but a heap of परमाणुs, is a mere name. Again, are the परमाणुs of a body conflicting with one another or are they at peace? In the former case, they would neutralize one another, and consequently there could be no body. In the latter case, we should not find such conflicting elements, as we so often do, of stable and unstable, red and not-red, matter composing a body. Next, does the body subsist in the atoms *wholly* or *partially*? In the former case, the whole body would be absorbed by a single atom and there would be no possibility of a body; also, the body being contained in each atom, there would be as many bodies as there are atoms! In the latter case, the body would lose its entirety or single wholeness. Besides, if the body is supposed to abide in the atoms by one set of parts, there will arise the question, how are these parts related to the atoms? If they are separate from the atoms, the old difficulties of the body residing in the atoms will revive. If they are one with the atoms, they have no existence, and the difficulties which they were called upon to solve remain intact. It is thus a mere superstition—a superstition caused and nourished by the वासनाs of innumerable lives—that we should believe in the existence of an external Reality. On the Theory of Atoms, cf. S'aṁkara's criticism of the Vais'eṣika doctrine in his Com. on Br. Sûtras II. ii.

अलङ्कारकारेण etc.—Quotation from प्रज्ञाकरगुप्त's प्रमाणवार्तिकालङ्कार, a work of Buddhist Metaphysics and Logic.

Criticism : ज्ञान is a क्रिया—an action,—and it, therefore, presupposes a कर्म—the object to which it is directed. Thus, the existence of an external world is a necessity involved in the very act of ज्ञान. It may be asked: Isn't a false appearance—an unreality—an object of ज्ञान, as in the case of 'the hair in the sky' (an optical delusion)? Answer: No; even in that case, one who has never seen a real hair cannot experience the delusion. Similarly, a dream implies the experience of a real world. Cf. S'rî-Bhâṣya (Khyâtis), S'âṁkara Bhâṣya and Advaita-siddhi. तथा च महाभाष्यकारः *i. e.* जिनभद्रगणि क्षमाश्रमण, author of a भाष्य called 'विशेषावश्यक' on a portion of the आवश्यकसूत्र (AMP—foot-note). The gâthâ अनुभूतदृष्टचिन्तितश्रुतप्रकृतिविकारदैविकानूपाः वा । स्वप्नस्य निमित्तानि पुण्यं पापं च नाभावः ॥—(1703). आशामोदक—Cf. the criticism of Hegelian Idealism: if thoughts were things, the thought of a hundred pounds in my pocket would be the same as the possession of those pounds!

न चामून्यर्थदूषणानि etc.—The Syâdvâdin admits the existence of both—the परमाणुs and the अवयविन्. As regards the proofs of परमाणुs, we have both प्रत्यक्ष and अनुमानः our प्रत्यक्ष, in the sense that we see the परमाणुs in seeing the घट; also the प्रत्यक्ष of Yogins. That we do not see the atoms (अनुपलब्धि) is due to their being too small. There is also अनुमान proving the existence of atoms. Thus,—Atoms exist, because without them we cannot explain the gross body. Of course, there is no such invariable rule that a gross body should be made of atoms. For, a gross body is sometimes made of gross parts, *e. g.*, a पट of तन्तुs. आत्मन् and आकाश are not made of any parts—पुद्गल matter at all. Where, however, a gross body springs from atoms, the atoms somehow get combined by such forces as time etc. and thereby cause the gross body.

यदपि किंचायमनेकावयवाधार etc.—As regards the criticism that the atoms of the body would be conflicting with one another and so on, we admit the fact, but we explain it on the principle of Anekântavâda, according to which, a body is one *and* yet manifold.

यच्चोपन्यस्तं etc.—Next, as regards the criticism that the body cannot exist in the atoms either wholly or partially and so on, we reject both the horns of the dilemma, and hold that the अवयविन् exists in the अवयवs inseparably.

किंच यदि बाह्योऽर्थो etc.—We would call upon you to explain how we happen to have a definite experience of नील etc. in the absence of a real external world of नील etc. You will perhaps explain that the external world which we experience is in the form of ज्ञान (विज्ञानाकारोऽयम्). But this is contrary to experience, in which the objective reality is perceived as outside the ज्ञान. If the objective reality were *in us*, our experience would have been '*I* am नील' not '*This* is नील". You will say : there are many forms of ज्ञान—one of them is the perception of अहम्, while another is the perception of इदम् e. g.—'This is नील,' in other words, both the external and the internal world are really *internal*—ज्ञानाकार. But this is wrong. अहम् and नील are not on the same footing : अहम् is not rigidly fixed like नील : what is अहम् to me is त्वम् to you; not so the नील—which is the *same for all*. No doubt, what is नील to one may be पीत to another owing to optical derangement. But this is obviously a case of भ्रान्ति, not प्रमा, and therefore outside our reckoning.

स्वयं स्वस्य संवेदने etc.—The Vijñânavâdin (the Idealist) explains : The ज्ञान of अहम् and the ज्ञान of नील are on the same level. The distinction drawn between अहम् and नील to the effect that the former is personal and shifting, while the latter is universal and fixed is untenable; for, when a man thinks of himself, the self is *always* presented as अहम्, and consequently there is no want of fixity in this case. To that the following answer can be made: You say when a man thinks of *himself*; but this implies that there is something other than himself (otherwise, where is the point in restricting the object of thinking to 'himself' ? A self is a correlative word, which carries with it the admission of a not-self. This is fatal to the Vijñânavâda. You will perhaps explain the not-self as nothing but the self, the perception of the distinction being pure hallucination. But we refuse to accept that explanation as sound. Here is प्रत्यक्ष bearing testimony to the distinction between self and not-self, between within and without, between subject and object,—and there is no room to think that it is a भ्रान्ति.

भ्रान्तं प्रत्यक्षं etc.—The Vijñânavâdin now endeavours to show that it is a भ्रान्ति, and he relies upon the following अनुमान to prove that ज्ञान and अर्थ are not separate : यद्येन सह etc. If A is invariably found with B, A is not separate from B,—as, for example, an illusory moon is not separate from the real moon. Now, अर्थ is invariably bound up with ज्ञान, and we, therefore, conclude that it is not separate from ज्ञान. The अनुमान may be shown to be valid as follows : In a good अनुमान, where there is no व्यापक, there should be no व्याप्य. सहोपलम्भ-अनियम which is the व्यापक of भेद (*e. g.* नील, पीत which are भिन्न, and are therefore not always सहोपलब्ध, that is, found together) is not found in the present case ; therefore its व्याप्य viz., भेद (भेद of ज्ञान and अर्थ) is not possible.

Criticism : The अनुमान is faulty. The rule on which it rests, viz. wherever there is सहोपलम्भ there is अभेद, is not invariable. This may be shown as follows : ज्ञान performs the double function of revealing itself and its objects (See Stanza and compare Râmânuja's view propounded in his S'rî-Bhâṣya against the S'âṁkara idealism). In its latter function, it reveals नील, in its former function, नीलज्ञान. Now, these two viz. नील and नीलज्ञान being disclosed together, there is सहोपलम्भ. But where is अभेद ? नील and नीलज्ञान are not the same. Thus, there is no such invariable law that wherever there is सहोपलम्भ there is अभेद. The अनुमान is thus shown to be based upon a doubtful rule and is therefore vitiated by—सन्दिग्ध-अनैकान्तिक हेत्वाभास. Secondly, it may be shown to be vitiated by असिद्ध-हेत्वाभास also—when the so-called हेतु is not really found in the पक्ष. Thus, सहोपलम्भ is not found in ज्ञान and अर्थ between which अभेद is attempted to be established by means of the अनुमान. The अर्थ is experienced *externally* in the form '*This* is नील' ; the ज्ञान which is experienced *internally* is not experienced at the same time as the अर्थ. Moreover, the अनुमान will be free from बाधित हेत्वाभास only if the प्रत्यक्ष of भेद can be shown to be misleading; and the प्रत्यक्ष can be accepted as misleading only if the अनुमान can be shown to be valid. Thus, there is अन्योन्याश्रय of the two प्रमाणs.

Then, again, if there is no external reality (अर्थ) to control our ज्ञान, we cannot assign definite localities to things. For, in the absence of the external reality there will be nothing compelling us to assign one thing to this place and another thing to that place, and so on. The Vijñânavâdin will try to explain this restriction by the hypothesis of वासनानियम, that is to say, by the supposition that we assign A to a fixed place in the external world not because A possesses that place as an independent reality, but because our वासना has determined that it should be assigned to that place and no other. In other words, the explanation of the restriction is to be sought not in the external world, but in the internal mind.

Criticism : The explanation will not do (See Ṣaḍ. Com. p. 40). The वासनाs cannot determine the places. There *is* the external world in which things have their definite places; our अनुभव obeys external facts, and our वासनाs are determined by the अनुभव. Thus, the final determining agent in our प्रमा is the external world. The Vijñânavâdin will perhaps attempt a clever escape from this difficulty in the following way : The specific characters of various experiences require to be explained. There is no external reality which we can draw upon for the explanation, for none exists. Therefore, the only possible hypothesis which will provide the explanation is the hypothesis of वासनावैचित्र्य.

Criticism : Is the वासनावैचित्र्य the same as ज्ञान ('बोधाकार') or different ? If it is the same as ज्ञान, how can there be वैचित्र्य ? For, in ज्ञान there is no वैचित्र्य. If it is different from ज्ञान, the principle of अद्वैत is sacrificed and there is no reason why you should admit वासनावैचित्र्य and cherish such inveterate prejudice against अर्थवैचित्र्य—to which our common sense bears witness.

तथा च प्रयोग : etc.—Mallisena next proceeds to lay down a syllogism to show that ज्ञान and अर्थ are two *distinct* realities. The syllogism is based upon the हेतु *that* अर्थ and ज्ञान do not possess the same character but are on the contrary opposed to each other. The points of opposition are the following: 1. ज्ञान is internal, अर्थ is external; 2. ज्ञान is posterior, अर्थ is prior; 3. ज्ञान springs from आत्मन्, अर्थ from its own causes in the external world; 4. ज्ञान is luminous (प्रकाश), अर्थ is dark (जड).

अत एवाह स्तुतिकारः etc.—M. in winding up his long commentary on this Stanza shows how to construe the third line in the light of the above remarks.

संविदद्वैतपक्षे—one compound word = ज्ञानाद्वैतपक्षे.

नार्थसंवित्—अर्थज्ञान cannot be satisfactorily explained.

विलूनशीर्णं—Another reading विलू(ली)नशीर्णं.

सुगतो मायापुत्रः—'माया'—the name of the mother of Gautama Buddha. On the significance of the name is founded the view that the whole story of the life of Buddha is an allegory. This view was accepted by certain old orientalists, but is not held now by any responsible thinker.

तत्तत्प्रमाण etc.—Reference to the three ways in which the Stanza has been interpreted by M. The doctrines criticised are:

1. **तत्तत्प्रमाण-तत्तत्फलाभेद**—The identity of प्रमाण and फल.
2. **क्षणक्षय**—Momentariness of all things.
3. **ज्ञानार्थ** etc.—Monism of ज्ञान arising from अर्थ and ज्ञान being inseparable and therefore one.

Reference Books.

1. Vijñânavâda in works of Yogâcâra and Mâdhyamika Buddhism.
2. Keith's "Buddhist Philosophy" Ch. XIV.
3. Examination of Vijñânavâda in S'aṃkara's Commentaries on the Br. Sûtrâs II. ii.
4. Criticism in Nyâya books and in S'aṃkara's Com.
5. Idealism and Criticism of Idealism in Western Philosophy.

Appendices.

1. तदेव च प्रत्यक्षं ज्ञानं प्रमाणफलमर्थप्रतीतिरूपत्वात्। अर्थसारूप्यमस्य प्रमाणं तद्वशादर्थप्रतीतिसिद्धेरिति।—N. Bindu. I.

2. यदेवानन्तरमुक्तं प्रत्यक्षं तदेव प्रमाणस्य फलम्। कथं प्रमाणफलमित्याह। अर्थस्य प्रतीतिरवगमः। सैव रूपं यस्य प्रत्यक्षज्ञानस्य तदर्थप्रतीतिरूपम्। तस्य भावः। तस्मादेतदुक्तं भवति। प्रापकं ज्ञानं प्रमाणम्। प्रापणशक्तिश्च न केवलादर्थाविनाभावित्वाद्भवति। बीजाद्यविनाभाविनोऽप्यङ्कुरादेरप्रापकत्वात्। तस्मादर्थादुत्पत्तावप्यस्य ज्ञानस्यास्ति कश्चिदवश्यकर्तव्यः प्रापकव्यापारः। येन कृतेनार्थः प्रापितो भवति। स एव च प्रमाणफलम्। यदनुष्ठानात्प्रापकं भवति ज्ञानम्। उक्तं च पुरस्तात्प्रवृत्तिविषयप्रदर्शनमेव प्रापकस्य प्रापकव्यापारो नाम। तदेव च प्रत्यक्षमर्थप्रतीतिरूपमर्थदर्शनरूपम्। अतस्तदेव प्रमाणफलम्।

यदि तर्हि ज्ञानं प्रमितिरूपत्वात्प्रमाणफलं किं तर्हि प्रमाणमित्याह। अर्थेन सह यत्सारूप्यं सादृश्यमस्य ज्ञानस्य तत्प्रमाणमिह। यस्माद्विषयाज्ज्ञानमुदेति तद्विषयसदृशं तद्भवति। यथा नीलादुत्पद्यमानं नीलसदृशम्। तच्च सादृश्यमाकार इत्याभास इत्यपि व्यपदिश्यते।

ननु च ज्ञानादव्यतिरिक्तं सादृश्यम्। तथा च सति तदेव ज्ञानं प्रमाणं तदेव प्रमाणफलम्। न चैकं वस्तु साध्यं साधनं चोपपद्यते। तत्कथं सारूप्यं प्रमाणमित्याह। तद्वशादिति। तदिति सारूप्यं तस्य वशात्सारूप्यसामर्थ्यात्। अर्थस्य प्रतीतिरवबोधस्तस्याः सिद्धिः। तत्सिद्धेः कारणात्। अर्थस्य प्रतीतिरूपं प्रत्यक्षं विज्ञानं यतस्तस्मान्नीलस्य प्रतीतिरवसीयते। येभ्यो हि चक्षुरादिभ्यो विज्ञानमुत्पद्यते न तद्वशात्तज्ज्ञानं नीलस्य संवेदनं शक्यतेऽवस्थापयितुम्। नीलसदृशं त्वनुभूयमानं नीलस्य संवेदनमवस्थाप्यते। न चात्र जन्यजनकभावनिबन्धनः साध्यसाधनभावः येनैकस्मिन्वस्तुनि विरोधः स्यात्। अपि तु व्यवस्थाप्यव्यवस्थापकभावेन। तत एकस्य वस्तुनः किंचिद्रूपं प्रमाणं किंचित्प्रमाणफलं न विरुध्यते। व्यवस्थापनहेतुर्हि सारूप्यम्। तस्य ज्ञानस्य व्यवस्थाप्यं च नीलसंवेदनरूपम्। व्यवस्थाप्यव्यवस्थापकभावोऽपि कथमेकस्य ज्ञानस्य चेदुच्यते। सदृशमनुभूयमानं तद्विज्ञानम्। यतो नीलस्य ग्राहकमवस्थाप्यते निश्चयप्रत्ययेन। तस्मात्सारूप्यमनुभूतं व्यवस्थापनहेतुः। निश्चयप्रत्ययेन च तज्ज्ञानं नीलसंवेदनमवस्थाप्यमानं व्यवस्थाप्यम्। तस्मादसारूप्यव्यावृत्त्या च नीलबोधरूपत्वं व्यवस्थाप्यम्। व्यवस्थापकश्च विकल्पप्रत्ययः प्रत्यक्षबलोत्पन्नो द्रष्टव्यः।

ननु निर्विकल्पकत्वात्प्रत्यक्षमेव नीलबोधरूपत्वेनात्मानमवस्थापयितुं शक्नोति। निश्चयप्रत्ययेनाव्यवस्थापितं सदपि नीलबोधरूपं विज्ञानमसत्कल्पमेव। तस्मान्निश्चयेन नीलबोधरूपं व्यवस्थापितं विज्ञानं नीलबोधात्मना सद्भवति।

—N. B. T. p. 18.

3. ननु यदि क्षणक्षयिण परमाणव एव तात्त्विकास्तर्हि किंनिमित्तोऽयं घटपटशकटलकुटादिस्थूलार्थप्रतिभास इति चेत्। निरालम्बन एवायमनादिवितथवासनाप्रवर्तितस्थूलार्थावभासो निर्विषयत्वादाकाशकेशवत्स्वप्नज्ञानवद्वेति। यदुक्तम्

बाह्यो न विद्यते ह्यर्थो यथा बालैर्विकल्प्यते।
वासनालुठितं चित्तमर्थाभासे प्रवर्तते ॥ १ ॥

नान्योऽनुभाव्यो बुद्ध्यास्ति तस्या नानुभवोऽपरः।
ग्राह्यग्राहकवैधुर्यात्स्वयं सैव प्रकाशते ॥ २ ॥ इति—Saḍ. p. 40.

4. अथ विनश्वरस्वभावः समुत्पद्यते। तथा च सति विघ्नाभावादायातमस्मदुक्तमशेषपदार्थजातस्य क्षणिकत्वम्। तथा चोक्तम्।

जातिरेव हि भावानां विनाशे हेतुरिष्यते।
यो जातश्च न च ध्वस्तो नश्येत्पश्चात्स केन वा।

नन्वनित्यत्वे सत्यपि यस्य घटादिकस्य यदैव मुद्गरादिसामग्रीसाकल्यं तदैव तद्विनश्वरमाकल्पते न पुनः प्रतिक्षणं, ततो विनाशकारणापेक्षाणामनित्यानामपि पदार्थानां न क्षणिकत्वमिति। तदेदतनुपासितगुरोर्वचः,। यतो मुद्गरादिसन्निधाने सति चोऽस्य घटादिकस्यान्त्यावस्थायां विनाशस्वभावः स स्वभावस्तस्यैवोत्पत्तिसमये विद्यते न वा। विद्यते चेत्, आपतितं तर्हि तदुत्पत्तिसमनन्तरमेव विनश्वरत्वम्। अथ न विद्यते स स्वभाव उत्पत्तिसमये, तर्हि कथं पश्चात्स भवेत्। अथेदृश एव तस्य स्वभावो यदुत कियन्तमपि कालं स्थित्वा तेन विनष्टव्यमिति चेत्, तर्हि मुद्गरादिसन्निधानेऽप्येष एव तस्य स्वभावः स्यात्। ततो भूयोऽपि तेन तावत्कालं स्थेयम् एवं च मुद्गरादिघातशतपातेऽपि न विनाशो भवेत्। जातं कल्पान्तस्थायित्वं घटादेः। तथा च जगद्व्यवहारव्यवस्था विलोपपातकपाङ्किलता। इत्यभ्युपेयमनिच्छुनापि क्षणक्षयित्वं पदार्थानाम्। प्रयोगस्त्वेवम्। यद्विनश्वरस्वभावं तदुत्पत्तिसमयेऽपि तत्स्वरूपं, यथान्त्यक्षणवर्तिघटस्य स्वरूपम्। विनश्वरस्वभावं च रूपरसादिकमुदयत आरभ्येति स्वभावहेतुः। तदेवं विनाशहेतोरकिंचित्करत्वात्। स्वहेतुत एव पदार्थानामनित्यानामेवोत्पत्तेः क्षणिकत्वमवस्थितमिति। ननु यदि क्षणक्षयिणो भावाः कथं तर्हि स एवायमिति ज्ञानम्। उच्यते। निरन्तरसदृशापरापरक्षणनिरीक्षणचैतन्योदयादविद्यानुबन्धाच्च पूर्वक्षणप्रलयकाल एव दीपकलिकायां दीपकलिकान्तरमिव तत्सदृशमपरं क्षणान्तरमुदयते। तेन समानाकारज्ञानपरंपरापरिचयाचिरतरपरिणामान्निरन्तरोदयाच्च पूर्वक्षणानामत्यन्तोच्छेदेऽपि स एवायमित्यध्यवसायः प्रसभं प्रादुर्भवति। दृश्यते च यथा लूनपुनरुत्पन्नेषु नखकेशकलापादिषु स एवायमिति प्रतीतिः तथेहापि किं न संभाव्यते स्वजनेन। तस्मात्सिद्धमिदं यत्सत्तत्क्षणिकमिति ॥ —Saḍ. pp. 29-30.

Stanza XVII.

In this Stanza, the author criticises the S'ûnyavâda—Nihilism or the doctrine of the Absolute Void—maintained by a certain school of Buddhists.

प्रमाणादिचतुष्टय॰ etc.—The S'ûnyavâdin denies the existence of (1) प्रमातृ, (2) प्रमेय, (3) प्रमाण and (4) प्रमिति.

शून्यः शून्यवादी etc.—The S'ûnyavâdin has not even the bare chance of endeavouring to establish his position, which other heretical schoolmen have, inasmuch as he rejects the validity of प्रमाणs altogether.

अथ चेत् etc.—Explanation of the third line. कुप्येत् कृतान्तः—If he accepts प्रमाणs to prove his own case, it will raise his Siddhânta against him, that is to say, it will conflict with his fundamental principle viz. शून्यवाद. If he relies upon आगम—the word of the master—even then he so far surrenders his S'ûnyavâda. Pun upon the word कृतान्त which means both (1) Siddhânta and (2) Yama, the God of Death.

किं च प्रमाणं प्रमेयं etc.—If प्रमाण be rejected, प्रमेय will go with it, thus enabling the only logical position, that of absolute silence. Even an assertion of S'ûnyavâda makes it प्रमेय, and so far contradicts the Sûnyavâda itself.

अत्र च स्पृशिधातुं etc.—कृतान्त means also Yama, the God of Death. Yamaraja will be angry with him, *i. e.*, he will fall dead, caught in the snare of निग्रहस्थानs—self-contradictions etc.

असूया etc.—We have both forms, असूयिन् and असूयु from असूया. The latter is used by Udyanâcârya, the author of the न्या. ता. परिशुद्धि also.

इह शून्यवादिनामियं etc.—The position which the S'ûnyavâdin endeavours to maintain is that the *four principles* generally asserted by other schoolmen viz. (1) प्रमातृ, (2) प्रमेय, (3) प्रमाण, and (4) प्रमिति have no more existence than 'the horn of a horse'—in other words, they are a pure fiction. This may be shown as under :—

1. *There is no* प्रमातृ *or* आत्मन्. For, there is no प्रमाण to prove him. (1) *Not* प्रत्यक्ष: Because आत्मन् is universally admitted to be outside the range of इन्द्रियs, and प्रत्यक्ष is the प्रमाण working through इन्द्रियs. Then, again, it is said that आत्मन् is known by *introspection*, through the consciousness of the ego (अहंप्रत्यय). But the argument goes too far. Such consciousness arises with reference to the body also when one says, 'I am fair, I am dark,' and so on. Moreover, if the ego-consciousness referred to आत्मन्, it would not be occasional, but perpetual, since आत्मन् is a reality which is ever present to us. But the ego-consciousness arises as an occasional phenomenon (when I enter upon an act of introspection), and therefore requires to be explained by an occasional cause, as does the percept of a lightning-flash. (2) *Not* अनुमान: Because there is no invariable mark from which one can infer the existence of आत्मन्. (3) *Not* आगम (शब्द): For आगमs are contradictory. Apart from the contradictions contained in the scriptures of each school, those which exist between the scriptures of the several schools must render this प्रमाण altogether precarious and unacceptable.

[For the language of this passage compare S'aṁkara's criticism of human reason.—Ved. Sû. Bh. II. i. 11.]

2. *There is no* प्रमेय i. e. the world of objective reality. The absurdity of an external world has been demonstrated already (See supra).

3. *There is no* प्रमाण. For प्रमाण is said to be 'knowledge which reveals itself and others' *i. e.* the world of objective reality. (Cf. "स्वपरव्यवसायि ज्ञानं प्रमाणम्" P. N. T. laṇkâra I. 2; also Râmânuja's Srî-Bhâṣya—I. i. 1.) But, where is the objective reality to render प्रमाण possible ?

किं चैतदर्थसमकालं etc.—Here is a dilemma for the Realist to meet: Is the प्रमाण synchronous with the अर्थ or is it subsequent ? In the former case, all the main existing अर्थs of the universe being synchronous with it will have a right to be treated as its अर्थs—which is absurd. In the latter case, the प्रमाण *i. e.* ज्ञान will have to be regarded as either निराकार or साकार. In the former case, for want of आकार, it will leave the nature of each particular object undetermined. In the latter case, the आकार will have to be regarded as either identical with or separate from the ज्ञान to which it belongs. If it is *identical* with the ज्ञान, it is simply ज्ञान and nothing more i. e. it will be the same as the hypothesis of निराकार ज्ञान which has been already dealt with and disposed of. If it is *separate* from ज्ञान, it should be either चिद्रूप or अचिद्रूप. If it is चिद्रूप, it would be वेदक i. e. in the position of ज्ञान, and would have to undergo the ordeal of the dilemma of निराकार and साकार which has been already shown to be unsurmountable. If it is अचिद्रूप, is it its revealer as अज्ञात or ज्ञात? In the former case, *i. e.* if it does not require to be known in order to be the revealer of the objective world, it would reveal the world to Mr. Maitra as well as to Mr. Chaitra, no matter whether one knows it or not. In the latter case, i. e. if it has to become the object of ज्ञान, it will raise the old problems of साकार and निराकार ज्ञान with all their attendant difficulties—अनवस्था.

4. *There is no* प्रमिति. तत्त्वोपप्लवसिंह seems to be a work similar to the खण्डनखण्डखाद्य of S'rî Harṣa, a Vedântin of the Anirvacanîyatâ or Mâyâ school.

Criticism: ननु यदिदं etc.—The usual criticism passed upon the S'ûnyavâda in Metaphysical Nihilism or the doctrine of a universal void. Cf. similar criticisms of modern Agnosticism in the West.

Dilemma: Is the Nihilistic proposition (शून्यवाद) itself *nil* (शून्य) or not? In the former case, it can prove nothing, it cannot even make a claim to establish itself. In the latter case, it will destroy itself, and the *Four Principles*–प्रमाण etc.—will stand unchallenged. सा भगवती=प्रमाणादितत्त्वचतुष्टयी व्यवस्था.

प्रामाणिकसमय etc.—In accordance with the established practice of logicians or philosophers. Strictly speaking, the above criticism is sufficient to dispose of the doctrine of Metaphysical Nihilism as unworthy of credence. Yet, out of courtesy to the opponent, and without prejudice to the argument above advanced, we shall enter upon a short criticism of each of the propositions laid down by him in the preceding paragraphs.

1. First, *as to the proposition that* प्रमातृ (आत्मन्) *is not proved by* प्रत्यक्ष. We agree on this point, in the sense that प्रमातृ lies beyond the reach of the external इन्द्रियs. But we demur to the proposition that आत्मन् is not perceived by मानस प्रत्यक्ष *i. e.* introspection, *i. e.* the internal consciousness of the ego (अहम्). For, such internal consciousness as 'I am happy', 'I am miserable' clearly refers to and proves the existence of आत्मन्.

तथा चाहुः etc.—The consciousness in "I am happy' is not a bare, general consciousness of happiness, but of happiness *belonging to the ego*. It is not a consciousness of the nature of 'इदं सुखम्' like that of 'अयं घटः', but it is a consciousness of the nature of 'अहं सुखी'.

यत्पुनरहं गौरः etc.—The consciousness of one's being fair or dark in 'अहं गौरः', 'अहं श्यामः' etc. does not necessarily prove अहम् to be really the body. It is a case of the secondary application of the word अहम् to the body, its primary signification being आत्मन्. Compare the master speaking of the servant as *himself*, in the secondary sense of the word 'self'.

यच्चाहंप्रत्ययस्य etc.—Malliṣeṇa explains how we happen to have occasional consciousness of the ego (See above).

आत्मन् is described as 'उपयोगलक्षण' *i. e.* possessing the characteristic of going forth in consciousness–'उपयोग'—which may be either साकार (as in शरीर, घट etc.) or निराकार (as in अहम्), and the consciousness of the ego (the अहंप्रत्यय) is one kind of the 'उपयोग' which characterizes आत्मन्. 'उपयोग'—a Jaina technical term.

तस्य च कर्म० etc.—This 'उपयोग'—in the shape of अहंप्रत्यय—is determined by a number of conditions such as इन्द्रिय, विषय

etc. which are regulated by the law of *Karma*, and is therefore occasional or caused; and not perpetual, although अहम् *i.e.* आत्मन् is perpetual. This may be illustrated by the example of बीज which *always* possesses the शक्ति of producing an अङ्कुर and yet puts forth the शक्ति only *occasionally*, when the accessories viz. water, soil etc. co-operate. Thus, because अङ्कुरोत्पादन is कादाचित्क (occasional) it does not follow that अङ्कुरोत्पादनशक्ति is कादाचित्की; in the same way, because अहंप्रत्यय (an उपयोगविशेष of आत्मन्) is कादाचित्क, it does not follow that अहम् (आत्मन्) is कादाचित्क.

2. Next, *as to the proposition that* आत्मन् *is not proved by* अनुमान, since there is no certain mark or लिङ्ग on which the अनुमान can be based, this is wrong. There are *numerous* marks or लिङ्गs to prove the existence of आत्मन्:—

(1) रूपाद्युपलब्धिः सकर्तृका क्रियात्वात् छिदिक्रियावत् (यश्चास्याः कर्ता स आत्मा). The perception of the objective world requires an agent of the act of perceiving; because, perception is an action, and all actions require an agent, as, for example, an action of cutting requires a cutter. This agent in the act of perceiving, *i. e.* the percipient, we call आत्मन्. Could the senses (इन्द्रियs) such as चक्षुः etc. be the agents in the present case? No. They are *instruments*—like the hatchet in the act of cutting—which are dependent upon one who could wield them. That they are instruments requiring to be wielded by a person, follows from the fact that they are made of matter (पौद्गलिक), and are therefore inanimate requiring to be put in motion by a चेतन without whose stimulus they are incapable of doing anything. If the इन्द्रियs were the real agents in the present case, the following three things would happen :—

1st. I could not *remember* the experiences of a particular sense after the sense happened to be destroyed, as in the case of subsequent blindness. For, the act of remembrance must belong to the same agent to whom the original experience belongs; and as the supposed agent of the experience viz. the sense is destroyed or has ceased to function, the act of remembrance has become impossible.

2nd. The various experiences of the different senses—viz. seeing, touching, smelling, tasting and hearing—could not then be referred to a common agent, the senses being different. Cf. Nyâya manuals.

3rd. रूप, रस etc.—the objects of the different senses—could not be apprehended *together*; whereas our experience of रूप followed by re-collection of रस and the attendant taste (flow of saliva) in the mouth would show that there is one person to whom belongs रूपग्रहण and रसस्मरण—a function which could not be preformed by any single इन्द्रिय. आत्मन् in this case acts like a man peeping out of different windows. Therefore, the इन्द्रियs are करणs and आत्मन् is their driver, the कर्तृ in the act.

(2) साधनोपादानपरिवर्जनद्वारेण etc.—रथक्रियावत्.

Our movements—by which we seek to acquire something or abandon something which we regard as good or bad for us, and which we direct towards acquiring or abandoning the means to that end—are not haphazard or involuntary movements but they are movements which imply an act of *volition* such as that shown in driving a chariot towards a definite goal and in a definite manner.

(3) Next, शरीरं च प्रयत्न......सारथिवत्. The body is ruled over by a voluntary agent, because it is the seat of a definite activity—*e. g.* a chariot.

(4) (शरीरं प्रयत्नवदधिष्ठितं) इच्छा...व्यापयितृवत्. Another argument by which शरीर could be shown to be ruled over by a voluntary agent—the आत्मन्—is the argument founded on the analogy of a pair of bellows—which is filled with a certain amount of air by the smith and worked to a definite end.

(5) इच्छाधीननिमेषोन्मिष.................................यन्त्रवत्—

Another argument by analogy is furnished by the example of a machine-toy which opens and shuts its eyes as regulated by a voluntary agent.

(6) "शरीरस्य वृद्धिक्षत..........................संरोहणवत".—

Moreover, the powers of growth and healing or repair clearly indicate the presence of an indwelling soul in the body. For, we observe that a house does not grow of itself or repair itself without the agency of a mason. A tree will perhaps be cited as an example of spontaneous growth and repair. But, as a matter of fact, the tree, too, is a living organism possessing one single organ and an indwelling soul. [For the doctrine of an indwelling soul in trees etc. M. refers the reader to Âchârâñga Sûtra.]

(7) तथा प्रेर्यं मनः..आत्मा.

मनः is capable of being directed towards a definite object, like a stone aimed by a boy at a target. That which thus directs the मनः is आत्मा.

(8) आत्मचेतन etc.......................................स आत्मा.

आत्मन्, चेतन, क्षेत्रज्ञ, जीव, पुरुष are synonymous terms, which denote something, some reality of which they are names. That something is आत्मा.

(9) अस्त्यात्मा etc...................................नम्भोरुहद्वयः

All simple terms such as घट etc. denote realities; खरविषाण, नभोऽम्भोरुह etc. are unrealities, but, then, they are compound terms.

(10) सुखादीनि.......................................स आत्मा.

सुख etc. are qualities, which must abide in some द्रव्य, and the only द्रव्य fit to hold them is आत्मन्.

3. *As to* आगमs, those that are self-contradictory are, of course, worthless. But those that are declared by आप्तs *i. e.* reliable authorities, can easily stand the tests of कष, छेद and ताप (See infra St. 32) and are therefore प्रमाण. (Cf. तापच्छेदान्निकषात् सुवर्णमिव पण्डितैः। परीक्ष्य भिक्षवो ग्राह्यं मद्वचो न तु गौरवात्.) It may be

argued that an आप्त is one who is free from all infirmities (दोष), and since there is no one of whom we could say this, there is no आप्त and, therefore no आगम प्रमाण. But the argument is based vitiated upon very narrow empiricism. No doubt, our minds are by रागादिदोषs *more or less*, but the very fact that the दोषs admit of being made more or less points to the possibility of their being eradicated altogether. An analogy is furnished in the thickening and thinning clouds which some time cover the sun.

निरवयवतया—Being deprived of all parts or limbs *i. e.* the forces which feed them.

अथाऽनादित्वाद्रागादीनां etc.—No doubt, the दोषs have had no beginning, but that is no reason why they should have no end. It is quite possihle to destroy them by means of रत्नत्रय *i. e.* ज्ञान, दर्शन and चारित्र.

क्षीणदोषस्य etc.—When the दोषs are destroyed there arises केवलज्ञान which means सर्वज्ञत्व. सर्वज्ञत्व is the acme of perfection in the matter of ज्ञान. Our imperfect ज्ञान is capable of growth in the direction of perfection and the highest point to which it can be carried will be the point of perfection. [For a similar argument in proof of the existence of God, see Pat. Yoga-Sûtras and Vyâsa Bhâṣya I, 24-25].

तथा सूक्ष्मान्तरित etc.—Besides, there are realities which are too fine or too remote tor ordinary sight, but they must be *present* (प्रत्यक्ष) to some minds, *e. g.* a fire in a mountain cave.

Moreover, how true are the astronomical predictions of authoritative writers! This fact may well be taken as one indication of सर्वज्ञत्व being possible in the case of great teachers.

एगे आया etc.—Quotation from Ṭhâṇaṅga I. l. to prove the existence of आत्मन्.

2. प्रमेयं etc.—This has been already established. (See p.)

3. प्रमाणम् or ज्ञानम् etc. A करण is necessarily implied in a क्रिया.

यच्चात्र समकालमित्युक्तं etc.—M. admits both the alternatives. प्रत्यक्ष takes note of objects which exist simultaneously with the ज्ञान. स्मरण deals with objects which belong to the past. शब्द and अनुमान treat of things belonging to all times, past, present and future.

निराकारं चैत्रद्—They are निराकार and yet the required definiteness in determining particular objects is possible owing to the law of ज्ञानावरण, वीर्यान्तराय, and क्षयोपशम which make our world what it is.

शेष० :—The remaining alternatives are discarded.

4. प्रमितिः etc.—It is the फल of प्रमाण and is revealed by self-revelation. What is directly experienced or revealed as consciousness needs no teaching or proof.

फलं च द्विधा etc.—The फल may be either immediate or mediate. अज्ञाननिवृत्ति is the immediate फल of all प्रमाणs. The mediate i. e. eventual or ultimate फल of the particular प्रमाण viz. केवलज्ञान is औदासीन्य *i. e.* freedom from worldly interest. That of the other प्रमाणs is हान, उपादान, उपेक्षा, तुष्टि. Cf. Tarkabhāṣā.

ततश्च—The Jaina philosopher rejects such absurd doctrines as " नासत्र "—"Reality neither *is*, nor *is not*; nor is it *both*, nor is it *neither*." He accords welcome to all and says Reality both *is* and *is not* etc.

किं चेदं प्रमाणादीनां etc.—Is the unreality of प्रमातृ etc.—if it is held to be the truth of philosophy—proved by प्रमाण or अप्रमाण ?—*i. e.* negation of प्रमाण can prove nothing. प्रमाण must be either itself real or unreal. If it is unreal, it can prove nothing real, not even the शून्यवाद. If it is real, it contradicts the शून्यवाद which is sought to be established.

संवृति lit. observation of the truth ; सांवृत—arising from the observation of truth ; untrue.

तदेव पक्षद्वये etc.— 'इतो व्याघ्रः इतस्तटी' between the tiger and the precipice.

Stanza XVIII.

Stanza : Greatly audacious is that opponent of yours who desires to hold (the doctrine of) क्षणभङ्ग (momentary perishing of everything), while remaining unmindful of the bad consequences which would thereby stare him in the face viz.:—

(1) कृतप्रणाश—what is done passing away into nothingness, leaving no consequence behind.

(2) अकृतकर्मभोग—experiencing the fruits of acts for which one has not been responsible.

(3) भवभङ्गदोष—impossibility of life hereafter.

(4) प्रमोक्षभङ्ग—impossibility of emancipation from Saṁsâra.

(5) स्मृतिभङ्ग—impossibility of memory.

I. A short explanation of the Stanza :

कृतप्रणाशदोष etc.—The दोषs or evil consequences arising from क्षणभङ्गवाद. Here four such are mentioned. There is a discrepancy, however, between this and the explanation in the sequel, where भव and प्रमोक्ष are taken as factors of a द्वन्द्व and not a षष्ठीतत्पुरुष compound.

साक्षात् etc.—Discarding direct experience in the interest of a mere theory.

गजनिमीलिका०—Shutting one's eyes to; not completely, but partially, like the elephant, who is supposed to keep only one eye open while looking this side or that. We say, 'partially,' because we are not unmindful of the partial truth which is embodied in the क्षणभङ्गवाद.

क्षणभङ्ग etc.—Annihilation immediately after truth.

वैनाशिक : etc.—The metaphysical Nihilist, follower of one of the schools of Buddhistic metaphysics. (See Kern's "Indian Buddhism" and Keith's "Buddhist Philosophy ")

अहो महासाहसिकः etc.—a great adventurer; a reckless combatent.

II. Fuller Exposition :

(1) and (2). बौद्धा बुद्धिक्षण etc.—आत्मन् according to the Buddhist is a plurality of discrete momentary ideas ; not the principle of synthesis and unity lying behind the ideas, like a string running through a number of pearls and making a single necklace of them.

तन्मते etc.—One consequence of that position would be that the idea which was responsible for a good or bad deed would pass away into nothingness, making the law of moral retribution impossible ; and, similarly, the idea which undergoes retribution would be so doing without having been the author of the deed of which it is supposed to be the retribution—which is contrary to the essence of the law of retribution.

अत्र कर्मशब्द etc.—The word 'कर्म' of 'अकृतकर्मभोग' in the first line should be connected in thought with 'कृत' of 'कृतप्रणाश' also.

(3) तथा भवभङ्गदोष: etc.—Moreover, there would be none to go to the other world in obedience to the law of Karma. भव-becoming, transmigration, not only to another life on the earth, but also to the other world of heaven and hell (परलोक:).

यच्च मोक्षाकरगुप्तेन etc.—Mokṣākaragupta, a Buddhist writer assigned to " about 1100 A.D. " by Dr. Satîs'candra Vidyâbhûṣaṇa. He wrote a work called Tarkabhâṣâ following the system of Dharmakîrti.

यच्चित्तं etc.—An argument advanced by the Buddhist to prove life after death : one चित्त (idea) refers to (प्रतिसन्धत्ते) another, as does the present चित्त ; and there is a चित्त at the moment of death, which must be referred to by another चित्त but this would be possible only on the assumption of a life after death.

Criticism.—The argument is faulty, inasmuch as one चित्त cannot refer to another चित्त if, as the Buddhist holds, it perishes absolutely leaving no trace behind. In the argument and the criticism, we have assumed that the word 'प्रतिसंधत्ते'

means 'begets'. If 'प्रतिसंधत्ते' means 'calls to mind', according to the usual acceptation of the word, the act of 'प्रतिसंधान' in that sense also will require an abiding principle to connect one चित्त with another.

न च प्रतिसंधत्ते etc.—It might be urged that 'प्रतिसंधत्ते' means जनयति 'begets'. It may be added that in truth 'प्रतिसंधत्ते' does not mean 'जनयति' *i. e.* 'begets.' For, in that case the argument would be an अनुमान from a कार्यहेतु, whereas it is given by the author as an argument from a स्वभावहेतु. (For the distinction between कार्यहेतु and स्वभावहेतु see Nyāyabindu II, also N. B. T. on the same). स्वभावहेतु presupposes तादात्म्य as in अयं वृक्षः शिंशपात्वात् where वृक्ष and शिंशपा are not two distinct entities, but *one*. But there cannot be तादात्म्य between two चित्तs which belong to different moments of time. If the two चित्तs belong to the same moment of time, how can they be divided as प्रतिसंधेय and प्रतिसंधायक *i. e.* that which is the object of and that which is the agent of प्रतिसंधान?

अस्तु वा प्रतिसंधानस्य etc.—Granting, however, that the word 'प्रतिसंधान' means begetting (जनन), the difficulty is not at all removed. For, how can there be a relation of the 'begetter' and the 'begotten' if the two चित्तक्षणs are simultaneous? If the two follow one another, still when the second is born the first is no more, which cannot therefore be the उपादान of the second.

4. तथा प्रमोक्षभङ्गदोषः etc.—For want of personal identity, there would be impossibility of that complete and final liberation from the bondage of कर्म which is the goal of all philosophies.

संतानस्तु etc.—An attempt is made by the Buddhist to tide over the difficulty by setting up a संतान or stream of consciousness to do duty for an abiding ego. But the attempt must fail. For, the संतान is either real, existing over and above the ideas, or is nothing in addition to the ideas. In the former case, it is but an *alias* of आत्मन्; in the latter, the position does not improve.

अपि च बौद्धा etc.—Further, some of the Buddhists hold that मोक्ष means the production of pure ज्ञान relieved of all the disturbance caused by the forms of विषयs when वासनाs are eradicated. But this must be impossible, for there can be no कार्यकारणभाव under the conditions of क्षणभङ्ग.

भावनाप्रचयो etc.—मोक्ष, says the Buddhist, can be brought about by the intensity of भावना (meditation or pondering) about the momentariness of things. But this, too, is impossible. For, according to the Buddhist, there is no abiding principle which can be the seat of the भावना. Moreover, an impure ज्ञान, according to the law of the homogeneity of cause and effect, can only produce another impure ज्ञान and not a pure ज्ञान—each lasting for a single moment of time only. And the series of impure ज्ञानs thus arising must go on endlessly unless it is to be ended abruptly which is impossible.

किंच समलचित्तक्षण etc.—Moreover, the impure चित्तक्षणs having perished of themselves and a pure चित्तक्षण having succeeded them, there is no continuity *i. e.* no संतान.

बन्धमोक्षौ च etc.—Besides, बन्ध and मोक्ष must belong to the same person in respect of the same विषयs, that is to say, the same person who is subject to बन्ध is to prepare for मोक्ष, and the same fetters which bind one in बन्ध have to be destroyed in मोक्ष. Thus, in a two-fold way, identity is required for मोक्ष.

(5) तथा स्मृतिभङ्गदोषः etc.—Syllogism: तथाहि पूर्वबुद्ध्यानुभूतेऽर्थे etc.—On the hypothesis of क्षणभङ्ग, recollection would become impossible. For, the ज्ञान that is experience has passed away, and there is nothing to connect it with the ज्ञान that is memory. If the author of experience and that of memory were not required to be identical. A would experience a thing and B would remember it; in other words, any man would remember anything irrespective of the need of previous experience. And, if the two have a common back-ground constituting identity, it means continuity from the point of experience to that of memory—and that is abandonment of the क्षणभङ्ग theory.

Moreover, if on the क्षणभङ्ग hypothesis, स्मृति (memory) becomes impossible, प्रत्यभिज्ञा (recognition of something that was experienced before) becomes impossible, too. For, प्रत्यभिज्ञा involves स्मृति in addition to अनुभव.

पदार्थप्रेक्षण etc.—The genesis and the nature of प्रत्यभिज्ञा.

अथ स्यादयं दोषः etc.—An attempt is made by the Buddhist to explain memory by admitting a causal connection—(in place of a continuing back-ground)—between experience and memory. If A experiences an object, it is not B that remembers it, because there is a causal connection between A's experience and A's memory and not between A's experience and B's memory. The Buddhist makes the admission that there is a causal connection between संतानिन्s (ज्ञानक्षणs) of the same संतान (continuance of consciousness) viz. अनुभवक्षण and स्मृतिक्षण.

तदप्यनवदातं etc.—*Criticism* : Apart from the impossibility of a causal connection between things that are absolutely separated by time, there is the want of identity between the author of अनुभव and of स्मृति according to that theory—which leaves the position *in quo ante.*

नहि कार्यकारणभावात् etc.—Call for a दृष्टान्त which is acceptable to both the parties and is thus capable of supporting an argument. (See न्या. सू. I. i. 25)

अथ यस्मिन्नेव etc.—A verse giving the required दृष्टान्त and quoted in many places. See Sûtrakṛitāṅga etc.

A [a particular stream of consciousness—संतान] experiences a thing and remembers it, and not B [a different stream of consciousness], because "that संतान on which कर्मवासना is laid becomes the seat of its फल (*i. e.* कार्य of कर्मवासना), and not any संतान : *e. g.* if you apply a red colour to a piece of cotton, the red colour will produce its effect in the same piece of cotton, and not anywhere else."

तदसाधीयः etc.—*Criticism* : The argument fails. For, the example you have cited does not prove your case, nor does it disprove mine. Thus, you cannot make कार्यकारणभाव the हेतु and argue as follows: यत्र यत्र कार्यकारणभावः तत्र तत्र स्मृतिः कर्पासे रक्ततावत् (the example is not a case of स्मृति), or यत्र यत्र स्मृतिर्न भवति तत्र तत्र कार्यकारणभावो न भवति.

असिद्धत्वाद्यनु० etc.—Recall the Syllogism. पूर्वबुद्ध्यानुभूतेऽर्थे नोत्तरबुद्धीनां स्मृतिः संभवति। ततोऽन्यत्वात् संतानान्तरबुद्धिवत्।

Now, let us see whether the Buddhist's example 'कर्पासे रक्ततावत्' affects the validity of the syllogism. It does not. यत्र अन्यत्वं तत्र स्मृतिर्न भवति is not invalidated by the example of 'कर्पासे रक्तता,' since the example is not a case either of स्मृति or of अनन्यत्व. That it is not a case of स्मृति is obvious. That it is not a case of अनन्यत्व is patent from the fact that under the क्षणभङ्ग doctrine there is incessant change and कार्पास too, according to the theory, is not the same for any two moments of time.

किंत्वभ्यस्त्वेऽपि etc.—Besides, if स्मृति could be produced by the causal relation without the necessity of recognizing a permanent background behind अनुभव and स्मृति, the causal relation which exists between the teaching of the master and the understanding of the pupil would make the latter स्मृति, which is absurd.

अथ नायं प्रसङ्गः etc.—Such an absurd consequence the Buddhist would try to avert by adding the condition of 'एकसंतानत्वे सति'. Thus, the understanding of the pupil does not become a case of स्मृति inspite of कार्यकारणभाव between it and the master's teaching, because the two are not parts of the same संतान or stream of consciousness, one belonging to the stream of consciousness which you call the master, and the other belonging to the stream of consciousness which you call the pupil.

भेदाभेदपक्षाभ्यां etc.—*Criticism*: You will substitute a stream of consciousness (संतान) for momentary ideas (ज्ञानक्षणs, the संतानिन्s) in order to connect अनुभव with स्मरण. But the old dilemma—Is the संतान the same as the

28

संतानिन्न or different?—and the difficulty of answering the question will soon dispose of the defence. Let us put the dilemma in detail: Is the संतान (continuous consciousness) the same as the series of ज्ञानक्षणs or something over and above them? In the former case (अभेदे), the position remains unimproved. In the latter case (भेदे), a question may be put whether the distinction of the संतान from the ज्ञानक्षणs–the क्षणपरम्परा—is real or unreal. If it is unreal (अपारमार्थिक), the position remains status in quo ante. If it is real (पारमार्थिक) we should like to know whether the संतान which is supposed to be really distinct from the क्षणपरम्परा is itself क्षणिक or otherwise. In the former case (क्षणिक), the position remains unimproved. (The attempt to seek shelter under a क्षणिक संतान is like that of going 'from one robber to another'). In the latter case (अक्षणिक), the संतान is only another word for a permanent आत्मन्.

तदभावे etc.—A consequence flowing from स्मृतिभङ्ग. That is to say, the क्षणभङ्गवाद not only sins against psychology by rendering स्मृति impossible, but it sins against logic also by rendering अनुमान impossible, for अनुमान proceeds on the basis of स्मृति.

अपि च स्मृतेरभावे etc.—Not only would psychology and logic be thereby outraged, but even our social and economic life would become impossible.

इत्येकनवतेः कल्पे etc.—Quoted in several other places. Gautama Buddha is there described as remembering one of his past lives.

एवमुत्पत्तिः etc.—A modified form of क्षणभङ्गवाद. Things last for *four moments* only viz. those of (1) उत्पत्ति, (2) स्थिति, (3) जरा, (4) विनाश.

क्षणचतुष्कानन्तर etc.—If things last for four moments only, why should you go to dig out a deposit which you have laid underground a long time ago? Is it not with the consciousness that the treasure you will find is the treasure you have buried?

Stanza XIX.

Stanza: That वासना (psychic impression) and that क्षणसंतति (series of ज्ञानs or ideas) do not fit in, whether they are supposed to be identical or distinct or neither. Therefore, the opponents should rest upon your words, on the analogy of the little birds who fly away from the mast of a ship, yet, unable to see land, return to the same.

I

सा शाक्यपरि० etc.—सा = That, *i. e.* the वासना maintained by the Buddhists, which is said to be like a thread running through the क्षणs which without it are like so many loose pearls. वासना is defined as ' पूर्वज्ञानजनिता उत्तरज्ञाने शक्तिः ' *i. e.* the power imparted by the anterior ज्ञान to the posterior ज्ञान.

सा च क्षणसंततिः etc.—सा = That, well-known in the Buddhist system.

क्षणसंततिः—A series of momentary ज्ञानs which *seem* to be the same, but which in reality are new every moment like the light-rays of a lamp.

(1) न तावदभेदेन etc.—The two viz. वासना and क्षणसंतति cannot fit in with each other as identical inter se. For, if they be identical, they are either वासना or क्षणसंतति; one must be merged in the other, it cannot enjoy separate existence *e. g.* घटस्वरूप which is identical with घट.

केवलायां वासनायां etc.—If there is वासना alone, it is an admission of the principle of persistence.

वास्याभावे etc.—Besides, if there is वासना alone, and no वास्य (क्षणसंतति) on which वासना is to operate, the वासना would be no वासना. If, on the other hand, you admit क्षणसंतति to be the sole reality, the old difficulties stand as before. (See the preceding Stanza and Com.)

(2) न च भेदेन ते युज्येते etc.—If वासना and क्षणसंतति are different, may we know whether the वासना is क्षणिक or अक्षणिक ? If it is क्षणिक, why should it be recognized at all ? The only reason for its recognition is to supply the principle

of permanence which is wanting in the क्षणसंतति. If it is अक्षणिक, it violates the doctrine of universal क्षणभङ्ग, and the assumption that other पदार्थs are क्षणिक becomes gratuitous.

अनुभयपक्षेणापि etc.—This alternative is impossible. There must be either भेद or अभेद between वासना and क्षणसंतति; because भेद and अभेद are mutually exclusive, and if one is not, the other must be there.

अथवाऽनुभव etc.—Besides, if the relation is neither भेद nor अभेद, it means it is unreal (अवस्तु). According to all those who do not endorse the अनेकान्तवाद of the Jainas, a thing must be either भिन्न or अभिन्न; a third alternative is not possible any more than the child of a barren woman.

एवं विकल्पत्रयेऽपि etc.—The author therefore concludes that the opponent must endorse the Jaina doctrine of both भेद and अभेद. (Note that this is not the same thing as अनुभय).

न च प्रत्येकं etc.—भेदाभेद is not a sum-total of भेद and अभेद, with all their difficulties only added together and remaining intact. [This is the weakness of the भेदाभेद doctrine which in maintained by a certain section of Vedântins.] It is a distinct category of existence—a kind of complex reality like a कुक्कुटसर्प or नरसिंह *i. e.* cock-serpent or man-lion.

नन्वार्हतानां etc.—चेन्नैवम् etc.—The Jaina does hold that a series of पर्यायs which are new every moment goes on occurring in every द्रव्य, while the द्रव्य is the permanent principle which connects the past, present and future पर्यायs. The series of पर्यायs—the पर्यायपरम्परा—is *in a way* identical with the constant factor viz., the द्रव्य, and is *in a way* distinct from it. Since the पर्यायs are designated by separate terms, and are the objects of separate cognitions, they are separate from the द्रव्य; and since the द्रव्य undergoes modification and assumes these various forms—the पर्यायs—they are one with the द्रव्य. Both propositions are true from different points of view. For further light on this doctrine see the exposition of सकलादेश and विकलादेश in the sequel.

अपि च बौद्धमते etc.—Furthermore in the Bauddha system there is no room for वासना. वासना, according to the Buddhist, may be defined as पूर्वक्षणेनोत्तरक्षणस्य वास्यता—*i. e.* an impression produced by an anterior क्षण on a posterior क्षण. But in a system where everything is momentary and the क्षणs are not synchronous and there is nothing to connect them, the relation of वास्य and वासक is impossible. Musk produces its वासना in a piece of cloth, because the cloth is an abiding substance and is connected with the musk.

अथ पूर्वचित्तसहजात् etc.—Another attempt on the part of the Buddhist to get over the difficulty. A certain चेतना (consciousness) born with an anterior चित्त (idea) produces a posterior चित्त possessing the power of the anterior चित्त, and this is वासना. In other words, वासना is the name of the particular चेतना which acts like a bridge between the anterior (वासक) and the posterior (वास्य) चित्त.

तथाहि पूर्वचित्तं etc.—The above definition of वासना is further explained: The पूर्वचित्त—the anterior चित्त—which has for its object रूप etc. is called प्रवृत्तिविज्ञान—which is of six kinds: viz. the five रूपादिविज्ञानs (sensuous cognitions) and the sixth विकल्पविज्ञान (conceptual विज्ञान). Synchronous with the पूर्वचित्त is born a certain consciousness of the ego, which is called आलयविज्ञान, and this आलयविज्ञान produces the next चित्त invested with the शक्ति of the former चित्त. The आलयविज्ञान is वासना. आलयविज्ञान *i. e.* 'receptacle intelligence' is so called because in it lie the प्रवृत्तिविज्ञानs (आलीयन्ते प्रवृत्तिविज्ञानान्यस्मिन्निति) and the प्रवृत्तिविज्ञानs are so called because they represent the active side of consciousness (See Keith's "Buddhist Philosophy" p. 253.).

तदपि न etc.—No amount of mere change of phraseology will help the Buddhist in his predicament. The difficulty of connecting the पूर्वचित्त with the उत्तरचित्त (call them प्रवृत्तिविज्ञानs) is not lessened by setting up an आलयविज्ञान (another name of वासना) between them, unless that आलयविज्ञान is admitted to be a permanent factor capable of connecting the two. But in the

Buddhist system of universal impermanence (क्षणभङ्ग) there is no room for a permanent factor of consciousness.

यश्चासौ चेतनाविशेषः etc.—Criticism: The particular चेतना which accompanies the anterior चित्त cannot influence a *present* चित्त, because the present—which according to the Buddhist lasts for a single moment only—can never be influenced in any way—it perishes just as it was born, without any change whatsoever,–for the plain reason that it lasts for a single moment only. Nor can the particular चेतना influence a future चित्त, inasmuch as it is unconnected with it, unless you suppose that the चेतना (आलयविज्ञान) is an abiding reality which in the Buddhist system it is impossible for it to be.

अत्र च स्तुतिकारेण etc.—In spite of the impossibility of वासना, the author of the Stanza discussed the alternatives of its भेद, अभेद etc.—This was only with a view to leading the reader to realise the necessity of recognizing an element of permanence in our consciousness.

II

अथोत्तरार्धं etc.—Second Half of the Stanza.

मायातनयाः—The Buddhists, the followers of Gautama, son of 'माया'; 'माया' the name of Gautama's mother. Pun upon the word 'माया' suggesting deceit.

पारावार—Ocean. प्रवहणकूपस्तम्भ—The mast of a ship.

नीति—The Science of Politics; political prudence.

इतरथाऽन्धगजन्यायेन etc.—Otherwise, there would be a grasp of half-truths only, such as the blind men had in the famous parable of the Elephant and the Blind Men. पल्लवग्राहिता–catching only a fringe of the total reality.

श्रयन्तीति etc.—Some read श्रयन्ति for श्रयन्तु.

Appendices.

1. तत्र यत्तावदुक्तं ज्ञानलक्षणप्रवाह इत्यादि [ज्ञानलक्षणप्रवाहव्यतिरेकेण कस्याप्यात्मनोऽभावात् कस्य मुक्तौ ज्ञानादिस्वभावः प्रसाध्यते ?] तदविचारितविलपितम् । ज्ञानक्षणप्रवाहव्यतिरिक्तं मुक्ताकणानुस्यूतसूत्रोपममन्वयिनमात्मानमन्तरेण कृतनाशाकृतागमादिदोषप्रसक्तेः स्मरणाद्यनुपपत्तेश्च ।......नहि कालान्तरावस्थाय्येकानुसंधातृव्यतिरेकेण भावनाद्युपपद्यते । तथा यो हि निगडादिभिर्बद्धः तस्यैव तन्मुक्तिकारणपरिज्ञानानुष्ठानाभिसंधिव्यापारे सति मोक्ष इत्यैकाधिकरण्ये सत्येव बन्धमोक्षव्यवस्था लोके प्रसिद्धा । इह त्वन्यः क्षणो बद्धोऽन्यस्य च तन्मुक्तिकारणपरिज्ञानमन्यस्य चानुष्ठानभिसंधेर्व्यापारश्चेति वैयधिकरण्यात् सर्वमयुक्तम् । किं च सर्वो बुद्धिमान् बुद्धिपूर्वं प्रवर्तमानः किंचिदिदमतो मम स्यादित्यनुसंधानेन प्रवर्तते । इह च कस्तथाविधो मार्गाभ्यासे प्रवर्तमानो मोक्षो मम स्यादित्यनुसंदध्यात् ? । क्षणः संतानो वा ? । न तावत् क्षणः । तस्यैकक्षणस्थायितया निर्विकल्पतया चैतावतो व्यापारान् कर्तुमसमर्थत्वात् । नापि संतानः । तस्य संतानिव्यतिरिक्तस्य सौगतैरनभ्युपगमात् । किं च निरन्वयविनश्वरत्वे च संस्काराणां मोक्षार्थः प्रयासो व्यर्थ एव स्यात्, यतो रागाद्युपरमो हि भवन्मते मोक्षः उपरमश्च विनाशः, स च निर्हेतुकतयाऽयत्नसिद्धः । ततस्तदर्थोऽनुष्ठानादिप्रयासो निष्फल एव ॥ Guṇaratna's Com. on Ṣaḍdars'ana-Saṃgraha pp. 194–95.

2. "उत्तरोत्पादे च पूर्वनिरोधात्"—क्षणभङ्गवादिनोऽयमभ्युपगम उत्तरस्मिन् क्षण उत्पद्यमाने पूर्वः क्षणो निरुध्यत इति । न चैवमभ्युपगच्छता पूर्वोत्तरयोः क्षणयोर्हेतुफलभावः शक्यते संपादयितुम् । निरुद्धमानस्य निरुद्धस्य वा पूर्वक्षणस्याभावग्रस्तत्वादुत्तरक्षणहेतुत्वानुपपत्तेः । अथ भावभूतः परिनिष्पन्नावस्थः पूर्वक्षण उत्तरक्षणस्य हेतुरित्यभिप्रायस्तथापि नोपपद्यते । भावभूतस्य पुनर्व्यापारकल्पनायां क्षणान्तरसंबन्धप्रसङ्गात् ॥ —S'aṃkara's Com. on Br. S. II. ii. 20.

"अनुस्मृतेश्च"—अपि च वैनाशिकः सर्वस्य वस्तुनः क्षणिकतामभ्युपयन्नुपलब्धुरपि क्षणिकतामुपेयात् । न च सा संभवति । अनुस्मृतेः । अनुभवमुपलब्धिमनूत्पद्यमानं स्मरणमेवानुस्मृतिः । सा चोपलब्ध्येककर्तृका सती संभवति । पुरुषान्तरोपलब्धिविषये पुरुषान्तरस्य स्मृत्यदर्शनात् ॥ Ibid Br. S. II. ii. 25.

Stanza XX.

एवं क्रियावादिनां etc.—The systems hitherto dealt with were those of the क्रियावादिन्s, and they, howsoever wrong in many important points, had one merit at least viz. that they all embraced क्रियावाद. The system which is next going to be examined is that of the *Cârvâkas*—the *Lokâyatikas* or *Nâstikas*—atheists and materialists, who are अक्रियावादिन्s.

What is meant by क्रियावाद and अक्रियावाद? One should have thought that क्रियावाद meant belief in the voluntary activity and therefore in the moral responsibility and future life of आत्मन्, and अक्रियावाद denial of the same, and in this sense the Cârvâka could well be called अक्रियावादिन्. Now, it is probable that the word did mean that originally. But the traditional explanation as given by the Jaina commentators is different, and the wording in the text would show that the same is followed by our author. By क्रिया they understand the *act of existence* (not a very probable meaning originally): thus, 'क्रियावादिन्' means he who asserts the existence of आत्मन्, and 'अक्रियावादिन्' he who denies it. Cf. etc. Sil. Com. on Utt. XVIII, 23, p. 442, Devchand Lalbhai Series—"क्रिया अस्तीत्येवंरूपा। अक्रिया तद्विपरीता ॥" Sil. Com. on Uttara XVIII. See Appendix.

See Jacobi, S. B. E. Jaina Sûtras, Part II Introduction p. xxxv, where 'क्रियावाद' is explained as the view of those who "maintain that the soul is directly affected by actions, passions etc."

For the name लोकायतिक etc. see Gunaratna's Introduction to the Section on Cârvâka in Ṣaḍ. 80-86; Max Müller's "Six Systems", and Sacred Books of the Buddhists Vol. II, pp. 166-172. According to Rhys Davids, in the old texts of Buddhism the word लोकायत means Nature-lore.

तन्मूलस्य etc.—The gravamen of the criticism is that the doctrine of the Laukâyatikas is based upon the recognition of प्रत्यक्ष as the only प्रमाण to the exclusion of even अनुमान.

Stanza: To the नास्तिक, who cannot know the mind of others for lack of अनुमान recognised as a प्रमाण, it is not open to speak: What a gulf between चेष्टा—a significant movement of limbs which implies अनुमान—and प्रत्यक्ष! Alas! what a folly to deny अनुमान!

प्रत्यक्षमेवैकं etc.—प्रत्यक्ष is the only प्रमाण, says Cârvâka. See Ṣaḍ. and Sarvadars'ana Saṁgraha.

For 'चार्वाक' See M. Bh. and Max Müller's "Six Systems of Indian Philosophy", and Guṇaratna's Com. on Ṣaḍ p. 300. चार्वाक from चारुवाक् (=one who speaks pleasantly and therefore temptingly) seems to be the more plausible derivation of the word.

संनह्यते from सं+नह् to bind, to gird up one's loins, to put on an armour and go to war.

अनु पश्चात् etc.—'अनुमान'-from अनु-after and मा—to measure, and hence to know—is so called because by means of that particular kind of knowledge, a thing, though remote in time, space and nature, is *measured* out to the mind, *after* one has recollected the relation of invariable concomitance (व्याप्ति) between लिङ्ग (हेतु *e. g.* धूम) and लिङ्गिन् (साध्य *e. g.* वह्नि).

प्रस्तावात्—The context requires that by 'अनुमान' in the first line we should understand स्वार्थानुमान. अनुमान is of two kinds: स्वार्थानुमान and परार्थानुमान. The former is the अनुमान which is conducted for one's own enlightenment; the latter for the enlightenment of others. See Tarka manuals; also Pr. N. T. iii. 9. (अनुमानं द्विप्रकारं स्वार्थं परार्थं च). The division is said to have originated in the Buddhist section of Indian Logic. See Keith's "Indian Logic and Atomism" and Vidyâbhûṣana's "History of Indian Logic".

अनुमानेन etc.—अनुमान paraphrased as लैङ्गिक प्रमाण *i. e.* प्रमाण based upon हेतु.

नास्ति परलोकः etc.—Etymology of the word नास्तिक. See Com. on Ṣaḍ. St. 81.

वचनं हि परप्रत्यायनाय etc.—Unless अनुमान is recognised as a प्रमाण there will be no possibility of our knowing what others know or do not know, and we cannot employ words to enlighten them, there being no objective in view. For want of such an objective all our talk will be as aimless and meaningless as that of a madman.

क्केति etc.—क्क—क्क signifies a vast gulf or difference as in क्क सूर्यप्रभवो वंशः क्क चाल्पविषया मतिः (Raghu.). See Apte's Guide to Sanskrit Composition.

दृष्टमात्रं etc.—प्रत्यक्षमात्रं etc.

नहि प्रत्यक्षेण etc.—By mere प्रत्यक्ष we cannot know the mind of others. But we do know it somehow from such marks as a cheerful face etc. Therefore, we must recognise a प्रमाण other than mere प्रत्यक्ष viz. अनुमान.

तथाहि etc.—This man desires to hear my words ; otherwise there would not have been such marks as I observe on his face.

अत्र च संपूर्वस्य etc.—How is it that सं-विद् which is Atmanepadin only when it is used intransitively is here so inspite of its being used transitively ? Answer : संविदानः one *able* to know, as per rule " वयः शक्तिशीले " (Hema-V. ii. 24).

तथा प्रकारान्तरेण etc.—Next follows a set of arguments to show that (1) we cannot determine the प्रामाण्य of प्रत्यक्ष without admitting the प्रामाण्य of अनुमान; and (2) that there is the same ground for admitting the प्रामाण्य of अनुमान and आगम as that which exists in the case of प्रत्यक्ष.

चार्वाकः कश्चित् etc.—The Cârvâka found certain cognitions—which are based on the senses—to be always in harmony with reality, and certain others—such as those based on inference or the word of a teacher—to be sometimes out of harmony with reality; and so, whenever after that experience he came across similar cognitions of the first type he considered himself justified in regarding them as true, and those of the second type as false. This could never be accomplished by mere प्रत्यक्ष—whose operations are confined to *present objects*, and has no power to relate cognitions belonging to different times. See Sarva. D. S., Criticism of the Cârvâka by the Bauddha (see Appendix).

न चायं स्वप्रतीति etc.—Besides, he cannot so much as ask another man to accept a proposition as true or false inasmuch as that proposition though प्रत्यक्ष to himself is not प्रत्यक्ष (but only अनुमेय) to the other person.

तस्माद्यथादृष्ट etc.—Therefore one must accept a प्रमाण called अनुमान whose business it will be to prove a certain present ज्ञान as true or false on the basis of its similarity to previous experience (प्रत्यक्ष).

परलोकादि etc.—On the mere ground of प्रत्यक्ष, you are not justified in denying life after death. For, प्रत्यक्ष can address itself to the *present* only, neither to the past nor to the future.

परलोकादिकं etc.—It is but a piece of childish folly to feel unhappy unless life after death is denied, and also to reject the validity of अनुमान. If the problem of life after death is to be discussed at all it can only be on the basis of अनुमान (or आगम) प्रमाण, the problem being outside the range of प्रत्यक्ष.

किं च प्रत्यक्षस्यापि etc.—Moreover, the very validity of प्रत्यक्ष will have to be established by अनुमान only. For, why is the water of a mirage which does not serve the purpose of bath, drink etc. regarded as false, inspite of its being प्रत्यक्ष ? The reason is—प्रत्यक्ष is reliable where it agrees with Reality, not everywhere. Thus, it is reliable where the water you perceive serves your purpose of bath and drink ; it is unreliable where it fails you, as the water of a mirage. Now, we want you to realise that the same applies to अनुमान and आगम. Where they agree with reality, they are reliable ; where they do not, they are not. In other words, प्रत्यक्ष, अनुमान and आगम all stand on the same level in the matter of reliability.

व्यभिचारिणोरप्यनयोः etc.—If you say that अनुमान and आगम are sometimes discovered to be discordant will Reality and are therefore unreliable, we reply that the same is the case with प्रत्यक्ष also. For, we do sometimes see (प्रत्यक्ष) *two* moons owing to disease in the eye. And just as we have a false प्रत्यक्ष, we may have a false अनुमान or a false आगम also.

एवं च प्रत्यक्षमात्रेण etc.—So you cannot rest your knowledge on the reliability of प्रत्यक्ष only, and so all your denials of जीव, पुण्य, अपुण्य, and परलोक based on प्रत्यक्ष must fall to the ground.

एवं नास्तिकाo etc.—Similarly, one may reject the doctrine of materialism held by the Cârvâkas.

तथा च द्रव्यालङ्कारकारः—Its criticism has been set forth very well by Râmachandra, author of *Dravyâlamkâra* (See Peterson's Report), while dealing with the subject of उपयोग *i. e.* consciousness which belongs to Âtman.

न चायं भूतधर्मः—Consciousness, says he, is not a property of matter. Were it a property of matter, we should have found it in every particle of matter, just as we observe the property of intoxication in intoxicating drugs.

कायाकारo etc.—Cârvâka: When matter assumes the form of a living body, consciousness originates therein. Criticism: If the modification of matter which you call the living body be matter itself and nothing more, then we should expect the living body to be continuous with matter, and not an occasional phenomenon in it. If, on the other hand, the living body be regarded as something other than matter, it amounts to a recognition of a non-material principle, and that would be only another name for आत्मन्. If आत्मन् had no causal connection with consciousness, consciousness would not necessarily be limited to the place where आत्मन् is. It would arise even in a dead body. If you say that certain conditions such as the presence of blood (as in a living body) is necessary, it may be replied that the blood exists in a dead body and yet there is no consciousness. Next, आत्मन् is not born. If you say आत्मन् exists and yet he is originated by the भूतs (a modified form of pure materialism), it would involve persistently recurring origination of आत्मन् in spite of its existence; for, existence is, then, no bar to origination. If, on the other hand, you hold that आत्मन् did not exist before and is only come into existence when matter is become a living body, the question arises: How can that which is a nonentity perform the act of coming into existence ? For, coming into existence is after all an act, and requires somebody or something to perform it. That which is not, and is, therefore, devoid of every conceivable power, cannot perform the act of coming into existence. Therefore उपयोग or consciousness is not a property of भूतs, that is, matter.

कुतस्तर्हि etc.—Explain how a man rising out of sleep comes to possess consciousness, while चैतन्य had been absent owing to want of consciousness during the sleep. Answer: We only *remember* what we had experienced before in the waking condition. The unconsciousness of sleep was due to the impediment caused by sleep. Then how is it, you will ask, that चैतन्य suffers with the suffering of the body? We answer: It is not the rule: A fine mind is often found in a wretched and diseased body. Even when the body remains the same we rejoice or grieve according to our mental attitude. The mind is distorted by grief and yet no change is observed in the body. There must be some cause, you will admit, to which the change of mind should belong, namely, the mind or आत्मन्. You will perhaps say: the matter undergoes change and becomes consciousness. Answer: It cannot, because the two are so unlike. Properties such as hardness etc. do not belong to it. The atoms when they become gross enough are apprehended by the इन्द्रियs.

तथा भवांश्च etc.—What is the definition of आत्मन् ? Answer: That which you attack. The आत्मन् is self-revealed. If आत्मन् were but matter, it would be presented as "this" (external), not as "I" (internal).

Books of Reference:

1. S'îlâṅka's Tîkâ on Sûtrakritānga II. 1. 1.
2. „ Uttarâ. XVIII, 23.
3. Ṣaḍdarsana Samuccaya, Guṇaratna's Commentary.
4. Pramāṇa-Naya-Tattvālokālaṁkāra.

Appendices.

1. ये तावत् क्रियावादिनस्तेऽस्तिक्रियाविशिष्टमात्मानं मन्यमाना अपि तस्य सदा विभुत्वाविभुत्वकर्तृत्वाकर्तृत्वादिभिर्विप्रतिपद्यन्ते । उक्तं हि वाचकैः— क्रियावादिनो नाम येषामात्मनोऽस्तित्वं प्रत्यविप्रतिपत्तिः, किंतु स विभुरविभुः कर्ताऽकर्ता क्रियावानितरो मूर्तिमानमूर्तिरित्येवमाद्या ग्रहोपहृतप्रीतयः ॥......... ये त्वक्रियावादिनस्तेऽस्तीतिक्रियाविशिष्टमात्मानं नेच्छन्त्येव, अस्तित्वे वा शरीरेण सहैकत्वान्यत्वाभ्यामवक्तव्यत्वमिच्छन्ति ।......अक्रियावादित्वं चैषां कथंचिद्भेदाभेदलक्षणप्रकारान्तराभावेन तदभावस्यैवावशिष्यमाणत्वात् । येऽप्युत्पत्त्यनन्तरमात्मनः प्रलयमिच्छन्ति तेषामपि तदस्तित्वाभ्युपगमेऽप्यनुपचरितपरलोकाद्यसंभवात् तत्त्वतस्तदसत्त्वमेवेत्यक्रियावादित्वम् । उक्तं हि वाचकैः—ये पुनरिहाक्रियावादिनस्तेषामात्मैव नास्ति न चावक्तव्यः शरीरेण सहैकत्वान्यत्वे प्रति, उत्पत्त्यनन्तरप्रलयस्वभावको वा, तस्मिन्ननिर्णिक्ते च कर्तृत्वादिविशेषमूढा एवेति ॥ S'îlânka's Com. on Uttarâdhyayana XVIII.

2. यदि कश्चित् प्रामाण्यमनुमानस्य नाङ्गीकुर्यात् तं ब्रूयात्—अनुमानं प्रमाणं न भवतीत्येतावन्मात्रमुच्यते तत्र न किंचन साधनमुपन्यस्यत उपन्यस्यते वा । न प्रथमः । अशिरस्कवचनस्योपन्यासे साध्यासिद्धेः । एकाकिनी प्रतिज्ञा हि प्रतिज्ञातं न साधयेत् इति न्यायात् ।...किं च प्रमाणतदाभासव्यवस्थापनं तत्समानजातीयत्वादिति वदता भवतैव स्वीकृतं स्वभावानुमानम् ॥

Ṣaḍdars'ana Saṁgraha, Bauddha Dars'ana.

3. गल चर्वं अदने । चर्वन्ति भक्षयन्ति तत्त्वतो न मन्यन्ते पुण्यपापादिकं परोक्षं वस्तुजातमिति चार्वाकाः ।......लोका निर्विचाराः सामान्या लोकास्तद्वदाचरन्ति स्मेति लोकायता लोकायतिका इत्यपि ॥—Guṇa. on Ṣaḍ. p. 300.

Stanza XXI.

Stanza : Oh Lord Jina! he who, while seeing before his eyes one Reality which is permanent as well as possessed of production and destruction every moment, disregards your teaching (which recognises all the three is either a fool or a devil.)

प्रतिक्षणं etc.—उत्पाद is but उत्तराकारस्वीकार, and विनाश पूर्वाकारपरिहार. स्थिरैक—objection to ईक्षमाणः.

स्थिरम् etc.—In the midst of change.

एकशब्दोऽत्र etc.—Here एक does not mean *numerically one*, but *identical.*

पर्यायाणां etc.—In view of this उत्पाद and विनाश, the पर्यायs (the changing modes or forms) are many; the द्रव्य is one.

आज्ञां etc.—आज्ञा, from आ = completely in all its varying forms + ज्ञा = to know, means the teaching which gives a complete knowledge of the पदार्थs—जीव, अजीव etc.—in all their numberless aspects or attributes. आज्ञा=आगम=शासन.

वातकी—Suffering from mental windiness or flatulence; a fool. For the grammatical formation of the word, see Hema. VII. ii. 61.

पिशाचकी—possessed by a पिशाच or devil.

एकान्तवादापस्मार etc.—Epilepsy of metaphysical 'one-sidedness' or absolutism.

नाथ—The Lord who accomplishes the 'योग-क्षेम' of the spiritual well-being of his followers. The 'योग' consists in furnishing new light to his followers, and 'क्षेम' in confirming the same by means of repeated sermons.

वस्तुतत्त्वं etc.—Reality consists of उत्पाद, व्यय and ध्रौव्य *i. e.* Production, Destruction and Permanence. ("उत्पादव्ययध्रौव्ययुक्तं सत्" Tatv. 39.) As द्रव्य, nothing is produced or destroyed: it persists, as is indicated by our sense of identity in the midst of change. It may be argued that a false sense of identity is sometimes experienced as in the case of hair and nails—which though replaced by new products of the same kind from time to time *appear* to remain identical. The answer to that objection is that in their case there is sufficient contrary evidence to show that the hair etc. are *not* the same; whereas in the case under consideration, the identity of द्रव्य in the midst of उत्पाद and विनाश is easily established by प्रत्यभिज्ञाप्रमाण *i. e.* the sense of recognition of a thing as the same as that which was seen before.

सर्वव्यक्तिषु etc.—Found quoted in the Tattva. Bh. on V. 29. (See Appendix). All individuals are certainly changing every moment, and yet there is no change, in the midst of production and destruction (चिति and अपचिति): this fact of change in the midst of permanence has its analogue in the relation of जाति and आकृति—wherein individuals (गोs) come and go, but not their °त्व (गोत्व) or universal which remains the same.

ततो द्रव्यात्मना etc.—Mark that permanence and change are not attributed to a thing in one and the same capacity, but in different capacities—'द्रव्यात्मना' and 'पर्यायात्मना'. Mark, further, that the Jaina does not regard change to be a mere show or illusion as does the Mâyâ-Vedântin; with him it is as much a reality as permanence which is the other half of the truth.

अस्खलित etc.—Because we perceive change of the पर्यायs and there is no reason to distrust the truth of the perception.

न चैव शुक्ले शङ्के etc.—That we have a certain perception may not be conclusive. For, do we not perceive a yellow colour in a white conchshell, when we are suffering from jaundiced eye? Answer: But that is because the perception itself is false. It is not so, however, in the case of the innumerable पर्यायs of हर्ष, अमर्ष etc.—which we experience in our soul.

नन्नूत्पादादयः etc.—Objection to the theory of the Three-in-One viz., उत्पाद, व्यय and ध्रौव्य in one Reality: Are the three different *inter se* or not? If they are, they are three in number; and, then, how can *one* be *three*? If they are not, they are not three, but one; and then one is one, not three is one.

तदयुक्तं कथंचित् etc.—Reply to the objection: They (उत्पाद etc.) are in a certain sense different from one another, because their लक्षणs or characters are different from one another.

उत्पादविनाश etc.—Syllogism to prove that उत्पाद, विनाश and ध्रौव्य are different *inter se*.

न च भिन्नलक्षणत्वं etc.—भिन्नलक्षणत्व is the हेतु which can be thus shown to be true of the पक्षः उत्पाद, व्यय and ध्रौव्य has each a nature of its own which is not the same as that of the other two. उत्पाद is defined as 'असत आत्मलाभः'—*i. e.* coming into being of a thing that was not; विनाश is defined as 'सत आत्मवियोगः' *i. e.* loss of existence in a thing that had it before; and ध्रौव्य is defined as 'द्रव्यतयानुवर्तनम्' *i. e.* persistence as the substance. The three definitions differ *inter se*, and so do the notions defined.

न चामी भिन्न०—Note that different as they are in their लक्षणs, the three are not mutually independent–उत्पाद can never be without विगम (विनाश) and स्थिति (ध्रौव्य) any more than hair could exist on the back of a tortoise; that is to say, उत्पाद without the others is a pure fiction, a nothing. The same as regards विनाश and स्थिति.

घटमौलि etc.—Âptamîmâṁsâ verse 59. A commentator relates a story to explain the meaning of the verse. A certain king had a son and a daughter. The latter possessed a jar made of gold, which at the instance of the prince the king ordered to be turned into a crown. This pleased the prince, but displeased the princess, the king himself remaining neutral all along, being the owner of so much gold whether in the form of a jar or a crown.

पयोव्रतो etc.—Âptamîmmâsâ verse 60. This is simple. He who has vowed to live on milk does not take curds; he who has vowed to live on curds does not take milk; he who has vowed to live on food other than that supplied by a cow takes neither milk nor curds—so there may be उत्पाद, विनाश or ध्रौव्य according to the several points of view.

Books of Reference :

1. Tattvârthâdhigama Bhâṣya on V. 29 and Commentaries thereon.
2. Pramâṇa-Naya-Tattvâlokâlaṁkâra.

Appendices.

1. सर्वव्यक्तिषु नियतं क्षणे क्षणेऽन्यत्वमथ च न विशेषः ।
सत्योश्चित्यपचित्योराकृतिजातिव्यवस्थानात् ॥ १ ॥
नरकादिगतिभेदो भेदः संसारमोक्षयोश्चैव ।
हिंसादिस्तद्धेतुः सम्यक्त्वादिश्च मुख्य इति ॥ २ ॥
उत्पादादियुते खलु वस्तुन्येतदुपपद्यते सर्वम् ।
तद्रहिते तदभावात् सर्वमपि न युज्यते नीत्या ॥ ३ ॥
निरुपादानो न भवत्युत्पादो नापि तादवस्थ्येऽस्य ।
तद्विक्रिययाऽपि तथा त्रितययुतेऽस्मिन् भवत्येषः ॥ ४ ॥
सिद्धत्वेनोत्पादो व्ययोऽस्य संसारभावतो ज्ञेयः ।
जीवत्वेन ध्रौव्यं त्रितययुतं सर्वमेवं तु ॥ ५ ॥

—Qutoed in Tatt. Bhâṣya V. 29. [This portion of the Bhâṣya, however, has been noticed in Haribhadra's Commentary but not in Siddhasena's].

2. "येनोत्पादव्ययध्रौव्ययुक्तं, यत्तत्सदिष्यते ।
अनन्तधर्मकं वस्तु तेनोक्तं मानगोचरः ॥"

ननु पूर्वमसतो भावस्योत्पादव्ययध्रौव्ययोगाद्यदि पश्चात्सत्त्वं, तर्हि शशशृङ्गादेरपि तद्योगात्सत्त्वं स्यात्। पूर्वं सतश्चेत्, तदा स्वरूपसत्त्वमायातं किमुत्पादादिभिः कल्पितैः ? । तथोत्पादव्ययध्रौव्याणामपि यद्यन्योत्पादित्रययोगसत्त्वं, तदानवस्थाप्रसक्तिः । स्वतश्चेत्सत्त्वं, तदा भावस्यापि स्वत एव तद्भविष्यतीति व्यर्थमुत्पादादिकल्पनमिति चेत् । उच्यते । न हि भिन्नोत्पादव्ययध्रौव्ययोगाद्भावस्य सत्त्वमभ्युपगम्यते, किंतूत्पादव्ययध्रौव्ययोगात्मकमेव सदिति स्वीक्रियते । तथाहि । उर्वीपर्वततर्वादिकं सर्वं वस्तु द्रव्यात्मना नोत्पद्यते विपद्यते वा, परिस्फुटान्वयदर्शनात् । लूनपुनर्जातनखादिष्वन्यदर्शनेन व्यभिचार इति न वाच्यं, प्रमाणेन बाध्यमानस्यान्वयस्यापरिस्फुटत्वात् । न च प्रस्तुतोऽन्वयः प्रमाणविरुद्धः, सत्यप्रत्यभिज्ञानत्वात् सर्वव्यक्तिषु नियतं क्षणे क्षणेऽन्यत्वमथ च न विशेषः, सत्योश्चित्यपचित्योराकृतिजातिव्यवस्थानादिति वचनात् । ततो द्रव्यात्मना सर्वस्य वस्तुनः स्थितिरेव, पर्यायात्मना तु सर्वं वस्तूत्पद्यते विपद्यते वा, अस्खलितपर्यायानुभवसद्भावात् । न चैवं शुक्ले शङ्खे पीतादिपर्यायानुभवेन व्यभिचारः, तस्य स्खलद्रूपत्वात् । न खलु सोऽस्खलद्रूपो येन पूर्वाकारविनाशोऽजहतोत्तराकारोपादानाविनाभावी भवेत् । न च जीवादौ वस्तुनि हर्षामर्षौदासीन्यादिपर्यायानुभवः स्खलद्रूपः, कस्यचिद्बाधकस्याभावात् । नन्वुत्पादादयः परस्परं भिद्यन्ते न वा । यदि भिद्यन्ते कथमेकं आत्मकं, न भिद्यन्ते चेत् तथापि कथमेकं त्र्यात्मकमिति चेत् । तदयुक्तं, कथंचिद्भिन्नलक्षणत्वेन तेषां कथंचिद्भेदाभ्युपगमात् । तथाहि ।

उत्पादविनाशध्रौव्याणि स्याद्भिन्नानि, भिन्नलक्षणत्वात्, रूपादिवत्। न च भिन्नलक्षणत्वमसिद्धं, असत आत्मलाभ उत्पादः, सतः सत्तावियोगो विनाशः। द्रव्यरूपतयानुवर्तनं ध्रौव्यमित्येवमसंकीर्णलक्षणानां तेषां सर्वैः प्रतीतेः। न चामी परस्परानपेक्षत्वेन भिन्ना एव, परस्परानपेक्षाणां खपुष्पवदसत्त्वापत्तेः। तथाहि। उत्पादः केवलो नास्ति, स्थितिविगमरहितत्वात् कूर्मरोमवत्; तथा विनाशः केवलो नास्ति, स्थित्युत्पत्तिरहितत्वात्, तद्वत्; एवं स्थितिरपि केवला नास्ति, विनाशोत्पादशून्यत्वात्, तद्वदेवेत्यन्योन्यापेक्षाणामुत्पादादीनां वस्तुनि सत्त्वं प्रतिपत्तव्यम्। तथा च कथं नैकं त्र्यात्मकम्। तथा चोक्तम्।

प्रध्वस्ते कलशे शुशोच तनया मौलौ समुत्पादिते
पुत्रः प्रीतिमुवाह कामपि नृपः शिश्राय मध्यस्थताम्।
पूर्वाकारपरिक्षयस्तदपराकारोदयस्तद्द्वया-
धारश्चैक इति स्थितं त्रयमयं तत्त्वं तथा प्रत्ययात्॥
घण्टमौलिसुवर्णार्थी नाशोत्पादस्थितिष्वलम्।
शोकप्रमोदमाध्यस्थं जनो याति सहेतुकम्।
पयोव्रतो न दध्यत्ति न पयोऽत्ति दधिव्रतः।
अगोरसव्रतो नोभे तस्माद्वस्तु त्रयात्मकम्॥

Stanza XXII.

Stanza: Reality is possessed of innumerable characters; it is not possible to explain it in any other way. So, your proofs are like roars of a lion which frighten away antelopes, namely, heretics.

तत्त्वं परमार्थभूतं etc.—तत्त्व in the stanza=परमार्थभूतं वस्तु *i. e.* Reality, viz., जीव and अजीव.

अनन्तधर्मात्मकमेव etc.—The word अनन्तधर्मात्मकम् explained: अनन्ताः—Belonging to the three times and therefore endless.

ये धर्माः etc.—धर्मs or attributes are of two kinds: सहभाविनः—synchronous or co-existing and क्रमभाविनः—successive.

त एवात्मा etc.—Which is characterized by endless attributes, some of which are सहभाविनः and some क्रमभाविनः.

एवकारः etc.—That is the character of Reality and no other,

अतोऽन्यथा etc.—Hence no other character can well be established in regard to the Reality.

अनेन साधनं etc.—The second line supplies the साधन or हेतु for the statement af the first line that Reality is essentially possessed of an endless number of attributes.

तथा हि—The syllogism will run thus :

तत्त्वम् (subject, minor term, पक्ष); अनन्तधर्मात्मकम् (predicate, major term, साध्य); सत्त्वान्यथानुपपत्तेः (reason, middle term, हेतु, साधन).

अन्तर्व्याप्त्यैव etc.—It will be noticed that no दृष्टान्त is given in the above syllogism. The reason is that no दृष्टान्त is possible as will be seen below. Yet the argument is sound, as it is based on 'अन्तर्व्याप्ति': the very idea of Being (सत्त्वम्) properly analysed yields the साध्य, viz., अनन्तधर्मात्मकत्व. Therefore, there is no need for examples to support the inductive reasoning which establishes the major premiss. Vide Siddhasena-Divâkara's Nyâyâvatâra 20 and Com. thereon:—"अन्तर्व्याप्त्यैव साध्यस्य सिद्धेर्बहिरुदाहृतिः । व्यर्था स्यात् तदसद्भावेऽप्येवं न्यायविदो विदुः ॥' अन्यदा हि स्मर्यमाणे वा संबन्धे प्रयुज्येत, अगृहीते वा । यद्याद्यः पक्षः,' सोऽयुक्तः । यदा सर्वत्र साध्याविनाभाविनं हेतुं स्मरति प्रतिपाद्यः, तदा पक्षेऽपि तमवबुध्य कथं साध्यं न प्रातिपद्येत ? । ततश्चान्तः पक्षमध्ये व्याप्तिः साधनस्य साध्याक्रान्तत्वमन्तर्व्याप्तिः । तयैव साध्यस्य गम्यस्य सिद्धेः प्रतीतेः । बहिर्विवक्षितधर्मिणोऽन्यत्र दृष्टान्तधर्मिण्युदाहृतिः व्याप्तिदर्शनरूपा व्यर्था निष्प्रयोजना । तत्प्रत्याय्यार्थाभावादिति । द्वितीयपक्षस्यापि निर्दोषतां निरस्यन्नाह—तदसद्भावेऽप्येवं संबन्धाग्रहणादन्तर्व्याप्त्यभावेऽप्येवमिति व्यर्थैव बहिरुदाहृतिः । न हि सहदर्शनात् क्वचित् सर्वत्र तद्रूपता सिध्यति । व्यभिचारदर्शनात् । तस्मादगृहीतसंबन्धे प्रतिपाद्ये प्रमाणेन प्रतिबन्धः साध्यः, तत्सिद्धौ तत एव साध्यसिद्धेरकिंचित्करी दृष्टान्तोदाहृतिरिति न्यायविदो विदुः अवबुध्यन्त इति ॥"

This doctrine of अन्तर्व्याप्ति in Buddhism, was intended to meet the necessities of the case in which statements were made about the totality of things on the ground of अनुमान. Obviously, there could be no दृष्टान्त in such a case, the दृष्टान्त being included in the पक्ष. The truth of the व्याप्ति was here justified *internally* (अन्तर्) between the हेतु and the साध्य and not sought externally, in a दृष्टान्त. What really arose from the necessities of a special case was applied generally to all cases of Inference, and that which was originally a generalisation from particulars was treated as a generalisation above and, therefore, independent of, particulars.

Earlier logicians, however, had continued to follow the older logic of अनुमान as based on generalisation from external data, viz. the दृष्टान्तs. This the new school rejects: "सत्त्वे [in क्षणिकं सत्त्वात्] केवलं जडधियामेव नियमेन दृष्टान्तसापेक्षः साधनप्रयोगः परितोषाय जायते। तेषामेवानुग्रहार्थमाचार्यो दृष्टान्तमुपादत्ते। यत् सत् तत् क्षणिकं यथा पट इति। पटुमतयस्तु नैवं दृष्टान्तमपेक्षन्ते ॥"—"अन्तर्व्याप्तिसमर्थनम्"
—by Ratnâkara S'ânti.

(See "The Six Buddhist Tracts" including one on अन्तर्व्याप्ति by Ratnâkara S'ânti, edited by M. M. Haraprasad S'âstri). "The work argues that the inseparable connection between the middle term and major term can be conceived without the aid of an example in which the things signified by the two terms co-abide, nay without the aid even of a minor term in which we are to prove the co-presence of the things, *e. g.* fiery because smoky." (Dr. Vidyâbhuṣaṇa's " H. I. L.").

" A further refinement of logical doctrine is contained in the *Antarvyâptisamarthana* of Ratnâkara S'ânti in the tenth century [? 1045 A.D. *i. e.* eleventh century—Dr. Vidyâbhûṣaṇa]. It is necessitated by considerations affecting the proof of the momentariness of things. Normally an inferenee gives us in the example the concomitance of the middle and the major in some object; for instance, fire on the mountain is proved from the presence of smoke with the aid of the example of the kitchen where smoke and fire co-exist. But this is impossible in the case of momentariness *ex vi termini*. Moreover, the conclusion in the normal case takes the form of the presence of the invariable relation in some subject, *e. g.* the relation of smoke and fire in the mountain, and the inference to establish momentariness cannot be given such a form. The new doctrine insists that it is possible to prove the relation within (antar) that is simply between the thing to be proved and the thing by which it is to be proved, without the intervention of something external (*bahis*) in which the relation is to exist." —Keith's " Buddhist Philosophy " pp. 316–17.

यदनन्तधर्मात्मकं etc.—A व्यतिरेकव्याप्ति *i. e.* a negative universal major premiss. Its example, however, by the very nature of the case cannot be real. Therefore, the example, ' वियदिन्दीवरम् '—a ' sky-lotus '. The हेतु here is केवलव्यतिरेकी *i. e.* capable of entering into a negative व्याप्ति (यत्र साध्याभावः तत्र साधनाभावः) only, अन्वय *i. e.* positive व्याप्ति being evidently impossible, since every दृष्टान्त that you can think of to illustrate the व्याप्ति-यत्र यत्र सत्त्वान्यथानुपपत्तिः (सत्त्वं) तत्र तत्र अनन्तधर्मात्मकत्वम्-will be found included in the पक्ष viz. वस्तु *i. e.* all Reality.

अनन्त० etc.—The list of सहभाविधर्मs of आत्मन्. हर्ष etc.—The list of the क्रमभाविधर्मs of आत्मन्. See Pravacanasāra and Dravyasaṁgraha.

धर्मास्तिकायादि०—

See जीवा पुग्गलकाया धम्माधम्मा तहेव आयासं ।
अत्थितह्मि य णियदा अणण्णमइया अणुमहंता ॥
(जीवाः पुद्गलकाया धर्माधर्मौ तथैव आकाशम् ।
अस्तित्वे च नियता अनन्यमया अणुमहान्तः ॥)

—Pañcâstikâya, 4.

असंख्येयप्रदेशात्मकत्वं—

See जीवा पोग्गलकाया धम्माधम्मा पुणो य आगासं ।
देसेहिं असंखादा णत्थि पदेस त्ति कालस्स ॥
(जीवाः पुद्गलकाया धर्माधर्मौ पुनश्चाकाशम् ।
प्रदेशैरसंख्याता न सन्ति प्रदेशा इति कालस्य ॥)

—Pravacanasâra II–43.

अत्र चात्मशब्देन etc.—In the predicate अनन्तधर्मात्मकम् of the line the आत्मन् (—त्मकम्) suggests that Reality is not a mere panorama or cinema show of पर्यायs, but that there is a principle of permanence (ध्रौव्य) also in the midst of change (उत्पाद and व्यय) Thus सत् or Reality may be defined as ' उत्पादव्ययध्रौव्ययुक्तं सत् ' (See Tattvârtha V. 29.)

शब्दस्त्वेपि etc.—A list of the धर्मs of शब्द. (See Prâtis'âkhyas).

अस्य हेतोः etc.—The author does not go into the tedious process of showing that the हेतु in the above syllogism is free from all the हेत्वाभासs viz., असिद्ध etc.

कुवादि etc.—The master is compared to the lion, the heretics to so many deer.

अत्र प्रमाणानि etc.—The plural number suggests that endless are the proofs which support the Lord's doctrine.

Stanza XXIII.

Stanza: When integrated, Reality is without characters; when differentiated, it is without a substance. You have fully seen the truth of Seven Modes which is expressed according to different points of view–a truth which is known by supremely wise men only.

अनन्तरं etc.—In the last stanza, Reality was described to be अनन्तधर्मात्मक *i. e.* possessed of an infinite number of predi. cates. The same truth is now going to be formulated in the shape of the great Jaina doctrine of सप्तभङ्गी or the Seven Modes. मुकुलितम्—in a brief or condensed form.

I

Reality described *synthetically* is a द्रव्य without reference to पर्यायs; the same described *analytically* is पर्यायs without reference to their द्रव्य.

अपर्ययं—अविवक्षितपर्यायं-devoid of पर्ययs or पर्यायs, that is to say, described without reference to पर्यायs, not that a thing can really exist without the पर्यायs.

वस्तु from वस् to dwell; that in which dwell the पर्यायs or properties, the Reality consisting of the six dravyas viz. धर्म etc.

अभ्यन्तरीकृत—in which the पर्यायs have been rolled up into a द्रव्य. When we say आत्मन् or घट, we think of the पर्यायs as non-distinct from the द्रव्य.

द्रव्यास्तिकनयाः शुद्धसंग्रहादयः etc.—The point of view of synthesis, which believes in द्रव्यs and treats पर्यायs as non-distinct from द्रव्यs. द्रव्यास्तिकनय is also called द्रव्यार्थिकनय *i. e.* the point of view of the reality (°आर्थिक) or existence (°आस्तिक) of द्रव्य. [For a full exposition of the नयs, see Tattvârtha Bhâṣya on I. 24-25.]

पर्यवः=पर्ययः=पर्यायः—more usually the last two. The first gives the Prākṛit पज्जव, and is itself a Prâkrit substitute for पर्यय.

च=पुनः—Whereas (पूर्वस्माद्विशेषद्योतने).

भिन्नक्रमः—Construe विविच्यमानं च.

अद्रव्यमेव—In which the underlying द्रव्य is ignored.

पर्यायास्तिकनयानुपातिनः—Those who adopt the पर्यायास्तिकनय *i. e.* the point of view of the existence of the पर्यायs only.

भागा एव हि भासन्ते etc.—Only the parts or modes appear located in different ways; there is no द्रव्य anywhere apart from the parts or modes.

ततश्च—So the statement depends upon what is going to be presented (अर्पित) or suppressed (अनर्पित). Sometimes the द्रव्य is presented and its पर्यायs suppressed ; sometimes, vice versa. अत एवाह अर्पितानर्पितसिद्धेः—See Tattvārtha-Sûtra V. 31.

ननु अन्याभिधानप्रत्यय etc.—Objection: The word द्रव्य is different from the word पर्याय; and so also the idea of one is different from the idea of the other. How can Reality be said to be both द्रव्य and पर्याय ?

आदेश°—The answer to that is to be found in the words of the text आदेश° *i. e.* owing to statements being of two kinds—सकलादेश and विकलादेश—synthetical statement and analytical statement* on which is based the doctrine of सप्तभङ्गी.

बुधरूपैर्वेद्यम्—which only the wisest can know. बुधरूपाः = उत्कृष्ट-बुधाः—Supremely wise cf. Pāṇ. V, iii, 66.

---

* Not used in the Kantian sense of synthetical and analytical propositions of Logic.

नैसर्गिक०—Right knowledge which is either innate or acquired.

न पुनः etc.—Teachers of other schools may be possessed of a highly trained intellect *i. e.* बुध, yet they are not बुधरूप—eminently wise.

तथा चागमः etc.—अज्ञान may arise from (1) failure to distinguish between true and false or right and wrong; (2) from the position which springs from the cause of Saṁsâra *i. e.* Karma; (3) from Jñâna not producing its fruit; and (4) from a false view (मिथ्यादृष्टि).

अत एव तत्परिगृहीतं etc.—Hence, in consequence of मिथ्यादृष्टि or wrong vision, even a study of the Twelve Jaina Scriptures [See "Outlines of Jainism" pp.135–146]; will become मिथ्याश्रुत *i. e.* wrong study in the case of heretics; whereas, even the study of heretical works will prove सम्यक्श्रुत or right study in the case of those who possess सम्यग्दृष्टि. The reason is that heretics when they read Jaina scriptures do not try to *understand* them (उपपत्तिनिरपेक्षं etc.), but interpret them in any way they *please* (यदृच्छया); whereas the followers of the Jaina Âgama bring to bear the right kind of vision upon the meaning even of heretical works. Thus, the latter have often succeeded in discovering the right विधिs and निषेधs in Brahmanical works, which have escaped the understanding of Brâhmaṇa commentators. दृष्टि=दर्शन, primarily meaning vision, comes to mean the faith which gives the vision. दर्शन=तत्त्वार्थश्रद्धान (Tattvârthâdhigama I. 2).

तथा हि etc.—A few examples may be given :

(1) There is a passage in the Veda 'अजैर्यष्टव्यम्'-which the Brâhmaṇas understand as referring to the sacrifice of goats (अजs). According to Jaina scholars, however, it refers only to the offering of corn which has become incapable of germination owing to lapse of time (अज=जन्मायोग्यं). Their reason for the latter interpretation is that it does not stand to moral reason to regard animal sacrifice as good—a point of view

which is given by सम्यग्दृष्टि *i. e.* faithful adherence to the Jaina creed and the consequent right vision.

(2) अत एव च भगवता etc.—Another example : There is the famous passage of the Br. Up. "विज्ञानघन etc.—"(" Full of consciousness, it springs from these material elements and sinks back into them : there is no consciousness after death.") which was the subject of a sermon by Vardhamâna (Mahâvîra) to Indrabhûti. The latter who before his conversion was a Brâhmaṇa understood the passage as denying the existence of Jîva (आत्मन्) and life after death and thus propounding materialism. Vardhamâna knew better, and he understood it as referring to the temporary eclipse of the soul's consciousness and not its absolute annihilation. S'ankara rejects the view that the passage is intended to teach materialism (See Br. Sûtra; Bhâṣya. See Hem. Tri. Ch. X, verses 77, 78; Sûtrakṛit Bk. II Brahmajâla Sutta, Ch. III; Avas'yaka with Har. Vṛtti.

(3) तथा स्मार्ता अपि. Next, there is a passage of the Manusmṛiti which runs as follows: न मांसभक्षणे दोषः etc. (Manu V. 56) Taken literally, it is self-contradictory. If there be no sin in meat-eating, how can abstention from it be declared to be 'महाफला'? If abstention from such a 'sinless' act as meat-eating is to be deemed highly beneficial, on the same principle abstention from other sinless acts such as worship, study, charity should also be deemed beneficial! So the passage requires to be interpreted in some other way. Take न मांसभक्षणे दोषः= न मांसभक्षणेऽ (अ–)दोषः (अ being elided according to sandhi rules), अपि तु दोषः; and प्रवृत्तिरेषा भूतानां etc.—not in the sense of 'It is the way of all creatures', but in the sense of "It is the breeding ground of animalculæ germs or bacteria." Malliṣeṇa next proceeds to show how an infinite number of animalculæ spring into life and then perish in the process of meat-making, wine-making and sexual enjoyment. [It is worthy of note how अहिंसा which was at first only one, even though the foremost, of the Five Vratas of the Jainas, along with those of the Brâhmaṇas and the Bauddhas, came to acquire the position of an all-embracing vrata with the Jaiṇas. Thus, in the Jaina Ethics, all the

other vratas including Brahmacarya are recommended not on their own account, but on account of their violating the great Law of Ahiṁsâ.]

Another suggestion made in order to remove the contradiction in Manu's verses and also to bring it into harmony with our moral reason is to take भूतानां=पिशाचप्रायाणाम्, (the way) of the devils ; तु=एव, alone (See Amara III, 239). This interpretation is further supported by other passages quoted from the Manusmṛti, M. Bhârata etc.

आमासु य पक्कासु etc.=आमासु च पक्कासु च विपच्यमानासु मांसपेशीषु । आत्यन्तिक उपपादो भणितस्तु निगोदजीवानाम् ॥ १ ॥ मद्ये मधुनि मांसे नवनीते चतुर्थके । उत्पद्यन्तेऽनन्तास्तद्वर्णास्तत्र जन्तवः ॥ २ ॥ मैथुनसंज्ञारूढो नवलक्षं हन्ति सूक्ष्मजीवानाम् । केवलिना प्रज्ञापिताः श्रद्धातव्याः सदाकालम् ॥ ३ ॥ —Quoted from the Sâṁbodha Saptatîka of Ratnas'ekhara Sûri (Gathās 66,65,63)—See AMP edition of the Syâdvâdamañjarî.

स्त्रीयोनौ संभवन्ति द्वीन्द्रियादिस्तु ये जीवाः। एको वा द्वौवा त्रयो वा लक्षपृथुत्वं चोत्कृष्टम् ॥ ४ ॥ पुरुषेण सहगतायां तेषां जीवानां भवति उद्रवणम् । वेणुकदृष्टान्तेन तप्तायसशलाकाज्ञातेन ॥ ५ ॥ पञ्चेन्द्रिया मनुष्या एकनरभुक्तनारीगर्भे । उत्कृष्टं नवलक्षा जायन्ते एकवेलायाम् ॥ ६ ॥ नवलक्षाणां मध्ये जायते एकस्य द्वयोर्वा समाप्तिः । शेषाः पुनरेवमेव च विलयं व्रजन्ति तत्रैव ॥ ७ ॥

—Some anticipation of modern sexual physiology.

II.

अथ केऽमी सप्तभङ्गाः etc.—It will be borne in mind that the discussion of the Ahiṁsâ and other texts was only by way of passing. The main point under consideration is the Doctrine of the "Seven Bhaṅgas or Modes" and the "Two Âdes'as" (See supra) to which we now revert.

एकत्र जीवादौ...सप्तभङ्गीति गीयते—See Pr. N. T. IV. 14 p. 59, Taken almost verbatim from its Commentary, Ratnâkarâvatârikâ.

"एकत्र जीवादौ etc.—" For a detailed exposition of the meaning, see further "भज्यन्ते etc....अभिहितम्" ibid pp. 59-60.

The point of the last remark in the passage above quoted will be explained in the sequel.

Saptabhangī is defined as a statement (वचनविन्यासः) in seven different ways (सप्तभिः प्रकारैः)—to be mentioned hereafter—of affirmation and negation (विधिनिषेधयोः), with the use of the word स्यात (स्याच्छब्दलाञ्छितः), singly and jointly (पृथग्भूतयोः समुदितयोश्च) without inconsistency such as that arising from conflict with प्रत्यक्ष (अविरोधेन=प्रत्यक्षादिबाधापरिहारेण), as the result of inquiry (प्रश्नवशात्) about each of the different predicates (धर्म) of a thing such as सत्त्व (existence) etc.

तद्यथा etc.—From स्यादस्त्येव सर्वम् to सप्तमः taken verbatim from Pr. N. T. III, 14 to 21:—

(1) स्यादस्त्येव सर्वम्—Statement of affirmation made singly (इति विधिकल्पनया प्रथमो भङ्गः).

(2) स्यान्नास्त्येव सर्वम्—Statement of negation made singly (इति निषेधकल्पनया द्वितीयः).

(3) स्यादस्त्येव स्यान्नास्त्येव (इति क्रमतो विधिनिषेधकल्पनया तृतीयः) Statement of affirmation and negation made conjointly, but in such a way as to avoid inconsistency which can be done by making the affirmation and the negation one after the other (क्रमतः).

(4) स्यादवक्तव्यमेव (इति युगपद् विधिनिषेधकल्पनया चतुर्थः) Statement of indescribability arising from making affirmation and negation conjointly, and also simultaneously,—thus involving a contradiction which can be got over by making the statement of indescribability.

(5) स्यादस्त्येव स्यादवक्तव्यमेव (इति पञ्चमः) Statement of affirmation and indescribability made conjointly, the latter, which arises from combining affirmation and negation simultaneously and yet without running into the absurdity of self-contradiction, being added to the former affirmation.

(6) स्यान्नास्त्येव स्यादवक्तव्यमेव (इति निषेधकल्पनया युगपद्विधिनिषेधकल्पनया च षष्ठः) Statement of negation and indescribability made conjointly, the latter, which arises from combining affirmation and negation simultaneously and yet without the absurdity of self-contradiction, being added to the former negation.

(7) स्यादस्त्येव स्यान्नास्त्येव स्यादवक्तव्यमेवेति (इति क्रमतो विधिनिषेध-कल्पनया युगपद्विधिनिषेधकल्पनया च सप्तमः) Statement of affirmation and negation made conjointly but successively, joined with that of indescribability arising from combining affirmation and negation simultaneously and yet without the absurdity of self-contradiction.

III.

Fuller Exposition.

(1) तत्र स्यात् कथंचित् etc.—From स्यात् कथंचित् to व्यवच्छेद-प्रयोजनतः taken verbatim from the Ratnākarâvatârikā except that M. omits स्यादित्ययमनेकान्तद्योतकं and inserts the prefatory तत्र.

A thing may *be* in one way, in view of its own द्रव्य (substance), क्षेत्र (place), काल (time) and भाव (nature or property); but the same may *not be*, in another way, in view of the द्रव्य, क्षेत्र, काल and भाव of another thing. Otherwise, the thing would lose its individuality, its own self. The illustration in the text is clear.

अवधारणं चात्र०—एव (=only, which expresses exclusion) means 'that, and that only,' that is, the particular statement which we wish to make and no other.

तथाप्यस्त्येव etc.—अस्ति would connote absolute, unrestricted existence, while what is meant to be conveyed is a particular existence, an existence of the thing as such and not as another thing. This is why we use the word स्यात् in stead of अस्ति. One connotes absolute, the other modal or relative existence. For it, another word is कथंचित्. In ordinary parlance, we do not use the words स्यात् or कथंचित् in every proposition, but it is always understood.

स्यात् कथंचित् etc.—A thing *is*, in its own substance, not in another's substance; *e. g.* घट is as a पार्थिव object, not as a जलीय object; that is to say, in a certain way and not in any other way. Hence कथंचित्, which is the same as स्यात्.

(2) Bhaṅga II. स्यात् कथंचित् नास्त्येव etc.—From स्यात् कथंचित् to तस्य साधनस्वाभावप्रसङ्गात् borrowed from the Ratn. iii, 16

(See also S. R.) with a few unimportant changes. स्वद्रव्यादिभिरिव परद्रव्यादिभिरपि वस्तुनोऽसत्त्वानिष्टौ.........वस्तुप्रतिनियमविरोधः......सिद्धमित्यभिधानीयम् । साधनाभासत्वप्रसङ्गात् । Ratnā. the rest being omitted by M.

The reading adopted in the Text belongs to most of the Mss. and is evidently the correct reading. For it agrees with its original of the Ratnâkarâvatârikâ and gives the sense as required by the author's exposition of the affirmation and negation as contained in the Syâdvâda doctrine. See supra note on Stanza XIV p. 165. "तत्र स्यात् कथंचित्...न पुनः परद्रव्य etc.—अन्यथेतररूपापत्त्या स्वरूपहानिप्रसङ्गः, where असत्त्व is predicated of a thing not 'स्वद्रव्यरूपेण' but 'परद्रव्यरूपेण'' which requires परद्रव्यादिभिरपि वस्तुनोऽसत्त्वानिष्टौ in the present passage. In fact, it is the very point which the critic of the स्याद्वाद often misses and which the Syâdvâdin makes out in defence of his position. Of course, it is not denied that in the Anekântavâda असत्त्व belongs to the thing itself and not to the other thing, and that is what distinguishes the Anekântavâda from Ekântavâda. But, be it noted that the असत्त्व is nowhere said to belong to the thing स्वद्रव्यरूपेण or 'स्वद्रव्यादिभिः' but only परद्रव्यरूपेण or 'परद्रव्यादिभिः'. Thus, does the Jaina Anekântavâda stand distinguished from the Buddhistic nihilism, and the Jaina may well claim that it is the only form in which the Buddhistic nihilism could justify itself to common sense.

A thing cannot be असत् 'स्वद्रव्यादिभिः' but if it is not going to be regarded as असत् even ' परद्रव्यादिभिः ', one thing would be every other thing *i. e.* anything would be anything, and there would be nothing like a thing's own nature.

न चास्तित्वैकान्तवादिभिः etc.—The necessity of recognising अस्तित्व and नास्तित्व alongside of each other (though in different capacities such as ' स्वद्रव्य ' and ' परद्रव्य ') may be thus shown: If you want to prove anything, say अनित्यत्व, by means of a साधन (हेतु), say सत्त्व, then that साधन will have to fulfil the condition of a good साधन viz. absence from the विपक्ष *e. g.* यत्र अनित्यत्वं नास्ति तत्र सत्त्वमपि नास्ति (व्यतिरेकव्याप्ति) quite as much as presence in the सपक्ष; thus involving नास्तित्व of the साधन alongside the अस्तित्व of the same, and vice versa. The doctrine of absolute अस्तित्व or नास्तित्व thus breaks down. Of course, we may wish to give prominence to one or the other, and so may mention one and remain silent about the other (अर्पितानर्पितसिद्धेः ' as Umâsvâti says Tattv. V. 31).

'अर्पितानर्पितसिद्धे':—For further explanation see the Tattvârtha Bhâṣya and the Râjavârtika (V. 31) and Ratnâ. IV. p. 61. अथ यदेव...लक्षणीयम्.

(3) तृतीयः स्पष्ट एव—See above द्वाभ्यामस्तित्व॰ etc.—From द्वाभ्यां to सामर्थ्याभावात् reproduced from the Ratnâ. on Pr. N. T. iii. 18; the rest of the passage substantially agrees with the rest of its original which is noted in the Appendix. The gist of the passage in the text is to show how अवक्तव्यत्व arises from attempting to combine simultaneously and with equal prominence the सत्त्व and the असत्त्व. There is no word in the language to do this: the word सत् will connote सत्त्व and not असत्त्व; the word असत् will connote असत्त्व and not सत्त्व. If may be asked: Is there no single word which could present both सत्त्व and असत्त्व, just as there is the single word पुष्पदन्त presenting both the sun and the moon. Answer: as a matter of fact, there is not. But supposing there were such a word, still it would present the two to the mind one after the other. Question: Does not the technical name सत् as declared in the Sûtra शतृशानयोः सत् (Pāṇ. III, ii, 27.) stand for both the शतृ and शान terminations? Answer: It does, but even then it does not present both the terminations to the mind simultaneously, but only *one after the other*. As there is no single word to express सत्त्व and असत्त्व *simultaneously* combined, so there is no Dvandva compound, nor Karmadhâraya compound, nor a sentence which could give expression to the idea of

---

* The paragraph in the Ratnâkarâvatârikâ concludes with an important piece of information that "अयं च भङ्गः कैश्चित् तृतीयभङ्गस्थाने पठ्यते तृतीयश्चैतस्य स्थाने। न चैवमपि कश्चिद्दोषः। अर्थविशेषस्याभावात्।"

simultaneous combination of सत्त्व and असत्त्व. वृत्ति=समास as in K. Pr. 'धर्मोपमानयोर्लोपे वृत्तौ वाक्ये च दृश्यते'.

न च सर्वथा etc.—This is a very important *nota bene.* The अवक्तव्यत्व here laid down is not *absolute* अवक्तव्यत्व—which would mean only अनभिधेयत्व, which is absurd—, but only अवक्तव्यत्व as an element in the Anekânta position.

शेषास्त्रयः सुगमाभिप्रायाः—The last three are explained in the Ratn. on Pr. N. T. iii. 19-20-21 : "स्वद्रव्यादिभिः etc."

न च वाच्यं एकत्र वस्तुनि etc.—As against the *seven* Bhangas, it may be urged, there will be an *infinite* number of भङ्गs about every thing in consequence of the infinite number of धर्मs which can be affirmed or denied about that thing (see also St. XIV "अनन्तधर्मात्मकमेव वस्तु—"). The answer to that objection is—Surely, if you take *all* the *infinite* number of पर्यायs or धर्मs, the number of भङ्गs will be infinite. But in respect of *each* of the पर्यायs, the भङ्ग will be *seven* only. That is the point. The passage in the Text from एकत्र वस्तुनि to संभवात् is reproduced from Pr. N. T. iii. 37-38. See Appendix.

यथा हि सदसत्त्वाभ्यां etc.—M. shows how the सप्तभङ्गी principle can be applied to धर्मs other than सत्त्व and असत्त्व also, such as सामान्य and विशेष. Of the सामान्य and the विशेष, the first may be taken as the affirmative and the latter as the negative ; if you treat the two correlatives as standing on an equal footing it may depend upon which of them is going to be made the principal and which the subordinate, the principal being presented as the affirmative and the subordinate as the negative.

प्रतिपर्यायेण etc. पत्तेरिति etc.—Reproduced from the Pr. N. T. iii, 39 to 42. See Appendix. The reason given for the number *seven* of the भङ्गs is that the पर्यनुयोगs (questions) in respect of each पर्याय are seven ; and the पर्यनुयोगs are seven because the जिज्ञासाs (curiosities) from which they spring are seven; and the जिज्ञासाs are seven because संदेहs (doubts) which give rise in them are seven ; and the संदेहs are seven because वस्तुधर्मs (characters of things) in regard to which doubts may exist are seven. See Saptabhangîtaranginî quoted in the Appendix.

इयं च सप्तभङ्गी सकलादेश etc.—The सप्तभङ्गी in respect of each of the भङ्गs is either *Synthetic* (सकलादेश०) or *Analytic* (विकलादेश०). The former refers to the entire, undivided Reality, and the latter to a fragment or aspect of the same thing. The former is, therefore, known as 'प्रमाणवाक्य' or Proposition of the Truth *i. e.* the whole Truth, while the latter is called 'नयवाक्य' or Proposition *leading* to the Truth *i. e.* the proposition of a particular view-point. (तत्र सकलादेशः प्रमाणवाक्यम्—विकलादेशो नयवाक्यम्). For the rejection of this view see Saptabhaṅgītaraṅgiṇī.

तल्लक्षणं चेदम् etc.—सकलादेश *i. e.* Statement of the entire, undivided Reality is thus defined : "प्रमाणप्रतिपन्नानन्तधर्मात्मकवस्तुनः कालादिभिः अभेदवृत्तिप्राधान्यात् अभेदोपचारात् वा यौगपद्येन प्रतिपादकं वचः सकलादेशः". The definition is taken verbatim from Pr. N. T. iii, 41, and so also its explanation कालादिभिः...सकलादेशः from Ratn. thereon. See Appendix.

The points to note in the definition are : (1) If we bring प्रमाण to bear upon the Reality before us (and be it noted that we are here dealing with Reality), we shall find that it is possessed of an infinite number of धर्मs (प्रमाणप्रतिपन्न०). (2) Now, these धर्मs can, by an act of synthesis, be united together, which is rendered possible by certain bonds of union among the धर्मs such as काल etc. (3) The synthesis may be due either to emphasis laid upon the identity of the common elements (काल etc.) or to a supposed identity of those elements in the case of all the धर्मs. (अभेदवृत्तिप्राधान्यात्—). Lastly (4) It is necessary that all the धर्मs should be viewed *together*, *simultaneously* (यौगपद्येन).

यौगपद्येन अशेषधर्मात्मकं वस्तु etc.—नयात्मकत्वात्—Reproduced from the Ratnā. (See Appendix) except the last word, which in the Ratnā. is "नयायत्तत्वात्." The points of difference between the two Ādes'as are : (1) In the former, the entire Reality is comprehended synthetically *i. e.* with all its धर्मs taken *simultaneously* ; in the latter, the Reality is treated analytically *i. e.* with its धर्मs taken *one by one*. (2) In the former, emphasis is laid on the *unity* of the object (अभेदवृत्त्या); in the latter, on the *difference* (भेदप्राधान्यात्), or the difference is superimposed upon the unity, so that the unity is lost in the difference (भेदोपचाराद्); or the unity is superimposed upon the difference, so that the difference is lost in the unity (अभेदोपचारेण). (3) सकलादेश depends upon प्रमाण *i. e.* the view of Truth or full-orbed Reality; विकलादेश on नय *i. e.* a single point of view which takes note of merely the broken lights or fragments of Reality.

कः पुनः क्रम ?...यौगपद्यम्—Taken verbatim from the Ratnā. (See Appendix). When one desires to emphasise the difference of the धर्मs such as अस्तित्व etc., in point of काल etc., he will find no single word to express the separate धर्मs, which will, therefore, have to be done by separate words, and therefore क्रम or *succession* in the use of words will be inevitable. If, however, it is not the difference of धर्मs to which attention is to be called, but their synthetic unity, one word may originally express a single धर्म but through that धर्म it will express the whole object with all its धर्मs taken *simultaneously*.

के पुनः कालादयः etc.—शब्देनाभेदवृत्तिः Now comes the much-awaited explanation of 'कालादिभिः' in the definition. This, again, is taken verbatim from the Ratnākarâvatârikâ where the manner in which अभेदवृत्ति or अभेदोपचार arises through काल (Time) etc. is thus shown :

(1) काल—Time. When we say स्याज्जीवादि वस्तु अस्त्येव (as in the first भङ्ग) we know that at the time (काल) when अस्तित्व is there, there are also numberless other qualities belonging to the object : thus, owing to the sameness of time, they may be all treated as one.

(2) आत्मरूप—Nature. That which is the nature of अस्तित्व viz. to be one of the धर्मs of the object, is also the nature of every other धर्म of the object; and so, owing to it, all the धर्मs may be treated as one.

(3) अर्थः—Substratum. That which is the substratum of अस्तित्व viz., the dravya, the same is the substratum of all the

other धर्मs; so, owing to this fact, all the धर्मs may be treated as one.

(4) संबन्ध—Relation, viz. that of identity with the object. As अस्तित्व is non-distinct from the object, so are all the other धर्मs. Thus, owing to the sameness of their relation to the object they may be all treated as one.

(5) उपकार—Influence. The influence which अस्तित्व exercises upon an object viz. to tinge it with its self, is also the influence which all the other धर्मs exercise upon that object. So, owing to the sameness of the influence, they may be all treated as one.

(6) गुणिदेश—The locality of the substance. Moreover, the locality of the substance of all the धर्मs is the same, and so, owing to it, they may be all treated as one.

(7) संसर्ग—Contact or relation. The relation which अस्तित्व bears to an object is also the relation which other धर्मs bear to it. So all the धर्मs may, owing to this fact, be treated as one.

[The distinction between संबन्ध (अविष्वग्भाव) and संसर्ग may be pointed out: The former leans towards अभेद, the latter towards भेद.]

(8) शब्द—Word. The word which denotes an object with the धर्म अस्तित्व, say घट, is the same as the word which denotes the object with the other धर्मs. So all the धर्मs may be treated as one, realising their unity in the घट.

पर्यायार्थिकनये etc.—अभेदोपचारः क्रियते. It must be carefully noted that this अभेदवृत्ति or recognition of unity is possible when emphasis is laid upon द्रव्यार्थिकनय as opposed to पर्यायार्थिकनय. The difference between the two is this: in द्रव्यार्थिकनय it is the central द्रव्य that is adverted to or kept in mind; in the पर्यायार्थिकनय, it is the पर्यायs. Now, when the द्रव्यार्थिकनय is subordinated to the पर्यायार्थिकनय, which is the same thing as saying—when the पर्यायs are considered rather than the द्रव्य, the principle of unity retires into the background, and since the पर्यायs are many, the अभेदवृत्ति (unity) in question is impossible. For, from this point of view, there cannot be many गुणs belonging to one and the same object at the same time. You will ask: Is this not contrary to our experience that many गुणs do belong to the same object at the same time? viz., Answer: No; not without creating a pro tanto breach in the unity of the object, which thus becomes really as many as the गुणs. This may be shown by a consideration of those points on which अभेदवृत्ति was shown to rest in the case of द्रव्यार्थिकनय.

(1) Take काल. The several गुणs do not belong to the same object *at the same time.* If they do, by that very act they would create a breach in the unity, and there would be as many different substrata as there were पर्यायs, and also as many moments of time characterising them. The guṇas being many, they cannot belong to the same object at the same time. If they did, they would create a breach in the unity of the object and also the time. Thus, there would be as many objects as there are पर्यायs characterising them, and these again would belong to different moments of time. So the unity of time on which the synthesis was based in the previous case (द्रव्यार्थिकनय) is not available in the present case (पर्यायार्थिकनय), and here therefore there is no possibility of अभेदवृत्ति (real synthesis).

(2) Next, take आत्मरूप. The आत्मरूपs, that is *selves*, being different, there is no possibility of the गुणs coming to unity. If they had all the same आत्मरूप, that would militate against their plurality.

(3) Similarly, the अर्थ or आधार of the several गुणs is not the same, every गुण having its own अर्थ or आधार. And so there is no possibility of अभेदवृत्ति.

(4) Moreover, the अर्थ or आधार of the several गुणs being not the same, this principle of unity is also wanting in the present case. If अर्थ or आधार of the several guṇas were the same, this would *ipso facto* make for the unity of the guṇas—which is contrary to our hypothesis of a plurality of guṇas.

(4) संबन्धs, too, are many, corresponding to the many संबन्धिन्s. For a plurality of संबन्धिन्s must involve a plurality of संबन्धs. So this principle of synthesis (unity of संबन्ध) is also wanting in the present case.

(5) Each गुण exercises its own peculiar उपकार (influence), and so there are as many उपकारs as there are गुणs (उपकारिन्s). Thus, there is no unity of उपकार to effect the required synthesis (अभेदवृत्ति).

(6) The गुणिदेशs, too, vary with the गुणs. And since they vary, this is another principle of unity which is wanting in the present case.

(7) संसर्ग, again, differs with the संसर्गिन्s. And, therefore, no unity of संसर्ग is possible in this case. So this is another principle of unity that is wanting for the synthesis.

(8) Lastly, शब्द differs with each object. All the गुणs could be expressed by a single word, one word in the language would do duty for all, and all the rest of the vocabulary would be superfluous. This is evidently absurd. Therefore, there are as many words as there are guṇas. And so the unity of word is also wanting in the present case to effect the synthesis.

तत्त्वतो etc.—Summary in the words of the Ratnakārāvatārikā with a slight variation. It means: Thus, the पर्यायs differ in काल, आत्मरूप etc., and, therefore, their unity cannot be real, but only superimposed upon their difference. The reader will now understand the reason for introducing 'अभेदोपचाराद्वा' in the definition of सकलादेश.

प्रमाणवाक्यापरपर्यायः—The सकलादेश is otherwise called प्रमाणवाक्य. See supra. Ratn. adds इति स्थितम्, and then concludes with a kârikâ giving the list of 'कालादि's. Thus :—

कालात्मरूपसंबन्धाः संसर्गोपक्रिये तथा ।
गुणिदेशार्थशब्दाश्चेत्यष्टौ कालादयः स्मृताः ॥

नयविषयीकृतस्य etc.—In this partial view of things which is called विकलादेश or नयवाक्य, भेदवृत्ति or difference is real and prominent, and even when there is अभेद, भेद is superimposed upon the अभेद, and the latter thrown into the background. With भेद comes also the succession (यौगपद्य), which characterizes the statement in a विकलादेश. Pr. N. T. has here a sûtra " तद्विपरीतस्तु विकलादेशः" (iv-45) and the definition is given in the Ratn. in the words which are reproduced in the Text.

Books of Reference.

1. Pramāṇa-naya-tattvālokālaṁkāra with Ratnākarāvatārikā.
2. Saptabhaṅgîtaraṅginî.
3. Prof. S. C. Chakravartin's Introduction to his edition of the Pañcastikāya.
4. " An Epitome of Jainism " by Messrs. Nahar and Ghosh Chs. VIII and IX.

Appendices.

I. एकत्र वस्तुन्येकैकधर्मपर्यनुयोगवशादविरोधेन व्यस्तयोः समस्तयोश्च विधिनिषेधयोः कल्पनया स्यात्काराङ्कितः सप्तधा वाक्प्रयोगः सप्तभङ्गी ।

एकत्र जीवादौ वस्तुन्येकैकसत्त्वादिधर्मविषयप्रश्नवशादविरोधेन प्रतिपक्षादिबाधापरिहारेण पृथग्भूतयोः समुदितयोश्च विधिनिषेधयोः पर्यालोचनया कृत्वा स्याच्छब्दलाञ्छितो वक्ष्यमाणैः सप्तभिः प्रकारैर्वचनविन्यासः सप्तभङ्गी विज्ञेयः । भज्यन्ते भिद्यन्तेऽर्था यैस्ते भङ्गा वचनप्रकारास्ततः सप्तभङ्गाः समाहृताः सप्तभङ्गीति कथ्यते । नानावस्त्वाश्रयविधिनिषेधकल्पनया शतभङ्गीप्रसङ्गनिवर्तनार्थमेकत्र वस्तुनीत्युपन्यस्तम् । एकत्रापि जीवादिवस्तुनि विधीयमाननिषिध्यमानानन्तधर्मपर्यालोचनयाऽनन्तभङ्गीप्रसक्तिव्यावर्तनार्थमेकैकधर्मपर्यनुयोगवशादित्युपात्तम् । अनन्तेष्वपि हि धर्मेषु प्रतिधर्मं पर्यनुयोगस्य सप्तधैव प्रवर्तमानत्वात् । तत्प्रतिवचनस्यापि सप्तविधत्वमेवोपपन्नमित्येकैकस्मिन् धर्मे एकैकैव सप्तभङ्गी साधीयसी । एवं चानन्तधर्मापेक्षया सप्तभङ्गीनामानन्त्यं यदायाति तदभिमतमेव । प्रत्यक्षादिविरुद्धसदाद्येकान्तविधिप्रतिषेधकल्पनयाऽपि प्रवृत्तस्य वचनप्रयोगस्य सप्तभङ्गीत्वानुषङ्गभङ्गार्थयमविरोधेनेत्यभिहितम् । अवोचाम च—

या प्रश्नाद्विधिपर्युदासभिदया बाधच्युता सप्तधा
धर्मं धर्ममपेक्ष्य वाक्यरचनाऽनेकात्मके वस्तुनि ।
निर्दोषा निरदेशि देव ! भवता सा सप्तभङ्गी यया
जल्पन् जल्परणाङ्गणे विजयते वादी विपक्षं क्षणात् ॥

इदं च सप्तभङ्गीलक्षणं प्रमाणनयसप्तभङ्ग्योः साधारणमवधारणीयम्। विशेषलक्षणं पुनरनयोरग्रे वक्ष्यते।

स्यादस्त्येव सर्वमिति विधिकल्पनया प्रथमो भङ्गः—

स्यादित्यव्ययमनेकान्तावद्योतकम्। स्यात् कथंचित् स्वद्रव्यक्षेत्रकालभावरूपेणास्त्येव सर्वं कुम्भादि, न पुनः परद्रव्यक्षेत्रकालभावरूपेण। तथाहि—कुम्भो द्रव्यतः पार्थिवत्वेनास्ति, न जलादिरूपत्वेन; क्षेत्रतः पाटलिपुत्रकत्वेन, न कान्यकुब्जत्वेन; कालतः शैशिरत्वेन, न वासन्तिकादित्वेन; भावतः श्यामत्वेन, न रक्तत्वादिना। अन्यथेतररूपापत्त्या स्वरूपहानिप्रसङ्ग इति। अवधारणं चात्र भङ्गोऽनभिमतार्थव्यावृत्त्यर्थमुपात्तम्। इतरथाऽनभिहिततुल्यतैवास्य वाक्यस्य प्रसज्येत, प्रतिनियतस्वार्थाभिधानात्। तदुक्तम्—

वाक्येऽवधारणं तावदनिष्टार्थनिवृत्तये।
कर्तव्यमन्यथाऽनुक्त समत्वात् तस्यकुत्रचित्॥

तथाप्यस्त्येव कुम्भ इत्येतावन्मात्रोपादाने कुम्भस्य स्तम्भाद्यस्तितनापि सर्वप्रकारेणास्तित्वप्राप्तेः प्रतिनियतस्वरूपानुपपत्तिः, स्यात् तत्प्रतिपत्तये स्यादिति प्रयुज्यते स्यात्, कथंचित् स्वद्रव्यादिभिरेवायमस्ति, न परद्रव्यादिभिरपीत्यर्थः। यत्रापि चासौ न प्रयुज्यते तत्रापि व्यवच्छेदफलैवकारवद् बुद्धिमद्भिः प्रतीयत एव। यदुक्तम्—

सोऽप्रयुक्तोऽपि वा तज्ज्ञैः सर्वत्रार्थात् प्रतीयते।
यथैवकारो योगादिव्यवच्छेदप्रयोजनः॥

अथ द्वितीयभङ्गोल्लेखं ख्यापयन्ति—

स्यान्नास्त्येव सर्वमितिनिषेधकल्पनया द्वितीयः॥ स्वद्रव्यादिभिरिव परद्रव्यादिभिरपि वस्तुनोऽसत्त्वानिष्टौ हि प्रतिनियतस्वरूपाभावाद्वस्तुप्रतिनियमविरोधः। न चास्तित्वैकान्तवादिभिरत्र नास्तित्व मसिद्धमित्यभिधानीयम्। कथंचित् तस्य वस्तुनि युक्तिसिद्धत्वात् साधनवत्। न हि क्वचिदनित्यत्वादौ साध्ये सत्त्वादिसाधनस्यास्तित्वं विपक्षे नास्तित्वमन्तरेणोपपन्नम्; तस्य साधनाभासत्वप्रसङ्गात्। अथ यदेव नियतं साध्यसद्भावेऽस्तित्वं तदेव साध्याभावे साधनस्य नास्तित्वमभिधीयते तत्कथं प्रतिषेध्यम्? स्वरूपस्य प्रतिषेधत्वानुपपत्तेः, साध्यसद्भावे नास्तित्वं तु यत्तत्प्रतिषेध्यम् तेनाविनाभावित्वे साध्यसद्भावास्तित्वस्य व्याघातात्तेनैव स्वरूपेणास्ति नास्ति चेति प्रतीत्यभावादिति चेत्, तदसत्। एवं हेतोस्त्रिरूपत्वविरोधात् विपक्षासत्त्वस्य तात्त्विकस्याभावात्। यदि चायं भावाभावयोरेकत्वमाचक्षीत तदा सर्वथा न क्वचित् प्रवर्तेत नापि कुतश्चिन्निवर्तेत। प्रवृत्तिनिवृत्तिविषयस्य भावस्याभावपरिहारेणासंभवात्, अभावस्य च भावपरिहारेणेति वस्तुनोऽस्तित्वनास्तित्वयो रूपान्तरत्वमेष्टव्यम्। तथा चास्तित्वं नास्तित्वेन प्रतिषेध्येनाविनाभावि सिद्धम्। यथा च प्रतिषेध्य मस्तित्वस्य नास्तित्वं तथा प्रधानभावतः क्रमार्पितोभयत्वादिधर्मपञ्चकमपि वक्ष्यमाणं लक्षणीयम्॥

अथ तृतीयं भङ्गमुल्लेखतो व्यक्तीकुर्वन्ति—

स्यादस्त्येव स्यान्नास्त्येवेति क्रमतो विधिनिषेधकल्पनया तृतीयः ॥

सर्वमिति पूर्वसूत्रादिहोत्तरत्र चानुवर्तनीयम्। ततोऽयमर्थः। क्रमार्पितस्वपरद्रव्यादिचतुष्टयापेक्षया क्रमार्पिताभ्यामस्तित्वनास्तित्वाभ्यां विशेषितं सर्वं कुम्भादि वस्तु स्यादस्त्येव स्यान्नास्त्येवेत्युल्लेखेन वक्तव्यमिति ॥

इदानीं चतुर्थभङ्गोल्लेखमाविर्भावयन्ति—

स्यादवक्तव्यमेवेति युगपद्विधिनिषेधकल्पनया चतुर्थः ॥

द्वाभ्यामस्तित्वनास्तित्वाख्यधर्माभ्यां युगपत्प्रधानतयाऽर्पिताभ्यामेकस्य वस्तुनोऽभिधित्सायां तादृशस्य शब्दस्यासंभवादवक्तव्यं जीवादि वस्त्विति। तथाहि—सदसत्त्वगुणद्वयं युगपदेकत्र सदित्यभिधानेन वक्तुमशक्यम्। तस्यासत्त्वप्रतिपादनासमर्थत्वात्। तथैवासदित्यभिधानेन न तद्वक्तुं शक्यम्। तस्य सत्त्वप्रत्यायने सामर्थ्याभावात्। सांकेतिकमेकं पदं तदभिधातुं समर्थमित्यपि न सत्यम्। तस्यापि क्रमेणार्थद्वयप्रत्यायने सामर्थ्योपपत्तेः। शतृशानचौ सदिति शतृशानचोः संकेतितसच्छब्दवत्। द्वन्द्ववृत्तिपदं तयोः सकृदभिधायकमित्यनेनापास्तम्। सदसत्त्वे इत्यादि पदस्य क्रमेण धर्मद्वयप्रत्यायने समर्थत्वात्। कर्मधारयादिवृत्तिपदमपि न तयोरभिधायकं तत एव वाक्यं तयोरभिधायकमनेनैवापास्तमिति सकलवाचकरहितत्वादवक्तव्यं वस्तु युगपत् सदसत्त्वाभ्यां प्रधानभावार्पिताभ्यामाक्रान्तं व्यवतिष्ठते। अयं च भङ्गः कैश्चित्तृतीयभङ्गस्थाने पठ्यते तृतीयश्चैतस्य स्थाने। न चैवमपि कश्चिद्दोषः। अर्थविशेषस्याभावात् ॥

अथ पञ्चमभङ्गोल्लेखमुपदर्शयन्ति, स्यादस्त्येव स्यादवक्तव्यमेवेति विधिकल्पनया युगपद्विधिनिषेधकल्पनया च पञ्चमः ॥ स्वद्रव्यादिचतुष्टयापेक्षयाऽस्तित्वे सत्यस्तित्वनास्तित्वाभ्यां सह वक्तुमशक्यं सर्वं वस्तु। ततः स्यादस्त्येव स्यादवक्तव्यमेवेत्येवं पञ्चमभङ्गेनोपदर्श्यत इति ॥

अथ षष्ठभङ्गोल्लेखं प्रकटयन्ति—स्यान्नास्त्येव स्यादवक्तव्यमेवेति निषेधकल्पनया युगपद्विधिनिषेधकल्पनया च षष्ठः। परद्रव्यादिचतुष्टयापेक्षया नास्तित्वे सत्यस्तित्वनास्तित्वाभ्यां यौगपद्येन प्रतिपादयितुमशक्यं समस्तं वस्तु। ततः स्यान्नास्त्येव स्यादवक्तव्यमेवेत्येवं षष्ठभङ्गेन प्रकाश्यते ॥

संप्रति सप्तमभङ्गमुल्लिखन्ति—स्यादस्त्येव स्यान्नास्त्येव स्यादवक्तव्यमेवेति क्रमतो विधिनिषेधकल्पनया युगपद्विधिनिषेधकल्पनया च सप्तम इति ॥

इतिशब्दः सप्तभङ्गीसमाप्त्यर्थः। स्वपरद्रव्यादिचतुष्टयापेक्षयाऽस्तित्वनास्तित्वयोः सतोरस्तित्वनास्तित्वाभ्यां समसमयमभिधातुमशक्यमखिलं वस्तु तत एवमनेन भङ्गेनोपदर्श्यते ॥ —P. N. Tattvālokalaṁkāra, and Ratnâkarâvatârikâ Ch. IV.

II. कथंचित् ते सदेवेष्टं कथंचिदसदेव तत् ।
तथोभयमवाच्यं च नययोगान्न सर्वथा ॥
क्रमार्पितद्वयाद्द्वैतं सहावाच्यमशक्तितः ।
अवक्तव्योत्तराः शेषास्त्रयो भङ्गाः स्वहेतुतः ॥

(१) विधिकल्पना, (२) प्रतिषेधकल्पना, (३) क्रमतो विधिप्रतिषेधकल्पना (४) सहविधिप्रतिषेधकल्पना च, (५) विधिकल्पना-सहविधिप्रतिषेधकल्पना च (६) प्रतिषेधकल्पना-सहविधिप्रतिषेधकल्पना च (७) क्रमाक्रमाभ्यां विधिप्रतिषेधकल्पना च— —Âptamîmaṁsâ with Com.

III. (a) "स्यादस्त्येव घटः (१), स्यान्नास्त्येव घटः (२), स्यादस्ति नास्ति च घटः (३), स्यादवक्तव्य एव (४), स्यादस्ति चावक्तव्यश्च (५), स्यान्नास्ति चावक्तव्यश्च (६) स्यादस्ति च नास्ति चावक्तव्यश्च"—इति एतत्सप्तवाक्यसमुदायः सप्तभङ्गीति कथ्यते । तल्लक्षणं तु प्राश्निकप्रश्नज्ञानप्रयोज्यत्वे सति एकवस्तुविशेष्यकाविरुद्धविधिप्रतिषेधात्मकधर्मप्रकारकबोधजनकसप्तवाक्यपर्याप्तसमुदायत्वम् ।............... । तदिदमाहुरभियुक्ताः "प्रश्नवशादेकत्र वस्तुन्यविरोधेन विधिप्रतिषेधकल्पना सप्तभङ्गी" इति ।......

(b) यद्यपि सत्यन्तनिवेशस्यातिव्याप्त्यव्याप्त्यादिदोषवारकत्वं न संभवति, तथापि प्रतिपाद्यप्रश्नानां सप्तविधानामेव सद्भावात् सप्तैव भङ्गा इति नियमसूचनाय तन्निवेशनम् । ननु प्रश्नानां सप्तविधत्वं कथमिति चेत्, जिज्ञासानां सप्तविधत्वात् । प्राश्निकनिष्ठजिज्ञासाप्रतिपादकवाक्यं हि प्रश्न इत्युच्यते ॥ ननु सप्तधैव जिज्ञासा कुत इति चेत् सप्तधा संशयानामुत्पत्तेः । संशयानां सप्तविधत्वं तु तद्विषयीभूतधर्माणां सप्तविधत्वात् । तादृशधर्माश्च--कथंचित् सत्त्वं, कथंचिदसत्त्वं क्रमार्पितोभयं, अवक्तव्यत्वं, कथंचित् सत्त्वविशिष्टावक्तव्यत्वं, क्रमार्पितोभयविशिष्टावक्तव्यत्वं चेति सप्तैव । एवं च दर्शितधर्मविषयकाः सप्तैव संशयाः ।...... ......इत्युक्तप्रणाल्या धर्मसप्तविधत्वाधीनं भङ्गानां सप्तविधत्वमिति बोधयितुं सत्यन्तनिवेश इति ध्येयम् । तदुक्तम्—

भङ्गाः सत्त्वादयः सप्त संशयाः सप्त तद्गताः ।
जिज्ञासाः सप्त सप्त स्युः प्रश्नाः सप्तोत्तराण्यपि ॥

(c) प्रथमे भङ्गे सत्त्वस्य प्रधानभावेन प्रतीतिः, द्वितीये पुनरसत्त्वस्य, तृतीये क्रमार्पितयोः सत्त्वासत्त्वयोः, चतुर्थे त्ववक्तव्यत्वस्य, पञ्चमे सत्त्वविशिष्टावक्तव्यत्वस्य, षष्ठे चासत्त्वविशिष्टावक्तव्यत्वस्य, सप्तमे क्रमार्पितसत्त्वासत्त्वविशिष्टावक्तव्यत्वस्येति विवेकः । **प्रथमभङ्गादावसत्त्वादीनां गुणभावमात्रं न तु प्रतिषेधः ।**

(d) इयं च सप्तभङ्गी द्विविधा—प्रमाणसप्तभङ्गी नयसप्तभङ्गी चेति । किं पुनः प्रमाणवाक्यम् । किंवा नयवाक्यमिति चेत्, अत्र केचित्—**सकलादेशः प्रमाणवाक्यं विकलादेशो नयवाक्यम् ।** अनेकधर्मात्मकवस्तुविषयक-

बोधजनकवाक्यत्वं सकलादेशत्वं, एकधर्मात्मकवस्तुविषयकबोधजनकवाक्यत्वं विकलादेशत्वम्—इत्याहुः। तेषां प्रमाणवाक्यानां नयवाक्यानां च सप्तविधत्वव्याघातः। प्रथमद्वितीयचतुर्थभङ्गानां सत्त्वासत्त्वावक्तव्यत्वरूपैकैकधर्मात्मकवस्तुविषयकबोधजनकानां सर्वथा विकलादेशत्वेन नयवाक्यत्वापत्तेः। तृतीयपञ्चमषष्ठसप्तमानामेकधर्मात्मकवस्तुविषयकबोधजनकानां सदा सकलादेशत्वेन प्रमाणवाक्यतापत्तेः। न च त्रीण्येव नयवाक्यानि चत्वार्येव प्रमाणवाक्यानीति वक्तुं युक्तम्। सिद्धान्तविरोधात्॥ यत्तु धर्मविषयकबोधजनकवाक्यत्वं सकलादेशत्वं, धर्म्यविषयकधर्मविषयकबोधजनकवाक्यत्वं विकलादेशत्वमिति। तन्न। सत्त्वाद्यन्यतमेनापि धर्मेणाविशेषितस्य धर्मिणः शाब्दबोधविषयत्वासंभवात्। धर्मिवृत्तित्वाविशेषितस्य धर्मस्यापि तथात्वादुक्तलक्षणस्यासंभवात्। न च स्याज्जीव एवेत्यनेन धर्मिमात्रविषयकबोधस्य जननात् स्यादस्त्येवेत्यनेन केवलधर्मविषयकबोधस्य जननाच्च नासंभव इति वाच्यम्। यतो जीवशब्देन जीवत्वरूपधर्मावच्छिन्नस्यैव जीवस्याभिधानं न तु केवलधर्मिणः, अस्तिशब्देन च यत्किंचिद्धर्मिवृत्तित्वविशेषितस्यैवास्तित्वस्याभिधानं न तु केवलधर्मस्येति सर्वानुभवसाक्षिकम्॥........

अपरे तु स्यादस्तीत्यादि वाक्यं सप्तविधमपि प्रत्येकं विकलादेशः, समुदितं सकलादेशः इति वदन्ति। अत्र चिन्त्यते। कुतः स्यादस्तीत्यादिवाक्यं प्रत्येकं विकलादेशः?। ननु सकलार्थप्रतिपादकत्वाभावाद्विकलादेश इति चेन्न। तादृशवाक्यसप्तकस्यापि विकलादेशत्वापत्तेः। समुदितस्यापि सदादिवाक्यसप्तकस्य सकलार्थप्रतिपादकत्वाभावात्। सकलश्रुतस्यैव सकलार्थप्रतिपादकत्वात्। एतेन सकलार्थप्रतिपादकत्वात् सप्तभङ्गीवाक्यं समुदितं सकलादेश इति निरस्तम्। समुदितस्यापि तस्य सकलार्थप्रतिपादकत्वासिद्धेः। सदादिसप्तवाक्येन एकानेकादिसप्तवाक्यप्रतिपाद्यधर्माणामप्रतिपादनात्। सिद्धान्तविदस्तु एकधर्मबोधनमुखेन तदात्मकानेकाशेषधर्मात्मकवस्तुविषयकबोधजनकवाक्यत्वं सकलादेशत्वम्। तदुक्तम्—'एकगुणमुखेनाशेषवस्तुरूपसंग्रहात् सकलादेश' इति। तस्यार्थः—यदा अभिन्नं वस्तु एकगुणरूपेणोच्यते गुणिनां गुणमन्तरेण विशेषप्रतिपत्तेरसंभवात् तदा सकलादेशः। एको हि जीवोऽस्तित्वादिष्वेकस्य गुणमन्तरेण विशेषप्रतिपत्तेरसंभवात् तदा सकलादेशः। एको हि जीवोऽस्तित्वादिष्वेकस्य गुणस्य रूपेण अभेदवृत्त्या अभेदोपचारेण वा निरंशः समस्तो वक्तुमिष्यते विभागनिमित्तस्य तत्प्रतियोगिनो गुणान्तरस्याविवक्षितत्वात्। कथमभेदवृत्तिः कथं चाभेदोपचार इति चेत् द्रव्यार्थत्वेनाश्रयणे तदव्यतिरेकादभेदवृत्तिः पर्यायार्थत्वेनाश्रयणे परस्परव्यतिरेकेऽप्येकत्वाध्यारोपादभेदोपचार इति। अभेदवृत्त्यभेदोपचारयोरनाश्रयणे एकधर्मात्मकवस्तुविषयबोधजनकं वाक्यं विकलादेश इति प्राहुः॥

(६) तत्र स्वरूपादिभिरस्तित्वमिव नास्तित्वमपि स्यादित्यनिष्टार्थस्य निवृत्तये स्यादस्त्येवेत्येवकारः। तेन च स्वरूपादिभिरस्तित्वमेव न नास्तित्वमित्यवधार्यते। तदुक्तम्—

वाक्येवधारणं तावदनिष्टार्थनिवृत्तये ।
कर्तव्यमन्यथानुक्तसमत्वात् तस्य कुत्रचित् ॥

Saptabhangī-taranginī pp. 2-21.

IV. एकत्र वस्तुनि विधीयमाननिषिध्यमानानन्तधर्माभ्युगमेनानन्तभङ्गीप्रसङ्गादसंगतैव सप्तभङ्गीति न चेतसि निधेयम् । विधिनिषेधप्रकाशापेक्षया प्रतिपर्यायं वस्तुन्यनन्तानामपि सप्तभङ्गीनामेव संभवात् । प्रतिपर्यायं प्रतिपाद्यपर्यनुयोगानां सप्तानामेव संभवात् । तेषामपि सप्तत्वं सप्तविधतज्जिज्ञासानियमात् । तस्या अपि सप्तविधत्वं सप्तधैव तत्संदेहसमुत्पादात् । तस्यापि सप्तप्रकारत्वनियमः स्वगोचरवस्तुधर्माणां सप्तविधत्वस्यैवोपपत्तेः ॥ इयं सप्तभङ्गी प्रतिभङ्गं सकलादेशस्वभावा विकलादेशस्वभावा च । प्रमाणप्रतिपन्नानन्तधर्मात्मकवस्तुनः कालादिभिरभेदवृत्तिप्राधान्यादभेदोपचाराद्वा यौगपद्येन प्रतिपादकं वचः सकलादेशः । तद्विपरीतस्तु विकलादेशः ॥

P. N. Tattvâlokâlaṁkâra Ch. IV, Sutra 37-45.

Stanza XXIV.

Next, the author shows how the Syâdvâda is sound, notwithstanding that it predicates such mutually contradictory concepts as सत्त्व and असत्त्व and अवक्तव्यत्व of one and the same subject. His explanation is that the different predicates refer to different aspects of the same subject (उपाधिभेद) and therefore the so-called contradiction is really no contradiction at all.

सदवाच्यते च—The 'ता' termination to be construed with सत् and अवाच्य. Therefore सदवाच्यते=सत्ता and अवाच्यता=अस्तित्व and अवक्तव्यत्व.

तथाहि—The supposed contradiction is, first, that which exists between अस्तित्व and नास्तित्व (अस्तित्वं नास्तित्वेन सह); secondly, that between विधि and निषेध, that is, affirmation and denial of the same predicate of the same subject—such as अस्ति and नास्ति —in which consists the अवक्तव्यत्व ('अवक्तव्यत्वमपि विधिनिषेधात्मकमन्योन्यं'); thirdly, that between अवक्तव्यत्व and वक्तव्यत्व-the वक्तव्यत्व which is necessarily implied in the very statement of Syâdvâda —स्यादस्ति etc. ('अथवा अवक्तव्यत्वं वक्तव्यत्वेन साकम्').

अनेन च नास्तित्वा etc.—Of the seven भङ्गीs *i. e.* forms or constituent propositions of the Syâdvâda, स्यादस्ति, स्यान्नास्ति and स्यादवक्तव्यः are the *three primary* भङ्गs; the rest are derived by compounding two or more of these three :

नन्वेते धर्माः परस्परं विरुद्धाः etc.—विशेषणद्वारेण—'उपाधिभेदोपहितं' is a हेतुगर्भविशेषण *i. e.* an adjective which constitutes the reason for the statement that the Syâdvâda involves no contradiction. The reason is that no predicate is affirmed or denied of the subject absolutely, but only under definite limiting conditions which thus provide the different standpoints from which the same subject may be viewed.

अयमभिप्रायः etc.—The test of contradiction is this: Do the two things *exclude* each other—as do शीत and उष्ण (cold and hot) which never subsist together? Applying this test, we do *not* find that सत्त्व and असत्त्व are contradictory. The सत्त्व in a घट does not exclude असत्त्व in that घट; if it did, we could not say घट *is not* पट, wherein we do predicate असत्त्व ('is not') of the same घट. But the fact is that the घट *exists* (सत्त्व) in *itself* and does *not exist* (असत्त्व) as *other-than-itself*—सत्त्व (existence) being predicated of it from one standpoint and असत्त्व (non-existence) from the other (that of things other than itself); and neither of them *absolutely*, without reference to definite aspects such as स्व-रूप and पर-रूप. The घट would not only exist as itself but as *everything*, even as things other than itself (पररूपेणापि) if existence were *absolutely* predicable of it; and in that case, no पट, प्रासाद etc. would be needed, घट being everything !

न चासत्त्वं etc.—If, on the other hand, you lay hold of the negative predicate (असत्त्व), as in घट *is not* पट, and regard it as *absolute*, the thing itself would be *nothing*, everything would be nothing, all a universal void ! But the fact is, you cannot regard it as absolute, the negation in the present case being only from the standpoint of its relation with other things ('पररूपेण'). See Dravyânuyoga xi, 13-14.

इदं लोकस्मिन् etc.—The view of the Naiyâyika on this point is different from both. He does not hold that the two colours belong to the two parts of the पट and there the story ends. Nor does he hold that contradictory as they are they belong to the same पट in its different aspects viz. the two parts. But he holds that the two colours produce *one* चित्ररूप and the latter belongs to the one—whole—पट, while the former belongs to the parts. See Tarka Saṁgraha Dīpikā p. 11.

तदा विरोधः स्याद् etc.—Cf. Ratnâk. p. 85. on P. N. T. iii. 8.

It should be noted that the Jaina doctrine of "Syâd-vâda" is not a statement of the absolute identity of Being and Non-Being, but only a statement of their relation to the same subject from *different viewpoints*. Thus, a thing *is* from one viewpoint viz. from the viewpoint of *itself*, and *is not* from another viewpoint, viz. the viewpoint of things *other-than-itself*. Mark that according to this explanation Being and non-Being are not implicitly contained in each other and so reconcileable—as in Hegel's system—, but are to be referred to different aspects of the thing, and so there is no contradiction whatsoever. According to the Syâdvâda, the contradiction is not a fact transcending or confounding the laws of logic, that is to say, a fact which because it is a fact has somehow to be accepted whatever the difficulties of thought—as is done in the *Anirvacanīyatâvâda* of the S'āṁkara school—; it is a fact perfectly amenable to the laws of logic, a fact which logic easily succeeds in showing to be no contradiction at all, inasmuch as the supposed contradictory elements refer to two different aspects of the same reality. Cf. तदा विरोधः स्यात्. (Text) Cf. नन्वत्र विरोधः Ratnâk. Pari. V pp. 85-86. Mark three points in the Jaina doctrine: (1) The Jaina does not hold that Being and Non-Being are *absolutely* the same "न खलु......" Ratn. iii. 8. p. 86. (2) Nor does he hold that Non-Being exists as inseparable from Being (ibid p. 86). (3) What he holds is that Being and Non-Being are predicable of the same subject. Cf. ननु अस्तित्वमेव etc. —Saptabhaṅgî-taraṅgiṇî, pp. 52-54, pp. 86-87.

The Jaina doctrine is illustrated in the text by the example of a 'मेचकरत्न' (many-coloured gem) and a 'चित्रपट' (a multicoloured piece of cloth) which may be at once red and black, red in one part and black in the other. Here both the colours are in the same पट even though in different parts of it. If you say that here a certain part is red and a certain other part is black, and so the two colours are not predicated of one and the same thing ('सत्त्वासत्त्वयोर्भिन्नदेशत्वप्राप्तिः'), it will be easy to reply that they are so predicated ('तत्रापि भिन्नदेशत्वासिद्धेः'), although with reference to particular parts *i. e.* कथंचित्, *somehow*, with reference to this part or that. If you think that this is only an ingenious escape from a difficult position and that the colours after all belong to different things (पटावयवs) and not to the same thing (चित्रपट) in its different aspects (पटावयवs),‡ we shall give you another illustration which is not open to any such objection. It is the illustration of *one man* bearing such mutually contradictory predicates as father, son, uncle, nephew etc., which are perfectly reconcileable in so far as they refer to different relationships of the same man. Cf. "अस्तित्वनास्तित्वयोरवच्छेदकभेदेनाप्यर्थमाणयोर्विरोधाभावात्। यथा—एकस्यैव देवदत्तस्यैकापेक्षया पितृत्वमन्यापेक्षया पुत्रत्वं च परस्परमविरुद्धम्—" Sapta. p.81. Cf. S'âṁkara Bhâṣya on Brahma Sûtra. II. i. 14.

Moreover the स्वरूप and the पररूप of a thing may refer to the द्रव्य, क्षेत्र, काल or स्वभाव of that thing. See Sapta. pp. 43–45.

तदेकान्तहताः—Struck down or confounded by their one-sided dogmatism. पतन्ति—lie low on the ground where they are liable to be trampled upon by every passer-by on the road.

पतन्ति—(1) err ; or, (2) fall down speechless like a man who has met with an accident on the road.

---

‡As to what one should take as the स्वरूप and the पररूप of a thing such as घट, different views are noticed in the Saptabhaṅgî-taraṅgiṇî, pp. 39 to 43; also in the Râjavârtika. pp. 24–26.

अत्र च विरोधस्यो० etc.—The charge expressly laid against the Syâdvâda and answered in the Stanza is that of विरोध or contradiction. It stands however for a host of other faults also ('उपलक्षणत्वात्') viz.—(2) वैयधिकरण्य, (3) अनवस्था, (4) संकर, (5) व्यतिकर, (6) संशय, (7) अप्रतिपत्ति, (8) विषयव्यवस्थाहानिः each of which is explained and answered in the sequel. (See Saptabhaṅgî-Taraṅgiṇî pp. 81–82).

वैयधिकरण्य–Dislocation, absence of a common abode : सामान्य and विशेष–one positive and the other negative in character—are opposed to each other and cannot have a common abode or location, any more than heat and cold which never subsist together. You will perhaps explain that in a certain aspect a thing is an abode of सामान्य, and in another aspect it is an abode of विशेष. But, then, we are entitled to ask : Is this done by a single nature of the thing, or has that thing two natures corresponding to the two aspects? In the former case, the difficulty of वैयधिकरण्य remains status quo. In the latter, if two natures are required for the two aspects, two again will be required for each of the two natures, and so on ad infinitum. This is the अनवस्था mentioned above as fault No. 3.

Moreover, there is संकर or confusion–fault No. 4—Thus : That nature by which the thing becomes an abode of सामान्य, by it it becomes an abode of both सामान्य and विशेष–which is absurd, for the reason that it involves संकर or confusion between सामान्य and विशेष, in a common abode. (" सर्वेषां युगपत्प्राप्तिः संकरः " S. T.).

Next there is the fault of व्यतिकर or exchange of natures. Thus: by that very nature by which a thing is the abode of सामान्य, it would be the abode of विशेष also, and vice versa. This, however, is absurd, since सामान्य and विशेष would in that exchange their natures and take each other's place. (परस्पर-विषयगमनं व्यतिकरः S. T.),

Next there is the fault of संशय (No. 6)—doubt arising from the difficulty of ascertaining the exact nature of a thing in regard to सामान्य and विशेष. And from the same arises अप्रतिपत्ति (No. 7) or failure to understand the position, thus throwing the whole science of logic into confusion विषयव्यवस्थाहानिः (No. 8).

The reader, if the carefnlly compares the explanation of संकर and व्यतिकर here given with those given in the Syâdvâda-taraṅgiṇî, he will perceive some slight difference.

All these faults fail to apply to स्याद्वाद which is a philosophy of a different kind altogether. For, the सामान्य and विशेष in Jaina philosophy are not independent concepts as in Nyâya and other systems. The word 'विरोध' in the stanza may primarily signify the particular दोष called 'विरोध' in the narrow sense of the term and then indicate by way of उपलक्षण the rest of the series of दोषs beginning with वैयधिकरण्य. Or, the word may be taken in the general sense of दोष, and may thus include the whole group of दोषs viz. विरोध, वैयधिकरण्य etc. For a full answer to the objections see Sapta-bhaṅgî-taraṅgiṇî pp. 81–82.

अतः स्याद्वाद etc.—For further elucidation of विरोध and its kindred दोषs vide the excerpts given in the Appendix from the Saptabhangî-taraṅgiṇî pp. 87-88.

Books of reference :

1. Âptamîmaṁsâ and Aṣṭasahasrî.
2. Saptabhaṅgî-taraṅgiṇî.
3. Râja–Vârtika with Commentary.
4. Ratnâkarâvatârikâ on Pr. N. T.
5. Guṇaratna's Com. on Ṣaḍdars'ana-samuccaya.
6. Anekântajayapatâkâ.

Appendices

1. प्रश्नवशादेकस्मिन् वस्तुनि अविरोधेन विधिप्रतिषेधकल्पना सप्तभङ्गी। अनेकान्ते तदभावादव्याप्तिरिति चेन्न, तत्रापि तदुपपत्तेः। छलमात्रमनेकान्त

इति चेन्न, छललक्षणाभावात्। संशयहेतुरिति चेन्न, विशेषलक्षणोपलब्धेः। विरोधाभावात् संशयाभावः। अर्पणाभेदादविरोधः पितृपुत्रादिसंबन्धवत्।

Râja-Vârtika pp. 24-26.

2. एवं घटस्य स्वद्रव्यं मृद्द्रव्यं, परद्रव्यं सुवर्णादि। घटो मृदात्मनास्ति, सुवर्णाद्यात्मना नास्ति। घटस्य स्वद्रव्यात्मनेव परद्रव्यात्मनाऽपि सत्त्वे घटो मृदात्मको न सुवर्णात्मक इति नियमो न स्यात् तथा च द्रव्यप्रतिनियमविरोधः।...... एवं घटस्य स्वक्षेत्रं भूतलादि, परक्षेत्रं कुड्यादि। घटः स्वक्षेत्रेऽस्ति, परक्षेत्रे नास्ति। घटस्य स्वक्षेत्र इव परक्षेत्रेऽपि सत्त्वे प्रतिनियतक्षेत्रत्वानुपपत्तिः। परक्षेत्र इव स्वक्षेत्रेऽप्यसत्त्वे च निराधारत्वापत्तिः। तथा घटस्य स्वकालो वर्तमानकालः, परकालोऽतीतादिः। तत्र स्वकालेऽस्ति परकाले नास्ति। घटस्य स्वकाल इव परकालेऽपि सत्त्वे प्रतिनियतकालत्वाभावेन नित्यत्वमेव स्यात्। परकाल इव स्वकालेऽप्यसत्त्वे सकलकालासंबन्धित्वेनावस्तुत्वापत्तिः। कालसंबन्धित्वमेव हि वस्तुत्वम्। एवं च घटो घटत्वेनास्ति, पटत्वेन नास्ति। मृद्द्रव्येणास्ति, सुवर्णद्रव्येण नास्ति। स्वक्षेत्रादस्ति, परक्षेत्रान्नास्ति। स्वकालादस्ति, परकालान्नास्तीति पर्यवसन्नम्।—Sapta. pp. 43-45.

3. ननु अस्तित्वमेव वस्तुनः स्वरूपं, न पुनर्नास्तित्वम्। तस्य पररूपाश्रयत्वात्। यदि च पररूपाश्रितमपि नास्तित्वं वस्तुनः स्वरूपं, तदा पटगतरूपादिकमपि घटस्य स्वरूपं स्यात्। इति चेन्न। उभयस्यापि स्वरूपत्वे प्रमाणसद्भावात्। तथाहि—घटस्य स्वरूपाद्यवच्छिन्नास्तित्वं पररूपाद्यवच्छिन्ननास्तित्वं च प्रत्यक्षेणैव गृह्यते। घटो घटत्वेनास्तीत्यबाधितप्रतीतेः। अनुमानप्रयोगश्च—अस्तित्वं स्वाभावेन नास्तित्वेनाविनाभूतं विशेषणत्वात् साधर्म्यवत्। यथा साधर्म्यं वैधर्म्येणाविनाभूतं तथास्तित्वं स्वाभावेन नास्तित्वेनाविनाभूतम्।.........। एवं नास्तित्वं स्वाभावेनास्तित्वेनाविनाभूतं विशेषणत्वात्। वैधर्म्यवत्। इत्यनुमानेन तयोर्विनाभावसिद्धिः—Sapta. pp. 52-53.

4. नन्वत्र विरोधः। कथमेकमेव कुम्भादि वस्तु सच्च असच्च भवति?। सत्त्वं ह्यसत्त्वपरिहारेण व्यवस्थितम्, असत्त्वमपि सत्त्वपरिहारेण, अन्यथा तयोरविशेषः स्यात्। ततश्च तद्यदि सत्, कथमसत्?। अथासत्, कथं सदिति?। तदनवदातम्। ततो यदि येनैव प्रकारेण सत्त्वं तेनैवासत्त्वम्, येनैव चासत्त्वं तेनैव सत्त्वमभ्युपेयेत, तदा स्याद्विरोधः। यदा तु स्वरूपेण घटादित्वेन, स्वद्रव्येण हिरण्मयादित्वेन, स्वक्षेत्रेण, नागरादित्वेन, स्वकालत्वेन वासन्तिकादित्वेन सत्त्वं, पररूपादिना तु पटत्वतन्तुत्वग्राम्यत्वग्रैष्मिकत्वादिनाऽसत्त्वम्। तदा क्व विरोधगन्धोऽपि?। ये तु सौगताः परासत्त्वं नाभ्युपयन्ति तेषां घटादेः सर्वात्मकत्वप्रसङ्गः। तथाहि—यथा घटस्य स्वरूपादिना सत्त्वं तथा यदि पररूपादिनापि स्यात्, तथा सति स्वरूपादित्ववत् पररूपादित्वप्रसक्तेः कथं न सर्वात्मकत्वं भवेत्?। परासत्त्वेन तु प्रतिनियतोऽसौ सिध्यति। अथ न नाम

नास्ति परासत्त्वं किं तु स्वसत्त्वमेव तदिति चेत् अहो नूतनः कोऽपि तर्कवितर्ककर्कशः समुल्लापः। न खलु यदेव सत्त्वं तदेवासत्त्वं भवितुमर्हति। विधिप्रतिषेधरूपतया विरुद्धधर्माध्यासेनानयोरैक्यायोगात्। अथ पृथक् तत्राभ्युपगम्यते न च नाभ्युपगम्यत एवेति किमिदमिन्द्रजालम्? ॥

—Ratnâkarâvatârikâ Pari. V. pp. 85–86.

5. ननु अनेकान्तवादे विरोधादयोऽष्टदोषाः संभवन्ति। तथाहि—एकत्रार्थे विधिप्रतिषेधरूपावास्तित्वनास्तित्वधर्मौ न संभवतः। शीतोष्णयोरिव भावाभावयोः परस्परं विरोधात्। अस्तित्वं हि भावरूपं विधिमुखप्रत्ययविषयत्वात्, नास्तित्वं च प्रतिषेधरूपं नञुल्लिखितप्रतीतिविषयत्वात्। यत्रास्तित्वं तत्र नास्तित्वस्य विरोधः, यत्र च नास्तित्वं तत्रास्तित्वस्य विरोधः। इति विरोधः (१)॥ अस्तित्वस्याधिकरणमन्यन्नास्तित्वस्याधिकरणमन्यदित्यस्तित्वनास्तित्वयोर्वैयधिकरण्यम् (२)॥ येन रूपेणास्तित्वं येन च रूपेण नास्तित्वं तादृशरूपयोरपि प्रत्येकमास्तित्वनास्तित्वात्मकत्वं वक्तव्यम्। तच्च स्वरूपपररूपाभ्यां, तयोरपि प्रत्येकमास्तित्वनास्तित्वात्मकत्वं स्वरूपपररूपाभ्यामित्यनवस्था (३) अप्रामाणिकपदार्थपरंपरापरिकल्पनाविश्रान्त्यभावश्चानवस्थेत्युच्यते॥ येन रूपेण सत्त्वं तेन रूपेणासत्त्वस्यापि प्रसङ्गः, येन रूपेण चासत्त्वं तेन रूपेण सत्त्वस्यापि प्रसङ्ग इति संकरः (४)। सर्वेषां युगपत्प्राप्तिः संकरः इत्यभिधानात्॥ येन रूपेण सत्त्वं तेन रूपेणासत्त्वमेव स्यान्नतु सत्त्वं, येन रूपेण चासत्त्वं तेन सत्त्वमेव स्यान्नत्वसत्त्वम् इति व्यतिकरः (५) परस्परविषयगमनं व्यतिकरः इति वचनात्॥ सत्त्वासत्त्वात्मके च वस्तुन इदमित्थमेवेति निश्चेतुमशक्तेः संशयः (६)। ततश्चानिश्चयरूपाऽप्रतिपत्तिः (७)॥ ततः सत्त्वासत्त्वात्मनो वस्तुनोऽभावः (८)॥

—Sapta. pp. 81–82.

For a reply to this set of objections, read:—

6. अत्र वदन्त्यभिज्ञाः। कथंचित् प्रतीयमाने स्वरूपाद्यपेक्षया विवक्षितयोः सत्त्वासत्त्वयोः प्रतीयमानयोर्न विरोधः। अनुपलम्भसाध्यो हि विरोधः। न हि स्वरूपादिना वस्तुनः सत्त्वे तदैव पररूपादिभिरसत्त्वस्यानुपलम्भोऽस्ति। स्वरूपादिभिः सत्त्वस्येव पररूपादिभिरसत्त्वस्यापि प्रतीतिसिद्धत्वात् न खलु वस्तुनः सर्वथा भाव एव स्वरूपं स्वरूपेणेव पररूपेणापि भावप्रसङ्गात्॥..............
ननु स्वरूपेण भाव एव पररूपेणाभावः, पररूपेणाभाव एव च स्वरूपेण भाव इति भावाभावयोरेकत्र वस्तुनि भेदाभावाद्वस्तुनः कुतस्तदुभयात्मकता इति चेत्, <u>भावाभावापेक्षणीयस्य निमित्तस्य भेदादिति ब्रूमः</u> स्वद्रव्यादिकं हि निमित्तमपेक्ष्य भावप्रत्ययं जनयत्यर्थः, परद्रव्यादिकं चाभावप्रत्ययम्, इत्येकत्वद्वित्वादिसंख्यावदेकवस्तुनि भावाभावयोर्भेदः॥..............

Incidentally a reply is given to the S'âmkara Vedântin :—

ननु सत्त्वासत्त्वयोरेकत्र वस्तुनि प्रतीतिर्मिथ्येति चेन्न। बाधकाभावात्। विरोधो बाधक इति चेन्न। परस्पराश्रयापत्तेः। सति हि विरोधे प्रतीतेस्तेन बाध्यमानत्वात् मिथ्यात्वसिद्धिः। ततश्च सत्त्वासत्त्वयोर्विरोधसिद्धिः इति ॥

किं च विरोधस्तावत्त्रिधा व्यवतिष्ठते, वध्यघातकभावेन सहानवस्थानात्मना वा प्रतिबध्यप्रतिबन्धकरूपेण वा। तत्राद्ये त्वहिनकुलाग्न्युदकादिविषयः। स चैकस्मिन् काले वर्तमानयोस्संयोगे सति भवति, संयोगस्यानेकाश्रयत्वात् द्वित्ववत्। नासंयुक्तमुदकमग्निं नाशयति सर्वत्राग्न्यभावप्रसंगात्। ततस्सति संयोगे बलीयसोत्तरकालमितरद्बाध्यते। न हि तथाऽस्तित्वनास्तित्वयोः क्षणमात्रमप्येकस्मिन्वृत्तिरस्तीति भवताभ्युपगम्यते, यतो वध्यघातकभावरूपो विरोधस्तयोः कल्प्येत। यदि चैकस्मिंस्तयोर्वृत्तिरभ्युपगम्यते, तदा तयोस्तुल्यबलत्वान्न वध्यघातकभावः॥ नापि सहानवस्थानलक्षणो विरोधः स चैकत्र कालभेदेन वर्तमानयोर्भवति यथा आम्रफले श्यामतापीततयोः। उत्पद्यमाना हि पीतता पूर्वकालभाविनीं श्यामतां नाशयति। न हि तथाऽस्तित्वनास्तित्वे पूर्वोत्तरकालभाविनि। यदि स्याताम्—अस्तित्वकाले नास्तित्वाभावाज्जीवसत्तामात्रं सर्वें प्राप्नुवीत। नास्तित्वकाले चास्तित्वाभावात्तदाश्रयो बन्धमोक्षादिव्यवहारो विरोधमुपगच्छेत्। सर्वथैवासतः पुनरात्मलाभाभावात्, सर्वथा च सतः पुनरभावप्राप्त्यनुपपत्तेर्नैतयोस्सहानवस्थानं युज्यते। तथास्तित्वनास्तित्वयोः प्रतिबध्यप्रतिबन्धकभावरूपविरोधोपि न सम्भवति। यथा-सति मणिरूपप्रतिबन्धके वह्निना दाहो न जायत इति मणिदाहयोः प्रतिबन्ध्यप्रतिबन्धकभावो युक्तः, न हि तथाऽस्तित्वकाले नास्तित्वस्य प्रतिबन्धः स्वरूपेणास्तित्वकालेपि पररूपादिना नास्तित्वस्य प्रतीतिसिद्धत्वात् इति।

यत्तु शीतोष्णस्पर्शयोरिवेति दृष्टान्तकथनं तदसत्। एकत्रधूपघटादाववच्छेदकभेदेन शीतोष्णस्पर्शयोरुपलम्भात्तयोरपि विरोधासिद्धेः।

यथैकत्र चलाचलात्मनोर्वृक्षादौ रक्तारक्तात्मनोर्घटादावावृतानावृतात्मनोः शरीरादौ चोपलम्भादविरोधस्तथा सत्त्वासत्त्वयोरपि।

एतेन वैयधिकरण्यमपास्तम्। सत्त्वासत्त्वयोरेकाधिकरणतया प्रतीति सिद्धत्वात्।

यच्चानवस्थानदूषणमुक्तम्, तदपि नानेकान्तवादिनां दोषः। अनन्तधर्मात्मकस्य वस्तुनः स्वयं प्रमाणप्रतिपन्नत्वेनाभ्युपगमात्। अप्रामाणिकपदार्थपरम्परापरिकल्पनाविरहात्॥ एतेन संकरव्यतिकरावपि निरस्तौ प्रतीतिसिद्धेऽर्थे कस्यापि दोषस्याभावात्। दोषाणां प्रतीत्यसिद्धपदार्थगोचरत्वात्॥ संशयादयश्च पूर्वमेव निरस्तप्रायाः। इत्यन्यत्र विस्तरः।

अथैवमुपपत्त्या विरोधादिदोषाभावे प्रतिपादितेऽपि मिथ्यादर्शनाभिनिवेशात्तत्त्वमप्रतिपद्यमानं पुरुषं प्रति सार्वलौकिकहेतुवादमाश्रित्योच्यते। स्वेष्टार्थसिद्धि-

मिच्छता प्रवादिना हेतुः प्रयोक्तव्यः, प्रतिज्ञामात्रेणार्थसिद्धेरभावात्। स च हेतुः स्वपक्षस्य साधकः परपक्षस्य दूषकश्च। येन रूपेण हेतोस्साधकत्वं येन च रूपेण दूषकत्वं न तादृशे रूपे हेतोरत्यन्तभिन्ने, तयोर्हेतुधर्मत्वेन हेत्वपेक्षया कथञ्चिदभिन्नत्वात्। न हि तयोर्हेत्वपेक्षयाऽनन्यत्वाद्येन रूपेण साधकत्वं तेन रूपेण दूषकत्वं च सम्भवतीति संकरः, येन रूपेण साधकत्वं तेन रूपेण दूषकत्वमेवेति व्यतिकरो वा, साधकत्वदूषकत्वयोर्विरोधो वा सम्भवति, तथाऽनेकान्तप्रक्रियाया-मपि विरोधादिदोषानवतारः।

वस्तुतस्तु—अनेकान्तप्रक्रियायां सर्वेषां प्रवादिनामपि प्रतिपत्तिरेव। एका-नेकात्मकस्य वस्तुनस्सर्वसम्मतत्वात्॥

—Sapta. pp. 81–90.

Stanza XXV.

स्यादित्यव्ययम्—स्यात्, originally pot. 3rd sing. of अस्, is here employed as an adverb. This means that the word will not change its form even if the subject and the predicate be in the plural number: thus स्यान्नित्यानि, not स्युर्नित्यानि. This conversion of a verb into an adverb seems intended for fixing the title by which the essential character of the doctrine may be designated.

अष्टस्वपि—स्यात् to be construed with—(1) नास्ति, (2) नित्यं, (3) सदृशं, (4) विरूपं, (5) वाच्यं, (6) न वाच्यं, (7) सत् and (8) असत्—which make four Syâdvâda propositions:

(1) स्यान्नित्यम्, स्यादनित्यम्—the two together making a single proposition.

(2) स्यात् सामान्यम्, स्याद्विशेषः ,,

(3) स्याद्वक्तव्यम्, स्यादवक्तव्यम् ,,

(4) स्यात् सत्, स्यादसत्. ,,

जरामरणाविपश्चितां नाथ=संख्यावतां मुख्य Chief of the wise. जरामरणापहारित्वात् etc.—This is why the Truth of Jaina philosophy is compared to nectar.

यथा हि कश्चिदाकण्ठं etc.—The utterances of the Master are compared to eructations which follow upon his having drunk to his fill the nectar of Truth. The suggestion is—When the very eructations of nectar are so fragrant, how much more fragrant must be the nectar!

अथवा—Perhaps the commentator realised that his analysis of the simile made it a bit coarse. मनोहृत्य—to their heart's fill.

एते चत्वारोऽपि—Of the propositions mentioned above, No. (1) in आदीपमाव्योम॰ St. V, No. (2) in अनेक॰ St. XIV, Nos. (3) and (4) in अपर्ययं वस्तु॰ St. XXIII which deals with the सप्तभङ्गी doctrine.

Stanza XXVI.

य एव दोषाः etc.—The destructive criticisms of the *Nityavâda* and the *Kṣaṇikavâda* destroy each other and thereby lead to a higher synthesis in the same way as the enemies of a king may destroy themselves by mutual warfare and thereby serve to bring about his undisputed sovereignty.

I Untenability of अनित्य (क्षणिक) वाद—नित्यवादी प्रमाणयति etc.—The *Nityavâdin's* (*Eternalist's*) *criticism of his opponent.* He thus argues his case: If all things be क्षणिक, the cause and the effect will fall on two different moments of time, and so at the moment when one *is*, the other *is not*. Now, how can that which *is* act upon that which *is not* ? And if a thing cannot *act*, it cannot *be*, for *to be* is *to act*. (अर्थक्रियाकारित्वं सत्त्वम्). Thus it may be shown that things can never be क्षणिक. That a क्षणिक thing is incapable of *acting* (अर्थक्रिया) may be thus shown by means of a dilemma : Is the क्षणिक thing सत् while it acts or is it असत्? Not the former. For in that case, the क्षणिक thing would be operating upon its contemporaneous effect which is impossible; for, if that were possible, all things being contemporaneous with one another would be causes of one another which is abswrd. Nor will the latter alternative do. For, how can a thing that is असत् possess causal power any more than a शशविषाण (the horn of a hare) ? And no third alternative is possible. Therefore the original hypothesis of क्षणिकत्व breaks down, and that of नित्यत्व rises in its place.

II Untenability of नित्यवाद—The *Kṣaṇikavâdin's criticism of Nityavâda :*

The Kṣaṇikavâdin argues his case thus :

सर्वं क्षणिकं सत्वात्—All things are क्षणिक because they are possessed of सत्व, क्षणिकत्व being a necessary condition of सत्व. That क्षणिकत्व is a necessary condition of सत्व may be thus proved: First, remember that सत्व means अर्थक्रियाकारित्व, (Cf. James's Pragmatic Theory of Truth), for that is the very definition of सत्व, and so when अर्थक्रिया is impossible सत्व is impossible. Now, let us consider whether a thing that is not क्षणिक, in other words what is नित्य, can ever be अर्थक्रियाकारिन्. That it can never be may be shown by means of the following dilemma: Does the thing that is supposed to be नित्य exercise अर्थक्रिया step by step (क्रम) or all at once (यौगपद्य)? It cannot do so *step by step*, for that involves the loss of नित्यत्व — the thing having already changed, i. e. ceased to be नित्य, the moment the first step has been taken. If the thing continues to be the same even after the first step is taken there will be no cessation of the acting suited to the first step and thus there will be no possibility of a second step ever being taken. If, on the other hand, the thing is supposed to change by the first step it loses its नित्यत्व by so doing. For, to be no longer in the former state means to be अनित्य. There is a possible way out of this difficulty. Suppose it is held that the thing remains the same all along the steps, but awaits the arrival of a सहकारिन् or auxiliary cause in going from step to step ; thus the changes are rung out not on the original thing which retains its sameness and therefore नित्यत्व, but only on the series of सहकारिन्s. But this makeshift does not really obviate the difficulty, but only pushes it a little further on. Thus, if the thing remains the same in spite of the arrival of the सहकारिन् it means the सहकारिन् has exercised no influence upon the original cause. Now, we ask: why has it not ? Is it that it was waiting for another सहकारिन् to come to its aid ? If so, it only launches you upon अनवस्था a regressus ad infinitum Let us now take the other alternative, viz., that of action *all at once* (यौगपद्य). It will be readily seen that this is impossible. Nothing can put forth activities in all directions and accomplish its effects all at once in a single moment of time. Supposing it can, all its work will be finished in the first instant of time, leaving the thing without क्रिया and therefore different from what it was before,—which amounts to a confession that the thing is अनित्य.

तदेवमेकान्तद्वयेऽपि etc.—The logical result of the above conflict is that the हेतुs put forward by each of the two parties is found to be vitiated by the हेत्वाभास called 'विरुद्ध' *i. e.* the हेतु ('सत्त्वात') which proves the very opposite of what it is intended to prove.

अत्र च नित्यानित्यैकान्त० etc.—The aobve line of reasoning with respect to नित्य and अनित्य is to be applied mutatis mutandis to the dogmas of सामान्य and विशेष as held by the other schools.

सुन्दोपसुन्दवत्—Mutual destruction like that of the two demon-brothers Sunda and Upasunda.

Here is the story: ततस्तिलोत्तमा तत्र वने पुष्पाणि चिन्वती। वेशमाक्षिप्तमाधाय रक्तेनैकेन वाससा ॥ नदीतीरेषु जातान् सा कर्णिकारान् प्रचिन्वती। शनैर्जगाम तं देशं यत्रास्तां तौ महासुरौ ॥ तौ तु पीत्वा परं पानं मदरक्तान्तलोचनौ। दृष्ट्वैव तां वरारोहां व्यथितौ संबभूवतुः ॥ तावुत्थायासनं हित्वा जग्मतुर्यत्र सा स्थिता। उभौ च कामसंमत्तावुभौ प्रार्थयतश्च ताम् ॥ दक्षिणे तां करे सुभ्रूं सुन्दो जग्रपाणिना। उपसुन्दोऽपि जग्राह वामे पाणौ तिलोत्तमाम् ॥ वरप्रदानमत्तौ तावौरसेन बलेन च। धनरत्नमदाभ्यां च सुरापानमदेन च ॥ सर्वैरेतैर्मदैर्मत्तावन्योन्यं भ्रुकुटीकृतौ। मदकामसमाविष्टौ परस्परमथोचतुः ॥ मम भार्या तव गुरुरिति सुन्दोऽभ्यभाषत। मम भार्या तव वधूरुपसुन्दोऽभ्यभाषत ॥ नैषा तव ममैवेति ततस्तौ मन्युराविशत्। तस्या रूपेण संमत्तौ विगतस्नेहसौहृदौ ॥ तस्या हेतोर्गदे भीमे संगृहीतामुभौ तदा। प्रगृह्य च गदे भीमे तस्यां तौ काममोहितौ ॥ अहं पूर्वमहं पूर्वमित्यन्योन्यं निजघ्नतुः। तौ गदाभिहतौ भीमौ पेततुर्धरणीतले ॥ रुधिरेणावसिक्ताङ्गौ द्वाविवार्कौ नभश्च्युतौ।

द्वादशाङ्गीरूपम्—For the Jaina canon and its divisions see Weber's article in Ind. Ant. (1888 and 1892), Enc. Rel. and Ethics, Art. on "Jainism", Jaini's "Outlines of Jainism.

शक्तार्हे कृत्याश्च—Hem. V, vi, 35.

Stanza XXVII

The doctrine of स्याद्वाद or अनेकान्तवाद, as it is otherwise called, is not a doctrine of mere speculative interest—one intended to solve a mere ontological problem—but has a bearing upon man's psychological and spiritual life. This is the point of Stanza XXVII in which the author shows how it is impossible to explain सुख-दुःख (भोग), पुण्य-पाप, and बन्ध-मोक्ष—except on the hypothesis of अनेकान्तवाद.

I

1. एकान्तनित्ये etc.—If आत्मन् be exclusively नित्य, the experiences of happiness and misery will thereby be rendered impossible. For, to be नित्य means to be unchangeable, and there cannot be experiences of happiness and misery one after another unless आत्मन् could pass (change) from one state to another. It will be said by way of a defence of the नित्यैकान्तवाद that the आत्मन् does not change, only its states change. This however, may be met by asking : Do the states remain separate from the आत्मन् or are they *one* with the आत्मन्? In the former case, how could they be associated with आत्मन्? Besides, they would be entire strangers to आत्मन्, as foreign to it as any other thing in the universe. In the latter case, they are as good as not, and the old difficulty of accounting for change consistently with the नित्यत्व of आत्मन् remains the same. Moreover, if आत्मन् is exclusively possessed of a particular nature, how can there be any difference or change of states such as one from दुःख to सुख ?

(2) पुण्य and पाप, too, are impossible on the hypothesis of exclusive नित्यत्व. For, the experience of सुख and दुःख are

brought about by पुण्य and पाप— which means that they should exercise a certain activity, and this is impossible if आत्मन् is कूटस्थ नित्य *i. e.* unchangingly eternal. Remember that the Jaina does not deny the eternality of आत्मन् provided it is eternality-with-change.

(3) बन्ध and मोक्ष are similarly impossible on the hypothesis of exclusive नित्यत्व. बन्ध is the union of karmic matter (कर्मपुद्गल s) with every portion of आत्मन्, like that of fire with a piece of iron; while मोक्ष is the annihilation of all कर्मन्s. Now, both of these would be impossible under the hypothesis of exclusive नित्यत्व. Thus:—बन्ध is a kind of संयोग and संयोग is अप्राप्तानां प्राप्तिः *i. e.* obtaining what has not been obtained already. Thus, there are two distinct states involved in the notion of संयोग—the previous absence and the later presence, which are inconsistent with the hypothesis of changeless नित्यत्व of आत्मन्. Moreover, we would ask: How does a changeless and uniformly enduring आत्मन् suddenly happen to incur the trammels of बन्ध? Again, was he not मुक्त before the chains of बन्ध came to be put on him? Then, again, does the बन्ध make any change in the आत्मन् or not? If it *does*, he is अनित्य, like any other mortal thing such as a piece of hide. If it *does not*, so as to keep the आत्मन् निर्विकार the presence or absence of the बन्ध matters nothing to him, who remains as unaffected as आकाश by the change

2. एवमनित्यैकान्तवादेऽपि etc.—The doctrine next criticised is the other side of the Truth regarded as the *whole* Truth viz. absolute अनित्यत्व of आत्मन्. An absolutely अनित्य thing is that which is 'अत्यन्तोच्छेदधर्मक' *i. e.* that which undergoes absolute annihilation.

(1) If आत्मन् is so absolutely अनित्य as to undergo such an annihilation it means an end to the law of Retribution—which requires personal identity of कर्तृ and भोक्तृ.

अथ यस्मिन्नेव etc.—Supposing the doctrine of the absolute अनित्यत्व of आत्मन् is so modified as to substitute संतान for आत्मन् *i. e.* continuity for identity: thus, not the identical आत्मन्, but the continuous stream of consciousness which we call आत्मन् is both कर्तृ and भोक्तृ, karma being transmitted from one life to another in the shape of कर्मवासनाs *i. e.* as impressions left on the आत्मन् by karmans—on the analogy of a colour which transmits itself from one piece of cloth to another. But the second position is no more tenable than the first. For, the संतान and the वासना which are substituted for आत्मन् and कर्म are pure fictions, and so they have been shown in the commentary on St. XVIII.

(2) Similarly, under the hypothesis of absolute अनित्यत्व of आत्मन्, the resulting lack of personal identity and the passing away of the original कर्म make पुण्य and पाप and their consequent सुखदुःखोपभोग impossible; in other words, they take away all sense from the law of Retribution. Moreover, if आत्मन् is अनित्य in the sense of क्षणमात्रस्थायी *i.e.* existing only for a single instant he cannot be the author of पुण्य and पाप. For the single instant is the length of time just sufficient for it to come into existence, and there is nothing left to spare for doing पुण्य or पाप. [Note that a क्षण is by hypothesis and definition an infinitesimal division of time, and so one क्षण, one act.] You will say: Suppose the आत्मन् of the first क्षण produced the आत्मन् of the next क्षण and so on, so that there is a continuity-mark, not the identity—of being. But this explanation will not do. The law of homogeneity of Cause and Effect would require that a happy आत्मन् should beget only a happy आत्मन्, and so the vicissitudes of happiness and misery in the आत्मन् would become impossible.

(3) Lastly, under the hypothesis of the absolute अनित्यत्व of आत्मन्, बन्ध and मोक्ष are correlates which have no meaning unless they are predicated of one and the same आत्मन्.

Thus, rejecting the doctrine of absolute नित्यत्व of आत्मन् on the one hand, and of absolute अनित्यत्व on the other, the Jaina philosopher lays down the doctrine of the परिणाम of आत्मन् which represents the synthesis of the two extremes

(अनेकान्तवाद). It is the doctrine of *identity-in-change*, of *unity-in-difference*, of *one-in-many*.

परिणामो etc.—परिणाम defined.

पातञ्जलटीकाकारोऽप्याह—See Yogasûtra Vyâsa Bhâṣya III–12. The quotation is made from Vyâsa's commentary on Patanjali's Sûtra, and so Malliṣeṇa is quite right in saying "पातञ्जलटीकाकारोऽप्याह." The foot-note in AMP edition of the Syâdvâda Mañjarî—अत्र ग्रन्थकृता 'टीकाकारोऽप्याह' इति यदुक्तं तच्चिन्त्यम् । यत इदं पातञ्जलसूत्रम् ।' is evidently a mistake.

एवं सामान्यविशेष०—Similary it may be shown that it would be impossible to explain सुखदुःख, पुण्यपाप and बन्धमोक्ष, if we held the doctrines of absolute सामान्य and absolute विशेष, absolute सत् and absolute असत्, absolute वक्तव्यत्व and absolute अव्यक्तव्यत्व.

II

अथोत्तरार्धव्याख्या—

परैः It has the double sense of "others" *i. e.* non-Jaina-heretical-philosophers, and of "enemies". The word has been used before in this double sense. नीति=नय; such doctrines as give only a part-view of Truth (नीयते एकदेशविशिष्टोऽर्थः प्रतीतिविषयमाभिरिति) दुर्नीति=दुर्नय.

अपिशब्दस्य० Construe अशेषमपि जगत्.

तात्स्थ्यात् तद्यपदेशः—By *lakṣaṇâ* as in 'मञ्चाः क्रोशन्ति' where मञ्चाः=मञ्चस्थाः पुरुषाः See Kâvya Pr. II.

सम्यग्ज्ञानादयो० etc.—सम्यग्ज्ञान and other psychic qualities are the 'भावप्राणs' of Siddhas *i, e.* the mental qualities which have become their very breath. Hence, Siddhas are classed among जीवs, not-withestanding the absence of ordinary vital airs ('द्रव्यप्राणs') in their case. The root जीव् means 'to possess vital airs or life.' The vital airs in the case of Siddhas are the सम्यग्ज्ञान and similar qualities.

दशविधद्रव्यप्राण—These have been enumerated in the foot-note of AMP edition: पञ्चेन्द्रियाणि, श्वासोच्छ्वास, आयुष्य, मनोबल, वचनबल and शारीरबल.

Stanza XXVIII.

सांप्रतं etc.—The author is next going to explain what is meant by (1) दुर्नय, (2) नय, and (3) प्रमाण.

प्रमाणनयैरधिगमः—Tattvârtha Sûtra I. 6.

जीवाजीवादितत्त्व०--These are (1) जीव, (2) अजीव, (3) आस्रव, (4) बन्ध, (5) संवर, (6) निर्जरा and (7) मोक्ष See Tattvârtha I. 4.

अर्थते etc.—अर्थ, derived from the root ऋ, means that which is determined or known; all knowables.

विधौ सप्तमी. Hema लिङ् लकार. विधौ, *i. e.* in the sense of commandment, that is, in the sense of 'must be', not-'may be'.

नया नैगमादयः—*Nayas* are the points of views which disclose only *partial* truths. See below.

प्रमीयते...प्रमाणम्—*Pramâṇa* is the doctrine of Syâdvâda, which lays bare the *whole truth* which is the synthesis of extremes and not absolute extremes or fragmentary truths. प्र in प्रमाण suggests completeness of view. For the two avrieties of प्रमाण, viz. प्रत्यक्ष and परोक्ष, see Tattvârtha VII, 12. Pr. N. T. Pari II, 2 etc. and III, 1 etc.

सदेव– When a partial truth is put forward as the whole truth *e.g.* सदेव—' It *is*, and *is only;* ' it is दुर्नय *i. e.* a false proposition.

अव्यक्तव्यत्वात् नपुंसकत्वम्—Neut. gend. That is in 'सत्'. When we do not know the sex (अवक्तव्यत्वात्) of the child we use the neut. gender *e. g.* when we say ' किं तस्या गर्भे जातम् ?'

सत्—When a partial truth is put forward as in the proposition "सत्"= "It is," without excluding, that is, denying, its contradictory by an ' एव', it is नय *i. e.* a partial truth: thus, ' अस्ति घटः' is an illustration of नय. But to say सदेव and thus exclude the element of असत् absolutely is दुर्नय. प्रमाण is a syntnesis of सत् and असत् which is expressed in the स्याद्वाद which is the only प्रमाण-view. Thus: (1) सदेव is दुर्नय; सत् is नय; स्यात् सत् is प्रमाण. गजनिमीलिका—One-sided vision of the elephant; the idea is that the elephant does not keep both his eyes open, but only one or the other as he turns this way or that.

स्यात् सत्—स्यात्=(कथंचित्) सत् (वस्तु). 'It *is*' from a certain point of view, implying that 'it *is not*' from another point of view. This is a statement of the *whole* Truth. There is nothing 'दृष्ट' or 'इष्ट' (which we see or which we should like to see) which contradicts it; while there are objections in the other case (विपक्षे) *i. e.* the case of laying down absolute propositions like those discussed in the preceding stanzas.

सदिति दिङ्मात्र०—Here we have exemplified दुर्नय, नय and प्रमाण in the case of (1) सत्त्व. Similar examples may be framed with respect to (2) असत्त्व (3) नित्यत्व (4) अनित्यत्व, (5) वक्तव्यत्व and (6) अवक्तव्यत्व (7) सामान्य and (8) विशेष. These are the eight पद्s mentioned supra—See St. XXV and Commentary.

तुशब्दस्य etc.—Construe the words in the Stanza thus: त्वमेव आस्थः. आस्थः from अस् to throw or cast off *i. e.* reject, refute. For the grammatical form see below. त्वमेव–you and you alone, न तीर्थान्तरदैवतानि, not even the gods of the other schools.

तीर्थान्तरशास्तारस्तु etc.—That is to say, they fail to see the whole truth through रागद्वेष.

इदमुक्तं भवति—यथा कश्चित् etc.—One who knows the Path of Truth and is benevolently disposed towards others makes travellers abandon the path which is beset with 'thieves' ('दुर्नय'); next, he shows them the Path which is possessed of at least the negative virtue of being not bad, though it is not positively good (*i. e.* नय); and, lastly, he points out to them the path which is not only not bad, but positively good (*i. e.* प्रमाण).

आस्थ इत्यस्य ते०—Aor. of अस् (Hema 78 दिवादिगण). See Hem III. iv. 60. IV. iii. 103; and IV. iv. 31. अद्यतनी–लकारः

मुख्यवृत्त्या etc.—Strictly speaking, प्रमाण alone is Truth and not नय. For, नय to the extent that it does not disclose the whole truth may be said to be Error.

अनुयोगद्वार०—In the journey from अनुयोगद्वार to प्रज्ञापना (names of Âgamas) *i.e.* from Inquiry to Establishment of Truth,

चत्वारि हि etc.—प्रवचनानुयोग--Exposition of the word.

एतेषां च स्वरूपं etc.—See विशेषावश्यक भाष्य on St. 77,1:

अणुगोद्दाराइं महापुरस्सेव तस्स चत्तारि। etc.

See also S'îl's Com. on Acâr. 1. i. p. 3.

अत्र चैकत्र कृतसमासान्तः etc.—Here are two words of the same form ('पथ'), one being a form of पथिन् at the end of the compound, the other a noun ending in अ. The commentator need not have made this attempt to explain away 'कथितपददोष' (See K. Pr. VII) which is after all not a very serious fault in a work of logic or philosophy.

तत्रापि प्रथमं नयस्वरूपं etc.—The author of the Stanza has arranged the three subjects दुर्नय etc. in the order of their degree of importance or ascending values; Malliṣeṇa's business as a commentator is to *explain* the terms, and so he will take up नय before दुर्नय, a knowledge of the latter being hardly possible without that of the former.

तत्र प्रमाणप्रतिपन्नार्थैकदेश०—Definition of नय. नय may be defined as "प्रमाणप्रतिपन्नार्थैकदेशपरामर्शः" *i.e.* apprehension of a part of the object, the whole of which is revealed only by प्रमाण. Take प्रमाणप्रतिपन्न with अर्थ, and not अर्थैकदेश; for, what distinguishes प्रमाण from नय is that it reveals tho *whole* truth while नय reveals but a *part* of the whole truth. In further support of this, see Devasûri's definition of नय (Pr. N. T. Ch VII) quoted in the sequel: "नीयते येन श्रुताख्यप्रमाणविषयीकृतस्यार्थस्यांशः तदितरांशौदासीन्यतः etc.—Where प्रमाणविषयीकृतस्य qualifies अर्थस्य and not अंशः. Note, further, that नय is not simply अर्थैकदेशपरामर्श but प्रमाणप्रतिपन्नार्थैकदेशपरामर्श, that is to say, knowledge of a part of the *Truth* and not merely of a part of any object whatsoever whether real or imaginary. Thus, नय, so far as it goes, deals with Reality, though with only a part of Reality: Is not नय, then, प्रमाण *pro tanto?* The question and the answer will be found in a passage of Pr, N. T. Ratna, quoted in the sequel,

एकदेशः— A part or a fragment, not necessarily one part or one fragment. 'अंशः'–'अत्रैकवचनमतन्त्रं तेनांशावशा वा' (Pr. N. T.)

अनन्तधर्माध्यासितं वस्तु—नय is so called because it conveys (from नी) to the mind Reality as possessed of that particular धर्म or धर्मs to which one desires to advert, although as a matter of fact that Reality is possessed of numberless धर्मs (cf अनन्तधर्मा ...Âcâr. I. i. p. 3). Since नय operates upon a Reality which has been already revealed by प्रमाण, नय follows प्रमाण. Cf. 'प्रमाण......' Râj. p. 65. Besides, numberless are the नयs, because numberless are the धर्मs belonging to a thing, and any one or more of them may be adverted to by the speaker.

According to the explanation here given नय conveys the Reality to the mind (वस्तु नयति प्रापयति संवेदनकोटिमारोहयति); in the Bhâsya, on Tv. Sûtra, नय is explained as conveying the mind to the Reality.

तथा च वृद्धाः—The quotation is made from the संमतिसूत्र of Siddhasena Divâkara.

जावइया etc.—As many are the statements of नय as are the ways of speaking about a thing.

तथापि चिरन्तनाचार्यैः etc.—The infinite number of नयs has been reduced to the following seven: नैगम etc. The Tatv. Sûtra enumerates five नयs viz. नैगम, संग्रह, व्यवहार, ऋजुसूत्र and शब्द ("नैगम-संग्रह-व्यवहार-र्जुसूत्र-शब्दा नयाः" T. V. i. 34) and afterwards divides नैगम into two and शब्द into three: (आद्यशब्दौ द्वित्रिभेदौ—Tv. i. 35). The two, says the Bhâsya, are 'देशपरिक्षेपी' and 'सर्वपरिक्षेपी'; the three are सांप्रत, समभिरूढ and एवंभूत. (For explanation, see below.)

कथमेषां सर्वसंग्राहकत्वम्—The अभिप्राय or the point of view of the speaker may have reference either to अर्थ or to शब्द *i. e.* thought, or the word in which the thought is expressed. Since these are the only ways in which the mind can approach Reality, we may take it that a division of नयs which is founded upon them, so far as their foundation is concerned, is exhaustive. The points of view which have reference to thought are all included in the first four नयs, while those which have reference to its verbal form in the last three.

The infinite number of नयs and their reduction to *seven types* procede upon the principle of 'व्यास' (Diffusion, or Detailed treatment) and 'समास' (Condensation, or Brief treatment) respectively, says Devasûri: "स व्याससमासाभ्यां द्विप्रकारः" (Pr. N. T. vii. 3); व्यासतोऽनेकाविकल्पः (vii. 4.); समासतस्तु द्विभेदो द्रव्यार्थिकः पर्यायार्थिकश्च (vii. 5.); आद्यो नैगमसंग्रहव्यवहारभेदात् त्रेधा (vii. 6.); पर्यायार्थिकश्चतुर्धा ऋजुसूत्रः, शब्दः, समभिरूढ, एवंभूतश्च (vii. 27.) [For explanation see below]. Here is adopted another principle of division besides that of अर्थ and शब्द adopted above, viz., द्रव्यार्थिक and पर्यायार्थिक, the first three नयs being referred to the former and the last four to the latter.

तत्र नैगमः etc.—The Naigama viewpoint takes note of (1) सत्ता—the highest सामान्य which groups together द्रव्यs, गुणs and कर्मन्s in one class; (2) the अवान्तर सामान्यs *i. e.* lower intermediate universals, such as द्रव्यत्व, गुणत्व and कर्मत्व which are confined to द्रव्यs, गुणs and कर्मन्s respectively (see supra), and are, therefore, lower than सत्ता, though higher than पृथ्वीत्व, रूपत्व etc.; (3) the ultimate विशेषs, each of which is unique in itself; and lastly (4) the अवान्तरविशेषs, which distinguish their abodes from other objects and are regarded as distinct from सामान्य, All these doctrines are well-known in the Nyâya-Vaiśeṣika system and so the author remarks later on "नैगमनयदर्शनानुसारिणौ नैयायिक-वैशेषिकौ."

Mark that the Naigama viewpoint recognises both सामान्य and विशेष, yet it does not amount to अनेकान्तवाद, inasmuch as it regards each of these as absolute and self-sufficient, whereas अनेकान्तवाद looks upon them as different aspects of the same reality. One exception, however, is admitted to the absolute distinction between सामान्य and विशेष in the Nyâya–Vaiśeṣika system: it is the rocognition of पृथ्वीत्व and ather अवान्तरसामान्यs as 'सामान्य-विशेषs' (see Vaiś. Sûtras and Bh., Tarka Bhâṣâ etc.).

प्रवचनप्रसिद्ध० Let us now turn to other works and see what explanations they give of this Naya. A different explanation

of नैगम will be found in the Tat. Sûtra-Bhâṣya and the Râjavārtika with its Com. where नैगम is said to be "अर्थसंकल्पमात्रग्राही नैगमः"—according to which a नैगम view consists in apprehending a thing which is intended. See also its illustration. A third explanation will be found in the passage quoted from Pr. N. T. of Devasûri, for which see infra. and Appendices. Dr. Satischandra's explanation agrees with the one expressed in the text, except in one point, for which see his History of Indian Logic.

2. संग्रहस्तु etc.—It is the view which ignores all विशेषs and takes note of सामान्य only.

3. व्यवहारस्तु etc.—The Vyavahâra view-point presents things as they appear to the 'vulgar' eye *i. e.* it does not care for the logical or scientific method of ascertaining Truth and does not believe in things unseen, that is, such as lie beyond the range of human experience. All प्रमाणs according to it must be subordinated to experience and that, too, common experience. Accordingly, it sees no reason to admit either सामान्य or विशेष, both of which it regards as contradicted by common experience. The category of सामान्य, if it existed, inasmuch as it embraces the whole world, would make us all omniscient! [The criticism would apply with special cogency to the Naiyâyika's doctrine of 'Sâmânyalakṣaṇâ-pratyâsatti' See Tarka-Kaumudi]. Nor is the category of विशेष justified by our actual experience; for, what we percieve is a घट, and not the ultimate particulars (विशेषs,) which are supposed to consist in§ or belong† to atoms or perish every minute.‡

The only reality is the reality of what actually exists, what we all feel and handle, what exists in the living present, not in the dead past or the imaginary future, both of which lie outside the range of प्रमाण and therefore of the real.

---

§ The Buddhist view. † The Nyâya-Vaiś. view.

‡ The Buddhist view. The atoms and their विशेषs are नित्य according to the Nyâya-Vaiśeṣika.

तथा च वाचकमुख्य: etc.—See the Tv. Sûtra Bhâṣya i. 35.

लौकिक etc.—It is the point of view such as belongs to the common folk; it is not strictly correct; it refers to reality such as is accepted and understood by the vulgar mind.

(4) ऋजुसूत्र: It agrees with the व्यवहार point of view in recognising the reality of the present only, neither of the past nor of the future, as the two latter are no more real than the 'horns of a hare'—which *do* nothing and therefore *are* nothing. Besides, the real is the simple—which does not admit of any division. Thus, the indivisible atoms are the only reals; they coagulate and act, and not the so-called bodies or gross reality. That which is its own, and not what is foreign to it, is the real in a thing.

(5) शब्द:—It is the point of view which finds a single object denoted by a variety of synonymous terms. At the same time, it recognises differences of objects arising from differences of gender, number, tense, agent (mood), person or—

(6) समभिरूढ—This view-point recognises differences of sense even in the case of synonymous terms, corresponding to the etymological suggestions of differing connotations, and is thus contrary to शब्द. For example, इन्द्र, शक्र, पुरन्दर—although synonymous, convey different senses owing to the differences of connotation suggested by their several etymologies. Thus, इन्द्र signifies the lord of gods, शक्र the powerful god, पुरन्दर the destroyer of the cities, and so on, notwithstanding they are एकार्थक from the शब्द point of view. In other words, while the शब्दनय considers the denotative aspect, समभिरूढ considers the connotative aspect of words.

(7) एवंभूत—This point of view recognises the propriety of applying a word to an object only while it is justified by the then character of the object. Thus, घट which means that which does (√घट्) *i. e.* performs the work of carrying water, is applicable to the object only while it is actually performing the work on the head of a water-carrier, not while it is lying idle.

The mere *capacity* to perform that work, such as belongs to a घट before it is used or after it has been used and laid aside, does not justify the application of the word to the घट in either of the two latter states. For capacity after all is nothing, no better than 'the horn of a hare'. It is the actuality that counts. If we were to allow such an extension of the correct explanation of the word, the word घट would apply to the shells or the lump of clay even before the घट has been actually made or after it has actually ceased to exist.

अत्र संग्रहश्लोकाः etc.—(1) The नैगमनय distinguishes between सामान्य and विशेष, and recognises both. The former is regarded as the principle of unity or co-ordination—'अभिन्नज्ञानकारणं' —by which we know things as one, belonging to the same class; the latter is its opposite.

(2) The संग्रहनय comprehends the whole universe in a single concept— that of Being or Existence—which covers everything.

(3) The व्यवहारनय accepts Existence as it finds it embodied in each particular object. Men in their daily avocations of life are guided by this point of view.

(4) The ऋजुसूत्रनय refers to the changing पर्यायs only as distinguished from the abiding द्रव्य. For, all Reality according to it is perishable, constantly departing from the state of existence.

(5) The शब्दनय recognises differences of connotation (but not of denotation) in accordance with the differences in the forms of words, such as इन्द्र, शक्र, पुरंदर etc.

(6) The समभिरूढनय goes further and recognises differences of अर्थ, that is, denotation, corresponding to those of their different etymologies.

(7) एवंभूतनय declares that a thing bears a particular name only while it performs the क्रिया which entitles it to bear that name, not always.

Note that these partial view-points become positively false and therefore 'दुर्नय' when they make not only statements of part-truths, but *go further and put forward part-truths as whole truths.*

नैगमनय etc.—Many heretical systems have glimpses of part-truths and are so far right. But they are narrow and deny the other sides of truth, and there lies their folly. The Nyâya and Vaiśeṣika systems fall under **नैगमनय**; the Vedânta and the Sâṁkhya are cases of **संग्रहनय**; the Cârvâka is largely based on **व्यवहारनय**; the Buddhists follow **ऋजुसूत्रनय**; the grammarians **शब्दनय**.

उक्तं च सोदाहरणं etc.—See Devasûri's Pr. N. T. and Ratnâ.

नीयते etc.—There, '**नय**' is defined as the particular point of view by which a part of the whole Truth—which only the Jaina scripture has declared—is apprehended.

स्वाभिप्रेतादंशात् etc.—The **नय** is **नय** so long as it confines itself to its limited area of truth; but it becomes '**दुर्नय**'—'**नयाभास**'—when it grows aggressive and ventures to deny other parts of the truth.

The question whether **नय** is **प्रमाण** *pro tanto* is thus discussed in the Ratn.:—

नयः प्रमाणमेव, स्वार्थव्यवसायकत्वादिष्टप्रमाणवत्। स्वार्थव्यवसायकस्याप्यप्रमाणत्वानभ्युपगमे प्रमाणस्यापि तथाविधस्य प्रमाणत्वं न स्यादिति कश्चित्। तदसत्। नयस्य स्वार्थैकदेशनिर्णीतिलक्षणत्वेन स्वार्थव्यवसायकत्वासिद्धेः। ननु विषयतया संमतोऽर्थैकदेशोऽपि यदि वस्तु तदा तत्परिच्छेदी नयः प्रमाणमेव। वस्तुपरिच्छेद लक्षणत्वात् प्रमाणस्य। स न चेद्वस्तु तर्हि तद्विषयो नयो मिथ्याज्ञानमेव स्यात् तस्यावस्तुविषयत्वलक्षणत्वादिति चेत्, तदवद्यम्। अर्थैकदेशस्य वस्तुत्वावस्तुत्वपरिहारेण वस्त्वंशतया प्रतिज्ञानात्। तथा चावाचि—

> नायं वस्तु न चावस्तु वस्त्वंशः कथ्यते बुधैः।
> नासमुद्रः समुद्रो वा समुद्रांशो यथैव हि ॥
> तन्मात्रस्य समुद्रत्वे शेषांशस्यासमुद्रता।
> समुद्रबहुता वा स्यात् तत्त्वे क्वास्तु समुद्रवित् ॥

यथैव हि समुद्रांशस्य समुद्रत्वे शेषसमुद्रांशानामसमुद्रत्वप्रसङ्गात् समुद्रबहुत्वापत्तेर्वा तेषामपि प्रत्येकं समुद्रत्वात्। तस्यासमुद्रत्वे वा शेषसमुद्रांशानामप्यसमुद्रत्वात् क्वचिदपि समुद्रव्यवहारायोगात्। समुद्रांशः समुद्रांश एवोच्यते, तथा स्वार्थैकदेशो नयस्य न वस्तु, स्वार्थैकदेशान्तराणामवस्तुत्वप्रसङ्गात् वस्तु-

बहुत्वादुपपत्तेर्वा; नाप्यवस्तु, शेषांशानामप्यवस्तुत्वेन क्वचिदपि वस्तुव्यवस्थानुपपत्तेः। किं तर्हि वस्त्वंश एवासौ तादृक्प्रतीतेर्बाधकाभावात्। ततो वस्त्वंशे प्रवर्तमानो नयः स्वार्थैकदेशव्यवसायलक्षणो न प्रमाणं नापि मिथ्याज्ञानमिति।

Taken individually, there is no end to नयs (व्यासतोऽनेकविकल्पः); but in a condensed form (समासतः), that is, generically they may be divided into two: (1) द्रव्यार्थिक and (2) पर्यायार्थिक. The former takes note of the द्रव्य, and the latter of the पर्यायs.

द्रवति द्रोष्यति अदुद्रुवत् तांस्तान् पर्यायानिति द्रव्यम्। तदेवार्थः। सोऽस्ति यस्य विषयत्वेन स द्रव्यार्थिकः। पर्येत्युत्पादविनाशौ प्राप्नोतीति पर्यायः स एवार्थः सोऽस्ति यस्यासौ पर्यायार्थिकः। एतावेव च द्रव्यास्तिकपर्यायास्तिकाविति, द्रव्यस्थितपर्यायस्थिताविति, द्रव्यार्थपर्यायार्थाविति च प्रोच्येते।

—Pr. N. T.; Ratnâ.

The first of these viz. द्रव्यार्थिकनय is subdivided into (1) नैगम, (2) संग्रह and (3) व्यवहार.

(1) धर्मयोर्धर्मि॰ etc.—नैगम—which may be said to be an abbreviated form of 'नैकगमः', says Devasûri,—is the statement in which, of two धर्मs or two धर्मिन्s or one धर्म and one धर्मिन्, one is subordinated to the other.

धर्मयोर्धर्मिणोर्धर्मधर्मिणोश्च प्रधानोपसर्जनभावेन यद्विवक्षणं स नैकगमो नैगमः। पर्याययोर्द्रव्यपर्याययोश्च मुख्यामुख्यरूपतया यद्विवक्षणं स एवंरूपः नैकगमामार्गो यस्यासौ नैगमो नाम नयो ज्ञेयः। —Pr. N. T.

सच्चैतन्यमात्मनि etc.—Illustration of नैगम in which, of two धर्मs one is principal and the other is subordinate. सच्चैतन्यमात्मनि *i. e.*—In आत्मन्, there is (सत्) consciousness (चैतन्यं): here चैतन्य and सत् both are धर्मs, but one of them, viz. चैतन्य is the subject and therefore principal. सत् (existing) is subordinated (being made a विशेषण that is, a predicate) to the other viz. चैतन्य (which is a विशेष्य—the subject) सच्चैतन्यमात्मनीति धर्मयोः।

अत्र चैतन्याख्यस्य व्यञ्जनपर्यायस्य प्राधान्येन विलक्षणम्। विशेष्यत्वात् सत्त्वाख्यस्य तु व्यञ्जनपर्यायस्योपसर्जनभावेन। तस्य चैतन्यविशेषणत्वात्। इति धर्मद्वयगोचरो नैगमस्य प्रथमो भेदः। —Pr. N. T.; Ratnâ.

वस्तुपर्यायवद्॰—Another illustration of नैगम in which of two धर्मिन्s one is principal and the other subordinate. The passage may be construed in two ways: (1) पर्यायवद्द्रव्यं वस्तु, or (2) वस्तु पर्यायवद्द्रव्यम्. In (1) द्रव्य and वस्तु are the two धर्मिन्s of which द्रव्य—the subject—is the principal and वस्तु—the predicate—is subordinate. Or, (2) of the two धर्मिन्s, वस्तु (Reality)—the subject-is principal and पर्यायवद्द्रव्यम् (द्रव्य with its attributes)—the predicate—is subordinate.

वस्तु पर्यायवद् द्रव्यमिति धर्मिणोः।

अत्र हि पर्यायवद् द्रव्यं वस्तु वर्तते इति विवक्षायां पर्यायवद् द्रव्याख्यस्य धर्मिणो विशेष्यत्वेन प्राधान्यम्। वस्त्वाख्यस्य तु विशेषणत्वं न गौणत्वम्॥ यद्वा। किं वस्तु पर्यायवद् द्रव्यमिति विवक्षायां वस्तुनो विशेष्यत्वात् प्राधान्यम्। पर्यायवद् द्रव्यस्य तु विशेषणत्वात् गौणत्वमिति धर्मियुग्मगोचरोऽयं नैगमस्य द्वितीयो भेदः। —Pr. N. T.; Ratnâ.

क्षणमेकं etc.—A third illustration of नैगम— in which of one धर्म and the other धर्मिन्, one is principal and the other subordinate. Here विषयासक्तजीवः—the धर्मिन्—is principal, and क्षणमेकं सुखी—the धर्म—is the predicate and therefore subordinate.

क्षणमेकं सुखी विषयासक्तजीव इति धर्मधर्मिणोः।

अत्र हि विषयासक्तजीवाख्यस्य धर्मिणो मुख्यता। विशेष्यत्वात्। सुखलक्षणस्य तु धर्मस्याप्रधानता। तद्विशेषणत्वेनोपात्तत्वात्। इति धर्मधर्म्यालम्बनोऽयं नैगमस्य तृतीयो भेदः। —Pr. N. T.; Ratnâ.

धर्मद्वया°—When the principal and the subordinate are regarded as *absolutely* separate, we drift into नयाभास.

धर्मद्वयादीनामैकान्तिकपार्थक्याभिसन्धिर्नैगमाभासः।

आदिशब्दाद् धर्मिद्वयधर्मधर्मिद्वययोः परिग्रहः। ऐकान्तिकपार्थक्याभिसन्धिरैकान्तिकभेदाभिप्रायो नैगमाभासो नैगमदुर्नय इत्यर्थः।

यथाऽऽत्मनि सत्त्वचैतन्ये परस्परमत्यन्तं पृथग्भूते इत्यादिः।

आदिशब्दाद्वस्त्वाख्यपर्यायवद् द्रव्याख्ययोर्धर्मिणोश्च सर्वथा पार्थक्येन कथनं तदाभासत्वेन द्रष्टव्यम्॥

नैयायिकवैशेषिकदर्शनं चैतदाभासतया ज्ञेयम्॥

यथा यत् सत् तद् द्रव्यं पर्यायो वेत्यादिः।

आदिशब्दादपरसंग्रहगृहीतार्थगोचरव्यवहारोदाहरणं दृश्यम्। यद् द्रव्यं तज्जीवादि षड्विधम्। यः पर्यायः स द्विविधः क्रमभावी सहभावी चेति। एवं यो

जीवः स मुक्तः संसारी च। यः क्रमभावी पर्यायः स क्रियारूपः अक्रियारूपश्चेत्यादिः। Pr. N. T.; Ratnâ.

यथात्मनि॰ etc.—Illustration of नयाभास. To regard सत्त्व and चैतन्य or सुख and जीव in the above illustrations as *absolutely* separate is नैगमनयाभास.

(2) सामान्यमात्र॰—सामान्यमात्रग्राही परामर्शः संग्रहः।

सामान्यमात्रमशेषविशेषरहितं सत्त्वद्रव्यत्वादिकं गृह्णातीत्येवं शीलः, सम् एकीभावेन पिण्डीभूततया विशेषराशिं गृह्णातीति संग्रहः। अयमर्थः स्वजातेर्दृष्टेष्टाभ्यामविरोधेन विशेषाणामेकरूपतया यद् ग्रहणं स संग्रह इति।

—P. N. T., Ratnâ.

संग्रहनय is one in which only the universal is taken note of, the particular being quietly overlooked.

अयमुभय etc.—It is of two kinds पर and अपर (corresponding to the पर and अपर सामान्यs of the Vaiśeṣikas).

परसंग्रहनय is one in which pure द्रव्य is apprehended in its highest universality, that is as pure सत्, all the विशेषs (particulars) being overlooked: अशेषविशेषेष्वौदासीन्यं भजमानः शुद्धद्रव्यं सन्मात्रमभिमन्यमानः परसंग्रहः Ill. विश्वमेकं सदविशेषात्.

सत्ताद्वैतं etc.—When, however, an aggressive statement is made denying the विशेषs we pass from नय to नयाभास.

Ill. सत्ताद्वैतं स्वीकुर्वाणः सकलविशेषान्निराचक्षाणस्तदाभासः। यथा सत्तैव तत्त्वं ततः पृथग्भूतानां विशेषाणामदर्शनात्। अद्वैतवादिदर्शनान्यखिलानि सांख्यदर्शनं चैतदाभासत्वेन प्रत्येयम्।

द्रव्यादीन्यवान्तर etc.—अपरसंग्रहनय is one in which a द्रव्य is apprehended under any of the lower universals. द्रव्यत्वादीन्यवान्तरसामान्यानि मन्वानस्तद्भेदेषु गजनिमीलिकामवलम्बमानः पुनरपरसंग्रहः।

धर्माधर्म॰—Ill: when the द्रव्यs viz. धर्म, अधर्म etc. are apprehended under the one head of द्रव्यत्व and their particular features viz. धर्मत्व, अधर्मत्व etc. are overlooked, it is a case of अपर-संग्रह.

द्रव्यत्वापारकं etc.—When, however, you do not rest content with grouping धर्म, अधर्म etc. together in one class viz. द्रव्य, but go a step further and deny their particular distinguishing traits (विशेष), you fall into अपरसंग्रहाभास.

यथा द्रव्यत्वमेव etc.—Ill. of the above: यथा–द्रव्यत्वमेव तत्त्वं ततोऽर्थान्तरभूतानां द्रव्याणामनुपलब्धेरित्यादिः । अयं हि द्रव्यत्वस्यैव तात्त्विकतां प्रख्यापयति तद्विरोधभूतानि तु धर्मादिद्रव्याण्यपह्नुते इत्यपरसंग्रहाभासनिदर्शनम् ।

(3) संग्रहेण...व्यवहारः etc.—When things which are brought together by संग्रहनय are affirmed and then distinguished as from an ordinary, conventional point of view—it is व्यवहारनय.

संग्रहगृहीतान् सत्त्वाद्यर्थान् विधाय, न तु निषिध्य, यः परामर्शविशेषस्तानेव विभजते स व्यवहारनयः ।

यथा यत् सत् etc.—Ill. That which exists (सत्-Reality) is either द्रव्य or पर्याय. Now, as a matter of whole truth, द्रव्य and पर्याय are not separable, and yet सत् (got by संग्रहनय) is here divided into the *two*—द्रव्य and पर्याय.

यः पुनः etc.—If you go further and insist upon an *absolute* distinction of द्रव्य and पर्याय, you commit व्यवहाराभास. For in reality there is no such absolute distinction. That is, from the ordinary or व्यवहार point of view we can allow you to speak of द्रव्य *and* पर्याय, but if you insist upon their *absolute* distinction we must point out that you are going beyond your rights. You are setting up व्यवहार for परमार्थ, that is, नय for प्रमाण.

The philosophy of the materialist (चार्वाकदर्शन) is a good example of व्यवहाराभास. For, while he adopts the common people's point of view in affirming the existence of matter (as constituting our self) we may not object; but when he goes further and claiming to be a philosopher he denies the existence of जीव (our spiritual self), he falls into व्यवहाराभास.

चार्वाको हि प्रमाणप्रतिपन्नं जीवद्रव्यपर्यायादिप्रविभागं कल्पनारोपितत्वेनापह्नुते । अविचारितरमणीयं भूतचतुष्टयप्रविभागमात्रं तु स्थूललोकव्यवहारानुयायितया समर्थयते । इत्यस्य दर्शनं व्यवहारनयाभासतयोपदर्शितम् ।—Ratnā.

पर्यायार्थिकश्चतुर्धा etc.—Four more varieties of नय are added. These are sub-divisions of पर्यायार्थिक :—(1) ऋजुसूत्र, (2) शब्द, (3) समभिरूढ and (4) एवंभूत.

(1) ऋजु वर्तमान etc.—ऋजुसूत्र point of view is one in which the *actual phenomena* (attributes or changes occurring in a substance) are principally recognised. It is called ऋजु-straight, because it does not bend towards the past or the future.

ऋजु अतीतानागतकालक्षणलक्षणकौटिल्यवैकल्यात् प्राञ्जलम्। अयं हि द्रव्यं सदपि गुणीभावान्नार्पयति पर्यायांस्तु क्षणध्वंसिनः प्रधानतया दर्शयतीति Pr. N. T.; Ratn.

यथा सुखविवर्तः etc.—Ill. "At present, there is a feeling of joy in me." अनेन हि वाक्येन क्षणस्थायि सुखाख्यं पर्यायमात्रं प्राधान्येन प्रदर्श्यते, तदधिकरणभूतं पुनरात्मद्रव्यं गौणतया नार्प्यते।

सर्वथा द्रव्यापलापी—When, however, you go further and deny the substance-the आत्मन्—to whom the joy belongs, you fall into the error of ऋजुसूत्राभास—as, for example, the Buddhist does. यथा तथागतमतम्। तथागतो हि प्रतिक्षणविनश्वरान् पर्यायानेव पारमार्थिकतया समर्थयते, तदाधारभूतं तु प्रत्यभिज्ञादिप्रमाणप्रसिद्धं त्रिकालस्थायिद्रव्यं तिरस्कुरुते।

(2) कालादिभेदेन (=कालकारकलिङ्गसंख्यापुरुषोपसर्गभेदेन) Thus we may distinguish between the क्रियाs—when we say बभूव or भवति etc.—according to the different terminations applied to the root—notwithstanding that there is a single क्रिया of Being behind them.

तद्भेदेन etc.—But if we go further and distinguish between the क्रियाs as if they were so many realities distinct from each other as पाक, पाठ etc. we fall into the error of शब्दाभास.

(3) पर्यायशब्देषु etc.—समभिरूढ is one in which meanings of words are distinguished in accordance with their different etymologies. Thus, इन्द्र etc. (See supra, and Pr. N. T.)

पर्यायध्वनीनां etc.—But if anybody thinks that corresponding to the different synonyms इन्द्र, शक्र etc. there are different individuals he commits समभिरूढाभास.

(4) शब्दानां स्वप्रवृत्ति etc.—When a word is taken to signify an object *with* the क्रिया connoted by its etymology, it is एवंभूतनय. (See supra and Pr. N. T.).

एतेषु चत्वारः etc.—Another principle of division: of the seven, the first four are अर्थनयs, and the last three शब्दनयs.

पूर्वः पूर्वः etc.—every preceding नय is wider than every succeeding नय; every succeeding नय is more limited in extent than every preceding नय. This may be shown as under:

सन्मात्रगोचरात् etc.—It may be objected that, according to the above, नैगम should be wider than संग्रह, but as a matter of fact, संग्रह is the widest, inasmuch as it deals with all that *is* (सन्मात्रs). But the objection can be easily met; संग्रह deals with only Being; नैगम with both non-Being and Being. नैगम is thus, wider.

सद्विशेष०—व्यवहार deals with particular forms or entities of Being; while संग्रह with general Being. संग्रह is, therefore, wider than व्यवहार.

वर्तमानविषय०—ऋजुसूत्र is concerned with the present only, व्यवहार with the past, present and future. व्यवहार is thus wider than ऋजुसूत्र.

कालादिभेदेन etc —शब्दनय deals with अर्थs which it regards as differing according to the differences of time (tense) etc. ऋजुसूत्र makes no such distinction, and is, therefore, wider.

प्रतिपर्याय०-समभिरूढ distinguishes between the अर्थs of even synonymous terms *e. g.* इन्द्र, शक्र etc. according to their varying etymologies. शब्द does not do that. शब्द is, therefore, wider than समभिरूढ.

प्रतिक्रियं०—एवंभूत is confined to अर्थs only while they perform a particular क्रिया, and thus it distinguishes between अर्थs according to the क्रियाs connoted by the term. समभिरूढ distinguishes पुरन्दर from शचीपति, but it applies the term to Indra even when he is not engaged in 'destroying cities.' समभिरूढ is thus wider than एवंभूत.

नयवाक्यमपि etc.—Just as there is प्रमाणसप्तभङ्गी, so also there is नयसप्तभङ्गी-the differerce being that the former is of the nature of सकलादेश, the latter of विकलादेश. (See ante.)

भाष्यमहोदधि etc.—Tattvārtha Bhāṣya etc. are the principal sources of information regarding नयs.

प्रमाणं तु etc.—प्रमाण or the view of the whole truth embraces all the नयs. The नयs become प्रमाण when 'स्यात्' is added unto them. cf. Samantabhadra : "नयास्तव...etc."

तच्च द्विविधं etc.—See Tattvârtha Sûtra, Bhâṣya and Com. I. 15–16.

- प्रमाण
  - प्रत्यक्ष
    - सांव्यावहारिक
      - इन्द्रियनिमित्त
      - अनिन्द्रिय०
        - (१) अवग्रह
        - (२) ईहा
        - (३) अवाय
        - (४) धारणा
    - पारमार्थिक
      - (आत्ममात्रापेक्ष)
        - क्षायोपशमिक
          - (१) अवधि
          - (२) मनःपर्यय
        - क्षायिक
          - (३) केवलज्ञान
  - परोक्ष
    - (१) स्मृति, (२) प्रत्यभिज्ञा, (३) ऊह, (४) अनुमान, (५) आगम.
      - अनुमान:
        - स्वार्थ
        - परार्थ

Appendices.

1. The authors of the संमतितर्क and its commentary divide the schools of नय into two kinds: (1) द्रव्यास्तिक and पर्यायास्तिक *i. e.* (1) those who believe in substance, and (2) those who believe in modes. The first believe in the principle of unity or permanence, the second in that of diversity or change—corresponding respectively to the two categories of सामान्य and विशेष—or to use the language of संमति०, संगह (संग्रह) and विसेस (विशेष). [संग्रहविशेषौ द्रव्यपर्यायौ सामान्यविशेषशब्दवाच्यौ—Com.]. These are the only two fundamental नयs, the other नयs

mentioned by other writers being subsidiary varieties of these: "परस्परविविक्तसामान्यविशेषविषयत्वात् द्रव्यार्थिकपर्यायार्थिकावेव नयौ, न च तृतीयं प्रकारान्तरमस्ति यद्विषयोऽन्यस्ताभ्यां व्यतिरिक्तो नयः स्यात्। तृतीयविषयस्य चासंभवो भेदाभेदविनिर्मुक्तस्य भावस्वभावस्यापरस्यानुपपत्तेः। ताभ्यामन्य एकस्तद्वानर्थोऽस्तीति चेत्, न; स्वभावान्तराभावात् प्रकृतविकल्पानतिवृत्तेः तत्स्वभावातिक्रमे वा खपुष्पसदृशत्वप्रसक्तेः॥" *i. e.* the principle of the main division is one of dichotomy and therefore no other variety is possible alongside of it, all the other varieties which are mentioned in other books falling under one or the other of these two: (दवट्ठिओ य पज्जवणओ य सेसा वियप्पा सिं द्रव्यास्तिकश्च पर्यायनयश्च शेषा विकल्पास्तयोः—Saṁmati. "शेषास्तु नैगमादयो विकल्पा भेदाः अनयोर्द्रव्यार्थिकपर्यायार्थिकयोः"—Com.)

The द्रव्यास्तिकनय is next divided into 'शुद्ध' or simple and 'अशुद्ध' or complex, represented respectively by the unitarian Vedântin and the trinitarian Sâṁkhya. Both these schools of द्रव्यास्तिक, while they criticise their opponents from their own standpoints, are themselves criticised by the पर्यायास्तिकनय. Before proceeding to subdivide the latter, it may be mentioned as noteworthy that the author of the Saṁmati does not mention नैगमनय. But the commentator notes it and gives a derivation which is more probable than that given by देवसूरि, the author of the P. N. Tattvâlokâlaṁkâra ("नैकगमो नैगमः") and others. Thus, he says: "येषां तु मतेन नैगमनयस्य सद्भावस्तैस्तस्य स्वरूपमेवं वर्णितम्—राश्यन्तरोपलब्धं नित्यत्वमनित्यत्वं च नयतीति निगमव्यवस्थाभ्युपगमपरो च नैगमनयः। निगमो हि नित्यानित्य-सदसत्-कृतकाकृतकस्वरूपेषु भावेष्वपास्तसांकर्यस्वभावः सर्वथैव धर्मधर्मिभेदेन संपद्यत इति । स पुनर्नैगमोऽनेकधा व्यवस्थितः प्रतिपत्त्रभिप्रायवशान्नयव्यवस्थानात्। प्रतिपत्तारश्च नानाभिप्रायाः।—" *i. e.* नैगमनय is the method of arriving at absolute conclusion regarding the nature of things, *e g.* something is नित्य, and something else is अनित्य. 'निगमन' a technical term of Indian Logic, which means deduction or arriving at a conclusion from premises. It is to be noted that according to नैगमनय different things have different natures, such as, नित्यत्व or अनित्यत्व, that is, some are नित्य and some are अनित्य not that *one* and the same thing may have different aspects such as नित्यत्व and अनित्यत्व. The latter is the 'प्रमाण' or whole view, while the former is only a नय or part-view.

'व्यवहारनय' is the common-sense or popularly accepted view of things. Thus the commonly accepted view which speaks of प्रमाण, प्रमेय, and प्रमिति is an example of व्यवहारनय. (लोकप्रतीतापथानुसारेण प्रतिपत्तिगौरवपरिहारेण प्रमाण-प्रमेय-प्रमिति-प्रतिपादनं व्यवहारप्रसिद्ध्यर्थं परीक्षकैः समाश्रितमिति व्यवहारनयाभिप्रायः —Com.): So far we have been dealing with द्रव्यास्तिकनय. Next we come to पाण्मासिक. ऋजुसूत्र is the naive view which takes note of what appears to be only now and here (देशकालान्तर-संबद्धस्वभावरहितं वस्तुतत्त्वं सांप्रतिकमेकस्वभावमकुटिलं ऋजु सूत्रयतीति ऋजुसूत्रः—Com.). The Buddhist क्षणभङ्गवाद view that all reality is क्षणिक, is an example of this kind. It arises from confining the attention to things here and now, that is, क्षणs. Similary विज्ञानमात्रवाद—another Buddhist view—which attempts to avoid all the difficulties of epistemology by regarding ideas as the only reals may be looked upon as ऋजुसूत्र. Or, one may get rid of even this trouble, that of affirming the reality of विज्ञान, and thus hold the simplest of all doctrines, viz. शून्यवाद. The first it the doctrine of Buddhist realists, सौत्रान्तिक and वैभाषिक; the second of the योगाचार; and the third of the माध्यमिक.

Next, शब्दनयः—"शब्दनयश्च ऋजुसूत्राभिमतपर्यायात् शुद्धतरं पर्यायं स्वविषयत्वेन व्यवस्थापयति । तथाहि—तटः, तटी, तटम् इति विरुद्धलिङ्गलक्षणधर्माक्रान्तं भिन्नमेव वस्तु, नहि तत्कृतं धर्मभेदमननुभवतस्तत्सम्बन्धो युक्तः। तद्धर्मभेदे वा स्वयं धर्मी कथं न भिद्यते ?......एकस्मिन्नुदकपरमाणौ आपः इति बहुत्वसंख्यया निर्देशोऽनुपपन्नः ॥ न ह्येकत्वसंख्यासमाध्यासितं तदेव विरुद्धबहुत्वसंख्योपेतं भवतीत्येकसंख्ययैव तन्निर्देष्टव्यम्। कालभेदाद्वस्तुभेदः ऋजुसूत्रेणाप्यभ्युपगम्यत एव ।...विरमति इति न युक्तः। आत्मार्थतायां हि विरमते इत्यस्यैव प्रयोगसंगतेः। न चैवं लोकशास्त्रव्यवहारविलोप इति वक्तव्यम्। सर्वत्रैव नयमते तद्विलोपस्य समानत्वात्। इति यथार्थशब्दनात् शब्दनयो व्यवस्थितः।"

It will be noticed that शब्दनय insists upon punctiliousness of language so much so that it would not permit the use of the plural 'आपः' for a drop of water or even 'विरमति' (although grammatically sound) instead of 'विरमते' where the क्रिया is आत्मने. Of course, this would involve a great deal of revolution in the use of words, but this is necessary if we are to avoid looseness of language and secure complete correspondence between language and things, expression and things expressed. ऋजुसूत्र recognises the distinctions made by time; शब्दनय recognises distinctions due to language. Moreover, it frankly admits that in doing so it has frequently to override व्यवहार.

समभिरूढ—carries the punctiliousness of language still further (शुद्धतर). It recognises differences of things corresponding to those of synonyms. "एकसंज्ञासमभिरोहणात् समभिरूढस्त्वाह यथा हि विरुद्धलिङ्गादियोगाद् भिद्यते वस्तु तथा संज्ञाभेदादपि। तथाहि—संज्ञाभेदः प्रयोजनवशात् संकेतकर्तृभिर्विधीयते न व्यसनितया। अन्यथाऽनवस्थाप्रसक्तेः। ततो यावन्तो वस्तुनः स्वाभिधायकाः शब्दास्तावन्तोऽर्थभेदाः। नैकस्यार्थस्यानेकेनाभिधानं युक्तम्।...क्रियाशब्दत्वाद्वा सर्वशब्दानां सर्वेऽप्यन्वर्था एव वाचकाः।"

"एवंभूतः शब्दाभिधेयक्रियापरिणतिवेलायामेव तद्वस्तु इति भूत एवंभूतः प्राह—यथा संज्ञाभेदाद् भेदवद् वस्तु तथा क्रियाभेदादपि। सा च क्रिया तद्रेत्री यदैव तामाविशति तदैव तन्निमित्तं तत्तद्व्यपदेशमासादयति नान्यदेत्यतिप्रसङ्गात्। "तथाहि यदा घटते तदैवासौ घटः॥" *i. e.* एवंभूत goes even beyond समभिरूढ. While the latter insists upon recognising distinctions of things corresponding to distinctions of synonyms, एवंभूत would confine the word to the thing just while it performs the क्रिया which it connotes.

2. नय is thus characterised in the Râja-Vârtika: "प्रमाणप्रकाशितोऽर्थविशेषप्ररूपको नयः" which is explained as follows: "प्रकर्षेण मानं प्रमाणं सकलादेश इत्यर्थः। तेन प्रकाशितानां न प्रमाणाभासपरिगृहीतानामित्यर्थः। तेषामर्थानामस्तित्वनास्तित्वनित्यत्वाद्यन्तात्मनां जीवादीनां ये विशेषाः पर्यायास्तेषां प्रकर्षेण रूपकः प्ररूपकः।" Its primary varieties are said to be 'द्रव्यास्तिक,' and 'पर्यायास्तिक', also called 'द्रव्यार्थिक' and 'पर्यायार्थिक' which practically convey the same meanings. The words are explained as follows: द्रव्यमस्तीति मतिरस्य द्रव्यभवनमेव नातोऽन्ये भावविकाराः नाप्यभावस्तद्व्यतिरेकेणानुपलब्धेरिति द्रव्यास्तिकः। पर्याय एवास्ति इति मतिरस्य जन्मादिभावविकारमात्रमेव भवनं न ततोऽन्यद् द्रव्यमस्ति तद्व्यतिरेकेणानुपलब्धेरिति पर्यायास्तिकः॥ अथवा द्रव्य-

मेवार्थोऽस्य न गुणकर्मणी तदवस्थारूपादिति द्रव्यार्थिकः । पर्याय एवार्थोऽस्य रूपाद्युत्क्षेपणादिलक्षणादिलक्षणो न ततोऽन्यद् द्रव्यमिति पर्यायार्थिकः । अथवा अर्यते गम्यते निष्पाद्यत इत्यर्थः । कार्यं द्रवति गच्छतीति द्रव्यं कारणम् । द्रव्यमेवार्थोऽस्य कारणमेव कार्यं नार्थान्तरं, न च कार्यकारणयोः कश्चिद्रूपभेदः तदुभयमेकाकारमेव पर्वाङ्गुलिद्रव्यवदिति द्रव्यार्थिकः । परि समन्ताद् आयः पर्यायः । पर्याय एवार्थः कार्यमस्य न द्रव्यमतीतानागतयोर्विनष्टानुत्पन्नत्वेन व्यवहाराभावात् स एवैकः कार्यकारणव्यपदेशभागिति पर्यायार्थिकः । अथवाऽर्थनमर्थः प्रयोजनं द्रव्यमेवार्थोऽस्य प्रत्ययाभिधानानुप्रवृत्तिलिङ्गदर्शनस्य निह्नोतुमशक्यत्वादिति द्रव्यार्थिकः । पर्यायोऽर्थः प्रयोजनमस्य वाग्विज्ञानव्यावृत्तिनिबन्धव्यवहारप्रसिद्धेरिति पर्यायार्थिकः ॥

Next the नयs are classified and defined as follows:

(1) अर्थसंकल्पमात्रग्राही नैगमः—which is explained thus: निगच्छन्त्यस्मिन्निति निगमनमात्रं वा निगमः, निगमे कुशलो भवो वा नैगमः तस्य लोके व्यापारः. निगम means that to which one goes, *i. e.* object aimed at, the idea of an object (अर्थसंकल्पमात्र) as distinguished from its accomplishment; the end, purpose, intention, objective. नैगमनय—is a statement with reference to the objective. It is illustrated thus: अर्थसंकल्पमात्रग्रहणं प्रस्थेन्द्रगृहगम्यादिषु—तद्यथा कंचित् प्रगृह्य परशुं पुरुषं गच्छन्तमभिसमीक्ष्याह किमर्थं गच्छति भवान् इति स तस्मै व्याचष्टे प्रस्थार्थमिति । तथा इन्द्रगृहादावपि । तथा कतरेऽत्र गमीत्युक्ते आचष्टे अहं गमीति संप्रत्यगच्छत्यपि गमीति व्यवहारः *e. g.* A man goes out, axe in hand, to fell a tree, take some wood out of it and make a प्रस्थ (a wooden measure for measuring grain). When asked 'why are you going?' he answers 'for a प्रस्थ.' Now here the immediate object of going is to cut a tree, but he says "for a प्रस्थ"—which is done with reference to the final purpose of going.

(2) स्वजात्यविरोधेनैकत्वोपनयात् समस्तग्रहणं संग्रहः—'संग्रह' is that in which many are *collected into one* without contradicting their own nature *e. g.* when one says सद्द्रव्यं घटः—the द्रव्यत्व (स्वजाति) of घट is not denied, but it is subsumed under the higher category of सत्; similarly, all the घटs whether made of gold or clay may be called by the class-name घट, which does not deny the individual natures of different घटs and yet brings

together all the घटs and calls them by a class-name, घट. (घट इति चोक्ते नामादिभेदान्मृत्सुवर्णादिकारणविशेषाद्वर्णसंस्थानादिविकाराच्च भिन्नानां घटशब्दवाच्यानां तदव्यतिरेकत्वेन संग्रहः ")

(3) अतो विधिपूर्वकमवहरणं व्यवहारः—When without denying the general (संग्रह) one specifies a particular, for that alone would serve his purpose, the नय is called व्यवहार. (वि=विधिपूर्वकम्+अवहरणम्)—taking out (अवहरणं) a part from the class, affirmatively (विधिपूर्वकम्) that is, without denying the truth of संग्रह. The necessity and scope of this नय are thus explained in detail: सर्वसंग्रहेण यत्संगृहीतं तच्चानपेक्षितविशेषं नालं संव्यवहारायेति व्यवहारनय आश्रीयते ।—यत् सत् तद् द्रव्यं गुणो वेति। द्रव्येणापि च संग्रहाक्षिप्तेन जीवाजीवविशेषानपेक्षेण न शक्यः संव्यवहार इति । जीवद्रव्यमजीवद्रव्यमिति वा व्यवहार आश्रीयते। जीवाजीवावपि च संग्रहाक्षिप्तौ नालं संव्यवहारायेति प्रत्येकं देवनारकादिर्घटादिश्च व्यवहारेणाश्रीयते। कषायो भैषज्यमित्युक्ते च सामान्यस्य विशेषात्मकत्वान्नैयग्रोधादिविशेषसामर्थ्यं नहि शक्यः प्रभुणापि चक्रभृता सर्वैः कषायसमाहारः कर्तुम्। नामस्थापनाद्रव्याणि च संग्रहोपात्तानि नालं व्यवहारायेति भाव एव गृह्यते। एवमयं नयस्तावद्वर्तते यावत् पुनर्नास्ति विभागः।

This detail shows that व्यवहार is the opposite of संग्रह, and takes note of the particular instead of the general which is the viewpoint of संग्रह.

(4) सूत्रपातवदृजुसूत्रः—यथा ऋजुः सूत्रपातस्तथा ऋजु प्रगुणं सूत्रयति तन्त्रयति ऋजुसूत्रः। सर्वांस्त्रिकालविषयानतिशय्य वर्तमानविषयकालमादत्ते। ऋजुसूत्र *i. e.* the straight or direct point of view, which takes note of the present only, for this alone is directly the object of knowledge.

(5) (शब्दः) स च लिङ्गसंख्यासाधनादिव्यभिचारनिवृत्तिपरः—'शब्द' is the नय which insists upon accuracy of language. It tolerates no looseness of language in point of gender, number etc. if it conflicts with reality, not even if it be allowed by grammar. (See the examples given above.)

(6) नानार्थसमभिरोहणात् समभिरूढः—यतो नानार्थान् समतीत्यैकमर्थमाभिमुख्येन रूढस्ततः समभिरूढः। कुतः वस्त्वन्तरासंक्रमेण तन्निष्ठत्वात्। .... एकस्यार्थस्यैकेन गतत्वात् पर्यायशब्दप्रयोगोऽनर्थकः शब्दभेदश्चेदस्ति अर्थ-

भेदेनाप्यवश्यं भवितव्यमिति । नानार्थसमभिरोहणात् समभिरूढः । इन्दनादिन्द्रः, शकनाच्छक्रः, पूर्दारणात् पुरन्दर इत्येवं सर्वत्र ॥ अथवा यो यत्राभिरूढः स तत्र समेत्याभिमुख्येनारोहात् समभिरूढः ।

Synonyms connote differences of meaning, and so they should be employed with strict adherence to their connotation. This is the point of view of 'समभिरूढ'—*i. e.* the presentation of the connotation before the mental eye.

(7) येनात्मनाभूतस्तेनैवाध्यावसाययतीत्येवंभूतः। which is explained: येनात्मना येनाभिधेयेन भूतः शब्दस्तेनैवाध्यवसाययति । यथेन्द्रशब्दः परमेश्वरत्वाभिधेयः स परिणामो यत्र यदा वर्तते तत्र तदैव युक्तो न नामस्थापनाद्रव्येषु तत्परिणामाभावात् । इत्येवमितरेष्वपि शब्देषु स्वाभिधेयक्रियापरिणतिक्षण एव युक्तिर्नान्यदेति ॥ अथवा येनात्मना येन स्वरूपेण भूतोऽर्थस्तेनैवाध्यवसाययति यथा गच्छतीति गौरिति यदैव गच्छति तदैव गौरिति न स्थितो न शायित इति । पूर्वोत्तरकालयोस्तदर्थाभावात् दण्डिवत् ॥ अथवा येनात्मना येन ज्ञानेन भूतः परिणतस्तेनैवाध्यवसाययति यथेन्द्राग्निज्ञानपरिणत आत्मैवेन्द्रोऽग्निश्चेत्येवं भूतार्थप्रत्यायनाच्छब्द एवंभूतः तत्कार्यीत्वाच्छब्दसिद्धेः ॥

3. The author of the Tattvârtha–S'loka–Vârtika observes:

सामान्यादेशतस्तावदेक एव नयः स्थितः ।
स्याद्वादप्रविभक्तार्थविशेषव्यञ्जनात्मकः ॥ I. 33.

—In its most general form, नय is but one, and it consists of the presentation of a particular truth—which is part of the comprehensive truth which is expressed in स्याद्वाद. He next divides them into two main types: संक्षेपाद् द्वौ विशेषेण द्रव्यपर्यायगोचरौ ॥ *i. e.* द्रव्य and पर्याय (the latter including गुण)—of which the first comprises the three नैगम, संग्रह and व्यवहार, and the second the remaining four, ऋजुसूत्र, शब्द, समभिरूढ and एवंभूत. The term 'नय' is explained thus: नीयते गम्यते येन श्रुतार्थांशो नयो हि सः ।—*i. e.* that by which *part* of the truth is conveyed. The different नयs mentioned in the Tattva-Sûtra (I. 33) spring from the two primary नयs, द्रव्य० and पर्याय० (प्रमाणगोचरार्थांशा नीयन्ते यैरनेकधा । ते नया इति व्याख्याता जाता मूलनयद्वयात्). The author rejects the view of those who hold that there are four नयs, सामान्य० and विशेष being added to द्रव्य० and पर्याय. The ground for the rejection is that they are included in द्रव्य and

पर्याय. Next, 'नैगम' is defined तत्र संकल्पमात्रस्य ग्राहको नैगमो नयः and is explained in two ways: (1) संकल्पो निगमस्तत्र भवोऽयं तत्प्रयोजनः *e.g.* तथा प्रस्थादिसंकल्पः तदभिप्राय इष्यते, and (2) यद्वा नैकंगमो योऽत्र स सतां नैगमो मतः। It is distinct from संग्रह and व्यवहार; for these refer only to a part of नैगम—संग्रहे व्यवहारे च नान्तर्भावः समीक्ष्यते। नैगमस्य, तयोरेकवस्त्वंशप्रवणत्वतः। नैगम being thus shown to be indispensable, the total number of नयs is seven and not six as some have urged. Others, again, speak of nine नयs thus:—पर्यायनैगमः, द्रव्यनैगमः, द्रव्यपर्यायनैगमश्चेति। तत्र प्रथमस्त्रेधा अर्थपर्यायनैगमो व्यञ्जनपर्यायनैगमोऽर्थव्यञ्जनपर्यायनैगमश्चेति। द्वितीयो द्विधा। शुद्धद्रव्यनैगमः, अशुद्धद्रव्यनैगमश्चेति। तृतीयश्चतुर्धा शुद्धद्रव्यार्थपर्यायनैगमः, शुद्धद्रव्यव्यञ्जनपर्यायनैगमः, अशुद्धद्रव्यार्थपर्यायनैगमः, अशुद्धद्रव्यव्यञ्जनपर्यायनैगमश्चेति नवधा नैगमः। संग्रहादयस्तु वक्ष्यमाणा षडिति पञ्चदश नयाः समासतः प्रतिपत्तव्याः।

Next coming to संग्रह, the term is thus defined and explained

एकत्वेन विशेषाणां ग्रहणं संग्रहो नयः।
सजातेरविरोधेन दृष्टेष्टाभ्यां कथंचन ॥
समेकीभावसम्यक्त्वे वर्तमानो हि गृह्यते।

Next is व्यवहार, which is defined and explained as in the Râjavârtika:—

संग्रहेण गृहीतानामर्थानां विधिपूर्वकः।
योऽवहारो विभागः स्याद्व्यवहारो नयः स्मृतः।

Next ऋजुसूत्र—

"ऋजुसूत्रं क्षणध्वंसि वस्तु सत् सूत्रयेदृजु।
प्राधान्येन गुणीभावाद्द्रव्यस्यानर्पणात् सतः।

Next शब्दनय—

"कालादिभेदतोऽर्थस्य भेदं यः प्रतिपादयेत्।
सोऽत्र शब्दनयः शब्दप्रधानत्वादुदाहृतः॥"

Lastly, समभिरूढ—

"पर्यायशब्दभेदेन भिन्नार्थस्याधिरोहणात्।"

नयः समभिरूढः स्यात्। *e. g.* इन्द्रः पुरन्दरः शक्र इत्याद्या भिन्नगोचराः। शब्दा विभिन्नशब्दत्वाद्वाजिवारणशब्दवत्—*i. e.* synonyms are really words with different meanings.

In conclusion, the division of नयs into शब्दनयs and अर्थनयs and their comparative extents are thus stated in the T. S'l. Vârtika:

तत्रर्जुसूत्रपर्यन्ताश्चत्वारोऽर्थनयाः स्मृताः ।
त्रयः शब्दनयाः शेषाः शब्दवाच्यार्थगोचराः ॥
पूर्वपूर्वनयो भूमविषयः कारणात्मकः ।
परः परः पुनः सूक्ष्मगोचरो हेतुमानिह ॥
सन्मात्रविषयत्वेन संग्रहस्य न युज्यते ।
महाविषयताभावाभावार्थान्नैगमान्नयात् ॥
यथा हि सति संकल्पस्तथैवासति वेद्यते ।
तत्र प्रवर्तमानस्य नैगमस्य महार्थता ॥
संग्रहाद्व्यवहारोऽपि सद्विशेषावबोधकः ।
न भूमविषयो शेषसत्समूहोपदर्शितः ॥
नर्जुसूत्रप्रभूतार्थो वर्तमानार्थगोचरः ।
कालत्रितयवृत्त्यर्थगोचराद्व्यवहारतः ॥
कालादिभेदतोऽप्यर्थमभिन्नमुपगच्छतः ।
नर्जुसूत्रान्महार्थोऽत्र शब्दस्तद्विपरीतवत् ॥
शब्दात् पर्यायभेदेनाभिन्नमर्थमभीप्सितः ।
न स्यात् समभिरूढोऽपि महार्थस्तद्विपर्ययः ॥
क्रियाभेदेऽपि चाभिन्नमर्थमभ्युपगच्छतः ।
नैवंभूतः प्रभूतार्थो नयः समभिरूढतः ॥

The Tattva S'l. Vârtika applies the principle of सप्तभङ्गी to the नयs—which is detailed in the commentary as follows:

इह तावन्नैगमस्य संग्रहादिभिः सह षड्भिः प्रत्येकं षट् सप्तभङ्ग्यः संग्रहस्य व्यवहारादिभिः सह वचनात् । पंच व्यवहारस्य । ऋजुसूत्रादिभिश्चतस्रः, ऋजुसूत्रस्य शब्दादिभिस्तिस्रः, शब्दस्य समभिरूढादिभ्यां द्वे, समभिरूढस्यैवंभूतेनैका, इत्येकविंशतिमूलनयसप्तभङ्ग्यः ।

4. Siddharṣi's commentary on the Nyâyâvatâra of Siddhasena Divâkara deals with the subject of नयs in full detail, and like the commentary on the Sammatitarka, it shows how the different systems of Brâhmaṇa and Bauddha philosophy represent particular नयs or partial viewpoints only, that is to say, they are नयs and not प्रमाण. See—

अनेकात्मकं वस्तु गोचरः सर्वसंविदाम् ।
एकदेशविशिष्टोऽर्थः नयस्य विषयो मतः ॥

Nyâyâvatâra, 29.

...एतेनास्य हेतोः कापिला अप्यसिद्धतादिदोषमभिधित्सवो मौक्यमानीताः .... ॥ तथा सुगतमतानुसारिणामपि मध्ये सौत्रान्तिकस्तावदस्य हेतोरसिद्धतामाविर्भावयितुं नोत्सहते, तदभ्युपगतिव्यतिरेकेण निजदर्शनव्यवस्थानुपपत्तेः......... ॥

तथोररीकृतयोगाचारमतमपि बलादनेकान्तप्रकाशरज्जुरावेष्टयति एकस्यापि ज्ञानस्यानेकवेद्यवेदकाकारतया प्रथनोपगतेः ।......... ॥

शून्यवादिनः समस्ताभावादसिद्धोऽनेकान्तप्रकाश इति चेन्न, तस्यापि प्रमाणप्रमेयाभावेन सर्वाभाववेदनं समस्ति, अन्यथाऽप्रमाणकं सर्वं सर्वत्र विद्यते इति परस्यापि वदतो न वदनभङ्गः स्यात्, तदभ्युपगमेऽभ्युपगमक्षतिः ।...........

नयस्तर्हि किंभूतं मन्यते इति वचनावकाशे सत्याह एक इत्यादि । अनन्तधर्माध्यासितं वस्तु स्वाभिप्रेतैकधर्मविशिष्टं नयति प्रापयति संवेदनमारोहयतीति नयः प्रमाणप्रवृत्तेरुत्तरकालभावी परामर्श इत्यर्थः । तस्य विषयो गोचरोऽभिमतः अभिप्रेतैकदेशेनानित्यत्वादिधर्मलक्षणेन विशिष्टः पररूपेभ्यो व्यवच्छिन्न इत्यर्थः॥...

ननु चादिवाक्यतः प्रमाणव्युत्पादनमात्रं प्रतिज्ञातं तत् किमयमप्रस्तुतोऽत्र नयगोचरः प्रतिपाद्यत इति ।

न नयः प्रमाणादत्यन्तं दूरयायी; किं तर्हि? तदंशभूत एव; नयसमुदायसंपाद्यत्वात् प्रमाणस्य, अतस्तद्व्युत्पादनप्रतिज्ञातेऽसावपि तन्मध्यपतितस्तद्ग्रहणेन गृह्यत इति न्यायाद् गृहीत एव तत्रायमप्रस्तुत इति तत्र प्रमाणप्रतिपन्नार्थैकदेशपरामर्शो नय इति लक्षणम् । सर्वनयविशेषानुयायित्वात् पररूपव्यावर्तनक्षमत्वाच्चास्य । संख्यया पुनरनन्ता इति । अनन्तधर्मत्वाद्वस्तुनः, तदेकदेशधर्मपर्यायावसिताभिप्रायाणां च नयत्वात् । तथापि चिरंतनाचार्यैः सर्वसंग्राहिसत्ताभिप्रायपरिकल्पनाद्वारेण सप्त नयाः प्रतिपादिताः । तद्यथा—नैगमसंग्रहव्यवहारर्जुसूत्रशब्दसमभिरूढैवंभूता नया इति । अतोऽस्माभिरपि त एव वर्ण्यन्ते । कथमेते सर्वाभिप्रायसंग्राहका इति चेत् उच्यते । अभिप्रायस्तावदर्थद्वारेण शब्दद्वारेण वा प्रवर्तेत, गत्यन्तराभावात् । अर्थश्च सामान्यरूपो विशेषरूपो वा । शब्दोऽपि रूढितो व्युत्पत्तितश्च । व्युत्पत्तिरपि सामान्यनिमित्तप्रयुक्ता तत्कालभाविनिमित्तप्रयुक्ता वा स्यात् । तत्र ये केचनार्थनिरूपणप्रवणाः प्रमात्रभिप्रायास्ते सर्वेऽप्याद्ये नयचतुष्टयेऽन्तर्भवन्ति । तत्रापि ये परस्पराविशकलितौ सामान्यविशेषाविच्छन्ति तत्समुदायरूपो नैगमः । ये पुनः केवलं सामान्यं वाञ्छन्ति तत्समूहसंपाद्यः संग्रहः। ये पुनरनपेक्षितशास्त्रीयसामान्यविशेषं लोकव्यवहारमवतरन्तं

घटादिकं पदार्थमभिप्रेयन्ति तन्निचयजन्यो व्यवहारः। ये सौगतास्तु क्षणक्षयिणः परमाणुलक्षणा विशेषाः सत्या इति मन्यन्ते तत्संघातघटित ऋजुसूत्र इति। तथा ये मीमांसकाः रूढितः शब्दानां प्रवृत्तिं वाञ्छन्ति तन्निबद्धसाध्यः शब्द इति। ये तु व्युत्पत्तितो ध्वनीनां प्रवृत्तिं वाञ्छन्ति नान्यथा, तद्द्वारजन्यः समभिरूढ इति। ये तु वर्तमानकालभाविव्युत्पत्तिनिमित्तमधिकृत्य शब्दाः प्रवर्तन्ते नान्यथेति मन्यन्ते तत्संघटितः खल्वेवंभूत इति। तदेवं न स कश्चन विकल्पोऽस्ति वस्तुगोचरो योऽत्र नयसप्तके नान्तर्यातीति सर्वाभिप्रायसंग्राहका एते इति स्थितम् ॥

Since the different systems of Bauddha and Brâhmaṇa philosophy arise, as shown above, from the fact that their teachers have failed to see things whole, it follows that their teachings are not प्रमाण. If so, a question arises: Why has the subject of partial viewpoints—called नय—been discussed here, in connection with प्रमाण? The answer given is: Because नयs, though wrong (अप्रमाण) as statements of whole truth, do deal with part truth, (प्रमाणप्रतिपन्नार्थैकदेशपरामर्शो नयः), and so come to be considered in the chapter on प्रमाण. Siddharṣi next proceeds to show how all 'अभिप्राय's or truths which the different systems purport to convey are embraced in the classification of नय which is here given. Thus, अभिप्राय-स्तावदर्थद्वारेण शब्दद्वारेण प्रवर्तेत। Next, अर्थश्च सामान्यरूपो विशेषरूपो वा। P. N. T. [These—सामान्य and विशेष—again may be taken as independent of each other (विशकलितौ—severed, distinct,) or only one of them may be recognised and the other overlooked, or only the popular view—as distinguished from the logical view—of सामान्य and विशेष—may be accepted.] Similarly, शब्दोऽपि रूढितो व्युत्पत्तितश्च। व्युत्पत्ति, again, may be सामान्यनिमित्त-प्रयुक्ता or तत्कालभाविनिमित्तप्रयुक्ता. Thus will arise the different नयs.

5. भवन्ति नैगमादयः—उक्तं च "नैगमसंग्रहव्यवहारऋजुसूत्रशब्दसमभिरूढैवंभूता नयाः"। एते च द्रव्यास्तिकपर्यायास्तिकलक्षणे नयद्वयेऽन्तर्भाव्यन्ते। द्रव्यमेव परमार्थतोऽस्ति न पर्याया इत्यभ्युपगमपरो द्रव्यास्तिकः। पर्याया एव वस्तुतः सन्ति न द्रव्यमित्यभ्युपगमपरः पर्यायास्तिकः। तत्राद्यास्त्रयो द्रव्यास्तिकाः, शेषास्तु पर्यायास्तिकाः। पुनर्द्रव्यास्तिकोऽपि सामान्यतो द्विविधो विशुद्धोऽविशुद्धश्च। तत्र नैगमव्यवहाररूपोऽविशुद्धः संग्रहरूपस्तु विशुद्धः। कथम्?। यतो नैगम-व्यवहारावनन्तपरमाण्वनन्तद्व्यणुकाद्यनेकव्यक्त्यात्मकं कृष्णाद्यनेकगुणाधारं त्रिकाल-

विषयं वाऽविशुद्धं द्रव्यमिच्छतः। संग्रहश्च परमाण्वादिकं परमाण्वादिसाम्यादेकं तिरोभूतगुणकलापमविद्यमानपूर्वापरविभागं नित्यं सामान्यमेव द्रव्यमिच्छति। एतच्च किलानेकताद्यभ्युपगमकलङ्केनाकलङ्कितत्वाच्छुद्धम्। ततः शुद्धद्रव्याभ्युगमपरत्वादयमेव शुद्धः॥—अनुयोगमलधारीया. Com. on अनुयोग. This illustrates the नयs in their relation to the problem of the nature of substance and forms or modes.

6. "निलयनप्रस्थके"त्यादि—तत्र निलयनं वसनमित्यनर्थान्तरम्। तद्दृष्टान्तो यथा—कश्चित् केनचित् पृष्टः क्व वसति भवान्? स प्राह—लोके। तत्रापि जम्बूद्वीपे, तत्रापि भरतक्षेत्रे, तत्रापि मध्यमखण्डे, तत्राप्येकस्मिन् जनपदे नगरे गृहे इत्यादीन् सर्वानपि विकल्पान् नैगम इच्छति॥ प्रस्थको धान्यमानविशेषः तद्दृष्टान्तो यथा —सद्योग्यं काष्ठं वृक्षावस्थायामपि तदनुकीर्तिकं स्कन्धे कृतं गृहमानीतमित्यादि सर्वास्वप्यवस्थासु नैगमः प्रस्थकमिच्छति। ग्रामोदाहरणं यथा—विवक्षितग्रामवास्तव्यप्रधानकतिपयपुरुषदर्शनेऽपि ग्रामोऽयावितीच्छति नैगमः॥ "भमराइ गाहा"। इह भ्रमरकोकिलादिः कृष्णतयोपलभ्यमानोऽपि निश्चयमतेन पञ्चवर्णः, शेषवर्णचतुष्टयं हि न्यग्भूतत्वात्तत्र न दृश्यते न पुनर्नास्तीति प्रतिपद्यतेऽसौ। तथा प्रज्ञप्तिः—"भमरेणं भंते! कइवण्णे कइगंधे कइरसे कइफासे? गौतमा—इत्थं दो नया कज्जंति। तं जहा—निच्छनए य वावहारियनए अ। वावहारिअनयस्स कालए भमरे, निच्छनयस्स पंचवण्णे दुगंधे पंचरसे अट्ठफासे" इत्यादि। एवं नीललोहितपीतशुक्लतया व्यवहारतोऽवगतेष्वपि वस्तुषु निश्चयतः पञ्चवर्णताऽवगन्तव्या। तदेवं भ्रमरादौ निश्चयनयमतेन पञ्चवर्णे निश्चिते सति व्यवहारस्य को निश्चयार्थ इत्याह—"सो विणिच्छयत्थोत्ति" स विनिश्चयार्थ इति ज्ञेयः।......। यस्मिन् वा कस्मिंश्चिदर्थे जनपदस्य गोपालाङ्गनादिरूपस्य नामस्थापनाद्रव्यभावानामन्यतररूपेण वा निश्चयः समुत्पद्यते स विनिश्चयार्थः।......। अन्येषु सत्स्वपि बहुष्वशेषगोपालाङ्गनादिजनपदस्योद्भूतशक्तितया यो ग्राह्योंऽशः स विनिश्चयार्थः। तदर्थं व्रजति व्यवहार इति गाथार्थः। यस्मिन्नेवांशे जनपदस्य निश्चयो भवति किमित्यसौ तमेव गमयति सतोऽपि शेषांशान् मुञ्चतीत्याह—'बहुतर उत्ति य' इत्यादि। स एव बहुतरांशो यत्र जनपदस्य निश्चय उत्पद्यत इति तमेवांशं गमयति व्यवहारपथमवतारयति। येषु त्वंशेषु लोकस्य निश्चयो न भवति तान् सतोऽपि मुञ्चति व्यवहारो नयः- किं कुर्वन्?। लोकं लोकव्यवहारमिच्छन्। कया?। संव्यवहारपरतया, संव्यवहारस्वरूपत्वादेव तस्येति गाथार्थः। "प्रति प्रति वोत्पन्नमिति"। एकैकं स्वामिनमाश्रित्योत्पन्नम्। एतदेवाह। "भिन्नव्यक्ती"त्यादि। भिन्ना व्यक्तयः स्वामिन्यो यस्य तत्तथाभूतम्। ऋजुसूत्रो हि वर्तमानक्षणभाव्येव वस्त्विच्छति तदपि भिन्नव्यक्तिस्वामिकम्। तन्मतेन हि यद्देवदत्तस्य वित्तं तद् यज्ञदत्तस्यावित्तमेव तदपेक्षया वित्तकार्याकारणाद् यज्ञदत्तस्यापि यद्वित्तं तद्देवदत्तस्याप्यवित्तमेव तत एव हेतोः। तस्माद् द्वयोरपि वित्तयोभिन्नस्वाम्यपेक्षयैव वित्तत्वमिति भिन्नव्यक्तिस्वामिता। "ऋजुसूत्रः ऋजुश्रुतो वेति"। शब्दद्वयस्य यथाक्रमं व्युत्पत्तिमाह-"तत्र ऋजुवर्तमान" मित्यादि॥ "नामस्थापनाद्रव्यविरहेण समानलिङ्गवचनेत्यादि" लिङ्गं च

वचनं च लिङ्गवचने येषां ते च ते पर्यायध्वनयश्च–इन्द्रः शक्रः पुरन्दर इत्यादयस्तद्वाच्यत्वेन च। तदनेनातिक्रान्तवक्ष्यमाणनयद्वयाद्भिन्नताऽस्य सूचिता। अतिक्रान्तनयो हि नामादिचतुर्विधमपि भिन्नलिङ्गवचनपर्यायध्वनिवाच्यमेव वस्त्विच्छति, अयं तु भावरूपमेव समानलिङ्गवचनपर्यायध्वनिवाच्यमेव च तदिच्छतीत्यनयोर्भेदः। वक्ष्यमाणस्त्वेकस्मिन् वस्तुन्येक एव ध्वनिः प्रवर्तते न समानलिङ्गवचना अपि बहव इत्यभिमंस्यते। अतो नयादप्यस्य भिन्नता। एवमन्येष्वपि नयेषु विशेषणानि यथासंभवपूर्वोत्तरनयाभिन्नता सूचकत्वेन द्रष्टव्यानि। "तस्यार्थपरिगहादि"त्यादि तस्य प्राधान्येनाङ्गीकृतशब्दस्य वाच्यत्वेन संबन्धी योऽर्थो घटादिलक्षणस्तं परिगृह्णाति नयो ज्ञानविशेष इत्युपचारात् सोऽपि ज्ञानस्वरूपो नयः शब्द इत्युच्यते। "न च भिन्नेत्यादि" ननु भिन्नवचनत्वादेकत्वाभावे कुटवृक्षवदित्युदाहरणमसंगतम् कुटश्च वृक्षश्च कुटवृक्षौ ताविव कुटवृक्षवदिति। न ह्यत्र क्वचिद्वचनभेदोऽस्ति। सत्यम्। स्यादेतद् यद्येकवचनान्तपदद्वयस्यात्र समासोऽभिप्रेतः स्यात्। किंतु कुटश्च वृक्षौ चेति समस्य वतिः क्रियते इत्यस्ति वचनभेदः। ननु भवत्वेवं तथाप्ययुक्तमिदमुदाहरणम्। न ह्यत्र वचनाभेदेऽपि कुटवृक्षशब्दयोः पर्यायता युज्यते। भिन्नजातीयवस्तुवाचकत्वात्। तथाहि—कुटशब्देन घट उच्यते वृक्षशब्देन तु शाखादिमान् पदार्थः तत्कुतो वचनाभेदेऽप्यनयोः पर्यायशब्दता?। नैवम्। भिन्नजातीयवस्तुवाचित्वादित्यस्यासिद्धत्वात्। यन्नः कौ पृथिव्यामटतीति व्युत्पत्तेः कुटशब्देन वृक्ष एवात्र विवक्षित इत्यनयोः पर्यायशब्दता। क्वचित्तु कूटवृक्षवदिति पाठस्तत्रनिर्विवादं कूटशब्देन वृक्ष एवाभिधीयत इति। अस्माकं तावदयं संप्रदायः, सुधिया त्वन्यथापि भाव्यमिति॥ "न स्थानभरणक्रियामि"ति—स्थानस्थस्यैव भरणक्रिया स्थानभरणक्रिया तां न विशेषयतीत्यर्थः। यदा स्थानस्थित एव जलादिना भ्रियते तदा घटो न भवति किंतु योषिन्मस्तकारूढो जलाहरणचेष्टां कुर्वन्नेवेति भावार्थः॥ समाप्ता नयाः॥

—आवश्यक-हारिभद्रटिप्पणे नयाधिकारः

The importance of this long extract lies in the fact that the doctrine of नयs is traceable to the Sûtras or Âgama. In the first few lines the illustrations of नैगमनय referred to in the Sûtras (see our Text p. 162–168 St. XXVIII) are explained in detail. These are old and obscure, but the commentator does his best to explain them. Next a very important point is introduced viz. the distniction between 'निश्चयनय' and 'व्यवहारनयः' that is the scientific view and the popular view. This corresponds to the distinction drawn in Vedânta betwen the points of view of परमार्थ and व्यवहार—which has also its parellel in Buddhism. A very interesting point, which is supported by an extract from the Prajnapati (one of the Âgamas), is the strange doctrine that as a matter of absolute or scientific truth every object—*e. g.* even a black bee—possesses all the five colours but only one of them is patent—the black in the case of the bee—while the rest are latent. A simlar doctrine regarding the constitution of matter is held by Ramânujâcârya who says that when a piece of mother-of-pearl is mistaken for silver, it is because the silver is in the mother-of-pearl; and so is even a serpent in a rope!

7. नत्थि नयेहिं विहूणं सुत्तं अत्थोय जिणमए किंचि।
आसज्ज उ सोयारं नयेणय विसारओ बुया॥
[=नास्ति नयैर्विहीनं सूत्रमर्थश्च जिनमते किंचित्।
आसाद्य तु श्रोतारं नयेन च विशारदो ब्रूयात्॥]

इति वचनाज्जिनमते सर्वेऽपि पदार्था नयैर्विचारणीयाः। इत्यतो द्रव्यमङ्गलमपि नयैर्विचारयन्नाह—

एगो मङ्गलमेगं णेगा णेगाइं णेगमनयस्स।
संगहनयस्स एक्कं सव्वं चिय मंगलं लोए॥
[=एको मङ्गलमेकमनेकेऽनेकानि नैगमनयस्य।
संग्रहनयस्यैकं सर्वमेव मङ्गलं लोके॥]

वक्ष्यमाणशब्दार्थस्य नैगमनयस्य मतेनैकोऽनुपयुक्तो मङ्गलशब्दार्थप्ररूपक एकं द्रव्यमङ्गलम्। अनेके त्वनुपयुक्तास्तत्प्ररूपका अनेकानि द्रव्यमङ्गलानि। अयं हि नयः सामान्यं विशेषांश्चाभ्युपगच्छत्येव। तत्र विशेषवादित्वपक्षे एकोऽनुपयुक्त एकं द्रव्यमङ्गलम् अनेके त्वनुपयुक्ता अनेकानि द्रव्यमङ्गलानीत्युपपद्यत एव, विशेषाणां पृथग् भिन्नत्वादिति। संग्रहनयस्य तु वक्ष्यमाणस्वरूपस्य केवलसामान्यवादिनो मतेन सर्वस्मिन्नपि लोके एकमेव द्रव्यमङ्गलम्। सर्वेषां द्रव्यमङ्गलत्वप्राप्तेः सामान्यस्य च त्रिभुवनेऽप्येकत्वात्। इति गाथार्थः॥

एक्कं निच्चं निरवयवमकियं सव्वगं च सामन्नम्।
निस्सामन्नत्ताओ नत्थि विसेसो खपुप्फं व॥
[=एकं नित्यं निरवयवमक्रियं सर्वगं च सामान्यम्।
निःसामान्यत्वान्नास्ति विशेषः खपुष्पमिव॥]

एकमद्वितीयत्वादेकसंख्योपेतं सामान्यम्। एकमपि क्षणिकं स्यात्। तत्राह— नित्यमनपायि। नित्यमप्याकाशवत् सावयवं स्यात्, तन्निरवयवत्वे सन्तिरुदया-स्तमनायोगात्। इत्यत्राह—निरवयवमनंशम्। पूर्वापरकोटिशून्यत्वादिति। निरवयवमपि परमाणुवत् सक्रियं स्यात्। अत आह—अक्रियं क्रियारहितं परिस्पन्द-विनिर्मुक्तत्वादिति। अक्रियमपि दिगादिवत् सर्वगतं न स्यात्। अत्राह—सर्वगं च सकललोकाऽवाप्तसत्ताकम्। इदमित्थंभूतं सामान्यमेवाऽस्ति, न तु विशेषः कश्चनाऽपि विद्यते। कुत इत्याह—निःसामान्यत्वात् सामान्यविरहितत्वात्, खपुष्पवत्, यच्चास्ति

तत् सामान्यविरहितं न भवति यथा घटः। तस्मादेकस्माद् द्रव्यमङ्गलसामान्याद्व्यतिरिक्तत्वाद् तद्व्यतिरेके चाद्रव्यमङ्गलताप्रसङ्गात् सामान्यस्य च त्रिभुवनेऽप्येकत्वादेकमेव संग्रहनयमते द्रव्यमङ्गलम् इति स्थितम् ॥ इति गाथार्थः ॥

अत्र विशेषवादिनयमतस्थितः कश्चिदाह--ननु कथमनेकानि द्रव्यमङ्गलानि न संभवन्ति यथा हि वनस्पतिरित्युक्ते वृक्ष-गुल्म-लता-वीरुदादयो विशेषा एव प्रतीयन्ते न पुनस्तदतिरिक्तः कश्चिद् वनस्पति एवमिहापि द्रव्यमङ्गलमित्युक्तेऽनुपयुक्ततत्प्ररूपकलक्षणा विशेषा एवावगम्यन्ते न तु तदधिकं किंचित् सामान्यम् अतः किं शून्य इवास्मिन् जगत्येवमभिधीयते--'निस्सामन्नत्ताओ नत्थि विसेसो खपुप्फं व' इति. इति विशेषवादिना प्रोक्ते सामान्यवादी संग्रहः प्राह--ननु यत एव वनस्पतित्युरिक्ते वृक्षादयः प्रतीयन्ते अत एव ते तदनर्थान्तरभूताः हस्तस्येवाङ्गुलयः इह यस्मिन्नुच्यमाने यत् प्रतीयते तत् ततो व्यतिरिक्तं न भवति यथा हस्त इत्युक्तेऽङ्गुल्यादयः प्रतीयमाना हस्ताद् न व्यतिरिक्ताः प्रतीयन्ते च वनस्पतिरित्युक्ते वृक्षादयः इत्यमी न वनस्पतिव्यतिरिक्ताः ततो न सामान्यदतिरिक्तः कोऽपि विशेषः समस्ति। इत्येकमेव सर्वत्र द्रव्यमङ्गलमिति। अथोपपत्त्यन्तरेणाऽपि सामान्यवाद्येव वृक्षादीनां सर्वेषामपि वनस्पतिसामान्यरूपतां समर्थयन्नाह--

चूओ वणस्सइच्चिय मूलाइगुणो त्ति तस्समूहो व्व।
गुम्मादओ वि एवं सव्वे न वणस्सइविसिट्ठे ॥
[=चूतो वनस्पतिरेव मूलादिगुण इति तत्समूह इव।
गुल्मादयोऽप्येवं सर्वे न वनस्पतिविशिष्टाः ॥]

'चूतः' आम्रो वनस्पतिरेव वनस्पतिसामान्यं न व्यभिचरतीत्यर्थः इति प्रतिज्ञा। मूल-कन्द-स्कन्ध-त्वक्-शाखा-प्रवाल-पत्र-पुष्प-बीजादिगुणत्वादिति हेतुः चूतसमूहवदिति दृष्टान्तः इह यो यो मूलादिगुणः स स वनस्पतिसामान्यरूप एव यथा चूतसमूहः, मूलादिगुणश्च चूतः तस्माद् वनस्पतिसामान्यरूप एव। गुल्मादयोऽप्येवं वाच्याः। तथाहि--विशेषवादिना विशेषतयाऽभ्युपगम्यमानो गुल्मोऽपि वनस्पतिसामान्यरूप एव मूलादिगुणत्वात् गुल्मसमूहवत् इति। एवमन्येषामपि लतादिविशेषाणां वनस्पतिसामान्यादव्यतिरिक्तत्वं साधनीयम्। तद्व्यतिरेके सर्वत्र मृण्मयत्वादिप्रसङ्गो बाधकं प्रमाणम्। तस्मात् सामान्यमेवास्ति न विशेषाः॥ इति गाथार्थः ॥

किं च—

सामन्नाउ विसेसो अन्नोऽणन्नो व होज्ज जइ अण्णो।
सो नत्थि खपुप्फं पिवऽणण्णो सामन्नमेव तयं ॥
[=सामान्याद् विशेषोऽन्योऽनन्यो वा भवेत् यद्यन्यः।
स नास्ति खपुष्पमिव, अनन्यः सामान्यमेव तत् ॥]

भो विशेषवादिन्! सामान्याद् विशेषोऽन्यो वा स्यात् अनन्यो वा इति विकल्पद्वयम्। यद्याद्यो विकल्पः तर्हि नास्त्येव विशेषः निःसामान्यत्वात् खपुष्पवत्—इह यद् यत्र सामान्यविनिर्मुक्तं तत् तद् नास्ति यथा गगनारविन्दम्

सामान्यविरहितश्च विशेषवादिना विशेषोऽभ्युपगम्यते तस्माद् नास्त्येवायमिति। अथानन्य इति द्वितीयः पक्षः कक्षीक्रियते हन्त तर्हि सामान्यमेवाऽसौ तदनन्यत्वात् सामान्यात्मवत् यद् यस्मादनन्यत् तत् तदेव यथा सामान्यस्यैवात्मा अनन्यश्च सामान्याद् विशेषः इति सामान्यमेवायमिति। यदि चातिपक्षपातितया सामान्येऽपि विशेषोपचारः क्रियते तर्हि न काचित् क्वचित् क्षतिः न ह्युपचारेणोच्यमानो भेदस्तात्त्विकमेकत्वं बाधितुमलम् तस्मात् सामान्यमेवास्ति न विशेषः। इति संग्रहनयमतेन सर्वत्रैकमेव द्रव्यमङ्गलम्॥ इति गाथार्थः॥

तदेवं संग्रहेण स्वाभिमते सामान्ये प्रतिष्ठिते विशेषवादिनौ नैगमव्यवहारावाहतुः-

न विसेसत्थंतरभूअमत्थि सामण्णमाह ववहारो।
उवलंभववहाराभावाओ खरविसाणं व॥
[=न विशेषार्थान्तरभूतमस्ति सामान्यमाह व्यवहारः।
उपलम्भव्यवहाराभावात् खरविषाणमिव॥]

ननु भोः सामान्यवादिन् भवताऽपि वनस्पतिसामान्यं बकुलाशोक-चम्पक-नाग-पुन्नागा-म्र-सर्जार्जुनादिविशेषेभ्योऽर्थान्तरं वाऽभ्युपगम्येत अनर्थान्तरं वा। यद्यर्थान्तरं तर्हि नास्त्येव तद् विशेषव्यतिरेकेण उपलब्धिलक्षणप्राप्तस्य तस्योपलम्भव्यवहाराभावात् खरविषाणवत्। क एवमाह व्यवहारानयः उपलक्षणत्वाद् विशेषवादी नैगमश्च। एतौ हि लोकव्यवहारानुयायिनौ तद्व्यवहारश्च प्रायो विशेषनिष्ठ एव इति विशेषानेव समर्थयत इति भावः। अथानुपलब्धिलक्षणप्राप्तं तदभ्युपगम्यते तथाऽपि नास्ति विशेषेभ्यः सर्वथाऽन्यत्वात् गगनकुसुमवदिति। अथ विशेषेभ्योऽनर्थान्तरं तदिति द्वितीयपक्षः तर्हि विशेषा एव तत् तेभ्योऽनर्थान्तरभूतत्वात् विशेषाणामात्मस्वरूपवदिति। यदि च विशेषेष्वपि सामान्योपचारः क्रियते तर्हि न काचित् क्षतिः न ह्यौपचारिकमेकत्वं तात्त्विकमनेकत्वं बाधते॥ इति गाथार्थः॥

एतदेव समर्थयते

चूयाईएहिंतो को सो अण्णो वणस्सई नाम।
नत्थि विसेसत्थंतरभावाओ सो खपुप्फं व॥
[चूतादिभ्यः कः सोऽन्यो वनस्पतिर्नाम।
नास्ति विशेषार्थान्तरभावात् स खपुष्पमिव॥]

चूतादिभ्यो विशेषेभ्योऽन्यः को नाम वनस्पतिः यो व्रण-पिण्डी-पादलेपादिके लोकव्यवहारे उपयुज्येत न कोऽपीत्यर्थः। तस्मात् समस्तलोकसंव्यवहारानुपयोगित्वाद् नास्ति सामान्यम् खपुष्पवत् इति पूर्वोक्तमेवार्थं निगमनद्वारेणाह—'नत्थीत्यादि' तस्माद् नास्त्यसौ सामान्यवादिनाऽभ्युपगम्यमानो वनस्पतिः सद्रूपेभ्यो हि विशेषेभ्योऽर्थान्तरभावात् खपुष्पवत्। सद्रूपेभ्यो हि विशेषेभ्योऽर्थान्तरं भवत् असद्रूपमेव भवति तथाभूतं च नास्त्येव खपुष्पवत्॥ इति गाथार्थः॥

किं पुनः कारणं येन नैगमव्यवहारौ विशेषान् समर्थयतः इत्याह—

जं नेगमववहारा लोअव्ववहारतप्परा सो य।
पाएण विसेसमओ तो ते तग्गाहिणो दो वि ॥
[=यद् नैगमव्यवहारौ लोकव्यवहारतत्परौ स च।
प्रायेण विशेषमयस्तस्मात् तौ तद्ग्राहिणौ द्वावपि ॥]

यद् यस्माद् नैगमव्यवहारौ लोकव्यवहारतत्परौ स च लोकव्यवहारस्त्यागादानादिकः प्रायेण विशेषमयो विशेषनिष्ठ एव दृश्यते सामान्यस्य व्रणपिण्ड्यादौ लोकेऽनुपयोगात्। 'वनं' 'सेना' इत्यादौ क्वचित् कश्चित् कथंचित् सामान्यस्यापि दृश्यते उपयोगः, इति प्रायोग्रहणम्। यत एवं तस्मात् तौ नैगमव्यवहारौ द्वावपि तद्ग्राहिणौ विशेषाभ्युपगमपरौ ॥ इति गाथार्थः ॥

—विशेषावश्यक Commentary.

8. सिद्धसेनीयाः पुनः षडेव नयानभ्युपगतवन्तः। नैगमस्य संग्रहव्यवहारयोरन्तर्भावविवक्षणात्। तथाहि—यदा नैगमः सामान्यप्रतिपत्तिपरस्तदा स संग्रहेऽन्तर्भवति सामान्याभ्युपगमपरत्वात्। विशेषाभ्युपगमनिष्ठस्तु व्यवहारे। आह च सिद्धसेनीयमतमुपसंजिघृक्षुर्भाष्यकृत्—" जो सामन्नग्गाही स नेगमो संगहं गओ अहवा इयरो ववहारमिओ जो तेण समाणनिद्देसो।" ततः सिद्धसेनीयाभिप्रायेण षड्भिरेव नयैरागमतो द्रव्यमङ्गलविचारः कर्तव्यः न सप्तभिरिति ॥—Com. on विशेषावश्यक सूत्र.

9. Malliṣeṇa's Commentary contains a reproduction of the following Sūtras of Pramāṇanaya-tattvālokālaṁkāra—

स्पष्टं प्रत्यक्षम्। अनुमानाद्याधिक्येन विशेषप्रकाशनं स्पष्टत्वम् (ii. 2,3)। तद् द्विप्रकारम्—सांव्यवहारिकं पारमार्थिकं च (ii. 4)। संव्यवहारो बाधारहितप्रवृत्तिनिवृत्ती प्रयोजनमस्येति सांव्यवहारिकं बाह्येन्द्रियादिसामग्रीसापेक्षत्वादपारमार्थिकम् अस्मदादिप्रत्यक्षमित्यर्थः। परमार्थे भवं पारमार्थिकं मुख्यम् आत्मसंनिधिमात्रापेक्षम् अवध्यादिप्रत्यक्षम्—Com. Note that सांव्यवहारिक is ordinary प्रत्यक्ष, while पारमार्थिक is extraordinary प्रत्यक्ष, no such distinction as that of the real and the unreal being implied, although the phraseology which is borrowed from Vedānta and Buddhism had this meaning.] तत्राद्यं द्विविधम्—इन्द्रियनिबन्धनमनिन्द्रियनिबन्धनं च (ii. 5)। एतद् द्वितयमवग्रहेहावायधारणाभेदादेकशश्चतुर्विकल्पम् (ii. 6)। The text omits the definitions of अवग्रह etc. as being too well-known ('सुप्रतीतत्वात्'), but they may well be reproduced here: विषयविषयिसंनिपातानन्तरसमुद्भूतसत्तामात्रगोचरदर्शनाज्जातमाद्यमवान्तरसामान्याकारविशिष्टवस्तुग्रहणमवग्रहः (ii. 7)। अवगृहीतार्थविशेषाकाङ्क्षणमीहा (ii. 8)।

ईहितविशेषनिर्णयोऽवायः (ii. 9) । स एव दृढतमावस्थापन्नो धारणा (ii.10) ॥ पारमार्थिकं पुनरुत्पत्तावात्ममात्रापेक्षम् (ii. 18) । [क्षय-क्षयोपशम-विशेषविशिष्टमात्मद्रव्यमेवाव्यवहितं समाश्रित्य पारमार्थिकमेतदवध्यादिप्रत्यक्ष-मुन्मज्जति न पुनः सांव्यवहारिकमिवेन्द्रियादिव्यवहितमात्मद्रव्यमाश्रित्येति भावः—Com.] तद्विकलं सकलं च (ii. 19) । तत्र विकलमवधिमनःपर्याय-ज्ञानरूपतया द्वेधा (ii. 20) । अवधिज्ञानावरणविलयविशेषसमुद्भवं भवगुणप्रत्ययं रूपिद्रव्यगोचरमवधिज्ञानम् (ii. 21) । संयमविशुद्धिनिबन्धनाद् विशिष्टावरण-विच्छेदाज्जातं मनोद्रव्यपर्यायालम्बनं मनःपर्यायज्ञानम् (ii. 22) । सकलं तु सामग्रीविशेषतः समुद्भूतसमस्तावरणक्षयापेक्षं निखिलद्रव्यपर्यायसाक्षात्कारिस्वरूपं केवलज्ञानम् (ii. 23) ।

The subject goes back to the Tattvārthādhigama-sûtra, (See T. Sûtra and T. Râja-Vārtika)—where मतिज्ञान is divided into इन्द्रियनिमित्त and अनिन्द्रियनिमित्त (तदिन्द्रियानिन्द्रियनिमित्तम्— i. 14); इन्द्रियनिमित्तं स्पर्शनादीनां पञ्चानां स्पर्शादिषु पञ्चस्वेव स्वविषयेषु अनिन्द्रियनिमित्तं मनोवृत्तिरोघज्ञानं च । This is further subdivided into अवग्रहेहावायधारणाः (i. 15), and each of these four is defined as follows: तत्राव्यक्तं यथास्वमिन्द्रियैर्विषयाणामालोचनावधारणमवग्रहः । अवग्रहो ग्रहो ग्रहणमालोचनमवधारणमित्यनर्थान्तरम् । निश्चयविशेषजिज्ञासा चेष्टा ईहा । ईहा ऊहा तर्कः परीक्षा विचारणा जिज्ञासेत्यनर्थान्तरम् । अवगृहीते विषये सम्यगसम्यगिति गुणदोषविचारणा अध्यवसायापनोदोऽवायः । अवायोऽपगम अपनोदः अपव्याधः अपेतमपविद्धमनुत्तमित्यनर्थान्तरम् । धारणा प्रतिपत्तिर्यथास्वं मत्यवस्थानमवधारणं च । धारणा प्रतिपत्तिरवधारणावस्थानं निश्चयोऽवमः अवबोध इत्यनर्थान्तरम् ।

स्मरणप्रत्यभिज्ञानतर्कानुमानागमभेदतस्तत् पञ्चप्रकारम् (P.N.T. iii. 2) ॥ तत्र संस्कारप्रबोधसंभूतमनुभूतार्थविषयं तदित्याकारं वेदनं स्मरणम् तत्तीर्थं-करबिम्बमिति यथा (iii. 3, 4) ॥ अनुभवस्मृतिहेतुकं तिर्यगूर्ध्वतासामान्यादि-गोचरं संकलनात्मकं ज्ञानं प्रत्यभिज्ञानम् । यथा तज्जातीय एवायं गोपिण्डः गोसदृशो गवयः स एवायं जिनदत्त इत्यादि ॥ (iii. 5,6) [तिर्यक्सामान्यं च गवादिषु गोत्वादिस्वरूपसदृशपरिणामात्मकम् । ऊर्ध्वतासामान्यं च परापरविवर्त-व्यापि मृत्स्नादिद्रव्यम् ।—Com. संकलनं विवक्षितधर्मयुक्तत्वेन वस्तुनः प्रत्यवमर्शनम्—Com.] उपलम्भानुपलम्भसंभवं त्रिकालीकलितसाध्यसाधन-संबन्धाद्यालम्बनमिदमस्मिन् सत्येव भवतीत्याद्याकारं संवेदनमूहापरनामा तर्कः (iii. 7, 8) । यथा यावान् कश्चिद् धूमः स सर्वो वह्नौ सत्येव भवतीति तस्मिन्न-सत्यसौ न भवत्येव । [उपलम्भानुपलम्भाभ्यां प्रमाणमात्रेण ग्रहणाग्रहणाभ्यां

संभव उत्पत्तिर्यस्येति कारणकीर्तनम्। त्रिकालीकलितयोः कालत्रयीवर्तिनोः साध्यसाधनयोर्गम्यगमकयोः संबन्धोऽविनाभावो व्याप्तिरित्यर्थः स आदिर्यस्याशेषदेशकालवर्तिवाचकसंबन्धस्यालम्बनं गोचरः यस्य तत्तथेति विषयाविष्करणम्। इदमस्मिन् सत्येव भवतीत्यादिशब्दादिदमस्मिन्न सति न भवत्येवाकारं साध्यसाधनसंबन्धालम्बनम्। एवंजातियः शब्दः एवंजातीयस्यार्थस्य वाचकः सोऽपि तथाभूतस्तथाभूतस्य वाच्य इत्याकारं वाच्यवाचकभावालम्बनं च संवेदनमिहोपादीयते इति स्वरूपप्रतिपादनम्। एवंरूपं यद्वेदनं स तर्क इति कीर्त्यते ऊह इति च संज्ञान्तरं लभते—Com.] अनुमानं द्विप्रकारं स्वार्थं परार्थं च (iii. 9)। तत्र हेतुग्रहणसंबन्धस्मरणकारकं साध्यविज्ञानं स्वार्थम् (iii. 10)। पक्षहेतुवचनात्मकं परार्थमनुमानमुपचारात् (iii. 23)। [पक्षहेतुवचनस्य च जडरूपतया मुख्यतः प्रामाण्यायोगे सति उपचारादित्युक्तम्। कारणे कार्योपचारादित्यर्थः। प्रतिपाद्यगतं हि यज्ज्ञानं तस्य कारणं पक्षादिवचनम्। कार्ये कारणोपचाराद्वा। प्रतिपादकगतं हि यत्स्वार्थानुमानं तस्य कार्यं तद्वचनमिति—Com.] आप्तवचनादाविर्भूतमर्थसंवेदनमागमः (iv. 1) उपचारादाप्तवचनं च (iv. 2).

The same subject will be found in Hemacandra's Pramâṇamîmâṁsâ. प्रमाणं द्विधा। प्रत्यक्षं परोक्षं च (I. i. 9,10) इन्द्रियमनोनिमित्तोऽवग्रहेहावायधारणात्मा सांव्यवहारिकम् (I i. 21)। अक्षार्थयोगे दर्शनानन्तरमर्थग्रहणमवग्रहः (I. i. 27)। अवगृहीतविशेषाकाङ्क्षणमीहा (I. i. 28)। ईहितविशेषनिर्णयोऽवायः (I. i. 29)। स्मृतिहेतुर्धारणा (I. i. 30).

अविशदः परोक्षम् (प्र· मी· १-२-१)॥ स्मृति-प्रत्यभिज्ञो-हा-नुमानागमास्तद्विधयः (१-२-२)॥ वासनोद्बोधहेतुका, तदित्याकारा, स्मृतिः(१-२-३)॥ दर्शनस्मरणसंभवं तदेवेदं तत्सदृशं तद्विलक्षणं तत्प्रतियोगीत्यादिसंकलनं प्रत्यभिज्ञानम् (१-२-४)॥ उपलम्भानुपलम्भनिमित्तं व्याप्तिज्ञानमूहः (१-२-५)॥ साधनात् साध्यविज्ञानमनुमानम् (१-२-७)॥ तद् द्विधा स्वार्थं परार्थं च (१-२-८)॥ स्वार्थं स्वनिश्चितसाध्यविनाभावैकलक्षणात् साधनात् साध्यज्ञानम् (१-२-९)॥ यथोक्तसाधनाभिधानजः [निर्णयः] परार्थम् (२-१-१)॥ वचनमुपचारात् (२-१-२)॥

Note 1. वासनोद्बोधहेतुका (प्र· मी·)='संस्कारप्रबोधसंभूतं' (Tex·) The text adds अनुभूतार्थविषयम्.

2. दर्शन-स्मरणसंभवं (प्र· मी·) अनुभव-स्मृतिहेतुकं (Text). The text omits the details तदेवेदं to तत्प्रतियोगि and inserts तिर्यगूर्ध्वतादिसामान्यगोचरम्.

3. उपलम्भानुपलम्भनिमित्तं (प्र· मी·)=उप ('पा' in the text is a misprint)-लम्भानुपलम्भसंभवं (Text). The text substitutes for

व्याप्तिज्ञान of (प्र. मी.) "त्रिकालीकलितसाध्यसाधनसंबन्धाद्यालम्बनमिदमस्मिन् सत्येव भवतीत्याद्याकारं संवेदनं" which is only an explanation of the nature of व्याप्तिज्ञान of प्र. मी. It adds that 'तर्क' is another word for 'ऊह'.

4. साधनात् साध्यविज्ञानम्—the definition of अनुमान given in प्र. मी. where अनुमान is characetrised as "अन्यथानुपपत्त्येकलक्षण" *i. e.* the conclusion or hypothesis without which the position becomes absurd.

वचनमुपचारात् (प्र. मी. २-१-२). If is thus explained by Hemacandra himself in his स्वोपज्ञवृत्तिः—"अचेतनं हि वचनं न साक्षात् प्रमितिफलहेतुरिति न निरुपचारेतप्रमाणभावभाजनं मुख्यानुमानहेतुत्वेन तूपचरितानुमानाभिधानपात्रतां प्रतिपद्यते। उपचारश्च कारणे कार्यस्य यथोक्त-साधनाभिधानात् तद्विषया स्मृतिरुत्पद्यते स्मृतेश्चानुमानं तस्मादनुमानस्य परंपरया यथोक्तसाधनाभिधानं कारणं तस्मिन् कारणे वचने कार्यस्यानुमानस्योपचारः समारोपः क्रियते। ततः समारोपात् कारणं वचनमनुमानशब्देनोच्यते। कार्ये वा प्रतिपादकानुमानजन्ये वचने कारणस्यानुमानस्योपचारः वचनमौपचारिक-मनुमानं न मुख्यमित्यर्थः॥ *i. e.* Two ways of understanding उपचार in the present case: (1) कार्य (अनुमान) used for the कारण (वचन) and (2) कारण (अनुमान=प्रतिपादक अनुमान) used for the कार्य (वचने).

अवग्रहेहा०—See Tv. Sûtra I.15. Bhāṣya, Rāj. Vārt. and Com.

क्षायोपशमिक— „ II. 5.

तिर्यगूर्ध्वतादि—See "एककाले नानाव्यक्तिगतोऽन्वयस्तिर्यक्सामान्यं भण्यते। तत्र दृष्टान्तो यथा—नानासिद्धजीवेषु सिद्धोऽयं सिद्धोऽयमित्यनुगताकारः सिद्धजातिप्रत्ययः। नानाकालेष्वेकव्यक्तिगतोऽन्वय ऊर्ध्वतासामान्यं भण्यते। तत्र दृष्टान्तो यथा—य एव केवलज्ञानोत्पत्तिक्षणे मुक्तात्मा द्वितीयादिक्षणेष्वपि स एवेति प्रतीतिः॥ अथवा नानागोशरीरेषु गौरयं गौरयमिति गोजातिप्रतीतिस्तिर्यक्सामान्यम्। यथैव चैकस्मिन् पुरुषे बालकुमाराद्यवस्थासु स एवायं देवदत्त इति प्रत्यय ऊर्ध्वतासामान्यम्—Com. on Pravacanasâra. सामान्य is of two kinds which are graphically described as *horizontal* (तिर्यक्सामान्य) and *vertical* (ऊर्ध्वतासामान्य); the former represents unity in the plurality of different individuals of the same class, the latter represents unity in the plurality of different conditions of the same individual. Cf. also तिर्यक्सामान्यं

च गवादिषु गोत्वादिस्वरूप सदृशपरिणामात्मकम्। ऊर्ध्वतासामान्यं च परापरविवर्तव्यापि मृत्स्नानादिद्रव्यम्। (Ratnâkarâvatârikâ on P.N.T. iii. 5).

उपलम्भानुपलम्भ०—Arising from the presence and absence.

त्रिकालीकलित०—resting upon the eternal relation of concomitance between साध्य and साधन. Pr. N. T. III. 7.

ऊहः—Otherwise called तर्क, *e. g.* whatever धूम there is is only when there is वह्नि; it is not when वह्नि is not. See Pr. N. T. with Ratna. III. 7.

अनुमानं द्विधा etc.—See Pr. N. T. with Ratn. III. 9.

आप्तवचनात्‌०—The primary sense of आगम is the knowledge of things which springs from the words of a reliable person (आप्त); its secondary sense is the word itself. Pr. N. T. with Ratn. IV. 1,2.

प्रमाणान्तराणां-Cf. Tarka books, Muktâvalî and Nîlakaṇṭhî etc.

Reference Books.

1. Tv. Sû. Bhâṣya. Sarvârtha-Siddhi.
2. ,, Râjavârtika.
3. Pramâṇa-Mîmaṁsâ.
4. Pr. N. Tattv. with Ratnâkarâvatârikâ.
5. ,, Syâdvâda-Ratnâkara.
6. Saptabhaṅgî T.
7. Sammatitarka with Commentary.
8. Nyâyâvatâra with Commentary.
9. Viśeṣâvaś'yaka.
10. "A History of Indian Philosophy"—by S. N. Dasgupta Vol. I pp. 176–179.
11. "Indian Philosophy"—by Radhakrishnan Vol. I pp. 299–302.
12. 'A History of Indian Logic"—by S. C. Vidyâbhûṣaṇa pp. 170–171.
13. "An Epitome of Jainism"—by Nahar and Ghosh Ch. VII pp. 78–102.

Stanza XXIX.

इदानीं सप्तद्वीप etc.—Refer also to the Brahmanical geography of seven islands and seven oceans. As against it, the Jaina holds that the oceans and the islands are infinite in number. For Brahmanical and Jaina cosmographies see Barnett's "Antiquities of India" pp. 196-99.

The Stanza: According to Jainas, souls are infinite in number. The stanza contains a criticism of the contrary doctrine.

इदमत्राकूतम् etc.—If there be only a finite number of souls, a time is conceivable when all the souls shall have achieved मुक्ति, leaving the world empty; or the once emancipated soul should return to the world to keep it ever populated! The second alternative is absurd, for all thinkers are agreed that emancipation once accomplished is accomplished for ever; in fact, it would be contrary to the notion of emancipation to suppose that emancipated souls are born again in the world and subjected to the round of births and deaths. For, is not emancipation an end of *all karmans*? And if *all karmans* have once ended, how can there be a return to bondage? Is not bondage a necessary result of karmans only? The first alternative is also impossible. For, it would be contrary to the very nature of the world (संसार) to be emptied of all souls.

दग्धे बीजे etc.—Quoted also in the Râj. Vārt. p. 361, which the editor traces to तत्त्वार्थसार.

आह च पतञ्जलिः—Vide Yogasûtras. II, 13.

एतट्टीका—The com. by Vyâsa on the same. 'वात्स्यायनभाष्य' in the AMP edition of the Syâdvâdamañjarî is a mistake for व्यासभाष्य.

सत्सु क्लेशेषु— While the root, viz. the passions, lasts, the abode of कर्म produces their fruition; but not when the root is eradicated. For example, paddy which is rice with their encasing husk will become the seed of the next paddy crop, but the paddy from which husk has been removed or which is scorched by fire will never do so.

तथा क्लेशावनद्ध etc.—In the same way the abode of karmans, while it is wrapped in passions, has the power to germinate into Saṁsāra, but when it is stripped of them, or the root is scorched, it is no longer capable of doing so. प्रसंख्यानदग्ध–burnt deliberately.

विपाकस्त्रिविधः etc.—The three varieties of the fruition of karman are: (1) जातिः (quality of birth) (2) आयुः (duration life) and (3) भोग (joy or suffering).

अक्षपादोऽप्याह—Vide Nyâyasûtras IV, i, 64. When the passions have been destroyed no action (कर्म) makes for fruition.

विभङ्गज्ञानिशिवराजर्षि—One whose wisdom was mutilated or incomplete, having been hindered by jñânâvaraṇîya karma.

भगवदुपज्ञम्—Discovered and taught by the master.

षड्जीवकायम् पृथिव्यब्वनस्पतयः स्थावराः; तेजोवायू द्वीन्द्रियादयश्च त्रसाः—Tv. Sûtra: II, 13-14. Souls of Earth, Water, and the Vegetable Kingdom are immobile; and those of Light, Air and those possessed of two or more senses are mobile.

अजीवन् etc.—Those that have lived, are living or will live, *i. e.* जीव connotes potential as well as actual life.

इन्द्रियादि—इन्द्रियs are called 'द्रव्यप्राणs', and ज्ञान etc. 'भाव-प्राणs'. By 'प्राण' we here understand not vital airs but vital energies manifested either on the physical or the mental plane. The former are called 'द्रव्यप्राणs', and the latter 'भावप्राणs'. The point of calling both of them 'प्राण' is to emphasise that one set of activities is as much a part of life as the other. That the प्राणs at first meant not the vital airs but all organs of vital activity may be seen in the सप्तप्राणसंवाद of the Upaniṣads. And this fact throws a new and interesting light on the meaning of 'प्राणायाम' as a spiritual exercise. It will not then mean a control of the vital airs of exhalation and inhalation, but a control of the very physical basis of life. The Jaina extends the meaning still further.

संघेनूर्ध्वे (Hema V, iii, 80)—काय=समूह; from the root चि.

पृथिव्यादि षण्णां etc.—'षड्जीवकायम्' a compound dissolved in two ways: (1) षण्णां जीवकायानां समाहारः षड्जीवकायम्; (2) षण्णां जीवानां कायः...तम्।

The six kinds of संसारि जीवs are those of (1) Earth, (2) Water, (3) Fire, (4) Air, (5) Vegetable Kingdom and (6) Ani al Kingdom, called respectively: (1) पृथ्वीकाय, (2) अप्काय, (3) तेजःकाय, (4) वायुकाय, (5) वनस्पतिकाय, and (6) त्रसकाय. See Âcârânga Sûtra 1. Adh. 2; Tattvârtha II, 13-14.

पृथिव्यादीनां पुनर्जीवत्वं etc.—अत्र च पृथिव्येव, कायो येषामिति विग्रहः Sîl. com on Âcâr. Sû. I. ii. 79, 84, 85, and Sîl. com. pp.30-31.

Mrs. Sinclair Stevenson asks us to note and rightly: "The Jaina believes that water itself (not as is so often supposed, the animalculæ living in it) is inhabited by Ekendriya Jîva called Apkâya ekendriya. See "Heart of Jainism" p. 98.

भगवन्मते हि etc.—The six classes of Jîvas may be arranged thus in the ascending order of their numbers:

त्रस-, तेजः-, पृथिवी-, अप्-, वायु-, and वनस्पति-कायिकs.

The तेजःकायिकs are infinitely more numerous than the त्रसकायिकs; similarly still more numerous are पृथिवीकायिकाः; still more numerous are अप्कायिकाः; still more are वायुकायिकाः infinitey multiplied in number are वनस्पतिकायिकs and so on.

ते च व्यावहारिकाः etc.—The वनस्पतिकायिकs are व्यावहारिक and अव्यावहारिक.

गोला etc.—Quoted partly in S'îl. com. Âcârânga. (p. 59) See Bhagavatî, X, XI.

अनाद्यनन्तेऽपि काले etc.—Even if we were to put together all the Jîvas who have attained निर्वाण (मोक्ष), who are now attaining it, and who will attain it hereafter, still their number falls infinitely short of the number of निगोदs. Hence the world will never get emptied of souls, and the Saṁsâra will never end. As many fresh souls are supplied from the reservoir of निगोद्s as pass out into मुक्ति.

अभिप्रेतं चैतद्—Certain Brahmanical Schools share this doctrine.

Mrs. Sinclair learns from a S'v. Sâdhu that *nigoda* is a kind of hell in which are thrown evil Jîvas who have committed specially heinous sins like murder, and who have no hope of ever coming out. See her " Heart of Jainism " p. 272.

Evidently this statement that they have " no hope of ever coming out " does not agree with the statement in the text. See also Herbert Warren, p. 45.

गोलाय असांखिज्जा etc. = गोलाश्च असंख्येया असंख्यनिगोदो गोलको भणितः। एकैकस्मिन् निगोदे अनन्तजीवा ज्ञातव्याः। सिध्यन्ति यावन्तः खलु इह संव्यवहारजीवराशेः। आयान्ति अनादिवनस्पतिराशेस्तावन्तस्तस्मिन् ॥

There are innumerable spheres (गोलs) in the Universe and in each sphere there are innumerable reservoirs (निगोद्s) of jîvas; and in each such, again, there are innumerable lives or souls (जीवs). From this infinite reservoir or rather from the particular part which lies immediately below animal life, that is, the vegetable kingdom (वनस्पतिराशि), there emerge souls to make up the deficiency caused by the emancipation of the souls that achieve मोक्ष from time to time.

" The storehouse of unevolved *Jîvas* is the region called *nigoda* where an infinite number of them exist from all eternity. The *nigoda* is the portion of the universe situated below the hells. Here evolution is almost at a stand-still and is proceeding so slowly as to be almost imperceptible. From this condition *jîvas* are constantly passing into the higher states of evolution."—Champat Rai Jain's " Key of Knowledge " p. 715.

अत्र च पृथिव्येव कायो येषामिति विग्रहः।........

कथं पुनरिदमवगन्तव्यं सन्ति पृथिवीकायिका इति । उच्यते—तदधिष्ठितशरीरोपलब्धेः। अधिष्ठातरि प्रतीतिर्गवाश्वादाविव इति । न हि उपयोगादीनि लक्षणानि पृथिवीकायेषु व्यक्तानि समुपलक्ष्यन्ते। सत्यमेतद्। अव्यक्तानि तु विद्यन्ते। यथा कस्यचित् पुंसः हृत्पूरकव्यतिमिश्रमदिरातिपानपित्तोदयाकुलीकृतान्तःकरणविशेषस्याव्यक्ता चेतना न चैतावता तस्याश्चिद्रूपता एवमत्राप्यव्यक्तचेतनासंभवोऽभ्युपगन्तव्यः । ननु चात्रोच्छ्वासादिकमव्यक्तचेतनालिङ्गमस्ति न चेह तथाविधं किंचिच्चेतनालिङ्गमस्ति। नैतदेवम्—इहापि समानजातीयलतोद्भेदादिकमर्शोमांसाङ्कुरवच्चेतनाचिह्नमस्त्येव । अव्यक्तचेतनानां हि संभावितैकचेतनालिङ्गानां वनस्पतीनामिव चेतनाऽभ्युपगन्तव्येति । वनस्पतेश्च चैतन्यं विशिष्टर्तुपुष्पफलप्रदत्त्वेन स्पष्टं साधयिष्यते च। ततोऽव्यक्तोपयोगादिलक्षणसद्भावात् सचित्ता पृथिवीति स्थितम् ।

S'îl. Com. on Acârânga I. ii. 84.

सचेतना आपः क्वचित् खातभूमिस्वाभाविकसंभवत्वात्। दर्दुरवत्। अथवा सचेतना अन्तरिक्षोद्भवा आपः स्वाभाविकव्योमसंभूतसंपातित्वात्। मत्स्यवत्।

सचेतनं तेजो यथायोग्याहारोपादानेन वृद्धिविशेषतद्विकारवत्त्वात् पुरुषवत् । एवमादिलक्षणेनाग्नेया जीवा निश्चेया इति ।

चेतनावान् वायुः अपरप्रेरिततिर्यगनियमितगतिमत्त्वात्। गवाश्वादिवत्। For त्रस see Sîlāṅkâ's Com. on Âcârânga I. vi. 50, and Sarvârthasiddhi on Tattvârtha II. 14. "त्रसत्वं च द्विविधं क्रियातो लब्धितश्च। तत्र क्रिया कर्म चलनं देशान्तरप्राप्तिः। अतः क्रियां प्राप्य तेजोवाय्वोस्त्रसत्वम्। लब्धिस्तु त्रसनामककर्मोदयो यस्माद्द्वीन्द्रियादीनां क्रिया च देशान्तराप्राप्तिलक्षणेति। लब्ध्या पृथिव्यप्तेजोवायुवनस्पतयः सर्वे स्थावरनामकर्मोदयात् स्थावरा एव । सास्नाविषाणादिसंघाता हि छेद्यभेद्योत्क्षेप्यभोग्याघ्रेयरसनीयस्पृश्यद्रष्टव्यत्वे सति जीवशरीरतया प्रसिद्धाः। पृथिव्यादीनां च छेद्यत्वादि दृष्टमपह्नोतुं न शक्यते जीवशरीरत्वेन निरूपितत्वात्। पाणिपादसंघातानामिव पृथिव्यादीनामपि कदाचिच्चैतन्यं न चात्यन्तमचित्ततेति कदाचित् किंचिदचेतनमपि शस्त्रोपहतत्वात् पाण्यादिवदेवेति।"

—Sarvârtha-Siddhi II. 13.

A similar doctrine of sentiency of matter held by a certain school of Vedântins on the basis of an Upaniṣad text is noticed by S'aṁkara in his Com. on Br. Sûtra II. i. 4.

———

Stanza XXX.

प्रकर्षेण etc.—प्रवादाः The blatant heresies.

अतिशायिने etc.—Hem.

मत्सरिणः Full of jealousies or angry passions. The poss. term. applied in the sense of excessiveness. Quoted in S. K. on Pâṇ. V. ii. 94.

अन्योन्यपक्ष etc.—पक्षः=पच्यते etc.—पक्ष is so called because it is put forth (पच्यते व्यक्तीक्रियते) as possessed of the साध्य by means of the हेतु. It is thus the presentation of the साधन (हेतु) in order to prove the साध्य (धर्म).

य एव मीमांसकानां etc.—The Mim. hold that शब्द is नित्य; the Buddhists on the other hand hold that शब्द is अनित्य. Here is an example of two schools diametrically opposed to each other.

सम्यगेति etc.—समय explained in different ways: "(1) सम्यगेति शब्दोऽनेनेति : संकेतः that by which the word goes well to the Reality; the teaching in whih the word harmonizes with truth. प्रज्ञाभिधे—Hem.

(2) यद्वा सम्यगवैपरीत्येनेयन्ते ज्ञायन्ते जीवाजीवादयोर्थां अनेनेति समयः=सिद्धान्तः. The doctrine which gives correct knowledge of the nine categories viz. जीव, अजीव etc.

(3) अथवा सम्यगयन्ते......समयः आगमः The teaching of the Master in which the above-mentioned categories come to their own, that is to say, appear in their true nature.

(4) अथवा...समयः—The doctrine of उत्पाद, व्यय and ध्रौव्य. (See supra Notes on St. V. pp.31–32) which has been declared by the Master as "the Mother" (cf. 'अष्टप्रवचनमाता') that is to say, good and kind like a mother.

न पक्षपाती :—Not leaning exclusively towards either side. When there are no passions such as jealousy and hatred, there is no partisanship.

तव समय इति etc.—'Yours' *i. e.* proclaimed by you. Has Mahâvîra proclaimed the Jaina Âgama ? Yes, in a way. For, although the Gaṇadharas have presented it in the form of the Sûtras, it is Mahâvîra who has been the real author of the teaching.

नयानशेषान् etc.—Welcoming all the नयs without distinction. His teaching is like a necklace of pearls, wherein every system has its proper place like a pearl. This synthetic teaching is the Syâdvâda. A similar claim can be made by the Vedântin of the Sâṅkara school who holds the doctrine of अनिर्वचनियता.

नतु प्रत्येकं नयानां etc.—In the Syâdvâda, discordant notes are blended so as to make a perfect harmony. In it all the 'little systems' find their great conciliator or peacemaker. As rivers mingle in the ocean, so do all systems mingle in the Syâdvâda.

न स्ववाच्यं तर्हि etc.—How is it that we do not see the Syâdvâda in the 'little systems'? The question has been answered by Siddhasena Divâkara who, identifying Mahâvîra with his great teaching, says: "Oh Lord ! all views find their place in you like rivers in the ocean; you do not appear in them just as an ocean does not appear in the rivers."

अन्ये etc.—Another way of construing the passage is to take पक्षपाती as an enlargement of the subject समयः, and make मत्सरी (corresponding to मत्सरिणः in the correlative passage) the predicate.

अत्र च क्लिष्टाक्लिष्ट०—The author seems a bit too anxious to avoid मत्सर and पक्षपात. So he would not say that the second explanation is क्लिष्ट.

Appendices.

(१) एते हि बौद्धादयः स्वयं स्याद्वादवादं युक्त्याभ्युपगच्छन्तोऽपि तं वचनैरेव निराकुर्वन्तो नूनं कुलीनताभिमानिनो मानवस्य स्वजननीमाजन्मतोऽप्यसतीमाचक्षाणस्य वृत्तमनुकुर्वन्ति। तथाहि—प्रथमतः सौगताभ्युपगतोऽनेकान्तः प्रकाश्यते। दर्शनेन क्षणिकाक्षणिकत्वसाधारणस्यार्थस्य विषयीकरणात् कुतश्चिद्भ्रमनिमित्तादक्षणिकत्वारोपेऽपि न दर्शनमक्षणिकत्वे प्रमाणं किंतु प्रत्युताप्रमाणम्। विपरीता-

ध्यवसायाक्रान्तत्वात् । क्षणिकत्वेऽपि न तदप्रमाणम् । अनुरूपाध्यवसायाजननात् । नीलरूपे तु तथाविधनिश्चयकरणात् प्रमाणमित्येवंवादिनां बौद्धानामेकस्यैव दर्शनस्य क्षणिकाक्षणिकत्वयोरप्रामाण्यं नीलादौ तु प्रामाण्यं प्रसक्तमित्यनेकान्तवादाभ्युपगमो बलादापतति ॥ १ ॥ तथा दर्शनोत्तरकालभाविनः स्वाकाराध्यवसायिन एकस्यैव विकल्पस्य बाह्येऽर्थे सविकल्पकत्वमात्मस्वरूपे तु सर्वचित्तचैत्तानामात्मसंवेदनं प्रत्यक्षमिति वचनान्निर्विकल्पकत्वं च रूपद्वयमभ्युपगतवतां तेषां कथं नानैकान्तवादापत्तिः ॥ २ ॥ तथा हिंसाविरतिदानादि चित्तं यदेव स्वसंवेदनगतेषु सत्त्वबोधरूपत्वसुखादिषु प्रमाणं तदेव क्षणक्षयित्वस्वर्गप्रापणशक्तियुक्तत्वादिष्वप्रमाणमित्यनेकान्त एव ॥ ३ ॥ तथा यद्वस्तु नीलचतुरस्रोर्ध्वतादिरूपतया प्रमेयं तदेव मध्यभागक्षणविवर्तादिनाप्रमेयमिति कथं नानेकान्तः ॥ ४ ॥ तथा सविकल्पकं स्वप्नादिदर्शनं वा यद्बहिरर्थापेक्षया भ्रान्तं ज्ञानं तदेव स्वस्वरूपापेक्षयाऽभ्रान्तमिति बौद्धाः प्रतिपन्नाः ॥५॥ तथा यन्निशीथिनीनाथद्वयादिकं द्वित्वेऽलीकं तदपि धवलतानियतदेशचारितादौ तेऽनलीकं प्रतिपद्यन्ते ॥ ६ ॥ कथं च भ्रान्तज्ञानं भ्रान्तिरूपतयाऽऽत्मानमसंविन्दत् ज्ञानरूपतया चावगच्छत् स्वात्मनि भावद्वयं विरुद्धं न साधयेत् ॥ ७ ॥ तथा पूर्वोत्तरक्षणापेक्षयैकस्यैव क्षणस्य जन्यत्वं जनकत्वं चाभ्युपागमन् ॥ ८ ॥ तथाऽर्थाकारमेव ज्ञानमर्थस्य ग्राहकं नान्यथेति मन्यमानाश्चित्रपटग्राहकं ज्ञानमेकमप्यनेकाकारं संप्रतिपन्नाः ॥ ९ ॥ तथा सुगतज्ञानं सर्वार्थविषयं सर्वार्थाकारं चित्रं कथं न भवेत् ॥ १० ॥ तथैकस्यैव हेतोः पक्षधर्मसपक्षसत्त्वाभ्यामन्वयं विपक्षेऽविद्यमानत्वाद्व्यतिरेकं चान्वयविरुद्धं ते तात्त्विकमूरीचक्रिरे ॥ ११ ॥ एवं वैभाषिकादिसौगताः स्वयं स्याद्वादं स्वीकृत्यापि तत्र विरोधमुद्भावयन्तः स्वशासनानुरागान्धकारसंभारविलुप्तविवेकदृशो विवेकिनामपकर्णनीया एव भवन्ति । किंच । सौत्रान्तिकमत एकमेव कारणमपरापरसामग्र्यन्तःपातितयानेककार्यकार्यो विद्यते यथा रूपरसगन्धादिसामग्रीगतं रूपमुपादानभावेन स्वोत्तरं रूपक्षणं जनयति रसादिक्षणांश्च सहकारितया तदेव च रूपं रूपालोकमनस्कारचक्षुरादिसामग्र्यन्तरगतं सत्पुरुषस्य ज्ञानं सहकारितया जनयति । आलोकाद्युत्तरक्षणांश्च तदेवमेकं कारणमनेकानि कार्याणि युगपत्कुर्वाणं किमेकेन स्वभावेन कुर्यात् नानास्वभावैर्वा । यद्येकेन स्वभावेन तर्ह्येकस्वभावेन कृतकत्वात् कार्याणां भेदो न स्यात् । अथवा नित्योऽपि पदार्थ एकेन स्वभावेन नानाकार्याणि कुर्वाणः कस्मान्निषिध्यते । अथ नित्यस्यैकस्वभावत्वेन नानाकार्यकरणं न घटते तर्ह्यनित्यस्यैकस्वभावत्वेन नानाकार्यकरणं न घटते तर्ह्यनित्यस्यापि तेषां करणं कथमप्यस्तु निरंशैकस्वभावत्वात् । सहकारिभेदाच्चेत् कुरुते तर्हि नित्यस्यापि सहकारिभेदात्तदस्तु । अथ नानास्वभावैरनित्यः कुर्यादिति चेत् नित्यस्यापि तथा तत्करणमस्तु । अथ नित्यस्य नानास्वभावा न संभवन्ति कूटस्थनित्यस्यैकस्वभावात् । तर्ह्यनित्यस्यापि नानास्वभावा न सन्ति निरंशैकस्वभावत्वात् । तदेवं नित्यस्यानित्यस्य च समानदोषत्वान्नित्यानित्योभयात्मकमेव वस्तु मानितं वरम् । तथा चैकान्तनित्यानित्यपक्षसंभवं दोषजालं सर्वं परिहृतं भवतीति ॥ १२ ॥ ज्ञानवादिनोऽपि ताथागताः स्वार्थाकारयो-

रभिन्नमेकं संवेदनं संवेदनाच्च भिन्नौ ग्राह्यग्राहकाकारौ स्वयमनुभवन्तः कथं स्याद्वादं निरस्येयुः ॥ १ ॥ तथा संवेदनस्य ग्राह्यग्राहकाकारविकलता स्वप्नेऽपि भवद्भिर्नानुभूयते । तस्या अनुभवे वा सकलासुमतामधुनैव मुक्ततापत्तेः । तत्त्वज्ञानोत्पत्तिर्मुक्तिरिति वचनात् । अनुभूयते च संवेदनं संवेदनरूपतया कथंचित् । तत एकस्यापि संवेदनस्यानुभूतानुभूततयानेकान्तप्रतिभासो दुःशंकोऽपह्नोतुमिति ॥ २ ॥ तथा सर्वस्य ज्ञानं संविद्रूपस्वसंवेदनेन ग्राह्यग्राहकाकारशून्यतयात्मानमसंविदत् संविद्रूपतां चानुभवद्विकल्पेतरात्मकं सदेकान्तवादस्य प्रतिक्षेपकमेव भवेत् ॥ ३ ॥ तथा ग्राह्याकारस्यापि युगपदनेकार्थावभासिनश्चित्रैकरूपता प्रतिक्षिपत्येवैकान्तवादमिति ॥४॥

(२) नैयायिकैर्वैशेषिकैश्च यथा स्याद्वादोऽभ्युपजग्मे तथा प्रदर्श्यते । इन्द्रियसंनिकर्षादेर्धूमज्ञानं जायते । तस्माच्चाग्निज्ञानम् । अत्रेन्द्रियसंनिकर्षादिः प्रत्यक्षं प्रमाणं तत्फलं धूमज्ञानं धूमज्ञानं चाग्निज्ञानापेक्षयानुमानं प्रमाणम् । अग्निज्ञानं त्वनुमानफलम् । तदेवं धूमज्ञानस्य प्रत्यक्षफलतामनुमानप्रमाणतां चोभयरूपतामभ्युपगच्छन्ति । एवमन्यत्रापि ज्ञाने फलता प्रमाणता च पूर्वोत्तरापेक्षया यथार्हमवगन्तव्या ॥ १ ॥ एकमेव चित्रपटादेरवयविनो रूपं विचित्राकारमभ्युपयन्ति । न च विरोधमाचक्षते । तदुक्तं कन्दलयाम् । विरोधादेकमनेकस्वभावमयुक्तमिति चेन्न । तथा च प्रावादुकप्रवादः ।

एकं चेत् तत्कथं चित्रं चित्रं चेदेकता कुतः ।
एकं चैव तु चित्रं चेत्येतच्चित्रतरं मतम् ॥

इति को विरोध इत्यादि । चित्रात्मनो रूपस्य नायुक्तता । विचित्रकारणसामर्थ्यभाविनस्तस्य सर्वलोकप्रसिद्धेन प्रत्यक्षेणैवोपपादितत्वादित्यादि ॥ २ ॥ एकस्यैव धूपकटच्छुकस्यैकस्मिन् भागे शीतस्पर्शः परस्मिंश्च भाग उष्णस्पर्शः । अवयवानां भिन्नत्वेऽप्यवयविन एकत्वादेकस्यैव द्वौ विरुद्धौ तौ स्पर्शौ यतस्तेषामेवं सिद्धान्तः एकस्यैव पटादेश्चलाचलरक्तारक्तावृतानावृतताद्यनेकविरुद्धधर्मोपलम्भेऽपि दुर्लभो विरोधगन्धः इति ॥ ३ ॥ नित्यस्येश्वरस्य सिसृक्षा संजिहीर्षा च रजस्तमोगुणात्मकौ स्वभावौ क्षितिजलाद्यमूर्तिता च सात्त्विकस्वभावाः परस्परं विरुद्धाः॥४॥ एकस्यामलकस्य कुवलयबिल्वाद्यपेक्षया महत्त्वमणुत्वं च विरुद्धे ॥ ५ ॥ एवमिक्षोः समिद्वंशापेक्षया ह्रस्वत्वदीर्घत्वे अपि ॥ ६ ॥ देवदत्तादेः स्वपितृसुतापेक्षया परत्वापरत्वे अपि ॥ ७ ॥ अपरं सामान्यं नाम्ना सामान्यविशेष इत्युच्यते । सामान्यविशेषश्च द्रव्यत्वगुणत्वकर्मत्वलक्षणः । द्रव्यत्वं हि नवसु द्रव्येषु वर्तमानत्वात् सामान्यं गुणकर्मभ्यो व्यावृत्तत्वाद्विशेषः । एवं गुणत्वकर्मत्वयोरपि सामान्यविशेषता विभाव्या । ततश्च सामान्यं च तद्विशेषश्चेति सामान्यविशेषः । तस्यैकस्य सामान्यता विशेषता च विरुद्धे ॥ ८ ॥ एकस्यैव हेतोः पञ्च रूपाणि संप्रतिपद्यते ॥ ९ ॥ एकस्यैव पृथिवीपरमाणोः सत्तायोगात् सत्त्वं द्रव्यत्वयोगाद्द्रव्यत्वं पृथिवीत्वयोगात् पृथिवीत्वं परमाणुत्वयोगात् परमाणुत्वम् अन्त्याद्विशेषात् परमाणुभ्यो भिन्नत्वं

चेच्छतां परमाणोस्तस्य सामान्यविशेषात्मकता बलादापतति, सत्त्वादीनां परमाणुतो भिन्नतायां तस्यासत्त्वाद्द्रव्यत्वापृथिवीत्वाद्यापत्तेः ॥ १० ॥ एवं देवदत्तात्मनः सत्त्वं द्रव्यत्वमात्मत्वयोगादात्मत्वमन्त्याद्विशेषाद्यज्ञदत्ताद्यात्मभ्यो भिन्नतां चेच्छतां तस्यात्मनः सामान्यविशेषरूपतावश्यं स्यात्। एवमाकाशादिष्वपि सा भाव्या ॥ ११ ॥ योगिनां नित्ये तु तुल्याकृतिगुणक्रियेषु परमाणुषु मुक्तात्मसु च प्रत्याधारं विलक्षणोऽयमिति प्रत्ययो येभ्यो भवति तेऽन्त्या विशेषा इत्यत्र तुल्याकृतिगुणक्रियत्वं विलक्षणत्वं चोभयं प्रत्याधारमुच्यमानं स्याद्वादमेव साधयेत् ॥ १४ ॥ एवं नैयायिकवैशेषिका आत्मनानेकान्तमुररीकृत्यापि तत्प्रतिक्षेपायोद्यच्छन्तः सतां कथं नोपहास्यतां यान्ति ? । किं च । अनेकान्ताभ्युपगमे सत्येव गुणः परस्परविभक्तेष्ववयवावयव्यादिषु मिथोवर्तनचिन्तायां यद्दूषणजालमुपनिपतति तदपि परिहृतं भवति । तथाहि । अवयवानामवयविनश्च मिथोऽत्यन्तं भेदोऽभ्युपगम्यते नैयायिकादिभिर्न पुनः कथंचित्। ततः पर्यनुयोगमर्हन्ति । अवयवेष्ववयवी वर्तमानः किमेकदेशेन वर्तते किं वा सामस्त्येन । यद्येकदेशेन, तदयुक्तम् । अवयविनो निरवयवत्वाभ्युपगमात्। सावयवत्वेऽपि तेभ्योऽवयवी यद्यभिन्नः, ततोऽनेकान्तापत्तिः। एकस्य निरंशस्यानेकावयवत्वप्राप्तेः । अथ तेभ्यो भिन्नोवयवी तर्हि तेषु स कथं वर्तेत इति वाच्यम् । एकदेशेन सामस्त्येन वा । एकदेशपक्षे पुनस्तदेवावर्तेत इत्यनवस्था । अथ सामस्त्येन तेषु स वर्तते, तदप्यसाधीयः । प्रत्यवयवमवयविनः परिसमाप्ततयावयविबहुत्वप्रसङ्गात् । ततश्च तेभ्यो भिन्नोऽवयवी न विकल्पभाग् भवति । नन्वभेदपक्षेऽप्यवयविमात्रमवयवमात्रं वा स्यादिति चेत् न । अभेदस्याप्येकान्तेनानभ्युपगमात् । किं तर्ह्यन्योन्याविश्लिष्टस्वरूपो विवक्षया संदर्शनीयभेदोऽवयवेष्ववयव्यभ्युपगम्यते । अबाधितप्रतिभासेषु सर्वत्रावयवावयविनां मिथो भिन्नाभिन्नतया प्रतिभासनात् । अन्यथा प्रतिभासमानानामन्यथा परिकल्पने ब्रह्माद्वैतशून्यतावादादेरपि कल्पनाप्रसङ्गात् । एवं संयोगिषु संयोगः समवायिषु समवायो गुणिषु गुणो व्यक्तिषु सामान्यं चात्यन्तं भिन्नान्यभ्युपगम्यमानानि तेषु वर्तनचिन्तायां सामस्त्यैकदेशविकल्पाभ्यां दूषणीयानि । तदेवमेकान्तभेदेऽनेकदूषणोपनिपातादनेकान्ते च दूषणानुत्थानादनेकान्ताभ्युपगमान्न मोक्ष इति । अतो वरमादावेव मत्सरितां विहायानेकान्तोऽभ्युपगतः । किं भेदैकान्तकल्पनया अस्थान एवात्मना परिक्लेशितेनेति ? ॥

(३) सांख्यः सत्त्वरजस्तमोभिरन्योन्यं विरुद्धैर्गुणैर्ग्रथितं प्रधानमभिदधान एकस्याः प्रकृतेः संसारावस्थामोक्षसमययोः प्रवर्तननिवर्तनधर्मौ विरुद्धौ स्वीकुर्वाणश्च कथं स्वस्यानेकान्तमतवैमुख्यमाख्यातुमीशः स्यात् ॥ ?

मीमांसकास्तु स्वयमेव प्रकारान्तरेणैकान्तेकाद्यनेकान्तं प्रतिपद्यमानास्तत्प्रतिपत्तये सर्वथा पर्यनुयोगं नार्हन्ति । अथवा शब्दस्य तत्संबन्धस्य च नित्यत्वैकान्तं

प्रति तेऽप्येवं पर्यनुयोज्याः। त्रिकालशून्यकार्यरूपार्थविषयविज्ञानोत्पादिकानोदनेति मीमांसकाभ्युपगमः। अत्र कार्यतायास्त्रिकालशून्यत्वेऽभावप्रमाणस्य विषयता स्यात्। अर्थत्वे तु प्रत्यक्षादिविषयता भवेत्। उभयरूपतायां पुनर्नोदनाया विषयतेति ॥

—Guṇaratna's Com. on Ṣaḍdarśana Samuccaya.

——:o:——

Stanza XXXI.

विभव एव॰—वैभव = विभव-Wealth 'प्रज्ञादिभ्योण्'. Pâṇ. V.iv. 38; 'प्रज्ञादिभ्यश्च' Hem. VII. ii. 165. विभोर्भावः कर्म etc.—Or वैभव=the quality and the act of विभु *i. e.* all-comprehensiveness.

हे महनीयमुख्य etc.—The best of the adorable viz. the Pañca Parameṣṭhins to whom obeisance is offered in the famous formula "णमो अरिहंताणम्" etc.

ननु सिद्धेभ्यो etc.—Why Arhats first? Are not they lower than the Siddhas? Do not the Arhats bow to the Siddhas on entering the life of asceticism? काऊण etc.=कृत्वा नमस्कारं सिद्धेभ्योऽभिग्रहं तु सोऽग्रहीत्.

मैवं etc.—They do. But it is the teaching of the Arhats that reveals the existence of the Siddhas. अरहन्तु etc.="अर्हदुपदेशेन सिद्धा ज्ञायन्ते तेनार्हदादिः"—विशेषावश्यकगाथा-३२१३.

लङ्घेमेत्यादि—Nidarśanālaṁkāra. अथवा लघु शोषणे etc.—लघ् लङ्घ् in the sense of 'to cross' being Âtm. pada लङ्घेम may have to be defended by the rule of elasticity of the rule as to padas (आत्मनेपदमनित्यम्); or it may be taken as a form of लघ्, लङ्घ् to dry up which M. seems to prefer.

अत्र चौद्धत्यपरिहारेण etc.—A very ingenious bit of commentary. Why is there the plural number in आशास्महे, लङ्घेम and वहेम, when the person to whom they refer is but one? Answer: It is intended to suggest that there are numberless souls in the position of the author who venture to describe the greatness of his teaching but fail to do it justice. Thus, the plural number instead of betraying egotism places 'a banner at the top of the palace of humanity'.

एषु एकत्रिंशति—Up to this, from I to XXXI stanzas, the metre was उपजाति. That in XXXII is शिखरिणी.

Stanza XXXII.

विप्रतारक—deceitful.

अव्यभिचारि—His teaching is in no point wrong, and consequently he is able to show that no other system which differs from it can claim to be altogether right (अव्यभिचारि).

अन्ययोग etc.—Exclusion of all the other systems from the laim of bringing salvation to mankind.

हतपरे—The wretched heretics.

मायाकाराः—Jugglers *i. e.* the deceitful teachers.

शाम्बरीयप्रयोग—Practice of the science tanght and practised by the demon शम्बर *i. e.* sorcery.

अन्धं करोति etc.—अन्ध, that which blinds + तमः darkness = अन्धतमसम्. For the affix अ applied to तमस्, see अवसमन्धेभ्यस्तमसः Pâṇ. V.iv. 79; Hem. VII.iii. 80.

यत्रान्धतमसे etc.—Twofold error of confounding तत्त्व with अतत्त्व and अतत्त्व with तत्त्व, A with not-A and not-A with A.

अनेन च विशेषणेन—Thus the Error is what is technically known in the Jaina S'âstras as मिथ्यात्व मोहनीय कर्मन्. मिथ्यात्व मोहनीय—See Tattvârtha Sûtra VIII.9. and Râj Vârt. मोहनीय कर्म is of two kinds: दर्शन° and चारित्र°. The former is of three kinds: (1) सम्यक्त्वदर्शन-मोहनीय ('which makes right faith or perception defective'), (2) मिथ्यात्वदर्शन-मोहनीय ('that which leads the soul away from right faith or perception') and (3) सम्यक्त्वमिथ्यात्व° ('mixed right and wrong faith ')—Jaini's "Outlines of Jainism" p. 92. On मिथ्यात्वमोहनीय° Mrs. Sinclair Stevenson writes: "The last of the eighty-two fruits of sin (मिथ्यात्व-मोहनीय) is the most terrible of all, for it deprives a man of the power of believing in the truth. He is forced by it to believe in a false instead of in a true god; and in an evil guru and not in a good one; and in a false creed instead of the true faith." ("The Heart of Jainism" —p. 139).

तथा च ग्रन्थान्तरे See Hem. Yogaśâstra II. 3.

अविसंवादिवचनः—Whose teaching never swerves from Truth, कष-च्छेद-ताप—the three tests of real gold. The same are explained in the Gâthâs "पाणव .... " See below.

कष—To avoid the life of sin such as Hiṁsâ, and practise Dhyâna, Adhyayana, *i. e.* meditation, study etc. Mark the homogeneity of Brâhmaṇa and Jaina religious disciplines and practices.

छेद—To see that the outward conduct is in harmony with the laws of धर्म and makes for purity.

ताप—To undergo pain and bondage connected with the the life of a Jîva.

पाणवहाई आणं etc.—

" प्राणवधादीनां पापस्थानानां यस्तु प्रतिषेधः ।
ध्यानाध्ययनादीनां यश्च विधिरेष धर्मकषः ॥
बाह्यानुष्ठानेन येन न बाध्यते तन्नियमात् ।
संभवति च परिशुद्धः स पुनर्धर्मे छेद इति ॥
जीवादिभाववादो बन्धादिप्रसाधक इह तापः ।
एतैः परिशुद्धो धर्मो धर्मत्वमुपैति ॥ "

—Traced to हरिभद्रसूरिकृत पञ्चवस्तुक चतुर्थद्वार by AMP.

तीर्थान्तरीयास्तु हि etc.—The teachers of the other schools of thought teach doctrines which cannot stand the test laid down above (कष, च्छेद and ताप), and are, therefore, not gold but base metal. They can only sink the world in the depths of false knowledge.

त्रातः—One who has saved himself and knows how to save others (त्रिभुवनपरित्राणप्रवीण).

त्वयि etc.—त्वयि = त्वय्येव, न देवान्तरे.

कृतधियः = कृता...संस्कृता...बुद्धिर्येषां ते कृतधियः चिद्रूपाः पुरुषाः—Those who have 'made' their intellect; those who have cultivated and refined their mind; the wise.

कृता in कृतधियः=परिकर्मिता *i. e.* refined, cultivated, adorned, *i. e.* adorned with wisdom; कृता in कृतसपर्याः=प्रकृता; कर्तुमारब्धा (प्रादिकं विनाप्यादिकर्मणो गम्यमानत्वात्).

S'l. 1. येषामुज्ज्वलहेतुहेति etc.—One shining with bright weapons consisting of arguments or reason.

प्रामाणिकाध्वस्पृशाम्—Those who tread the path which is 'प्रामाणिक' or which belonged to those who are 'प्रामाणिक'. Not much difference in sense. It means—those who tread the path of reason or those who follow reason.

हेमाचार्य—Who have a powerful friend in the shape of thought arising from this Song of Praise addressed by Hemâcârya to Jina Mahâvîra.

तेषां दुर्नयदस्यु॰—They are never afraid of the robbers, namely, false systems of philosophy.

आयासेन विना—They easily reach the city of जिनागम—the scriptures or teaching of Jaina.

Sl. 2. चातुर्विद्य—(1) लक्षण (Grammar), (2) आगम (Scriptures), (3) साहित्य (Literature and Rhetoric) and (4) तर्क (Logic). See Note on p. 7 and in the Supplementary Notes.

Hemācārya's works in all these branches are well known. (See Introduction).

Read गम्भीरार्थविलोकने and द्राघीयःसमया॰.

द्राघीयःसमया॰—Where many an evil has been averted by insistent regard for a long time. द्राघीयःसमय has been interpreted as 'महान् सिद्धान्त' (See Hiralal Hansraj's Gujarati translation). But I do not think द्राघीयः means 'महान्' and समय=सिद्धान्त here.

सिद्धाञ्जनम्—The miraculous application which gives a new power to the eye.

S'l. 3. अन्यान्यशास्त्रतरु...इचधां मया—

Let those whose hearts are pure wear this commentary on the praise of the last Tirthaṁkara (Lord Mahâvira) like a garland made of a few dotrines which have been gathered here and which are like tempting flowers resting on the trees of different systems of philosophy.

प्रमाणसिद्धान्त—A good expression of modesty.

उर्व्यामेष सुधाभुजां गुरुरिति—to be construed with अनुमिति in the second line. It means: the inference that he is the t^acher of gods on this earth. त्रैलोक्यविस्तारिणो to be construed with प्रतिभाभरात्—from the rich imagination which extends throughout the three worlds. निर्दम्भम्—rightly, honestly, सुधेति वचनोद्गारं=वचनोद्गारं सुधेति·

संवादमेदस्विनीम्—Construe with सुधा—full of consistency or agreement with truth. The verse is a relative clause, to be construed with ते विश्ववन्द्याः of the next line.

S'l. 6. नागेन्द्रगच्छ०—Who is in the नागेन्द्रगच्छ like the Kaustubha gem on the breast of Vishnu.

नन्द्यासुः—May he (उदयप्रभसूरि-the guru of मल्लिषेण) rejoice

S'l. 7. मनुरविमितशाकाब्दे—*i. e.* in the S'aka year 1214. मनु=१४ (चतुर्दश मनवः); रवि=१२ (द्वादश आदित्याः).

दीपमहसि—On the day of Divâli the thirtieth day of Âśvina.

S'l. 8. साहाय्यो०—Composed and made particularly 'fragrant' by the co-operation or rather help of जिनप्रभसूरि.

S'l. 9. बिभ्राणे कलिनिर्जयात्—One who has been like Jina (Lord Mahâvîra) owing to his achieving victory over Kali.

मिषात्—This is a commentary on the Song of Praise composed by Hemācārya; but, truth to say, it is not intended to be so much a literary composition as an expression of 'bhakti' towards Hemacandra.

निर्णेतुं etc.—'I do not submit it to the judgment of scholars.'

तस्यास्तित्वम् etc.—The author is confident that there is plenty of spontaneous thought in his work.

Supplementary Notes.

कलिकालसर्वज्ञ—A title well deserved by one who was 'probably the most learned man of his time'.

अन्ययोगव्यवच्छेदिका—The name of the text commented upon by Malliṣeṇa. If means: the work in which the claims of other (non-Jaina) systems of philosophy as expressions of Truth (*i. e.* the whole Truth) are disproved.

स्याद्वादमञ्जरी—The name of the commentary. In disproving the claims of other systems, the Jaina does not allege that they are wholly untrue, but maintains that they are broken lights of one entire Truth for which Jainism stands in its doctrine of Syâdvâda—*i. e.* the doctrine of 'May-be' or partial truths.

सारस्वतः......मन्त्रः—

श्रीरैवतावतारे च तीर्थे श्रीनेमिनामतः ।
सार्थे साधुमते तत्रावात्सीदवहितस्थितिः ॥
निशीथेऽस्याविनिद्रस्य नासाग्रन्यस्तचक्षुषः ।
आराधनात् समक्षाऽभूद् ब्राह्मी ब्रह्ममहोनिधिः ॥
वत्स स्वच्छमते यासीर्मास्य देशान्तरं भवान् ।
तुष्टा त्वद्भक्तिपुष्ट्याहं सेत्स्यतीहितमत्र ते ॥
इत्युक्त्वा सा तिरोधत्त देवी वाचामधीश्वरी ।
स्तुत्या तस्या निशां नीत्वा पश्चादागादुपाश्रयम् ॥
सिद्धसारस्वतोऽक्लेशात् सोमः सीमा विपश्चिताम् ।
अभूदभूमिरुन्निद्रान्तरवैरिकृतद्रुहः ॥

—Prabhâvakacarita of Candraprabhasûri, Hema. Prabandha vv. 42-46.

उदयप्रभः—Author of धर्मशर्माभ्युदय, a महाकाव्य. See Introduction.

दुःषमार—See Hemacandra's Abhidhânacintâmaṇi I. 42.

रैवत—Girnar, made holy by its association with the name of Neminâtha, twenty-second Tirthamkara, said to be a contemporary and kinsman of Kṛṣṇa.

ब्राह्मी=सरस्वती. The name points to the original solidarity of Jaina and Brâhmaṇa beliefs.

सोमः=सोमचन्द्रः, the name of हेमचन्द्र before he became a 'सूरि'.

सिद्धसारस्वतः—सिद्धः सारस्वतो (मन्त्रः) यस्य, to be construed with अभूत्.

चातुर्विद्यनिर्माणैकब्रह्मणा—Like Brahmâ who made the four Vedas, Hemacandra made the four vidyâs viz. लक्षण, आगम, साहित्य and तर्क. In earlier Gujarat inscriptions 'चातुर्विद्य' is often used for 'the four Vedas' declared by Brahmâ.

For चातुर्विद्य—Cf. Prabāvakacarita:—

"सोमचन्द्रस्ततश्चन्द्रोज्ज्वलप्रज्ञाबलादसौ ।
तर्कलक्षणसाहित्यविद्याः पर्यच्छिनद्द्रुतम् ॥

—Hema. 37.

Cf. also श्रीसिद्धराजेन वादनिष्णाततां पृष्टाः श्रीहेमाचार्याश्चतसृषु विद्यासु परं प्रावीण्यं बिभ्राणं............कर्णावतीस्थितं श्रीदेवाचार्यं प्राहुः—Prabodhacintâmaṇi, where 'the four branches of Knowledge' are, according to Tawney, "त्रयी, the triple Veda; आन्वीक्षिकी, logic and metaphysics; दण्डनीति, the science of government; and वार्ता, practical arts." This meaning does not seem likely, in view of the consensus of explanation given by Jaina writers that the word means लक्षण (Grammar), आगम (Canon), साहित्य (Literature including Poetics) and तर्क (Logic including Metaphysics.)

Bhoja, King of Mâlava, is said to have composed a set of four विद्याs which differed from the above in two. They are s'âstras of (1) शब्द, (2) अलङ्कार, (3) दैवज्ञ-(ज्योतिर्विद् or ज्यौतिष-) and तर्क.

Cf. " असौ हि मालवाधीशो विद्वच्चक्रशिरोमणिः ।
शब्दालङ्कारदैवज्ञतर्कशास्त्राणि निर्ममे ॥ "

Prabhâvaka-Hema. 76.

For the meaning of 'लक्षण' cf. ibid:—

संक्षिप्तश्च प्रवृत्तोऽयं समयेऽस्मिन् कलापकः ।
लक्षणं तत्र निष्पत्तिः शब्दानां नास्ति तादृशी ॥

पाणिनेर्लक्षणं वेदस्याङ्गमित्यत्र च द्विजाः।
अवलेपादसूयन्ति कोर्थऽस्तैरुन्मनायितैः ॥

— „ 82-83.

श्रीहेमसूरयोऽप्यत्रालोक्य व्याकरणव्रजम्।
शास्त्रं चक्रुर्नवं श्रीमत् सिद्धहेमाख्यमद्भुतम् ॥
मौलिं लक्षणशास्त्रेषु विश्वविद्वद्भिराद्दतम् ॥

— „ 96-98.

For the origin of the use of the word 'लक्षण' in this sense, Cf. कथं पुनरिदं भगवतः पाणिनेराचार्यस्य लक्षणं प्रवृत्तम्?— Vyâkaraṇa Mahâbhâṣya, Introduction. The reason for the word लक्षण as applied to Grammar will be found in the following passage which precedes it: "अथैतस्मिञ्शब्दोपदेशे सति किं शब्दानां प्रतिपत्तौ प्रतिपदपाठः कर्तव्यः? I.........I कथं तर्हीमे शब्दाः प्रतिपत्तव्याः? किंचित्सामान्यवल्लक्षणं प्रवर्त्यम्।—M. Bhâṣya *i. e.* Grammar lays down general rules, and does not deal with each individual word in the language. Cf. also" तस्मात् स्वतन्त्रमेवेदं विद्यास्थानमर्थनिर्वचनम् व्याकरणं तु लक्षणप्रधानमिति विशेषः—Durga's Com. on Yâska's Nirukta, where लक्षण=forms in accordance with different senses.

अभयदानाभिधानजीवातु°—Vide "प्रभोरादेशाचाज्ञाकारिष्वष्टादशदेशेषु चतुर्दशवत्सरप्रमितां सर्वभूतेषु मारिं निवारितवान्"—Prabandhacintâmaṇi, Kumârapâla Prabandha; also, "श्रीकुमारपालदेवे तु द्वासप्तति सामन्ताः स्वाज्ञां ग्राहिताः। अष्टादशदेशेष्वमारिपटहो दापितः। चतुर्दशदेशेषु मैत्रीबलेनार्थबलेन च जीवरक्षा कारिता"—Kumārapāla Prabandha of Jinamaṇḍana gaṇi.

विज्ञान—See Hemacandra's Abhidhānacintāmaṇi II. 224:—
"पण्डा तत्त्वानुगा मोक्षे ज्ञानं, विज्ञानमन्यतः।
शुश्रूषा श्रवणं चैव ग्रहणं धारणं तथा ॥"

अष्टादशदोषसंक्षय—Cf. अन्तराया दानलाभवीर्यभोगोपभोगगाः। हासो रत्यरती भीतिर्जुगुप्सा शोक एव च ॥ कामो मिथ्यात्वमज्ञानं निद्रा चाविरतिस्तथा। रागो द्वेषश्च नो दोषास्तेषामष्टादशाप्यमी ॥—Abhidhāna I. 72-73.

अपायापगम—Destruction of अन्तरायकर्म, one of the *Karmans*, the eighth on the list, which impedes ज्ञान.

महाप्रातिहार्यसपर्या—This consists of the following: "कंकिल्लि कुसुमवुट्ठि देवज्झुणि चामरा सणाइं च। भावलय भेरि छत्तं जयन्ति जिण पाडि-

हेराइं ॥" (Pravacana Sâroddhâra XXXIX, 440.) *i. e.* अशोकवृक्ष, कुसुमवृष्टि, दिव्यध्वनि, चामरs, आसनs, भावलय (प्रभामण्डल) भेरी and छत्र.

Cf. "अशोकवृक्षः सुरपुष्पवृष्टिर्दिव्यो ध्वनिश्चामरमासनं च। भामण्डलं दुन्दुभिरातपत्रं सत्प्रातिहार्याणि जिनेश्वराणाम्।"—Quoted in नन्दिसूत्र हारिभद्रीयवृत्ति. The whole section on जिनस्तुति, in Haribhadra's Com, on Nandisûtra, will be found interesting in this connection.

जे एगं जाणइ etc.—Âcârâṅga I. iii. 1–4. Sûtra 122.

आत्ममात्रतारक etc.—Who brings about his own salvation only. अन्तकृत्—Who puts an end to his karmans. केवली is 'अतीतानागतसूक्ष्मव्यवहितपदार्थवेदी' and is described as 'द्रव्यभावमुण्डनप्रधानस्तथाविधबाह्यातिशयशून्यः।', that is, leading a life of asceticism, with the outward symbol and the inner mentality of the shaven-headed. मुण्डकेवली is thus described: "संविग्नो भवनिर्वेदादात्मनिःसरणं तु यः। आत्मार्थं संप्रवृत्तोऽसौ सदा स्यान्मुण्डकेवली॥" —Intense as is the asceticism of the मुण्डकेवलिन्, he still aims at *his own* salvation, and not of the world of living beings, as does the Tîrthaṁkara. Compare the distinction between अर्हत् and बोधिसत् or बुद्ध in Buddhism.

चतुस्त्रिंशदतिशयाः—Thirty-four excellences; 4 सहोत्थाः (सहजन्मानः) congenital, 11 कर्मघातजाः *i. e.* accruing from the destruction of karmans, and 19 दैव्याः (देवकृताः) made by gods. For further details see the footnote on p. 22 of Ârhata-Mata-Prabhâkara edition of प्रमाणमीमांसा.

निशीथचूर्णौ etc.—In the Nisîthacûrṇi, 17th Uddesa.

गुणस्थान—*i. e.* 'Stages in the evolution of the soul' (Jaini), These are thus enumerated in Gommaṭasâra Jîvakâṇḍa, verses 9–10:—मिच्छो सासणमिस्सो अविरदसम्मो य देसविरदो य। विरदापमत्त इदरो अपुव्व अणियट्ट सुहमो य॥ उपसंतखीणमोहो सजोगकेवलिजिणो अजोगी य। चउदस जीव समासा कमेण सिद्धा च णादव्वा॥—*i. e.* There are fourteen stages of the soul (गुणस्थानs): (1) False belief (मिच्छो or मिच्छे= मिथ्यात्व). (2) Backsliding (सासण=सासादन or सास्वादन); (3) Mixed right and wrong belief (मिस्सो=मिश्र); (4) Right faith, not acted on, that is, lacking in विरति or abstention (अविरदसम्मो अविरतसम्यक्त); (5) Beginning of right conduct (देसविरदो=देशविरतः

i. e. partial renunciation). (6) Slight negligence as to right conduct (विरदापमत्त=प्रमत्त-विरत i. e. विरत and yet प्रमत्त occasionally), (7) Right conduct free from all negligence (इदरो= इतरः the other i. e. right conduct without negligence अप्रमत्त°) (8) Initiation to the higher life (अपुव्व=अपूर्वकरण i. e. unprecedented or unique); (9) Incessant pursuit of the higher life (अणियट्ट अणिवृत्तिकरण); (10) Condition almost devoid of desires (सुहमो=सूक्ष्मसंपराय); (11) Condition entirely devoid of desires (उवसंत=उपशान्ति). i.e. (12) Infatuationlessness (खीणमोहो=क्षीणमोहः); (13) Omniscience in the embodied condition (सजोग केवलि=सयोग केवलिन्); and lastly, (14) Omniscience (अजोगी=अयोगकेवलिन्). When this perfection is reached the soul is called Siddha or Perfect. (See Jaini's "Outlines of Jainism" pp. 105-106, and for a fuller account, Mrs. Sinclair Stevenson's "Heart of Jainism" pp. 185 to 192, section on "the fourteen steps to Liberation from Karma").

श्रुतकेवल्यादिषु—Kevalins who were versed in all the parts of the Jaina Canon. These are six and they are enumerated in the Abhidhânacintâmaṇî Ch. I, 33-34—अथ प्रभवः प्रभुः । शय्यंभवो यशोभद्रः संभूतविजयस्ततः । भद्रबाहुः स्थूलभद्रः श्रुतकेवलिनो हि षट् ॥

श्रीवर्धमानाभिधमात्मरूपम् etc.—The whole stanza in the अयोगव्यवच्छेदद्वात्रिंशिका runs as follows:—" अगम्यमध्यात्मविदामवाच्यं वचस्विनामक्षवतां परोक्षम् । श्रीवर्धमानाभिधमात्मरूपमहं स्तुतेर्गोचरमानयामि ॥"

For वर्धमान and the age in which he lived cf. "भगवान् ऋषभस्वामी सुषमदुष्षमारकपर्यन्ते समुदपादि, एकोननवतिपक्षेषु शेषेषु सिद्धिमगमत् । वर्धमानस्वामी तु भगवान् दुष्षमसुषमारकपर्यन्तेषु एकोननवतिपक्षेषु शेषेषु मुक्तिसौधमध्यमाध्यास्त ।.........। उत्सर्पिण्यामपि च प्रथमतीर्थकरो दुष्षमसुषमाया-मेकोननवतिपक्षेषु व्यतिक्रान्तेषु जायते, यतो भगवद्वर्धमानस्वामिसिद्धिगमनस्य भविष्यन्महापद्मतीर्थकरोत्पादस्य चान्तरं चतुरशीतिवर्षसहस्राणि सप्तवर्षाणि पञ्च मासाः पठ्यन्ते ।......। तत उत्सर्पिण्यामपि प्रथमतीर्थकरो यथोक्तकालमान एव जायते । तथा उत्सर्पिण्यां चतुर्विंशतितमः तीर्थकरः सुषमदुष्षमायामेकोननवति पक्षेषु व्यतिक्रान्तेषु जन्मासादयति । एकोननवतिपक्षाधिकचतुरशीतिपूर्वलक्षातिक्रमे च सिध्यति । तत उत्सर्पिण्यामवसर्पिण्यां वा दुष्षमसुषमसुषमदुषमयोरेव तीर्थकृतां जन्मनिर्वाणं च ॥"—Malayagiri's Com. on Nandî-sûtra.

St. III.

रूसउ वा परो वा etc.—Cf. " परो रुष्यतु वा मा वा विषवत् प्रतिभातु वा । भाषितव्या हिता भाषा स्वपक्षगुणकारिणी "—quoted in the footnote in A.M.P. edition of Syadvâdamañjarî p. 12 from Hemacandra's S'reṇikacaritra II 32.

न भवति धर्मः etc.—Tattvârtha-Sûtra-Sambandha-Kârika 29, attributed to Umâsvâti by Malliṣeṇa (For the quotation and the authorship of the work see Introduction p. 4 of AMP. editon of तत्त्वार्थ°).

St. VI.

In Notes p. 68 on Page 28 ll. 175-178 of the text read: " The passage that follows is reproduced verbatim in Guṇaratna's T. R. D. pp. 261-62 ". for " ....is taken verbatim from......" शिपिविष्ट—S'iva. See " स्याद्व्योमकेशः शिपिविष्टभैरवौ ". - Abhidhânacintâmaṇi II. 112.

शम्भोरष्टगुणाधिकरणत्वे etc.—बुद्धि, इच्छा, प्रयत्न, संख्या, परिमाण, पृथक्त्व, संयोग and विभाग.

St. VIII.

किं शिखण्डिना सत्तायोगेन—Possession of सत्ता which is fruitless. The allusion is to the famous character (शिखण्डिन्) in the Mahâ-Bhârata, whom Bhîṣma refused to fight because he was originally a girl. शिखण्डिन् was thus neither a male nor a female and, therefore, the word stands for what is fruitless. The whole passage is borrowed from Hemacandra's Pramâṇa-Mîmâṃsâ I. i. 33: यदि द्रव्यादत्यन्तविलक्षणं सत्त्वं तदा द्रव्यमसदेव भवेत् । सत्तायोगात् सत्त्वमस्त्येवेति चेत् असतां सत्त्वयोगेऽपि कुतः सत्त्वम् । सतां तु निष्फलः सत्तायोगः । स्वरूपसत्त्वं भावानामस्त्येवेति चेत् तर्हि किं शिखण्डिना सत्तायोगेन । सत्तायोगात् प्रागभावो न सत्राप्यसन् । सत्तासंबन्धात्तु सन्निति चेत् वाङ्मात्रमेतत् सदसद्विलक्षणस्य प्रकारान्तरस्यासंभवात्—see pp. 49-50.

लाक्षणिकाः—Grammarians.

नट्ठंभि etc.—उत्पन्नेऽनन्ते नष्टे च छाद्मस्थिके ज्ञाने । रात्र्यां संप्राप्तो महासेनवनमुद्यानम्—छाद्मस्थिकज्ञान is the state immediately preceding केवलज्ञान.

दानादिलब्धिवत्—See तत्त्वार्थसूत्रभाष्य on II. 5:—लब्धयः पञ्चविधा दानलब्धिर्लाभलब्धिर्भोगलब्धिरुपभोगलब्धिर्वीर्यलब्धिरिति—where लब्धि is something like the सिद्धि of Yoga. See Syâdvâda-Ratna.

St. IX.

द्रव्यालङ्कारकारः—Râmacandragaṇi. See Jainagranthâvali p. 73.

गन्धहस्त्यादिषु—गन्धहस्तिभाष्य is said to have been a commentary by Samantabhadra on तत्त्वार्थसूत्र, which is lost. आप्तमीमांसा of Samantabhadra is its Introduction, which has two commentaries one short (अष्टशती) and the other long (अष्टसहस्री) by Akalaṅka and Vidyânandin respectively. The last three are available and have been printed.

St. X.

वैशेषिकनैयायिकयोः समानतन्त्रत्वात्—For the latest discussion on the relative chronology of the Vaiśeṣika and the Nyâya Sûtras see Dr. H. N. Randle's "Indian Logic in the Early Schools" pp. 6-8. I agree in his conclusion.

यौगमत—The Nyâya system of Akṣapâda Gautama. The kinship of Nyâya and Vaiśeṣika is paralleled by the close connection of their religious schools, viz. 'शैव' and 'पाशुपत' which both belong to S'aivism. Guṇaratna observes: "परं शास्त्रेषु नैयायिकाः सदा शिवभक्तत्वात् शैवा इत्युच्यन्ते वैशेषिकास्तु पाशुपता इति ॥" The practice of योग, perhaps in a striking form, which seems to have given the name 'यौगs' to the Naiyâyikas (the school of गौतम अक्षपाद) was, however, no less a feature of the Vaiśeṣika school. Thus, Praśastapâda, a great Vaiśeṣika, concludes his Bhâṣya as follows:

"योगाचारविभूत्या यस्तोषयित्वा महेश्वरम् ।
चक्रे वैशेषिकं शास्त्रं तस्मै कणभुजे नमः ॥"

For "the whole text from छलं तत्त्रिधा to इति निग्रहस्थानम् is taken verbatim from Guṇaratna's Tarkarahasyadîpikâ" read "The whole text from छलं तत्त्रिधा to इति निग्रहस्थानम् is reproduced verbatim in Guṇaratna's Tarakarahasyadîpikâ."

In the Bibliography suggested at the end, add Hemacandra's Pramâṇamîmâṃsâ.

अर्थोपलब्धिहेतुः प्रमाणम्—Vâtsyâyana Bhâṣya on the Nyâya-Sûtras, p. 94, l. 5. Quoted also in the Pramāṇamîmāṃsâ I. i. 8, p. 11.

St. XI.

चातुर्गतिकसंसारं etc.—नारक, तिर्यञ्च्, मानुष and देव, enumerated here in the ascending order—perhaps with the exception of Tirthaṃkaras who though men are reckoned as superior to gods. For the classification see Tattvârtha-Sûtra.

त्रेताग्निः—The three fires viz. दक्षिण, आह्वनीय and गार्हपत्य.

आरनालः—तन्दुलजातिविशेषः and

धूमांशः—सालवृक्षः साग इति भाषायाम्—says AMP.—I do not know on what authority.

ग्लानाद्यसंस्तरः—'संयमानिर्वाहः' AMP.=failure to observe the vow.

आधाकर्मादि०—आधाय साधूंश्चेतसि प्रणिधाय यत् क्रियते भक्तादि तदाधाकर्म । पृषोदरादित्वादिति यल्लोपः । आधानं साधुनिमित्तं चेतसः प्रणिधानं यथा मुक्तस्य साधोः कारणेन मया भक्तादि पचनीयमिति । आधया कर्म पाकादिक्रिया आधाकर्म । तद्योगाद् भक्ताद्यपि आधाकर्म । *i. e.*—Preparing a dinner with the object of serving it to a Sâdhu.

नवकोटि etc.—"१ स्वयं हननं, २ अन्येन घातनं, ३ अपरेण हन्यमानस्यानुमोदनं, ४ स्वयं पचनं, ५ अन्येन पाचनं, ६ अपरेण पाच्यमानस्यानुमोदनं, ७ स्वयं क्रयणं, ८ अन्येन क्रायणं, ९ अपरेण क्रीयमाणस्यानुमोदनम्—इति मलयगिर्याचार्यकृतायां पिण्डनिर्युक्तिविवृतौ उद्गमद्वारे गा. ४०२"—AMP. footnote on p. 88.

पञ्चकादियतनया etc.—"तत्थेव अन्यगामेवुच्छन्तर असंभरंत जयणाए। संथरणे सणमादि छन्नं कडजोगी गीयत्थे"—प्रथमतस्तत्रैव ग्रामे प्रायोग्यमन्वेषणीयम्। तत्र यदि न लभ्यते तदान्यग्रामेऽपि। अथासावन्यग्रामो दूरतरस्ततोऽन्तरालेऽन्तरालग्राम उषित्वा द्वितीये दिने आनयन्ति। अथैवमप्यसंस्तरणं भवति ततः अकारप्रश्लेषादसंस्तरतोग्लानस्यार्थाय यतनया पञ्चपरिहारिण्या गृह्णन्ति। अथ ग्लानार्थं व्यापृतानां परिचारकाणां संस्तरणं तत एषणादोषेषु आदिशब्दादुद्गमादिदोषेषु च पञ्चकपरिहाण्या यतितव्यम्। अथ प्रतिदिवसं ग्लानप्रायोग्यं न लभ्यते ततश्छन्नमप्रकटं कृतयोगी गीतार्थो वा प्रायोग्यं द्रव्यं परिवासयन्ति। यथाकार्णितछेदश्रुतार्थः प्रत्युच्चारणासमर्थः कृतयोगी यस्तु छेदश्रुतार्थं श्रुत्वा प्रत्युच्चारयितुमीशः स गीतार्थ उच्यते।"—बृहत्कल्पसूत्रे उद्देशे बृहच्छालीयश्रीक्षेमकीर्तिसूरिकृतटीकायाम्। समासार्थोऽपि तत्रैव।"—AMP. footnote on p. 89.

Add as an Appendix to the discussion relating to हिंसा versus अहिंसा the following interesting and parallel passage from Kumârapāla Prabandha of Jinamaṇḍanagaṇi:—

1. न विना जीवघातेन मांसं भवति कुत्रचित्। जीवघातस्तु न श्रेयांस्तस्मान्मांसं परित्यजेत्॥ १॥ न भक्षयति यो मांसं न हन्यान्न च घातयेत्। स मित्रं सर्वभूतानां मनुः स्वायंभुवोऽब्रवीत् ॥२॥ इति मनुस्मृतौ॥ वर्षे वर्षेऽश्वमेधेन यो यजेत शतं समाः। मांसानि च न खादेत तयोः पुण्यफलं समम्॥ स्कन्दपुराणे—"भोक्ताऽनुमन्ता संस्कर्ता क्रयिविक्रयिहिंसकाः। उपकर्ता घातयिता हिंसकश्चाष्टधाऽधमाः॥ १॥ यः स्वार्थं मांसपचनं कुरुते पापमोहितः। यावन्ति पशुरोमाणि तावत्स नरकं व्रजेत्॥२॥ परप्राणैस्तु ये प्राणान् स्वान् पुष्णन्ति हि दुर्धियः। आकल्पं नरकान् भुक्त्वा ते युज्यन्तेऽत्र तैः पुनः ॥३॥ जातु मांसं न भोक्तव्यं प्राणैः कण्ठगतैरपि। भोक्तव्यं तर्हि भोक्तव्यं स्वमांसं नेतरस्य च ॥४॥ क्व मांसं क्व शिवे भक्तिः क्व मद्यं क्व शिवार्चनम्। मद्यमांसरतानां हि दूरे तिष्ठति शङ्करः ॥ ५॥ स्कन्दपुराणे—धनेन क्रायको हन्ति उपभोगेन खादकः। घातको वधबन्धाभ्यामित्येष त्रिविधो वधः॥

यदि वेदेषु जीवदयाऽस्ति तर्हि सकलशास्त्रसंवादशुद्धां जीवदयां कुर्वाणाः कथं वेदबाह्याः। यदाहुः—अहिंसा प्रथमो धर्मः सर्वशास्त्रेषु विश्रुतः। यत्र जीवदया नास्ति तत्सर्वं परिवर्जयेत् ॥ १॥ श्रूयतां धर्मसर्वस्वं, श्रुत्वा चैवावधार्यताम्। आत्मनः प्रतिकूलानि परेषां न समाचरेत्॥ २ ॥ सर्वे वेदा न तत् कुर्युः सर्वे यज्ञाश्च भारत। सर्वे तीर्थाभिषेकाश्च यत्कुर्यात् प्राणिनां दया॥ ३ ॥ ध्रुवं प्राणिवधो यज्ञे नास्ति यज्ञस्त्वहिंसकः। सर्वसत्त्वेष्वहिंसैव दयायज्ञो युधिष्ठिर॥ ४ ॥ अथ वेदेषु दया नास्ति तर्हि न प्रमाणं वेदाः नास्तिकधर्मशास्त्रवत्। जीवो यत्र शिवस्तत्र न भेदः शिवजीवयोः॥ "न हिंस्यात् सर्व भूतानि" इति॥ न वेदैर्नैव दानैश्च न तपोभिर्न चाध्वरैः। कथंचित्सद्गतिं यान्ति पुरुषाः प्राणिहिंसकाः॥ इत्यादि धर्मशास्त्राणि जानद्भिः पठद्भिश्च वेदाः सर्वजीवहिंसा मातृपितृगोमेधादियज्ञप्ररूपकाः यैः

प्रमाणीक्रियन्ते तैर्नास्तिकशास्त्राणि कस्मान्निराक्रियन्ते ॥ अन्धे तमसि मज्जामः पशुभिर्ये यजामहे । हिंसा नाम भवेद्धर्मो न भूतो न भविष्यति ॥ ....अथ भगवन् । यज्ञार्थं पशवः सृष्टाः स्वयमेव स्वयंभुवा । यज्ञोऽस्य भूत्यै सर्वस्य तस्माद्यज्ञे वधोऽवधः ॥ औषध्यः पशवो वृक्षास्तिर्यञ्चः पक्षिणस्तथा । यज्ञार्थं निधनं प्राप्ताः प्राप्नुवन्त्युच्छ्रितिं पुनः । इत्यादि वदन्तो द्विजा वेदोक्तहिंसाया धर्मसाधनत्वं प्राहुः तत्कथम् । सूरिः—राजन् । नैतत् सत्यम् । यतः स्कन्दपुराणे—अग्निषोमीयमिति या पश्वालम्भनकारिका । सा न प्रमाणं ज्ञातॄणां भ्रामका सा सतामिह ॥ वृक्षांश्छित्त्वा पशून् हत्वा कृत्वा रुधिरकर्दमम् । दग्ध्वा वह्नौ तिलाज्यादि चित्रं स्वर्गोऽभिलष्यते ॥ तथा श्रीभागवतपुराणे त्रयोविंशत्यध्याये शुकः—"ये त्विह दाम्भिका दम्भयज्ञेषु पशून् विशसन्ति तानमुष्मिन् लोके वैशसे नरके पतितान् निरयपतयो यातयित्वा विशसन्ति" इत्यादि ॥ मीमांसायाम् "अन्धे तमसि मज्जामः पशुभिर्ये यजामहे । हिंसा नाम भवेद्धर्मो न भूतो न भविष्यति ॥" श्रीभागवतपुराणे एकादशाध्याये ब्राह्मण उवाच "तथैव राजन्नुरुगार्हमेधवितानविद्योरुविजृम्भितेषु । न वेदवादेषु हि तत्त्ववादः प्रायेण शुद्धोऽनुचकास्ति साधुः" ॥ किंच "यज्ञार्थं पशवः सृष्टा यदीति वदति स्मृतिः । तन्मांसमश्नतः स्मार्ता वादयन्ति न किं नृपान् ॥ यदि यज्ञार्थं पशवः सृष्टास्तर्हि व्याघ्रादिभिर्देवाः किं न तृप्यन्ते । अहिंसासंभवो धर्मः स हिंसातः कथं भवेत् ॥ न तोयजानि पद्मानि जायन्ते जातवेदसः ॥ तथाच धर्मसमुद्देशे—"आत्मवत् सर्वजीवेषु कुशलवृत्तिचिन्तनम् । धर्मस्याधिगमोपायः शक्तितस्त्यागतोऽप्ययम् ॥ इति ॥ श्रीभोजराजाग्रे धनपालवाक्यम्—"नाहं स्वर्गफलोपभोगतृषितो नाभ्यर्थितस्त्वं मया । संतुष्टस्तृणभक्षणेन सततं साधो न युक्तं तव । स्वर्गं यान्ति यदि त्वया विनिहता यज्ञे ध्रुवं प्राणिनो यज्ञं किं न करोषि मातृपितृभिः पुत्रैस्तथा बान्धवैः ॥" इत्यादिहेमसूरिवाक्यामृतसिक्तहृदयः श्रीचौलुक्यो वेदोक्तमार्गस्याप्रमाणत्वममन्यत ॥

—Kumârapâlaprabandha.

2. अविशेषश्चोभयोः ॥ १, ६ ॥—उभयोरेव दृष्टादृष्टयोरत्यन्तदुःखनिवृत्त्यसाधकत्वे यथोक्ततद्धेतुत्वे चाविशेष एव मन्तव्य इत्यर्थः । एतदेव कारिकायामुक्तम्—दृष्टवदानुश्रविकः स ह्यविशुद्धिक्षयातिशययुक्तः इति । गुरोरनुश्रूयत इत्यनुश्रवो वेदः तद्विहितयागादिरानुश्राविकः । स दृष्टोपायवदेवाशुध्द्या हिंसादिपापेन विनाशिसातिशयफलकत्वेन च युक्त इत्यर्थः । न न वैधहिंसायाः पापजनकत्वे बलवदनिष्टाननुबन्धेष्टसाधनत्वरूपस्य विध्यर्थस्यानुपपत्तिरिति चेन्न । वैधहिंसाजन्यानिष्टस्येष्टोत्पत्तिनान्तरीयकत्वेनेष्टोत्पत्तिनान्तरीयकदुःखाधिकदुःखजनकत्वरूपस्य बलवदनिष्टाननुबन्धित्वस्य विध्यंशस्याक्षतेः । यत्तु वैधहिंसातिरिक्तहिंसाया एव पापजनकत्वमिति तदसत् । संकोचे प्रमाणाभावात् । युधिष्ठिरादीनां स्वधर्मेऽपि युद्धादौ ज्ञातिवधादिप्रत्यवायपरिहाराय प्रायश्चित्तश्रवणाच्च । तस्माद्यास्यामहं तात दृष्ट्वेमं दुःखसंनिधिम् । त्रयीधर्ममधर्माढ्यं किंपाकं फलसंनिभम् । इति मार्कण्डेयवचनाच्च । अहिंसन् सर्वभूतान्यन्यत्र तीर्थेभ्य इति श्रुतिस्तु वैधातिरिक्तहिंसानिवृत्तेरिष्टसाधनत्वमेव वक्ति न तु वैधहिंसाया अनिष्टसाधनत्वाभावमपीत्यादिकं योगवार्तिके

द्रष्टव्यमिति दिक् ॥ दुःखाद् दुःखं जलाभिषेकवन्न जाड्यविमोकः ॥ ८४ ॥ आनुश्रविकात्तु हिंसादिदोषेण दुःखात्मकभोगेन च दुखाद् दुःखं दुःखधारैव भवति, न तु जाड्यविमोकोऽविवेकनिवृत्तिः । दुःखविमोकस्त्वतिदूर एव तिष्ठति । यथा जाड्यार्तस्य जलाभिषेकाद् दुःखनिवृत्तिरेव भवति न तु जाड्यविमोक्ष इत्यर्थः । तदुक्तम्--
यथा पङ्केन पङ्काम्भः सुरया वा सुराकृतम् । भूतहत्यां तथैवैकां न यज्ञैर्मार्ष्टुमर्हति ।

—Sâṁkhya-sûtras with Bhâṣya.

3. A few texts bearing on the subject of अहिंसा will also be found in Mâṭhara-Vṛtti on the Sâṃkhya Kârikâs.

4. For a fairly long list of texts bearing on अहिंसा and यज्ञ and translated in the various volumes of the "Sacred Books of the East" see "*Ahiṃsâ*" in (a) Jaina religion, (b) in Buddhism and (c) in Brahmanism on pp. 30–32 and "Sacrifice—(d) Relative value or wortnlessness of sacrifice, and symbolical sacrifice" on pp. 182–83 in Winternitz' "Concise Dictionary of Eastern Religion."

5. A most interesting and instructive treatment of the subject with a long list of quotations made from the MBh and the Puraṇas and the Smṛtis will be found in the edition of the Sâṁkhya Kârikas with Sâṃkhya-Tattvakaumudi annostated by Bâlârama Udâsîna of Benares.

The texts of S'ruti, Smṛti, Mahâbhârata and Purâṇas, as well as the views of Sâṁkhya, Vedânta and Bhakti schools of religion cited in the Syâdvâdamañjari and in the extracts given above leave no doubt that there was a strong body of opinion even in Brahmanism which revolted against हिंसा, even वैधहिंसा (*i. e.* हिंसा prescribed in S'âstras, such as animal slaughter in a sacrifice). This trend of thought seems to have come down from times earlier than the rise of Jainism and Buddhism, mainly in the Bhakti and Jñâna schools as distinguished from the ritualist school of Brahmanism.

St. XII.

भीमांसकभेदभट्टानाम्—The school of Kumârila Bhaṭṭa is one of the two famous schools of Mîmâṃsâ *i. e.* Pûrva Mîmâṃsâ;

the other being that of Prabhâkara or 'Guru' as he is generally styled. The differences of the two schools on certain problems of philosophy are radical. See Dr. Ganganath Jha's thesis on the "Prabhâkara School."

यौगानां—see supra.

लब्ध्युपयोगं—लब्धिः=अर्थग्रहणशक्तिः, उपयोगः=अर्थग्रहणव्यापारः
(Footnote in AMP. p. 95).

"**लब्ध्युपयोगौ भावेन्द्रियम्—लब्धिरुपयोगश्च भावेन्द्रियं भवति। लब्धिर्नाम गतिजात्यादिनामकर्मजनिता तदावरणीयकर्मक्षयोपशमजनिता चेन्द्रियाश्रयकर्मोदयनिर्वृत्ता च जीवस्य भवति। सा पञ्चविधा। तद्यथा। स्पर्शनेन्द्रियलब्धिः, रसनेन्द्रियलब्धिः, घ्राणेन्द्रियलब्धिः, चक्षुरिन्द्रियलब्धिः श्रोत्रेन्द्रियलब्धिरिति**"—Tattvârtha Sûtra II. 18 and Bhâṣya. **भावेन्द्रियs** *i. e.* subjective senses. Sense-faculties are of two kinds: (1) **लब्धि** (it is the attainment of manifestation of the sense-faculty by the partial destruction, subsidence and operation of the knowledge-obscuring karma relating to that sense.); (2) **उपयोग** (the conscious attention of the soul directed to that sense.)—Tattvârtha translated by Mr. J. L. Jaini in "The Sacred Books of the Jainas." More briefly, "**इन्द्रियनिर्वृत्तिहेतुः क्षयोपशमविशेषो लब्धिः तन्निमित्तः परिणामविशेष उपयोगः।**" (Headnote to the Tattvârtha-S'loka-Vârtika on T. S. II. 18).

भट्टास्तावदिदं वदन्ति—Partly drawn from Ratnaprabhâcârya's Ratnâkarâvatârikâ on P. N. T. (p. 37) and simplified: Cf. **अत्रेयं भट्टचट्टघट्टना—ननु न स्वसंवेदनं वेदनस्य सुन्दरम्, स्वात्मनि क्रियाविरोधात् इत्यस्य पारोक्ष्यमेवाक्षुण्णं कक्षीकरणीयम्। तदेतदरमणीयम्। यतः—किमुत्पत्तिः ज्ञप्तिर्वा स्वात्मनि विरुध्येत?। यद्युत्पत्तिः, सा विरुध्यताम्। न हि ज्ञानमात्मानमुत्पादयतीति वयमध्यगीष्महि। अथ ज्ञप्तिः, नेयमात्मनि विरोधमदीधरत्। तदात्मनैव ज्ञानस्य स्वकारणकलापादुत्पादात् प्रकाशात्मनेव प्रदीपाकलिकालोकस्य। अथ प्रकाशात्मनैव प्रदीपालोकोऽयमुदयमाशिश्रायदिति परप्रकाशकोऽस्तु, आत्मानमप्येतावन्मात्रेणैव प्रकाशयतीति तु कौतुस्कुती नीतिः? इति चेत्। तत् किं तेनाप्रकाशितेनैव वराकेण स्थातव्यम् आलोकान्तराद् वा प्रकाशेनास्य भवितव्यम्?। प्रथमे, प्रत्यक्षबाधा। द्वितीयेऽपि, सैवानवस्थापत्तिश्च। अथ नाऽसौ स्वमपेक्ष्य कर्मतया चकास्ति, इत्यप्रकाशकः स्वीक्रियते, प्रकाशरूपतयानूत्पन्नत्वात् स्वयं प्रकाशत एवेति चेत् अनेनैव सुधामहि। नहि वयमपि ज्ञानं कर्मतयैव प्रतिभासमानं स्ववेद्यमावेदयामहि, ज्ञानं स्वयं प्रतिभासत इत्याद्यकर्मकस्य तस्य**

चकासनात्। यथा तु ज्ञानं जानामीति कर्मतयापि तद् भाति यथा प्रदीपः स्वं प्रकाशयतीत्ययमपि तथा प्रथत एव।.........

सत्संप्रयोगे.........इत्येवं त्रिपुटीकल्पना भट्टानां प्रयासफलैव॥ Cf. Hemacandra's Pramâṇamîmâṃsâ for the necessary grounds: येऽपि "तत्संप्रयोगे पुरुषस्येन्द्रियाणां बुद्धिजन्म सत्प्रत्यक्षं यद्विषयं ज्ञानं तेन संप्रयोगे इन्द्रियाणां पुरुषस्य बुद्धिजन्म। सत्प्रत्यक्षं यदन्यविषयं ज्ञानमन्यसंप्रयोगे भवति न तत्प्रत्यक्षम्"—इत्येवं तत्सर्वतो व्यत्ययेन लक्षणमनवद्यमित्याहुः—तेषामपि क्लिष्टकल्पनैव संशयज्ञानेन व्यभिचारानिवृत्तेः। तत्र हि यद्विषयं ज्ञानं तेन संप्रयोग इन्द्रियाणामस्त्येव। यद्यपि चोभयविषयं ज्ञानं तथापि तयोरन्यतरेणेन्द्रियेण संयुक्तमेव। उभयावमर्शित्वाच्च संशयस्य। तेन संयुक्ते चक्षुस्तद्विषयमपि तज्ज्ञानं भवत्येवेति नातिव्याप्तिपरिहारः। अव्याप्तिश्च चाक्षुषज्ञानस्येन्द्रियसंप्रयोगत्वा-भावात्। अप्राप्यकारि च चक्षुरित्युक्तप्रायम्॥

यौगास्त्वाहुः—The whole of this is substantially and almost verbatim taken from Ratnaprabhācārya's Ratnākarāvatārikā. Cf. "अथ यौगाः संगिरन्ते—अहो आर्हताः नास्मिन् मीमांसके वराके व्यपाकृतेऽपि संवेदने स्वसंवेदनदोहदः पूरयितुं पार्यते। तथाहि—ज्ञानं स्वान्यप्रकाश्यम् ईश्वरज्ञानान्यत्वे सति प्रमेयत्वात् यदेवं तदेवं यथा घटः तथा चेदं तस्मात्तथा। समुत्पन्नं हि ज्ञानमेकात्मसमवेतानन्तरसमयसमुत्पादिष्णुमानसप्रत्यक्षेणैव लक्ष्यते न पुनः स्वेन। न चैवमनवस्थावल्लेरुल्लासः अथावसायिवेदनोत्पादमात्रेणैवार्थसिद्धेः तद्धि पदार्थपरामर्शस्वभावमेवइत्युत्पन्नमात्रमेव पदार्थप्रथामनोरथस्थितं कृतार्थयति प्रमातारम्। अर्थज्ञानजिज्ञासायां तु तत्रापि ज्ञानमुत्पद्यत एवेति।

तदेतदेतेषां मतेस्तरलतां तनोति। प्रकटितप्रयोगे पक्षस्यानुमानेन मानखण्डनात्। तथा च तावक्राकूतेन तत्र हेतोः कालात्ययापदिष्टत्वनिष्टङ्कनाच्च। तथाहि—विवादास्पदं ज्ञानं स्वसंविदितं ज्ञानत्वात् ईश्वरज्ञानवत्। बाधासिद्धमेतन्निदर्शनम् जैनैरीश्वरास्वीकारेण तज्ज्ञानस्य तेषामप्रसिद्धेः इति चेत्। तदचतुरस्रम्। अनवद्यविद्याविद्याधरीबन्धुरपरिष्वङ्गस्य पुरुषातिशेषविशेषस्य खण्डपरशोः स्वीकारात् त्रिविष्टपघटनलम्पटपटिम्नः सकलावलोकनकौशलशालिन एव चास्य तिरस्कारात्। व्यर्थविशेष्यश्चात्र हेतुः। समर्थविशेषणोपादानेनैव साध्यसिद्धेः धूमध्वजसिद्धौ धूमवत्त्वे सति द्रव्यत्वादितिवत्। न हीश्वरज्ञानादन्यत् स्वसंविदितमप्रमेयं चास्ति यदपोहाय प्रमेयत्वादिति क्रियते। अप्रयोजकश्चायं हेतुः। सोपाधिकत्वात्। साधनाव्यापकः साध्येन समव्याप्तिकः खलूपाधिरभिधीयते तत्पुत्रत्वादिना श्यामत्वे साध्ये शाकाद्याहारपरिणामवत्। कः पुनरुपाधिरत्र सूक्ष्मेक्षणैरीक्षाञ्चक्रे इति चेत् उच्यते—निबिडजडिमन् जडिमलक्षणः। तथाहि—ईश्वरज्ञानान्यत्वे प्रमेयत्वे सत्यपि यदेव जडिमपात्रं पात्रादि तदेव स्वस्मादन्येनैव प्रकाश्यते। स्वप्रकाशे

परमुखोत्प्रेक्षित्वं हि जडस्य लक्षणम्। न च ज्ञानं जडस्वरूपम् इति सिद्धं साधनाव्यापकत्वं जाड्यस्य साध्येन समव्याप्तिकत्वं चास्य स्पष्टमेव जाड्यं विहाय स्वप्रकाशाभावस्य तं च त्यक्त्वा जाड्यस्य क्वचिदप्यदर्शनादिति ॥

यच्चोक्तं समुत्पन्नं हि ज्ञानमेकात्मसमवेतेत्यादि तदपि नावितथम्। इत्थमर्थज्ञानतज्ज्ञानयोरुत्पद्यमानयोः क्रमानुपलक्षणात्। आशूत्पादादत्र क्रमानुपलक्षणमुत्पलपत्रशतव्यतिभेदवदिति चेत्। तदचारु। जिज्ञासाव्यवहितस्यार्थज्ञानज्ञानस्योत्पादप्रतिपादनात्। न च जिज्ञासासमुत्पाद्यत्वं संवेदनानां संगच्छते। अजिज्ञासितेष्वपि योग्यदेशेषु गोचरेषु तदुत्पादप्रतीतेः। न चायोग्यदेशमर्थज्ञानम्। आत्मसमवेतस्यास्य समुत्पादात् इति जिज्ञासामन्तरेणैवार्थज्ञाने ज्ञानोत्पादप्रसङ्गः। बाढमुत्पद्यतां नामेदम्। को दोषः इति चेत्। नन्वेवमेव तज्ज्ञानज्ञानेऽप्यपरज्ञानोत्पादप्रसङ्गः। तत्रापि चैवमेवायम्। इत्यपरापरज्ञानोत्पादपरम्परायामेकात्मनो व्यापाराद् न विषयान्तरसंचारः स्यात्। इति न ज्ञानस्य ज्ञानान्तरज्ञेयताऽपि युक्तिमार्गमवगाहते ॥

1. The position of the Jainas on the problem, whether ज्ञान is स्वतोग्राह्य (स्वयंप्रकाश) or परतोग्राह्य (परप्रकाश) is thus stated in the P. N. T. स्वपरव्यवसायिज्ञानं प्रमाणम् (I. 2.) ज्ञानादन्योऽर्थः परः (I. 15.) तदुभयमुत्पत्तौ परत एव, ज्ञप्तौ तु स्वतः परतश्च (I. 20).

2. See on a kindred point, Anantavîrya's लघुवृत्ति on Mâṇikyanandin's परीक्षामुखसूत्रः—

अत्र भवतु नाम उक्तलक्षणलक्षितं प्रमाणं तथापि तत्प्रामाण्यं स्वतः परतो वा। न तावत् स्वतः अविप्रतिपत्तिप्रसङ्गात्। नापि परतोऽनवस्थाप्रसङ्गात्। इति मतद्वयमाशङ्क्य तन्निराकरणेन स्वमतमवस्थापयन्नाह ॥...... अभ्यासदशायां स्वतोऽनभ्यासदशायां च परत इति। तेन प्रागुक्तैकान्तद्वयनिरासः। न चानभ्यासदशायां परतः प्रामाण्येऽप्यनवस्था समाना। ज्ञानान्तरस्याभ्यस्तविषयस्य स्वतः प्रमाणभूतस्याङ्गीकरणात् ॥

In a portion of his commentary Malliṣeṇa has drawn upon Hemacandra's gloss on his (Hemacandra's) own work—प्रमाणमीमांसाः—

नन्वनुभूतेरनुभाव्यत्वे घटादिवदननुभूतित्वप्रसङ्गः। मैवं वोचः। ज्ञातुर्ज्ञातृत्वेनेवानुभूतेरनुभूतित्वेनैवानुभवात्। न चानुभूतेरनुभाव्यत्वं दोषः। अर्थापेक्षयानुभूतित्वात्, स्वापेक्षयाऽनुभाव्यत्वात्। स्वपितृपुत्रापेक्षयैकस्य पितृत्वपुत्रत्ववद्विरोधाभावात्। न च स्वात्मनि क्रियाविरोधः। अनुभवसिद्धेऽर्थे विरोधासिद्धेः। अनुमानाच्च स्वसंवेदनसिद्धिः। तथाहि—ज्ञानं प्रकाशमानमेवार्थं प्रकाशयति प्रकाशकत्वात् प्रदीपवत् संवेदनस्य प्रकाशकत्वात्। प्रकाशकमसिद्धमिति चेत्

न। अज्ञाननिरासादिद्वारेण प्रकाशकत्वोपपत्तेः। न च नेत्रादिभिरनैकान्तिकता। तेषां भावेन्द्रियरूपाणामेकमेव प्रकाशकत्वात् भावेन्द्रियाणां च स्वसंवेदनरूपतैव न व्यभिचारः। तथा संवित् स्वप्रकाशा अर्थप्रतीतित्वात्। यः स्वप्रकाशो न भवति नासावर्थप्रतीतिर्यथा घटः तथा यज्ज्ञानं तदात्मबोधं प्रत्यनपेक्षितपरव्यापारं यथा गोचरान्तरग्राहि ज्ञानप्राग्भाविगोचरान्तरग्राहि ज्ञानप्रतिबन्धस्यान्त्यज्ञानम्। ज्ञानं च विवादाध्यासितं रूपादिज्ञानमिति संवित् स्वप्रकाशे स्वावान्तरजातीयं नापेक्षते वस्तुत्वात् घटवत्। संवित् परप्रकाश्या वस्तुत्वात् घटवदिति चेत् न। अस्याप्रयोजकत्वात्। न खलु घटस्य वस्तुत्वात् परप्रकाश्यता अपि तु बुद्धिव्यतिरिक्तत्वात्॥

Cf. also Hemacandra: स्वपराभासी परिणाम्यात्मा प्रमाता॥ Pr. M. स्वमात्मानं परं चार्थमाभासयितुं शीलं यस्य स स्वपराभासी स्वोन्मुखतया चावभासनात् घटमहं जानामीति कर्मकर्तृक्रियाणां प्रतीतेः। अन्यतरप्रतीत्यपलापे प्रमाणाभावात्। न च परप्रकाशकत्वस्य स्वप्रकाशकत्वेन विरोधः प्रदीपवत्। नहि प्रदीपः स्वप्रकाशे परमपेक्षते। अनेनैकान्तस्वाभासिपराभासिवादिनिरासः॥ (Pr. Mîm. 1.1.43 & Com.)

Note that Hemacandra's definition of प्रमाण differs from that of the authors of the Parîkṣâmukha Sûtra and its Vṛitti. He says: ननु च परिच्छिन्नधर्मं परिच्छिन्दता प्रमाणेन पिष्टं पिष्टं स्यात् तथा च गृहीतग्राहिणां धारावाहिकज्ञानानामपि प्रामाण्यप्रसङ्गः। ततोऽपूर्वार्थनिर्णय इत्यस्तु लक्षणम्। यथाहुः स्वापूर्वार्थव्यवसायात्मकं ज्ञानं प्रमाणम् इति। तथा अपूर्वार्थविज्ञानम्–इति च तत्राह—ग्रहीष्यमाणग्राहिण इव गृहीतग्राहिणोऽपि नाप्रामाण्यम्। (१-१-४)॥

अयमर्थः द्रव्यापेक्षया वा गृहीतग्राहित्वं विप्रतिषिध्येत पर्यायापेक्षया वा। तत्र पर्यायापेक्षया धारावाहिकज्ञानानामपि गृहीतग्राहित्वं न संभवति। क्षणिकत्वात् पर्यायाणाम्। तत्कथं तन्निवृत्त्यर्थं विशेषणमुपादीयते। अथ द्रव्यापेक्षया। तदप्ययुक्तम। द्रव्यस्य नित्यत्वादेकत्वेन गृहीतग्रहीष्यमाणावस्थयोर्न भेदः। ततश्च कं विशेषमाश्रित्य ग्रहीष्यमाणग्राहिणः प्रामाण्यं न गृहीतग्राहिणः। अपि च अवग्रहादीनां गृहीतग्राहित्वेऽपि प्रामाण्यमिष्यत एव॥

प्रमाणं स्वपराभासि ज्ञानं बाधविवर्जितम्।—Nyā·āvatāra 1.

—इह च व्यवच्छेद्यापेक्षया लक्षणे विशेषणप्रवृत्तेः स्वपराभासि इत्यनेन ये स्वाभास्येव ज्ञानं मन्यन्ते ज्ञानवादिनो बौद्धविशेषाः ये च पराभास्येव मीमांसकनैयायिकादयः ते निरस्ताः॥—Com. by Siddharṣi.

सर्वज्ञानमनध्यक्षं प्रत्यक्षोऽर्थः परिस्फुटः।
इति केचिदनात्मज्ञाः प्रमाणव्याहतं विदुः॥

प्रत्यक्षमात्मनि ज्ञानमपरत्रानुमानिकम् ।
प्रत्यात्मवेद्यमाहन्ति तत्परोक्षत्वकल्पनाम् ॥
विज्ञानस्य परोक्षत्वे प्रत्यक्षोऽर्थः स्वयं कथम् ।
सर्वदा सर्वथा सर्वैः सर्वस्य न तथा भवेत् ॥
ततः परं च विज्ञानं किमर्थमुपकल्प्यते ।
कादाचित्कत्वसिध्यर्थमर्थज्ञप्तेर्न सा परा ॥
विज्ञानादित्यनध्यक्षात् कुतो विज्ञायते परः ।
लिङ्गाचेत् तत्परिच्छित्तिरपि लिङ्गान्तरादिति ।
क्वावस्थानमनेनैव तयार्थापत्तिराहता ।
अविज्ञातस्य सर्वस्य ज्ञापकत्वविरोधतः ॥
स्वसंवेद्यान्तरादन्याद्विज्ञानं किं करिष्यते ।
करणेन विना कर्तुः कर्माणि व्यावृतिर्न चेत् ॥
स्वसंवित्तिक्रिया न स्यात् स्वतः पुंसोऽर्थवित्तिवत् ।
यदि स्वात्मा स्वसंवित्तावात्मनः करणं मतम् ॥
स्वार्थवित्तौ तदेवास्तु ततौ ज्ञानं स एव नः ।
ज्ञानं ज्ञानान्तराद्वेद्यं स्वात्मज्ञप्तिविरोधतः ।
प्रमेयत्वाद्यथा कुम्भ इत्यप्यश्लीलभाषितम् ॥
ज्ञानान्तरं यदी ज्ञानादन्यस्मात्तेन विद्यते ।
तदानवस्थितिप्राप्तेरन्यथा ह्यविनिश्चयात् ॥
अर्थज्ञानस्य विज्ञानं नाज्ञातमवबोधकम् ।
ज्ञापकत्वाथाक्षलिङ्गलिङ्गिनो नान्यथा स्थितिः ॥

4. नान्यथा ह्यर्थसद्भावो दृष्टः सन्नुपपद्यते ।
ज्ञानं चेन्नेत्यतः पश्चात् प्रमाणमुपजायते ॥
—S'l. Vârt. V. S'ûnyavâda 182.

तत्र केचिदाहुः। सर्वथा तावदस्ति ज्ञानम्। तथा हि विद्यमान एव हि घटः कस्यचिदेव व्यवहारयोग्यतामापद्यते न सर्वेषां, नापि सर्वदा; तदवश्यं यो यदा तेन व्यवहरति तस्य तद्व्यवहारानुगुणः कश्चिदतिशयः संजात इति कल्पनीयम् स ज्ञानम् इति ॥ सत्यम्। एवं सिध्यति ज्ञानं किंतु प्रागपि व्यवहारादवगम्यते ज्ञानम् अव्यवहरन्नपि ज्ञातोऽयमर्थो मयेति आत्मनाऽर्थस्य ज्ञातत्वमनुसंधत्ते इति सर्वजनीनमेतत्। न च ज्ञानमविदुषां ज्ञातत्वरूपत्वं शक्यं वेदितुम् यदेव प्रागेव व्यवहारादुपजायमानो ज्ञातत्वावगमोऽसति ज्ञानस्य प्रत्यक्षत्वे कथमुपपद्यते ॥ अत्राहुः। ज्ञानजन्योऽर्थगतः कश्चिदतिशयः प्रकाशनभासनादिपर्यायपदवाच्यः। स च पाकगन्धौनादिगतातिशयवदनवरातेऽपि ज्ञाने शक्यतेऽवगन्तुम्। अतः ज्ञानस्य कल्पक इति। सत्यम् अस्त्यतिशयः, स च प्रत्यक्षेऽर्थे प्रत्यक्षावगतः कल्पयेदपि ज्ञानम्। अनुमानादिषु तु तस्या-

प्रत्यक्षत्वात् प्राग्व्यवहारात्तु ह्याप्तलिंगाभावादप्रमितस्य चाकल्पकत्वान्न ज्ञानं कल्पयेत्। अनुमितेऽपि चार्थे ज्ञातो मयाऽग्निरिति अग्निं ज्ञातमनुसंधत्ते। अतस्तत्त्वं वक्तव्यम्। ज्ञाने प्रमाणमुच्यते। ज्ञानक्रियाजनितो ज्ञातुर्ज्ञेयेन सहाप्तत्वसंबन्धः। स मानसप्रत्यक्षावगतो ज्ञानं कल्पयति सत्यां जिज्ञासायाम्। यत्रापि च काश्चिदर्थमनुभूय तद्विषयं ज्ञानमकल्पयित्वैव कालान्तरे तमर्थं स्मरामि तत्रापि स्मृतिज्ञानेनैवात्मनोऽर्थस्य च दृश्यदृष्टत्वसंबन्धे निष्पन्ने मानसप्रत्यक्षेण चावगते तद्बलेन च ज्ञाने कल्पिते तस्य ज्ञानस्येन्द्रियादिप्रत्युत्पन्नकारणाऽसंभवेन स्मृतित्वं निश्चित्य तदनुपपत्त्या पूर्वानुभवः कल्प्यते। यथोक्तं तदैव ह्यस्य संवित्तिरर्थापत्त्योपजायते इति। कः पुनरसौ संबन्धः? उक्तं प्राप्तिरिति। येऽपि च स्वप्रकाशां संविदं मन्यन्ते तेषामपि स्वोत्पत्तिसमये संवित्तिः स्वात्मानं कर्तारं वेद्यं च भासयति न तु स्वस्य वेत्तुर्वा संवेद्यसंबन्धः तस्य तदाऽनिष्पन्नत्वेनासत्त्वात् ततो निष्पन्नायां संवित्तौ तस्याः कर्तुश्च तद्द्वारा विषयसंबन्धे जाते ततो मानसेनैव प्रत्यक्षेणाऽर्थेन सह संवित्तेः संवेत्तुश्च संबन्धोऽवभासते इति अङ्गीकर्तव्यम्। संविदन्तरोत्पत्तिसमये च पूर्वसंविदा नष्टत्वान्न तद्धर्मत्वेन संवेद्यसंबन्धः शक्यते प्रत्यक्षेण ग्रहीतुमिति संवेत्तृधर्मभूत एव संवेद्यसंबन्धः कोऽपि नाम सर्वजनीनः प्राप्तिपर्यायो गृह्यत इति तत एव संवित्तिरूपक्रियाकल्पनासिद्धेरलं स्वप्रकाशतया। तत्सिद्धमुत्पत्तिवेलायामर्थस्य दृष्टत्वाभावेन फलांशाभावात् न ज्ञानं गृह्यते पश्चात्तु दृष्टत्वांशेन गृह्यत इति॥

—Nyâyaratnâkara pp. 319–21.

In the Bibliography given at the end of the Notes on this Stanza, add Catuh–Sûtrî, Sûtra I, after S'rî-Bhâṣya on अनुभूति.

To the list add:

4. Tattvârtha S'loka-Vârtika I. Sûtra 10. Verses 35 etc.

And, for S'loka Vârtika on Sûtra 2–4 substitute Kumârila's S'loka Vârtika on प्रत्यक्षसूत्र relevant verses; more especially S'l. Vârt. on 182 etc. on Sûtra V.

St. XIII.

"सर्वं खल्विदं ब्रह्म etc." and "आहुर्विधातृप्रत्यक्षं etc." are quotations which seem to have been borrowed from Devasûri's Syâdvâda–Ratnâkara, the author's own commentary on P.N.T. where they are quoted.

आहुर्विधातृप्रत्यक्षं etc.—This verse, with a difference, occurs in the Tattvârtha S'loka Vârtika as a reply to the verse as it stands here. (See Aṣṭasahasrî, Gândhi Nâthâraṅga Jaina Granthamâlâ, pp. 94–95.) Thus:—

आहुर्विधातृप्रत्यक्षं न निषेद्धृ विपश्चितः ।
न नानात्वागमस्तेन प्रत्यक्षेण विरुध्यते ।

भवतु नाम विधातृप्रत्यक्षमनिषेद्धृ च तथापि तेन नानात्वविधायिनो नागमस्य [सन्त्यनन्ता जीवा इत्यस्य] विरोधः संभवति एकत्वविधायिन इव । विधायकत्वाविशेषात् । कथमेकत्वमनिषेधत् प्रत्यक्षं नानात्वमात्मनो विदधातीति चेत्, नानात्वमनिषेधदेकत्वं कथं विदधीत ? । तस्यैकत्वविधानेन नानात्वप्रतिषेधकत्वमिति चेत् तदेकत्वस्य किम् ? । न ह्यस्मदादिप्रत्यक्षामिन्द्रियजं मानसं वा स्वसंवेदनमेक एवात्मा सर्वं इति विधातुं समर्थं नानात्मभेदेषु तस्य प्रवृत्तेः । योगिप्रत्यक्षसमर्थमिति चेत्, पुरुषनानात्वमपि विधातुं तदेव समर्थमस्तु तत्पूर्वकागमश्चेत्यविरोधः । स्वसंवेदनमेवास्मदादेः स्वैकत्वस्य विधायकमिति चेत्, तथान्येषां स्वैकत्वस्य तदेव विधायकमनुमन्यताम् । कथं—

यथैव च ममाध्यक्षं विधातृ न निषेद्धृ वा ।
प्रत्यक्षत्वात्तथान्येषामन्यथैतत्तथा कुतः ॥

परेषां प्रत्यक्षं स्वस्य विधायकं परस्य न निषेधकं वा, प्रत्यक्षत्वात्, मम प्रत्यक्षवत् । विपर्ययो वा अतिप्रसङ्गविपर्ययाभ्यां प्रत्यात्मसंवेदनस्यैकत्वविधायित्वासिद्धेरात्मबहुत्वसिद्धिरात्मैकत्वासिद्धिर्वा । न च विधायकमेव प्रत्यक्षमिति नियमोऽस्ति निषेधकत्वेनापि तस्य प्रतीयमानत्वात् ॥

It will be noticed that while the verse in the text is the Vedântic plea, the verse in the T. S. Vârtika is a reply to it in the same language taking up the contrary position.

अस्ति ह्यालोचनाज्ञानं etc.—This verse (Mîm. S'l. Vārtika on Sûtra IV (Pratyakṣa), 112) has been explained thus by Pārthasārathi in his commentary: यस्तु........सर्वमेव ज्ञानं शब्दानुविद्धत्वात् सविकल्पकमेव न किंचिन्निर्विकल्पकमस्तीति मन्यते तं प्रत्याह—अस्तीति । बालानामिवाव्युत्पन्नानामस्माकमपि चक्षुःपातानन्तरं सविकल्पकात् प्रथममस्ति निर्विकल्पकं प्रतीतिसिद्धमालोचनविज्ञानं शुद्धवस्तुविषयं, तदभावे हि निर्निमित्तं शब्दस्मरणं स्यात् अस्मृतशब्दस्य च शब्दानुविद्धो विकल्पो न संभवतीति शुद्धवस्तुजमित्येतद्विवृणोति । न विशेषो न सामान्यं तदानीमनुभूयते । तयोराधारभूता तु व्यक्तिरेवावसीयते ॥

प्रत्यक्षाद्यवतारः स्यात्—This is the Mîmāṃsaka's and Vedāntin's plea for refusing to admit **अभाव** as a **विषय** of **प्रत्यक्ष** or any of the other **प्रमाण**s recognised by the Naiyâyika, and consequently for setting up a special **प्रमाण** for apprehending **अभाव**, called **अनुपलब्धि**. The verses on this point run as follows in Mîm. S'l. Vârt. V. 17–18:—

प्रत्यक्षाद्यवतारस्तु भावांशो गृह्यते यदा ।
व्यापारस्तदनुत्पत्तिरभावांशे जिघृक्षिते ॥

—*i. e.* **प्रत्यक्ष** is possible when something positive, or the positive aspect of a thing, is apprehended; but when **अभाव**—a negation or negative aspect of a thing—has to be apprehended, the method by which this is done is the fact of '**तदनुत्पत्ति**'—*i. e.* **प्रत्यक्ष** etc. do not arise here to testify to anything positive. This is made clear in the next verse in the Mîm. S'l. Vârt.

न तावदिन्द्रियैरेषा नास्तीत्युत्पद्यते मतिः ।
भावांशेनैव संयोगो योग्यत्वादिन्द्रियस्य हि ॥

निर्विशेषं हि सामान्यं etc.—The preceding verse (Mîm. S'l. Vārt. V.-आकृतिवाद, 9) will explain this:

अन्योन्यापेक्षिता नित्यं स्यात् सामान्यविशेषयोः ।
विशेषाणां च सामान्यं ते च तस्य भवन्ति हि ॥

—समानानां हि भावः सामान्यं तत्कथमस्तु बहुषु विशेषेषु स्यात् इदं च विशेषाणां विशेषत्वं यत्समानात्मनो भावात् विशिंषन्ति । तेनान्यतरेण विनेतरस्यात्मलाभाभावात् तस्यापि सिद्धिरिति—

तदेवमुपपादितं द्व्याकारत्वं प्रयोगेण दर्शयति—निर्विशेषं न सामान्यं भवेच्छशविषाणवत् । सामान्यरहितत्वाच्च विशेषास्तद्वदेव हि ॥ निर्विशेषं परकल्पितं सामान्यं धर्मि; नास्तीति साध्यं, तथा निःसामान्या विशेषा न सन्तीति; विशेषरहितत्वात् सामान्यरहितत्वादिति हेतुद्वयम् ॥......

तेन नात्यन्तभेदोऽपि स्यात् सामान्यविशेषयोः ।

The reader will notice how the Mîmâṃsaka, in recognising this aspect, admits the Jaina doctrine of **अनेकान्त**.

निर्विशेषं हि सामान्यम्—This occurs in Kumârila's S'l. Vârt. Âkṛti. Cf. **सर्ववस्तुषु बुद्धिश्च व्यावृत्यनुगमात्मिका । जायते द्व्यात्मकत्वेन**

विना सा च न सिध्यति ॥ (S'l. Vârt. Âkṛti-vâda 5) विशेषमात्र इष्टे च न सामान्यमतिर्भवेत्। सामान्यमात्रबोधेन न निर्निमित्ता विशेषधीः ॥ (ibid. 6) —"यदि तावदसाधारणं स्वलक्षणमेव वस्तु स्यान्न सामान्यं यथा सौगतैरुच्यते ततोऽयं गौरयमपीति सामान्यबुद्धिर्न स्यात्। यदि तु गोत्वादिशाबलेयादिविशेषानुवृत्तव्यावृत्तात्मनोऽपह्नुत्य महासामान्यं सन्मात्रमेव वस्त्वङ्गीक्रियते यथा वेदान्तवादिभिरुच्यते ततो गौरयमश्वोयं शाबलेयोयमिति विशेषबुद्धिर्न स्यात् ॥" —Nyâyaratnâkara, Com. on S'l. Vârt.

Kumârila makes a very close approach to the Jaina view on the subject when he says: "अन्योन्यापेक्षिता नित्यं स्यात् सामान्यविशेषयोः। विशेषाणां च सामान्यं ते च तस्य भवन्ति हि। निर्विशेषं न सामान्यं भवेच्छशविषाणवत्। सामान्यरहितत्वाच्च विशेषास्तद्वदेव हि ॥" (S'l. Vârt-Âkṛti 9–10); and further on, in answering the objection of विरोध, Kumârila says: "विरोधस्तावदेकान्ताद्वक्तुमत्र न युज्यते। सामान्यानन्यविज्ञाते विशेषे नैकवृत्तिता। सामान्यानन्यवृत्तित्वं विशेषात्मैकभावतः। एवं च परिहर्तव्या भिन्नाभिन्नत्वकल्पना ॥ केनचिद्व्यात्मनैकत्वं नानात्वं चास्य केनचित्। सामान्यस्य तु यो भेदं ब्रूते तस्य विशेषतः ॥ दर्शयित्वाऽभ्युपेतव्यं विशेषैक्यं च जातितः। यथा कल्माषवर्णस्य यथेष्टं वर्णनिग्रहः ॥ चित्रत्वाद्वस्तुनोप्येवं भेदाभेदावधारणम्। सामान्यांशे तु निष्कृष्य भेदो येन प्रसाध्यते ॥" (S'l. Vârt. Âkṛti 54-57)—which N. R. elucidates in words which remind us of the Jaina doctrine of सामान्य and विशेष regarded as two aspects of one reality: "यदि ह्यनेकवृत्त्येव सामान्यं स्यात् अनन्यवृत्तय एव विशेषाः तयोरेकत्वं विरुध्यते। यदा तु विशेषा अपि सामान्यात्मनाऽनेकवृत्तयः सामान्यं च विशेषात्मनानान्यवृत्ति तदा को विरोध इति। यत्त्वन्याऽनन्यतैव कथमेकस्येत्युक्तं—तत्राह एवमिति। एतदेव दर्शयति केनचिदिति। गोत्वं हि शाबलेयात्मना बाहुलेयाद्भिद्यते। स्वरूपेण च न भिद्यते। तथा व्यक्त्यन्तरादपि व्यक्तिः जात्यात्मना न भिद्यते स्वरूपेण च भिद्यते इति अपेक्षाभेदादविरोधः। समाविशन्ति हि विरुद्धान्यपि एकत्वापेक्षाभेदात्। एकमपि हि किंचिदपेक्ष्य ह्रस्वं किंचिदपेक्ष्य दीर्घं यथैकोऽपि चैत्रो द्वित्वापेक्षया भिन्नोऽपि स्वात्मापेक्षया न भिद्यते। अनेनैकानेकत्वमपि परिहर्तव्यम्। तदेव हि वस्तुस्वरूपेण सर्वत्र सर्वदा चैकमपि शाबलेयादिरूपेणाऽनेकं भवतीति न विरोधः इति।……… नानावर्णे हि वस्तुनि य एव वर्णो निष्कृष्य दर्शयितुमिष्यते स एव शक्यो दर्शयितुम्। एवं नानारूपे वस्तुनि सर्वस्य भेदाभेदादेः संभव इति।"

हेतोरद्वैतसिद्धिश्चेत् etc.—(Âptamîmâṃsâ 26) is thus explained in अष्टसहस्रीः—तत्सिद्धिर्यदि साधनात् साध्यसाधनयोस्तर्हि द्वैतं स्यात्।

अन्यथाऽद्वैतसिद्धिवद्द्वैतसिद्धिः कथं न स्यात् ?। स्वाभिलाषमात्रादर्थसिद्धौ सर्वं सर्वस्य सिध्येत् ॥

कर्मद्वैतं फलद्वैतं etc.—(Âptamîmâṃsâ 25) is thus explained in अष्टसहस्री:—लौकिकं वैदिकं च कर्मेति वा कुशलमकुशलं च कर्मानुष्ठानमिति वा, पुण्यं पापं च कर्मेति वा कर्मद्वैतं न स्यात्। तदभावात् इहामुत्र च श्रेयःप्रत्यवायलक्षणं फलद्वैतं न स्यात्, कारणाभावे कार्यस्यानुत्पत्तेः। तत एव इहलोकपरलोकलक्षणं लोकद्वैतं न स्यात्। कर्मादिद्वैतस्यानाद्यविद्योपदर्शितत्वाददोष इति चेन्न। धर्माधर्मद्वैतस्याभावे विद्याविद्याद्वयस्यासंभवाद् बन्धमोक्षद्वयवत्। पूर्वविद्योदयादेव विद्याविद्याद्वयं बन्धमोक्षद्वयं च परमार्थतस्तदसंभवात् 'न बन्धोऽस्ति नैव मोक्ष इत्येषा परमार्थता' इति प्रवचनात् प्रतिभासमात्रस्य परब्रह्मण एव तात्त्विकत्वादिति चेन्न। नैरात्म्यस्यापि तात्विकत्वापत्तेस्तत्कल्पनाया नैष्फल्याविशेषात् ॥

St. XIV

न सोऽस्ति प्रत्ययो लोके यः शब्दानुगमादृते। अनुविद्धमिव ज्ञानं सर्वं शब्देन भासते ॥—Bhartṛhari's Vâkyapadîya I. 124, which the commentator explains as follows: "काचिदेव सा ज्ञानावस्था सविकल्पाख्या.........शब्दानुविद्धेन शब्दशक्त्यनुपातिना ज्ञानेनोपगृह्यमाणो वस्त्वात्मा ज्ञानानुगतो व्यक्तरूपप्रत्यवभासो ज्ञायत इत्यभिधीयेत तादृश एव च स्मृतिविषयो भवति। अनुभवसमानाकारत्वात्तस्याः।......" Cf. Max-Müller's view that there can be no thought without language. Note, however, that Bhartṛhari's dictum is intended to apply to सविकल्पक consciousness (in the sense of 'सविकल्पक' as used in the Yoga-S'āstra) only. Cf. Vyākaraṇa Mahābhâṣya (I. i. 1):—"सिद्धे शब्दार्थसंबन्धे—सिद्धे शब्दे अर्थे संबन्धे च—with Kaiyyaṭa's gloss—त्रयाणामात्यन्तिकाविश्लेषप्रदर्शनाय समाहारनिर्देश इति बोध्यम्।...शब्दार्थयोः संबन्धश्च शक्तिरूपं तादात्म्यमेवेत्यन्यत्र प्रपञ्चितम् ॥

ते च द्रव्यास्तिकनयानुपातिनः etc.—For a full exposition of the नयs, see notes on Stanza XXVIII and the books of reference mentioned therein. The Jaina claims that all the different philosophical systems, except his own, embody *partial* truths, while his system is the only one which presents the *Whole* Truth. Thus, Reality which is the primary synthesis of द्रव्य (substance) and पर्याय (mode) is grasped only fragmentarily by the other schools, some apprehending and emphasising one aspect and some the other.

ते च द्रव्यास्तिकनयानुपातिनः etc.—For the best exposition of this subject, see the section on नयमीमांसा in Abhayadeva's commentary on Siddhasena Divâkara's Saṃmati-tarka. (Purâtattva-mandira Edition, Vol. II, pp. 271–310).

ते च द्रव्यास्तिकनयानुपातिनो मीमांसकभेदाः—I was wondering what could be the point of 'भेदाः' in 'मीमांसकभेदाः'—I then remembered the passages which I have quoted above from Kumârila and his commentator. In view of these passages, Kumârila and his commentator certainly deserve to be assimilated with the Syâdvâda school and not classed as mere 'द्रव्यास्तिकनयानुपातिनः'. For a full exposition of द्रव्यास्तिकनय and पर्यायास्तिकनय and the schools which severally fall under them, see Abhayadeva's Commentary on Saṃmatitarka, Chapters on Naya-Mîmâṃsâ.

तथा च पठन्ति—एतासु पञ्चस्ववभासनिषु etc.—I think the title of this work by "Pandita Aśoka" (as the colophon runs)—who is assigned to circa 900 A. D., is really "सामान्यदूषण(सिद्धि)दिक्" and not "सामान्यदूषणदिक्प्रसारिता" as found in M. M. Dr. Haraprasâda S'âstri's edition of "Six Buddhist Nyâya Tracts" published by the A. S. Bengal and accepted in AMP. edition of the Syâdvâda-mañjarî footnote, 'प्रसारिता' there being only a predicate of '°दिक्' and meaning has been 'set forth'.

The concluding verse which follows this as a summary of the book is as follows: "प्रत्यक्षप्रतिभासि वत्र्मै (corrected in the Preface into–धर्मेषु) न पञ्चस्वङ्गुलीषु स्थितं सामान्यं प्रतिभासते न च विकल्पाकारबुद्धौ तथा। ता एवास्फुटमूर्तयोऽत्र हि विभासन्ते न जातिस्ततः सादृश्यभ्रमकारणौ पुनरिमावेकोपलब्धिध्वनी ॥ *i. e.* "Generality is not found residing in the five fingers whose attributes (or states or phenomenal being) we apprehend by perception; nor does it appear in the idea of form which is apprehended by conception. What is perceived is the same fingers distinctly (then in निर्विकल्पक, now in सविकल्पक ज्ञान). Therefore there is no such thing as Generality (जाति or सामान्य). That several reals produce one idea and are denoted by one word arises from our confounding likeness with unity or sameness." The general line of reasoning is thus indicated in the opening portion of the work: व्यापकं नित्यमेकं च सामान्यं यैः प्रकल्पितम्। मोहग्रन्थिच्छिदे तेषां तदभावः प्रसाध्यते। कथमिदमवगम्यते। परस्परविलक्षणक्षणेषु प्रत्यक्षसमीक्ष्यमाणेष्वभिन्नधीध्वनिप्रसवनिबन्धनमनुयायिरूपं सामान्यं न मान्यं मनीषिणामिति। साधकप्रमाणविरहात् बाधकप्रमाणसंभवाच्चेति ब्रूमः। तथाहि यदिदं सामान्यसाधनमनुमानमभिधीयते परैः। यदनुगताकारं ज्ञानं तदनुगतवस्तुनिबन्धनं यथा बहुषु पुष्पेषु स्रक् स्रगिति ज्ञानम्। अस्ति च परस्परसंपर्कविकलकलासु कार्यादिव्यक्तिष्वनुगताकारं विज्ञानं तदप्यनैकान्तिकतादोषाक्रान्तशरीरत्वान्न तद्भावसाधनायालम्। यतो भवति बहुषु पाचकेषु पाचकः पाचक इति एकाकार परामर्शप्रत्ययः। न च तेष्वनुगतमेकं वस्तु समस्ति। तद्भावे हि प्रागेव तथाविधप्रत्ययोत्पादप्रसङ्गो दुर्वारप्रचारः॥

यच्चास्य पौद्गलिकत्वनिषेधाय स्पर्शशून्याश्रयत्वात् अतिनिबिडप्रदेशे प्रवेशनिर्गमयोरप्रतिघातात् पूर्वं पश्चाच्चावयवानुपलब्धेः सूक्ष्ममूर्तद्रव्यान्तराप्रेरकत्वात् गगनगुणत्वाच्चेति पञ्चहेतवो यौगैरुपन्यस्ताः—The word "यौगैः" denotes both the Nyâya and the Vaiśeṣika systems although more often in this work, the Nyâya. But I have not been able to trace to their source these hetus, which look like sûtras either of the Nyâya or the Vaiśeṣika system, but are not found in their existing sûtras. Cf. एवं विभागसंयोगौ तद्भावादन्ययोगवत्। जैनकापिलनिर्दिष्टं शब्दश्रोत्रादिसर्पणम्—S'l. Vârt. VI. 106, where the commentator presents the Jaina doctrine as follows: "जैनैर्हि शब्दस्यागमनं, परिमाणं, स्पर्शः, तेषां चाभिभवः स्पर्शवत्त्वेऽपि च त्वगिन्द्रियाग्राह्यत्वं, सूक्ष्माश्च भागा पुद्गलरूपाः कल्पिताः॥"

"In Kârikâs 106–122 [of this section of the S'l. Vârt.] we find a refutation against the Jainas, who believe sound to be material and tangible, to travel from its place of origin to our auditory organ, and to consist of component parts (pudgalas). [This is criticised in the following verse.]

शब्दस्यागमनं तावददृष्टं परिकल्पितम्।
मूर्तिस्पर्शादिमत्त्वं च तेषामभिभवः सताम्॥

(VI. 107–108).

This belief in the substantiality of sound must have had originally more supporters than the Jainas. In Europe too it has been upheld for a long time and is expressed by Lucretius in his De natura rerum."—"The Vaiśeṣika System" by Dr. Faddegon, p. 189.

In connection with the passage on शब्दार्थसंबन्ध contained in this Stanza and its commentary, consult particularly शब्दनित्यताधिकरण in Kumârila's S'loka Vârtika, the Nyâya Sûtras II. ii, and शब्दार्थतत्संबन्धयोर्मीमांसा in Abhayadeva's commentary on Saṃmatitarka (Gujarat Purā-tattva-mandira edition Vol. II.)

On p. 165 of the Notes with reference to "यौगास्तु—The Vaiśeṣikas would say" please note that the term 'यौगाः' very often stands for Naiyâyikas, but may apply sometimes to Vaiśeṣikas also. Here, the subject is more in the line of the Vaiśeṣikas than of the Naiyâyikas; and therefore I have said "The Vaiśeṣikas" etc.

विकल्पयोनयः शब्दाः—Quoted in Ratnâkarâvatârikâ I. 9.

सर्वमस्ति स्वरूपेण (p. 91 of the Sanskrit text)—The verse has been quoted by Hemacandra in Pramâṇamîmâṃsâ p. 44. Before him, it was quoted by Siddharṣi in his commentary on the Nyâyâvatâra. (Siddharṣi, the author of Upamitibhava-Prapañcakathâ, completed it in 906 A.D.).

अभिहाणं अभिहेयाउ etc.—Quoted also by Devabhadra who lived in the second half of the twelfth century, that is about a hundred years before Malliṣeṇa.

Cf. 'शब्दानां न परमार्थतः किंचिद्वाच्यं वस्तुस्वरूपमस्ति । सर्व एव शाब्दप्रत्ययो भ्रान्तः। भिन्नेष्वर्थेष्वभेदाकाराध्यवसायेन प्रवृत्तेः। यत्र तु पारंपर्येण वस्तुप्रतिबन्धस्तत्रार्थसंवादो भ्रान्तत्वेऽपि तत्र यत् तदारोपितं विकल्पबुद्ध्यार्थेष्वभिन्नं रूपं तद् अन्यव्यावृत्तपदार्थानुभवबलायातत्वात् स्वयं चान्यव्यावृत्ततया प्रतिभासनाद् भ्रान्तैश्चान्यव्यावृत्तार्थेन सहैक्यैनानध्यवसितत्वात् अन्यापोढपदार्थाधिगतिफलत्वाच्च अन्यापोह इत्युच्यते । अतः अपोहः शब्दार्थ इति प्रसिद्धम्' —Com. on Saṃmatitarka p. 173, Purātattva Edition. अपोह

or the doctrine of negative denotation is a logical necessity of S'ûnyavâda. The doctrine is endorsed by other schools of Buddhism also. Cf. Stcherbatsky's "Conceptions of the Buddhist Nirvâṇa," p. 155 footnote 3; " But the school of Dignâga have a special theory of their own about the meaning of words according to which words express only relations, or mutual negation (अपोह = परस्परपरिहार = अन्यव्यावृत्ति = व्यवच्छेद = परिच्छेद) between point-instants." For an exposition of this subject see Ratnakîrti's " Apoha Vada ", one of the " Six Buddhist Tracts " collected and published by Haraprasâda Sâstri (A. S. Bengal Series). Note, however, that the doctrine is not always put forward in the extreme form in which it has been taken by its critics: cf. " नास्माभिरपोहशब्देन विधिरेव केवलोऽभिप्रेतः नाप्यन्यव्यावृत्तिमात्रं, किंत्वन्यापोहविशिष्टो विधिः शब्दानामर्थः ततश्च न प्रत्येकपक्षोपनिपातिदोषावकाशः "—Ratnakîrti's "Aphohasiddhi" p. 3.

The subject of अपोह was hotly discussed by the Buddhists, the Jainas and the Brâhmaṇas in the age of Kumârila, and also in the few centuries before and after him. See Kumârila's S'loka-Vârtika, which contains a special section on the criticism of अपोह. Both the criticism and the original doctrine have been examined at great length in the section on " शब्दार्थ-तत्संबन्धमीमांसा " in Abhayadeva's commentary on Saṃmatitarka pp. 173–270, which refers also to the contributions of Uddyotakara and numerous other logicians to the discussion of this great question. See also S'ântarakṣita's " Tattva-saṁgraha " with Kamalaśîla's " Pañjikâ "; and for a brief discussion, Siddharṣi's commentary on Nyâyâvatâra pp. 4–5. The subject has been also fully discussed from the Naiyâyika (Brâhmaṇa) point of view in the Nyâya-mañjarî of Jayanta. See Vol. I, pp. 290–327.

अपरे सामान्यमात्रमेव etc.—As Kumârila contends: "अगोनिवृत्तिः सामान्यं वाच्यं यैः परिकल्पितम्। गोत्वं वस्त्वेव तैरुक्तमगोऽपोहगिरा स्फुटम् ॥" Note, however, that in Kumârila's philosophy सामान्य is only the other side of विशेष, both of them being aspects of the same reality.

विधिवादिनस्तु etc.—These are different from the विधिवादिन्s referred to in the com. on Sammatitarka "अत्र विधिवादिनः प्रेरयन्ति etc." whose "विधिरेव शब्दस्यार्थः" means that the denoted object is a positive reality, and not an empty negation (अपोह). The विधिवादिन्s, the नियोगवादिन्s and the प्रैषवादिन्s are different forms of one common doctrine that every proposition (वाक्य) is a positive or negative *mandate*, (आम्नायस्य क्रियार्थत्वात्-Pûrva Mîm. Sûtra) no proposition being, in its ultimate effect, a mere statement of fact. Even sentences with a verb in the indicative mood are understood by them as subordinate to some other sentence which has a verb in the imperative mood. Thus all such texts as तत्त्वमसि, सर्वं खल्विदं ब्रह्म, ऐतदात्म्यमिदं सर्वम् are subordinate to such central texts as तद्विजिज्ञासस्व, सोऽन्वेष्टव्यः विजिज्ञासितव्यः etc. (See the concluding paragraphs of Râmânuja's S'rî-Bhâṣya on 'जिज्ञासाधिकरण' (I. i. 1) and his exposition of 'समन्वयाधिकरण' (I. i. 4). This logical attitude may be compared with that of the present-day Pragmatists in American and European philosophy. The following passage in L. P. Jack's "The Education of the Whole Man." on 'disguised imperatives' will be found interesting: "Then it was that it flashed upon me with the force of a revelation that all philosophies and sciences, without exception —both those I agreed with and those I disagreed with—were *injunctions to live in a particular way and avoid living in other ways*. They all come to their spear-point, so to speak, in some kind of *injunction*. They were all disguised imperatives. Behind the information was the *command*, which took the form, "Live in this way and avoid living in that." Commands disguised as information." On the subject of वाक्यार्थवैविध्य, क्रियावाक्यार्थत्वं, विधि, नियोग etc. see Nyâyamañjarî of Jayanta Vol. I.

St. XV.

एवमन्यासामपि etc.—Cf. पञ्चविपर्ययभेदा भवन्त्यशक्तिश्च करणवैकल्यात्। अष्टाविंशति भेदा तुष्टिर्नवधाऽष्टधा सिद्धिः ॥—S. K. 47. पञ्चविपर्ययभेदाः=अविद्याऽस्मिता-राग-द्वेषा-भिनिवेशाः यथासंख्यं तमो-मोह-महामोह-तामिस्रान्धतामिस्रसंज्ञकाः पञ्चविपर्ययविशेषाः S. T. K. ibid. The latter are the technical terms of Sâṁkhya philosophy for अविद्या etc. of Yoga which are thus defined in Patañjali's Sûtras: (1) अनित्या-शुचि-दुःखा-नात्मसु नित्य-शुचि-सुखा-त्मख्यातिरविद्या (Pat. Yoga sûtras II. 5); (2) दृग्दर्शनशक्त्योरेकात्मतेवास्मिता (II. 6); सुखानुशयी रागः (II. 7); दुःखानुशयी द्वेषः (II. 8); स्वरसवाही विदुषोऽपि तथारूढोऽभिनिवेशः (II. 9). For further light on each of these which are collectively called "क्लेश" by Patañjali, and "विपर्यय" by Vyâsa by way of giving a synonym of क्लेश, see Vyâsa-Bhâṣya.

ब्राह्मप्राजापत्य etc.—Cf. "अष्टविकल्पो दैवः तैर्यग्योनश्च पञ्चधा भवति। मानुषश्चैकविधः समासतो भौतिकः सर्गः ॥" (S. K. 53) As regards details cf. Tattva-Kaumudi, Mâṭhara-Vṛtti and Sâṁkhya-Candrikâ give पैत्र or पित्र्य for सौम्य of our text and place it after ऐन्द्र; तैर्यग्योन is the same. The hetu in the note of Vācaspatimiśra on "मानुषश्चैकविधः" will be fonnd interesting: "ब्राह्मणत्वाद्यवान्तरजातिभेदाविवक्षया संस्थानस्य चतुर्ष्वपि वर्णेष्वविशेषात्।"

बाधिर्यकुष्ठता etc.—अशक्ति (Infirmity) which is second on the list after विपर्यय is of twenty-eight kinds, of which eleven are इन्द्रियवधs, and seventeen बुद्धिवधs, nine of the latter being the opposites of nine तुष्टिs (Complacencies) and eight the opposites of eight सिद्धिs (Attainments) (एकादशेन्द्रियवधाः सहबुद्धिवधैरशक्तिरुद्दिष्टा। सप्तदशवधा बुद्धेर्विपर्ययात् तुष्टिसिद्धीनाम्—S. K. 49). S. T. K.:—"बाधिर्यं कुष्ठितान्धत्वं जडताजिघ्रता तथा। मूकता कौण्यपङ्गुत्वे क्लैब्योदावर्तमन्दताः"—thus mentioning मन्दता instead of मत्तता as found in our text.

तुष्टिनवकविपर्ययसिद्ध्यष्टकविपर्यय etc.—The nine तुष्टिs (Complacencies) are thus classified in the S. K. "आध्यात्मिक्यश्चतस्रः प्रकृत्युपादानकालभागाख्या बाह्या विषयोपरमात् पञ्च च नव तुष्टयोऽभिमताः" While accepting that आत्मन् is distinct from प्रकृति, if a man stops there and does not strive to realise the distinction by

श्रवण, मनन etc. he suffers from तुष्टि (Complacency) regarding the Self (आध्यात्मिकी). This is of four kinds: (1) प्रकृति (Nature), (2) उपादान (Means), (3) काल (Time) and (4) भाग (Luck).

(1) The first is thus explained in S. T. K. " कस्यचिदुपदेशे विवेकसाक्षात्कारो हि प्रकृतिपरिणामभेदः तं च प्रकृतिरेव करोतीति कृतं ध्याना-भ्यासेन तस्मादेवमेवास्स्व वत्स इति येयमुपदेष्टव्यस्य शिष्यस्य तुष्टिः प्रकृतौ सा तुष्टिः प्रकृताख्या अम्भ इत्युच्यते"—It is the attitnde of complacently resting in प्रकृति instead of rising to the realisation of the true nature of पुरुष—the result of a kind Natural Fatalism. It is esoterically known as 'अम्भः' (2) The second: " या तु प्रकृत्यपि विवेकख्यातिर्न सा प्रकृतिमात्राद्भवति, मा भूत् सर्वस्य सर्वदा तन्मात्रस्य सर्वान् प्रत्यविशेषात्, प्रव्रज्यायास्तु सा भवति, तस्मात् प्रव्रज्यामुपाददीथाः कृतं ते ध्यानाभ्यासेनायुष्मन् इत्युपदेशे या तुष्टिः सोपादानाख्या "—One may accept the view that Natural Fatalism (प्रकृति) is wrong, because Nature is the same for all, and consequently the विवेकख्याति of one who is content with the fatalism of Nature is no good. But if he thinks that Asceticism is all that one has to add he is mistaken. For without the practice of ध्यान, mere asceticism is useless. (3) The complacency of such a man is complacency in regard to Means (उपादान). This complacency is esoterically known as 'सलिल'. " या तु प्रव्रज्याऽपि सद्यो न निर्वाणमेति सैव कालपरि-पाकमपेक्ष्य सिद्धिं ते विधास्यति अलमुत्तप्ततया तव ' इत्युत्पदेशे या तुष्टिः सा कालाख्या—ओघ इत्युच्यते ॥ " To imagine that प्रव्रज्या in the fulness of time with bears its fruits and therefore ध्यान is unnecessary is wrong. This kind of complacency—a pathetic belief in the potency of time—is कालाख्या तुष्टि which is esoterically known as 'ओघ'. (4) "या तु प्रकृतेर्न कालान्नाप्युपादानाद्विवेकख्यातिः अपि तु भाग्यादेव, अत एव मदालसापत्यान्यतिबालानि मातुरुपदेशादेव विवेकख्याति-मन्ति मुक्तानि बभूवुः तस्माद् भाग्यमेव हेतुर्नान्यद् इत्युपदेशे या तुष्टिः सा भागाख्या सा वृष्टिरित्युच्यते ॥ " When the realisation of the distinction between पुरुष and प्रकृति (विवेकख्याति) is regarded as a matter of pure luck (*e. g.* the children of मदालसा who practised neither प्रव्रज्या nor ध्यान before realising the distinction), it is a kind of तुष्टि which is called ' भाग ', and is esoterically known as ' वृष्टि '. Next comes the group of five बाह्यतुष्टिs, which with the four internal (आध्यामिकी) mentioned above make up *nine* in all. (1) The वैराग्य (cessation of attachment to worldly life) is necessary for realising the distinction between प्रकृति and पुरुष, but it is not all. There are some people, however, who imagine that the renunciation of the five विषयs—शब्द, रूप, रस, गन्ध and स्पर्श is enough; or if they renounce objects of comfort and enjoyment (विषयs) for any of the following reasons, it is all that they need do. These reasons are: (1) The trouble and the humiliation involved in earning wealth—अर्जन. The renunciation caused by this motive is esoterically known as 'पार'; (2) The trouble involved in protecting it from the depredations of robbers and from accidental loss. This is renouncing a thing in order to escape the trouble of protecting it (रक्षण),—which in esoterical language is called 'सुपार'. (3) To cease to care for wealth for the reason that after all it will be exhausted is the kind of renunciation arising from the sense of प्रक्षय and is esoterically known as 'पारापार'. The thought that enjoyment of विषयs after all whets the desire of enjoyment all the more may be the reason for renunciation in some cases. This, which arises from reflecting on the nature of भोग is not, however, all that is needed. It is called भोग (दोषदर्शन) तुष्टि, and in esoteric language ' अनुत्तमाम्भः ' (5) Lastly, all enjoyments involve हिंसा. Desisting from विषयs with this idea, is तुष्टि from the idea of हिंसा—called esoterically 'उत्तमाम्भः'.

त्रयो दुःखविघाताः etc.—Next, we come to सिद्धिs (Attainments). These are enumerated as follows: " ऊहः शब्दोऽध्ययनं दुखविघातास्त्रयः सुहृत्प्राप्तिः । दानं च सिद्धयोऽष्टौ सिद्धेः पूर्वोऽङ्कुशस्त्रिविधः " ॥ (S. K. 51)—S. K. T. adopts its own order for explanation. (1) अध्ययनम्=विधिवद्गुरुमुखादध्यात्मविद्यानामक्षरस्वरूपग्रहणम्—*i.e.* Study of the letter of the Sâstra under a teacher. This is called 'तारम् (2) शब्दः—' शब्द इति पदं शब्दजनितमर्थज्ञानमुपलक्षयति—Study of the meaning of the S'âstra, (3) ऊहः=तर्क आगमाविरोधिन्यायेनागमार्थ-परीक्षणम्—also called मनन as distingnished from the first two which constitute श्रवण. ऊह = Reasoning in harmony with the Scriptures. It is called 'तारतारम्' in mystic lanuage. (4) सुहृत्प्राप्तिः

—Discussion with friends: = स्वोत्प्रेक्षितं मननममननमेव आसुहृत्संमतम् न्यायेन स्वयंपरीक्षितमप्यर्थं न श्रद्धधते, न यावद् गुरुशिष्यसब्रह्मचारिभिः संवाद्यते अतः सुहृदां गुरुशिष्यसब्रह्मचारिणां संवादकानां प्राप्तिः सुहृत्प्राप्तिः This is known in mystic lore as 'रम्यक'. (5) दानं = शुद्धिर्विवेकज्ञानस्य (From दैप् शोधने, to purify) One's own ज्ञान has to be confirmed by discussion with friends. This purification takes place when the विवेकख्याति is absolutely freed from संशय and विपर्यास together with their वासना or संस्कार. (अविप्लवः शुद्धिः सा च सवासनसंशयविपर्यासानां परिहारेण विवेकसाक्षात्कारस्य स्वच्छप्रवाहेऽवस्थापनम्"—This सिद्धि is known in esoteric language as 'सदामुदितम्'. In addition to these five, there are three principal सिद्धिs consisting of the distinction of the three kinds of दुःख viz. आध्यात्मिक, आधिभौतिक and आधिदैविक. These are called प्रमोद, मुदित and मोदमान.

संवरप्रतिसंवर—For this reading of the AMP. edition, one may read संचरप्रतिसंचर—which are used elsewhere for evolution and involution respectively.

For "the whole passage from 'सांख्यमते' to पञ्चविंशतिः is extracted from Guṇaratna's com. p. 97 on Ṣad. D. Samuccaya 34" in the Notes p. 169 read: "The whole passage ......is reproduced in Guṇaratna's com. ......" For the Note on महत्तत्त्व—generally understood as Cosmic Intelligence—consult Keith's "Sâṁkhya System" p. 79 where the earlier view is distinguished from that of the Sâṁkhya Kârikâ where "Stress is laid on the intellect as psychological." On p. 171 of the Notes read "The same are reproduced in Guṇaratna's com." instead of "The same as in......On p. 174 of the Notes, for "The slip was originally Guṇaratna's etc." read "The slip was originally Malliṣeṇa's, which has been repeated by Guṇaratna .... Could it be that in the time of Malliṣeṇa (read this for 'Guṇaratna')" On p. 175 ll. 1-2 for "The whole passage......is reproduced from Guṇaratna's commentary" read "The whole passage is reproduced in Guṇaratna' commentary".

वादमहार्णवोऽप्याह—In the AMP. edition p. 123 footnote 'वादमहार्णव' is said to be 'वेदान्तग्रन्थविशेषः' Evidently this is a mistake, arising from the figure of बिम्बप्रतिबिम्ब which as a matter of fact is as much a property of Sāṁkhya as of Vedânta. वादमहार्णव seems to be a work of Sāṁkhya, as is clear from the context, where a number of authorities are quoted in support of the Sāṁkhya theory: Patañjali (This should be Vyâsa, the commentator of Patañjali who may well be regarded as an authority on Sāṁkhya which is a sister science of Yoga), Vâcaspati Miśra, Âsuri and Vindhyavâsin. Âbhayadeva Sûri, a Jaina writer, is also said to have composed a work of the same name (see the Praśasti of Prabhâvakacarita, verse 4: शिष्योऽस्याभयदवेसूरिरभवत्......ग्रन्थो वादमहार्णवोऽस्य विदितः."

विन्ध्यवासी त्वेवं भोगमाचष्टे—Vindhyavâsin is well known as a contemporary of Vasubandhu who lived in the third century A. D. As regards his indentification with Iśvarakṛṣṇa, the author of the Sâṁkhya Kārikas, see J. R. A. S. 1905. But this hypothesis is now definitely rejected, and we know that the name of this 'dweller in the Vindhyas' was Rudrila, as we see from a verse cited by Kamalaśîla in his commentary on the Tattva-Saṁgraha of S'ântarakṣita which runs as follows: "यदेव दधि तत्क्षीरं यत्क्षीरं तद्दधीति च । वदता रुद्रिलेनैव ख्यापिता विन्ध्यवासिता"—*i. e.* The Sāṁkhya philosopher—Rudrila—who identifies cause and effect in his सत्कार्यवाद—is indeed a man of the jungle of the Vindhya mountain, who does not know what is milk and what is curds and how one differs from the other.

तथा चासुरिः—आसुरि was a direct pupil of कपिल. For the Sāṁkhya गुरुशिष्यपरम्परा vide—एतत् पवित्रमग्र्यं मुनिरासुरयेऽनुकम्पया प्रददौ । आसुरिरपि पञ्चशिखाय तेन बहुधा कृतं तन्त्रम् ॥—S. K. 70. Mâṭhara supplies the later names betwen पञ्चशिख and ईश्वरकृष्ण as follows: पञ्चशिखेन तस्मात् भार्गवोलूकवाल्मीकिहारीतदेवलप्रभृतीनागतम् । See also p. 39 of Keith's "Sâṃkhya System."

St. XVI.

द्विषसंबन्धसंवित्तिः etc.—Quoted in Ratnâkarâvatârika (Pariccheda I. p. 4. 2).

एवं यौगाभिप्रेतः etc.—Note that this doctrine of the Naiyâyikas which is the opposite of that of the Buddhist logician Dharmakîrti is similarly rejected. This is in order to establish the resulting अनेकान्तवाद of the Jainas. अथवा पूर्वार्धमिदमन्यथा... व्याख्येयम्। सौगताः किलेत्थं प्रमाणयन्ति-सर्वं सत् क्षणिकं etc. cf. यत्सत्तत्क्षणिकं यथा जलधरः सन्तश्च भावा इमे सत्ताशक्तिरिहार्थकर्मणि मिते सिद्धेषु सिद्धा च सा। नाप्येकैवविधान्यदापि परकृन्नैव क्रिया सा भवेत् द्वेधापि क्षणभङ्गसंगतिरतः साध्यैव विश्राम्यति ॥ For a statement of क्षणभङ्गवाद see Ratnakîrti's Tract on 'क्षणभङ्गसिद्धि,' and Keith's "Budhist Philosophy" pp. 181–184, also S'âutarakṣita's Tattva-Saṃgraha with Kamalas'îla's Pañjikâ—Section on स्थिरभावपरीक्षा. (G.O.S.Tattvasaṃgraha Vol. I). For its criticism, see Sâṁkara Bhâṣya on Br. Sûtras II, ii, 19–22. The Jaina position is thus argued and summed up by Hemacandra who quotes " अर्थक्रिया न युज्येत नित्यक्षणिकपक्षयोः। क्रमाक्रमाभ्यां भावानां सा लक्षणतया मता ॥" cf. also Guṇaratna's com. on क्षणिकाः सर्वसंस्काराः Saḍ. Darśana Sam. verse 7. pp. 30–31. On p. 195 of the Notes, in l. 3 from the bottom read " Br. Sûtras II, ii, 11–17 and in the last line: " Prajnâkara Gupta's date is given in Dr. Vidyâbhûṣana's H. I. L. about 940 A. D." On p. 199 of the Notes—for " if there is " and " we cannot " in ll. 6 and 7, read " if there were " and " we could not " respectively. For " S'ad. Com." read " Ṣaḍ. Com." of Guṇaratna; and the same for " S'ad " on p. 202. To the list of Reference Books add: 6 Abhayadeva's Com. on Sammatitarka, 7. Nyâyabindu of Dharmottara with Nyâyabinduṭîkâ of Dharmakîrti 8. S'ântarakṣita's Tattva-Saṃgraha with Kamalaśîla's Pañjika, 9. " Six Buddhist Tracts ", 10. Mahâyâna Sûtrâlaṁkâra Mâdhyamikâ Vṛtti, 11. Vijnaptimatratâsiddhi, 12. Account of Buddhist schools in Kern's " Indian Buddhism ", 13. Keith's "Buddhist Philosophy", 14. Sogen's "Systems of Buddhist Thought", 15. Suzuki's "Outlines of Mahâyâna Buddhism ", 16 and Stcherbatsky's Introduction to his " The Conception of Buddhist Nirvāṇa ".

St. XVII.

इह शून्यवादिनामयमभिसन्धिः—For S'ûnyavâda see Madhyamikâvṛtti, Stcherbatsky's "Buddhist Concept of Nirvâṇa" and Keith's "Buddhist Philosophy" Ch. XIII:—" The Negativism of the Madhyamaka ".

For an examination of the doctrine from the Brâhmaṇa point of view see Kumârila's S'lokavârtika, sections on निरालम्बनवाद and शून्यवाद. For the Jaina examination, See Com. on Saṃmatitarka, नयमीमांसा.

सुखादि चेत्यमानं हि—Quoted in Ratnâkarâvatârikâ on P.N.T. VII 55 p. 142. The whole commentary on "प्रमाता प्रत्यक्षादि-प्रसिद्ध आत्मा" and "चैतन्यस्वरूपः परिणामी कर्ता साक्षाद्भोक्ता स्वदेहपरिमाणः प्रतिक्षेत्रं भिन्नः पौद्गलिकादृष्टवांश्चायमिति" (P. N. T. VII. 55,56), both in Ratnâkara and Avatârikâ, contains a good dissertation on the nature of Âtman according to the Jainas. See in this connection, Pravacanasâra. For the Buddhist examination of rival doctrines see "Tattvasaṃgraha" with Pañjikâ Vol. I., section on आत्मपरीक्षा S'l. 171–349 pp. 79–130.

For the interesting question of the nature of Âtman according to other schools, consult Jayanta's Nyâyamañjarî, Râmânuja's Srîbhâṣya etc. On p. 211 of the Notes in ll. 3 & 4 from the bottom "observation" is a wonderful misprint for "obscuration." It puzzled me for a few minutes to find out with what word it could have been confounded. On संवृति *i. e.* 'concealment' or 'obscuration,' see Suzuki's "Outlines of Mahâyâna Buddhism." 'संवृति' corresponds to "व्यावहारिकी सत्ता" which conceals (by the आवरणशक्ति of अविद्या or माया) the "पारमार्थिकी सत्ता" which lies beyond it.

स्वज्ञानावरणवीर्यान्तराय etc.—"पढमं ज्ञाणावरणं, बीयं पुण दंसणस्स आवरणं । त इयं च वेयणियं, तहा चउत्थं च मोहणीयं"—*i. e.* ज्ञानावरण, which is the first of the four obscuring Karmans. वीर्यान्तराय—कर्मविशेषः यस्योदये उत्साहप्रतिघातो भवति *i. e.* the Karman which obstructs the exercise of moral will; moral weakness. See A. M. P.'s edition of Pramâṇamîmâṃsâ pp. 18–19, footnotes.

क्षयोपशम—Wearing out and ultimate cessation of karman. न सन्नसदसन्न......तत्त्वमाध्यात्मिका जगुः—I have no doubt the correct reading is "तत्त्वं माध्यमिका जगुः"—the reference being to the famous Madhyamaka or Mâdhyamika school of Buddhism.

" The relation between mental and material things is a case of causation but of a special kind since it may be said to be simultaneous, in lieu of subsequent. This raises a difficulty as suggesting the Vijñânavâda theory that there is no real externality in things, but a mistaken and illusory attribution of externality to that which is internal, as can be shown from the fact that we always experience an object and its cognition together. The Sautrântikas reject this view; the facts are, they argue, clearly that what we see are objects, as external, not merely internal modifications of consciousness, to which in point of fact we do not in everyday life attend as such. The idealist admission that things appear as if external undermines their whole position, for the conception of externality could not rise without real ground. There is no real difficulty as to simultaneity between the object and the perception of it; we do not, as the objection to this possibility seems to imply, first know the object and then know the perception, but the object by contact with the sense organ impresses its form on the cognition, and then from the form we conclude by inference the existence of an external object which causes it, just as we infer nourishment from a thriving appearance, nationality from language, and love from emotion. The object moulds our knowledge without ceasing to be itself. Cognition cannot explain our objects; in itself it is the same and there would be no differentiation of objects if objects were derived from it. The diversity of cognitions in an observer, himself remaining the same, is explicable only by the operation on him of external things, a fact which gives us the realization of the self as the conscious subject (ālaya-vijñāna) in whom individual cognitions (pravṛtti-vijñāna), caused by external things appear from time to time.

The Vaibhāṣikas, though realists, object to this doctrine of the Sautrāntikas–indeed a fanciful etymology gives them their name because of their habit of styling the doctrine of inferability 'contradictory chatter (viruddha bhāṣā)'. If knowledge is thus reduced to inferability, then there is no object of perception, and, this being so, there is no basis for the observation of the invariable concomitance, which is the essential ground of inference, and we shall have a complete contradiction with all actual experience. Knowledge, in fact, is of two kinds; perception as indeterminate, that is free from the operation of imagination, which is authoritative, and determinate perception which is worked up by imagination and so is not directly authoritative, although what is inferred serves as a basis for action and common acceptance; we can verify by action the truth of inferences, and we can accept statements on authority as resting ultimately on perception."

—Keith's "Buddhist Philosophy" pp. 161–162.

St. XVIII.

Add as an Appendix:—

बौद्धा बुद्धिक्षणपरंपरा etc.—This has a parallel both in language and in thought in the following paragraph of P. N. T. Ratnâkarâvatârikâ Pari. VII, p. 142 :—

बौद्धास्तु बुद्धिक्षणपरंपरामात्रमेवात्मानमाम्नासिषुः, न पुनर्मौक्तिककण-निकरनिरन्तरानुस्यूतैकसूत्रवत् तदन्वयिनमेकम्। ते लोकायतलुण्टाकेभ्योऽपि पापीयांसः। तद्भावेपि तेषां स्मरणप्रत्यभिज्ञानाद्यघटनात्। तथाहि—पूर्वबुद्ध्यानु-भूतेऽर्थे नोत्तरबुद्धीनां स्मृतिः संभवति ततोन्यत्त्वात् संतानान्तरबुद्धिवत्। न ह्यन्य-दृष्टोऽर्थोऽन्येन स्मर्यते। अन्यथैकेन दृष्टोऽर्थः सर्वैः स्मर्येत। स्मरणाभावे च कौतस्कुती प्रत्यभिज्ञाप्रसूतिः। तस्याः स्मरणानुभवोभयसंभवत्वात्। पदार्थप्रेक्षणप्रबुद्ध—प्राक्तनसंस्कारस्य हि प्रमातुः स एवायमित्याकारेणेयमुत्पद्यते। अथ स्यादयं दोषो यद्यविशेषेणान्यदृष्टमन्यः स्मरतीत्युच्यते। किंत्वन्यत्वेपि कार्यकारणभावादेव स्मृतिः। भिन्नसंतानबुद्धीनां तु कार्यकारणभावो नास्ति तेन संतानान्तराणां स्मृतिर्न भवति। न चैकसांतानिकीनामपि बुद्धीनां कार्यकारणभावो नास्ति येन पूर्वबुद्ध्यनुभूतेऽर्थे तदुत्तरबुद्धीनां स्मृतिर्न स्यात्। तदप्यनवदातम्। एवमपि नानात्वस्य तदवस्थत्वात्।

अन्यत्वं हि स्मृत्यसंभवे साधनमुक्तम्। तच्च कार्यकारणभावाभिधानेपि नापगतम्। न हि कार्यकारणभावाभिधाने तस्यासिद्धत्वादीनामन्यतमो दोषः प्रतिपद्यते। नापि स्वपक्षसिद्धिरनेन क्रियते। नहि कार्यकारणभावात् स्मृतिरित्यत्रोभयप्रसिद्धोस्ति दृष्टान्तः। अथ—"यस्मिन्नेव हि संतान आहिता कर्मवासना। फलं तत्रैव संधत्ते कर्पासे रक्तता यथा॥" इति कर्पासरक्ततादृष्टान्तोऽस्तीति चेत् तदसाधीयः। साधनदूषणासंभवात्। अन्वयाद्यसंभवान्न साधनम्। नहि कार्यकारणभावो यत्र तत्र स्मृतिः कर्पासे रक्ततावदिति अन्वयः संभवति। नापि यत्र न स्मृतिस्तत्र न कार्यकारणभाव इति व्यतिरेकोऽस्ति। असिद्धत्वाद्यद्भावनाच्च न दूषणम्। नहि ततोऽन्यत्वादित्यस्य हेतोः कर्पासे रक्ततावदित्यनेन कश्चिद्दोषः प्रतिपाद्यते। किं च। यद्यन्यत्वेपि कार्यकारणभावेन स्मृतेरुत्पत्तिरिष्यते तदा शिष्याचार्यादिबुद्धीनामपि कार्यकारणभावसद्भावेन स्मृत्यादि स्यात्। अथ नायं प्रसङ्गः। एकसंतानत्वे सतीति विशेषणादिति चेत् तदयुक्तम्। भेदाभेदपक्षाभ्यां तस्योपक्षीणत्वात्। क्षणपरंपरातस्तस्याभेदे हि क्षणपरंपरैव सा तथा च संतान इति न किंचिदतिरिक्तमुक्तम्। भेदे तु पारमार्थिकोऽपारमार्थिको वासौ स्यात्। अपारमार्थिकत्वे त्वस्य तदेव दूषणम्। पारमार्थिकत्वे स्थिरो वा स्यात् क्षणिको वा क्षणिकत्वे संतानिनिर्विशेष एवायमिति किमनेन स्तेनभीतस्य स्तेनान्तरशरणस्वीकरणकारिणा। स्थिरमथ संतानमभ्युपेयाः प्रथयन्तं परमार्थसत्स्वरूपम्। अमृतं पिब पूतयाऽनयोक्त्या स्थिरवपुषः परलोकिनः प्रसिद्धेः॥' —P. N. T. Ratnâkarâvatârikâ. Ch. VII pp. 142–143.

Cf. a similar line of argument in S'âmkara Bhâṣya on Br. Sû. II. ii. 25—अनुस्मृतेश्च.

Appendices

1. "In Hindu and Jaina accounts of Buddhist philosophy, we find mention of only four schools, viz. (1) the Mâdhyamikas, or nihilists, (2) the Yogâcâras, or subjective idealists, (3) the Sautrântikas or representationists and (4) Vaibhâshikas or presentationists. The chief tenets of each of these schools are supposed to be summed up in the well-known stanza:—

अर्थो ज्ञानसमन्वितो मतिमता वैभाषिकेणोच्यते
प्रत्यक्षो नहि बाह्यवस्तुविसरः सौत्रान्तिकैराश्रितः॥
योगाचारमतानुगैरभिमता साकारबुद्धिः परा
मन्यन्ते बत मध्यमाः कृतधियः स्वस्थां परां संविदम्॥

These four probably represented the principal classes of Buddhists who flourished in India at a time when militant

Vedântism was hurling the missiles against the moribund faith of Sugata."

—Sogen's "Systems of Buddhist Thought".

Malliṣeṇa does not mention any of these four schools by name, but they are just those which have been criticised by him. The doctrine attributed to the Madhyamaka in the last line of the Stanza makes it identical with the doctrine of "Para-Brahma" as maintained in the S'ânkara school. The Jaina, like the other schoolmen, takes it be the doctrine of शून्यता in the sense of Universal Void or Emptiness which is the very opposite of S'ankara's Universal Plenum (पूर्ण—cf. "पूर्णमिदं पूर्णमदः पूर्णात् पूर्णमुदच्यते । पूर्णस्य पूर्णमादाय पूर्णमेवावशिष्यते ।" Upaniṣad.)], and yet it is curious that as a representative text of the शून्यवाद Malliṣeṇa quoted a passage (" सर्व एवायमनुमानानुमेयव्यवहारो न बुद्ध्यारूढेन धर्मधर्मिभावेन न बहिः सदसत्त्वमपेक्षते ") which has been attributed to Diṅnâga (See Randle's " Fragments from Diṅnâga " and Pârthasārathi on Mîm. S'l. Vârt. and Uddotakara's Nyâya-Vârtika and Vâcaspati's N. V. Tâtparya) who was certainly not a Mâdhyamika S'ûnyavâdin.

S'abarasvâmin and Kumârila—the great Bhâṣyakâra and Vârtikakâra respectively of the Mîmâṃsâ Darśana—, however, use the word 'शून्य' not in the sense of Universal Void, but as a negation of distinction between ज्ञान and अर्थ, the आकार *i.e.* the particular form, being one which cannot be said to be either that of ज्ञान or that of अर्थ. The शून्यवाद is thus different from निरालम्बनवाद in which only one of the two, viz. ज्ञान is supposed to possess the आकार, thus rendering the reality of the other superfluous. Both these have been considered apart from the शून्यवाद of Stanza XVII.

Cf. " ननु सर्व एव निरालम्बनः स्वप्नवत् प्रत्ययः। प्रत्ययस्य हि निरालम्बनतया स्वभाव उपलक्षितः स्वप्ने । जाग्रतोऽपि स्तम्भ इति वा कुड्य इति वा प्रत्यय एव भवति । तस्मात् सोऽपि निरालम्बनः ॥ उच्यते । स्तम्भ इति जाग्रतो बुद्धिः सुपरिनिश्चिता कथं विपर्यसिष्यतीति । स्वप्नेऽप्येवमेव सुपरिनिश्चितासीत् । प्राक् प्रबोधनात् न कश्चिद्विशेष इति । न । स्वप्ने विपर्ययदर्शनात् । अविपर्ययस्य

इतरस्मिन्। तत्सामान्यादितरत्रापि भविष्यतीति चेत् यदि स्वप्नप्रत्ययस्य मिथ्याभावः जाग्रत्प्रत्ययस्यापि तथा भवितुमर्हति। अथ प्रतीतिस्तथाभावस्य हेतुः न शक्यते प्रत्ययत्वाद् अयमन्य इति वक्तुम्। अन्यतस्तु स्वप्नप्रत्ययस्य मिथ्याभावो विपर्ययादवगतः। कुत इति चेत्। सनिद्रस्य मनसो दौर्बल्यात् निद्रा मिथ्याभावस्य हेतुः स्वप्नादौ स्वप्नान्ते च। सुषुप्तस्याभाव एव। अचेतयन्नेव हि सुषुप्त इत्युच्यते। तस्माज्जाग्रतः प्रत्ययो न मिथ्येति। ननु जाग्रतोऽपि करणदोषः स्यात्। यदि स्यात् अवगम्येत। स्वप्नदर्शनकालेऽपि नावगम्यत इति चेत्। तत्र प्रबुद्धो ह्यवगच्छति निद्राक्रान्तं मे मन आसीदिति ॥

शून्यस्तु कथम्—अर्थज्ञानयोराकारभेदं नोपलभामहे। प्रत्यक्षा च नो बुद्धिः। अतस्तद्भिन्नमर्थरूपं नाम न किंचिदस्तीति पश्यामः॥ स्यादेतदेवं यद्यर्थाकारा बुद्धिः स्यात् निराकारा तु नो बुद्धिः आकारवान् बाह्योऽर्थः। स हि बहिर्देशसंबद्धः प्रत्यक्षमुपलभ्यते। अर्थविषया। हि प्रत्यक्षबुद्धिः न बुद्ध्यन्तरविषया। क्षणिका हि सा न बुद्ध्यन्तरकालमवस्थास्यत इति। उत्पद्यमानैवासौ ज्ञायते। ज्ञापयति च अर्थान्तरप्रदीपवदिति यदुच्यते तन्न। न ह्यज्ञातेऽर्थे कश्चिद् बुद्धिमुपलभते। ज्ञाते तु अनुमानादवगच्छति। तत्र यौगपद्यमनुपपन्नम्। नन्वुत्पन्नायामेव बुद्धौ ज्ञातोऽर्थ इत्युच्यते नानुत्पन्नायाम्। अतः पूर्वं बुद्धिरुत्पद्यते पश्चाज्ज्ञातोऽर्थः। सत्यम्। पूर्वं बुद्धिरुत्पद्यते न तु पूर्वं ज्ञायते। भवति हि कदाचिदेतद् यज्ज्ञातोऽप्यर्थः सन् अज्ञात इत्युच्यते। न चार्थव्यपदेशमन्तरेण बुद्धे रूपोपलम्भनम्। तस्मादव्यपदेश्या बुद्धिः अव्यपदेश्यं च नः प्रत्यक्षम्। तस्मादप्रत्यक्षा बुद्धिः। अपि च काममेकरूपकत्वे बुद्धेरेवाभावः नार्थस्य प्रत्यक्षस्य सतः। न चैकरूप्यम्। अनाकारामेव बुद्धिमनुमिमीमहे। साकारं चार्थं प्रत्यक्षमेवावगच्छामः। तस्मादर्थालम्बनः प्रत्ययः। अपि च नियतनिमित्तस्तन्तुष्वेवोपादीयमानेषु पटप्रत्ययः। इतरथा तन्त्वादानेपि कदाचिद् घटबुद्धिरविकलेन्द्रियस्य स्यात्। न चैवमस्ति। अतो न निरालम्बनः प्रत्ययः। अतो न व्यभिचरति प्रत्यक्षम् ॥"

—S'abara Bh. on P. Mîm. I. i. 5.

—Note that the second paragraph begins with "शून्यस्तु" and yet ends with "निरालम्बनः प्रत्ययः"—thus making little distinction between शून्यवाद and निरालम्बनवाद. The same is the case with the Vârtika also.

See also Kumârilâs S'l. Vârt on निरालम्बनवाद and शून्यवाद, and S'ânkara Bh. on II. ii. "वैधर्म्याच्च न स्वप्नादिवत्."

2. "The fundamental doctrine of this Mādhyamika school has been imperfectly understood and grossly misrepresented by the so-called scholars of Buddhism in Europe, and latter-

day India. Most of them give the appellation of 'Nihilism' to this school, simply because Nâgârjuna applied the terms 'S'ûnyatâ' or emptiness to express his conception of human life and truth. S'ûnyatâ, however......does not imply 'nothingness; it simply expresses "the everchanging state of the phenomenal world" or absolute restrictedness of the noumenal side of the universe"—Sogen's "Systems of Buddhistic Thought"—p. 194. Sogen approvingly cites the following passage from Suzuki's "Outlines of Mahâyâna Buddhism":—"*Sûṇyatâ* simply means conditionality or transitoriness of all phenomenal existence. It is a synonym for *anitya* or *pratîtya* Therefore, 'emptiness', according to the Buddhists, signifies negatively the absence of particularity, the non-existence of individuals as such, and positively the ever-changing state of the phenomenal world, a constant flux of becoming, an eternal series of causes and effects. It must never be understood in the sense of annihilation or absolute nothingness; for nihilism is as much condemned by Buddhism as *naïve* realism".

Similarly, in regard to the क्षणभङ्गवाद, Mr. Sogen says that it asserts the "momentariness" of the phenomenal world only, leaving the noumenal reality untouched. I agree that the original teaching of Gautama Buddha probably amounted to this only, but I am not sure whether the later Buddhists did not go further. If Mr. Sogen's interpretation of क्षणभङ्गवाद is correct, it concides with the Jaina's "उत्पादव्ययध्रौव्यं सत्।"

St. XIX.

लौकायतिकानाम्—The word 'लोकायत' originally meant scientists who based their conclusions on observation or 'Nature-lore' (see Rhys David's note in his Introduction to Kûṭadanta Sutta, in "Dialogues of Buddha" Vol. II. S. B. B. p. 166. See also Haraprasâd Sastri's "Lokâyata," a Bulletin of the Dacca University.

St. XX.

चार्वाकः—Now derived by some from 'चारुवाक्'=Sweet-tongued has been derived in Siddharṣi's commentary on Nyâyâvatâra and elsewhere thus: चर्व अदने चर्वन्ति भक्षयन्ति तत्त्वतो न मन्यन्ते पुण्यपापादिकं परोक्षं वस्तुजातमिति चार्वाकाः (Hema. Uṇâdi 37.)

Borrowed, in some parts almost verbatim with a change of order in some lines from Hemacandra's Commentary on his प्रमाणमीमांसा. cf. "व्यवस्थान्यधीनिषेधानां सिद्धेः प्रत्यक्षेतरप्रमाणसिद्धिः १-१-११ ।.........चार्वाको हि काश्चिज्ज्ञानव्यक्तीः संवादित्वेनाव्यभिचारिणीरुपलभ्यान्याश्च विसंवादित्वेन व्यभिचारिणीः पुनः कालान्तरे तादृशीतराणां ज्ञानव्यक्तीनामवश्यं प्रमाणेतरते व्यवस्थापयेत्। न चायं स्वप्रतीतिगोचराणामपि ज्ञानव्यक्तीनां परं प्रति प्रामाण्यमप्रामाण्यं वा व्यवस्थापयितुं प्रभवति । तस्माद्यथादृष्टज्ञानव्यक्तिसाधर्म्यद्वारेणेदानीन्तनज्ञानव्यक्तीनां प्रामाण्याप्रामाण्यव्यवस्थापकं परप्रतिपादकं परोक्षान्तर्गतमनुमानरूपं प्रमाणान्तरमुपासीत। अपि च अप्रतिपित्सितमर्थं प्रतिपादयन्नायं लौकिको न परीक्षक इत्युन्मत्तवदुपेक्षणीयः स्यात्। न च प्रत्यक्षेण परचेतोवृत्तीनामधिगमोऽस्ति । चेष्टाविशेषदर्शनात्तदवगमे च परोक्षस्य प्रामाण्यमनिच्छतोऽप्यायातम्। परलोकादिनिषेधश्च न प्रत्यक्षमात्रेण शक्यः कर्तुम्। संनिहितमात्रविषयत्वात्तस्य । परलोकादिकं चाप्रतिषिध्य नायं सुखेनास्ते प्रमाणान्तरं च नेच्छतीति डिम्भहेवाकः । किं च प्रत्यक्षस्याप्यर्थाव्यभिचारादेव प्रामाण्यं तच्चार्थः प्रतिबद्धलिङ्गशब्दद्वारा समुन्मज्जतः परोक्षस्याप्यर्थाव्यभिचारादेव किं नेष्यते। व्यभिचारिणोऽपि परोक्षस्य दर्शनादप्रामाण्यमिति चेत्। प्रत्यक्षस्यापि तिमिरादिदोषादप्रामाण्यस्य दर्शनात् सर्वत्राप्रामाण्यप्रसङ्गः। प्रत्यक्षाभासं तच्चेत् इत्यत्रापि तुल्यमेतदन्यत्र पक्षपातात् ॥"

Cf. Sâṃkhya tattvakaumudi: "नानुमानं प्रमाणमिति वदता लौकायतिकेन अप्रतिपन्नः संदिग्धो विपर्यस्तो वा पुरुषः कथं प्रतिपद्येत । न च पुरुषान्तरगता अज्ञानसंदेहविपर्ययाः शक्या अर्वाग्दृशा प्रत्यक्षेण प्रतिपत्तुम्। नापि प्रमाणान्तरेण । अनभ्युपगमात्। अनवधृताज्ञानसंशयविपर्यासस्तु यं कंचन पुरुषं प्रति वर्तमानोऽनवधेयवचनतया प्रेक्षावद्भिरुन्मत्तवदुपेक्ष्येत । तदनेनाज्ञानादयः परपुरुषवर्तिनोऽभिप्रायभेदाद्वचनभेदाल्लिङ्गादनुमातव्या इत्यकामेनाप्यनुमानं प्रमाणमभ्युपेयम् ॥"—*i. e.* in short, all our social intercourse, including the discussion of a proposition with the opponent, depends upon the assumption that अनुमान is a valid form of thought (प्रमाण).

As regards the unreliability of अनुमान as a प्रमाण Guṇaratna narrates an interesting story alluded to in the following couplet of Ṣaḍdarśana-samuccaya of Haribhadra: "एतावानेव लोकोऽयं यावानिन्द्रियगोचरः। भद्रे वृकपदं पश्य यद्वदन्त्यबहुश्रुताः॥ (8D) अत्रायं संप्रदायः—कश्चित् पुरुषो नास्तिकयवासनावासितान्तःकरणो निजां जायामास्तिकमतनिबद्धमतिं स्वशास्त्रोक्तयुक्तिभिरभियुक्तः प्रत्यहं प्रतिबोधयति। सा तु यदा न प्रतिबुध्यते तदा स इयमनेनोपायेन प्रतिभोत्स्यत इति स्वचेतसि विचिन्त्य निशायाः पश्चिमे यामे तया समं नगरान्निर्गत्य तां प्रत्यवादीत्—प्रिये य इमे नगरवासिनो नराः परोक्षविषयेऽनुमानादिप्रामाण्यमाचक्षाणा लोकेन च बहुश्रुततया व्यवह्रियमाणा विद्यन्ते पश्य तेषां चारुविचारणायां चातुर्यमिति। ततः स नगरद्वारादारभ्य चतुःपथं यावन्मन्थरतरप्रसृमरसमीरणसमीभूतपांशुप्रकरे राजमार्गे द्वयोरपि स्वकरयोरङ्गुष्ठप्रदेशिनीमध्यमाङ्गुलित्रयं मीलयित्वा स्वशरीरस्योभयोः पक्षयोः पांशुषु न्यासेन वृकपदानि प्रचक्रे। ततः प्रातस्तानि पदानि निरीक्ष्यास्तोको लोको राजमार्गेऽमिलत्। बहुश्रुता अपि तत्रागता जनान् प्रत्यवोचन् भो भो वृकपदानामन्यथानुपपत्त्या नूनं निशि वृकः कश्चन वनतोऽत्रागच्छत् इत्यादि। ततः स तांस्तथाभाषमाणान्निरीक्ष्य निजां भार्यां जजल्प हे भद्रे प्रिये वृकपदं पश्य निरीक्षस्व॥"

The principles of the school are thus summarised in the Ṣaḍdarśana-Samuccaya.

"लोकायता वदन्त्येवं नास्ति जीवो न निर्वृतिः। धर्माधर्मौ न विद्येते न फलं पुण्यपापयोः॥ एतावानेव लोकोऽयं यावानिन्द्रियगोचरः॥ भद्रे वृकपदं पश्य यद्वदन्त्य(v.l. न्ति)बहुश्रुताः॥ पिब खाद च चारुलोचने यदतीतं वरगात्रि तु तन्न ते। नहि भीरु गतं निवर्तते समुदयमात्रमिदं कलेवरम्॥" (vv. 80–82).

Appendix.

"यत्तावदुक्तं प्रत्यक्षमेवैकं प्रमाणं नानुमानादिकमित्येतदनुपासितगुरोर्वचः। तथाहि–अर्थाविसंवादकं प्रमाणमित्युच्यते। प्रत्यक्षस्य च प्रामाण्यमेवं व्यवस्थाप्यते। काश्चित् प्रत्यक्षव्यक्तीर्धर्मित्वेनोपादाय प्रमाणयति–प्रमाणमेताः अर्थाविसंवादकत्वात् अनुभूतप्रत्यक्षव्यक्तिवत्। न च ताभिरेव प्रत्यक्षव्यक्तिभिः स्वसंविदिताभिः परं व्यवहारयितुमयमीशः तासां स्वसंविन्निष्ठत्वात्। मूकत्वाच्च प्रत्यक्षस्य। तथा नानुमानं प्रमाणमित्यनुमानेनैवानुमाननिरासं कुर्वंश्चार्वाकः कथं नोन्मत्तः स्याद्। एवं ह्यसौ तदप्रामाण्यं प्रतिपादयेत् यथा–नानुमानं प्रमाणं विसंवादकत्वात् अनुभूतानुमानव्यक्तिवदिति। एतच्चानुमानम्। अथ परप्रसिद्धयैतदुच्यते। तदप्ययुक्तं यतस्तत्परप्रसिद्धमनुमानं भवतः प्रमाणमप्रमाणं वा। प्रमाणं चेत्कथमनुमानमप्रमाणमित्युच्यते। अथाप्रमाणं कथमप्रमाणेन सता तेन परः प्रत्या-

घ्यते । परेण तस्य प्रामाण्येनाभ्युपगतत्वादिति चेत् तदप्यसांप्रतम् । यदि नाम परो मौढ्यादप्रमाणमेव प्रमाणमित्यध्यवस्यति किं भवताऽतिनिपुणेनापि तेनैवासौ प्रतिपाद्यते । यो ह्यज्ञो गुडमेव विषमिति मन्यते किं तस्य मारयितुकामेनापि बुद्धिमता गुड एव दीयते । तदेवं प्रत्यक्षानुमानयोः प्रामाण्याप्रामाण्ये व्यवस्थापयतो भवतोऽनिच्छतोऽपि बलादायातमनुमानस्य प्रामाण्यम् ।—Śîlâṁka's Commentary on Sûtra-Kṛtâṁga p. 17.

एवं नास्तिकाभिमतो भूतचिद्वादोऽपि निराकार्यः—Cf. S'îl. Com. on Sûtra-Kṛtâṁga pp. 15–17: न पृथिव्यादिव्यतिरिक्त आत्मास्ति तद्ग्राहकप्रमाणाभावात् ।...यत्तु चैतन्यं तेषूपलभ्यते तद्भूतेष्वेव कायाकारपरिणतेष्वभिव्यज्यते मद्याङ्गेषु समुदितेषु मदशक्तिवदिति...। तदेवं भूतव्यतिरिक्तस्यात्मनोऽभावाद्भूतानामेव चैतन्याभिव्यक्तिः जलस्य बुद्बुदाभिव्यक्तिवदिति ।......। ननु च यदि भूतव्यतिरिक्तोऽपरः कश्चिदात्माख्यः पदार्थो न विद्यते कथं तर्हि मृत इति व्यपदेश इत्याशङ्क्याह ।—अथैषां कायाकारपरिणतौ चैतन्याभिव्यक्तौ सत्यां तदूर्ध्वं तेषामन्यतमस्य विनाशे अपगमे वायोस्तेजसश्चोभयोर्वा देहिनो देवदत्तस्याख्यस्य विनाशः अपगमो भवति ततश्च मृत इति व्यपदेशः प्रवर्तते ।...। इति भूताव्यतिरिक्तचैतन्यवादिपूर्वपक्षः ॥...यत्तावदुक्तं यथा भूतेभ्यः परस्परसव्यपेक्षसंयोगभाग्भ्यश्चैतन्यमुत्पद्यते तत्र विकल्पयामः किमसौ संयोगः संयोगिभ्यो भिन्नोऽभिन्नो वा । भिन्नश्चेत् षष्ठभूतप्रसङ्गः ।...अभिन्नो भूतेभ्यः संयोगः तत्राप्येतच्चिन्तनीयम्—किं भूतानि प्रत्येकं चेतनावन्त्यचेतनावन्ति वा ।...। यदप्यत्रोक्तं यथा मद्याङ्गेष्वविद्यमानापि प्रत्येकं मदशक्तिः समुदाये प्रादुर्भवतीति तदप्ययुक्तं यतस्तत्र किण्वादिषु या च यावती च शक्तिरुपलभ्यते...। किं च भूतचैतन्याभ्युपगमे मरणाभावः ... नैतदस्ति । तत्र मृतकाये वायोस्तेजसो वाऽभावान्मरणसद्भावः इत्यशिक्षितस्योल्लापः । तथाहि मृतकाये शोफोपलब्धेर्न वायोरभावः कोथस्य च पक्तिस्वभावस्य दर्शनान्नाग्नेरिति । अथ सूक्ष्मः कश्चिद्वायुविशेषोऽग्निर्वा ततोपगत इति मतिरिति एवं च जीव एव नामान्तरेणाभ्युपगतो भवति ॥

To the list of Books of Reference add: 5 Nyâya Sûtras. 6 Praśastapâda Bhâṣya with Nyâyakandalî.

St. XXI.

घटमौलि etc.—Cf. "प्रध्वस्ते कलशे शुशोच तनया मौलौ समुत्पादिते पुत्रः प्रीतिमुवाह कामपि नृपः शिश्राय मध्यस्थताम् । पूर्वाकारपरिक्षयस्तदपराकारोदयस्तद्द्वयाधारश्चैक इति स्थितं त्रयमयं तत्त्वं तथाप्रत्ययात् ॥"—Ratnākarāvatārikā.

St. XXII.

अन्यथानुपपत्त्येकलक्षणत्वाद्धेतोः—'अन्यथानुपपत्ति'—Otherwise-inexplicability; impossibility except on a particular hypothesis; *e.g.* the existence of धूम is impossible except on the assumption that there is वह्नि also. Cf. "साध्याविनाभावित्वेन निश्चितो हेतुः"—Pratijñâmukha-Sûtra, where अविनाभाव is divided into two varieties, अविनाभाव of co-existence and अविनाभाव of succession:—सहक्रमभावनियमोऽविनाभावः. We are further told how the former, *i. e.* सहभाव can be सहभाव of two companions or that of the pervader and the pervaded: सहचारिणोर्व्याप्यव्यापकयोश्च सहभावः. The क्रमभाव similarly may be क्रमभाव of mere antecedent and consequent or of cause and effect: पूर्वोत्तरचारिणोः कार्यकारणयोश्च क्रमभावः. This relation is determined by तर्क (तर्कात्तन्निर्णयः). The P. N. T. states that according to Jainas only two अवयवs are necessary in a syllogism viz पक्ष and हेतु, and thus distinguishes the Jaina view from that of other schools: "एवं च यद् व्याप्त्युपेतं पक्षधर्मतोपसंहाररूपं सौगतैः, पक्षहेतुदृष्टान्तस्वरूपं भाट्टप्राभाकरकापिलैः, पक्षहेतुदृष्टान्तोपनयनिगमनलक्षणं नैयायिकवैशेषिकाभ्यामनुमानमाम्नायि तदपास्तम् ॥ Next, P. N. T. mentions how the हेतु may be stated: हेतुप्रयोगस्तथोपपत्त्यन्यथानुपपत्तिभ्यां द्विप्रकारः। सत्येव हेतोरुपपत्तिस्तथोपपत्तिः, असति साध्ये हेतोरनुपपत्तिरेवान्यथानुपपत्तिः। यथा कृशानुमानयं पाकप्रदेशः सत्येव कृशानुमत्त्वे धूमवत्त्वस्योपपत्तेः असत्यनुपपत्तेर्वा। अनयोरन्यतरप्रयोगेणैव साध्यप्रतिपत्तौ द्वितीयप्रयोगस्यैकत्रानुपयोगः ॥ (P. N. T. III. 29-82.)

अन्तर्व्याप्त्यैव—Cf. अन्तर्व्याप्त्या हेतोः साध्यप्रत्यायने शक्तावशक्तौ च बहिर्व्याप्तेरुद्भावनं व्यर्थम् ॥ (ibid. 37) अयमर्थः अन्तर्व्याप्तेः साध्यसंसिद्धिशक्तौ बाह्यव्याप्तेर्वर्णनं वन्ध्यमेव। अन्तर्व्याप्तेः साध्यसंसिद्ध्यशक्तौ बाह्यव्याप्तेर्वर्णनं व्यर्थमेव ॥

On p. 237 in l. 14 from the bottom, for the words in the rectangular brackets read:—[It should be eleventh century, according to the date given by Dr. Vidyâbhûṣaṇa which is 1045 A. D.]

St. XXIII.

न च पुष्पदन्तादिवत्—I am afraid the AMP. footnote "पुष्पदन्ताख्यो गन्धर्वविशेषः........" has missed the point. For the correct explanation cf. "पुष्पदन्तौ पुष्पवन्तावेकोक्त्या शशिभास्करौ"—Hema. Kośa.

St. XXIV.

Cf. तस्य [प्रमाणस्य] विषयः सामान्यविशेषाद्यनेकान्तकं वस्त्विति P. N. T. ५-१. See the same author's—Devasûri's—Commentary Syâdvâda-Ratnâkâra Pt. 5, pp. 736. After stating the objections of the यौगs (Naiyâyikas and Vaiśeṣikas) the writer quotes the following verse which enumerates them "तदुक्तम्—संशय-विरोध-वैयधिकरण्य-संकर-मथोभयं दोषः। अनवस्थाव्यतिकरमपि जैनमते सप्त दोषाः स्युः।" These are answered in detail and the section concludes as follows:

"ततो घटादेः प्रतिनियतरूपव्यवस्थामिच्छता नाऽनुपजायमानः संशयो बलादापादयितुं शक्यः ॥ १ ॥ ...तदित्थं विरोधस्य परामृश्यमानस्याघटमानत्वात्रायं भेदाभेदयोः परिकल्पयितुं युक्तः ॥ २ ॥ नापि वैयधिकरण्यम्। एकाधारतया निर्बाधबोधे भेदाभेदयोः प्रतिभासमानत्वात् ॥ ३ ॥ नापि उभयदोषानुषङ्गः। तस्करपारदारिकाभ्यामतस्करपारदारिकवद्भेदात्मकवस्तुनः केवलभेदाभेदाभ्यां जात्यन्तरत्वात्। न खलु भेदाभेदयोरन्योन्यनिरपेक्षयोरेकत्वं जिनपतिमतानुसारिभिरिष्टं येनायं दोषः स्यात्। तत्सापेक्षयोरेव तदभ्युपगमात् तथाप्रतीतेश्च ॥ ४ ॥ नापि संकरव्यतिकरौ—। स्वरूपेणैवार्थे तयोः प्रतीयमानत्वात् ॥ ५, ६ ॥ नाप्यनवस्था। धर्माणां परधर्मासंभवात्। धर्मिणोऽनेकरूपत्वं न धर्माणां कथंचन इत्यभिधानात् ॥ ७ ॥—P. N. T. Ratnâkara pp. 740-743.

Appendices.

अत्र च विरोधस्योपलक्षणत्वात् वैयधिकरण्यम् etc.—Much of the commentary of this stanza has been borrowed from Hemacandra's Com. on his Pramâṇa-Mîmâṃsâ and the same recurs in the later Saptabhaṅgi-Taraṅgiṇi. cf.—

1. "द्रव्यपर्याययोरैकान्तिकभेदाभेदपरिहारेण कथंचिद्भेदाभेदवादः स्याद्वादिभिरुपेयते। न चासौ युक्तो विरोधादिदोषात्। विधिप्रतिषेधरूपयोरेकत्र वस्तुन्य-

संभवात् नीलानीलवत् ॥ १ः—अथ केनचिद्रूपेण भेदः केनचिदभेदः । एवं सति भेदस्यान्यदधिकरणम् अभेदस्य चान्यद् इति वैयधिकरण्यम् ॥ २ः—यं वात्मानं पुरोधाय भेदो यं चाश्रित्याभेदस्तावप्यात्मानौ भिन्नाभिन्नौ अन्यथैकान्तवाद-प्रसक्तिः तथा च सत्यनवस्था ॥ ३ः—येन रूपेण भेदस्तेन भेदश्चाभेदश्च येन चाभेद-स्तेनाप्यभेदश्च भेदश्चेति संकरः ॥ :—येन रूपेण भेदस्तेनाभेदो येनाभेदस्तेन भेद इति व्यतिकरः ॥ ५ः—भेदाभेदात्मकत्वे च वस्तुनो विविक्तेनाकारेण निश्चेतुमशक्तेः संशयः ॥ ६ः—ततश्चाप्रतिपत्तिरिति न विषयव्यवस्था ॥ नैवम्—प्रतीयमाने वस्तुनि विरोधस्यासंभवात् । यत्संनिधाने यो नोपलभ्यते स तस्य विरोधीति निश्चीयते । उपलभ्यमाने च वस्तुनि को विरोधगन्धावकाशः । नीलानील-योरपि यद्येकत्रोपलभ्योऽस्ति तदा नास्ति विरोधः । एकत्र चित्रपटीज्ञाने सौगतै-र्नीलानीलयोर्विरोधाभ्युपगमात् । एकस्यैव पटादेश्चलाचलरक्तारक्तावृतानावृतादि-विरुद्धधर्माणामुपलब्धेः प्रकृते को विरोधशङ्कावकाशः। एतेन वैयधिकरण्यदोषोऽप्य-पास्तः । तयोरेकाधिकरणत्वेन प्रागुक्तयुक्तिदिशा प्रतीतेः । यदप्यनवस्थानं दूषण-मुपन्यस्तं तदप्यनेकान्तवादिमतानभिज्ञेनैव तन्मतम् । द्रव्यपर्यायात्मके वस्तुनि द्रव्यपर्यायावेव भेदः भेदध्वनिकौ तयोरेवाभिधानात् द्रव्यरूपेणाभेदः इति द्रव्य-मेवाभेदः एकानेकत्वाद्वस्तुनः ॥ यौ च संकरव्यतिकरौ तौ मेचकज्ञाननिदर्शनेन सामान्यविशेषदृष्टान्तेन च परिहृतौ ॥ अथ तत्र तथा प्रतिभासः समाधानं पर-स्यापि तदेवास्तु प्रतिभासस्यापक्षपातित्वात् । निर्णीते चार्थे संशयोऽपि न युक्तः तस्य सम्यक्प्रतिपत्तौ दुर्घटत्वात् । प्रतिपन्ने च वस्तुन्यप्रतिपत्तिरिति साहसम् । उपलब्ध्यभिधानादनुपलम्भोऽपि न सिद्धस्ततो नाभाव इति दृष्टेष्टाविरुद्धं द्रव्य-पर्यायात्मकं वस्त्विति ॥

2. ननु द्रव्यपर्यायात्मकत्वेऽपि वस्तुनः कथमर्थक्रिया नाम । सा हि क्रमा-क्रमाभ्यां व्याप्ता । द्रव्यपर्यायैकान्तवदुभयात्मकादपि व्यावर्तताम् । शक्यं हि वक्तु-मुभयात्मा भावो न क्रमेणार्थक्रियां कर्तुं समर्थः । शक्यं हि वक्तुमुभयात्मा भावो न क्रमेणार्थक्रियां कर्तुं समर्थः । समर्थस्य क्षेपायोगात् । न च सहकार्यपेक्षा युक्ता । द्रव्यस्यापि कार्यत्वेन सहकारिकृतोपकारनिरपेक्षत्वात् । पर्यायाणां च क्षणिकत्वेन पूर्वापरकार्यकालाप्रतीक्षणात् । नाप्यक्रमेण युगपद्धि सर्वकार्याणि कृत्वा पुनर-कुर्वतोऽनर्थक्रियाकारित्वादसत्त्वं कुर्वतः क्रमपक्षभावी दोषः ॥ द्रव्यपर्यायवादयोश्च यो दोषः स उभयवादेऽपि समानः । प्रत्येकं यो भवेद्दोषो द्वयोर्भावे कथं न सः इति वचनादित्याह—

पूर्वोत्तराकारपरिहारस्वीकारस्थितिलक्षणपरिणामेनास्यार्थक्रियोपपत्तिः ॥ १. १. १४. ॥—

पूर्वोत्तरयोराकारयोर्विवर्तयोर्यथासंख्येन यौ परिहारस्वीकारौ ताभ्यां स्थितिः सैव लक्षणं यस्य स चासौ परिणामश्च। एतेनास्य द्रव्यपर्यायात्मकस्यार्थक्रियोपपद्यते। अयमर्थः। न द्रव्यरूपं न पर्यायरूपं नोभयरूपं वस्तु येन तत्पक्षभावी दोषः स्यात्। किंतु स्थित्युत्पादव्ययात्मकं शबलं जात्यन्तरमेव वस्तु। तेन तत्तत्सहकारिसंनिधाने क्रमेण युगपद्वा तां तामर्थक्रियां कुर्वतः सहकारिकृतां चोपकारपरंपरामुपजीवतो भिन्नाभिन्नोपकारादिनोदनानुमोदनाप्रमुदितात्मनः उभयपक्षभाविदोषशङ्काकलङ्कान्दिशीकस्य भावस्य न व्यापकानुपलब्धित्वेनार्थक्रियाया नापि तद्व्याप्यस्य सत्त्वस्य निवृत्तिरिति सिद्धं द्रव्यपर्यायात्मकं वस्तु प्रमाणस्य विषयः॥
—Com. on Pramâṇa-Mîmâṃsâ pp. 45-46.

Stanza XXV.

Note that reference is here made to those fundamental problems of Ontology on which the philosophers, not only of India but of the whole world, are divided, and which, therefore, provide suitable principles for their classification. (1) Some are "*Eternalists*" in regard to *all* things; they believe that everything is *permanent*. Some are "*Non-Eternalists*"; they believe that *everything changes*. Intermediate between the two are "*Semi-Eternalists*"; they believe that some things are permanent, while others not; in other words, some change, while others do not. To the first category belong Vedântins of the Śâṁkara school, who believe that one eternal principle, Brahman, is the only reality. They have, however, to recognise the fact of change or impermanence, even if they may not consider it necessary to explain it, change, according to them, being unreal and irrational and, therefore, by its very nature, incapable of explanation. To the second category belong the Buddhists who believe in impermanence or change of all things. All the other schools of thought fall between these two extremes, which are represented in the history of Greek Philosophy by Parmenides and Heraclitus, and in Modern European Philosophy by Spinoza and Hume. Between the two fall all other schools of thought, which accept both the extremes in one way or another. In the Nyâya-Vaiśeṣika school, some things are regarded as permanent, and others as impermanent. Things, accordingly, fall in two distinct classes; nothing being at once permanent and impermanent, as with the Jainas. The Sâṁkhya school maintains the doctrine of Prakṛti and Vikṛti, that is to say, of one eternally changing Prakṛti. Virtually, this makes the nearest approach to the Jaina doctrine of द्रव्य and पर्याय, but it still differs from it, inasmuch as in the Sâṁkhya view, the two, viz., Prakṛti and Vikṛti, are not regarded as *two aspects of one Reality from different points of view*, as in the Jaina Philosophy. I do not know, however, whether this difference should be regarded as substantial and essential, or as formal and of no moment. Patañjali's Yoga and those schools of Vedânta which are known as Bhedâbheda and Viśiṣṭâdvaita belong to this intermediate class, as far as they endorse the view of the Sâṁkhya.

(2) Another principle of the classification of philosophers is their attitude regarding the problem of the *Universal* and the *Particular*, or the One and the Many. The differences among philosophers in this matter run on parallel lines to those which divide them on the question of Permanence and Change. Compare on the problem of the Universal and the Particular the controversies of Realism, Nominalism and Conceptualism in the history of European Philosophy.

(3) The third point on which Philosophers are divided is the competence or incompetence of words to capture the nature of Reality, when it is found to be consisting of contradictories from opposite points of view. All philosophers agree that Reality cannot contain contradiction from one and the same point of view. But the Jaina maintains that it can and it does contain contradiction, although from different points of view. According to the Vedânta of the Śâṁkara school this only points to unreality and irrationality (Mâyâ, Avidyâ, Anirvacanîyatâ), or contradiction in Reality or Truth.

(4) *Being vs. Non-Being* is another problem which divides philosophers. This division also, like No (2) runs parallel to that in No (1). The two are not only reconcileable, but always coexist, although as viewed from different view-points, according to Jainas. The two extremes were harmonised by Heraclitus in the category of Becoming, which however, sinks back into that of non-Being.

Stanza XXVI.

These controversies of नित्यवाद and अनित्यवाद go back to the Brahmajâla Sûtta of the Buddhist canon where a record is made of the various schools of "Brâhmaṇas and recluses" who hold different views. Among them are Eternalists ('Sassatikâ'), Non-eternalists (' Asassatikâ'), Semi-eternalists, Annihilationists (Ucchedavâda). Thus some are reported as holding—"Eternal is the soul; and the world, giving birth to nothing new, is steadfast as a mountain peak, as a pillar firmly fixed; and though these living creatures transmigrate and pass away, fall from one state of existence and spring up in another, yet they are for ever and ever." Again, it is said "There are, brethren, some recluses and Brâhmaṇas who are Eternalists with regard to some things, and in regard to others Non-eternalists." "Some recluses and Brâhmaṇas are Semi-eternalists, and maintain that the soul and the world are in some respects eternal, and in some not." (S. B. B. Brahmajâla Sutta).

In some of these doctrines, one may see Anekântavâda of the Jainas. Also, "This world is neither finite nor yet infinite."

अवस्थितस्य द्रव्यस्य पूर्वधर्मनिवृत्तौ etc.—On it the commentator, Vâcaspatimiśra, puts a note: "**धर्मशब्द आश्रितत्वेन धर्मलक्षणावस्था-वाचकः**" i. e. **धर्म** includes, besides itself, **लक्षण** and **अवस्था**.

Stanza XXVII.

"अप्राप्तानां प्राप्तिः":—Definition of संयोग as given in Praśastapâda-Bhâṣya.

वर्षातपाभ्यां etc.—and यस्मिन्नेव हि संताने etc.—Quoted in the Ratnâkarâvatârikâ Ch. VII 57, pp. 145 and 143 respectively.

Stanza XXVIII.

" षाण्मासिक "—This is a strange misprint in the Notes on p. 293 for पर्यायास्तिक.

नैगम—None of the commentators' explanations of the word seems to be satisfactory, and there is, besides, no certain tradition on the point. Probably it originally meant the point of view involved in coming from the general to the particular, in which both the general and the particular get equal recognition. Compare 'निगमन' of the Nyâya school in which one comes to the particular from the general or universal, both of which are equally real.

संग्रह—The viewpoint of the comprehension and consequent merging of particulars in the universal. (com. सम्, prehendere-to take-ग्रह्).

ऋजुसूत्र—Superficial point of view. Probably, applied at first to those who read the Sûtras superficially without the light of the commentary.

शब्द, समभिरूढ and एवंभूत—In these nayas exaggerated importance is attached to the form of expression, in the ascending order. शब्द—In it differences of grammatical forms make realities different. समभिरूढ—In it differences implied by different synonyms cause differences of Reality. एवंभूत—It takes note of the present condition only, and unless an object is possessing the kriyâ at the time, the name will not be applied to it.

Stanza XXIX.

यथा चोक्तं वार्तिककारेण—अत एव च विद्वत्सु मुच्यमानेषु etc.—" अयं ग्रन्थो न विज्ञायते"—A. M. P. But Śrîdhara quotes this in his Nyâyakandalî p. 88. "यथाहुर्वार्तिककाराः" etc.

पृथिव्यादीनां जीवत्वमित्थं साधनीयम् etc.—I cannot agree with Jacobi* and other writers who see primitive animism in the Jaina doctrine of Universal sentiency. To me it appears to be a conscious and deliberate expression of sympathy with all Nature which is based on the belief that all its objects are endowed with life. I would rather go without the early date, if it rests only on this ground, than accept this humiliating characterisation of its great religious tenet.

Stanza XXX.

अन्ये त्वेवं व्याचक्षते—Evidently Malliṣeṇa seems to know earlier glosses on the Dvâtriṁśikâ, written or oral.

अन्योन्यपक्ष etc.—The derivation of the word पक्ष given by M. and found elsewhere also (see Commentary on the "Nyâya-praveśa") is clearly far-fetched. पक्ष implies the metaphor of one wing of the bird as opposed to the other wing, this word having originated in the atmosphere of debate.

यथा हि समीचीनं etc.—Unlike the Vedântin who demonstrates अनिर्वचनीयता and gives rise to agnosticism—although unintentionally—the Jaina establishes harmony among all the darśanas by recognising that all are partially right, rather than that every one is partially wrong.† This implies, however, that the Jaina steps in only after other systems have done their work, it may be, even of mutual recriminations.

---

* S. B. E. Vol. XLV Introduction, p. xxxiii.

† That the present work displays the latter feature shows how difficult it is to live up to one's ideal.

Appendix

वस्तुतस्तु—अनेकान्तप्रक्रियायां सर्वेषां प्रवादिनामपि प्रतिपत्तिरेव। एकानेकात्मकस्य वस्तुनः सर्वसंमतत्वात्। सांख्यास्तावत् सत्त्वरजस्तमसां साम्यावस्था प्रधानमित्याहुः। तेषां मते प्रसादलाघवशोषतापवारणादिभिन्नस्वभावानामनेकात्मनामेकप्रधानात्मकस्वीकारिणैकानेकात्मकवस्तुनः स्वीकृतत्वात्। ननु प्रधानं नामैकं वस्तु नास्ति। साम्यावस्थामापन्नाः सत्त्वरजस्तमोगुणा एव प्रधानम्। सत्त्वरजस्तमसां समूहे प्रधानपदशक्तेः स्वीकारात्। इति चेन्न॥ तथाप्येकानेकात्मकवस्तुस्वीकारस्याक्षतत्वात्। समुदायसमुदायिनोरभेदात् समुदायिनां गुणानामनेकेषां समुदायस्य चैकस्याभेदाभ्युपगमात्॥

नैयायिकास्तु—द्रव्यत्वादिकं सामान्यविशेषमभ्युपगच्छन्ति। अनुवृत्तिव्यावृत्तिप्रत्ययविषयत्वाद् द्रव्यत्वादिकं सामान्यविशेषः। द्रव्यं द्रव्यमित्यनुगतबुद्धिविषयत्वात् सामान्यम्। गुणो न द्रव्यं कर्म न द्रव्यमिति व्यावृत्तिबुद्धिविषयत्वाद्विशेष इति। एवं च सामान्यविशेषात्मकत्वमेकस्याभ्युपगतम्। एवं गुणत्वं कर्मत्वं च सामान्यविशेष इति बोध्यम्॥

सौगतास्तु—मेचकज्ञानमेकमनेकाकारमभ्युपगच्छन्ति। पञ्चवर्णात्मकं रत्नं मेचकम्। तज्ज्ञानं नैकप्रतिभासात्मकमेव। चित्रज्ञानत्वविरोधात्। नीलपीतादिनानाकारज्ञानं हि चित्रज्ञानं न त्वेकाकारमेव। नापि मेचकज्ञानमनेकमेव। मेचकज्ञानमिदमित्यनुभवविरोधात्। इमानि मेचकज्ञानानीत्यनुभवप्रसङ्गाच्च। ततश्च तदेकानेकात्मकं चित्रज्ञानं सौगतानामभिमतम्॥

चार्वाकास्तु—'पृथिव्यापस्तेजोवायुरिति चत्वारि तत्त्वानि। तेभ्यश्चैतन्यं किण्वादिभ्यो मदशक्तिवत्।' इति बार्हस्पत्यसूत्रानुरोधात् पृथिव्यादिभूतचतुष्टयपरिणामश्चैतन्यमिति वदन्ति। तच्च न पृथिव्याद्यपेक्षयाऽतिरिक्तमेकं तैरभ्युपगम्यते। तत्त्वान्तरप्रसङ्गात्। भूतचतुष्टयवादव्याघातात्। नापि पृथिव्यादिकमेकैकमेव तत्। घटादेरपि चेतनत्वापत्तेः। किं तु पृथिव्याद्यनेकात्मकमेकं चैतन्यमिति॥

मीमांसकास्तु—प्रमातृप्रमितिप्रमेयाकारमेकं ज्ञानम्। घटमहं जानामीत्यनुभवात्। ज्ञानानां स्वतः प्रकाशत्वात्। इति वदन्ति। तत्रानेकपदार्थनिरूपितविषयताशाल्येकं ज्ञानं स्वीकृतम्। विषयतानां च ज्ञानस्वरूपत्वात्तादृशविषयतात्रयात्मकमेकं ज्ञानं स्वीकृतमिति। एवं रीत्या मतान्तरेष्वनेकान्तप्रक्रिया बुद्धिमद्भिरूह्येति सर्वमनवद्यम्॥—Saptabhaṅgîtaraṅgiṇî.

प्रज्ञप्त्यस्तितया वाच्यः मुद्गलो द्रव्यतो न तु—यतश्च प्रज्ञप्तितोऽस्तीति वक्तव्यो द्रव्यतो नास्तीति वक्तव्यः। एवमनेकांशवादपरिग्रहे नैवास्तित्वे दोषावकाशो न नास्तित्वे॥—Mahâyânasûtrâlamkâra pp. 155.

सदसत्ख्यातिर्बाधाबाधात्—(Sâṁkhyasûtra V. 56) । न च सदसत्त्वयोर्विरोध इति वाच्यम् । प्रकारभेदेनाविरोधात् । यथाहि लौहित्यं बिम्बरूपेण सत् स्फटिकगतप्रतिबिम्बरूपेण चासदिति दृष्टम् । यथा वा रजतं वणिग्वीथीस्थरूपेण सच्छुक्त्यध्यस्तरूपेण चासत् तथैव सर्वं जगत् स्वरूपतः सत् चैतन्याद्यावध्यस्तरूपेण चासदिति ।...एवमेवावस्थाभेदेनापि सदसत्त्वमविरुद्धम् । यथा हि वृक्षादिः प्ररूढाद्यवस्थाभिः सन्नप्यङ्कुराद्यवस्थाभिरसन् भवति तथैव प्रकृत्यादिकं सदसदात्मकमिति ॥—Sâṁkhya Pravacana Bhâṣya.

Stanza XXXI.

जङ्घालतया=जाङ्घिकतया=वेगवत्तया. जङ्घालता literally means, the state of being possessed of good, powerful thighs, hence of powerful legs.

दुर्लभं परस्मैपदम्—I think Malliṣeṇa is wrong in rejecting the better known √लङ्घ् to cross (अतिक्रमणार्थे लङ्घि) and preferring the obscure √लघु to dry up (लघु शोषणे). The reason which he assigns for his preference of the latter (दुर्लभं परस्मैपदम्) is not very weighty, being rightly countered by his second thought—" अनित्यं वा आत्मनेपदम् ".

Stanza XXXII.

सिद्धाञ्जन—Cf. the titles " न्यायसिद्धाञ्जन ", and " सिद्धान्तसिद्धाञ्जन " of Kṛṣṇânanda.

उदयप्रभ—author of " धर्माभ्युदय ", not of " धर्मशर्माभ्युदय ". The supplementary note occurring on p. 328 is a slip, which has been corrected on p. xiii of the Introduction.

Appendix A : Various Readings.

I.

Page 1.

A. B. E. Cm. begin with उँ नमः सर्वज्ञाय; C. उँ नमो वातगणाय; H. उँ नमः श्रीसर्वज्ञाय नमः, D. F. G. अर्हं;

3. B. F. K. read रागद्वेषमुखद्विषां

10. E. G. श्रयन्ति for श्रयन्ते

Page 2.

17. A. C. E. F. °दुष्षमारजनि, Bm. Cm. Dm. Em. H दुःखमा-रजनि; B दुःषमारजनि.

19. G. Bm. भूपाल for क्ष्मापाल; H omits क्ष्मापाल; G. reads जीवानुसंजीवित°

20. Bm. °कल्पावधिस्थिरीकृत for °कल्पावधिस्थायि.

21. H adds लक्षणसाहित्यतर्कागमाः after निरवद्य.

22. Am. omits द्वात्रिंशत् after विरचित.

23. G. reads रूपमयोग्यव्यवच्छेदा°

26. A. Bm. etc. परिषद् for H's पर्षद्.

29. Am. Bm. Cm. omit विषय after पर्याय

30. A. omits यस्य सोऽनन्तविज्ञानः

31. B. adds अतीतदोषमिति after तथा

33. Am. reads अशक्यसिद्धान्तः; Am. लक्षणोऽस्य

31.—40. H. omits from तथाऽतीता to वचनातिशयः

Page 3.

40. G. omits भणनात् after प्रणयन.

50. Am. omits अपि after तीर्थिनिकारदर्शने.

52. D. अवशं for अवश्यं; Am reads °विज्ञानस्य for °विज्ञानत्वस्य; H. नैवं for न.

56. D. E. H. read सर्वं पश्यतु वा मा वा इष्टमर्थं तु पश्यतु। for तस्मादनुष्ठानगतम् etc.; but H. notes the latter on margin as पाठान्तरम्.

57. D. F. H read एतान् गृध्रान् for एते गृध्रान्.

Page 4.

76. Am. omits अनेन after विशेषणेन.

80. G. omits विशेष्यपदमपि after श्रीवर्धमानमिति.

Page 5.

81. Am. Bm. Cm. Dm. Em. अनुभावात्मक for अनुभवात्मक.

82. Am. omits सिद्धान्ते प्रसिद्धत्वात्.
84. Am. and D. read बाह्यलक्षणत्वेन for बाह्यलक्षणसंख्याया उपलक्षणत्वेन
85. A omits लक्षणानां after अन्तरंग०
89. A omits प्राप्ति after गुणस्थान०
93. A. B. C. F. G. H. read अभ्रादित्वान्मत्वर्थीयोऽच्प्रत्ययः for अर्शादित्वा०.
95. and मुख्यादेर्यः for शाखादेर्यः
98. C. omits स्वयंभूः after भवतीति.
99. G. बुद्धः for संबुद्धः.
100. G. स्तोत्रविषयीकर्तुं for स्तुति०
104. Am. परोपदेशानुवर्त्यादि for परोपदेशान्यानुवृत्त्यादि०

Page 6.

106. Am reads श्रीवर्धमानत्वविशेषणेन
107. H. reads हेतुमद्भावेन for हेतुहेतुमद्भावेन
110. G. H. चतुष्टय for चतुष्क०
111. C. omits वर्धमानत्वमुपचर्यते; यद्यपि च after अवस्थानयोगात्.
115. F. reads विज्ञानतत्त्वं for विज्ञानत्वम्
117. A. C. D. E. F. G. अपि केवलदर्शनापरपर्यायस्य for केवलज्ञानापरपर्यायस्य Bm. परार्थम् for पारार्थ्यम्.
119. H. निरूपयति for प्ररूपयति.
121. Am reads ज्ञानमात्रतायाः for ज्ञानमात्रायाः.
122. Am omits समता.

Page 7.

134. H लक्षणत्वेन for लक्षणेन. Am reads संबुद्धगुणत्वेन.
135. Am omits इति after श्रीवर्धमानम्
137. D. reads श्रीवर्धमानाभिधमात्मरूपमिति विशेष्यपदम् प्रकृष्ट आत्मा आत्मरूपस्तं परमात्मानमिति and omits from विशेष्यमनुवर्तमानम् to व्याख्येयमिति.
138. A. C. E. F. G. H. and Am. add प्रकृष्ट (Am. प्रकृष्टम्.) आत्मा आत्मरूपस्तं परमात्मानमिति यावत् after विशेष्यपदम्; but Am omits from यावत् to व्याख्येयमिति.
140. G. काव्यार्थः for वृत्तार्थः

II.

2. A. आप्तान्यवच्छेदः for आप्तत्वान्यवच्छेदः.
3. Am reads प्रामाण्यमुच्यते स्तुतेः for प्रामाण्यमश्नुते

5. Am. Bm. वस्तुवादिवाख्य० for वस्तुवादित्वाख्यम्; Am. omits एव after गुणविशेषम्.

Page 8.

10. E. reads लक्षणाच्चतुर्थी.

12. D. E. and Am Em. read तत्किं तान्यपि स्तोष्यसे उत नेत्याशंक्य for तत्किमर्थं तत्रोपेक्षेत्याशङ्क्य.

13. Am. C. H. add पूर्वक before विशेष०; H एकं for एकमेकम्.

15. D. अस्मिन् for तस्मिन्; Am. reads तस्मिन्नपि कस्मिन्नपि for तस्मिन्नेकस्मिन्नपि.

21. G. Am परीक्षा for परीक्षणम्.

24. A. स्वरूपत्वात् for रूपत्वात्

III.

1. D. E H. कुतीर्थिकाः for कुतीर्थ्याः

Page 9.

4. A. C. G. Cm. omit अदसस्तु विप्रकृष्टे इति वचनात्.

6. H मा शिष्यन् for मा शिश्रियन्.

10. A. C. E and Am भगवान् for भवान्। F खण्डम् for काण्डम्.

11. D निषिध्य for प्रतिषिध्य.

12. Am. उपदर्शयति for उपदिशति.

13. Am. Dm. read सत्ययुक्तियुक्तम्.

16. Am. omits नयपथ० after अवितथ० Bm. Cm. Dm. Em. read नयपथविचारणायाः

17. D. adds च before तत्फलम्.

18. E. लोचनानि for विलोचनानि.

20. C. omits ततः before अस्वदमानः.

23. G. omits यदि before पारमेश्वरे.

24. D. किमर्थं स्वान्। for किमर्थं तान्.

Page 10.

25. D. E. अनवेक्ष्य for अनपेक्ष्य.

26. F स्वार्थेन for स्वार्थत्वेन.

27. A. हितोपदेशापरः हितोपदेशादपरः.

30. H adds तथा before उवाच; F. वाचस्पतिः for वाचकमुख्यः

IV.

2. Am. Bm. Cm. Dm. Em. तत्काण्य for तावत्काण्य; Dm. omits अभिमत before तत्त्वानि

Page 11.

7. E reads आत्मस्वरूपात् for आत्मीयस्वरूपात्

9. A. D. E. G. add व्यावृत्तिः before विजातीयेभ्यः
10. Am. Bm. Cm. Dm. Em. read संमिलिते for संवलिते
15. A. C. D. E व्यावृत्ति for व्यतिवृत्ति॰
19. D. स्वरूपतया for रूपतया
22 Am. omits न before सामान्यविशेषयोः; F reads सामान्यविशेषणयोः, and omits पृथक् before पदार्थान्तरत्व॰
24. Cm. omits विशेषण after एकान्तभेदे॰
26. H omits एव after एकस्मिन्
27. Am. Bm. Cm. Dm. Em. read अनन्तधर्मात्मकत्वाद्वस्तुन;

Page 12.

33. E. omits कस्मादेतत्प्रत्ययद्वयं वदन्तः before इत्याह॰
36. G. इति for इत्यनेन॰
37. A. नाभूत् for मा भूत्; E. G. omit मा भूत् पराभिमतस्य सत्यरूपतेति विशेषणमिदम्॰
39. A. F. G. H. परिकल्पितं for प्रकल्पितम्; Am. reads यथा स्यात्तथा॰
40. Am. अविष्वग्भावे॰
44. C. D. E. F. H. नोपपद्यते for नोपपद्येत.
45. Am. एकान्तताभेदे; C. G. वा for च
46. Am. Dm. omit वस्तुनः प्रमाणेन॰
47. पक्ष after निरपेक्ष॰
48. Am. उपहसनत्वं for उपहसनीयत्वम्॰
49. Dm. omits स्वरूप after वस्तु॰

V.

Page 13.

1. D. omits अथ तदभिमतावेकान्तनित्यानित्यपक्षौ दूषयन्नाह॰
3. Am. रूपम् for स्वरूपम्॰
4. Am. omits च after किम्; A. C. B. E. F. H. आत्मकम् for आत्मकत्वम्।
8. E. omits धर्म before शबलैकवस्तु.
10. Am. Dm. तथाहि for यथाहि॰
12. A. एव for एवम्॰
15. A. F. G. स्वभावत् for स्वभावत्व॰.
18. Am. reads तत्रैकान्ता नित्यानित्यया॰

Page 14.

21. D. E. H. आश्रयन्तः for आसादयन्तः
22. A. C. D. E. G. H omit द्रव्य after पुद्गल॰.

24. A. and Am. Bm. Cm. Dm. Em. Fm. स्थास्य for स्थासक.
28. C. G. तमसः for तमः G. चाक्षुषत्वम् for चाक्षुषम्.
32. Am. आलोकमपेक्षदर्शनाः for आलोकापेक्षदर्शनाः.
34. B. C. D. E. G. H. शैत्यस्पर्श for शीतस्पर्श०; E. शैत्येस्पर्श०.
38. E. G. प्रतिषेध्यति F निषेध्यानि for प्रतिषेध्यानि; H omits च before वाच्यम्.
41. C. omits रूप after धूम०.
42. A. B. C. E. यदापि for यद्यपि.

Page 15.

47. E reads अवकाशमाकाशम्.
49. C. अस्य for तस्य.
53. C. E. G. omit विनाश० after संयोग०.
54. D. परिमाण० for परिणाम०.
55. A. B. C. D. E. F. G. H. एकाधिकरणत्वम् for एकाधिकरणम्.
57. Am. reads तद्भावाव्ययनित्यम्.
58. Cm. सद्भावात्। C. H. यन्नव्येति for नव्येति.
60. Am. यदाहि for यदिाहि। एष्यति for इष्यते.
64. A. B. E. G. H. omit नचाकाशं न द्रव्यम्.
68. Am. Em. read मुख्यार्थस्य स्पर्शत्वात्.

Page 16.

69. A. B. C. D. E. read घटादि for घटपटादि.
70. F. नियति for नियत०। A. B. E. F. G. परिणामवशात् for परिमाणवशात्.
71. A. E. omit पटाकाश० after घटाकाश०.
73. F omits अवस्थाभेदे before अवस्थावतः.
74. A. E. G. नित्यानित्यं व्योम F व्योम नित्यानित्यम् for नित्यानित्यत्वं व्योम्नः.
75. A. H. स्वयंभुवापि for स्वायंभुवा अपि.
77. Am. धर्मः for धर्मी.
79. C. H. वर्धमानः for वर्धमानकः.
86. Am. ध्रौव्यात्मक for ध्रौव्यात्मकत्वे; F adds अपि after ध्रौव्यात्मकत्वे.
87. Am. B. read आकाशादिकम् for आकाशात्मादिकम्.
88. Am. omits हि after इत्थम्.
90. Cm, धर्म्यसमर्थन० for धर्मसमर्थन०.

Page 17.

93. Am. अथ च for अत्र च; G. परसिद्धया for परप्रसिद्धया.

94. A. reads एव for एवम्.

96. H. धरायाम् for पृथिव्याम्.

98. B. नित्या चानित्या च for नित्यानित्या च.

99. B. E. F. द्रव्यकार्यलक्षण॰ for कार्यद्रव्यलक्षण॰; Am लक्षणः॰; H. omits विषय॰ after लक्षण॰.

101. A. H. जलादिषु for अबादिषु.

103. Dm. विभागाविति नित्यानित्यपक्षम्.

109. Am. omits तावत् before क्रमेण.

111. H. reads कालक्षेपिणोऽसामर्थ्यप्राप्तेः। Cm. omits क्रिया after प्रथम॰.

113. B. C. D. E. F. G. H. सामर्थ्यं for समर्थम्.

116. A. C. D. E. F. G omit समर्थो वा.

117. Em. reads ननु सर्वमपि बीजम्; C. E. F. G. H. उपेक्षते for अपेक्षते.

Page 18.

118. A. C. E. G. H. reads जलानलानिलादि Am. reads इलाजलानिलादिसहितम्.

121. D. reads किन्नासार्थक्रियायामुदास्ते, F किन्न सोऽर्थक्रियायामुदास्ते for किं न तदाप्यर्थक्रियायामुदास्ते.

125. K. विन्ध्यादेः for विन्ध्याद्रेः; Am. उपकारकः for उपकारः.

134. Am. omits भावः after क्रमेणार्थक्रियाम्.

Page 19.

143. Am. omits अपि after अनित्यपक्षः.

152. Am. omits अपि after वस्तुत्वे; Am. F क्षणिकत्वे for क्षणिकत्वम्.

155. C. E. G. H. omit रूपादि after पूरादि; Bm. Cm. Dm. read बीजपूररूपादिक्षणः.

158. F. G. H. K. इति ते for इति चेत्।

161. Am. Dm. स्वभावानामेकत्वं प्रसह्यते; H. प्रसह्येत for प्रसज्येत.

164. Am Em D. E. कार्यसांकार्यं for कार्यसांकर्यम्.

165. Am. reads रूपत्वादक्रमं न क्रमाच्च क्रमिणाम्.

167. B. C. G. H. K. add लक्षणात् before कारणात्.

Page 20.

172. Dm. omits सत्त्वमपि before व्यापकानुपलब्धिबलेन; Dm. निर्वर्तते for निवर्तते.

175. F एकस्मिन् for एकत्र.
176. Am. Bm. Dm. read नित्यपक्षानित्यपक्षविलक्षणस्य; A. लक्षणस्य, F. विचक्षणस्य for विलक्षणस्य.
177. F. adds इति after अनुभवात्.
181. H. विशेषकैः for वैशेषिकैः; Am. विचित्ररूपस्य for चित्ररूपस्य
182. E. adds पटापट० after चलाचल०; A. B. C. D. H. वृत्तानावृत्तत्वादि for वृत्तानां वृत्त्वादि०.
188. A. B. D. F. G. H. K. Bm. Cm. यद्यपि, E यद्यपि, for यद्यापि and तदपि for तदापि.
189. F. omits वस्तु.

VI.

Page 21.

4. K. reads स्रष्टा विद्यतेऽस्ति.
6. D. तत्सर्वम् for तत्तत्सर्वम्.
9. A. C. E. read भूभूधरादेः स्वकारण०
12. B. E. F. G. H. प्रतिपादित्वात् for प्रतिपादितत्वात्.

Page 22.

22. A. B. C. E. K. समापनीपद्येत.
31. Am. omits स before स्ववशः.
36. E. अनीश्वरापत्तिः for अनीश्वरत्वापत्तिः
38. F कृतकत्वापत्तिः for कृतकत्वप्राप्तिः.
40. Em. omits स्यात् after अनित्यो वा.
42. C. G. K. नित्यानित्यकल्पनायाम्, B नित्यानित्यविकल्पकल्पनायाम्.

Page 23.

46. Am. Dm. add च after एव
51. A. B. C. D. E. F. G. H. K. भवन्ति for वदन्ति। चैकम् for चैवम्; F omits स्तुतिकारः;
52. Am. Cm. Em. omit इति before एकवचनम्
53. B. D. F. H. add इतरशास्तॄणामसाधारणम् before अद्वितीयम्
56. Am. Bm. Cm. Dm. Em. omit वाचम् before आचष्टे
57. Cm. reads पापकर्मबंधकल्माषितात्मनाम्; A. C. D. H. कल्मषित Bm. Dm. B. E. G. K कल्माषित and E. कल्मिषित० for कलुषित०; Bm. reads अपुनर्बंधमुक्तकारि.
60. A. B. D. E. H. गणः for गुणः
63. Am. दुष्ट Dm. E. G. दृष्ट C. reads द्रष्ट for दष्ट०

64. उपालभनीयः for उपालम्भनीयः
65. Am. H. read भासयंतो न भानवीया भानवः
66. Dm. कौशिकालोकहेतु०; Am. D. कौशिकस्यालोकहेतु०; F. कौशिकस्यावलोकहेतु०

Page 24.

72. Dm. reads रूपत्वमेवैते ब्रूमः
87. Am. reads वैषम्यात् for वैषम्यम् and adds विरुद्धो हेतुः before घटादयः; F. omits तदादृष्टान्तदार्ष्टान्तिकयोर्वैषम्यम् after अशरीरश्चेत् and reads अशरीरश्चेद्विरुद्धो हेतुर्घटादयः
91. Bm. reads धर्मैकदेशस्य.

Page 24.

103. A. तव for तेषाम्.
107. Am. सेवनमिवाभासते.
111. F. परपुरुषस्य for परमपुरुषस्य; H reads क्रोडीकृतजगत्त्रयस्याभ्युपगमात्.
112. Dm. वेदेन न विरोधः.
115. Am. पदार्थसार्थानाम्.

Page 26.

120. D. F. H. add यद्वा देहस्य सर्वगतत्वे नावकाशं विना व्यापारासंभवात् before द्वितीयपक्षे; Am. omits तु Am. D. read उचितकार्य कल्पनायाम्.
122. Am. reads संकल्पमात्रेण च तत्कार्यम्.
124. A. H. स्थानेषु for स्थलेषु; Bm. सर्वगतत्वेऽपि; F. omits from तथा चानिष्टापत्तिः to संभावनात्
129. A. स्वस्थ०, C. D. E. G. H. K. स्वस्थानस्थ० for स्वस्थलस्थ; D. अवकिरणम् for अवकरणम्
130. A. H. न हि for तर्हि
131. Bm. reads अंगनागहरस०
132. H reads वेदनमात्रेणैव तृप्तिप्राप्तौ for चिन्तनमात्रेणैव तृप्तिसिद्धौ.
135. A. तस्यात्मना सर्वगतत्वेन for तस्यात्मधर्मत्वेन.
143. D. श्रीहरिभद्रसूरिपादाः for श्रीहरिभद्राचार्यपादाः.

Page 27.

157. B. omits लिङ्गग्रहणेन.
164. K. कर्मपरिपाकविशेषणेनैव for कर्मपरिपाकवशेनैव.

Page 28.

168. Am. omits स्व before गुणोत्कीर्तनस्य.

169. Am. omits एव after कर्तृत्वम्.

181. A. B. F. H. K. read अनृतभाषणं प्रथमं निषिध्य and omit नानृतं ब्रूयादित्यादिना.

Page 29.

194. G. H. कृष्णाः for कृपणाः.

197. F. omits पश्चादपि before कर्तव्यनिग्रहान्

214. A. D. E. F. K. हानेः for हानिः

Page 30.

218. G. omits from सृजेत्स्वभावायोगात् to स्वभावेन जगन्ति

219. H. सृष्टिरिव for सृष्टिवत्

220. C. reads तानि संहरेण वा and omits तानि संहरेत्स्वभावान्तरेण वा K. रूपत्वे for स्वरूपत्व.

223. K. रूपत्वान्नित्यत्वहानिः for रूपत्वहानिः

227. K. अवस्थितौ for स्थितौ; B. K. क्षितिः for क्षतिः; G. adds इति after केन वार्यतेः; K. omits केवलम् before बलवत्.

VII.

Page 31.

4. A. B. C. D. E. F. G. H. K. add इति after अश्नुवते

5. B. C. F. K. add अतिभेदे after अतीवभेदे

7. H. adds स्वभावहानिः after अङ्गीक्रियमाणे

10. B. omits अपि after भिन्नत्वे.

12. D. reads अपृथक् for अयुत.

13. A. B. C. D. E. F. G. H K. समवायनात् for समवयानात्.

Page 32.

14. Am. H. व्याख्यायते for आख्यायते.

17. Am. F. मितिः for मतिः.

22. D. प्रतिभासनं for प्रतिभानं; D. omits from किंतु द्वयोरेव to न ज्ञाने प्रतिभानं

25. Cm. omits न before पटे D. H. K. add घटे before. तसमव

26. Am. reads व्यापकत्वे; C omits नित्यत्व after एकत्व; D. E. F.

27. G. H. K. read यथाकाशमेकं नित्यं व्यापकममूर्तं च तत् (G K.) सत्) सर्वैः संबन्धिभिः &c etc.

35. G. K. तत्तत् for तत् in some.

30. Am. reads स्वभावाभेदादिति

31. Am. ज्ञाने न for न ज्ञाने.
F. reads अथ कथं न समवायस्य प्रतिभानं for अथ कथं समवायस्य न ज्ञाने प्रतिभासनं.
H. प्रतिभासनं for प्रतिभानं.

36. A. इहेदमिति मति for इहेदमिति इहेदमिति.
B. F. G. H. K. read इहेदमितिमतिरिहेदमिति.

Page 33.

38. D. तथा च for यथा.

40. E. omits वस्त्वन्तरं after नापरं.

45. H. reads इति व्यक्त एव समवाय इह समवायत्वं for इह समवाये समवायत्वं.

47. A. B. C. D. E. F. G. H. K. add एवं after समवेतं.
A. B. C. D. E. omit एवं after समवायत्वं.

50. Cm. reads महासाहसिक्य for साहसिक्य.
Am. Bm. Cm. Dm. Em. omits पुनः after आलस्य.

52. Dm. reads त्वतलाभिव्यङ्ग्यस्य for त्वतलादिप्रत्ययाभिव्यङ्ग्यस्य.

56. Reading of A. B. C. D. E. F. G. H. K.; some add विपश्चित् before चेतः Am. reads जातिरुद्रवतीति केन. B. reads जातिरुत्पद्यन्ती for जातिरुद्रवन्ती. D. adds इति after उद्रवन्ती

61. Am. reads उभयत्रापि व्यभिचारात्.

Page 34.

69. D. reads प्रसाधन for साधन.

VIII.

Page 35.

18. G. omits from गुणकर्मभ्यो to गुणत्वं सामान्यं.

20. F. घटादिकं for घटत्वादिकं.

Page 36.

27. D. E. G. H. K. द्रव्यं न भवति । F. द्रव्यत्वमेव न भवति.

35. B. omits तथा before न सत्ता कर्म.
D. F. G. H. K. भावः for सत्ता.

43. A. आकृति for तुल्याकृति.

49. Cm. Dm. द्रवत्वादिवत् for द्रव्यत्वादिवत्.

Page 37.

54. C. omits कारणं after असाधारणं.
H. वचो युक्तिः for वाचो.

61-65. C. omits from तत्रैव सत्ता to अनुवृत्तिप्रत्ययः and from स एव सदिति to त्वमपि विद्यते.

71. F. स्वरूपसत्त्वहानिः; K. स्वरूपत्वहानिः; लक्षणत्व for लक्षण.

Page 38.

85. C. आत्मनो वैशेषिकगुणानां for आत्मविशेषगुणानां

91. A. D. विशेषगुणानां for वैशेषिकगुणानां.

Page 39.

109. B. मोक्ष for मुक्त.

122. Am. Dm. G. H. तच्छास्त्रोपनिबन्धनः कृतः; E. शब्दार्थ for शास्त्रार्थ.

123. Am. अथ for अत्र

125. Am. adds सुसूत्रमिति चोपहासवचनं before उपहसनीयता etc.

Page 40.

130. Dm. विशेषेषु for अशेषेषु.

134. C. omits from बहुत्वादयमपि to सत्सदित्यनुगम.

136. A. F. G. H. K. स्वरूपसत्व Am. स्वपररूपसत्त्व for स्वरूपत्व.

139. F. adds नैवं before असति.

142. C. मुख for मुख्य.

144. Am. H. omit पुनः after विशेषेषु.

Page 41.

166. Am. reads सर्वत्रवृत्तेरेव विशेषतः

168. Am. H. omit च after विनाशे.

Page 42.

179. F. G. H. read स्वपरप्रकाशस्वभावता.

181. B. H. प्रकाशत्वं for प्रकाशकत्वं

182. E. G. संबन्धन for संबन्ध. H. स्वसंबन्धनस्वभावौ for स्वपर etc.

184. C. F. H. K. निबन्धनस्य for निबन्धस्य.

187. Am. reads तथेहात्मन्यपि ज्ञानम्

195. Dm. omits आन्तरं before एकान्तेन.

198. B. D. E. F. G. H. K. some omit दीपेन before चक्षुषा.

199. Reading of D. F. G. H. some omit सति after तथा च

201. A. B. C. D. E. परिणामे च or परिणामेन.

202. Am. reads गृहीत्वा तमर्थं व्यवस्यति.

Page 43.

213. Am. Cm. read वेष्टयतीत्यत्र अथ परिकल्पितः

213. A. B. C. D. E. F. G. H. K. अभेदे यथा कर्तृकरणभावस्तथात्रापि.

216. B. कल्पना for परिकल्पना.

217. Am. omits अपि after अभेदे.

226. F. समानाधिकरण for समानाधिकरणतया.

Page 45.

257. Am. Cm. A. C. G. H. साधनविकलो for साध्य.

263. F. adds श्रैव्य after व्यय.

269. C. omits परस्परानुषक्तयोः after प्रियाप्रिययोः

Page 46.

286. Am. शिलाशकलकल्पं for शिलाकल्पं

287. Bm. Em. C. H. K. add दुःखसंवेदनरूपत्वादस्य सुखदुःखयोरेकस्याभावेऽपरस्यावश्यं भावात् after उपपादयितुं यतेत.

298. Am. reads विचारयन्ति for विवेचयन्ति

Page 47.

305. B. D. F. H. K. add इहापि विषयनिवृत्तिजं सुखमनुभवसिद्धं तद्यदि मोक्षविशिष्टं नास्ति ततो मोक्षो दुःखरूप एव आपद्यते इत्यर्थः after लिप्सूनामेव.

311. A. B. C. D. E. F. G. H. K. add स्यात्तदा न प्रेक्षावतां (K. अत्र न) प्रवृत्तिः स्याद्भवति चे(K. वे)यं ततः सिद्धो मोक्षः after त्वदभिमतो मोक्षः

Page 48.

331. A. G. H. K. पापक्षये for पापक्षयः

337. Dm. मोक्षस्यैव योगात्

340. G. omits युक्तिरिक्तेयमुक्तिरिति काव्यार्थः

IX.

1. D. omits स्वयं before संवेद्यमानं। and adds च after आत्मनः

2. A. B. C. D. E. F. G. H. K. add अपि after संवेद्यमानम्
A. C. D. F. G. H. K. add शास्त्र after कुशास्त्र. A. B. C. D. E. F. G. H. K. read विनष्टसद्दृष्टयः for विनष्टदृष्टयः

6. K. अध्यारोहः for अध्याहारः

Page 49.

26. E. F. आत्मस्वरूपं for आत्मरूपं

Page 50.

36. D. अन्यथा for इतरथा.

37. Reading of G. H. K.; some read उत्पाद्यन्ते for उत्पद्यन्ते
39. F. omits साधने after सर्वगतत्व.
40. D. अदृष्टकारित्वं for अदृष्टकारितम्
41. H. दाहशक्तिवत् for दहनशक्तिवत्
42. A. C. D. G. सैव H. K. स एव for तदेव.
43. C. D. F. G. H. K. विरुद्धः for विरोधः
48. Am. D. H. add ततः after व्यापकः
49. G. reads परस्परानुरोधे H. परस्परानुबन्धे K. परस्परानुवेधे.
51. B. F. read समञ्जसमापनीपद्येत.
53. B. D. read शुभाशुभकर्मविपाकेन. Am. omits संवेदन । B. C. D. F. G. H. K. सम्बन्धिन for संबन्धेन D. दुःखितत्वं for दुःखित्वं

Page 51

61. A. B. C. H. read अभ्युपगमेनायं दोषः
63. G. मताङ्गीकारः for अभिमता° ।
65. H. omits दिक् before देशान्तर.
68. Cm. नियमाभावात् for नियमासंभवात्
72. Am. संयुक्तस्याकर्षणे for संयुक्तस्याप्याकर्षणे.
78. Dm. omits सजातीये.

Page 52.

81. Dm. A. B. C. E. F. omit आत्मा after आत्मभिः
88. A. B. C. E. F. G. H. K. read द्रव्यालंकारकारः
94. A. B. C. D. E. F. G. read संयोगारभ्यत्वं for संयोगात्मत्वं
98. Cm. omits अपि स्यात् after आत्मा.
101. D. reads अनित्यतानुषङ्गात्
102. Am. adds आत्मनः before प्रतिसंधानम्
103. D. स्पृशामि for स्मरामि.

Page 53.

106. A. कृतिः B. F. G. H. K. क्षितिः E. C. क्षतिः for क्षतेः
107. A. B. C. D. G. परिमाणत्वे; some परिणामत्वे.
109. B. परिणामत्वं for परिमाणत्वं
113. D omits from आकाशकालदिगात्मनां to प्रतिषेधनात्
117. K. reads प्रवेशानुपपत्ति for अनुप्रवे°
118. D. तत्रापि प्रतिषिध्यते for तत्रासौ
122. H. omits परिमान before परित्यागे.

126. A. F. G. K. omit अथ before आत्मनः

128. B. C. D. F. read शरीरसंबद्धात्म for शरीरसंबन्धात्म etc.

X.

Page 54.

4. H. बाध्ये for वाच्ये.

Page 55.

11. D. K. reads जातावेकवचनात् for जातावेकवचनप्रयोगात्

13. Am. reads स्वतत्त्वातत्त्वसाधनाव्यभिचारितया. D. reads स्वाध्यस्वतत्त्वसाधना etc.

14. D. omits अपि after साधनोपन्यासः

17. B. कुत्र for कस्मिन्. D. reads मायामुपदिष्टवान् for मायामयमुप°

19. Am. तत्वविमर्श A. B. C. E. F. G. H. K. तत्वावमर्श and D. तत्वाविमर्श for तत्वातत्वविमर्श.

21. A. omits वादः after अधिक्षेपदक्षः F. omits दक्षः after अधिक्षेप. F. reads श्रीभगवान्

25. D. F. read इव for एव after ग्रहगृहीत.

27. D. H. K. read तथा प्रतिपक्षस्थापनाहीनवाक्यं वितण्डा for तथा वितण्डा etc.

Page 56.

37. Am. Dm. Fm. A. E. व्यवस्थापन for व्यवस्थापना. D. मतस्थापनविशंस्थुलो for व्यवस्थापनाविसंस्थुलो.

40. Am. घृताद्याहुति for घृताहुति.

43. D. K. कुशिक्षित for दुःशिक्षित.

44. A. B. C. D. E. F. G. H. K. पण्डिताः for मण्डिताः

47. Am. adds वैराज्य after कारुणिकत्वं D. omits उक्तं after युक्तं

49. A. B. C. D. E. F. G. H. सूचासूत्रं for सूचनासूत्रं

52. Dm. E. omit समस्तानां A. omits व्यस्तानां

Page 57.

58. F. सहिते for संहते । K. adds भवति after मुक्तिः

59. D. omits तत् before ज्ञानक्रिययोः

61. D. reads आसूत्रितं

61. D. तत् for एतत् E. अर्थोपलब्धिः for अर्थोपलब्धिहेतुः

62. D. H. निमित्तमात्रं for निमित्तत्वमात्रं

65. D. omits च before इंद्रियसंनिकर्षादि

66. C. omits from ज्ञानाभावे to तत्र after सत्यपि.

67. A. B. C. D. E. F. add च after अव्यवहितफलं F. कारणं for करणं।

69. अत्र for अन्यत्र.

73. Am. reads स्वपरव्यवसायज्ञानं

Page 58.

79. E. omits प्रमेयत्वाभावः after करणत्वात् and reads दुःखप्रमेयाभावः

79. D. F. A. C. F. प्रमेयाभावः for प्रमेयत्वाभावः

79. Bm. Dm. add असूया after मोह.

82. K. व्यापारकत्वात् for व्यापारात्मकत्वात्

83. F. फलेन for फलं

87. Am. reads लक्षणं द्वादशविधं प्रमेयमिति तु समीचीनं

88. E. F. G. H. K. अनुप्रेक्षणीयं for अनुपेक्षणीयं

90. D. ग्रन्थान्तरं for ग्रन्थान्तरताम्

93. A. omits कपट after प्रकट.

102. F. प्रेतार्था for प्रेतादर्था.

103. F. omits कथिते after विवक्षया.

104. K. निषेधितं H. निषेधयति.

106. G. omits ब्राह्मणः after असौ.

Page 59.

108. E. ब्राह्मणस्य for ब्राह्मणत्वस्य.

112. D. F. G. add तु after मञ्चस्थाः

113. A. B. झगिति for झटिति.

114. E. reads हेतुप्रतिबन्धनप्रायं for हेतुप्रतिबिम्बनप्रायं

114. C. adds यद्यनित्यघटसाधर्म्यात्कृतकत्वादनित्यः शब्द इष्यते तर्हि नित्याकाशसाधर्म्यादमूर्तत्वान्नित्यः प्राप्नोति। after प्रत्यवस्थानं

115. Am. reads साधर्म्येण प्रत्यवस्थानं

125. H. प्रयुज्य for प्रयुज्यते.

125. A. B. H. add घटस्य हि निरवयत्वं वैधर्म्यं स्वयं सावयवत्वात् after प्रयुज्यते.

127. Cm. reads न पुनर्वैधर्म्यात्

130. D. किंचित् for कंचित्

131. D. F. add अपि after मूर्तेः

132. A. omits अपि after अनित्यः

Page 60.

138. G. omits दूषणाभासे before दूषणबुद्धि

144. A. B. E. G. H. निरनुयोग्यानुयोगः

146. D. F. K. add भवति after विग्रहस्थानं

147. Bm. Em. ऐन्द्रियकत्वमपि for ऐन्द्रियकमपि.

149. Cm. omits सः before एव ब्रुवाणः

153. A. G. add यत् before सामान्यं

153. Am. omits तद्धि before सर्वगतं

156. D. omits इति after एव.

Page 61.

158. Am. Dm. उपदेशतः for उपदिशतः

159. D. वैराग्यवर्णनं for वैराग्यव्यावर्णनं; D. प्रकाशात्मक for प्रकाशात्मकत्व.

XI.

13. H. reads प्रीणितात्मनाम्

15. D. विधा for विधान.

16. Bm. reads श्रोत्रियार्थं

Page 62.

19. B. omits आचार्यः before प्रतिविधत्ते.

23. D. omits श्रुत्वा चैवावधार्यतां after धर्मसर्वस्वं

23. F. omits श्रूयतां.........इत्यादिः after कथं

27. G. omits प्रातीतिकं and reads भवतीति किं

28. A. अकरणत्व F. अकारकत्व for अकारणत्व.

34. H. omits प्रत्युत हा कष्टमास्त । न कोपि कारुणिकः ....तेपु वदन.

37. B. C. D. E. F. G. read अयस्पिण्डः

41. A. B. C. D. E. F. G. K. दहति for प्रदहति

Page 63.

43. Cm. reads लोकपूज्यत्वदर्शनात्

44. K. वैधर्म्येण for वैषम्येण.

45. A. B. C. D. E. F. G. अयस्पिण्डादयः

47. Dm. reads वदेनानुत्पादादि.

47. D. अनुदयादिरूपा F. G. अनुत्पादिरूपा for अनुत्पादादिरूपा.

48. D. omits चेत् after इति.
52. C. गतार्थत्वात् for गतार्थत्वं.
53. K. विधापने for विधाने.
57. Am. reads अनन्योपायत्वेन सयतनया.
61. Am. reads प्रतिपादितेषु नियमादिषु.
62. A. C. D. F.G. H. K. शौनिकाधिकं; some शौनिकाधिकाधिकं.
64. D. साधर्म्यमात्रेण for साधर्म्यद्वारेण.
65. D. जिनभवन for जिनायतन.

Page 64.

72. Am. Bm. Cm. Dm. and D. मिमाणं; some ममाणं.
75. B. वैदिकविधिविधाने for वैदिकवधविधाने.
77. D. पुण्यार्जन for पुण्योपार्जन.
81. D. भूरिकामः for भूतिकामः.
82. Cm. K. साध्यमानत्वात् for साध्यत्वात्.
87. F. omits पक्षिणस्तथा after तिर्यञ्चः.
88. B. C. K. उच्छ्रितिं, H. उदितिं for उच्छ्रितं.
91. B. उपचारः for उपकारः.

Page 65.

93. A. B. D. F. G.H.K. पारमर्षाः, C.परमर्शाः, another परमार्याः.
95. F. स्वर्गो नरकः for स्वर्गे नरके.
97. H. K. मातृपित्रादिव्यापादनेन.
98. C. तथा for अथ.
99. H. मणिमन्त्रमहौषधानाम्.
101. K. omits विवाह before गर्भाधान.
105. Dm. omits क्रिया before वैगुण्यं.
108. Am. omits यथा before युष्मन्मते.
109. G. adds समाहिलाभं after बोहिलाभं.
114. Am. reads विवाहादीनामिव.
116. A. वेदस्यापर्यवसित; another वेदस्य पर्यवसित.
K. कन्दलत्वं for कन्दत्वं.

Page 66.

121. K. शुद्धेः for विशुद्धेः.
134. Am. reads ज्ञात्वा हि विमले.
136. G. adds युग्मं after कुरूत्तमं.

137. K. नाशनैः for नाशकैः

138. A. B. D. E. F. G. H. K. °हृतैः; another °हुतैः.

139. Cm. K. च for तु.

Page 67.

147. D. H. प्रतिगृहीतौ; another प्रगृहीतौ for °हृतिगृहीतौ.

153. A. B. C. add इति after अस्मदादिवत्.

157. D. E. H. देवतानां for देवानां.

158. K. omits भुक्ति before प्रसङ्गः.

166. A. D. F. G. add भवन after त्रिभुवन.

Page 68.

166-67. Am. Cm. °मतिसूर्या। Dm. reads मतिपस्तर्या. On the margin of Cm. there is a note explaining this reading by the word अतिचर्चया। A. अतिविस्तरेण B. C. D. E. G. अतिचस्तर्या F. H. अति च सूर्या K. इत्यलं चस्तर्या। for अतिचर्चया.

177. A. H. जंगल for जांगल.

178. H. पारितोषिकानुमानम्। H. omits from तत्र to परितोषः.

179. A. B. D. प्रत्यिंगकारात् for प्रत्यंगीकारात्.

180. A. B. कटुतैल for कटुकतैल; one MS. reads उपभुक्त्या for भुक्त्या.

182. K. समवाय for समवधान.

184. Cm. omits तु after अतिथिनां. K. पक्वान्नौदनापि.

185. K. महाजकल्पनम्.

186. A. K. विधाने for विधानेन.

189. B. omits स्वकृत; another reads सुकृत for कर्म.

Page 69.

192. E. यौथ्येन पठितं for यूथिनः पठन्ति.

193. Am. D. E. read तृप्तिकारकम्.

195. H. आवर्जितं for अर्जितं F. G. K. omit तदन्यकृतत्वात् after तस्य.

196. Am. omits अथ before तेषां.

197. K. omits पुण्यं.

199. Cm. reads विलीनः for विलीनं. A. F. G. omit किंतु पापानुबंधिपुण्यत्वात्तत्वतः पापमेव after त्रिशंकुज्ञातेन.

200. F. adds अन्नं after तेभ्यः.

203. B. अनुपलंभात् for अनवलोकनात्.
204. K. adds भुञ्जाना after आकुलतरं and omits भक्षयन्तः before प्रेतप्रायाः.
205. Cm. reads यदि च for यदपि.
206. Am. विभङ्गज्ञाने.
214. A. B. D. add यत् before वचनं.

Page 70.

232. F. omits अपवादः after अपवादयोः.
233. D. बलवान् for बलीयान्.
234. Cm. D. read अनुज्ञातत्वात् for अनुज्ञानात्.
235. B. ग्लानाद्यर्थमसंस्तरे.
239. F. omits वाक्येन after प्रयुक्तेन. A. अनापोद्यते.
240. Cm. वर्तेते for प्रवर्तेते.

Page 71.

248. Am. सुव्वइ for सुच्चइ.
256. Cm. कालावरोधि for कालाविरोधि. Cm. ज्वरादि for ज्वरादा.
256. Dm. पथ्यं परिहारः.
262. K. omits पितृ after अतिथि.

Page 72.

268. D. स्वर्गहेतुत्वं for सुगतिहेतुत्वं.
272. A. C. H. K. वाच्यस्य; one reads वाच्यत्वस्य.
274. D. omits भावाग्निहोत्रं before ज्ञानपाली.
276. A. प्रवचन for वचन। D. भगवत् for भवत्.
280. D. H. कलङ्कः for कलङ्कपङ्कः.
281. Am. and K. read एवं श्रूयतां धर्मसर्वस्वमित्यादि स्वोत्पन्नवचनरूपनिजसुतनिपातेन वेदविहिता हिंसाया मुग्धपुरुषस्वामिवत् क्षुद्रदेवतादिप्रीतिसिद्धावपि.
282. K. कर्म for दुष्कृतं.
283. B. omits तादृक् after असदृश.
284. Am. and H. read °मात्रमेव स्वपुत्रपतित्वाभावे पुरुषपतित्वस्याप्यभावात्तत्वतो न पुनस्तत्सिद्धिः.
285. A. G. H. add नृपूज्यत्वे before देवतादि. K. परितोषेण for परितोषणे.
G. H. add एवं श्रूयतां धर्मसर्वस्वमित्यादिवाक्योत्पन्नवचनरूपनिजसुतनिपातनेन मुग्धपुरुषस्वक्षुद्र before वेदविहितहिंसा.

286. A. K. प्रीतिः for तृप्तिः. C. adds पितृपूज्यत्वे. B. C. D. E. F. omit उत्तमजनपूज्यत्वं इंद्रादिदिवौकसां च before तृप्तिः। D. G. H. प्रीतिः for तृप्तिः. K. देवतानां for दिवौकसां.

Verse XII.

Page 73.

2. H. योगानां for यौगानां।
4. A. reads अर्थस्य पदार्थस्य च।
5. D. F. omit from इति क्रियया to बोधस्यापि तत्सिद्धिः।
6. G. omits सर्वप्रकाशानां and reads सर्वप्रकाशकत्वेन for स्वार्थ प्रकाशकत्वेन। A. adds तु after प्रकाशानां।
10. H. reads वस्तुस्वरूपम्।
17. B. एतत् for यस्य तत्।
18. D. न स्वसंविदितं for अस्वसं०।

Page 74.

22. G. भद्राः for भट्टाः।
24. B. H. नटबटुः; one MS. नवबटुः; G. नटः for नवबटुः A. C. D. E. K. read only बटुः
29. Am. Dm. read प्रकाशात्मनैव for °नैव
32. D. भाव्यम् for स्थातव्यम्
46. K. omits दोषः.

Page 75.

49. Dm. omits अपि after स्वोन्मुखतया.
50. Cm. reads स्वसंवेदितत्वं।
55. G. adds अनुभाव्यात्वनुभूतित्वात्प्रदीपवत् यथा प्रदीपस्यार्थापेक्षया प्रकाशकत्वं स्वापेक्षया च प्रकाश्यप्रकाशकत्वमिति after स्वापेक्षया, and omits अनुभाव्यत्वात्।
56. B. संवेदसिद्धिः for संवेदन°।
57. D. स्वसंवेदनस्य for संवे°।
59. Cm. F. read प्रकाशकत्वात् for °पपत्तेः.
60. H. reads प्रकाशत्वहेतोः।
61. F. लक्षणता for लक्षणभाव।
63. B. प्रकाशकः for प्रकाशः।
65. Bm. Em. read तत्संप्रयोगे।
67. F. भावानां for भट्टानां।
71. C. D. E. F. G.H.K. कृतार्थत्वात् for कृतकत्वात् of one Ms.

Page 76.

73. Dm. omits पक्षस्य before प्रत्यनुमान° ।

76. A. B. C. प्रसिद्धिः for प्रसिद्धेः ।

79. Am. reads विशेषश्च for विशेष्यश्च ।

79. A. C. अप्रमेयं च for °वा.

81. D. सोपाधिकत्वात् for सोपाधित्वात् ।

84. Am. omits च after प्रमेयत्वे ।

94. Am. reads °यज्जिज्ञासामन्तरेण ।

96. H. reads न त्वेतत् for नन्वेवमेतत् ।

Page 77.

102. Am. reads तत्रापि न चायमित्यपरापर° ।
Cm. reads तत्रापि चैवायमित्यपरापर° ।
K. add न्यायः after अयं ।

Verse XIII.

2. H. omits वर्ति after विश्वत्रय

11. H. उपप्रदर्शने for उपदर्शने

13. D. सर्वोपेक्षाविरहितस्य for सर्वोपाख्या°

Page 78.

19. D. E. F. मायैव चेत्यादि.

22. D. adds अव्याक्षेपो भविष्यन्त्याः कार्यसिद्धि(द्धे?)र्हि लक्षणम् after आदिपूरुषः

23. D. काव्यार्थः for वाक्यार्थः

25. Dm. माशङ्क्यं

35. A. H. add वै after सर्वं

36. A. B. Dm. read पश्यामि for पश्यन्ति. A. B. E. G. K. omit आरामं तस्य पश्यन्ति न तत्पश्यति कश्चन.

37. C. reads इति समयात् for इति न्यायात् । A. B. C. E. G. H. अर्थप्रपञ्चः for अयं तु° ।

43. B. H. omits असत्ख्याति after अन्यतरार्थत्वे.

46. B. omits स before प्रपञ्चः ।

53. D. reads प्रतिषेधयति ।

56. Dm. reads °मन्तरेण तत्स्वरूपनिषेधमन्तरेण तत्स्वरूपपरि° ।

58. B. omits प्रतिपत्ति after प्रतिषेध ।

62. D. reads वस्तुव्यवस्थितः for सुव्यवस्थितः ।

64. H. सिद्धिः K. सिद्धः for सिद्धं ।

Page 80.

65. F. अनुबाधित for अनुमानबाधित ।

68. Am. A. G. omit तेषां before श्रेयसी ।

72. D. reads अद्वैत for अद्वैतवाद ।

76. Am. reads परब्रह्मण एवैकस्य परमार्थसतो विधिरूपस्य विद्यमानत्वात् प्रास्ताविकत्वं स्यात् ।

77. D. Cm. read इदं च वादस्थलं काव्यार्थव्याख्यानुरोधेन नियंत्रितमिवोपन्यस्तं सांप्रतमुत्कलमेवोपन्यस्यामो ननु परब्रह्मण एवैक for अथवा प्रकारान्तरेण etc.; but H. adds this before अथवा.

79. Dm. A. E. omit द्वितियस्य after अपरस्य ।

81. F. विकल्पकभावात् for सविकल्पकभेदात् ।

82. Cm. reads प्रत्यक्षात्सन्मात्रस्यैव तस्यैकस्यैव ।

87. Am. reads यच्च सविकल्पं प्रत्यक्षं B. यथा for यच्च ।

Page 81.

101. E. adds तस्मात् after पदार्थाः ।

105. D. omits from उतामृतत्वस्य to सर्वस्यास्य बाह्यतः ।

107. A. K. omit मन्तव्यः after श्रोतव्यः.

113. A. Cm. D. K. read सत्तैकरूपेणा° ।

Page 82.

117. C. D. H. K. गद्गदोदित for गद्गदोद्गदित ।

118. Am. omits हि after सर्वं ।

118. C. D. E. G. K. read वस्तुप्रमाणसिद्धं सिद्धं ।

121. B. C. स्वन्मते; some तन्मते for स्वन्मते.

122. Cm. omits नित्य before निरंशस्य

124. F. omits from प्रत्यक्षं to सविकल्पकेन
G. omits from आबालगोपालं to सर्वस्यापि ।

125. Dm. reads एवं च for एतच्च

131. B. omits परमब्रह्मणः after एकस्य ।

Page 83.

141. B. C. साधनयालं for साधनायालं ।

Verse XIV.

2. Cm. reads परिकल्पित for प्रकल्पित ।

3. H. omits अभावं after वैभव

5. H. एकं for एकात्मकं । Dm. reads सामान्यरूपत्वात् for °रूपतया

6. Cm. Fm. omit रूपं after अनेक ।

8. A. C. E. F. G. विशेषात्मकत्वात् for विशेषोभयात्मकत्वात्

10. H. reads एकात्मकत्वं for एकानेकात्मकत्वं ।

20. F. adds शब्दार्थतया after वाच्यतया ।

Page 84.

22. F. omits वाच्यं before निर्वचन्ति ।

28. Am. reads सत्तात्मकत्वात् for सत्ताकत्वात्

35. C. omits व्यावृत्तिप्रत्ययहेतुत्वं लक्षणम्

38. Dm. reads स्वरूपात् for स्वरूपसत्त्वात्.

45. K. reads कथं न व्यावृत्तिः.

Page 86.

48. H. omits अन्यथा before अनुपपत्ते.

53. C. E. F. G. H. K. read सामान्यैकान्तः for वादः

67. Dm. reads भेदाद्भिन्नत्वात्.

Page 87.

71. D. कदाचित् for काचित्. Dm. reads °मेवोपचारात् for °मेवोपयोगात्.

75. Am. Dm. Fm. read तथा instead of तथा हि.

85. Dm. reads यावेवेतावेवमभ्युपगन्तव्यः । एवं सामान्यस्थाने विशेषशब्दं विशेषस्थाने च सामान्यशब्दं प्रयुञ्जानेन सामान्येऽपि यथा पाथः etc.

93. D. omits सास्ना after ककुद्

Page 88.

99. K. omits सकल before शबल.

101. Dm. Fm. विशेषरूपकत्वे for विशेषात्मकत्वे.

107. A. C. D. E. F. G. विभिन्नं for अभिन्नं C. D. F. G. omit कथंचिदभिन्नं.

112. D. reads सामान्यविशेषता for °रूपता.

114. D. reads व्यपदेशभावत्त्वात् for व्यपदेशादिभाक्त्वात्

115. Cm. ततः for यतः ।

Page 89.

122. A. K. read, some omit it: सदृशपरिणामरूपस्य विसदृशपरिणामवत् before कथंचित्.

123. D. omits कथंचित् ।

124. F. omits कथंचिद्धर्माध्यासितत्वं.
125. H. reads कक्षाप्रदेशः for °प्रवेशः ।
126. H. reads पावकस्वरूप.
129. C. reads विपरीतं for वैपरीत्यं.
130. H. सुव्यक्तं for सुष्ठूक्तं.
141. A. पराणुवत् for परमाणुवत्.

Page 90.

145. K. निर्गमौ for निष्क्रमौ.
147. A. असिद्धिः for असिद्धः.
154. E. अनुभूतः for अनुभूयते.
162. K. omits शब्दैकत्वैकान्ताऽनित्यशब्दवाद्यभिमतः.
165. D. omits अभ्युपगमात् after तादात्म्य.

Page 91.

176. Cm. reads सतत्त्वं.
180. Dm. reads सकलं काव्यमिदं व्याख्यायते.
183. H. omits विजातीय.
185. A. D. reads जलधारणादिसमर्थः; some others जलधारणाहरणादिक्रियासमर्थः. B. C. E. F. G. H. K. omit क्रिया before समर्थः.
190. D. भावात्मकत्वेन for भावात्मकत्वे K. omits तस्मात् before स्वरूपेण.

Page 92.

196. Am. adds रूपं before अन्तरेण.
204. A. B. D. G. read स्वरूपादित्ववत् for °सत्त्ववत्.
205. Cm. सर्वात्मकं for सर्वात्मकत्वं.
216. Cm. reads पटाभावात् for घटाभावात्.
247. Am. पूर्वोक्त for यथोक्त. Cm. अर्थोक्त.
230. A. B. E. F. G. omit कल्प before व्यवहारः. Cm. reads जीवितव्यवहारानुसारात् for जीतकल्प°
231. Cm. omits तु after शास्त्रापेक्षया.
232. F. अलिपदेन for अलिशब्देन.
235. H. कालादौ for देशकालादौ.
237. H. दुर्जित for दुर्जय.
239. Am. omits तु after प्रतिभाप्रमादः.

Page 94.

246. Dm. reads °चेदिति ब्रूमः.

247. Am. reads शब्दगोचरः.

248. Dm. reads लिङ्गानां.

250. C. adds रूप after प्रतिपन्न.

251. Cm. omits न पुनः before विशेषाः.

257. Am. reads फलवदभिलाष°.

Verse XV.

3. B. omits चित् before चैतन्यशक्तिः.

6. D. omits व्योम before प्रभृति.

Page 95.

8--9. D. reads अनात्मनः for अनात्मकस्य; and omits आत्मनः.

15 16. C. परिबद्धं for उपनिबद्धं. C. गर्भि for गर्भे.

Page 96.

34. Cm. reads °मित्यर्थान्तरम्.

36. Am. reads °दित्यपरपर्याया उत्पद्यते.

41. Dm. reads ससत्त्वोऽमुं हनिष्यामि.

43. Am. reads तन्मात्रादीनि विशेषरूपाणि.

49. A. B. C. D. E. F. G. H.K. Dm. omit तद्यथा before शब्दं.

Page 97.

62. C. G. H. K. अतदात्मा; some अतदात्मकः.

68. B. D. F. H. K. अवभासते for आभासते.

Page 98.

86. Dm. reads विषयविषयपरिच्छेदशून्या.

91. C. सक्रियाकता for सक्रियात्मकता.

100. Dm. reads अनुपादेयः प्रतिसंक्रमः and omits एवायम्.

Page 99.

108. C. E. Dm read चेतनावतीवाभासते.

113. B. omits अपि after तस्य.

123. C. D. E. G. K. यचोक्तं; some यथोक्तं for यच्चोक्तं.

130. Dm. omits तेषां before प्राकृतिको बन्धः.

Page 100.

141. A. E. G. H. K. omit इति चेत् before न.

142. some read एवं before प्रवृत्ते°

149. C. विख्यातौ for ख्यातौ.
151. A. निवृत्य for निवृत्ता.
153. A. E. omits पुनः before कथं.

Page 101.

164. Dm. reads उपरतपश्चर्जिन Am. उपरतपश्चार्जन.
165. A. E. अपदेश्यः for व्यपदेश्यः.

XVI.

Page 102.

5. Cm. omits ज्ञानं after तदेव.
6. Am. omits फलं before कार्यं.
9. A. C. reads भिन्नाधिकरणत्वात्
11. Am. reads घटे घटत्वं for घटेन घटत्वं.
13. D. F. G. H. read स चैकान्तभेदे न घटते.
K. omits तयोः after उत्पद्यमानयोः.
19. K. omits हेतौ विलीने न फलस्य भावः इति.
22. K. °प्रसक्तत्वात् for °प्रसङ्गात्.
25. Am. reads ग्रहणात्तदसंभवात्.

Pge 103.

30. A. B. C. D. E. F. G. H. K. read विज्ञानं यतः तस्मान्नीलस्य प्रतीतिरवसीयते येभ्यो हि after नीलनिर्भासं हि and before चक्षुरादिभ्यः; some others omit it.
32. Dm. नीलसंवेदनम्.
40. Am. Bm. F. read सारूप्यमर्थाकारं तच्च.
43. D. व्यवस्थाने for व्यवस्थापने.
49. G. adds घटाद्याकाररहितत्वं यदा व्यावृत्तं तदा तच्च सारूप्यं आकारोपलब्धेः after असारूप्यव्यावृत्तिः and before सारूप्यं.
K. °प्रसक्तेः for °प्रसङ्गात्
56. A. B. C. D. E. F. G. H. K. read नैवं after व्यवस्थेति चेत्.
B. C. G. add अपि before अनुपपत्तेः.

Page 104.

58. H. व्यवस्था चेत् for व्यवस्थावत्.
55. A. B. C. D. E. F. G. H. K. read सजातीयादपि before व्यावृत्तत्वात्; some others omit it.
63. Am. Dm. read प्रसजत इत्यलम्.

70. A. B. C. D. E. F. G. H. K. omit एष after सन्निधानेपि.
72. Cm. reads पत्रप्रतिलिखित.
74. A. B. C. D. E. F. H. K. add क्षणद्वयस्थायित्वात्पुनरपि before क्षणद्वय.

Page 105.

82. E. F. अनश्वरत्वे for अविनश्वरत्वे.
84. F. omits तत् before विनश्यति; some read it.
86. Dm. omits विनश्वरस्वरूपं.
102. A. omits पादयोः before प्रागेव.

Page 106.

104. D. omits नाश before वर्जं.
107. H. K. read स्याद्वादवादिनां.
114 H. अन्यथा for अपरथा.
121. D. अनुयुज्यते for अनुषज्यते.

Page 107.

130. F. omits from निर्मूलमेव to ज्ञानजनकत्वात् after अतीतत्वात् and before नचान्वयव्यतिरेकाभ्यां; D. reads ज्ञानोत्था स्यात्.
133. A. B. C. F. G. K. omits अन्यथा तत्प्रवृत्तेरसंभवात् after जलज्ञानोत्पादात्.
134. D. adds एवमन्यतरेष्वप्यर्थेषु भावनीयं after असंभवात्.
135. C. अर्थजं for अनर्थजं.
141. Gm. reads वेव for णेव.
150. Dm. reads अर्थज्ञानयोः नियतव्यवस्था प्रकाशकभावसंभवान्न ज्ञान निमित्तत्वमर्थस्य.

Page 108.

153. K. omits नैवं after प्रसज्येत.
156. Cm. adds अपि after अर्थसान्निध्ये; H. K. omit अशेषार्थ-सान्निध्ये. D. omits तत्तदर्थसान्निध्ये.
157. F. omits from जन्मेति to अमूर्तस्य after ज्ञानस्य.
159. Cm. D. G. जडत्व for साकारत्व. Dm. omits ज्ञानस्य.
167. Cm. reads °सद्भावात् ज्ञानरूपत्वैतच्च.
169. C. adds ज्ञान before ग्राहकत्वं.
171. K. व्याख्यानं for व्याख्यातुं.
172. C. मन्यन्ते for मन्वते.

Page 109.

179. H. K. omit अयं परमाणुः.

184. H. स्वभावभेदात् for स्वभावभेदेन.

185. B. C. E. F. G. H. असत्त्वप्राप्तिः for असत्त्वापत्तिः.

187. E. omits निरपेक्षत्वात्

188. C. adds भावानां after अपेक्षातो हि.

Page 110.

206. C. reads प्राग्विरोधे दुर्गन्धः.

210. A. B. C. D E. F. G. H. K. read वाङ्मात्रं किञ्चायमनेकावयवाधार इष्यते ते चावयवा यदि विरोधिनस्तर्हि नैकः स्थूलावयवी before विरुद्धधर्माध्यासात् and after प्रचयरूपः स्थूलावयवी; some omit it. A. B. C. E. G. Fm. बाधः; some विरोधः for बाधः.

225. B. H. K. निरालम्बः for निरालम्बन एव.

226. Cm. omits ज्ञान after आकाशकेश.

Page 111.

244. E. H. विलीना for प्रलीना.

Page 112.

256. A. B. C. D. E. F. G. H. K. Dm. अपुद्गलत्व° for अपुद्गलकार्यत्व° of others.

258. D. H. अविरुद्धा for अवितथा.

264. B. omits अवयविनः before अवयवेषु.

265. D. इदं for इदानीम्.

266. K. adds प्रतीतिः before चेत्.

271. H. धत्तूरादिभिः for हत्पूरादिभिः

Page 113.

284. A. D. E. F. G. H. K. omit भिन्नयोः before नीलपीतयोः.

292. Cm. reads नीलानुभवस्यानुभवा° ।

295. Am. Bm. read प्रत्यक्षस्याभ्रान्तत्वे.

296. H. omits विवक्षितदेशे.

297. C. adds स नियमः । अथास्ति तावत् after वासनानियमात्तदा.

299. D. बाह्याभावे for बाह्यार्थाभावे.

Page 114.

311. Am. reads °मञ्चति for °मङ्गति.

316. A. B. G. H. K. read तात्त्विकं after एकं; some omit it.

322. A. C. विधातृत्वात् for विधायित्वात् of some.

327. C. D. E. F. G. H. K. दुर्विधं for दुर्विदग्धं.

Page 115.

332. A. B. C. उपदिशन्ति for उशन्ति.

Verse XVII.

7. F. omits किंवत्

10. Cm. स एवायं.

11. A. B. C. F. अप्रमाणकः; some अप्रमाणिकः.

15. D. reads प्रत्यक्षान्यतमत्

Page 116.

21. C. H. अङ्गीकारात् F. प्रमाणांगीकरणात्

23. C. D. K. ताण्डवडम्बरं.

26. F. सर्वेषां for सर्वथा. C. omits तदा after विद्यते ।

31. D. लक्षणतया for लक्षणया.

38. Dm. omits पर before परिकल्पितं.

Page 117.

50. A. omits च after प्रमेयं.

51. Cm. reads प्रतिक्षेपणे निर्लोठितः.

52. Am. reads ज्ञानमेव वाच्यं.

Page 118.

67. D. अवसेयं for अवलोकनीयं.

69. D. प्रतिविधी विधीयते for प्रतिविधीयते.

71. Am. reads किञ्चित्स्वत्साधनं.

76. Am. Cm. omit न before सिद्धिः.

79. A. D. E. G. आत्मालम्बन° for आत्मावलम्बन°

81. B. C. F. G. K. अनुबोधात् for अनुवेधात्

89. °इन्द्रियालोके° ।

Page 119.

101. A. C. G. H. Dm. omit हि after यदि.

103. A. E. Fm. प्रतीतेः for प्रतिपत्तेः.

106. D. H. K. गवाक्षयोः for गवाक्षकयोः.

109. Cm. सामर्थ्यचेष्टा.

Page 120.

122. Dm. Fm. पुरुषादयः for पुद्गलादयः.

123. C. G. पदार्थाः for पर्यायाः.
126. Bm. Dm. Em. read घटादिव्यतिरे°

130. D. adds after अम्भोरुहादयः–

आगमो ह्याप्तवचनं आप्तदोषक्षयं विदुः ।
क्षीणदोषोऽनृतं वाक्यं न ब्रूयादेवसम्भवात्

131. D. adds after स प्रमाणमेवः–

तापाच्छेदान्निकषात्सुवर्णमिव पण्डितैः ।
परीक्ष्याभीक्ष्य वो ग्राह्यं मद्वचो न तु गौरवात् ॥

135. C. जलपटलवत्.
139. C. क्षय for प्रक्षय.
141. D. रागद्वेषाणां for रागादिदोषाणां.

Page 121.

144. D. omits आकाश before परिणामतारतम्यवत्.
161. D. omits अस्य before नैयत्येन.
161. B. विषयवशात् for विशेषवशात्.
166. A. read हानोपेक्षाबुद्धयः.

Page 122.

170. A. C आध्यात्मिकं for आध्यात्मिका.
176. A. B. C. omit तदसिद्धौ च.

XVIII.

5. Cm. reads क्षणभङ्ग उदया...विनाशरूपक्षण .

Page 123.

16. K. adds परकृतस्य after स्वयमकृतस्य.
25. C. नाशिनां for विनाशिनां. Cm. reads प्रतिसन्धानयोगात्.

Page 124.

44. C. omits इत्याहुः.
52. Bm. यत एतदर्थं प्रयतते Cm. यं एतदर्थं प्रयतते.
K. प्रतियतते for प्रयतते.
55. K. omits प्राप्नोति.

Page 125.

73. Cm. omits हि after तथा.
72. C. कर्पासदृष्टान्तः for कर्पासरक्ततादृष्टान्तः
78. K. स्मृतिरिष्यते for स्मृतेरुत्पत्तिरिष्यते.

XIX.

Page 126.

1. D. H. तथागताः
2. A. E. F. G. H. read यत्पदार्थानां.
7. A. B. C. D. E. F. G. H. अकामान् for अकामयमानान्.

Page 127.

12. A. B. C. read सुसदृश०
14. K. reads वासना स्यात्.
17. A. C. D. E. F. G. वितिष्ठते B. K. अवतिष्ठते; some व्यवतिष्ठते.
22. Cm. reads न घटते.

Page 128.

44. B. reads पूर्वलक्षणेन for पूर्वक्षणेन.
46. B. reads स्थिरसंबद्धस्य.

Page 129.

59. Dm. Fm. read भेदादिचर्चा.
61. K. omits संवाद Cm. भूतानि, Am. स्यूतानि for पूतानि.
70. K. reads प्रतिपद्यन्ते.
73. B. अनेकवाद for अनेकान्तवाद
75. K. omits सर्वस्य before वस्तुनः
77. F. omits श्रयन्तीति.

XX.

Page 130.

1. A. B. C. D. E. F. कुग्राहनिग्रहं; G. कतिकुग्राहानिग्रहं; H. K. कुग्राहनिग्रहणं.

Page 131.

14. B. G. लौकायितकस्य; C लोकायतिकस्य.
17. B. H. अविधेय for अवधेय.
28. Cm. ततश्च for अतश्च

Page 132.

51. K. reads प्रतिबद्धलिङ्गद्वारा°; Am समुत्पद्यतो for समुन्मज्जतो.
61. K. adds भूतेभ्यः after परिणतेभ्यः
62. B. C. E. F. G. H. K. omit आत्मनः उपयोगस्य before अहेतुत्वे. A. B. C. E. G. H. K. omit उपयोगः before स्यात्; some read it.

Page 133.

71. F. Am. read कायविकारदर्शनात्.

73. A. B. C. E. F. G. H. K. read परिणमन्ते.

76. B. omits तत् and reads for तस्य for अस्य.

78. A. B. C. D. E. G. H. read प्रमाणस्य for प्रामाण्यस्य.

XXI.

Page 134.

12. C. E. G. जैत्र (c तृ) त्वात् for जैत्र.

13. A. B. C. E. F. G. H. जीवादयः for जीवाजीवादयः

25. D. विगत for विगलित. A. B. E. H. अविधेय° for अवधेय°.

Page 135.

32. D. प्रतिपालन for परिपालन.

35. D. reads अन्वयिदर्शनात्.

43. G. reads पीतादिपर्यायानुभवः स्वलद्रूपः and omits from अनुभवेन to परम्परा°.

50. A. B. G. E. F. K. त्र्यात्मकं for त्रयात्मकं.

54. A. B. C. D. E. F. G. H. K. omit इति after रूपादिवत्.

Page 136.

56. G. omits लक्षणानि.

60. A. C. G. K. omit तद्वत् after रहितत्वात्

XXII.

3. C. G. H. read उपन्यसन् for उपन्यस्यन्.

Page 137.

10. E. उत्पद्यते, F. H. उपपद्यते for उपपाद्यते.

24. D. पक्त्वं E. पाकजरूपादित्वं for पाकजरूपादिमत्त्वम्.

25. A. C. E. and Dm. हरणादि K. हारणादि for हरण°

26. Cm. reads °नियमता for °नयमता.

Page 138.

34. A. B. E. F. H. K. read साक्षात्साक्षात्

36. F. and Cm. एकदेश for एकांश.

37. D. omits मृगाः.

40. A. B. C. E. F. G. H. K. and Dm. त्रासं for त्रस्तुतां.

43. E. F. G. read बहुवचनेषु.

44. D. omits सूत्रस्य.

46. Cm. omits बहु before वचनान्ता°.

49. D. reads सर्वविन्मूलतया प्रमाणत्वादिति काव्यार्थः and omits from अथवा to बहुवचनम्.

XXIII.

Page 139.

5. A. B. C. E. F. G. K. read गुणाः पर्यायाः.

24. A. पर्यार्पणया for पर्यायनयार्पणया.

26. H. इत्यर्थः for इति.

Page 140.

30. Some omit एकं.

47. A. B. C. D. E. F. G. K. परिणमते; H. परिणमन्ते.

Page 141.

55. A. B. C. D. E. F. G. K. इत्यादिकाः; some इत्यादयः.

Page 142.

97. D. H. सूक्तयनुवादैः F.K. and Am. सूक्तानुवादैः for सूत्रानुवादैः.

98. A. B. C. G. E. omit अति before प्रसङ्गेन.

101. G. C. K. and Cm. read एकसत्त्वादि.

Page 143.

115. Cm. अनलादि° D. जलादि° for आप्यादि°

117. B. रूपादित्वापत्त्या: for रूपापत्त्या.

120. A. B. C. D. E. F. G. H. K. तदुक्तं for यदुक्तं.

Page 144.

127. D. and Am. फलैवकारः for फलैवकारवत्.

151. B. सत्त्वाभ्यां A. C. E. F. G. K. सदसत्त्वाभ्यां for सत्त्वा सत्त्वाभ्यां.

Page 145.

164-5-6. B. H. D. add इतरस्य निषेधरूपता A. E. G. F. K. इतरस्य च निषेधरूपता C. इति निषेधरूपता before एवं सर्वत्र etc. C. रूपता for विधिरूपता.

176. B. E. G. H. K. omit प्राधान्य and read अभेदवृत्त्या A. C. प्रधान for प्राधान्य.

Page 146.

195. A. G. D. and Dm. read अविष्वग्भावः.

196. G. and Bm. लक्षणसम्बन्धः.

200. C. D. H. add प्रधान after अभेद.

Page 147.

225. H. reads सप्तभङ्गीम् C. D. E. भेदोदितः सप्तभङ्गम्.

5

XXIV.

Page 148.

2. B. आत्मकं for आत्मकत्वं B. प्ररूपेण for प्ररूपणेन.
7. Am. reads नास्तित्वेन सहविरोधं.
12. E. उद्भावयति for उद्वहति.
13. B. reads अनास्तित्व for अस्तित्व; D. omits अस्तित्व.

Page 149.

27. Am. reads अथ न चासत्त्वं.
30. Bm. omits तु after अन्योपाधिकं; some read तु.
34. A. B. C. E. मेचकरत्केपि Bm. मेचके रत्नेपि.
35. Bm. इहाग्भिः for एभिः.
40. Am. omits भ्रातृव्यत्व.
41. Bm. प्रसिद्धौ for प्रसिद्धिदर्शनात्.

Page 150.

45. A. B. C. E. K. H. read यः विरोधः and omit वा.
60. A. E. H. K. उद्भावनीयाः for उद्भाविताः.
    D. reads °परोद्भाविता दोषाः स्याद्वादमर्मवेदिभिरुद्धरणीयास्तदुपपत्तिभिरिति काव्यार्थः and omits from अभ्यूह्यः to निरवकाशा एव and from स्वतन्त्रतया to the end.
65. Bm. omits भवति after वैयधिकरण्यं.
69. B. C. omit तावपि स्वभावान्तराभ्यां.

XXV.

Page 151.

2. Am. Bm. °स्वादे for °स्वाद.

Page 152.

25. A. E. K. omit भेद and read वादचतुष्टयी.
    H. reads वादनादचतुष्टयी.
32. Bm. एतेन A. H. K. एते च for एते.

Page 153.

33. B. C. E. F. H. omit प्रदर्शितः.
34. A. B. C. D. E. F. H. omit संसूचितः.
35. A. B. C. D. E. F. H. omit चर्चितः.

XXVI.

1. E. F. H. read बद्धलक्षणतया.
2. Am. विधिहेतु for विविधहेतु.

Page 154.

22. Dm. and D. F. omit क्रमेण after क्रियायां.
24. Am. and D. F. H. K. read अनित्यलक्षणत्वात्.
39. D. omits एकान्तवादिषु.
40. Am. and K. read द्वादशाङ्गीमयं for द्वादशाङ्गीरूपं.

Page 155.

42. A. B. D. E. omit अपराभवनीयम्.
A. C. K. read पराभावुकानां for पराभिभावुकानां.
D. omits पराभिभावुकानां.
42. D इति विधानात् for इति कृत्यविधानात्.
43. D. reads धर्षितुमर्हं जयति and omits अशक्यं धर्षितुमनर्हं वा.
45. D. शत्रुषु for द्विषत्सु.

XXVII.

3. D. H. omit उद्धृत्त after उद्भावकतया.
7. A. B. C. D. E. F. G. H. K. नञ् प्रयोगः for नञः प्रयोगः.
11. D. अपि भुङ्क्ते for उपभुङ्क्ते.
13. D. omits एवं and reads परं दुःखं.

Page 156.

16. A. B. C. D. E. F. G. H. K. add ननु after तास्ततः and omit न.
18. D. reads एकान्तरूपत्वे for एकान्तैकरूपत्वे.
19. A. omits अपि after अवस्थाभेदः.
31. D. H. भवेत् for अभवत्.
33. Bm. reads नाप्यस्य विशेषः.
38. Bm. and F. H K. अनुपपत्तेः for अनुपपत्तिः.

Page 157.

41. D. reads अपि after क्रियाकारिणः.
42. Am. निरवयवं विनष्टत्वात् H. निरन्वयविनाशे for निरवयवनाशे.
56. D. पूर्वलक्षण° for पूर्वक्षण°.

58. D. उपपद्यते F. H. K. उत्पद्येत for उत्पद्यते.
63. A. E. F. H. K. स्वीक्रियमाणे for स्वीक्रियमाणं.

Page 158.

67. Bm. adds सर्वस्य before द्रव्यस्य.
72. B. अर्थतः for अथ च.
74. D. रूपं for विषयं.
77. D. स एव for तदेव.
77. H. omits शक्ति before युक्तत्वात्.
78. D. reads असिरिव खड्गेन एवं etc. and omits from असिः to हेवाक.
78. A omits दुर्नीतिवादव्यसनासिस्तेन after कृपाणः.
81. D. reads त्रैलोक्यं...विलुप्तं etc. and omits तात्स्थ्यात् to जन्तुजातम्.
85. Dm. अनुविधीयते E. अधीयते for अभिधीयते.
86. Dm. अजीवतत्त्व° for अजीवत्त्व°.
87. D. omits द्रव्य after दशावध.

XXVIII.

Page 159.

2. A. C. D. E. G. omit तेषां before प्रमाणनयानां.
F. H. K. omit प्रमाणनयानां.
Am. Bm. read प्रमाणनयानानां तेषां प्रतिपादयितुः.
7. A. D. G. E. F. H. K. omit परिच्छिद्यते after नीयते.
9. Some read नैगमादयः for नैगमाद्याः.
11. D. प्रमाणानि for प्रमाणे.
15. D. omits एकान्तास्तित्वमेव to स्वाभिमतं in line 19.

Page 160.

24. C. D. E. K. दर्शनार्थं for देशनार्थं.
27. H. व्याख्याय for आख्याय.
29. Bm. निराकुर्वन् for निराकृतवान्.
31. D. omits from यथार्थोऽस्ति to यथार्थदर्शी.
36. H. सम्यग्मार्ग° for सन्मार्ग°.
44. H. reads प्रज्ञापनार्थं and omits प्रज्ञापनाङ्गज्ञापनार्थं before चत्वारि.

Page 161.

47. C. D. omit कृत before समासान्तः.

50. D. दुर्नयप्रमाणस्वरूपं.

54. Bm. omits प्रापयति.

70. D. जल्पितं for क्षुण्णं.

D. omits from प्रवचन to अयम् line 70–71 on p. 162.

Page 162.

89. Bm. reads °लोकबाधितं प्रमाणं सिद्धं for °लोकाबाधितं प्रमाण-प्रसिद्धं.

87. A. उपचरयन्ति Bm. उपचरन्ति for उपरचयन्ति.

92. Am. omits वर्तमान before क्षणविवर्त्यें°.

Page 163.

108. Bm. omits अर्थ before अभिप्रैति.

109. D. omits from तथैव to प्रतीयन्ते lines 109–11.

109. C. K. एकत्वं for एक.

110. H. पुरन्दराद्याः for पुरन्दरादयः.

111. C. प्रत्ययते for प्रतीयन्ते.

113. A. C. एकैकं for एक.

113. K. पर्यायध्वनीनां for पर्यायशब्दानां.

Page 164.

130. Bm. omits एवं भाषते.

131. D. विवर्तते for प्रवर्तते.

138. D. repeats from चेष्टावत्यपि to अविकलमस्ति in line 140.

138. C. D. H. K. and Dm. omit तदा after प्रयुज्येत.

Page 165.

157. Dm. प्रवाहित for प्रभावित.

170. Bm. reads क्षणमेकसुखी.

Page 166.

179. C. D. omit जीव before द्रव्याणां.

180. D. प्रतिपद्यमानः for प्रतिजानानः.

181. Am. Bm. यच्च for यथा.

Page 167.

200. H. वस्तुतच्छब्दं for वस्तु शब्द°

212. C. and Dm. वर्तमानं for प्रवर्तमानं.

213. H. विधिनिषेधाभ्यां for विधिप्रतिषेधाभ्यां.

215. F. omits टीका.

218. A. B. C. G. H. K. read समन्त भद्रः.

Page 168.

221–22. F. सव्यवहारिकं for सांव्यवहारिकं

223. A. B. C. G. K. एकैकशः D. एकत्वात् for एकशः.

234. A. B. D. E. F. H. K. तर्कापरपर्यायः for अपरनामा तर्कः.

236. D. omits द्विधा after अनुमानं.

243. H. खलीकृतः for खिलीकृतः.

XXIX.

Page 169.

A. B. C. D. E. F. G. H. K. षड्जावकायं for षट्कायजीवं in l. 3 of the St.

5. Fm. निर्वृत्तिप्राप्तः A. E. D. F. K. निर्वृतिप्राप्तः C. H. निर्वृतिं प्राप्तः G. निर्वृत्तिप्राप्तः for निर्वृतिमाप्तः.

13. Bm. omits स after खलु.

A. B. C. D. K. निर्वृतिः; some निर्वृत्तिः

Page 170.

27. A. B. C. D. E. F. G. H. K. प्ररोहण° for प्ररोह°.

28. Bm. विपाकारम्भी भवति; some विपाकप्ररोही भवति.

29. A. B. C. D. E. F. G. H. K. omit प्रसंख्यान and क्लेश and read नापनीतक्लेशो न दग्धबीजभावो वेति.

34. A. B. C. E. F. G. H. omit तथा तेन प्रकारेण before अनन्तसंख्यं.

42. D. omits मर्यादया before प्ररूपितवान्.

48. A. B. C. E. F. G. H. K. जीवत्वं for जीवं.

48. D. सात्मकाः; some सात्मिकाः.

Page 171.

49. Bm. reads समानधानात्थानादर्शाङ्कुरवत्.

55. A. B. C. D. E. F. G. K. म्लान्यादि; H. मालिन्यादि for ग्लान्यादि.

59. A. B. C. E. G. H. भगवदुपज्ञे; some भगवदुपक्रमे.

60. Bm. सर्वस्तोकायिका: H. सर्वस्तोकात्रसा: for सर्वस्तोकात्रसकायिका:.

64. D. F. omit अव्यवहारिकाश्च.

70. D. तावत्तावता for तावता.

72. D. K. अवसेयं for अवगन्तव्यं.

XXX.

Page 172.

6. Am. असहनशीलिन: Ac. मत्सरशालिन: for असहनताशालिन:

8. F. omits from स्वकक्षीकृतपक्ष to हेत्वादिभिरिति पक्ष: in line 10.

10. D. विशिष्टेन A. C. E. विशिष्ट्येन for वैशिष्ट्येन.

Page 173.

12–13. A. D. omit पक्षप्रतिपक्षभाव: after तस्य भाव: and omit पक्ष after परस्परं य:

K. omits पक्ष after तस्य भाव:.

17. Bm. एवं सर्वत्र प्रयोगेषु C. एवं सर्वत्र योगेषु.

24. Dm. omits हि after पक्षपातित्वं.

31. D. रूपतया H. पाठरूपतया for पदरूपतया.

36. Bm. °शब्दस्य for °वादस्य.

Page 174.

40. D. omits मध्यस्थं before न्यायनिर्णेतारं.

XXXI.

Page 175.

4. Dm. निगमयन्नाह for निगमनमाह.

8. D. omits संबन्धिनं before निखिलं.

15. Am. H. omit परि before ज्ञानात्

Page 176.

34. A. B. C. D. F. G. H. K. add विकार: after अहंकार.

Bm. omits बहु before वचनमात्रेण.

Bm. न न खल्वहङ्कार: for न खल्वहङ्कार:.

34–35. D. omits स्तोतारि प्रभौ and reads प्रढौकनीय: for शङ्कनीय:,

XXXII.

Page 177.

13. F. व्यतिकीर्णताख्य for व्यतिकीर्णताव्यामिश्रता.

D. K. omit स्वभावविनिमयः.

A. E. omit व्यामिश्रता.

C. reads व्यतिकीर्णता विनिमयः.

17. Bm. लक्षत्वात् for लक्षणत्वात्

19. Bm. reads:–तथा च श्रीजिनवल्लभसूरयः.

देवीयत्युरुदोषिणः क्षतमहो दोषान्न देवीयति
सर्वज्ञीयति मूर्खमुख्यमवहं तत्त्वज्ञमज्ञीयति
उन्मार्गीयति जैनमार्गमपथं सम्यक्पथीयत्यहो
मिथ्यात्वग्रहिलो जनः स्वगुणाग्रण्यं कृतार्थीयति ॥ १ ॥

after तथा च ग्रन्थान्तरे.

24. Dm. and A. K. उपदिश्य for उपदर्श्य.

Page 178.

42. A. B. F. G. H. K. omit कुतः कारणात्.

45. A. B. C. D. F. G. and Dm. देवतान्तरे for देवान्तरे.

48. Dm. reads प्रादिकर्मणः for आप्त्यादिकर्मणः

D. omits प्रादिकं विना° to कृतसपर्याः in line 50.

Page 179.

80. In टीकाकारस्य प्रशस्तिः–D. reads राजिष्णो कलिनिर्जयाजिन इव for बिभ्राणे कलिनिर्जयाजिनतुलां and A. B. C. D. E. F. G. H. K. मयाविष्कृता for मया विस्तृता.

K. omits Verses 1 to 5 (both inclusive) in the टीकाकारप्रशस्ति and also Verse 9.

Appendix B: Quotations & References

Stanza I.

ज्ञानिनो धर्मतीर्थस्य कर्तारः परमं पदम् ।
गत्वाऽऽगच्छन्ति भूयोऽपि भवं तीर्थनिकारतः —Untraced.

सर्वं पश्यतु वा मा वा तत्त्वमिष्टं तु पश्यतु ।
कीटसंख्यापरिज्ञानं तस्य नः क्वोपयुज्यते ॥ —Untraced.

Called "वैशेषिकवचनम्" by Malliṣeṇa. Quoted also in Pārthasārathi's Commentary (न्यायरत्नाकर) on Mîm. Śl. Vārtika on Mîm. Sûtra II.

तस्मादनुष्ठानगतं ज्ञानमस्य विचार्यताम् ।
प्रमाणं दूरदर्शी चेदेते गृध्रानुपास्महे ॥ —Untraced.

Probably this too "वैशेषिकवचनम्".

जे एगं जाणइ से सव्वं जाणइ ।
जे सव्वं जाणइ से एगं जाणइ ॥

—Àcārāṅga, Śruta Skandha (I), Adhyayana III, Uddeśa iv, Sûtra 122.

एको भावः सर्वथा येन दृष्टः सर्वे भावाः सर्वथा तेन दृष्टाः ।
सर्वे भावाः सर्वथा येन दृष्टा एको भावः सर्वथा तेन दृष्टः ॥
—Untraced.

यथा निशीथचूर्णौ......... —Niśîthacûrṇi, Udd. 17.

अभ्रादित्वात् [अभ्रादिभ्यः]–Hema Śabdānuśāsana VII. ii. 46.

शाखादेर्यः --Hema S'abda VII. i. 114.

श्रीवर्धमानाभिधमात्मरूपम् [अगम्यमध्यात्मविदामवाच्यं वचस्विनाम-क्षवतोऽपरोक्षम् । श्रीवर्धमानाभिधमात्मरूपमहं स्तुतेर्गोचरमानयामि ॥]
—Ayogavyavaccheda St. I.

Stanza II.

तादर्थ्ये चतुर्थी --Hema S'abda II. ii. 54.

स्पृहेर्व्याप्यं वा --Hema S'abda II. ii. 26.

Stanza III.

अदसस्तु विप्रकष्टे [इदमस्तु संनिकृष्टे समीपतरवर्ति चैतदो रूपम् ।
अदसस्तु विप्रकृष्टे तदिति परोक्षे विजानीयात् ॥]

रुसऊ वा परो मा वा विसं वा परियत्तऊ ।
भासियव्वा हिया भासा सपक्खगुणकारिया ॥
(रुषतु मा वा परो मा वा विषं वा पर्यटतु (विषवत् प्रतिभातु वा) ।
भाषितव्या हिता भाषा स्वपक्षगुणकारिका (कारिणी) ॥
Cf. परो रुष्यतु वा मा वा विषवत् प्रतिभातु वा ।
भाषितव्या हिता भाषा स्वपक्षगुणकारिणी ॥)

—Hema-S'reṇikacaritra II. 32.

वाचकमुख्यः—न भवति धर्मः श्रोतुः सर्वस्यैकान्ततो हितश्रवणात् ।
ब्रुवतोनुग्रहबुध्द्या वक्तुस्त्वेकान्ततो भवति ॥

—Umāsvāti ('Vācakamukhya')'s Tatt. Sûtra-Sambandha-Kārikā 29.

Stanza IV.

गम्ययपः कर्माधारे —Hema S'abda II. ii. 74.

Stanza V.

उत्पादव्ययध्रौव्ययुक्तं सत् —Tattvārtha Sûtra V. 29.

अवकाशदमाकाशम् —Bhāvavijayagaṇi's Vṛtti on Uttarādhyayana Adh. XXVIII. 9.

अयमेव हि भेदो भेदहेतुर्वा यद्विरुद्धधर्माध्यासः कारणभेदश्चेति

—Untraced.

अप्रच्युतानुत्पन्नस्थिरैकरूपं नित्यम् ,,

तद्भावाव्ययं नित्यम् —Tatt. Sûtra V. 30.

द्रव्यं पर्यायवियुतं पर्याया द्रव्यवर्जिताः ।
क्व कदा केन किंरूपा दृष्टा मानेन केन वा ॥
[Cf. दव्वं पज्जव विज्जुअं दव्वविउत्ताय पज्जवा नत्थि

—Sammati I. 12.]

त्रिविधः खल्वयं धर्मिणः परिणामो धर्मलक्षणावस्थारूपः ।

—Yoga Sûtra III. 13, Vyāsa-Bhāṣya.

सा तु द्विविधा–नित्याऽनित्या च......

—Praśastapāda Bhāṣya, Section on पृथ्वी.

शब्दकारणत्ववचनात् संयोगविभागौ—Section on आकाश.

अच्युतानुत्पन्न......नानाकार्याणां कथमुत्पत्तिः

—Taken substantially and almost verbatim from Hemacandra's com. on his own Pramāṇa-Mîmāṃsā.

सापेक्षसमर्थम्—A nyāya of in Hema Śabdanuśāsana and noted in the collection of nyāyas made by Hemahaṃsagaṇi.

यो यत्रैव तत्रैव यो यदैव तदैव सः ।
न देशकालयोर्व्याप्तिर्भावानामिह विद्यते ॥ —Untraced.

Attributed to Âjîvakas in A. M. P. edition.

भागे सिंहो नरो भागे योऽर्थो भागद्वयात्मकः ।
तमभागं विभागेन नरसिंहं प्रचक्षते ॥ —Untraced.

सर्वे गत्यर्था ज्ञानार्थाः—A nyāya from Hema.44.(see supra).

Stanza VI.

ईश्वरप्रेरितो गच्छेत् स्वर्गं वा श्वभ्रमेव वा (v. l. नरकमेव वा)
अज्ञो(न्यो)जन्तुरनीशोऽयमात्मनः सुखदुःखयोः ॥

—Mahābhārata. Attributed to Vyāsa (and rightly) by the author of the Parîkṣāmukha Sûtra Laghuvṛtti. Found quoted in S'abara-Bhāṣya on Mîm. Sûtra I. ii. 4. Also in Māṭhara Vṛtti on Sāṃkhyakārikā 61.

अपगतमले हि मनसि......शूलमभव्यस्य

—Kādambari-Pûrvārdha, Peterson's edition p. 103.

सद्धर्मबीजवपनानघकौशलस्य
यल्लोकबान्धव तवापि खिलान्यभूवन् ।
तन्नाद्भुतं खगकुलेष्विह तामसेषु
सूर्यांशवो मधुकरीचरणावदाताः ॥

—Siddhasena's Dvātriṃśikā II, 13.

विश्वतश्चक्षुरुत विश्वतोमुखो विश्वत:पाणिरुत विश्वतःपाद् ।

—S'ukla Yajurveda Saṁhita XVII. 19.

किरणा गुणा न दव्वं तेसि पयासो गुणो, न वा दव्वं ।
जं णाणं आयगुणो कहमदव्वो स अन्नत्थ ॥ १ ॥
गन्तूण न परिछिंदइ णाणं णेयं तयम्मि देसम्मि ।
आयत्थं चिय, नवरं अचिंतसत्ती उ विण्णेयं ॥ २ ॥
लोहोवलस्स सत्ती आयत्था चेव भिन्नदेसंपि ।
लोहं आगरिसंती दीसइ इह कज्जपच्चक्खा ॥ ३ ॥
एवमिह नाणसत्ती आयत्था चेव हंदि लोगंतं ।
जइ परिछिंदइ सव्वं कोणु विरोहो भवे तत्थ एत्थं ॥ ४ ॥

—Dharma–Sāṁgrahiṇî of Haribhadrācārya 370–373.

न हिंस्यात् सर्वा भूतानि । —Untraced.

Often quoted

षट्शतानि नियुज्यन्ते पशूनां मध्यमेऽहनि ।
अश्वमेधस्य वचनात् न्यूनानि पशुभिस्त्रिभिः ॥
(v. l. यज्ञस्य नवभिश्चाधिकानि च)

—Quoted in Mahîdhara-Bhāṣya on Yajus Saṁhitā Adh.24, and in Māṭhara Vṛtti on S. Kārikās.

अग्नीषोमीयं पशुमालभेत । —Aitareya Âraṇyaka VI. 3.

सप्तदश प्राजापत्यान् पशूनालभेत । —Taittirîya Saṁhitā I. 4.

ब्राह्मणार्थेऽनृतं ब्रूयात् । —Âpastamba.

न नर्मयुक्तं वचनं हिनस्ति न स्त्रीषु राजन्न विवाहकाले ।
प्राणात्यये सर्वधनापहारे पञ्चाऽनृतान्याहुरपातकानि ॥
Cf. उद्वाहकाले इति संप्रयोगे प्राणात्यये सर्वधनापहारे ।
विप्रस्य चार्थे ह्यनृतं वदेयुः पञ्चानृतान्याहुरपातकानि ॥

—Vasiṣṭha Dharma Sûtra XVI. 36.

ब्राह्मणानां तु दौर्बल्यात् वृषलाः परिभुञ्जते ।
(आनृशंस्याद् ब्राह्मणस्य भुञ्जते हीतरे जनाः ॥

—Manu Smṛti I. 101 b.

स्वमेव ब्राह्मणो भुङ्क्ते स्वं वस्ते स्वं ददाति च ।

Cf. Bhāgavata. —Manu Smṛti I. 101 a.

अपुत्रस्य गतिर्नास्ति । —Devî Bhāgavata.

अनेकानि सहस्राणि कुमारब्रह्मचारिणाम् ।
दिवं गतानि विप्राणामकृत्वा कुलसंततिम् ॥ —Âpastamba.

Stanza VII.

आवर्जिता किंचिदिव स्तनाभ्याम् ।
—Kumārasaṃbhava III. 54.

उद्वृत्तः क इव सुखावहः परेषाम् । —S'iśupālavadha.

प्राप्तानामेव प्राप्तिः समवायः ।
—Vide Praśastpāda's 'अप्राप्तानां प्राप्तिः संयोगः' and S'rîdhara's comment thereon: अप्राप्तयोरिति समवायव्यवच्छेदार्थम् ।

अव्यभिचारी मुख्योऽविकलोऽसाधारणोऽन्तरङ्गश्च ।
विपरीतो गौणोऽर्थः, सति मुख्ये, धीः कथं गौणे ॥ —Untraced.

ईहाद्याः प्रत्ययभेदतः । —Hema Liṅgānuśāsana पुंस्त्री० 5.

Stanza VIII.

पृथिव्यापस्तेजो वायुराकाशः कालो दिगात्मा मनः इति नव द्रव्याणि ।
—Vaiś. Sûtra I. i. 5 and Praśasta.

रूपरसगन्धस्पर्शसंख्यापरिमाणानि पृथक्त्वं संयोगविभागौ परत्वापरत्वे बुद्धिः सुखदुःखे इच्छाद्वेषौ प्रयत्नश्च ।—Vaiś. Sûtra I. i. 6 and Praśastapāda Bhâṣya.

अन्त्येषु भवा अन्त्याः; स्वाश्रयविशेषकत्वाद् विशेषाः । विनाशारम्भरहितेषु नित्यद्रव्येष्वण्वाकाशकालदिगात्ममनःसु–प्रतिद्रव्यमेकैकशो वर्तमाना अत्यन्तव्यावृत्तिबुद्धिहेतवः । यथाऽस्मदादीनां गवादिष्वश्वादिभ्यस्तुल्याकृतिगुणक्रियावयवोपचयावयवविशेषसंयोगनिमित्ता प्रत्ययव्यावृत्तिर्दृष्टा–गौः शुक्लः शीघ्रगतिः पीनः ककुद्मान् महाघण्ट इति; तथाऽस्मद्विशिष्टानां योगीनां–नित्येषु तुल्याकृतिगुणक्रियेषु परमाणुषु, मुक्तात्मनःसु चाऽन्यनिमित्तासंभवाद् येभ्यो निमित्तेभ्यः प्रत्याधारं विलक्षणोऽयमिति प्रत्ययव्यावृत्तिः, देशकालविप्रकृष्टे च परमाणौ स एवायमिति प्रत्यभिज्ञानं च भवति, तेऽन्त्या विशेषाः ।
—Praśastapāda Bhāṣya p. 168.

व्यक्तेरभेदस्तुल्यत्वं सङ्करोऽथानवस्थितिः ।
रूपहानिरसम्बन्धो जातिबाधकसङ्ग्रहः ॥

—Udayanācārya's Dravya Kiraṇāvali p. 161.

न हि वै सशरीरस्य प्रियाप्रिययोरपहतिरस्ति ।
अशरीरं वाव सन्तं प्रियाप्रिये न स्पृशतः ।

—Chāndogya VIII. 12.

यावदात्मगुणाः सर्वे नोच्छिन्ना वासनादयः ।
तावदात्यन्तिकी दुःखव्यावृत्तिर्न विकल्प्यते ॥ १ ॥
धर्माधर्मनिमित्तो हि संभवः सुखदुःखयोः ।
मूलभूतौ च तावेव स्तम्भौ संसारसद्मनः ॥ २ ॥
तदुच्छेदे च तत्कार्यशरीराद्यनुपप्लवात् ।
नात्मनः सुखदुःखे स्त इत्यसौ मुक्त उच्यते ॥ ३ ॥
इच्छाद्वेषप्रयत्नादि भोगाऽऽयतनबन्धनम् ।
उच्छिन्नभोगायतनो नात्मा तैरपि युज्यते ॥ ४ ॥
तदेवं धिषणादीनां नवानामपि मूलतः ।
गुणानामात्मनो ध्वंसः सोपवर्गः प्रतिष्ठितः ॥ ५ ॥
ननु तस्यामवस्थायां कीदृगात्मावशिष्यते ।
स्वरूपैकप्रतिष्ठानः परित्यक्तोखिलैर्गुणैः ॥ ६ ॥
ऊर्मिषट्कातिगं रूपं तदस्याहुर्मनीषिणः ।
संसारबन्धनाधीनदुःखक्लेशाद्यदूषितम् ॥ ७ ॥
कामक्रोधलोभगर्वदम्भहर्षा—ऊर्मिषट्कमिति ।"

—Nyāyamañjarî of Jayanta.

करणं द्विविधं ज्ञेयं बाह्यमाभ्यन्तरं बुधैः ।
यथा लुनाति दात्रेण मेरुं गच्छति चेतसा ॥

—Attributed to grammarians—Untraced.

न हि वै सशरीरस्य सतः प्रियाप्रिययोरपहतिरस्ति"

—Chāndogya VIII. 12.

सुखमात्यन्तिकं यत्र बुद्धिग्राह्यमतीन्द्रियम् ।
तं वै मोक्षं विजानीयाद् दुष्प्रापमकृतात्मभिः ॥ —Untraced.

—The first line is found also in the Bhagavadgîtā.

वरं वृन्दावने रम्ये क्रोष्टुत्वमभिवाञ्छितम् ।
न तु वैशेषिकीं मुक्तिं गौतमो गन्तुमिच्छति ॥ —Untraced.

मोक्षे भवे च सर्वत्र निःस्पृहो मुनिसत्तमः । —Untraced.

नट्ठं मिय छाउमत्थिए नाणे ।
(उपण्णंमि अणंते नट्ठं मिय छाउमत्थिए नाणे ।
राईए संपत्तो महक्षेणवणंमि उज्जाने ।
उत्पन्नेऽनन्ते नष्टे च छाद्मस्थिके ज्ञाने ।
रात्र्यां संप्राप्तो महासेनवनं उद्यानम् ॥

—Âvasyaka Purvavibhāga 539.

पुण्यपापक्षयो मोक्षः —Untraced.

said to be ' आगमवचन '.

सर्वगतत्वेऽप्यात्मनो देहप्रदेशे ज्ञातृत्वम् । नान्यत्र । शरीरस्योपभोगायतनत्वात् । अन्यथा तस्य वैयर्थ्यात् ।

—Srîdhara's Nyāyakandalî.

नाना त्मानो व्यवस्थातः
आकाशोऽपि सदेशः, सकृत्सर्वभूतात्रिर्सबन्धार्हत्त्वात् "

—Attributed in the text to the author of Dravyālaṁkāra.

इम कारके —Hema S'abda III. ii. 121.

बहुभिरात्मप्रदेशैरधिष्ठिता देहावयवा मर्माणि— ?

गुणादस्त्रियां नवा— —Hema S'abda II. ii. 77.

लब्धिख्यात्यर्थिना तु स्याद् दुःस्थितेनामहात्मना ।
छलजातिप्रधानो यः स विवाद इति स्मृतः ॥

—Haribhadrasûri's Aṣṭaka XII. 4.

Cf. वादं च निर्णयफलार्थिभिरेव शिष्यसब्रह्मचारिगुरुभिः सह वीतरागैः ।
न ख्यातिलाभरभसप्रतिवर्धमानस्पर्धानुबन्धविधुरात्मभिरारभेत ॥

—Jayanta's Nyāyamañjarî.

अभ्युपेत्य पक्षं यो न स्थापयति स वैतण्डिक इत्युच्यते ॥

—Uddyotakara's Nyāya-Vārtika I. i. 1.

दुःशिक्षितकुतर्कांशलेशवाचालिताननाः ।
शक्याः किमन्यथा जेतुं वितण्डाटोपमण्डिताः ॥

गतानुगतिको लाकः कुमार्गं तत्प्रतारितः !
मागादिति छलादीनि प्राह कारुणिको मुनिः ॥ —Untraced.

प्रमाणप्रमेय.........निःश्रेयसाधिगमः ॥
—Gautama's Nyāyasûtra I. i. 1.

अर्थोपलब्धिहेतुः प्रमाणम् —Vātsyāyana Bhāṣya.

सम्यगनुभवसाधनं प्रमाणम् —Bhāsarvajña's Nyāyasāra which has a commentary called Nyāyabhûṣaṇa.

स्वपरव्यवसायि ज्ञानं प्रमाणम् —Pramāṇanaya-tattvālokālaṁkāra of Devasûri and Pramāṇamîmāṃsā of Hemacandra.

प्रवृत्तिदोषजनितं सुखदुःखात्मकं मुख्यं फलं तत्साधनं तु गौणम्
—Jayanta's Nyāyamañjarî.

द्रव्यपर्यायात्मकं वस्तु प्रमेयम्
—Pramāṇanaya-tattvālokālaṁkāra.

साधर्म्यवैधर्म्य.........समा —Gautama's Nyāyasûtra.

Stanza XI.

महोक्षं वा महाजं वा श्रोत्रियाय प्रकल्पयेत्
—Yajñavalkya Smṛti, Âcāra 109.

द्वौ मासौ मत्स्यमांसेन त्रीन् मासान् हरिणेन तु ।
औरभ्रेणाथ चतुरः शाकुनेनेह पञ्च तु ॥ —Manusmṛti III. 268.

श्रूयतां धर्मसर्वस्वं श्रुत्वा चैवावधार्यताम् —Cāṇakya I. 7.
also M. Bh.

संबद्धं वर्तमानं च गृह्यते चक्षुरादिना—
—Kumārila's Mîm. Sl. Vārtika IV. 84.

पुढवाइयाण जइवि हु होइ विणासो जिणालयाहिन्तो ।
तव्विसया वि सुदिट्ठिस्स णियमओ अत्थि अणुकंपा ॥
एयाहिंतो बुद्धा विरया रक्खन्ति जेण पुढवाई ।
इत्तो निव्वाणगया अबाहिया आभवमिमाणं ॥
रोगिसिरावेहो इव सुविज्ज किरिया व सुप्पउत्ताओ ।
परिणामसुंदरच्चिय चिट्ठासे बाहजोगे वि ॥

[=पृथिव्यादीनां यद्यपि भवत्येष विनाशो जिनलयादिभ्यः ।
तद्विषयापि सुदृष्टेर्नियमतोऽस्त्यनुकम्पा ॥

एताभ्यो बुद्धा विरता रक्षन्ति येन पृथिव्यादीन् ।
अतो निर्वाणगता अबाधिता आभवमेषाम् ॥

रोगिशिरावेध इव सुवैद्यक्रिया इव सुप्रयुक्ता तु ।
परिणामसुन्दर इव चेष्टा सा बाधयोगेपि ॥—

—Jinapatisûri's Pañcalingî 58-59-60.

श्वेतं वायव्यमजमालभेत भूतिकामः।—S'atapatha Brāhmaṇa(?)

औषध्यः पशवो वृक्षास्तिर्यञ्चः पक्षिणस्तथा ।
यज्ञार्थं निधनं प्राप्ताः प्राप्नुवन्त्युच्छ्रितं पुनः ॥

—Quoted in Hema-Yogaśāstra.

यूपं (v.l. वृक्षं) छित्वा पशून् हत्वा कृत्वा रुधिरकर्दमम् ।
यद्येवं गम्यते स्वर्गे नरके केन गम्यते ॥
—Found quoted in Māṭhara Vṛtti on Sāṁkhyakārikā.

आरोग्ग बोहिलाभं समाहिवरमुत्तमं दिंतु ।
[=आरोग्यं बुद्धिलाभं समाधिवरमुत्तमं ददतु]

—Avaśyaka XXIV. 6.

देवोपहारव्याजेन यज्ञव्याजेन येऽथवा ।
घ्नन्ति जन्तून् गतघृणा घोरां ते यान्ति दुर्गतिम् ॥ —Untraced.

अन्धे तमसि मज्जामः पशुभिर्ये यजामहे ।
हिंसा नाम भवेद् धर्मो न भूतो न भविष्यति ॥ —Untraced.

अग्निर्मामेतस्माद्धिंसाकृतादेनसो मुञ्चतु । —Untraced.
Pâraskara (?)

ज्ञानपालिपरिक्षिप्ते ब्रह्मचर्यदयाम्भसि ।
स्नात्वातिविमले तीर्थे पापपङ्कापहारिणि ॥

ध्यानाग्नौ जीवकुण्डस्थे दममारुतदीपिते ।
असत्कर्मसमित्क्षेपैरग्निहोत्रं कुरूत्तमम् ॥

कषायपशुभिर्दुष्टैर्धर्मकामार्थनाशकैः ।
शममन्त्रहुतैर्यज्ञं विधेहि विहितं बुधैः ॥

प्राणघातात् तु यो धर्ममीहते मूढमानसः ।
स वाञ्छति सुधावृष्टिं कृष्णाहिमुखकोटरात् ॥
—Attributed in the Text to Vyāsa (Mahābhārata).

चतुर्थ्यन्तं पदमेव देवता । —Pûrvamîmāṃsā.

शब्देतरत्वे युगपद्भिन्नदेशेषु यष्टृषु ।
न सा प्रयाति सांनिध्यं मूर्तत्वादस्मदादिवत् ॥ —Mṛgendra (?)

अग्निमुखा वै देवाः । —Âśvalāyana Gṛhyasûtra 4.

मृतानामपि जन्तूनां श्राद्धं चेत्तृप्तिकारणम् ।
तन्निर्वाणप्रदीपस्य स्नेहः संवर्द्धयेच्छिखाम् ॥ —Untraced.

अतीन्द्रियाणामर्थानां साक्षाद् द्रष्टा न विद्यते ।
नित्येभ्यो वेदवाक्येभ्यो यथार्थत्वविनिश्चयः ॥
(प्र. l. तस्मादती०, द्रष्टुरभावतः)
—Haribhadrasûri's Ṣaḍdarśana Sammuccaya.

ताल्वादिजन्मा ननु वर्णवर्गो वर्णात्मको वेद इति स्फुटं वः ।
पुंसश्च ताल्वादिरतः कथं स्यादपौरुषेयोऽयमिति प्रतीतिः ॥
—Untraced.

अग्निहोत्रं जुहुयात् स्वर्गकामः —Taittirîya Saṁhitā (?)

न हिंस्यात् सर्वा भूतानि —Untraced.

उत्सर्गापवादयोरपवादो विधिर्बलीयान् ।
—Hemahaṃsagaṇi's Hema. Nyāya.

सव्वत्थ संजमं संजमाओ अप्पाणमेव रक्खिज्जा ।
मुच्चइ अइवायाओ पुणो विसोही नयाऽविरई ॥
[सर्वत्र संयमं संयमादात्मानमेव रक्षेत् ।
मुच्यतेतिपातात्पुनर्विशुद्धिर्नचाविरतिः ।] —Untraced.

उत्पद्यते हि सावस्था देशकालामयान् प्रति ।
यस्यामकार्यं कार्यं स्यात्, कर्म कार्यं तु वर्जयेत् ॥ —Untraced.

कालाविरोधि निर्दिष्टं ज्वरादौ लङ्घनं हितम् ।
ऋतेनिलश्रमक्रोधशोककामकृतज्वरान् ॥

पूजया विपुलं राज्यमग्निकार्येण संपदः ।
तपः पापविशुद्ध्यर्थं ज्ञानं ध्यानं च मुक्तिदम् ॥

—Attributed to Vyāsa (Mahābhārata).

Stanza XII.

सत्संप्रयोगे इन्द्रियबुद्धिजन्मलक्षणं ज्ञानं, ततोऽर्थप्राकट्यं, तस्मादर्थापत्तिः, तया प्रवर्तकज्ञानस्योपलम्भः —Based on Jaiminisûtra I. i. 45.

Stanza XIII.

ते च प्रापुरुदन्वन्तं बुबुधे चादिपूरुषः । —Raghu X. 6.

सर्वं खल्विदं ब्रह्म नेह नानाऽस्ति किञ्चन ।
आरामं तस्य पश्यन्ति न तत्पश्यति कश्चन ॥

—Chāndogya Upaniṣad III. 14.

आहुर्विधातृ प्रत्यक्षं न निषेद्धृ विपश्चितः ।
नैकत्व आगमस्तेन प्रत्यक्षेण प्रबाध्यते ॥

—Tattvārtha S'loka-Vārtika I. 36, and quoted in Jayanta's Nyāyamañjarî.

अस्ति ह्यालोचनाज्ञानं प्रथमं निर्विकल्पकम् ।
बालमूकादिविज्ञानसदृशं शुद्धवस्तुजम् ॥

—Mîmāṃsā S'loka-Vārtika (Pratyakṣa) 112.

यदद्वैतं तद् ब्रह्मणो रूपम् । —Vedānta(?)

प्रत्यक्षाद्यवतारः स्याद् भावांशो गृह्यते यदा ।
व्यापारस्तदनुत्पत्तेरभावांशे जिघृक्षिते ॥

—Mîmāṃsā S'l. Vārtika V. (Abhāva) 17.

पुरुष एवेदं सर्वं यद्भूतं यच्च भाव्यम् ।
उतामृतत्वस्येशानो यदन्नेनातिरोहति ।

—Yajurveda's variant of Ṛg. X.

यदेजति यन्नैजति, यद्दूरे यदन्तिके ।
यदन्तरस्य सर्वस्य यदुत सर्वस्यास्य बाह्यतः ।—Îśāvāsya-Upaniṣad.

अयमात्मा श्रोतव्यो मन्तव्यो निदिध्यासितव्यानुमन्तव्यः ।

—Bṛhadāraṇyaka Upaniṣad (without 'अनुमन्तव्यः').

सर्वं वै खल्विदं ब्रह्म नेह नानाऽस्ति किञ्चन ।
आरामं तस्य पश्यन्ति न तत् पश्यति कश्चन ॥ (See Supra).

निर्विशेषं हि सामान्यं भवेत् खरविषाणवत् ।
सामान्यरहितत्वेन विशेषास्तद्वदेव हि ॥

—Mîmāṃsā S'l. Vārtika V. (Âkṛti) 10. (with न for हि and °रहितत्वाच्च for °रहितत्वेन.

हेतोरद्वैतसिद्धिश्चेद् द्वैतं स्याद् हेतुसाध्ययोः ।
हेतुना चेद् विना सिद्धिर्द्वैतं वाङ्मात्रतो न किम् ॥

—Âptamîmâṃsā II. 26.

कर्मद्वैतं फलद्वैतं लोकद्वैतं विरुध्यते ।
विद्याविद्याद्वयं न स्याद् बन्धमोक्षद्वयं तथा ॥

—Âptamîmāṃsā II. 25.

Stanza XIV.

न सोऽस्ति प्रत्ययो लोके यः शब्दानुगमादृते ।
अनुविद्धमिव ज्ञानं सर्वं शब्देन भासते ॥

—Bhartṛhari's Vâkyapadîya I. 124.

एतासु पञ्चस्ववभासिनीषु प्रत्यक्षबोधे स्फुटमङ्गुलीषु ।
साधारणं रूपमवेक्षते यः शृङ्गं शिरस्यात्मन ईक्षते सः ॥

—Aśoka's Sāmānyadûśaṇadik.

अभिहाणं अभिहेयाउ होई भिण्णं अभिण्णं च ।
खुरअग्गिमोयगुच्चारणम्हि जम्हा उ वयण सवणाणं ॥
नवि छेओ न वि दाहो ण पूरणं, तेण भिन्नं तु ।
जम्हा य मोयगुच्चारणम्हि तत्थेव पच्चओ होइ ॥
न य होइ स अन्नत्थ तेण अभिन्नं तदत्थओ
(=अभिधानमभिधेयाद् भवति भिन्नमभिन्नं च ।
क्षुरा-ग्नि-मोदकोच्चारणे यस्मात्तु वदनश्रवणयोः ।
नापिच्छेदो नापि दाहो न पूरणं तेन भिन्नं तु ।
यमाच्च मोदकोच्चारेण तत्रैव प्रत्ययो भवति ।
न च भवति अन्यार्थे तेनाभिन्नं तदर्थात्.)

—Bhadrabāhu (where ?).

विकल्पयोनयः शब्दा विकल्पाः शब्दयोनयः ।
कार्यकारणता तेषां नार्थं शब्दाः स्पृशन्त्यपि ॥ —Untraced.

सर्वमस्ति स्वरूपेण, पररूपेण नास्ति च ।
अन्यथा सर्वसत्त्वं स्यात्, स्वरूपस्याप्यसंभवः ॥ —Untraced.

जे एगं जाणइ से सव्वं जाणइ ।
जे सव्वं जाणइ से एगं जाणइ । —See supra. St. I.

एको भावः सर्वथा येन दृष्टः सर्वे भावाः सर्वथा तेन दृष्टाः ।
सर्वे भावाः सर्वथा येन दृष्टा एको भावः सर्वथा तेन दृष्टः ॥
—See Supra. St. I.

स्वाभाविकसामर्थ्यसमयाभ्यामर्थबोधनिबन्धनं शब्दः ।
—Pramāṇanaya IV. 11.

अपोहः शब्दलिङ्गाभ्यां न वस्तु विधिनोच्यते । —See Diṅnāga.

Stanza XV.

तस्माद् न बध्यते नापि मुच्यते नापि संसरति कश्चित् ।
संसरति बध्यते मुच्यते च नानाश्रया प्रकृतिः ॥
—Sāṁkhyakārikā 62.

मूलप्रकृतिरविकृतिर्महदाद्याः प्रकृतिविकृतयः सप्त ।
षोडशकश्च विकारो न प्रकृतिर्न विकृतिः पुरुषः ॥
—Sāṃkhyakārikā 3.

अमूर्तश्चेतनो भोगी नित्यः सर्वगतोऽक्रियः ।
अकर्ता निर्गुणः सूक्ष्म आत्मा कापिलदर्शने ॥ —Untraced.

शुद्धोऽपि पुरुषः प्रत्ययं बौद्धमनुपश्यति, तमनुपश्यन् अतदात्मको तदाऽऽत्मक इव प्रतिभासते । —Vyāsa Bhāṣya.

सर्वो व्यवहर्ता आलोच्य—मन्वहमत्राधिकृत इत्यभिमत्य, कर्तव्यमेतन्मया, इत्यध्यवस्यति । ततश्च प्रवर्तते, इति लोकतः सिद्धम् । तत्र कर्तव्यमिति योऽयं निश्चयश्चितिसन्निधानापन्नचैतन्याया बुद्धेः सोऽध्यवसायो बुद्धेरसाधारणो व्यापारः।
—Sāṁkhyatattva Kaumudī on S. K. Verse 23.

बुद्धिदर्पणसंक्रान्तमर्थप्रतिबिम्बकं द्वितीयदर्पणकल्पे पुंस्यध्यारोहति; तदेव भोक्तृत्वमस्य न त्वात्मनो विकारापत्तिः। —Vādamahārṇava (?)

विविक्ते दृक्परिणतौ बुद्धौ भोगोऽस्य कथ्यते।
प्रतिबिम्बोदयः स्वच्छे यथा चन्द्रमसोऽम्भसि॥ —Âsuri.

पुरुषोऽविकृतात्मैव स्वनिर्भासमचेतनम्।
मनः करोति सान्निध्यादुपाधिः स्फटिकं यथा॥ —Vindhyavāsin.

अपरिणामिनी भोक्तृशक्तिरप्रतिसंक्रमा च परिणामिन्यर्थे प्रतिसंक्रान्ते च तद्वृत्तिमनुभवति। —Vyāsa on Patañjali's Yogasûtra.

शब्दगुणमाकाशम्। —Vaiś. sûtra.

नानाश्रयायाः प्रकृतेरेव बन्धमोक्षौ संसारश्च; न पुरुषस्य।
—Based on Sāṁkhyakārikā 62.

इष्टापूर्तं मन्यमाना वरीष्ठं नान्यच्छ्रेयो येऽभिनन्दन्ति मूढाः।
नाकस्य पृष्ठे ते सुकृतेन भूत्वा इमं लोकं हीनतरं वा विशन्ति॥
—Muṇḍaka Upaniṣad I. 2. 10.

रङ्गस्य दर्शयित्वा निवर्तते नर्तकी यथा नृत्यात्।
पुरुषस्य तथात्मानं प्रकाश्य विनिवर्तते प्रकृतिः॥
—Sāṁkhyakārikā 59.

तमोमोहमहामोहतामिस्रान्धतामिस्रभेदात् पञ्चधाऽविद्यास्मितारागद्वेषाभिनिवेशरूपो विपर्ययः।
—Sāṁkhyakārikā 47; Gauḍapāda and Vācaspati 53,49, 50, 51.

उभयत्र तदेव ज्ञानं प्रमाणफलमधिगमरूपत्वात्।
(=तदेव च प्रत्यक्षं ज्ञानं प्रमाणफलमर्थप्रतीतिरूपत्वात्।)
—Nyāyabindu I. 18.

द्विष्ठसंबन्धसंवित्तिर्नैकरूपप्रवेदनात्।
द्वयोः स्वरूपग्रहणे सति संबन्धवेदनम्॥ —Untraced.
—See however P. N. Tattva-Ratna p. 42.

अर्थसारूप्यमस्य प्रमाणं तद्वशादर्थप्रतीतिसिद्धेः।
—Nyāyabindu I 19, 20.

नीलनिर्भासं हि विज्ञानं यतस्तस्माद् नीलस्य प्रतीतिरवसीयते ।

येभ्यो हि चक्षुरादिभ्यो ज्ञानमुत्पद्यते न तद्वशात् तज्ज्ञानं नीलस्य संवेदनं शक्यतेऽवस्थापयितुम् । नीलसदृशं त्वनुभूयमानं नीलस्य संवेदनमवस्थाप्यते । न चात्र जन्यजनकभावनिबन्धनः साध्यसाधनभावः । येनैकस्मिन् वस्तुनि विरोधः स्यात् । अपि तु व्यवस्थाप्यव्यवस्थापकभावेन, तत एकस्य वस्तुनः किंचिद्रूपं प्रमाणं किंचित् प्रमाणफलं न विरुध्यते । व्यवस्थापनहेतुर्हि सारूप्यं तस्य ज्ञानस्य व्यवस्थाप्यं च नीलसंवेदनरूपम् । —Nyāyabinduṭīkā.

नाऽकारणं विषयः —Untraced.

ण णिद्दाणगया भग्गा पुंजो णत्थि अणागए ।
णिव्वुया णेव चिट्ठंति आरग्गे सरिसवोवमा । — ,,
न विधानगता भग्नाः पुञ्जो नास्त्यनागते ।
निर्वृत्ता नैव तिष्ठन्ति आराग्रे सर्षपोपमाः ।

अर्थेन घटयत्येनां न हि मुक्त्वाऽर्थरूपताम् ।
तस्मात् प्रमेयाधिगतेः प्रमाणं मेयरूपता ॥ — ,,

भूतिर्येषां क्रिया सैव कारणं सैव चोच्यते । — ,,

प्रत्येकं हि भवेद्दोषो द्वयोर्भावे कथं न सः । ॥ — ,,

स्वाकारबुद्धिजनका दृश्या नेन्द्रियगोचराः । — ,,

यदि संवेद्यते नीलं कथं बाह्यं तदुच्यते ? ।
न चेत्संवेद्यते नीलं कथं बाह्यं तदुच्यते ? ॥
—Pramāṇa Vārtikālaṁkāra of Prajnākaragupta.

नान्योऽनुभाव्यो बुध्याऽस्ति तस्या नानुभवोऽपरः ।
ग्राह्यग्राहकवैधुर्यात् स्वयं सैव प्रकाशते ॥
बाह्यो न विद्यते ह्यर्थो यथा बालैर्विकल्प्यते ।
वासनालुठितं चित्तमर्थाभासे प्रवर्तते ॥ —Untraced.

अणुहूयदिट्ठचिंतियसुयपयइविचारदेवयाणूवा ।
सुविणस्स निमित्ताइं पुण्णं पावं च णाभावो ॥
(=अनुभूतदृष्टचिन्तितश्रुतप्रकृतिविकारदैविकानूपाः ।
स्वप्नस्य निमित्तानि पुण्यं पापं च नाभावः)
—Jinabhadragaṇi Kṣamāśramaṇa's Mahābhāṣya on Viśeṣāvaśyaka 1703.

आशामोदकतृप्ता ये ये चास्वादितमोदकाः ।
रसवीर्यविपाकादि तुल्यं तेषां प्रसज्यते ॥ Untraced.

Stanza XVII.

सर्व एवायमनुमानानुमेयव्यवहारो बुध्द्यारूढेन । धर्मधर्मिभावेन न बहिस्सदसत्त्वमपेक्षते ।—Quoted in the Nyāyavārtika and attributed by Pārtha-Sārathi to Dinnāga.

यथा यथा विचार्यन्ते विशीर्यन्ते तथा तथा ।
यदेतद् स्वयमर्थेभ्यो रोचते तत्र के वयम् ॥ —Untraced.

सुखादि चेत्यमानं हि स्वतन्त्रं नानुभूयते ।
मतुबर्थानुवेधात्तु सिद्धं ग्रहणमात्मनः ॥
इदं सुखमिति ज्ञानं दृश्यते न घटादिवत् ।
अहं सुखीति तु ज्ञप्तिरात्मनोऽपि प्रकाशिका ॥ —Nyâyamañjarî.

देशतो नाशिनो भावा दृष्टा निखिलनश्वराः ।
मेघपङ्क्त्यादयो यद्वत् एवं रागादयो मताः ॥ —Untraced.

रागाद् वा द्वेषाद् वा मोहाद् वा वाक्यमुच्यते ह्यनृतम् ।
यस्य तु नैते दोषास्तस्याऽनृतं कारणं किं स्यात् ॥ ,,

एगे आया —Ṭhaṇâṅga I. i.

नासन्न सन्न सदसन्न चाप्यनुभयात्मकम् ।
चतुष्कोटिविनिर्मुक्तं तत्त्वं माध्यमिका विदुः ॥

v. l. °माध्यात्मिका; but माध्यमिका is evidently the correct reading.

Stanza XXVIII.

यच्चित्तं तच्चित्तान्तरं प्रतिसंधत्ते यथेदानीन्तनं चित्तं चित्तं च मरणकालभावि ।
—Mokṣâkaragupta.

निखिलवासनोच्छेदे विमतविषयाकारोपप्लवविशुद्धज्ञानोत्पादो मोक्षः ।
—Untraced.

यस्मिन्नेव हि संताने आहिता कर्मवासना ।
फलं तत्रैव संधत्ते कर्पासे रक्तता यथा ॥—Untraced. Quoted in

इत एकनवते कल्पे शक्त्या मे पुरुषो हतः ।
तेन कर्मविपाकेन पादे विद्धोऽस्मि भिक्षवः। —Untraced.

Stanza XIX.

प्रत्येकं यो भवेद् दोषो द्वयोर्भावे कथं न सः । —Untraced.

Stanza XX.

नास्तिकास्तिकदैष्टिकम् ॥ —Hema S'abdānu. VI. iv. 66.

वयः शक्तिशीले ॥ —Hema S'abdānu. V. ii. 24.

न चायं भूतधर्मः सत्त्वकठिनत्वादिवत् । मद्याङ्गेषु भ्रम्यादिमदशक्तिवद् वा प्रत्येकमनुपलम्भात् ।

धर्मः फलं च भूतानामुपयोगो भवेद्यदि ।
प्रत्येकमुपलम्भः स्यादुत्पादो वा विलक्षणात् ॥
—Dravyālaṁkārakāra (?)

Stanza XXI.

वातातीसारपिशाचात्कश्चान्तः ॥ —Hema S'abdâ. VII. ii. 61.

सर्वव्यक्तिषु नियतं क्षणे क्षणेऽन्यत्वमथ च न विशेषः ।
सत्योश्चित्यपचित्योराकृतिजातिव्यवस्थानात् ॥ —Untraced.

यद्युत्पादादयो भिन्नाः कथमेकं त्रयात्मकम् ।
अथोत्पत्त्यादयोऽभिन्नाः कथमेकं त्रयात्मकम् ॥
घट–मौलि–सुवर्णार्थी नाशोत्पादस्थितिष्वयम् ।
शोक–प्रमोद–माध्यस्थ्यं जनो याति सहेतुकम् ।
पयोव्रतो न दध्यत्ति न पयोऽत्ति दधिव्रतः ।
अगोरसव्रतो नोभे तस्माद् वस्तु त्रयात्मकम् ॥
—Āptamîmâṃsâ 59, 60.

Quoted in P. N. T. Ratn.

Stanza XXII.

उत्पादव्ययध्रौव्ययुक्तं सत् । —Tattvârtha V. 29.

Stanza XXIII.

भागा एव हि भासन्ते संनिविष्टास्तथा तथा ।
तद्वान् नैव पुनः कश्चिन्निर्भागः संप्रतीयते ॥ —Untraced.

अर्पितानर्पितसिद्धेः । —Tattvārtha V. 31.

सदसदऽविसेसणाउ भवहेउ जदिच्छि ओवलंभाउ ।
णाणफलाभावाउमिच्छादिट्ठिस्स अण्णाणं ॥
(=सदसदविशेषणोद्भवहेतुयदृच्छोपलम्भात् ।
ज्ञानफलाभावान्मिथ्यादृष्टेरज्ञानम् ॥) —Viśeṣāvaśyaka 115.

अजैर्यष्टव्यम् ।

विज्ञानघन एवैतेभ्यो भूतेभ्यः समुत्थाय तान्येवानुविनश्यति, न प्रेत्य-संज्ञाऽस्ति । —Bṛhadâraṇyaka Upaniṣad II. iv. 12.

न मांसभक्षणे दोषो न मद्ये न च मैथुने ।
प्रवृत्तिरेषा भूतानां निवृत्तिस्तु महाफला ॥ —Manusmṛti V. 56.

आमासु य पक्कासु य विपच्चमाणासु मंसपेसीसु ।
आयंति अमुववाओ भणियो दुणिगोअजीवाणं ॥
मज्जे महुम्मि मंसंम्मि णवणीयम्मि चउत्थए ।
उप्पज्जन्ति अणंता तव्वण्णा तत्थ जंतूणो ॥
मेहुण सण्णारूढो णवलक्ख हणेइ सुहुम जीवाणं
केवलिणा पण्णत्ता सद्दिहियव्वा सयाकालं ॥
इत्थीजोणीए संभवंति बेइंदिया उ जे जीवा ।
इक्को व दो व तिण्णि व सक्खपुहुत्तं उ उक्कस्सं ॥
पुरिसेण सह गयाए तेसिं जीवाण होइ उद्दवणं ।
वेणुगदिट्ठंतेणं तत्तायासिलागणाएणं ॥
पंचिंदियामणुस्सा एगणरभुत्तणारिगब्भम्मि ।
उक्कस्सं णवलक्खा जायंति एगवेलाए ॥
णवलक्खाणं मज्झे जायइ इक्कस्स दुण्हे य समत्ती ।
सेसा पुण एमेव य विलयं वचंति तत्थेव ॥
—Sambodhasaptaṭīkā of Ratnaśekhara 66, 65, 63.

आमासु च पक्वासु च विपच्यमानासु मांसपेशीषु ।
आत्यन्तिकमु पपादो भणितस्तु निगोदजीवानाम् ॥

मद्ये मधुनि मांसे नवनीते चतुर्थके ।
उत्पद्यन्तेऽनन्तास्तद्वर्णास्तत्र जन्तवः ॥
मैथुनसंज्ञारूढो नवलक्षं हन्ति सूक्ष्मजीवानाम् ।
केवलिना प्रज्ञपिताः श्रद्धातव्याः सदाकालम् ॥
स्त्रीयोनौ संभवन्ति द्वीन्द्रियादिस्तु ये जीवाः ।
एको वा द्वौ वा त्रयो वा लक्षपृथुत्वं चोत्कृष्टम् ॥
पुरुषेण सह गतायां तेषां जीवानां भवति उद्रवणम् ।
वेणुकदृष्टान्तेन तप्तायसशलाकाज्ञातेन ॥
पञ्चेन्द्रिया मनुष्या एक नरभुक्तनारीगर्भे ।
उत्कृष्टं नवलक्षा जायन्ते एकवेलायाम् ॥
नवलक्षाणां मध्ये जायते एकस्य द्वयोर्वा समाप्तिः ।
शेषाः पुनरेवमेव विलयं व्रजन्ति तत्रैव—

निवृत्तिस्तु महाफला । —Manu. V. 56.

तु स्याद् भेदेऽवधारणे —Amarakośa III. 239.

वर्षे वर्षेऽश्वमेधेन यो यजेत शतं समाः ।
मांसानि च न खादेद्यस्तयोस्तुल्यं भवेत् फलम् ॥—Manu. V. 53.

एकरात्रोषितस्याऽपि या गतिर्ब्रह्मचारिणः ।
न सा क्रतुसहस्रेण प्राप्तुं शक्या युधिष्ठिर ॥
वाक्येऽवधारणं तावदनिष्टाऽर्थनिवृत्तये ।
कर्तव्यमन्यथाऽनुक्तसमत्वात् तस्य कुत्रचित् ॥
—Tattvârtha Śl. Vārtika I. vi. 53.

सोऽप्रयुक्तोपि वा तज्ज्ञैः सर्वत्राऽर्थात्प्रतीयते ।
यथैवकारोऽयोगादिव्यवच्छेदप्रयोजनः ॥
Tattvârtha S'l. Vārtika I. vi. 56.

अर्पिताऽनर्पितसिद्धेः । —Tattvārtha Sûtra V. 31.

Stanza XXVI.

शक्तार्हे कृत्याश्च । —Hema S'abdānu. V. iv. 35.

Stanza XXVII.

अप्राप्तानां प्राप्तिः —Praśastapāda.

वर्षाऽऽतपाभ्यां किं व्योम्नश्चर्मण्यस्ति तयोः फलम् ।
चर्मोपमश्चेत्सोऽनित्यः खतुल्यश्चेदसत्फलः ॥ —Untraced.
Quoted in P. N. T. Ratnâkarâvatârîkâ.

यस्मिन्नेव हि संताने आहिता कर्मवासना ।
फलं तत्रैव संधत्ते कर्पासे रक्तता यथा ॥ „

परिणामोऽवस्थान्तरगमनं न च सर्वथा ह्यवस्थानम् ।
न च सर्वथा विनाशः परिणामस्तद्विदामिष्टः ॥ „

अपस्थितस्य द्रव्यस्य पूर्वधर्मनिवृत्तौ धर्मान्तरोत्पत्तिः परिणामः ।
—Vyāsa on Patañjali's Yogasûtra III. 13.

प्रमाणनयैरधिगमः । —Tattvārtha sûtra I. 6.

Stanza XXVIII.

शास्त्यसूवक्तिख्यातेरङ् । —Hema III. iv. 60.

श्वपन्यसूवचपतः श्वास्थवोचपप्तम् । —Hema IV. iii. 103.

स्वरादेस्तासु । —Hema IV. iv. 31.

जावइआ वयणपहा तावइहा चेव हुंति नयवाया । —Untraced.
लौकिकसम उपचारप्रायो विस्तृतार्थो व्यवहारः ।
—Tattvārtha Bhāṣya I. 35.

यदेवाऽर्थक्रियाकारि तदेव परमार्थसत् । —Untraced.

अन्यदेव हि सामान्यमभिन्नज्ञानकारणम् ।
क्रियाभेदेन भिन्नत्वादेवंभूतोभिमन्यते —Untraced.

नीयते येन श्रुताख्यप्रमाणविषयीकृतस्य अर्थस्य अंशस्तदितरांशौदासीन्यतः स प्रतिपत्तुरभिप्रायविशेषो नयः ॥ —Taken from P. N. T. of Devasûri.

नयवाक्यमपि स्वविषये प्रवर्तमानं विधिप्रतिषेधाभ्यां सप्तभङ्गमनुव्रजति ॥
—Pramāṇanaya VII.

नयास्तव स्यात्पदलञ्छना इमे रसोपविद्धा इव लोहधातवः ।
भवन्त्यभिप्रेतफला यतस्ततो भवन्तमार्याः प्रणता हितैषिणः ॥
—Vimalanāthastava of Samantabhadra,

तच्च द्विविधं—प्रत्यक्षं परोक्षं च...... —Pr. N. T. II. 5, 6.

पारमार्थिकं पुनरुत्पत्तौ आत्ममात्रापेक्षम् —Pr. N. T. II. 18.

परोक्षं च स्मृति...आप्तवचनं च—Pr. N. T. II.1,2,3,4,10,23.

Stanza XXIX.

दग्धे बीजे यथात्यन्तं प्रादुर्भवति नाङ्कुरः ।
कर्मबीजे तथा दग्धे न रोहति भवाङ्कुरः ॥ —Untraced.

सति मूले तद्विपाको जात्यायुर्भोगाः ।—Pat. Yoga Sûtra II. 13.

स सुक्लेशेषु...भोगः ॥ —Vyāsa Bhāṣya on the same.

न प्रवृत्तिः प्रतिसंधानाय हीनक्लेशस्य
—Akṣapāda (Gautama) IV. i. 64.

गोला य असंखिज्जा असंखणिगोअगोलओ भणिओ ।
इक्किक्कम्मि णिगोए अणन्तजीवामुणे अव्व ॥
सिज्झंति जत्तिया खलु इह संववहार जीवरासीओ ।
एंति अणा इवणस्स इरासिओ तत्तिआ तम्मि ॥
(= गोलाश्च असंख्येयाः असंख्यनिगोदो गोलको भणितः ।
एकैकस्मिन् निगोदे अनन्तजीवा ज्ञातव्याः ॥
सिध्यन्ति यावन्तः खलु इह संव्यवहारजीवराशेः ।
आयान्ति अनादिवनस्पतिराशेस्तावन्तस्तस्मिन् ॥)
अत एव च विद्वत्सु मुच्यमानेषु संततम् ।
ब्रह्माण्डलोकजीवानामनन्तत्वादशून्यता ॥
अन्त्यन्यूनातिरिक्तत्वैर्युज्यते परिमाणवत् ।
वस्तुन्यपरिमेये तु नूनं तेषामसम्भवः ॥
—Attributed to 'वार्तिककारमिश्र' in S'rîdhara's Nyāya-Kandalî.

Stanza XXX.

पुन्नाम्नि घः । —Hema V. ii. 130.

अत्थं भासइ अरहा सुत्तं गंथंति गणहरा णिउणं ।
—Viśeṣāvaśyaka 1119.

उप्पज्जेइ वा विगमेइ वा धुवेइ वा । —Untraced.

उदधाविव सर्वसिन्धवः समुदीर्णास्त्वयि नाथ दृष्टयः ।
न च तासु भवान् प्रदृश्यते प्रविभक्तासु सरित्स्विवोदधिः ॥
—Dvātriṃśaddvātriṃśikā No. IV. 15.

का ऊण नमुक्कारं सिद्धाणम भिग्गहं तु सो गिण्हे ।
भरहन्तुवएसेण सिद्धा णज्झंति तेण अरिहाई ।
(=कृत्वा नमस्कारं सिद्धेभ्योऽभिग्रहं तु सोऽग्रहीत् ।)
अर्हदुपदेशेन सिद्धा ज्ञायन्ते तेनार्हनादि
—Viśeṣāvaśyaka on 3213.

Stanza XXXII.

समवान्धात् तमसः । —Hema VII. iii. 80.

अदेवे देवबुद्धिर्या गुरुधीरगुरौ च या ।
अधर्मे धर्मबुद्धिश्च मिथ्यात्वं तद्विपर्ययात् ॥
—Hemacandra's Yoga-S'āstra II. 3.

पाणवहाईआणं पावट्ठाणाण जो उ पडिसेहो ।
झाणऽज्झयणाईणं जो य विही एस धम्मकसो ॥ १ ॥
बज्झाणुट्ठाणेणं जेण ण बाहिज्जए तयं णियमा ।
संभवइ य परिसुध्धं सो पुण धम्मम्हि छेउ त्ति ॥ २ ॥
जीवाइ भाववाओ बंधाइ पसागहो इह तावो ।
एएहिं परिसुध्धो धम्मो धम्मत्तणमुवेइ ॥ ३ ॥
(=प्राणवधादीनां पापस्थानानां वस्तुप्रतिषेधः ।
ध्यानाध्ययनादीनां यश्च विधिरेष धर्मकषः ॥
बाह्यानुष्ठानेन येन न बाध्यते तन्नियमात् ।
संभवति च परिशुद्धः स पुनर्धर्मे छेद इति ॥
जीवादिभाववादो बन्धादिप्रसाधक इह तापः ।
एतैः परिशुद्धो धर्मो धर्मत्वमुपैति ॥)
—Haribhadra's Pañcavastukacaturthadvâra.

Note:—Most of these quotations I have traced to their sources with the help of the Ârhata-Mata-Prabhâkara edition of the Syâdvâdamañjarî published at Poona by Sheth Motilal

Ladhaji. Even when many of them I could have traced easily, I have unhesitatingly utilized the work done by my predecessor as I found it both handy and on the whole reliable. I have corrected, however, a few mistakes, and have traced certain passages which had been declared untraceable. The sources of a few of these quotations as given in the A.M.P. edition, have appeared to me doubtful, but I regret that I have not been able to verify them, being often far away, while doing this work, from my private, public and University libraries.

Appendix C : Authors and Works quoted, referred to or borrowed from.

A. *Brâhmaṇa authors and works quoted, referred to or borrowed from :*

(1) सांख्यः—

आसुरि—a direct pupil of कपिल, a prehistoric figure. See Intr. p. xxxvi.

पञ्चशिख—Referred to in the M. Bhârata. See Intr. p. xxxvii.

ईश्वरकृष्ण and his सांख्यकारिका 1st cent. B. C. See Intr. p. xlix.

माठर—1st Century A. D. See Intr. pp. xlix to li.

विन्ध्यवासिन्—Contemporary of वसुबन्धु, 3rd or 4th century A. D. See Intr. pp. xlvi, li.

गौडपाद भाष्य—G. grand-preceptor of Saṁkarâcârya; consequently he belongs to early 8th century A. D.

वाचस्पति and his सांख्यतत्त्वकौमुदी—About 850 A. D. See Intr. p. lvi.

वादमहार्णव—?

(2) योगः—

पतञ्जलि—150 B. C. See Wood's Introduction to the "Yoga-Sûtras" and Das-Gupta's "Yoga and Patañjali" in the "History of Indian Philosophy" Vol. I.

व्यास (पातञ्जल टीकाकार)—1st century B. C. Earlier than Vâtsyâyana, the author of the Nyâya-Bhâṣya, for whose date see Introduction pp. xlix and li.

(3) वैशेषिकः—

वैशेषिकसूत्रs of कणाद—Their nucleus, some centuries B. C. the lower limit of their date 1st century A. D. See Intr. pp. xli–xlvii.

प्रशस्तकर (पाद)—Earlier than Diṅnâga who lived in the 4th century A. D. Latest date assigned 450 A. D. See Intro. pp. liv–lv, and my Intro. to the Nyâyapraveśa Part I (Gaekwad Oriental Series).

श्रीधर—author of the न्यायकन्दली, a commentary on Praśastapâda-Bhâṣya—A. D. 991. See Intr. p. lvii.

(4) न्यायः—

अक्षपाद—or गौतम, author of the Nyâyasûtra. I refer the nucleus of the work to second century B. C. See Intr. pp. xlvii–liv. For a fuller discussion, see my paper on "त्रिविधमनुमानं पूर्ववत् शेषवत् सामान्यतोदृष्टं च", read at the First Oriental Conference.

वात्स्यायनभाष्य—1st century A. D. but generally referred to the 3rd or 4th century. See Intr. pp. xlviii–lv.

उद्योतकर—author of न्यायवार्तिक 1st half of the 7th century A. D. See Intr. p. lv.

भासर्वज्ञ—न्यायभूषणसूत्र(न्यायसार)कार—Beginning of the 10th century A. D. See Intr. p. lvi.

उदयन—author of a Vaiśeṣika work called किरणावलि and also of न्यायतात्पर्यपरिशुद्धि which is a commentary on Vâcaspati's न्यायतात्पर्यटीका which is a commentary on Uddyotakara's न्यायवार्तिक first half of the written in defence of the न्यायसूत्रs of Akṣapâda against the attacks of Buddhists such as Diṅnâga etc. Latter half of the 10th century A. D. See Intr. pp. lv–lvii.

जयन्त and his न्यायमञ्जरी—880 A. D., a little later than Vâcaspatimiśra.

(5) पूर्वमीमांसाः—

A system earlier than न्याय and as old as the oldest S'rauta sûtras.

शबरभाष्य—400 A. D. See Introduction pp. lviii–lix.

कुमारिलभट्ट—the author of the S'lokavârtika—first part of the 8th A. D. See Intr. lix.

(6) वेदान्त—

उपनिषद्s—छान्दोग्य and बृहदारण्यक. Some centuries before Gautama Buddha.

(7) ब्राह्मण-स्मृति-तन्त्र.

मनु and his मनुस्मृति.

याज्ञवल्क्यस्मृति.

व्यास—the author of the Mahâbhârata.

ऐतरेयब्राह्मण.

तैत्तिरीयारण्यक.

त्रिपुरार्णव.

B. *Buddhist authors and works:*—

न्यायबिन्दु of धर्मकीर्ति—first part of the 7th century A. D. (635 A. D.)

न्यायबिन्दुटीका of धर्मोत्तर—middle of the 9th century A. D. (847 A. D.)

मोक्षाकरगुप्त—about 1100 A. D. See Dr. S. C. Vidyâbhûṣaṇa's "History of Indian Logic".

मृगेन्द्र—?

तत्त्वोपप्लवसिंह ?

C. *Jaina authors and works :*—

आचाराङ्ग—

ठाणाङ्ग—

आवश्यकगाथा

तत्त्वार्थभाष्य

गन्धहस्तिटीका

धर्मसंग्रहणी

निशीथचूर्णी

न्यायकुमुदचन्द्र

न्यायावतार

जीतकल्प

भद्रबाहुस्वामिन्—8th in the line of teachers after Mahâvîra-svâmin. 4th century B. C.

उमास्वाति ('वाचकमुख्य')—author of तत्त्वार्थाधिगमसूत्र and भाष्य—1st century A. D. See Intr. p. lxxix-lxxx.

सिद्धसेनदिवाकर—author of न्यायावतार, संमति तर्क etc. 6th or 7th century A. D. See Intr. p. lxxx.

समन्तभद्र—author of आप्तमीमांसा believed to be the author of the lost गन्धहस्तिभाष्य according to Digambaras. Contemporary of Siddhasena Divâkara. See Intr. p. lxxx.

हरिभद्र—about the same time.

देवसूरि—author of प्रमाणनयतत्त्वालोकालङ्कार, and its com. रत्नाकर.

हेमचन्द्र—author of प्रमाणमीमांसा etc. See Introduction.

English Index.

Sanskrit Index.